The Printed Homer

To my parents
who nurtured in me
a love for books and for antiquity;

and to my dear wife, Nancy,
who nurtures in me
an Achillean love of life
and an Odyssean longing for the hearth

The Printed Homer

*A 3,000 Year Publishing
and Translation History of
the* Iliad *and the* Odyssey

PHILIP H. YOUNG

McFarland & Company, Inc., Publishers
Jefferson, North Carolina, and London

ALSO BY PHILIP H. YOUNG

Children's Fiction Series: A Bibliography, 1850–1950
(McFarland, 1997)

ON THE TITLE PAGE:
Marble bust thought to represent Homer;
second century C.E. copy of earlier original (Piazza Museum, Naples)

LIBRARY OF CONGRESS CATALOGUING-IN-PUBLICATION DATA

Young, Philip H., 1953–
The printed homer : a 3,000 year publishing and translation
history of the *Iliad* and the *Odyssey* / by Philip H. Young.
        p.   cm.
Includes bibliographical references and index.

ISBN 0-7864-1550-9 (illustrated case binding : 50# alkaline paper)

1. Homer. Iliad.   2. Homer. Odyssey.   3. Homer—Translations—
History and criticism.   4. Homer—Translations—Bibliography.
5. Epic poetry—Publishing—History.   6. Epic poetry, Greek—
Bibliography.   7. Transmission of texts—History.
8. Homer—Bibliography.   I. Title.
PA4037.Y68   2003   883'.01—dc22   2003013979
British Library cataloguing data are available

On the cover and title page: Ancient bust of Homer
(Museo Archeologico Nazionale, Naples)

Manufactured in the United States of America

McFarland & Company, Inc., Publishers
Box 611, Jefferson, North Carolina 28640
www.mcfarlandpub.com

TABLE OF CONTENTS

PREFACE

It is surely hubris to consider adding another book on Homer to the legions that exist, but perhaps the Fates will forego my nemesis if I explain my reasons adequately. First: There is no overview for the non-specialist to showcase the recent advances that classicist scholars have made in understanding the remarkable story of the creation, transmission, permutation, and ultimate preservation of these remarkable poems.* Second: The creation of computer databases of library holdings has only very recently permitted digital access to book collections, and computers also permit the sorting and processing of lists in ways not possible just a few years ago. Third: At the turn of the second to the third millennium C.E.,† we stand at the door of a revolution in the storage, availability, and organization of information, literature, and, indeed, all human knowledge. This new era is due to the advent of widespread digitalization of previously printed texts, the development of hypertext, and computerized speech synthesis and recognition.

The times seem right, at the end of the almost three thousand year history of the written book, to review one of the most celebrated texts in Western civilization. This Homeric text was created orally, preserved in writing through manuscript and printed books, and is making the transition into digital format where, ironically, it can again be appreciated aurally as in the era of its creation. However, there are questions about whether it will have a future. This book in its entirety is an argument that the answer should be an emphatic "yes"!

I would like to thank the University of Indianapolis for a sabbatical leave to begin work on this project and, especially, the staff of the Krannert Memorial Library who continued their fine work in my absence as library director.

Philip H. Young
June 2003

---

* *The recent four volume work* Homer: Critical Assessments *edited by Irene J. F. de Jong (New York: Routledge, 1999) is an anthology of articles and book excerpts from the eighteenth century to 1996.*
† *For dating notation I follow the nonreligious convention, which uses "B.C.E." for "Before Common Era" and "C.E." for "Common Era" instead of the older "B.C." and "A.D." designations.*

INTRODUCTION

Why bother to study Homer in this day and age when for some years it has been trendy to deride or intentionally ignore the deeds and especially the written words and ideas of dead, white, European men? In this book I will provide an answer to this question and, more than that, try to persuade you, the reader, that the history of the Homeric poems should be ongoing because it speaks to basic human questions and, in fact, is intellectually interesting—and even fun! It is a treasure hunt, a whodunnit and a discovery of archetypal stories. But, first, I must persuade you that the treasure is worth pursuing. Ours is an era when study of the classical Greeks and Romans has been significantly reduced in scale from what it was a generation or two ago, even to the extent that a recent book on this topic was titled, appropriately, *Who Killed Homer?* For some reason, however, Homer has been considered almost a demi-god for nearly three millennia—a wise person might want to consider why this has been so. I would like to whet your appetite to learn more about this ancient Greek poet and the history of his text by illustrating with a few quotes the acclaim he has received from antiquity to modern times:

> Our earliest infancy was intrusted to the care of Homer, as if he had been a nurse, and while still in our swaddling clothes we were fed on his verses, as if they had been our mother's milk. As we grew to youth we spent that youth with him, together we spent our vigorous manhood, and even in old age we continued to find our joy in him. If we laid him aside we soon thirsted to take him up again. There is but one terminus for men and Homer, and that is the terminus of life itself.
>
> — Heraclitus (*ca.* 500 B.C.E)

> [Homer] was the teacher of all Hellas ... [and] the best and the most divine of poets....
>
> — Plato (*ca.* 429–347 B.C.E)

> ...Homer is pre-eminent among poets ... the transcendent excellence of Homer is manifest.
>
> — Aristotle (384–322 B.C.E)

> Homer because of his outstanding excellence made the common name "poet" his own proper name.
>
> — Cicero (106–43 B.C.E)

3

I have read him [Homer] again and again because he tells me what I need to know better and more plainly than any academic.

— Horace (65–8 B.C.E)

Homer is first, middle, and last for every boy, for every man in vigor, and for every man in old age.

— Dio Chrysostom (*ca.* 40–115 C.E.)

And Homer will be all the books you need.

— John Sheffield, Duke of Buckingham (1648–1721)

Be Homer's works your study and delight,
Read them by day, and meditate by night,
Thence form your judgments, thence your maxims bring,
And trace the Muses upward to their spring.

— Alexander Pope (1688–1744)

As we advance in life ... things fall off one by one, and I suspect we are left at last with Homer and Virgil, perhaps with Homer alone.

— Thomas Jefferson (1743–1826)

All Greek gentlemen were educated by Homer, all Roman gentlemen by Greek literature, all Italian, French, and English gentlemen by Roman literature and its principles. It does not matter how much or how little one may have read of Homer — everything has been moulded by him.

— John Ruskin (1819–1900)

In the front of all poetry stands the poetry of Hellas, and in its foremost rank stands the epic of Homer. If we were offered the unhappy choice whether we should lose Homer and keep the rest of Greek poetry, or keep the rest and lose Homer, there could be little doubt as to our choice. We would rescue the Iliad and the Odyssey.

— Andrew Lang (1844–1912)

...Homer was the Greek Bible — an inspired book containing perfect wisdom on all things, human and divine....

— J. P. Mahaffy (1881)

But the variousness of critical effort points to the greater miracle — to the truth that Homer, after some twenty-seven hundred years, continues to be as alive, as challenging, and as crucial to our imaginings as he was to the ancient Greeks.... And although there are many books by which men have ordered their lives, I wonder whether any can do more than the Homeric poems to make us endure the exactions of mortality.

— George Steiner (1962)

Greece, ancient Greece, exercised a mysterious fascination over me. It was the Iliad that made Greece my paradise.... When I read the finest passages of the Iliad, I am conscious of a soul-sense that lifts me above the narrow, cramping circumstances of my life. My physical limitations are forgotten — my world lies upward, the length and breadth and the sweep of the heavens are mine.

— Helen Keller (1965)

[The Iliad is] the most famous story of the Western world, the prototype of all tales of human conflict, the epic that belongs to all people and all times since — and even before — literacy began.... All of human experience is in the tale of Troy, or Ilium, first put into epic form by Homer.... Although the gods are its motivators, what it tells us about humanity is basic, even though — or perhaps because — the circumstances are ancient and primitive. It has endured deep in our minds and memories for twenty-eight centuries because it speaks to us of ourselves, not least when least rational. It mirrors, in the judgment of another storyteller, John Cowper Powys, "what happened, is happening and will happen to us all, from the very beginning until the end of human life upon this earth."

— Barbara W. Tuchman (1984)

So, where do we begin our study of the history of Homer? First, we have to try to find out who wrote or otherwise created the poems — what scholars since antiquity have called "the Homeric question." That will lead us to consider when and how the poems were created, in the process reviewing the trends of Homeric criticism and scholarship through the ages. We will follow Homer's text through classical antiquity, the Byzantine world, the Middle Ages, the Renaissance, and into early modern and modern times. From the fifteenth century on our study will highlight the explosive results for the Homeric text (as for all others) of the invention of the printing press. We will look at the translations of the Homeric poems and the successes and failures of the many who attempted this feat. Finally, we will think about the future of written texts, Homer's included, and ponder whether Homer is relevant to this and future generations.

As indicated in the preface, this book is addressed not to Homeric scholars whose knowledge exceeds anything written here but, rather, to the educated public and students of the past who want to study the world's most famous epic poet, about whom more writers have spilled ink and created theories than any other. Because my book is a general synthesis based on the detailed scholarship of classicists, I have quoted some of them at length in order to give the reader a flavor of their verbiage. I wish to show the reader that learning more about the ancient Homeric poems is fun even today — an intellectual treasure hunt set in the mists of time, with the enticing challenge to read or reread two of the earliest and best works in the literature of Western civilization with an added understanding of how we possess these texts today and why they still speak to us.

PART I

HOMER AND THE HOMERIC TEXT

1

WHO WAS HOMER?

Even in classical (Greek and Roman) antiquity the great poet Homer was shrouded in the mists of the past, and from the beginning of written history readers of the remarkable poems called the *Iliad* and the *Odyssey* have, naturally, wondered about the person who composed them. This search has even come to have its own name — "the Homeric question." Unfortunately, from the earliest eras of historical information, facts about Homer were mixed up with fictional information created to fill the void of actual knowledge. To make matters worse, misinformation was often intentionally created by families, guilds of rhapsodes (performers of epic poetry),[1] and even cities trying to enhance their own reputations by claiming access to hidden knowledge about Homer or to historical association with the famous poet. The romantic story that he had been a poor, blind, wandering singer of poems became attached to Homer as people tried to humanize the poet — the man who had created such wonderful poems that cities contended for the honor of having been his birthplace, as indicated in the following two eighteenth-century couplets based on sayings going back to antiquity:

> Seven cities warr'd for Homer, being dead,
> Who, living, had no roof to shroud his head.
>
> — Thomas Heywood,
> *Hierarchie of the Blessed Angels*

> Seven wealthy towns contend for Homer dead,
> Through which the living Homer begg'd his bread.
>
> — Thomas Seward, *On Homer*

The history of Homer must begin not with the later traditions that grew up around the poet, but with the surviving writings of ancient Greece. According to M.L. West, "There is only one (probable) seventh-century reference to 'Homer,' and there he is associated not with the *Iliad* or *Odyssey* but with a lost epic, the *Thebaid*."[2] The name "Homer" next appears in fragments of texts written by the Greek poets Xenophanes of Colophon and Simonides dated to the late sixth century B.C.E., but they also provide no evidence about the person. Actually, it was not common to associate authors' names with writings in ancient literature, as evidenced by the Bible (except for the letters of Paul). In fact, the

9

titles of the two famous epic poems ascribed to Homer were first given as the *Iliad* and *Odyssey* by Herodotus, the "father of history," writing in the second half of the fifth century. At that time (and even into modern times) it was generally thought that Homer had composed many epic poems; in fact, it is fair to say that in early Greece virtually *all* epic poems were ascribed to Homer. It was only the scholars working in the famous Museum in Alexandria in the second century B.C.E. who separated the authorship of the *Iliad* and the *Odyssey* from the others, and by that time there was widespread belief that the *Odyssey* was created later than the *Iliad* due to its tighter organization of plot and technique (as well as time frame) and perhaps even composed by another author than Homer.

It is clear from their writings that the historical Greeks did not know any true facts about the life of this poet Homer, and they also did not have a good idea of when he had lived, simply assigning him to some past era before their own time. The historian Herodotus, without citing his evidence, calculated that Homer had lived some 400 years previous to his day (i.e. 850 B.C.E.), but the garrulous historian knew no other biographical details. References to Homer prior to the last third of the sixth century are probably misunderstandings or interpolations, but at this time there suddenly appeared many valid references to Homer as an epic poet, including an inscription from the ancient Athenian Agora dateable to ca. 475 B.C.E. About the second century B.C.E. an anonymous author wrote a short biography or "Life" of Homer, in which he put his birth at 622 years before the invasion of Greece by Xerxes (480 B.C.E.), resulting in a date of 1102 B.C.E.

By the fifth century several cities (including Chios, Smyrna, and Kolophon) were claiming to be Homer's birthplace, but none was universally accepted as correct; the incentive for these fabrications is as obvious as it is for the plethora of modern claims for beds slept in by George Washington. By the fifth century there was on the Greek island of Chios a guild of poets who called themselves the *Homeridai* (Sons of Homer), but there is no evidence whether they actually were connected with the real Homer or had just adopted his name and poems to enhance their own reputation.[3] The so-called Homeric Hymn to Apollo, probably actually written by a member of the *Homeridai* for the famous festival on the island of Delos held in 523 B.C.E.,[4] includes the following not-so-subtle lines in purported reference to its composer:

> But now may Apollo and Artemis be propitious;
> and all you maidens farewell. I ask you to call me to mind
> in time to come whenever some man on this earth,
> a stranger whose suffering never ends, comes here and asks:
> "Maidens, which of the singers, a man wont to come here,
> is to you the sweetest, and in whom do you most delight?"
> Do tell him in unison that I am he,
> a blind man, dwelling on the rocky island of Chios,
> whose songs shall all be the best in time to come.[5]

Following in the footsteps of this ancient tradition, a curious epic poem (an "Epopee" according to the subtitle) was published in 1891 under the title *Homer in Chios* in which the author has Homer return to his birthplace in his old age and tell about his life:

So spake aged Homerus, the bard, as he sat in his settle,
Where grew a garden of fruit, the fig and the pear and the citron,
Grapes suspended in clusters and trees of the luscious pomegranate.
He had returned to his home with a life full of light and of learning;
Wandering over the world, he knew each country and city,
Man he had seen in the thought and the deed, the Gods he had seen too;
Home he had reached once more, the violet island of Chios,
Blind, ah blind, but with sight in his soul and a sun in his spirit.[6]

Unfortunately, it must be concluded from this search in the early Greek sources that for the real Homer's life and date no conclusions can be reached from authority external to the poems themselves. The frustrating dearth of evidence for the man named Homer has led some writers to deny his very existence. However, it is clear that "all the early Greeks took him as much for granted and as familiar as their own mountains and streams, so that they seemed to feel no mystery concerning him and rarely made a conjecture regarding his age, his nativity, or his genius,"[7] and many modern scholars in a similar way simply accept his existence in some period before the earliest known historical personalities and leave it at that. "There are two centuries going back from Pindar — whose flesh-and-blood existence has not yet been called on question — of written record, in which we do not find Homer. Homer is spoken of, followed, completed, but he is not there himself. He was earlier, he is looked back to."[8] He was a famous poet of the past about whose life so little was known that when the Greek historian Diodorus Siculus visited Egypt about 60 B.C.E., local priests could claim without fear of refutation that along with other famous Greek personages of the past Homer had actually studied in their country. That claim would be easily refuted today.[9]

What about the poems themselves? Do they reveal anything about their composer's own life? Many ingenious deductions from the surviving texts and traditions have been made from ancient to modern times by writers trying to recover some biographical details for Homer. The fact that the epics are written in the Ionic Greek dialect is cited as evidence that Homer lived in the Greek East, perhaps Chios as claimed by its inhabitants from an early era. The *Iliad*'s detailed and accurate descriptions of the landscape around the site of Troy would seem to demonstrate that the poet was personally familiar with the area. The *Odyssey* showcases a remarkable knowledge of Mediterranean geography from the Black Sea to the Near East to Crete and Italy and, on the surface, would seem to reveal that the author traveled widely before writing the epics, a supposition supported by the accurate description of ships and sea-going techniques. The persistent tradition that Homer was blind has been much debated. Some writers (such as the writer called pseudo–Herodotus) have argued that the name itself means, in fact, "blind," but anyone reading the masterful, visual details of the epics cannot imagine them the product of a congenitally blind person — perhaps he went blind after returning from his travels? It has been creatively argued that the reputed blindness was developed by later apologists in their embarrassment that Homer was an oral poet who could not read and write, but this theory betrays an anachronistically modern negative view of illiteracy.[10] It is more likely that the tradition of Homer's blindness arose from the reference in the *Odyssey* to a blind minstrel whom Odysseus entreated during his stay on the island of the Phaeacians to sing about Troy and the deeds of the Achaeans (a general term used in the *Iliad* and *Odyssey* for the Greeks). The name "Homeros" has sometimes been thought to mean "captive" or "hostage" because of its similarity to the Greek word *homera* with that meaning. "Ephorus, the historian from Cyme, who wanted Homer to be a Cymaean, claimed that *homeros* was a Cymaean word for 'blind,' and that Homer was named for that reason. But there is no supporting evidence for the existence of such a word...."[11] Recently, "Homeros" (hom-ar-os) has been analyzed etymologically as having Indo-European roots meaning "man" (*homo*) and "joiner" (*ar-*) in the sense of a master carpenter or wheel-maker; if so, the very meaning of the name is evidence for one theory of the poems' creation technique which will be reviewed below.[12]

The lack of actual information about him did not prevent ancient authors from writing "lives" of Homer, which in fact were commonly included with manuscript and printed editions of the *Iliad* and the *Odyssey* up until relatively modern times.[13] The two most authoritative of the Lives (of which eight have survived) were mistakenly attributed to Plutarch and Herodotus, and thus are known today as pseudo–Plutarch and pseudo–Herodotus. Despite realistic-sounding family trees and other supposed details "most of the information they contain does not reach the level of historical fact...."[14] It is likely that some of the lives date only to the first century C.E., a period when spurious biographical notes about Homer were appearing in the works of writers such as Pausanias and Lucian. However, even if some of the lives may date to the classical Greek period (fifth and fourth centuries B.C.E.), they still reveal only a wishful desire to know facts about Homer. "I think these biographies should be taken as an indication that wandering epic singers were still a familiar phenomenon in the fourth century B.C.; when the lack of a biography of Homer was felt, the natural model for his life was the life of contemporary wandering bards."[15] It must be included that the details in the lives are at best useless and at worst purposely misleading, even to the point of being created for humorous purposes. "The whole 'tradition' ... contains much that is laughable.... Possibly we have at work less of the people's naive delight in storytelling ... and more of the satire of an intelligent wag who is mischievously making fun of the conventional forms of the tradition of a poet's *Life* (and the credulity of the masses). Be that as it may, this is not a seriously meant biography. Such a work could serve for entertainment, not instruction (the term *folk book* has been applied to it with justice and it has been compared to the *Till Eulenspiegel* [a medieval German tale of a merry prankster]."[16]

In a similarly humorous spirit, mention should be made of the alleged discovery of Homer's actual tomb on the Greek island of Ios in 1773 by Graaf Pasch Baron van Krienen, who claimed to be a Dutch count.[17] Pasch reported that after a month of digging he found a marble sarcophagus, which he opened with astonishing results. Sitting on a stone bench inside was the fully preserved body of Homer himself! Unfortunately, his workmen then dropped the heavy coffin lid which caused the remains to crumble into dust. The tomb was also said to have contained a marble inkstand, pen, and pen-sharpener, coins and gems with his image on them, and a marble bust of him. Curiously, all the evidence, including an epigram inscribed on Homer's bench, subsequently vanished, and initial scholarly excitement turned into incredulity. If there is any truth to the account of Pasch (who was later found to be a story-teller of the likes of Baron von Munchausen), it might be that the islanders had fabricated a tomb of Homer to try to solidify an ancient tradition that Homer had died on Ios. Similarly, the modern residents of Chios, following a tradition based on the pseudo–Herodotean Life of Homer, still point tourists to a carved rock at the town of Vrontados called Homer's Stone, which is said to be where the poet taught students in a school (although the site is probably actually a sanctuary of the goddess Cybele).[18]

From this study it must be concluded that the ancient world knew no more factual biographical details about a real Homer than does the modern; there is only the Homeric text as evidence for his existence. "He is a shadow, or rather a voice, and the only thing we can hope to know of him, the only reality we can give him, is the unique quality of this voice."[19] The few and conflicting ancient references reveal that in antiquity nothing certain was known about the life of Homer, although they do reveal a driving need to try to fill this gap in their knowledge. "Homer is so hidden by his own creations that we cannot get a glimpse of him, except as these creations reveal his greatness."[20] Perhaps all that can concluded is that there existed "…a strong impression for the Greeks of the period down to about 450 B.C. [that] Homer was a real person who had lived [perhaps] in the early seventh century and had composed a large number of narrative poems of the highest quality which were still being recited by professional rhapsodes, and especially by a group of people who lived in Chios and called themselves *Homeridae*, thus claiming to be the poet's descendants."[21] "As Homeric scholars are well aware…, their poet resembles nothing so much as Churchill's definition of the Soviet Union: a riddle wrapped in a mystery inside an enigma."[22]

For the remainder of this book the name "Homer" will be used in two ways: to refer to the unknown creator(s) of the two poems called the *Iliad* and *Odyssey*; and as a general term for the text of the poems themselves. Thus, in the sentence "Homer may have lived in the eighth century" the name would refer to the unknown creator(s); and in the sentence "Homer is not read much in schools today" the name would refer generally to the text of the two poems.

THE CREATION OF THE HOMERIC TEXT

The *Iliad*'s theme is ostensibly the terrible consequences caused by the wrath of Achilles, the Achaean hero, who was wronged by their leader Agamemnon when he appropriated a captured woman allotted to Achilles after he had to give up his own to appease the gods. The time frame of the poem is only a few weeks during the ninth year of the ten-year Trojan War, in which the Achaeans, in a mighty army raised from all over Greece, retaliated against the city of Ilion, or Troy, in the Levant (present Turkey) because its prince Paris had stolen away Helen, the wife of the Spartan king Menelaus. The poem's audience is assumed already to know the events leading up to the war and during its first nine years, as well as how the war ended with the sack of Troy following the ruse of the famous Trojan horse, an episode not included in the *Iliad* either. In the poem mighty deeds of fighting occur by heroes on both sides, but the absence of the sulking Achilles inevitably gives the advantage to the Trojans, led by their hero Hector. The Achaeans are driven back to their ships, which are in danger of being burned despite the erection of a wooden wall to protect them. Achilles still refuses to come to his army's assistance, but he relents to the supplications of his bosom friend Patroclus to wear his distinctive armor of divine origin in hopes of frightening the Trojans. The ruse succeeds for a while, but the Trojans become wise to it and kill Patroclus. This outrage energizes Achilles to reenter the conflict after reconciling himself to Agamemnon. Achilles rages against the Trojan forces with such ferocity that the local river Scamander overflows and tries to fight him. Only Hector stays outside the strong walls of Troy to oppose Achilles, but the Achaean hero has the assistance of the gods and kills him, dragging his body around and around the city in his continuing anger over the death of Patroclus. Finally, in one of the most touching scenes in all literature, Hector's father Priam comes to Achilles to beg for the return of his son's body so that he can bury it. Achilles at last comes to his senses and complies, knowing that his own destiny is also to die at Troy. The poem ends with the celebration of funeral games in honor of Patroclus, foreshadowing those for the doomed but glorious Achilles himself.

"The tragic course of Achilles' rage, his final recognition of human values—this is the guiding theme of the poem, and it is developed against a background of violence and death. These two poles of the human condition, war and peace, with their corresponding aspects of human nature, the destructive and the creative, are implicit in every situation and statement of the poem...."[1] In some ways the *Iliad* is unsettling. "A great work of art is likely to be challenging and even subversive of almost anyone's peace.... Homer celebrated remorseless cruelty, and loathed the results of remorseless cruelty. The *Iliad* in its ambivalence about glory and death challenges most of our current ideas about what is right and wrong, what is true, what is heroic, and finally, what is human."[2] The *Iliad* is a poem about what it means to be a hero and to achieve what the Greeks called *kleos* ("fame" or "glory"). "The hero is between god and man. Men die, while the gods live forever; the hero, however, does both. After death he is immortal in two different senses: immortal in cult and immortal in song. He receives *time*, cultic observance, and *kleos*, the fame of those whose stories are told by the bards."[3] Thus, the Homeric text itself, representing the telling of the tales of the heroes, is a player in the actual action it relates!

The *Odyssey* is the story of the ten-year efforts of Odysseus, one of the Achaean heroes from Troy, to return home to his wife Penelope and son Telemachus on the small island of Ithaca. Although the goddess Athena is his patroness, he and his men run afoul of other gods, especially the sea-god Poseidon, and are delayed by a series of monstrous beings and disastrous events. They are almost eaten by the one-eyed Cyclops Polyphemus, but the crafty Odysseus, whose cunning is demonstrated over and over, gets him drunk, rams a sharpened stake into his eye, and succeeds in spiriting his men away from his island safely. Their next encounter involves an enchantress, Circe, who turns Odysseus' men into pigs. However, he succeeds in getting her to reverse her spell, and the sailors spend a year in comfort on her island before their homesick captain convinces them to move on. Next Odysseus and his men sail into Hades, where he converses with the shades of the famous dead. Being forewarned of the island of the Sirens with their deadly songs, Odysseus has his men put wax in their ears, and soon thereafter they avoid the twin dangers of a shore with a multi-headed monster, Scylla, and the sea passage with a violent whirlpool, Charybdis. The sailors then land on an island where live the Cattle of the Sun, property of the gods and, famished, they eat one despite being warned. As they sail away, a terrible storm strikes and the ship and crew are all destroyed except Odysseus, who floats on the mast and keel for nine days before arriving at an island on which the nymph Calypso lives. Despite her love for him, Odysseus convinces her (with divine help) to free him and allow him to build a new ship, but this ship also founders. Odysseus is washed up on an island where he is rescued by the king's daughter Nausicaa and brought to the court of King Alcinous. Meanwhile, Odysseus' now-grown son Telemachus and his wife Penelope have been contending with a rapacious group of suitors who have almost eaten them out of house and home. Telemachus makes an expedition to Greece to try to find news of his father, but despite meeting old King Nestor, Menelaus, and other heroes of the Trojan War, his quest for news is unsuccessful and he returns home. Finally, Odysseus reaches Ithaca with assistance from his erstwhile hosts. He disguises himself, revealing his identity only to his faithful shepherd and to Telemachus. They hatch a plan which results in the massacre of the suitors and Odysseus' reunion with Penelope. The epic poem ends with Odysseus again undertaking his duties as king of the island.

"The *Odyssey* is an after-the-war poem, a plea for relief and gratification, and it turns, at times, into a sensual, even carnal celebration. ... The gigantic poem is built around an excruciating paradox: The temptation to rest, to fill your stomach is almost overwhelming, yet the instant you rest, you are in danger of losing consciousness or life itself. In the end, short of death or oblivion, there *is* no rest, a state of being that might be called the Western glory and the Western disease."4 "Between them, then, the Iliad and the Odyssey express the two great archetypal conditions of human nature: war and peace, worlds static and dynamic, moral conservatism and radical pragmatism, old aristocratic tribal ways slowly yielding to a new and self-reliant colonial expansiveness, rational thought making inroads on hallowed heroic myth. Both are valid, both are important as partial reflections of human nature. Yet it remains true — and I'm not sure what this tells us about the scholarly mind — that academic aficionados of the Iliad have tended to despise the Odyssey, carefully cloaking their contempt in literary terms. The entry on Homer in the recently published third edition of the Oxford Classical Dictionary is typical, briskly dismissing the Odyssey as 'a romance, enjoyable at a more superficial level than the heroic/tragic Iliad.' It would be about as reasonable to describe the Iliad as the longest and bloodiest narcissistic sulk in literature…. People are always saying how modern the Odyssey is, and in many ways they are right. There is more scope for the development of personal (as opposed to public) relationships once the constraints of battle and siege are removed…. The most striking contrast is in the treatment of Helen. Whereas in the Iliad she is simply a disruptive femme fatale, the irresistible and disastrous embodiment of sex, in the Odyssey she is drawn, with sly comic brilliance, as a kind of Marin County hostess, handing out hash (or the equivalent) to guests, and reminiscing, in postwar wicked-old-me mode, about life among all those big handsome Trojans."5

And now the search for Homer reaches the central issue — who created these wonderful epics? When? Why? How? With, as discussed previously, no certain facts from antiquity about a person "Homer" or the circumstances and date of his epic creations, it is no surprise that since antiquity scholars have debated the proverbial "Homeric question." In fact, the single question of "who" evolves into several, each of which when pursued "grow like Topsy" (or, perhaps, a better allusion would be to Brer Rabbit's Tar Baby, easy to attack but hard to escape!) The core issues can be laid out as follows:

1. Were the Homeric epics composed by one person "Homer" as monumental works, or are they the result of some other process?
2. When were the epics composed and when were they first written down, for what reason, and by whom; and, when did a standardized text become dominant?
3. Regardless of their date of composition, what epoch is reflected in their narrative content (or are they a hodgepodge of eras)?
4. To what extent do the epics reflect historical events and geographical realities, and to what extent are they fictional?

The last question, being historical and archaeological, is the least relevant to the study of the Homeric text. In the *Iliad*, the city of Ilion (Troy) is clearly located just south of the strait called in antiquity the Hellespont and today the Dardanelles, that narrow body of water connecting the Aegean with the Black Sea. The location of Homer's Troy at the hill called Hissarlik, which fits the poem's geographical references quite well, has been assumed from ancient times, as the classical Greek and Roman inscriptions referring to the site as "Ilion" found there attest, although other hills in the vicinity have sometimes been suggested. This identification is almost certainly the location of Homer's Troy, despite the curious, recent book titled *Where Troy Once Stood,* which boldly locates the venerable city in East Anglia in England of all places.[6] For Homer, Troy was a great city of large size, defended by mighty walls and towers, with nearby coastal beaches where the Achaeans drew up their "dark ships" and an intervening plain where the heroes fought. Some scholars up to the nineteenth century argued that the city was, in fact, a literary invention of Homer, but others assumed that there was such a place, even if the characters and events were fictional.

In 1865, Frank Calvert was the first scholar to put the site at Hissarlik to the test of the neonatal discipline of archaeology, and his trial trench recovered enough antiquities to whet the appetite of the famous (or infamous) Heinrich Schliemann. This German businessman and self-taught linguist later promoted himself as the only person to believe literally in Homer and, *Iliad* in hand, to have walked the area and discovered the real Troy. From 1870 to 1890 he excavated at Hissarlik, removing great quantities of earth and archaeological finds, including a hoard of rich objects (probably not actually found together) which he advertised as the "Treasure of Priam." Despite his tendency to fabricate and embellish the truth, Schliemann can be credited with publicizing the site to both scholars and the general public so that, with his subsequent work at Mycenae in Greece, he essentially discovered the Bronze Age Greek civilization now referred to as "Mycenaean."

Schliemann's exploratory work at Troy was continued by the qualified archaeologist Wilhelm Dörpfeld — who managed to make some sense out of Schliemann's findings — and, in the 1930s, by Carl Blegen and a team from the University of Cincinnati. Schliemann and Dorpfeld identified not one city but nine different cities, represented by distinctive layers. Blegen refined this sequence and the dating of each layer and discovered that the city corresponding in date to the Greek Late Bronze Age was, in fact, Troy VII, in Schliemann and Dorpfeld's system whereby the lowest and earliest was labeled Troy I. The sub-period Troy VIIa was thought by them to be the exact time period when Homer's Trojan War took place, but recent work has modified these dates; the massive city called Troy VI, which was destroyed in a cataclysm, is now thought to be the corresponding layer. Doubters, however, pointed out that even Troy VI seemed far too small to be Homer's massive city, and that there was not really a plain for the fighting or a coastline for the Achaean ships. It happens that archaeological excavations currently under way are discovering a large area of houses outside the walls which now shows the walled area to be a stronghold, rather than the entire city. The archaeologists have also found that the coastline was more distant and longer in the Bronze Age than it is now.[7]

Was this, then, the very city outside whose walls Achilles and Hector fought? It is important not to forget that the *Iliad* is primarily a work of literature, and readers must restrain themselves from reading too much factual information into it. Recent scholarship, especially in the realms of archaeology, "suggests that poetic memory owes more to imagination than to history."[8] However, the new discoveries tend at least to support the theory that the author of the *Iliad* was very familiar with the topography of this area and may have been reflecting some actual war that took place far before his time, perhaps about 1200 B.C.E. towards the close of the Bronze Age. The location of Troy at a spot well sited to protect the entrance to the Hellespont is suggestive of a place expansionists, such as the Bronze Age Mycenaean Greeks, would want to control before moving towards the rich Black Sea area and which indigenous people would defend to the last man to prevent their advance. In a fascinating recent book the scholar J. V. Luce undertook a detailed comparison of the landscapes of Troy and Ithaca, Odysseus' home island, taking into account the new archaeological and topographic information about changes in the Trojan coastline; his important conclusion is that "Homer was well informed about the terrain in both regions, that his account provides an authentic setting for the action in both epics, and that he does not arbitrarily invent landmarks to suit his poetic purposes. In short, [his book is] ... a comprehensively illustrated vindication of the overall accuracy of Homeric topography."[9]

Unfortunately, this does not equate to proving the historicity of Homer's Trojan War, the personages involved, or the supposed reasons for its occurrence, although there is a great amount of popular enthusiasm for trying to make such a connection, as demonstrated by the recent success of Michael Wood's book and television series *In Search of the Trojan War*. Tempting references in Hittite documents to *Ahhiyawa* (Achaeans?), *Wilusa* (Ilion?), *Ataksandus* (Alexander/Paris?) make us want to find Homer to be historical, but even if these references should equate to Homeric characters, they would not prove the events of the *Iliad* to be true. We now know that the source of the Homeric epics is oral poetry, but recent research indicates that this type of composition favors the rapid mythologizing and distortion of historical facts instead of careful preservation and handing down of actual incidents. Such transformations are readily obvious in the more recent epics the French *Song of Roland* and the German *Nibelungenlied,* where the actual historical facts are known from other sources. "Myths and oral traditions are important to society because they help explain and legitimize present conditions. They *can* transmit historical memories; they can also be constructs that are retrojected into the past without having any grounding in the past."[10] Unless remarkable new evidence is discovered by archaeologists in the future, it is probably best to place the Homeric epics firmly in the literary realm while allowing for a few instances of past memories to have been inserted.

Let us now move to the questions central to an understanding of the text itself, those having to do with how it was composed, at what date, and to what time period it refers. A suitable place to begin is with the observation that despite the moving nature of the stories told in the Homeric poems, readers from antiquity to modern times have noticed a number of oddities about their text and have striven mightily to explain these anomalies, as will be seen below. Even from the plot outlines of the two poems given above, it is evident that the tone and structure of the works is greatly different, that of the *Iliad* ponderous and brooding about the fate of men, the tragedy of war, the consequences of wrong actions, etc. while that of the *Odyssey* is more upbeat as Odysseus foils one monster after another and finally comes home to his faithful wife. The *Iliad* "proceeds with inhuman calm" and its focus is not on pathos but on the joys of being alive and being on an adventure, even in a situation of gruesome slaughter; the Homeric heroes are "less afraid of the terrors of combat than of the long boredom of the hearth."[11] In opposition to the straightforward narrative of the *Iliad*, the *Odyssey*'s story comes in waves and episodes, with the overarching theme of marital fidelity never far from the surface; it has been argued on this kind of basis that the composer of the *Odyssey* was a woman, in fact, the character Nausicaa. "There is not a line in the *Odyssey* which a woman might not perfectly well write, and there is much beauty which a man would be almost certain to neglect. Moreover there are many mistakes in the *Odyssey* which a young woman might easily make, but which a man could hardly fall into…."[12]

From ancient times, careful readers of the poems have noticed a number of seeming errors, narrative contradictions, illogical repetitions of passages, etc. They have also identified references to social institutions and objects of widely differing time periods. Commentators have deemed some passages of significantly inferior quality to others. Following is a list and discussion of some of these oddities:

1. Objects and customs of quite disparate eras appear in the poems. The most striking evidences of early date are the references to a boar's tusk helmet, known archaeologically to belong to the Mycenaean Bronze Age (ca. 1400 B.C.E.) and Ajax's so-called tower shield, which covered his whole body and is also known archaeologically to be of Mycenaean date. But other references to armor, the use of iron, and a knowledge of Mediterranean geography cannot predate the era of Greek colonization of the eighth century and later.

2. There are traces of very early language forms within the much later dialect of the poems. From antiquity, linguists have noticed obscure vocabulary and grammatical forms; in fact, the early references to the Homeric poems are dictionaries and grammatical commentaries to assist classical readers. Peculiarities in line scansion puzzled scholars until the realization by the 18th-century clergyman and classicist Thomas Bentley that certain words in the written text were missing a lost letter and sound called a "digamma," which, when added back, explain certain scansion oddities. For example, the word *anax* was originally *wanax*.

3. The story lines of the poems reveal factual contradictions and repetitions of narrative. In Book 21 of the *Iliad* Achilles lays down his spear, but several lines later he is wielding it in battle. The minor warriors Schedios, Pylaimenes, and Chromios are killed in battle but later are alive and well; similarly, in Book 5 Palaemenes, king of the Paphlagonians is killed by Patroclus but in Book 13 is alive and mourning the death of his son Harpalion. In Book 7 the Greeks are frantically building a wall to protect their ships from the raging Hector just when Diomedes is blithely forecasting a speedy overthrow of Troy. In Book 15 Zeus decrees that Hector will pursue the Greeks all the way to the ship of Achilles, but their progress only goes to the ship of Protesilaus. The regular Achaean troops are sent out of battle in one passage in Book 15 but fourteen lines later are still fighting and dying. Near the beginning of the *Iliad* readers are told of the division of the Achaean troops (Book 2) and a duel between Paris and Menelaus (Book 3), while Helen stands on the walls of Troy and identifies the unknown Achaean heroes to King Priam. But this is supposed to be the ninth year of the war — surely these events took place at its start! At the beginning of the *Odyssey* (Book 1), there is a council of the gods in which after some squabbling it is decided

to send Hermes to tell Calypso to release Odysseus, but later (Book 5) there is another council of the gods having the same debate and seemingly ignorant of the first one. Also in Book 1, Athena advises Telemachus that if from his trip to Pylos he learns that his father, Odysseus, is dead he should give his mother, Penelope, away in marriage; but, then, the goddess tells him to consider how to slaughter the suitors in his house (there would be no suitors if Penelope is remarried!) In the *Odyssey* (Book 7) Odysseus asks the Phaeacians for dinner, but he has already eaten. In Book 13 Athena transforms Odysseus into a crippled old beggar, but a few lines later he is inexplicably a strong boxer.

4. Some passages seem interpolated and confusing for good narrative flow. The most likely examples of these inserts are: (a) the *Iliad*'s "Catalog of Ships," which is a point where the poem suddenly stops and a long list of cities which supplied ships to the Achaean effort is inserted without obvious reason; (b) the whole of *Iliad* Book 10, often termed the "Doloneia," which describes a night-spying adventure by a few Achaeans in which the Trojan Dolon is captured and killed, an episode seemingly a separate poem unto itself as Book 9 ends with planning before going to bed and Book 11 begins with dawn's implementation of the plans; (c) the visit to Hades in the *Odyssey*, in which the sailors who have visited and will visit various island and lands, all identifiable as real places in the Mediterranean Sea, suddenly drop off the map and visit a non-real place whose inhabitants are more a catalog of famous dead people than actors in the poem; and (d) the last section of the *Odyssey* which has been criticized from antiquity as an add-on because it seems that the poem should end after Odysseus' slaughter of the suitors and reunion with Penelope but, instead, it continues with his dealings with local affairs on Ithaca, a story without epic significance. In the most recent authoritative edition 166 lines, in addition to the "Doloneia," are identified as being interpolations.[13]

5. Periodically, it seems that the poems have passages of inferior poetic quality, although such criticisms are subjective. The funeral games in *Iliad* Book 23 are excellently written until at line 798 the quality suddenly declines as Ajax and Diomedes are peculiarly encouraged to wound one another. In the same book there is described an archery contest, which requires a virtually impossible shot to cut the string tethering a pigeon to a ship's mast — "such miracles are common in some later non–Greek heroic traditions, but are foreign to the Greek taste."[14] Even ancient writers noticed various passages of inferior quality; for example, the Roman poet Horace wrote: "I too am indignant when good Homer nods, but in a long work it is permitted to snatch a little sleep"[15] from which comes the saying that "even Homer nods."

6. The poems, compared to other Greek literature, are written in a contrived, old-fashioned poetic language. "It contains too many alternative forms, too many synonyms, too many artificial forms for it to be in any sense a vernacular."[16] Most notably, there is continued repetition of noun-epithet formulas, such as "swift-footed Achilles," "rosy-fingered dawn," and "owl-eyed Athena." Longer formulas may be "several complete lines, composing a passage which is repeated whenever a typical scene, like the preparation of a meal or sacrifice or the launch-

ing or beaching of a ship, is to be described."[17] It has been calculated that "about one-third of the entire poem [the *Iliad*] consists of lines or blocks of lines which occur more than once in the work, and the same is true of the *Odyssey*."[18] Although there is a wide range of these formulas, they are sometimes repeated without obvious narrative purpose.

So, how can these apparent errors and other oddities in the Homeric text be explained? How could their composer have not noticed them and corrected them? In the nineteenth century some scholars, most notably those in Germany, argued that the poems were not the product of one person's creation at all but resulted instead from the editing together of many separate tales. Led by the German Friedrich August Wolf (1759–1824) who published his influential *Prolegomena ad Homerum* in 1795,[19] these scholars believed that the poems could be teased apart into their original, separate sources or folk "lays" and were, thus, termed "analysts"; their opinion was largely accepted up to about 1930. Wolf argued that the Homeric poems were composed orally about 950 B.C.E. and handed down orally for about four hundred years before being written down, a process which resulted in the accidental and intentional changes from the original text to which they were overlays. He believed that the artistic unity observable in the existing text resulted from the work of editors when the poems were eventually written down. "Previous expressions of doubt about the authenticity of the Homeric poems had been passed over, either as mere *obiter dicta* [passing comments] or as the work of amateurs; but Wolf's closely reasoned and highly professional argument could not be so easily disregarded."[20] The reaction to the *Prolegomena* and the arguments of the analysts was profound, either pro or con, but all subsequent interpreters have had to consider the possibility that the Homeric texts were created through a process of evolution and, if they concur, have to decide where in that evolution to place Homer.

Unfortunately, the analysts in their zeal to discover an original core text, presumably the true words of Homer, edited out various parts of the existing text using as their guide the subjective "principle of the inerrancy of great poets."[21] Parts that were factually contradictory or just seemed inferior in quality were excised, a process clearly fallacious. "The analysts, who believe that the *Iliad* and *Odyssey* consist of older and younger layers and are the work of different poets, use amongst other things aesthetic criteria to distinguish between these poets. The rule of thumb employed is that what is good poetry derives from the original poet, and what is bad poetry from a second-rate *Bearbeiter* [editor] who added various interpolations to the original text. The desire to distinguish between good and bad poetry makes analytic literary criticism a rather subjective affair, which tells us more about the literary principles of the nineteenth century—catchwords here are unity, coherence, and relevance — or the personal taste of the scholar involved, than about the Homeric text."[22] In 1847, Karl Lachmann (1793–1851) published *Betrachtungen über Homers Ilias* (Observations on Homer's Iliad) in which he proposed that the original kernel consisted of eighteen separate and distinct lays. Although the technique of the analysts to judge passages based on quality assessment is clearly dangerous, the concept that the Homeric poems could have resulted from multiple authorship does explain some of the oddities discussed above, including the narrative inconsistencies, variation of internal dates, seemingly interpolated passages, and the more obvious variations of poetic quality. The philosopher Goethe jokingly reworked the old aphorism quoted in chapter 1 to read:

> "Sieben Städte zankten sich drum, ihn geboren zu haben;
> Nun da der Wolf ihn zerriss, nehme sich jede ihr Stuck."
> [Seven cities fought among themselves to have been his birthplace
> But now that Wolf has destroyed him, each can take their piece.][23]

Alarmed at the carving up of the Homeric poems (and the questioning of the existence of a single composer Homer) and at the assumption that the poems as they exist are poor-quality collections of earlier material carelessly thrown together, a counterthrust against the Analysts was mounted by scholars who stressed the artistic unity of the poems, which could only derive from a single act of composition. It is this so-called "unitarian" theory of the epics' creation, promulgated by Andrew Lang (1895), that many scholars find most satisfying because it preserves a "Homer" and views the poems as self-contained creations instead of accreted layers. "The Unitarian position, which seeks to defend the unity of the *Iliad* and *Odyssey*, is by its very nature more promising where literary criticism is concerned. However, the earliest Unitarian responses to the Analytic attack often made use of the same kind of subjective aesthetic comments: they simply proclaimed beautiful what their opponents had considered bad poetry ... [and] explained them away, not by ascribing them to a *Bearbeiter* but by forgiving Homer.... Later, Unitarians adopted the far more fruitful position of simply taking the text as their point of departure and analyzing the compositional and literary techniques to be found within that text."[24]

It is possible to study the use of humor, the descriptions of fighting, characterization, and infinitely many other aspects of the poems as whole entities from the unitarian position, just as scholars study other works of literature known to have been written by a single person. Aristotle himself in the *Poetics* praised the poems for their superiority to other epic poems due to their unity of action. (It should be noted, however, that the unitarian theory does not itself address the question of whether the *Iliad* and the *Odyssey* were created by the same poet.) The balance of most accepted opinion swung from the analysts to the unitarians with the 1938 publication of *Iliasstudien* by Wolfgang Schadewaldt, "a study rivaling in minuteness those of the analysts [in which he] sought to establish numerous correlations, references back and forth, economy of narrative or deliberate slowing up of the action, as indications of the conscious design of a single creative artist."[25] Some scholars hoped for a compromise between the two opposing schools of opinion — "we must part company with simple-minded unitarians who imagine Homer creating in a vacuum and with those analysts who ... ply their scalpels in an endless vivisection of the living body of the *Iliad*."[26]

Homeric studies, which had reached a deadlock between the analysts and unitarians in the early twentieth century, were revolutionized (and made even more complex) by the work of Milman Parry and his student Albert Lord who, essentially, discovered and defined a new concept — oral poetry.[27] Starting with an analysis of the noun-epithet formulas in the Homeric poems, Parry and Lord built their argument: that the poems were composed orally in a long tradition of oral poetry which had its own rules and structure that differ from those of written literature. The formulas are, in fact, mnemonic devices which along with already known story lines assist the poets as they create their epics during actual performances. "He [the poet] creates his epic as he chants it, using a vast stock of traditional motifs and formulas to sustain his invention or his variations on a given epic theme."[28] Parry and Lord built their work on the ethnographic study of living oral poets in what was then Yugoslavia and Albania, and subsequently similar work in other surviving oral poetry traditions elsewhere, especially Africa and India, has confirmed their observations.

It was discovered that oral poets have a repertoire of repetitive formulas in their memory which they draw upon to make their lines conform to their poetic meter and to give themselves mental pauses to prepare for the next lines. "Oral conditions indicate three main directions in which composition is affected. First, the actual conditions of performance impose on the poet certain obligations which are not expected to be found in written books. Secondly, the poet has behind him a large mass of stories, among which there may be several variations of a single story, and from these he has to make his choice. Thirdly, the time available for the recitation of a story or an episode affects the manner of telling it."[29] Oral poets believe that they tell the same poem time after time but, in fact, the actual lines and narrative differ because the oral presentation is actually the moment of creation or recreation, even if the general plot is not new; they do not memorize their poems. "An oral poem is composed not *for* but *in* performance."[30]

The circumstances of the oral presentation dictate many aspects of the resultant poem because the poet is eager to please his audience and responds to it. Thus, passages which may flatter the particular listeners of the moment may be elaborated, and passages which may be uncomplimentary or just thought uninteresting to the audience may be pared down, altered, or omitted. Oral poets consider themselves to be entertainers of the moment and do not have a feeling that their poems are creations to be preserved past the moment of presentation; they are proud of having learned the poems from older poets and assume the preservation of them will come by teaching them to younger oral poets.

When the elements of oral poetry are applied to the Homeric text, there are eye-opening results, especially in explaining many of the oddities discussed above, and it is now virtually impossible to deny at least an element of orality in the composition of these poems. Oral composition clearly explains the recurrent use of noun-epithet formulas as devices for the oral poet to select from to complete a line's meter correctly and, while doing so, to have a few seconds to plan his next line. The conservative nature of oral poetry in preserving formulas, phrases and plots from earlier poets explains the presence in the Homeric texts of descriptions of physical objects and grammatical forms of much older time periods, mixed together with those of more recent eras, and it explains the old-fashioned language of the poems. Oral poetry techniques can also be used to explain the narrative contradictions, repetitions and interpolations. A poet might purposely or accidentally repeat a descriptive section, and he might forget minor details as he recreates his poem, resulting in factual contradictions when studied and analyzed as a written document. The oral technique also explains the flow of the poems and their creator's obvious tendency to linger over descriptions of objects and nature; these are elements of orally developed stories without an interest in literary balance. "An oral poet spins out a tale; he likes to ornament, if he has the ability to do so, as Homer, of course, did. It is on the story itself, and even more on the grand scale of ornamentation, that we must concentrate, not on any alien concept of close-knit unity. The story is there and Homer tells it to the end. He tells it fully and with a leisurely tempo, ever willing to linger and to tell another story that comes to his mind. And if the stories are apt, it is not because of a preconceived idea of structural unity which the singer is self-consciously and laboriously working out, but because at the moment when they occur to the poet in the telling of his tale he is so filled with his subject that the natural processes of association have brought to his mind a relevant tale. If the incidental tale or ornament be, by any chance, irrelevant to the main story or to the poem as a whole, this is no great matter; for the ornament has a value of its own, and this value is understood and appreciated by the poet's audience."[31]

Of course, the observation that oral poets essentially recompose their epics with each retelling does not preclude memorization of special passages to be inserted, just as their general story lines are memorized; this would account for the retention of certain sections in the Homeric text that closely reflect Mycenaean realities, such as the "Catalog of Ships." Most important for the Homeric oral theory is that many ancient writers (and, in fact, the Homeric poems internally) make reference to a world where oral poets provided entertainment. "We have a picture of archaic and early classical Greece with many singers, some of them professional, with a great variety of songs of considerable length, with a wide interest in the art, and with occasions where people gathered together from some distance to participate in a celebration."[32] The meter and verse length of the Homeric epics is dactylic hexameter, each line having six "dactyls" or "feet" (oral sections) composed of one long and two short elements with the final one a "spondee" with two even beats. The poems when viewed through the lens of oral poetry are seen almost certainly to have been composed to be sung or chanted to the accompaniment of a musical instrument, such as a lyre. "The hexameter remains not only a powerful instrument of narrative poetry, such as is to be found hardly anywhere else in the world, but in its own way a precise and careful means for keeping language at an impressive level of music and movement. It has its skillfully devised rules, and these illustrate what mastery Homer had of it and what versatility he displayed in combining an elaborate technique with a straightforward manner of telling a story."[33]

To the strict model of oral poetry created in each performance the scholar Gregory Nagy has recently proposed an important addendum suggesting that the texts of orally produced epics became less and less original over time. He describes "as *text-fixation* or *textualization* the process whereby each composition-in-performance becomes progressively less changeable in the course of diffusion — with the proviso that we understand *text* here in a metaphorical sense."[34] In Nagy's hypothetical process there would be a slow transition from the true oral poetry model of Parry and Lord in which *aoidoi* recreated the poems in each retelling towards an actual memorization of established oral texts which rhapsodes performed verbatim, a situation known to have existed by the late sixth century in the Panathenaic and other festivals and contests. Nagy elaborates: "I apply this notion of textual fixation to oral traditions with an emphasis on gradual patterns of fixity in an ongoing process of recomposition in diffusion, and without presupposing that the actual composition of the 'text' required the medium of writing."[35] So, where does Nagy find the monumental poet Homer in this process? It has already been shown that in the early historical period and, to some extent, throughout antiquity, virtually all epic poetry was attributed to Homer and that no factual information was actually known about the life of this person. The oral poetry tradition and Nagy's addendum indicate that the oral epics were not each the creation of an individual poet but were evolving stories which, over time, grew more and more restricted in wording. Putting all these observations together, Homer is lost as a single person but is instead found as a legendary forefather. "With Homeric poetry ... the notion of composer is drastically retrojected, from the standpoint of the performers themselves, to a protopoet whose poetry is reproduced by an unbroken succession of performers...."[36] Nagy does admit the possibility of a poet named Homer whose name got attached to the poems somewhere along the oral to textual fixation process but for whom all factual information has been lost. "The Panhellenic tradition of oral poetry appropriates the poet, potentially transforming even historical figures into generic ones who represent the traditional functions of their poetry. The wider the diffusion and the longer the chain of recomposition, the more remote the identity of the composer becomes. Extreme cases are Homer and Hesiod."[37]

One of the arguments which has been brought against oral composition of the Homeric poems is their length (*Iliad, ca.* 16,000 lines; *Odyssey, ca.* 12,000 lines), which greatly exceeds most of the oral poems collected in modern ethnographic research. A plausible counter-argument is that what is extant as the *Iliad* and the *Odyssey* is not the text of one oral performance which, as noted above, would have included selections from the poet's full repertoire. Instead of these usual "weightings" of certain incidents over others depending on the perceived interest of the audience, what has survived is the full repertoire of the poet without the biases caused by performance.[38] Thus, the extant Homeric text would represent an "unweighting" in which each segment of the poet's repertoire is represented more fully than in any single performance, although in the *Iliad* the Achilles theme has remained dominant. There is also a complementary explanation for the length of the poems, which is to assume that the extant Homeric text is actually a collection of independent oral poems by different composers over the years edited together at some later point. The ancient writer Aelian (170–235 C.E.) provided remarkable support for this idea when he wrote "that the ancients used to sing the poetic utterances of Homer in separate parts: for example, they spoke of 'The Battle of the Ships,' 'A Story of Dolon,' 'The Greatest Heroic Moments of Agamemnon,' 'The Catalogue of Ships,' 'The Story of Patroklos,' 'The Ransom,' 'The Funeral Games over Patroklos,' and 'The Breaking of the Oaths.' These were in place of the *Iliad*. In place of the other poem there were 'The Happenings in Pylos,' 'The Happenings in Sparta,' 'The Cave of Calypso,' 'The Story of the Raft,' 'The Stories Told to Alkinoos,' 'The Story of the Cyclops,' 'The Spirits of the Dead,' 'The Story of Circe,' 'The Bath,' 'The Killing of the Suitors,' 'The Happenings in the Countryside,' and 'The Happenings at Laertes' Place.'" Interestingly, the concept of oral composition tends to reconcile the old debate between the analysts and the unitarians; in an oral framework, neo-analysts can argue for separate epic poems being stitched together (by Homer?), while neo-unitarians can argue for one great poet (Homer?) who drew upon the repertoire of multiple stories to create the poems. "That [Homeric question] of single or multiple authorship has been obviously and elegantly solved by the theory of Parry: analytics and unitarians were both right, the authorship is multiple at the level of tradition, single at that of individual performance."[39]

However, doubts linger about both the supposition of completely oral composition of the Homeric text and about multiple authorship due to the high literary quality and unity of the poems. Artistic and literary genius is to be found in "the desire and ability to compose judiciously, to construct logically but not plainly or simplemindedly, to motivate rationally and yet with exquisite discrimination, to delineate complete characters of diverse complexity, to devise conflicts and to resolve them convincingly — in short, to reflect the world in all its characteristics ... and to explain it meaningfully."[40] The ethnographic studies have not, for the most part, found poetry of this complex organization and beauty of narrative, and some scholars, therefore, argue that because the *Iliad* especially is an epic poem of "dazzling intricacy" and shows "a design of extreme complexity and formal control" that its creation is beyond that of an oral performance and must have involved writing.[41] "It is the opinion of not a few of these skeptics that the artistry, cohesiveness, and sheer monumentality of the *Iliad* and the *Odyssey* rule out the role of oral poetics — and supposedly prove that such marvels of artistic achievement must have required the technology of writing."[42] However, other scholars who have studied living epic oral traditions argue that although the poems studied by Parry and Lord were of humbler types, there are in Africa oral poets whose compositions approach the complexities of quality and internal organization of themes that appear in the Homeric poems.[43] Even parallel scenes separated by great distance in the poems need only be proof of a talented oral poet and not that the poems were composed in writing. "The demonstration [of oral composition] is fraught with methodological snares and confronts an apparent paradox. On the one hand the formular aspects of Homer's style, contemplated by themselves, are so relentlessly systematized as to resemble a machine that runs by itself — or at least allows a minimal freedom to the poet at the controls.... On the other hand, it is equally clear that the Iliad and Odyssey alike were shaped by a poetic imagination of the first order, both on the monumental level and down into the details of scene after scene."[44]

Narrative unity is said to be proof of a single author. "The inner unity of the *Iliad* thus lies in the mirror opposition of the two heroes. Achilles and Hector represent the two aspects of war, aggressive and defensive, something suffered and something done. What is necessary and yet unjustifiable in fact justifies itself, at the end, as an object of poetic knowledge. What is incomprehensible in experience becomes patterned and even beautiful in the imitation of experience. And since poetic imitation, which claims to stand outside experience, is itself a human achievement, poetry claims for itself a place both outside and within the human world, as it recovers for man a tragic meaning in the experience of meaninglessness.

> Zeus sent this evil portion, so that later,
> For men to come, we should be themes for song [VI.357–58].[45]

The argument that the unity and style of the poems require a single creator can be looked at as evidence of just the opposite: "An examination of the epic style, moreover, with its stock epithets, its unerring tact in suiting the means to the effect, its elaborate and fixed dialect, and, above all, its rhythmical perfection, forces us to the conclusion that we have in these poems the last fruit of a long development. Hundreds of poets must have worked to bring the hexameter to its perfection; ever in touch with an intelligent audience, whose unconscious criticism gradually perfected the art and created the atmosphere necessary for the rise of great poets."[46] Nagy gives his "general opinion about the *Iliad* and the *Odyssey*: the structural unity of such epics results, I think, not so much from the creative genius of whomever achieved a fixed composition but from the lengthy evolution of myriad previous compositions, era to era, into a final composition."[47]

So, was Homer working within an oral tradition or outside it? "Even a superficial analysis of the Iliad is enough to show that it did not come to be by means of free improvisation. This ability, which in earlier times was the special merit of the poet and brought him great fame, became, with the creation of a work such as the Iliad, almost irrelevant. The Iliad is the result of long and careful planning. In it the single episodes are not placed one after the other in loose sequence, but are integrating elements in an organized structure."[48] Perhaps there is a compromise between oral and written explanations. "By applying the procedures of modern narrative theory to the Homeric epics, scholars have sought to reconcile the difference between oral and written compositional methods. They have paved the way to the insight that Homer, even within the parameters of his oral technique, followed universal norms of narration. In view of this, the very plausible supposition presents itself that the *Iliad* and the *Odyssey* are in fact the well-planned monumental compositions of a single hand."[49] In light of these problems in understanding the creation of the Homeric poems an important trend in recent literary scholarship has been not to worry about their probably oral composition and the questions about the person and time period of "Homer" but to study the content of the poems, just as is done with other written pieces of literature. "The Iliad and the Odyssey must be treated as independent entities, proper sources in themselves of verification for literary critical assertions. They may legitimately be viewed as poetic texts rather than exclusively as oral performances, for the former they patently are, the latter they can never again be (if indeed they ever were)."[50] However, studying them just as literature will not address the creation and dating issues of classicists.

Outside of the debate about one creator versus many, most scholars have accepted that the Homeric poems to some extent reflect the techniques of oral poetry.[51] "It is now clear, chiefly through the examination of their formular language, that they are substantially constructed from traditional elements: traditional vocabulary, traditional fixed phrases, traditional themes and episodes. Yet these were worked together and expanded so as to form the two great epics, each of which displays as a whole an undeniable unity of technique, purpose and effect."[52] The argument over single or multiple oral poets brings up perhaps the central question in studying the Homeric texts, a question that is implicit even if the oral composition of the Homeric poems is accepted—*how, when* and *why* were they eventually written down? It should be clearly noted that "it is unnecessary to assume that the poems were composed in writing; if both language and style point to oral composition, the simplest theory to explain the facts must be that they actually were orally composed."[53] "The question is no longer whether the poems are composite, but whether the composition is good and the pieces of which it is composed are well chosen, well shaped, and well arranged—mosaic can be a great art, and even the humble patchwork quilt may be beautiful."[54]

"Consequently, the transitional process itself *from orality to literality*, necessarily to be assumed, has for a considerable time now held the position as the chief cause of controversy between Oralists and Neo-Unitarians, to both of which groups it remains mandatory to come up with a convincing answer to the question: from a fluid oral tradition realized in small-scale performances to a fixed written text of monumental proportions— what happened?"[55] Scholars have surmised that there are three possible scenarios to explain how this orally composed text was written: a scribe present at an oral poet's performance; a scribe taking dictation from an oral poet; or a literate poet himself writing down his own "orally" created text.[56] It seems impossible for an ancient scribe to record an actual oral performance, as ethnographic experiments have shown. The existence of narrative inconsistencies and probable interpolations and bad transitions would seem to rule out a fully written creation whose author would, presumably, edit out obvious problems, and the studies of the oral poetry, as noted above, show that oral poets are normally uninterested in preservation of their work in writing. Thus, many scholars from Lord on have theorized a compromise conclusion that the Homeric text was *dictated* orally to a writing scribe; this supposition has important consequences for understanding the content of the poems and, most importantly, their date. And it explains the artistic unity which is so critical to the poems' importance: "It is on the narrative strategy and the character-drawing (both unsurpassed in later times) of the Homeric poems that the claim of their author (or authors) to a place among the great poets finally rests."[57]

The dictation theory is very seductive because it answers the questions of the unusual length of the poems and their high literary quality, yet preserves the oral explanations for its textual oddities. A dictating poet would have to slow down for the scribe, which would have permitted more careful choice of formulas and the luxuriating in descriptions and building up of episodes that a poet in a normal oral performance would not have the luxury of doing. Most importantly, the dictating poet would have the opportunity of unweighting, including many more aspects of a story than would be done for a particular audience. Parry and Lord experimented with dictation and received poor results, but other ethnographers have found that an oral poet can get used to the slower dictation process by considering it a type of performance. The quality of the interaction of the scribe and poet is extremely important, and in a good relationship mutual inspiration results in added stimulation to the poet and lengthening of the poem, as well as careful orthography and recording of wording and meter by the scribe.[58]

It has even been suggested by the scholar Minna Skafte Jensen that the dictation theory is supported by the fact that the texts of the *Iliad* and *Odyssey* as they exist today are each divided into twenty-four songs (*rhapsoidiai*) or books, a fact which has puzzled many scholars because the breaks do not seem to come at obvious change points in the text's narrative. A subscriber to this theory would "interpret the arrangement of each poem into twenty-four songs as resulting from the process of dictation. It would be the scribe's idea, not the singer's, that there are exactly twenty-four, each called after one of the letters of the Ionic [Greek] alphabet."[59] Traditional explanations have been that the books represent performance units, *i.e.* the amount one later rhapsode could memorize to give at a recital, or much later divisions by booksellers or editors,[60] but this theory suggests that, in fact, they represent the amount of material originally dictated in one day. Accepting the general dictation theory, some scholars have "declare[d] the *Iliad* and *Odyssey* 'post-oral': while they display obvious relics of an oral tradition they were composed with the aid of writing and hence are of a high literary sophistication."[61] One scholar has gone so far as to conclude that Homer's genius, as opposed to other epic poets, consisted primarily in his realization of the value of writing to preserve his works. "I venture to guess that Homer was the first great poet in Western literature because he was the first to have understood the infinite resources of the written word. In the zest of the Homeric narrative, in its superb architecture, flashes the delight of a mind which has discovered that it need not deliver its creation into the fragile trust of memory. The harsh gaiety of the *Iliad* and its constant equivocation between shortness of life and eternity of fame mirror the poet's new and proud sense of his own survival. In the beginning of poetry is the word, but very near the beginning of poetry on the scale of the *Iliad* is writing."[62]

When was the Homeric text written down? It is known for certain that there was a written text by the fourth century B.C.E., because it was studied by Aristotle and others, and references suggest written texts in the fifth century and perhaps earlier. When the Bronze Age Mycenaean linear B script of *ca.* 1600 to 1100 B.C.E. was deciphered by Michael Ventris in 1952 and turned out to be an early form of Greek, it seemed that perhaps the Homeric texts could have been written very early. Unfortunately, all known linear B texts are of an administrative nature, not literary, which almost certainly rules out the Bronze Age script for use in writing the Homeric text. It would seem likely that the writing down was a major event given the great length of the *Iliad* and *Odyssey*. Not only would the writing have been time consuming, but it would also have been expensive given the cost of a sufficient amount of papyrus, leather or parchment to contain the lengthy text. Some scholars have assumed that there was an initial writing in the eighth century B.C.E. in the Aeolic Greek dialect with a later transliteration into the Ionic dialect that is preserved in the extant Homeric text, although the few Aeolic survivals could reflect only the travels of the composing poet or his familiarity with earlier Aeolic epics.[63] "There is general agreement that the Homeric epics are examples of oral poetry and that they were composed and written down — essentially in the present form — in the second half of the eighth century B.C., the *Odyssey* somewhat later than the *Iliad*."[64] Thus, "Homer" was the poetic genius who stood at the end of a long oral epic poetry tradition and, drawing on its form and on the wealth of preexisting Trojan War stories, tapped the muse and composed two magnificent epics of a quality never before seen and which he dictated for permanent preservation. Nagy concludes that "[the artistic] intent must be assigned not simply to one poet but also to countless generations of previous poets steeped in the same traditions. In other words, I think that the artistry of the Homeric poems is traditional both in diction and in theme. For me the key is not so much the genius of Homer but the genius of the overall poetic tradition that culminated in our *Iliad* and *Odyssey*."[65]

There are two lines of reasoning not yet discussed which must be considered for answering the question of when the Homeric text was written down, an act which, presumably, fixed the previously oral text. These areas of inquiry involve archaeologically and historically dating the cultural details described in the poems and also the level of writing competency of the Greeks to be able to write such lengthy texts. As mentioned above, study of the poems by scholars has shown that they include descriptions of objects and cultural situations from widely varying time periods, which indicates that the composer was not describing one particular time period but a "heroic" past that does not correspond to any one historical era. Because the subject of the poems is the Trojan War, an event certainly in the misty past for the composer, it is likely that he included archaizing elements to indicate the antiquity of the events in the poems. The stability of the oral tradition made possible the inclusion even of Bronze Age details, the most obvious being that the weapons used by the combatants were made of bronze, not iron. However, there are much later objects and situations described in the poems which show that the composer was using more recent or even contemporary information to fill the gaps in his knowledge of the epic era he purports to be describing. Logically, the latest dateable item that scholars can find in the poems provides a *terminus post quem,* a point after which the poems must have been composed and written. Such studies have discovered elements in the poems dating from the Bronze Age, Iron Age, and Archaic periods which, chronologically, span the years from about the sixteenth to the sixth centuries B.C.E. This information disproves the argument that heroic poetry typically describes an era not too distant and, therefore, because the Homeric poems are set in the Bronze Age, they must have been composed and written soon thereafter, *i.e.* in the tenth or ninth centuries B.C.E.[66]

Despite the setting of the poems ostensibly in the Bronze Age (bronze weapons, use of chariots), the simple warrior society of the Homeric poems does not jibe with the complex socio-political realities of the Mycenaean world as revealed in the linear B tablets. The epic heroes move in a world of luxurious palaces and kings but, oddly, the Trojan king Priam's sons still have to do the harnessing of his chariot, the Phaeacian king must solicit gifts for Odysseus from his nobles, and reaping and plowing imagery are found throughout the poems.[67] Archaeology increasingly reveals that the centuries following the Greek Bronze Age (a period once referred to as the Dark Ages) were not the poor and backward era traditionally thought to have resulted from the collapse of the high culture of the Mycenaean palaces under waves of uncivilized invaders. It appears that by the eighth and seventh centuries there were great developments in the Greek world that seem closer to the Homeric picture than earlier periods do. It was in this period that narrative art tradition evolved, overseas explorations and trading began to develop along with colonization, and there was an explosion of religious activity and temple building. In the Archaic period of the seventh and sixth centuries these developments blossomed, the quintessentially Greek concept of the city-state or *polis* was formed, and the Phoenician alphabet was adopted for use in writing Greek.

The first Greek contact with Italy and Sicily is seen archaeologically at the site of Pithekoussai and is datable from pottery to ca. 750 B.C.E;— in the *Odyssey* the people of Ithaca are engaged in commerce with the Sicilians, and some of the locations in the poem seem to refer to this area of the Mediterranean. The founding of a colony as described in the *Odyssey,* Book 6 must be paralleling known colonization efforts in the Greek west known to date to the eighth century or later. "We may conclude that the interrelationships between the Aegean and the eastern Mediterranean, which archaeological and other evidence suggest flourished during the ninth and especially eighth centuries B.C., are paralleled by the data in the Homeric poems. What is more, in many respects the information from both sources corresponds in striking detail."[68] Some scholars have argued that the Homeric poems reflect the urban realities of the *polis,* the quintessentially Greek cultural unit of the city-state, which is known historically to date to the eighth century or later: "The city is a model for the construction of the *Iliad*, as well as its essential theme. It is not the individual *oikos* (household) but the collective polis that is the social nucleus around which life in the Homeric poems acquires meaning."[69] Many Archaic period elements seem explicit or implicit in the Homeric poems, and it has been argued that "information derived from archaeological sources, when compared with internal evidence in the *Iliad* and *Odyssey*, supports the notion that Homer's heroic age is modeled on the poet's own eighth- (or even seventh-) century world...."[70] Comparative evidence from the study of modern oral poetry makes it almost certain that the conclusion is correct, that an oral poet largely describes the world of his own day (whenever that is) even if he introduces scattered memories of earlier times.[71]

The study of the introduction of Greek alphabetic writing is very important for providing the earliest possible date for the writing down of the Homeric text. At least one scholar has recently argued that the very "invention" of the Greek alphabet occurred for the specific purpose of writing down epic poetry including the Homeric text![72] However, this theory has a serious flaw because "it implies that one of the very first things that the alphabet was used for was the writing of two huge poems, which would be materially very problematic, and which inside a culture that was predominately oral would be a very unlikely project."[73] Epigraphers have shown that the adoption of the Phoenician letter forms to create a Greek alphabet must have occurred ca. 800 B.C.E. because there exist primitive inscriptions on Greek pottery which are externally datable from artistic decoration to as early as ca. 775 B.C.E.[74] The Semitic letter forms on which the Greek alphabet is based were evolving independently, and it has been determined that the forms adopted by the Greeks could not have been borrowed before ca. 800 B.C.E.[75] However, it is a long step from a few words scratched on pottery to the writing of the massive Homeric poems, so it must have been in the seventh or more likely the sixth century that writing had developed to that level. It was only ca. 600 B.C.E. that standardization of writing from left to right occurred (previously writing could also go right to left, called "retrograde" or even back and forth, called "boustrophedon," meaning as an ox plows a field); this standardization probably shows the introduction of writing on soft materials with ink which would smear if written other than left to right (assuming right-handed writers). The use of writing for long inscriptions (*e.g.* laws) and for literary manuscripts is documented only after ca. 550 B.C.E.[76] So, the evidence from study of Greek writing would best support a sixth century date for the written Homer.

Much ink has been spilled over two references in the *Iliad* which imply knowledge of writing by the composer and his audience. This first is the story of Bellerophon (Book 6) who is forced to carry to the king of Lycia a diptych on which are written "baneful signs" telling the king to kill him. Does this prove knowledge of alphabetic writing, or could the signs have just been drawings of some sort? The second reference is to an imagined epigram for a fallen warrior (Book 7) but, again, proof of knowledge of writing is not positive. Of course, a poet setting his scene in an imagined past might purposely omit references to writing which he knew to be more modern. Classicists who study the evolution of Greek dialects and literary forms are divided about the origin of the dactylic hexameter meter. Traditionally, it has been thought that it evolved from Bronze Age Mycenaean forms and, therefore, was the obvious choice for all epic poetry of subsequent periods. However, others have argued that it derives from Aeolic syllable-counting metrics and was adopted into the Ionic dialect of the Homeric poems as evidenced by remnants of an Aeolic proto-hexameter, which would be an internal argument for an early date of composition.[77]

An exciting possibility for dating the Homeric text from outside the epics themselves exists in the field of Greek art, specifically the medium of vase painting, and the scholar Anthony Snodgrass has recently studied this possibility in great detail.[78] There was an evolution of interest in figural representations on Greek Iron Age pottery which by the Late Geometric (LG) period (ca. 750 B.C.E.) had become narrative enough to permit possible identification of scenes, some of which scholars have identified as Homeric in content. If true, the high accuracy of the vase painting dating sequence would provide a powerful and independent proof of a *terminus ante quem* (time before which) for Homer, and it happens that the eighth century is the traditional date for the great poet. But there are two major problems with the accurate identification of a Homeric scene in vase painting: is the content clearly Homeric? or is it just a generic heroic/mythological scene? And, if the image clearly concerns the Trojan War, is it specifically Homeric or possibly from another story in the Trojan cycle (for most of which the text is lacking)? It is worth considering some examples. The photograph below shows an Athenian bowl decorated in the Geometric style (*ca.* 700 B.C.E.) with a large ship with banks of rowers ready to put to sea; on the shore are a large-scale man and woman, and he holds her by the wrist. This striking scene has been widely identified as one of an abduction, and many scholars have seen in it the Trojan prince Paris abducting the Spartan queen Helen. The first problem for using this scene to date Homer is that this action occurs not in the Homeric *Iliad* but in the lost epic called the *Cypria*. Even more importantly, art historians who have studied the convention of gesture in Greek art have discovered that the clutching of the wrist has the meaning of greeting or farewell and not, as seen by modern eyes, that of abduction. Thus, this vase painting probably represents the departure of a warrior from his wife; the artist may have had a specific myth in mind, or it could be no more than a stock scene.

Another Athenian Geometric vase painting (see photograph on page 33) shows a person clinging to an overturned ship while other bodies float in the sea, and the scene in the *Odyssey* (Book 12) where Odysseus' ship is wrecked and all his men drowned immediately comes to mind as its subject. But, again, close analysis indicates this scene is not

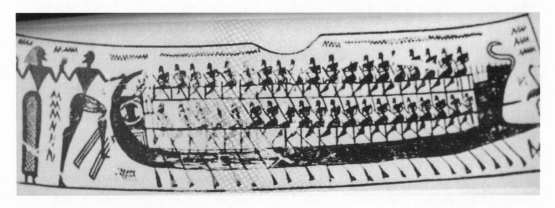

Ship scene with a man departing from a woman, frequently misidentified as Paris stealing Helen and preparing to take her to Troy; Late Geometric vase ca. 700 B.C.E. (The British Museum).

Shipwreck scene showing a man on the hull of an overturned ship; he is frequently misidentified as Odysseus; Late Geometric vase ca. 700 B.C.E. (Stoatl. Antikensammlungen und Glyptot, Munich).

Homeric either — the ship is not broken into pieces as described in the *Odyssey*; and careful observation of the figures in the sea shows each one touching another with gestures that indicate the men are alive and trying to rescue one another. A Cycladic relief amphora (*ca.* 700 B.C.E.) shows the famous Trojan Horse with Greek warriors exiting from the trap door in its belly and, oddly, seen in profile through windows in the horse's neck and side (see photograph on page 34). This is a clear example of early Greek art illustrating the Trojan Cycle — but not Homer, because this scene does not occur in the *Iliad* or *Odyssey* (probably having been told in the epic called the *Iliou Persis*). In the seventh century B.C.E., Greek artists invented a new vase painting technique which is called "black-figure" because images were painted solidly in black paint on a light background and a pointed tool was used to create the interior details of the images by scratching through the paint into the lighter clay below. The artists also began to paint labels and messages on the vases, and these captions are of great help in identifying scenes. About 650 B.C.E., there are several vase paintings (see photograph on page 35) of the blinding of Polyphemus, clearly a story told in the *Odyssey*. But, again, close analysis shows that the details of these scenes do not match the Homeric description; the scenes show an iron spit or spear as the weapon, but Homer describes a wooden stake; and the scenes show a sitting Polyphemus whereas Homer has him asleep on his back with head turned to the side. It is therefore

Embossed storage vessel neck with a scene showing the non–Homeric Trojan Horse; ca. 650 B.C.E. (Mykonos 70; photograph by E.M. Czako. German Archaeological Institute [DAI], Athens).

likely that there was a folklore tale which is the source of both the vase paintings and of Homer's story, and the poet has made some changes which are unique to his account; thus, it must be concluded that these vase paintings of Polyphemus were not influenced by the Homeric text as might initially be assumed.

A vase fragment of *ca.* 600 B.C.E. in the new black-figure technique and signed by an artist named Sophilos, shows men in bleachers watching a footrace and a chariot race (see photograph on page 36). This would appear to be a stock scene, except that Sophilos has written a caption which says "The Games for Patroclus." Some scholars had previously hypothesized that Patroclus was a character invented by Homer and, if so, this scene has to be inspired by the Homeric text (*Iliad* 23); but it must be wondered whether, in fact, other Trojan War epics could also have included this scene. One of the most famous of all Archaic Greek pots is the krater (wine-mixing bowl) called the François Vase, a name reflecting its discoverer (see photograph on page 36). Dated *ca.* 575 B.C.E., this amazing vessel is covered with scenes from Greek mythology, including no less than four from the Trojan War stories, and it also includes a plethora of labels which clearly identify the action. Surprisingly, only one of the Trojan scenes has subject matter relating to the Homeric text and, again, it is a chariot race from the games for Patroclus that is represented. A close analysis shows this scene does not derive from Homer — the artist

Black-figure scene of a non–Homeric blinding of Polyphemus; Odysseus offers a cup of wine while the sitting Cyclops holds the legs of a man he has eaten; 560 B.C.E. (Cliché Bibliothèque nationale de France, Paris).

has shown Odysseus as the winner and Automedon as second, neither of whom even participated in the Homeric race; Diomedes, whom Homer describes as the winner, is shown coming in third on the vase. These and similar examples point to the remarkable conclusion that although there are a few possible examples, it is not until the late sixth century and later that scenes which are clearly Homeric appear in Greek vase painting, a time when it is known that the Homeric text was already written down and in circulation.[79] Snodgrass' conclusion from his detailed study is "that the innumerable surviving portrayals of legendary scenes in the art of early Greece, thousands of which undoubtedly relate to the saga of the Trojan War and its aftermath, and some hundreds apparently to the very action of the *Iliad* and the *Odyssey*, were in fact seldom if ever inspired

Top: Black-figure potsherd by the printer Sophilos showing a non–Homeric horse race; ca. 575 B.C.E. (National Archaeological Museum, Athens). *Bottom:* The "François Vase" with Trojan War related scenes, including a non–Homeric horse race in the second register from the top; ca 570 B.C.E. (Museum of Archaeology, Florence).

by the Homeric poems."[80] The implication for dating the creation of the Homeric poems is clear — there is no unquestionable work of art dating before the late sixth century! This conclusion provides a stunning confirmation of the radical downdating for the creation of the Homeric text being proposed by some literary researchers studying the text itself.

This review of dating for the Homeric text from internal cultural details and external study of the transmission of the alphabet to Greece indicates that it is most likely that the *Iliad* and the *Odyssey* derive from oral poetry going back perhaps to the eighth century, Homer's traditional date, but that they were not written down and, thus, fixed until the sixth century or later, maybe even after *ca.* 550 B.C.E. "This school of thought holds that Homer was the contemporary, not the model, of the early lyric poets; that he worked in a deliberately archaizing manner which, for long passages on end, disguises this fact; that the gestures of homage to Homer in seventh-century poetry are illusory; and that Homer's own reflections of seventh-century Greece are neither few nor trivial, but widespread and pervasive."[81] Remember, however, that unless Homer himself wrote down the poems or, in fact, dictated them to a scribe their creation could have been much earlier than the actual writing down, if a robust oral tradition capable of diachronic transmission of such lengthy works is assumed. But such an assumption is a shaky one given the literary complexity of the poems, or else it implies a long period of great fluidity given oral poetry traditions which would beg the question of who, then, composed the final version which is extant today.

Athens has long been recognized as having played an important role in establishing an early text of the *Iliad*, and attempts have even been made to reconstruct it by removing lines thought to have been added later.[82] There is sketchy, and much debated, evidence that the early Homeric text was in some way manipulated by the Peisistratid tyrants of Athens who ruled that city from 560 to 510 B.C.E. In Archaic Greece the government of many cities was taken

Red-figure cup showing an actual Homeric scene of King Priam's embassy to Achilles to recover the body of his slain son Hector, shown sprawled under the hero's bed; 490 B.C.E. (Kunsthistorisches Museum, Vienna).

over by strong men outside the usual political process, and these rulers who in many cases were quite popular were termed "tyrants" without the later pejorative meaning that still pertains to the English word today. In many cases the tyrants drew their support from the non-aristocratic class, which led them to sponsor projects of interest to the general populace, such as building temples, water systems and other public works. Many tyrants also sought to legitimize their power by supporting the arts, and in Athens Peisistratus' son Hipparchus was remembered as a "culture-vulture" who erected stones (herms) around the Athenian countryside inscribed with positive aphorisms in elegiac hexameter for the moral improvement of the citizenry and who brought famous poets (*e.g.* Simonides and Anakreon) to the city. And it seems that Hipparchus may have had some involvement with the Homeric text!

In the fourth century B.C.E. dialogue called *Hipparchus* ascribed to the philosopher Plato (*ca.* 429–347 B.C.E.) there is the statement that the tyrant's son "first brought the poems of Homer to this land [Athens], and compelled the rhapsodes at the [Festival of the] Panathenaia to perform them according to the cues in due order, as they still do to this day." Diogenes Laertius (third century C.E.) made a similar statement about an early law requiring a sequence for the recitation of the Homeric poems, but he incorrectly ascribed it to Solon, a shadowy early Athenian lawgiver: "he proposed that Homer's poems should be recited from a cue, so that where the first stopped, from there the next should start." Cicero, the great Roman orator, stated (*de Oratore* iii.137) that Peisistratus was the first to arrange the Homeric poems as they were then known. Plutarch, writing ca. 100 C.E., wrote that the Spartan lawgiver Lycurgus collected the full Homeric epics in Ionia and brought them back to mainland Greece and that, later, the Athenians Solon and Peisistratus both interpolated lines favorable to Athens. Scholars have taken these clearly garbled and typically late references in various ways, but most have admitted that as a whole they indicate that the Peisistratids were involved in some way with the Homeric text. They would certainly have had the financial resources for the task.

One conclusion is that the tyrants in some way created a "Panathenaic rule" which organized the order of the recitation of the poems at the quadrennial all–Athenian festival called the Panathenaia which included both athletic and artistic (musical and rhapsodic) competitions. This implies that the various parts of the poems as previously recited could be sung in any order, a notion supporting the oral theorists who believe the various Trojan War stories were originally independent, some of which were edited together into the Homeric poems. It also implies something very important for the present search for Homer—the existence or creation of a written text establishing the "correct" order of the poems, *i.e.* an *Iliad* and *Odyssey* much as they are known today. Scholars have dubbed this hypothetical version the "Panathenaic text" and this editing of it the "Peisistratid recension." "The evolution of rhapsodic performance [from being able to perform any epic scene to those specific to the *Iliad* and *Odyssey*] is more or less consistent with the mythological repertoire of Attic vase painting in the sixth century. In the middle and third quarter of the century, there was a burst of interest in epic subjects, but it focussed on a small number of favorite episodes, the kind that might have formed the subject for a single recitation.... The *Iliad* and *Odyssey* did not yet have the imprimatur of geniune Homer, so they got no special treatment in the choice of subject, either by rhapsodes or painters, but neither were they entirely neglected. Only from the 520's, then, in the wake of Hipparchos' activity, did many new Iliadic subjects—and a few from the *Odyssey*—enter the painters' repertoire."[83]

If the accusation that the Peisistratids tinkered with the Homeric text is true, the writing down of the "Panathenaic text" would have provided an obvious opportunity to do so and the vase painting evidence provides striking confirmation. The pseudo–Herodotean *Life* of Homer has the poet feel sorry that he celebrated Argos so much in the *Iliad* and has him add a reference to Athens to make up for it; this sounds like a garbled memory of the Peisistratid interpolation alleged by other writers. Jensen argues that the Panathenaic rule is "the missing link" between oral poetry and the written text because it supplies the special circumstances for writing oral poetry that have been discussed previously: "an initiative from somebody who is interested in the tradition and possesses the necessary means and authority, but is not himself a full 'member' of the tradition."[84]

If a "Panathenaic text" sponsored by the Peisistratids is accepted, the central question is what source did they use for it. Was it copied from some earlier text or dictated orally by a rhapsode? There is no evidence for the former, and if the latter is true it raises a very big question—was this the *first* writing down of the Homeric text? Most scholars have argued that the earliest written version of the Homeric poems occurred in the eighth century B.C.E., some two hundred years before the Peisistratids, but as discussed above, the date when Greek alphabetic writing would have permitted such a massive undertaking and the vase painting evidence would seem to preclude this traditional date for a Homeric dictation. The sixth century tyrant's regime in Athens occurred at about the right time frame in the evolution of Greek writing, when a long text might have been written down. The problem of the lack of internal dating evidence after the seventh century is easily explained by assuming the Homeric poems had reached a stability or fixation in their oral format by the seventh century and for a century were just passed down with few new additions, a process defined by Nagy. His textual fixation model, which has the text becoming slowly more set over time, shows how the writing down of the Homeric poems can be divorced from the discussion of their creation, and the Peisistratid period seems the most likely time for a first written version. If this were their first writing down, it would explain the Ionic dialect and obviate the need to hypothesize the transliteration of an initially Aeolic text, but textual fixation would explain the remnant of Aeolic dialect. "Lord's theory that the poems are oral dictated texts is confirmed, and it is underlined that the initiative for recording oral epic poetry in writing normally comes from outside the tradition; the story of a recension undertaken by Pisistratus gives just such an out-side initiative."[85]

This remarkable new theory proposed by Dr. Jensen also explains that the persistent ancient accusations that Peisistratus in some way added pro–Athenian details to the Homeric text show two things: he had a written text in hand; and, more importantly, there was no other written text (or the additions solely in his own Athenian text would have carried no weight). In fact, the Athenians on at least two historical occasions are reported by Herodotus to have turned to the *Iliad* for political support: in 480 B.C.E. to argue that Athenians should lead the fight against the Persians because they were cited by Homer as good leaders in the Trojan War; and in the fourth century to "prove" ownership of Mytilene, a city near Troy, and of the island Salamis near Athens. "From Herodotus onwards Greeks seem to have found it completely natural that it was Athens who made reference to Homer; thus the very existence of this kind of story seems to be based on a common knowledge that the authoritative text of Homer was Athenian."[86] Jensen even argues that the name of the rhapsode hired by Peisistratus to do the dictation is known and, thus, the man who created the final version of the Homeric poems! *Scholia* (learned annotations) on Pindar's Nemean Ode refer to a Chian Homerid named Cynaethus who added verses into Homer's poetry, was the real author of the *Hymn to Apollo* attributed to Homer, and was the first rhapsode to recite the Homeric poems in Syracuse, a feat done in the sixty-ninth Olympiad (504–500 B.C.E.). "If the poems are oral dictated texts, the initiative of Peisistratus and/or Hipparchus will have consisted in their engaging the most famous Homerid of their day to dictate the Panathenaic text — here he is!"[87]

The theory that the creation of the *Iliad* and *Odyssey* through the first writing of their texts occurred in the Athens of the Peisistratids has received further support recently from a perceptive reanalysis of the *Odyssey* against the background of the growth of Athenian ritual and myth by the scholar Erwin F. Cook.[88] He argues that the performance tradition crystallized into the text of the *Odyssey* at the same time that the Athenian state was being formed and, along with that development, the establishment of the city myths which each Greek held as symbolic of its origins. For Athens, Cook explains that the city's origin was understood as an interplay between the concepts of *bie* (violent force) and *metis* (cunning intelligence) which are analogous to the terms "nature" and "culture" as used in anthropology. In the creation myth of Athens the goddess Athena and the god Poseidon struggled for control and identity of the city, and Athena was declared victorious when her gift of a domesticated olive tree was deemed superior to Poseidon's gift of a salt-spring. After her victory, Poseidon erupted in anger but eventually came to an accommodation with Athena and her Athenians. Their contest was the subject of the western pediment sculpture on the famous classical temple of Athena called the Parthenon (dedicated to Athena *Parthenos* or "virgin"). The original cult site on the Athenian Acropolis, however, was not on the site of the later Parthenon but north of it either in a peculiar building called the Erechtheion (after the mythological first king of Athens, named Erechthius) or in the adjacent remains of the old temple of Athena Polias; it was said that the mark of Poseidon's trident and the living olive tree of Athena remained visible somewhere in this vicinity. Cook interpreted the myth in terms of a victory of *metis* over *bie* followed by a fusion of the two out of which Athens was created. "The victorious goddess, champion of culture, redefines that culture through her victory over the elemental forces of nature, championed by the defeated god. Through Athena's accommodation with Poseidon, culture now includes nature and is thus reinvented in Athens."[89]

It has long been known that the two primary ritual objects housed either in the Erechtheion of the old Athena temple, in addition to an ancient wooden statue of Athena, were a lamp and an olive tree, both important in the foundation myth. Cook has shown that these two objects are also significant in the *Odyssey, e.g.* Odysseus' use of an olive-tree staff, the olive-tree bedpost in his palace, and the golden lamp used by Athena to guide Odysseus and Telemachus as they plan the slaughter of the suitors. "As Cook argues, the innermost sanctum of Athena at Athens can be viewed as the ritual and mythological impetus for the poetics of the epic that is the *Odyssey*," and the annual sacred festival of Athens, the Panathenaia, replays the creation of civil order in which the former rule is dissolved by violence and then renewed in the same way that Odysseus slew the usurping suitors in his house and restored his proper kingship.[90] Applying Nagy's theory of textual fixation over time with its three-stage transition from performance-creative *aoidai* to memorizing rhapsodes to writing, Cook concludes that in Athens the second stage was reached *ca.* 675–650 B.C.E. and became a written text by 550. B.C.E. "It is my contention that the *Odyssey* and Athenian ritual grew up together and continued to write each other — often in ways no longer recoverable — until the text of our poem achieved canonical status."[91] He argued that for an ancient listener the epic poem would be understood as a parallel to their city's rituals: "For Athenian audiences of Homeric per-

Vase painting detail showing a man with a lyre, perhaps an *aoidos*; ca 700 B.C.E. (National Archaeological Museum, Athens).

Red-figure vase painting of a rhapsode; ca. 460 B.C.E. (© The British Museum).

formance the *Odyssey* was a ritual mimesis of their most important civic cults."[92]

How exciting it is that there is now enough scholarly evidence to put together all the clues and "solve" the puzzle of the first stage in the 2,500-year search for Homer—who created the Homeric poems, how and when? When the newest developments in Homeric research, such as low dates for content in the poems, increasing evidence of Peisistratid involvement along with newly recognized Athenian content of the poems, and the striking new analysis of figural vase painting are incorporated into the 20th-century discoveries about oral poetry the resulting picture of the creation of the Homeric text becomes clear.[93] The new proposal is for an evolutionary oral theory which, as with the general oral theory, assumes that oral poetry began in the Bronze Age and that its various stories and cycles continued into the Iron Age repertoire of rhapsodes. Among the multitude of stories were many about the Trojan War, embellishing a core historical event which may have been caused by Mycenaean exploration and expansionism up the Hellespont near Troy towards the Black Sea. Centuries of separate stories about the Trojan War were invented, repeated, and enhanced by oral poets from the very end of the Bronze Age (*ca.* 1050 B.C.E.) down to the late sixth century alongside the creation and repetition of many other epic stories on other topics. This continuous tradition preserved some details from the Bronze Age and incorporated later ones as the poets updated the stories.

At first the texts of these stories were very fluid, just as if ten people today were asked to tell the story of Little Red Riding Hood they likely could do so and get the general narrative gist but would not use the same words or sentences in their telling. Over time, however, the Trojan War stories as presented by certain poets and their rhapsodic descendants came to be the preferred versions, and over time these versions became more and more fixed. The listeners came to have expectations of certain story lines and wording, and the *aoidoi* (singers)[94] wanted to tell the stories in the most popular forms. Perhaps, by the eighth or seventh centuries, the texts of many of these epic stories had become secure enough that the *aoidoi* added or subtracted less and less material as they performed them, explaining why many features of the poems seem to date to this period. Both the oral poetry tradition and the desire of *aoidoi* to create a heroic feel for the poems caused a tendency to archaize the stories by preserving snatches of earlier material culture and language. Over time, some of the Trojan War stories were joined together and became even more concretized by the natural evolution of storytelling. Of course, the *aoidoi* could still select from quite a large menu of stories and variants, depending on the wishes of the audience or their own desire to tell one that might impress or honor their specific host. For example, someone might say "Sing us tales of Achilles," and the *aiodos* might decide to start with the wedding of Peleus and Thetis, his parents, and continue with his birth and dipping in the River Styx, his arming with immortal armor made by Hephaistos for his father, his argument with Agamemnon at Troy, his glorious fight against Hector, and his tragic death and funeral there.

By the sixth century the Greeks began to wonder who had "created" the epic cycles which were being performed at many cities, and they hypothesized a blind poet "Homer" to whom they could be ascribed; the Chian poets claimed descent from him. By the late sixth century, the epic poems that were the most panhellenic had been polished by much repetition of peripathetic rhapsodes, unlike the local stories. The important final step in this process was the "Peisistratid dictation."[95] The Athenian tyrant realized that the developing technology of writing could be used to set down the oral Homeric poems in such a way that his personal reputation and that of his city would be enhanced as *owners* of the text, especially since they would have used their financial resources to purchase the significant amount of papyrus which would have been needed for the project. Their selection of these two specific poems was due to the fact that the prominence of the goddess Athena in them would, by extension, enhance the glory of their city Athens. The Peisistratids must have considered the large number of possible epic stories but, unfortunately, Athens had not been important in the era described by the epic poems. So, the tyrants decided on stories in which their patron goddess Athena played a large role (the fighting at Troy where she was patroness of the Greeks and the return home of Odysseus, the goddess' favorite); the Peisistratids probably also suggested including the Catalog of Ships so that they could slip in an Athenian contingent. They hired the best rhapsode they could find, perhaps from Chios, to dictate the Homeric poems to a scribe. The process of dictation permitted the rhapsode to build unusually lengthy and stylistically organized creations by the careful weaving together of several poems from the Trojan War cycles and fleshing out (unweighting) episodes to the extent not done in actual performances, but the narrative mistakes which he made were not edited out and remain in the text. The Peisistratids proclaimed the result to be the "official" Homeric text and required that the teams of rhapsodes who performed it at the Panathenaia follow its order, a rule surviving in the historical accounts.

By the fourth century this written version and the copies made from it began to be understood as separate works from the other epic poem cycles that were still around to a greater or lesser degree. With time it was accepted that the legendary forefather of all epic poetry called Homer had, in fact, authored these poems especially, and perhaps a few other lesser ones as well. Slowly, the poems were differentiated as the *Iliad* and *Odyssey* and achieved primacy throughout Greek culture. Written copies of this text began to circulate for the use of rhapsodes and so that other cities could have their own texts, but the one authoritative "original" remained in Athens. Sponsorship of the two poems by Athens, the most powerful state militarily and culturally during the fifth century, assured their survival while the oral creations of other poets waned in popularity in an age of written texts, a discrepancy which is clear even by the fourth century. Of course, as derivative copies of the Peisistratid original were made, minor errors were added and "helpful" scribes even padded the text somewhat in a few places, thus accounting for the variants known from papyri fragments. But it was essentially the Peisistratid text that came to the Hellenistic scholars at the Museum in Alexandria who, as will be seen, created from it a "Vulgate" which is, essentially, the text which has survived to modern times.

A general review of how understanding of Homer and the creation of his poems has changed through centuries of scholarship is presented in the chart on page 44. Row A on the chart illustrates the traditional understanding of mainstream readers and scholars from antiquity to the nineteenth century and can be labeled "Homer, the Lone Ranger." It was hypothesized that perhaps two to four hundred years after whatever was the reality of the Trojan War, a single man named Homer composed two monumental epic poems drawing on memories passed down from the Bronze Age. His unparalleled works were accurately passed down by memory until writing permitted their permanent recording, perhaps in the eighth century, and this text was preserved with few variations through antiquity and to modern times. This traditional theory, of course, has the advantage of postulating a real person "Homer" as most of the ancients assumed, but it also requires belief in the remarkable memories of generations of rhapsodes to pass on with very few errors lengthy and elaborate poems for a very long time. It also fails to incorporate what are now known to be the principles of oral poetry which explain so many aspects of the poems, and it has essentially been disproved by the mounting evidence for a later date of composition.

Row B on the chart shows what has been the mainstream theory during the twentieth century, termed here "Homer, Prince of Poets." It incorporates the new understanding of oral poetry technique and form, as well as more accurate dating of items mentioned in the Homeric text. This theory supposes that oral poetry developed far back in the Greek past, even well into the Mycenaean Bronze Age. When a triggering event took place, in this case early Greek trading and expansionism towards the Black Sea which resulted in a war over the strategic Hellespontine city of Ilion/Troy (modern Hissarlik), poets worked the deeds of brave warriors into their existing oral epic presentations and created new ones about them. Some of these details were retained in the oral tradition which survived the end of the Bronze Age, and stories of the Trojan War were included in the cycles of oral epics that developed during the early centuries of the Iron Age (eleventh to ninth B.C.E.). There were tales of specific heroes, such as Agamemnon, Ajax, and Diomedes, and of events, such as the anger of Achilles, the funeral games for Patroclus, the Trojan Horse, the return home of various heroes, Telemachus' voyage, and the slaughter of the suitors by Odysseus. In the eighth century, a genius poet probably named Homer reworked and built on the various Trojan War stories long in use by his predecessors and created two spectacular poems which, although clearly based on oral poetry forms, were so splendid as to almost rise above the oral tradition. It has been suggested that in this process the poet was knowledgeable of other epic poetry, made reference to it and built on it, and may even have incorporated direct quotes.[96]

HOMERIC TEXT CREATION THEORIES

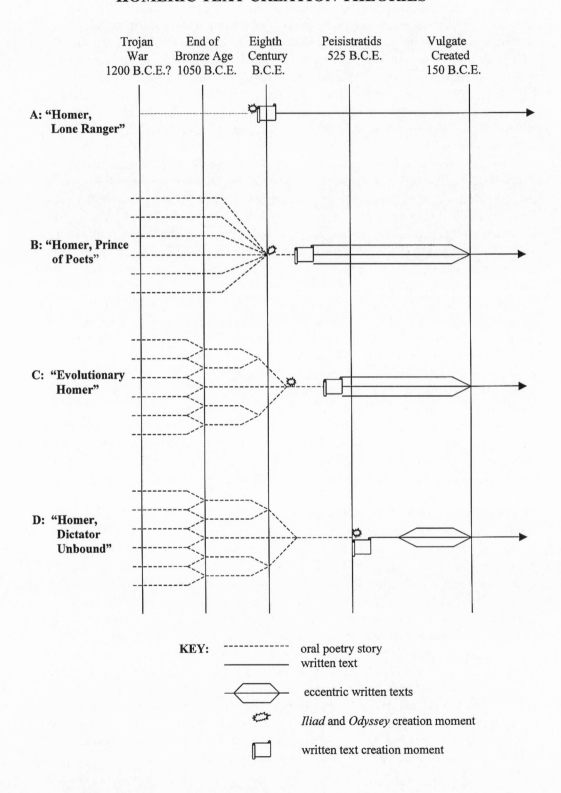

The assumption shown in Row B is that at some point (downdated from the traditional theory) several slightly differing versions of Homer's poems were written down in various locations, which accounts for the fact that fragments of ancient manuscripts have been found with slightly variant wording to our canonical Homeric text (termed by scholars "eccentric texts"). Perhaps the creation of the poems by Homer either inspired the actual importation of an alphabet for the specific purpose of recording the poems or made use of a writing system just getting started. Some advocates of this idea have argued that Homer himself dictated the poems, while others have suggested that he may have learned to write himself in order to record his masterpieces, which are too long and intricate to be taken down in performance. The most important feature of the version of this theory shown in Row B is that it retains the monumental creator but situates him within and at the end of an oral poetry tradition, which permits the nature of oral poetry to explain the oddities in the poems but has him rising above its restrictions and creating monumental works beyond it. The theory's main shortcoming is the eighth-century writing date which requires belief that such a long and expensive project as writing down the Homeric poems could have been undertaken at such an early stage of Greek writing. The theory also fails to give a reason for such an undertaking, which is outside observed norms of oral poets. It does not explain why only certain Trojan tales and specific variants were selected by Homer from the plethora evidently available at that time. It also fails to explain the lack of specifically Homeric art representations among the many showing Trojan War scenes and why the Greeks knew no facts about the person Homer.

Row C on the chart shows Nagy's variant oral composition theory, termed here "Evolutionary Homer," in which the independent Trojan War stories as hypothesized in the "Homer, Prince of Poets" theory became increasingly fixed in form over time in a naturally evolving selection process and were, essentially, fossilized in the oral tradition at the time of writing. It does have an implicit shortcoming of not giving a specific reason for the writing down of the poems or why they appear biased towards Athenian interests, although its downdating of the transcription is more compatible with newer understandings of the development of the Greek alphabet. The "Evolutionary Homer" theory adds to the supporting evidence for the previous oral theory an explanation of why various themes within the Homeric texts appear to be self-contained units. However, it has the emotional shortcoming of losing the person "Homer," a loss perhaps remediated by understanding Homer in a broader, mythic sense than as one man who personally created the poems. "For the ancient Greeks ... Homer was not just the creator of epic par excellence: he was also the culture hero of epic itself. Greek institutions tend to be traditionally retrojected, by the Greeks themselves, each to a proto creator, a culture hero who is credited with the sum total of a given cultural institution. It was a common practice to attribute any major achievement of society, even if this achievement may have been realized only through a lengthy period of social evolution, to the episodic and personal accomplishment of a culture hero who is pictured as having made his monumental contribution in an earlier era of the given society."[97] The "Evolutionary Homer" theory explains why there was no valid biographical information known about the poet and also the multiplicity of art representations of non–Homeric Trojan War scenes.

The final theory, shown in Row D and labeled for convenience "Homer, Dictator Unbound" is based on Jensen's persuasive arguments to explain the creation of the

Homeric text as the result of an oral process that culminated in a monumental act of dictation performed for the Athenian Peisistratid tyrants at the end of the sixth century B.C.E. This theory incorporates all the preexisting explanations for the oddities in the Homeric text as resulting from a long oral development and is compatible with Nagy's textual fixation hypothesis which increases our understanding of the story selections. Its premise of a premier, dictating poet having the time to "unweight" or elaborate on details of objects, characters and situations would seem to put the final touch on explaining the peculiarities of the text. The "Homer, Dictator Unbound" theory, which lowers the writing date further than previous theories, is also supported by Snodgrass' important rejection of earlier art representations as specifically Homeric and explains the texts' important connection (both in content and historically) to Athens. It also jibes with Cook's juxtaposition of the epics' creation with the late-sixth-century Athenian growth in civic awareness. Homer, as in the previous theory, becomes the mythical father of poetry, representing the Greek understanding that these epic poems in some special way derived from their own ancient past and the modern understanding of their evolutionary passage through a long oral and an abrupt written process.

Perhaps we should think in terms of several "Homers" as we search for answers to the Homeric question.[98] Clearly, the origins of the epics lie in oral poetry, but what we have is a formalized and selective piece somewhat removed from the raw aspects of oral composition. Close analysis of the text reveals inconsistencies of cultural descriptions and poetic formatting that demonstrates the multivariate nature of the epics, which include blurred memories, political undercurrents, and echoes of competing stories. But the final "Homer" that we have is a unified, carefully worked text far removed from spontaneous oral poetry and largely reworked to conceal its complex origins, and this unification requires the action of a person or persons and, more importantly, the overt intention to set down the texts into two books, each with twenty-four chapters (or songs). In a broad sense, each one of these stages and all of them together can be considered the "Homer" that we seek.

3

THE HOMERIC TEXT IN
CLASSICAL ANTIQUITY

Whether the work of a monumental creator, the creation of a talented composer hired by the Peisistratids, or the result of normal evolution of oral epic poetry, it is known that by the fifth century B.C.E. there were written versions of the Homeric text throughout the Greek world, although the poems were still being recited orally as well. Although writers of the classical Greek and Roman eras knew no reliable facts about the poet Homer whose name was attached to many oral epics of the past, they were fascinated especially by the two great Homeric poems, studying their odd vocabulary, commenting on obscure details, and writing at length about Homer's treatment of various topics. "No other poet, no other literary figure in all history, for that matter, occupied a place in the life of his people such as Homer's. He was their pre-eminent symbol of nationhood, the unimpeachable authority on their earliest history, and a decisive figure in the creation of their pantheon, as well as their most beloved and most widely quoted poet."[1]

The impact of the Homeric texts from the fifth century B.C.E. to the fifth century C.E. was tremendous but, interestingly, the text itself was so fixed that there were few variations. The legend of Homer as an almost divine poet grew steadily through antiquity, and the adoption of his text for educating young boys assured its equation with learning and literature. On a broken relief carving of the second century B.C.E. is illustrated the allegorical scene of Homer's "apotheosis" which means "becoming a god" (see photograph on page 48). He sits on a throne as two deities crown him while mortals bring sacrifices to an altar in front of him. Homer the poet as revealed in the Homeric texts evolved into a personification of Greek culture itself, and Plato's well-known comment that he was "the teacher of all Hellas" (*i.e.* of all Greeks) put this pervasive influence into words. In the fourth century B.C.E., the Greek orator Aeschines was making a speech before the jury in an Athenian court and at one point turned to the clerk of the court and asked him to recite certain Homeric passages extemporaneously — and he was able to do it! The poet Theocritus (*ca.* 300–250 B.C.E.) said that it was useless to try to rival Homer. Scholars and the reading public enjoyed debating whether the *Iliad* and the *Odyssey* had been written by the same person. The Roman emperor Nero emulated a Homeric bard as he sang to harp music after dinner (to the dismay of conservative

Detail from a relief sculpture called "The Apotheosis of Homer" in which the seated poet is crowned by Oikumene (the civilized world) and Chronos (Time); his chair is flanked by personifications of the Iliad (with a sword) and the Odyssey (with a steering oar); ca 125 B.C.E. (© The British Museum).

Romans), and an ugly rumor circulated after the great fire in Rome in 64 C.E. that Nero had taken to the outdoor stage of his mansion during the conflagration and recited his own poem on the fall of Troy with the city of Rome in flames as his backdrop! The Homeric poems have been called the Bible of the Greeks, not because they prescribed a religious stance, but because they permeated Greek culture, dealt with the interaction of humans and deity, and were thought to embody moral lessons for the conduct of life.

As noted in chapter 1, by the late sixth century references to Homer began to appear in written sources, such as those of the poets and philosophers Xenophanes, Heraclitus, Stesichorus, and Simonides, fragments of which survive today. Along with indirect references to Homeric poetry "they create a strong impression that for the Greeks of the period down to about 450 B.C. Homer was a real person who had ... composed a large number of narrative poems of the highest quality which were still being recited by professional rhapsodes...."[2] However, even these early commentators were beginning to question the factuality of everything that Homer mentioned; in a surviving fragment, the Athenian lawgiver Solon (sixth century B.C.E.) is quoted as remarking that "poets lie a great deal." Xenophanes (ca. 500 B.C.E.) complained about Homer's anthropomorphizing of the gods, making them as fallible as humans, and Heraclitus (ca. 500 B.C.E.) attacked the philosophical authority of Homer and other poets. Early writers considered Homer and other poets to have had extraordinary knowledge about the world and about human behavior, but Heraclitus said that Homer and the poet Archilochus deserved to be expelled from poetic contests and flogged for misleading people. It is reported that Theagenes of Rhegium (ca. 500 B.C.E.) was the first person to write about Homer's life and poetry, and it seems that he was already applying allegory to Homer's narrative, a defense of the Homeric content that would have a long life, as will be seen.

The lyric poet Pindar (ca. 518–438 B.C.E.), who wrote odes in honor of athletic and musical victors in the Olympic and other panhellenic games, referred to the dilemma of separating fact from fiction in epic poetry and accused Homer of expanding of the truth: "I think that the story of Odysseus was exaggerated beyond what he experienced, because of the sweet words of Homer: For there is an impressive dignity about his fictions and winged craft, and poetic skill deceives, leading astray with fables: The generality of men has a blind heart."[3] However, he believed in a reciprocity between the heroes of the past and the victors being honored in the present which paralleled a reciprocity between Homer as the idealized poet of the past and himself as the poet of the present.[4] In his *Pythian* ode 4 he wrote:

> Of all the words of Homer, understand and apply the saying that I now tell you: the best messenger, he said, wins as a prize the greatest honor for everything. And the Muse too becomes greater by way of the correct message.

In this rather confusingly worded passage Pindar is saying that just as the Muse of poetry gives honor, so she receives it; and just as a poet either of the past or present wins a prize or honor for his poetry, so does the subject of the poem who has done a glorious deed win honor conferred by the continuum of poets back to the time of heroes. It has been noticed that Pindar explicitly omits references to the Homeric poems in his odes, which seems odd when he substitutes lesser-known myths when Homeric ones would have been more pertinent. The answer seems to be that Pindar's goal was to create a monument of praise to his patrons, and if he had cited Homeric stories everyone would have recognized the reference due to the ubiquitous knowledge of the Homeric poems and this would have overshadowed Pindar's aim of singular laud for one individual.[5]

The historians Herodotus (*ca.* 480–425 B.C.E.) and Thucydides (*ca.* 460–400 B.C.E.) mentioned Homer, the former trying to assign him a date and discounting the story of Helen because the Trojans would surely have returned her rather than be defeated; and the latter questioning the historical nature of the Trojan War itself while believing Homer was a useful source to study early Greek society.[6] "Thucydides' respect for Homer as a source is striking, although there is a strong note of disparagement in the historian's reconstruction of the famous Athenian Pericles' funeral speech, where he says that Athens does not need a Homer to sing her praises, nor any poet whose verses will give a momentary pleasure, only to be contradicted by the truth of history."[7] This statement, by the way, could be taken to imply that Thucydides knew that Athens had had a special hand in sponsoring "Homer," as hypothesized in chapter 2, a boost which he is saying is unnecessary due to her evident glories. It is interesting that the earlier historian, Herodotus, understood his treatise on the Persian Wars in a similar way that Pindar felt about his odes— they both related back to Homer because for a man to have *kleos* (fame) required his deed to be celebrated in public acclamation, as Homer did for the ancient heroes, Pindar for the later victors, and Herodotus for the Greeks in their eventual success against the Persians. Herodotus went even further in relating his history to Homer's epics. He understood that the *Iliad* is the story of the conflict between Achilles and Agamemnon, set in the larger context of the Trojan War which in a larger context is a conflict between Greeks and foreigners, the very theme of Herodotus' history! "Herodotus is in effect implying that the events narrated by the *Iliad* are part of a larger scheme of events as narrated by himself."[8] The historian's claim that he has special knowledge of the world due to his wider travels parallels the *Odyssey,* in which crafty Odysseus is wise beyond his years due to his own travels.

The independence-loving Greeks never achieved a state-level society, preferring local allegiance to their *polis* or city-state. However, they had a keen sense of the commonality of their culture, even if politically divided, and this sense of superiority to other cultures is evident in their literature and art, where foreigners are often the butt of jokes and caricature. To the Greek ear, other languages sounded like gibberish, as if the speakers were simply repeating a nonsense syllable "bar, bar, bar," and from this elitist view they coined a word for anyone non–Greek — "barbarian" — meaning someone repeating nonsense foreign words. The common feeling of "Greekness" was strongly reinforced by the Homeric poems, in which the ancient cities of Greece had banded together to avenge the wrong done to one of their kings, and in which another Greek king struggled for ten years through foreign waters and against supernatural events to return home to his Greek wife and homeland, be it ever so humble. Isocrates appealed to the Panhellenic patriotism of Homer in his vain efforts to get the Greeks to unite against their northern aggressors, the Macedonian kings Philip II and his son Alexander, later to become "the Great." "Homer was the greatest single force in making of the Greeks a kindred people and in giving them a mutually understandable language and common ideas. This poetry not only permeated all classes of society and reached the utmost confines of Greek civilization, but its influence continued throughout the entire Greek period."[9]

It should be noted that by the later fifth century the casual references to Homer by many writers underscore the fact that the Homeric text was freely available, and this speaks to what must have been widespread copying of the text. By the end of the fifth century, writers who commented on the Homeric poems were becoming interested in trying to interpret or explain details of the text, such as the meaning of words, and in arguing about its morality. The philosophic school of the Sophists continued to explore the interpretation of Homer in allegorical terms, the most extreme example being Metrodorus of Lampsacus who apparently interpreted the whole of the *Iliad* in terms of Anaxagoras's cosmology, making Agamemnon the *aether,* Achilles the sun, Helen the earth, Paris the air, and Hector the moon.[10] Plato has Protagoras say that Homer and other early poets were really Sophists (known for being able to argue any side of an issue without revealing their own feelings) who used poetry to conceal their real knowledge of practical wisdom in order to avoid unpopularity.[11] Other writers studied the positive aspects of Homer for illustrating military valor and moral rectitude. "This kind of moralizing approach is echoed by Niceratus in Xenophon's *Symposium* (3.5), when he says that his father Nicias made him learn the whole of Homer's poetry by heart, as part of the education of a gentleman. Later on he claims him as a source of information on all kinds of ethical and practical subjects (4.6–7), as does the rhapsode Ion in Plato's dialogue (*Ion* 537a ff.)."[12] With the increase of interest in the Homeric poetry, especially by philosophers, and their questioning assumptions about it there are the foundations of textual criticism and Homeric scholarship that blossomed in the later Hellenistic period and became the basis for modern study.

In *The Republic* the philosopher Plato admitted that Homeric adulation was widespread but argued that his poems lacked morality and should be banished from his hypothetical utopian republic, which would be based on justice. He was seeking to replace poetic fiction, however beautiful, with philosophical truth and, thus, attacked poetry in all forms. He had Socrates, interviewing Polemarchus, say:

> The just man, then, as it seems, has come to light as a kind of robber, and I'm afraid you learned this from Homer. For he admires Autolycus, Odysseus' grandfather on his mother's side, and says he surpassed all men "in stealing and in swearing oaths." Justice, then, seems, according to you and Homer and Simonides, to be a certain art of stealing, for the benefit, to be sure, of friends and for the harm of enemies [334b].

Plato's detailed knowledge of the Homeric text is clear, and the same was assumed for his readers. The philosopher disliked Homer's portrayal of the Olympian deities. He had Adeimantus remark to Socrates that writers and poets such as Homer witness to the perversion of the gods because they portray them as being swayed to alter their actions by prayers, sacrifices, and offerings, and Socrates agrees, calling their stories about the gods "lies." Plato, through Socrates, rejected mythology for his perfect city but in doing so revealed how widespread it really was in the Greek world:

> Above all ... it mustn't be said that gods make war on gods, and plot against them and have battles with them — for it isn't even true — provided that those who are going to guard the city for us must consider it shameful to be easily angry with one another. They are far from needing to have tales told and embroideries woven about battles of giants and the many diverse disputes of gods and heroes with their families and kin. But if we are somehow going to persuade them that no citizen ever was angry with another and that to be so is not holy, it's just such things that must be told the children right away by old men and women; and as they get older, the poets must be compelled to make up speeches for them which are close to these. But Hera's bindings by her son, and Hephaestus' being cast out by his father ... and all the battles of the gods Homer made, must not be accepted in the city, whether they are made with a hidden sense or without a hidden sense [378d].

Note the last comment, which implies that already in Plato's time Homer's poems were being interpreted allegorically, *i.e.* seen to have hidden meanings, a trend which continued almost to the modern era. Plato admitted that Homer was not all bad, but he rejected interference by the gods in human affairs described by poet or playwright: "So, although we praise much in Homer, we'll not praise Zeus sending the dream to Agamemnon, nor Thetis' saying in Aeschylus that Apollo sang at her wedding..." (383a). Plato did not want Hades to be praised in his republic nor men to be permitted to show emotions because both might produce effeminate soldiers, and this required censoring the poets:

> So, we'd be right in taking out the wailings of renowned men ... [and] then, again, we'll ask Homer and the other poets not to make Achilles, son of a goddess "Now lying on his side, now again/ On his belly, and now on his side,/ Then standing upright, roaming distraught along the shore of the unharvested sea" nor taking black ashes in both hands and pouring them over his head, nor crying and lamenting as much as, or in the ways, Homer made him do; nor Priam, a near offspring of the gods, entreating and "rolling around in dung, calling out to each man by name." And yet far more than this, we'll ask them under no conditions to make gods who lament ... [388a-b].

He would not permit Homer to have gods laughing uncontrollably either. Not understanding the culture of the heroic society Homer was describing, Plato took exception to

Homer's depiction of Achilles' apparent disrespect for deities, his cruelty and his greediness for rewards and gifts, and rejects such poetic imagery in his republic:

> Nor shall we agree that he was such a lover of money as to take gifts from Agamemnon, or, again, to give up a corpse when getting paid for it, but otherwise not to be willing.... And, for Homer's sake..., I hesitate to say that it's not holy to say these things against Achilles and to believe them when said by others; or, again, to believe that he said to Apollo, "You've hindered me, Far-Darter, most destructive of all gods, and I would revenge myself on you, if I had the power;" and that he was disobedient to the river, who was a god, and ready to do battle with it; and that he said about the locks consecrated to another river, Spercheius, "To the hero Patroclus I would give my hair/ To take with him," although he was a corpse. It must not be believed that he did. The dragging of Hector around Patroclus' tomb, the slaughter in the fire of the men captured alive: we'll deny that all this is truly told. And we'll not let our men believe that Achilles—the son of a goddess and Peleus, a most moderate man and third from Zeus, Achilles who was reared by the most wise Chiron—was so full of confusion as to contain within himself two diseases that are opposite to one another—illiberality accompanying love of money, on the one hand, and arrogant disdain for gods and human beings, on the other [390e–391a].

The extent to which the Homeric texts were commonly known is evident not only by the liberal direct quotes by Plato but also in this speech put into the mouth of Socrates, who is still interrogating Adeimantus:

> Tell me, do you know the first things in the Iliad where the poet tells of Chryses' begging Agamemnon to ransom his daughter...?

and upon receiving an affirmative answer from his student,

> Then you know that up to these lines, "And he entreated all the Achaeans, but especially Atreus' two sons, the marshallers of the host," the poet himself speaks and doesn't attempt to turn our thought elsewhere... [393a].

Plato wanted the soldiers of his ideal republic to be physically fit and to eat a proper diet:

> From Homer too ... one could learn things very much of this sort. For you know that, during the campaign, at the feasts of the heroes, he doesn't feast them on fish—and that, although they are by the sea at the Hellespont—nor on boiled meats but only roasted.... Nor does Homer, I believe, ever make mention of sweets [404b-c].

When Plato began his diatribe against poets whom he says are "imitative" and, thus, "seem to maim the thought of those who hear them and do not have knowledge of how they [the soul's forms] really are as a remedy," he found that he must apologize to Homer whom he, like all other Greek boys, had studied since youth:

> And yet, a certain friendship for Homer, and shame before him, which has possessed me since childhood, prevents me from speaking. For he seems to have been the first teacher and leader of all these fine tragic things. Still and all, a man must not be honored before the truth, but, as I say, it must be told [595b].

Plato, through his mouthpiece, Socrates, proceeded to deconstruct Homer, who even by the fourth century had achieved the reputation of knowing all things:

Then, next, ... tragedy and its leader, Homer, must be considered, since we hear from some that these men know all arts and all things human that have to do with virtue and vice, and the divine things too.... Do you suppose that if a man were able to make both, the thing to be imitated and the phantom, he would permit himself to be serious about the crafting of the phantoms and set this at the head of his own life as the best thing he has? ...But, I suppose, if there were in truth a knower of these things that he also imitates, he would be far more serious about as memorials of himself and would be more eager to be the one who is lauded the deeds than the imitations and would try to leave many fair deeds behind rather than the one who lauds.... Well, then, about the other things, let's not demand an account from Homer or any other of the poets by asking, if any one of them was a doctor and not only an imitator of medical speeches.... Nor, again, will we ask them about the other arts, but we'll let that go. But about the greatest and fairest things of which Homer attempts to speak — about wars and commands of armies and governances of cities, and about the education of a human being — it is surely just to ask him and inquire, "Dear Homer, ... tell us which of the cities was better governed thanks to you.... What city gives you the credit for having proved a good lawgiver and benefited them?" ...[I]s any war in Homer's time remembered that was well fought with his ruling or advice? ...[A]s is appropriate to the deeds of a wise man, do they tell of many inventions and devices for the arts or any other activities...? ...[W]ell, then, if there is nothing in public, is it told that Homer, while he was himself alive, was in private a leader in education for certain men who cherished him for his intercourse and handed down a certain Homeric way of life to those who came after...? ...[I]f Homer were really able to educate human beings and make them better because he is in these things capable not of imitating but of knowing, do you suppose that he wouldn't have made many comrades and been honored and cherished by them? ...Then do you suppose that if he were able to help human beings toward virtue, the men in Homer's time would have let him or Hesiod go around being rhapsodes and wouldn't have clung to them rather than to their gold? ...Shouldn't we set down all those skilled in making, beginning with Homer, as imitators of phantoms of virtue and of the other subjects of their making? ...He himself doesn't understand; but he imitates in such a way as to seem, to men whose condition is like his own and who observe only speeches, to speak very well.... When even the best of us hear Homer or any other of the tragic poets imitating one of the heroes in mourning and making quite an extended speech with lamentations, or, if you like, singing and beating his breast, you know that we enjoy it and that we give ourselves over to following the imitation; suffering along with the hero in all seriousness, we praise as a good poet the man who most puts us in this state.... But when personal sorrow comes to one of us, you are aware that, on the contrary, we pride ourselves if we are able to keep quiet and bear up, taking this to be the part of a man and what we then praised to be that of a woman. ...When you meet praisers of Homer who say that this poet educated Greece, and that in the management and education of human affairs it is worthwhile to take him up for study and for living, by arranging one's whole life according to this poet, you must love and embrace them as being men who are the best they can be, and agree that Homer is the most poetic and first of the tragic poets; but you must know that only so much of poetry as is hymns to gods or celebration of good men should be admitted into a city. And if you admit the sweetened muse in lyrics or epics, pleasure and pain will jointly be kings in your city instead of law and that argument which in each instance is best in the opinion of the community [595a–607d].

Plato has been quoted at some length in order to demonstrate not only his objections to Homer's poetry but to reveal how pervasive that very poetry was in Greek culture by the fourth century. "Homer's poetry was well-known, and any portion of it could, for the educated audience, bring its context along. And with the context comes

Painting by Rembrandt called "Aristotle Contemplating the Bust of Homer (the Metropolitan Museum of Art, New York).

the intellectual and emotional associations of a lifetime of listening to Homer. Plato's attack on Homer is, in part, an attempt to supplant Homer's cultural hegemony."[13]

Plato's attacks on Homer were rebutted in a defense of Homer by another great philosopher, Aristotle (384–322 B.C.E.), who frequently quoted Homer in support of his ideas and even edited a special edition of the Homeric text. Among his many writings was a work, now lost, called *Homeric Problems;* references exist in the works of other writers which show that this was a list of questions about Homer which Aristotle then answered. The style is hinted at by this fragment from a summary of the work: "'Aristotle asks' how Polyphemus came to be born a Cyclops, given that his father was a god and his mother a sea nymph, and 'it is solved' from the nature of myth: Comparanda are mustered to show that Boreas fathered horses in myth and Pegasus was born to Poseidon and Medusa."[14] Clearly, Aristotle studied the Homeric text in great detail, along with the discussions of those who came before him, in order to solve the problems noticed by others and from his own observations. In the *Poetics* "he states the fundamental principle, so often ignored by both earlier and later critics, that poetry is not subject to the same criteria as are other arts and sciences (1460b13–15). If a scene achieves the kind of effects that are described in the *Poetics* as desirable, then minor faults of accuracy, coherence, and so on are irrelevant. With this simple observation most of the trivial objections of earlier pedants ... are swept away.... Moral criticisms (such as those raised by Plato and others) can be answered by appealing to historical context or the conventions of the poet's day.... Religious beliefs may simply reflect those of Greek society at that stage of development, and so to attack them from a modern viewpoint is misguided.... Alternatively, if something is untrue or historically impossible, it may be justified as idealization. Finally, many minor problems of interpretation and consistency can be solved by adopting a more flexible approach to the text and considering alternative ways of taking it, instead of assuming that the first or most obvious interpretation must be correct. To us these principles may seem largely obvious, but it is surprising how easily they can be forgotten by modern as well as ancient critics."[15]

Aristotle praised Homer's poems in the *Poetics* even though he concluded that tragedy was superior to epic poetry because it achieves a better emotional catharsis (although they both bring similar kinds of pleasure). "Aristotle's admiration for Homer is focused especially on the extraordinary skill with which he creates a single, unified story out of a vast and highly diversified body of material, incorporating many subsidiary episodes without allowing us to lose sight of the main theme."[16] Ironically, as has been seen, this is the very dilemma of trying to understand the oral poetry tradition and the presence or lack of a monumental poet in reconstructing the origin of the Homeric epics. In defending Homer, Aristotle turned the arguments away from fact versus fiction and from the contempt for his portrayal of the gods and morality.

In the fourth century B.C.E., writers began to question the Homeric text itself in addition to arguing about its moral and philosophical content, and this questioning continued throughout antiquity. As noted in the last chapter, allegations of Peisistratid tampering with the text were raised. More seriously, questions about the inconsistencies in the text began to emerge under the scrutiny of critical readers such as the Cynic philosopher Zoilus of Amphipolis, who on account of his bitter attacks became known as "the scourge of Homer." Surviving references show that many scholars studied the Homeric text and wrote works about it. Of these, four important works have been preserved with the *scholia* added to the Homeric text itself: Didymus, *On the Edition of Aristarchus* (ca. 20 C.E.); Aristonicus, *On the Signs of the Iliad and Odyssey* (ca. 20 C.E.); Nicanor, *On Punctuation* (ca. 130 C.E.); and Herodian, *Prosody of the Iliad* (ca. 160 C.E.). The Neoplatonist philosopher Porphyry (*ca.* 232–305 C.E.) wrote a work called *Homeric Questions* in the spirit of Aristotle and others who questioned the Homeric text. He was mainly interested in the meanings of words and phrases, but he also made observations on Homer's use of metaphor and simile which seem rather modern.

It must be supposed that the copies of the Homeric text prior to the second century B.C.E. "were produced in an extremely haphazard way"[17] resulting in copyist misspellings, reversal of lines, substitution of words, and other unintentional errors which would be multiplied with subsequent copyings. Quotations in earlier writers, including Herodotus, Thucydides and Plato, are very close to what eventually became the standard text, and variances can be explained as mistakes resulting from quoting from memory. Oddly, quotes by later writers, such as Strabo, Galen and Plutarch, show further variances from the standard text, and this may be due to their being indirect

Boeotian cup caricaturing Odysseus and the enchantress Circe; ca. 350 B.C.E. (Ashmolean Museum, Oxford).

quotations or, more likely, because well-to-do families maintained old libraries with older and less accurate editions of Homer.[18] *Scholia* refer to revisions of the text by various individuals, including the poet Antimachus of Colophon (ca. 400 B.C.E.), but the first extensive reworking was undertaken by Aristotle (ca. 330 B.C.E.). This text was called the Narthex edition, according to the biographer Plutarch and the geographer Strabo, because it was given to the philosopher's famous pupil, Alexander the Great, who later kept it in a richly decorated box ("narthex" in Greek). Plutarch tells us that after the battle of Issus when Alexander's army finally routed that of the Persian King Darius III, from the spoils

> a box ("narthex") was brought to him which was regarded by those who were in charge of Darius' baggage and treasure as the most valuable item of all, and so Alexander asked his friends what he should keep in it as his own most precious possession. Many different suggestions were put forward, and finally Alexander said that he intended to keep his copy of the *Iliad* there.

Apparently, this very edition was the one taken by Alexander on his conquest of the eastern world and which he kept under his pillow at night for inspiration, so it is not known whether its text was ever disseminated. When he conquered mainland Greece (thus unifying it for the Greeks) and turned his attentions east to the Persian Empire, he presented himself as a champion of Greece wreaking vengeance on the Persians for their aggression during the Persian Wars some 150 years earlier. His first act after crossing into Asia Minor in 334 B.C.E. was to visit Troy to see the actual site of the events of the *Iliad*, and at the tomb of Achilles the ambitious young man is said to have cried out: "Oh fortunate Achilles who didst find in Homer a herald of thy glory!"[19] In fact, it has been suggested that "the career of Alexander the Great was largely an attempt to realize the Homeric ideal and to duplicate the glory of Achilles" and that "many of that conqueror's acts would have little meaning, if we did not know that he was imitating both the passion and the extravagance of the Homeric hero."[20]

It has generally been believed that Stoic philosophers beginning with Zeno about 300 B.C.E. considered Homer to have been something of a "crypto–Stoic," *i.e.* concurring with their view of the world.[21] To do so requires the assumption, as has been so frequently done previously and subsequently, that the Homeric narrative was actually allegorical with underlying meanings acceptable to the Stoic philosophy. This theory, however, is unlikely as the Stoics were practical and straightforward and would have considered the idea of Homer foreshadowing their philosophy centuries before their own time ridiculous. In addition, they would not have had a motive to defend Homer's portrayal of the gods. It is known that Zeno wrote a lengthy treatise on Homeric problems, but this work (which is now completely lost) is likely to have been concerned with wording, interpolations, grammar, vocabulary, etc., like other contemporary studies of the Homeric text.[22]

Throughout antiquity, commentators on the *Iliad* and the *Odyssey* struggled with the issue of whether or not Homer's text should be read factually or allegorically; the answer was critical for it determined whether the poems contained value or were to be rejected. Strabo, the Greek geographer (*ca.* 63 B.C.E.–*ca.* 21 C.E.), studied Homer's geographical details and concluded that they were not total fictions, as had been alleged by the polymath and poet Eratosthenes (*ca.* 275–194 B.C.E.). Strabo decided that Homer often combined truth with myth in order to give his narrative extra interest, and he felt that he could tease out the facts from the mythical overburden.[23] In other words, he was using the Homeric text for research much as a modern scholar would study a primary document, looking for factual information while being aware of the author's biases. "The *Odyssey*, then for the geographer, is like a mine. The good ore of truth is to be found there, but a great deal is present as well that is a function of the poetry itself and has nothing to do with the truth."[24] Plutarch, the famous biographer (*ca.* 50–120 C.E.), wrote an essay called *On How to Study Poetry* in which he rejected astrological or cosmological allegory as mechanisms for defending Homer from charges of immoral representations of the gods. The scholar Crates, who was the first director of the library at Pergamon in the second century B.C.E., focused on Homer's descriptions of the shields of Agamemnon and Achilles to expound allegorical readings which he felt were descriptions of the cosmos.

From the third century B.C.E. there are actual surviving fragments of papyrus copies of the Homeric text that have been found in the ever-preserving sands of Egypt. "The enormously greater frequency of Homer, compared with other writers, among the surviving literary papyri makes it clear that there *was* a general reading public for Homer...."[25] In one catalog of some 3,026 Graeco-Roman Classical texts on papyri fragments from Egypt the Homeric numbers are as follows: *Iliad*—467; *Odyssey*—138; "Homerica"[26]—76. For comparison, the other most numerous Greek authors were: Euripedes—77; Hesiod—49; Thucydides—33; Aeschylus—30; and the most numerous Roman authors: Virgil—18; Cicero—9.[27] From these and similar counts of surviving papyri it is clear that "if a Greek owned any books—that is, papyrus rolls—he was almost as likely to own the *Iliad* and *Odyssey* as anything from the rest of Greek literature."[28] The most recent count of Homeric papyri fragments has risen to 1,543; the scholar who has collected their references noted their widespread existence among ancient examples and frequency of new discovery, commenting that "there is no end to them"![29]

When these earliest surviving original manuscripts of the Homeric text were first discovered in the nineteenth century, it was soon apparent after comparison with the standard text of Homer that the early papyri showed unexpected variances. "The distinctive feature of the early Homeric papyri is the high proportion of additional lines which they contain, and which do not survive in the later tradition."[30] Many of the added lines are simply copies of lines or formulae found elsewhere, but a large number have no close parallel either in the Homeric text or in other known texts. Scholars dubbed these texts "eccentric" to distinguish them from the standard text which, as noted above, the earlier writers had but which the later writers did not. The extra lines have minimal effect on the narrative flow and none have completely unknown episodes or plot changes. "A few are clearly superior to the traditional text; many are just as good. But a large number are obviously secondary, and arise from tendencies which were active at all stages of the tradition—simplification of difficult expressions, modernization and vulgarization of the text, elimination of hiatus, and so on."[31] It would seem, then, that there was an original text, bastardized over the centuries by errors and interpolations of copyists, which was again standardized into a form that survived antiquity and was passed to the present.

It was in this period (ca. 283 B.C.E.) that the famous Museum or Library at Alexandria was founded by Ptolemy Soter, and its scholars began collecting and studying the literature of the known world. Many manuscripts of the Homeric poems were procured, and the textual variations that had crept in through centuries of copying were discovered by comparison among them. The scholars responded by, essentially, inventing the field of textual criticism to try to determine the most accurate text. "The impressive textual, grammatical, metrical, and lexicographic studies of the great Alexandrian scholars laid the foundation on which all European literary and philological studies have been built."[32] Zenodotus of Ephesus became head of the Library about 250 B.C.E. and is reported to have done a severe revision of the Homeric text in which he excised large portions of it, apparently declaring them to be un-Homeric. "Zenodotus's drastic measures were natural in the circumstances; he was the first major scholar to contend against the corruptions of the current texts of Homer, and if he used the scalpel more freely than was strictly justifiable, the fault was clearly on the right side."[33] The *scholia* often quote an edition of Homer by Aristophanes of Byzantium, head of the Library from 195 to 180 B.C.E., who also was trying to sort out derivative additions from original text. "So far as we can see Aristophanes, like Zenodotus, was still struggling to make critical sense of the many divergent texts in the library, and had failed to find an Ariadne's clue to guide him through the labyrinth."[34]

The scholar Aristarchus of Samothrace (ca. 215–ca. 145 B.C.E.) seems to have been connected with the successful establishment of a generally accepted version of the Homeric text, a version that was subsequently taken to be the best possible and was not changed; modern scholars refer to this text, created about 150 B.C.E., as the Vulgate. It seems that this text was actually a copy of some earlier version to which scholars added commentary, diacritical accent marks to show proper pronunciation of words, and notations of which lines and sections they felt were spurious. The question then becomes: Where did this authoritative text derive from that the Alexandrian scholars felt compelled not to edit but just to add notations to? "The text which, from Aristarchus's time down to Wolf [the early-19th-century analyst], held the field against all comers, must, as its orthography shows, have come to Alexandria by way of Athens..." and may actually have been the so-called Panathenaic text.[35] It is known that Aristarchus considered Homer to have been an Athenian, and there is a surviving story that the Alexandrian Library borrowed the Athenian official copies of the text of the great tragedians to copy but, instead, forfeited their deposit and kept the originals. It is reported that the Alexandrian scholars were able to consult state or public copies of the Homeric text from the cities of Sinope, Chios, Argos, and Marseilles, but Athens is not listed. A clever explanation is that when one compares multiple copies of one text, the simplest way to do so is to take what is likely to be the best copy and compare the others to it. Thus, the Panathenaic text is not mentioned because it was the "official" copy to which the other cities' copies were compared.[36] "If the Alexandrian scholars had before them the official Attic [Athenian] text, it explains why they showed it so much respect, restraining the results of their scholarly work to commentaries and monographs without imposing their readings on the text."[37] It should be noted that many scholars do not subscribe to this explanation, but it does help explain the amazingly rapid conquest of the vulgate text over all variants, as shown by the papyri fragments. Detailed study and dating of the papyri have shown that the ones with eccentric texts end about 150 B.C.E. and that the ones dated later conform to the Vulgate. "It cannot be proved, but seems extremely probable, that Aristarchus was in some way responsible for the obsolescence of the eccentric texts. The change comes at about the time when he died; in antiquity he was generally held to have exercised a decisive influence on the text of Homer."[38] With the establishment of a standard text "one may say that from the time of Aristarchus onwards to the ninth century A.D. our interest in the history of the text shifts away from scholarship and criticism to the question of the physical transmission of the text."[39]

Until the late first or second century C.E., literature was mostly written on papyrus rolls which would have been cumbersome for long texts such as the Homeric poems. About this time a new format was invented, that of the codex or book which continues in use today. At the same period the widespread use of parchment (prepared animal skins) came into practice, a material especially useful for codices and which survived longer than papyrus. In Epigram 14 the Roman poet Martial (*ca.* 40–103 C.E.) marveled at the ability of a lifeless object to enclose such a lively poet as Homer:

> Homer on parchment pages!
> The *Iliad* and all the adventures
> Of Ulysses, foe of Priam's kingdom!
> All locked within a piece of skin
> Folded into several little sheets!

It has been suggested that the book trade may have led to the creation of the Vulgate itself from Aristarchus' scholarly edition: "The booksellers and proprietors of scriptoria accordingly fell in with popular demand, which may well have originated with students at the Museum: they canceled lines rejected by Aristarchus, but did not alter the wording of their texts" because they wanted the new, updated edition but without the scholarly apparatus.[40] Of course, it is possible that book producers themselves also noticed the unnecessary repetition of lines and other variants in the manuscripts they were working from, and it has been argued that "the new degree of textual 'standardization' in the era after 150 B.C.E. reflects not the authority of Alexandrian scholarship but other factors—including the advances being made in the kind of minimalist quasi-editing techniques that would be needed for large scale commercial copying of manuscripts."[41] The establishment of standard editions of Homer and other famous authors by the Alexandrian scholars and, perhaps, by the producers of books would have improved the copying standards of book production in which, previously, accuracy was considered secondary to providing just the general sense of passages. "The classics were now fossilized: even if what the author wrote appeared to be unmetrical, ungrammatical, factually incorrect, obscure, and improper, this was what must be transmitted. This may appear self-evident to us: a fifth-century Athenian would have thought otherwise."[42]

Interest in Homer during the Hellenistic period (third to first centuries B.C.E.) continued to pervade the Greek world even beyond the search for the most accurate version. "The texts themselves were subjected to rigorous critical attention, Homer's primacy in all fields of knowledge was expressed in a religious cult in which he was heroised, and his influence continued to pervade every branch of literature, including that of the Alexandrian movement."[43] Poets again wrote epics, such as the *Argonautica* of Apollonius Rhodius which told the story of Jason and the Argonauts, *i.e.* the quest for the Golden

Fleece. In this work and others of the period, as those by Theocritus and Callimachus, there were frequent allusions to the *Iliad* and *Odyssey* because by this time such references had become a necessary ingredient of the epic itself. "It is of course possible to read and enjoy the *Argonautica* without noticing the allusions to Homer. However, this is not to read it as an ancient reader would have done, since Homer was second nature to educated Greeks and the technique of allusion was so fundamental to classical literature that the reader would automatically be sensitive to it."[44]

Apollonius' poem is the only surviving epic from this period, but surviving papyrus fragments reveal that there were many written at the time. In the *Argonautica* he used Homeric devices frequently, such as "typical scenes," extended similes, and intervention by the gods, and there are parallels of scenes and language. In fact, it is possible to match the adventures of Odysseus and those of Jason one for one. The *Argonautica* is clear evidence that Hellenistic poets had no choice but to reflect Homer in their works, and their creative methods for so doing were their particular genius. "The relationship of Alexandrian poets to Homer can be summarized as follows: they acknowledge his supremacy, do not try to usurp his unique position in Greek literature but are influenced by him and exploit the reader's knowledge of him, even when writing in genres which are apparently very different from epic. The result is neither slavish imitation nor complete independence. Not surprisingly, the Alexandrian poets responded to Homer in different ways, according to the genres they used or developed, and their own poetic interests.... The relation of the *Argonautica* to Homer is 'intertextual' in the true sense that it is possible to transpose the systems of the *Iliad* and *Odyssey* into the later poem; the Homeric text is present at every level in Apollonius ... [and] it is clear that Homeric allusion is not a detachable extra, but permeates the *Argonautica* in all its aspects. Instead of concealing the debt of epic to Homer, the *Argonautica* celebrates it, constantly inviting the reader to recall the earlier poems."[45] The Homeric epics were imitated, embellished, "improved upon," parodied and otherwise copied by other poets as well, such as Quintus of Smyrna, whose *Posthomerica* completed the history of the Trojan War.

Prose works, especially the incipient novel, were also heavily influenced by the Homeric epics, and even Jewish works, such as the Book of Tobit, borrowed from them. A thought-provoking and potentially stunning argument has recently been made that the New Testament gospels, especially the oldest one, which goes under the name of Mark, show heavy Homeric influence.[46] The explanation is that Mark's gospel is a "hypertext" in which stories from the epics are "transvalued," which is to say that the general forms of many Markan stories about Jesus follow story lines from *Iliad* or *Odyssey* episodes but with twists to proclaim a theological message that Jesus was the supernatural Messiah. Jesus is frequently cast in the image of Odysseus: a wise but suffering figure with dolts as followers who fail their hero at critical times, so that he must face his foes alone at the end. Both Jesus and Odysseus are beset by temptations, devils, storms and other adversities as they work their ways home (Ithaca for Odysseus; Jerusalem, the location of the temple, for Jesus). Each warns the few faithful believers who realize their true identities (rightful king for Odysseus; Messiah for Jesus) that they must keep silent about him until the right moment when the sinners who have defiled his house will be punished and he will be seen for who he really is. In an example of transvaluation Odysseus successfully kills his opponents and regains his status while Jesus himself is killed by his opponents—

his triumph and punishment of his tormentors is to come later. Many specific stories in Mark could derive from Homeric ones, such as Jesus's "cleansing of the temple" from Odysseus' slaughter of the suitors; and the recovery of and burial of Jesus's dead body from that of the slain Hector, both heroes sinless themselves but killed to save their followers according to the will of their god(s), although both bodies remained inviolate despite attempts by their killers to defile them. How ironic it would be if the thesis of this biblical scholar should prove correct, because it would mean that the New Testament of the Bible would be seen as founded on the so-called Bible of the Greeks, the Homeric epics!

The history of the rise of the people of Rome to take over Italy, and even their subsequent conquest of the Mediterranean world and beyond, can to some extent be attributed to their search for safe borders and their capable administration of lands and peoples overtaken in that quest. Culturally, the Romans always felt a little inferior to the ancient civilizations they conquered to their east, although in their acquisition of cultural forms they always remolded them with a Roman flair. A poet quipped that, although the Romans took military and political possession of all the former Greek world, "captive Greece took her captor captive." The Romans were especially fascinated with Greek culture, from art and architecture to literature, and they thus inherited and magnified the tradition that Homer was the best of all poets, although this tradition was a cause of anxiety for Roman poets who wondered how they could compete. In his *Annals* the poet Quintus Ennius (born 239 B.C.E.) decided to confront the problem directly by presenting himself as Homer reincarnated! One of the earliest works of Latin literature which has been preserved is Livius Andronicus' version of Homer's *Odyssey*, dated *ca.* 200 B.C.E., but it was an adaptation, not a true translation (*e.g.* Apollo was turned into *filius Latonas* and the Muses became fountain goddesses). The *Iliad* was only truly translated into Latin at the end of the second century B.C.E. The great Roman orator and writer Cicero in the last century B.C.E. was fond of Homer, translating passages and quoting him in most of his private letters which have been preserved. In fact, all well-educated Romans were wont to quote Homer to show off their education. It is said that as Brutus was preparing to leave Italy his wife happened to see a painting of the parting of Hector and his wife Andromache (note the presence of Homeric themes in Roman art) and burst into tears at the parallel to their own situation; appropriately, both Brutus and a friend attempted to ease the situation with other, more comforting Homeric quotes.[47]

During the reign of Rome's first emperor Augustus at the beginning of the Christian era, the best work of Latin literature was written with its foundation built firmly on the greatest of ancient poets, Homer. As part of the glorification of the Augustan regime Publius Vergilius Maro, commonly known as Virgil, composed a great epic poem called the *Aeneid;* it begins with the flight of the Trojan hero Aeneas from the burning city of Troy with his elderly father Anchises on his back. Virgil has Aeneas become the ancestor of the Romans; he and his descendents settle in Italy and beget the line of none other than Augustus, thus legitimizing him and his family as proper rulers. In the *Aeneid* Rome becomes the new Troy that, unlike its predecessor, will last forever. The poem is an intentional parallel to Homer's *Odyssey*, as Virgil details the tribulations of the fleeing Trojans in their maritime search for a new home. This is especially clear when the prophetic words of the dying Hector in the *Iliad*, "There will come a day when the holy city of Troy will fall" are echoed in the early *Aeneid* as Virgil has the priest Panthus on the night of Troy's sacking say "Troy's final day and its inevitable hour has come."[48] "For the ancient commentators on Homer, the *Odyssey* was the *anaplerosis*, the completion or fulfillment, of the *Iliad*, not merely its narrative continuation. Through an extraordinary complex web of verbal repetitions such as this, the *Aeneid* not only establishes its identity as an epic but offers itself in turn as the *anaplerosis*, generic no less than narrative, of the Homeric poems."[49]

Virgil carefully followed Homer's dactylic hexameter verse and heroic style and was successful in making reference to the Homeric text throughout his own epic creation. Homer's *Iliad* opens with the words, "Sing, goddess, the destructive wrath of Achilles" and the *Odyssey* with "Tell me, Muse, of that man who wandered far and wide"; for Virgil, "the opening words of the poem... (*arma virumque cano*, 'I sing of arms and the man,' *Aen.* 1.1) famously signal a return to Homer and a combination within a single poem of the themes of the *Iliad* and the *Odyssey*."[50] In Virgil there are descriptions of games with rich prizes, as are so popular in Homer, and gods intervene in human affairs in both epics. When the Trojans eventually land in central Italy they must fight with an enemy Turnus, who almost conquers them but is vanquished by the hero Aeneas returning from a foray; this theme clearly parallels Homer's Achaeans, likewise landed on a foreign shore, who are almost defeated by the local hero Hector until the great Achilles returns to the fray. As the local people called the Rutuli prepare to attack the Trojan camp in Book Nine, the leader refers somewhat contemptuously to the *Iliad* by saying that he does not need arms made by Vulcan (those of Achilles were made by Hephaistos) or a thousand ships or a wooden horse to win the day. "The last part of this book, by its need to improve on the Iliad and compress it, reads like a compendium of Homer exaggerated."[51] These comparisons to Homer continue throughout the *Aeneid*: "In his final lines Virgil encompasses the whole of the *Iliad*, from the anger of Achilles against Agamemnon and later against Hector to the pleading words of Priam to Achilles transformed into Turnus' prayer of supplication."[52]

It could be said that Virgil "chose to imitate and adapt the works of Homer in a Latin form."[53] The result was the creation of a national literary work of epic proportions. "Homer provides the closest ancient parallel for the combination of literary prestige and popular recognition that characterizes Virgil's reputation in Antiquity."[54] Scholars and critics would debate the merits of the two poets until the end of the Roman world, but in the Middle Ages, due to the loss of the Greek language in Europe, it was assumed that Virgil had been the greatest of all ancient poets. If imitation is the highest form of flattery, Homer would have been honored! "The fact that a people who had gained empire without creating a single piece of pure literature which they cared to preserve should take over a foreign poet from a conquered people, adopt his meter, and make his poetry the ideal and the foundation for their own is the highest possible tribute which any nation could pay to a great poet."[55]

In the first or second century C.E. an otherwise unknown writer named Heraclitus wrote a work titled *Homeric Problems — Homer's Allegories Concerning the Gods* for the purpose of defending Homer from charges of blasphemy by Plato and others. "He states his primary point in his second sentence: 'If Homer was no allegorist, he would be completely impious.' That is to say, if Homer's apparent meaning is his real meaning, his gods are violent, sexually corrupt, the very reverse of moral exemplars."[56] Heraclitus believed that Homer's characters were cosmological entities; for example, Apollo is the sun, Poseidon is sea-water, Hera is air, etc. The pestilence of Apollo's arrows is really solar rays, and fighting among the gods is the struggle of virtues against vices, so that Athena's opposition to Ares and Aphrodite is wisdom versus passion and Apollo versus Poseidon is solar fire against the sea. For him, these are not meanings interpolated by a reader but are, in fact, Homer's original intentions. Heraclitus' basic theme is to defend Homer from Plato and other critics who labeled him an impious blasphemer. *"Homère [a été] universellement aimé et admiré, sauf par quelques esprits moroses* [Homer (was) universally loved and admired except by certain morose spirits]."[57]

The Neoplatonists also heavily used allegory for interpretation of Homer. As has been seen, Plato brutally attacked Homer as a worthless source of any truths, so "it is indeed surprising that the later pagan Platonists should have so blatantly violated the founding principles of their school as to embrace the poetry of Homer ... as texts of extraordinary authority."[58] One of them, Porphyry (*ca.* 232–305 C.E.), wrote an allegorical *Essay on the Cave of the Nymphs* that focuses on fifteen lines in the *Odyssey* which describe how Odysseus was returned to his homeland Ithaca by the Phaeacians. They left him with much treasure, which Athena tells him to hide in a cave so that he can return home disguised as an elderly beggar. Porphyry's interpretation provides a good example of the use of allegory[59]:

> Homer says that all outward possessions must be deposited in this cave and that one must be stripped naked and take on the attire of a beggar and, having withered the body away and cast aside all that is superfluous and turned away from the senses, take counsel with Athena, sitting with her beneath the olive, to learn how he might cut away all the destructive passions of his soul [79, 19–80].

A later Neoplatonist, Proclus (410–485 C.E.), head of the Platonic school in Athens, wrote a *Commentary on the Republic* in which he defended Homer against Plato's attacks, again using allegory as his weapon.

> [This] is why Homer told the tale of the most beautiful woman in the world [Helen]—to project onto his screen of poetic narrative an account of what draws souls into this world—and the war itself, on the highest level of generality, is a metaphor for the state that they are drawn into.[60]

In another example he interpreted the cosmic adultery of Ares and Aphrodite as a necessary "harmony and order of the opposites" in the universe, here of Love and War. From the later Neoplatonist period the allegorical approach to interpreting Homer took root and was prevalent through Greek antiquity and well into the Latin Middle Ages. It was to be understood that "each episode bristles with a proliferation of levels of reference, all contributing to the cumulative force of, first, the poem as a whole, and second, the greater myth beyond the epics, the Troy tale itself. For readers such as Porphyry in the third century and Proclus in the fifth, the true subject of the *Iliad* and *Odyssey* was the fate of souls and the structure of the universe. The first poem recounted the descent of souls into this world of strife, represented in the screen of the fiction by the metaphor of war, a descent triggered by the powerful attraction of the beauty of the cosmos (Helen). The second related the difficult return of one of these souls, plunged into the sea of matter and embroiled with the deities presiding over it, until he at last would achieve the state of 'dryness' promised by Teiresias and finally free himself of all memory of the material universe."[61] Although modern readers are not usually impressed with the late antique interpretations of Homer, their work did have the very important result of keeping interest in his works alive and, especially in the preservation of their text: "we owe an incalculable debt to the scholars who from the time of Herodian (second half of the second century A.D.) to that of Georgius Choeroboscus (about 600), maintained the study of Homer in spite of all difficulties...."[62]

In the late sixth century C.E., Gregory, bishop of Tours, discovered a lost manuscript called *The Acts of Andrew* which was labeled apocryphal but of sufficient interest that he wrote a summary or epitome of it which survives today to give us an idea of the full work, which was subsequently lost. Homeric interest in this obscure Christian text written *ca.* 300 C.E., which purported to narrate the missionary career and martyrdom of the New Testament disciple Andrew, arises because the plot can be interpreted as a Christianizing of Homer, especially the *Odyssey.* "The author selected Andrew as the protagonist because the Gospels had equipped him better than any of the Twelve to be an evangelizing Odysseus."[63] He was a former fisherman, his name means "manliness" in Greek, and he left home to rescue Matthias and then returned home (like Odysseus to Troy to rescue Helen and return to Ithaca). "Like Odysseus, Andrew endures storms, enters the netherworld, and escapes demons, cannibals, and monsters."[64] Jesus plays Homer's roles of Athena and Hermes in support of the hero, and the Devil plays Poseidon and the other Homeric gods causing the hero grief as the two sides give advice, inspiration and strength to their opposing human champions. But the author has not written a blind copy of the Homeric epics—he replaced the virility, violence and wealth of Odysseus with Andrew's celibacy, gentleness, and penury which shows a careful reworking of the originals to achieve a Christian purpose. One might ask why the author bothered to rewrite Homer and not just write an original narrative. The answer is that "the author wanted to claim the best of classical Greek antiquity for the Christian cause, and to distance it from the worst."[65] Although the author also incorporated other sources than Homer in his narrative, clearly the story was largely a rewriting of Homer, an interesting reuse of the earliest pagan epic for very Christian purposes.

It has already be seen that the *Odyssey* was imitated in antiquity by Apollonius and others, and it would also be imitated in early modern and modern times, the most famous example being *Ulysses* by James Joyce. The *Odyssey* more than the *Iliad* was susceptible to allegorizing, as has been seen, both in pagan and in Christian contexts. "Platonists had viewed Odysseus as a cipher for the soul adrift in the ocean of matter, bedeviled by monsters, beautiful temptresses, and shipwrecks, yet resolutely headed for its heavenly home and kindred. Christian Platonists ... saw in Odysseus's mast a resemblance to Christ's cross, by which he returned to his heavenly *patria* [homeland]."[66] The author of *The Acts of Andrew* shows us how the Homeric text, still so culturally pervasive a thousand years after it was composed, could be adapted in such as way as to draw on its knowledge by readers to encourage rejection of the past and acceptance of a new religious future. "He urged the reader to compare the worst of traditional pagan religion with the best of Christianity and to choose the latter over the former. Ought one worship gods

Page of Homeric text from the Bankes Papyrus, second century C.E. (© The British Museum).

who blind, maim, fornicate, and murder, or the God of Andrew, who heals and revives? Ought one choose a life of violence and wanton sex, or a life of peace and chastity?"[67]

The ubiquity of the Homeric text throughout the whole span of the Graeco-Roman era cannot be overemphasized. This fact is so admirably expressed by Heraclitus in his statement which was first quoted in the introduction:

> Our earliest infancy was intrusted to the care of Homer, as if he had been a nurse, and while still in our swaddling clothes we were fed on his verses, as if they had been our mother's milk. As we grew to youth we spent that youth with him, together we spent our vigorous manhood, and even in old age we continued to find our joy in him. If we laid him aside we soon thirsted to take him up again. There is but one terminus for men and Homer, and that is the terminus of life itself.

As students, young Greek and Roman boys learned to read Homer and memorize passages, and adult scholars and philosophers studied his poems for content and textual peculiarities. Statesmen quoted Homer, generals studied his descriptions of warfare, poets and dramatists overtly addressed Homeric themes and made covert allusions. Plato was referred to as the "Homer of Philosophers," Aesop the "Homer of Fable Writers," Sophocles the "Tragic Homer," and Sappho "the female Homer." Homer was known even in the "backwoods province" of Roman Pisidia (now Turkey).[68] A funerary inscription of Hellenistic date includes an epigram for the deceased written in Homeric style, and numerous inscribed statue bases from the city of Oinoanda have Homeric features. A mosaic of the second century C.E. from the ancient city of Seleukeia has a panel showing Homer as a father enthroned between two daughters who are labeled "Ilias" and "Odysseia." As late as ca. 500 C.E. an epitaph for a Christian woman from the city of Tyana includes a verse from the Iliad. In addition to their pervasive literary influence throughout antiquity, the Homeric epics functioned "as encyclopedias of religion, history, and culture"[69] of the classical world.

4

THE HOMERIC TEXT IN MEDIEVAL EUROPE AND THE BYZANTINE EMPIRE

The fall of the Roman Empire is traditionally dated to 476 C.E. with the destruction of the city of Rome itself by the Vandals but, in fact, Roman culture in western Europe had already been eroding for some time and would continue to flicker in various ways for some time to come. However, in the eastern, Greek half of the Roman world there was no conquest by an outside culture until 1453 C.E., and during this thousand years Roman civilization slowly evolved into a new one which is called the Byzantine Empire. In the medieval Latin West the Homeric text did not survive the collapse of Roman culture. Homer would not be translated into Latin until 1444 C.E. during the Renaissance, and the ability of the few learned men in the West to read Greek slowly dissipated over time until it was lost altogether. Thus, the story of the history of the Homeric text diverges at this point, following two paths to modern times: one through the medieval West and the other through the Byzantine East.

In medieval western Europe the Homeric text was essentially lost as literary knowledge and education retreated to the monasteries, and it is very difficult to trace the textual history of the manuscripts which survive. "If an adequate history of the medieval transmission of the Homeric *Iliad* is ever written, it will be a wonderful achievement, but a poor return for the substantial portion of a human life that its production will cost."[1] For the most part, little more of Homer was remembered than his name and a vague notion of the Trojan War preserved by the Latin text of Virgil's *Aeneid* and a summary of the *Iliad* known as the *Ilias Latina*. The great poet Dante Alighieri (1265–1321) knew something of Homer, calling him *poeta sovrano* when his shade appears in the underworld in the great poem, the *Divine Comedy*, but his six quotations from Homer all derive from the Latin version of Aristotle or from Horace.[2] Garbled information about the Trojan War largely derived from the forged Latin "eyewitness accounts" *De Excidio Troiae Historia* (History of the Destruction of Troy) attributed to Dares of Phrygia, a priest of Hephaestus at Troy (*Iliad* 5.9), but probably dating to the fifth century C.E. and

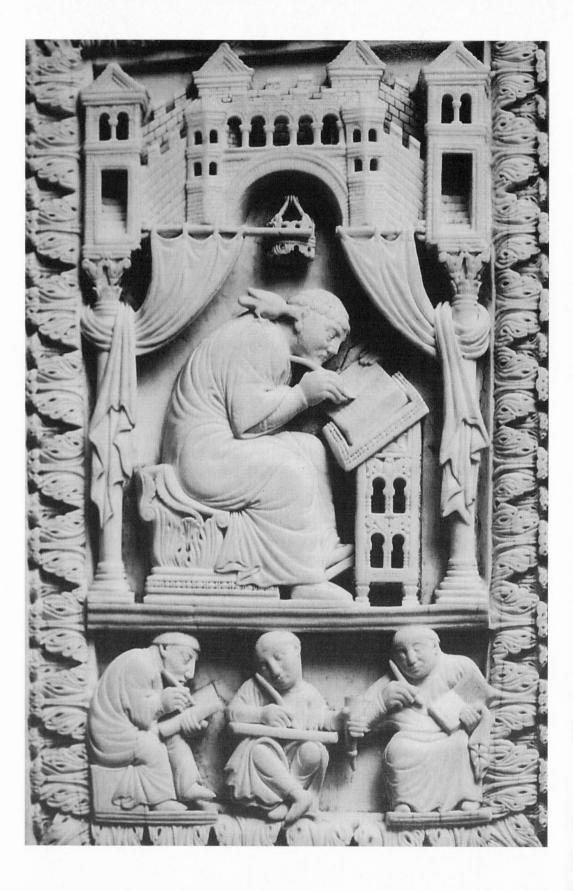

DARETIS
PHRYGII POETARVM ET
Historicorum omnium primi, de bello
Troiano, in quo ipse militauit, Libri
(quibus multis seculis caruimus) sex, à
CORNELIO NEPOTE Latino
carmine Heroico donati, & CRISPO
SALLVSTIO dedicati,
nunc primùm in luce
æditi.

Item,

PINDARI THEBANI HOME-
ricæ Iliados Epitome, suauissimis numeris exarata.

Adhæc,

HOMERI POETARVM PRIN-
cipis Ilias, quatenus à Nicolao
Valla, & V. Obsopœo car
mine reddita.

BASILEAE

Opposite: Carved ivory plaque showing a medieval manuscript writer (Pope Gregory I) and copyists; tenth century C.E. (Kunsthistorisches Museum, Vienna). *Above:* Title page of Dares' book printed in 1541 reflecting the medieval misunderstanding that he was more important than Homer: "On the Trojan War, by Dares of Phrygia, First among all Poets and Historians.... And also the Iliad of Homer, First among Poets."

Ephemeris Belli Troiani (Diary of the Trojan War) attributed to Dictys, a warrior at Troy, but probably dating to the second or third century C.E. A modern writer's assessment of these texts is that they were "wretched little compilations from earlier compilations in Greek."[3]

Trojan War stories turned up periodically in the literature of medieval Europe. One of the romances based on Dictys and Dares was the *Roman de Troye* (*ca.* 1200) by Benoit de Sainte-Maure which Guido delle Colonne adapted as *Historia Destructionis Troiae* later in the thirteenth century. It was the source of three English versions of the tale: *The "Gest Hystoriale" of the Destruction of Troy, The Laud Troy Book,* and *Troy Book* by John Lydgate (1513). The English printer and writer, William Caxton, incorporated Lydgate's work in his famous *Recuyell of the Historyes of Troye* printed at Bruges in 1475. Another medieval Latin epic based on the Trojan story was *De Bello Trojano* by Joseph of Exeter. These "sub-Homeric" stories inspired the visual arts in the latter Middle Ages, such as the Tale of Troy tapestries by Pasquier Brenier at Tournai.[4] The plot was reworked by Giovanni Boccaccio (1313–75) in *Il Filostrato*, by Geoffrey Chaucer (*ca.* 1385) in *Troylus and Criseyde*, and by Shakespeare in a play by the same name. The plot of the romance concerned Troilus, a son of Priam, and his lover, Criseyde, a Trojan girl sent to the Greeks in a prisoner exchange, after which she fell in love with the Greek hero Diomedes. At this point the writers are a long way from the Homeric text!

The non–Homeric story (from the Trojan epic cycle) of the tragic love between Achilles and the Amazon queen Penthesilea was central to the Trojan story in the Middle Ages, which thrived on romance. The ancient Greek vase painters had also been fond of showing the moment when the great Achilles thrust the mortal blow into Penthesilea's body, the same moment that their eyes met and they fell in love. The chronicler Geoffrey of Monmouth (d. 1155 C.E.) in his famous book *Historia Regum Britanniae* (History of the Kings of Britain) invented the founder of Britain as the Trojan-Italian Brutus, the great-grandson of Aeneas. His story was later expanded by Robert Wace in *Roman de Brut* (1155) and again in the romance-chronicle *Brut* by the twelfth century Layamon, an early Middle English poet. It might be noted as an aside that these works were instrumental in creating the legend of King Arthur and his knights of the round table.

Medieval writers continued to use allegory to sanitize the Homeric text. St. Basil of Caesarea (*ca.* 329 C.E.–379 C.E.) believed that the whole of Homer's poetry should be understood as the praise of virtue, as in the case of the encounter of Odysseus with the Sirens, which he interpreted as a story of a virtuous man shunning the world's temptations.[5] From St. Augustine (d. 604 C.E.) to St. Thomas Aquinas (1224/5–1274) it was felt that the classical thinkers had developed reason to its fullest, but in lacking the true faith of Christianity had fallen short of the mind's full potential. Thus, the classical texts were not of interest. It was not until Francesco Petrarch (1304–74) in the early Renaissance that this assumption was questioned. The Humanists of the Renaissance (who will be studied in the next chapter) based their newly found interest in the classics on texts copied in medieval monasteries, where the candle of ancient writing flickered but was kept burning. In the Middle Ages both Greek and Latin were hard to learn, both then being "dead" languages, but Latin was needed for church liturgy. There was some Greek preserved in chants and hymns, but, for the most part, it was considered an obscure but sacred language from which only a few words and symbols remained, such as Jesus's words, "I am the alpha and the omega." Only a very few tried to go beyond Latin to learn the dying Greek language.[6]

There were no bilingual (Greek and Latin) texts of Homer and, in fact, it seems that there were few texts of Homer at all preserved among the ancient manuscripts in medieval monasteries; memory of his works was virtually gone. "For the Latin Middle Ages, it was not Homer but Dionysius [the Areopagite] who was the 'seer' for whose sake it was thought worthwhile to undertake the study of Greek."[7] Even St. Augustine preferred Latin writers, despite his Greek education, because he felt that Homer lacked substance. At the Frankish Carolingian court there was reverence for Greek as an aspiration to the glories of the past, and Homer was revered as a great name. A major change in the attitude of the West towards Greek came in the eleventh century in a movement called Reform Monasticism which sought to impose the kingdom of God, a kingdom envisioned as a Latin one. The rift between Latin and Greek East had opened too wide for closing. "It is an open question whether it was the official schism (1054), the first crusade (1095)—in which the Greek Christians were often regarded as at least as foreign as the Moslems—or only the conquest of Constantinople by the Latins (1204) that opened the chasm that no attempts at reunification during the late Middle Ages and modern period have been able to bridge."[8] Greek was considered unimportant in the cathedral schools of the West out of which the universities later grew. Hardly a nod was made towards the ancient Greek world. About 1170, the French poet Chretien de Troyes, who is best known for his romances which spread the legend of King Arthur to Europe, wrote: "Our books teach us that Greece had the first and greatest renown for chivalry and also for learning. Then chivalry came to Rome, and the sum of learning did likewise, which thereafter came to France."[9]

Unlike the historical development of western Europe, the continuity of culture in the Greek East continued without break following the establishment *ca.* 330 C.E. of a new Roman capital at Byzantium on the Bosphorus by the Emperor Constantine, which he renamed Constantinople. As Homeric studies faded in the Latin West, Syria, Egypt, and the Byzantine cities of Constantinople and Salonica in northern Greece became centers for its study and initiated the first period of what may be considered Byzantine scholarship. The Homeric text continued to serve as school material for learning to read, and an elementary grammatical commentary, the *Epimerismoi*, was composed probably in the sixth century. "Michael, Bishop of Ephesus early in the eleventh century, ...mentions that boys learned Homer by heart at school, thirty lines a day for the average pupil, up to fifty lines a day for the brightest."[10] The Homeric text was also used by rhetoricians as a model of eloquence, and it provided the most ancient description of pagan Greek religion.

As has been seen, criticisms of Homer on moral grounds, especially in a new Christian world, had been met by interpreting the poems allegorically, holding hidden meanings "that comprised either appropriate moral precepts, or a description of the workings of the physical universe, or an allusion to historical events."[11] Homer's text had achieved an authority like no other except the Bible itself, which assured its preservation throughout the Byzantine period. "Moreover, the systematic search by the Neoplatonists for a deep and hidden meaning in the poems marks the climax of a long process of elevation of Homer from the status of an inspired poet to that of an equally inspired — and infallible — prophet, a man who had privileged access not only to the secrets of the universe

but to the mind of God, in the sense in which this term is used by a modern cosmolo-
gist such as Stephen Hawking."[12] However, *ca.* 400 C.E. the emperor banned Christians
from teaching Homer and Hesiod, not because their writings were outdated but because
they were subversive to Christianity in that they encouraged knowledge on its own ethical terms instead of those imposed by God. The historian Theodoret said that he
lamented: "We are shot with arrows feathered from our own wings for they make war
against us armed from our own books." After the ban there was an outpouring of Christian poetry, but Homer was not forgotten — the Gospel of John was rewritten in Homeric hexameters; Apollinarius of Laodicea wrote a Homeric-style epic on the antiquities
of the Hebrews in twenty-four books (like Homer); and there were other adaptations and
reuses of the Homeric text in the Christian context.[13]

   In the mid-fifth century C.E., a very unusual poem of a type called a "Homeric
cento" was written by Eudocia Augusta, the wife of the Byzantine emperor Theodosius
II. (Apparently, she had been exiled to Jerusalem by her husband for having an affair with
his most trusted advisor and found herself with time on her hands.) The word "cento"
meant "stitching" or "needlework" in the sense of making a patchwork quilt, and so the
term Homeric cento refers to an epic poem "made up entirely of verses lifted verbatim,
or with only slight modification, from the *Iliad* and *Odyssey*."[14] The resultant narrative
would be entirely Christian without any overt reference to the verses' origin — a true
"cut-and-paste" job! Several of these Homeric centos have survived, but that of the
Empress Eudocia is the longest, running to nearly 2,400 lines. The poem was clearly
intended to be performed orally and even used Homeric techniques such as formulae,
with the result that it reflected "both the mechanics and the esthetics of Homeric diction."[15] It seems that this poem was intended to be performed before audiences which
were very familiar both with the Homeric text and the Bible, because often understanding of the new biblical narrative is enhanced by knowing from where in Homer the original line was taken. What at first seems rather like the literature of juvenile plagiarism
or, at best, pedantic adult game playing is now understood to be quite a complex and
erudite literary format. The newly created biblical-based stories are neither Homer nor
the Bible. Thus, it could be said that the texts of two great works are destroyed in this
process, but a new literary work is created, phoenix-like from their ashes and, for the
well-educated, bearing evidence of its former incarnations.

   For example, there is a scene dealing with the theme of bereavement as the Virgin
Mary experiences the death of her son, Jesus, and the cento poem cleverly appropriates
material from *Iliad* Books 22 and 24, which deals with Priam's emotions upon the death
of his son Hector, to express the same emotions. In another example the poem describes
the Wedding at Cana using Homeric type-scenes of feasts, with the result that at Cana
there is dancing by bachelors and maidens, a minstrel, acrobats, and animal sacrifices,
none of which appears in the biblical account. When Judas is described entering the
Upper Room for the Last Supper, the centos poem appropriates lines from Homer's
description of the Trojan hero Sarpedon storming the wall protecting the Greek ships:
"He came on like a mountain lion when he's gone without meat for a spell and his strong
heart compels him to make an attempt on the sheep and go for the sheepfold." When
Jesus's disciples take down his body from the cross, lines from Homer's descriptions
of the fallen heroes Teucer and Patroclus are used: "And then, supporting him, two

faithful companions placed him on the bier, while his companions, his friends, stood around grieving; and a fresh tear fell from their cheeks." The dead Jesus is compared to the dead Hector in that both die naked and taunted, and both of their bodies are miraculously preserved after dying. Mary's lamentation over Jesus is actually Briseis, the concubine of Achilles, weeping for the dead Patroclus; Mary delivers a moving elegy for Jesus in the words of Andromache speaking of her dead husband Hector.[16]

"Eudocia's Centos comprise a single, continuous poem on a biblical theme that recounts the creation of the world, the temptation and fall of man, and the birth, life, death, resurrection, and ascension of Christ."[17] To create such a poem must have required remarkable patience, memory, and creativity, but the result was a literary work only recently appreciated by scholars who had tended to ignore it as a torn-up reflection of real literature. "Indeed, the semiotic magic at work in this poem is pervasive, for beneath the apparent mismatch of material on the Cento surface, the two source texts are strongly bound by theme and structure. As stories of quest, cunning, suffering, recognition, and return, the tales of Christ and Odysseus are compatible ... and their literary *Nachleben* [survival] attests to the adaptability of these two polytropic heroes."[18]

It has been noted that in the Byzantine Empire the practice of schoolboys learning to read, write and recite using the Homeric text continued, and aids for more learned men to read it more thoroughly remained available. Oddly, for a thousand years a profoundly Christian society retained the antiquated, pagan Homeric *Iliad* for use in schools instead of adopting or creating a more up-to-date Christian text; of course, Homer had been used for education for the previous thousand years, and it would have been hard to alter this tradition. In addition, a knowledge of Homer was equated with cultural sophistication and, perhaps more importantly, continued to be a symbol of the "superior" Greek world as opposed to the non–Greek, even though that Greek world was now a Christian one.[19] Writers and socialites explicitly adorned their writings and speech with Homeric quotes and they also made reference to people and events of their own day using Homeric terms. For example, "when [the emperor] Constantine IX introduced his mistress Skleraina to the court for the first time, a bystander murmured *ou nemesis*, echoing the words of the Trojan elders when Helen passed by."[20] Byzantine teachers produced a variety of reading aids, "in particular the line-by-line and sometimes word-by-word paraphrases of the poetic text, which are often found written interlinearly."[21] In the ongoing tradition of manuscript production the Homeric text was copied over and over, both completely and in part for collections of great writers.

Many paraphrases of Homer were made throughout the Byzantine period by scholars such as Procopius of Gaza, Manual Moschopoulos, and Michael Psellus. There was a great mass of mythological, grammatical, and allegorical material which survived from antiquity, and the Byzantine scholars used it as sources for marginal *scholia* in research manuscripts of Homer. Up until the eleventh century these sources were cited as authoritative, and they excluded Christian viewpoints; however, from this time on, writers began to question or quarrel with their sources, and Christian allegorizing interpretations crept into the *scholia*. As non-scholars began to read Homer, mostly in summaries, they wondered about the context of the stories within the larger picture of the Trojan War and even more about their meaning. "The Byzantines were not the first to see a hidden meaning in Homer. Those who replied to the criticisms of Xenophanes probably already had recourse to this method of avoiding the horns of a dilemma. The Stoics systematized the allegorical interpretation of Homer. And the Neoplatonists made it readily available in handbooks. All that was needed to make Homer entirely acceptable to the most orthodox Byzantine taste was to combine pagan Homeric allegory with Christian Old Testament allegory. And this is precisely what we find happening."[22]

The earliest surviving manuscript of Homer is called the *Venetus Marciannus* because it was discovered in the Marcian Library in Venice in 1779. It is written in early-tenth-century script designated as "minuscule" and contains details of the work of Aristarchus along with the Homeric text. Known to scholars as "A," this earliest text was published in 1788 by the French scholar J. B. G. d'Ansse de Villoison and became very important to the analyst F. A. Wolf whose *Prolegomena* was published in 1795. Another interesting manuscript of this period is called the *Ilias Ambrosiana* from its location in the Ambrosiana Library in Milan.[23] Originally it was a vellum codex of the whole *Iliad* written in Greek majuscule uncial script, but all that is left are fifty-two folio sheets containing 788 verses, about half of the total, and fifty-eight marvelous miniature paintings of a possible original two hundred created to illustrate the Homeric text.

During the Iconoclast movement, which outlawed all religious images from the time of Emperor Leo III in 718 until 843 C.E., there "was a period of complete stagnation, if not of actual persecution, for Classical studies."[24] Following the fall of Iconoclasm, there was a second period of Byzantine Homeric scholarship which ended in the sack of Constantinople during the Fourth Crusade (1204 C.E.). This period is commonly called the Comnenian Renaissance, and there was a general flowering of literature and the arts and specific interest in classical scholarship by the royal house. "Alexius Comnenus, at the beginning of the century, had written classical iambics of *Advice to a Son*. [In] his daughter Anna Comnena's great work, the *Alexias* ... her quotations from Homer are almost as frequent as her quotations from the Bible, and they are more accurate. ...Her brother, Isaac actually writes essays on Homer, as well as original poetry in classical and Byzantine meters."[25] Isaac's tracts on Homer were directed to the general reader and included such titles as *What Homer Left Out, Descriptions of the Greeks and Trojans at Troy*, and a *Preface to Homer*.[26]

There are twelve surviving manuscripts of the Homeric text from this period, during which the best Homeric scholars were John Tzetzes (*ca.* 1110–1180) and Eustathius of Salonica (*ca.* 1110–1192). About 1140 Tzetzes wrote an erudite commentary on the *Iliad*, intended as a schoolbook. It seems, however, that he tended to hurt his advancement opportunities by being too outspoken, especially against people who held power. In a letter he called those who failed to understand his erudition "ignorant abominations, babble-twisters, men who have barbarized the art of letters by not minding books, where all wealth lies. Their nectar is the stink of the dunghill — pigs do not want to eat the bread of angels."[27] In 1146 he received a commission to compose a treatise called *Homeric Allegories* for Berta-Eirene, the young German consort of the emperor Manual I, to familiarize her with Greek culture, and it included summaries of the Homeric poems and interpretations of passages from them. However, before he finished it, Tzetzes seems to have bungled the well-paying opportunity by assuming that since he was being paid by the amount of pages produced he might as well double- and triple-space his work; unfortunately, the secretaries of the Imperial Treasury were not amused and the contract was cancelled. Tzetzes also wrote the *Carmina Homerica*, three hexameter poems in which he covered the whole Trojan War cycle, drawing material from Homer and others. He earned his living primarily by teaching and not by selling his books, and the following lines from a letter to a father reveal this side of his work and the continuing use of the Homeric text to teach the young: "I feel it a wound in *my own* heart; I am deeply sorry for you ... his fellow-students construed five whole books [of Homer], and he was left completely behind, as I said to you personally. Since he made a second start, the other students have been working on another three books; some have got to the end, some to the middle, and some at least well away from the beginning, but *he* has not construed anything at all."[28]

Probably, the greatest scholar in Byzantine Homeric studies was Eustathius, who was the bishop of Salonica in northern Greece and who wrote the most massive *Commentary* on the *Iliad* and *Odyssey* that has ever been attempted. "He had read everything — or so he would have us believe."[29] Not only did he collect every scrap of previous commentary or tradition he could find but "the spoken Greek of his time, the customs of peasants and townsmen around him, popular beliefs, recent events, are all made to shed light on the poems. Homer in a sense belonged to the same world as Eustathios, and his poetry could be understood by accumulation of information and exercise of reasoning."[30] Fortunately, this encyclopedic work of antiquarianism and criticism has been preserved completely and even today is referred to by Homeric scholars, since it is the best source for trivia, stories, and comments on the Homeric text not only from the Byzantine era, but also some which had survived from antiquity. Eustathius made it clear in his preface that "the commentary is not a text-book but rather a companion to the *Iliad*, to be read with or without the Homeric text, by adults as well as by schoolboys, and for many different purposes."[31] He criticized those who had treated Homer allegorically, preferring to look for factual information or to accept unbelievable portions as myths, and it is clear that he loved the poems as great works of literature. Eustathius also attributed to Homer access to superhuman knowledge of the world through philosophy and believed that his poems were designed to lead them to it. "Homer's myths are not there for fun. They are shadows, or veils, of noble thoughts.... He weaves his poetry with myths to attract the multitude. The trick is to use their surface appearance as a bait and charm for men who are frightened of the subtleties of philosophy, until he traps them in the net. Then he will give them a taste of truth's sweetness, and set them free to go their ways as wise men, and to hunt for it in other places."[32] Homer was seen as a pagan Moses, revealing the divine mind.

The third period of Byzantine scholarship, called the Palaeologian Renaissance, began with the reestablishment of the capital of Constantinople in 1261. Homer's poems continued to be appreciated as great literature, as is shown by a thirteenth-century monk's note on Nonnus's hexameter *Paraphrase of the Gospel of John*: "One must know, moreover, that the reading of Greek literature is always something lovely and desirable for lovers of learning, and most of all that of the writings of Homer, on account of his eloquence and variety of diction. For this reason, the present paraphrase was written in heroic verse, for the delight of lovers of learning and of language."[33] By the fourteenth century, however, Byzantine scholars began to turn their attention to Athenian drama and Pindar and away from Homer who continued, nevertheless, to play his age-old role in the schoolroom. Some scholars did write new commentaries on the Homeric poems, and there were new works written for the general public about the Trojan War. In the fourteenth century, an anonymous writer translated into vernacular Greek the Old French *Roman de Troie* by Benoit de Sainte-Maure, who had written this adaptation of the Homeric poems from Latin versions preserved in the West.

5

HOMER, RENAISSANCE HUMANISM, AND THE PRINTING PRESS

The intellectual horizon of western Europe opened up in the late Middle Ages and early Renaissance due to a flood of refugee scholars, "a veritable diaspora,"[1] fleeing to the West from the collapsing Byzantine Empire and due to the relearning of the Greek language with their assistance. There was a resurgence of Hellenism in Norman Sicily from the eleventh to thirteenth centuries and this spread into Italy. By the middle of the fourteenth century there was a renewal of interest in the classical world, which began in Italy and later expanded to northern Europe; in 1453 C.E. the Byzantine Empire was snuffed out by the conquest of the Ottoman Turks—but the Homeric legacy had been preserved there long enough to live on in the West. Actually, the survival of the Homeric text through antiquity and the Middle Ages is somewhat of a miracle given that for most ancient authors no texts survive at all, and even for famous ones only a few titles were preserved (for example, seven of the over one hundred plays written by the Greek tragedian Sophocles). Homer's wide preservation in the manuscript tradition allowed him to reemerge in the new world of print. "The complete manuscripts of Homer are almost without number, so many are they that the Oxford Edition of Homer is based on nearly one-hundred-and-fifty manuscripts, most of which are good, so good that almost any two or three would suffice to establish the Homeric text."[2] "It may be concluded ... that the origins of the Western interest in Greek owed far less to the native traditions of rhetorical practice or medieval precedents than to direct or indirect contact with the Byzantine East."[3]

Venice established itself as the center of Greek scholarship *ca.* 1500 due to her schools, including the nearby university of Padua, the many printers producing first editions of the Greek classics, and the necessity for its colonial administrators to learn to read Greek. Previously, the Greek language, lost in most of western Europe during the Middle Ages, had been preserved in southern Italy and Sicily, for example in the Hohenstaufen and Angevin courts of Naples and Palermo. The Arabs in Spain, Sicily and northern Africa had been transmitters back to the West, from the eleventh to thirteenth centuries, of the works of Aristotle and other Greek scientific and philosophical writings. These versions, which were translated into Latin, were often preferred to translations directly from the Greek texts preserved in Byzantium, due to anti–Byzantine feelings. Progress in learning of Greek came in the fourteenth century in Florence, Ferrara and Rome, but by 1500 Venice succeeded the Florence of the famous Medici family as the intellectual center of the Renaissance. Venice had become a great colonial empire by participating in the shameful Latin conquest of Constantinople in 1204. Thus, her administrators now had to deal with Greek-speaking and -writing officials in the old Greek world, and as the dominant city Venice was the place to which many of the fleeing Greek scholars came. The University of Padua became a center for the new Renaissance humanism, a movement promoting full development of human virtue based on classical models, and learned Byzantine dignitaries visited Venice. By the late fifteenth century, Venetian aristocrats were including intellectual pursuits, such as studying Greek writers, in their training, which had previously been focused on commerce and navigation as was appropriate to an imperial naval power. In 1463 the Venetian Signoria established a chair of Greek letters with a fixed stipend at the University of Padua; the first occupant was the Athenian Demetrius Chalcondylas, whose excellent instruction spurred on Greek enthusiasts.[4]

The revival of interest in Greek writers initially focused on ones dealing with the natural sciences, especially Aristotle, but about 1200 there was a shift of interest to other ancient texts with the rise of humanism. "The humanistic shift of axes has begun in Western consciousness— away from theology and philosophy, toward poetry, history, the epistolary art, rhetoric; away from all despicable Scholastic scholarship, toward the artistic freedom of the individual; away from the 'Middle Ages,' toward antiquity!"[5] The humanist scholar Francesco Petrarch (1304–74) was the first northern European scholar to turn from medieval models of literature to classical ones, rising above the typical medieval assumption that classical writers had exhausted the possibilities of the mind but lacked the Christian truths in doing so. Petrarch, like all fourteenth-century Westerners, held the Greeks of his time in contempt, but in studying Latin authors he began to find quotes and references to ancient Greek writers and became interested. In doing so he rediscovered a body of literature that had been passed over in the West since late antiquity, and found it to be very exciting. "To study the lives of the ancients, for Petrarch, was like learning how to live."[6] He found that classical writers could help him struggle with human issues, such as grief and fear, which medieval thinkers had assumed only Christianity could address. As he worked his way through the ancient writers he decided that the best was the Latin poet Virgil, but he put Homer second even though at that time in the West he could not have read his works. In 1354 Petrarch acquired from his friend Nicholas Sigerus, an envoy in Constantinople, a Greek manuscript of Homer, and his response to the sender is remarkable for showing the early Renaissance eagerness to get an actual text of Homer, even if it was still unreadable:

> You have sent me from the confines of Europe a gift than which nothing could be more worthy of the donor, more gratifying to the recipient, or more noble in itself. Some make presents of gold and silver, others again of jewelry and the goldsmith's work. You have given me Homer, and, what makes it the more precious, Homer pure and undefiled in his own tongue. Would, however, that the donor could have accompanied his own gift! for, alas! your Homer is dumb in my presence, or rather I am deaf in his! Yet I rejoice at the mere sight of him alone, and I often embrace him and say with a sigh, "O great man, how I long to hear you."[7]

Both Petrarch and the humanist scholar Boccaccio wanted to read the Greek texts in the original and turned to two south Italian Greeks, Barlaam and Leontius Pilatus, to teach them. Petrarch was, however, unsuccessful in his studies and convinced Boccaccio to have his codex of Homer translated into Latin by their teacher Pilatus. Unfortunately, Pilatus used the method employed for translating scientific texts, that of copying the text with wide spacing to permit the insertion of a word-for-word translation in-between. This method is adequate for scientific works but unsuitable for poetry, and it seems that Pilatus's Greek and Latin were hardly up to the great task put before him. "But the spirits had been awakened: Homer had returned to Western consciousness. Now it was clear that there was no way to avoid a systematic study of Greek if one wished to find 'the source and origin of all divine invention' (Petrarch, with Macrobius, on Homer) among the Greeks."[8] This translation was superseded in the mid-fifteenth century by the Latin translation of Lorenzo Valla (1407–1457), and about the same time the first translations of Homer into modern vernacular languages began, as will be discovered in the next chapter.

Petrarch's friend Boccaccio (1313–1375) had been more successful at learning Greek, and he took up the old practice of inserting Greek quotations into Latin text. In his *Genealogiae Deorum Gentilium* he put long quotes from Homer in Greek characters into the text and inserted Pilatus' translation in the margin. About 1400, Plutarch was rediscovered and translated, another important ancient writer to be recovered by the early humanists. An impetus for Greek studies in the West came when the Byzantine emperor Manuel II Palaeologus sent Manuel Chrysoloras to implore the West for aid against the Turks; afterwards, Chrysoloras came and taught Greek in Florence, and his work began an era of great Greek translations and studies which was important for the growth of humanism. "Manuel Chrysoloras represents an exordium of the Greek school tradition in the West, of the 'discovery' of Greek authors and their large-scale translation into Latin."[9] Earlier medieval or late antique translations were considered barbaric and new ones were done with style in mind, not just meaning. Among these new translations into elegant Virgilian Latin were Homer's *Iliad* and *Odyssey*. The older Latin word for "translation" had been "transferre" and it was now deemed primitive and medieval; the word "traducere" was used in its place, and it was thought to mean translation with the classical spirit and embellishments. The humanists sought far and wide for new Greek texts to translate, abandoning medieval religious authors for ancient Greek ones. "When Dionysius the Areopagite disappeared from the purview of Greek studies in the West, he was replaced not by the Bible, but rather by Homer, and the Greek Fathers saw their rank contested by the ancient Greek epic poets, historians, and dramatists."[10] The humanists began to conceive of an idealized Greco-Roman antiquity that they considered they had newly discovered; any surviving medieval threads were forgotten and the Middle Ages were dismissed as "Dark Ages" of ignorance.[11]

It would seem logical that the humanists would have rejected allegorical interpretations of classical literature in favor of understanding the proper historical distinctions of the pagan and Christian past. "Even at the start of the Northern Renaissance, allegory seemed a survival of the fusty late-medieval world of the classicizing friars."[12] But this opinion actually triumphed only in the eighteenth and nineteenth centuries, as modern classical scholarship showed the ancient and medieval *scholia* to be appropriate subjects

for critical study without subscribing to their allegorical overburdens. The early humanists, in contrast, were still liable to fall into the trap of interpretative allegory. "Those
who despised ancient and medieval interpreters so thoroughly could hardly imagine that
they had been primary models for the first modern scholars in the fifteenth and sixteenth
centuries."[13] The great fifteenth-century scholar Angelo Poliziano wrote *scholia* on the
Iliad which were full of allegorical interpretations. Scholars in general and even the early
translators, such as George Chapman, continued to view Homer as all-knowing because
through allegory his poems seemed to reveal him as the premier moralist, scientist and
theologian. "An international consensus recognized Homer as a sage and saw allegoresis
as the Ariadne's thread that could lead the reader through the maze of his poems to the
core of truth."[14]

The Renaissance humanists were as often influenced by the ancient allegorists as by
the ancient texts themselves, and their failure to distinguish the two led to sincere reading and study of the later interpretations with the same reverence as given to the original poetry. Those who did reject moralizing, allegorical readings were often receptive to
the astronomical ones, due to their own new interest in the cosmos. "It was not until the
very end of the eighteenth century that Wolf definitively relegated ancient allegorical
readings of Homer to the realm of history. Before his time even the sharpest critics of
some forms of allegory — like his own teacher C. G. Heyne — were normally not modern
Aristarchuses, opponents of all allegories, but modern Porphyrys, who thought that they
themselves knew where to draw the obscure but vital line that the targets of their criticism overstepped."[15]

Some of the Renaissance scholars, in puttering around with late antiquity's views
of Homer's omniscience so frequently quoted, began to develop a better understanding
not of Homeric poetry itself necessarily but of the methods, contexts, and purposes of
those doing the quoting. Some scholars attacked Homer on all fronts, such as Julius Cae-
sar Scaliger, whose *Poetics,* published in 1561, took the diametrically opposed position to
that of the sympathetic Aristotle's ancient treatise by the same name. Others, such as
Obertus Giphanius and Isaac Casaubon, defended Homer, the former supposing that oral
transmission had corrupted the poems and introduced errors, and the latter reading the
poems in the context of a primitive society instead of judging their details in comparison to modern practices. In many ways these arguments were followed by the seventeenth-century scholars whose long-lasting debate about the superior merits of classical
versus recent literature was called the Quarrel of the Ancients and Moderns. "Defenders of modernity ... would follow Scaliger's lead and abuse Homer for his lapses in eti-
quette and taste, his princesses who did their own laundry and his palaces that had dung
piles before them. Defenders of Homer would emulate Giphanius and Casaubon, arguing that the epics had been corrupted in transmission and in any event imitated the realities of a simpler and a purer world."[16]

The problems for Renaissance scholars included dealing with a hodgepodge of peculiar texts associated with the great poet's works and also the odd interpretations which
had survived from antiquity. The early printed editions of Homer were so burdened
down with a variety of treatises, "lives," notes, etc. that it was hard for Renaissance
humanists to avoid being influenced and to see the actual text plainly. "The earliest editions of Homer, like the manuscripts on which they were based, were encumbered with

introductory essays of an interpretive nature ranging from the richly imaginative essay on the case of the Nymphs in *Odyssey* 13 by the Neoplatonist Porphyry to the ponderous encomium that went under the name of Plutarch and the title *On the Life and Poetry of Homer*.[17] Early printed editions of Homer usually appended some of these odd treatises to the actual text of the poet himself, but since the eighteenth century the trend has been to strip out these extra materials. Princeton University Library owns the copy of the first printed edition of Homer (1488) which belonged to the Renaissance scholar Guillaume Bude. His marginal notes are as extensive for the appended text of pseudo–Plutarch's *The Life and Writings of Homer* as they are for the *Iliad* and *Odyssey* and clearly show how the scholars of this time were as influenced by ancient allegorical interpretations as by the actual Homeric text. And so he is found, for example, accepting "Athena's restraint of Achilles as a physical allegory of the bipartite soul and a moral one of the opposition between prudence and anger."[18] Bude was, however, a serious scholar whose work, if not personality, was well respected. It would be a slight on the gods of humor to leave him without noting that "his rather chilly formality emerges well from the famous remark that he made to the servant who came to tell him, at his wife's request, that their house was on fire, 'Kindly inform your mistress that domestic matters are her affair.'"[19]

The use of allegory to sanitize Homer for a Christian world continued in use into the Early Modern era. In 1660, James Duport, Regius professor of Greek at Cambridge University, wrote a book titled *Homeri Gnomologia,* in which his parallels between Homeric maxims and the Bible show the height of silliness to which allegorical interpretation can reach. A sympathetic reader of the book declared of Homer: "tis certain his Work was a kind of New Gospel to the Pagans, couch'd according to the Customs of those Times under Fables, Parables and Allegories, and every where carries a visible conformity with Holy Scripture both in Phrase and Sentiments."[20] About the same time, Joshua Barnes, also a Cambridge University classicist, published a treatise "proving" that the Homeric poems were, in fact, written by King Solomon! Fortunately, it would only be a century before the birth of modern critical literary analysis.

An important development was the appropriation of Homer for the creation of individual national epics in his footsteps. The first serious epic after the medieval mock-heroic poetry was *Gerusalemme Liberata,* written in Latin by Tasso (1575) using the heroic theme of the First Crusade and done in a Homeric manner. The epic poem called *The Luciads*, written by Portugal's great national poet Luis Vaz de Camoens (1525–80) used an *Aeneid/Odyssey* model to treat the voyage to India of Vasco da Gama. In France a group of seven writers called the Pleiade devoted themselves to classical literature, especially Homer, who now began to eclipse Virgil in the estimation of critics. The Pleide greatly influenced Edmund Spenser, whose famous *Faerie Queene* (1590–96) was actually more related to Tasso's epic than to Homer, who still was available only in poor Latin translations. Eventually, John Milton resolved to write an English epic rivaling Virgil and Homer, and the resultant *Paradise Lost* (1667) was greatly influenced by both ancient works: "Except for the subject ... *Paradise Lost* is only less Homeric than the *Aeneid* itself."[21]

One of the most important inventions of the Renaissance was the printing press, an epochal development in human history. In the new era of printed books the history of Homer turns away from the manuscript transmission tradition to how the Homeric text

The Papermaker

The Typefounder

The printing of a book by hand required several operations: making paper, casting type, setting the type and inking it before pulling the lever of the press, and binding the resultant sheets into a book. (From an engraving by Jost Anman, 1568.)

made the pivotal transmutation into the printed word. About 1450 C.E., an entrepreneur in Mainz, Germany, named Johann Gutenberg realized that the technologies of engravers and wine-press makers could be combined in an innovative way to dramatically speed up the production of formerly manuscript texts. He could not have imagined how his invention of a printing press that used individually cut and, thus, moveable type would be the most significant turning point in information storage since the beginning of writing itself! Within a very few years the technology of the printing press spread all over Europe, and books of every sort were being mass-produced.

The printing press had profound, permanent effects upon scholarship and literature, including the Homeric text, as the lower cost and greater number of printed editions resulted in widespread access to works previously available only to a privileged few. From the fifteenth century to the present, Homer has become increasingly accessible to readers of all types with myriad results, the most direct of which (improved texts and vernacular translations) form the basis of Part II of this book. Increasing numbers of writers began to undertake the challenges of incorporating Homeric stories into their works while scholars searched for the "best" text and translators rendered them into the modern languages of the world. Responses to a text can take many forms: "They range from admiration to mockery, from preservation to elimination, from translation to transformation, from imitation to creative alteration.... The translations are themselves creative works, reflecting the culture of their times."[1] With options available, personal taste determines preferences for one translation of Homer over another. And translators, as will be seen, have varied tremendously in their approaches to the Homeric text. In his or her own way, each translator must undertake a personal search for Homer.

Personal aesthetic tastes also began to govern preferences among the printed format of the many editions available. Some had small print and were almost miniature in size, while others had large, easy-to-read print with wide margins and were almost of the size of a pulpit Bible. Some were bound in vellum, some in crude, plain leather, and others were lovingly bound in gold-tooled morocco leather with personalized markings. The format of a person's edition of Homer can influence his or her opinion of him — people sometimes do judge a book by its cover (or by its font and layout). As Marshall McLuhan, the well-known communications theorist of the 1960's, would say two hundred years later: "The medium is the message." Various presses outdid their rivals at different times, and popularity shifted.

6

THE HOMERIC TEXT IN THE MODERN WORLD: TRANSLATIONS AND EDITIONS

On Translating Homer

In this chapter, which is broken up into sections by date ranges, the highlights of printed editions of Homer from the true *editio princeps* (first edition) in 1488 to the end of the twentieth century will be studied. Each section will begin with commentary on significant or interesting printings from that period. In most sections there will be samples of translations of the first lines of the *Iliad*, along with biographical information about the most important and most interesting translators. Part II is a thorough bibliographic checklist of every known printing of the Homeric text. Appendix A is a discussion of how this list was achieved with notes on format, scope, etc. Included in the list are not only editions of the *Iliad* and the *Odyssey*, but also the other works thought until recently also to derive from a historical Homer: the *Epigrams*, the *Hymns*, the *Centones*, and the *Battle of the Frogs and Mice* (*Batrachomyomachia* in Greek; *Frosch- und Mauskrieg* or *Froschmausekampf* or *Krieg der Mause* in German; and *Les Fantastiques Batailles des Grans Rois Rodilardus et Croaeus* or *Le Grand Combat des Ratz et des Grenouilles* in French). The latter is the most interesting of these works and, as will be seen, was highly prized in various periods.

The detailed study of Homeric texts on a year-to-year basis provides a useful basis to follow its development and spread through time and space. In fact, such an analysis represents the modern evolution of Western culture as a whole with its foundation firmly on its ancient roots. The graph of the number of printings of Homer by year shown in Appendix A provides direct evidence of this remarkable development.

Before looking at the printed texts and translations from the fifteenth through twentieth centuries, it is worth pausing to consider the concept of translation itself. At first blush, especially to persons unschooled in languages other than their own, translation seems simple — "Just tell me what it says…" But the human mind is very complex, resulting in the fact that words often have many levels of meaning, and for the translator it is important to know as much as possible about the author as well as the receiver of a text to be able to make an adequate translation. "The translation process is, of course, an extremely difficult one, and in some sense impossible, if one keeps in mind Dante's maxim that 'the translator is a traitor.' The Italian poet warned us 700 years ago that any writer seeking to carry belles lettres over from one language to another, in anything but the most stupefying way, would be faced with a universe of compromises. Decisions must be made about what elements of the poem need to be retained and which ones can be slightly changed without *entirely* betraying the original."[2] Some misogynist wag has observed that, as with wives, there is an inverse relationship between beauty and fidelity in a text and its translation.

Literal translations from one language to another are not truly possible because of the nuances of meanings when certain word groups are associated, when words are given a special and meaningful order which only one language can interpret, and when reference is made to a cultural artifact appropriate only to one of the two language cultures. "The translator has a double responsibility. He must be faithful to the meaning of the original, but he must also be faithful to the nature of his own language."[3] If an English speaker in France is being plied with too much food by a gracious host, he or she might directly translate the words "I am full" into their French equivalents "Je suis plein." However, this French phrase has a higher level of meaning which linguists call an idiom; to a French person it means "I am pregnant" in the sense, particularly, of a female animal being pregnant! And there would be even higher levels of meaning for this phrase depending on who said it and who heard it. Consider, for example, the variant meanings coming from a man versus a woman; or from a married lady versus a teenaged girl. Could there be other levels of meaning here? For example, perhaps the speaker actually knew the idiomatic meaning and was making a joke against "stupid" Americans who were ignorant of it. Could the phrase be a quotation from a commonly known book or movie to which the speaker is referring? A translator must know as much as possible about the context, the author, and the hearer or reader to translate a seemingly simple text correctly by rendering the various levels of meaning.

Similarly, in considering a translation of Homeric poetry, a translator must conduct his or her own search for Homer by considering both the time frame of the poem, for whom the original was composed, and for whom the translation is intended. If a translator envisions Homer as the prince of poets weaving his tale for aristocratic courtiers, his or her translation is likely to use more highbrow verbiage than the translator who believes Homer to have been an impoverished, peripatetic bard wandering from city to city telling stories in the town square. If the translation is intended for pleasurable reading by the general public, the translator might edit the wording to improve understandability, use archaic sounding words to make it sound old-fashioned, or use flowery wording to reflect the Greek poetic style. Many scholars who read Homeric Greek have considered translation impossible, preferring that everyone should learn to read Homer in the original Greek: "The poetry of Homer is so melodious in meter, vocabulary, and inflection that it is impossible to give even a faintly adequate idea of its beauty by means of paraphrase or translation"; and "The essential thing with Homer ... is the magical, bewitching, irresistible, intoxicating sweep of the music of his meter. There is no meter in the world, there never has been, that can equal the hexameter of Homer."[4]

There has been, however, no dearth of translators and pundits on translation in different eras who have looked to a variety of models to try to reproduce Homer. For example, one wrote: "In the first place, the syntax must be simple and natural. For models the student can find nothing better than the English Bible, Chaucer, Latimer, Bunyan, and other writers who have lived not amongst books but in close contact with human life and with nature.... A fine style, noble yet simple, is not impossible to hope for; the real difficulty is the verse."[5] Another tried to boil down the problems of translation of poetry in general: "Poetry, to be savagely brief, is metrical speech. The translation of metrical speech can take one of two forms: the literal, in which one attempts to give as close a rendering of the original as possible and in which verse will most conveniently be abandoned for prose, since the exigencies of meter will of necessity force the translator either to expand or to contract the matter he is attempting to transfuse in as unadulterated a state as possible; and the poetic, in which one's primary concern is not literalness but is rather the attempt to convey in verse, through stylistic equivalents, selected stylistic qualities of the original."[6]

Trying to translate the poetry of Homer is especially hard. "The poetic translator is in a doubly difficult position, then; for he must be constantly aware of the fusion of style and meaning in his original and constantly aware of the fact that just because it is a fusion he cannot reproduce it. At the same time, furthermore, he must remain aware of his duty to his own language; for he is claiming to shape it in such a way that it is somehow related to the original poem and at the same time related in a more complex way than that of the literal translation. It is this complexity of relation, ultimately, which restrains us from making any abstract and theoretical judgment about what a poetic translation should do. We are forced instead to consider rather carefully what it has done and then, with reference to the original, to note its virtues and defects as well as its independent interest. If an *Iliad* translation should turn out to be in no sense a heroic poem, it seems likely that it would be unsatisfactory in a number of other ways as well. But it might turn out to be a very different sort of heroic poem from its original and still have legitimate claims as a poetic translation."[7] Of course, this focus on the beauty of the Homeric verse overlooks the beauty of the masterful plot narration and characterization which can, of course, be translated. In the final analysis a translation can never be the same as the original and cannot help but be heavily influenced not only by the time and cultural norms of the translator but also by those who have gone before. In fact, a translation stands as a work of literature on its own, bearing a greater or lesser dependence on the original through voluntary and involuntary choices of the translator. "There is no possibility of neutrality in translation."[8]

The stalwart person daring to attempt a new translation would initially have to make a major decision as to whether to try to craft a version in verse to parallel the original format of Homer or whether to transform its content into prose, which is more readable. If the translation is intended for use by students of ancient history, the translator would probably sacrifice line structure and flow in order to maintain accuracy of meaning from the original; the result would be a better resource for understanding the Homeric text and the culture portrayed in the original but would not be as good an "armchair read" as a translation crafted for ease and flow of style. As has been seen, however, Homer was not portraying one actual historical period or culture — rather, the poems describe a fictional, heroic culture that is an amalgam of various time periods and literary creativeness. A translator of Homer must "know Homeric culture" in this broader-than-historical sense, even though there is a circular argument involved. "We should not speak of the 'background' of the poems, as though we could reconstruct Homeric society and then apply this reconstruction to interpretation of the poems. On the contrary: we discover the society by interpreting the poems, just as we learn Homeric Greek, not in order to read Homer, but by reading Homer."[9]

The translator must not sacrifice accuracy in making his rendering readable. A simple example of a translator's dilemma is found in the New Testament parable (Mark 12:42) usually referred to as "The Widow's Mite." The point of the story is that the woman was extremely poor but still made a gift of her last two lowest value coins. But how to translate the name of the coin? In the Greek, its actual name is *lepton* (plural *lepta*), but using this word in a translation would confuse the modern reader. The name of the parable comes from the fact that early translators of the Bible decided to substitute the name for the lowest value coin in the sixteenth century England, a "mite"; today in America the word would be "penny." Notice how whatever word the translator selects is either an unintelligible archaism useful to scholars only or else a paraphrase of the original text with the value of making the text's meaning understandable but sacrificing exactness. Multiply this type of problem thousands of times over, and you can see the difficulties facing the translator of Homer. And how should a translator render the names of the characters when some have come to have spellings that are not exact transliterations of the Greek letters? For example, should it be the more accurate "Achilleus" or the more familiar "Achilles"? "Hektor" or "Hector"? The names of the gods pose a further problem in that many are better known by Roman names instead of Greek ones — should it be "Hera" or "Juno"? "Zeus" or "Jupiter" or "Jove"? And should the translator call the invasion force at Troy "Greeks," a word never used by the Greeks themselves either today, in antiquity or in the poems? William Cowper in a prefatory note to his translation (1791) solved the problem thusly: "The English reader will be pleased to observe, that by Achaians, Argives, Danai, are signified Grecians. Homer himself having found these various appellatives both graceful and convenient, it seemed unreasonable that a translator of him should be denied the same advantage." But should the more accurate "Achaians" be used or the more commonly used "Achaeans"; the older sounding "Grecians" or "Greeks" if the decision is made to go that route?

In the 1960s it was observed that "of the contemporary translations of Homer most are inadequate, not because of any lack of scholarship in the part of the translators, but because, in their effort to bring Homer within the purview of modern understanding, they have sacrificed much of the poet's antique flavor and much of his majesty."[10] However, more recent translators have done well to overcome these problems, even though in the final analysis "perhaps no translation can enable us to understand Homer as the Greeks understood him...."[11] Is it possible, in fact, to translate Homer? "To translate Homer — what does that mean? As to what it ought to mean (if only we could define it), there would, no doubt, be general agreement. But we find that what it actually does mean is Chapman or Pope, Cowper or Lord Derby. These are the names Maurice Hewlett chose to illustrate his doctrine that 'every age has the translation which it deserves'; they are names which might equally well illustrate the theorem that, in style and spirit, in manner and atmosphere, to translate Homer may mean anything: and the throng of minor versions enforces the theorem…. It ought to mean, a version equivalent to the whole of him, the whole of his manner as well as the whole of his matter. But it would seem that poetry will never again be capable of combining all the qualities which Homer contains. However Homeric the things may be the translator brings over into his English, he is sure to leave out things equally Homeric…."[12]

The best-known commentary on how the Homeric text should be translated was written by the Victorian poet and literary and social critic Matthew Arnold in 1861, with many subsequent editions and reprintings. "His lectures on translating Homer were the first adequate estimate, at least in English, of the literary qualities of the *Iliad* and *Odyssey* and did much to destroy the notion of a native genius or inspired folk-poet. Homer was now seen to be a conscious artist and took his place once and for all as the chief poet of antiquity, as Dante was of the Middle Ages and Shakespeare of modern times."[13] In his book Arnold reviewed most of the existing English translations (and some of his comments will appear below). From this review and his own observations he extrapolated several rules for translating Homer. First, a translator should be "faithful" to the original, an ideal that Arnold noted requires the translator to choose between producing a text so smooth that the reader does not realize it is a translation versus reproducing certain oddities of the original language to remind the reader of its origin. Second, a translator should seek to reproduce Homer's style and effect on the reader. "The translator of Homer should above all be penetrated by a sense of four qualities of his author; — that he is eminently rapid; that he is eminently plain and direct, both in the evolution of his thought and in the expression of it, that is, both in his syntax and in his words; that he is eminently plain and direct in the substance of his thought, that is, in his matter and ideas; and, finally that he is eminently noble…."[14] Arnold argued against attempts to translate Homer's poetry into rhyming lines because it adds an unoriginal and modern poetic form. Because of the impossibility of reproducing the Homeric poetic meter, prose translations are to be preferred. Other commentators have agreed with this last observation: "In spite of the translator's fine sense of epic poetry and great prosodic ingenuity, it remains a sad fact that the hexameter is a medium unsuited to the English language."[15]

Arnold made an important point about literal translation versus reproduction of the poet's intent within the original language: "the translator must without scruple sacrifice, where it is necessary, verbal fidelity to his original, rather than run any risk of producing, by literalness, an odd and unnatural effect." For example, when dealing with names a translator rendering into English a Greek line with the name "Philippos" should realize that it is a name and simply make it "Philip," not "Lover of Horses" which it actually means; this is a mistake routinely made with the names of American Indians, such as "Sitting Bull" whose name was actually "Tatankayotake." And, finally, Arnold argued that only Classical scholars who read Homeric Greek can judge the quality of a translation of Homer, although he added that "no translation will seem to them of much worth compared with the original…."[16] This rather elitist position was championed by the famous poet and translator Alexander Pope: "[The translator of Homer] must hope to please but a few, those only who have at once a Taste of Poetry, and competent Learning. For to satisfy such as want either, is not in the Nature of this Undertaking; since a mere Modern Wit can like nothing that is not *Modern*, and a Pedant nothing that is not *Greek.*"[17] Fortunately, modern democratic society would disagree with these assessments; yes, only a classically trained scholar can evaluate the literal accuracy of the translation if that is its goal, but anyone with a sense of literary quality can judge how successful a rendering is which has been created for the purpose of readability.

W. H. D. Rouse, writing an introduction to a late edition of Arnold's book, noted that the goal of a translator should be to produce a "translation [that] must seem natural in rhythm, style and idiom, and intelligible without pause; it must please him as a similar composition in his own language would please; and its effect must not fall short of the author's reputation."[18] But he immediately noted: "Judged by this high standard, all translations are failures." In fact, no work of literature can be faithfully translated from one language to another because to do so would require it to be magically transformed from one culture to another, an impossibility given the infinite cultural details, implications and understandings unique to any given culture. At best, a reader can peer into a window and view the action, but the reader can never be inside the room unless he or she is truly bilingual and bicultural. The bottom line and most important realization in looking at any translations from one language to another, including Homer, is that, unless its sole purpose is a literal rendering for scholars or students, a translation is really a work of literature in the language of the translation. Thus, when Homer is read in the translation of, for example, Alexander Pope, it must be realized that this is, in fact, a permutation or reaction to the Homeric text resulting in the creation of something new in a new language; and, thus, it must be agreed that, in the words of one commentator: "Pope's *Homer* is one of the most illustrious books of English authorship."[19] It has been argued further that in some sense even scholars must be involved with translation: "Nobody can know enough of the Greek that Homer spoke to be in intimate possession of his poem. Therefore to read the original at all worthily is to fill out with hints and guesses. The leap the imagination must take is into creative translation. Successful translation is therefore the condition for knowledge. Hence the ultimate validating authority is the translator's not the scholar's."[20]

Cowper described the problems and goals of translation as follows: "There are minutiae in every language, which transfused into another will spoil the version. Such extreme fidelity is in fact unfaithful; such close resemblance takes away all likeness. The original is elegant, easy, natural; the copy is clumsy, constrained, unnatural. To what purpose is this owing? To the adoption of terms not congenial to your purpose, and of a context such as no man writing an original work would make use of. Homer is everything that a poet should be. A translation of Homer so made, will be everything that a translation of Homer should not be; because it will be written in no language under heaven; — it will be English, and it will be Greek; and therefore it will be neither. ...[H]e is the man best qualified as a translator of Homer, who has drenched, and steeped, and soaked himself in the effusions of his genius, til he has imbibed their colour to the bone; and who, when he is thus dyed through and through, distinguishing between what is essentially Greek, and what may be habited in English, rejects the former, and is faithful to the latter, as far as the purposes of fine poetry will permit, and no further: this, I think, may be easily proved. Homer is everywhere remarkable either for ease, dignity, or energy of expression; for grandeur of conception, and a majestic flow of numbers. If we copy him so

closely as to make every one of these excellent properties of his absolutely unattainable —
which will certainly be the effect of too close a copy, — instead of translating we murder
him ... an English manner must *differ* from a Greek one, in order to be graceful, and for
this there is no remedy."[21]

The translator E. V. "Rieu expressed the hope that he would not 'fall into the most
heinous crime a translator can commit, which is to interpose the veil of his own personality between his original and the reader.' But this is of course what no translator can
escape, whether what is interposed is the translator's own personality or the literary
convention of the time, or, most likely, a combination of both, for the translator is engaged
in the often thankless task of remolding the original in terms intelligible and acceptable
to the translator's idea of the appropriate literary style."[22] At the start of the introduction to the Earl of Derby's translation the editor wrote: "To praise Homer is the delight
of all who have ever attempted to translate him, and the despair."[23] Perhaps he was right!

So, every translator of the Homeric text has had to face and has had to try to overcome the dilemmas of translation in general and the specific challenges in translating
Homer; each one has come to a different solution. In the following sections a number of
translators through the centuries will be reviewed with accounts of their work and what
critics have thought of it. In several cases, the translator's life was very important or
interesting, and a more lengthy discussion of it has been provided than for others. For
many of the translations, the translator's rendering of the *Iliad*'s first lines, or proem
(prelude), an invocation frequently found in epic poetry which gives an invocation to
the Muse of poetry and a statement of the theme of the poem, will be quoted. Just reading the proem to each translation provides a feel for the translator's style and verbiage,
and it gives an understanding of the comments by critics.

The *Iliad*'s proem is a masterpiece of literary composition — the very first word
is *menin* which is often translated into English as "anger," and it sets the stage for the
whole epic. However, in Greek this is a powerful term, having the significance of
long-term, festering antagonism and, thus, "wrath" is a closer translation. The first
word of line 2, which reaches back to modify *menin* in line 1, is *oulomenen* which means
"destructive" — together these words lay out the whole poem's theme, the "destructive
wrath" of Achilles. Here is a raw, word-for-word, interlinear translation of the *Iliad*'s
proem without any alteration of the word order to make it sound better in English:

> *Menin aeide, thea, Peleiado Achilleos*
> Wrath sing, O goddess, of Peleus' son Achilles,
>
> *oulomenen, [h]e muri Achaiois alge etheken,*
> destructive, which to many Achaians pains caused
>
> *pollas d'iphthimous psychas Aidi proiapsen*
> many and brave souls to Hades sent
>
> *[h]eroon, autous de [h]eloria teuche kunessin*
> of heroes, them and prey prepared for dogs
>
> *oionoisi te daita — Dios d'eteleieto boule —,*
> for birds and feasts — of Zeus and was fulfilling will —,

ex [h]ou de ta prota diasteten erisante
from which they first parted contended

Atreides te anax andron kai dios Achilleus.
son of Atreus king of men and godlike Achilles.

The first problem for a translator is immediately evident — the English speaker wants to put the imperative verb at the sentence's beginning to read, "*Sing*, O goddess, the wrath...." Unfortunately, this removes the critical word "wrath" from the first position. The translator must decide whether to go ahead anyway for better English grammar or to preserve the primary location by turning his English around a bit awkwardly, such as "The wrath of Peleus' son Achilles sing, O goddess."

The translator's second problem is that in uninflected English — which relies on word position rather than word endings to tell the reader which adjectives modify which nouns — there is the need to put "destructive" next to "wrath" to get: "Sing, O goddess, the *destructive* wrath...." But this loses the primacy of the word "destructive" at the beginning of the second Greek line. Another decision the translator must make in the very first line is how to translate the word *thea*, which literally means "goddess." Some translators

The wrath of Achilles flares when he learns of Agamemnon's decision to take away his concubine, Briseis; a scene from the famous engravings by John Flaxman.

have left it as "goddess," but many have felt the need to make it more directly refer to a specific deity of poetry and, thus, translate it as "Muse" or something even more creative. In the second half of the first line there is the previously discussed name problem — should the translator use "Peleus' son Achilles" (or some variation), or write "Achilles Peleusson"? (After all, the thirty-sixth American president was called "Lyndon Johnson," not "Lyndon, son of John"!) Similarly, in the second half of the second line the translator encounters the problem with "Achaians"— should it be Latinized to "Achaeans" or changed to "Greeks" which might be clearer to general readers?

In the last line of the proem, should the translator change "Atreides" which literally means "son of Atreus," into the person referred to, *i.e.* Agamemnon, to help out modern readers without the prior knowledge of the characters that ancient listeners had? And what should a translator make of the adjective *dios* modifying Achilles? Related to the Latin word *deus* and the English derivative "deity," should the translator stay literal and make Achilles "godlike" or "holy" or perhaps back off a little and use "brave" or "great" or "noble"? It is important to remember that his mother Thetis was a goddess, although his father Peleus was mortal. Before leaving the proem, it is worth trying to read the transliterated Greek words of the last line aloud; it will be noted that it is hard to move smoothly from the second word *te* to the third word *anax*. This is an example of the lost digamma, a letter with the sound of the letter *w*, and it will be recalled that the rediscovery of the missing digamma was important in the recovery of Homer's metrical verse. Thus, the Greek word *anax* was originally *wanax* when the line was composed — reading the line this way makes the difference evident.

The previous paragraphs have only looked at a few issues confronting a translator of the *Iliad*'s first seven lines— there are only sixteen thousand left to go! Meter, rhyme, prose versus blank verse, and various other decisions which the poor translator has to confront as he or she proceeds into the Homeric text have not even been considered. The rest of this chapter will show how some of the more famous translators have undertaken the search for Homer and their successes and failures.

1470 to 1500

The first books printed by Gutenberg's apprentices, K. Sweynheym and A. Pannartz, were a Latin grammar, Cicero's *De Oratore*, Lactantius' *De Divinis Institutionibus*, and St. Augustine's *De Civitate Dei*, a selection of titles clearly showing that the early market for printed books was focused on grammar, rhetoric, and patristics. Consequently, in the first decades following the invention of the printing press (ca. 1455) few classical texts were printed, and no edition of Homer appeared in these earliest years of the new technology. These first printed books sometimes needed Greek type when a Latin author being printed used a Greek quote, but for the most part the early printers lacked Greek type and simply used Latin letters similar to the Greek ones to simulate them. The first book to be printed fully in ancient Greek characters was Constantine Lascaris' *Erotemata*, a grammar of the Greek language printed in Milan in 1476; the preface was written by the Athenian Demetrius Chalcondylas from the University of Padua, who would become the editor of Homer's *editio princeps*. Interestingly, the first book to be printed in modern Greek was a translation of the *Iliad* published in Venice in 1526.[24]

The study of Greek texts was hampered by a shortage of Greek and Latin grammars and dictionaries, as well as accurate textual editions, until the establishment of the famous Aldine Press in Venice which, with its learned academy, began in the sixteenth century to print the needed texts and resources in cheap editions useful for scholars and students. The influx of classical manuscripts from Byzantium and the invention of the printing press had fueled the growth of humanism. As a result, many commentaries on classical works began to be produced, but it took awhile to establish accurate texts for them to be based on. Usually, printers hired scholars to prepare clean written versions of classical texts to be printed since they could not read them, but there was no incentive for the scholar to compare manuscripts and study variants to produce the most accurate text. In 1471 this rush to publication of classical texts without concern for quality led Niccolò Perotti to criticize the error-filled editions and to propose the following rules for scholar-editors: do not make additions to clarify passages; study whether an obscure passage is clarified later in the text and, then, fix the first instance; check whether unclear passages are imitations of passages from other authors and check those authors for clarification; and investigate whether a garbled passage might represent a Greek word that has been poorly transcribed into Latin characters. As the search for manuscripts widened, newly discovered manuscripts were often of better quality than those used to print the early editions, and humanist commentaries on texts began to include discussions of textual variants. With the goals of getting as close as possible to the original text and of clarifying passages difficult to understand, the humanists laid the foundations of modern textual criticism.[25]

The first printing efforts of the Homeric text, however, were not stellar. "Homer re-enters the European tradition in the fourteenth century as the man behind Virgil, possibly a greater Virgil ... [and] the Renaissance scholars [who] attempted to rehabilitate Homer ... were disappointed with what they were able to find in the poet."[26] Much of the problem was the poor state of the Homeric text, which had received little interest for improvement. "...[T]he line-by-line version thrown together by Leonzio Pilatus in 1369 [for Petrarch] survived without much change until the Cambridge edition of 1689."[27] The Latin interlinear translations of Pilatus and P. C. Decembrio (1439–44) were improved upon by the prose translation of Lorenzo Valla (1440–44), but these efforts gave a distorted and remote view of the Greek original. A few attempts toward a verse translation had a definite Virgilian character but, as noted above, were considered to be inferior to Virgil himself. In the printed *editio princeps* of 1488 Chalcondylas seems to have done little to improve the Byzantine manuscript version's text quality. Some of the minor *scholia* were used for textual improvement after their publication in 1517, but they did little to improve the generally poor quality of the Homeric texts being printed for a century.

The very first printing of a "Homeric" text in Verone, Italy in 1470 was, in fact, neither the *Iliad* nor the *Odyssey* but the lightweight story of the Battle of the Frogs and Mice called in Greek the *Batrachomyomachia*. Its plot, which is built on parodies of epic scenes and formulae, concerns a war between frogs and mice caused when the king of frogs, Cheekpuffer, who was carrying a mouse named Crumbsnatcher on his back across a lake when a water snake arrived, instinctively dove down, resulting in the mouse's death. Sadly, it would be a long time until textual study demonstrated that this "Homeric" work, as well as the *Hymns*,

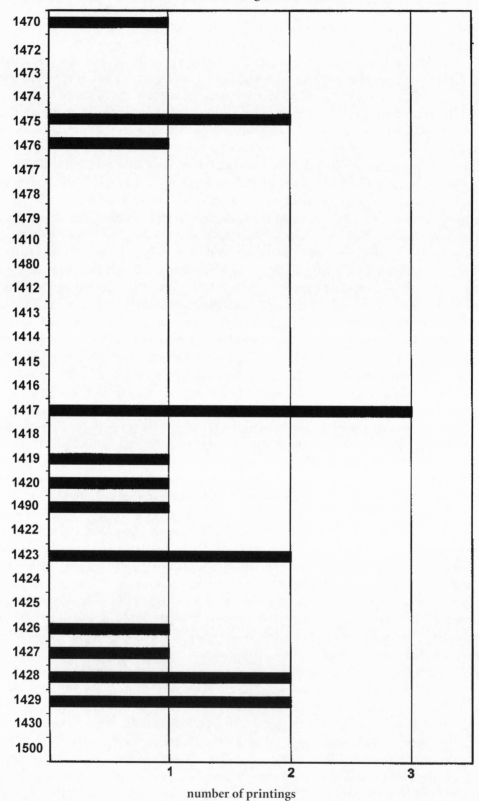

Homeric Printings, 1470–1500

number of printings

ΙΛΙΑΔΟϹ Α ΟΜΗΡΟΥ ΡΑΨΩΔΙΑϹ·

ΑΙ

The first page of the *editio princeps* of Homer (1488). Note how the early printers cut their type to resemble manuscript calligraphy.

Epigrams, and *Centones,* does not derive from the same ancient tradition of the "real" Homer. In 1474 Lorenzo Valla's Latin translation of the *Iliad* (essentially an epitome) was printed in Rome and Brescia, and in 1486 there was another printing of the *Batrachomyomachia* (this one in Venice), but the Homeric text itself remained unprinted. It is interesting to note the flattering terms used to identify Homer in these earliest works: *clarissimus poete* (most famous poet) and *poetarum supremus* (greatest of the poets); and in a 1496 printing *Grecorum poetarus clarissimus* (the most famous poet of the Greeks). These types of descriptors reflect the embers of a glow of respect from the classical past and would continue to be used for many centuries as the text itself was recovered and found to deserve the accolades.

Finally, in the year 1488 the actual Homeric text of the *Iliad* and the *Odyssey* as preserved by manuscript copyists for two thousand years met the marvelous new technology of the printing press, and the *editio princeps* was printed: "…[F]or Homer a new age begins in 1488…!"[28] As has been seen, many scholars had fled the Byzantine Empire around 1400 as its end approached, and Greek manuscripts of Homer were brought to Italy by these teachers. In fact, it was the Byzantine scholar Chalcondylas, born in Athens, educated in Constantinople, and whose appointment to a chair at Padua has been discussed, who in 1488 prepared the text for the first printed edition of the *Iliad* and *Odyssey*. After his stint in Padua, Chalcondylas moved to Florence to take up a chair there. The two-volume first edition of Homer, dedicated to Lorenzo de Medici, was printed in Florence by another Greek, Antonios Damilas from Crete. The manuscript used to print this book does not survive and may have been destroyed in the process of typesetting, although it is also possible that Chalcondylas' assertion that he had created his own copy from Eustathius and other commentaries is true.

Books printed before the year 1501 are denoted "incunabula" (a Latin word that means "in the cradle") in recognition of their having been printed in the first fifty years after Gutenberg's invention. Studying the subjects of incunabula provides an excellent source as to what topics and authors the first printers thought would be the most popular. For us, the placement of the Homeric text among the other classical authors that were printed in this period is a litmus test of its popularity within this group. One survey of incunabula indicates that there are twenty-five editions of the Homeric text, although the listing here counts nineteen; these small counts compare to 552 for Aristotle (the most popular classical writer in the Middle Ages) and 457 for Aelius Donatus, the famous grammarian and teacher of rhetoric at Rome in the fourth century C.E.[29] The lists of top Greek and Roman authors with their numbers of incunabula editions are:

Greek	*Roman*
Aristotle — 552	Aelius Donatus — 457
Homer — 25	Cicero — 389
Plato — 18	Virgil — 202
Hesiod — 9	Ovid — 181
Euclid — 4	Aesop — 161
Herodotus — 3	Cato — 137

It is clear that, despite the accolades noted above in Homeric incunabula titles, in this period Homer was not the most popular survivor from antiquity.

1501 to 1600

In the sixteenth century Homer was "rediscovered" and the text's popularity soared from then on, as can be seen in the listings in Part II. A total of 246 printings in the sixteenth century gives an average of two and a half titles per year. The demand for Homer started early in the century, as witnessed by the three editions printed by the famous Aldine Press of Venice in 1504, 1517, and 1524; Giunta in Florence 1519 and soon thereafter in Rome; four editions in Strassburg between 1525 and 1550; two editions in Basel in 1535 and 1541. The first printing in London did not occur until 1591.[30] "Homer at once took his place as the leading Greek author in the new classical curriculum of the Renaissance, and was assigned much the same primacy in the neo-classical literary criticism of the sixteenth and seventeenth centuries as he had enjoyed in the literary criticism of antiquity...."[31]

The first Aldine text (1504) set the standard for what was included in "the complete Homer": *Iliad, Odyssey, Batrachomyomachia, Hymns,* and "Lives" attributed to Herodotus,

Left: Title page of an edition of the *Iliad* printed in 1538 in Lugdunum (Lyons), France. Note that it includes the spurious "Life of Homer" wrongly attributed to the historian Herodotus. *Above:* Homer begins a new "life" in the world of the printed text.

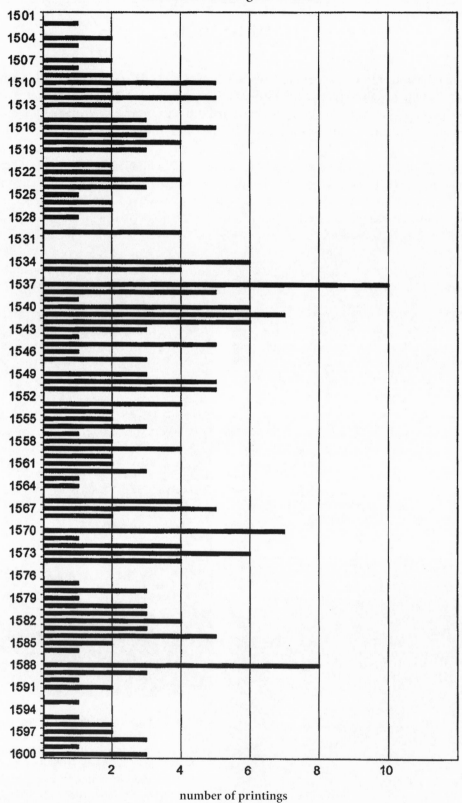

Homeric Printings 1501–1600

number of printings

Dione and Plutarch. The Homeric text became the basis for teaching students to read Greek, such as the 1523 edition of the first two books of the *Iliad* printed in Paris with educational annotations; there would be a long history of this type of usage, even to present times. Printings of Homer were now being produced in all of the major cities of western Europe, including Venice, Rome, Pisaro, Paris, Strasbourg, Leipzig, Leiden, Munich, Basel, Cologne, Nurenberg, and Leiden. And, finally, both Gutenberg's art and the Homeric text made it to England. Printing of the texts themselves were preceded by those of the popular medieval stories about Troy: "[Through] … Lydgate's celebrated Troy Book and Caxton's Recuyell of the Historyes of Troye…, the 'matter of Homer' informs not only the foundations and growth of the arts of English narrative in verse and in prose, but the origins and dissemination of printing itself. Printing comes to England via a 'Troye Booke.'"[32]

The first actual translation of the Homeric text itself into English consisted of the

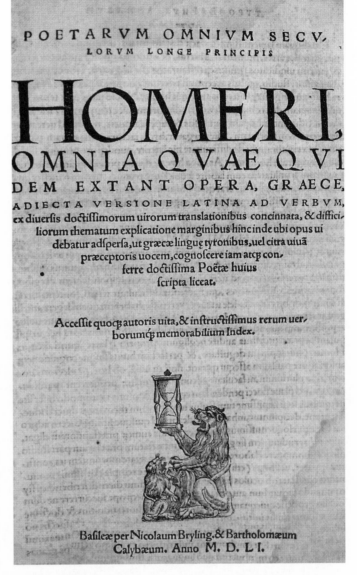

Title page from an edition of all of Homer's works, printed 1551 in Basel, Germany: "All the Works Which Exist of Homer, First for a long time Among Secular Poets, in Greek, To Which is Added a Word-for-Word Latin Version…."

first ten books by Arthur Hall in 1581, although instead of using the Greek text he "translated" it from the French text of Hugues Salel printed in 1555. "Hall was a landed gentleman and briefly a Member of Parliament before being barred from the House after a series of misdemeanours which included making 'sundry lewd speeches' inside and outside the House, serious affray, criticism of the Speaker, over-argumentiveness, and debt. His motivation for undertaking the task [of translation] seems to have been to please his patrons, the Cecil family, as protection in a life which was notorious for troubles with the law; and it is possible that some of the translation was undertaken while he was in prison."[33] Hall's translation did not reach the level of beautiful literature, as would Chapman's soon to follow. His biographer declared that "many lines suggest the monotonous jog-trot of a Middle English epic rather than the great body of verse which inevitably presents itself to our minds on hearing the word 'Elizabethan.'"[34]

The printings listed for this period show quite a popularity for the *Batrachomyomachia* printed both by itself, with other Homeric works, and in anthologies of fables and other antique stories such as those printed in Basel in 1518 and in Bologna in 1522. The actual Homeric text was now translated from Greek into Latin, and following is the *Iliad*'s *proem* in the Latin of Andreas Divus printed first in 1534:

> *Iram cane, Dea, Pelidae Achillis*
> *Perniciosam: quae infinitos Achivis dolores inflixit*
> *Multus aut fortes animas inferis misit*
> *Heroum, ipsos aut laniameta fecit canibus*
> *Auibusque, omnibus. Jovis autem perficiebatur voluntas*
> *Ex quo sane primum divis: sunt contendentes*
> *Atridesque, Rex virorum, et divus Achilles.*

During the years 1544 to 1550, the massive commentary of Eustathius was produced which stimulated improvement of the Homeric texts that were being printed, beginning with that of A. Turnebus in Paris (1554). Some slight improvements on Turnebus were made in the text of H. Stephanus, first printed at Geneva in 1566; this version became standard for some time and was used by the famous English translator George Chapman in 1611 and 1614, as will be seen below. One of the most important developments during the sixteenth century was the addition to the steady stream of Homeric printings in Greek and Latin of new, vernacular translations, which laid the foundations for the explosion of editions in a multitude of languages which was to follow. In 1526 in Venice the first edition was printed in modern Greek, and this book was also the first printed Homer to have woodcut illustrations. The first French translation was printed in Paris in 1530 with the title *Les Iliades de Homère, Poete Grec et Grant Hystoriographe* (The Iliads of Homer, Greek Poet and Great Historiographer) showing what will be a recurrent tendency to make the word *Iliad* plural and to heap titular accolades on the poet. In 1537 Simon Schaidenraisser's German translation of the *Odyssey* was issued with the fascinating subtitle: *die allerzierlichsten und lustigsten vier und zwaintzig bücher des eltisten kunstreichesten Vatters aller Poeten Homeri von der zehenjärigen irrfart des weltweisen Kriechischen Fürstens Ulyssis* (the most elegant and merry twenty-four books of Homer, the eldest artistic father of all poetry, concerning the ten year wandering of Ulysses, the philosophical Greek prince).

In 1550 the first Spanish translation of the Homeric text was made in Antwerp, Belgium and reprinted in Salamanca, Spain. Shortly thereafter, in 1553, the first translation was printed in the Spanish dialect Castilian. A Dutch edition was printed in 1561, an Italian in 1564, and a Florentine dialect version in 1581. The first English printing, as previously noted, did not appear until 1581. Often in this period and in the following ones, the same text was reprinted over and over with few or no changes—for example, from

1540 to 1550 the new Latin translation of the *Iliad* by Helius Eobanus Hessus was printed six times. It also had an interesting title: *Poetarum Omnium Seculorum Longe Principis Homeri Ilias, Hoc Est, de Rebus ad Trojam Gestis Descriptio* (The Iliad of Homer, Longtime Prince of all Secular Poets; that is, a Description of the Things that Occurred at Troy). One of the funniest derivatives of Homer was printed in 1596 with the title: *Penelope's Complaint; or, A Mirrour for Wanton Minions, Taken out of Homers Odissea and Written in English Verse*!

The century ended with great promise as the first part of Homer's *Iliad* by George Chapman became available.

1601 to 1700

In the seventeenth century there were 189 Homeric printings, giving an average of 1.9 per year, which is a decrease from the sixteenth century. George Chapman (1559–1634) was the first renowned translator of Homer into English (*Iliad* 1598 to 1611 and *Odyssey* 1616), and reprintings of his translations have continued right up until today. Although Chapman had the Greek in front of him, he was using the edition of Jean de Sponde published in Basel in 1583 which, like many early editions, had a Latin translation paralleling the Greek.[35] He also lexicons, commentaries, and translations in other languages with the result that despite his titles including the phrase "translated according to ye Greeke," in fact "his translation of Homer was a collation of these various sources, rather than an engagement with Homer's Greek text."[36] Here is the beginning of his *Iliad*:

> Achilles' baneful wrath resound, O Goddesse, that imposd
> Infinite sorrowes on the Greeks, and many brave soules losd
> From breasts Heroique — sent them farre, to that invisible cave
> That no light comforts; and their lims to dogs and vultures gave.
> To all which Jove's will gave effect; from whom first strife begunne
> Betwixt Atrides, king of men, and Thetis' godlike Sonne.

Although Chapman's Elizabethan spellings and vocabulary are outdated and his meter for the *Iliad* (which was called "the fourteener"; the *Odyssey* was done in a ten-syllable meter) somewhat odd, his results still remain intelligible and usually pleasing.

Even in the proem quoted above, the reader gets a feel for Chapman's uninhibited embellishment and outright addition of words and phrases to the actual Homeric text. For example, "Hades" becomes "the invisible cave that no light comforts," and "From breasts heroique" is added to the text's "souls." His translation "is by turns obscure and clear, forced and natural, periphrastic and compact. Its irregularity is the more remarkable because it fails in attempting to do in some places what it succeeds brilliantly in doing in others. The failures are not, therefore, indications of areas of weakness in style, but merely local instances of its breakdown."[37] "The strangely uneven style of Chapman's *Homer* has never been better described than in [Charles] Lamb's well-known remark that 'the great obstacle of Chapman's Translations being read is their unconquerable

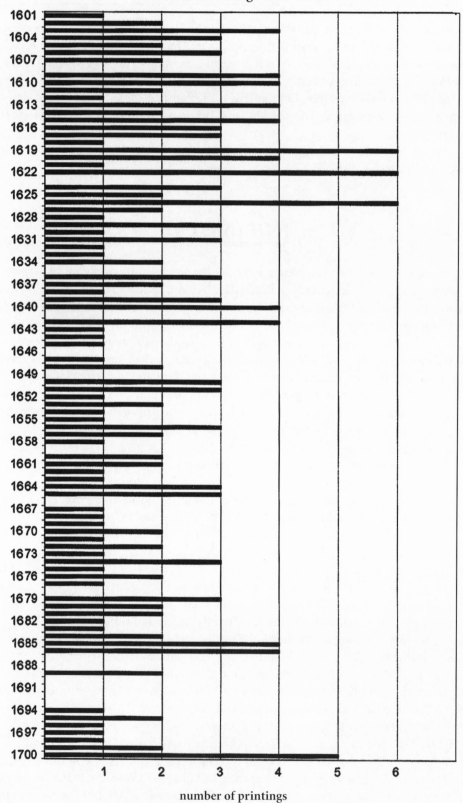

Homeric Printings 1601–1700

number of printings

quaintness. He pours out in the same breath the most just and natural and the most violent and forced expressions.'"[38] In 1598 he first published a translation of *Seauen Bookes of the Iliades* and most of Book XVIII of the *Iliad* under the title *Achilles Shield*; the title continued the conception of "Iliads" being plural that has been noted previously. In 1609 the first twelve books were published, and in 1611 all twenty-four books appeared under the title *The Iliads of Homer, Prince of Poets, Never Before in Any Language Truly Translated*. In 1614 the *Iliad* and the *Odyssey* together appeared, and it is interesting that Nathaniel Butter, the publisher of this edition titled *The Whole Works of Homer, Prince of Poets*, was also an early publisher of news tracts which makes him "the *de facto* father of English journalism."[39] When Chapman finished his translation, he is said to have exclaimed: "The work that I was born to do is done!"[40]

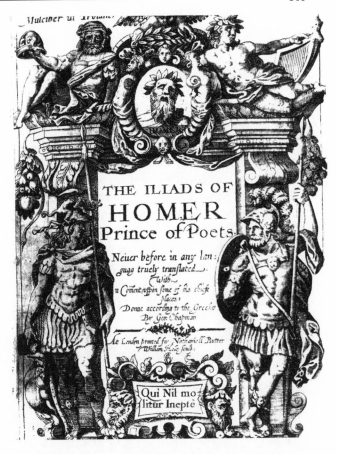

Elaborate title page from one of Chapman's first editions of Homer's "Iliads," printed in 1611 in London.

Thanks in no small part to the sonnet written by the poet John Keats, George Chapman's translation of Homer has received tremendous renown:

On First Looking into Chapman's Homer

Much have I travell'd in the realms of gold,
And many goodly states and kingdoms seen;
Round many western islands have I been
Which bards in fealty to Apollo hold.
Oft of one wide expanse had I been told
That deep-brow'd Homer ruled as his demesne;
Yet did I never breathe its pure serene
Till I heard Chapman speak out loud and bold:
Then felt I like some watcher of the skies
When a new planet swims into his ken;
Or like stout Cortez when with eagle eyes
He star'd at the Pacific — and all his men

Look'd at each other with a wild surmise —
Silent, upon a peak in Darien.

If Achilles had his Homer, Chapman had his Keats; and, someday, Johnson would have his Boswell! It seems that Keats was so enamored with Chapman's text that, after he borrowed the author's copy, he kept it for years despite its owner's frequent appeals by letter for its return.[41] A scholar has appropriately remarked: "one who has both Homer and Chapman before him must regret that Keats could not have written another sonnet upon reading Homer in Homer's own language."[42]

Chapman understood Homer in his own way, although his love of these works was evident from what he wrote in his preface: "Of all books extant in all kinds, Homer is the first and best." In the age-old tradition of interpreting Homer allegorically, Chapman viewed the great characters morally, although his personal opinion of them changed over time. He initially considered Achilles the true ideal, but as he worked his opinion of Achilles waned and his lofty position was replaced by Hector and Odysseus. "Chapman, in fact, saw Ulysses as an emergent dynamic character, one beset by passions that constantly threatened to destroy him, but struggling through repeated failures toward an ideal which he very gradually discovered in the process. Far from idealizing Homer's hero in the traditional manner, Chapman sometimes took pains to emphasize his faults."[43] "The inner meanings which Chapman saw in the *Odyssey* found their chief expression … in moral apophthegm, explicit statement, and in amplification of Homeric symbol and allegory, but they are also reflected in the austere, precipitate, lofty, and involved poetry he created for them."[44] Chapman claimed to have a peculiar and unique insight into Homer, perhaps even that he himself was mystically inspired by his soul! "His notes, especially in the *Iliad*, resound with scathing criticisms of earlier translators and scholars, while his introductory comments to the different translations reflect a jealous and proprietary attitude devoid of humility except when he contemplates the greatness of his original."[45] "Chapman saw in Homer the divinely inspired poet whose gift of poetry had been given him by the Muses. The translator would in the act of translation enter this secret sphere of poetic inspiration so that the translation itself would be poetry divinely inspired."[46]

Chapman was not above adding his own comments and additions to the Homeric text, which tends to add literary vigor but to reduce accuracy; note, for example, in the last line of his proem the insertion of the name of Achilles' mother, Thetis, which is not in the original text. He did this throughout his translations, such as making the text's venerable character "Nestor" into "the good old Nestor"; sometimes, whole lines were added. But his interpolations are more than just a word or phrase here and there — they were done with an overall purpose. "The most conspicuous alteration of the literal meaning of the original is found in Chapman's effort to reduce, as far as possible, the apparent discords inherent in the polytheistic system of Homer in order to produce, for Christian readers, the impression of a consistent and harmonious divine purpose and a consistent and harmonious moral law."[47] Chapman saucily responded to critics who pointed out his textual additions by writing a note "To the Reader" in which he compared his translation with its added elements to literal ones (of other authors):

Custome hath made even th'ablest Agents erre
In these translations : all so much apply
Their paines and cunnings word for word to render
Their patient Authors, when they may as well
Make fish with fowle, Camels with Whales engender,
Or their tongues' speech in other mouths compell.

Their word-for-word traductions (where they lose
The free grace of their naturall Dialect
And shame their Authors with a forced Glose)
I laugh to see — and yet as much abhorre
Their full compression and make cleare the Author.
From whose truth if you thinke my feet digresse
Because I use needfull Periphrases.

In the sixteenth century England had begun to participate in the European passion for classical literature, including the somewhat belated stirring of interest in Homer. In Sir Thomas More's *Utopia* (1516) his senate decreed that everyone must study the Greek language. In fact, the study of Greek became part of the standard English university curriculum and texts of Greek authors were published in London. Chapman's early-seventeenth-century translation of Homer ignited the English passion, and it became a classic. For three hundred years it could be said that "from this time to the present a knowledge of the contents of both the *Iliad* and the *Odyssey* has been part of the training of all educated Englishmen."[48] A poem published in 1651 began:

What none before durst ever venture on
Unto our wonder is by Chapman done,
Who by his skill hath made Great Homer's song
To vail its bonnet to our English tongue,
So that the learned well may question it
Whether in Greek or English Homer writ?[49]

However, later translators and critics liked to throw barbs at Chapman's translation in favor of their own or that of one of their contemporaries. The poets John Dryden, A. C. Swinburne, and T. S. Eliot had especially harsh opinions.[50] Alexander Pope considered Chapman to have been an arrogant man for boasting that he had translated the second half of the *Iliad* in less than fifteen weeks; proof, wrote Pope, that the translation had been done with negligence. Matthew Arnold criticized his translation for not being plain and direct in thought and ideas. He said that "between Chapman and Homer there is interposed the mist of the fancifulness of the Elizabethan age, entirely alien to the plain directness of Homer's thought and feeling...." Although he did not like the fourteen-syllable line that Chapman chose to use, he said that "Chapman's style is not artificial and literary like Pope's nor his movement elaborate and self-retarding like the Miltonic movement of Cowper. He is plain-spoken, fresh, vigorous, and, to a certain degree, rapid; and all these are Homeric qualities." His biggest defect is "the want of literal faithfulness to his original, imposed upon him, it is said, by the exigencies of rhyme."

Arnold smugly criticized Chapman's translation by saying that "Pope has been sneered at for saying that Chapman writes 'somewhat as one might imagine Homer himself to have written before he arrived to years of discretion.' But the remark is excellent: Homer expresses himself like a man of adult reason, Chapman like a man whose reason has not yet cleared itself." Arnold went on: "The Elizabethan poet [Chapman] fails to render Homer because he cannot forbear to interpose a play of thought between his object and its expression. Chapman translates his object into Elizabethan, as Pope translates it into the Augustan of Queen Anne; both convey it to us through a medium. Homer, on the other hand, sees his object and conveys it to us immediately." Differing with Arnold, his editor Rouse pointed out that the Elizabethan style used by Chapman may seem torturous to us today but would have seemed natural in the time of the translation. "It is alive, vigorous, pleasant to read aloud, generally quick and idiomatic, and omits little of the original." Some would conclude that "it is hard now to grasp the reasons for the great repute gained by Chapman's Homer, as it is so unlike and so much more difficult than the original...."[51] However, "from the time they appeared Chapman's translations of Homer received widespread attention from poets, critics, and scholars. ...Yet Chapman's translations make large claims not only as interpretations of Homer but as English epics."[52]

Seventeenth-century interest in Homer and all classical literature throughout Europe was an important influence upon how people thought about the era in which they were living. "While the [sixteenth-century] humanists had seen a possibility of creating a new ... hellenism through a return to Greek antiquity, the seventeenth century believed in the myth of a 'grand siecle': men compared their own age with the illustrious periods of classical antiquity and saw its greatness exemplified in the art and literature of the age of Louis XIV."[53] However, French and English critics, while recognizing Homer as "the father of poetry" still considered him a bit vulgar in comparison to the more sophisticated Virgil. This ambivalence can be seen in the 1601 title *Actio Tragicomica, ex Libro Primo Iliados Homeri* (Tragicomic Deeds from Book I of Homer's Iliad), the 1631 title *Les Travaux d'Ulysse, Tragé-Comedie Tirée d'Homère* (The Travails of Ulysses; Tragic-Comedy Taken from Homer), and in the fact that Chapman himself considered the bastardized "Homeric" story of the *Batrachomyomachia* to be "The Crowne of all Homers Workes" in his 1624 translation.

The English translations of Chapman were followed by better ones by John Ogilby (1669) and Thomas Hobbes (1673–77). Ogilby (1600–1676) had an early career as a theater owner in Ireland, but he returned to England after having his business ruined in the English Civil War. It was in this period of his life that he decided to learn Greek and Latin and he published translations of both Homer and Virgil. At the Restoration, his recognition as a poet was such that Charles II entrusted him with "the poetical part" of the coronation ceremonies. Ogilby turned his attentions to cartography and became known as a pioneer in the making of road atlases. After the Great Fire of London in 1666, he set up a printing shop and styled himself "king's cosmographer and geographical printer." That he saw in Homer more than just literature is clear from his comment that the *Odyssey* is "the most Ancient and Best Piece of Moral and Political Learning." Ogilby hired the best artists and engravers to illustrate his translation and also included scholarly annotations. When Thomas Hobbes made his own translation somewhat later he explained why he omitted any learned commentary: "Because I had no hope to do it better than it is already done by Mr. Ogilby."

Hobbes (1588–1679) is best remembered as one of England's greatest political thinkers, known for his writings on individual security and the social contract. After attending Oxford, he decided to become a classical scholar; his most famous translation in this period was of the Greek historian Thucydides. Hobbes' interests then turned to Euclid and mathematics as related to human cognition. He moved on to political philosophy and evolved the belief that absolute monarchy is the best government but that monarchs must be just because subjects have given up their individual rights in his/her support. His major book, *Leviathan, or, The Matter, Form, and Power of a Commonwealth, Ecclesastical and Civil* (1651) got him into trouble with the loyalists during the Cromwell era because they took it to support switching political allegiances if a monarch was inept or cruel, but after the Restoration Charles II brought

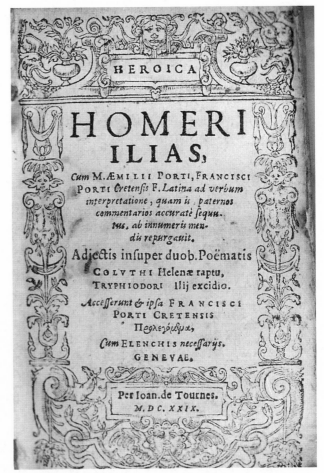

Decorated title page of an edition of the *Iliad* printed in Geneva in 1629. Note that the book also includes two other poems (non–Homeric) called "The Rape of Helen" and "The Siege of Troy."

him to court. In his later years Hobbes returned his thoughts to classical studies, and this was when he translated the *Iliad* and the *Odyssey*, more likely because he was tired of debating with opponents than trying to use the epics for continued anticlerical sentiments as has recently been alleged.[54] One of his final writings was an autobiography written in Latin verse. The proem to the *Iliad* illustrates his abbreviated and direct style:

> O goddess sing what woe the discontent
> Of Thetis' son brought to the Greeks: what souls
> Of heroes down to Erebus it sent,
> Leaving their bodies unto dogs and fowls.

It was at the age of eighty-five, when his philosophical writings had been banned in England, that Hobbes undertook to write his translation of Homer. In explaining himself, the crusty old fellow wrote: "Why then did I write it? Because I had nothing else to do. Why publish it? Because I thought it might take off my Adversaries from shewing their folly upon my more serious Writings and set them upon my Verses to shew their wisdom."[55] It seems that his *Odyssey*, which was published in 1674, was so well received that he was inspired to translate the *Iliad* as well. Alexander Pope, however, was more critical as indicated by comments published in the preface to his own subsequent translation: "Mr. Hobbes in his Version, says he, has given a correct explanation of the sense in general, but for particulars and circumstances he continually lops them, and often omits the most beautiful. As for its being esteemed a close translation, I doubt not many have been led into that error by the shortness of it, which proceeds not from his following the original line by line, but from the contractions abovementioned. He sometimes omits whole similes and sentences, and is now and then guilty of mistakes, into which no writer of his learning could have fallen, but through carelessness. His poetry as well as Ogilby's is too mean for Criticism." The modern commentator George Steiner says of his translation: "It is the work of a philosopher in his mid-eighties, with no poetic talent, but a fierce insight into Homeric politics and homicidal war."[56]

The new English translations of Homer and the important discovery of the Homeric digamma by Thomas Bentley (1699), discussed in Chapter 2, shifted the focus of Homeric scholarship to England by the beginning of the eighteenth century. However, it would be less than a hundred years until the German scholar F. A. Wolf's *Prolegomena* changed the way the world viewed Homer and made Germany the center of Homeric scholarship. Another famous Englishman who contributed a Homeric translation in the late seventeenth century was John Dryden (1631–1700). The son of a gentleman, he was classically educated as a boy and then attended Cambridge. He wrote excellent poetry for public consumption, such as poems lauding the return of Charles II and his restored monarchy, and he also had a long career as a playwright. Late in life, Dryden fell out of favor with James II and turned to writing non-political poetry and to translating classical authors, including Juvenal and Virgil. His last work was a collection of verse adaptions from Ovid, Chaucer, Boccaccio and Homer called *Fables Ancient and Modern*.

Not all the seventeenth-century printings of Homer were serious translations. There were also playful burlesques on the text, such as the Italian parody *L'Iliade Giocosa* by S. Gio. Franc. Loredano (1653), the French *L'Odyssée d'Homère, ou Les Avantures d'Ulysse en Vers Burlesques* by Hughes de Picou (1653), and *Homer à la Mode, a Mock Poem* by Lord Scudamore James (1664).

1701 to 1800

In the eighteenth century there were 455 Homeric printings, an average of 4.6 per year. A major battle arose in later-seventeenth- and eighteenth-century Europe, especially in France and England, among literary scholars who debated the merits of studying and copying the style of the ancient authors versus more modern ones. In France this discussion was called the *Querelle des Anciens et des Modernes* (Quarrel of the Ancients and Moderns). Issues included: "the problem of poetic genius and the kindred problem of originality"; "the question of realism...: how accurate did a poet need to be in depicting scenes and events"; "the question ... of the relative merits of primitive and sophisticated society"; and "the 'Homeric Question' itself; whether the *Iliad* and the *Odyssey* were or were not compilations from a number of separate poems, and the results of deliberate editing and interpolation."[57] The Moderns, led by Charles Perrault (also the collector of fairy tales published as the *Mother Goose Stories*), ridiculed Homer for content which seemed to be silly when taken out of cultural context, such as having his warriors boast to one another before fighting or having the gods behave like spoiled humans. They attacked the Homeric style, with its similes, epithets, and repetitions, and they argued that Homer's characters, led by Achilles, were brutal, cruel unjust, and capricious.

Some of the most violent attacks on Homer came from François Hédelin, abbé d'Aubignac. "In 1664 d'Aubignac delivered before [his] academy his *Conjectures académiques ou dissertation sur l'Iliade*, in which he attacked the Homeric poems for

Title page of an academic edition of the *Iliad* and the *Odyssey* in both Greek and Latin with *scholia* and textual notes, printed in Cambridge, England in 1711. Also included are the *Battle of the Frogs and Mice*, the *Homeric Hymns*, and the *Epigrams* (all now known to be non–Homeric).

bad morality, bad taste, bad style, and inconsistencies in the conduct of the narrative, from all of which, combined with the ancient reports of Homer's illiteracy, he concluded that there had never been such a person as Homer, and that the *Iliad* and *Odyssey* were the patchwork creations of a late and incompetent editor."[58] "It is hardly an oversimplification to say that the *querelle* itself was the most crucial intellectual struggle in the early development of modern Europe. During the *querelle* values derived from classical antiquity were for the first time set in opposition to progress, and the late seventeenth and early eighteenth centuries hence marked the beginning of a new phase in the history of thought."[59]

Anne LeFevre Dacier (1647–1720), or as she styled herself in her books, M[adame]

Homeric Printings 1701–1800

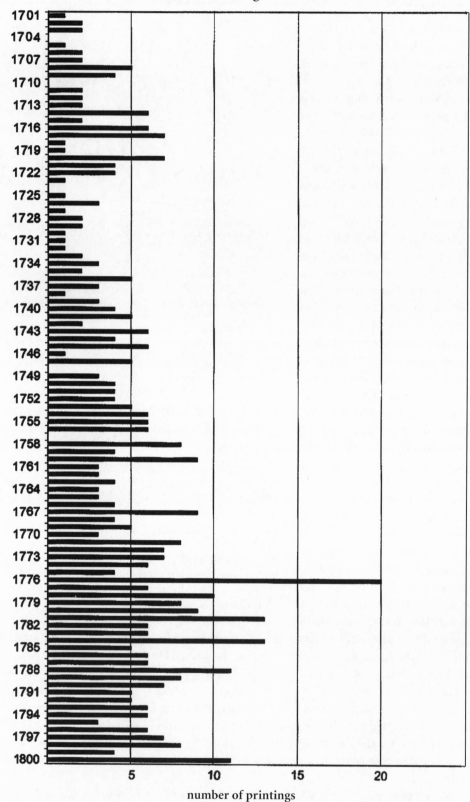

number of printings

Dacier, was one of the earliest professional women in European scholarship, and her translation of Homer into French set a high standard and had tremendous influence both on the continent and in England. Dacier and other writers in the France of Louis XIV, such as the dramatic poet Jean Racine, wanted to copy and make available to the public the good sense, good taste and sublimity that they saw in Homer. The writer of this age who did the most for Homer was François de Salignac de La Mothe-Fénelon, whose novel *Les Aventures de Télémaque* (1699) was widely read. In it he made the *Odyssey*'s Telemachus (son of Odysseus) "the hero of an edifying romance, full of mildly agreeable episodes which gave readers the impression that there was nothing 'barbaric' about Homer."[60] As a humanist scholar focused in classics, Dacier was a woman working in a man's world, and it was only her bourgeois origins that permitted her to publish under her own name when an aristocratic woman would have felt degraded for doing so. Dacier's Homer had a great impact on the English translation by Alexander Pope. "Her translation of Homer, which is her finest work, left a permanent impress on English literature. Through it she touched a creative chord in Pope. That his great translation of Homer owed so much to her sensitive response to Homer's beauties, as well as to her scholarship, is one of her most obvious claims to our attention."[61]

As a child Anne Le Fevre was infected with a love of Greek literature by her father, Tenneguy Le Fevre, who tutored students in their home; it is likely that in an age when girls were not educated in the classics, Anne learned her Greek from listening while he taught students and her two brothers. "Certainly the Le Fevre household, with its intimate connections with the [French] Academy, provided an ambiance in which a clever little girl could dream about and prepare to enter a new world, brave in its antiquity, and far beyond the small circle of understanding in which most women of the period were imprisoned."[62] Her reputation began with her publication of editions of Callimachus and Florus in a series of Delfhin books created for the education of the Dauphin. In 1681 she published a French translation of Anacreon which began her career in publishing ancient authors in French translation. This was the trend of the period, to make public the works of ancient writers which previously had been available only in their original languages to scholars. "Now ancient literature was to reach a wider public by way of attractive texts which had been clarified with the aid of abundant notes; by fresh and more accurate translations into the vernacular; by imitation; and finally in the more subtle and original from of emulation."[63] Because of her work on the Delfin editions of which she did five, she became acquainted with Andre Dacier, also a Delfin editor, and they married in 1683. Both were Protestants but converted to Catholicism due to the increasing persecution of Protestants (Huguenots) in France with the revocation of the Edict of Nantes.

Anne continued her translation work, despite being married. In 1684 she published the first French edition of the Greek comic dramatist Aristophanes, and in 1691 she and her husband jointly published a translation of the *Meditations* of the Roman emperor Marcus Aurelius. Madame Dacier pushed on with her work even though she bore several children, who died one by one causing her great grief. In working on a translation of the Latin poet and dramatist Terence she succeeded in viewing a manuscript in the King's Library, which required great personal courage because women were normally prohibited from entering. By the last years of the seventeenth century the two married classicists were at the center of the intellectual life of Paris, and Madame Dacier's fame especially was spreading. When in 1695 Andre Dacier was admitted to the French Academy, he was welcomed for his own work but praised for having a wife that brought such honor not only to her sex but to the century; many people thought Anne should have had the seat, but women were not permitted.

The groundwork had been laid for Madame Dacier's translation of Homer. Her *Iliad* was published in 1711, but this was the end of happy time for the Daciers, as their last daughter had died in the previous year. In the preface to the *Iliad* she wrote: "I have lost a friend and a faithful companion; we had never been separated for a single moment since her childhood."[64] Although she had done much work on the *Odyssey*, she could not bear to complete it until attacks on her dearly beloved Homer drew her again into the intellectual fray. The preface to her *Iliad* clearly shows that she undertook the difficult translation of Homer for the specific purpose of making accurate versions available instead of the existing ineffective French editions which distorted the original beauty. "Dacier's primary objective was pedagogical: not a customization, but a popularization (or ver-nacularization) of the ancients. Focusing on the reader, she envisioned her translation as a bridge — spacial and temporal —from antiquity to modernity. A close analysis of Dacier's preface reveals how her intimate knowledge and admiration of Homer's poetry inspired her to spread the good word about his art to non-believers in order to convert them."[65] Dacier decided to do her translation of Homer in prose in order to make the texts accessible, apologizing to her readers that the French language just was inadequate in render-ing the Greek poetry in verse. Her goals, thus, presented a "paradox ... in the tension between the aristocratic classicist anxious to maintain the pure and sacred character of primitive poetry and the bourgeois modernist eager to disseminate the Word through prose."[66]

Dacier's Homer achieved renown because it was the most accurate French transla-tion to date, despite its limitations of rejecting Homer's epithets and otherwise misun-derstanding the formulaic style as well as overly ennobling the characters. As was typical in her day, Dacier saw Christian moral and religious meanings in almost every episode and considered Homer's world controlled by the gods as an allegory for the Christian God and his angels, although she carefully kept these opinions in her notes and, as the good scholar she was, out of the text. "Her notes, however outmoded they may seem [today], are the first serious attempt to set Homer in a matrix of world literature and to keep before the general reader a historical awareness of the early Mediterranean world, theological as well as factual. Anne Dacier's intimate acquaintance with the earliest crit-ics of Homer and her ability to read them in the original tongues gave substance to what might otherwise have been empty speculation."[67] Like other translations of the period, her translation was made from the Latin text, not the Greek, and included textual errors as a result. "Her own translations inevitably bear the mark of her period, but they are so superior to all that had gone before as well as to much that came after that she fully deserves to be ranked ... among those who made a solid contribution to the glories of the reign of Louis XIV."[68]

Madame Dacier emerged as a major champion of the Ancients in the Quarrel of the Ancients and Moderns that was raging in French literary circles. She published a defense of Homer that attacked the Moderns and in two years finished the *Odyssey* and published a second defense of Homer. "Dacier's chief adversary in France was Antoine Houdar de

La Motte who answered her [translation of the] *Iliad* with a quaint French version of the poem divested of monotony, repetition, and all that smacked of bad manners in the narrative."[69] La Motte called his work an "imitation," believing that a new work of art is created by translation that establishes a new context for a contemporary message; this concept was opposite to that of Dacier, who believed fanatically in loyalty to the original meaning.[70] Dacier wrote a book *Des Causes de la Corruption du Goût* (Causes of the Corruption of Taste) vehemently attacking La Motte and alleging that his and the Moderns' positions threatened civilization as then known. La Motte wrote a book *Réflexions sur la Critique* to answer her, but in 1716 they agreed to end their ugly debate. In England John Ozell also responded to Dacier by translating his own *Iliad* in blank verse, writing in the preface that the French tongue was too timid and needed his version's "Sinews and Strength to allay the excessive softness of it."[71] In putting her tremendous work in perspective it must be realized that "Anne Dacier's Homer, like Pope's in England, represents the culmination of what has been called the 'Prince of Poets' tradition. Homer was accepted as not only the first but the greatest poet who ever lived, a tradition which goes back to Aristotle, was given substance by Horace, and was reinforced by later defenders such as Macrobius and the twelfth-century Archbishop of Thessalonica, Eustathius, a commentator dear to Madame Dacier."[72] On her career it can be concluded that "her contribution to the *Grand Siècle* of France, that period which teems with intellectual energy and artistic expression not merely in literature, but in all the arts, would have been noteworthy for a man. For a woman of her time it was unique."[73]

Beginning in 1715 the English poet Alexander Pope (1688–1744) produced translations of Homer's *Iliad* and *Odyssey* in iambic pentameter couplets which have been the most successful English versions of all time, as is evident from the multitudinous editions which have been published. Unfortunately, as a person Pope was not a very pleasant individual. From childhood he suffered from tuberculosis of the spine (Pott's disease) which resulted in physical deformity and stunted growth. Not surprisingly, he had low self-esteem which was exacerbated by the fact that his contemporaries attributed his twisted body to psychological effeminacy and too much studying. He was also insecure about his father's (and, therefore his own) social class which was not as high as he wished, a fact which he often obscured or actually lied about. Being a Catholic barred him

Engraved portrait of Alexander Pope from one of the many editions of his translations.

from attendance in British universities or from taking a naval or military commission, even if his physical deformities would have permitted it. His poor health and his family's financial problems due to penalties imposed on Catholics prevented him from attending an overseas university.

To make matters worse, Pope was a Tory in an era of long Whig political dominance. "All of these major facts of Pope's biography suggest a man who was an outsider in his own society and in an adversarial relationship to it, struggling for acceptance and deeply critical when the struggle failed."[74] A recent scholar studying Pope concluded that his peculiar behaviors and lifestyle resulted from his complete focus on his literary art and less on the unfortunate facts about his life: "where most readers coming to Pope for the first time are struck by the fact that he was a cripple, and ambitious, and a genius (in that order), I would put it the other way around—that Pope was a genius, who was therefore ambitious, and who happened to be a cripple."[75]

As a boy of about eight years, Pope had read Ogilby's translation of Homer and later wrote that "Homer ... was the first author that made me catch the itch of poetry."[76] In 1715 he wrote a poem called *The Temple of Fame* in which his growing respect for Homer is seen in these lines:

> Father of Verse! in holy Fillets drest,
> His Silver Beard wav'd gently o'er his Breast;
> Tho' blind, a Boldness in his Looks appears,
> In Years he seem'd, but not impair'd by Years...
> A strong Expression most he seemed t'affect,
> And here and there disclos'd a brave Neglect.

As an adult Pope was fixated on overcoming the negative strikes against him, and his intellectual genius provided an avenue to do so. "Pope's circumstances deprived him of any chance to 'make a man of himself' financially and socially except by publishing a translation of Homer, yet made it almost impossible for him to do even that."[77]

It seems clear that Pope used his poetry and epic writings to create a self-image other than the reality of his sickly body: "Pope's *Homer* masks the translator's personal deficiencies, conveying him into realms made accessible only by the authority of his original."[78] Before he undertook Homer, Pope had already achieved an outstanding presence as a top poet of his time, with many works, including the one for which he is best remembered, "The Rape of the Lock." In 1713 he accepted a handsome financial offer to translate the *Iliad*, a vast, twelve-year undertaking even though he frequently sought assistance with the text and grammar because he was not a Greek scholar; it was printed in volumes issued from 1715 to 1720 with an immediate second edition being printed and a third in 1732. His *Odyssey* (1725–26) was substantially ghost-written by two university-educated clergymen, Elijah Fenton and William Broome. "Nevertheless, the care with which Pope organized, supervised, and corrected every stage of the undertaking ensured that the final product was Pope's *Homer*."[79] Here is his proem to the *Iliad*:

> *Achilles'* wrath, to *Greece* the direful spring
> Of woes unnumber'd, heav'nly Goddess, sing!

That Wrath which hurl'd to *Pluto's* gloomy reign
The souls of mighty Chiefs untimely slain;
Whose limbs unbury'd on the naked shore
Devouring dogs and hungry vultures tore:
Since Great Achilles and Atrides strove,
Such was the sov'reign doom, and such the will of *Jove*!

Due to criticism Pope rewrote his first two lines which from the 1736 edition on appear as above; in the first edition of 1720, however, they appeared as follows:

The Wrath of *Peleus'* Son, the direful spring
Of all the *Grecian* Woes, O Goddess, sing!

Pope's method for translating the *Iliad* is reminiscent of Chapman's: "Pope read his Greek the way every other educated man of the period did, save the professional scholars: in a bilingual edition, with the Greek on one page and a Latin crib on the other — the Latin operates as a translator's Esperanto that imitated the Greek grammar and compound words, and enabled the reader to read into the original what he saw must be there. In addition, Pope sifted all the available translations for whatever they could supply — notes, formulations, or insight — and waded through the voluminous commentaries in Greek, Latin and French that had been accumulating on Homer ever since that of Eustathius, Bishop of Thessalonica, in the twelfth century. ...From these materials he extracted the annotations on Homer's geography, history, customs and morals which were an important part of his offer to the subscribers."[80] "The psychological background of Pope's Homeric enterprise had the complexity of that of a work of art. He attempted to lift the status of translation to the level of an original work, giving it a large measure of autonomy with regard to the original. He chose to take considerable liberties with the Homeric text, and to use the poetic language and form

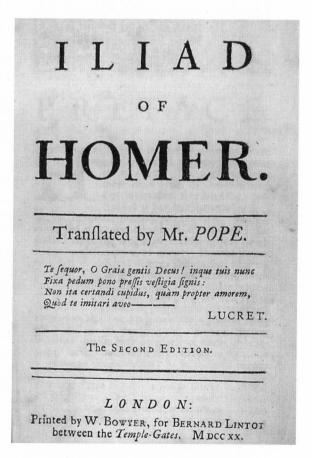

I L I A D

O F

HOMER.

Tranſlated by Mr. *POPE.*

Te ſequor, O Graiæ gentis Decus! inque tuis nunc
Fixa pedum pono preſſis veſtigia ſignis:
Non ita certandi cupidus, quàm propter amorem,
Quòd te imitari aveo——————
LUCRET.

The SECOND EDITION.

L O N D O N:
Printed by W. BOWYER, for BERNARD LINTOT
between the *Temple-Gates,* M DCC XX.

Title page of the second edition of Alexander Pope's *Iliad.* Volumes I and II of the second edition were printed in London in 1720, the same year that the last volume of the first edition appeared

which he and his contemporaries found the most congenial, namely the heroic couplet."[81]

The success of Pope's translations was phenomenal and ensured him the financial wherewithal to buy the life of high society which he had always sought. "When Pope began the *Iliad* translation, he was a rising young poet from a country background, with some famous friends and protectors; when he ended it, he was the country's unofficial laureate, rich, independent, and in a position (as he liked to say) to 'fling off Lords by dozens.'"[82] His translations sold so well not only due to their literary merit but also to Pope's strong-arm marketing by seeking patronage from his aristocratic associates and, then, pressuring them to purchase sets for themselves and friends. "The subscription list makes interesting reading, a regular 'Who's Who' of fashionable society. Her Royal Highness the Princess is listed, along with seventeen dukes, three marquises, fourty-nine earls, seven duchesses, 1 marchioness, and eight counteses."[83] Pope's contract with Lintot, his printer, permitted him to design the book's layout which he made lavishly illustrated and on fine paper to be sure to appeal to subscribers. "The production of Pope's translation of the *Iliad* is revolutionary both commercially and aesthetically, and in some respects commerce and aesthetics interact. It appeared at a time when the publication of works in weekly or monthly parts was becoming popular, and the idea of publishing it in six annual volumes rather than in one or two large volumes, as had previously been usual, meant a similar reduction in the working capital employed. In principle, [the printer] Lintot had only to pay for the production of one volume, the sales of which would in turn provide the money for the second volume, and so on to the end. ...In order to make part publication possible, and extract the maximum profit from it, the work had to be swelled out by the use of large formats and large type, even for the annotations to each book, which occupy almost as many pages as the text. What Mme Dacier printed in three volumes, duodecimo [a small format], Pope and Lintot swelled to six volumes in quarto or folio."[84] The publication in the quarto format by Pope was an important break with the tradition of publishing major works in the larger folio format. "In its day and its own terms, Pope's Homer was one of the wonders of its age."[85]

After 1729, Pope became more political and his poems reflected the issues and people of the day, especially through satire. Not surprisingly, he made enemies in the government who retaliated against him, which resulted in Pope's publication of *Epistle to Dr. Arbuthnot* in which he defended his use of personal satire and his status as a public figure. In *The Dunciad* Pope launched a comprehensive attack on professional writers who have to earn their living by writing, underlining his own (new) status as a wealthy, aristocratic writer. "As a very rich man, he could now afford to disparage those who wrote for bread and to equate professionalism with corruption and bad writing...."[86] Pope also became embroiled in the Quarrel of the Ancients and Moderns that had been so viciously fought in French intellectual circles. Jonathon Swift's *The Battel of the Books* had introduced the quarrel to England in 1704; he envisioned the "modern" books trying to depose the "ancients" of their more elevated shelf space. For Pope the quarrel also took on an aspect of a class issue involving amateur versus professional writers. "The gradual professionalism of historical, antiquarian and literary scholarship led to a backlash from the gentlemanly amateurs whose preserve it had been formerly."[87] This last-ditch attempt to preserve the past, both in supporting non-professional writers and in favoring the

Ancients over the Moderns, made him a strange colleague of Madame Dacier. Like her, he considered works by the Moderns to be "Cavils" and plagiarism: "One would imagine by the course of their Parallels, that these Criticks never so much as heard of Homer's having written first."[88] The eighteenth-century quarrel was indecisive, but, as was seen in chapter 2, by the end of that century the roots of modern critical analysis of Homer were growing with new techniques for looking at the Homeric question, championed by Wolf's *Prolegomena*.

Pope's *Iliad* and *Odyssey* were outstanding successes, not only financially, but also as literature. "He used the term 'fire' to describe what happened in the act of reading and hearing poetry, and linked this with the poet's experience of the act of creation. ...Pope insisted that the Homeric translator should see as his most important task the rendering of the Homeric fire, that elusive and inimitable element, a compound of rhythm, sound values and meanings which so affected him in his role as reader that he was carried away."[89] Sir Thomas Fitzosborne lauded Pope's translation: "To say of this noble work that it is the best which ever appeared of the kind, would be speaking in much lower terms than it deserves; the world perhaps scarce ever before saw a truly poetical translation."[90] The poet Samuel Taylor Coleridge referred to "that astounding product of matchless talent and ingenuity, Pope's *Iliad*."[91] Samuel Johnson's judgment was that it is "certainly the noblest version [translation] of poetry which the world has ever seen; and its publication must therefore be considered as one of the great events in the annals of learning."[92] Edward Young in "Night Thoughts" praised the translation of Pope (whom he calls Maeonides)[93]:

> Dark, though not blind, like thee, Maeonides!
> Or Milton, thee! Ah could I reach your strain,
> Or his who made Maeonides our own,
> Man too he sung.

Pope, himself, was more interested in the sound of his translation than in scholarship, as had been the classicist Madame Dacier whose notes he frequently quoted whole cloth without attribution. "His *Iliad* is full of the antitheses and literary conceits which are hallmarks of his style."[94] Pope relied on Dacier's work both for annotations and textual translation, more than he was willing to admit, but openly took an attacking posture towards the senior woman despite their agreement in the quarrel. "Pope's discontent was not ultimately aroused by Madame Dacier's mistakes; if she had been consistently misguided he could safely have ignored her. His difficulty lay in formulating an appropriate response to the frequent instances when she was irrefutably and indispensably right. She played Thetis to his Achilles: an obtrusively feminine presence, without whose aid he could achieve neither glory among his peers nor personal survival."[95] But debating with Dacier over details of Homeric scholarship was secondary to Pope's focus on the literary quality and verve of his work. "It was Pope's intention to make Homer appear as elevated, as fiery an author as good English would allow."[96]

Scholars and critics have debated Pope's translations ever since their original publication, but the multitude of reprints through the centuries and up to the present day evidence a long-lasting love for them. However, Pope's works have major flaws which were immediately seen by critics. A contemporary wrote: "Pope's version of Homer is rather a paraphrase than a translation; but its poetical merits are universally acknowl-edged. The notes, which he and his co-adjutors annexed to it, are sometimes trifling, but are frequently useful; and the work may be read with pleasure by the scholar, and with improvement and instruction by the unlearned."[97] Pope often added to and embellished Homer's text in order to increase its ornate verbiage in English, but this resulted in an "artificiality and stilted elegance that stand at the other end of the horizon from Homer's noble plainness."[98] Addressing an admirer of the wit in Pope's *Iliad*, a contemporary critic pretended to address Pope on his "improvements" to the Homeric text: "For what are you in Love with Homer? Speak, / And own the Wit is *English*, and not Greek."[99]

As seen in the *Iliad* proem above, Pope did his translation in rhyming couplets of blank verse, not everyone's favorite. A contemporary wag wrote: "could the Wretch, in Rhime, pretend / To give us *Homer*, plain, majestick, great[?]"[100] William Cowper remarked that Pope "who managed the bells of rhyme with more dexterity than any man, tied them about Homer's neck."[101] Matthew Arnold admitted that "there is a swing and a movement in many parts of Pope which might rival Homer himself"[102], but he cor-rectly complained that his translation failed at being plain and direct: "between Pope and Homer there is interposed the mist of Pope's literary artificial manner, entirely alien to the plain naturalness of Homer's manner...." His heroic and flowery style works well in passionate passages but is poor for rendering ordinary ones, such as relating the build-ing of a campfire. "He has missed 'the grand style of Homer' utterly and in scenes of sim-ple narrative he is too ornate, often bombastic and absurd."[103] Another contemporary wrote: "For HOMER translated, first in English, *secondly* in Rhyme, *thirdly*, not from the Original, but, *fourthly*, from a *French Translation*, and that in *Prose*, by a *Woman* too, how the Devil should it be Homer?[104] (Note the caustic gibe about Pope's reliance on Madame Dacier!) The most famous comment on Pope's translations and the one which most directly and tersely summarized their style was made by Richard Bentley, the great-est classical scholar of the day who said: "It is a pretty poem, Mr. Pope, but you must not call it Homer."[105]

However, Pope's poetic translation retains value in helping readers understand Homer, as was argued in the 1972 book *To Homer Through Pope*: "Thanks to Pope we who search for the epics by way of translations can look beyond our noses and see that Homer has an indefinite future among us as exhibiting not only what humanity has been but what it once again might become. ...But what above all comes over us if we approach the epic through Pope is that the deep vein of great humanity in Homer is always crop-ping out in passages by which men's hearts have never ceased to be touched, from Homer's days to ours. Very often these supreme touches come to us in direct speech, and here Pope has grasped and shown us the chief problem and task of a translator as being to find *credible speech*. ...Yet, if we can learn anything from Pope, a ... 'lift' is the very fea-ture by which we should know that a modern verse translation had begun to justify itself."[106]

Many of the critics of Pope's translation have been guilty of not understanding a translator's dual responsibility to the original text within its literary format but also to contemporary readers, responsibilities overtly understood by Pope. "The poetic task which [was] accepted by Pope — that of making his translation deal in some way with Homer, with the heroic tradition, and with the broader tradition of English poetry —

[took] two chief and familiar forms. Pope [would] have to be responsible simultaneously to the local structures and to the complete meaning of his version of the *Iliad*."[107] The translator Sir John Herschel wrote: "the magnificent adumbration of [the translation of] Pope (for whatever may be said against it, and with all its faults, which are not a few, I for one regard Pope's *Iliad*, *taken per se*, as one of the most magnificent, if not *the* most magnificent poem extant)...." A recent assessment of Pope's translation puts it into perspective: "The influence of Pope's *Homer* on English minds and poetic diction in the eighteenth century was certainly very great. Though probably little read now, it filled a whole century with the fame of Pope and Homer."[108] "it would be difficult to refute Johnson's claim that Pope's *Iliad* is 'the noblest version of poetry the world has ever seen'; it remains, certainly, the greatest verse translation of the *Iliad* in English. ...In Pope's version we find, for the last and perhaps the only time in the history of English verse, a traditional and viable poetic style that can be held answerable to the demands of the Homeric hexameter. And it was a style that was managed by a poet — great imitator and verbal genius that he was — who was very nearly equal to the impossible task."[109]

In 1715, two days after the appearance of Pope's first volume, Thomas Ticknell (1686–1740), a man of letters, published the start of his own translation of the *Iliad*. Pope, who was associated with the Tory party, suspected that Ticknell had been encouraged by Joseph Addison, the famous essayist and co-contributor (with Richard Steele) to the powerful periodicals *The Tatler* and *The Spectator*, due to Addison's Whig leanings. Pope was especially angered when Addison termed Ticknell's version "the best that ever was in any language." However, the court of public opinion did not concur, and another commentator did not mince words in reference to Ticknell's attempt: "This translation was published about the same time with Mr. Pope's. But it will not bear a comparison; and Mr. Ticknell cannot receive a greater injury, than to have his verses placed in contradistinction to Pope's."[110] Ticknell's translation was doomed and never proceeded past Book I due to the overwhelming preference of readers for Pope's version, although in 1779 it did get included (along with Pope's full work) in an anthology series called *Johnson's Works of the English Poets*.

Meanwhile, the eighteenth century was an important time for developments in Homeric studies. Although the concept was initially scoffed at by his peers, most difficulties in understanding the meter of the Homeric poems were solved by the discovery of the missing digamma by Bentley (1732). It was soon realized that "the importance of this discovery [was] enormous; for the first time a step had been made beyond the text as it had been fixed by the Alexandrian grammarians and their followers in later ancient and medieval times."[111] "In 1735 Thomas Blackwell (the younger), Regius Professor of Greek and Principal of Marischal College at Aberdeen, published anonymously the first modern book by a professional scholar which is entirely devoted to Homer, under the title *An Enquiry into the Life and Writings of Homer*."[112] Coming out of the Enlightenment's ideas that worldly phenomena are based on natural causes and artistic creativity does not derive from divine inspiration, it discussed the primitive conditions of Homer's time and his own personal intelligence as the explanations for the genius of his poetry. The next contributor to modern Homeric scholarship was Robert Wood (1717–1771) who wrote after a trip to Greece and Asia Minor his *Essay on the Original Genius and*

Title page of a German edition of the *Iliad*, printed in Leipzig in 1771.

Writings of Homer in which he discussed the geographical, historical and social background of the poems. Wood's conclusion that Homer had been illiterate and that the poems were originally preserved by memory had a strong effect on the school of Homeric studies at Gottingen, Germany founded by C. G. Heyne, who was the teacher of the analyst Wolf. About the same time, the proto-archaeologist Schliemann would soon be probing a hill called Hissarlik in northeast Turkey where the ruins of an ancient city, probably Homer's Ilion/Troy, are still being uncovered; and at Mycenae in Greece, spade in hand, he would claim to have gazed on the face of Agamemnon.

One amusing response to a text, as noted previously, is mockery. For a century or more burlesques of Homer had been appearing, in varying degrees of bawdiness. About one of them published in 1762 a reviewer wrote: "This work is by no means destitute of humour; and with those who are fond of this kind of versification, it might have passed off very well, had not the bounds of decency been, in many places, so insufferably transgressed."[113] A few lines of the proem from another one show just how far these burlesques could get from the Homeric text:

> So did great *Jove*, the King of Gods,
> Make *Aggy*, King of Men, at odds
> With *Peleus'* Son, and make them roar
> And rant and rave about a Whore.[114]

Thomas Bridges' burlesque translation became widely popular in the late eighteenth century but included so much vulgarity that it was not republished for a hundred years, and then only with serious revisions to keep it within the bounds of Victorian decency. Here is his saucy proem:

> Come, Mrs. Muse, but, if a maid,
> Then come Miss Muse, and lend me aid!
> Ten thousand jingling verses bring,
> That I Achilles' wrath may sing,
> That I may chant in curious fashion
> This doughty hero's boiling passion,
> Which plagu'd the Greeks; and gave 'em double
> A Christian's share of toil and trouble,
> And, in a manner quite uncivil,
> Sent many a Broughton[115] to the devil.
> Leaving their carcasses on rows,
> Food for great dogs and carrion crows.
> To this sad pass the bully's freaks
> Had brought his countryfolks the Greeks!
> But who the devil durst say no,
> Since surely Jove would have it so?
> Come tell us then, dear Miss, from whence
> The quarrel rose: who gave th'offence?
> Latona's son, with fiery locks,
> Amongst them sent both plague and *knocks*,
> And prov'd most *terribly* obdurate,
> Because the king had vex'd his curate;
> For which offence the god annoy'd 'em,
> And by whole wagon-loads destroy'd 'em.

In 1741 Edward Vernon made use of the now familiar Homeric form for a political satire which he immodestly called "The Vernon-iad of Homer." If Homer had been an actual person, he surely would have turned over in his grave at these developments!

Perhaps at the opposite end of the spectrum were printers honoring the Homeric text with the best of the printing arts. Edward Gibbon, author of the famous *Decline and Fall of the Roman Empire*, had a favorite edition of the Greek text of Homer: "As the eye is the organ of fancy, I read Homer with more pleasure in the Glasgow edition [of 1756–1758]. Through that fine medium, the poet's sense appears more beautiful and transparent." A reviewer commenting on the publication of the final volumes of this edition agreed with Gibbon on its fine quality of presentation and correctness of text: "We have the pleasure to observe, that the two last volumes are equal in merit with the two former, as to the beauty of the paper and type, and the accuracy and correctness of the work; which renders it not only as elegant and splendid, but perhaps as valuable an impression, as ever appeared in the Greek, or any other language."[116] The most famous illustrations of the Homeric text were produced in the late eighteenth century by the Englishman John Flaxman. In the 1770s his designing expertise was channeled into art pottery through work for Josiah Wedgwood, but by the 1790s he was in Rome sculpting

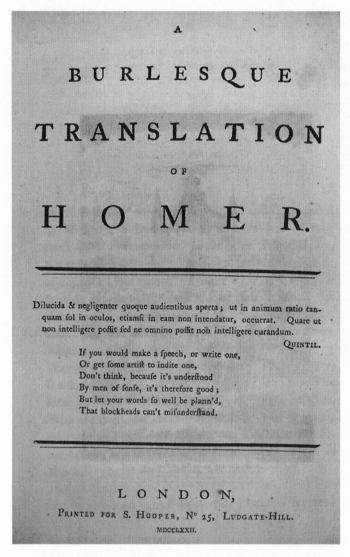

A

BURLESQUE

TRANSLATION

OF

HOMER.

Dilucida & negligenter quoque audientibus aperta; ut in animum ratio tan-
quam fol in oculos, etiamfi in eam non intendatur, occurrat.   Quare ut
non intelligere poffit fed ne omnino poffit non intelligere curandum.

QUINTIL.

If you would make a fpeech, or write one,
Or get fome artift to indite one,
Don't think, becaufe it's underftood
By men of fenfe, it's therefore good ;
But let your words fo well be plann'd,
That blockheads can't mifunderftand.

LONDON,
PRINTED FOR S. HOOPER, Nº 25, LUDGATE-HILL.
MDCCLXXII.

Title page of Thomas Bridges' burlesque rendering of
Homer, printed in London in 1772. The translation of the
Latin quote from the Roman writer Quintilian provides a
sense of the author's comic style.

large works in the neoclassical style, which imitated ancient art. His popular fame, however, came from his illustrations of the *Iliad* and *Odyssey* (1793) which led to other illustrating and sculptural commissions. His creative images of Homeric scenes with clear, neoclassical, linear rhythms were so successful that editions of Homer for two centuries, and even some current reprints, announce on their title pages that they include Flaxman's designs.[117]

One development of the eighteenth century was the printing of short translation pieces by "gentlemen scholars," examples of which can be seen in 1716, 1726, 1750 and 1753; persons with academic, poetic, or blue-blood pretensions continued to dabble with the Homeric text in the following centuries. Along with them, literary figures continued to attempt Homer as well. The poet William Cowper (1731–1800) created a translation of the *Iliad* and the *Odyssey* in blank verse which was first printed in 1791. For a sense of his style, here is his proem to the *Iliad*:

Sing, Muse, the deadly wrath of Peleus' son
Achilles, source of many thousand woes
To the Achaian host, which numerous souls
Of heroes sent to Ades premature,
And left their bodies to devouring dogs
And birds of heaven (so Jove his will perform'd)
From that dread hour when discord first embroil'd
Achilles and Atrides king of men.

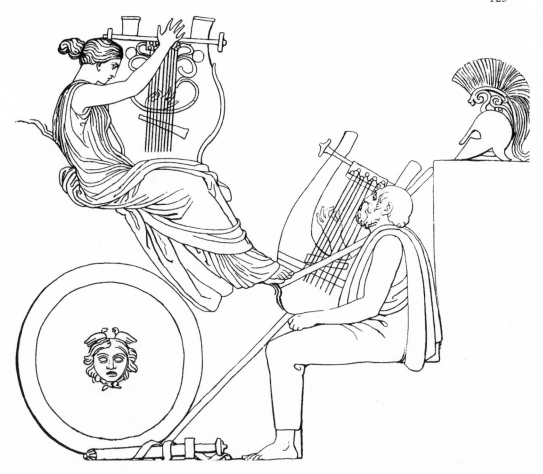

"Homer Invoking the Muse"; engraving by John Flaxman reflecting the famous first line of the *Iliad*'s famous proem.

Cowper insisted on his fidelity to the Homeric text, especially as opposed to the inventiveness of Pope: "my chief boast is that I have adhered closely to the original" and "the matter found in me, whether the reader like it or not, is found also in Homer; and the matter not found in me, how much soever the reader may admire it, is found only in Mr. Pope." A later commentator wrote about him: "As a translator of Homer, Cowper had many qualifications. Nothing is more characteristic of him than the sweet brightness of his inborn nature, — and nothing more touching to see under the dark cloud of melancholy that hung threatening his brain, — and this natural brightness united as it was to perfect delicacy of touch, a delicious humour, and a quivering sensitiveness, rendered him singularly responsive at once to the clear humanity, tenderness, and depth of the Homeric feeling, and to the charm and vividness of the Homeric fancy. What he lacked was perhaps energy and fire, and hence he is not quite so successful in the battle-pieces and fierce quarrels of the *Iliad*, and more at home in the romance and humour and mystery of the *Odyssey*, in the homely comfort of the swineherd's hut or in the sunny distant land where Nausicaa stood to greet Ulysses...."[118] A contemporary critic was less accepting: "We respect Mr. Cowper's abilities; some passages are executed with great

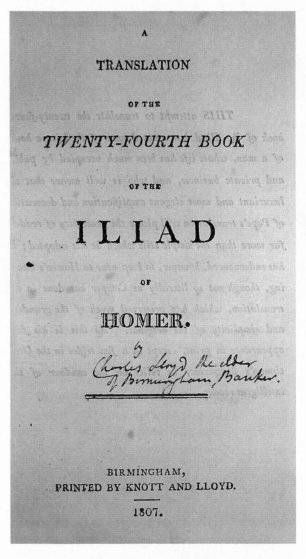

A

TRANSLATION

OF THE

TWENTY-FOURTH BOOK

OF THE

ILIAD

OF

HOMER.

by
Charles Lloyd the Elder
of Birmingham, Banker.

———————

BIRMINGHAM,
PRINTED BY KNOTT AND LLOYD.
———
1807.

Title page from a gentleman dabbler's translation of one book of Homer's *Iliad*, published in 1807. Note the handwritten attribution to "Charles Lloyd the Elder of Birmingham, Banker."

taste and spirit, and many that were difficult he has happily elucidated; yet, on the whole, the performance appears to us, considered as a poetical work, flat, heavy, and uninteresting."[119]

In another contemporary source, a critic wrote: "To the general praise of fidelity, Mr. Cowper is eminently entitled. Instances, however, occur, not infrequently, (and how could it be otherwise?) in which he has offended against the rigorous law that he professes to have imposed on himself; sometimes by mistaking the meaning of his author, at others by adding what is not to be found in the original Greek, or by omitting what really does exist there. The giant strength of Homer is sometimes presented by the feebleness of a pygmy: — his translator at one time soars into bombast, and at another, sinks into vulgarity. In many instances he happily exemplifies the coincidence of the Greek and English idioms; but, in others, his violent attempts to reconcile them, render his language affected and uncouth."[120] Matthew Arnold concluded that the translation failed at following Homer's rapidity and that "between Cowper and Homer there is interposed the mist of Cowper's elaborate Miltonic manner, entirely alien to the flowing rapidity of Homer." He noted that "the translation by Cowper is far superior to either Chapman's or Pope's as an interpretation of the poet, but it lacks a certain fire and swing essential to winning great poetic renown."

The eighteenth century also saw in 1729–40 the first of many printings of new and improved Homeric texts edited by Samuel Clarke and by the great Friedrich August Wolf. The first Homeric translations were made into Hungarian (1788) and Polish (1780), and there was an explosion of translations into various types of prose and verse and dialects: "paraphrastically translated" (1700), "in lingua Napoletano" (1700's), Tuscan dialect "in Ottava rima" (1703), "in Nederduitsch Heldendicht" (1709), "in rime Anacreontiche" (1741), "in versi Sciolti" (1742), "in imitation of the style of Milton"

(1750), "attempted by way of essay" (1750), "in Lombardia" (1788), and "in versi Milanesi" (1793).

The most lasting of German translations was published in 1793 by Johann Heinrich Voss (1751–1826), a professor of classical philology, poet, and lyricist, whose fame rests primarily on his *Odyssey* (1781) and *Iliad* (1793).

> Singe, Göttin, den Zorn des Peleiaden Achilleus,
> Der zum Verhängnis unendliche Leiden schuf den Achaiern
> Und die Seelen so vieler gewaltiger Helden zum Hades
> Sandte, aber sie selbst zum Raub den Hunden gewährte
> Und den Vögeln zum Frass— so wurde der Wille Kronions
> Endlich erfüllt —, nachdem sich einmal im Zwiste geschieden
> Atreus' Sohn, der Herrscher des Volks, und der edle Achilleus.

About the translations Arnold noted: "In Voss's well-known translation of Homer, it is precisely the qualities of his German language itself, something heavy and trailing both in the structure of its sentences and in the words of which it is composed, which prevent his translation, in spite of the hexameters, in spite of the fidelity, from creating in us the impression created by the Greek."[121] Sir John Herschel, however, argued the opposite, that the German language, especially that of Voss, permits better translation than English: "it has been found practicable to produce in German, what may be regarded as *fac similes* of the Iliad and Odyssee, in which every individual line, with every nicety of the meaning, and for the most part hardly any transposition in the order of the words, is rendered with a precision little short of miraculous, and which must for ever leave far behind it every other possible attempt of the kind. It is the fidelity with which an excellent photograph reproduces on paper a magnificent piece of architecture, in all its proportions and with even the most minute detail, while yet possessing (with perhaps some degree of unpleasing hardness) the air of a picture. For, after all, such *is* the impression which Voss's version produces."[122]

1801 to 1850

In the first half of the nineteenth century there were 704 Homeric printings, resulting in an average of 14.1 per year. During this significant increase in printings, translators continued experimenting with the Homeric text. Interesting efforts included a "Specimen of an English Homer in blank verse" (1807); a "metrisch ubersetzen" (1814); an *Odyssey* as a "freie Nachbildung in gereimten Strophen nach Homer" (1826); an *Iliad* "in terza rime" (1827); and *Iliad*s in "English accentuated hexameters" and "faithfully rendered in Homeric verse" (both 1844). The earlier burlesques of Homer also continued, such as this French one attributed to rather remarkable authors: *L'Iliad Travestie, par une Société de Gens de Lettres, de Savants, de Magistrats* (Iliad Travesty, by a Company of Men of Letters, Savants, and Judges) (1832).

The first half of the nineteenth century was also an important period for children's books, which had been very rare previously, and the new increase in production of these

Homeric Printings 1801–1850

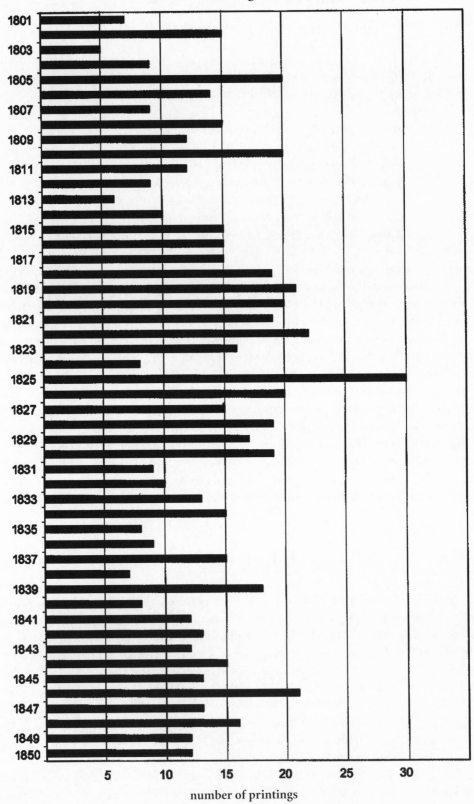

number of printings

works is seen in the list of Homeric titles. From 1802 to 1815 Karl Becker published his *Erzahlungen aus der alten Welt fur die Jugend* (Stories from the ancient World for Children) which included paraphrased passages from both the *Iliad* and the *Odyssey*. And the Homeric text began to be used in textbooks to teach the Greek language, such as this one (with text in Latin!) published in Avignon, France in 1820: *Introductio ad Linguam Graecam; Complectens Regulas Grammatices, Radices Vocum, et Exercitationem, seu Poema (Odusseus) in quo Regulae Radicesque Omnes ad Usum et Praxim Rediguntur; ad usum III. Classis et in eorum Gratiam qui Brevi Tempore Graecos Libro* (Introduction to the Greek Language; Containing Grammatical Rules, Roots of Voice, and Exercises; or, a Poem (Odyssey) in which all the Rules and Voices are Drawn into Use and Usefulness; Thanks to the Use of the Third Class whom I Raise up as Greeks for a Brief Time). *Iliad*s of 1842 and 1846 show the new trend of Homer as textbook in their subtitles: *zum Gebrauche für Schulen besorgt* (provided for the use of schools); and *comprising an accurately collated text, critical and explanatory notes and indices of words, subjects and authors.*

Homeric studies were dominated by the Germans throughout the nineteenth century, and this fact is evident in the list of printings. The important texts of Christian Gottlob Heyne and William Dindorf were published, texts destined to be used in countless future editions and translations. At Leipzig the firm of B. G. Teubner began its longlasting series of excellent editions of the classics, including Homer, the academic validity of which was underscored by the famous subtitle: *ad Optimorum Librorum Fidem Expressa* (Faithfully Rendered from the Best Books). Even today, scholars cite "the Teubner text" when rigorous standards are required. With rapid developments in textual criticism printings began to advertise that they included the "Urtext" or original, fundamental text and that they showed the restored digamma.

Non–German classicists were not too far behind. In Dublin in 1821 a scholarly text of the *Iliad* edited by Jacob Kennedy was printed with a subtitle similar to Teubner's: *ex Optimis Editionibus Fideliter Expressa*. In London the title of a translation by W. Trollope indicates how Homeric studies in general were affecting printings of the text: *The Iliad of Homer, Chiefly from the Text of Heyne, with Copious English Notes Illustrating the Grammatical Construction, the Manners and Customs, the Mythology and Antiquities of the Heroic Ages, and Preliminary Observations on Points of Classical Interest and Import* (1827). New vernacular translations appeared in Bohemian (1801), Icelandic (1829), Russian (1829), Slavic (1829), Norwegian (1835), Portuguese (1835), and Armenian (1843). A significant development in 1810 was the first appearance of the standard Italian translation of the *Iliad* done by the poet Vincenzo Monti. Here is his proem:

> Cantami, o Diva, del Pelide Achille
> L'ira funesta, che infiniti addusse
> Lutti agli Achei, molte anzi tempo all'Orco
> Generose travolse alme d'eroi,
> E di cani e d'augelli orrido pasto
> Lor salme abbandono (cosi di Giove
> L'alto consiglio s'adempia), da quando
> Primamente disgiunse aspra contesa
> Il re de'prodi, Atride, e il divo Achille.

It is also interesting that the English poet Percy Bysshe Shelley (1792–1822) who was, in fact, a serious student of ancient Greece, was inspired to translate the Homeric Hymns, published in 1821. Shelley and his comrade Lord Byron, the quintessential philhellenes, actually went to Greece to fight in their war to throw off Turkish control.

In 1841 an anonymous translator, identified only as a "graduate of the University of Oxford," published a prose edition of the *Iliad*, the proem of which follows:

> Sing, Goddess, the destructive wrath of Achilles, son of Peleus, which
> brought myriad [fn: i.e. Very many] disasters upon the Achaeans, and
> sent many gallant souls of heroes to Hades, and made themselves [fn:
> Their carcases] a prey to dogs and all birds *of prey* (for so the counsel
> of Jove was fulfilled), from the time when, first, Atrides, king of men,
> and the godlike Achilles, quarrelling with each other, separated.

That the translator's focus was on literally rendering the Greek text is clear from the proem's wording and also from his title and subtitle: *The* Iliad *of Homer, translated into English Prose, as literally as the different idioms of the Greek and English languages will allow; with explanatory notes.* He defended his decision in the preface: "There is nothing more common, among a certain class of scholars, than to cry out with vehemence against every literal translation. ...To translate the poetry of one language into the prose of another, is, to say the least of it, an irksome task, and necessarily obliges the translator to lay aside every idea of elegance in his composition. With respect to Homer, in particular, these objectives are peculiarly strong." He argued that unless the original text's epithets are fairly and literally given the result is not authentic, even if including them results in a "style [that] is always pompous, and not infrequently bombastic." In this translation he intended to follow the text faithfully "with the sole view of conveying more strictly and closely the construction, as well as the sense, of the noble original." The footnotes quoted above in the proem and the underlining of the words "of prey" to show that they are added for clarification are evidence of this careful rendering of the original text.

1851 to 1900

The second half of the nineteenth century was a high point for Homeric scholarship and for famous and infamous translations of the Homeric text. There were a remarkable 1,374 Homeric printings, an average of 25.5 per year, the highest for any period in history. New languages were added to the Homeric repertoire, including Platt-Deutsch (1869), Dutch (1880), Turkish (1887), and Arabic (1900). Here is the *Iliad*'s proem in a more modern Turkish version, that of Azra Erhat and A. Kadir (1967):

> Soyle, tanrica, Peleusoglu Akhilleus'un ofkesini soyle.
> Aci ustune aciyi Akhalara o kahreden ofke getirdi,
> ulu canlarini Hades'e atti nice yigitlerin,
> govdelerini yem yapti kurda kusa.

Buyrugu yerine geliyordu Zeus'un,
ilk acildigi gunden beri aralari
erlerin basbugu Atreusogluyle tanrisal Akhilleus'un.

Although the *Odyssey* had appeared in Portuguese in 1835, it was 1874 before a Portuguese *Iliad* was published, by Manoel Odorico Mendes, whose proem follows:

Canta-me, o deusa, do Peleio Achilles
A ira tenaz, que, luctuosa aos Gregos,
Verdes no Orco lancon mil fortesalmas,
Corpos de heroes a caes e abutres pasto:
Lei foi de Jove, em rixa ao discordarem
O de homens chefe e o Myrmidon divino.

F. W. Newman (1805–97) published his English translation of the *Iliad* in 1856, using an antiquated idiom with echoes of Anglo-Saxon poetry and alliterative verse to try to communicate Homer's strangeness and remoteness. Unfortunately for him, his effort became the impetus for Matthew Arnold's famous treatise on translation that has been reviewed in a previous section of this book. Arnold criticized Newman's work for failing to achieve a tone of nobility and said that "between Mr. Newman and Homer is interposed a cloud of more than Egyptian thickness, — namely, a manner, in Mr. Newman's version, eminently ignoble, while Homer's manner is eminently noble." Arnold, warming to his attack, continued: "Mr. Newman joins to a bad rhythm so bad a diction that it is difficult to distinguish exactly whether in any given passage it is his words or his measure which produces a total impression of such an unpleasant kind." And, at last, Arnold delivered the coup de grace: "I will by no means make search in Mr. Newman's version for passages likely to raise a laugh; that search, alas! would be far too easy." In the

Typically decorated front cover of a late-nineteenth-century *Iliad* printed for general public consumption.

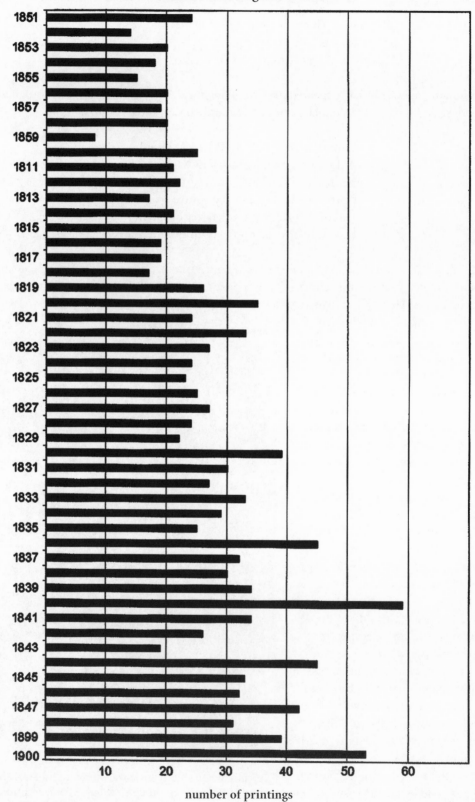

Homeric Printings 1851–1900

number of printings

1905 edition of Arnold's book the editor wrote: "Mr. Newman's translation of Homer ... is dead, and probably no one ever looks at it now except out of curiosity."[123] No wonder, after such criticism!

In 1887 the craftsman, poet, and printer William Morris (1834–96), who was part of the Pre-Raphaelite movement in arts and crafts, which promoted the styles of the fifteenth century, published a translation of the *Odyssey*. His interest in idealized medieval, Pre–Raphaelite ideals is evident in these comments by a critic of the translation: "It is composed in rhyming verse of varying syllabic lengths, and in verse-paragraphs interconnected by varying rhyme-schemes. The Spenserian stanza inhabits, as it were, Morris's technique of narrative rhyme. The idiom is often characteristic of Victorian medievalism. The influence of Tennyson's Arthurian narrative is patent. In this text we learn far more of Morris than we do of Homer."[124] Other critics were likewise unimpressed. His *Odyssey* was criticized by Rouse for having too many syllables per line with the result that it sounds slurred: "It is hard to believe that a poet with so wide a reputation could have an ear so deaf to the music of verse.... It is impossible to read Morris's translation aloud, without gabbling. Nor is ugly sound the only fault [— there are also mistranslations.] Add to this the false archaisms, and you have another Newman, although one who is less obtrusive. We need not search for any traces of the grand style in Morris."[125] The artist was especially interested in creating books that were beautiful works of art in the style of the Gothic past in contrast to the cheaply printed, ugly books of his time. Unfortunately, his *Odyssey*, initially published by the Kelmscott Press using his personally designed Golden Type, was not an especially successful effort in this field either, as it lacked much decoration in the type and lacked illustrations altogether.

One of the best translations of Homer was achieved by a collaboration of the scholars Samuel Henry Butcher (1850–1910), Andrew Lang (1844–1912), Walter Leaf (1844–1912), and Ernest Myers (1844–1921); Butcher and Lang's *Odyssey* first appeared in 1879, and Lang, Leaf and Myers' *Iliad* in 1882. As a sample, here is their proem:

Sing, goddess, the wrath of Achilles Peleus' son, the ruinous wrath that
brought on the Achaians woes innumerable, and hurled down into Hades
many strong souls of heroes, and gave their bodies to be a prey to dogs
and all winged fowls; and so the counsel of Zeus wrought out its accomplishment
from the day when first strife parted Atreides king of men
and noble Achilles.

These prose translations followed the Greek word order and syntax, and their verbiage was modeled on the Authorized Version of the Bible. Addressing the obvious question of how translation can be divided up among several persons, three in this case for the *Iliad*, they wrote in the prefatory remarks: "Each Translator is therefore responsible for his own portion; but the whole has been revised by all three Translators, and the rendering of passages or phrases recurring in more than one portion has been determined after deliberation in common." Many critics liked their translations; for example, one wrote: "in my opinion, no translation has surpassed, or will ever surpass the magnificent Victorian translation of Leaf, Lang, and Myers for the *Iliad*, and Butcher and Lang for the *Odyssey*."[126] Rouse said that they were the best translations in his generation: "Their style is modeled upon the English Bible, and is not free from false archaism. On the whole, however, they deserve their reputation; for the readers are used to the style, and the scholarship is excellent."[127]

Other critics, however, were less gracious: "But their slavish imitation of the syntax and idiom of the Greek brought their prose more than once to the very border of intelligibility.... And their language never approached the poetry of their model at its best...."[128] Arnold had argued that translations should be done for scholars, and the texts of Butcher and Lang probably come the closest to meeting this notion in that they tried to reproduce Homer's epic dignity by using King James archaisms while sticking closely to the word order and syntax of the original to keep their translation accurate.[129] A later commentator noted the dilemma for translators balancing accuracy versus poetry: "The prose translations of the *Odyssey* by Messrs. Butcher and Lang, and of the *Iliad* by Lang, Leaf, and Myers, are invaluable for any one who wishes, without the knowledge of Greek, to gain an accurate knowledge of the detailed matter in the poems. But, as the writers would be the first to admit, a close translation in prose of what was essentially a diction framed for poetry must always produce a certain unnaturalness of effect, and this does inevitably detract from the directness of appeal which is the supreme quality of Homer."[130] The importance of these translations was especially due to their usefulness in education: "For generations of schoolboys, university undergraduates and general readers, 'Lang, Leaf & Myers' became synonymous with 'Homer.' Even today, verse-translations and twentieth-century prose have not altogether superseded this fine battle-horse."[131]

Samuel Butler (1835–1902) is best known as a novelist through his two books, the Utopian satire *Erewhon* and the autobiographical novel *The Way of All Flesh*. However, he is also known in Homeric studies as the author of the book mentioned in chapter 1 (titled *The Authoress of the Odyssey)* proposing that Homer, or at least the creator of the *Odyssey*, was a woman. Reacting against the purposely antiquated prose of the versions of Lang et al., he decided to translate Homer (*Iliad* 1888; *Odyssey* 1900) to provide a version in "such prose as we write and speak among ourselves" and to "exterminate" the problems caused by the oral transmission of the poems. However, a critic complained that "Samuel Butler, a rebel against Victorian primness, made a prose version that he claimed was plain English but that ended up with the worst of both alternatives. Not only is his prose still mottled with fancy archaisms and inversions, his tone can range from indecorous to downright vulgar."[132]

Edward George Geoffrey Smith Stanley, 14th Earl of Derby (1799–1869) had a long political career in English government, serving as leader of the Conservative Party from 1846 to 1868 and three times as prime minister, although he was overshadowed by the famous politician Benjamin Disraeli. Lord Derby, as he is more efficiently referred to, was typical of the highest successful aristocrats of the nineteenth century, owning race-horses, overseeing his lands, and — of interest here — translating Homer. The proem of his frequently reprinted *Iliad*:

> Of Peleus' son, Achilles, sing, O Muse,
> The vengeance, deep and deadly; whence to Greece
> Unnumber'd ills arose; which many a soul

> Of mighty warriors to the viewless shades
> Untimely sent; they on the battle plain
> Unburied lay, a prey to rav'ning dogs,
> And carrion birds; but so had Jove decreed,
> From that sad day when first in wordy war,
> The mighty Agamemnon, King of men,
> Confronted stood by Peleus' godlike son.

"The version of the *Iliad* by Lord Derby, first published in 1864 ... has the great merits of simplicity, dignity, and sincerity, and its ease of style makes it eminently readable."[133] In his preface he wrote that he was trying for a literal translation but one which would convey the spirit of the original. He admitted his fear that readers of Greek would not want a translation and that non–Greek readers would prefer "the harmonious versification and polished brilliancy of Pope's translation...." However, he could not let the opportunity pass without noting: "But, admirable as it is, Pope's Iliad can hardly be said to be Homer's Iliad...." Lord Derby, like other translators, felt that the act of translating Homer was intoxicating: "It has afforded me, in the intervals of more urgent business, an unfailing, and constantly increasing source of interest; and it is not without a feeling of regret at the completion of my task, and a sincere diffidence as to its success, that I venture to submit the result of my labours to the ordeal of public criticism." The translation was afforded this balanced assessment by the author Sir Walter Scott: "A poetic translation of the *Iliad* has been made by the Earl of Derby, which is accurate, dignified, and poetic. This seems to me to reproduce Homer more nearly than any other English verse translation, but even these verses in the heroic measure of Milton bear little resemblance to the majestic and flowing hexameters of the original."

The English astronomer Sir John Frederick William Herschel (1792–1871), son and scientific successor of the famous astonomer Sir William Frederick Herschel, was also a translator of Homer. He spent most of his life contributing to research on double stars and observing nebulae from the Cape of Good Hope, which resulted in great publicity in the scientific world and his being named a baronet in 1838. In his final years he set himself the task of translating the *Iliad* into "English accentuated hexameters." Here is his proem from the initial publication in 1866:

> Sing, celestial Muse! the destroying wrath of Achilles,
> Peleus' son: which myriad mischiefs heaped on the Grecians,
> Many a valiant hero's soul dismissing to Hades;
> Flinging their corpses abroad for a prey to dogs *and to vultures*
> And to each bird of the air. Thus Jove's high will was accomplished.
> Ev'n from that fateful hour when opposed in *angry* contention
> Stood forth Atreides, King of men, and godlike Achilles.

In the preface to his translation Herschel wrote that although others had contended that translation of the Homeric text into English hexameter results in lines which are "utterly uncouth and barbarous," it could be done. He admitted that in his attempt he occasionally had to insert words to fill out the hexameters, but the trade-off was that he put these additions in italics. He also decided to leave out epithets except when he felt they were relevant to the narrative: "There is no denying that the continual recurrence of these epithets, in season and out of season, in Homer, has a very oppressive effect on the modern ear." His translation effort, unfortunately, was not successful in winning critical approval.

Another relatively unsuccessful translation of the *Iliad* was published in 1871 by John Graham Cordery. Here is his attempt at the proem:

> Sing, Goddess, of Achilles, Peleus' son
> The Wrath that rose disastrous, and the cause
> Of woes unnumber'd to Achaia's host,
> Casting to Hades many a mighty soul
> Of hero ere his time, and many a limb
> Prey to the dogs and all the fowls of heaven!
> Yet was the will of Zeus fulfill'd thereby;
> Then first, what time asunder stood in strife
> Achilles from Atrides king of men.

Cordery's pessimistic comments about translation were stated in his preface: "no really independent translator of Homer can be like another. As with the painting of nature, so it is with the attempted transfer of the master-pieces of poetry into a new language. …The two qualities which I have desired most to retain are those of rapidity of movement and directness of speech. …A translator cannot, indeed, like a poet, have his 'eye upon the object' only; it suffices for him to have it upon that image of the object which is presented to him on the mirror from which he is reading. …I concur with those who hold that the sonorous march of the ancient hexameter lies beyond the reach of the English tongue…."

In 1875 the first American translator of note, William Cullen Bryant (1794–1878), threw his hat into the ring. A native of New England, he is best known as a Romantic poet whose works glorified the beauty of nature seen in the Berkshire hills and streams. He also had a fifty-year career as a journalist editing New York's *Evening Post*, in which his liberal views in favor of free trade, workers' rights, free speech, and abolition were expounded. Like many other learned men, Bryant translated the *Iliad* and, in fact, produced quite a successful result. The recent commentator Steiner noted that written "by a Boston brahmin, poet, scholar and man of letters … this is a thoroughly readable 'Homer.' Quite often, it is more than that."[134] Here is his proem:

> O Goddess! Sing the wrath of Peleus' son,
> Achilles; sing the deadly wrath that brought
> Woes numberless upon the Greeks, and swept
> To Hades many a valiant soul, and gave
> Their limbs a prey to dogs and birds of air, —
> For so had Jove appointed, —from the time
> When the two chiefs, Atrides, king of men,
> And great Achilles, parted first as foes.

Like many translators of Homer, Bryant, as he noted in his preface, was somewhat regretful when his time spent with the *Iliad* was over: "I am not sure that, when it shall be concluded, it may not cost me some regret to part with so interesting a companion as the old Greek poet, whose thoughts I have, for four years part, been occupied, though with interruptions, in the endeavor to transfer from his own grand and musical Greek to our less sonorous but still manly and flexible tongue." Also in the preface he explained his approach to Homer and his translation technique: "I have endeavored to be strictly faithful in my rendering; to add nothing of my own, and to give the reader, so far as our language would allow, all that I found in the original. ...[B]ut in a very few cases, where they [epithets] embarrassed the versification, I have used the liberty taken by Homer himself, and left them out. ...I have endeavored to preserve the simplicity of style which distinguishes the old Greek poet, who wrote for the popular man and according to the genius of his language, and I have chosen such English as offers no violence to the ordinary usages and structures of our own. I have sought to attain what belongs to the original, — a fluent narrative style, which shall carry the reader forward without the impediment of unexpected inversions and capricious phrases, and in which, if he find nothing to stop at and admire, there will at least be nothing to divert his attention from the story and the characters of the poem, from the events related and the objects described. ...I have chosen blank-verse for this reason among others, that it enabled me to keep more closely to the original in my rendering, without any sacrifice either of ease or of spirit in the expression. The use of rhyme in a translation is a constant temptation to petty infidelities...." Sir Walter Scott deemed his translation "careful and successful."

The 1886 line-for-line verse translation of the *Iliad* by Arthur S. Way was also well received, as had been his previously published *Odyssey* offered under the pseudonym "Avia." Here is his proem to the *Iliad*:

> The wrath of Achilles the Peleus-begotten, O Song-queen, sing,
> Fell wrath, that dealt the Achaians woes past numbering;
> Yea, many a valiant spirit to Hades' halls did it send,
> Spirits of heroes, and cast their bodies to dog to rend,
> And to fowls of ravin, — yet aye Zeus' will wrought on to its end
> Even from the hour when first that feud of the mighty began,
> Of Atreides, King of Men, and Achilles the godlike man.

A reviewer wrote "Mr. Way is more careful than some of his contemporaries, perhaps by reason of his long practice in blank verse; and he shows in many places a true feeling for sound." Following the publication of the first volume, a writer for the *Saturday Review* gushed: "A translation of the Iliad into English remains, like the Quest of the Grail or the Fleece of Gold, an adventure hardly to be achieved. ...Now, Mr. Way in very many passages does offer us a version at once close, spirited, swift in movement, and simple. We have read much of his translation with great pleasure. ...If Mr. Way could keep his whole translation on this level, so rapid, distinct, close to Homer, and unaffected, we might look no further, but declare that the quest was ended, and the Fleece of Gold brought home." The *London Quarterly Review* reported that "he is unquestionably the most Homeric of English translators of Homer since Chapman."

The 1891 prose translation by John Purves was doomed, however, to oblivion for reasons evident even in his lackluster proem:

> Sing, O goddess, the fatal wrath of Peleus' son Achilles, which
> brought ten thousand troubles on the Achaeans, and sent to Hades
> many valiant souls of heroes, and made themselves a prey to dog
> and every foul — such was the will of Zeus — after that day when
> first Atrides, king of men, and divine Achilles, quarreled and were parted.

A similar fate awaited the translation by Prentiss Cummings initiated by the following uninspiring proem:

> Sing, O goddess, the song that tells of the WRATH of ACHILLES —
> Wrath to Achaians accursed, and fraught with sorrows unnumbered:
> Many a mighty soul to Hades it hurried untimely,
> Many a hero dead made prey to dogs, and a banquet
> Fed to the birds of air, — but the will of Zeus was accomplished: —
> Take up the song where first that great twain parted in quarrel,
> Even Atreides, of heroes the lord, and Achilles the godlike.

1901 to 1950

Along with humanity itself, in the first half of the twentieth century the Homeric text survived two world wars and an international business depression. There were 1,047 Homeric printings, averaging 20.9 per year; the decrease from the previous half-century illustrates the worldwide damage to civilization done by the wars, financial depression, and widespread cultural changes. With the sweeping away of the aristocratic European past, translators of Homer tended to be academicians and not poets, politicians, philosophers, or gentleman farmers. But there was no dearth of new editions, as well as a growing industry of reprinting those of the past. With new worldwide communications came translations into new languages, including: Czech (1904), Slovenian (1911), Serbo-Croatian (1915), Indian (1920), Yiddish (1924), Farsi (1925), Welsh (1928), Chinese (1929), Esperanto (an invented language promoted for international communication) (1930), Hebrew (1932), Lettish (1936), Gaelic (1937), Albanian (1941), and Croatian (1950).

The Homeric stories, redone for children, continued in popularity. Examples included: Walter Copland Perry, *The Boy's Iliad* (1902), Agnes Spofford Book Gale, *Achilles and Hector: Iliad Stories Retold for Boys and Girls* (1903); Helene Otto, *Ilias, in der Sprache der Zehnjährigen Erzählt* (Iliad, Presented in the Language of a Ten-Year Old) (1904); and, Maria Luz Morales, *La Iliada; o, El Sitio de Troya, Relatada a los Nianos* (1926). Michael West made the rather unorthodox association of Homer with the world's most famous liar in the 1935 book *Travellers' Tales from the Odyssey and Baron Munchausen*. This trend of separating individual stories out of the full epic poems was very popular. Examples of these Homeric derivatives include the play *Nausicaa, Pièce en un Acte, en Vers, Tirée de l'Odyssée* by Maurice Bouschor (1903); Hugh Woodruff Taylor, *The Women of the Iliad: a Metrical Translation of the First Book and of Other Passages in Which Women Appear* (1912); Henry Bertram Lister, *The Bride of Achilles; a Garland of Lines from Homer* (1932); *Odysseus und Nausikaa; ein Idyll aus Homer* (1949); and, Philip Dorf, *The Coming of Ulysses; a Play in Four Acts* (1949). In 1931 two especially fine editions of Pope's translations were published as limited editions for collectors by the Limited Editions Club and the Nonesuch Press. Unusual presentations included: Julius Schultz, *Das Lied vom Zorn Achills; aus Unserer Ilias Hergestellt und in Deutsche Nibelungenzeilen ubertragen* (The Ballad of Achilles' Wrath; Produced from our Iliad and Translated into German Nibelung lines) (1901); Ewen Maclachlan, *Gaelic Verse, Comprising a Translation of Homer's Iliad, Books I-VIII, and Original Compositions* (1937); and, Pierre Albert-Birot, *Les Amusements*

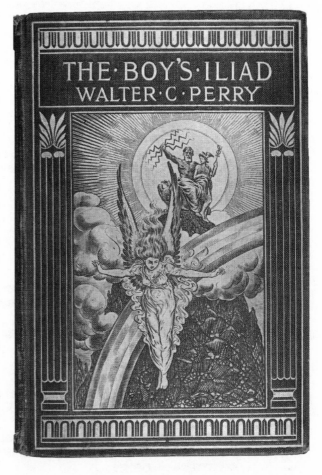

Art Nouveau style cover of an *Iliad* edition for boys, 1902.

Naturels, l'Iliade, les Eumenides, le Mystere d'Adam et Cent Cinquante Poems Nouveaux (Natural Amusements, the Iliad, the Eumenides, the Mystery of Adam and 150 New Poems) (1945).

John William Mackail (1859–1945) was born on the British Isle of Bute and attended Edinburgh University and then Balliol College, Oxford, pursuing classical studies where he was the top undergraduate student of his time. He wrote poetry, such as a prizewinning poem on the famous Greek battle at Thermopylae, and during his career as an academician wrote on Greek and Latin literature. Mackail's special interest was Virgil, and he published translations of all his works culminating with the *Aeneid* in 1930. However, he also contributed translations from Greek writers, including Homer's *Odyssey* (in three volumes: 1903, 1905, 1910) for which he used the rhyming quatrain of Edward Fitzgerald's *Omar Khayyam* with interesting but unsuccessful results: "The graceful and elegant style gives this translation an abiding charm; but the general effect of the recurrent rimes is dreamy, and the vigorous parts of it lose something in consequence. These quatrains cannot move fast, and speed is essential."[135] In 1906 Mackail became professor of poetry at Oxford and,

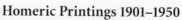

Homeric Printings 1901–1950

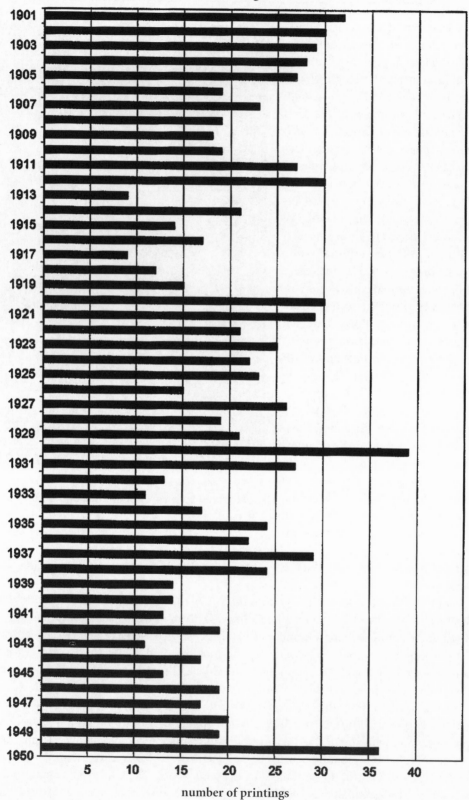

number of printings

subsequently, wrote extensively about other periods of poetry and also wrote biographies, including an excellent one of William Morris.

Another hopeful Homeric translator was Arthur Gardner Lewis whose proem to the *Iliad* follows:

> Sing thou the Wrath, O Muse! the baleful wrath
> Of Peleus' son, Achilles; wrath which heaped
> Unnumbered woes upon Achaea's band.
> And hurled to Hades countless mighty souls
> Of heroes, and their bodies gave for spoil
> To dogs and birds of prey, that the design
> Of Zeus might be fulfilled thus. These things all
> Found origin that day when parted first
> In jealous bick'ring Agamemnon, lord
> Of warriors, and Achilles the divine.

Lewis' 1911 translation into blank verse did not receive much fame, despite the good intentions written in his preface about himself in the third person: "His aim has been to produce a rendition which should be smooth, harmonious, and pleasing to the ear, so far as consistent with an adequate and literal interpretation of the poet's meaning; observing also, so far as lay in his power, the rules of simplicity, rapidity, and dignity, laid down by Matthew Arnold as essential. ...The absolutely ideal translation of Homer will never be written; yet perhaps each new attempt may contribute a little new truth, a little added beauty, just a new felicitous touch here and there, which shall be characteristic and all its own...."

In 1922 George Ernle published a translation of the *Iliad* whose proem follows:

> Sing me that Anger, Goddess, which blinding royal Achilleus
> Balefully, brought sufferings untold to the army of Argos,
> Sent many souls of mighty Achaeans into the darkness
> And flung abroad the bodies to the wild dogs and to the vultures
> And to the fowls of Heaven, till Zeus had duly accomplished
> All he decreed. Sing of it from where Agamemnon Atrides
> And the gallant Achilleus first fought and parted asunder.

The translation was accomplished in "quantitative hexameters." In his preface Ernle described his reasons for attempting this difficult meter: "There have been many attempts to write English verse in quantity but none to my knowledge has achieved popular success or diminished the prejudice which is naturally felt against any tampering with the established metrical system. ...He [the reader] will concede that the attempt to naturalize so glorious a metre is a worthy one, however desperate; that the hexameter is the only metre in which one may hope to give any adequate rendering of the swift, rolling, and magnificent music of Homer. The difference in form between hexameter and iambic is a difference of spirit; and I cannot think that blank verse, couplets, or stanzas, however beautiful, will ever be found satisfactorily to reproduce the spirit of the original." Unfortunately, Ernle's attempt was not received with overwhelming success.

The Loeb Classical Library of ancient authors is a series of Greek or Latin texts with translations published by Harvard University that is well known to every student of the classics. Greek authors are bound in green cloth and Latin in red, and rows of the diminutive volumes line the shelves of almost every college library. Classics scholars have sometimes complained about their quality (at least one drily calling them the "low ebb" editions), but their usefulness in making ancient texts readily available cannot be questioned. In 1919 Homer's *Odyssey* and in 1924 the *Iliad* were first published in this series, with prose translations by A(ugustus) T(aber) Murray (1866–1940). As stated in his introduction, his intent was "to give a faithful rendering ... that preserves in so far as possible certain traits of the style of the original." He noted that "such a rendering should be smooth and flowing and should be given in elevated but not in stilted language. In particular the recurrent lines and phrases which are so noticeable in the original should be preserved." The result was, not surprisingly, rather workmanlike, but many a student has pored over the Loeb editions comparing the Greek text on the left side with Murray's rendition on the right. The shortcomings of the translation are clearly evident in his stilted and outdated- sounding (even for its day) proem:

> The wrath do thou sing, O goddess, of Peleus' son, Achilles, that baneful
> wrath which brought countless woes upon the Achaeans, and sent forth to
> Hades many valiant souls of warriors, and made themselves to be a spoil
> for dogs and all manner of birds; and thus the will of Zeus was being
> brought to fulfilment; — sing thou thereof from the time when at the first
> there parted in strife Atreus' son, king of men, and goodly Achilles.

A contrast academically and aurally, Maurice Hewlett's blank verse translation of the *Iliad* was published in 1928. It began:

> Sing, Muse, the ruinous wrath of Peleus' son
> Achilles, which brought woes innumerable
> Upon the Greeks, casting great souls to Hell
> Great flesh to dogs and crows— so to fulfil
> The plans of Zeus—from that first strife which sunder'd
> Atreus' son, King of Men, from great Achilles.

Hewlett modestly explained his choice of blank verse, his omission of certain passages, and the lure of Homer: "Chapman, Pope, Cowper, Lord Derby. I may say of mine that I have added nothing to the feast, and have only omitted such of the standing garnish of Homer's table as tended to obscurity, redundancy, or other kind of nuisance. ...But suppose one could get one's blank verse as close to the original, as sensitive to atmosphere, as remote from, say, *The Light of Asia,* or other explicitly blank verse narrative as this book succeeds in getting prose — and yet push on with the tale, get something of Homer's effect of a river-flood, of unstaying, streaming, irresistible flow — would that not be worth trying after? That is what I have tried to get here. ...What precisely I have attempted in this translation may be stated thus: to communicate to the reader of it the same quality of intellectual pleasure which the English reader of Homer may be supposed to get. No more than that, for we don't know certainly what kind of pleasure the Greek reader or hearer got from him, seeing that we don't know certainly how the Greek read him. No more than that, but no less; for any difficulties which the text may present are better solved by a prose translation, and are in any case not to be solved by me who have no pretensions to Homeric scholarship. Now, what is the quality of intellectual pleasure obtainable by an English reader of Homer? First, certainly, the sense of heroic enterprise, the sense of being in touch with great men, great places, and great endeavour; the sense of sharing a tradition, of being uplifted into a great and keen air; of being borne swiftly, smoothly and irresistibly along on the tide of great events. All these must inhere in rhythm and in the diction alike. Secondly — and *pari passu* with the first — a sense of reality, of being in the open air with real people, of being in the hands of a poet who knows what he is writing about, who knows the landscape, the weather, the time of day, as well as the characters of his personages."[136]

Hewlett had his definite opinions about Homer — that he was not intending a work of grand style and that his intention was to be businesslike and direct. He wrote: "Grand manner — I don't find. I find idiom — racy language — great directness and simplicity — much seriousness and much humour." In the preface to a later edition Lascelles Abercrombie described Hewlett's meter and style: "Having disposed of these [eight-syllable, hexameter, and rhyming verse], his argument simply assumes (what is surely the fact) that blank verse is the natural equivalent in English of hexameters in Greek. But that equivalence is not very evident in the way he actually uses his blank verse. Continually its adventurous modulations make it more dramatic in its movement than narrative; the effect of the occasional half-lines is curiously un–Homeric; and in general he seems little concerned to develop whatever affinity there may be between blank verse rhythm and hexameter rhythm. This seems to call for some explanation. I have no doubt that the extreme freedom of his verse is simply another aspect of his refusal to see the Grand Manner in Homer. ...Hewlett composed his blank verse for the sake of the meaning he was giving — to invigorate by every stimulus of which versification is capable the sense of his English: that is to say, the sense which his instinct took over out of Homer to be the stuff of his version. Thus it is the same with his metre as with his diction. If he ignores Homeric majesty, it is precisely in order to render qualities which he valued infinitely more. And they are the qualities which make for liveliness and excitement. At all costs, his verse must show surprising and abrupt flexibility; only thus could its movement answer to every emphasis of the passion, every access of the energy, every sparkle of the zest and sting of the relish for life, which were for him the meaning of Homer."

A famous person of this period who might seem an unlikely translator of Homer was T(homas) E(dward) Lawrence (1888–1935), better known as Lawrence of Arabia, whose "translation of the *Odyssey* has ... earned a place in English literature, as one of the most successful renderings addressed to the general public" according to his recent biographer Jeremy Wilson.[137] Lawrence's worldwide travels, military experience, and participation in archaeological excavations at the ancient site of Carchemish gave him special insight into the central figure in the *Odyssey* and has led a recent commentator to label him "Odysseus of Arabia"![138] Because Wilson's "authorized biography" provides the texts of many personal letters relevant to this translation, it is possible to follow the translator's mind as he proceeded on the project, how he felt about previous translations,

T.E. Lawrence dressed as "Lawrence of Arabia."

and how he interacted with his sponsor.

Lawrence had already added literary pursuits to his well-publicized military ones by authoring the very successful *Seven Pillars of Wisdom* when he was approached (through their mutual acquaintance Ralph Isham) by the famous typographer Bruce Rogers to translate the *Odyssey*. In 1927, Random House had commissioned Rogers to print a fine edition of any book he chose. Having selected the second Homeric poem, "he began reading the various English renderings, but concluded 'that all the available translations were lacking in speed, primarily, however admirable they might be in other respects'" (p. 813).[139] On behalf of Rogers, Isham wrote to Lawrence, then stationed in Karachi, India and proposed the project as Rogers had outlined it: "They want to get away from the old translation; they want this to be a free translation — rather a new interpretation of the *Odyssey*. You will be glad to know that it is not your name they want but your translation. They are willing either to give the name you now use, as translator, or to give no name at all, whichever you wish. I do not know how you are at Greek but I thought this scheme might just fit into your present scheme of things and the honorarium of 800 pounds is not to be grown on every tree in India" (pp. 813–814).

When Lawrence received the letter his response was positive, as he was in the process of completing his second book, *The Mint*, and had considered finding another literary project. Fortunately, Lawrence was already a Homeric enthusiast and had a copy of the Greek text of the *Odyssey* at hand! The project tempted him, but he was open-eyed about the time it would take and the pressure to produce a good product, considering his amateur status in the world of classical studies. He wrote back to Isham that the offer had "knocked me out, temporarily.... The money suggested is wonderful, but that only shows how well they expect it to be done: and I have no trust whatever in my writing....

When your letter came, I took the *Odyssey* down from the shelf, (it goes with me, always, to every camp, for I love it) and tried to see myself translating it, freely, into English. Honestly, it would be most difficult to do. I have the rhythm of the Greek so in my mind, that it would not come readily into straight English. Nor am I a scholar; I read it only for pleasure, and have to keep a dictionary within reach. I thought of the other translators, and agreed that there was not a first-rate one. Butcher and Lang ... too antique. Samuel Butler ... too little dignified, tho' better. Morris ... too literary. That only shows the job as it is. Why should my doing be any better than these efforts of the bigger men? ... My strongest advice to you is to get someone better, to do you a more certain performance: I am nothing like good enough for so great a work of art as the *Odyssey*. Nor, incidently, to be printed by Bruce Rogers" (pp. 814–815).

Despite his admission of personal doubts and perceived shortcomings, Lawrence agreed to the translation project. His terms were that he be given two years, that it would be published anonymously or under a "virgin name," and that if the publishers were not satisfied with his work they could cancel the project and only pay him for the percentage done at that point. It was clear that Lawrence was warming to the task ahead. He wrote: "Translating Homer is playing with words, which, as you know, have always fascinated me: playing with them like a child with bricks..." (p. 819). He began corresponding directly with Rogers who wrote that he liked the "well-known rendering into colloquial English" by Samuel Butler (who was the proponent of the idea that Homer was a young woman) but, then, was swayed by the translation of George Herbert Palmer "which at once seemed to me superior to Butler's while not quite so 'literary' as Leaf and Myers.... But still his translation didn't march, and was pretty dull in spots.... Then it suddenly came to me that if the swing and go of your English in the *Seven Pillars* which held me to it when I was not specially interested in some of your expeditions, could be applied to the *Odyssey*, we would get a version that would out-distance any existing translations" (p. 813).

In May 1928, Lawrence was transferred to Miranshah to join the smallest R.A.F. detachment in India where he began working in earnest on Book I of the *Odyssey*. How bizarre it must have been to be translating an ancient Greek poem for an English audience while living under military conditions in rural India! Lawrence described his fellows and the surroundings: "We are only twenty-six, all told, with five officers, and we sit with seven hundred India Scouts (half regulars) in a brick and earth fort behind barbed wire complete with searchlights and machine guns. Round us, a few miles off, in a ring are low bare porcelain-coloured hills, with chipped edges and a broken-bottle skyline. Afghanistan is ten miles off. The quietness of the place is uncanny—ominous, I was nearly saying: for the Scouts and ourselves live in different compartments of the fort, and never meet: and so there's no noise of men: and no birds or beasts—except a jackal concert for five minutes about 10 P.M. each night, when the searchlights start. The India sentries flicker the beams across the plain, hoping to make them flash in the animals' eyes. So sometimes we see them. We are not allowed beyond the barbed wire, by day, or outside the fort walls, by night" (p. 828).

Fortuitously, the translation project helped Lawrence alleviate the boredom, and after five drafts of Book I he sent it to England. He noted his feelings and observations at this point: "If there is a spare hour it goes on the *Odyssey*.... The first pages are the hardest, for I have to find my style. Butler has missed, I find, all the picturesque side: the bric-a-brac: and most of the poetry has evaporated with Homer's queer, archaic, dignity. He or she [as Butler had argued] was not telling a contemporary story, any more than I am.... Only the unusual size of the translation fee would reconcile me to doing twenty-four Books like this: and I shall, on the whole, be glad if they call it not sound enough. Homer is a very great and exacting leader" (p. 829).

But Lawrence was not to get out of the project, as the publishers liked his first effort. Rogers wrote that "it is just the vein I hoped for and I am most enthusiastic over it" (p. 832). In fact, he decided to quit the Random House connection and, instead, to print a limited edition with the assistance of Emery Walker, a founding partner of the famous Doves Press who was working with Wilfred Merton. Rogers tried to console the unsure Lawrence: "I am not surprised at what you say of the difficulties of the job — it is probably the most difficult thing in the world to translate — you literally have to build the book over with Homer as raw material — but your opening book — or at least what I have by me — doesn't *show* the labour, and that to me is the main thing. It reads as though it were a new tale — fresh and unstudied" (p. 833).

Lawrence tentatively and defensively wrote back: "Also, I am not a scholar. If I read Greek, it is for pleasure. I fear my version will inevitably try harder to convey my pleasure, than to be an exact mould of the Greek. Yet accuracy is a good thing, in its way. Will you try to find a hidebound scholar, and ask him to snout through the sample chapter for literal errors? I'd like to avoid howlers.... The finding a style is hard, and it is not yet fully found. But remember that it is done after I have done the usual day's work of an airman in the workshop or office, and that on days when the R.A.F. gives me overtime to do, I shall not be able to touch the Greek. It is a common tale that no fellow in the Services works: — but I think it is not true. We go to bed very tired, as a rule" (pp. 833–834).

As he continued to translate, Lawrence began to get the feel of the *Odyssey*, although his confidence in his ability remained low: "The tale is very dignified: told for chiefs, and masters of households, to pass dark evenings. Butler is too parlour-like. Morris wanted to avoid the idea of translation. His version is neither free enough nor bound enough. He does not help me: for I want to keep the mediaeval city-state feeling out of it. The thing is Greek island, I feel sure.... [I]t is an impossible job to do well, and a heart-breaking job to botch... I'm a man buried 125,000 words deep in the ground, who's got to scrape his way to daylight and the sunny face of the earth.... If my *Odyssey* is no good, I shall be no worse for having lived so tightly with a great book all these months. It is a great book: and I am a very small creature, whose trotting up and down is not important except to itself" (p. 837).

Lawrence tried for a "mannered" style that would be readable but would seem archaic. He continued to marvel at the poem he was getting to know so well and worked to get in touch with its creator's methods and intentions. And he continued to keep one eye on previous translations. "The *Odyssey* is very difficult. It is clever, in the real sense, which held no derogatory meaning. A very skilful literary performance, not simple, not primitive: very, very artful and artificial. It's full of tags out of the *Iliad*, but is not epic at all. It's a narrative, and all its persons have character. That in itself would save it from epic, for the person of an epic should be on the stupid scale and the grandeur of it come from a relentless march of events. Nor is there much poetry about the story, so far as it has gone. The author writes in metre, as that was the consecrated form of the early novel, or *chanson de geste*. He was a poet — oh yes, a great poet, I fancy: but this was a story he was telling. He was also an antiquarian and filled in his background with lots of quaint furniture, to give it the antique feel ... with the modern bones showing through the fancy fleshings. His naivety is sham too: he laughs in his sleeve at his puppets. Line after line is ironical, as if he wasn't sure if it should be 'Sir Topas' [Chaucer's mock-heroic knight] or not. Perhaps the first part of *Don Quixote* is a nearer parallel....I think my version is richer, on the whole, than the original: as Samuel Butler's version is balder. Butler was the realist, telling a tale. Thereby I think he did the *Odyssey* too much honour. The author was picking flowers on the way, also. He or she? Honestly I don't care. No great sexualist, either way: no great lover of mankind. Could have been written by a snipped great ape. A marvellous crafty tale, mixed just to the right point with all the ingredients which would mix in. The translators aren't Catholic, like their master. Each of us leans towards his private fancy" (p. 842).

At this time, events in Afghanistan heated up, and hard-working Lawrence was accused of being a secret agent. Stories in the world press had followed him for some time, alleging seditious activities as one American newspaper reported: "Disguised in Arab garb, but known to every chieftain in the desert plains and hills between the Suez Canal and the Afghanistan frontier, the former Colonel Lawrence is continuing his peregrinations in the Middle East." Not many translators of Homer have had to face these kind of charges! The British government decided to bring the controversial figure home, and on January 12, 1929, Lawrence set sail with the prospect of a long voyage and, thus, good translating time ahead. When he arrived in England, he was stationed at the seaplane depot Cattewater, Plymouth which put him in easy traveling range of London. He finally met Rogers face-to-face, and the publisher's high opinion of Lawrence was not disappointed. He wrote to a friend: "Lawrence has four books done and they are in my hands—a whacking translation, I think—the best ever. He has two more books pretty well roughed out, but he goes over it and re-writes six or eight times..." (p. 849).

However, a small disaster was about to unfold. In April 1929, a weekly scandal-sheet published an article hostile to Lawrence and included the information that he was translating the *Odyssey*. Lawrence was furious, both at the tone of the article and in its revelation of his translation. He fired off a letter to Rogers in which he wrote: "I had not expected this trouble, before publication. *After*, yes: but somehow that didn't matter. You'll realize, I hope, that I can't carry on as it is" (p. 853). Rather than panic, Rogers replied: "Arn't you a little too heedful of the rumour and gossip that must necessarily attend the doings of anyone who has attracted the attention of the public at large...? ...I don't suppose that one person in a thousand who reads newspapers of the *John Bull* type has ever even heard of the *Odyssey*.... I think we shall have to go on, somehow. If you cannot produce any more at present, let it rest for a time. We have already enough copy to go on with for some time..." (p. 854).

The bullet had been dodged, and Lawrence had been pacified, although he was still whining about his work load. Looking past his threat to quit the project, he replied to Rogers: "I understand, and shall complete the translation as well as I can do it.... Only they put extra jobs on me here, one after the other, and so I have little spare time. I have not done anything since I wrote you that letter trying to get off the job" (p. 854). By the winter of 1929-30, Lawrence was fully at work again on his translation and both praising and griping at Homer: "I am so bored with the resourceful Odysseus: yet these two books ... have been better done than any of the earlier ones. With [Book] nine we get over the chit-chat and begin the adventures of Odysseus, as he tells them. I am trying to increase the rapidity of the style, here and there to feel like a narration. *Odyssey*-Homer is worse than [George] Borrow, as described by Sidney Webb. He (or she) does describe every cup of wine, every man, every wave, of the world. Intolerably slow, and yet so delicate, so subtle, so sophisticated, so civilized…. [W]hat a set of worms the ancient Greeks paint themselves to be. In my version I underline all strong words, and fade away the weakness, so that my translation will be not so much a copy as an intensification, dramatically. I try to make the poor yarn take up its bric-a-brac and walk. Vainly, I think: but that is meeter than Butler who threw all the muck out of the window before he began to English it" (p. 861).

Some of Lawrence's literary friends were not supportive about the *Odyssey* project, which they viewed as a work not his own, but others helped with verbal support and the reading of drafts. Lawrence's focus on his work and his perfectionism are made clear in these lines from a letter responding to a reader's remark on the difficulty of the work:

"What you say about it is about what I feel: a sense of effort, of hard work: of course there must be this. I never wrote (for printing) an easy line in my life. All my stuff is tenth-thoughts or twentieth-thoughts, before it gets out. Nice phrases in letters to you? Perhaps: only the differences between nice phrases in a letter (where one nice phrase will carry the thing) and an *Odyssey* where one phrase not nice will spoil it all, is too great to carry a comparison…. 'Don't,' you say, 'work too hard at it, all at once.' Why it has to be finished this year! I am at Book XII, only half-way…. Last night I spent five hours doing five lines— not doing them, for they were already on paper, but re-grouping and re-tensing and re-mooding them, to make them stand up: it's deadly hard. There cannot be any of my own exciting little adjectives or words: for I am translating Homer, most word-for-wordly, and Homer has been too long the possession of the educated world for any surprise to remain in him. We know all Homer: digested him generations back…. Other news? Why none at all. Homer covers all that. I do not think there will be any other news till next Christmas, when I may be a free man again" (p. 863).

But Lawrence's R.A.F. duties were requiring more and more of his time, and proofs sent to him by Rogers interfered with his translating. He was also taking time to try to bring his book *The Mint* to press, but financial difficulties and other delays kept getting in the way. It was clear that he would not make his two-year deadline for translating the *Odyssey*; by August, 1930 he was only to Book XV. The apologetic tone of his letter to Rogers adds to the disappointment his words stated about what he feared would be the final result: "I am so sorry: but having begun trying to do it very well I feel that it would be dishonest now to spare pains upon it. Alas & alack! I am not going to be really proud of my *Odyssey*" (p. 869). His depression was not eased by reports in the German press that he was, in fact, in Kurdistan fomenting Afghan revolt! In November, Rogers wrote to Lawrence about the problems his delays were causing, and the translator dutifully returned to his work again, refusing to give it anything but his best effort and vowing to take no vacation until done. He wrote: "I wish I felt its [the translation's] standard rise as it goes forward: but all I can hope is that it does not perceptibly worsen, through my being tired" (p. 876). In the spring, Lawrence was again delayed by a visit from his mother, his assistance to fellow writers, and the crash of a flying boat to which he was a witness and had to testify. Again, Lawrence wrote to Rogers with the bad news that his estimates of completion would have to be pushed back. Then came an intense period of testing of a boat for which Lawrence was responsible, and, again, the translation was moved to the back burner. "Homer finds life difficult. I have the books here, and my eyes smart too much, by night fall, with spray to welcome the crabbed Greek characters or my pencil drafts" (p. 882).

The testing of the special boat for the R.A.F. continued to take Lawrence's energies until August 1930 when, with twenty-eight days of leave, he at last was able to complete the huge task of translation. On the final page he summed up his feelings about the endeavor: "This last page of my version of the *Odyssey* upon which I have spent almost as long as Odysseus and traveled further.... Which has furnished me with luxuries for five years and so wholly occupied my hours off duty that I have had no leisure to enjoy them ... is affectionately, kindly, gratefully and gladly and with enormous relief and glee *presented*" (p. 887).

The intrepid translator had fulfilled his personal and professional commitment. The trade edition published in the U.S. was successful with eleven thousand copies sold by the next February, having gone through five printings, but the artistic edition issued in England received little public notice, despite its having been printed in Rogers' personally designed Centaur type on special hand-made paper and decorated with gold roundels. The ever self-effacing Lawrence wrote of it: "This is a good-looker, this book. The binding is very chaste. I tried to read a page of it, but failed. Awful muck, the text, alas" (p. 897). "His difficulties stemmed from his decision to avoid a pedestrian style, to aim at a prose that would suggest performance, a heightened decorum for a formal, public occasion."[140] However, "Lawrence's translation of the *Odyssey* will always have its admirers. It is the work of a writer with a vigorous individual style, a writer who had lived and fought for two strenuous years by the side of men who, in their devotion to war and plunder, their passionate self-esteem and prickly sense of personal honor, in their code of hospitality for the stranger as well as in their cunning and unpredictability, were not unlike the heroes of the world Homer created in his two great epic poems."[141]

The 1944 translation of William Benjamin Smith and Walter Miller was not much of a success, as might be guessed by the oddities of the wording of their proem:

> Sing, O Goddess, the wrath of Achilles, scion of Peleus,
> Ruinous wrath, that afflicted with numberless woes the Achaeans,
> Hurling headlong to Hades souls many and brave ones — of heroes
> Slain — ay, gave unto dogs, unto all birds lonelily flying
> *Them* as a prey; and the counsel of Zeus moved aye to fulfilment
> E'en from the time when first stood parted in quarrel asunder
> Atreus' son, the monarch of men, and godlike Achilles.

Smith and Miller were inspired to translate in the original meter by the famous German translation of Johann Heinrich Voss, as described in their preface: "The present translation of the *Iliad* is, as far as I can discover, the first attempt to reproduce in English Homer's great epic line for line in the metre of the original. Other translations of the *Iliad* have been made into English dactylic hexameters but neither complete nor line for line."

Born in London, the son of the Keeper of Oriental Manuscripts at the British Museum, E[mile] V[ictor] Rieu (1887–1972) studied classics at Oxford, and in 1910 joined the Oxford University Press. Subsequently, he became associated with the publishing firm of Methuen & Co. and became editor for a new series, Penguin Classics In Translation, which by the time of his retirement in 1964 included over two hundred authors. In 1946 Rieu's own translation of the *Odyssey* was published in this series and the *Iliad* in 1950 (along with other titles). Both Homeric translations were wildly successful, the *Odyssey* having sold over two million copies by his retirement and over three million in fifty years. "In Shaw's Homer, Odysseus, Homer, and Lawrence of Arabia vie for the reader's attention. E. V. Rieu, by contrast, is concerned to maintain the anonymity of both translator and author, from the use of his initials onwards."[142] His conviction was that translations should be into contemporary prose with the common reader as audience, and his proem to the *Iliad* illustrates this clearly:

> The wrath of Achilles is my theme, that fatal wrath, in fulfillment of the will of Zeus, brought the Achaeans so much suffering and sent the gallant souls of many noblemen to Hades, leaving their bodies as carrion for the dogs and passing birds. Let us begin, goddess of song, with the angry parting that took place between Agamemnon King of Men and the great Achilles son of Peleus.

Rieu's work has been criticized because he "adopted a plain, low-key style that avoided Butler's inelegancies but had no other aim than to tell the story in the simplest and most direct way possible in idiomatic English. It was, of course, a great success, a prodigious best-seller in fact, but over the years its plain style has lost much of its original appeal as poetic versions, those of Lattimore and Fitzgerald prominent among them, have restored to Homer some of his poetic brilliance."[143] Adam Parry, the son of the discoverer of oral poetry, complained that "to pretend that Homer talked as we do leads to translation as unreal as to pretend that he spoke — or composed — like the Jacobean translators of the Bible."[144] "Other writers have been even more dismissive, referring to Rieu's prose as 'cliché-ridden,' 'excessively informal,' 'devastatingly bathetic,' and 'banal and vulgar.'"[145] Scholars might have been unimpressed, but Rieu's goal of addressing the common reader was achieved and his translations became ubiquitous in the exciting new post-war era. "Intended to make Homer 'easy reading for those who are unfamiliar with the Greek world,' Rieu's prose version proved immensely successful. Customs officials stopped Rieu on a trip to the Continent to thank him for the wonders of a sea-story of which they took him to be the author. Denounced by some as 'the Agatha Christie version of Homer,' Rieu's rendition has become dated by its very contemporaneity. But it marks the new era of the pocket-book classic, obtainable at airports or railway newsstands."[146] Rieu's advice to fellow translators, which he sedulously followed himself, was "Write English" and then "Read it aloud" to be sure of easy comprehension and pleasant word flow. The success of his own translations and of the Penguin Classics in general bears witness to this good advice.

The 1950 prose edition of the *Iliad* published by I[vor] A[rmstrong] Richards (1893–1979) was a "shortened" translation which left it open to criticism on that account:

"If a knowledge of the *Iliad* you require could be equally well supplied by a digest, the 'potted' version by I. A. Richards will save you the trouble of following out the leisurely breadth and particularity of Homer. This version is suitable for the reader who habitually skips."[147] Here is his proem:

> Sing, goddess, the anger of Achilles, the anger which caused so many sorrows to the Greeks. It sent to Hades many souls of heroes and gave their bodies to be food of dogs and birds. So the design of Zeus was worked out from the time when, first, Agamemnon, king of men, and great Achilles were parted in anger.

In his introduction Richards explained his reasons for choosing this format: "The style of this version has been shaped by many aims. I hope and believe that they have settled their worst differences behind the scenes. But no one who has ever thought about the translation of remote texts can suppose that there is an ideal version for any *general* purpose. My compromise has at least tried to be conscious, to know what it is giving up for what, and to accept consistently its own limitations. ...to be undistracted, I will give up any] attempt to reflect the *language* of the *Iliad*: its archaism; its decorative stylized figuredness; its artificiality, and most of its characters as a medium for oral extempore composition ... before there can be a much wider knowledge and appraisal of the influences it sustains, a cleaning away of irrelevant incidents and insignificant accretions is necessary. The *Iliad* is choked with dense thickets of reported play-by-play fighting and celestial politics which commonly prevent the main sources of its power from being approached. I have tried to make such a clearance, to bring the plot out into the fullest clarity, and at the same time to parallel this clarification of the action with a simplification of the English I have used. ... I have therefore been appropriately ruthless in cutting down the text in the interest of the action. Four whole Books (2, 10, 13, 17) and passages long and short from many of the others have been omitted." Richards' unorthodox comments are characteristic of his career. Educated at Cambridge, he subsequently taught there and at Harvard where he polished his philosophy that poetry in general represents an extremely complex form of communication and requires correction and mastery. His preoccupation with poetry generalized into a crusade for a worldwide, simple language which he labeled "basic English." Richards was also an accomplished mountain climber, challenging the natural world with the same enthusiasm with which he challenged the literary one.

1951 to 2000

In the second half of the twentieth century the world underwent the struggles of a "Cold War" bisection between two paranoid superpowers with the eventual economic victory of capitalism; however, instead of unity as a result new divisions arose among ethnic, religious, and political groups. There were 1,552 Homeric printings making an average of thirty-one per year. Western civilization continued the donation of its great

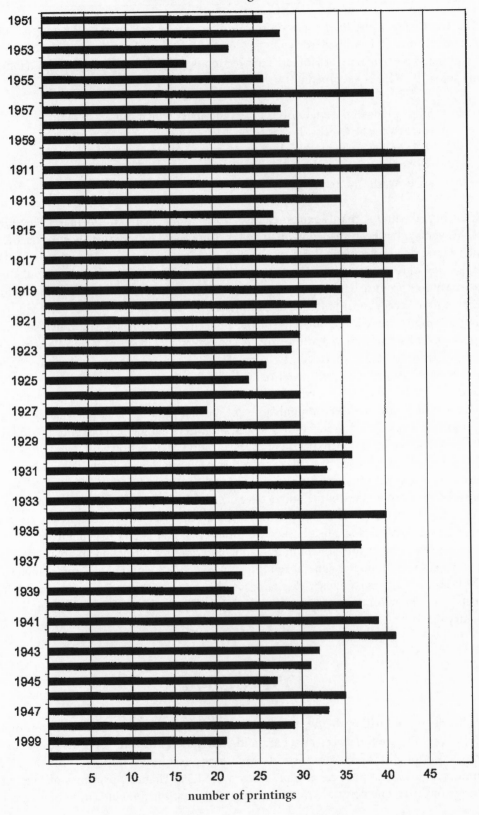

Homeric Printings 1951–2000

number of printings

Homeric ancestor to the entire world, as translations into new languages made the text available to speakers of almost any language. Specialists using new insights and techniques brought new understanding to the epic poems. "Since the 1960's, when the bibliography in Homeric scholarship was already huge, it has grown exponentially, with hundreds of books and thousands of articles. Critical methodology has passed through feminism, structuralism, deconstruction, new historicism, and post-colonialism."[148] Although questions were raised as to whether the new, postmodern public world was still interested in Homer, the printing presses continued to reprint older editions and new translators continued to step forward, a sure sign that not only scholars remained focused on the epics. The century ended with a new critical Teubner edition (1998), completed by K. G. Saur publishers.

Dust jacket of Rosemary Sutcliff's reworking of the *Iliad* for children (1993). (From *Black Ships Before Troy* by Rosemary Sutcliff, copyright 1993 by Rosemary Sutcliff, illus. © 1993 by Alan Lee. Used by permission of Dell Publishing, a division of Random House, Inc.)

Excellent editions of Homer for children were still popular, especially with improved printing quality for color illustrations, such as Barbara Leonie Picard, *The Iliad and Odyssey of Homer, Retold for Children illustrated by Joan Kiddell-Monroe* (1986), Rosemary Sutcliff, *Black Ships Before Troy: the Story of the Iliad, Illustrated by Alan Lee* (1993), and Padraic Colum *The Children's Homer* (1994). A new but related medium was that of the comic book, and the Homeric stories were transformed into this new art with minimal text; editions included *The Iliad of Homer* drawn by Alex A. Blum (1950), *The Odyssey of Homer* (Classics Illustrated No. 81, 1951), *The Iliad by Homer* drawn by Yong Montano (Marvel Comics, 1977), *The Odyssey by Homer* drawn by Jess Jodloman (Marvel Comics, 1977), *La Odisea Homero* (Pendulum Press, 1980), *The Odyssey of Homer* (Academic Industries, 1984), *L'Odyssee, Desnario Seron et Homere* (Dupuis, 1984), *The Iliad and the Odyssey* drawn by Marcia Williams (1966), and *Ao-ti-sai Ho-ma* drawn by David Oliphant (1998).

It is interesting that many early editions of Homer were republished in the second half of the twentieth century. In 1975 Madame Dacier's famous French translation was presented with original lithographs by the artist Marc Chagall. Other historic translations which were reprinted included: Thomas Hobbes (1975), Luis Segala y Estalella (1980 — 20th edition), "Lawrence of Arabia" (1992), Johann Voss (1995 — 19th edition), George Chapman (1998), Paul Mazon (1998) and Vincenzo Monti (1998). New and unusual languages to receive the Homeric text included: Afrikaans (1952), Bengali (1954), East Armenian (1957), Romanian (1955), Twi (1957), Tamil (1961), Schabian (1966), Slovak (1966), Latvian (1967), Albanian (1971), Japanese (1971), Kannada (1978), Korean (1973), Bulgarian (1976), Kurdish (1981), Urdu (1983), Marathi (1984), Basque (1985), Azerbaijani (1986), Persian (1990), Galician-Portuguese (1990), Tadzhik (1990), Irish (1990), Scottish (1992), Gujarati (1993), and Luxembourgish (1995).

The Homeric stories appeared in Braille editions, dramas, radio plays, sound recordings and in every other medium and format. Derivatives from Homer, including retellings, adaptations and novels based on Homer, multiplied with the general expansion of printed books in general, such as: Nikos Kazantzakis *Odysseia* (1957) written as a sequel to Homer; Kenneth McLeish *Odysseys Returns: Homer's Odyssey Retold* (1977); Gregory Falls, *The Odyssey: a Dramatization* (1978); and Richard Byers, *Andomache's Hector and Helenus: a Trojan War Novel Based on Homer's Iliad* (1989). Christopher Logue published several "free adaptations" of Homeric episodes in what can be called a modernist translation approaching paraphrase or free imitation: *Patrocleia* (1962), *Pax* (1963), *War Music* (1981), and *The Husbands* (1995).[149] An interesting adaptation by Paul Fleischman (1996) called *Dateline Troy* was a retelling of the Trojan War stories interleaved with reproduced modern news clippings to create parallels between the Homeric and modern worlds. "The publication of these numerous versions raises questions about demand and readership. Perhaps the spirit which prompted the extraordinary sales of Rieu's version is still abroad. More specifically, there might be an explanation in the massive growth of the higher education system in the United States in the late 1950's and early 1960's and the growing acceptance of classical civilization as an academic discipline, using translations rather than the original texts as source material."[150]

In 1951 Richard Lattimore published a new translation of the *Iliad* using a free, six-beat line which is not really an English hexameter. He avoided poetic dialect, arguing that it does not exist in the United States of his era, despite Matthew Arnold's historic desire for it. The proem to this very successful translation follows:

> Sing, goddess, the anger of Peleus' son Achilleus
> and its devastation, which put pains thousandfold upon the Achaians,
> hurled in their multitudes to the house of Hades strong souls
> of heroes, but gave their bodies to be the delicate feasting
> of dogs, of all birds, and the will of Zeus was accomplished
> since that time when first there stood in division of conflict
> Atreus' son the lord of men and brilliant Achilleus.

Lattimore wrote in A Note on the Translation: "Subject to such qualification [of avoiding mistranslation], I must render Homer into the best English verse I can write; and this will be in my own 'poetical language,' which is mostly the plain English of today." His work was deemed by Mason "more readable and less offensive than any of the prose versions" of W. H. D. Rouse, E. V. Rieu, A. H. Chase and W. G. Perry, I. A. Richards, and S. O. Andrew and M. J. Oakley, all of which are criticized for failure to assimilate Homer into the living culture of English-speaking people.[151] Lattimore seemed to have achieved a good balance between an understandable vernacular and the academic need for faithfulness to the Homeric text itself. "But perhaps the most striking feature of Lattimore's translation, which he does not mention in his explanatory text, is that the content of each line in the English corresponds to the content of each line in the Greek: in its way this is a remarkable achievement, but the line as translation unit, coupled to Lattimore's scholarly approach, imposes great constraints on his scope to bring the order of ideas and phrases into line with contemporary usage."[152] The recent commentator Steiner wrote: "The Iliad of Homer is the translation of a distinguished scholar, drawing on the latest Homeric scholarship. Formulae are preserved wherever possible, but the idiom is that of the American English of Lattimore's own day. The lines run to six beats but are much freer and more various than would be any strict English hexameter. Lattimore's Iliad exercised great influence via its use in schools and universities."[153] It is this last fact, the widespread use of this edition, that assured its dominance in the latter twentieth century. It could still be said in 1987 that "as for the *Iliad*, the best-known and most admired verse translation is Richmond Lattimore's."[154]

Robert Ranke Graves (1895–1985), educated at Oxford, made his name as a writer of historical novels, the best known of which is probably *I, Claudius* about the Roman emperor. However, he was also a poet and considered this his highest calling, as evidenced in his declaration in the preface to his *Poems 1938–45*: "I write poems for poets, and satires or grotesques for wits. For people in general I write prose, and am content that they should be unaware that I do anything else." Graves was also active as a literary critic, and in 1959 his aspirations turned to Homer, the proem of whose *Iliad* follows:

> Sing, MOUNTAIN GODDESS, sing through me
> That anger which most ruinously
> Inflamed Achilles, Peleus' son,
> And which, before the tale was done,
> Had glutted Hell with champions—bold,
> Stern spirits by the thousandfold;
> Ravens and dogs their corpses ate.
> For thus did ZEUS, who watched their fate,
> See his resolve, first taken when
> Proud Agamemnon, King of men,
> An insult on Achilles cast,
> Achieve accomplishment at last.

In the introduction to his translation Graves expressed his unusual model for dealing with the Homeric poetry: "A solemn prayer, a divine message, a dirge, or a country song disguised as a simile — they sound all wrong when turned into English prose: just as wrong as when muster-rolls and long, detailed accounts of cooking a meal or harnessing a mule are kept in verse. I have therefore followed the example of the ancient Irish and Welsh bards by, as it were, taking up my harp and singing only where prose will not suffice. This, I hope avoids the pitfall of either an all-prose or an all-verse translation, and restores something of the *Iliad's* value as mixed entertainment. But so primitive a setting forbids present-day colloquialisms, and I have kept the diction a little old-fashioned." Unfortunately, his effort was not widely appreciated, and he remains known solely as a novelist.

The 1971 translation of selections of the *Iliad* by M. L. West is titled *Sing Me, Goddess* with the subtitle *Being the First Recitation of Homer's Iliad*. Thus, it was intended for oral presentation, and its words flow appropriately well for this purpose, as evidenced by the proem:

> Sing me, goddess, of the anger
> of Achilles, son of Peleus,
> bane that brought to the Achaeans
> countless woe, and hurled to Hades
> countless mighty hero spirits,
> left to dogs and birds their carrion,
> and the will of Zeus accomplished.
> Sing from when they first made quarrel,
> Agamemnon, king of peoples,
> and the noble-born Achilles.

In the preface is a description of the unusual form chosen for the translation and why it was chosen: "The idea that the metre of the *Kalevala* [the Finnish national epic] might be the best medium for translating Homer lodged in my mind several years before I started doing it. Personally, I find ordinary blank verse, and long lines generally, wearisome to read in any quantity; the short verse of the *Kalevala*, with its trochaic rhythm, has a rapidity that leads one on painlessly. It also has the advantage of being a metre familiar to English readers in association with formulaic language, if not from the *Kalevala*, from Longfellow's imitation, *Hiawatha*. I have found it a manageable instrument, and good friends have encouraged me to think that the result is worth exhibiting in public."

The recent blank verse translations of the *Iliad* and the *Odyssey* by the Princeton professor and poet Robert Fagles have been received very positively. Here is his proem to the *Iliad*:

> Rage — Goddess, sing the rage of Peleus' son Achilles,
> murderous, doomed, that cost the Achaeans countless losses,
> hurling down to the House of Death so many sturdy souls,
> great fighters' souls, but made their bodies carrion,
> feasts for the dogs and birds,
> and the will of Zeus was moving toward its end.
> Begin, Muse, when the two first broke and clashed,
> Agamemnon lord of men and brilliant Achilles.

The critic Peter Levi proclaimed his translations "an astonishing performance" and wrote that they "should now become the standard translation for a new generation." A writer in *The Wall Street Journal* echoed his sentiment: "Mr. Fagles can claim to be the twentieth-century champion." His *Iliad* won the 1991 Harold Morton Landon Translation Award of the Academy of American Poets. As is appropriate in the modern era, Fagles' translations have won renown in a new, or perhaps, ancient medium — oral presentation! "Via its brilliant recording on audiotape this version has reached a wide public. It aims at narrative pace and oral resonance. A loose five-or-six-beat line, sometimes lengthening to seven, seeks to render the interplay of norm and variety in the original. Fagles cites the magic of 'mass and movement both,' of 'so much grace and speed in Homer.'"[155] However, the British scholar Steiner has complained about liberties with the original text and with Americanisms: "Robert Fagles has Achilles testing whether or not his heroic limbs 'ran free' in his new armour, where 'running free' helps define his method as translator. 'Gear' is American in flavour; Roan Beauty and Charger even more so. The bristling panoply worn in American football and the Kentucky stud-farms are close to hand."[156]

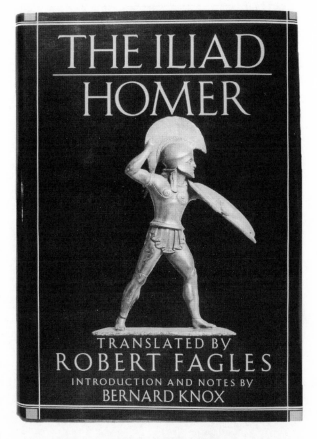

Dust-jacket of the recent translation of the *Iliad* by Robert Fagles (1990). (Cover by Penguin Putnam; bronze hoplite held by Staatliche Musean zu Berlin-Preussicher Kulturbesitz, Antikensammlung. Photograph of hoplite by Ingrid Geske.)

The recent (1994) translation of the *Iliad* by Michael Reck has not received the accolades of that of Fagles but is evidence of the ongoing search for Homer. His proem reads:

> Sing, Goddess, Achilles' maniac rage:
> Ruinous thing! It roused a thousand sorrows
> And hurled many souls of mighty warriors
> To Hades, made their bodies food for dogs
> And carrion birds— as Zeus' will foredoomed—
> From the time relentless strife came between
> Atreus' son, a king, and brave Achilles.

This proem is illustrative of several pros and cons about translations. The useful term "maniac rage" which, as discussed previously, denotes the profound meaning of the Greek

Homeric Printings 1470–2000

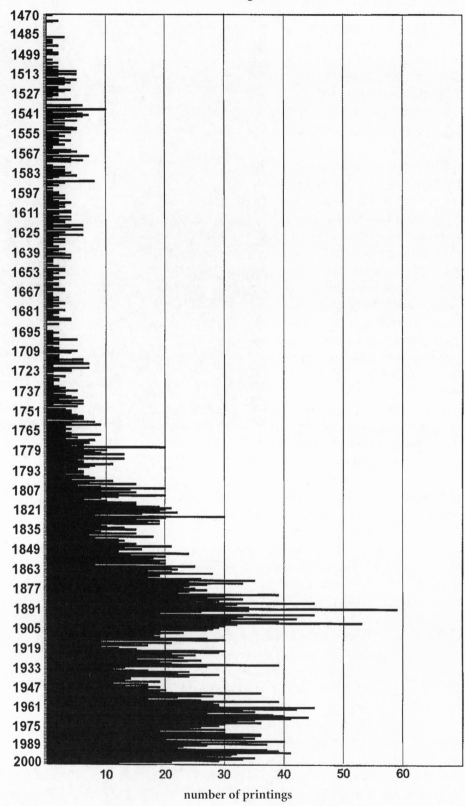

number of printings

word menis, properly connotes more than "anger" or just "rage." The nearly literal but yet poetically interesting lines that follow and the use of "Atreus' son" which is the true meaning of the Greek name which so many translators just give as "Atrides" (thus obscuring the patronymic) are good. But, then, Reck missteps—Achilles is not just "brave" but specifically "godlike" in the Greek text, and this distinction is crucial — although his father was mortal, his mother was a goddess, and in an effort to give her son immortality too she dipped him in the River Styx. In fact, a crucial theme throughout the *Iliad* is the fact that Achilles has chosen to fight at Troy and achieve glory beyond any other mortal (*i.e.* almost like a god) despite knowing that his choice will lead to his death instead of leading a safe and long, but dull, life at home.

One of the first observations that must strike anyone after this survey of just a few of the translators of Homer is the diversity of people who have undertaken to do so. There are poets (Percy Bysshe Shelley), playwrights, novelists, philosophers (Thomas Hobbes, I. A. Richards), thinkers on society (William Morris, Samuel Butler), master publishers (William Caxton, E. V. Rieu), prime ministers of England (Edward Earl of Derby, William Gladstone who published fragments of translations in his 1858 *Studies on Homer and the Homeric Age*), a courtier to a king (William Ogilby), ecclesiastics, headmasters, military men (T. E. Lawrence, Robert Graves), a French lady (Anne Dacier), as well as scholars galore. A second observation that is reinforced by a look at the list of printed editions in Part II is the overwhelming interest in Homer shown from the medieval period until today by the British. Dr. Steiner has speculated on this fact, noting the spurious identification of the indigenous Britains with Roman refugees from Troy which goes back to the Middle Ages. He underscores the British association of masculinity and warfare and the similar inclination towards male-only institutions such as boys schools and men's clubs; the British approval of both sporting winners and good losers, as can be observed in the *Iliad* where there are the victorious Achaeans and the noble underdogs Hector and Priam; and the British identification with sea-faring due to their island existence with its closeness to the sea and storms. "The light from Achilles' helmet, from the eyes of the 'cat-like Penelope' (T. E. Lawrence's epithet), 'screams … across three thousand years.' That dizzying phrase is out of Christopher Logue's transmutation of the Patrocleia. It 'screams' in English as it does in no other language after Greek."[157]

In these samples of proems can be seen translators struggling with the many issues discussed above in the section on the art of translating Homer, each one convinced that his or her new version of Homer is in some particular better than previous ones. In 1983 a scholar studying Pope's translation wrote: "there is no satisfactory contemporary translation of Homer's *Iliad*, largely because our modern versions, which are often more 'accurate' renditions than are their Augustan predecessors, tend to be written in a verse that is too loose with respect to meter and too colloquial with respect to diction to be capable of simulating, in English, Homer's formal and elevated style. For a poet writing at the beginning of the eighteenth century, however, formality and elevation were still within reach."[158] A recent writer reaffirmed frustration with existing translations in the ongoing search for Homer: "A translator should aim to reproduce the spirit and manner of the original no less faithfully than he renders the words. Few of the versions of Homer that have been served upon the public in recent years, and apparently received with much acclaim, fulfill this requirement. Flavourless, uncertain prose, prose interspersed with jingly verse, prose divided up as if it were itself verse, will not do, however lively or contemporary it may be. Homer is poetry, rhythmical poetry, stylistically remote from any prose ever written. His Greek was not, even to his original audience, contemporary or colloquial: it was archaic and elevated. If modern English poetry has turned its back on archaism and elevation, and for that matter rhythm, the translator must look elsewhere for models. After all, he is not trying to contribute to modern English poetry, he is trying to give an idea of what early Greek poetry was like."[159]

Each reader of a translation of Homer should select a version suitable for his or her purpose, and as these purposes vary so will the translation selected. Someone wanting beautiful language might select Pope, for example, while someone seeking literal meaning to study "Homeric society" might select Lattimore or Fagles. Teachers struggle whether to use for their students a verse or prose translation in a tension between an effort to reflect the meter and tone of the original poetry versus better understanding of the action. In one survey, "nearly three quarters of those polled prefer verse over prose translations of Homer's epics."[160] In this survey, published in 1987, Lattimore's verse translation of the *Iliad* was the most widely used version, preferred by more than three-fourths of the respondents. For the *Odyssey*, the translation of Fitzgerald was the most preferred, with Lattimore's verse rendition and that of Rieu in prose tying for distant seconds. One wonders what the results of this survey would be if taken today; in fact, it has been seen that every generation has a favorite version so it would be a moving target.

In the section on translating Homer the question was asked whether it is actually possible to translate Homer. The answer, of course, depends on how one defines "translate." As has been seen above, the ways to react to the Homeric text through translations are many and varied — but the effort is certainly not wasted. "The fact is, Homer offers to the imagination a world of such endlessly varied opportunity, that the exploiting of it calls for an effort as individual as the exploiting of nature herself. If the translator is a poet, he cannot sink himself in the work; rather, he must distinctly reveal himself in it. He must reveal himself by the mere necessity of having to make out of the multitude offered him decisive choice of that kind of opportunity which suits his personal temper. And of the result, as well say 'You must not call this nature,' as say 'You must not call this Homer.' The proper question is not, Is this Homer? But, Is this an individual response to Homer? One man's mind peculiarly responds to that extraordinary kindling of the fantasy which Homer's style provokes: and the result is Chapman. Another responds to that exquisite nicety of his, that consummate tact of his highly cultivated artifice: and the result is Pope. It may be true that, in either case, 'You must not call this Homer.' But it is certainly true that, in either case, such peculiar and selective response to Homer is exactly what we should look for in a translation of Homer."[161]

7

HOMER, PRESENT
AND FUTURE

We have come a long way in our study of the Homeric text and have seen how its history was in fact, that of Western civilization. The popularity of the Homeric texts from the Renaissance to the present is well illustrated by the 5,586 total printings that have averaged, an incredible ten and a half per year over the five and a half centuries since the invention of printing.

I began this book by trying to tempt you, the reader, with quotations from thinkers through the ages praising the eternal and universal themes in the Homeric texts, and now it is time to consider whether there will or should be a future for Homer and, if so, in what format. I will place my cards openly on the table — I believe that the *Iliad* and the *Odyssey* are remarkable literary works, no matter who created them or how or when, and that they can help us struggle with issues relevant not only to Western culture but to the whole world — and, perhaps most importantly, to realize that people throughout history just like us have been struggling with what it means to be human. "The scene in which Priam and Achilles, after all the pangs of battle, all the grief and cruelty of unmeasured vengeance, learn to understand and respect each other as men, is at once the culmination of the *Iliad* and the starting-point of the western conception of humanity."[1]

The Homeric poems, especially the *Iliad*, force the reader to think about life and death but give no easy answers. Someone who recently reread the *Iliad* wrote: "Reading the poem in its entirety is like fronting a storm that refuses to slacken or end. ...No one tells us how to react to the brutalities or to anything else. We are on our own. ...I don't mean to imply that the Iliad's power can be measured by the distress it causes.... A great work of art is likely to be subversive of almost anyone's peace. The Iliad contests most of our current ideas about what is right and wrong, what is true, what is heroic, and, finally, what is human. If the West enjoys a moral advantage over other cultures, the advantage lies in placing a high value on the experience of being unsettled. It esteems self-criticism perhaps as much as self-confirmation...."[2] The *Iliad* has even been used as a backdrop for understanding the very modern problem called post-traumatic stress disorder in a recent book by the psychiatrist Jonathan Shay titled *Achilles in Vietnam: Combat Trauma and the Undoing of Character.*[3]

159

Homer Reciting the Iliad (popular nineteenth-century engraving).

So, what are these universal themes of human life that Homer deals with? If I had to make a list, I might start as follows:

- Is it better to undertake a difficult and uncertain project and risk the outcome or take the easy way out and do nothing? (Achilles)
- Is it better to live life to the fullest or hope for a better afterlife? (Achilles)
- How does a leader do his or her job, even if he or she has personal imperfections and is not liked or appreciated by subordinates? (Agamemnon)
- How should a person react when personal pride and image is publically insulted, and can the reaction have lasting consequences? Is it possible to recover gracefully after having handled an insult poorly? (Achilles)
- How can a person conduct himself or herself honorably when playing second fiddle to a superstar? (Ajax)
- Can intelligence and crafty vision win out over brute strength? (Odysseus; Penelope)
- To what lengths should a friend go to help out a friend? (Patroclus)
- To what depths can the loss of a close friend send a person? (Achilles)
- How strong can love be between a husband and wife? (Hector and Andromache; Odysseus and Penelope) Between a son and father? (Telemachus and Odysseus)
- How ugly can overstepping social rules become, especially in a mob scene? (Penelope's suitors)
- How long should a cause deemed to be a just one be pursued, especially when things are not going well? (the war)

- Should we attribute unexpected events in our lives to supernatural, unearthly forces? (the gods)
- Are fighting and war glorious? Are they the best solutions to problems? (the *Iliad*)

And this is just a start — anyone else could make his or her own list. At the core of the *Iliad* lies the remembrance "of one of the greatest disasters that can befall man: the destruction of a city. A city is the outward sum of man's nobility; in it, his condition is most thoroughly humanized. When a city is destroyed, man is compelled to wander the earth or dwell in the open fields in partial return to the manner of a beast. That is the central realization of the *Iliad*."[4]

It seems to me that the Homeric poems, if read thoughtfully, deal with how one should live one's life, knowing that in the end we all face the inevitable finality of death. We can address this fact under the heading of religion, philosophy, or biology, and we can react to it as comedy or tragedy. But, despite the omnipresence of death in the *Iliad* and its foreshadowing for Achilles and the Trojans, the real theme of the poem is the joy of living and the desire to do something important with one's short life to achieve memory by later generations, good lessons for all people who also must live in the reality of death's inevitability. "War and mortality cry havoc, yet the center holds. That center is the affirmation that actions of body and heroic spirit are in themselves a thing of beauty, that renown shall outweigh the passing terrors of death, and that no catastrophe, not even the fall of Troy, is final."[5] The Homeric poems challenge us to overcome the vicissitudes of life either by achieving lasting results in some small arena of life or just by being the best people we can be. The *Iliad* "leaves the reader stunned by its beauty and force, and in a state of melancholy admiration of the poet's penetrating understanding of the tragedy of all human life.... We are pursued by the same relentless destiny, each one of us, even though we deceive ourselves into believing that we are sheltered by the superficial cooperative forces of a complex social structure. A single crisis can prove to us that we are alone before our fate and that we have to face that fate. Do we possess Achilles' sense of honor — that strong feeling of human dignity — to sustain us? I wonder."[6] For Homer "'the monkeyshines of the Olympians' form a comic screen hiding the unthinkable Fate that waits even for them — a screen against which whatever might seem futile in the brief dance of the mortals can gain its due dignity and its pitiful grandeur, undwarfed by astronomic unsearchables."[7]

On a lighter note, it is interesting that, unrecognized by many people, a number of terms and expressions from Homer are alive and well in modern language. Most obvious, especially to American youth who presently are immersed in sports activities from the time they can walk, is "Achilles' heel." Actually, the story of the hero's divine mother Thetis dipping her mortal son in the River Styx to give him immortality and, thus, leaving only the heel where she gripped him accessible to a deadly wound does not appear in the *Iliad*; as we have learned, it comes from the greater Trojan cycle of stories from which the Homeric ones were selected. Similarly, the poorly shot arrow from the bow of Paris which hit Achilles in that vulnerable heel and fulfilled his fate by killing him is not narrated in the *Iliad*; it also derives from the Trojan cycle. A second term associated with Homer that lives on in modern speech is "Trojan Horse" and its partner phrase "Beware of Greeks bearing gifts." The fall of Troy is not told in the *Iliad* either, although it is referred to in the *Odyssey*. Several modern names derive from Homer, both for people and products. We have a cleanser called "Ajax" and prophylactic condoms called "Trojans," both presumably indicative of strength. I wonder whether their parent companies considered that Ajax committed suicide because he was shown not to be the best and that the protective wall of the Trojans was breached! "Troy" is frequently used as a first name, and it occurs as a city name, such as Troy, New York. Even people who have not read Homer are familiar with the phrase "the face that launched a thousand ships," but not all of them can name its owner as Helen, the ships as Achaean, or the event as the Trojan War! Even the names of Homer's poems are used as vocabulary words in English, "odyssey" being more common as a term for any long trip. "Iliad" has been used in titles of books, such as the biography of General Douglas MacArthur titled *An American Iliad*.

Homer lives on in our speech because he is invested in Western culture. "It is nearly impossible to assess just how influential his position is in our literature and art. A glance at the small handbooks ... reveals hundreds of works from the Middle Ages down to the present that revolve around themes from the *Iliad* and the *Odyssey*— paintings, dramas, stories, novels; cantatas, operas, ballets; and nowadays films and television programs. ... In reality Homer's influence is much more pervasive, and all these individual works are only crystallization points within a broad tradition that has for centuries repeatedly given new stimulus to Western sculpture, painting, music, and literature. ...The true history of Homer's influence remains to be written."[8] Napoleon, encamped in Lombardy, is said to have brooded over the fate of Achilles.[9] Wordsworth told of his love of Homer in the introduction to his *Ode to Lycoris*. We have read Keats's sonnet on Chapman's translation; he also wrote one called "To Homer," and his *Hyperion* is full of Homeric mythology. The favorite poet of the Victorian age was Tennyson who took a copy of Homer with him on his travels, translated the *Odyssey* aloud to his wife, called his English Idyls "faint Homeric echoes, nothing-worth," and wrote short poems "On Translations of Homer" and "To Ulysses." Ruskin was enamored with Homer, and in his writings quoted every book of the *Iliad* but one and all of the *Odyssey* but three (for a total of forty-four books), and he wrote that all men are educated by Homer, as quoted in my introduction. The writers of the romantic movement were influenced by ancient classics, and there were some attempts to imitate Homer, such as Tennyson's *Ulysses* and *Morte d'Arthur* and Matthew Arnold's *Balder Dead* in which "Arnold has given us something more like Homer in English than any other poet."[10] Homer has even spawned theories that most would admit were over the edge, such as the recent book *Homer's Iliad: The Night Skies Decoded*[11] in which it is claimed that the meaning of the epic is astronomical and that its characters can be found among the constellations!

It is possible to follow the influence of just one Homer character through the literature of the ages: "The unsurpassed versatility of Homer's *Odysseus polytropos* is demonstrated, for example, in the metamorphoses he has undergone in such figures as Pindar's plausible cheat, the cynical tempter of Neoptolemus in *Philoctetes*, the sinister rogue Sinon described in the *Aeneid*, Plutarch's Stoic, Dante's politician, Shakespeare's statesman, Tennyson's insatiate adventurer, or Joyce's bourgeois Dubliner, to mention some of the better-known ones."[12] Homer as Plato's "Educator of the Greeks" can be seen as a modern "teacher of teachers" as well because he is an educator in that he informs his audience, moves and delights it and, especially, teaches it how to think.[13] It has been said that "at the sources of Western civilization, themselves its main source, stand two poems on the grand scale which for sustained beauty and splendour have found no superior, perhaps no equal, in all the poetry that has followed them. This is the most remarkable fact in the history of literature."[14]

Many modern authors have been influenced by Homer, one of the most obvious being James Joyce who wrote the novel *Ulysses* (1922). In an interview he commented on the relationship of his book and the works of Homer: "I am now writing a book based on the wanderings of Ulysses. The *Odyssey*, that is to say, serves me as a ground plan. Only my time is recent time and all my hero's wanderings take no more than eighteen hours." Later, after Joyce had commented that other characters in literature were incomplete, including Goethe's Faust about whom the reader knows nothing personal such as his age, the interviewer asked: "Your complete man in literature is, I suppose, Ulysses?" Joyce: "Yes. No-age Faust isn't a man. But you mentioned Hamlet. Hamlet is a human being, but he is a son only. Ulysses is son to Laertes, but he is father to Telemachos, husband to Penelope, lover of Calypso, companion in arms of the Greek warriors around Troy, and king of Ithaca. He was subjected to many trials, but with wisdom and courage came through them all. Don't forget that he was a war dodger who tried to evade military service by simulating madness. He might never have taken up arms and gone to Troy, but the Greek recruiting sergeant was too clever for him and, while he was ploughing the sands, placed young Telemachus in front of his plough. But once at the war the conscientious objector became a *jusqu'auboutist*. When the others wanted to abandon the siege he insisted on staying till Troy should fall. Another thing, the history of Ulysses did not come to an end when the Trojan War was over. It began just when the other Greek heroes went back to live the rest of their lives in peace."[15]

In 1990 Derek Walcott published a modern epic poem with the telling title *Omeros*. Although set in a Caribbean milieu instead of Mediterranean, it presents interesting questions about its relationship to the Homeric epics—is it an original poem or an imitation? "Poetic influence flows both ways; all poetic worlds are reversible. *Omeros* certainly belongs to an epic tradition defined in large part by the *Iliad* and the *Odyssey*, but Walcott's poem supplements and reshapes that tradition in turn, helping us learn 'to read Homer' again. His fusion of Homeric, Caribbean, and African traditions (among others) opens up the ancient and authoritative Homeric texts and gently chides us for our previous lack of imagination about them."[16]

I hope that I have been convincing about Homer's importance to Western and, in fact, to world culture, not just of the past but also for today and the future. "In the pantheon of poets of all cultures and centuries, Homer (however we respond to the Homeric question) has a unique place. His primacy is due to the fact that his two epic poems encapsulated Hellenic culture, both for the Greeks themselves, and for others steeped in the 'European tradition' whether in antiquity or in subsequent ages."[17] Will we always search for and learn from the great poet? We have looked at the eighteenth-century Quarrel of the Ancients and Moderns as a historical oddity, but essentially the same argument—whether students should study the classics—continues today. Why should an African-American girl in the Bronx, a Latino boy in Florida, or an Asian-American teenager in California read Homer? I would argue that the answer is the same reason that a white boy in Georgia should read Chinua Achebe's *Things Fall Apart*, Erica Jong's *Fear of Flying*, and other classics of non–Western, non-male literature — to struggle with what it means to be human! As the author of a recent introductory book on Homer wrote: "my goal has been to make modern readers so familiar with a great poetic work of the past that they might better understand their own lives."[18] Besides, as Voltaire wrote in a satirical pamphlet titled *Concerning the Horrible Danger of Reading*: "Books dissipate ignorance, the custodian and safeguard of well-policed states."

But some will still complain that a twenty-first-century reader cannot relate to ancient Greek situations. The Russian playwright Leo Tolstoy addressed this criticism as he stressed the universal accessibility of Homer which makes the poems so useful to all people of all cultures: "However distant Homer is from us we can without the slightest effort transport ourselves into the life he describes. And we are thus transported chiefly because, however alien to us may be the events Homer describes, he believes in what he says and speaks seriously of what he is describing, and therefore he never exaggerates and the sense of measure never deserts him. And therefore it happens that, not to speak of the wonderfully distinct, lifelike, and excellent characters of Achilles, Hector, Priam, Odysseus, and the eternally touching scenes of Hector's farewell, of Priam's embassy, of the return of Odysseus, and so forth, the whole of the *Iliad* and still more the *Odyssey*, is as naturally close to us all as if we had lived and were now living among the gods and heroes."[19] Some people might ask why Homer surpasses other great literary masterpieces, and I must agree with John Cowper Powys who wrote an answer to this question in defense of the primacy of the Homeric text: "I will tell you at once. By being more realistic and more natural. In other words, it is more like what has happened, is happening, and will happen to us all, from the very beginning, in our history in this world until the end of human life upon this earth."[20]

Already in the late nineteenth century Matthew Arnold, our translation analyst, wrote: "The study of classical literature is probably on the decline; but, whatever may be the fate of this study in general, it is certain that, as instruction spreads and the number of readers increases, attention will be more and more directed to the poetry of Homer, not indeed as part of a classical course, but as the most important poetical monument existing."[21] By the end of the twentieth century, his optimism had been shown to be ill-founded: "Today our literary curriculum is under attack by educational reformers who, though expressing themselves in language more arcane than the plain speech of Henry Ford, are planning to abolish the cultural tradition on which the West's sense of its unity and identity is founded. They propose, in the name of multiculturalism, feminism, and political correctness, to replace such patriarch and racist texts as Homer, the Bible, Plato, Dante, Shakespeare, Goethe, and Flaubert with works that presumably direct the eyes of the young forward to the new world of universal sister- and brotherhood."[22]

I wonder how a "Homer-less" reader of the future will interpret Emerson's line "Some figure goes by which Thersites too can love and admire" or Longfellow's couplet "Better like Hector in the field to die / Than like a perfumed Paris turn and fly"? (Or will they be ignorant of Emerson and Longfellow too?) Spenser, Shakespeare, Milton, Dryden, Pope, Auden — and on and on — the history of Western literature is filled with Homeric references or style. In 1843, Sir Charles Napier won smashing victories in Sind, a region along the lower reaches of the Indus River in what is now Pakistan; knowing that British public officials were routinely expected to know Latin, he simply wired home the word *peccavi* (I have sinned) as his report.[23] It has been said that "a society that turns its back on its past, abolishes its traditions and tries to replace them overnight with new-fangled substitutes geared to a new ideology, is headed, history seems to suggest, for catastrophe."[24] True, we cannot let cultural traditions ossify — they must be continually renewed and expanded. But let's do it hand in hand with tradition!

It has been noticed by more than one classicist that there is much evidence on the educational front that Western culture is abandoning its classical roots, of which Homer is the mainstay. "On one [front], in the academy itself, the world of scholarship and research, we fight to maintain the value and establish the necessity of our discipline for the humanities, which are themselves under pressure and losing territory rapidly. On the other, we compete in the marketplace for undergraduate students, for the numbers which will establish our credentials with the university administration. On both fronts we bear the brunt of a general assault on the loss of interest in the humanities as an academic pursuit. It is only logical that in such a situation our discipline should take heavy punishment; our texts *are* the humanities, the original humanities, the humanities in their most concentrated and genuine form. Without the two languages and literatures which are our province the humanities are hardly conceivable — without the Latin which preserved the heritage of civilization through the Dark Ages and beyond, without the Greek which came west to fuel the driving forces of the Renaissance and Reformation. And it is only to be expected that in this age of cultural dilution, of plastic substitutes, of mindless television shows, not to mention television dinners and instant coffee, the genuine article is no longer valued. It is too expensive; too much work has gone to produce it. To the general public we are an unknown entity; when identified, we are regarded as a freak."[25] This alarm has been captured and discussed in the recent (1998) book by Victor Davis Hanson and John Heath, shockingly titled *Who Killed Homer? The Demise of Classical Education and the Recovery of Greek Wisdom.* They contrapose what they call the "utility of the Greeks" versus "the timidity of Classicists," and they bewail the perceived fact that "in general it is fair to say that few Americans now know anything about Classics and could not care less" (p. xvii).

Hanson and Heath underscore the importance of the ancient Greeks for all of Western civilization, as I have done more specifically for Homer. They point out that many basic Western notions that we today take for granted were invented by the Greeks, such as constitutional and consensual government; free speech; individual rights; civilian control over the military; separation of religious and political authority; middle-class egalitarianism; private property and free economic activity; free abstract and rational scientific inquiry; free exchange of ideas; pursuit of knowledge for its own sake; permissibility of dissent and open criticism of religion, government and the military; leadership drawn from human peers and not divine or inherited; faith in the average citizen; and the belief in rationalism. These are, indeed, concepts we care about! Hanson and Heath point out that Western culture is not dying out; rather, thanks to mass media and other factors it is becoming worldwide. But in some cases the concepts listed above get misunderstood and misinterpreted. Hanson and Heath warn that the Greeks had their own cultural balance to deal with these situations, as have Western societies until recently, through their study of classical culture, a study that is dying out. "At the very moment in our history when Homer might be helping to remind us of who we are, why we got here, and where we should go, only a handful of Americans know the Greeks—or care that Classics is dying" (p. 5).

Hanson and Heath, as well as others, put some of the blame on classicists themselves, who have kept themselves in their ivory towers studying academic minutiae without ever relating their love of the Greeks and the importance of their thinking to the general public and to students in particular. In the 1960s the first shoe dropped as college students termed classical studies (and many other "traditional" courses) "irrelevant." In the 1980s and 1990s the second shoe dropped in the form of "multiculturalism," defined by Hanson and Heath as the idea that all cultures are equal "*except* the West, which is uniquely imperialistic, hegemonic, nationalistic, sexist, and patriarchal and therefore to be studied only as an exemplar of what is *wrong* with the present world" (p. 86). Another writer defines the debate succinctly: "What role should the Western classics and a 'Eurocentric' curriculum play in a country whose population was made up of people from many other places besides Europe—for instance, descendants of African slaves and American Indians? Should groups, formerly without much power—women, as well as minorities—be asked to read through a curriculum dominated by works written by Dead White European Males?"[26]

I think that there are two parts to the answer to this pointed and important question. First, I would argue that the answer is "yes" because I believe that anyone living in the West should expect to understand and participate in Western culture, whatever their ethnic background and the vagaries of fate that brought them here. To varying degrees in the modern world all people are mongrels, both genetically and culturally. Western civilization should evolve gracefully with input from everyone but not repudiate the achievements of the people of the past upon whose shoulders we stand. The truism about America is true about Western culture as well—we are less a melting pot, as we used to think, and more a beef stew with every piece retaining some of its own identity but all working together for the good of the whole. The second part of the answer to the question, it seems to me, is "yes, but..." The Western-based curriculum of the past must be supplemented with study of texts and other aspects of cultures whose origins are non–Western, non-male, and current. They will only add flavor to our beef stew and, by contrast to its original ingredients, remind us that it is, indeed, beef stew that we are making!

And what about Homer specifically? I have argued that this remarkable text addresses issues of general human concern but especially for anyone living in the Western culture. The author of the question quoted above would agree: "One can reject the injustices of the past without rejecting the flower of those sinful old civilizations—an obvious enough idea, though one that has grown increasingly rare in contemporary American universities, where the past seems under perpetual suspicion and even the art of the past is treated as if complicit in evil. Should Homer be dropped from college courses? No, he should not. Doing so would deprive students not only of the poetry, which flows in overwhelming waves, rendering the social view secondary, but of an experience they could not possibly get from a proper modern book—the heartrending impression of the sweetness of life and the misery of life intertwined."[27]

An excellent example of the continuing usefulness of Homer is a recent study showing how the popular 1992 cowboy movie *Unforgiven*, written by David Webb Peoples and directed and starred in by Clint Eastwood, can be understood in terms of the *Iliad*: "in this interrogation of the conventions and ideology of the Western, Eastwood is rewriting that famous ur–Western, the *Iliad*, even as he imitates it. This is not to imply that either Eastwood or Peoples refers consciously to the *Iliad*. But they belong to the cultural and ideological tradition that the *Iliad* has helped to shape, as evidenced by popular culture as well as high art."[28] In the movie, which is set in the mythical time frame of the American Old West, Eastwood plays the role of a retired gunslinger who, when his best friend is murdered, revives his murderous skills to wreak revenge on a cowboy who has disfigured a prostitute. The Homeric parallel is to Achilles, who abandons the Trojan War and its mission to punish the mishandlers of a woman (Helen) but returns to the violence of which he is an expert when his best friend (Patroclus) is murdered. Both epics end with the revitalized hero killing the opposing champion (Hector, Troy's champion, and the reformed cowboy, now become protector of his town). "The distance between the genres of Homeric epic and the American Western film is not so great as one might suppose. Both genres offer a carefully circumscribed view of human existence, foregrounding certain fundamental issues and values. Like archaic Greek epic, the Western presents its audience with an idealized period from its people's past, a time when 'simpler values than those of today' prevailed. The classic Western movie thus stands in a similar relation to the viewer as the Homeric epic did to its original audience. It is, in fact, the modern American epic and, as such, performs an equivalent cultural role. Above all, both works—like their respective genres—are vehicles of the ideology of manhood."[29]

As students who are the future of the world flee from classes in the humanities and from classics in particular and flock to courses in business, computers, and hands-on health fields (which they assume will lead to high-paying jobs upon graduation), class offerings in classics go unfilled and open faculty positions are left vacant. "No wonder boards of trustees, university regents, and budget efficiency experts look with moistening lips at departments which attract few students and whose members are engaged in research which, unlike the equally arcane investigations carried on by economists, social scientists, and physicists, can boast no special relevance."[30] Classicists have not helped the situation by making their work inaccessible to outsiders by including untranslated quotes from ancient and foreign languages and the use of discipline-specific jargon, and they have focused on minuscule topics and published too much. The result is "learned obscurity."[31]

What about the future and Homer? Let's talk about the Homeric text first because its potential future is bright. When writing was invented, people worried that humans would lose their memory. When printing was invented, calligraphically focused monks were put out of business and potentates could not control the spread of ideas and communication. In 1950, I. A. Richards wrote: "The reign of writing looks like it is drawing soon to a close. The radio may be restoring to the ear some of its original priority in 'literature.'" Today's widespread misunderstanding is that any information worthwhile has been digitized and is free to everyone on the Internet. In fact, we are, indeed, living in a transition period between two fundamental methods of mass communication—print and electronic, digital media. It is likely that, as the radio did not destroy writing, electronic communication will not do so either. Old and new technologies tend to have a long period of overlap, and in the case of printed books it is unlikely that it will ever become cost-effective to transfer every book that has ever existed into electronic format.

However, the "classics" are already making that transition, even though the technology for using them is still lagging the printed book in usefulness. Anyone can, indeed, now access the Homeric text via the Internet! And many classical scholars have argued that Hanson and Heath's fears are mostly unfounded and that Homer remains useful in liberal studies. "In the world of work and civic responsibility in which we live, and which our students are going to enter, access to such a broad range of approaches ideally allows for an equally broad range of creative responses to problems. If, like Odysseus, we 'learn the minds of many people,' we can become 'skilled in all ways of contending.' That is not a bad functional definition of liberal learning, and it is a partial but significant warrant for continuing to read Homer throughout the twenty-first century and beyond."[32]

One of the ironies of the coming era of electronic, digital text is that it has characteristics that, in some ways, permit interaction between human and text closer to that of an oral poet and his audience than that of a printed book and its reader. As we have seen, an oral poet has an outline in his head of the story he will tell, but the circumstances and especially the characteristics of a given audience on a given occasion dictate which parts of the story line will be expanded and dwelt upon and which glossed over without expansion. Similarly, with electronic text the reader/audience can dictate which parts of the text he or she wants expanded and which not because of the concept of "hypertext" by which each electronic word can have linked to it more information or a related story line which remains invisible unless selected by the reader. At present, this capability is usually used in an educational context. For example, a student reading an electronic textbook might use a mouse-click to select an unknown word, and the definition for the word, perhaps accompanied by a picture or paragraph of information, would pop up on the screen; the reader would then return to the text and continue in a linear, book-like fashion.

However, the implications of hypertext linking go far beyond this simple example. Why not create a novel that would free the reader entirely from the linear requirements of a book? The reader could select any entry point into the novel to begin, could move about randomly within its text, and could quit whenever he or she felt finished. For example, let's say the novel is a story of a person's life. The reader could start with the person's parents and birth and go on chronologically to his or her death. Or, perhaps the reader is interested in the person's marriage troubles and chooses to begin there. In the midst of reading about how the person's insecurity ruined marriage after marriage, he or she might "click" to the person's youth and explore the background of the person's psychological problems that would cause so much future grief. And then, it might be interesting to "click" to the end and find out whether the person dies happy, in the course of which the reader discovers that a life-altering visit to Africa has changed the person's outlook, and this period must now be explored. Along the way, the reader is presented with various characters in the main person's life, and to learn what forces made them what they are the reader has the option to "click" on them and explore their lives. Hyperlinkage theoretically permits infinite connections and in the order of the reader's whim. A reader could read the same "text" various ways over and over and not tread on the same ground! In fact, we already have something similar to this—the Internet. In the process of "surfing the Internet" a person can begin, say, with coin collecting, research coins of King George III, jump to the British royal family in general, look for a picture of the future king, Prince William, connect to the singing star formerly named Prince, and so on. The trail can go on indefinitely.

Well, what will the possibilities of electronic text do to the old, linear texts, such as Homer? An information expert writes: "we must abandon conceptual systems founded upon ideas of center, margin, hierarchy, and linearity and replace them with one of multilinearity, nodes, links, and networks. Almost all parties to this paradigm shift, which marks a revolution in human thought, see electronic writing as a direct response to the strengths and weaknesses of the printed book. This response has profound implications for literature, education, and politics."[33] Another curiosity about the coming age of all-electronic information is that we will communicate with our computers by voice — what would the ancient oral poets have thought! "With this giant step forward into the past, we're about to recreate oral culture on a more efficient and reliable technological foundation."[34] The prognosticators even see an improved stage in the evolution of the human mind through these developments. "The spatio-temporal qualities of the computer encourage the use of intuition and visualization. Digital writing ... escapes the psychic framework of the book and 'recaptures some of the immediacy — the apparent near-identity of thought and symbolization — that characterized oral culture.'"[35]

But what about Homer in this brave new world? Will anyone still read him, study him, and learn from him what Hanson and Heath call "Greek wisdom," the foundation of Western civilization? Will anyone in the future still undertake a "search for Homer"?

PART II

Printed Editions of the Homeric Texts, 1470 to 2000 c.e.

How to Read the Entries

The following is a comprehensive list of all known editions of the Homeric texts of the *Iliad* and *Odyssey*, as well as other works at one time attributed to Homer, including the *Battle of the Frogs and Mice, Epigrams,* and *Hymns.* In various languages and editions these texts have been termed "songs", "Gesange," "canti," "carmina," "ballads," "reliquiae," and so forth, or just "Works" ("Werke," "Les Oeuvres," etc.). In many languages the title of the *Odyssey* is derived from the Latinized name of its hero, e.g., *La Ulyxea de Homero* (Spanish). It is fascinating to see the variations published through the centuries. First, a few notes will assist the non-specialist in understanding the entries.

I have attempted to transcribe the title pages of these editions as completely as possible in terms of wording, but capitalization and punctuation has been standardized to some degree. Diacritical and accent marks used in non–English languages have not been included, and non-roman characters have been romanized for readability. For example, the title of the *Odyssey* in Chinese is given as "Ao-te-sai." Rough-breathing marks in Greek have been transcribed using the letter "h" in brackets, e.g., "[H]omerou." Many editions, especially in the earlier centuries, had the title printed first in Greek and then in Latin; in these cases, I have used an equals mark to show the parallel content which makes them look overly similar when the Greek letters are romanized, e.g., "[H]omerou Ilias = Homeri Ilias." Where known, I have added information in brackets, such as "first edition by this translator" or "reprint of the Antwerp edition of 1541." Wherever possible, I have kept spelling faithful to the original title page, e.g. *The Seaven Bookes of the Iliades of Homere* or *Fables Antient and Modern.*

Many titles include similar information, and this fact will assist readers trying to decipher unknown languages. A generic example in Latin might read: "*Homeri Poetarum Omnium Principis Ilias et Odyssea; cum brevi annotatione curante; ex recensione et cum notis Samuelis Clarkii,*" which translates as "The Iliad and Odyssey of Homer Prince of Poets; with short running annotations; from the edition and with notes of Samuel Clark." Even without reading Norwegian, a reader can understand *Forste Bog af Homers Odyssee* as "First Book of Homer's Odyssey."

Editions of the Homeric text frequently included a wide variety of information about themselves just on the title-page. Here are the types of information frequently found there, along with illustrative samples:

Date of Publication, given or transliterated into Arabic numerals [I have shown a few with a question mark if date is likely but not sure]

Title (either the full Homeric text or a portion; or other new title or an adaptation)
—*The Iliad of Homer; the first three books*
—*Hector's Ransoming: a translation of Iliad XXIV*
—*[H]omerou Iliados Rhapsodia Theta* [the books in the *Iliad* and *Odyssey* are usually given in Roman numerals, as above, but in Greek they are "numbered" with the letters of the Greek Alphabet — thus, this title comprises Book VIII]
—*Homeri Hymnus in Cererem* [*The Homeric Hymn to Ceres*]
—*La Guerre de Troie* [*The Trojan War*]

Translation Type (if a direct text)
—"von neuem metrisch übersetzt" ("newly translated metrically")
—"L'Iliade tradui en verse" ("The Iliad translated into verse")
—"done into English prose"
—"literally translated in Spencerian stanza"
—"a burlesque translation of Homer, in verse"

Text Editor, i.e. the person who established this version of the text
—"edidit Guilielmus Dindorf, correctior quam curavit C. Hentze" ("edited by William Dindorf, corrected with great care by C. Hentze")
—"edited by C[ornelius] C[onway] Felton" (I have supplied the full name which does not appear on the title page)
—"according to the text of Wolff"
—"texte établi et traduit par Victor Bérard" ("text established and translated by Victor Bérard")
—"nunc primum editus a Davide Ruhnkenio" (now edited for the first time by David Ruhnken)
—"ad novissimae Heynii editionis textum expressa" ("copied from the text of the newest edition of Heyne")

Illustrations, sometimes with a note of the format of the illustrations
—"with twenty-four illustrations from Flaxman's designs"
—"mit 6 original-Compositionem"
—"4 planches hors texte en couleurs et 50 compositions en noir par Henri de Nolhac"
—"illustrated by Alan Lee"
—"adorned with sculpture"

Edition; editions subsequent to the initial one may be simple reprints or may include new and updated material and corrections of previous errors
—"9th edition"
—"corrected edition"
—"new edition"
—"edizone critica"

—"ad optimas editiones castigate" ("printed from the best editions")
—"ad praestantissimas editiones accuratissime expressa" ("most accurately copied from the most distinguished editions")

Intended audience, e.g. students, general public, textual scholars
—"for the use of schools and colleges"
—"for beginners"
—"in freier Umdichtung fur das deutsche Haus" ("in a free adaptation for the German household")
—"for boys and girls"

Translation or Publication Format
—"burlesque translation"; "abridgement"; "retold"; "adaptation"
—"translated into English prose as literally as the different idioms of the Greek and English languages will allow"
—"traduite en prose"; "traduite en verse"
—"with an interlinear translation"
—"metrisch ubersetzt"
—"traduction literale avec le texte en regard"
—"faithfully translated into English hexameters according to the style and manner of the original"

Added Material
—"vita Homeri" (with a Life of Homer)
—"Homeri vita fidelissime continens" ("containing a most trustworthy life of Homer")
—"con note e analisi critiche di M. Valgimigli" ("with notes and critical analysis of M. Valgimigli")
—"mit Worterbuch, Noten fur Anganger, und einer Homerischen Vorschule fur Lehrer" ("with dictionary, notes for beginners, and a Homeric introduction for readers")
—"with notes for the use of schools and colleges"
—"avec des remarques et un discours sur Homere" ("with notes and an essay about Homer")
—"with explanatory notes and references to the grammar of Goodwin and Hadley"

Author or Translator's Intention, i.e., why he or she undertook this publication
—"fur den Schulgebracht" ("for school use")
—"[H]omerou Odysseia Mikra; erster Schul-Homer" ("A Small Odyssey of Homer; a first school-Homer")
—"Versuch einer Ubersetzung des Ilias; die zwanzigste Gesang der Ilias; Adieux d'Hector et d'Andromache" ("Attempt at a Translation of the Iliad; the twentieth Book of the Iliad; the Farewells of Hector and Andromache")
—"Esperimento di Traduzione delle Iliade" ("Experiment at Translating the Iliad")

Language of text and translation
—"Graece et Latine" ("in Greek and Latin")

II. Printed Editions of the Homeric Texts, 1470 to 2000 C.E.

176

—"in Nederlandsche hexameters overgebracht" ("translated into Netherlands hexameters")

—"translated into Latin elegiacs"

—"done into English prose"

—"volgarizzata litteralment in prosa e recata poeticamente in verso sciolto Ital...." ("literally translated into prose and reworked into free Italian verse")

Series of which book is a part
   —"Works of the Greek and Roman Poets"
   —"White's Grammar School Texts"
   —"The Works of Alexander Pope, Esq."

Number of Volumes
   —"in zwei Banden" ("in two volumes")
   —"in unum volumen digesti" ("arranged in one volume")
   —"Vol. III"
   —"Vol. I, Books I–XII"

Translator or Author (if a direct text, the author is, obviously, Homer and is not given in the entry; if a translation or an adaptation, a translator or author's name appears)
   —*The Iliad of Homer; translated by Alexander Pope*
   —*Iliade di Omero; traduzione Vincenzo Monti*
   —*The Iliads of Homer, Prince of Poets; never before in any language truly translated; done according to the Greek by George Chapman*
   — Ellen Stuart, *The Golden Sandals; a Play for Young People Adapted from Homer's Odyssey)*
   — Rosemary Sutcliff, *Black Ships Before Troy: the Story of the Iliad*

Place of Publication— usually straightforward (I have given modern names for ones given in Latin; see Appendix C)

Printer or Publisher – straightforward for most editions, but sometimes difficult to ascertain roles in early printings (e.g. "Baptista Fargengus for Franciscus Laurinus") and in modern publications with name-marks subsidiary to publishing houses (e.g. Mentor Books published by New American Library)

1470 to 1500

1400s— Muobatrachomachia [recto of each leaf has Greek text with Latin version interlinear; verso has Latin text in verse by Ch. Aretin] (Greek; Latin).

1470— Batrachomyomachia; id est Ranarum Murum [sic] Pugna Homeri poete clarissimi per Georgiu summaripam ueronensem in uernaculum sermonem traducta ad sp. Nicolaum pontanum patauinum iur. Cosultum; La Batracomiomachia d'Omero, tradotta in terze rimi (Latin; Italian). *Translator or author:* George Summaripa, Giorg. Sommaripa. Verona, Italy.

1474— Homeri Poetarvm Svpremi Ilias per Laurentivm Vallens[em] in Latinvm Sermonem Traducta (Latin). *Translator or author:* Lorenzo Valla. Brescia, Italy: Coloniensis, Henricus; Statius Gallicus.

1474— Incipiunt Aliqui Libri ex Iliade Homeri; translati p dnm Nicolau de Valle, etc. quos coplere aut emedare no potuit iprouisa morte preuentus [contains Books 3, 4, 5, 13, 18, 19 (20 verses), 20 (fragments), 22 (fragments), 23, 24] (Latin). *Translator or author:* Nicolaus deValle. Rome, Italy: Philippi, Johannis, de Lignamie.

1475— The Destruction of Troy (French) *Translator or author:* Lefevre, Raoul.

1486— [H]omerou Batrachomyomachia Endetisiti Gretos Tou Karos = Homeri Batrachomyomachia... [lines alternatively printed in red and black] Venice, Italy: Leonicus Cretensis.

1486— Cy Finist la Destruction de Troye la Grant; mise par personnages (French). *Translator or author:* Jacques Milet. Lyon, France: Huss, Matthias.

1486— Muobatrachomyomachia (Greek; Latin). London, England.

1488— [H]e tou [H]omerou Poesis [h]apasa Entupotheisa peras eilephen ede sun theo en phlorentia, analomasi men, ton eugenon kai agathon andron, kai peri logous [H]ellenikous spoudaion beruardou kai Neriou tanaidos tou Neriliou Phlorevtinoin. Pono de kai dexio (Greek). *Translator or author:* Demetrios Chalcondyle Florence, Italy: Nerlius, Bernard and Nerlius; Demetrius Damilas.

1489— Hystoria Troiana Guidonis (Latin). *Translator or author:* Guido delle Colonne, Strasbourg, France: Husner, Georg.

1490?— Archomenos proton mouson; textus Graecus cum versione interlineari in pagina recta legitur, et in pagina versa versio metrica Caroli Marsuppini dicti Aretini: Ranarum Muriumque simul crudelia bella (Greek). Venice, Italy.

1492— Homerus de Bello Troianorvm; Pyndarus hunc librum fecit sectatus Homerum Graecus Homerus erat sed Pyndarus iste Latinus; Homeri historici clarissimi traductio exametris uersibus Pyndari haud indocti ad institutionem filii sui Parmae impressa est (Latin). Parma, Italy: Ugoleti, Angelus.

1492— Homeri Poetae Clarissimi Batrachomyomachia per Karolum Aretinum traducta ad Marasium Siculum Poetam clarissimum (Latin). *Translator or author:* Karolus Aretinus. Parma, Italy: Ugoletus, Angelus.

1495— I: De Salute Corporis; II: De Salute Anime; III. De Amore Contra Luxuriosos et Lascivos [also contains: Homer's Descriptio Troianae Historiae] *Translator or author:* Guglielmoda Saliceto. Antwerp, Belgium: Godfridum Back.

1496?— Iliados: Homeri Grecorum Poetaruz Clarissimi Yliadum open per Pindarum Thebanu; e Greco in Latinum traductum [includes the Epitaphium Hectoris and Epitaphium Achilles] (Latin). *Translator or author:* Silius Italicus; Tiberius Catius. Leipzig, Germany:Landsberg, Martin.

1497— Homeri Poetarvm Svpremi Ilias per Laurentium Vallen. in Latinvm Sermonem Traducta (Latin). *Translator or author:* Lorenzo Valla. Brescia, Italy: Fargengus, Baptista for Franciscus Laurinus.

1497— Homeri Odyssea per Raphaelem Volaterranum in Latinum Versa (Latin). *Translator or author:* Raffaele Maffei Volaterrano. Brescia, Italy.

1498— Homerus de Bello Troiano.

1498— Homeri Poetae Clarissimi Batrachomyomachia; per Karolum Aretinum traducta ad Marasium Siculum Poetam clarissimum [with Alex. Gabuardi Tursellani notes; reprint of 1492 edition printed in Parma] *Translator or author:* Karolus Aretinus. Modena, Italy: Domin. Rocociolum.

1501 to 1600

1502— Homeri Poetae Clarissimi Ilias per Laurentiu Vallensem Romanum e Graeco in Latinum Translata (Latin). *Translator or author:* Lorenzo Valla. Venice, Italy: Ioannis Tacuini de Tridino.

1504— Homerus de Bello Troiano. Leipzig, Germany: Jacobus Thanner.

1504— Homeri Opera Omnia [Ilias, Vlyssea, Batrachomyomachia, Hymni, XXXII] cum vita Homeri ex Herodoto, Dione et Plutarcho, Graece [1st Aldine edition]. Venice, Italy: Aldus Pius Manutius.

1505— Pyndari Bellum Troianum ex Homero; Maphaei Vegii Astyanax; epigrammata quaedam. Fanestri.

1507— Homeri Yliadum Opus per Pindarum Thebanum e Greco in Latinum traductum (Latin). Leipzig, Germany: Martinus Herbiploenses.

1507—[H]omerou Batrachomyomachia; operoso huic opusculo, extremam imposuit manum Egidius Gourmontius ... primus ... Graecarum litterarum Parisiis impressor [actually 2nd Greek book printed in Paris] (Greek). *Translator or author:* Pierre Tissard. Paris, France: Gilles de Gourmont.

1508—Homeri Batrachomyomachia; a Karolo Aretino Latinitate donata, cum Alexandri Gabuardi Tursellani notis [reprint of 1492 edition printed in Parma]. *Translator or author:* Karolus Aretinus. Pesaro, Italy: Hieronymus Soncinam.

1509—Homeri Iliadum Opus per Pindarum Thebanum e Greco in Latinum Traductum (Latin). Leipzig, Germany: Martinus Herbipolenses.

1509—Batrachomyomachia; cum notis. *Translator or author:* Alex Gobuardi Tursellani. Pesaro, Italy: Hieronymus Soncinam.

1510—Homeri Batrachomyomachia Johanne Capnione Phorcensi Metaphraste (Latin). *Translator or author:* Johanne Capnione. Vienna, Austria.

1510—Homeri Poetarum Clarissimi Odyssea de Erroribus Vlyxis (Latin). *Translator or author:* Georgius Maxillus alias Ubelin. Strasbourg, France: Joannis Schott.

1510—Homeri Batrachomyomachia Johanne Capnione Phorcensi metaphraste. *Translator or author:* Johanne Capnione Phorcensi. Vienna, Austria: Hier. Vietor.

1510—Homeri Iliados 3. 4. 5. 14. 18. 20. 22. 23. 24. Et initium 19 a Nicolao Valla in Lat. Vers. Translati. (Latin). *Translator or author:* Nicolaus Valla. Paris, France: Badius Ascensius.

1510—Homeri Odissea per Raphaelem Volaterranum in Latinum conuersa [reprint of 1497 edition printed at Brescia] (Latin). *Translator or author:* Raffaele Maffei Volaterrano. Rome, Italy: Iacobus Mazochius.

1511—Ilias Homeri Quatenus ab Nicolao Valla Tralata est; Iodocus Badius Ascensious Iacobo Fabro Stapulen. Philosophiae decori et Compatri cum primis observando S. D. Wittenburg, Germany: Joannem Gronenberg.

1511?—Batrachomyiomachia (Latin). *Translator or author:* Servatius Aedicollius. Pauli Gulpen.

1512—Homeri Yliadum Opus e Versione Pindari Thebani. Leipzig, Germany: Wolfgang Monacenses.

1512—Croacus Elisii Calentii Amphraten; De Bello Ranarum [An imitation by E. Calenzio]. Strasbourg, France: Schurerianis.

1512—Homeri Poetae Clariss. Batrachomyomachia; per Karolum Aretimum traducta ad Marasium Siculum Poetam clarissimum [reprinted from edition printed at Padua in 1492]. *Translator or author:* Karolus Aretinus. Florence, Italy: Bernard Zucchettas.

1512—Homeri Poetae Clarissimi Ilias per Laurentium Vallensem Romanum e Graeco in Latinum translata, et nuper accuratissime emendata (Latin). *Translator or author:* Lorenzo Valla. Leipzig, Germany: Melchior Lotterus.

1512—Homeri Odysssea per Raphaelem Volaterranum in Latinum Sermonem Versa [reprint of editions printed at Brescia in 1497 and Rome in 1510] (Latin). *Translator or author:* Raffaele Maffei Volaterrano. Rome, Italy: Iacobus Mazochius.

1513—Pindari Viri Doctissimi Bellum Troianum; ex Homeri longo opere decerptu et castigatissime impressum. Vienna, Austria: Hieronymu Vietorem.

1513—Batrachomyomachia Homeri, Philymno interprete, et Eulogia funebria G. S; Daripinus poeta laureatus ad lectorem. I Der Beer ist Ghestochen (Greek, Latin). *Translator or author:* Philymno. Wittenburg, Germany: Jean de (Wittemberg) Wiridimontanus or Frunenberger.

1515—Homeri, Grecorum Poetarum Clarissimi Iliadus Opus per Pindarum Thebanum in Latinum traductum (Latin). Leipzig, Germany: Valentius Schuman.

1515—Pyndarvs de Bello Troiana; Astyanax maphaei Laudensis epigrammata quaedam diversorum autoru. Fani: Hieronymo Sincino.

1515—Homerocentra: hoc est, carmen ex diversis Homeri versibus & hemistichiis consarchinatum, continens descriptionem Veteris & Novi Testamenti; una cum interpretatione Latina. *Translator or author:* Patricius (Bishop).

1516—Homeri Liber Primus Iliados, Graece (Greek). Strasbourg, France: Joannis Schott.

1516—Homeri Opera e Graeco traducta. Theodori Gazae epistola qua Homerum ac Nicolaum Valle ... Iliados Homeri interpretem summopere commendat; Homeria vita auctore Plutarcho per Guarinum Veronensem Latina facta; Orationes Homeri per Leonardum Arretinum traducta (Latin). Venice, Italy: Bernardinum Benetum de Vitalibus.

1516—Batrachomyomchia; per Servatium Aedicollium Agrippinum in Latinos versus tralata

(Latin). *Translator or author:* Servatius Aedicollius. Daventrie [location?]: Albertus Paefraed.

1516— Batrachomyomachia Homeri (Latin). *Translator or author:* Servatius Aedicollius. Paris, France: J. Badii.

1516— Homeri Batrachomyomachia; hoc est Bellum Ranarum et Murum; Iohanne Capnione Phorcensi metaphraste; sequitur aliud carmen Iocis et facetiis refertissimum [reprint of 1510 edition by same printer]. *Translator or author:* Johanne Capnione Phorcensi. Vienna, Austria: Hieronymus Vietorus.

1517— Homeri Interpres Pervetustus seu scholia Graeca in Iliadem, addita ipsa Iliade praemissis duobus Jani Lascaris epigrammatibus; in integrum restituta, edita jussa Leonis X. Pont. Max.) (Greek). Rome, Italy: Angelius Collitius.

1517— [H]omerou Ilias (Odysseia; Batrachomyomachia; [H]umnoi lb) = Homeri Ilias (Vlyssea; Batrachomyomachia; Hymni XXXII [2nd Aldine edition] (Greek, Latin). Venice, Italy: Aldus Pius Manutius; Andreae Asvlani soceri.

1517— Le Premier Livre de l'Iliade (Greek). Strasbourg, France: Joannis Schott.

1518— Homeri de Murum Felisque Bello Comoedia; ab Hieronymo Soncino diligenter Graecanicis Latininque litteris impressa et ab Olivario interpretata (Greek; Latin). Ortona.

1518— Homeri Batrachomyomachia; musaeus de Herone et Leandro; Agapeti scheda regia, etc. Graece et Latine, Galeomyomachis, Graece (Greek, Latin). Basel, Switzerland: Johann Froben.

1518— Homeri Graecorum Poetarum Clarissimi Yliadum Opus per Pindarum Thebanum; e Greco in Latinum traductum (Latin). Leipzig, Germany: Valentinus Schuman.

1518— Aesopi Phrygis; vita et fabellae cum Latina interpretatione … [incl.] Homeri Batrachomyomachia, hoc est, Ranarum & murium pugna Graece & Latine…. (Greek, Latin). Basel, Switzerland: Johann Froben.

1519— [H]omerou Ilias; Homeri Ilias; [with Vlyssea, Batrachomyomachia, Hymni xxxij and lives of Homer by Herodotus and Plutarch at end] (Greek, Latin). *Translator or author:* Antonio Francino. Florence, Italy: Philip Giunta.

1519— Esta es la Iliada de Homero en romance traducida (Spanish). *Translator or author:* Juan de Mena. Valladolid, Spain: Arnao Guillen de Brocar.

1519— Opusculum de Herone & Leandro. Orphei argonautica. Eiusdem hymni. Orpheus de lap-

idibus. Sententiae ex uarijs poetis. Homeri batrachomyomachia (Greek, Latin). *Translator or author:* Musaeus; Marcus Musurus. Florence, Italy: Philip Giunta.

1521— Homeri Iliados Libri Primus et Secundus, Graece; cum Demosthenis Olynthiacis orationibus (Greek). Leuven (Louvain)Belgium: Theodoricus Martinus.

1521— Homeri Batrakomyomachia; seu Bellum ranarum in mures; per Elisium Calentium Latino sermone donata. *Translator or author:* Elisius Calentius. Paris, France: Gilles de Gourmont.

1522— Plutarchi Cheronei philosophi libellus; quibus modis ab inimicis iuuari possimus Ioanne Pannonio…. Fabula ex Homero, De Glauci et Diomedis armorum permutatione per Io. Pannonium latinitate donata [included Iliad, Book VI]. *Translator or author:* Io. Pannonium. Bologna, France: Hieronymus de Benedictis.

1522— Homeri Ilias per Laurent. Vallensem Latina facta (Latin). *Translator or author:* Lorenzo Valla. Cologne, Germany: Heronem Alopecium.

1523— Iliadis Libri I et II, Graece; cum annotatiunculis (Melch.) Volmarii passim suis locis adpositis [printed for student use]. Paris, France: Gilles de Gourmont.

1523— Homeri Ilias (Vlyssea, Batrachomyomachia, Hymni XXXII; Graece. ["[H]ypothesis tes G. [H]omerou rapsodias". Omits books I and II] (Greek). Leuven (Louvain), Belgium: Theodoricus Martinus.

1523— Hymnus in Apollinem; studiorum pariter ac studiosorum omnium exemplar, ordine conscriptum alphabetico a D. Jo. Alexandro Brassicano conversus atque scholiis illustratus. *Translator or author:* D. Jo. Alex. Brassicano. Strasbourg, France: Joh. Knoblouch.

1523— Homeri Odyssea Latine; metaphraste Raphaele Volaterrano, Quam diligentissime excusa (Latin). *Translator or author:* Raffaele Maffei Volaterrano. Cologne, Germany: Euchahrius Cervicornus.

1524— [H]omerou Ilias = Homeri Ilias [vol. 1]. Odysseia. Batrachomyomachia. [H]ymno lb. Vlyssea. Batrachomyomachia. Hymni. XXXII. [vol. 2] (Greek). Venice, Italy: Aldus Pius Manutius; Andreae Asvlani soceri.

1524— Homeri Ilias per Laur. Vallam Latina Facta (Latin). *Translator or author:* Laurentius Valla. Cologne, Germany.

1524— Homeri Odyssea; metaphraste Raphaele Volaterrano, quim diligentissime excusa; cvm indice (Latin). *Translator or author:* Raffaele Maffei Volaterrano. Cologne, Germany: Heronem Alopecium.

1525—[H]omerou Ilias (also: Odysseia, Batrachomyomachia, [H]ymnoi, lb-[H]omerou bios) [Iliad reproduces Aldine text] (Greek). *Translator or author:* Johann Lonitzer. Strasbourg, France: Wolfgang [Vuolffgangus Cephalaeus] Capito.

1526—[H]omerou Ilias; metabletheisa palai eis koinen glossav, nun de diorthotheisa; introduction by Frances R. Walton [1st edition in modern Greek; has woodcuts which are the earliest printed illustrations to the Iliad] (Greek, Modern). *Translator or author:* Nikolaos Loukanes. Venice, Italy: Stefanos da Sabio.

1526—Sensuyt la Destruction de Troye la Grant; par personnages, faicte par les Grecz, auec les merueilleux faitz dupreux Hector de Troye, filz du grant roy Priam (French). *Translator or author:* Jacques Milet; Joseph Thouvenin. Paris, France: Philippe le Noir.

1527—Homericae Iliados Libri Duo, Secundus et Nonus, Latinitate don. per Vinc. Obsopoeum (Latin). *Translator or author:* Vinc. Obsopoeum. Nuremberg, Germany: Frid. Peypus.

1527—Homeri Poetae Clariss. Ilias (Latin). *Translator or author:* Lorenzo Valla. Cologne, Germany: Euchahrius Cervicornus.

1528—Homeri Poetarum Principis, cum Iliados, tum Odysseae libri XLVIII; Laur. Vallen. & Raph. Volaterrano interpr.; his recend access; Ausonii poetae in singulos libros argumenta; item Batrachomyomachia is est Ranarum et Murium Pugna, Aldo Manutio interprete; (Latin). *Translator or author:* Lorenzo Valla; Raffael Volaterranus. Antwerp, Belgium: Io. Grapheum.

1530—[H]omerou Ilias, Odysseia, Batrachomyomachia, [H]ymnoi (Greek). Strasbourg, France.

1530—Homeri Iliadis LL. I-X, Graece (Greek). Paris, France: Chrest. Wechel.

1530—Aesopi Phygis Fabellae Graece & Latine; cum alijs opusculis, quorum index proxima refertur pagella [includes Batrachomyomachia] (Latin). *Translator or author:* Aldo Manuzio. Basel, Switzerland: Johann Froben.

1530—Les Iliades de Homere, Poete Grec et Grant Hystoriographe; avecque les premisses ou commencemens de Guyot de Coulones, souverain hystoriographe, additions et sequences de Dares Phrigius et de Dictys de Crete; translatees en partie de Latin en langaige (French). *Translator*

or author: Jehan Samxon. Paris, France: Jehan Petit.

1534—Ilias (Odysseia. Batrachomyomachia, [H]ymnoi. lb.) (Greek). Strasbourg, France: Petrus Brubacchius.

1534—Homeri ... Ilias (Latin). *Translator or author:* Andrea Divo; Conrad Heresbach. Venice, Italy: D. Iacob a Burgofrancho.

1534—Les Fantastiques Batailles des Grands Rois Rodilardus & Croacus; translate de Latin en Francois (French). *Translator or author:* Elisius Calentius. Lyon, France: Francois Juste.

1534—[H]omerou Ilias; [H]e tes autes polyplokos anagnosis [reprinted from Lonitzer's 1525 edition] (Greek). *Translator or author:* Johann Lonitzer. Strasbourg, France: Wolfgang [Vuolffgangus Cephalaeus] Capito.

1534—Odysseia. Batrachomyomachia. Hymnoi. lb. Vlyssea. Batrachomyomachia. Hymni xxxii (Greek). *Translator or author:* Philipp Lunicer. Strasbourg, France: Wolfgang [Vuolffgangus Cephalaeus] Capito.

1534—Homeri Hymni XXXII; e Graeco Latine redditi per Iodocum Velareum. *Translator or author:* Iodocus Velareus. Cologne, Germany: Euchahrius Cervicornus.

1535—Homeri Odysseae Libri Quinque Priores; Graece (Greek). Paris, France: Chrestiani Wechel.

1535—Homeri Ilias; Graece. Ulyssea, Batrachomyomachia, et Hymni XXXIII (Greek). Leuven (Louvain), Belgium: Rutg. Rescius.

1535—[H]omerou Ilias kai Odysseia meta tes exegesios = Homeri Ilias et Ulyssea cum interpretatione. [h]e ton auton polyplokos anagnosis = Variae lectiones in utroq[ue] opere, annotatio (Greek, Latin). Basel, Switzerland: Ioan. Hervagius.

1535—Les Fantastiques Batailles des Grands Roys Rodilardus, & Croaeus translates de Latin en Francois [an imitation, by E. Calenzio, rather than a translation] (French). *Translator or author:* Elisius Calenzio. Poitiers, France; Lyon, France: L'Enseign du Pelican.

1537—Homeri Poetarvm Omnivm Principis Ilias, Andrea Diuo Iustinopolitao interprete, adverbu translata; Herodoti Halicarnassei continens, Conrado Heresbachio interprete; cum indice copiosissimo (Latin). *Translator or author:* Andreas Divus. Venice, Italy: Aldus Pius Manutius.

1537—Homeri Poetarvm Omnivm Principis Ilias (Latin). *Translator or author:* Andreas Divus. Venice, Italy: Melchior Sessa.

1537— Homeri Poetae Clarissimi Odyssea [includes Batrachomyomachia and Hymni] (Latin). *Translator or author:* Andreas Divus; Aldus Manutius; Georgius Dartona. Venice, Italy: Melchior Sessa; Georgius Dartona.

1537— Homeri Ilias et Odyssea; ad verbum transtulit Andreas Divus Iustinopolitanus; addita est Batrachomyomachiae versio ab Aldo Manutio et Hymnorum a Georgio Dartona, Cretensi, composita (Latin). *Translator or author:* Andreas Divus; Aldus Manutius; Georgius Dartona. Venice, Italy: D. Iacob a Burgofrancho; Georgius Dartona.

1537— Homeri Poetae Clarissimi Odyssea;, Andrea Diuo Iustinopolitano interprete, adverbu translata. Eivsdem Batrachomyomachia, id est, ranaru muriu pugna, Aldo Manutio Romano interprete; eivsdem Hymni Deorum (Latin). *Translator or author:* Andreas Divus; George Darton. Venice, Italy: Aldus Pius Manutius.

1537— Homeri Ilias, Odyssea, Batrachomyomachia, Hymni XXXII; eorundem multiplex lectio (Greek). *Translator or author:* Antonio Francini. Venice, Italy: Luca Antonius Junta.

1537— Homeri Omnium Poetarum Principis Ilias; Andrea Diuo Iustinopolitao interprete, ad verbu translata; Herodoti Halicarnassei libellus, Homeri vita fidelissime continens, Conrado Heresbachio interprete; cum indice copiosissimo (Latin). *Translator or author:* Conrad Heresbach. Venice, Italy: D. Iacob a Burgofrancho.

1537— Odyssea. *Translator or author:* Simon Schaidenraisser. Munich, Germany.

1537— Odyssea; das seind die allerzierlichsten und lustigsten vier und zwaintzig bucher des eltisten kunstreichesten Vatters aller Poeten Homeri von der zehenjarigen irrfart des weltweisen Kriechischen Furstens Ulyssis … durch Maister Simon Schaidenraisser, ge. *Translator or author:* Simon Schaidenraisser. Augsburg, Germany: Alexander Weissenhorn.

1537— Odyssea; das seind die allerzierlichsten und lustigsten vier und zwanzig Bucher der eltisten Kunstreichesten Vatters aller Poeten Homeri, von der zehenjarigen Jrrfahrt des Weltweisen Kriechischen Furstens Vlyssis, beschriben, und erst durch Maister Simon (German). *Translator or author:* Simon Schaidenraisser. Leipzig, Germany: E. Avenarius.

1538— Commentarius Explicationis Primi Libri Iliados Homeri; Ioachimi Camerarij; eiusdem libri primi Iliados conuersio in Latinos uersus, eodem autore; his Graeco etiam ediecta sunt (Greek; Latin). *Translator or author:* Joachim Camerarius. Strasbourg, France: Cratonis Mylius.

1538— Homeri Ilias, Latine; Andrea Divo, Iustinopolitano, interprete ad verbum; accessit Herodoti libellus de Homeri vita Conr. Heresbachio interprete (Latin). *Translator or author:* Andreas Divus. Leiden (Leyden), Netherlands: Vinc. de. Portonariis.

1538— Homeri Ilias; ad verbum translata, Andrea Divo, Iustinopolitano, interprete; Batrachomyomachia, Aldo Manutio interprete; Hymni, Geo. Dartona Cretense, interprete (Latin). *Translator or author:* Andreas Divus. Paris, France: Chrestiani Wechel.

1538— Homeri Odyssea ad verbum translate, Andrea Diuo Iustinopolitano interprete; eivsdem Batrachomyomachia, .i. Ranarum & Murium Pugna, Aldo Manutio interprete; eivsdem Hymni deorvm XXXII; Georgio Dartona Cretense interprete (Latin). *Translator or author:* Andreas Divus; Aldus Manutius; Georgius Dartona. Paris, France: Chrestiani Wechel; Georgius Dartona.

1538— Homeri Omnium Poetarvm Principis Ilias (Latin). *Translator or author:* Andreas Divus; Conrad Heresbach. Leiden (Leyden), Netherlands: Jacobus Giunta.

1539— Odysseae Homeri Libros.IX.X.XI et XII; Latino carmine elegiaco expr. Iohannes Prassinus (Latin). *Translator or author:* Joh. Prassinus. Wittenburg, Germany.

1540— Homeri Batrachomyomachia; hexametris Latinis prope expressa (Latin). Venice (?).

1540— Commentarii Explicationum Secundi Libri Homericae Iliados; item conuersio uersuum in Latinos; autore I. Camerario (Greek; Latin). *Translator or author:* Joachim Camerarius. Strasbourg, France: Cratonis Mylii.

1540— Homeri Ilias; ad verbum translata (Latin). *Translator or author:* Andreas Divus. Salingiaci [location?]: Ioannes Soter.

1540— Poetarvm Omnivm Secvlorvm Longe Principis Homeri Ilias; hoc est, de rebvs ad Trojam gestis descriptio, jam recens Latino carmine reddita, Helio Eobano Hesso interprete (Latin). *Translator or author:* Helius Eobanus Hessus. Basel, Switzerland: Robert Winter.

1540— Le Grand Combat des Ratz et des Grenovilles; lisez Francoys ce petit livre neuf traduit du Grec l'an mil cinq cens trente-neuf (French). *Translator or author:* Ant. Macault. Paris, France: Chrestiani Wechel.

1540— L'Iliade d'Homere; traduction en prose Francoise par S. de Souhait [1st printing by this translator] (French). *Translator or author:* S. de Souhait. Paris, France.

1541—[H]omerou Odysseia (Greek). Paris, France: Conr. Neobarius.

1541—Odyssea, Graece (Greek).

1541—[H]omerokentra = Homerocentra; quae et centones, Graece et Latine, Probae Falconiae centones ex Virgilio; Nonnou Poietou metabole tou kata Ioannen [h]agiou euangeliou; Nonni paraphrasis evangelii secondum Joannem, Graece (Greek, Latin). Frankfurt am Main, Germany: Petrus Brubacchius.

1541—Poieseis [H]omerou Ampho etc. = Opvs vtrvmqve Homeri Iliados et Odysseae (Graece cum scholiis Graecis) dilig. op. Jac. Micylli et Joa. Camerarii recogn; Porphyrii philosophi Homericarum quaestionum liber; ejd. de Nympharum antro in odyssea opusculum (Greek). *Translator or author:* Jacobus Micyllus; Joachim Camerarius. Basel, Switzerland: Ioan. Hervagius.

1541—Daretis Phrygii … De Bello Troiano, in quo ipse militauit, libri … sex, a Cornelio Nepote Loatino carmine heroico donati … nunc primum in luce[m] aediti; item Pindari … Homericae Iliados epitome, suauissimis numeris exarata; ad haec, Homeri … Ilias, quatenus (Latin). *Translator or author:* Albanus Torinus. Basel, Switzerland.

1541—Homeri, Poetarum Omnium Principis, Ilias (Latin). *Translator or author:* Lorenzo Valla. Leiden (Leyden), Netherlands: Sebastian Gryphius.

1541—Odysseae Homeri Libri XXIIII; Raphaele Regio Volaterrano interprete; ejusdem Batrachomyomachia, Aldo Manutio & Hymni Deorum; Iodoco Velaraeo interpretibus; item Herodoti Halicarnassei libellus de vita Homeri, per Conradum Heresbachium Latinitate donatus (Latin). *Translator or author:* Raffaele Maffei Volaterrano. Leiden (Leyden), Netherlands: Sebastian Gryphius.

1542—Galeomyomachia, Tragoedia, Graece; Batrachomyomachia; cum scholiis Phil. Melanchthionis (Greek). Basel, Switzerland.

1542—Homeri Ilias; Odyssea; Batrachomyomachia; Hymni XXII; eorundem multiplex lectio (Greek). Venice, Italy: Giovanni de Farraeus; et Fratres.

1542—[H]omerou Ilias. Strasbourg, France: Wolfgang [Vuolffgangus Cephalaeus] Capito.

1542—Moralis Interpretatio Errorum Vlyssis Homerici; commentation Porphyrii Philosophi de nympharum antro, &tc… *Translator or author:* Konrad Gesner.

1542—Ranarum et Murium Pugna; Batrachomyomachia, Graece cum scholiis Phil. Melanchthonis; a studioso quodam ex ore ipsius jam alim exceptis (Greek). *Translator or author:* Philip Melanchthon. Paris, France: Ioannes Lodoicum Tiletanum.

1542–50—Eustathiou archiepiskopou Thessalonikes Parekbolai eis ten [H]omerou Iliada kai Odysseian; Eustathii, archiepisc. Thessalonicensis, commentarii in Homeri Iliadem et Odysseam, (edidit N. Majoranus; cum indice Math. Devarii) [1st ed.] (Greek). *Translator or author:* Eustathius. Rome, Italy: Antonius Asulanus Bladus; Giuntam.

1543—Homeri Batrachomyomachia; e Graeco in Latinum carmen verse (Latin). *Translator or author:* Franciscus Villerius Confiniacus. Paris, France: Sim. Colinaeus.

1543—Il Primo Libro de l'Iliade d'Homero; tradotia di Greco in volgare per M. Franc. Gussano (Italian). *Translator or author:* M. Franc. Gussano. Venice, Italy: Comin da Trino di Monferrato.

1543—Homeri Iliados Libri I,II,III; Latino carmine redditi per Helio Eobano Hesso interprete. *Translator or author:* Helius Eobanus Hessus. Paris, France: Iac. Bogard.

1544—Homeri Ilias; iam recens Latino carmine reddita, Helio Eobano Hesso interprete (Latin). *Translator or author:* Helius Eobanus Hessus. Basel, Switzerland: Robert Winter.

1545—Homeri Odysseae; libri octo Latine carmine, per Franciscum Floridum Sabinum (Latin). *Translator or author:* Franciscus Sabinus Floridus. Paris, France: Michael Vascosanus.

1545—Poetarum Omnium Seculorum Longe Principis Homeri Ilias; hoc est, de rebus ad Troiam gestis descriptio; iam recens Latino carmine reddita, Helio Eobano Hesso interprete (Latin). *Translator or author:* Helius Eobanus Hessus. Paris, France: Carolas Guillard.

1545—Les Dix Premiers Livres de l'Iliade d'Homere, Prince des Poetes; traduitz en vers Francois (French). *Translator or author:* Hugues Salel. Paris, France: Jehan Loys.

1545—Homeri Odysseae Liber XI; Latino Carmine redditus a I. Stigelio (Latin). *Translator or author:* I. Stigelio. Wittenburg, Germany.

1545—Odissea; liber undecimus Latino carmine redditus a I. Stigelio. *Translator or author:* I. Stigelio. Wittenburg, Germany: Viti Crucerij.

1546—Homeri Batrachomyomachia per Elisium Calentium Amphratensem Latino carmine donata, quem Croacum inscripsit (Greek). *Translator or author:* Elisius Calentius. Paris, France: Ioannes Lodoicus Tiletanus.

1547—[H]omerou Ilias = Homeri Ilias. Venice, Italy: Melchior Sessa.

1547—Poetarum Omnium Seculorum Longe Principis Homeri Ilias; hoc est, de rebus ad Troiam gestis descriptio, jam recens Latino carmine reddita; interprete Helio Eobano Hesso. Paris, France: Gazellum.

1547—Odyssea; Batrachomyomachia; Hymni xxxij. (and Homeri Vita) (Greek). Venice, Italy: sumptu Melchioris Se Petrus de Nicolinis de Sabio.

1549—Homeri Batrachomyomachia; Graece et Latine; a Leonh. Lycio emendatius edita; accedunt Phil. Melanchthonis et H. Stephani annotationnes, et Sim. Lemnii conversion versibus heroicis (Greek; Latin). Leipzig, Germany: Ernesti Voegelini.

1549—Homeri Iliados; de rebvs ad Troiam gestis, libri XXIIII; nuper Latino carmine elegantiss. Redditi (Latin). *Translator or author:* Helius Eobanus Hessus. Basel, Switzerland: Johannes Oporin.

1549—Odyssea Homeri Libri.XXIV; a Sim. Lemnio heroico carmine Latine facta, et a mendis quibisdam priorum translationum repurgata; accedit Batrachomyomachia ab eodem secundum Graecum hexametrum Latinitate donata (Latin). *Translator or author:* Simon Lemnius. Basel, Switzerland: Johannes Oporin.

1550—[H]omerou Ilias. Odysseia. Batrachomyomachia. [H]ymnoi ex tes tetartes diagnoseos. Cum indice nunc primum adiecto. Strasbourg, France: Wolfgang [Vuolffgangus Cephalaeus] Capito.

1550—Homeri Ilias; Latino carmine reddita, Helio Eobano Hesso interprete [reprint of edition printed in Basel in 1540] (Latin). *Translator or author:* Helius Eobanus Hessus. Paris, France: Guil. Morelium.

1550—Batrachomyomachia; Graece et Latine, a Leonharto Lycio emendatius edita et illustrata, nunc rec—- et perpurgata; accedunt Phil. Melanchthonis et Henr. Stephani annotationes, et Sim. Lemnii conversio versibus heroicis (Greek; Latin). *Translator or author:* Leonhart Lycio. Leipzig, Germany: Ernesti Voegelini.

1550—De la Vlyxea de Homero XIII. Libros [1st Spanish edition of Homer] (Spanish). *Translator or author:* Gonzalo Perez. Antwerp, Belgium: Juan Steelsio.

1550—De la Vlyxea de Homer. XIII. Libros [reprint of Antwerp edition, same year] (Spanish). *Translator or author:* Gonzalo Perez. Salamanca, Spain: Andrea de Portonariis.

1551—[H]omerou Ilias = Homeri Ilias; noua recognitione castigata (Greek; Latin). Venice, Italy: Melchior Sessa.

1551—Homeri Ilias. Odyssea. Batrachomyomachia. Hymni XXXII. Omnia nova recognitione castigata (Greek). Venice, Italy: sumptu Melchioris Se Petrus de Nicolinis de Sabio.

1551—Odyssea = Batrachomyomachia = Hymni xxxij; [Vitae by Herodotus and Plutarch]; omnis noua recognitione castigata (Greek). Venice, Italy: Melchior Sessa.

1551—Poieseis [H]omerou Ampho Ete Ilias kai [h]e Odysseia…; opvs vtrvmqve Homeri Iliados et Odysseae, diligenti opera Jacobi Micylii & Joacimi Camerarii recognita; adiecta etiam est eiusdem Batrachomyomachia; Porphyrii Homericarum quaestioneum liber, et de n (Greek). *Translator or author:* Jacobus Micyllus; Joachim Camerarius. Basel, Switzerland: Ioan. Hervagius.

1551—Poetarum Omnium Seculorum Longe Principis Homeri; omnia qvae qvidem extant opera, Graece, adiecta uersione Latina ad uerbum ex diuersis doctissimorum uirorum translationibus concinnata, & difficilium thematu[m] explicatione marginibus hinc inde ubi opus (Greek, Latin). *Translator or author:* Heinricus Pantaleon. Basel, Switzerland: Nicolaus Bryling; Bartholomaeus Calybaeus.

1553—Poetarum Omnium Seculorum Longe Principis Homeri (Greek; Latin). Basel, Switzerland: Nicolaus and Barthol. Calybaeus Bryling.

1553—The Faythfull and True Storye of the Destruction of Troye (English). *Translator or author:* Thomas Paynell; Mathurin Heret; Dares. London, England: John Cawood; Dares.

1553—La Vlyxea de Homero; repartida en XIII libros, traduzida en romance Castellano (Spanish). *Translator or author:* Gonzalo Perez. Venice, Italy: Gabriel Giolito de Ferrari; y sus Hermanos.

1553—La Vlyxea de Homero; repartida en XIII libros, traduzida en romance Castellano [reprint of Venice edition of same year] (Spanish). *Translator or author:* Gonzalo Perez. Antwerp, Belgium: Juan Steelsio.

1554—[H]omerou Ilias = Homeri Ilias; id est, de rebus a Trojam gestis… (Greek). Paris, France: Adrian Turnebus.

1554—Les Unzieme & Douzieme Livres de l'Iliade d'Homere; traduitz de Grec en Francois; avec le commencement du trezieme; l'umbre dudict Salel par Olivier de Maigny; & autres vers mis sur son tombeau par divers poetes de ce tems (French). *Translator or author:* Hugues Salel. Paris, France: Vincent Sertenas.

1555—Les Dix Premiers Livres de l'Iliade d'Homere; traduicgtz en vers Francois (French). *Translator or author:* Hugues Salel. Paris, France: Estienne Grouleau.

1555—Homeri Sententiae; nunc recens ex omnibus ipsius monumentis ordine collectae, per Boetium Rordahusamum (Greek; Latin). *Translator or author:* Boetius Rordahusanus. Leuven (Louvain), Belgium: P. Colonaeum.

1556—Ilias (Greek; Italian). *Translator or author:* Nicolaus Lucanus. Venice, Italy.

1556—Coriolani Martirani Cosentini episcopi Sancti Marci. Tragoediae. VIII. Medea, Electra, Hippolytus, Bacchae, Phoenissae, Cyclops, Promethevs, Christvs. Comoediae II. Plvtvs, Nvbes.; Odysseae Lib. XII. Batrachomyomachia. Argonavtica. *Translator or author:* Coriolanus Martiranus. Naples, Italy: Simonetta.

1556—La Vlyxea de Homero; repartida en XIII libros, traduzida en romance Castellano [from the Antwerp edition of 1550] (Spanish). *Translator or author:* Gonzalo Perez. Antwerp, Belgium: Juan Steelsio.

1557—Opus Utrumque Homeri, Iliados et Odysseae [from the 1541 edition]. Basel, Switzerland: I. Hervagius.

1558—Les Dix Premiers Livres de l'Odyssee. Paris, France: Chrest. Wechel.

1558—v. I: Keras Amaltheias, [h]e Okeanas ton exegeseon [H]omerkon, ek ton tou Eusatheiou parekbolon synermosmenon. Cornu copiae sive oceanvs enarrationvm Homericarvm ex Eustat. v. II: [H]e tou [H]omerou Odisseiu meta ton Exegeseon sintonoete kai anagkaion (Greek). *Translator or author:* Eustathius. Basel, Switzerland: Johann Froben; Nikolaus Episkopus.

1559—Le Grand Combat des Ratz et des Grenouilles; en vers Francois (French). Lyon, France.

1559—[H]omerou Ilias = Homeri Ilias, id est, De rebus ad Trojam gestis. [H]omerou Odysseia, Homeri Odyssea, id est, De rebus ab Ulysse gestis. Ejusdem Batrachomyomachia et Hymni, Latina versione ad verbum e regione apposita (Greek; Latin). *Translator or author:* Adrian Turnebus. Geneva, Switzerland: Ioannis Crispinus.

1559—[H]omerou Odysseia = Homeri Odyssea, id est de rebus ab Vlysse gestis; eiusdem Batrachomyomachia & Hymni. *Translator or author:* Adrian Turnebus. Geneva, Switzerland: Ioannis Crispinus.

1559-60—Homeri Opera; Eustathii archiepiscopi Thessalonicae, in Homeri Iliadis et Odysseae (Greek). *Translator or author:* Eustathius. Basel, Switzerland: Johann Froben.

1560—Batrachomyomachia [reprint of 1542 edition printed in Paris; with scholia of Philip Melanchthon] (Greek). Paris, France: Richard.

1560-67—Homeri Ilias, Odyssea, Batrachomyomachia & Hymni; Latina versione ad verbum e regione apposita. Geneva, Switzerland: Crisp. Atrebatius.

1561—Homeri Opera Graeco-Latina; quae quidem nunc extant, omnia; hoc est: Ilias, Odyssea, Batrachomyomachia, et Hymni; praeterea Homeri uita ex Plutarcho, cum Latina item interpretatione … omnibus in utrius linguae Tyronum usum Graece & Latine simul eregione (Greek, Latin). *Translator or author:* Sebastien Castelion. Basel, Switzerland: Nicolaus Bryling.

1561—D'eerste (en tweede) Twaelf Boecken Odysseae; dat is de Dolinghe van Vlyssee, bescreue in't Griecx doer den poeet Homerum, vaderer ende fonteyne alder poeten, ny eerstmal wten Latyne in rijm verduytscht door D. Coornhert (Flemish). *Translator or author:* Dirk Volkertszoon. Haarlem, Netherlands: Jan van Zuren.

1562—Homeri Batrachomyomachia; Graece, cum scholiis Phil. Melanchthonis (Greek). Paris, France: Thd. Richardus.

1562—Homeri Ilias, Graece (Greek). Paris, France: Guil. Morelius.

1562—La Ulyxea de Homero; repartida en 13 libros, traduzida en romance Castellano [reprint of Venice edition of 1553] (Spanish). *Translator or author:* Gonzalo Perez. Venice, Italy: Francesco Rampazato.

1563—[H]omerou Ilias. Odysseia. Batrachomyomachia. [H]ymnoi. Ek tes pemptes kai epimelezeras avagnoseos. Cum indice (Modern Greek). Worms, Germany: Wolfgang [Vuolffgangus Cephalaeus] Capito.

1564—L'Iliade d'Homero [Books 1-5]; tradotta in lingua Italiana da Paolo Badessa Messinese (Italian). *Translator or author:* Paolo La Badessa. Padova (Padua), Italy: Gratioso Perchacino.

1566—Batrachomyomachia = Homeri poema de ranarum cum muribus pugna; opera Leonh. Lycii cum eiusdem annotationibus; additit Ph. Melanchthonis scholia quaedam; Graece et Latine (Greek; Latin). Leipzig, Germany: Ernesti Voegelini.

1566— Homeri Odyssea, Graece (Greek). Paris, France: Guil. Morelium.

1566— Henrici Stephani Annotationes in libellos Herodoti, Plutarchi, Porphyrii de Homero scriptos, & a se illus editioni praetixos [series: Poetae Graeci Principes]. Geneva, Switzerland: Henricus Stephanus.

1566— Liber IX, X,XI et XII Odyseae Homeri; elegiaco carmine redditus a M. Abraham Rockenbach Zeapolitano. *Translator or author:* M. Abraham Rockenbach Zeapolitano. Wittenburg, Germany.

1567— Odyssea; eiusdem Batrachomyomachia, Hymni, aliaq; eius opuscula, seu catalecta, omnia Graece et Latine (Greek; Latin). Strasbourg, France: Theodosius Rihelius.

1567—[H]omerou Odysseia = Homeri Odyssea, id est de rebus ab Vlysse gestis; eiusdem Batrachomyomachia & Hymni (Greek; Latin). Geneva, Switzerland: Ioannis Crispinus.

1567—[H]omerou Ilias = Homeri Ilias, id est, De rebus ad Trojam gestis. [H]omerou Odysseia, Homeri Odyssea, id est, De rebus ab Ulysse gestis. Ejusdem Batrachomyomachia et Hymni, Latina versione ad verbum e regione apposita (Greek; Latin). Geneva, Switzerland: Ioannis Crispinus.

1567— General, grundlich und kurtze Ordnung, oder Methodus, wieder diess pestilentialische Feber, itziger Aeit sehr notig, mit trostlichen Experimenten, so zuvor heimlich gehalten, nuhn in Druck neben etlichen Epistolis de Peste vorfertiget [includes Iliad I, (Latin). *Translator or author:* Joachim Baudis. Neyss [location?]: Johann Creutziger.

1567— Homeri Opera Graeco-Latina; quae quidem nunc extant, omnia; hoc est, Ilias, Odyssea, Batrachomyomachia, et Hymni. In haec operam suam contulit Sebastianus Castalio; edition tertia superioribus longe et emendatior et auctior; adjectris etiam, qui in prior (Greek; Latin). *Translator or author:* Sebastien Castelion. Basel, Switzerland: Nicolaus Bryling.

1568— Ranarvm et Mvrivm Pvgna Homeri, a Joanne Stariconio Semusovio versu latino donata; conflictus ad Nevelam Polonorum cum Moschis, auctore Jo. Stariconio Semusovio (Latin). *Translator or author:* Joanne Stariconio Semusovio. Bologna, France: Jo. Rossium.

1568— Virgilius Collatione Scriptorum Graecorum Illustratus; opera et industria Fulvii Ursini [includes passages from Homer]. *Translator or author:* Fulvius Ursinus. Antwerp, Belgium: Christopher Plantin.

1570— L'Achille et l'Enea, dove egli tessendo l'historia della Iliade d'Homero, a quella dell'Eneide di Vergilio, ambedue l'ha ridotte in ottava rima da L. Dolce (Italian). Venice, Italy: Gabriel Giolito de' Ferrari.

1570— Il primo libro della Iliade d'Homero; trad. da Lu. Groto Cieco d'Hadria (Italian). *Translator or author:* Lu. Cieco d'Hadria. Venice, Italy: Simon Rocca.

1570— Homeri Ilias; Graece et Latine per Mich. Neandrum (Greek; Latin). *Translator or author:* Mich. Neandrum. Geneva, Switzerland: Ioannis Crispinus.

1570—[H]omerou Ilias kai Odusseia = Homeri Ilias et Odyssea; 2nd ed. (Batrachomyomachia and Hymni, and Quaedam epigrammata.) (Greek; Latin). *Translator or author:* Franciscus Portus. Geneva, Switzerland: Ioannis Crispinus.

1570— Les Iliades d'Homere; augmentees outre les precedentes impressions de l'umbre du dit Salel par Olivier de Magny, du 11. livre de l'Iliade par le meme Salel et du commencement du 12. par le meme, avec le 1. et le 2. Livre de l'Odyssee par Jaques Pelletier (French). *Translator or author:* Hugues Salel. Paris, France.

1570— Homeri des aller hoch berumbsten und Griechischen Poeten Odissea; ein schone nutzliche vnd lustige Beschreibung von dem Leben, Gluck un Vngluck des dapffern klugen vnnd anschlegigen Helden Vlyssis... (German). *Translator or author:* Simon Schaidenraisser. Frankfurt am Main, Germany: Johannes Schmidt.

1570?— Batrachomyomachia, Poema de Ranarum cum Muribus Pugna (Greek; Latin). *Translator or author:* Leonhart. Lycio; S. Lemnius. Leipzig, Germany: Ernesti Voegelini.

1571— L'Achille et l'Enea; dove egli tessendo l'historia della Iliade d'Homero, a quella dell'Eneide di Vergilio, ambedue l'ha ridotte in ottava rima (Italian). *Translator or author:* L. Dolce. Venice, Italy: Giolito.

1572— L'Achille et l'Enea de messer Lodovico Dolce; dove egli tessendo l'historia della Iliade d'Homero a qvella dell'Eneide di Vergilio, ambedve l'ha ... ridotte in ottava rima ... Aggivntovi nel fine vna oratione del s. Andrea Menechini, sopra le lodi della poes. *Translator or author:* Lucovico Dolce. Venice, Italy: Gabriel Giolito de' Ferrari.

1572—[H]omerou Ilias, [h]e mallon apanta ta sozomena = Homeri Ilias, seu potius omnis eius quae extant opera; studio et cura Oberti Giphanii J. C. quam emendatiss, ed. c. ejd scholiis et indd. novis. [only Iliad included, despite title]. *Translator or author:* Obertus Giphanius [Hubert von Giffen]. Strasbourg, France: Theodosius Rihelius.

1572—[H]omerou Odysseia = Homeri Odyssea, id est, de rebus ab Vlysse gestis; eiusdem Batrachomyomachia & Hymni (Greek, Latin). *Translator or author:* Obertus Giphanius [Hubert von Giffen]. Strasbourg, France: Theodosius Rihelius.

1572—L'Iliade volgare di Franc. Nevizano (Italian). *Translator or author:* Francesco Nevizano. Torino (Turin), Italy: Martin Cravotto.

1573—Homeri Iliados Metaphrasis; a Nic. Valla et Obsopaeo composita et ex Helii Eobani Hessi versione metrica suppletra; cum Darete Phrygio aliisque (Latin). Basel, Switzerland.

1573—[H]omerou kai Hesiodou Agon = Homeri et Hesiodi Certamen; nunc primum luce donatum; Matronis et aliorum parodiae, ex Homeri versibus parva immutatione lepide detortis consutae; Homericorum heroum epitaphia; cum duplici interpretatione Lat. [a parody] (Greek; Latin). Geneva, Switzerland: Henricus Stephanus.

1573—Dell'Iliade d'Homero, tradotta da M. Bernardino Leoda Piperno, libri dodeci all' illustrissimo & referendissimo Monsignor il Signor Ferdinando Medici Cardinale di Fiorenza (Italian). *Translator or author:* Bernardino Leo da Piperno. Rome, Italy: Bartholomeo Toso Bresciano.

1573—Homeri Batrachomyomachia e Graeco in Latinum carmen verse per Franc. Villerium Confiniacum. *Translator or author:* Franc. Villerius Confiniacus. Paris, France: Sim. Colinaeus.

1573—L'Vlisse di M. Lodovico Dolce, da lvi tratto dall'Odissea d'Homero et ridotto in ottava rima, nel qvale si raccontano tvtti gli errori, & le fatiche d'Vlisse dalla partita sua di Troia, fino al ritorno alla patria per lo spatio di uenti anno... (Italian). *Translator or author:* Lucovico Dolce. Venice, Italy: Gabriel Giolito de Ferrari.

1573—Belli Troiani Scriptores Praecipvi, Dictys Cretensis, Dares Phrygius & Homerus, omnes iampridem latio iure donati, nunc vero a mendis expurgati, & in vnum volumen digesti. Additae sunt quoque Libanij & Aristidis declamationes quaedam, historias Troiani be. *Translator or author:* Georg Henisch. Basel, Switzerland: Petrus Pernas.

1574—Odyssea, Batrachomyomachia & Hymni; Latina versione ad verbum & regione apposita; 2nd ed. (Greek; Latin). Geneva, Switzerland: Eustathius Vignon.

1574—La Continuation de l'Iliade d'Homere; ou les XII. XIII. XIV. XV. & XVI. livres; trad. En vers Francois (French). *Translator or author:* Amadis Jamyn. Paris, France: Lucas Breyer.

1574—Premier & Second Livre de l'Odyssee d'Homere; traduits en vers Francois (French). *Translator or author:* Jacques Peletier. Paris, France: Cl. Gautier.

1574–80—Homeri Ilias [Odyssea ... Batrachomyomachia, & Hymni]; Latine omnia ad verbum exposita; et a F. Porto Cretensi innumeria in locis emendata; postreme editio (Greek; Latin). *Translator or author:* Aemilius Portus. Geneva, Switzerland.

1577—Les XXIIII Livres de l'"Iliade d'Homere, Prince des Poetes Grecs; traduicts du Grec en vers Francois; les XI premiers par M. Hvgves Salel, et les XIII derniers par Amadis Lamin; avec le premier & second de l'Odissee d'Homere, par laques Peletier du Mans; l (French). *Translator or author:* M. Hygyes Salel; Amadis Lamin. Paris, France: Lucas Brayer.

1578—Eis [H]omerou Epigrammata Palaia Diaphoron. Paris, France: Frederici Morelli.

1578—Homerici Centones, a Veteribus Vocati [H]omerokentra; Virgiliani centones, vtrique in quaedam historiae sacrae capita scripti; nonni paraphrasis evangelii Ioannis, Graece & Latine (Greek; Latin). Geneva, Switzerland: Henricus Stephanus.

1578—Il Nono et Decimo Libro dell'Odissea di Omero; che contengono parte di quel Ragionamento che fece Vlisse astretto da Alcinoo re di Corfu, dal giorno, che parti da Troia insin che peruenne a quella isola, dato in Parafrasi alle Toscane Muse da Ferrante Car (Italian). *Translator or author:* Ferrante Carrafa. Naples, Italy: Marino d' Alessandro.

1579?—Homeri Odyssea: eiusdem Batrachomyomachia, Hymni, aliaq; eius opuscula, seu catalecta; omnia Graece & Latine edita quam emendatissime, cum praefatione, scholijs, & indice D. Giphanij [undated reprint of 1572 edition by same printer] (Greek; Latin). *Translator or author:* Obertus Giphanius [Hubert von Giffen]. Strasbourg, France: Theodosius Rihelius.

1580—Les XXIIII Libres de l'Iliade d' Homere, Prince des Poetes Grecs; traduicts du Grec en vers Francois (French). *Translator or author:* Amadis Jamyna; Hugues Salel. Paris, France: Lucas Breyer.

1580—Batrachomyomachia; id est Ranarum et Murium Pugna, Latino uersu donata ex Homero, a Christophero Ionsono interprete (Latin). *Translator or author:* Christopher Johnson. London, England: Thomas Purfoote.

1580—[H]omerou Ilias, Homeri Ilias; postrema editio, cui originem et exitum belli Trojani addidimus, Coluthi Helenae raptum, et Thryphiodori Ilii excidium, Latine omnia ad verbum expecta; et a Fr. Porto Inumeris in locis emendata. *Translator or author:* Inumeris Portus. Geneva, Switzerland: Eustathius Vignon.

1581—Ten Books of Homers Iliades [in Verse Alexandrine]; translated out of French, by Arthur Hall of Grantham, M. P. [1st translation of Iliad into English] (English). *Translator or author:* Arthur Hall. London, England: Ralph Nevvbarie.

1581—Odyssea Homeri Libri.XXIV; nuper a Simone Lemnio, Emporico Rheto Curiensi, heroico Latino carmine facti & a mendis quibusdam priorum translationum repurgati; accessit Batrachomyomachia Homeri ab eodem secundum Graecum hexametro Latinitate donata (Latin). *Translator or author:* Simon Lemnius. Paris, France: Martin Juvenum.

1581–89—[H]omerou Iliados Rhapsodia Alpha—Lambda (Greek). Antwerp, Belgium: Christopher Plantin.

1582—Homeri, Quae Exstant, Omnia; praeter operam Seb. Castalionis, nunc ad postremam H. Stephani ac aliorum quorundam editionem collata; acced. Plutarchi liber de Homero. Basel, Switzerland: Brylinger.

1582—Odyssea, Graece (Greek). Paris, France: Steph. Prevosteau.

1582—L'Odissea d'Homero; tradotta in volgare Fiorentino da M. Gir. Baccelli [1st printing by this translator] (Italian). *Translator or author:* Girolamo Baccelli. Florence, Italy: Sermartelli.

1582—[H]omerou Odysseia; Homeri Odyssea eiusdem Batrachomyomachia, Hymni, aliaq eius opuscula, seu catalecta, omnia Graece & Latine, una cum locupletissimo indice (Greek; Latin). *Translator or author:* Sebastien Castelion. Basel, Switzerland: Nicolaus Bryling.

1583—Homeri Graecorum Poetarum Clarissimi Yliadum Opus per Pindarum Thebanum; e Greco in Latinum traductum (in I. Spondani versioni Homeri). Basel, Switzerland.

1583—Odyssey, Books I–XII (English). Oxford, England: Clarendon Press.

1583—Homeri Quae Extant Omnia, Ilias, Odyssea, Batrachomyomachia, Hymni, Poematia aliquot.; Cum Latina uersione omnium quae circumferuntur, emendatiss. aliquot locis jam castigatiore, perpetuis item justisque in Iliada simul et Odysseam Jo. Spondani Mauleonens (Greek; Latin). *Translator or author:* Jean de Sponde. Basel, Switzerland: Eusebius Episcopius.

1584—Homeri Odysseae Libri Quinque Priores, Graece (Greek). Paris, France: Christian Wechel.

1584—Fabulae Graece et Latine [includes Batrachomyomachia] (Greek; Latin). *Translator or author:* Aesop. Basel, Switzerland: Nicolaus Bryling.

1584—Commentarii in Librvm Primvm [et secvndvm] Iliados Homeri (Greek; Latin). *Translator or author:* Joachim Camerarius. Frankfurt am Main, Germany: John Wechel.

1584—Les Vingt-Quatre Livres de l'Iliade d'Homere; trad. du Grec en vers Francois, par Hugues Salel et Amadis Jamyn; avec les trois premiers livres de l'Odyssee, par Jamyn [from the 1580 edition printed by Lucas Breyer] (French). *Translator or author:* Hugues Salel; Amadis Jamyn. Paris, France: Abel L'Angelier.

1584—Batracomyomachia Politico-rhythmicis versibus, Graecobarbaro Idiomate Versa (in Martini Cruisii Turcograeciae libris octo) (Greek, Modern). *Translator or author:* Demeterio Zeno. Basel, Switzerland: Leonardum Ostenium Sebastiani Henricpetri.

1585—[H]omerou Iliados Rhapsodia delta, Graece (Greek). Antwerp, Belgium: Christopher Plantin.

1585—[H]omerou Iliados Rhapsodia epsilon, Graece (Greek). Antwerp, Belgium: Christopher Plantin.

1586—[H]omerou Odysseia=Homeri Odyssea, id est, De rebus ab Ulysse gestis; eiusdem Batrachomyomachia & Hymni. Cui praeter versionem Latinam innumeris locis a docto quodam viro emendatam, accessit. Tertia editio. Heraclidis Pontici de fabulis Homericis libellus (Greek; Latin). *Translator or author:* Konrad Gesner. Geneva, Switzerland: Eustathius Vignon.

1588—[H]omerou Iliados Rhapsodia Eta, Graece (Greek). Leiden (Leyden), Netherlands: Christopher Plantin.

1588—Iliados [H]omerou R[h]apsodias Bibloi Treis: K, L, M; Iliados Homeri libri tres: decimvs, vndecimvs, et dvodecimvs (Greek). Cologne, Germany: sumptibus Arnoldi Mylij Birckmannica.

1588—[H]omerou Iliados Rhapsodia Iota, Graece (Greek). Leiden (Leyden), Netherlands: Christopher Plantin.

1588—[H]omerou Iliados Rhapsodia Theta, Graece (Greek). Leiden (Leyden), Netherlands: Christopher Plantin.

1588—[H]omerou Iliados Rhapsodia Beta, Graece (Greek). Antwerp, Belgium: Christopher Plantin.

1588—Homeri Poemata Duo, Ilias et Odyssea; alia item Carmina ejd. cum interpretatione Latina repurgata; adjucti Homerici Centones, item proverbialium Homeri versuum libellus, Graece et Latine [also includes Batrachomyomachia and Hymns] (Greek; Latin). Paris, France: Henricus Stephanus.

1588—[H]omerou Iliados Rhapsodia Zeta, Graece (Greek). Leiden (Leyden), Netherlands: Fr. Rapheleng.

1588—Batrachom.; przekladania (Polish). *Translator or author:* Paul Zaborowskiego. Zabomyszwoyna, Poland.

1589—[H]omerou Iliados Rhapsodia Kappa, Graece (Greek). Leiden (Leyden), Netherlands: Christopher Plantin.

1589—[H]omerou Iliados Rhapsodia Lambda, Graece (Greek). Leiden (Leyden), Netherlands: Christopher Plantin.

1589—Homeri Poemata Duo: Ilias et Odyssea; sive Ulyssea: alia item carmina eiusdem, de quibus vide pag. sequenti proximam: cum interpretatione Lat. ad verbum, post alias omnes editiones repurgata... (Greek; Latin). *Translator or author:* Franciscus Portus. Geneva, Switzerland: Henri Estienne.

1590—Homeri Ilias. Geneva, Switzerland: Eustathius Vignon.

1591—[H]omerou Ilias = Homeri Ilias, id est, de rebus ad Trojam gestis [oldest edition of Homer printed in England] (Greek). London, England: George Bishop.

1591—Sexta Odysseae pars Latinis Versibus. *Translator or author:* Simon Stenius. Heidelberg, Germany: Abraham Smesmannus.

1593—Fabellae Graece et Latine; cum aliis opusculis, quorum index proxima refertur pagelle [includes Batrachomyomachia] (Greek, Latin). *Translator or author:* Aesop. Venice, Italy: J. Varisci.

1595—Les Vingt-Quatre Livre de l'Iliade d'Homere; traduit du Grec en vers Francois, par Hugues Salel et Amadis Jamyn; avec les trois premiers livres de l'Odyssee par Jamin [reprint of Paris edition of 1580] (French). *Translator or author:* Hugues Salel; Amadis Jamyn. Rouen, France.

1596—Penelope's Complaint; or, A Mirrour for wanton Minions; taken out of Homers Odissea, and written in English verse (English). *Translator or author:* Peter Colse.

1596—The Ancient Historie of the Destruction of Troy (English). *Translator or author:* Raoul Lefevre; William Caxton. London, England: Thomas Creede.

1597—Homeri Ilias; ab Eobano Hesso Latino carmine expressa (Latin). Ingolstadt, Germany.

1597—Les Vingt-Quatre Livres de l'Iliade d'Homere [reprint of Paris edition of 1584] (French). *Translator or author:* Hugues Salel; Amadis Jamyn. Paris, France: Abel L'Angelier.

1598—Seauen bookes of the Iliades of Homere, Prince of Poets; translated according to the Greeke, in iudgement of his best commentaries; Achilles Shield, translated as the other seuen bookes [I–II, VII–XI] of Homer, out of his eighteenth book of Iliades (English). *Translator or author:* George Chapman. London, England: John Windet.

1598—D'eerste (en tweede) XII boecken Odysseae; d. i. de Dolinghe van Ulyssee, beschr. in't Griecx doer den poet Homerum, vadere ende fonteyne alder poeten, ny eerstmal wten Latyne in rijm verduytscht door D. Coornhert (Flemish). *Translator or author:* Dirk Volkertszoon Coornhert. Delft, Netherlands: B. Hz. Schinckel.

1598–01—Homeri Odysseae liber primus [secundus & tertius] in Hannoueranae scholae vsum seorsum excusi (Greek, Latin). Helmstedt, Germany: Jacob Lucius.

1599—Les Vingt-Quatre Livres de l'Iliade d'Homere; traduit du Grec en vers Francois, par Hugues Salel et Amadis Jamyn; avec les trois premiers livres de l'Odyssee par Jamin [reprinted from Paris edition of 1580] (French). *Translator or author:* Hugues Salel; Amadis Jamyn. Paris, France.

1600—Iliados Homeri Lib. XXIII (Greek; Latin). Mainz, Germany: Ioannes Albinus.

1600—The First Twelve Books of Homer's Iliad (English). *Translator or author:* George Chapman. London, England.

1600?—Homeri Odysseae; libri vinintiquatuor (Greek, Latin).

1601 to 1700

1601— Actio Tragicomica, ex Libro Primo Iliados Homeri; Graeco-Latina, publice recitata (Greek; Latin). Strasbourg, France: Antonius Bertramus.

1602— Fabulae, Elegantissimis Iconibus, Veras Animalium Species ad Viuum Adumbrantibus ... Batrachomyomachia Homeris, hoc est Ranarum & Murium Pugna ... Haec omnia cum Latina interpretatione; accesserunt Avieni antiqui auctoris fabulae; editio postrema, caeteris omni (Latin). Lyon, France: Jacques Roussin.

1603— Homeri Graecorum Poetarum Clarissimi Yliadum Opus per Pindarum Thebanum; e Greco in Latinum traductum (in I. Spondani versioni Homeri). Basel, Switzerland.

1603— Les Fantastiques Batailles des Grands Rois Rodilardus & Croaeus translates de Latin en Francois [reprinted from Lyons edition of 1535] (French). Rouen, France: Anth. Boutier.

1603— The Strange and Wonderfull and Bloudy Battel Between Frogs and Mise; paraphrastically done into English Heroycall verse by W. F. (English). *Translator or author:* William Fouldes.

1603–14— The Iliads of Homer, prince of poets, never before in any language truely translated; with a comment vpon some of his chiefe places; donne according to the Greeke by Geo. Chapman (English). *Translator or author:* George Chapman. London, England: Nathaniell Butter.

1604— Homeri Opera Omnia; adjecta sunt Coluthi de Helenae raptu et Tryphiodori de Ilii excidio poemata; Graece cum Latina ad verbum interpr ... Paul Stephanus.

1604— Homeri Batrachomyomachia; Graece et Latini; opera Leonh. Lycii, cum notis Ph. Melanchthonis et H. Stephani; accedit Io. Ab Hoeckelshouen dispositio poematis [reprint of 1550 edition printed in Leipzig] (Greek; Latin). Frankfurt am Main, Germany.

1604— L'Odysee d'Homere de la Version de Sal. Certon en Vers Francois (French). *Translator or author:* Salomon Certon. Paris, France: Abel L'Angelier.

1605— D'eerste (en tweede) XII boecken Odysseae d. i. de Dolinghe van Ulyssee, beschr. in't Griecx doer den poet Homerum, vadere ende fonteyne alder poeten, ny eerstmal wten Latyne in rijm verduytscht door D. Coornhert (Flemish). *Translator or author:* Dirk Volkertszoon Coornhert. Amsterdam, Netherlands.

1605— Les XXIV Libres de l'Iliade d'Homere; trad; avec les trois premiers livres de l'Odyssee, traduits en Francois; precedees d'une Epitre de Dame Poesie au tres-Chretien Roi de France, Francois I (French). *Translator or author:* Hugues Salel; Amadis Jamyn. Rouen, France.

1606— [H]omerou [H]apanta [in Iac. Lectii Corpore Poetarum Graecor., Aurel Allobr.] (Greek; Latin). Geneva, Switzerland.

1606— D'eerste (en tweede) XII boecken Odysseae d. i. de Dolinghe van Ulyssee, beschr. in't Griecx doer den poet Homerum, vadere ende fonteyne alder poeten, ny eerstmal wten Latyne in rijm verduytscht door D. Coornhert (Flemish). *Translator or author:* Dirk Volkertszoon Coornhert. Delft, Netherlands.

1606— Homeri Qvae Extant Omnia Ilias, Odyssea, Batrachomyomachia, Hymni, Poematia aliquot Cum Latina versione omnium quae circumferuntur emendatiss. Aliquot locis iam castigatiore, perpetuis item iustisque in Iliada simul & Od. [reprint of 1583 Basel edition] (Greek; Latin). *Translator or author:* Jean de Sponde. Basel, Switzerland: Sebastianus Henricpetrus.

1607— Aesopi Phrygis Fabulae; elegantissimis iconibus, veras animalium species ad viuum adumbrantibus ... haec omnis cum Latina interpretatione; editio postreme, caeteris omnibus castigatior (Greek, Latin). Lyon, France: Paulus Frellon.

1607–22— Homeri Batrachomyomachia; opera Leonh. Lycii, cum notis Phil. Melanchthonis et Matth. Dresseri. Leipzig, Germany.

1609— Homeri Opera; Graece et Latine ex versione Aemilii et Franc. Porti (Greek; Latin). Geneva, Switzerland: Eustathius Vignon.

1609— Homeri Opera; Graece, una cum Colutho et Tryphiodoro (Greek). Geneva, Switzerland: Eustathius Vignon.

1609— D'eerste (en tweede) XII boecken Odysseae; d. i. de Dolinghe van Ulyssee, beschr. in't Griecx doer den poet Homerum, vadere ende fonteyne alder poeten, ny eerstmal wten Latyne in rijm verduytscht door D. Coornhert (Flemish). *Translator or author:* Dirk Volkertszoon Coornhert. Amsterdam, Netherlands: H. Barentz.

1609?— Homer Prince of Poets; translated according to the Greek, in twelue bookes of his Iliads (English). *Translator or author:* George Chapman. London, England: H. Lownes.

1610— Homer Prince of Poets; tr. in twelve bookes of his Iliads; 2nd ed. (English). *Translator or author:* George Chapman. S. Macham.

1610— Homeri Qvae Extant Omnia: Ilias, Odyssea, Batrachomyomachia, Hymni, poematia aliquot cum Latina versione omnium quae circumferuntur emendatissim; aliquot locis iam castigatiore perpetuis item iustisque in Iliada simul & Odysseam Io. Spondani Mauleonensi (Greek, Latin). *Translator or author:* Jean de Sponde. Geneva, Switzerland: Caldoriana Societas.

1610— Ilias Homeri; das ist, Homeri dess vralten furtrefflichen Griechischen Poeten XXIIII Bucher, von dem gewaltigen Krieg der Griechen, wider die Trojaner auch langwirigen Belagerung, vnnd Zerstorung der Koni Statt Troja; desgleichen die XII Bucher Aeneidos d (German). *Translator or author:* Johannes Sprenger. Augsburg, Germany: Christoph Mangen.

1610–27— [H]omerou Odysseias A (-omega); Homeri Odyssea, id est, de rebus ab Ulysse gestis (Greek). Paris, France: Ioannes Libert.

1611— Homeri Batrachomyomachia, Graece et Latine (in Casp. Dornavii Amphitheathro Sapientiae Socraticae iocoseriae (Greek; Latin). Hannover, Germany.

1611— De eerste 12 boeken van de Ilyadas, beschreven in't Griecks door Homerum; wt Grieks in Franschen dicht vertaeld door Mr. Huges Salel, ende nu vyt Francoyschen in Nederduydschen dicht, door K. v. Mander (Flemish). *Translator or author:* K. v. Mander. Haarlem, Netherlands: A. Rooman.

1612— The Whole Works of Homer, Prince of Poetts; in his Iliads, and Odysses; translated according to the Greeke (English). *Translator or author:* George Chapman.

1613— Speculum Heroicum; principis omnium temporum poetarum Homeri (Latin; French). Utrecht, Netherlands: Cr. Passaei.

1613— Les Vingt-Quatre Livres d'Homere reduits en tables demonstratives, figurees par Crespin de Passe; chaque livre redige en argument poetique par J. Hilaire Sieur de la Riviere (French). *Translator or author:* Crespin de aPasse. Utrecht, ???.

1613— The Whole Works of Homer, Prince of Poets; Iliads and Odysses, translated according to ye Greke, by George Chapman (English). *Translator or author:* George Chapman. London, England: Nathaniell Butter.

1613— The Strange, Wonderfull, and Bloudy Battell Betweene Frogs and Mise; done into Eng. Heroycall verse interlaced with diuers pithy and morall sentences ... paraphrastically done into English heroycall verse (English). *Translator or author:* William Fouldes. London, England: S. Stafford.

1614— Homer's Odysses (the XII first bookes), translated according to ye Greeke by G. Chapman (English). *Translator or author:* George Chapman. Rich. Field.

1614— L'Iliade d'Homere; traduction en prose Francoise par S. de Souhait; avec la vie d'Homere, tiree d'Herodote, le ravissement d'Helene, tiree de Dictys de Crete et de Dares Phrygien et une imitation de l'Iliade en vers Alexandrins (French). *Translator or author:* S. de Souhait. Paris, France.

1615— Les Opvscvles d'Homer; qui sone La Batrachomyomachie, Les Hymnes, Les Epigrammes (French). Paris, France: T. Blaise.

1615— Les Oeuvres d'Homere, Prince des Poetes; traduit du Grec en vers Francois assavoir l'Iliade, l'Odyssee revue et corrigee, la Batrachomyomachie, les Hymnes et les Epigrammes; le tout de la version de Salomon Certon [Odyssey reprinted from 1604 Paris ed.] (French). *Translator or author:* Salomon Certon. Paris, France: Nic. Hameau.

1615— L'Odyssee d'Homere; de la version de Salomon Certon (French). *Translator or author:* Salomon Certon. Paris, France: T. Blaise.

1615— Homer's Odysses, translated according to ye Greeke, by Geo. Chapman [Bks. i–xxiv.] (English). *Translator or author:* George Chapman. R. Field.

1616— Histoire Facetieuse de la Guerre des Rats Contre les Grenouilles, Imitation d'Homere; second edition, augmentee de figures (French). Paris, France: J. Sara.

1616— La Batrachomyomachie d'Homere; traduit du Grec en vers Francois par Sal. Certon [reprint of edition of Paris, 1615] (French). *Translator or author:* Salomon Certon. Paris, France.

1616— The Whole Works of Homer, Prince of Poetts; in his Iliads and Odysses, translated according to the Greeke, by Geo. Chapman [reprint of 1612 edition] (English). *Translator or author:* George Chapman. London, England: R. Field.

1617— Homeri Opera, Graece et Latine (Greek; Latin). Geneva, Switzerland: Iac. Stoer.

1617— [H]omerou Epsilon Odysseias Rhapsodias; Homeri Odysseae liber V (Greek). Paris, France: Ioannes Libert.

1617— Ilias Homeri; das ist Homeri, dess vralten,

furtrefflichen Griechischen Poeten XXIIII Bucher. *Translator or author:* Johannes Sprenger. Augsburg, Germany: Christoff Mangen; Elias Willers.

1618— Constantij Pulcharellij a Massa Lubrensi e Societate Iesu Carminum libri quinque; his adiecti Dialogus de uitijs senectutis; et Homericae Iliadis libri duo (Latin). *Translator or author:* Giovanni Paolo Caccavello. Naples, Italy: Tarquinius Longus.

1619— Constantij Pulcharellii a Massa Lvbrensi e Societate Iesv Carminvm Libri Quinque; his adiecti Dialogus de vitiis senectutis, et Homericae Iliados libri duo e Graeco in Latinum conuersi (Latin). La Fleche, France: Georgius Griveav.

1619— Aesopi Phrygis Fabvlae...; [Batrachomyomachia] Homeri, hoc est, Ranarvm & Murium Pugna.... Geneva, Switzerland: Joannus Tornaesivs.

1619— Tes [H]omerou Iliados [h]e sigma Rhapsodia (Greek). Paris, France: Sebastian Cramoisy; Sebastian Chappelet.

1619— Homeri Batrachomyomachia, Graece et Latine (in Casp. Dornavii Amphitheatro Sapientiae Socraticae iocoseriae (Greek; Latin). Hannover, Germany.

1619— Tes [H]omerou Iliados [h]e Chi Rhapsodia (Greek). Paris, France: Sebastian Chappelet.

1619— L'Odyssee d'Homere traduit de Grec en Francois par Cl. Boitel (French). *Translator or author:* Cl. Boitel. Paris, France: Math. Guillemot.

1620— L'Iliade di Homero tradotta in ottava rima dal Gio. Batt. Sebaldi detto l'Elicona (Italian). *Translator or author:* Gio. Batt. Sebaldi detto l'Elicona. Ronciglione, Italy: Lodovico Grignani; Lorenzo Lupis.

1620— L'Iliade d'Homere; traduction en prose Francoise [reprint of edition of Paris, 1614] (French). *Translator or author:* S. de Souhait. Paris, France.

1620— Ilias Homeri [reprint of edition of Augsburg, 1610] (German). *Translator or author:* Johannes Sprenger. Frankfurt am Main, Germany.

1620–28— [H]omerou Ilias A (-omega) = Homeri Ilias, id est, de rebus ad Trojam gestis liber primus (-XXIV) (Greek). Paris, France: Claudius Morellus; Ioannes Libert.

1621— Homeri Opera, Graece et Latine (Greek; Latin). Geneva, Switzerland: Math. Berjon.

1622— [H]omerou Iliados Rho; Homeri Iliados liber XVII (Greek). Paris, France: Sebastian Cramoisy; Sebastian Chappelet.

1622— Odysseae Homeri Libri Priores III; separatim editi, cum prooemio Matth. Dresseri (Greek). Leipzig, Germany: Johannes Gluck; Bartholomaei Voigt.

1622— Homeri Iliadis Libri III; separatim editi, cum prooemio Matth. Dresseri (Greek). Leipzig, Germany: Johannes Gluck; Bartholomaei Voigt.

1622— Batrachomyomachia. Leipzig, Germany.

1622— Homeri Opera, Graece et Latine (Greek; Latin). Math. Berjon.

1622–24— Homeri Ilias, Odyssea et alia Carmina cum Interpretatione Latina. Accedunt Homerici centones et proverbialium Homeri versuum libellus; Editio postrema, diligenter recognita a I.T.P... Paris, France: Ioannes Libert.

1624— Tou [H]omerou duo poiemata, [h]e Ilias kai [h]e Odysseia; Homeri poemata duo, Ilias et Odyssea, sive Ulyssea (Greek). Paris, France: Ioannes Libert.

1624— The Crowne of all Homers Workes: Batrachomyomachia, or the Battaile of Frogs and Mice, his Hymn's and Epigrams; translated according to ye originall by George Chapman [1st collected edition of Chapman's translations] (English). *Translator or author:* George Chapman. London, England: John Brill.

1624–50— Homeri Odyssea, Graece Latine; e castigatione Stephani, adiecti sunt Homerici Centones, Graece, et proverbialium Homeri versuum libellus; edition postrema recognita per I. T. P. (Greek; Latin). Paris, France; Amsterdam,.

1625— [H]omerou Iliados lambda; Homeri Iliados liber XI (Greek). Paris, France: Sebastian Cramoisy.

1625— Ilias Homeri [reprint of edition printed in Augsburg in 1610] (German). *Translator or author:* Johannes Sprenger. Frankfurt am Main, Germany.

1626— Homeri Iliadis Graece; in usum scholarum Hollandiae & West-Frisiae (Greek). Bonaventura and Abraham Elzevir.

1626— [H]omerou Iliados [h]e Tau Rhapsodia; Homeri Iliados lib. XIX (Greek). Paris, France: Ioannes Libert.

1626— Homeri Batrachomyomachia, Graece et Latine; cum solis figuris; cum Aesopi fabulis (Greek; Latin).

1626— Tes [H]omerou Iliados [h]e Nu Rhapsodia; Homeri Iliados liber XIII (Greek). Paris, France: Sebastian Chappelet.

1626—[H]omerou Odys. M = Homeri Odysseae XII (Greek). Paris, France: Sebastian Chappelet.

1626—[H]omerou Odys. Lambda = Homeri Odysseae XI (Greek). Paris, France: Sebastian Cramoisy.

1627—[H]omerou Batrachomyomachia = Homeri Ranarum et Murium Pugna (Greek). Paris, France: Ioannes Libert.

1627—L'Iliade d'Homere; traduction en prose Francoise [reprint of translation printed in Paris in 1614] (French). *Translator or author:* S. de Souhait. Paris, France.

1628—Hymnos eis Apollona (Greek). Paris, France.

1629—Epigrammatum Opusculum, duobus libellis distinctum; ad iecta est Homeri Batrachomyomachia Latino carimine reddita, varisque in locis aucta et illustrata. London, England: Huntindon Plumtre.

1629—The Crowne of all Homer's workes: Batrachomyomachia, his Hymns and Epigrams, translated by George Chapman [reprinted from 1624 edition] (English). *Translator or author:* George Chapman. London, England.

1629—[H]eroika; [H]omerou Ilias= Homeri Ilias; cum M. Aemilij Porti, Francisco Porti Cretensis f. Latina ad verbum interpretatione, quam is, paternos commentarios accurate sequutus, ab innumeris mendis repurgauit; adiectis insuper duob. Poematis Coluthi Helena (Greek, Latin). *Translator or author:* Aemilius Portus. Geneva, Switzerland: Ioan. de Tournes.

1630—Ilias Homeri [reprint of edition printed in Augsburg in 1610] (German). *Translator or author:* Johannes Sprenger. Frankfurt am Main, Germany.

1631—Iliados [H]omerou Eta; Homeri Iliadis liber septimus (Greek). Paris, France: Ioannes Libert.

1631—Les Travavx d'Vlysse; trage-comedie tiree d'Homere (French). Paris, France: Pierre Menard.

1631—Homer's Odes [Hymns]; translated (English). *Translator or author:* T. Hawkins. London, England.

1632—Fabulae Aesopi, Graece et Latine; nunc denuo selectae; eae item quas Avienus carmine expressit; accedit Ranarum & Murium Pugna, Homero olim asscripta; cum elegantissimis in utroque libello figuris, & utriusque interpretatione plurimis in locis emendata (Greek, Latin). Leiden (Leyden), Netherlands: Ioannis Maire.

1633—The Whole Works of Homer … in his Iliads and Odysses (English). *Translator or author:* George Chapman. London, England: Thomas Harper.

1634—Batrachomyomachia, or The Strange, Wonderfull and Bloudy Battell betwene Frogs and Mise, paraphrastically done into English verse [reprint of the London, 1603 edition] (English). *Translator or author:* William Fouldes. London, England: Thomas Harper.

1634—L'Iliade d'Homere; traduction en prose Francoise par S. de Souhait [reprint of the Paris, 1614 translation] (French). *Translator or author:* S. de Souhait. Paris, France: Nic. Grasse.

1636—Homeri Iliadis Liber II, Graece (Greek). Paris, France: Ioannes Libert.

1636—Batrachomiomachia ofte den wonderlijken Veldslagh tusschen de Muysen ende de Kickverschen (Flemish). *Translator or author:* Kickvorschen. Leiden (Leyden), Netherlands: Js. Burchoorn.

1636—The Ancient Historie of the Destruction of Troy; divided into III bookes, the I shewing the founders, and … how it was … first destroyed by Hercules; the II how it was re-edified, and how Hercules … destroyed it … the III how Priamus … rebuilded Troy againe … a (English). *Translator or author:* Raoul Lefevre; William Caxton; William Phiston. London, England: B. and T. Fawcet Alsop; William Phiston.

1637—[H]omerou Batrachomyomachia = Homeri Ranarum & Murium Pugna (Greek). Paris, France: Ioannes Libert.

1637—Batrachomyomachia Homeri tuba Romana cantata a Iacobo Balde , Societ. Iesv (German). *Translator or author:* Jakob Balde. Ingolstadt, Germany: Gregorius Haenlinius.

1638—Homeri Ilias ad verbum (Latin). *Translator or author:* Andreas Divus. Paris, France: Chrest. Wechel.

1639—Iliados [H]omerou Epsilon Rhapsodia; Iliados Homeri liber quintus (Greek). Paris, France: Sebastian Chappelet.

1639—L'Odyssee d'Homere traduit de Grec en Francois par Cl. Boitel [reprint of edition printed at Paris in 1619] (French). *Translator or author:* Cl. Boitel. Paris, France: Math. Guillemot.

1639—Ilias cum M. Aemilii Porti, Francisci Porti Cretensis F. Latina ad vesouns interpretatione, quam is paternos commentarios accurate sequutus, ab innumeris mendis repurgavit, adiectis insuper duob; poematis (Latin). *Translator or author:* Aemilius Portus. Geneva, Switzerland: Ioan. de Tournes.

1640—The Whole works of Homer, Prince of Poetts; in his Iliads and Odysses [comprised of reprints of 1612 and 1615 editions] (English). *Translator or author:* George Chapman. London, England: Nathaniell Butter.

1640—Ilias in versus Graecos vulgares translata a Nic. Lucano [2nd edition by this translator—1st was Venice edition of 1526] (Greek). *Translator or author:* Nic. Lucano. Venice, Italy: P. Pinelli.

1640—[H]omerou Ilias metatypotheisa eis koinen glossan enetiesin par Ioanne petro to pinello (Greek, Modern). *Translator or author:* Ioannes Petro to Pinello.

1640?—[H]omerou Iliados [h]e zeta Rhapsodia (Greek). Paris, France: Jean-Baptiste Brocas.

1642—Homer; I Iliadis, Graece; cum indice alphabetico et exegetico omnium fere vocum (Greek). Elzevie.

1642—Homeri Odysseae Liber Primus; Graece, cum versione interlineari & vocum explicatione, in usum iuventutis (Greek). Paris, France: Ioannes Libert.

1642—L'Iliade di Homero trasportata dalla Greca nella Toscana lingua da Fed. Malipiero, Nobile Veneto; Libri XXIV; aggiontovi in fine il Ratto di Elena (Italian). *Translator or author:* Federico Malipiero. Venice, Italy: Paulo Baglioni.

1642—L'Iliade di Homero; l'Odissea d'Homero etc. (Italian). *Translator or author:* Federico Malipiero. Venice, Italy: Taddeo Pavoni.

1643—L'Odissea trad. in prosa da F. Malipiero (Italian). *Translator or author:* Federico Malipiero. Venice, Italy: Gasparo Corradicci.

1644—Tes [H]omerou Odysseias [h]e Theta Rhapsodia; Homeri Odysseae liber VIII (Greek). Lemovicis: Antonius Barbou.

1645—Homeri Iliados Rhapsodiae Quatuor; cum interlineari versuum expositione. Leiden (Leyden), Netherlands: C Prost; J. Bapt De Venet.

1647—Homeri Batrachomyomachia tuba Romana cantata etc. a Jac. Balde [reprint of edition printed in Ingolstadt in 1637]. *Translator or author:* Jakob Balde. Munich, Germany.

1648—[H]omerou Ilias = Homeri Ilias (English). Cambridge, England: Roger Daniel.

1648—Homeri Opera cum Interpretatione Latina. Accedunt Homeri in centones et proverbialium Homeri versuum libellus. Editio postreme diligenter recognita a I.T.P. (Greek, Latin). Amsterdam, Netherlands: Henricus Laurentius.

1650—L'Odyssee d'Homere; ou les avantures d'Ulysse en vers burlesques (French). *Translator or author:* Henri de Picou. Paris, France: Toussaint Quinet.

1650—Homeri Opera Omnia; cum interpretatione Latina ad verbum, etc. ut Latius in Epist. ad lectorem; adjucti sunt Homerici Centones, proverbial; versuum Homeri libellus, et breves notae marginales; editio Novissima (Greek). *Translator or author:* Henricus Stephanus. Amsterdam, Netherlands: Joannes Ravenstein.

1650?—Iliados [H]omerou [H]e Gamma Rhapsodia (Greek). Paris, France (?).

1651—Homeri Omnia, Graece et Latine; accedunt auctoris vita et instructissimus rerum et verborum index (Greek; Latin). Basel, Switzerland.

1651—De Dooling van Ulisses, in 24 Boecken Door; Homerus beschreven en van G. V. S. vertaalt (Flemish). *Translator or author:* G. V. S. Amsterdam, Netherlands.

1651—Ilias; vertaeld door Glazemaker (Flemish). *Translator or author:* Glazemaker. Amsterdam, Netherlands.

1652—Matth. Jay Excerpta in sex priores Homeri Iliados libros. *Translator or author:* Matthew Jay. London, England.

1653—L'Iliade Giocosa del S. Gio. Franc. Loredano, nobile Veneto [this is a burlesque parody] (Italian). *Translator or author:* S. Gio. Franc. Loredano. Venice, Italy: Henrico Giblet Cavalier.

1653—L'Odyssee d'Homere; ou les aventures d'Ulysse en vers burlesques [reprint of the edition printed in Paris in 1650] (French). *Translator or author:* Henri de Picou. Leiden (Leyden), Netherlands: Jean Sambix.

1654—L'Iliade Giocosa del S. Gio. Franc. Loredano, nobile Veneto [reprint of the Venice 1653 edition, with corrections] (Italian). *Translator or author:* S. Gio. Franc. Loredano.

1655—Porphyrii Fragmentum de Styge ad Illustranda Loca Homeri, Iliad. et Odyss; e Graece cum Luc. Holstenii Lat. Interpretatione, et aliis Porphyrii libris. Cambridge, England.

1656—[H]omerou Ilias kai Odysseia = Homeri Ilias & Odyssea, et in Easdem Scholia; sive interpretation Didymi, cum Latina versione accuratissima, indiceque Graeco locupletissimo rerum ac variantium lection.; accurante Corn. Schrevelio (Greek, Latin). Amsterdam, Netherlands: Ludovicus Elzevir; Franciscus Hackius.

1656—[H]omerou Ilias kai Odysseia = Homeri

Ilias & Odyssea, et in Easdem Scholia; sive interpretation Didymi, cum Latina versione accuratissima, indiceque Graeco locupletissimo rerum ac variantium lection.; accurante Corn. Schrevelio (Greek; Latin). Lyons, France: Fr. Hackius.

1656— Homers Iliads and Odisses; translated, adorned with sculptures and illustrated with annotations [1st printing by this translator] (English). *Translator or author:* John Ogilby.

1657— L'Iliade en Vers Burlesques (French). Paris, France.

1657— Fabulae Aesopi Graece ac Latine; quibus adduntur Ranarum Muriumque Pugna, & Epigrammata quaedam ex anthologia selecta (Greek, Latin). *Translator or author:* Maximus Planudes. London, England: Roger Daniel.

1658— La Batrachomyomachie en vers burlesques; traduit du Grec d'Homere en vers burlesques (French). Paris, France: Thierry le Chasseur.

1660— Homeri Gnomologia; duplici parallelismo illustr., uno ex locis s. scripturae, altero ex gentium scriptoribus; insertis observationibus ethico-politicis et notis criticis per Jac. Duportum (Greek, Latin). *Translator or author:* Jac. Duport. Cambridge, England: Johannes Field.

1660— Homer: his Iliads Translated; adorned with sculpture & illustrated with annotations [reprinted from the 1656 edition] (English). *Translator or author:* John Ogilby. London, England: Thomas Roycroft.

1661— Homeri Iliadis Liber IX; in usum studiosae juventutis seorsum editus; accesserunt de Homeri vita et scriptis ex optimis Graecis ac Latinis scriptoribus collectanea, cura Ionnis Sanderi Brunsvicensis, Opt. Art. Magistri, & Ludi Magdegurgensium Rectoris. Magdeburg, Germany: Johann Muller.

1661— L'Iliade d'Homero; trad. in verso Ital. da D. Franc. Velez e Bonanno (Italian). *Translator or author:* Francesco Velez; Bonanno. Palermo, Sicily, Italy: Bisagni.

1662— L'Iliade Giocosa del S. Gio. Franc. Loredano, Nobile Veneto [reprint of Venice, 1653 edition, with corrections] (Italian). *Translator or author:* S. Gio. Franc. Loredano.

1663— The Destruction of Troy (English). *Translator or author:* Raoul Lefevre; William Caxton. London, England: Samuel Speed.

1664— Homer a la Mode; a mock poem, upon the first and second books of Homer's Iliads (English). *Translator or author:* James Scudamore. Oxford, England.

1664— La Granaoul-Ratomacheo; o la furiouso e descardo bataillo des rats, e de las grenouillos, couts le regne de Rodilard e Croacus, a l'imitacio del Grec d'Homero, poemo burlesco [rough paraphrase of Batrachomyomachia into Languedoc verse] (Languedoc). *Translator or author:* Bernard Grimau Toulousain. Toulouse (Toloso), France: Bernat Bosc.

1664–65— Homeri Ilias cum Interpr. Latine; adje sunt breves notae marginales. ed. noviss.; Homeri Odyssea cum interpr. Latine ad verbum post alias omnes edd. repurg. plurimis erroribus (et quidem crassis alicubi) partim ab Henr. Stephano partim ab aliis; adj. Sun (Greek; Latin). Cambridge, England: Joannes Field.

1665— [H]omerou Iliados, [h]e 2 Rhapsodia: Homeri Iliadis, liber secvndvs, cum versione & vocum omnium explicatione (Greek, Latin). Paris, France: Sebastian Cramoisy.

1665— Homer a la Mode; a mock poem, upon the first and second books of Homer's Iliads [reprint of the 1664 edition] (English). *Translator or author:* Lord Scudamore James. Oxford, England.

1665— Homer his Odysses translated adorn'd with sculpture and illustrated with annotations by J. Ogilvie [reprinted from the 1656 edition] (English). *Translator or author:* John Ogilby. London, England.

1667— Batrachomyomachia Homeri; 2nd ed. (Latin). *Translator or author:* Jakob Balde. Munich, Germany: L. Straub.

1668— L'Iliade Giocosa del S. Gio. Franc. Loredano, Nobile Veneto [reprint of the Venice, 1653 edition] (Italian). *Translator or author:* S. Gio. Franc. Loredano.

1669— Homer, his Odysses translated; Homer, his Iliads translated [set reprinted from the 1660 and 1665 editions for King Charles II] (English). *Translator or author:* John Ogilby. London, England: James Fletcher.

1670— Ilias et Odyssea, cum Scholiis Didymi. Oxford, England.

1670— The Destruction of Troy; in three books; 8th ed. (English). *Translator or author:* Raoul Lefevre; William Caxton. London, England: T. Passenger.

1671— Aisopou Mythoi; sun tois epigrammasin en tes Anthologias eklektois: Fabulae Aesopi, Graece et Latine; quibus adduntur Ranarum Muriumque Pugna & Epigrammata quaedam ex anthologia selecta (Greek, Latin). London, England: John Redmayne.

1672—[H]omerou Ilias [1st ed.] (Greek, Latin). Cambridge, England: Johannes Hayes.

1672—Fabulae Aesopi Graece et Latine Nunc Denuo Selectae; ex item, quas Avienus carmine expressit; accedit ranarum & murium pugna, Homero olim asscripta; cum elegantissimis in utroque libello figuris, & utriusque interpretatione, plurimis in locis emendata; ex (Greek; Latin). Amsterdam, Netherlands: Joannes Ravesteyniuni.

1673—The Travels of Ulysses; as they were related by himself in Homer's ninth, tenth, eleventh, and twelfth books of his Odysses, to Alcinous, king of Phaeacia; translated into English verse [beginning of editions by this translator] (English). *Translator or author:* Thomas Hobbes. London, England: William Crook.

1674—[H]omerou Odysseai A = Homeri Odyssea, id est, de rebus ab Ulysse gestis, liber primus (Greek). Paris, France: Simon Benard.

1674—[H]omerou Iliados [h]e Gamma Rhapsodia (Greek). Paris, France: Sebastian Cramoisy.

1674—The Travels of Ulysses; 2nd ed. [reprint of 1673 edition] (English). *Translator or author:* Thomas Hobbes. Oxford, England.

1675—The Iliads and Odysses of Homer; translated out of Grek into English by Thomas Hobbes of Malmsbury; with a large preface concerning the vertues of an heroick poem, written by the translator (English). *Translator or author:* Thomas Hobbes. London, England: William Crook.

1676—[H]omerou Ilias kai eis auten scholia Didymou; Graece (Greek). Oxford, England: Sheldon Theatre.

1676—The Destruction of Troy; in three books; The I. Shewing the founders and foundation of the said city, with the causes and manner how it was sacked and first destroyed by Hercules; The II. How it was re-edified, the second time: and of Hercules his worthy (English). *Translator or author:* Raoul Lefevre. London, England: T. Passenger.

1677—The Iliads and Odysses of Homer; translated by Th[omas] Hobbes of Malmesbury; 2nd ed. [from the 1675 edition] (English). *Translator or author:* Thomas Hobbes. London, England: William Crook.

1679—Fabulae Aesopi, Graece ac Latine; quibbus adduntur Ranarum Muriumque Pugna & Epigrammata quaedam ex Anthologia selecta (Greek, Latin). London, England: John Redmayne.

1679—Homeri Opera, Graece et Latine; post aliorum editiones repurgata...; Adiecti sunt Homeri centones... (Greek, Latin). Cambridge, England: Johannes Hayes.

1679—The Destruction of Troy, a Tragedy; acted at His Royal Highness the Duke's Theatre (English). *Translator or author:* John Bankes. London, England: A. G. and J. P.

1680—Tes [H]omerou Iliados= Homeri Iliadis vigintiquatuor libri (Greek, Latin).

1680—The Destruction of Troy; in three books; 10th ed. (English). *Translator or author:* Raoul Lefevre; William Caxton. London, England: T. Passenger.

1681—Homer a la Mode; the second part, in English burlesque; or a mock poem upon the ninth book of Iliads; invented for the meridian of Cambridge, where the Pole of Wit is elevated by several degrees (English). London, England: D. Newman.

1681—L'Odyssee d'Homere; traduit de Grec en Francois [reprint of edition printed at Paris in 1619] (French). *Translator or author:* Cl. Boitel. Paris, France: Math. Guillemot.

1682—L'Iliade et l'Odyssee d'Homere; nouvelle traduction suivant la copie imprimee a Paris (French). *Translator or author:* M. de la Valterie. Paris, France; Barbin, Holland: Claude Barbin.

1683—Homer's Odysses [reprint of 1675 edition] (English). *Translator or author:* Thomas Hobbes.

1684—The Iliads and Odysses of Homer (English). *Translator or author:* Thomas Hobbes. London, England: William Crook.

1684—The Destruction of Troy; in three books; 11th ed. (English). *Translator or author:* Raoul Lefevre. London, England: T. Passenger.

1685—Homeri Iliados Liber Primus; in quo singularum vocum significationes, compositiones ac derivationes annotantur; dialecto clare et distincte exponuntur; synonima multis locis adiiciuntur; particularum varii ac elegantes usu demonstrantur; phrases et senten. London, England: George Sylvanus.

1685—Fabulae Aesopi, Graece et Latine, nunc denuo selectae (Greek, Latin). *Translator or author:* Rufius Festus Avienus. Utrecht, Netherlands: Georgius a Poolsum.

1685—Homer's Odysses [reprint of 1675 edition] (English). *Translator or author:* Thomas Hobbes.

1685—Homeri Iliados Liber Primus; in quo singularum vocum significationes, compositiones ac derivationes annotantur; dialecti clare et distincte exponuntur; synonima multis locis adiiciuntur; particularum varii ac elegantes usus demonstrantur; phrases et sente. *Translator or author:* George Sylvanus. London, England: Samuel Smith.

1686—Homeri Graecorum Poetarum Clarissimi Yliadum Opus per Pindarum Thebanum; e Greco in Latinum traductum (in I. Spondani versioni Homeri). Basel, Switzerland.

1686—[H]omerou Ilias (Greek). Cambridge, England: Johannes Hayes.

1686— The Iliads and Odysses of Homer translated out of Greek into English by Tho. Hobbes of Malmsbury; 3rd ed. [reprint of 1675 edition] (English). *Translator or author:* Thomas Hobbes. London, England: William Crook.

1686— Homeri Iliados Liber Primus [2nd ed. of 1685 printing] (English). *Translator or author:* George Sylvanus. London, England: Samuel Smith.

1689—[H]omerou Ilias kai eis auten szolia tov palaion = Homeri Ilias et veterum in eam scholia, quae vulgo appellantur Didymi; totum opus cum plurimis, vetustissimis et optimis editionibus collatum; et luculenter ex eadum fide restitutum. [Anr. ed.] (Greek; Latin). Cambridge, England: Johannes Hayes.

1689— The Iliads and Odysses of Homer; translated by Thomas Hobbes of Malmesbury; 4th ed. (English). *Translator or author:* Thomas Hobbes. London, England.

1694—Patroclus's Request to Achilles for his Arms; imitated from the beginning of the sixteenth Iliad of Homer by Thomas Yalden, D.D. in the annual miscellany for the year 1694,a being the fourth part of miscellany poems published by John Dryden, Esq. (English). *Translator or author:* Thomas Yalden. London, England.

1695—[H]omerou Ilias [2nd ed.] (Greek). Oxford, England: Johannes Hayes.

1695—[H]omerou Ilias kai eis Auten Scholia Pseudepigrapha Didymou = Homeri Ilias, et in Eam Scholia, Quae Perperam Didymo Tribui Solent (Greek; Latin). Oxford: Sheldon Theatre.

1696–98— Homeri Ilias, Graece et Latine (Greek; Latin). Oxford, England.

1697—[H]e tou [H]omerou Batrachomyomachia, seu Ranarum et Murium Pugna (Greek; Latin). Paris, France: Viduam Claudii Thiboust; Petrum Esclassan.

1698— Homeri Ilias, Graece et Latine [reprint of 1696 ed.] (Greek; Latin). Oxford, England.

1699—Fabulae Aesopi, Graece et Latine, Nunc Denuo Selectae: eae item, quas Avienus carmine expressit; accedit Ranarum & Murium Pugna, Homero olim ascripta, cum … figuris, & … interpretatione, plurimis in locis emendata (Greek, Latin). *Translator or author:* Rufius Festus Avienus. Utrecht, Netherlands: Georgius a Poolsum.

1699—L'Iliade et l'Odyssee d'Homere; nouvelle traduction suivant la copie imprimee a Paris [reprint of 1682 edition] (French). *Translator or author:* M. de la Valterie. Paris, France.

1700—Fables Antient and Modern; translated into verse from Homer [Book I], Ovid, Baccace and Chaucer; with original poems; 1st ed. (English). *Translator or author:* John Dryden. London, England: Jacob Tonson.

1700—Batrachomyomachia (Latin; Russian). *Translator or author:* Il'ya Fedorovich Kopievich.

1700— Homer in a Nut-shell, or his War Between the Froggs and the Mice; paraphrastically translated in three cantos (English). *Translator or author:* Samuel Parker. London, England.

1700—Die Listige Juno; wie solche von dem grossen Homer im 14 B. der Ilias abgebildet, hachmals von Eustachius ausgelaget, nunmehr in teutschen Versen vorgestellet und mit Anmerkungen erkahret (German). *Translator or author:* Christ. Henr. Postel. Hamburg, Germany.

1700—Le Premier Libre de l'Iliade en Vers Francois; avec une dissertation et quelques autres pieces detachees, traduites du Grec par l'abbe Regnier (French). *Translator or author:* Regnier. Paris, France: Jean Anisson.

1700— The New History of the Trojan Wars and Troy's Destruction (English). *Translator or author:* Elkanah Settle. London, England: J and J. Fuller Hodgeson.

1700 to 1800

1701—Le Premier Livre de l'Iliade d'Homere; traduit en vers Francois (French). *Translator or author:* M. de la Motte. Paris, France: Pierre Emery.

1702—Homeri Odyssea, Graece (Greek). Oxford, England.

1702—The Destruction of Troy; 12th ed. (English). London, England.

1703—L'Omero Toscano Cioe l'Iliade d'Omero; trad. in Ottava rima (Italian). *Translator or author:* Bernardino Bugliazzini. Lucca, Italy: Venturini.

1703—L'Omero Toscano Cioe l'Ulissea d'Omero, o Gli errori d'Ulisse, in Ottava rima (Italian). *Translator or author:* Bernardino Bugliazzini. Lucca, Italy: D. Ciuffetti.

1705—[H]omerou Odysseia (Greek). Oxford, England: Sheldon Theatre.

1706—Homeri Odyssea, Graece [reprint of the 1702 edition] (Greek). Oxford, England.

1706—[H]omerou Ilias = Homeri Ilias; id est de rebus ad Trojam gestis; ex anthologia vet. Epigrammatum (Greek, Latin). London, England: William Redmayne.

1707—Opera Quae Extant Graece et Latine; Graeca ad princ. Henr. Stephani ut et ad primam omnium Demetrii Chalcondylae ed. atque insuper ad Codd. Mss. sunt excussa; ex Latine selecta sunt optima, verum ita interpol., ut plurimis longe locis, praesertim totius O (Greek; Latin). *Translator or author:* Stephan Bergler. Amsterdam, Netherlands: J. de Wetstein.

1707—Batrachomyomachia; a Demetrio Zeno Zacynthio in vulgarem linguam Graecam rhythmice conversa [with Latin translation by B. Martin Crusius] (Latin; Modern Greek). *Translator or author:* Demetrius Zeno Zacynthius; B. Martin Crusius. Altdorf, Germany: J. G. Kohles.

1708—Homeri Odyssea, Graece [reprint of the 1702 edition] (Greek). Oxford, England.

1708—L'Odyssee; 3rd ed. (French). Paris, France: Claude Barbin.

1708—L'Iliade; 3rd ed. (French). Paris, France: Claude Barbin.

1708—The Destruction of Troy; in three books (English). *Translator or author:* Raoul Lefevre. London, England: E. Tracey.

1708–09—L'Iliade et l'Odyssee d'Homere; nouvelle traduction suivant la copie imprimee a Paris [reprint of the 1682 edition] (French). *Translator or author:* M. de la Valterie. Paris, France: Brunet.

1709—L'Iliade et l'Odyssee; traduites en prose, avec des notes et des figures de Picard (French). *Translator or author:* Anne LeFevre Dacier. Paris, France: Rigaud.

1709—Sarpedon's Speech to Glaucus, in the XIIth book of the Iliad of Homer, translated into English, by Sir John Denham, Knight of the Bath, in his Poems and Translations, with the Sophy (English). *Translator or author:* John Denham. London, England.

1709—Batrachomyomachia in Nederduitsch Heldendicht Overgrbracht (Flemish). *Translator or author:* L. Schermer. Haarlem, Netherlands.

1709—L'Odyssee d'Homere; traduite en Francois (French). *Translator or author:* de la Valterie. Paris, France: Michel Brunet.

1711—Homeri Ilias et Odyssea, Graece et Latine, et in Easdem Scholia; sive interpretation veterum; item notae perpetuis in textum et scholia, variae lectiones etc. cum vers. Lat. emendatiss.; acc. Batrachomyomachia, Hymni et Epigrammata una cum fragmentis et g (Greek; Latin). *Translator or author:* Joshua Barnes. Cambridge, England: Corn. Crownfield.

1711–20—L'Iliade et l'Odyssee d'Homere; traduites en Francais, avec des remarques, par Mad. Dacier en prose, avec des notes et des figures de Picard (French). *Translator or author:* Anne LeFevre Dacier. Paris, France: Rigaud.

1712—The Iliad; with notes, to which are prefixed a preface of the life of Homer by Madame D'Acier, done from the French by Mr. Oldsworth, Mr. Broome and Mr. Ozell etc.; to which are added some grammatical notes by Mr. Johnson and a large poetical index to the (English). London, England: Bernard Lintot.

1712–17—L'Iliade et l'Odyssee d'Homere; novelle edition revue & corrigee, ou l'on a mis les remarques sous le texte (French). *Translator or author:* Anne LeFevre Dacier. Amsterdam, Netherlands: De La Compagnie.

1713—[H]omerou Ilias = Homeri Ilias; id est, de rebus ad Trojam gestis [reprint of the 1706 edition] (Greek, Latin). London, England: John Redmayne.

1713—Fables Antient and Modern; translated into

II. Printed Editions of the Homeric Texts, 1470 to 2000 C.E.

198

verse from Homer [Book I], Ovid, Baccace and Chaucer; with original poems [2nd ed.] (English). *Translator or author:* John Dryden. London, England: Jacob Tonson.

1714—Homeri Ilias, Graece (Greek). London, England: William Bowyer.

1714—Homeri Ilias, Odyssea, Graece (Greek). Oxford, England: Sheldon Theatre.

1714—[H]omerou Ilias; ek theatrou en Oxonia (Greek). London, England: J Bowyer and H. Clements.

1714—Ilias Graece, sine scholiis (Greek). Oxford, England: Sheldon Theatre.

1714—L'Iliade, Poeme en Vers Francois; avec un discours sur Homere par Houdart de la Motte (French). Paris, France: Greg. Dupuis.

1714—L'Iliade; trad. (French). *Translator or author:* M. de la Motte. Amsterdam,.

1715—The First Book of Homer's Iliad; translated by Mr. Ticknell (English). *Translator or author:* Thomas Ticknell. London, England.

1715–20—The Iliad of Homer; translated, with notes [1st edition by this translator] (English). *Translator or author:* Alexander Pope. London, England: William Bowyer.

1716—L'Homere Travest ou l'Iliade en Vers Burlesques; orne de fig. en taille-douce (French). *Translator or author:* Carlet de Marivaux. Paris, France: Pierre Prault.

1716—Homerides; or, Homer's First Book Moderniz'd [written in doggerel] (English). *Translator or author:* George Duckett. London, England: R. Burleigh.

1716—Le Premier Livre de l'Iliade d'Homere; traduit en vers Francois (in Oeuvres) (French). *Translator or author:* Francois Seraphim Regnier.

1716—The First Book of Homer's Odyssey translated, with notes (English). *Translator or author:* Lewis Theobald. London, England.

1716—The First Book of Homer's Iliad (English). *Translator or author:* Thomas Ticknell. Dublin, Ireland: S. Powell.

1716–20—L'Iliade et l'Odyssee; traduit par Mad. Dacier en prose, avec des notes et des figures de Picard; reprint of 1711–16 edition] (French). *Translator or author:* Anne LeFevre Dacier. Paris, France.

1717—Homer's Battle of the Frogs and Mice (English). Dublin, Ireland: Thomas Hume.

1717—Homeri Batrachomyomachia, Graece et Latine; cum commentario Herm. Von der Hardt (Greek; Latin). Helmst, Germany.

1717—La Batrachomyomachie d'Homere, ou Combat des Rats et des Grenouilles, en vers francois, par le docteur Junius Biberius-Mero, et les Cerises renversees, poeme heroique (French). *Translator or author:* Jean Boivin. Paris, France: Giffart.

1717—L'Odyssee d'Homere; tr. en Francois, avec des remarques (French). *Translator or author:* Anne LeFevre Dacier. Amsterdam, Netherlands: De La Compagnie.

1717—Odyssey [Book 11, published in his Poetical Works] (English). *Translator or author:* Elijah Fenton.

1717—Homer's Battle of the Frogs and Mice; with the remarks of Zoilus (English). *Translator or author:* Thomas Parnell. London, England: Bernard Lintot.

1717—The Odyssey, Book I (English). *Translator or author:* Lewis Theobald. London, England: J. Roberts.

1718—The Iliad of Homer (English). *Translator or author:* Alexander Pope. London, England: T. J.

1719—L'Iliade d'Homere…avec quelques reflexions sur la preface Angloise de M. Pope; 2nd ed (French). *Translator or author:* Anne LeFevre Dacier. Paris, France.

1720—The Iliad of Homer (English). London, England: George Routledge.

1720—De Dooling van Ulisses, in 24 Boecken Door; Homerus beschreven en van G. V. S. vertaalt (Flemish). *Translator or author:* G. V. S. Amsterdam, Netherlands: Jac. Verheyden.

1720—L'Iliade, Poeme en Vers Francois; avec un discours sur Homere par Houdart de la Motte [reprint of the 1714 edition] (French). *Translator or author:* M. de la Motte. Paris, France.

1720—The Iliad of Homer; 2nd edition (English). *Translator or author:* Alexander Pope. London, England: William Bowyer.

1720—The Iliad of Homer (English). *Translator or author:* Alexander Pope. London, England: Frederick Warne.

1720—The Iliad of Homer (English). *Translator or author:* Alexander Pope. London, England: J. F. Dove.

1720–26—The Iliad and Odyssey of Homer [reprint of the 1715–20 edition] (English). *Trans-*

lator or author: Alexander Pope. London, England.

1721—Homeri Ilias, Graece et Latine (Greek, Latin). London, England: Jacob Tonson; J. Watts.

1721—Homeri Batrachomyomachia; Graece, ad veterum exemplarium fidem recusa; glossa recusa, variant. lectionibus versionibus Latinis et comment. necnon indd. illustrata (st. Mich. Maittaire) (Greek, Latin). London, England: William Bowyer.

1721—The Iliad of Homer; 2nd ed. (English). London, England: J. Bettenham.

1721—Fables Antient and Modern; translated into verse from Homer [Book I], Ovid, Baccace and Chaucer; with original poems [3rd ed.] (English). *Translator or author:* John Dryden. London, England: Jacob Tonson.

1722—[H]omerou Ilias = Homeri Ilias; id est, de rebus ad Trojam gestis (Greek, Latin). London, England: J. R. Prostant.

1722—Homeri Hymnus in Apollinem, Graece et Latine; Fed. Morello interprete, cum notis Mich. Maittaire, in illius miscellaneis Graecorum aliquot scriptorum carminibus (Greek, Latin). London, England.

1722—The Iliad of Homer; Books X and XI, with notes by Madam Dacier; 3rd ed. (English). *Translator or author:* William Broome. London, England: H. Woodfall.

1722—Ilias; adjic. in calce interpr. Latina (Greek). *Translator or author:* Mich. Maittaire. London, England: Jacob Tonson; J. Watts.

1723—Iliade d'Omero tradotta dall'originale in versi sciolti; Odissea ed altre poesie d'Omero, etc. Ed. II, in cui si e aggiunta una nuova traduzione della Batracomiomachia (Italian). *Translator or author:* A. M. Salvini. Florence, Italy: Gio. Gaetano Tartini e Santi Franchi.

1725–26—The Odyssey of Homer; a general view of the epic poem, and of the Iliad and Odyssey, extracted from Bossu; postscript, by Mr. Pope; Homer's Battle of the Frogs and Mice, corrected by Mr. Pope (English). *Translator or author:* Alexander Pope. London, England: Bernard Lintot.

1726—Batrachomyomachia (Greek). *Translator or author:* Mich. Maittaire. London, England: G. Bowyer.

1726—Homeri Iliados Liber Primus (Latin). *Translator or author:* George Sylvanus. London, England: Samuel Smith.

1726—The Iliad in a nutshell (English). *Translator or author:* Wesley. London, England.

1727—Homer's Battle of the Froggs and the Mice; translated with the remarks of Zoilus and the life of Zoilus by Dr. Th. Parnell (English). *Translator or author:* Thomas Parnell. London, England.

1728—[H]omerou Ilias = Homeri Ilias (Greek, Latin). London, England: Wood.

1728—Homer's Iliad; in English verse; a new edition, carefully revised & corrected by the author in a great many places (English). *Translator or author:* Alexander Pope. London, England: T. J.

1729—The Iliad of Homer (English). *Translator or author:* Alexander Pope.

1729–40—Homeri Ilias Graece et Latine; annotatt. in usum Sereniss. Princ. Buil. Aug. ducis de Cumberland etc. regio jussu scripsit atque ed. Sam. Clarke [1st ed.] (Greek, Latin). London, England: Jac. And Joa. Knapton.

1730–35—Eustathii diac. etc. commentarii in Homeri Iliadem, Graece, Alex. Politius nunc primum Lat. vertit, rec., notis perpet. illustravit; acced. notae Ant. Mar. Salvini (Latin). *Translator or author:* Alex. Politius. Florence, Italy: Bern. Paperinium.

1731—L'Iliade et l'Odyssee, traduct. d'Homere, par Mad. Dacier, avec un supplement par Banier, les remarques et la preface de Pope (French). *Translator or author:* Anne LeFevre Dacier. Amsterdam, Netherlands: J. de Wetstein.

1732—The Iliad and Odyssey of Homer [reprint of the 1715–20, 1725–26 editions] (English). *Translator or author:* Alexander Pope.

1733—The Odyssey (English). *Translator or author:* Alexander Pope. Edinburgh, Scotland: A. and W. Creech and J. Balfour Kincaid.

1733—Homeri Iliados Liber Primus. *Translator or author:* George Sylvanus. London, England: Samuel Smith.

1734—Ilias [edited by Samuel Clarke] (Greek, Latin). Amsterdam, Netherlands.

1734—The Iliad; with notes, to which are prefixed a preface of the life of Homer by Madame D'Acier, done from the French by Mr. Oldsworth, Mr. Broome and Mr. Ozell etc.; to which are added some grammatical notes by Mr. Johnson and a large poetical index to the (English). London, England.

1734—Fables Antient and Modern; translated into verse from Homer [Book I], Ovid, Baccace and Chaucer; with original poems; 4th ed.

(English). *Translator or author:* John Dryden. London, England: Jacob Tonson.

1735—Homers Batrachomyomachia; Griechisch mit Deutschen Anmerkungen von Ch. Tob. Damm.; vollstand. Registern u. einer freyen deutschen Uebers (Greek). Berlin, Germany.

1735—Homers Krieg der Mause; Griechisch, mit Griechisch Deutschen vollstandigen Registern und einer freyen Deutschen Ubersetzung (Greek; German). Berlin, Germany.

1736—Homeri Batrachomyomachia, Graece; cum indice Graeco et Latino (Greek). Berlin, Germany.

1736—Il Primo Canto dell'Iliade d'Omero tradotto in versi Italiani (Italian). *Translator or author:* Scipione Maffei. Londra [Italy?]: Giovanni Brindley.

1736—The Iliad and Odyssey [reprint of the 1715–20, 1725–26 editions] (English). *Translator or author:* Alexander Pope.

1736—Batrachomyomachia; or the Battle of the Frogs and Mice; translated from Homer by a Landwaiter in the Port of Poole. *Translator or author:* H. Price. London, England: J. Wifford.

1736–43—[H]omerou Ilias = Homeri Ilias; id est de rebus ad Trojam gestis; ex anthologia vet. Epigrammatum [reprint of the 1706 edition] (Greek; Latin). London, England.

1737—Il Primo Canto dell'Iliade d'Omero (Italian). Verona, Italy: Jacopo Vallarsi.

1737—The Iliad of Homer (English). Dublin, Ireland: P. Crampton.

1737—Die Ilias des Homerus, Erstes Buch; ubersetzt (German). *Translator or author:* Gottsched.

1738—The Iliad of Homer [reprint of the 1715–20 edition] (English). *Translator or author:* Alexander Pope. London, England.

1739—Introductio ad Linguam Graecam; complectens regulas grammaticae radices vocum, et exercitationem, seu poema in quo regulae radicesque omnes ad usum & praxim rediguntur [includes Odyssey Books 1–6] (Greek, Latin). Rome, Italy: Haeredum Ferri.

1739—Phaedri Augusti liberti [includes Batrachomyomachia]. *Translator or author:* David van Hoogstraten. Venice, Italy: F. Pitteri.

1739—Destruction of Troy; the sequel of the Iliad (Greek; English). *Translator or author:* Tryphiodorus; James Merrick. Oxford, England: Sheldon Theatre.

1740—Homeri Ilias; Graece et Latine; annota-tions...scripsit atque editit Samuel Clarke [3rd ed.] (Greek, Latin). London, England: John and Paul Knapton.

1740—Homeri Batrachomyomachia; cum Phaedro et Avieni fabulis. Padova (Padua), Italy.

1740—Homeri Odyssea; Graece et Latine item Batrachomyomachia, Hymni, et Epigrammata, Homero vulgo ascripta; editit...a Samuel Clarke (Greek; Latin). London, England: John and Paul Knapton.

1740—Phaedri Augusti liberti, et Fl. Aviani Fabulae; cum adnotationibus ad utrumque; accedunt fabulae Graecae Latinis respondentes, et Homeri Batrachomyomachia in usum scholarum Seminarii Patavini. *Translator or author:* David van Hoogstraten. Padova (Padua), Italy: Joannes Manfre.

1741—Le Combat des Rats et des Grenouilles, Tire d'Homere, Poeme Heroique (French). Avignon, France.

1741—Graeca Scholia Scriptoris Anonymi in Homeri Iliados Librum I; Ant. Bongiovanni ex vet. cod. bibl. Venet. D. Marci eruit, Lat. interpr. est notisque illustr. *Translator or author:* Ant. Bongiovanni. Venice, Italy.

1741—La Guerra de' Ranocchi e de' Topi; tradotta in rime Anacreontiche da Angiol Maria Ricci [1st printing by this translator]; etc. con altri ameni Volgarizzamenti e un' appendice di placevoli Poosie (Italian). *Translator or author:* Angiol Maria Ricci. Florence, Italy: Gaetano Albrizzini.

1741—Tes [H]omerou Vernon-iados, rhapsodia [h]e gramma A: The Vernon-iad [a political satire in Homeric form]. *Translator or author:* Edward Vernon. London, England: Charles Corbett.

1741–56—L'Iliade et l'Odyssee; traduit par Mad. Dacier en prose, avec des notes et des figures de Picard [reprint of the 1711–16 edition] (French). *Translator or author:* Anne LeFevre Dacier. Paris, France.

1742—Le Combat des Rats et des Grenouilles; tire d'Homere; poeme heroique (French). Cologne, Germany: Antoine Frick.

1742—Iliade d'Omero; trad. in versi Sciolti da A. M. Salvini; Odissea ed altre poesie d'Omero, etc. in cui si e aggiunta una nuova traduzione della Batracomiomachia; 2nd ed. [from edition printed at Florence in 1723] (Italian). *Translator or author:* Anton Maria Salvini. Padova (Padua), Italy: Giovanni Manfre.

1743—Ilias et Odyssea (Greek). Oxford, England.

1743—Homeri Ilias, Graece [from the 1736 edition] (Greek). London, England.

1743—[H]omerou Ilias = Homeri Ilias; edition altera (Greek). Oxford, England: Sheldon Theatre.

1743—Homeri Opera Omnia Quae Exstant; Graece et Latine iuxta editionem emendat. Et accurat. Samuelis Clarke [reprint of 1707 Amsterdam edition] (Greek, Latin). *Translator or author:* Stephan Bergler. Amsterdam, Netherlands: J. de Wetstein.

1743—The Last Parting of Hector and Andromache; from the sixth book of the Iliad [in his Original Poems and Translations, Vol. II] (English). *Translator or author:* John Dryden. London, England.

1743—The Iliad and Odyssey [reprint of the 1715–20, 1725–26 editions] (English). *Translator or author:* Alexander Pope.

1744—Homeri Opera Quae Extant Omnia, Graeca, etc. (Greek, Latin). Paris, France: Jean-Baptiste Brocas.

1744—La Batracomiomachia d'Omero Greca, Latina, e Italiana (Greek, Latin, Italian). Venice, Italy: Gio. Battista Albrizzi q. Girolamo.

1744—Iliade et Odissea d'Omero [includes Batrachomyomachia translated by Ricci reprinted from the 1707 Amsterdam edition] (Italian). *Translator or author:* Stephan Bergler. Padova (Padua), Italy.

1744—La Batracomiomachia di Omero; Greca, Latina ed Italiana (Greek, Latin, Italian). *Translator or author:* Ant. Lavagnoli. Venice, Italy: Albrizzi.

1745—Incerti Scriptoris Graeci Fabulae aliquot Homericae de Ulixis erroribus; ethice explicatae (Greek, Latin). Lyon, France: P. Bonk; J. W. de Groot.

1745—The Odyssey of Homer [reprint of the 1726–26 edition] (English). *Translator or author:* Alexander Pope; W. Broome; E. Fenton.

1745—Fables Antient and Modern; translated into verse from Homer [Book I], Ovid, Baccace and Chaucer; with original poems; 5th ed. (English). *Translator or author:* John Dryden. London, England: Jacob and R. Tonson; S. Draper.

1745—Versuch einer Ubersetzung der Ilias des Homers (German). *Translator or author:* Gf. Ephr. Muller. Dresden, Germany.

1745—Homeri Batrachomyomachia in Latinum translata a Petro Rossi (Greek; Latin). *Translator or author:* Petrus Rossi. Lucca, Italy.

1745–53—[H]omerou Ilias = Homeri Ilias, Graece et Latine, ad praestantissimas editiones accuratissime expressa (Greek, Latin). *Translator or author:* Johann Georg Hager. Chemnitz, Germany: Fratres Stoesselios.

1746—Traduzioni Poetiche; o sia Tentativi per ben tradurre in verso esemplificati col Volgarrizzamento del primo libro dell'Iliade, del primo dell'Eneide, e di alcumi Cantici della Scrittura, e d'un Salmo (Italian). Verona, Italy: Stamperia del Seminario.

1747—Homeri Ilias [edited by Samuel Clarke] (Greek, Latin). Glasgow, Scotland: Robert and Andrew Foulis.

1747—Homeri Ilias; adjic. in calce interpr. Latina [reprint of the 1722 edition] (Greek, Latin). *Translator or author:* Mich. Maittaire. London, England: Jacob. Tonson; J. Watts.

1747—Batracomiomachia d'Omero; azzoe la vattaglia ntra le ranonchie e li surece de lo stisso autore per Gianfr. Paci (Italian). *Translator or author:* Gianfr. Paci. Naples, Italy.

1747—Hectoris interitus; carmen Homeri, sive Iliadis liber XXII, cum scholiis vetustis Porphrii et aliorum, Graece, evulgavit Lud. Casp. Valckenaerius. *Translator or author:* Lud. Casp. Valkenaer. Leovardiae: Coulon.

1747–48—Homeri Opera, Graece et Latine; ex edit. Sam[uel] Clarke (Greek; Latin). Paris, France: Jean-Baptiste Brocas.

1749—Li Due Primi Canti dell'Iliade, e Li Due Primi dell'Eneide; tradotti in versi Italiani; si aggiunge la traduzione di un'Elegia di Catullo in Greco fatta dal Signor Anton (Italian). Verona, Italy: Dionigi Ramanzini.

1749—Iliad, Book I (English). *Translator or author:* H. Fitz-Cotton.

1749—Homeri Iliados. *Translator or author:* George Sylvanus. London, England.

1750—The Eighth Book of the Iliad of Homer; attempted by way of essay (English). *Translator or author:* Samuel Ashwick. London, England: J. Brindley.

1750—Iliad; parts of books X and XI, in imitation of the style of Milton [in his Poems on Several Occasions] (English). *Translator or author:* William Broome. London, England.

1750—Der Anfang des ersten und ein Stuck aus dem zweiten Gesange der Ilias; ubersetzt (in

Neuer Buchersaal) (German). *Translator or author:* Fromm. Leipzig, Germany.

1750–58—[H]omerou Odysseia = Homeri Odyssea [edited by Samuel Clarke] (Greek). Oxford, England: Sheldon Theatre.

1751—The New History of the Trojan Wars and Troy's Destruction; in four books...to which is added, The Seige of Troy, a tragi-comedy (English). London, England: J.and J. Fuller Hodges.

1751—L'Odissea d'Omero Trasportata in Istile Eroicomico in Ottava Rima (in Opere Varie di Monsignor Bali Gregorio Redi Aretino) (Italian). *Translator or author:* Bali Gregorio Redi Aretino. Venice, Italy: Battista Recurti.

1751—Homers Ilias; in Deutsche Verse uberset-zet; I. II. III. Buch. (German). *Translator or author:* Diet. Blohm. Altona, Germany.

1751—The Iliad of Homer [reprint of the 1715–20 edition] (English). *Translator or author:* Alexander Pope. London, England.

1752—Fables Ancient and Modern; translated into verse, from Homer [Book I], Ovid, Boccace, & Chaucer; with original poems (English). *Translator or author:* John Dryden. Glasgow, Scotland: Robert and Andrew Foulis.

1752—Homers Ilias in Deutsche Verse ubersetzt und mit Anmerkungen begleitet; erstes und zweytes Bucher (German). *Translator or author:* Adolph Peter Gries. Altona, Germany.

1752—Poesie del Sig. Marchese Scipione Maffei Volgari e Latine Parte non piu raccolte, e parte nonpiu stampate, tomo primo (includes the three first books of the Iliad in verse) (Italian). *Translator or author:* Marchese Scipione Maffei. Verona, Italy: Antonio Andreoni.

1752—The Odyssey of Homer [reprint of the 1725–26 edition] (English). *Translator or author:* Alexander Pope. London, England.

1753—Ilias [edited by Samuel Clarke] (Greek, Latin). London, England.

1753—Traduzione in Verso Sciolto Italiano del Libro Primo della Iliada d'Omero da Recitarsi nell'Aula del Collegion di Brera (Italian). Milan, Italy: Francesco Malatesta.

1753—Homer's Hymn to Venus; translated into English verse [in his Works, Vol. 3] (English). *Translator or author:* William Congreve. London, England.

1753—Priam's Lamentation and Petition to Achilles, for the Body of his Son Hector; and the

lamentation of Hecuba, Andromache and Helen, over the dead body of Hector; translated from the Greek of Homer [in his Works, Vol. 3] (English). *Translator or author:* William Congreve. London, England.

1753—The Iliad and Odyssey [reprint of the 1715–20, 1725–26 editions] (English). *Translator or author:* Alexander Pope. Glasgow, Scotland.

1754—Homeri Odyssea, Graece et Latine, Item Batrochomyomachia, Hymni, Epigrammata, Homero; vulgo adscripta [reprinted from the 1740 editions edited by Samuel Clarke] (Greek; Latin). London, England.

1754—Homeri Ilias; Graece et Latine; scriptsit atque editit Samuel Clarke [2nd ed.] (Greek, Latin). London, England: John and Paul Knapton.

1754—Das Beruhmteste Uberbleibsel aus dem Griechischen Alterthum Homers Ilias, oder Beschreibung der Eroberung des Trojanischen Reichs; den Deutschen Lesern mitgetheilet von einer Gesellschaft gelehrter Leute, mit einer Landkarte versehen und mit 24 saubern Ku (German). Frankfurt und Leipzig, Germany.

1754—Homers Ilias; in Deutsche Verse uberset-zet IV und V Bucher (German). *Translator or author:* Diet Blohm. Altona, Germany.

1754—Fables Antient and Modern; translated into verse from Homer [Book I], Ovid, Baccace and Chaucer; with original poems [reprint of 1700 edition] (English). *Translator or author:* John Dryden.

1754—The Iliad (English). *Translator or author:* Alexander Pope. Glasgow, Scotland: R. Urie.

1755—[H]omerou Ilias = Homeri Ilias, Graece et Latine; 5th ed. [edited by Samuel Clarke] (Greek, Latin). London, England: G. Innys and J. et al. Richardson.

1755—Das Beruhmteste Uberbleibsel aus dem Griechischen Alterthum: Homer Odyssea; oder Reisegeschichte des Ulysses etc. mit 24 saubern Kupferstichen nach Picartischer Zeichnung gezieret (German). Frankfurt and Leipzig, Germany.

1755—Introductio ad Linguam Graecam; complectens Iliadis Homericae quatuor priores libros Graeco-Latinos; cum duplici indice vocum, cum Graecarum tum Latinarum ad usum rhetoricae (Greek; Latin). La Rochelle, France: R. J. Desbordes.

1755—Des Ulysses Wiederkunft zu seinem Vater; Telemachs Besuch beim Nestor; Telemach beim

Menelaus; Des Ulysses Abschied von der Kalypso [in Fragmente in der erzahlended Dichtart] (German). *Translator or author:* Johann Jakob Bodmer. Zurich, Switzerland: C. Orell.

1755— Fables Antient and Modern; translated into verse from Homer [Book I], Ovid, Baccace and Chaucer; with original poems; 6th ed. (English). *Translator or author:* John Dryden. London, England: Jacob and R. Tonson; S. Draper.

1755— An Essay Towards a Translation of Homer's Works; [excerpts translated] in blank verse (English). *Translator or author:* Joseph Nicol Scott. London, England: Thomas Osborne; and Shipton.

1756— Versuch einer gebundenen Ubersetzung der Iliad des Homers (German). *Translator or author:* Dieterich Blohm. Altona.

1756— Les Oeuvres d'Homere; de la version de Salomon Certon (French). *Translator or author:* Salomon Certon. Paris, France.

1756— Iliade (French). *Translator or author:* Anne LeFevre Dacier. Paris, France.

1756— Odysee (French). *Translator or author:* Anne LeFevre Dacier. Paris, France.

1756— The Iliad of Homer (English). *Translator or author:* Alexander Pope. London, England: Henry Lintot.

1756–58— Ta tou [H]omerou, sozomenon apavion tomoi tessares. Tes tou [H]omerou Iliados. Tes tou [H]omerou Odysseias, cui subiuncta sunt reliqua, quae vilgo adtributa sunt Homero (Greek). *Translator or author:* James Moor; George Muirhead. Glasgow, Scotland: Robert and Andrew Foulis.

1758— Homeri Odyssea; Graece et Latine; edidit, annotationesque, ex notis nonnullis MStis Samuele Clarke [2nd ed.] (Greek, Latin). London, England: A. Millar.

1758—[H]omerou Ilias = Homeri Ilias Graece; 3rd ed. (Greek). Oxford, England: Sheldon Theatre.

1758—[H]e tou [H]omerou Ilias = Homeri Ilias; ad optimas editiones castigata; adiecta est interpretatio Latina (Greek, Latin). Edinburgh, Scotland: Wal. Ruddimann.

1758— Homeri Ilias et Odyssea, Graece [reprint of the 1743 edition] (Greek). Oxford, England.

1758— The Odyssey of Homer [reprint of the 1725–26 edition] (English). *Translator or author:* Alexander Pope; W. Broome; E. Fenton.

1758— Ton tou [H]omerou Sesosmenon [h]apanton Tomoi Tessares (Greek). *Translator or author:* James Moor; George Muirhead. Glasgow, Scotland: Robert and Andrew Foulis.

1758— Tes tou [H]omerou Odysseias (Greek). *Translator or author:* James Moor; George Muirhead. Glasgow, Scotland: Robert and Andrew Foulis.

1758— The Odyssey of Homer; translated from the Greek (English). *Translator or author:* Alexander Pope. London, England: Henry Lintot.

1759— Homers Hymne auf den Kriegsgott; Bacchus oder die Rauber; Hymne an die Minerve; Hymne an Venus; Hynme auf dem Sonnengott (in Lyrische, Elegische Poesien) (German).

1759— Homers Froschmausekrieg; ein episch Gedicht, von einem Ungenannten (in Lyrische, Elegische und Epische Poesien) (German). Halle an der Saale, Germany.

1759— The Iliad and Odyssey [reprint of the 1715–20, 1725–26 edition] (English). *Translator or author:* Alexander Pope.

1759–64—[H]omerou Apanta = Homeri Opera Omnia; ex recensione et cum notis Samuelis Clarkii; accessit varietas lectionum mss. Lips. et edd. vet. cura Jo. Aug. Ernesti qui et suas notas adspersit [edited by Jo. Aug. Ernesti] (Greek, Latin). Leipzig, Germany: G. Thphi Georgius; impr. Vdalr. Ch. Saalback.

1760— Iliade d'Omero; 3rd ed. (Spanish). Padova (Padua), Italy: Joannes Manfre.

1760— Iliados (Greek). London, England.

1760— Fr. Xav. Alegrii Ilias, Latino Carm. Expressa; acc. ejd. Alexandrias s. de expurgatione Tyri ab Alexandro Macedone LL.IV (Latin). *Translator or author:* Xav. Alegrius. Pesaro, Italy.

1760— Vierter Gesang und sechster Gesang der Ilias; in hexametern ubersetzt (German). *Translator or author:* Johann Jakob Bodmer. Zurich, Switzerland: Orell.

1760— Homer's Battle of the Frogs and Mice (English). *Translator or author:* Thomas Parnell. London, England: Charles Rivington; T. Osborne.

1760— Poems on Several Occasions [includes Batrachomyomachia] (English). *Translator or author:* Alexander Pope. London, England: Jacob and R. Tonson.

1760— The Iliad and Odyssey of Homer [reprint of the 1715–20, 1725–26 edition] (English). *Translator or author:* Alexander Pope. London, England.

1760—The Iliad of Homer (English). *Translator or author:* Alexander Pope. London, England: Charles Rivington; T. Osborne.

1760–68—Opera, Graece et Latine; ex edit. Sam[uel] Clarke; 6th ed. (Greek; Latin). London, England.

1761—Parte della Iliade di omero in lingua Napoletana [inVarie Poesie di Niccolo Capasso; includes the first 6 books and part of the 7th of The Iliad, in Neopolitan dialect] (Italian). *Translator or author:* Nicc. Capasso. Naples, Italy.

1761—The Iliad of Homer (English). *Translator or author:* Alexander Pope. Edinburgh, Scotland: Hamilton; Balfour; Neill.

1761—The Odyssey of Homer; translated from the Greek (English). *Translator or author:* Alexander Pope. Edinburgh, Scotland: E. and J. Robertsons.

1762—Traduction Libre de l'Iliade (French). *Translator or author:* Paul Jeremie Bitaube. Berlin, Germany: Samuel Pitra.

1762–64—The First Volume of a New Translation of Homer's Iliad, adapted to the capacity of honest English roast beef and pudding eaters; by Caustic Barebones, a broken apothecary; to which is prefixed some small account of the abovesaid Mr. Barebones himself (English). *Translator or author:* Robert Seymour Bridges. London, England.

1762–64—A New Translation of Homer's Iliad; adapted to the capacity of honest English roast beef and pudding eaters; by Caustic Barebones, a broken apothecary; v. 2: Homer travestie; being a new Burlesque Translation of the ten first books of the Iliad (English). *Translator or author:* Thomas Brydges. London, England.

1763—La Bataglia delle Rane; e de topi di Omero tradotta; in Ottava rima (in Italica Phaedri Fabularum) (Italian). *Translator or author:* D. Antonio Migliarese. Naples, Italy: Abbaziana.

1763—The Iliad and Odyssey (English). *Translator or author:* Alexander Pope. London, England: Thomas Osborne.

1763—The Iliad and Odyssey of Homer (English). *Translator or author:* Alexander Pope. Edinburgh, Scotland: Alexander Donaldson; J. Reid.

1763—Ein Stuck aus dem dritten Buche der Ilias; ubersetzt (in Theater der Griechen) (German). *Translator or author:* Steinbrychel. Zurich, Switzerland.

1764—L'Iliade d'Homere; traduit nouvelle prec. de reflexions sur Homere par Bitaube (French). *Translator or author:* Paul Jeremie Bitaube. Paris, France: Perault.

1764—A Burlesque Translation of Homer, in Verse [from the 1762 edition] (English). *Translator or author:* Thomas Brydges. London, England.

1764—Fables Antient and Modern; translated into verse from Homer [Book I], Ovid, Baccace and Chaucer; with original poems [reprint of the 1700 edition] (English). *Translator or author:* John Dryden.

1765—Canzoni Scelte d'Anacreonte; con tre pezzi scelti dell'Iliade d'Omero il tutto nuovamente tradotta dall'Original Testo Greco (Italian). Venice, Italy: Simone Occhi.

1765—Homeri Batrachomyomachia; ex recensione et cum notis I. A. Ernesti recudi curavit suisque notis auxit I. Ad. Schier (Greek; Latin). Leipzig, Germany.

1765—Homeri Ilias, Graece (Greek). Oxford, England: Sheldon Theatre.

1766—Homeri Graecorum Poetarum Clarissimi Yliadum Opus per Pindarum Thebanum; e Greco in Latinum traductum (in Collectione Pisaurensi Omnium Poematum).

1766—L'Iliade et l'Odyssee; traduit par Mad. Dacier en prose, avec des notes et des figures de Picard [reprint of the 1711–16 edition printed in Paris] (French). *Translator or author:* Anne LeFevre Dacier. Leiden (Leyden), Netherlands: J. de Wetstein and Son.

1766—The Odyssey of Homer (English). *Translator or author:* Alexander Pope. London, England: M. Cooper.

1766–70—L'Iliade d'Homere, traduite en vers, avec des remarques (French). *Translator or author:* Guillaume Dubois de Rochefort. Paris, France: Saillant.

1767—Homeri Ilias, Graece et Latine; ad praestantissimas editiones accvratissime expressa (Greek, Latin). Chemnitz, Germany: Stoesselios.

1767—[H]omerou Odysseia; syn tois scholiois; Batrachomyomachia, [H]ymnoi, Epigrammata, Leipsana (Greek). Oxford, England.

1767—Die sechs ersten Gesange der Ilias von Bodmer (in his Callippe) (German). *Translator or author:* Johann Jakob Bodmer. Zurich, Switzerland.

1767—A Burlesque Translation of Homer, in Verse [from the 1762 edition] (English). *Translator or author:* Thomas Brydges. London, England.

1767—Homers Iliade; erster Gesang, v. 1–304; sechster Gesang, v. 1–65; ubersetzt (in Klotzii Bibliothek) (German). *Translator or author:* Gottfried August Burger.

1767—Iliad; translated from the Greek into blank verse; with notes, pointing out the peculiar beauties of the original and the imitations of it by succeeding poets; with remarks on Mr. Pope's admired version; Book I, being a specimen of the whole, which is to (English). *Translator or author:* Samuel Langley. London, England: Dodsley.

1767—La Ulyxea de Homero, reparatida en XIII libros, traduzida en romance castellano [reprint of the 1553 edition printed in Venice] (Spanish). *Translator or author:* Gonzalo Perez. Madrid, Spain: Francisco Xavier Garcia.

1767—The Iliad of Homer (English). *Translator or author:* Alexander Pope. Glasgow, Scotland: Robert and Andrew Foulis.

1767—The Iliad and Odyssey of Homer [reprint of the 1715–20, 1725–26 editions] (English). *Translator or author:* Alexander Pope. Edinburgh, Scotland: Alexander Donaldson.

1768—Homeri Ilias (Greek, Latin). London, England.

1768—The Odyssey of Homer [reprint of the 1725–26 edition] (English). *Translator or author:* Alexander Pope; W. Broome; E. Fenton.

1768—[H]omerou [Hymnos] eis Apollona = Homers Gesang auf den Apollo mit Deutschen Anmerkungen also verfertiget.... d. K. Ldw. Kohler. *Translator or author:* K. Ldw. Kohler. Leipzig, Germany: Buschel.

1768—The Odyssey of Homer (English). *Translator or author:* Alexander Pope. Glasgow, Scotland: Robert and Andrew Foulis.

1769—Phaedri Augusti liberti; et Fl. Aviani fabulae cum adnotationibus ad utrumque (Latin). Padova (Padua), Italy: Joannes Manfre.

1769—The Odyssey of Homer [reprint of the 1725–26 edition] (English). *Translator or author:* Alexander Pope. London, England.

1769—The Iliad and Odyssey [reprint of the 1715–20, 1725–26 editions] (English). *Translator or author:* Alexander Pope. Edinburgh, Scotland.

1769–70—L'Iliade d'Omero; tradotta in Ottava Rima dal Giuseppe Bozoli della Compagnia di Gesu; con le annotazioni del medecimo (Italian). *Translator or author:* Guiseppe Bozoli. Rome, Italy: Salomoni.

1769–71—Des Homerus Werke; aus dem Griechis-

chen neu ubersetzt und mit einigen Anmerkungen erlautert von Christian Tobias Damm (German). *Translator or author:* Christian Tobias Damm. Lemgo, Germany: Meyer.

1770—A Burlesque Translation of Homer, in Verse [from the 1762 edition, with additions and corrections] (English). *Translator or author:* Thomas Brydges. London, England.

1770—The Iliad of Homer; 6th ed. (English). *Translator or author:* Alexander Pope. Dublin, Ireland: W. and W. et al. Smith.

1770–71—Versuch einer Ubersetzung der Ilias des Homer; womit zugleich zu einer offentlichen Redeubung einladet (German). *Translator or author:* Helfr. Bernh. Wenk. Darmstadt, Germany.

1771—Les Oeuvres d'Homere (French). Leiden (Leyden), Netherlands: J. de Wetstein and Son.

1771—Homers Batrachomyomachie; ubersetzt (in Journal fur Liebhaber der Litteratur) (German). Leipzig, Germany.

1771—The Odyssey of Homer (English). *Translator or author:* Alexander Pope; W. Broome; E. Fenton.

1771—Fables Ancient and Modern; translated into verse, from Homer [Book I], Ovid, Boccace and Chaucer, with original poems [reprint of the 1700 edition] (English). *Translator or author:* John Dryden. Glasgow, Scotland: Robert and Andrew Foulis.

1771—The Iliad and Odyssey of Homer (English). *Translator or author:* Alexander Pope. London, England.

1771—Der Krieg der Frosch- und Mause; aus dem Griechischen (German). *Translator or author:* J. G. Willamow. St. Petersburg, Russia.

1771–72—The Iliad and Odyssey [reprint of the 1715–20, 1725–26 editions] (English). *Translator or author:* Alexander Pope. Glasgow, Scotland: Robert and Andrew Foulis.

1771–73—Homers Iliad (German). *Translator or author:* C. A. Kuttner. Leipzig, Germany: Dyk.

1772—[H]omerou Ilias; syn tois scholiois pseudepigraphois Didimou [reprint of the 1714 edition] (Greek). Oxford, England: Sheldon Theatre.

1772—Homers Hymne aud die Sonne (in Treue Ubersetzungen) (German). *Translator or author:* K. G. Anton. Leipzig, Germany.

1772—L'Odissea d'Omero; trad. in ottava rima da Gius. Bozoli (Italian). *Translator or author:* Guiseppe Bozoli. Rome, Italy.

II. Printed Editions of the Homeric Texts, 1470 to 2000 C.E.

206

1772—A Burlesque Translation of Homer, in Verse (English). *Translator or author:* Thomas Brydges; Francis Grose. London, England: S. Hooper.

1772—Fables Antient and Modern; translated into verse from Homer [Book I], Ovid, Boccace and Chaucer, with original poems [reprint of the 1700 edition] (English). *Translator or author:* John Dryden.

1772—Homer's Battle of the Frogs and Mice; with the remarks of Zoilus [reprint of the 1717 London edition] (English). *Translator or author:* Thomas Parnell.

1772–77—L'Iliade d'Homere; tradui en vers avec des remarques et un discours sur Homere; nouv. ed. augm. d'un examen de la philosophie d'Homere par M. Guill. de Rochefort. L'Odyssee d'Homere, trad. en vers, par le meme, suivie d'une dis. sur les voyages d'Ulysse (French). *Translator or author:* Guillaume Dubois de Rochefort. Paris, France.

1773—Bacchus, oder die Seerauber, aus dem Griechischen des Homer (in Belustigungen fur allerlei Leser) (German). Leipzig, Germany.

1773—Fables Antient and Modern; translated into verse from Homer [Book I], Ovid, Baccace and Chaucer; with original poems (English). *Translator or author:* John Dryden. London, England: T. et al. Davies.

1773—The Iliad of Homer; translated; 2nd ed. (English). *Translator or author:* James Macpherson. London, England: T. Becket; P. A. De Hondt.

1773—The Iliad of Homer; 2nd ed. (English). *Translator or author:* James Macpherson. Dublin, Ireland: Thomas Ewing.

1773—The Iliad and Odyssey [in series: British Poets] (English). *Translator or author:* Alexander Pope.

1773—The Iliad (English). *Translator or author:* Alexander Pope. Edinburgh, Scotland: J. Robertson.

1773—The Odyssey of Homer (English). *Translator or author:* Alexander Pope. Edinburgh, Scotland: J. Robertson.

1774—Homeri Ilias [edited by Samuel Clarke; reprint of the 1729–40 edition]. Oxford, England.

1774—Homeri Ilias; 8th ed. [edited by Samuel Clarke]. London, England: Charles Rivington.

1774—Fables Antient and Modern; translated into verse from Homer [Book I], Ovid, Baccace and Chaucer; with original poems (English).

Translator or author: John Dryden. London, England: T. et al. Davies.

1774—The Iliad and Odyssey (English). *Translator or author:* Alexander Pope.

1774—The Iliad of Homer (English). *Translator or author:* Alexander Pope. Aberdeen, Scotland: John Boyle.

1774—Homeri Batrachomyomachia; Griechisch und Deutsch (von Willamovitz (Greek; German). *Translator or author:* Willamovitz. Petersburg and Leipzig, Germany: Breitkopf.

1775—The Beauties of Homer Selected from the Iliad (Greek). Oxford, England: J. and J. Fletcher (sold by J&J Rivington in London).

1775—Der Frosch- und Mausekrieg; ein scherzhaftes Heldengedicht aus dem Griechischen in Prosa ubersetzt, mit beigefugten Anmerkungen (in Leipzig Musen-Almanach) (German). *Translator or author:* Theophilus Calestinus Piper. Leipzig, Germany.

1775–76—The Odyssey; translated from the Greek (English). *Translator or author:* Alexander Pope. London, England: Bernard Lintot.

1775–87—L'Iliade di Omero; recato dal testo Greco in versi Toscani (Italian). *Translator or author:* Hyac. Ceruti. Torino (Turin), Italy: Brislo.

1776—Gnomiai Homerikai. Schweden [location?]: Biorckegranianis.

1776—Fr. Xav. Alegrii Ilias, Latino Carm. Expressa; acc. ejd. Alexandrias s. de expugnatione Tyri ab Alexandro Macedone LL.IV [reprint of edition printed in Pesaro in 1776] (Latin). *Translator or author:* Xav. Alegrius. Bonn, Germany.

1776—Homers Ilias, sechster Gesang; ubersetzt (in Deutscher Merkur) (German). *Translator or author:* Gottfried August Burger.

1776—Homers Ilias; funfter Gesang; ubersetzt (in Deutsches Museum) (German). *Translator or author:* Gottfried August Burger.

1776—Iliade; traduccion (Italian). *Translator or author:* Ceruti. Venice, Italy.

1776—Homeri Ilias; Latinis Versibus Expressa a Raym. Cunichio (Latin). *Translator or author:* Raymundo Cunichio. Rome, Italy: Zempel.

1776—Fables Antient and Modern; translated into verse from Homer [Book I], Ovid, Baccace and Chaucer; with original poems (English). *Translator or author:* John Dryden. Glasgow, Scotland: Andreas Foulis.

1776—Le Commencement de l'Iliade; traduit en vers Francois (French). *Translator or author:* St. Ange Ferian. Paris, France.

1776—Der zwanzigste Gesang der Ilias (in Deutsche Museum) (German). *Translator or author:* F. L. Graf. Stolberg, Germany.

1776—Les Adieux d'Hector et d'Andomache (French). *Translator or author:* Gruet. Paris, France.

1776—L'Iliade d'Homere [1st edition by this translator] (French). *Translator or author:* Charles-Francois Lebrun. Paris, France.

1776—Traduction d'un Morceau du 24 Chant de l'Iliade, Priam qui redemande le corps d'Hector (French). *Translator or author:* J. R. T. de Maizieres. Rheims, France.

1776—Les Adieux d'Hector et d'Andromaque: Iliade d'Homere, Livre Vie; piece qui a partage le prix de l'Academic Francoise en 1776 (French). *Translator or author:* Murville. Paris, France: Demonville.

1776—Priam aux Pieds d'Achille; morceau tire du 24 livre de l'Iliade (French). *Translator or author:* Doigne de Ponceau. Paris, France.

1776—The Odyssey of Homer [reprint of the 1725–26 edition] (English). *Translator or author:* Alexander Pope. Frankfurt am Main, Germany: J. G. Garbe.

1776—Extracts [by William Holwell Carr] from Mr. Pope's Translation Corresponding with the Beauties of Homer (English). *Translator or author:* Alexander Pope. Oxford, Engand;London, England: J. and J. Fletcher (sold by J&J Rivington in London).

1776—L'Iliade di Omero; tradotta in versi sciolti e la Batracomiomachia in ottave da Cristof. Ridolfi (Italian). *Translator or author:* Cristof. Ridolfi. Venice, Italy.

1776—L'Iliade (French). *Translator or author:* Jean Jacques Rousseau. Paris, France.

1776—L'Odissea; trad. (Italian). *Translator or author:* P. G. Salimbeni. Naples, Italy: Morelli.

1776–77—Homeri Odyssea; una cum Batrachomyomachia, Hymnis et Epigrammatibus, Graece et Latine, cura I. G. Hageri (Greek; Latin). Chemnitz, Germany.

1777—Homeri Odyssea: Batrachomyomachia, Hymni, & Epigrammata, Graece et Latine; Graeca ad principen H. Stephani, ut & ad primam, omnium Demetrii Chalcondylae editionem atque insuper ad codd. mss. sunt excussa; ex Latiniis

iditis selecta sunt optima, verum ita (Greek; Latin). Padova (Padua), Italy: Joannes Manfre; Typis Seminarii.

1777—The Iliad of Homer (English). *Translator or author:* Alexander Pope. London, England: J Buckland; T. Longman.

1777—The Iliad (English). *Translator or author:* Alexander Pope. Edinburgh, Scotland: Charles Elliot.

1777—L'Iliade et l'Odyssee d'Homere (French). *Translator or author:* Guillaume Dubois de Rochefort. Paris, France: Brunet.

1777—Odusseus Erzahlung von dem Kuklopen aus dem neunten Gesang der Odyssee von J. H. Voss (in Deutsches Museum) (German). *Translator or author:* Johann Heinrich Voss.

1777—Homeri Odyssea; Latinis versibus expressa a Bernardo Zamagna, Ragusino (Latin). *Translator or author:* Ben. Zamagna. Senis [location?]: Pazzini Caroli Fratres.

1778—Homeri Ilias, Graece [edited by Samuel Clarke; reprint of the 1747 edition] (Greek; Latin). Glasgow, Scotland: Andreas Foulis.

1778—The Odyssey of Homer [reprint of the 1725–26 edition] (English). *Translator or author:* Alexander Pope; W. Broome; E. Fenton.

1778—Homers Werke; aus dem Griechischen ubersetzt von dem Dichter der Noachide (German). *Translator or author:* Johann Jakob Bodmer. Zurich, Switzerland: Orell.

1778—L'Odissea d'Omero; trad. in ottava rima da Gius. Bozoli [reprint of the 1772 edition] (Italian). *Translator or author:* Guiseppe Bozoli. Mantova (Mantua), Italy.

1778—Dell' Iliade (Italian). *Translator or author:* Giacomo Casanova. Venice, Italy: Modesto Fenzo.

1778—The Odyssey of Homer (English). *Translator or author:* Alexander Pope. Edinburgh, Scotland: Charles Elliot.

1778—The Odyssey of Homer (English). *Translator or author:* Alexander Pope. Edinburgh, Scotland: Alexander Donaldson.

1778—The Iliad of Homer (English). *Translator or author:* Alexander Pope. Edinburgh, Scotland: Alexander Donaldson.

1778—The Odyssey of Homer (English). *Translator or author:* Alexander Pope. Aberdeen, Scotland: John Boyle.

1778—Homers Ilias; verdeutscht (German). *Translator or author:* Friedrich Leopold Graf zu Stolberg. Flensburg and Leipzig, Germany: Korte.

1779—Homeri Ilias et Odyssea, nec non Batrachomyomachia, Hymni, Epigrammata; 9th ed. [edited by Samuel Clarke] (Greek, Latin). London, England.

1779—Auserlesene Stellen der Iliade; ubersetzt, metrisch und prosaisch (in Allgem. Deut. Bibl.) (German) .

1779—Homeri Opera, Graece et Latine; ad optimas editiones expressa (Greek; Latin). Basel, Switzerland: Eman. Thurneisen.

1779—Oeuvres d'Homere (French). *Translator or author:* Anne LeFevre Dacier. Geneva, Switzerland: Du Villard Fils and Nouffer.

1779—The Poetical Works of Elijah Fenton; with the life of the author (English). *Translator or author:* Elijah Fenton. Edinburgh, Scotland: at the Apollo Press Martins.

1779—The First Book of Homer's Iliad [reprint of the 1715 edition; in series: Johnson's Works of the English Poets] (English). *Translator or author:* Thomas Ticknell.

1779–81—Hymn to Venus (English). *Translator or author:* William Congreve.

1779–81—The Iliad and Odyssey [reprint of the 1715–20, 1725–26 editions; in series: Johnson's Works of the English Poets (English). *Translator or author:* Alexander Pope.

1780—Homeri Hymnus in Cererem (Greek). Leiden (Leyden), Netherlands: Samuel and Joann. Luchtmans.

1780—Iliados; in usum scholarum Belgicae (Greek). Brussels, Belgium: Typis Regiae Academiae.

1780—La Ulyxea de Homero (Polish). Warsaw, Poland.

1780—Homeri Ilias, Odyssea, Batrachomyomachia, etc.; Graece, cum scholiis pseudepigraphis Didymi (Greek). Oxford, England: Clarendon Press.

1780—Homeri Ilias et Odyssea. Graece cum scholiis pseudepigraphis Didymo (Greek). Oxford, England: Clarendon Press.

1780—Auserlesene Ubersetzungen aus Homers Werken (German). Frankfurt am Main, Germany.

1780—Probe der verdeutschten Odyssee, nebst Ankundigung (German). *Translator or author:* L. T. Kosegarten.

1780—Homers Hymnus an Damatar (in Deitscher Musenalmanach) (German). *Translator or author:* Ch. Graf zu Stolberg.

1780–85—L'Iliade et l'Odyssee d'Homere; traduit et avec des remarques sur Homere (French). *Translator or author:* Paul Jeremie Bitaube. Paris, France.

1781—L'Iliade d'Homere; traduite en vers Francois par le baron de Beaumanoir (Greek, French). *Translator or author:* Beaumanoir. Paris, France.

1781—Homer's Hymn to Ceres; translated into English verse (English). *Translator or author:* Richard Hole. London, England: Dilly.

1781—Homer's Hymn to Ceres (English). *Translator or author:* Richard Hole. Exeter, England: B. Thorn and Son.

1781—Aus dem ersten Buch der Ilias; ubersetzt (in Ephem. Inscr. Der Greis) (German). *Translator or author:* Klopstock.

1781—Homers Ilias; ubersetzt (German). *Translator or author:* C. A. Kuttner. Leipzig, Germany: Dyk.

1781—Homers Odyssee, sechster Gesang; eine metrische Ubersetzung (German). *Translator or author:* Gli. Ch. O. Link. Altdorf, Germany.

1781—Homer's Hymn to Ceres; translated into English verse, with notes critical and illustrative; to which is prefixed a translation of the preface of the editor, D. Ruhnkenius (English). *Translator or author:* Robert Lucas. London, England: J. Robson.

1781—Homeri Batrachomyomachia, Graece; ad veterum exemplarium fidem recusa; glossa Graece; variantibus lectionibus, versionibus Latinis et commentariis, nec non indicibus illustrata; 2nd ed. (Greek). *Translator or author:* Mich. Maittaire. London, England.

1781—Homers Odyssee; 1st ed. (German). *Translator or author:* Johann Heinrich Voss. Basel, Switzerland: Birkhauser.

1781—Homers Odussee; ubersetzt (German). *Translator or author:* Johann Heinrich Voss. Hamburg, Germany.

1781–82—L'Iliade d'Homere; trad. en vers avec des remarques et un discours sur Homere; nouv. ed. augm. d'un examen de la philosophie d'Homere par M. Guill. de Rochefort. L'Odyssee d'Homere, trad. en vers, par le meme, suivie d'une diss. sur les voyages d'Ulysse (French). *Translator or author:* Guillaume Dubois de Rochefort. Paris, France.

1781–87—Homers Iliade; von neuem metrisch ubersetzt (German). *Translator or author:* E. Wilh. De Wobeser. Leipzig, Germany: Kummer.

1781–93—Homers Werke; in zwei Banden (German). *Translator or author:* Johann Heinrich Voss. Stuttgart, Germany: J. G. Cotta Buchhandlung.

1782—Opera (Greek). Oxford, England.

1782—[H]omerou Ilias; 3rd ed. (English). London, England: Johannes Hayes.

1782—Homeri Hymnus in Cererem; nunc primum editus a Dav. Ruhnkenio; accedunt duae epistolae criticae ex editione altera multis partibus locupletiore (Greek, Latin). Leiden (Leyden), Netherlands: Samuel and Joann. Luchtmans.

1782—Homer XXX Humnen aus dem Griechischen ubersetzt (in Gedichte) (German). *Translator or author:* Ch. Graf zu Stolberg. Hamburg, Germany.

1782—Erster, zweiter und dritter Gesang aus Homers Odyssee, ubersetzt (German). *Translator or author:* Vincent. Munich, Germany: Coppenrath.

1782–85—Nouvelle traduction de l'Iliade (French). *Translator or author:* L. G. R. Cordier de Launay-Valeris. Paris, France: Theoph. Barrois.

1783—Ilias, Latinis Versibus Expressa [reprint of the 1776 edition] (Latin). Rome, Italy: Zempel.

1783—Homeri Odyssea Latinis Versibus; expressa a Ben. Zamagna, ragusino [reprint of 1777 edition] (Latin). *Translator or author:* Ben. Zamagna. Vienna, Austria.

1783—Homers Iliade, erster Gesang, v. 1–304; funfter Gesang, v. 1–296; sechster Gesang, v. 1–65; ubersetzt (in Sammlung der Besten Zerstreuten Ubersetzungen) (German). *Translator or author:* Gottfried August Burger.

1783—The Iliad and Odyssey of Homer [reprint of the 1715–20, 1725–26 editions] (English). *Translator or author:* Alexander Pope. London, England.

1783—L'Iliade; trad. (French). *Translator or author:* Rochefort. Paris, France.

1783—Iliadis Libri I et II; cum paraphrasi Graeca, hucusque ined. et Graecorum veteribus commentariis magnum partem nunc primum in lucem prodeunti ed. Ever. Wassenbergh (Greek). *Translator or author:* Ever. Wassenbergh. Frankfurt am Main, Germany.

1784—Odyssea, Latinis Versibus Expressa a

Ragusino [reprint of 1777 edition] (Latin). Senis [location?]: Fr. Carli.

1784—Homeri Odyssea cum Batrachomyomachia, Hymnisque, Ceterisque Poematiis Homero; vulgo tributis etiam nuper reperto Hymno in Cererem ad exemplar maxime Glasg. In usum Scholarum diligentissime expressa (cura F. A. Wolfii) (Greek). Halle an der Saale, Germany: Orphan.

1784—Homers Ilias, Erster bis Vierter Gesang (in Journal von und fur Deutschland) (German) .

1784—Homers Ilias; ad exemplar maxime Glasgoviense, in usum scholarum diligentissime expressa (cura F. A. Wolfii). Halle an der Saale, Germany: Orphan.

1784—Homeri Ilias Latinis versibus expressa a Raym. Cunichio [reprint of 1776 edition printed at Rome] (Latin). *Translator or author:* Raym. Cunichio. Vienna, Austria.

1784—L'Iliade d'Homere; traduite en vers Francois, avec des remarques a la fin de chaque chant par M. Dobremes (French). *Translator or author:* M. Dobremes. Paris, France: Cabinet du Roi.

1784—Batracomiomachia; volgarizz. in versi sciolti (Italian). *Translator or author:* Fel. Fontana. Milan, Italy.

1784—Oeuvres Completes d'Homere; traduit en Francois par A. Gin; avec des notes historiques, geographiques, et litteraires, dont la partie qui rapproche la geographie ancienne des noms modernes a ete dirigee par M. Mentelle, suivie des imitations des poetes a (French). *Translator or author:* A. Gin. Paris, France: Servieres.

1784—The Iliad of Homer [reprint of the 1715–20 edition] (English). *Translator or author:* Alexander Pope. London, England.

1784—Homers Frosch- und Mausekrieg (in Deutsches Museum) (German). *Translator or author:* Ch. Graf von Stolberg.

1784—Batrachomyomachie, die blutige und muthige Schlacht der Mause und Frosche, mit Fleisse beschrieben und lustig zu lesen (German). *Translator or author:* J. H. Woltersdorf. Hamburg, Germany.

1784–85—Traduction de l'Iliade; nouvelle edition, revue, corrigee, augmentee des plusiers notes par l'auteur, et precedee de Recherches historiques et philosophiques sur Homere (French). *Translator or author:* L. G. R. Cordier de Launay-Valery. Paris, France: chez Laurent Valade.

1784–90—Homeri Ilias; cum variis lectionibus et

notis A. Herm. Niemeyer. Halle an der Saale, Germany: Gebauer.

1785— Homeri Ilias [edited by Samuel Clarke; reprint of the 1729–40 edition]. London, England.

1785— Homeri Odyssea; cura I. G. Hageri (Greek; Latin). Chemnitz, Germany.

1785— Traduction de l'Iliade (French). *Translator or author:* L. G. R. Cordier de Launay-Valery. Paris, France.

1785— La Ulyxea de Homero; repartida en 13 libros, traduzida en romance Castellano, por Goncalo Perez [reprint of the 1553 Venice edition] (Spanish). *Translator or author:* Gonzalo Perez. Madrid, Spain.

1785— Volgarizzamento del Inno a Cerere con testo Greco (Greek; Italian). *Translator or author:* Ippolito Pindemonte. Bassano, Italy.

1786— Homers Ilias; im Auszuge. Curia, Germany.

1786— Homeri Ilias, I–VI r Gesang; Griechisch mit Anmerkungen und einem vollstandigen Worterbuch zum Gebr. Der Schulen herausgegeben von Casp. Conr. Brohm (Greek). Stendal, Germany: Franz.

1786— Homeri Graecorum Poetarum Clarissimi Yliadum Opus per Pindarum Thebanum; e Greco in Latinum traductum (in Wernsforfii Poetis Lat. Min.).

1786— Oeuvres completes d'Homere; traduction nouvelle, dediee au roi; avec des notes ... suivies des imitations des poetes anciens et modernes par A. Gin [only contains The Iliad] (French). *Translator or author:* A. Gin. Paris, France: Ambrosio Firmin Didot.

1786–88— L'Iliade et l'Odyssee d'Homere; traduit etc. avec des remarques sur Homere [reprint of 1780–85 edition] (French). *Translator or author:* Paul Jeremie Bitaube. Paris, France.

1786–94— L'Iliade d'Omero;recata poeticamente in verso sciolto Ital. dal abb. Mich. Cesaiotti insieme col volgarizzamento litterale dal testo in prosa, ampiamente ellustr. da una scelta dell osservaz. orig. de' piu celebri critici antichi e moderni e da quelle (Italian). *Translator or author:* Melchiorre Cesarotti. Padova (Padua), Italy: Penada.

1787— Homeri Ilias [edited by Samuel Clarke] (Greek; Latin). Dublin, Ireland.

1787— Ilias. *Translator or author:* Ceruti. Torino (Turin), Italy.

1787— Homeri Hymnus in Cererem; ad codicum mosq. denuo collatum recensuit et animadversionibus illustravit Cha. W. Mitscherlich. *Translator or author:* Ch. W. Mitscherlich. Leipzig, Germany: Weidmann.

1787— Homers Ilias; verdeutscht [reprint of the 1778 edition] (German). *Translator or author:* Friedrich Leopold Graf zu Stolberg. Flensburg and Leipzig, Germany: Korte.

1787— Los Quatro Primeros Libros de la Iliada (in Colecion de Obras en Verso y Prosa) (Spanish). *Translator or author:* Th. De Yriarte. Madrid, Spain.

1787–88— L'Iliade et l'Odyssee; avec des remarques sur Homere (French). *Translator or author:* Paul Jeremie Bitaube. Paris, France: Didot l'Aine.

1788— Francisci Xaverii Alegre Mexicani Veracrucensis Homeri Ilias Latino Carmine Expressa (Latin). Rome, Italy: Tipographum Vaticanum Salvionem.

1788— Initia Homerica; sive excerpta ex Iliade Homeri, eum locorum omnium Graeca metaphrase, ex codicibus Bodleianis et novi collegii Mss. Maiorem in partem nunc primum edita Thomas Burgess (Greek). Oxford, Engand;London, England: Prince; Elmsley.

1788— Homerus Iliassa; forditasanak peldajat Kiadta Molnar Janos Tudos Szepesi Kanonok a Magyar Musaeum (Hungarian). Kotet. [Hungary?]: Gyorb.

1788— Ilias, Graece; ad vet. codicis Veneti fidem recensita; scholia in eam antiquissima ex. eod. cod. aliisque nunc primum edidit cum asteriscis, obeliscis aliisque signis criticis J. Bapt. Casp. d'Ansse de Villoison (Greek). Venice, Italy: Coleti.

1788— Fr. Xav. Alegrii Ilias; Latin carm. expressa; acc. ejd. Alexandrias s. de expugnatione Tyri ab Alexandro Macedone LL.IV [reprint of the 1776 edition] (Latin). *Translator or author:* Xav. Alegrius. Venice, Italy.

1788— Omero in Lombardia [idiom of dialects of northern Italy]; dell' abb. Franc. Boaretti; Iliade tomi II (Italian). *Translator or author:* Francesco Boaretti. Venice, Italy: Dom. Fracassi.

1788— La Batracomiomachia di Homero; volgarizzata da Ant. Lavagnoli, si aggiungono due Elegie di Callilmaco, volgarizzate d'un altro traduttore [based on the edition printed in Venice in 1744] (Italian). *Translator or author:* Ant. Lavagnoli. Verona, Italy: Romangini.

1788— La Iliada de Homero, traducida del Griego

en verso Castellano (Spanish). *Translator or author:* Ignacio Garcia Malo. Madrid, Spain: Castilla.

1788— Homer's Hymn to Venus, translated from the Greek, with notes (English). *Translator or author:* Is. Rittson. London, England: Johnson.

1788— La Guerra di Topi e di Ranocchi; poema eroi-comico (Italian). *Translator or author:* Andr. Di Sarto. Florence, Italy.

1788–93— Ilias; cum excerptis ex Eustathii commentariis et scholiis minoribus [issued in 24 parts (1 for each book) from 1788 to 1813, each part titled in the form: Iliados Rhapsodia xx, Sive Libri yy]. *Translator or author:* Johann August Muller. Meissen, Germany: F. W. Goedsche.

1789— Iliade de Omero; tradotta in compendio ed in prosa (Italian). Rome, Italy.

1789— Homeri Ilias [edited by Samuel Clarke; reprint of the 1729–40 edition]. London, England.

1789— Die Batrachomyomachie und Galeomyomachie, griechisch, mit einer Einleitung, Anmerkungen, und einem Wortregister fur junge Leute von A. Ch. Borheck (Greek). *Translator or author:* Borbeck. Lemgo, Germany: Meyer.

1789— Oeuvres complettes d'Homere; traduit en Francois par A. Gin; avec des notes historiques, geographiques, et litteraires, dont la partie qui rapproche la geographie ancienne des noms modernes a ete dirigee par M. Mentelle, suivie des imitations des poetes a (French). *Translator or author:* A. Gin. Paris, France: Didot.

1789— Homera Batrachomyomachia; czyli Bitwa zab z Myszami wierszem oyczystym wylozona przez Jacka Przybylskiego (Polish). *Translator or author:* Hiacynth. Przybylskiego. Krakow, Poland.

1789— Homers Odussee (German). *Translator or author:* Johann Heinrich Voss. Vienna, Austria.

1789— Odusseus und Menelaus, IL. III. 191–224; der Mauerkampf, Il. XII 417 sqq; der Schild des Achilleus, Il. XVIII, 468; ubersetzt (in Musenalmanach) (German). *Translator or author:* Johann Heinrich Voss.

1789–94— Homeri Ilias, Odyssea, etc., Graece et Latine; ad codicem Vindobonensem expressae; recensuit Fr. -Car. Alter; cum varietate lectionis ex codicibus vindobon (Greek; Latin). *Translator or author:* Car. Alter. Vienna, Austria: Trattner.

1790— Ilias [edited by Samuel Clarke] (Greek, Latin). London, England.

1790— Eine Stelle aus dem achtzehnten Gesang der Ilias v. 468–489; ubersetzt (German). *Translator or author:* F. Sav. Grater.

1790—(English). *Translator or author:* Alexander Pope. Edinburgh, Scotland.

1790— L'Odyssea d'Omero; transp. in Ottava rima (Italian). *Translator or author:* Bali Greg. Redi. Rome, Italy: Prato.

1790—[H]e tou [H]omerou Odysseia Rapsod. A = Homers Odyssee, Ir Gesang, herausgegeben und erklart von C. S[tolzenburg]; ein Versuch (Greek; German). *Translator or author:* C. Stolzenburg. Leipzig, Germany: Crusius.

1790— The First Book of Homer's Iliad [reprint of 1715 and 1779 editions; in series: Johnson's Works of the English Poets] (English). *Translator or author:* Thomas Ticknell.

1790— Probe einer Ubersetzung der Ilias (neunter Gesang) (in Neues Deutsches Museum) (German). *Translator or author:* Johann Heinrich Voss.

1791— Hymni Homerici cum Reliquis Carminibus Minoribus Homero Tribui Solitis et Batrachomyomachia; addita est Demetrii Zeni versio Batrachomyomachiae dialecto vulgari et Theodori Prodromi Galeomyomachia; textum recensuit et animadversionibus criticis illustravi. Halle an der Saale, Germany: Schwetschke Hemmerde.

1791— The Iliad and Odyssey of Homer, to which is added, The Battle of the Frogs and Mice; translated into English blank verse; the Battle of the Frogs and the Mice translated into English blank verse by the same hand (English). *Translator or author:* William Cowper. London, England: J. Johnson.

1791— Iliada Homera; przekladania (Polish). *Translator or author:* Francziskiego Xaweriusa Dmochowskiego. Warsaw, Poland.

1791— Inni di Omero; volgarizz. (Italian). *Translator or author:* Gius. Pagnini. Pistoia, Italy.

1791— The New History of the Trojan Wars and Troy's Destruction (English). *Translator or author:* Elkanah Settle. Berwick, England: W. Pharson.

1792— The Iliad and Odyssey (Greek). *Translator or author:* William Cowper. Dublin, Ireland.

1792— The First Book of the Iliad of Homer; verbally rendered into English verse; being a specimen of a new translation of the poet; with critical annotations (English). *Translator or author:* Alexander Geddes. London, England: Debrett.

1792— The Iliad of Homer (English). *Translator or author:* Alexander Pope. Edinburgh, Scotland.

1792—The Iliad of Homer; translated into English (English). *Translator or author:* William Tremenheere. London, England: Faulder.

1792–97—Homeri Ilias, Odyssea, Batrachomyomachia et Hymni, Graece cum Scholiis Didymi (Greek). Oxford, England.

1793—Homerocentra, sive Homerici Centones, etc., Graece et Latine; denuo edidit L. H. Teucherus (Greek; Latin). Leipzig, Germany.

1793—Opere di Omero; tradotte (Italian). *Translator or author:* Giacinto Ceruti; Gius. Bossoli. Venice, Italy: Zatta.

1793—Batracomiomachia; trad. in versi Milanesi col testo al fronte (Italian). *Translator or author:* P. Garioni. Milan, Italy.

1793—Homers Ilias; verdeutscht (German). *Translator or author:* Friedrich Leopold Graf zu Stolberg. Flensburg and Leipzig, Germany: Korte.

1793—Homers Werke; in zwei Banden (German). *Translator or author:* Johann Heinrich Voss. Stuttgart, Germany: J. G. Cotta Buchhandlung.

1793—Homers Werke [1st edition of this translator] (German). *Translator or author:* Johann Heinrich Voss. Altona, Germany.

1794—Homeri Odysseae Rhapsodia A; cum integris scholiis minoribus edidit I. A. Muller. Hamburg, Germany: Vollmer.

1794—Inni di Omero trad. (Italian). Venice, Italy.

1794—Ilias; 12th ed. [edited by Samuel Clarke] (Greek, Latin). London, England.

1794—Homeri et Homeridarum Opera et Reliquiae; ex veterum criticorum notationibus optimorumque exempl. fide rec. F.A. Wolf [2nd ed.] (Greek; Latin). Halle an der Saale, Germany: Orphan.

1794—Der Schild des Achilles aus dem achtzehnten Buche (in Hesiods Schild) (German). *Translator or author:* J. D. Hartmann.

1794—The New History of the Trojan Wars, and Troy's Destruction; in three books (English). *Translator or author:* Elkanah Settle. Philadelphia, PA: M. Carey.

1795—Ubersetzung des Homerischen Hymnus auf den Apoll (in Horen) (German).

1795—Traduction de l'Iliade; nouvelle edition, revue, corrigee et augmentee des plusieurs notes par l'auteur (French). *Translator or author:* L. G. R. Cordier de Launay-Valery. Paris, France: Michel.

1795—The Iliad of Homer; translated from the Greek (English). *Translator or author:* Alexander Pope. Philadelphia, Pa.: J. Crukshank.

1796—Batrachomyomachie (French).

1796—L'Iliade et l'Odyssee d'Homere; traduites en Francois; avec des remarques sur Homere [3rd ed.; reprint of 1780–85 edition] (French). *Translator or author:* Paul Jeremie Bitaube. Lyon, France.

1796—Opuscules d'Homere; traduction nouvelle par J. M. L. Coupe [contains Batrachomyomachia and 27 Hymns] (French). *Translator or author:* Elisabeth Sopie Cheron. Paris, France: Giffart and Honnert.

1796—Hymni Homerici; cum reliquis carminibus minoribus Homero tribui solitis, et Batrachomyomachia; addita est Demetrii Zeni versio Batrachomyomachiae dialecto vulgari, et Theodori Prodromi Galeomyomachia; textum recensuit et animadversionibut (Greek). *Translator or author:* C. D. Jlgen. Halle an der Saale, Germany.

1796—The Iliad and Odyssey of Homer; a new edition with additional notes, critical and illustrative by Gilbert Wakefield (English). *Translator or author:* Alexander Pope. London, England: Longman.

1796—Hymne an Aphrodite (in Gedichte) (German). *Translator or author:* H. W. F. Uelzen. Bremen, Germany.

1797—Ilias, Odysseia, Batrachomyomachia et Hymni, Graece, cum Scholiis Didymi (Greek). Oxford, England.

1797—A Burlesque Translation of Homer, in Verse; 4th ed. [from the 1762 edition] (English). *Translator or author:* Thomas Brydges. London, England.

1797—The Odyssey; translated into English prose, as literally as the different idioms of the Greek and English languages will allow; with explanatory notes; by a member of the University of Oxford [a burlesque translation] (English). *Translator or author:* Henry Francis Cary. Oxford: T. A. Buckley.

1797—Hymnus an den Hermes, ubersetzt (in Lyceum der schonen Kunste) (German). *Translator or author:* F. A. Eschen. Berlin, Germany.

1797—Hymne an die Erde, ubersetzt (in Allgem. Geschichte d. Poesie) (German). *Translator or author:* I. D. Hartmann.

1797—Homeri Batrachomyomachia; la guerre des grenouilles et des souris d'Homere, traduite, mot pour mot, de la version Latine d'Etienne Berglere, imprimee vis-a-vis; par Mr. Franc Cohen de Kentish Town, age de huit ans (auhourdhui Sir Franc. Palgrave); a quoi. *Translator or author:* Frank Palgrave. London, England: M. Pope.

1797— The Iliad and Odyssey of Homer; translated by Pope, with additional notes by G. Wakefield (English). *Translator or author:* Alexander Pope. London, England.

1798— Homeri Iliados Rhapsodia I. Hafn: Laur. Sahl.

1798— Hymnus an den Delischen Apoll, von einem Ungenanntem (in Neuer deut. Merkur) (German).

1798— Homeri Ilias Prima; Graece et Latine ex recensione Sam. Clarkii; adiecta clave Sam. Patrik.; edition noua. Havn: Pelt.

1798— L'Iliade d'Omero (Italian).

1798— Die Batrachomyomachie und Geleomyomachie, Griechisch mit ein. Einl., Anmerk. u. e. Wortreg. von A. Ch. Borheck (Greek). *Translator or author:* A. Ch. Borheck. Lemgo, Germany.

1798— Der Froschmausekampf; aus dem Griechischen (in Berlinische Blatt) (German). *Translator or author:* F. A. Eschen. Berlin, Germany.

1798— Hymnos an Dionysos (oder die Rauber) (in Berliner Blatt m. Mart.) (German). *Translator or author:* F. A. Eschen. Berlin, Germany.

1798–02— Iliade d'Omero; volgarizzata litteralmenta in prosa e recata poeticamente in verso sciolto Ital. da Melch. Cesarotti [reprint of the 1786–94 edition] (Spanish). *Translator or author:* Melchiorre Cesarotti. Padova (Padua), Italy: Brandolese.

1799— Homer's Battle of the Frogs and Mice [reprint of the 1717 edition] (English). Dublin, Ireland: Thomas Hume.

1799— Odyssea [edited by Samuel Clarke] (Greek, Latin). Glasgow, Scotland.

1799— An die Musen und Apollo; an Aphrodite; an Dionysos; an Artemis; an die Mutter aller (in Schilleri Musenalmanach) (German). *Translator or author:* F. A. Eschen. Tubingen, Germany.

1799— Erster Gesang der Ilias des Homers ubersetzt in Deutschen Hexametern (German). *Translator or author:* J. Jak. Hofmann. Erlang, Germany: Junge.

1800— Homeri Odyssea, Graece et Latine; ad praestantissimas editiones expressa (Greek; Latin). Upsalla.

1800— [H]omerou Ilias kai Odysseia; estin alethos basilikon pragma [h]e [H]omerou poiesis; ex ergasteriou tupogr. Akademias tes en Oxonia (Greek). Oxford, England.

1800— Iliade; vingt-quatre grandes compositions (French). Paris, France: Maison Quantin.

1800— Homeri Ilias et Odyssea, Graece (editio impensis CC. Buckingham et Grenville excusa, curis Th. Grenville, R. Porson, Randolph, Cleaver et Rogers (Greek). *Translator or author:* D. D. Buckingham; et al. Oxford, England: Clarendon Press.

1800— Iliada Homera; przeklad (Polish). *Translator or author:* Franciszek Ksawery Dmochowski. Warsaw, Poland.

1800— Nouvelle traduction de l'Iliade [reprint of the 1782 edition] (French). *Translator or author:* L. G. R. Cordier de Launay-Valery. Paris, France.

1800— The Iliad and Odyssey [reprint of the 1715–20, 1725–26 editions] (English). *Translator or author:* Alexander Pope.

1800— Homers Froschmausekampg (in Bluthen griech. Dichter) (German). *Translator or author:* F. K. L. Frnhn. Von Seckendorf. Weimar, Germany.

1800— Homers Odyssee (German). *Translator or author:* Johann Heinrich Voss. Vienna, Austria; Prague, Chechoslavakia: F. Haas.

1800–13— Opere [chpts. 6–16 are La Iliade di Omero] (Italian). *Translator or author:* Melchiorre Cesarotti. Pisa, Italy: Tipografia della Societa Lett.

1800–75— Homer: The Iliad (English). *Translator or author:* William Lucas Collins. Philadelphia, Pa.: J. B. Lippincott.

II. Printed Editions of the Homeric Texts, 1470 to 2000 C.E.

214

1801–1850

1801— Homers Werke (German). Stuttgart, Germany: J. G. Cotta Buchhandlung.

1801— L'Iliade et l'Odyssee (French).

1801— Homere Grec, Latin, Francois; ou, oeuvres completes d'Homere, accompagnees de la traduction Francoise, de la version interlineaire Latine et suivies d'observ. litt. et crit. et de la clef d'Homere per J. B. Gail (Greek, Latin, French). *Translator or author:* Jean-Baptiste Gail. Paris, France.

1801— Homerowa Iliada; Zpew prwnf od J. Nejedleho (Bohemian). *Translator or author:* J. Nejedleho. Praze [location?].

1801— Iliad and Odyssey; new edition (English). *Translator or author:* Alexander Pope. London, England: J. Johnson.

1801— [H]omerou Ilias kai Odysseia; estin alethas [h]asilikon pragmae [H]omerou poiesis (Greek). *Translator or author:* Richard Porson. Oxford, England: Ergasteriou typographikou.

1801— Select translations from the works of Homer [Iliad] and Horace; with original poems (English). *Translator or author:* Gilbert Thompson.

1802— Homeri Ilias; 13th ed. [edited by Samuel Clarke] (Latin). London, England: John and Paul Knapton.

1802— Homeri Ilias, Graece et Latine; annotationes in usum serenissimi principis Gulielmi Augusti, ducis de Cumberland etc. [edited by Samuel Clarke] (Greek, Latin). London, England: Luc. Hansard.

1802— [H]omerou Ilias; syn tois scholiois pseudepigraphois Didymou (Greek). Oxford, England.

1802— Homeri Ilias, Graece et Latine; annotationes... [edited by Samuel Clarke] (Greek, Latin). London, England: Bye and Law.

1802— L'Iliade; volgarizzata litteralmente in prose e recata poeticamente in verso da Melsh. Cesarott, ediz. 2nd, coll'aggiunta del testo Greco [reprint of the 1786–94 edition] (Spanish). *Translator or author:* Melchiorre Cesarotti. Padova (Padua), Italy.

1802— L'Iliade d'Omero recata poeticamente in verso sciolto ital. dal abb. Mich. Cesarotti insieme col volgarizzamento letterale dal testo in prosa, ampiamente ellustr. da una scelta dell osservaz. orig. de' piu celebri critici antichi e moderni e da quelle (Italian). *Translator or author:* Melchiorre Cesarotti. Pisa, Italy.

1802— L'Iliade d'Omero recata poeticamente in verso sciolto ital. dal abb. Mich. Cesarotti insieme col volgarizzamento letterale dal testo in prosa, ampiamente ellustr. da una scelta dell osservaz. orig. de' piu celebri critici antichi e moderni e da quelle (Italian). *Translator or author:* Melchiorre Cesarotti. Padova (Padua), Italy.

1802— The Iliad and the Odyssey of Homer; translated into English blank verse; second edition with copious alterations and notes prepared for the press by the translator and now published with a preface by his kinsman J. Johnson; 2nd ed. (English). *Translator or author:* William Cowper. London, England: J. Johnson.

1802— The Odyssey of Homer; 2nd ed. (English). *Translator or author:* William Cowper. London, England: Bunney and Gold.

1802— The Iliad and the Odyssey of Homer (English). *Translator or author:* Alexander Pope. London, England: Bensley.

1802— Homeri Hymnus in Cererem (Latin). *Translator or author:* David Ruhnken. Leiden (Leyden), Netherlands: Samuel and Joann. Luchtmans.

1802— Homers Werke [2nd edition] (German). *Translator or author:* Johann Heinrich Voss. Konigsburg [location?].

1802— The First Book of the Iliad of Homer; translated into blank verse, with notes (English). *Translator or author:* P. Williams. London, England.

1802–15— Erzahlungen aus der alten Welt fur die Jugend... (German). *Translator or author:* Karl Friedrich Becker. Halle an der Saale, Germany: Waisenhaus.

1802–22— Homeri Carmina cum Brevi Annotationes; accedunt variae lectiones et observationes veterum grammaticorum cum notrae aetatis critica; curante Ch. Glb. Heyne (Greek, Latin). Leipzig, Germany; London, England: Weidmannsche Buchhandlung.

1803— Extraits d'Homere, de Sophocle et de Theocrite, accompagnes d'observations grammaticales et critiques, ou, seconde partie de l'anthologie poetique grecque (French). *Translator or author:* Jean-Baptiste Gail. Paris, France.

1803— La Mort d'Hector; traduction en vers de

l'Iliade (in Amours epiques) (French). *Translator or author:* Perceval Grand-Maison. Paris, France.

1803—[H]omerou Ilias; syn tois scholiois pseudepigraphois Didymou (Greek). *Translator or author:* Spyridon Vlantes. Venice, Italy: Nikolaos Glykus.

1803—[H]omerou Odysseia, syn tois scholiois pseudepigraphois Didymou (Greek). *Translator or author:* Spyridon Vlantes. Venice, Italy: Nikolaos Glykus.

1803-4—L'Iliade; ossia, La Morte di Ettore, poema Omerico; ed. cor. (Italian). Venice, Italy: Pasquali q. Mario.

1804—[H]omerou Batrachomyomachia; sun te metaphrasei; Theod. Gazae. Florence, Italy; Leipzig, Germany.

1804—The New History of the Trojan Wars and Troy's Destruction; in four books (English). Wilmington, DE: Bonsal and Niles.

1804—Ilias; curante C. G. Heyne. Payne.

1804—Homeri Ilias; cum brevi annotatione, curante Ch. Glo. Heyne. Leipzig, Germany: Weidmann.

1804—L'Iliade et l'Odyssee d'Homere; traduit; avec des remarques sur Homere [reprint of the 1780–85 edition] (French). *Translator or author:* A. Gin. Paris, France: J. G. Dentu.

1804–05—Grec-Latin-Francais ou Oeuvres Completes d'Homere; accompagnees de la traduction Francaise, de la version interlineaire Latine, et suivies d'observations litteraires et critiques (Greek, Latin, French). Paris, France.

1804–05—Dziela Homera T. I. II. III. przez Franc. Dmochowskiego; Iliada, tamze w druk. XX (Polish). *Translator or author:* Franciszek Ksawery Dmochowski. Piiarow, Poland.

1804–07—Homeri et Homeridarum Opera et Reliquiae; ex veterum criticorum notationibus, optimorumque exemplarium fide novis curis recensuit F. A Wolfius (Greek). Leipzig, Germany; Goshen [Germany?]: G. I. Goschen.

1804–07—L'Iliade d'Omero recata poeticamente in verso Sciolto Ital. dal abb. Mich. Cesarotti insieme col volgarizzamento letterale dal testo in prosa, ampiamente ellustr. da una scelta dell osservaz. orig. de' piu celebri critici antichi e moderni e da quelle (Italian). *Translator or author:* Melchiorre Cesarotti. Florence, Italy.

1805—Homeri Odyssea; editio nova in usum scholarum librorum summariis aucta; accedit Batrachomyomachia. Halle an der Saale, Germany: Orphan.

1805—[H]omerou Ilias kai Odysseai eis to [H]ellenikon meta ton tou Didymou scholion (Greek, Modern). Enetiesin [location?]: Nikolaos Glykus.

1805—[H]omerou [H]ymnos eis ten Demetran (Greek). Parma, Italy: Bodoni.

1805—Pars Iliados Libri XVI; Rossice verse (in Ephem. Inscr., Freund der Aufklar) (Russian). Leipzig, Germany.

1805—L'Odyssea d'Omero; trad. (Italian). *Translator or author:* Girol. Baccelli. Livorno, Italy.

1805—L'Iliade; trad. in Ottava rima in dialetto Veneziano da F. Boaretti (Italian). *Translator or author:* Francesco Boaretti. Venice, Italy.

1805—Iliade e Odissea (Italian). *Translator or author:* Ceruti.

1805—Opere di Omero; tradotte in volgare da varii [this is a collection of translations overseen by Poggiali: Il by Giac. Ceruti, Ody by Gir. Baccelli [1582 ed], Bat by Franc. Fontana, Ang. Maria Ricci and Ant. Lavagnoli, Hymns by A.M. Salvini and Dion. Str] (Italian). *Translator or author:* Giacinto Ceruti; Gius. Bossoli. Livorno, Italy: Massi.

1805—L'Iliade, o la Morte di Ettore (Italian). *Translator or author:* Melchiorre Cesarotti. Venice, Italy: Santini.

1805—L'Iliade d'Homere (French). *Translator or author:* Anne LeFevre Dacier. Avignon, France: F. Sequin.

1805—The Iliad of Homer (English). *Translator or author:* John Flaxman. London, England: Longman, Hurst, Rees, Orme, etc.

1805—Inno di Omero a Cerere; Fr. e Ital., trad. (Greek, Italian). *Translator or author:* Luigi Lamberti. Parma, Italy: Bodoni.

1805—Homeri Hymni et Batrachomyomachia; denuo recensuit auctario animadversionum et varietate lectionis instruxit et interpretatus est Augustus Matthiae (Latin). *Translator or author:* Augustus Matthias. Leipzig, Germany: Weidmann.

1805—The Iliad of Homer (English). *Translator or author:* Alexander Pope. London, England: W. Suttaby; C. Corral.

1805—Odyssey; translated into English verse by Pope, etc. (English). *Translator or author:* Alexander Pope. London, England: Evance Suttaby.

1805—Ilias (English). *Translator or author:* Alexander Pope. Birmingham, England: Knott and Lloyd.

1805—Odissea di Omero; trad. in versi Ital. da Fr. Soave (Italian). *Translator or author:* Francesco Soave. Pavia, Italy.

1805—Homers Froschmausekampf; ubersetzt (German). *Translator or author:* Weinzierl. Munich, Germany: Lentner.

1805—Aus Homers odyssee ubersetzt (German). *Translator or author:* Weinzierl. Munich, Germany: Lentner.

1805–06—Homer; works in English (English). *Translator or author:* Alexander Pope. London, England: F. J. Du Roveray.

1806—Homeri et Homeridarum Opera et Reliquiae; ex recens. Frid. Aug. Wolfii (Greek). Leipzig, Germany; Goshen [Germany?]: G. I. Goschen.

1806—Ilias; ed. nova in usum scholarum summariis aucta; accedunt Hymni Homeridarum et Epigrammata (Latin). Halle an der Saale, Germany: Orphano.

1806—Homeri Iliad, Graece et Latine (Greek, Latin). London, England: Luc. Hansard.

1806—Homeri Odyssea, Graece et Latine; 4th ed. (Greek, Latin). Aberdeen, Scotland: Chalmers.

1806—Ilias, Graece et Latine; 14th edition [edited by Samuel Clarke] (Greek; Latin). London, England: J. Johnson.

1806—Homeri Hymni et Epigrammata; edidit Gf. Hermann (Greek). *Translator or author:* Godofr. Hermann. Leipzig, Germany: Weidmann.

1806—Incerti auctoris vulgo Pindari Thebani epitome Iliadas Homericae (Latin). *Translator or author:* Theodorus van Kooten. Amsterdam, Netherlands: A. F. Boehme.

1806—Vorschule des Homer; enthaltend eine Sammlung einiger vorzuglichen Stellen aus der Homerischen Iliade, mit untergelegter Analyse und Worterklarungen; nebst einem Praparationsbuche zum ersten und zwelten Gesange der Homerischen Iliad (German). *Translator or author:* Albert Christian Meinecke. Erfurt, Germany: Hennings.

1806—Homer's Battle of the Frogs and Mice (English). *Translator or author:* Thomas Parnell. London, England: Bye and Law.

1806—The Iliad and the Odyssey; with additional notes, critical and illustrative, by Gilb[ert] Wakefield [from the 1715–20, 1725–26 editions] (English). *Translator or author:* Alexander Pope. London, England: J. Johnson.

1806—The Iliad of Homer (English). *Translator or author:* Alexander Pope. Boston, Mass.: Edward Cotton; Joseph Cushing.

1806—The Odyssey of Homer (English). *Translator or author:* Alexander Pope. Edinburgh, Scotland: Thomas Turnbull.

1806—Homers Werke [reprint of the 1793 edition printed at Altona] (German). *Translator or author:* Johann Heinrich Voss. Tubingen, Germany.

1806—The Iliad of Homer; translated into blank verse (English). *Translator or author:* P. Williams. London, England: Allen Lackington.

1807—[H]omerou Epe = Homeri et Homeridarum Opera et Reliquiae; ex veterum criticorum notationibus optimorumque exemplarium fide novis curis recensita (Greek, Latin). Leipzig, Germany: G. I. Goschen.

1807—Specimen of an English Homer; in blank verse [Iliad I, 1–222 and VI 404–496] (English).

1807—Esperimento di traduzione della Iliade di Omero di Ugo Foscolo (Italian). *Translator or author:* Ugo Foscolo. Brescia, Italy: Nicolo Bettoni.

1807—Esperimento di traduzione della Iliade di Omero (Italian). *Translator or author:* Ugo Foscolo; Melchiorre Cesarotti; Vincenzo Monti. Parma, Italy: Edizioni Zara.

1807—A translation of the twenty-fourth book of the Iliad of Homer (English). *Translator or author:* C. Lloyd. Birmingham, England: Knott and Lloyd.

1807—Ilias (English). *Translator or author:* Alexander Pope. Berwick, England: H. Richardson.

1807—Works of Homer (English). *Translator or author:* Alexander Pope. London, England: Samuel Bagster.

1807—The Iliad and the Odyssey of Homer [reprinted from the 1715–20, 1725–26 editions] (English). *Translator or author:* Alexander Pope. London, England: Walker.

1807—Homers Ilias (German). *Translator or author:* Johann Heinrich Voss. Frankfurt am Main, Germany.

1808—Homeri Ilias, Odyssea, Batrachomyomachia...; Graece [reprint of 1780 edition] (Greek). Oxford, England: Clarendon Press.

1808—Les Carmina Homerica Repurgata. London, England: Bulmer.

1808—Homeri Ilias, Graece; edited by Aloys. Lamberti (Greek). Parma, Italy: Bodoni.

1808—Hymnus in Cererem; editus a D. Ruhnkenio; accedunt C. G Mitscherlichii adnotationes (Greek, Latin). Leiden (Leyden), Netherlands: Luchtmans.

1808—Homeri Ilias, Interpretatio Latina; adjecta est es editione S. Clarke (Greek). Edinburgh, Scotland.

1808—The Adventures of Ulysses (English). *Translator or author:* Charles Lamb. London, England: T. Davison.

1808—The Iliad of Homer; translated [reprint of edition printed in London in 1773] (English). *Translator or author:* James Macpherson. Dublin, Ireland.

1808—The Iliad of Homer (English). *Translator or author:* Alexander Pope. London, England: W. Suttaby; Crosby et al.

1808—The Iliad of Homer; translated; ornamented with wood cuts, originally designed and engraved by A. Anderson, of New-York (English). *Translator or author:* Alexander Pope. New York, N.Y.: William Durell; J. Seymour.

1808—The Odyssey of Homer; translated; ornamented with wood cuts originally designed and engraved by G. Lansing (English). *Translator or author:* Alexander Pope. Boston, Mass.: Etheridge and Bliss Hastings.

1808—The Iliad of Homer (English). *Translator or author:* Alexander Pope. Boston, Mass.: Etheridge and Bliss Hastings.

1808—The Iliad of Homer (English). *Translator or author:* Alexander Pope. London, England: J. et al. Walker.

1808—The Odyssey of Homer (English). *Translator or author:* Alexander Pope. New York, N.Y.: William Durell; Elliot's Press.

1808—Proeve Eener Dichterlyke Vertaling van de Ilias. *Translator or author:* Siegenbeek. Amsterdam, Netherlands.

1808—Homer Odyssee (German). *Translator or author:* Johann Heinrich Voss. Cologne, Germany: Neuen Verlagsbuchhandlung und Buchdruckerei.

1809—Homeri Ilias, Graece et Latine; annotationes... [edited by Samuel Clarke] (Greek, Latin). Edinburgh, Scotland: William et al. Creech.

1809—Homeri Opera; I. G. Hageri. Edit nova. Chemnitz, Germany.

1809—Incerti Auctoris Vulgo Pindar Thebani

Epitome Iliadas Homericae e recensione (Latin). Amsterdam, Netherlands: L. A. C. Hesse.

1809—L'Iliade d'Homere; traduite en vers Francais [1st edition by this translator] (French). *Translator or author:* E. Aignan. Paris, France.

1809—Incerti Auctoris Vulgo Pindari Thebani Epitome Iliados Homericae; e recensione et cum notis Theodori van Kooten, edidit, praefatus est, suasque animadversiones adjecit Henricus Weytingh, apud Campenses Gymnasii publ. Rector (Latin). *Translator or author:* Theodorus van Kooten. Leiden (Leyden), Netherlands; Amsterdam, Netherlan: Luchtmanniensis and Holtropianis.

1809—L'Iliade d'Homere [2nd printing of this translator, heavily reworked (1st was 1776)] (French). *Translator or author:* Charles-Francois Lebrun. Paris, France: Bossange.

1809—The Iliad of Homer; translated into English blank verse; by the Rev. James Morrice, A.M. (English). *Translator or author:* James Morrice. London, England: White.

1809—Traduzione de Due Primi Canti dell'Odissea e di Alcune Parti delle Georgiche; con due epistole (Italian). *Translator or author:* Ippolito Pindemonte. Verona, Italy.

1809—The Iliad of Homer (English). *Translator or author:* Alexander Pope. London, England: W. et al. Suttaby.

1809—The Odyssey of Homer (English). *Translator or author:* Alexander Pope. London, England: C. Whittingham; J. Sharpe.

1809—The Iliad of Homer (English). *Translator or author:* Alexander Pope. London, England: J. Sharpe.

1809-14—Homeri Ilias; cum excerptis ex Eustathii commentariis et scholiis minoribus edidit I. A. Muller; denuo edidit A. Weichert. Meissen, Germany: Godsche.

1810—A Translation of the First Seven Books of the Odyssey (English). Birmingham, England: Knott and Lloyd.

1810—Odyssey, Graece et Latine; 4th ed. [edited by Samuel Clarke] (Greek; Latin). Edinburgh, Scotland: Bell and Bradfute.

1810—Ilias et Odyssea (Greek). Oxford, England: Bliss.

1810—L'Iliade et l'Odyssee d'Homere; traduit etc. avec des remarques sur Homere par P. Jer. Bitaube [reprint of the Paris edition of 1780–85] (French). *Translator or author:* Paul Jeremie Bitaube. Lyon, France.

1810— L'Odyssee d'Homere, avec des remarques; precedee d'observations sur l'Odyssee, et de reflexions sur la traduction des poetes; 4th ed. (French). *Translator or author:* Paul Jeremie Bitaube. Paris, France: J. G. Dentu.

1810— Iliade d'Omero; volgarizzata litteralmente in prosa e recata poeticamente in verso sciolto Ital. da Melch. Cesarotti [reprint of the 1786–94 edition] (Italian). *Translator or author:* Melchiorre Cesarotti. Padova (Padua), Italy: Brandolese.

1810— The Iliad and Odyssey of Homer; translated into English blank verse by W. Cowper, second edition with copious alterations and notes prepared for the press by the translator and now published with a preface by his kinsman J. Johnson [reprint of the 1791 e (English). *Translator or author:* William Cowper. London, England.

1810— Iliad and Odyssey; plates by Fusell, Howard, Stothard etc. (English). *Translator or author:* William Cowper. J. Johnson.

1810— The Poems of John Dryden [includes translations from Homer] (English). *Translator or author:* John Dryden. London, England.

1810— Homer Beka-Eger Hartz f. Nagy Ferentz (Hungarian). *Translator or author:* Nagy Ferentz.

1810— The Battle of the Frogs and Mice; from the Batrachomyomachia; with miscellaneous translations (English). *Translator or author:* Francis Howse. Cambridge, England: F. Hodson.

1810— Iliade di Omero; trad. in versi Toscani da Vinc. Monti (Italian). *Translator or author:* Vincenzo Monti. Brescia, Italy: Nicolo Bettoni.

1810— The Batrachomuomachia: or, The Battle of the Frogs and Mice; with the Hymns and Epigrams of Homer. *Translator or author:* Thomas Parnell. London, England: Whittingham and Rowland.

1810— The Iliad and Odyssey of Homer (English). *Translator or author:* Alexander Pope. London, England: T. Bensley.

1810— Hymns and Epigrams; translated (English). *Translator or author:* H. J. Pye.

1810— Ilias (Greek). *Translator or author:* Albrecht Schaeffer. Leipzig, Germany: Car. Tauchnitz.

1810— Odyssea (Greek). *Translator or author:* Albrecht Schaeffer. Leipzig, Germany: Car. Tauchnitz.

1810— L'Iliade d'Homere; nouv. traduction en prose par M. M. Thomas, A. Renouvier et A. C. (French). *Translator or author:* M. M. Thomas; A.

Renouview; A. de Cambis. Paris, France: F. Schoell.

1810— Homerus; vertaald door F. E. Turr. (Flemish). *Translator or author:* F. E. Turr ... Hage, Germany: Deel I.

1810–12— [H]omerou Ilias meta palaias paraphraseos ex idiocheirou tou Theodorou Gaze nun proton tupois ekdotheises, [h]e prostithetai kai Batrachomyomachia sun te idia paraphrasei ekdidomene to deuteron, para Nik. Theseos. (Greek). *Translator or author:* Theodorus Gaze. Florence, Italy: Nic. Carli.

1811— Odyssea, Graece (Greek). Oxford, England: N. Bliss.

1811— Homeri Ilias et Odyssea, Graece; cum scholiis Didymi et Seberi indice (Greek). Oxford, England: Clarendon Press.

1811— Clavis Homerica. Patrick.

1811— Odyssey (English).

1811— Homeri Ilias, Graece et Latine; annotationes in usum serenissimi principis Gulialmi Augusti, duois de Cumberland, &c. Regio jussu scripsit atque edidit Samuel Clarke ... editio quinta decim (Greek; Latin). London, England: F. C. and J. Rivington; J. Walker.

1811— L'Iliade et l'Odyssee; traduit par Mad. Dacier en prose, avec des notes et des figures de Picard [reprint of the 1711–16 edition] (French). *Translator or author:* Anne LeFevre Dacier. Paris, France.

1811— L'Iliade et l'Odyssee; trad. (French). *Translator or author:* Anne LeFevre Dacier. Avignon, France: Offray.

1811— The Odyssey of Homer (English). *Translator or author:* Alexander Pope. London, England: Evance Suttaby; Crosby.

1811— The Odyssey of Homer (English). *Translator or author:* Alexander Pope. London, England: W. Lewis; J. Walker.

1811— The Odyssey of Homer [reprint of the 1725–26 edition] (English). *Translator or author:* Alexander Pope; W. Broome, E. Fenton.

1811–20— Iliadis Libri I–IV, Graece [no more ever printed] (Greek). Paris, France: Dr. Coray.

1811–20— [H]omerou Iliados; met' ezegeseon palaion kai neon (Greek). *Translator or author:* Adamantios Koraes. Paris, France: I. M. Everartos.

1812— L'Iliade d'Homere; traduite en vers Francais; nouvelle edition, suivie de notes critiques, de morceaux empruntes d'Homere par les poetes anciens et modernes les plus celebres et de tables red. sur un nouveau plan [from the 1809 edition] (French). *Translator or author:* E. Aignan. Paris, France: Treuttel and Wurtz.

1812—Homer's Iliade; travestirt (German). *Translator or author:* Blumauer. Jena, Germany.

1812—Iliade en Octaves Ital (Italian). *Translator or author:* Eust. Fiocci. Pavia, Italy.

1812—L'Iliade de Homere; traduite en prose [3rd ed.] (French). *Translator or author:* Charles-Francois Lebrun. Paris, France: Bossange and Masson.

1812—Iliade di Omero; trad. in versi Toscani da Vinc. Monti [reprint of the edition printed in Brescia in 1810] (Italian). *Translator or author:* Vincenzo Monti. Milan, Italy.

1812—The Iliad of Homer (English). *Translator or author:* Alexander Pope. New York, N.Y.: William Durell; C. S. Van Winkle.

1812—The Iliad of Homer (English). *Translator or author:* Alexander Pope. Baltimore, Md.; New York, N.Y.: Philip H. et al. Nicklin.

1812—The Odyssey of Homer (English). *Translator or author:* Alexander Pope. New York, N.Y.: William Durell; D. and G. Bruce.

1812—The Iliad of Homer (English). *Translator or author:* Alexander Pope. Philadelphia, Pa.: Fry and Kammerer.

1813—[H]e tou [H]omerou Ilias = Homeri Ilias (Greek, Latin). Aberdeen, Scotland; London, England: A. Brown; Longman, Hurst et al.

1813—Homeri Odyssea, Graece et Latine; ad praestantissimas editiones accuratissime expressa (Greek, Latin). *Translator or author:* Johann Georg Hager. Chemnitz, Germany: William Starkium.

1813—The Odyssey of Homer; translated from the Greek (English). *Translator or author:* Alexander Pope. Georgetown, D.C.; Philadelphia, Pa.: Richards and Mallory; P. H. Nicklin.

1813—The Iliad and Odyssey [reprint of the 1715–20, 1725–26 editions in the series: Works of the Greek and Roman Poets] (English). *Translator or author:* Alexander Pope.

1813—The Iliad of Homer; new ed. (English). *Translator or author:* Alexander Pope. London, England: F. J. Roveray.

1813—Batrachomyomachie; trad. (French). *Translator or author:* F. Seguier.

1814—Ilias; Graece et Latine, cum annotation-ibus Samuelis Clarke [1st American edition]. New York, N.Y.: Duyckinck.

1814—Homeri Opera Omnia; Graece et Latine, ex recensione Jo. Aug. Ernesti; notis S. Clarkii; acc.; varietas lectt. ms. Lips. et edd. vett. cura ;J. A. Ernesti qui et suas notas adspersit (Greek; Latin). Glasgow, Scotland: Andr. Duncan.

1814—Homeri Ilias, Odyssea, Batrachomyomachia et Hymni, Graece cum scholiis Didymi [reprint of 1792–97 edition] (Greek). Oxford, England.

1814—Opera Omnia ex recensione et cvm notis Samuelis Clarkii accessit varietas lectionvm ms. Lips. Et edd. Veterum (Greek). Leipzig, Germany.

1814—The Iliad and Odyssey (English). *Translator or author:* William Cowper. Boston, Mass.

1814—Homers Hymnen; metrisch ubersetzt (German). *Translator or author:* A. Follenius; Conr. Schwenck. Giessen, Germany: Heyer.

1814—Werke (German). *Translator or author:* Johann Heinrich Voss. Stuttgart, Germany.

1814—Iliad, von 1ten bis 24ten Gesang (German). *Translator or author:* Johann Heinrich Voss. Vienna, Austria: Haasische Buchhandlung.

1814–15—Homaros Ilias; ofvers. af Marcus Wallenberg (Swedish). *Translator or author:* Marcus Wallenberg. Stockholm, Sweden: Grahn.

1814–16—Pamiatka Dziejow Bohatyrskich z Wieku Grayskotroskiego w spiewach Homera i Kwinta wedlug pierwotworow greckich Slawianom dochowana (Polish). *Translator or author:* Hiacynth. Przybylskiego. Krakow, Poland.

1815—[H]omerou Batrachomyomachia, Graece et Latine; edente I. B. Gail (Greek; Latin). Paris, France: Aug. Delalain.

1815—Homeri Ilias, Graece et Latine (Greek, Latin). Chemnitz, Germany: William Starkium.

1815—Homeri Ilias; Graece et Latine; annotationes in usum Serenissimi Principis Gulielmi Augusti, Ducis de Cumberland, etc. Regio (Greek; Latin). Dublin, Ireland: Johannes Exshaw.

1815—Proeve Eener Dichterlyke Vertaling van de Ilias (in W. Bilderdyk). Haarlem, Netherlands.

1815—Homer Iliad; Graece et Latine ex recensione et cum notis Samuelis Clarke; 16th ed. (Greek, Latin). London, England; Edinburgh, Scotland; York, England: J. Cuthell; J. Nunn, Lackington et al.

1815—Odysseia (Greek). Oxford, England.

II. Printed Editions of the Homeric Texts, 1470 to 2000 C.E.

220

1815—Odyssea, Graece et Latine; edidit, annotationesque, ex notis nonnullis manuscriptis a Samuele Clarke, S.T. P., relictis, partim collectas, adjecit Samuel Clarke, S.R.S. 5th ed. (Greek, Latin). London, England: J. Cuthell.

1815—L'Iliade et l'Odyssee; traduit par Mad. Dacier en prose, avec des notes et des figures de Picard [reprint of the 1711–16 edition] (French). *Translator or author:* Anne LeFevre Dacier. Paris, France: Plancher.

1815—Homers Hymnen, Epigramme und Batrachomyomachie; ubersetzt und mit Anmerkungen begleitet (German). *Translator or author:* F. Kammerer. Marburg [Germany?]: Krieger.

1815—Iliade di Omero; trad. in versi Toscani da Vinc[enzo] Monti [reprint of the 1810 edition printed in Brescia] (Italian). *Translator or author:* Vincenzo Monti. Naples, Italy.

1815—L'Iliade d'Omero; trad. (Italian). *Translator or author:* Vincenzo Monti. Naples, Itlay.

1815—Odysseia przekladania J. Przybylskiego. *Translator or author:* Hiacynth. Przybylskiego. Krakow, Poland.

1815—L'Odissea; tradotta in versi Ital. con annotazioni; aggiuntavi la Batrachomiomachia (Italian). *Translator or author:* Francesco Soave. Milan, Italy.

1815—Homers Froschmausekempf; ubersetzt; herausgegeben und mit einer Einleitung und Inhaltsanzeige versehen von C. F. W. Solbrig und Seeger (German). *Translator or author:* M. Str. Salzwedel, Germany.

1815–18—Oeuvres d'Homere; traduit nouvelle (French). *Translator or author:* M. Jean-Baptiste Dugas-Montbel. Paris, France: A. A. Renouard.

1816—Odyssea; ad editionem recensionis Wolfianae Lipsiensem expressa, curante Niclao Schow.

1816—Homero Poema de Ranarum cum Muribus Pugna, Graece (Greek). Paris, France: Aug. Delalain.

1816—Ilias (Greek). London, England.

1816—Homeri Odyssea. Glasgow, Scotland.

1816—Homeri Odyssea, Graece et Latine; edidit, annotationesque, ex notion nonsullis [?] manuscriptis a Samuele Clarke, S.T.P. defuncto ralictis, partis collectas, adjecit Samuel Clarke, S.R.S.; 4th ed. Edinburgh, Scotland; London, England: Bell and Bradfute; Silvestram Doig; J. Nunn; Longman.

1816—Iliade di Omero; recata dal testo Greco in versi Italiani (Italian). *Translator or author:* Melchiorre Cesarotti. Torino (Turin), Italy: Vedova Pomba e Figli.

1816—L'Iliade d'Homere; traduction litterale avec le texte, en regard, a l'usage des personnes qui, ayant les premiers elements du Grec, veulent entendre Homere dans sa propre languq; et de celles qui, ne sachant pas le Grec, veulent connaitre, autant que poss (French). *Translator or author:* Anne LeFevre Dacier. Paris, France: Verdiere.

1816—L'Iliade di Omero; trad. in Ottava rima dall'abb. Eust. Fiocchi (Italian). *Translator or author:* Eustathius Fiocchi. Milan, Italy.

1816—La Batracomiomachia; trad. ined. dal Greco (Italian). *Translator or author:* C. Leopardi. Milan, Italy.

1816—The Iliad of Homer; translated from the Greek (English). *Translator or author:* Alexander Pope. London, England: J. et al. Nichols.

1816—The Odyssey of Homer; translated from the Greek (English). *Translator or author:* Alexander Pope. Georgetown, D.C.: Richards and Mallory, etc.

1816—Commentatio de extrema Odysseae parte — — rhaps. [psi] versu CCXCVII, aevo recentiore ort — — - homerico, a F. -A -G Spohn. *Translator or author:* F. A. G. Spohn. Leipzig, Germany: Weidmannsche Buchhandlung.

1816—Homers Odyssee; ubersetzt (German). *Translator or author:* Johann Heinrich Voss. Vienna, Austria: Haasische Buchandlung.

1816–17—The Odyssey of Homer; translated into English blank verse, with copious alterations and notes prepared for the press by the translator and published by his kinsman, J. Johnson; 4th ed. (English). *Translator or author:* William Cowper. London, England: C. Whittingham; J. Sharpe.

1816–18—Homeri Ilias; edidit J. B. Gail (Greek). Paris, France: Aug. Delalain.

1817—Homeri Ilias; ex recensione C[hristian] G[ottlob] Heynii, fere impressa; in usum scholarum. London, England: Valpianis.

1817—Ilias. Robbins.

1817—Ilias; scholiis Didymi [reprinted from the 1797 edition]. Oxford, England: Clarendon Press.

1817—Homeri Ilias, Graece; cum brevi annotatione curante C[hristian] G[ottlob] Heyne; accedunt excursus in Homerum; necnon index nominum et rerum; in usum scholae Wintoniensis (Greek; Latin). London, England; Winton [England?]: J. B. Whittaker; G. Cowie; Robbins and Wheeler.

1817—L'Iliade d'Homere en Grec; avec des sommaires Latins et Franc. soigneusement corriges d'apres la dern. ed. de Wolf par Ch. M. E(berhart) (Greek). Paris, France: Nyon.

1817—Odyssea cum Scholiis, Batrachomyomachia, Hymnis et Reliquis Carminibus Minoribus. Oxford, England.

1817—[H]omerou Epe: Homeri et Homeridarum Opera et reliquiae [reprint of the 1807 edition] (Greek, Latin). Leipzig, Germany: G. I. Goschen.

1817—Homeri et Homeridarum Opera et Reliquiae; ex recensione Frid. Aug. Wolfii; nova recognito multis locis emendatior (Greek).

1817—The Odyssey of Homer; translated into English blank verse, with copious alterations and notes prepared for the press by the translator and published by his kinsman, J. Johnson; 4th ed. (English). *Translator or author:* William Cowper. London, England: Baldwin, Cradock and Joy.

1817—Odyssee: Poeme; traduit du Grec d'Homere (French). *Translator or author:* Anne LeFevre Dacier. Paris, France: Menard and Desenne.

1817—L'Iliade et l'Odyssee; trad. (French). *Translator or author:* A. Gin. Nantes, France: Mellinet-Malassis.

1817—L'Odissea; tradotta (Italian). *Translator or author:* Ippolito Pindemonte. Milan, Italy: G. Silvestri.

1817—The Iliad of Homer; translated (English). *Translator or author:* Alexander Pope. London, England: Walker and Edwards et al.

1817—The Iliad and Odyssey of Homer [series: Works of the Greek and Roman Poets] (English). *Translator or author:* Alexander Pope. London, England.

1817—Ilias (Greek). *Translator or author:* Rousiades. Vienna, Austria.

1818—Odyssea; ad optimorum librorum fidem accurate edita (Greek). Leipzig, Germany: Car. Tauchnitz.

1818—Homeri Ilias, Graece et Latine; annotationes in usum serenissimi principis Gulielmi Augusti, Ducis de Cumberland, etc.; scripsit atque edidit Samuel Clarke; 16th ed. (Greek; Latin). London, England: F. C. and J. Rivington etc.

1818—Homers Batrachomyomachie und Hymnen; zum Schulgebrauch. Bamberg, Germany: Wesche.

1818—L'Iliade d'Omero; recata poeticamente in verso Sciolto Ital. dal abb. Mich. Cesarotti insieme col volgarizzamento letterale dal testo in prosa, ampiamente ellustr. da una scelta dell osservaz. orig. de' piu celebri critici antichi e moderni e da quelle (Italian). *Translator or author:* Melchiorre Cesarotti. Venice, Italy.

1818—The Hymns, the Batrachomyomachia and Two Original Poetical Hymns by George Chapman; with an introductory preface by S. W. Singer [reprint of the 1624 edition] (English). *Translator or author:* George Chapman. Chiswick, England.

1818—L'Iliade et l'Odyssee traduit; avec le texte Grec en regard (Greek; French). *Translator or author:* Anne LeFevre Dacier. Paris, France: Aug. Delalain.

1818—L'Iliade et l'Odyssee; traduit par Mad. Dacier en prose, avec des notes et des figures de Picard [reprint of the 1711–16 edition] (French). *Translator or author:* Anne LeFevre Dacier. Paris, France.

1818—L'Odyssee d'Homere; traduit nouvelle suivie de la Batrachomyomachie, des Hymnes, de divers petits poemes, attribues a Homere [reprint of the 1815 edition] (French). *Translator or author:* M. Jean-Baptiste Dugas-Montbel. Paris, France: A. A. Renouard.

1818—Hector: Tragedie, Suivie de Plusieurs Fragmens Imites de l'Iliade, et d'une Scene du Role d'Helene que l'Auteur a Supprime; representee, pour la premiere fois, sur le theatre Francais (French). *Translator or author:* J. -Ch. -J. Luce de Lancival. Paris, France: Barba.

1818—L'Iliade; traduz. epica in ottava rima [1st printing of this translator]. *Translator or author:* Lorenzo Manzini. Florence, Italy.

1818—Homers Hymnus an Demeter, ubersetzt (German). *Translator or author:* H. L. Nadermann. Munich, Germany: Theissing.

1818—Ilias (English). *Translator or author:* Alexander Pope. London, England: Evance Suttaby.

1818—The Iliad and Odyssey of Homer [reprint of the 1804 edition] (English). *Translator or author:* Alexander Pope. London, England: Walker.

1818—The Iliad of Homer; translated from the Greek (English). *Translator or author:* Alexander Pope. Paris, France: Cordier.

1818— Odyssee (German). *Translator or author:* Johann Heinrich Voss. Stockholm, Sweden: E. Bruzelius.

1818— Anfang der Odyssee (v.1–100) metrisch ubersetzt (in Litterarische analekten) (German). *Translator or author:* Friedrich August Wolf.

1818–19— Ilias; ed by J. A. Mueller; denuo ed. A. Weicherth; cum excerptis ex Eustathii Commentariis et Scholiis Minoribus in Usum Scholarum (Greek). Meissen, Germany: F. W. Goedsche.

1818–19— The Iliad of Homer; translated (English). *Translator or author:* James Macpherson. Dublin, Ireland: Graham & Son.

1818–19— De Ilias van Homerus; naar het Grieksch, in Nederduitsche verzen gevolgd. *Translator or author:* Jan Van Gravenweert. Amsterdam, Netherlands: Hey.

1819— [H]omerou Ilias = Homeri Ilias; ex recensione C[hristian] G[ottlob] Heyne fere impressa; cum notis Anglicis (Greek). London, England: Longman etc.

1819— Ilias, Greek and Latin (Greek; Latin). Glasgow, Scotland: Duncan.

1819— Homeri Ilias, curante C[hristian] G[ottlob] Heyne [reprint of the 1817 edition]. London, England: Priestley.

1819— Odyssea; edidit J[ohann] G[eorg] Hager (Greek, Latin). Chemnitz, Germany: Starke.

1819— Ilias, with notes; with Latin translation [edited by Samuel Clarke] (Greek; Latin). Rivington.

1819— Homeri Ilias; ad optimorum fidem accurate edita (Greek). Leipzig, Germany: Car. Tauchnitz.

1819— Homeri Odyssea (Greek). Berlin, Germany: Librariis Orphanotrophei.

1819— L'Iliade et l'Odyssee [reprint of the 1804 edition] (French). *Translator or author:* Paul Jeremie Bitaube. Paris, France: Ledoux and Tenre.

1819— L'Iliade et l'Odyssee [reprint of the 1804 edition] (French). *Translator or author:* Paul Jeremie Bitaube. Paris, France: Lequien.

1819— L'Iliade et l'Odyssee [reprint of the 1804 edition] (French). *Translator or author:* Paul Jeremie Bitaube. Paris, France: Coste.

1819— L'Iliade et l'Odyssee d'Homere; traduit etc. avec des remarques sur Homere [reprint of Paris edition of 1780–85] (French). *Translator or author:* Paul Jeremie Bitaube. Lyon, France.

1819— L'Iliade et l'Odyssee; traduit par Mad. Dacier en prose, avec des notes et des figures de Picard [reprint of Paris edition of 1711–16] (French). *Translator or author:* Anne LeFevre Dacier. Avignon, France: F. Seguin.

1819— The Eight First Books of Homer's Ilias; literally translated, with notes (English). *Translator or author:* D. B. Hickie. Dublin, Ireland: J. at the Hibernia Press Cumming.

1819— The Adventures of Uiysses (English). *Translator or author:* Charles Lamb. London, England: J. J. Godwin and Co.

1819— L'Odyssee d'Homere; traduit en prose [1st edition of The Odyssey by this translator] (French). *Translator or author:* Charles-Francois Lebrun. Paris, France: Bossange and Masson.

1819— The Iliad of Homer; translated from the Greek (English). *Translator or author:* Alexander Pope. Baltimore, Md.: R. Lucas; N. G. Maxwell.

1819— The Iliad of Homer; translated (English). *Translator or author:* Alexander Pope. Chiswick, England: C. Whittingham.

1819— Iliada Homera; przekladania (Polish). *Translator or author:* Stanisl Staszic. Warsaw, Poland.

1819— Homers Ilias; ubersetzt (German). *Translator or author:* Johann Heinrich Voss. Reutlingen, Germany: Comptoir der Deutschen Classiker.

1819— Odyssee; ubersetzt (German). *Translator or author:* Johann Heinrich Voss. Reutlingen, Germany: Comptoir der Deutschen Classiker.

1819–20— Homeri Opera Quae Exstant Omnia, Graece et Latine (Greek; Latin). Padova (Padua), Italy: Typographia Seminarii.

1820— Hektors Abschied von Andromache aus Iliad VI 464 sqq. (in Lyra, Eine Sammlung von Ubersezz a. d. klass. Alterth.) (German). Meissen, Germany: Godsche.

1820— Initia Homerica (excerpta ex Iliade); cum locorum omnium Graeca metaphrasi, ex. codd. Bodlej. nunc primum edita a Th[omas] Burgess; editio nova accedunt Popii versio Anglica, cum annotationes; versio Latina; initiorum Homericorum grammatica [2nd edition] (Greek). London, England: Priestley.

1820— Homeri Odyssea. Leipzig, Germany; Leiden (Leyden), Germany: J. A. G. Weigel; S et J. Luchtmans.

1820— Homeri Odyssea et Hymni Fere Omnes (Greek; Latin). Padova (Padua), Italy: Typographia Seminarii.

1820—Homeri Ilias. Halle an der Saale, Germany: Librariis Orphanotrophei.

1820—[Works of Homer] (English). London, England: W. Wilson.

1820—Batrachomyomachia [H]omerike; fur Anganger mit Zurechtweisungen und einem Wortregister versehen (Greek). Hildurgh, Germany: Kesselring.

1820—L'Iliade et l'Odyssee; trad. (French). *Translator or author:* Paul Jeremie Bitaube. Avignon, France: Chambeau.

1820—L'Iliade et l'Odyssee d'Homere; traduit etc. avec des remarques sur Homere [reprint of the 1780–85 edition] (French). *Translator or author:* Paul Jeremie Bitaube. Lyon, France.

1820—La Traduction de l'Iliade par Ceruti [reprint of the 1776 edition] (Italian). *Translator or author:* Ceruti. Milan, Italy.

1820—The Iliad and the Odyssey (English). *Translator or author:* William Cowper. London, England: Walker.

1820—The Odyssey of Homer; translated into English blank verse, with notes, by William Cowper, esq. Fifth edition (English). *Translator or author:* William Cowper. London, England: Cradosk and Joy Balwin.

1820—Introductio ad Linguam Graecam; complectens regulas grammatices, radices vocum, et exercitationeem, seu poema (Odusseus) in quo regulae radicesque omnes ad usum et praxim rediguntur; ad usum III. classis et in eorum gratiam qui brevi tempore Graecos libro (Greek; Latin). *Translator or author:* Bonaventure Giraudeau. Avignon, France: F. Sequin.

1820—Batrochom.; Polonice vertit (Polish). *Translator or author:* Bruno Comes Kicinshki.

1820—Carmina Homerica, Ilias et Odyssea; a rhapsodorum interpolationibus repurga et in prist. formam, quatenus recuperanda esset, tam e vett. monumentorum fide et auctori quam ex antiqui sermo indole ac rat. red; cum notic ac prolegg. in quibus de eorum origin. *Translator or author:* Richard Payne Knight. London, England; Paris, France; Strasbourg, France: Treuttel and Wurz.

1820—Iliade di Omero; traduzione; 3rd ed. (Italian). *Translator or author:* Vincenzo Monti. Milan, Italy: Societa Tipografica dei Classici Italiani.

1820—Batracomiomachia d'Omero; volgarizzata (Italian). *Translator or author:* Ant. Pazzi. Florence, Italy.

1820—The Odyssey of Homer; to which is added The Battle of the Frogs and Mice; translated (English). *Translator or author:* Alexander Pope. London, England: W. Wilson; J. Bumpus.

1820—The Odyssey, and the Hymns, Odes and Epigrams of Homer (English). *Translator or author:* Alexander Pope; Richard Hole; Henry J. Pye. Chiswick, England: C. Whittingham.

1820—Homers Hymnus an Demeter; Griechisch mit metrischer Ubersetzung und ausfuhrlichen Word- und Sach- Erklarungen durch Auflosung der altesten Mysterien- und Templesprache in Hellas vermittelt; nebst einem Briefe an Hrn. Geh. Hofrath Creuzer in Heidelberg (Greek, German). *Translator or author:* F. K. Sickler. Hildburghausen, Germany: F. K. L. Sickler.

1821—Homeri Ilias, Graece et Latine; ex recensione et cum notis Samuelis Clarke; 17th ed. (Greek; Latin). London, England: J. Cuthell etc.

1821—Iliadd; translated into English prose, by a graduate of Oxford (English). Oxford, England: Munday & S; Whittaker.

1821—Clavis Homerica. London, England: Walker.

1821—[H]omerou Ilias = Homeri Ilias; cum brevi annotatione curante C[hristian] G[ottlob] Heyne; accedunt scholia minora necnon Heraclidis allegoriae Homericae (Greek; Latin). Oxford, England: Clarendon Press.

1821—[H]omerou Polemos ton Pontikobatrachon; eis [h]aplen phrasin (Greek, Modern). *Translator or author:* George Astobek. Venice, Italy: Nikolaos Glykus.

1821—Batrachomiomachia (Flemish). *Translator or author:* Bilderdijk. Leiden (Leyden), Netherlands.

1821—In Apollinem Hymnus Homericus Svethice Redditus; quem praeside mag. Josepho Ott. Hoejer (Greek; Swedish). *Translator or author:* Johan Albert Butsch; Johannes Lundblad; et al. Uppsala, Sweden: Regiae Acad. Typographi.

1821—The Iliad of Homer; translated into English prose, with explanatory notes (English). *Translator or author:* Henry Francis Cary. Oxford, England.

1821—[Homers Krieg der Mause] (German). *Translator or author:* K. M. Ph. Marx. Carlsruhe, Germany.

1821—Iliade di Omero; traduzione; 3rd ed. (Italian). *Translator or author:* Vincenzo Monti. Florence, Italy: L. Ciardetti.

1821—Homeric Hymns (English). *Translator or author:* Percy Bysshe Shelley.

1821—Iliade; tradotta e compendiata in prose; ed illustrata con brevi annotazione le quali accennano I luoghi omnessi o abbreviati, espongono il preciso testo letterale, e facilitano la intelligenza del poema (Italian). *Translator or author:* Alessandro Verri. Milan, Italy: G. Silvestri.

1821—Homers Werke in Zwei Banden; ubersetzt; mit einer literarhistorischen Einleitung von Joseph Lautenbacher [reprint of the 1781–93 edition] (German). *Translator or author:* Johann Heinrich Voss. Stuttgart, Germany: J. G. Cotta Buchhandlung.

1821–22—Homeri Ilias; ex optimis editionibus fideliter expressa; accedunt illustrationes ex scholl. vet. et probatissimis editoribus desumtae, necnon indices absoluti, et curae secundae, studio et impensis Jacobi Kennedy. Dublin, Ireland: Typis Academicis.

1821–22—Ilias, Graece et Latine; Opera M. Ioan. Georg. Hageri; 5th ed. (Greek; Latin). Chemnitz, Germany: William Starkium.

1821–22—The Iliad of Homer; translated (English). *Translator or author:* Alexander Pope. London, England: F. C. and J. Rivington.

1821–25—The Iliad of Homer; translated into English prose, as literally as the different idioms of the Greek and English languages will allow (English). Oxford, England.

1821–28—Opere del Cavaliere Vincenzo Monti (Italian). *Translator or author:* Vincenzo Monti. Bologna, France: Stamperia delle Muse.

1821–34—Homeri Ilias cum Brevi Annotatione; accur. Ch. Gl. Heynio; accedunt scholia minora passim emendata et Heraclidis Pont. allegoriae e ms. locupl. (Greek). Oxford, England.

1822—The Odyssey of Homer (English). Philadelphia, Pa.: Ashmead.

1822—[H]omerou Odysseia mixra; oder, sechs Bucher der Odysse, enthaltend die vollstandige Reisebeschreibung der Ulysses fur den ersten Schulgebrauch; Griechisch, mit grammatischen Anmerkungen, erklar. Worterverzeichnisse, und einer historisch-kritischen Einle (Greek). Marburg, Germany: Krieger.

1822—Homeri Ilias et Batrachomyomachia; Graece (Greek). Halle an der Saale, Germany: Orphan.

1822—Medea [incl. Batrachomyomachia and Hymni]; ex recensione Petri Elmsleii; in usum scholarum. Leipzig, Germany: C. H. F. Hartmann.

1822—Opera Omnis; Graece et Latine ex rec. et cum notis Sam. Clarke accessit varietas lect. ms. Lips. et edd. vett. cura J. A. Ernesti qui et suas notas adspersit; adnexa sunt F. A. Wolfii proless. (Greek; Latin). London, England: Priestley.

1822—Libri Novem Priores Librique XVIII. et XXII [Homer]. Andover, Mass.: Codmoniano.

1822—L'Iliade et l'Odyssee d'Homere; traduit etc. avec des remarques sur Homere [reprint of the Paris edition of 1780–85] (French). *Translator or author:* Paul Jeremie Bitaube. Lyon, France.

1822—L'Iliade et l'Odyssee [reprint of the Paris edition of 1804] (French). *Translator or author:* Paul Jeremie Bitaube. Paris, France: Crapelet.

1822—Probe einer neuen (metrischen) Ubersetzung der Odysee (in Seebodii Krit Bibl) (German). *Translator or author:* K. L. Kannegiesser.

1822—Der erste Gesang der Odyssee, ubersetzt (German). *Translator or author:* K. L. Kannegiesser. Leipzig, Germany: Brockhaus.

1822—Oeuvres d'Homere; traduits du Grec (French). *Translator or author:* Lebrun. Paris, France.

1822—L'Odissea di Omero; tradotta [reprint of the Milan edition of 1817] (Italian). *Translator or author:* Ippolito Pindemonte. Verona, Italy: Soc. tipogr.

1822—L'Odissea di Omero, tradotta [reprint of the Verona edition, also of 1822] (Italian). *Translator or author:* Ippolito Pindemonte. Livorno, Italy.

1822—The Odyssey of Homer; translated from the Greek (English). *Translator or author:* Alexander Pope. New York, N.Y.: Myers and Smith.

1822—The Iliad and Odyssey [reprint of the 1715–20, 1725–26 editions; in the series: Sandford's Works of the British Poets] (English). *Translator or author:* Alexander Pope.

1822—Iliadis (Greek). *Translator or author:* Robinson. Catskill [location?].

1822—Homers Odyssee; ubersetzt; 10r Gesang; als erste Probe (German). *Translator or author:* Konrad Schwenck. Bonn, Germany: Weber.

1822—Werke von Homer; ubersetzt; 5th ed. (German). *Translator or author:* Johann Heinrich Voss. Stuttgart, Germany; Tubingen, Germany: J. G. Cotta Buchhandlung.

1822–23— Homers Iliade; prosaisch ubersetzt und kurz erlautert (German). *Translator or author:* E. F. Ch. Oertel. Munich, Germany: Fleischmann.

1822–24— Odyssea; cum interpretatione Eustathii quorum grammaticorum delectu, commentariis edidit D. Baumgarten, Crusiae (Greek). *Translator or author:* Crusius Baumgarten. Leipzig, Germany: C. H. F. Hartmann.

1822–25— Homeri Carmina. Halle an der Saale, Germany: Orphan.

1822–28— Odyssea; Gr. ed. et annot. perp. ill. G. Ed. Lowe (Greek). *Translator or author:* G. Ed. Lowe; F. A. Ad. Heinichen. Leipzig, Germany.

1823— L'Iliade d'Homere; en Grec; edition collationnee sur les textes les plus purs, par Jos. Planche; precede stereot. De MM. le marquis de Paroy et Durouchail (Greek). Paris, France: Lesage.

1823— Odyssey; translated into English verse, etc. (English). George Bell Whittaker.

1823— Homeri Opera Omnia, Graece et Latine; ex recensione et cum notis Sam. Clarke; accessit varietas lectionum Mscr. Lips. Et editionum veterum cura I. A. Ernesti, qui et suas notas adspersit; adnexa sunt F. A. Wolfii prolegomena (Greek; Latin). London, England: Priestly.

1823— La Batrachomyomachie, en Grec; edition stereotype d'apres le procede de MM le marquis de Paroy et Durouchail (Greek). Paris, France: Lesage.

1823— La Batrachomyomachie d'Homere; traduite en vers Francais; avec le texte en regard (Greek; French). Paris, France: L'Avocat.

1823— The Odyssey (English). London, England.

1823— Homeri Ilias. Leipzig, Germany; Leiden (Leyden), Germany: Samuel and Joann. Luchtmans.

1823— La Batrachomyomachie d'Homere; traduite en Francois (French). *Translator or author:* Jules Berger de Xivrey. Paris, France: Arth. Bertrand.

1823— The Odyssey; translated into English prose, as literally as the different idioms of the Greek and English languages will allow; with explanatory notes; by a member of the University of Oxford (English). *Translator or author:* Henry Francis Cary. Oxford, England.

1823— Odyssey (Italian). *Translator or author:* Eust. Fiocci. Pavia, Italy.

1823— Iliade di Omero; traduzione (Italian).

Translator or author: Vincenzo Monti. Florence, Italy: P. Caselli.

1823— Odissea di Omero; tradotta (Italian). *Translator or author:* Ippol. Pindemonte. Livorno, Italy.

1823— L'Odissea (Italian). *Translator or author:* Ippolito Pindemonte. Florence, Italy: L. Ciardetti.

1823— Homers Ilias; verdeutscht (German). *Translator or author:* Friedrich Leopold Graf zu Stolberg. Hamburg, Germany: Perthes.

1823— Homers Ilias; text und deutsche Ubersetzung; eine Ubersetzungsprobe in achtzeiligen Stanzen, von Waldhauser (in Zeitschrift fur Studirendevon K. F. Loose and J. M. Waldhauser} (German). *Translator or author:* Waldhauser. Passau: Pustet.

1823–24— Homeri Opera, Graece (Greek). *Translator or author:* J. Fr. Boissonade. Paris, France: Lefevre.

1823–25— L'Iliade de'Omero; volgarizzata in versi Sciolti (Italian). *Translator or author:* Mich. Leoni. Torino (Turin), Italy.

1824— Homeri Ilias et Odyssea (Greek). London, England.

1824— Ilias; 16th ed [edited by Samuel Clarke] (Greek, Latin). London, England.

1824— Homeri Opera Omnia; 2nd ed [edited by Jo. Aug. Ernesti based on Samuel Clarke's; reprint of the 1759–64 edition] (Greek, Latin). Leipzig, Germany: Weidmann.

1824— [H]omerou Ilias = Homeri Ilias; ad novissimae Heynii editionis textum expressa (Greek; Latin). London, England: Robertson.

1824— L'Iliade di Omero; traduz. epica in ottava rima [from the 1818 edition] (Italian). *Translator or author:* Lorenzo Mancini. Florence, Italy: Molini.

1824— The Iliad of Homer; translated (English). *Translator or author:* Alexander Pope. London, England: J. F. Dove.

1824— The Poetical Works of Alexander Pope, esq.; including his translation of Homer; with the life of the author by Dr. Johnson (English). *Translator or author:* Alexander Pope. London, England: Jones and Company.

1824–61— [H]omerou Epe = Homeri Carmina; ad optimorum librorum fidem expressa, curante Guilielmo Dindorio. Leipzig, Germany: B. G. Teubner.

1825— The Iliad of Homer; translated into

English prose, as literally as the different idioms of the Greek and English languages will allow; with explanatory notes; by a graduate of the University of Oxford; 2nd ed. (English). London, England: George Bell Whittaker.

1825— Iliade (Greek). Florence, Italy.

1825— Ilias, Graece et Latine; ex recens. S[amuel] Clarke (Greek; Latin). Nunn.

1825— Homeri Ilias; accedunt Hymni et Epigrammata. Halle an der Saale, Germany: Orphan.

1825— Ilias; new translation, with notes by Blank Blank, Esq., pt. 1 [books 1 and 2] (English). Robertson.

1825— Homeri Ilias Graece et Latine; ex recensione et cum notis Samuelle Clarke; 16th ed. (Greek; Latin). London, England: J. Cuthell.

1825— Homeri Ilias. 16th ed [edited by Samuel Clarke] (Greek, Latin). London, England.

1825— The Iliad of Homer; translated into English prose, with explanatory notes; by a graduate of the University of Oxford (English). Oxford, England.

1825— Inni di Omero; trad. (Italian). Venice, Italy.

1825— Batracomiomachia ed Inni di Omero; tradotti da varj autori (Italian). Macerata, Italy.

1825— Oeuvres d'Homere, traduites du Grec (French). Paris, France: Masson and Son.

1825— La Batrachomyomachie; edition collationnee sur les textes les plus purs, avec des sommaires nouveaux, par J. Planche (Greek). Paris, France: Lasneau.

1825— Iliade d'Homere; edition collationnee sur les textes les plus pures, avec des sommaires nouveaux, par Jos. Planche. Paris, France: Lanneau.

1825— Batrchomiomachia ed Inni di Omero; tradott da varj autori (Italian). Macerata, Italy.

1825— Carmina; secondum recensionem Wolfii, cum praefat. Godofr. Hermanni (Greek). Leipzig, Germany: Car. Tauchnitz.

1825— L'Iliade; trad. (French). *Translator or author:* Paul Jeremie Bitaube. Paris, France: Castel de Courval.

1825— La Traduction de l'Iliade par Ceruti [reprint of the Milan edition of 1825 from the 1st edition in 1776] (French). *Translator or author:* Ceruti. Florence, Italy: L. Ciardetti.

1825— L'Iliade et l'Odyssee; traduit par Mad.

Dacier en prose, avec des notes et des figures de Picard [reprint of the 1711–16 edition] (French). *Translator or author:* Anne LeFevre Dacier. Paris, France.

1825— Oeuvers d'Homere; trad. (French). *Translator or author:* M. Jean-Baptiste Dugas-Montbel. Paris, France: Sautelet.

1825— Homers Odysseens I-III Sang overs. af P. G. Fibiger (Danish). *Translator or author:* P. G. Fibiger. Copenhagen, Denmark.

1825— Oeuvres d'Homere; trad. (French). *Translator or author:* Lebrun. Paris, France: Bossange.

1825— Homers Odysseens VI ferste Boger, metrick. overs af P. M. Moller (Danish). *Translator or author:* P. M. Moller. Copenhagen, Denmark.

1825— Iliade di Omero; trad. in versi Toscani [reprint of the Brescia edition of 1810] (Italian). *Translator or author:* Vincenzo Monti. Milan, Italy: Stella.

1825— Iliade di Omero; tradotta (Italian). *Translator or author:* Vincenzo Monti. Milan, Italy: Nicolo Bettoni.

1825— Iliade di Omero; traduzione; 5th ed. (Italian). *Translator or author:* Vincenzo Monti. Bologna, France: Veroli e comp. Presso Turchi.

1825— Iliade di Omero; traduzione (Italian). *Translator or author:* Vincenzo Monti. Naples, Italy: Stamperia Francese.

1825— The Odyssey of Homer; translated; to which is added the Battle of the Frogs and Mice [by Thomas Parnell] (English). *Translator or author:* Alexander Pope. London, England: etc. Baynes.

1825— The Iliad of Homer (English). *Translator or author:* Alexander Pope. New York, N.Y.: W. Barradaile.

1825— The Iliad of Homer; translated (English). *Translator or author:* Alexander Pope. Chiswick, England: C. & C. Whittingham.

1825— Die Homerischen Hymnen metrisch ubersetzt und mit Anmerkungen begleitet (German). *Translator or author:* Konrad Schwenck. Frankfurt am Main, Germany: Bronner.

1826— Homers Batrachomyomachie; in metrischer Deutscher Ubersetzung mit dem Urtexte von Jos. Helm. (German). Mannheim, Germany: Loffler.

1826— Homeri Opera; nova editio iteratis curis castigata et expolita. Leipzig, Germany: Tauchnitz.

1826—[H]omerou Odysseia mixra; oder sechs Bucher der Odyssee, enthaltend die vollstandige Reisebeschreibung des Ulysses, fur den ersten Schulgebrauch Unbemittelter herausgegeben von Ch. Kock (Greek). Marburg, Germany: Krieger.

1826—Iliad; with English notes to the first six books. London, England: Valpy.

1826—L'Iliade et l'Odyssee [reprint of the 1804 edition] (French). *Translator or author:* Paul Jeremie Bitaube. Paris, France: Castel-Courval.

1826—Ilias; 2nd ed [edited by Samuel Clarke] (Greek, Latin). *Translator or author:* Clarke. New York, N.Y.

1826—L'Iliade d'Homere; traduite (French). *Translator or author:* Anne LeFevre Dacier. Avignon, France: Fils Aine Offray.

1826—Irrfahrten des Odysseus; in vier und zwanzig Gesangen; freie Nachbildung in gereimten Strophen nach Homer (German). *Translator or author:* Hedwig Hoffmeier Hulle. Bremen, Germany: Heyse.

1826—Homers Ilias und Odyssee (German). *Translator or author:* K. G. Kelle. Leipzig, Germany.

1826—L'Iliade et l'Odyssee d'Homere [1st uniting of this translator's The Iliad of 1776 and 1809 and The Odyssey of 1819] (French). *Translator or author:* Charles-Francois Lebrun. Paris, France: Bossange.

1826—Iliade di Omero; trad. in versi Toscani da Vinc[enzo] Monti [reprint of the Brescia edition of 1810] (Italian). *Translator or author:* Vincenzo Monti. Florence, Italy: L. Ciardetti.

1826—Homers Heldengesange; ubersetzt (German). *Translator or author:* C. G. Neumann. Dresden, Germany: Arnold.

1826—The Iliad and Odyssey of Homer; translated; to which is added The Battle of the Frogs and Mice (English). *Translator or author:* Alexander Pope. London, England: Jones and Company.

1826—Homers Odysse, ubersetzt; 5r Gesang; als zweite Probe (German). *Translator or author:* Konrad Schwenck. Frankfurt am Main, Germany: Bronner.

1826—[H]ymne an Demeter; ubersetzt und erlautert; mit dessen Bildniss (Greek; German). *Translator or author:* Johann Heinrich Voss. Heidelberg, Germany: C. F. Winter.

1826–27—Homeri Carmina; secundum recensionem Wolfii cum praefatione Godoredi Hermanni. Leipzig, Germany: Car. Tauchnitz.

1826–27—Homers Werke; prosaisch ubersetzt (German). *Translator or author:* Josef Stanislav Zauper. Prague, Czechoslavakia: Calve.

1826–28—Homeri Odyssea, Graece; in usum scholarum edidit et annotatione perpetus illustravit E. Lowe (Greek). Leipzig, Germany: Kayser.

1826–28—L'Iliade et l'Odyssee; text Grec, d'apres l'edition de Wolf; nouvelle edition, avec sommaires, arguments, notes en Francais, et tables des matieres (Greek). Paris, France: Aug. Delalain.

1826–69—Homeri Carmina; ad optimorum librorum fiden expressa curante Guilielmo Dindorfio. Leipzig, Germany: B. G. Teubner.

1827—The Iliad of Homer, chiefly from the text of Heyne; with copious English notes illustrating the grammatical construction, the manners and customs, the mythology and antiquities of the heroic ages; and preliminary observations ... by William Trollope. London, England: Rivington.

1827—Odyssea; cum scholiis, et variis lect. accedunt Batrachomyomachia, Hymni, fragmenta (Greek). Oxford, England: Clarendon Press.

1827—Hymnus in Cererem; editus a D. Ruhnkenio; accedunt C. G. Mitscherlichii adnotationes (Latin). Leipzig, Germany: C. H. F. Hartmann.

1827—L'Iliade d'Homere par Jos. Planche. Paris, France; Berlin, Germany: Mandar; Devaux.

1827—L'Iliade d'Homere; texte Grec d'apres l'edition de Wolf; nouvelle edition, avec sommaire, arguments, notes en Francais et une table des matieres (Greek). Paris, France.

1827—Oeuvres d'Homere; trad. (French). *Translator or author:* Paul Jeremie Bitaube. Paris, France: Aug. Delalain.

1827—Homers Iliaden overs.; orig. Versemaal af P. G. Fibiger I H. (I–VI Sang.) (Danish). *Translator or author:* P. G. Fibiger. Copenhagen, Denmark.

1827—La Iliada de Homero; traducida del Griego en verso Castellano [reprint of the 1788 edition] (Spanish). *Translator or author:* Ignacio Garcia Malo. Madrid, Spain.

1827—Iliade di Omero; trad. in terza rima (Italian). *Translator or author:* L. B. Novara.

1827—Odissea di Omero; tradotta; prima edizione Milanese, a cui si aggiugne le tavole delle cose notabili e dei nomi propri in essa contenuti [reprint of the 1817 edition, with corrections] (Italian). *Translator or author:* Ippolito Pindemonte. Milan, Italy: Silvestri.

1827—The Odyssey (English). *Translator or author:* Alexander Pope. London, England.

1827—The Iliad of Homer; chiefly from the text of Heyne, with copious English notes illustr. the grammatical construction, the manners and customs, the mythology and antiquities of the heroic ages, and prelim. observ. on points of classical interest and import (Greek). *Translator or author:* W. Trollope. London, England.

1827–28—Ilias, Book I; with literal translation on the plan recommended by Mr. Locke, 2 parts (English). J. Taylor.

1827–28—L'Iliade et l'Odyssee d'Homere; traduit etc. avec des remarques sur Homere [reprint of the Paris edition of 1780–85] (French). *Translator or author:* Paul Jeremie Bitaube. Lyon, France.

1827–28—Homers Odyssee; erlautert von I. St. Zauper. IrBd. Abthl. I–IV. Rhaps. I–XXIV. Mit der homerischen Welttafel. *Translator or author:* Josef Stanislav Zauper. Vienna, Austria: Volke F.

1828—Homers Odyssee; erlautert von J. St. Zauper. Vienna, Austria: F. Volke.

1828—[H]omerou Odysseia = L'Odyssee d'Homere; texte Grec-Latin avec analyses et notes en Francais (Greek; Latin). Paris, France: Aug. Delalain.

1828—La Batrachomyomachie; texte Grec, avec sommaires et des notes en Francais, suivie d'un lexique Grec-Francois (Greek). Paris, France: Aug. Delalain.

1828—Homeri Odyssea; Graece et Latine; edidit annotationesque ex notis nonnullis Mss. A Sam[uel] Clarke; 6th ed. (Greek; Latin). London, England: Longman.

1828—L'Odyssee d'Homere, en Grec; avec des sommaires Latins et Francais, soigneusement corriges d'apres la derniere edition de M. Wolf, par Ch. M. E[erhart] (Greek). Paris, France: Nyon.

1828—L'Iliade d'Homere, en Grec; nouvelle edition, enrichie de nombreuses imitations d'Homere, qui se trouvent dans Virgile; par Fl. Lecluse; Chants I–IV (Greek). Toulouse, France: Vieusseux.

1828—Iliade d'Homere; traduction (French). *Translator or author:* Paul Jeremie Bitaube. Paris, France: Gauthier Freres.

1828—Oeuvres d'Homere; avec des remarques; precedees de reflexions sur Homere et sur la traduction des poetes (French). *Translator or author:* Paul Jeremie Bitaube. Paris, France: Ledentu.

1828—Oeuvres d'Homere; trad. (French). *Translator or author:* Paul Jeremie Bitaube. Besancon, France: Deis.

1828—The First Six Books of the Iliad of Homer; literally translated into English prose, with copious explanatory notes, and a preliminary dissertation on his life and writings; by a member of the University (English). *Translator or author:* Henry Francis Cary. Cambridge, England: Hall.

1828—Homeri Carmina Minora; Hymni, Epigrammatica Fragmenta et Batrachomyomachia; ad optimarum editionum fidem recensuit et notis instruxit F. Franke. *Translator or author:* F. Franke. Leipzig, Germany: Teubner.

1828—Hymnus auf Aphrodite in Metrischer Deutscher Ubersetzung mit dem Urtexte (Greek; German). *Translator or author:* F. J. Grieser.

1828—Odyssea (Greek). *Translator or author:* Loewe. Leipzig, Germany.

1828—Iliade di Omero; trad. in versi Toscani [reprint of the Brescis edition of 1810] (Italian). *Translator or author:* Vincenzo Monti. Naples, Italy.

1828—Iliade di Omero; trad. in versi Toscani [reprint of the Brescia edition of 1810] (Italian). *Translator or author:* Vincenzo Monti. Bologna, France: Masi.

1828—Odyssey (English). *Translator or author:* Alexander Pope. Philadelphia, Pa.

1828–29—[H]omerou Ilias = The Iliad of Homer; from the Text of Wolf; with English notes and Flaxman's illustrative designs edited by C[orneliu] C[onway] Felton [1st ed] (Greek). Leipzig, Germany: Car. Tauchnitz.

1828–34—Les Oeuvres d'Homere; traduit nouvelle en francais; L'Odyssee d'Homere, suivie de la Batrachomyomachie, des Hymnes, de divers petits poemes, attribues a Homere; Nouv. ed (avec le texte en regard); 2nd ed. (Greek; French). *Translator or author:* M. Jean-Baptiste Dugas-Montbel. Paris, France: Ambrosio Firmin Didot.

1828–36—[Opera] (German). *Translator or author:* E. Schaumann. Benzlau, Germany.

1829—L'Iliade d'Homere, en Grec; traduction interlineaire; Chants I–IV (French). Paris, France: Aug. Delalain.

1829—Homeri Ilias; Graece cum notis Latinis (Greek). Paris, France: Hachette.

1829—Homeri Iliados Prima Series, Libris I–IV; constans, expressa versibus Latinis, cum notis, a N. F. L. C. D. L. G. (Latin). Paris, France: Hachette.

1829—Odysseae Homericae Rhapsodiae Sex; notis et indicibus discipulorum usui adcommodatis instruxit G. J. Bekker (Greek). Leuven (Louvain), Belgium: G. Cuelens.

1829—L'Iliade d'Homere en Grec; expliquee en Francais suivant la methode des colleges par deux traductions l'une litterale et interlineaire avec la construction du Grec dans l'ordre naturel des idees, l'autre conforme au genie de Franc.; Chants I–VIII (Greek; French). *Translator or author:* Paul Jeremie Bitaube. Paris, France: Aug. Delalain.

1829—L'Iliade et l'Odyssee d'Homere; traduit etc. avec des remarques sur Homere [reprint of the 1780–85 edition] (French). *Translator or author:* Paul Jeremie Bitaube. Paris, France: Philippe.

1829—L'Iliade d'Homere; texte en regard, avec deux traductions, l'une interlineaire et l'autre correcte; Chants I–IV; par E. Boutmy (Greek; French). *Translator or author:* E. Boutmy. Paris, France: Mansut.

1829—Iliada Gomera; perevedennaia (Russian). *Translator or author:* Nikolaaei Ivanovich Gnedich. St. Petersburg, Russia: Imperatorskoi Rossiiskoi Akademii.

1829—Iliade di Omero; trad. in versi Toscani [reprint of the Brescia edition of 1810] (Italian). *Translator or author:* Vincenzo Monti. Milan, Italy.

1829—Odissea di Omero; tradotta (Italian). *Translator or author:* Ippolito Pindemonte. Torino (Turin), Italy: G. Pomba.

1829—L'Odyssea di Omero; trad. (Italian). *Translator or author:* Ippolito Pindemonte. Milan, Italy.

1829—Odissea di Omero; trad.; con aggiunta della Batracomiochia e di alcuni Inni, tradotta da altri autori [reprint of the Verona edition of 1822] (Italian). *Translator or author:* Ippolito Pindemonte. Milan, Italy.

1829—Homeri Iliados Lib. I. V. 1–91; Latinis versibus redditus a Schulze (in Seebodii Archiv fur Philologie und Paedagogik., no. 34) (Latin). *Translator or author:* Schulze.

1829—Catullus; ubers von Konrad Schwenck; Anhang: Sechster Gesang der Odysee (German). *Translator or author:* Konrad Schwenck. Frankfurt am Main, Germany: J. D. Sauerlander.

1829–30—Homere, Iliade; texte en regard, avec deux traductions, l'une interlineaire et l'autre correcte (French). *Translator or author:* E. Boutmy. Paris, France: Chez Mansut Fils Librarie Classique.

1829–31—Homerus Slavicis Dialectis Cognata Lingua Scripsit; ex ipsius Homeri Carmine Ostendit Gregorius Dankovsky, Folium I–V, Iliados, Lib.I.1–303; Slavice et Graece idem sonans et significans, adjecta nova versione Latina et commentario Graeco-Slavico (Slavic; Greek; Latin). *Translator or author:* Gregor Dankowszky. Presburg [?]: Landes.

1829–40—Fyrsta [-tuttugasta og fjoroa] bok af Homeri Odyssea; a Islenzku utlogd (Icelandic). *Translator or author:* Sveinbjorn Egilsson. Videyar Klaustri, Iceland: Kostnao Bessastaoa Skola.

1830—[H]omerou Odysseia; zum drittenmal herausgegeben von C. Kock (Greek). Leipzig, Germany: Nauck.

1830—The Hymns of Homer; translated into verse from the original Greek; with notes, critical and explanatory; to which is prefixed, an inquiry into the life of Homer by Columbus C. Conwell (Greek; English). Philadelphia, Pa.: Mifflin and Parry.

1830—Homeri et Homeridarum Opera et Reliquiae (Greek). Hilpertohusae [location?].

1830—L'Iliade d'Homere en Grec; nouvelle edition, collationnee sur le texte de Wolf, enrichie de sommaires nouveaux et de notes historiques, mythologiques, archeologiques et grammaticales; par V. Parisot et Liskenne; Chants I–IV (Greek). Paris, France: Poilleux.

1830—Ilias; ex recensione F. A. Wolfii edidit notisque in usum scholarum instruxit Ch. F. Ingerslev (Greek). Havn [location?]: Gyldendal.

1830—Opera (Greek). London, England: William Pickering.

1830—La Batrachomyomachie en Quatres Langes: Grecque ancienne et moderne [from the 1707 edition], Latine [edited by Fl. Lecuse] et Francaise [by Boivin] (Greek, Modern Greek, Latin, French). Toulouse (Toloso), France: Fl. Lecluse.

1830—L'Iliade et l'Odyssee d'Homere; traduction nouvelle en vers Francais, precedee d'un essai sur l'epopee Homerique (French). *Translator or author:* M. Anne Bignan. Paris, France: Belin-Mandar.

1830—Oeuvres d'Homere; avec des remarques, precedees de reflexions sur Homere et sur la traduction des poetes (French). *Translator or author:* Paul Jeremie Bitaube. Paris, France: Philippe.

1830—Iliade di Omero; tradotta (Italian). *Translator or author:* Vincenzo Monti. Milan, Italy: Gaetano Schiepatti.

1830—Iliade di Omero; trad. in versi Toscani

[reprint of the Brescia edition of 1810] (Italian). *Translator or author:* Vincenzo Monti. Venice, Italy.

1830— Odissea do Omero; tr. (Italian). *Translator or author:* Ippolito Pindemonte. Milan, Italy: Gaetano Schiepalli.

1830— The Poetical Works of Alexander Pope; to which is prefixed the life of the author, by Dr. Johnson (English). *Translator or author:* Alexander Pope. Philadelphia, Pa.: J. J. Woodward.

1830— Collezione delle Similitudini Contenute nella Iliade di Omero Estratte Fedelmente dalle Due Piu'Celebri Versioni, l'Una Latina del P. Raimondo Cunich, l'Altra Italiana del Cav. Vincenzo Monti (Latin; Italian). *Translator or author:* P. Raimondo; Vincenzo Monti. Rome, Italy: Mercuri e Robaglia.

1830— Homers Werke; ubersetzt, mit einer Einleitung und erklarenden Anmerkungen versehen (German). *Translator or author:* E. Schaumann. Prenzlau: Ragoczy.

1830— Sechster Gesang der Odyssee; ubersetzt; cum eiusdem versione Catulli carminum (German). *Translator or author:* Conrad Schwenk. Frankfurt am Main, Germany: Sauerlander.

1830— The First Book of the Iliad; the parting of Hector and Andromache; and the Shield of Achilles; specimens of a new version of Homer (English). *Translator or author:* William Sotheby. London, England: John Murray.

1830— Gesandtskabet til Achilles; eller Iliadens niende sang, oversat med indledende bemaerkninger om an Dansk Homerisk oversaettelse og om det heroiske versemaal (Danish). *Translator or author:* Christian Frederik Emil Wilster. Soroe, Denmark.

1830–43— Homers Werke; im Versmass der Urschrift ubersetzt (German). *Translator or author:* Ernst Wiedasch. Stuttgart, Germany: Metzler.

1831— Homeri Ilias et Odyssea (Greek). London, England.

1831— Iliad and Odyssey (Graece); Diamond edition (Greek). London, England: Pickering.

1831— L'Iliade et l'Odyssee d'Homere; trad. en vers Francais (French). *Translator or author:* M. Anne Bignan. Paris, France.

1831— Ilias, Books I and II; Battle of Frogs and Mice, etc. *Translator or author:* William John Blew. Oxford, England: Talboys; Pickering.

1831— La Iliada; traducida (en verso y con notas) (Spanish). *Translator or author:* D. Jose Gomez Hermosilla. Madrid, Spain.

1831— La Iliada de Homero; traducida del Griego al Castellano (Spanish). *Translator or author:* Jose Gomez Hermosilla. Madrid, Spain: Imprenta Real.

1831— Odissea di Omero; trad. [reprint of the edition printed in Verona in 1822] (Italian). *Translator or author:* Ippolito Pindemonte. Milan, Italy.

1831— Homer's Iliad; translated into English verse (English). *Translator or author:* William Sotheby. London, England: John Murray.

1831–32— L'Illiade di Omero; testo Greco arricchito della traditione letterale in Latino dell'Heyne, della versione metrica del Cunich parimente in Latino, e delle piu accredite nelle cinque principali lingue d'Europa [Italian of Vincenzo Monti, German of Johann V (Greek; Italian). Florence, Italy: Borghi Passigli.

1832— Homere, Hymne a Ceres; texte Grec, avec sommaires et notes en Francais, par E. G. (Greek). Paris, France: Aug. Delalain.

1832— Ilias (Greek). New York, N.Y.

1832— [H]omerou Ilias = Homeri Ilias; ex recensione C. G. Heynii fere impressa; in usum scholarum; 4th ed. (Greek). London, England: Valpianis; Longman, Whittaker, Simpkin etc.

1832— Ilias, Graece et Latine; ex recens S[amuel] Clarke (Greek; Latin). London, England: Baldwin.

1832— L'Iliade travestie; par une societe de gens de lettres, de savants, de magistrats (French). *Translator or author:* L. Dumoulin; A. Goujon, Ch-Martin Rousselet. Paris, France: A. Goujon.

1832— Iliadis Homericae Prima Rhapsodia, Fennice Reddita; quam Praeside Carolo Nicolao Keckman, publico examini modeste offert auctor Ericus Alexander Ingman (Finnish). *Translator or author:* Karl Niklas Keckman. Helsinki, Finland: J. C. and Son Frenckell.

1832— Inni; trad. (Italian). *Translator or author:* A. Venanzio. Padova (Padua), Italy.

1832–33— Iliad and Odyssey [series: Family Classical Library] (English). *Translator or author:* Alexander Pope. Valpy.

1832–35— Carmina; recognovit et explicuit Fridericus Henricus Bothe (Greek). *Translator or author:* Fridericus Henricus Bothe. Leipzig, Germany: Hahn.

1832–36— Homeri Ilias; recensuit et brevi annotatione instruxit Francisc. Spitzner Saxo (Greek). *Translator or author:* Francisc. Spitzner. Gotha, Germany; Erfurt, Germany: Guil. Hennings.

1833— Ilias, Graece et Latini; illustrated by critical and explanatory notes, indices, etc. by Dr. James Kennedy Baillie [from the 1821–22 edition] (Greek; Latin). Dublin, Ireland: J. Cumming (at University Press).

1833— The Iliad of Homer; translated into English prose; with explanatory notes, by a graduate of the University of Oxford; 3rd ed. (English). London, England: Whittaker, Treacher & Co..

1833— Ilias; first six books, with literal prose translation (Greek; English). Cambridge, England: Hankin and Hall.

1833— The Odyssey of Homer; translated into English prose, as literally as the different idioms of the Greek and English languages will allow, with explanatory notes, by a member of the University of Oxford (English). *Translator or author:* Henry Francis Cary. London, England: Whittaker; Longman, Rees, Orme etc.

1833— The Iliad of Homer; translated into English prose, with explanatory notes; by a graduate of the University of Oxford [reprint of edition of 1821, with corrections by J. A. Buckley] (English). *Translator or author:* Henry Francis Cary. Oxford, England.

1833— The Iliad of Homer; from the text of Wolf. With English notes (English). *Translator or author:* Cornelius Conway Felton. Boston, Mass.; Cambridge, Engand: Gray Hilliard; Brown, Shattuck.

1833— L'Iliade; trad. (Italian). *Translator or author:* Mich. Leoni. Torino (Turin), Italy.

1833— Omero; Col Supplimento do Quinto Calabro, Virgilio, Volume Unico (Italian). *Translator or author:* Vincenzo Monti. Naples, Italy: Tipografia della Sibilla.

1833— Iliade di Omero; trad. in versi Toscani [reprint of edition printed at Brescia in 1810] (Italian). *Translator or author:* Vincenzo Monti. Milan, Italy.

1833— The Iliad and Odyssey of Homer [series: Sandford's Works of the British Poets] (English). *Translator or author:* Alexander Pope. London, England.

1833— The Iliad and Odyssey of Homer; translated; illustrated by the designs of Flaxman (English). *Translator or author:* William Sotheby. London, England: G. and W. Nicol; J. Murray.

1833— L'Odyssee d'Homere; tr. en Francais (French). *Translator or author:* Jean Baptista Sugas-Montbel. Paris, France: Ambrosio Firmin Didot Freres.

1833— Homers Werke (German). *Translator or author:* Johann Heinrich Voss. Stuttgart, Germany.

1834— Homeri Odyssea; cum versione Latina ex recensione et cum notis Samuelis Clarkii, et Io. Augusti Ernesti; edidit suasque notulas adspersit Johannes Walker (Greek; Latin). Dublin, Ireland: R. Graisberry.

1834— [H]omerou Ilias = Homeri Ilias; cum brevi annotatione curante C[hristian] G[ottlob] Heyne; accedunt scholia minora passim emendate (Greek). Oxford, England: Clarendon Press.

1834— [H]omerou = The Iliad of Homer; from the Text of Wolf; with English notes and Flaxman's illustrative designs edited by C[orneliu] C[onway] Felton; 2nd ed. [reprint of the edition printed in Leipzig in 1828–29] (Greek). Boston, Mass.: Gray Hilliard.

1834— Odyssey, Book XI, literally translated (English). Cambridge, England.

1834— [H]omerou Ilias = Homeri Ilias; cum brevi annotatione curante Chr[istian] Gottl[ob] Heyne (Greek). London, England: Priestley.

1834— [H]omerou Ilias = Homeri Ilias; ex recensione C[hristian] G[ottlob] Heynii fere impressa; cum notis Anglicis, in usum scholarum; curante J[ohn] D[avid] Ogilby (Greek). New York, N.Y.

1834— Ilias; with English notes by Dr. Ja[me]s Kennedy. *Translator or author:* James Kennedy. George Bell Whittaker.

1834— The Iliad; translated (English). *Translator or author:* Alexander Pope. London, England: T. Allman.

1834— Specimen Interpretationis Odysseae Latinis Numeris Adstrictae (Latin). *Translator or author:* G. T. Scheibner.

1834— Odyssee VII; ubersetzt (German). *Translator or author:* Konrad Schwenck.

1834— The Odyssey of Homer (English). *Translator or author:* William Sotheby. Nicol.

1834— Iliad and Odyssey; translated (English). *Translator or author:* William Sotheby. London, England: John Murray.

1834— Alexander's Casket (English). *Translator or author:* Tufts. Lexington.

1834— Homerics; attempted by Archdeacon

Wrangham [Odyssey V and Iliad III] (English). *Translator or author:* Wrangham. Chester, England.

1834–35—Die Sage von Odysseus nach Homer (German). *Translator or author:* Ed. Eyth. Karlsruhe, Germany.

1835—Burgers Sammtliche Werke; hrsg. von August Wilhelm Bohtz; einzig rechtmassige gesammt-ausgabe in einem bande; mit dem sauber in stahl gestochenen bildnisse des dichters und einem facsimile seiner handscrift (German). *Translator or author:* Gottfried August Burger. Gottingen, Germany: Dieterich'sche Verlagsbuchhandlung.

1835—The Iliad of Homer (Greek). *Translator or author:* Cornelius Conway Felton. Boston, Mass.

1835—Batrachomyomachia, ou Guerra dos Ratos e das Raas: Poemeto Heroe-Comico por Homero; traduzido do Grego em verso solto Portuguez (Portuguese). *Translator or author:* Antonio Maria do Couto. Lisbon, Portugal: R. D. Costa.

1835—Etudes Epiques et Dramatiques; ou, novelle traduction en vers des chants les plus celebres des poemes d'Homere, de Virgile, du Camoens et du Tasse; avec le texte en regard et des notes (French). *Translator or author:* Victor de Perrodil. Paris, France: B. et Blanc Cormon.

1835—The Poetical Works of Alexander Pope, esq.; to which is prefixed the life of the author, by Dr. Johnson (English). *Translator or author:* Alexander Pope. Philadelphia, Pa.: J. J. Woodward.

1835—Odyssee 2; ubersetzt (German). *Translator or author:* Konrad Schwenck. Frankfurt am Main, Germany.

1835—Forste Bog af Homers Odyssee, overs. til Veiledning for dem, der forberede sig til examen artium af W. Thrane (Norwegian). *Translator or author:* W. Thrane. Christ. [Norway?].

1835–40—Homeri Odysea; a Islanzku utlagoar (Icelandic). *Translator or author:* Sveinbjorn Egilsson. Vioey, Iceland: Vioeyjar Klaustri.

1836—Ilias, Hamiltonian System. Aylott.

1836—Ilias; with notes by William Trollope; 2nd ed. Rivington.

1836—Oeuvres d'Homere; traduits en Francais (French). *Translator or author:* Paul Jeremie Bitaube.

1836—The Iliad and Odyssey of Homer [reprint of 1791 edition] (English). *Translator or author:* William Cowper.

1836—l'Iliade et l'Odyssee d'Homere; traduit du Grec (French). *Translator or author:* Charles-Francois Lebrun. Paris, France: Lefevre.

1836—The Poetical Works of A. Pope; to which is prefixed the life of the author, by Dr. Johnson (English). *Translator or author:* Alexander Pope. Philadelphia, Pa.: J. J. Woodward.

1836—The Odyssey of Homer, with, The Battle of the Frogs and Mice; translated, with explanatory notes and index (English). *Translator or author:* Alexander Pope. London, England: Scott, Webster, and Geary.

1836—Homer (English). *Translator or author:* Alexander Pope. New York, N.Y.

1836—Homers Iliaden; overs. (Danish). *Translator or author:* Christian Frederik Emil Wilster. Copenhagen, Denmark.

1837—Ilias, Graece; from the text of Wolf with English notes ed. by C. C. Felton, with Flaxman's designs on a reduced scale (Greek). Boston, Mass.

1837—Homeri Carmina et Cycli Epici Reliquiae (ex recensione Guiliemus Dindorf); cum indice nominum et rerum [series: Bibliothecque Grecque] (Greek; Latin). Paris, France: Ambrosio Firmin Didot Freres.

1837—Homeri Ilias Graece; quam vertebant Latine soluta oratione C. G. Heyne, versibus item Latinis R. Cunich, Italicis V. Monti, Germanicis Voss, Anglicis Pope, Gallicis, Aignan, Ibericis Gracia-Malo (Greek). Florence, Italy: V. Batelli and Sons.

1837—Homeri Iliadis Primi Duo Libri; recognovit et delectis veterum grammaticorum scholiis suisque commentariis instructos ed. Theodorus Fridericus Freytagius. Leipzig, Germany: L. Vossium.

1837—La Batrachomyomachie d'Homere; traduite en Francais (le texte Grec en regard), par J. Berger de Xivrey; 2nd edition, augmentee d'une dissertation sur ce poem, trad. de l'Italien du comte Leopardi; et de la guerre comique, ancienne imitation en vers burles (Greek, French). *Translator or author:* J. Berger de Xivrey. Paris, France: Arth. Bertrand.

1837—The Odyssey of Homer; translated into English blank verse (English). *Translator or author:* William Cowper. London, England: Baldwin and Cradock.

1837—Iliadis Primi Duo Libri; recognitos et delectis vett. grammaticorum scholiis suisque commentariis instr. edidit Theod. Frideric. Freytagius. *Translator or author:* Theod. Frideric. Freytagius. St. Petersburg, Russia.

1837—Iliade di Omero; trad. in versi Toscani da Vinc[enzo] Monti [reprint of edition printed at Brescia in 1810] (Italian). *Translator or author:* Vincenzo Monti. Venice, Italy.

1837—Odissea di Omero; trad. [reprint of edition printed in Verona in 1822] (Italian). *Translator or author:* Ippolito Pindemonte. Venice, Italy.

1837—Homer (English). *Translator or author:* Alexander Pope. New York, N.Y.

1837—The Odyssey of Homer; translated (English). *Translator or author:* Alexander Pope. London, England: T. Allman.

1837—Homers Odysseen; overs. (Danish). *Translator or author:* Christian Frederik Emil Wilster. Copenhagen, Denmark.

1837—Demetrii Zeni paraphrasis Batrachomyomachiae; vulgari Graecorum sermone scripta, quam collatis superioribus editionibus recensuit, interpretatione Lat., instruxit et commentariis illustravit Fr. Guil. Aug. Mullachius (Greek, Latin). *Translator or author:* Zenos. Berlin, Germany: Fincke.

1837–38—Poemata kai tou kyklon Leipsana; Homeri carmina et cycli epici reliquiae; Graece et Latine cum ind. nom. et rerum (Greek, Latin). Paris, France: Ambrosio Firmin Didot.

1837–39—Homeri Odyssea; mit erklarenden Anmerkungen von Gottl[ieb] Christ[ian] Crusius (Greek). Hannover, Germany: Hahn.

1838—Homeri Ilias, Graece et Latin; ex recensione et cum notis Samuelis Clarke (Greek; Latin). London, England: J. [etc.] Duncan.

1838—The Iliad of Homer; from the text of Wolf, with English notes; edited by C[ornelius] C[onway] Felton (Greek). Boston, Mass.: Gray Hilliard.

1838—The Iliad of Homer (English). *Translator or author:* William Cowper. Philadelphia, Pa.

1838—La Batracomiomachi, val a dir, La Guerra di Ranucc' cun I Pondg; e La seccia ruba del Tasson; componimenti in dialetto Bolognese (Italian (Bolognese dialect)). *Translator or author:* Francesco Maria Longhi. Bologna, France: Chierici.

1838—Homers Odyssee (German). *Translator or author:* Johann Heinrich Voss. Vienna, Austria: Michael Lechner.

1838–40—Odyssea [B. 9–12, 16, 18–24] a Islansku Utlagdar af Sveinbirni Egilssyni, Adjunkt. Videyar Klaustri, Iceland: Helgason.

1838–43—Odyssea; mit erklarenden Anmer-

kungen von Gottl[eib] Christ[ian] Crusius (Greek).

1839—Homeri Hymnus in Cerrerem; nunc primum editus a Davide Ruhnkenio;; accedunt duae epistolae criticae, ex editone altera, multis partibus locupletiores. Leipzig, Germany: Lehnhold.

1839—Odyssea (Greek). Leipzig, Germany.

1839—[H]omerou Ilias = The Iliad of Homer; from the text of Wolf; with English notes; edited by C[ornelius] C[onway] Felton (Greek). Boston, Mass.: Gray Hilliard.

1839—Ilias (Greek). Leipzig, Germany.

1839—Homeri Ilias; ex recensione C[hristian] G[ottlieb] Heynii; cum notes anglicis; 6th ed. London, England: Lonman, Orme, Brown, Green, and T. & W. Longman.

1839—Ilias. Munich, Germany: Sumptibus Librariae Scholarum Regiae.

1839—Der Homerische Hymnus auf den Delischen Apollo; Vorwort, Grundtext u. Ubers. von Gu. Assmann. *Translator or author:* Gu. Assman. Leonica (Liegnitz), Poland.

1839—Homeri Iliadis L.XXIII; Latinis versibus interpretatus est F. W. Gliemann (Latin). *Translator or author:* F. W. Gliemann. Halle an der Saale, Germany: Gebauer-Schwetschkeschen Buchdruckerei.

1839—Iliada Gomera; perevedennaia N. Gnedichem; posviashchena Ego Velishestvu Gosudariu Imperatoru Nikolaiu Pavlovichu; 2nd ed. (Russian). *Translator or author:* Nikolaaei Ivanovich Gnedich. St. Petersburg, Russia: U Izdatelia Knigoprodavtsa Lisenkova.

1839—The English Works of Thomas Hobbes of Malmesbury (English). *Translator or author:* Thomas Hobbes. London, England: John Bohn.

1839—The Iliad; 3rd ed. (Greek). *Translator or author:* James Kennedy. Dublin, Ireland.

1839—The Adventures of Ulysses (English). *Translator or author:* Charles Lamb. London, England: William Smith.

1839—Iliade di Omero; trad. in versi Toscani da Vinc[enzo] Monti [reprint of edition printed in Brescia in 1810] (Italian). *Translator or author:* Vincenzo Monti. Milan, Italy.

1839—Iliade di Omer; trad. in versi Toscani da Vinc. Monti [reprint of edition printed in Brescia in 1810] (Italian). *Translator or author:* Vincenzo Monti. Bologna, France.

1839—The Iliad of Homer; translated (English).

Translator or author: Alexander Pope. Philadelphia, Pa.: R. W. Pomeroy.

1839—The Iliad of Homer; translated, with explanatory notes and index; to which is prefixed an essay on the life, writings, and genius of Homer (English). *Translator or author:* Alexander Pope. London, England: Scott, Webster, and Geary.

1839—The Poetical Works of Alexander Pope, esq.; to which is prefixed the life of the author, by Dr. Johnson (English). *Translator or author:* Alexander Pope. Philadelphia, Pa.: J. J. Woodward.

1839—Homers Werke [reprint of 1833 edition] (German). *Translator or author:* Johann Heinrich Voss. Stuttgart, Germany.

1840—Initia Homerica: the First and Second Books of the Iliad of Homer; with parallel passages from Virgil, and a Greek and English lexicon (Greek; Latin). London, England: B. Fellowes.

1840—Homers Odysee, Sechster Gesang, Lucanus, Marcus Annaeus, Pharsalis, Erster Gesang; ubersetzt (German). *Translator or author:* G. S. Falbe.

1840—Iliade di Omero; trad. in versi Toscani da Vinc[enzo] Monti [reprint of edition printed in Brescia in 1810] (Italian). *Translator or author:* Vincenzo Monti. Milan, Italy.

1840—Der Schild des Achilleus, Ilias SVIII ges. V.478–608 in 9 darstellungen erfunden und metallographert (German). *Translator or author:* L. Nauverk. Berlin, Germany.

1840—The Odyssey of Homer; translated; with explanatory notes and index (English). *Translator or author:* Alexander Pope. London, England: Scott, Webster, and Geary.

1840—Homer; translated (English). *Translator or author:* Alexander Pope. New York, N.Y.: Harper and Brothers.

1840—Homers Werke (German). *Translator or author:* Johann Heinrich Voss. Stuttgart, Germany.

1840–42—Ilias; mit erklar. Anmerk. von G[ott]l[ie]b Ch[ri]st[ian] Crusius (Greek). *Translator or author:* Gottlieb Christian Crusius. Hannover, Germany.

1841—Iliad; translated into English prose (English). Longman.

1841—The First Six Books of Homer's Iliad; with interpaged translation (Greek, English). London, England: Walton.

1841—The Iliad of Homer; from the text of Wolf; with English notes; edited by C[ornelius] C[onway] Felton (Greek). Boston, Mass.: Gray Hilliard.

1841—L'Iliade et l'Odyssee d'Homere; traduit en vers Francais (French). *Translator or author:* M. Anne Bignan. Paris, France.

1841—L'Iliade d'Homere; traduit; revue et corr. sur les dernieres editions Grecques par M. H. Trianon (French). *Translator or author:* Anne LeFevre Dacier. Paris, France: Lefevre.

1841—La Batracomiomachia; vers. (Italian). *Translator or author:* C. Grossi. Torino (Turin), Italy.

1841—Iliade di Omero; trad. in versi Toscani da Vinc[enzo] Monti [reprint of edition printed in Brescia in 1810] (Italian). *Translator or author:* Vincenzo Monti. Milan, Italy.

1841—L'Odissea; volgarizzamento in prosa (Italian). *Translator or author:* Cornelia Sale-Mocenigo-Codemo. Treviso, Italy.

1841—Ilias XXII Gesang; ubersetzt und mit einem Vorwort (German). *Translator or author:* H. E. Sauppe.

1841—Odyssee XI (German). *Translator or author:* Konrad Schwenck. Frankfurt am Main, Germany.

1841—Ilias, Litera Digamma Restituta; ad metri leges redegit et notatione brevi illustravit Th. Shaw Brandreth (Greek). *Translator or author:* Brandreth Shaw; Thomas Shaw. London, England.

1841–44—The Adventures of Ulysses; to which is added Mrs. Leicester's school, or, The history of several young ladies, related by themselves (English). *Translator or author:* Charles Lamb. London, England: Edward Moxon.

1842—Ilias; Greek and Latin with English notes (Greek, Latin). Marshall Simpkin.

1842—Odyssea, Greek and Latin; cura Ernesti et Walker (Greek; Latin). George Bell Whittaker.

1842—Homeri Ilias; zum Gebrauche fur Schulen besorgt und mit Deutschen Inhaltsanzeigen versehen; von Gottl[ieb] Christ[ian] Crusius (Greek). Hannover, Germany: Hahn.

1842—Homeri Odyssea; mit erklarendon Anmerkungen von Gottl[ieb] Christ[ian] Crusius; 2nd ed. *Translator or author:* Gottlieb Christian Crusius. Hannover, Germany: Hahn.

1842—Iliade di Omero; trad. in versi Toscani da

Vinc[enzo] Monti [reprint of edition printed in Brescia in 1810] (Italian). *Translator or author:* Vincenzo Monti. Milan, Italy.

1842—Iliad and the Odyssey (English). *Translator or author:* Alexander Pope. New York, N.Y.

1842—The Odyssey of Homer; translated (English). *Translator or author:* Alexander Pope. London, England: T. Allman.

1842—Homeri Odyssea; suethice reddita; praeside Axelio Gabriele Sjostrom (Swedish). *Translator or author:* Axelius Gabr. Sjostrom. Helsinki, Finland: J. C. and Son Frenckell.

1842—Homeros Ilias; Fran Grekiskan af J. Traner; T. I–III. 2nd ed. (Swedish). *Translator or author:* J. Traner. Oerebro, Sweden.

1842—Homers Werke [reprint of 1833 edition] (German). *Translator or author:* Johann Heinrich Voss. Stuttgart, Germany.

1842—Ilias. *Translator or author:* Williams. London, England: John Murray.

1842—Homerowna Iliada, prelozenim Wlckowskeho (Bohemian). *Translator or author:* Wlckowskeho. Praze [location?].

1842–43—L'Iliade; traduction nouvelle accompagnee de notes, par Eugene Bareste, illustrees par de Villy et Titeaux; l'Odyssee traduit par le meme et illustree par A. Lemud (French). *Translator or author:* Eugene Bareste. Paris, France: Lavigne.

1843—[H]omerou Odysseias VI, VII; from the text of Lowe; with English notes, &c., &c. by D. B. Hickie (Greek). Cambridge, England: Grant.

1843—Homeri Carmina et Cycli Epici Reliquiae, Graece et Latine; cum indice nominum et rerum (Greek; Latin). Paris, France: Ambrosio Firmin Didot.

1843—Odyssea; ex recogn. Imm. Bekker (Greek). Berlin, Germany.

1843—Ilias; ex recogn. Imm. Bekker (Greek). Berlin, Germany.

1843—Iliads; with notes by Taylor [reprint of 1611–14 edition] (English). *Translator or author:* George Chapman. London, England: C. Knight.

1843—The Iliad and Odyssey of Homer; with commentary [reprint of 1791 edition] (English). *Translator or author:* William Cowper. Harvey.

1843—Homer's Sammtliche Werke ubers. v. Fr. Leop. Grafen zu Stolberg u. Joh. H. Voss (German). *Translator or author:* Leop. Grafen; Joh. Heinr. Voss. Leipzig, Germany: Abr. Voss.

1843—The Iliad and Odyssey of Homer; translated out of Greek into English; with a preface concerning the virtures of an heroic poem, written by the translator; now first edited by William Molesworth [reprint of the 1677 edition] (English). *Translator or author:* Thomas Hobbes. London, England: John Bohn.

1843—[Iliad and Odyssey; with 40 woodcuts by Flaxman] (English). *Translator or author:* W. C. Taylor. London, England.

1843–47—L'Iliade et l'Odyssee; traduit du Grec en vers Armeniens (Armenian). *Translator or author:* P. E. Thomadjan. Venice, Italy.

1843–49—Homeri Odyssea; mit erklarenden Anmerkungen von Gottl[ieb] Christ[ian] Crusius. Hannover, Germany: Hahn.

1843–79—Chant[s] [I, IV, VI, IX–X, XXIV] de l'Iliade (French). *Translator or author:* C. Leprevost. Paris, France: L. Hachette.

1844—The First Three Books of Homer's Iliad; according to the ordinary text, and also with the restoration of the digamma, to which are appended English notes, critical and explanatory, a metrical index, and Homeric glossary (English). *Translator or author:* Charles Anthon. New York, N.Y.: Harper and Brothers.

1844—Gottfried August Burgers Sammtliche Werke (German). *Translator or author:* Gottfried August Burger. Gottingen, Germany: Dieterich'sche Verlagsbuchhandlung.

1844—[Iliad] (German). *Translator or author:* Alb. De Carlowitz. Leipzig, Germany.

1844—The Iliad of Homer (Greek). *Translator or author:* Cornelius Conway Felton. Boston, Mass.

1844—The Iliad of Homer; translated into English accentuated hexameters (English). *Translator or author:* John Frederick William Herschel. London, England; Cambridge, England: Macmillan.

1844—Odyssee (German). *Translator or author:* A. W. L. Jacobi. Berlin, Germany.

1844—Homerowa Odyssea (Bohemian). *Translator or author:* Ant. Liska. Praze [location?].

1844—L'Iliade di Omero; traduzione (Italian). *Translator or author:* Vincenzo Monti. Florence, Italy: Tipografia Fraticelli.

1844—Homer; translated (English). *Translator or author:* Alexander Pope. New York, N.Y.: Harper.

1844—The Iliad of Homer; faithfully rendered in Homeric verse [Books 1–9] (English). *Translator or author:* Lancelot Shadwell. London, England.

1844— Homers Werke (German). *Translator or author:* Johann Heinrich Voss. Stuttgart, Germany; Tubingen, Germany: J. G. Cotta Buchhandlung.

1844— Homers Werke (German). *Translator or author:* Johann Heinrich Voss. Vienna, Austria: R. Sammer.

1844–45— Homeros Odysseia; Fran Grekiskan af J. Fr. Johansson; I–XXIV (Swedish). *Translator or author:* J. Fr. Johansson. Oerebro, Sweden.

1844–53— Homeri Odyssea; mit erklarenden Anmerkungen von Gottl[ieb] Christ[ian] Crusius; 3rd ed. (Greek; German). *Translator or author:* Gottlieb Christian Crusius. Hannover, Germany: Hahn.

1844–69— An t'Iliad: Air Cogad na Troige Ro Can Homear; air drigte, o Greag-bearla go ran Gaoidilge, le Seagan, Ard-Easbog Tuama (Greek; Irish). *Translator or author:* John MacHale. Dublin (Baile Atha Cliath), Ireland: Gudmhain.

1845— Homeri Ilias Graece et Latine; ex recensione et cum notis Samuelis Carke (Greek; Latin). Edinburgh, Scotland: R. Martin.

1845— Ilias Graece; the three first books with the restoration of the digamma, English notes, glossary, etc. by C. Anthon (Greek). *Translator or author:* Charles Anthon. New York, N.Y.

1845— L'Iliade d'Homere; traduction; revue et corrigee par M. H. Trianon (French). *Translator or author:* Anne LeFevre Dacier. Paris, France: Charpentier.

1845— Carmina (Greek, Latin). *Translator or author:* Didot. Paris, France.

1845— The English Works of Thomas Hobbes of Malmesbury [reprint of the 1839 edition; series: Goldsmith-Kress Library of Economic Literature] (English). *Translator or author:* Thomas Hobbes. London, England: John Bohn.

1845— Odissea; trad. (Italian). *Translator or author:* Paolo Maspero. Milan, Italy.

1845— Iliade d'Omero; con la versione poetica di Vincenzo Monti; e con la letterale di Melchiorre Cesarotti; accompagnata da note illustrative desunte de quelle stresso Cesarotti e di altri (Italian). *Translator or author:* Vincenzo Monti. Florence, Italy: V. Batelli.

1845— Odyssey (Greek). *Translator or author:* Owen. New York, N.Y.

1845— Odissea di Omero; trad. [reprint of the edition printed at Verona in 1822] (Italian).

Translator or author: Ippolito Pindemonte. Florence, Italy.

1845— The Odyssey of Homer; translated (English). *Translator or author:* Alexander Pope. Philadelphia, Pa.: J. Crissy.

1845— The Iliad of Homer; translated (English). *Translator or author:* Alexander Pope. New York, N.Y.: A. S. Barnes.

1845— The Iliad of Homer; translated (English). *Translator or author:* Alexander Pope. London, England: George Bell Whittaker.

1845–49— Homeri Ilias; mit erklarenden anmerkungen von Gottl[ieb] Christ[ian] Crusius; 2nd ed. Hannover, Germany: Hahn.

1846— The First Three Books of Homer's Iliad; with a glossary, and English notes by Charles Anthon; edited by J[ohn] R[ichardson] Major (Greek). London, England: John W. Parke.

1846— Ilias; Greek and Latin; literally translated, with notes by Baillie (Greek; Latin). London, England: Henry G. Bohn.

1846— The First Six Books of Homer's Iliad; with English notes, critical and explanatory, a metrical index, and Homeric glossary by Charles Anthon (Greek). New York, N.Y.: American Book Company.

1846— Homeri Odyssea, Graece et Latine; edidit, annotationesque ex notis nonnullis manuscriptis a Samuele Clarke; relictis, partim collectas, adjecit Samuel Clarke; 6th ed. (Greek; Latin). Edinburgh, Scotland: R. Martin.

1846— [H]omerou Ilias = Homeri Ilias; ex recensione C[hristian] G[ottlob] Heynii; fere impressa in usum scholarum (Greek). London, England: Longman, Brown, Green, and T. and W. Longman.

1846— The First Three Books of Homer's Iliad; according to the ordinary text, and also with the restoration of the digamma, to which are appended English notes, critical and explanatory, a metrical index, and Homeric glossary by Charles Anthon (Greek). New York, N.Y.: Harper and Brothers.

1846— The Odyssey of Homer; according to the text of Wolf; with notes; for the use of schools and colleges; by John J[ason] Owen; 4th ed. (Greek). New York, N.Y.: Trow Leavitt.

1846— The Iliad of Homer, Books I–VIII; comprising an accurately collated text, critical and explanatory notes and indices of words, subjects and authors; by James Kennedy Bailie; 4th ed. Dublin, Ireland: Cumming and Ferguson.

1846—[H]omerou Ilias = The Iliad of Homer; from the text of Wolf; with English notes by C[ornelius] C[onway] Felton (Greek). Boston, Mass.: James Munroe.

1846—Ilias, Greek; Libri I–III (Greek). *Translator or author:* Anton; Davies. London, England: W. Tegg.

1846—Homer's Iliad; translated (English). *Translator or author:* T. S. Brandreth. London, England.

1846—L'Odyssee d'Homere; suivi du Combat des Rats et des Grenouilles, des Hymnes, des Epigrammes, et des Fragments; traduits (French). *Translator or author:* Anne LeFevre Dacier; Mm. Trianon; E. Falconnet. Paris, France: Charpentier.

1846—Ilias Graece; the three first books with the restoration of the digamma [reprinted from the edition printed in New York in 1845] (Greek). *Translator or author:* J. Davies. London, England.

1846—[Iliad] (German). *Translator or author:* A. W. L. Jacobi. Berlin, Germany.

1846—Homeros Ilias; Fran Grekiskan at J. F. Johannson; I–XXIV (Swedish). *Translator or author:* J. Fr. Johannson. Oerebro, Sweden.

1846—Ilias (German). *Translator or author:* Monje. Frankfurt am Main, Germany.

1846—[Iliad] (German). *Translator or author:* Herm. Monse. Frankfurt am Main, Germany.

1846—Homer's Iliad (English). *Translator or author:* William Munford. Boston, Mass.: C.C. Little and J. Brown .

1846—Homer; translated (English). *Translator or author:* Alexander Pope. New York, N.Y.: Harper.

1846—The Iliad and Odyssey of Homer (English). *Translator or author:* Alexander Pope. London, England.

1846—Homer Odysseaja (Hungarian). *Translator or author:* Istvan Szabo. Pest, Hungary.

1847—Iliad; literally translated into English prose with short notes by a bachelor of arts (English). Dublin, Ireland.

1847—The First Six Books of Homer's Iliad. New York, N.Y.: Harper and Brothers.

1847—The Iliad of Homer; translated into English prose, as literally as the different idioms of the Greek and English languages will allow; with explanatory notes; by a graduate of the University of Oxford (English). Princeton, N.J.: George Thompson.

1847—[H]omerou Ilias = The Iliad of Homer; with a carefully corrected text, with copious English notes, illustrating the grammatical construction, the manners and customs, the mythology and antiquities of the heroic ages. by the Rev. William Trollope; 3rd ed. (Greek). London, England: F. & J. [etc.] Rivington.

1847—Homer's Iliad; translated. *Translator or author:* Bryce. Marshall Simpkin.

1847—The Iliad and the Odyssey [reprint of the 1791 edition] (English). *Translator or author:* William Cowper.

1847—The Iliad of Homer (Greek). *Translator or author:* Cornelius Conway Felton. Boston, Mass.

1847—Odissea; trad. con un disc. estet. del Pr. A. Zondada [reprint of the 1845 edition] (Italian). *Translator or author:* Paolo Maspero. Milan, Italy.

1847—Iliade di Omero; traduzione ad uso de' giovanetti; per cura del canonico Domenico Rossi (Italian). *Translator or author:* Vincenzo Monti. Milan, Italy: Pirotta.

1847—Odyssea, Gr.; with notes for the use of schools by J. J. Owen (Greek). *Translator or author:* J. J. Owen. New York, N.Y.

1847—The Poetical Works of Alexander Pope, esq.; to which is prefixed the life of the author, by Dr. Johnson (English). *Translator or author:* Alexander Pope. Philadelphia, Pa.: J. J. Woodward.

1847—Odisakan Homeros; t'argmaneats' I Hellenakane (Armenian). *Translator or author:* Eghiay T'omachean. Venetik [location?]: I Tparani Srboyn Ghazaru.

1847—Homers Werke. *Translator or author:* Johann Heinrich Voss. Stuttgart, Germany; Tubingen, Germany: J. G. Cotta Buchhandlung.

1848—The First Six Books of Homer's Iliad; with English notes, critical explanatory, a metrical index and Homeric glossary, by Charles Anthon (Greek). New York, N.Y.: Harper and Brothers.

1848—Homeri Odyssea; ad optima exemplaria recognovit et in usum scholarum, edidit Georg Aenotheus Koch. Leipzig, Germany: Philipp Reclam jun.

1848—Odyssea, Greek; Wolf's text, notes by J. J. Owen. 6th edition (Greek). Wiley.

1848—[H]omerou Ilias = The Iliad of Homer; from the text of Wolf; with English notes by C[ornelius] C[onway] Felton (Greek). Boston, Mass.: James Munroe.

1848—Ilias; juxta Wolf. et Heyn. edd., Lat. notas

ex Heynii comment. plerumque desumtas add. L. Quicherat; lib. IX (Greek). Paris, France.

1848—[H]omerou Ilias = L'Iliade d'Homere; texte revu avec sommaires et notes en Francais par Fr[iedrich] Dubner (Greek). Paris, France: Librairie de Jacques Lecoffre et Cie.

1848—Pytho's Grundung, ein nomischer Hymnos aus dem Homerischen Hymnos auf Apollon; ausgeschieden und ubersetzt von Gymnasiallehrer C. F. Creuzer (Greek; German). *Translator or author:* C. F. Creuzer. Hersfeld.

1848—The Iliad (Greek). *Translator or author:* Cornelius Conway Felton. Boston, Mass.

1848—La Iliada; traducida; 2nd ed. (Spanish). *Translator or author:* D. Jose Gomez Hermosilla. Paris, France: Libreria Castellana.

1848—[Homers Krieg der Mause] (German). *Translator or author:* Joh. Kern. Breslau (Wroclaw), Poland.

1848—Neuvieme Chante de l'Iliade. *Translator or author:* M. C. Leprevost. Paris, France: L. Hachette.

1848—Iliade di Omero; tradotta (Italian). *Translator or author:* Vincenzo Monti. Torino (Turin), Italy: Fontana.

1848—Homer; translated (English). *Translator or author:* Alexander Pope. New York, N.Y.: Harper and Brothers.

1848—Translations of the Iliad and the Odyssey of Homer; with valuable notes and commentaries, and several incidental literary papers, not contained in any other edition; edited by W[illiam] C. Armstrong; 5th ed. (English). *Translator or author:* Alexander Pope. Hartford, Conn.: S. Andrus.

1848—The Iliad and the Odyssey of Homer; translated; with valuable notes and commentaries, and several incidental literary papers, not contained in any other edition; edited by W. C. Armstrong (English). *Translator or author:* Alexander Pope. New York, N.Y.: Leavitt and Allen.

1848–57—Homeri Ilias; mit erklarenden Anmerkungen von Gottl[ob] Christ[ian] Crusius. Hannover, Germany: Hahn.

1849—Ilias [series: Oxford Pocket Classics]. John Henry and Jacob Parker.

1849—The Odyssey of Homer; according to the text of Wolf; with notes for the use of schools and college by John J. Owen (Greek). New York, N.Y.: Leavitt and Company.

1849—Odyssey, I–III, VIII–XII; translated into English (English). Washbourne.

1849—Ilias. *Translator or author:* Immanuel Bekker. John Henry and Jacob Parker.

1849—Ilias. *Translator or author:* T. S. Brandreth. Pickering.

1849—The Iliad of Homer; translated into English blank verse; edited by Robert Southey, with notes by M[ary] A[nn] Dwight (English). *Translator or author:* William Cowper. New York, N.Y.: David Appleton.

1849—Homeric Ballads; with translations and notes (English). *Translator or author:* W. Maginn. Parker and Son.

1849—The Iliad of Homer; translated (English). *Translator or author:* Alexander Pope. New York, N.Y.: A. S. Barnes.

1849—Translation of the Odyssey of Homer; with Pope's postscript to the Odyssey, and "Conclusion of the Notes" by Broome, &c. (English). *Translator or author:* Alexander Pope. Hartford, Conn.: S. and Son Andrus.

1849—Homere, Chants I a IV de l'Odyssee (Greek; French). *Translator or author:* Edouard Sommer. Paris, France: L. Hachette.

1849–50—Homers Odyssee; erklart von J[ohann] U[lrich] Faesi (Greek). Leipzig, Germany: Weidmannsche Buchhandlung.

1849–57—Homeri Odyssea; mit erklarenden Anmerkungen von Gottl[ieb] Christ[ian] Crusius; 3rd ed. Hannover, Germany: Hahn.

1850—[H]omerou Odysseias = The Odyssey of Homer, according to the text of Wolf; with notes, for the use of schools and colleges, by John J[ason] Owen; 7th ed. (Greek). New York, N.Y.: Leavitt and Company.

1850—Odyssee d'Homere; texte Grec; revu sur les meilleures editions et accompagne de notes en Francais par E[douard] Sommer (Greek). Paris, France: L. Hachette.

1850—Ilias, Greek, Books I–IV (Greek). *Translator or author:* Arnold. Rivington.

1850—Poems, Original and Translated, Including the First Iliad of Homer (English). *Translator or author:* William George Thomas Barter. London, England: W. Pickering.

1850—The Iliad of Homer; translated into English blank verse; edited by Robert Southey; with notes by M. A. Dwight (English). *Translator or author:* William Cowper. New York, N.Y.: G. P. Putnam.

1850—L'Iliade d'Homere; traduction; revue et corrigee sur les dernieres editions Grecques par H. Trianon (French). *Translator or author:* Anne LeFevre Dacier. Paris, France: Lefevre.

1850—Homeric Ballads [from the Odyssey]; with translation and notes by the late W. Maginn (Greek; English). *Translator or author:* W. Maginn. London, England.

1850—Iliade (Greek). *Translator or author:* Planche. Paris, France.

1850—The Poetical Works of Alexander Pope, esq; to which is prefixed the life of the author by Dr. Johnson (English). *Translator or author:* Alexander Pope. Philadelphia, Pa.: Crissy and Markley.

1850–55—[H]omerou Epe: Homeri Carmina ad Optimorum Librorum Fidem Expressa; curante Guilielmo Dindorfio; 3rd ed. (Greek). Leipzig, Germany: B. G. Teubner.

1850s—Iliad of Homer; with notes, by T[heodore William] A[lois] buckley (English). *Translator or author:* Alexander Pope. Chicago, Il.: Henneberry.

1851–1900

1851—Operon Odysseias = The Odyssey of Homer; according to the text of Wolf; with notes for the use of schools and colleges by John J. Owen; 8th ed. (Greek). New York, N.Y.: Trow and Company.

1851—Homeri Iliadis, Rhapsodia I; recensuit et critica annotatione auctam ed. Iacobus Marinus van Gent. Leiden (Leyden), Netherlands: E. J. Brill.

1851—The Iliad of Homer; according to the text of Wolf; with notes for the use of schools and colleges by John J[ason] Owen (Greek). New York, N.Y.: Leavitt and Allen.

1851—The Odyssey of Homer; according to the text of Wolf; with notes for the use of schools and colleges by John J. Owen; 8th ed. (Greek). New York, N.Y.: Leavitt and Company.

1851—Iliadis; curante Guilielmo Dindorfio; 3rd ed. (Greek). Leipzig, Germany: B. G. Teubner.

1851—[H]omerou Odysseia Mikra; erster Schul-Homer, mit Worterbuch, Noten fur Anganger und einer Homerischen Vorschule fur Lehrer, herausgeben von Dr. Christian Koch (Greek). Leipzig, Germany: Nauck.

1851—The First Six Books of Homer's Iliad; with English notes, critical and explanatory, a metrical index, and Homeric glossary; by Charles Anthon (Greek). New York, N.Y.: Harper and Brothers.

1851—Ilias [von] Homer; edited by Wolf, Friedrich August (Greek). New York, N.Y.: New York Free Academy.

1851—The Battles of the Frogs and Mice, after Homer; by the Singing Mouse; illustrated with coloured drawings and numerous woodcuts by the same (English). London, England: Hope.

1851—Ilias, Books I–VI, XX, and XXI; vocabulary by Ferguson (Greek). Marshall Simpkin.

1851—Ilias for beginners; Greek, Libri I–III, edited by Arnold (Greek). Rivington.

1851—Odyssea, Greek [series: Oxford Pocket Classics] (Greek). John Henry and Jacob Parker.

1851—Iliad, Books I–VIII; translated literally from the text of Heyne (English). Marshall Simpkin.

1851—The Odyssey of Homer (English). *Translator or author:* Theodore Alois Buckley. London, England.

1851—Iliad; translated into English prose (English). *Translator or author:* Theodore Alois Buckley. London, England: Henry G. Bohn.

1851—Odyssey, Hymns etc. *Translator or author:* Theodore Alois Buckley. London, England: Henry G. Bohn.

1851—[Iliad] (German). *Translator or author:* Ed. Eyth. Stuttgart, Germany.

1851—La Odisea de Homero; traducida (Spanish). *Translator or author:* Antonio Gironella y Syguals. Barcelona, Spain: T. Gorchs.

1851—The Iliad (Greek). *Translator or author:* Owen. New York, N.Y.

1851—Iliad of Homer; translated (English). *Translator or author:* Alexander Pope. New York, N.Y.: A. S Barnes.

1851—The Odyssey of Homer; with Pope's postscript to the Odyssey, and "Conclusion of the Notes," by Broome, &c.; carefully revised, expressly for this edition by W. C. Armstrong (English). *Translator or author:* Alexander Pope. Hartford, Conn.: S. Andrus.

1851—Translation of the Iliad of Homer; carefully revised, expressly for this edition by W. C. Armstrong (English). *Translator or author:* Alexander Pope. Hartford, Conn.: S. Andrus.

1851—Homers Werke [reprint of the 1833 edition] (German). *Translator or author:* Johann Heinrich Voss. Stuttgart, Germany.

1851–53—Homeri Carmina ad Optimorum Librorum Fidem Expressa; curante Guilielmo Dindorfio; 3rd ed (Greek). Leipzig, Germany: B. G. Teubner.

1852—Iliad (Greek). *Translator or author:* Arnold. London, England.

1852—Batrachomyomachia Homero; vulgo attrib. textum ad fidem codd. rec. var. lect. adj. prolegg. crit. scripsit Aug. Baumeister (Greek). *Translator or author:* Augustus Baumeister. Gottingen, Germany.

1852—Homers Iliades; tre forste Boger, oversatte ogi kortfattede Anmaerkninger oplyste af Fr. M. Bugge (Norwegian). *Translator or author:* M. Bugge. Bergen, Norway.

1852—L'Iliade travestie; par une societe de gens de lettres, de savants, de magistrats (French). *Translator or author:* L. Dumoulin; A. Goujon, Ch. -Martin Rousselet. Paris, France: A. Goujon.

1852—The Iliad (Greek). *Translator or author:* Cornelius Conway Felton. Boston, Mass.

1852—[Iliad] (Greek; German). *Translator or author:* K. Frenzel. Leipzig, Germany.

1852—Iliade di Omero; trad. in versi Toscani da Vinc[enzo] Monti [reprint of the edition printed at Brescia in 1810] (Italian). *Translator or author:* Vincenzo Monti. Torino (Turin), Italy.

1852—Ilias. *Translator or author:* Owen. Delf.

1852—[Iliad] (German). *Translator or author:* Ernst Wiedasch. Stuttgart, Germany.

1852–55—Homer's Iliad [reprint of the 1846 edition] (English). *Translator or author:* William Munford. Richmond, Va.

1852–55—The Iliad of Homer [reprint of the 1715–20 edition] (English). *Translator or author:* Alexander Pope. Hartford, Conn.

1852–55—The Odyssey of Homer [reprint of the 1725–26 edition] (English). *Translator or author:* Alexander Pope; W. Broome; E. Fenton. Hartford, Conn.

1852–64—Ilias (Greek). *Translator or author:* Gottlieb Christian Crusius. Hannover, Germany.

1852–72—Odyssea. 4th ed. (Greek). *Translator or author:* Gottlieb Christian Crusius. Hannover, Germany.

1853—The Iliad of Homer; with a carefully corrected text with copious English notes, illustrating the grammatical construction, the manners and customs, the mythology and antiquities of the herioc ages; and preliminary observation...by William Trollope; 4th ed. (Greek). London, England: F. & J. Rivington.

1853—[H]omeroy Ilias = The Iliad of Homer; according to the text of Wolf; with notes for the use of schools and colleges by John J. Owen (Greek). New York, N.Y.: Leavitt and Allen.

1853—Carmina et Cycli Epici Reliquiae (Greek). Paris, France.

1853—The Odyssey of Homer, with the Hymns, Epigrams, and Battle of the Frogs and Mice; literally translated, with explanatory notes (English). *Translator or author:* Theodore Alois Buckley. London, England: Henry G. Bohn.

1853—The Iliad of Homer; literally translated, with explanatory notes (English). *Translator or author:* Theodore Alois Buckley. London, England: Henry G. Bohn.

1853—The Iliad and Odyssey of Homer; with notes by T[heodore Alois] Buckley (English). *Translator or author:* William Cowper. London, England.

1853—Iliade d'Homere; traduit en Francais; precedee de l'histoire des poesies homeriques; 3rd ed. (French). *Translator or author:* M. Jean-Baptiste Dugas-Montbel. Paris, France: Ambrosio Firmin Didot Freres.

1853—Odyssee et Poesies Homeriques; traduites en Francais; 3rd ed. (French). *Translator or author:* M. Jean-Baptiste Dugas-Montbel. Paris, France: Ambrosio Firmin Didot Freres.

1853—Homers Odyssee; erklart; 2nd ed. *Translator or author:* Johann Ulrich Faesi. Leipzig, Germany: Weidmannsche Buchhandlung.

1853—Iliade di Omero; trad. in versi Toscani da Vinc[enzo] Monti [reprint of the edition printed at Brescia in 1810] (Italian). *Translator or author:* Vincenzo Monti. Livorno, Italy.

1853—Odissea di Omero [reprint of the edition printed at Verona in 1822] (Italian). *Translator or author:* Ippolito Pindemonte. Livorno, Italy.

1853—The Odyssey of Homer (English). *Translator or author:* Alexander Pope. London, England.

1853—Odyssey in English (English). *Translator or author:* Alexander Pope. Griffin.

1853—The Poetical Works of Alexander Pope, Esq.; to which is prefixed the life of the author, by Dr. Johnson (English). *Translator or author:* Alexander Pope. Philadelphia, Pa.: Crissy and Markley.

1853—The Odyssey of Homer; translated; with notes, by the Rev. Theodore Alois Buckley; with Flaxman's designs, and other engravings (English). *Translator or author:* Alexander Pope. New York, N.Y.: T. Y. Crowell.

1853—Translations of the Iliad and the Odyssey of Homer by Alexander Pope; with valuable notes and commentaries, and several incidental literary papers, not contained in any other edition; edited by W. C. Armstrong; 5th ed. (English). *Translator or author:* Alexander Pope. Hartford, Conn.: S. Andrus.

1853—The Iliad of Homer (English). *Translator or author:* Alexander Pope. London, England.

1853—Homers Werke (German). *Translator or author:* Johann Heinrich Voss. Stuttgart, Germany; Tubingen, Germany: J. G. Cotta Buchhandlung.

1853—Homers Ilias; im Versmass der Urschrift ubersetzt (German). *Translator or author:* Ernst Wiedasch. Stuttgart, Germany: J. B. Metzler.

1853–56—Odysseae; curante Guilielmo Dindorfio; 3rd ed. (Greek). Leipzig, Germany: B. G. Teubner.

1854—Homeri Odyssea; edidit Guilelmus Baeumlein; edition stereotypa. Leipzig, Germany: Bernhardi Tauchnitz.

1854—Homers Iliade; erklart von J[ohann] U[lrich] Faesi (Greek). Leipzig, Germany: Weidmannsche Buchhandlung.

1854—The First Six Books of Homer's Iliad; with English notes, critical and explanatory, a metrical index, and Homeric glossary (Greek). *Translator or author:* Charles Anthon. New York, N.Y.: Harper and Brothers.

1854—The First Three Books of Homer's Iliad, According to the Ordinary Text; and also with the restoration of the digamma. *Translator or author:* Charles Anthon. London, England: W. Tegg.

1854—Opera (Greek). *Translator or author:* Baeumlein. Leipzig, Germany.

1854—Homer's Iliad; translated in Spenserian stanza, with notes by W. G. T. Barter (English). *Translator or author:* William George Thomas Barter. London, England: Longman.

1854—The Iliad of Homer; literally translated, with explanatory notes (English). *Translator or author:* Theodore Alois Buckley. London, England: Bohn.

1854—The Iliad of Homer; from the text of Wolf; with English notes (Greek). *Translator or author:* Cornelius Conway Felton. Boston, Mass.: James Munroe.

1854—L'Iliade et l'Odyssee; traduction nouvelle, suivie d'un essai d'Encyclopedia Homerique; 3rd ed. (French). *Translator or author:* Pierre Giguet. Paris, France: V. Lecou.

1854—Homers Odysseifs-kvaeoi, Gefio ut af Hinu Islenzka Bokmentafelagi. *Translator or author:* Benedikt Sveinbjarnar Grondal. Kaupmannahofn [location?]: S. L. Mollers.

1854—L'Iliade di Omero; traduzione (Italian). *Translator or author:* Vincenzo Monti. Florence, Italy: P. Fraticelli.

1854—The Odyssey of Homer; translated; with notes, by the Rev. Theodore Alois Buckley; with Flaxman's designs, and other engravings; 2nd ed. (English). *Translator or author:* Alexander Pope. London, England: Nathaniel Cooke.

1854—Translation of the Odyssey of Homer; with Pope's postscript to the Odyssey, and "Conclusion of the Notes" by Broome, etc.; revised by W. C. Armstrong (English). *Translator or author:* Alexander Pope. Hartford, Conn.: S. Andrus.

1854—Homer's Iliad, First Three Books; adapted to the Hamiltonian system; with analytical interlineal translation and notes; 3rd ed. (Greek; English). *Translator or author:* John William Underwood. London, England: Charles H. Law.

1854—Homer' Werke [reprint of the 1833 edition] (German). *Translator or author:* Johann Heinrich Voss. Stuttgart, Germany.

1854–55—Homers Iliade; erklart von J[ohann] U[lrich] Faesi (Greek). Berlin, Germany.

1854–56—[Opera] (German). *Translator or author:* Johannes Minckwitz. Leipzig, Germany.

1854–59—Homere, Chants I a XXIV de l'Odyssee (French). *Translator or author:* Edouard Sommer. Paris, France: L. Hachette.

1855—The First Six Books of Homer's Iliad; with English notes, critical and explanatory, a metrical index, and Homeric glossary, by Charles Anthon (Greek). New York, N.Y.: Harper and Brothers.

1855—Homeri Odyssea; ex recognitione Guilielmi Dindorfii (Greek). Oxford, England: Typographeo Academico.

1855—The Odyssey of Homer (English). *Translator or author:* Theodore Alois Buckley. London, England.

1855—Odyssey; translated; edited by Robert Southey (English). *Translator or author:* William Cowper. London, England: Bohn.

1855—The Iliad of Homer; translated into English blank verse; edited by Robert Southey; with notes by M. A. Dwight (English). *Translator or author:* William Cowper. New York, N.Y.: David Appleton.

1855—L'Odyssee d'Homere, Suivie de Combat des Rats et des Grenouilles, des Hymnes, des Epigrammes, et des Fragments; traduits (French). *Translator or author:* Anne LeFevre Dacier; Mm. Trianon; E. Falconnet. Paris, France: Charpentier.

1855—Ilions-kvios Homers (Icelandic). *Translator or author:* Sveinbjorn Egilsson. Reykjavik, Iceland: Th Johnsen; E. Poroarson; E. Jonsson; J. Arnason.

1855—Odyssey; 9th ed. (Greek). *Translator or author:* Owen. New York, N.Y.

1855—Homer; translated (English). *Translator or author:* Alexander Pope. New York, N.Y.: Harper.

1855–56—Ilias et Odyssea (Greek). Oxford, England: H. Parker.

1855–56—Odyssee erklart von J. M. Faesi (Greek). *Translator or author:* Johann Ulrich Faesi. Berlin, Germany.

1855–57—Homeri Carmina ad Optimorum Librorum Fidem Expressa; curante Guilielmo Dindorfio; praemittitur Maximiliani Sengebusch Homerica dissertatio prior; 4th ed. (Greek). Leipzig, Germany: B. G. Teubner.

1855–58—Homeri Ilias; edidit Guilielmus Dindorf; 4th ed. (Greek). Leipzig, Germany: B. G. Teubner.

1855–58—The Iliad and Odyssey of Homer [reprint of the 1791 edition] (English). *Translator or author:* William Cowper. New York, N.Y.

1855–58—Homer's Iliad; with an interlinear translation (English). *Translator or author:* Hamilton and Clark. Philadelphia, Pa.

1855–73—Homere, L'Odyssee (French). *Translator or author:* Edouard Sommer.

1856—Ilias, notes by Wheeler (Greek). Marshall Simpkin.

1856—Homeri Ilias; ex recognitione Guilielmi Dindorfi (Latin). Oxford, England: Typographeo Academico.

1856—Odyssee d'Homere; texte Grec; nouvelle edition publiee avec des arguments et des notes en Francais par E[douard] Sommer (Greek). Paris, France: L. Hachette.

1856—Homer's Iliad, Books IX, XVIII; with concise notes, grammatical and exegetical; also a paper on the Homeric controversy, by George B. Wheeler (Greek). Dublin, Ireland: McGlashan and Gill.

1856—The First Six Books of Homer's Iliad; with English notes, critical and explanatory, a metrical index and Homeric glossary, by Charles Anthon (Greek). New York, N.Y.: Harper.

1856—[H]omerou Poiemata kai ta tou Kuklou Leipsana = Homeri Carmina et Cycli Epici Reliquiae; Graece et Latine, cum indice nominum et rerum (Greek; Latin). Paris, France: Ambrosio Firmin Didot.

1856—Odyssee fur den Schulgebr. erkl. von L. Fr. Ameis (Greek). *Translator or author:* L. Fr. Ameis. Leipzig, Germany.

1856—Iliad; 2nd ed (Greek). *Translator or author:* Arnold. London, England.

1856—The Iliad of Homer; literally translated, with explanatory notes [reprint of the 1851 edition] (English). *Translator or author:* Theodore Alois Buckley. New York, N.Y.: Harper.

1856—Odyssee; mit erklar. Anm. von Glb. Ch. Crusius; nebst der Batrachomyomachie. *Translator or author:* Gottlieb Christian Crusius. Hannover, Germany.

1856—Odysseifs-kvaedi, gefid ut af hinu islenzka bokmentafelagi (Icelandic). *Translator or author:* Sveinbjorn Egilsson. Reykjavik, Iceland: E. Thordason.

1856—Ilions-Kvaeoi, I–XII; kvioa, gefio ut af hinu Islanzka bokmentafelagi (Icelandic). *Translator or author:* Benedikt Sveinbjarnar Grondal. Reykjavik, Iceland: I Prentsmioju Islands E. Boroarson.

1856—Homeric Ballads [from the Odyssey] and Comedies of Lucian (English). *Translator or author:* W. Maginn. Andover, Mass.

1856—Homeric Ballads and Comedies of Lucian (English). *Translator or author:* W. Maginn. New York, N.Y.

1856—Homer's Iliad; translated into unrhymed English metre (English). *Translator or author:* F. W. Newman. London, England: Walton.

1856—The Iliad (Greek). *Translator or author:* Owen. New York, N.Y.

1856—Homers Werke [reprint of the 1833 edition] (German). *Translator or author:* Johann Heinrich Voss. Stuttgart, Germany.

1856—Iliad (Greek). *Translator or author:* Wheeler. Dublin, Ireland.

1856—Homers Odyssee; im Versmass der Urschrift ubersetzt von E. Wiedasch (German). *Translator or author:* Ernst Wiedasch. Stuttgart, Germany: J. B. Metzler.

1856–58—Homers Odyssee; prosaisch ubersetzt; 3rd ed. (German). *Translator or author:* Josef Stanislav Zauper. Prague, Czechoslavakia: F. F. Tempsky.

1857—[H]omerou Ilias = Iliade d'Homere; text Grec d'apres l'edition de Wolff, avec des sommaires Francais, et des remarques generales sur les licenses poetiques et les dialectes les plos usites dans Homere (Greek). Nantes, France: Merson.

1857—Homer, for Beginners: Iliad, Books 1–3; with English notes by Thomas Kerchever Arnold (Greek). London, England: Rivingtons.

1857—Ilias, Greek, Libri I–III. *Translator or author:* Charles Anthon; Major. Parker and Son.

1857—Iliad (Greek). *Translator or author:* Arnold. London, England.

1857—The Iliad of Homer; literally translated in Spencerian stanza (English). *Translator or author:* W. G. T. Barter. Longman.

1857—The Iliad of Homer (English). *Translator or author:* Theodore Alois Buckley. London, England.

1857—The Odysseys of Homer [reprint of the 1843 edition] (English). *Translator or author:* George Chapman. London, England: J. R. Smith.

1857—The Iliads of Homer, Prince of Poets, Never Before in any Language Truly Translated; with a comment on some of his chief places done according to the Greek by George Chapman; with an introduction and notes by Richard Hooper (English). *Translator or author:* George Chapman. London, England: J. R. Smith.

1857—The Iliad (Greek). *Translator or author:* Cornelius Conway Felton. Boston, Mass.

1857—Oeuvres Completes d'Homere; traduction nouvelle, avec une introduction et des notes (French). *Translator or author:* Pierre Giguet. Paris, France: L. Hachette.

1857—Ilions Kvaeoi. I–XII; kvioa; gefio ut ut hinu islenzka bokmentofelagi B. Grondahl izlenzkaoi (Icelandic). *Translator or author:* Benedikt Sveinbjarnar Grondal. Copenhagen, Denmark.

1857—The Odyssey; 13th ed (Greek). *Translator or author:* Owen. New York, N.Y.

1857—Homer; translated (English). *Translator or author:* Alexander Pope. New York, N.Y.: Harper and Brothers.

1857—The Iliad of Homer; translated; with observations on Homer and his works and brief notes, by the Rev. J[ohn] S[elby] Watson; illustrated with the entire series of Flaxman's designs (English). *Translator or author:* Alexander Pope. London, England: Henry G. Bohn.

1857—Homer Odysseaja; Hellenbol. *Translator or author:* Istvan Szabo. Pest, Hungary: Kilian Gyorgy.

1857–58—The Whole Works of Homer, Prince of Poetts; in his Iliads and Odysseys; translated according to the Greeke [includes volume of lesser works and notes by Richard Hooper; reprint of the 1612 edition] (English). *Translator or author:* George Chapman; R. Hooper. London, England.

1857–59—The Iliad; with English notes critical and explanatory, drawn from the best and latest authorities, with preliminary observations and appendices [edited by] T[homas] H[umphrey] L[indsay] Leary (Greek). London, England: John Weale.

1857–59—Carmina ad Optimorum Librorum Fidem Expressa [4th ed] (Greek). Liiae [location?].

1857–59—Works (Greek). *Translator or author:* T. H. L. Leary. London, England.

1858—The Odyssey of Homer According to the Text of Wolf; with notes for the use of schools and colleges, by John J[ason] Owen; 14th ed. (Greek). New York, N.Y.: Leavitt and Allen.

1858—Iliade (Greek). Berlin, Germany.

1858—Carmina Homerica; Imm. Bekker. emend. et annot. Bonn, Germany.

1858—Hymni Homerici Accedentibus Epigrammatis et Batrachomyomachia Homero; vulgo attributis ex recensione Augusti Baumeister (Greek). Leipzig, Germany: B. G. Teubner.

1858—Ilias, Books III–IV (Greek). George Bell Whittaker.

1858—Odyssea, Greek, Books I–VI, VII–XII, XIII–XVIII (Greek). *Translator or author:* Baeumlein. John Weale.

1858—Odyssey (English). *Translator or author:* Theodore Alois Buckley. London, England.

1858—Batrachomyomachia and Hymns [edited

by J. R. Smith; reprint of the 1624 edition]. *Translator or author:* George Chapman; R. Hooper.

1858—The Iliad of Homer; translated into English blank verse; ed. By Robert Southey; notes by M. A. Dwight; 2nd ed. (English). *Translator or author:* William Cowper. New York, N.Y.: David Appleton.

1858—Homers Odyssee; Deutsch in der Versart der Urschrift (German). *Translator or author:* Johann Jakob Christian Donner. Stuttgart, Germany: Hoffmann.

1858—Odyssea, Greek, Books I–II (Greek). *Translator or author:* Dr. Giles. London, England: James Cornish.

1858—Odyssee, I Gesang; Deutsch im Vermasse der Urschrift (German). *Translator or author:* P. J. Holl.

1858—The Iliad of Homer; translated (English). *Translator or author:* Alexander Pope. London, England: T. Allman.

1858—Odyssey in English (English). *Translator or author:* Alexander Pope. George Routledge.

1858—Odyssey in English; with Flaxman's designs (English). *Translator or author:* Alexander Pope. London, England: Henry G. Bohn.

1858—Werke (German). *Translator or author:* Johann Heinrich Voss. Stuttgart, Germany.

1858—Iliad, Books I–XII; in English verse (English). *Translator or author:* J. C. Wright. Macmillan.

1858–59—The First Three Books [and the fourth, fifth and sixth books] of Homer's Iliad; according to the ordinary text, and also with the restoration of the digamma; to which are appended English notes, critical and explanatory, a metrical index, and Homeric glos (Greek). *Translator or author:* Charles Anthon; B. Davies. London, England: W. Tegg.

1858–60—The Works of Homer According to the Text of Baeumlein; with English critical and explanatory notes by the Rev. T. H. L. Leary (Greek). London, England: John Weale.

1858–60—Iliadis I–XXIV; 4th ed. (Greek). Leipzig, Germany: B. G. Teubner.

1859—Die Homerische Odyssee und Ihre Entstehung, Text und Erlauterungen von A. Kirchhoff (Greek). Berlin, Germany: W. Wertz.

1859—Ilias. *Translator or author:* Arnold. Rivington.

1859—Iliad (English). *Translator or author:* Theodore Alois Buckley. New York, N.Y.

1859—The Iliad of Homer; translated; with observations on Homer and his works, and brief notes by J[ohn] S[elby] Watson (English). *Translator or author:* Alexander Pope. London, England: Henry G. Bohn.

1859—The Odyssey of Homer; translated; to which are added the Battle of the Frogs and Mice by Parnell, and the Hymns by Chapman and others; with observations and brief notes by J. S. Watson (English). *Translator or author:* Alexander Pope. London, England: Henry G. Bohn.

1859—Homer's Iliad; translated into English verse; books I–VI (English). *Translator or author:* J. C. Wright. Cambridge, England.

1859—Homers Werke; prosaisch ubers.; 3rd ed. (German). *Translator or author:* Josef Stanislav Zauper. Prague, Czechoslavakia: J. C. Calve (F. Tempsky).

1859–60—The First Six Books of Homer's Iliad; with English notes, critical and explanatory, a metrical index, and Homeric glossary by Charles Anthon (Greek). New York, N.Y.: Harper and Brothers.

1860—New Readings of the Iliad. James Backwood.

1860—Ilias, Greek; Books I–VI; with short English notes for schools [series: Greek Texts] (Greek). John Henry and Jacob Parker.

1860—Premier Chant de l'Iliade [d']Homere (Greek; French). Paris, France: L. Hachette.

1860—Carmina ad Optimorum Librorum Fidem Expressa; 4th ed (Greek). Liiae [location?].

1860—The Iliad of Homer; from the text of Wold; with English notes by C[ornelius] C[onway] Felton (Greek). Boston, Mass.: James Munroe.

1860—Ilias, Greek; Libri I–III [reprint of the 1846 edition] (Greek). *Translator or author:* Charles Anton; B. Davies. London, England: W. Tegg.

1860—Opera; in Greek (Greek). *Translator or author:* Baeumlein. John Weale.

1860—Hymni Homerici (Greek). *Translator or author:* Augustus Baumeister. Leipzig, Germany.

1860—Iliad; translated (English). *Translator or author:* Theodore Alois Buckley. New York, N.Y.: Harper.

1860—The Iliad of Homer; with an interlinear translation (Greek; English). *Translator or author:* Thomas Clark. Philadelphia, Pa.: C. De Silver.

1860—Ilias, Greek and English; Books I–VI (Greek; English). *Translator or author:* Eton. George Bell Whittaker.

1860—Oeuvres Completes d'Homer [reprint of the 1857 edition] (French). *Translator or author:* Pierre Giguet. Paris, France: L. Hachette.

1860—Iliad, Books I–VI; construed literally. *Translator or author:* Dr. Giles. London, England: James Cornish.

1860—Carmen Homeri Fornacale (Greek). *Translator or author:* Goettling. Lenae [location?].

1860—Carmina d'Homere; traduite en Francais; 4th ed. (Greek). *Translator or author:* Dugas Montbel. Paris, France: Ambrosio Firmin Didot.

1860—L'Iliade di Omero; tradotta (Italian). *Translator or author:* Vincenzo Monti. Naples, Italy.

1860—Iliad [from the 1715–20 edition] (English). *Translator or author:* Alexander Pope. George Routledge.

1860—Iliad (English). *Translator or author:* Alexander Pope. Rivington.

1860—The Iliad of Homer; translated (English). *Translator or author:* Alexander Pope. Halifax, England: Milner and Sowerby.

1860—Iliad (English). *Translator or author:* Alexander Pope. London, England: Henry G. Bohn.

1860—Ilias, VI. Gesang; in Stanzen und zugleich in freien Nibelungenstrophen ubersetzt (German). *Translator or author:* F. Rinne.

1860—Ilias. *Translator or author:* Veitch. Marshall Simpkin.

1860–61—Homers Ilias; Deutsch in Strophenform (German). *Translator or author:* W. O. Gortzitza. Elk (Lyck), Poland: Im Velage des Verfassers.

1860–62—Odyssee; 4th ed (Greek). Berlin, Germany.

1860s—The Odyssey of Homer; translated; with notes and introduction by Rev. T[heodore] A[lois] Buckley, and Flaxman's designs (English). *Translator or author:* Alexander Pope. New York, N.Y.: John W. Lovell.

1861—Ilias; with English notes by Valpy (Greek). Longman.

1861—The Iliad; with a carefully corrected text; with copious notes by the Rev. William Trollope; 5th ed. (English). London, England: etc. Rivington.

1861—Carmina et Cycli Epici Reliquiae, Graece et Latine; cum indice nominum et rerum (Greek; Latin). Paris, France: Firmin Didot Amrosio.

1861—[H]omerou Ilias = Homeri Ilias (Greek). Oxford, England: John Henry and Jacob Parker.

1861—The Odyssey of Homer in English Hendecasyllable Verse (English). *Translator or author:* Henry Alford. London, England: Longman, Green, and Roberts.

1861—The Iliad of Homer; literally translated, with explanatory notes (English). *Translator or author:* Theodore Alois Buckley. New York, N.Y.: Harper and Brothers.

1861—Odyssey (English). *Translator or author:* Theodore Alois Buckley. New York, N.Y.

1861—Oeuvres Completes d'Homere; 6th ed. (French). *Translator or author:* Pierre Giguet. Paris, France: L. Hachette.

1861—Iliadis Carmina XVI (Greek). *Translator or author:* Koechly. Leipzig, Germany.

1861—Ilias. *Translator or author:* Mattaire. Longman.

1861—L'Iliade di Omero; traduzione (Italian). *Translator or author:* Vincenzo Monti. Florence, Italy: Felice Le Monnier.

1861—Homere, Iliade; traduction nouvelle avec arguments et notes explicatives (French). *Translator or author:* Emile Pessonneaux. Paris, France: Charpentier.

1861—The Iliad of Homer; the first three books faithfully translated into English hexameters, according to the style and manner of the original (English). *Translator or author:* Frederick Henry James Ritso. London, England: Rivington.

1861—Metrische Ubersetzung des Ersten Buches von Iliade (German). *Translator or author:* E. Schunck.

1861—Homers Gedichte; im Versmasse der Urschrift ubersetzt (German). *Translator or author:* Karl Uschner. Berlin, Germany: A. Hofmann.

1861–62—The Iliad of Homer (English). London, England: James Cornish.

1861–62—The Odyssey of Homer; translated into English verse in the Spenserian stanza (English). Edinburgh, Scotland: William Blackwood.

1861–62—The Odyssey of Homer translated into Spenserian stanza [1st ed.] (English). *Translator or author:* Philip Stanhope Worsley. Edinburgh, Scotland: William Blackwood and Sons.

1861–63—Carmina ad Optimorum Librorum Fidem Expressa; curante G. Dindorfio; praemittutur M. Sengebusch Homerica dissertatio duplex; 4th ed. (Latin). Leipzig, Germany.

1861–65—Homers Odysee; fur den Schulge-brauch erklart von Karl Friedrich Ameis; 2nd ed. (German). *Translator or author:* Karl Friedrich Ameis. Leipzig, Germany: B. G. Teubner.

1861–65—The Iliad (English). *Translator or author:* Wright. Cambridge, England.

1862—The First Six Books of Homer's Iliad; with English notes, critical and explanatory, a metrical index, and Homeric glossary, by Charles Anthon (Greek). New York, N.Y.: Harper and Brothers.

1862—Ilias, Books XX, XXI, XXII; with English notes and literal translation (Greek; English). Hamilton.

1862—The Iliad of Homer, According to the Text of Wolf; with notes for the use of schools and colleges by John J[saon] Owen (Greek). New York, N.Y.: Leavitt and Allen.

1862—[H]omerou Poiemata kai ta tou Kyklou Leipsana = Homeri Carmna et Cycli Epici Reliquiae [ex recens. Guil. Dindorf], Graece et Latine; cum indice nominum et rerum (Greek; Latin). Paris, France: Ambrosio Firmin Didot.

1862—Iliad, Books I–III; VIII, IX and XVIII, literally translated; notes by Wheeler (English). Marshall Simpkin.

1862—Odyssea, Greek, Books I–XII; with Latin translation, notes by Walker (Greek). Marshall Simpkin.

1862—Iliad; literally translated into English hexameters (English). London, England: Bell and Daldy.

1862—Ilias, Books I–VIII; notes by Fausset (Greek). W. Allan.

1862—Homer's Iliad, Book First; translated into English hexameters (English). *Translator or author:* J. Inglis Cochrane. London, England: Hardwicke.

1862—The Iliad of Homer; translated (English). *Translator or author:* William Cowper. New York, N.Y.: David Appleton.

1862—Iliad, Books I–XII; in English hexameter verse (English). *Translator or author:* J. H. Dart. London, England: Longman.

1862—Translations of Poems, Ancient and Modern, Not Published (English). *Translator or author:* Edward George Geoffrey Smith Stanley, Earl of Derby. London, England: Hatchard.

1862—Loci Homerici Totidem Versibus Latine Redditi (Latin). *Translator or author:* H. Gebhardt.

1862—Book I of the Iliad; translated in the hexameter metre (English). *Translator or author:* John Frederick William Herschel. London, England.

1862—The Iliad, Book I; in English hexameters according to quantity (English). *Translator or author:* John Murray. London, England: Walton and Maberly.

1862—Odyssey in English dramatic blank verse (English). *Translator or author:* Thomas Starling Norgate. Williams and Norgate.

1862—The Odyssey; 16th ed (Greek). *Translator or author:* Owen. New York, N.Y.

1862—The Odyssey of Homer; translated; to which are added the Battle of the Frogs and Mice by Parnell; and the Hymns by Chapman and others; with observations and brief notes by the Rev. J[ohn] S[elby] Watson; illustrated with the entire series of Flaxman's designs (English). *Translator or author:* Alexander Pope. London, England: Henry G. Bohn.

1862—Homer's Odyssey; translated; to which is added The Battle of the Frogs and Mice, translated by Parnel[l] and corrected by Pope (English). *Translator or author:* Alexander Pope. Halifax, England: Milner and Sowerby.

1862—Gradus ad Homerum, or, The A. B. C. D. of Homer; being a heteroclite translation of the first four books of the Iliad into English heroics with notes, by X. Y. Z. [i.e. William Purton] (English). *Translator or author:* William Purton. Oxford, Engand;London, England: T. & B. Shrimpton; Whittaker; Ward and Lock.

1862—Ilias; new edition. *Translator or author:* Trollope. Rivington.

1862–67—Homers Odysee; erklart von J[ohann] U[lrich] Faesi (Greek). Berlin, Germany: Weidmannsche Buchhandlung.

1863—Ilias; mit erklarenden Anmerkungen von G. C. Crusius; in neuer Bearbeitung von Victor Hugo G. Hildebrand Koch; 3rd ed. (Greek). Hannover, Germany: Hahn.

1863—The Odyssey of Homer, According to the Text of Wolf; with notes for the use of schools and colleges by John J[ason] Owen (English). New York, N.Y.: Leavitt and Allen.

1863—Iliade; edition collationee sur les textes les plus purs, avec sommaires en Francais par J. Planche (Greek). Paris, France: E. Belin.

1863—The Iliad of Homer; with an interlinear translation; for the use of schools and private learners on the Hamiltonian system as improved by Thomas Clark (Greek; English). Philadelphia, Pa.: C. De Silver.

1863— The First Six Books of Homer's Iliad; with English notes, critical and explanatory, a metrical index, and Homeric glossary by Charles Anthon (Greek). New York, N.Y.: Harper and Brothers.

1863— The Iliad of Homer; literally translated, with explanatory notes (English). *Translator or author:* Theodore Alois Buckley. New York, N.Y.: Harper and Brothers.

1863— The Odyssey of Homer, with the Hymns, Epigrams, and Battle of the Frogs and Mice; literally translated, with explanatory notes (English). *Translator or author:* Theodore Alois Buckley. London, England: Henry G. Bohn.

1863— Oeuvres Complete d'Homere; traduction nouvelle, avec une introduction et des notes (French). *Translator or author:* Pierre Giguet. Paris, France: L. Hachette.

1863— Nausikaa, VI. Gesang der Odyssee des Homer; in freie Stanzen ubersetzt (German). *Translator or author:* L. Korodi.

1863— Homer Iliad B; literally translated into English hexameters (English). *Translator or author:* James T. B. Landon. Oxford, England: J. Vincent.

1863—[H]omerou Ilias; methermeneutheisa eia ten Kathomiloumenen pros chresin (Greek, Modern). *Translator or author:* Demetros Nikolaides; Gregoras, Chr. Istanbul, Turkey: N. Heptalophou.

1863— The Odyssey; or, The Ten Years' Wandering of Odusseus, After the Ten Years' Siege of Troy; reproduced in dramatic blank verse (English). *Translator or author:* Thomas Starling Norgate. London, England: Williams and Norgate.

1863— The Iliad of Homer; translated; with brief notes by J[ohn] S[elby] Watson; and index; to which is prefixed, an essay on the life, writings, and genius of Homer (English). *Translator or author:* Alexander Pope. London, England: Henry G. Bohn.

1863–64— Ilias (Greek). *Translator or author:* Doederlein. Leipzig, Germany.

1863–64— Odyssee (Greek). *Translator or author:* Duntzer. Paderborn, Germany.

1863–66— L'Iliade d'Omero; con note Italiane di Giuseppe Rigutini (Greek). Prato, Italy: Alberghetti.

1863–72— Homerische Blatter (German). *Translator or author:* Immanuel Bekker. Bonn, Germany: Adolph Marcus.

1864—[H]omerou Ilias = Homeri Ilias (Greek). Oxford, England: John Henry and Jacob Parker.

1864— Carmina ad Optimorum Librorum Fidem Expressa; 4th ed (Greek). Leipzig, Germany.

1864— The First Six Books of Homer's Iliad; with English notes, critical and explanatory, a metrical index, and Homeric glossary by Charles Anthon (Greek). New York, N.Y.: Harper and Brothers.

1864— Homer's Iliad; with English notes and grammatical references edited by Thomas Kerchever Arnold; 3rd ed. (Greek). London, England: Rivingtons.

1864— Homeri Odyssee, Sang I–VI; med forklarande anmarkningar utgifna (Swedish). *Translator or author:* Lars Axel Alfred Aulin. Stockholm, Sweden: P. A. Norstedt.

1864— Iliakan Homeri; han I hay H. Arsen Komitas Bagratuni I Mkhit'ariants' (Armenian). *Translator or author:* Arsen K. Bagratuni. Venetik [location?]: Vans Srboyn Ghazaru.

1864— The Iliad; rendered into English blank verse [1st ed.] (English). *Translator or author:* Edward George Geoffrey Smith Stanley, Earl of Derby. London, England: John Murray.

1864— The Iliad of Homer; rendered into English blank verse [1st ed.] (English). *Translator or author:* Derby Edward George Geoffrey Smith Stanley, Earl of Derby. London, England: George Routledge.

1864— Der Homeridische Hymnus auf Demeter; metrisch ubersetzt und mieiningen Bemerkungen uber die Griechischen Mysterien begleitet (German). *Translator or author:* E. Doehler.

1864— Ilias, Lib. I–VIII. *Translator or author:* Fausset. George Bell Whittaker.

1864— Einundzwansigstes und zweiundzwansigstes Buch der Ilias; nach Handschriften und den Scholien hrsg. Von Carl August Julius Hoffmann (Greek). *Translator or author:* Hoffmann. Clausthal, Germany.

1864— Poems and Translations (English). *Translator or author:* Edward Vaughan Kenealy. London, England: Reeves and Turner.

1864— Ilias, Lib. I–VI. *Translator or author:* T. H. L. Leary. John Weale.

1864— Die Ilias des Homer; verdeutscht; 2nd ed. (German). *Translator or author:* Johannes Minckwitz. Leipzig, Germany: W. Engelmann.

1864— Odyssee et Poesies Homeriques; traduites en Francais; 3rd ed. (French). *Translator or au-*

thor: Dugas Montbel. Paris, France: Ambrosio Firmin Didot.

1864— The Iliad; or Achilles' Wrath at the siege of Ilion; translated into dramatic blank verse (English). *Translator or author:* Thomas Starling Norgate. Williams and Norgate.

1864— Homer's Iliad; translated (English). *Translator or author:* Alexander Pope. London, England; New York, N.Y.: Routledge; Warne and Routledge.

1864— The Odyssey of Homer; translated; to which is added, The Battle of the Frogs and Mice (English). *Translator or author:* Alexander Pope. London, England: Routledge, Warne, and Routledge.

1864— Iliad, Books XIII–XVIII. *Translator or author:* J. C. Wright. Macmillan.

1864–65— Iliade (Greek). Berlin, Germany.

1864–74— Homer' Werke; Deutsch, in der Versart der Urschrift (German). *Translator or author:* Johann Jakob Christian Donner. Stuttgart, Germany; Nubling [Germany?]: Krais and Hoffmann.

1865— Homeri Ilias Lib. I–XII; emendavit et illustravit D. Ludovicus Doederlein (Greek). Leipzig, Germany; London, England: Dorffling & Francke; Williams & Norgate.

1865— Homers Iliade; 4th ed. Berlin, Germany: Weidmannsche Buchhandlung.

1865— The Odyssey of Homer; according to the text of Wolf; with notes for the use of schools and colleges by John J[ason] Owen; 16th ed. (Greek). New York, N.Y.: Leavitt and Allen.

1865— Hymni Homerici; ex recensione A. Baumeister (Greek). Leipzig, Germany.

1865— Iliade; imprimee en gros caracteres, precedee d'une etude sur Homere, et accompagnee de sommaires et de notes philologiques, litteraires et grammaticales en Francais par M. P. -A Brach (Greek). Paris, France: E. Belin.

1865— Homeri Ilias, Sang I–VI; med forklarende anmarkningar utgifna (Swedish). *Translator or author:* Lars Axel Alfred Aulin. Stockholm, Sweden: P. A. Norstedt.

1865— The Whole Works of Homer; with a comment on some of his chief places; done according to the Greek; with introduction and notes, by the Rev. Richard Hooper; 2nd ed. [series: Library of Old Authors] (English). *Translator or author:* George Chapman. London, England: J. R. Smith.

1865— Iliad; hexameter verse. *Translator or author:* J. H. Dart. London, England: Longmans.

1865— The Iliad of Homer; rendered into English blank verse [2nd ed.; reprint of the 1864 edition] (English). *Translator or author:* Edward George Geoffrey Smith Stanley, Earl of Derby. New York, N.Y.: Charles Scribner.

1865— The Iliad of Homer; rendered into English blank verse; 5th ed. (English). *Translator or author:* Edward George Geoffrey Smith Stanley, Earl of Derby. Philadelphia, Pa.: Porter and Coates.

1865— The Iliad; rendered into English blank verse; 5th ed., revised (English). *Translator or author:* Edward George Geoffrey Smith Stanley, Earl of Derby. London, England: John Murray.

1865— La Batrachomyomachie ou Combat des Grenouilles et des Rats: Poeme du Cycle Homerique; suivi du Moretum et de la premiere Eglogue de Virgile; traduis en vers Francais avec le texte Latin en regard de la traduction du Moretum & de la 1re Eglogue (French). *Translator or author:* A. Dethou. Marseilles, France: Chez tous les libraries.

1865— [H]omerou Ilias = L'Iliade d'Homere; texte revu avec sommaires et notes en Francais (Greek). *Translator or author:* Friedrich Dudner. Paris, France: Jacques Lecoffre.

1865— Iliad, Books I and II. *Translator or author:* William Charles Green. London, England: Bell and Daldy.

1865— The Odyssey of Homer; rendered into English blank verse (English). *Translator or author:* George Musgrave. London, England: Bell and Daldy.

1865— Odyssey; in dramatic blank verse. *Translator or author:* Thomas Starling Norgate. Williams and Norgate.

1865— Hymnum Tertium (Greek). *Translator or author:* Oesterheld. Jena, Germany.

1865— Iliade [d']Homere; traduction nouvelle avec arguments et notes explicatives; 2nd ed. (French). *Translator or author:* Emile Pessonneaux. Paris, France: Charpentier.

1865— The Iliad of Homer; translated; with explanatory notes and index; to which is prefixed, an essay on the life, writings, and genius of Homer (English). *Translator or author:* Alexander Pope. London, England: Henry G. Bohn.

1865— Iliad (English). *Translator or author:* Alexander Pope. New York, N.Y.

1865— Homers Ilias, Serios und Comisch in Ein und Zwanzig Radirtern Blattern; mit erklarung von Dr. Rietschel; 2nd ed. *Translator or author:* J. H. Ramberg. Hannover, Germany: Wedekind.

1865—Iliad, Books V, VI. *Translator or author:* Selwyn. London, England: Bell and Daldy.

1865—Homer's Iliad; translated from the original Greek into English hexameters (English). *Translator or author:* Edwin W. Simcox. London, England: Walford and Hodder Jackson.

1865—Homers Iliade; oversat; 3rd ed. (Danish). *Translator or author:* Christian Frederik Emil Wilster. Copenhagen, Denmark: C. A. Reitzel.

1865—Iliad; blank verse (English). *Translator or author:* J. C. Wright. Longmans.

1865–68—The Iliad (English). *Translator or author:* Philip Stanhope Worsley. Edinburgh, Scotland.

1865–71—Homers Odysee; fur den Schulgebrauch erklart von Karl Friedrich Ameis; 3rd ed. (Greek). Leipzig, Germany: B. G. Teubner.

1865–77—Carmina ad Optimorum Librorum Fidem Expressa (Greek). Leipzig, Germany.

1866—Iliad, Books XXIII & XXIV; the Greek text, with an accurate English version, notes grammatical, critical and explanatory, and short prolegomena, edited by E[dmund] S[amuel] Crooke (Greek; English). Cambridge, England: J. Hall.

1866—Petite Odyssee: Chants et Episodes Choises; avec une introduction, des notes et un vocabularie par E. Ragon (French). Paris, France: Ch. Poussielgue.

1866—Odyssee d'Homere; texte revu avec arguments et notes en Francais par Fr. Dubner (Greek). Paris, France: Jacques Lecoffre.

1866—Ilias Homeri; Latino carmine reddita interprete J. P. J. Lallier, editio altera aucta et emendata, cura et sumptibus F. Lallier (Latin). Paris, France: Jacques Lecoffre.

1866—The Odyssey of Homer, According to the Text of Wolf; with notes for the use of schools and colleges by John J[ason] Owen (Greek). New York, N.Y.: David Appleton.

1866—The Iliad of Homer. New York, N.Y.: Charles Scribner.

1866—[H]omerou Ilias = The Iliad of Homer; with a carefully corrected text, with copious English notes by William Trollope; 6th ed. (Greek). London, England: J. & F. H. Rivington.

1866—Homers Ilias; erklarende Schulausgabe von Heinrich Duntzer (Greek). Paderborn, Germany: Ferdinand Schoningh.

1866—The Iliad of Homer; rendered into English blank verse; 3d ed. (English). *Translator or author:* Edward George Geoffrey Smith Stanley, Earl of Derby. New York, N.Y.: Charles Scribner.

1866—Oeuvres Completes d'Homere; traduction nouvelle avec une introduction et des notes (French). *Translator or author:* Pierre Giguet. Paris, France: L. Hachette.

1866—The Iliad of Homer; translated into English accentuated hexameters (English). *Translator or author:* John Frederick William Herschel. London, England: Macmillan.

1866—Iliade d'Homere; traduite en Francais; precedee de l'histoire des poesies Homeriques; 3rd ed. (French). *Translator or author:* Dugas Montbel. Paris, France: Ambrosio Firmin Didot.

1866—Odyssee [d']Homere; traduction nouvelle avec arguments et notes explicatives (French). *Translator or author:* Emile Pessonneaux. Paris, France: Charpentier.

1866—Iliad [from the 1715–20 edition] (English). *Translator or author:* Alexander Pope. Marshall Simpkin.

1866—The Odyssey of Homer; translated; to which are added the Battle of the Frogs and Mice by Parnell and the Hymns by Chapman and others; with observations and brief notes by the Rev. J. S. Watson; illustrated with the entire series of Flaxman's designs (English). *Translator or author:* Alexander Pope. London, England: Bell and Daldy.

1866—Iliad, Book I (English). *Translator or author:* C. S. Simms.

1866–71—Ilias = The Iliad of Homer; edited with English notes by F[rederick] A[pthorp] Paley (Greek). London, England: George Bell Whittaker.

1866–82—The Odyssey of Homer; edited with marginal references, various readings, notes and appendices by Henry Hayman (Greek). London, England: David Nutt.

1866–98—Homers Odyssee; Deutsch in der Versart der Urschrift von J[ohann] J[akob] C[hristian] Donner (German). Berlin, Germany: G. Langenscheidt.

1867—The First Six Books of Homer's Iliad; with English notes, critical and explanatory, a metrical index, and Homeric glossary by Charles Anthon (Greek). New York, N.Y.: Harper and Brothers.

1867—The Iliad; with English notes, critical and explanatory by T. H. L. Leary; text of Baumlein (Greek). London, England: Strahan.

1867—The Odyssey of Homer According to the Text of Wolf; with notes for the use of schools and colleges by John J[ason] Owen (Greek). New York, N.Y.: David Appleton.

1867—Odyssea Homeri Latino Carmine Reddita Interprete J. P. J. Lallier; edita F. Lallier (Latin). Paris, France: Jacques Lecoffre.

1867—[H]omerou Odysseia; methermeneutheisa eis ten kathomiloumenen pros chresin; meta ton anankaion semeioseon (Greek, Modern). *Translator or author:* N. Argyriades. Istanbul, Turkey: N. Heptalophou.

1867—Homer's Iliad; literally translated; with exegetical notes, and an introductory essay on the peculiarities of the Homeric dialect (English). *Translator or author:* Charles William Bateman. Dublin, Ireland: Kelly.

1867—The Odyssey of Homer, with the Hymns, Epigrams, and Battle of the Frogs and Mice; literally translated, with explanatory notes (English). *Translator or author:* Theodore Alois Buckley. London, England: George Bell.

1867—Homer's Iliad; translated into English hexameters (English). *Translator or author:* James Inglis Cochrane. Edinburgh, Scotland.

1867—The Iliad of Homer; rendered into English blank verse; with a biographical sketch, by R. Shelton Mackenzie; 5th ed, from the 9th English ed. (English). *Translator or author:* Edward George Geoffrey Smith Stanley, Earl of Derby. Philadelphia, Pa.: Henry T. Coates.

1867—The Iliad of Homer; rendered into English blank verse; 3rd ed. From the 5th English ed. (English). *Translator or author:* Edward George Geoffrey Smith Stanley, Earl of Derby. New York, N.Y.: Charles Scribner.

1867—The Iliad; rendered into English blank verse [6th ed.] (English). *Translator or author:* Edward George Geoffrey Smith Stanley, Earl of Derby. London, England: John Murray.

1867—The Adventures of Ulysses (English). *Translator or author:* Charles Lamb. London, England: Groombridge and Sons.

1867—Iliade [d']Homere; traduction nouvelle (French). *Translator or author:* Leconte de Lisle. Paris, France: Alphonse Lemerre.

1867—The Odyssey (Greek). *Translator or author:* Owen. New York, N.Y.

1867—The Iliad of Homer; translated; with observations on Homer and his works, and brief notes, by the Rev. J[ohn] S[elby] Watson; illustrated with the entire series of Flaxman's designs (English). *Translator or author:* Alexander Pope. London, England: Bell and Daldy.

1867—La Bataille Fantastique des Roys Rodilardus et Croacus; traduction du Latin d'Elisius Calentius; attribuee a Rabelais; avec une notice bibliographique par M. P. L. (French). *Translator or author:* Francois Rabelais. Geneva, Switzerland: J. Gay.

1867–68—Odyssea Ad Fidem Librorum Optimorum (Greek). *Translator or author:* La Roche. Leipzig, Germany.

1867–69—Homers Odyssee; fur den Schulgebrauch erklart von Dr. Karl Friedrich Ameis; 4th ed. (Greek). Leipzig, Germany: B. G. Teubner.

1867–73—Odyssee; erklart von J[ohann] U[lrich] Faesi; 5th ed. (Greek). Berlin, Germany: Weidmannsche Buchhandlung.

1868—The Odyssey of Homer According to the Text of Wolf; with notes for the use of schools and colleges by John J[ason] Owen (Greek). New York, N.Y.: David Appleton.

1868—Ilias Homeri (Greek). Leipzig, Germany; Paris, France: Otto Holtze; Haar & Steinert.

1868—[H]omerou Odysseia = Homeri Odyssea (Greek). Oxford, England: J. Parker.

1868—Odyssee; nouvelle edition precedee d'une etude sur Homere et accompagnee de sommaires analytiques et de sommaires analytiques et de notes philologiques, litteraires et grammaticales en Francais par M. P. -A. Brach (Greek). Paris, France: E. Belin.

1868—The First Six Books of Homer's Iliad (Greek). *Translator or author:* Charles Anthon. New York, N.Y.

1868—L'Iliade (French). *Translator or author:* Barthelemy St.-Hilaire. Paris, France.

1868—The Iliad of Homer; rendered into English blank verse; 3rd ed. from the English 5th, revised ed. (English). *Translator or author:* Edward George Geoffrey Smith Stanley, Earl of Derby. New York, N.Y.: Charles Scribner.

1868—The Iliad of Homer; rendered into English blank verse, to which are appended translations of poems ancient and modern; 7th ed. (English). *Translator or author:* Edward George Geoffrey Smith Stanley, Earl of Derby. London, England: John Murray.

1868—Odyssee, Hymnes, Epigrammes, Batrakhomyomakhie; traduction nouvelle (French). *Translator or author:* Leconte de Lisle. Paris, France: Alphonse Lemerre.

1868—The Iliad (Greek). *Translator or author:* Owen. New York, N.Y.

1868—L'Odissea di Omero; tradotta (Italian). *Translator or author:* Ippolito Pindemonte. Florence, Italy: G. Barbera.

1868—The Iliad of Homer; translated (English). *Translator or author:* Alexander Pope. New York, N.Y.: A. S. Barnes.

1868—Homeric Studies (English). *Translator or author:* Edmund Lenthal Swifte. London, England: J. Madden.

1868—The Odyssey of Homer translated into Spenserian stanza [2nd ed.; reprint of the 1861–62 edition] (English). *Translator or author:* Philip Stanhope Worsley. Edinburgh, Scotland: Blackwoods.

1868–70—Iliade (Greek). *Translator or author:* Koch. Hannover, Germany.

1868–71—Odyssee; 4th ed. (Greek). *Translator or author:* Karl Friedrich Ameis. Leipzig, Germany.

1868–86—Ilias, Pt. 1–8 (German). *Translator or author:* Karl Friedrich Ameis. Leipzig, Germany.

1869—Homeri Odyssea (Greek). Leipzig, Germany: Otto Holtze.

1869—[H]omerou Ilias = The Iliad of Homer, According to the Text of Wolf; with notes for the use of schools and colleges, by John J[ason] Owen (Greek). New York, N.Y.: David Appleton.

1869—The First Six Books of Homer's Iliad; with explanatory notes, intended for beginners in the epic dialect; accompanied with numerous references to Hadley's Greek grammar, to Kuhner's larger Greek grammar, and to Goodwin's Greek moods and tenses (Greek). Chicago, Il.: S. C. Giggs.

1869—Homerische Untersuchungen. Leipzig, Germany: B. G. Teubner.

1869—Iliad of Homer, Books One to Eight; chiefly according to the text of Dr. Kennedy; with original notes, philological and exegetical; examination questions, &c.; comprising also the various readings and comments of the most eminent critics on Homer; by A[ndrew] R[obert] Fausset (Greek). Dublin, Ireland: McGlashan.

1869—L'Iliade d'Homere; texte Grec, revu et corrige d'apres les documents authentiques de la recension d'Aristarque accompange d'un commentaire critique et explicatif precede d'une introduction et suivi des prolegomenes de Villoison, des prolegomenes et des pr (Greek). Paris, France: L. Hachette.

1869—A Nearly Literal Translation of Homer's Odyssey into Accentuated Dramatic Verse (English). *Translator or author:* Lovelace Bigge-Wither. Oxford, Engand;London, England: J. Parker.

1869—First Six Books of Homer's Iliad (Greek). *Translator or author:* Boise. Chicago, Il.

1869—Hymnus Celeris Homericus (Greek). *Translator or author:* Bucheler. Leipzig, Germany.

1869—Iliad [series: Ancient Classics]. *Translator or author:* William Lucas Collins. Blackwoods.

1869—The Iliad of Homer; rendered into English blank verse; 5th ed. from English 9th (English). *Translator or author:* Edward George Geoffrey Smith Stanley, Earl of Derby. New York, N.Y.: Winston.

1869—The Iliad of Homer; rendered into English blank verse; 3rd ed. (English). *Translator or author:* Edward George Geoffrey Smith Stanley, Earl of Derby. New York, N.Y.: Charles Scribner.

1869—Odyssey; translated into blank verse (English). *Translator or author:* G. W. Edgington. Longmans.

1869—L'Iliade et l'Odysee d'Homere; abregees et annotees par A. Feillet sur la traduction de P[iere] Giguet, et illustrees par Olivier (French). *Translator or author:* Pierre Giguet. Paris, France: L. Hachette.

1869—[Odyssea; Platt-Deutsch, ubersetzt] (Platt-Deutsch). *Translator or author:* H. Lehmann. Neustettin [Germany?].

1869—Homer's Iliad; rhymed verse (English). *Translator or author:* Charles Merivale. London, England: Strahan.

1869—Odyssey in blank verse. 2nd ed. [reprint of the 1865 edition] (English). *Translator or author:* George Musgrave. London, England: Bell and Daldy.

1869—[H]o Polemos ton Pontilobatrachon (Greek). *Translator or author:* Ostobek. Athens, Greece.

1869—Odyssee; traduction nouvelle, avec arguments et notes explicatives; 3rd ed. (French). *Translator or author:* Emile Pessonneaux. Paris, France: Charpentier.

1869—L'Iliade (Greek). *Translator or author:* Pierron. Paris, France.

1869—Diomede: from the Iliad of Homer. *Translator or author:* William R. Smith. New York, N.Y.; London, England: David Appleton.

1869—Homers Werke (German). *Translator or author:* Johann Heinrich Voss. Stuttgart, Germany: J. G. Cotta Buchhandlung.

1869—The Fifth and Ninth books of the Odyssey (English). *Translator or author:* E. D. Witt. London, England.

1869–72—Odyssee. 4 aufl (Greek). *Translator or author:* Karl Friedrich Ameis; Carl Hentze. Leipzig, Germany.

1869–73—Homers Odyssee; erklart von J[ohann] U[lrich] Faesi; 5th ed. (Greek). Berlin, Germany: Weidmannsche Buchhandlung.

1869–75—[Oeuvres d'Homere]; texte Grec, revu et corrige par Alexis Pierron (Greek). Paris, France: L. Hachette.

1870—Homers Ilias; fur den Schulgebrauch erklart von J[acob] La Roche (Greek). Berlin, Germany: H. Ebeling & C. Plahn.

1870—The Iliad of Homer, According to the text of Wolf; with notes for the use of schools and colleges by John J[ason] Owen (Greek). New York, N.Y.: David Appleton.

1870—Homer's Iliad, Books I, VI, XX, and XXIV; with a copious vocabulary for the use of schools and colleges, by James Fergusson; 6th ed. (Greek). Edinburgh, Scotland: Oliver and Boyd.

1870—The First Six Books of Homer's Iliad (Greek). *Translator or author:* Charles Anthon. New York, N.Y.

1870—Carmina; vol. III: Hymni Homeriei Accedentibus Epigrammatis et Batrachomyomachia Homere vulge attributis; ex recensione Augusti Baumeister [series: Bibliotheca Teubneriana]. *Translator or author:* Augustus Baumeister. Leipzig, Germany: B. G. Teubner.

1870—The Iliad and the Odyssey; translated into English blank verse (English). *Translator or author:* William Cullen Bryant. Boston, Mass.: Houghton.

1870—The Odyssey of Homer, with the Hymns, Epigrams, and Battle of the Frogs and Mice; literally translated with explanatory notes (English). *Translator or author:* Theodore Alois Buckley. London, England: Bell and Daldy.

1870—The Odyssey of Homer, with the Hymns, Epigrams and Battle of the Frogs and Mice; literally translated, with explanatory notes (English). *Translator or author:* Theodore Alois Buckley. New York, N.Y.: Harper and Brothers.

1870—The Iliad of Homer; translated into English verse (English). *Translator or author:* W. G. Caldcleugh. Philadelphia, Pa.: J. B. Lippincott.

1870—Iliados papsodia (Greek). *Translator or author:* Christopoulos. Athens, Greece.

1870—Odyssey [series: Ancient Classics]. *Translator or author:* William Lucas Collins. Blackwoods.

1870—Iliad [reprint of the 1869 edition] (English). *Translator or author:* William Lucas Collins. Philadelphia, Pa.

1870—Iliad; blank verse (English). *Translator or author:* John Graham Cordery. Rivingtons.

1870—The Iliad of Homer; rendered into English blank verse; 5th ed. from English 9th (English). *Translator or author:* Edward George Geoffrey Smith Stanley, Earl of Derby. New York, N.Y.: Porter and Coates.

1870—Oeuvres Completes d'Homere/Homero; 19th ed. *Translator or author:* Pierre Giguet. Paris, France: L. Hachette.

1870—The Iliad (Greek). *Translator or author:* T. H. L. Leary. London, England.

1870—Ilias metabetheisa palau eis koinen glossan (Greek). *Translator or author:* Loukanos. Athens, Greece.

1870—Odyssey (English). *Translator or author:* Alexander Pope. Low.

1870—The Iliad (Greek). *Translator or author:* Richard Williams Reynolds. London, England: Rivingtons.

1870—Homers Odyssee; 5th ed. *Translator or author:* Ferdinand Schmidt. Berlin, Germany.

1870—Die Homeridischen Dichtungen; ubers. (German). *Translator or author:* Georg Thudichum. Stuttgart, Germany: J. B. Metzler.

1870—Odyssee (German). *Translator or author:* Johann Heinrich Voss. Leipzig, Germany.

1870—Odyssee (German). *Translator or author:* Johann Heinrich Voss. Berlin, Germany: G. Hempel.

1870—Ilias (German). *Translator or author:* Johann Heinrich Voss. Leipzig, Germany.

1870—Homers Iliade; erklart von Dr. V. H. Koch.

1870–71—Ilias, Pt. 1–6 (Greek). *Translator or author:* La Roche. Berlin, Germany.

1870–72—Homers Ilias; fur den Schulgebrauch erklart von Karl Friedrich Ameis; 2nd ed. (Greek). Leipzig, Germany: B. G. Teubner.

1870–74—Homeri Ilias; edidit Guilielmus Dindorf; 4th ed. (Greek). Leipzig, Germany: B. G. Teubner.

1870–76— Homeri Iliadis Epitome; in usum scholarum; edidit Franciscus Hochegger (Greek). Vienna, Austria: Caroli Filii Gerold.

1870–78— Odyssey [of] Homer; with introduction, notes, etc. by W[illiam] W[alter] Merry; 1st ed. (Greek). Oxford, England: Clarendon Press.

1870–84— Ilias; 2nd ed. (German). *Translator or author:* Karl Friedrich Ameis. Leipzig, Germany.

1870s— The Iliad and Odyssey of Homer; translated (English). *Translator or author:* Alexander Pope. New York, N.Y.: Leavitt and Allen.

1870s— The Poetical Works of Alexander Pope, esq.; to which is prefixed the life of the author, by Dr. Johnson (English). *Translator or author:* Alexander Pope. Philadelphia, Pa.: H. T. Coates.

1870s— The Odyssey of Homer; translated; with notes by the Rev. Theodore Alois Buckley; and Flaxman's designs (English). *Translator or author:* Alexander Pope. New York, N.Y.: Welford and Armstrong Scribner.

1870s— The Iliad of Homer; translated; with notes and introduction by Theodore Alois Buckley and Flaxman's designs (English). *Translator or author:* Alexander Pope. New York, N.Y.: John W. Lovell.

1871— Odyssea, Book I–XII, &c.; edited by William Walter Merry (Greek). Macmillan.

1871— Homeri Carmina et Cycli Epici Reliquiae, Graece et Latine; cum indice nominum et rerum (Greek; Latin). Paris, France: Ambrosio Firmin Didot.

1871— Carmina ad Optimorum Librorum Fidem Expressa; 4th ed (Greek). Leipzig, Germany.

1871— Odysseia (Greek). Oxford, England.

1871— Iliad, Book I; rendered into English hexameters (English). *Translator or author:* T. F. Barham.

1871— The Odyssey of Homer; translated into English blank verse; 12th ed. (English). *Translator or author:* William Cullen Bryant. Boston, Mass; New York, N.Y.: Houghton Mifflin.

1871— The Iliad of Homer; translated into English blank verse (English). *Translator or author:* William Cullen Bryant. Boston, Mass.: James R. Osgood.

1871— The Odyssey of Homer, with the Hymns, Epigrams, and Battle of the Frogs and Mice; literally translated, with explanatory note (English). *Translator or author:* Theodore Alois Buckley. New York, N.Y.: Harper.

1871— The Whole works of Homer; notes by Richard Herne Shepherd [reprint of the 1612 edition] (English). *Translator or author:* George Chapman.

1871— The Odyssey (English). *Translator or author:* William Lucas Collins. Edinburgh, Scotland.

1871— The Iliad of Homer; translated (English). *Translator or author:* John Graham Cordery. London, England: Rivington.

1871— The Iliad of Homer; rendered into English blank verse; 4th ed. (English). *Translator or author:* Edward George Geoffrey Smith Stanley, Earl of Derby. New York, N.Y.: Charles Scribner.

1871— The Iliad of Homer; rendered into English blank verse; to which are appended translations of poems ancient and modern; 8th ed. (English). *Translator or author:* Edward George Geoffrey Smith Stanley, Earl of Derby. London, England: John Murray.

1871— Dalla Rapsidia IX dell'Iliade la Risposta di Achille; nella versione indedita (Italian). *Translator or author:* Ugo Foscolo. Livorno, Italy: Francesco Vigo.

1871— Homere, Iliade; traduction nouvelle, accompagnee de gravures d'apres Marillier et d'un portrait d'Homere tire d'une medaille antique; notice par J. Janin (French). *Translator or author:* P. Lagrandville. Paris, France.

1871— Iliad; translated in unrhymed English metre [reprint of the 1856 edition] (English). *Translator or author:* F. W. Newman. Teubner.

1871— The Iliad of Homer; translated; with observations on Homer and his works; and brief notes, by the Rev. J[ohn] S[elby] Watson; illustrated with the entire series of Flaxman's designs (English). *Translator or author:* Alexander Pope. London, England: Bell and Daldy.

1871— [H]omerou Ilias; metenechtheisa eis ten Kathomiloumenen (Greek, Modern). *Translator or author:* A. Skalides. Athens, Greece: N. G. Passare.

1871— Odisseia Gomera; perevod (Russian). *Translator or author:* Vasilii Andreevich Zhukovskii. Moscow, Russia: T. Ris.

1871–72— The Odyssey of Homer; translated into English blank verse (English). *Translator or author:* William Cullen Bryant. Boston, Mass.: James R. Osgood.

II. Printed Editions of the Homeric Texts, 1470 to 2000 C.E.

254

1871–73—Homers Odyssee; fur den Schulgebrauch erklart von Karl Friedrich Ameis; 5th ed. (Greek). Leipzig, Germany: B. G. Teubner.

1871–74—Odyssee; 5th and 6 eds. (Greek). Berlin, Germany.

1871–74—Homeri Odyssea; tekst c Slovarem I prilozheniem o Gomerovskom dialektie. *Translator or author:* I. A. Kremerom. Moscow, Russia: T. Ris.

1871–77—Iliade; 5th ed. (Greek). Berlin, Germany.

1872—Iliade; new ed. (French). Paris, France: P. A. Brach.

1872—The First Six Books of Homer's Iliad; with explanatory notes, intended for beginners in the epic dialect; accompanied with numerous references to Hadley's Greek grammar, to Kuhner's larger Greek grammar, and to Goodwin's Greek moods and tenses; by James R (Greek). Chicago, Il.: S. C. Griggs.

1872—The First Six Books of Homer's Iliad, with English notes, critical and explanatory, a metrical index and Homeric glossary (Greek). *Translator or author:* Charles Anthon. New York, N.Y.: Harper and Brothers.

1872—Dasz Elfte Lied vom Zorne des Achilleus nach Karl Lachmann ausz dem Zwolften Buche der Iliad; hrsg. Von Hans Karl Benicken (Greek; German). *Translator or author:* Hans Carl Benicken. Barmen, Germany: D. B. & T. G. Wiemann.

1872—The Odyssey of Homer; translated into English blank verse (English). *Translator or author:* William Cullen Bryant. Boston, Mass.: Houghton Mifflin.

1872—The Iliad of Homer; translated into English blank verse (English). *Translator or author:* William Cullen Bryant. Boston, Mass.: Osgood Fields.

1872—The Odyssey of Homer, with the Hymns, Epigrams, and Battle of the Frogs and Mice; literally translated with explanatory notes (English). *Translator or author:* Theodore Alois Buckley. New York, N.Y.: Harper.

1872—The Odyssey of Homer, with the Hymns, Epigrams, and Battle of the Frogs and Mice; literally translated, with explanatory notes (English). *Translator or author:* Theodore Alois Buckley. London, England: Bell and Daldy.

1872—The Iliad of Homer; with an interlinear translation, for the use of schools and private learners, on the Hamiltonian system as improved by Thomas Clark (Greek; English). *Translator or author:* Thomas Clark. Philadelphia, Pa.: C. Desilver.

1872—L'Iliade; traduction; nouv. ed., rev., cor., et precedee d'une introduction par M. [Leon] Crousle (French). *Translator or author:* Anne LeFevre Dacier. Paris, France: Garnier Freres.

1872—Il Libro Io della Iliade di Omero; parodia nel dialetto Veneziano (Italian (Venetian dialect)). *Translator or author:* Luigi de Giorgi. Parma, Italy: Fiaccadori.

1872—The Minor Poems of Homer; The Battle of the Frogs and Mice; Hymns and Epigrams; translated by Parnell, Chapman, Shelley, Congreve and Hole; with introductions by Henry Nelson Coleridge, and a translation of the life of Homer attributed to Herodotus (English). *Translator or author:* Parnell, Chapman, Shelley, Congreve, Hole. New York, N.Y.: A. Denham.

1872—The Iliad and Odyssey; ed. by Henry Francis Cary [reprint of the 1715–20, 1725–26 editions] (English). *Translator or author:* Alexander Pope. New York, N.Y.

1872—The Iliad…[and The Odyssey]; edited by the Rev. H[enry] F[rancis] Cary, A.M.; with a biographical notice of the author [in Collected Works of Alexander Pope] (English). *Translator or author:* Alexander Pope. London, England: George Routledge and Sons.

1872—Odysseias Rapsodia VII; metaphrastheisa eis demotikous stichous hypo D. Vikela; Odysseias rapsodia hepta (Greek, Modern). *Translator or author:* Demetrios Vilelas. Athens, Greece: Andreas Koromela.

1872—Homers Odyssee Vossische Ubersetzung; mit 40 Original-Compositionen von Friedrich Preller, in Holzschnitt ausgefuhrt von R. Brend'Amour und K. Oertel (German). *Translator or author:* Johann Heinrich Voss. Leipzig, Germany: A. Durr.

1872—Homers Werke (German). *Translator or author:* Johann Heinrich Voss. Stuttgart, Germany: Philipp Reclam jun.

1872–73—Iliad (English). *Translator or author:* Alexander Pope. Marshall Simpkin.

1872–74—Homeri Odyssea; edidit Guilielmus Dindorf; 4th ed. (Greek). Leipzig, Germany: B. G. Teubner.

1872–75—Iliade; erklart von Victor Hugo Koch; 2nd ed. (Greek). Hannover, Germany: Hahn.

1872–76—Odyssee; 2nd ed. (Greek). *Translator or author:* Karl Friedrich Ameis; Carl Hentze. Leipzig, Germany.

1872–76—Iliad and Odyssey [reprint of the 1851 edition] (English). *Translator or author:* Theodore Alois Buckley. New York, N.Y.

1872–76—Odyssey [reprint of the 1870 edition] (English). *Translator or author:* William Lucas Collins. Philadelphia, Pa.

1872–76—The Iliad and Odyssey of Homer [reprint of the 1791 edition] (English). *Translator or author:* William Cowper. New York, N.Y.

1872–76—Achilles' Wrath: A Composite Translation of Book I of the Iliad (English). *Translator or author:* P. Roosevelt Johnson. Boston, Mass.: Colby and Rich.

1872–76—Iliad [reprint of the 1869 edition] (English). *Translator or author:* Charles Merivale. New York, N.Y.

1872–76—The Iliad of Homer; ed by J. S. Watson [reprint of the 1715–20 edition; series: Bohn Library] (English). *Translator or author:* Alexander Pope. New York, N.Y.; Philadelphia, Pa.

1872–76—The Iliad of Homer [reprint of the 1715–20 edition; series: Scribner's Popular Library] (English). *Translator or author:* Alexander Pope. New York, N.Y.: Scribner's.

1872–76—The Iliad of Homer; edited by J. S. Watson [reprint of the 1715–20 edition; series: Chandos Classics] (English). *Translator or author:* Alexander Pope; W. Broome. New York, N.Y.

1872–76—The Odyssey of Homer [reprint of the 1725–26 edition; series: Chandos Library] (English). *Translator or author:* Alexander Pope; W. Broome; E. Fenton; J.S. Watson. New York, N.Y.

1872–76—The Odyssey of Homer; edited by J. S. Watson [reprint of the 1725–26 edition; series: Bohn Library] (English). *Translator or author:* Alexander Pope; W. Broome; E.Fenton. Boston, Mass; Philadelphia, Pa.

1872–80—Odyssey. *Translator or author:* Kelly. London, England: James Cornish.

1872–93—Homers Odyssee; erklart von Dr. Victor Hugo Koch (Greek). Hannover, Germany; Leipzig, Germany: Hahn.

1873—The Odyssey of Homer; according to the text of Wolf; with notes for the use of schools and colleges by John J[ason] Owen (Greek). New York, N.Y.: David Appleton.

1873—Homers Odyssee; Vossische ubersetzung mit 40 original-compositionem von Friedrich Preller; in holzschnitt ausgefuhrt von R. Brend'amour und K. Oertel; 2nd ed. (Greek). Leipzig, Germany: Alphonse Duvv.

1873—Homer's Iliad...edited by T. K. Arnold (English). London, England: Rivingtons.

1873—Ilias, ad Fidem Librorum Optimorum; ed. J[acob] La Roche (Greek). Leipzig, Germany: G. B. Teubner.

1873—Homers Odyssee; erklart von J[ohann] U[lrich] Faesi; besorgt von W[ilhelm] C[arl] Kayser; 6th ed. (Greek). Berlin, Germany: Weidmannsche Buchhandlung.

1873—Odyssey, Books I–XII; with introduction, notes, etc. by W[illiam] W[alter] Merry; 3rd ed. (Greek). Oxford, England: Clarendon Press.

1873—Homeri Carmina ad Optimorum Librorum Fidem Expressa; curante Guilielmo Dindorfio; 4th ed. (Greek). Leipzig, Germany: B. G. Teubner.

1873—The First Book of the Iliad, translated into English hexameters (English). *Translator or author:* W. Marsham Adams. London, England.

1873—Das zweite Lied vom Zorne des Achilleus (Greek). *Translator or author:* Hans Carl Benicken. Leipzig, Germany.

1873—Das funfte Lied vom Zorne des Achilleus (Greek). *Translator or author:* Hans Carl Benicken. Halle an der Saale, Germany.

1873—The Odyssey of Homer; translated into English blank verse (English). *Translator or author:* William Cullen Bryant. Boston, Mass.: James R. Osgood.

1873—The Iliad of Homer; translated into English blank verse (English). *Translator or author:* William Cullen Bryant. Boston, Mass.: James R. Osgood.

1873—The Iliad of Homer; literally translated with explanatory notes (English). *Translator or author:* Theodore Alois Buckley. London, England: Bell and Daldy.

1873—Iliad, Books XXIII and XXIV; with English version, notes by Crooke (Greek: English). *Translator or author:* E. S. Crooke. Marshall Simpkin.

1873—Iliad; first book of Pope's, translated into Latin elegiacs (Latin). *Translator or author:* G. Denman. London, England: George Bell and Sons.

1873—The Iliad of Homer; rendered into English blank verse; 5th ed. (English). *Translator or au-*

thor: Edward George Geoffrey Smith Stanley, Earl of Derby. New York, N.Y.: Porter and Coates.

1873—Oeuvres Completes d'Homere; traduction nouvelle avec une introduction et des notes; 11th ed. (French). *Translator or author:* Pierre Giguet. Paris, France: L. Hachette.

1873—The Narrative of Odysseus (Greek). *Translator or author:* Mayor. London, England.

1873—Iliade di Omero; tradotta; 2nd ed. (Italian). *Translator or author:* Vincenzo Monti. Florence, Italy: G. Barbera.

1873—L'Odissea di Omero (Italian). *Translator or author:* Ippolito Pindemonte. Milan, Italy: M. Guigoni.

1873—The Iliad of Homer; translated, with observations on Homer and his works, and brief notes, by the Rev. J. S. Watson; illustrated with the entire series of Flaxman's designs [reprinted from the 1715–20 edition] (English). *Translator or author:* Alexander Pope. London, England: George Bell and Sons.

1873—The Odyssey of Homer [reprint of the 1725–26 edtion] (English). *Translator or author:* Alexander Pope; W. Broome; E. Fenton.

1873—Iliad; six books, translated into fourteen-syllable verse (English). *Translator or author:* C. S. Simms. Stanford.

1873–74—Homers Odyssee; fur den Schulgebrach erklart von Dr. Karl Friedrich Ameis; 5th ed. (Greek). Leipzig, Germany: B. G. Teubner.

1873–75—Initia Homerica; 1st and 2nd books of the Iliad; new edition. B. Fellowes.

1873–76—Homer Ilias, ad Fidem Librorum Optimorum; edidit I[acob] LaRoche; 4th ed. (Greek). Leipzig, Germany: B. G. Teubner.

1873–78—Homers Ilias; erklarende Schulausgabe von Heinrich Duntzer; 2nd ed. (Greek). Paderborn, Germany: Ferdinand Schoningh.

1874—Hymni Homerici Accedentibus Epigrammatis et Batrachomyomachia Homero; vulgo attributis ex recensione Augusti Baumeister (Greek). Leipzig, Germany: B. G. Teubner.

1874—Odyssey; 4th ed. (Greek). Oxford, England.

1874—Homers Iliad; fur den Schulgebrauch erklart von Karl Friedrich Ameis; besorgt von K[arl] Hentze; 4th ed. (Greek). Leipzig, Germany: B. G. Teubner.

1874—Homeri Quae Fertur Batrachomyomachia;

edidit Ioannes Draheim. Berlin, Germany: Nicolai Stricker.

1874—Odyssey; book I; notes for candidates of the Oxford exam (Greek). *Translator or author:* Almack. Longmans.

1874—The First Six Books of Homer's Iliad; with English notes, critical and explanatory, a metrical index and Homeric glossary (English). *Translator or author:* Charles Anthon. New York, N.Y.: Harper.

1874—Das dritte und vierte Lied vom Zorne des Achilleus (Greek). *Translator or author:* Hans Carl Benicken. Halle an der Saale, Germany.

1874—Odyssey; book VI, modern Greek (Modern Greek). *Translator or author:* D. Bikelos. Williams and Norgate.

1874—The First Six Books of Homer's Iliad (Greek). *Translator or author:* Boise. Chicago, Il.

1874—The Odyssey of Homer, with the Hymns, Epigrams, and Battle of the Frogs and Mice; literally translated, with explanatory notes (English). *Translator or author:* Theodore Alois Buckley. New York, N.Y.: Harper.

1874—The Odyssey of Homer, with the Hymns, Epigrams, and Battle of the Frogs and Mice; literally translated, with explanatory notes (English). *Translator or author:* Theodore Alois Buckley. London, England: George Bell and Sons.

1874—The Odysseys of Homer, Translated According to the Greek; with introduction and notes by the Rev. Richard Hooper; 2nd ed. (English). *Translator or author:* George Chapman. London, England: Reeves and Turner; Smith.

1874—The Whole Works of Homer [reprint of the 1612 edition] (English). *Translator or author:* George Chapman.

1874—The Iliad of Homer; rendered into English blank verse; to which are appended translations of poems ancient and modern; 9th ed. (English). *Translator or author:* Edward George Geoffrey Smith Stanley, Earl of Derby. London, England: John Murray.

1874—Homer (German). *Translator or author:* Johann Jakob Christian Donner. Berlin, Germany; Schoneberg, Germany: G. Langenscheidt.

1874—La Iliada; Obras de Homero; new ed. (Spanish). *Translator or author:* Jose Gomez Hermosilla. Paris, France: A. Bouret.

1874—Iliada de Homero; em verso Portuguez; edictor e revisor Henrique Alves de Carvalho (Portuguese). *Translator or author:* Manuel

Odorico Mendes. Rio de Janeiro, Brazil: Typographia Guttemberg.

1874— The Iliad (English). *Translator or author:* Pope; Buckley. London, England.

1874— Homer's Iliad (English). *Translator or author:* John Benson Rose. London, England: Clowes.

1874–18— Homers Ilias; fur den Schulgebrauch erklart von Karl Friedrich Ameis; besorgt von K[arl] Hentze; 3rd ed. (Greek). Leipzig, Germany: B. G. Teubner.

1874–75— Iliad and Odyssey, translated; with notes by Theodore Alois Buckley; and Flaxman's designs (English). *Translator or author:* Alexander Pope. Frederick Warne.

1874–77— Homeri Ilias [et] Odyssea; cum potiore lectionis varielate; ed. Augustus Nauck (Greek, Latin). Berlin, Germany: Weidmannsche Buchhandlung.

1874–77— Odyssee; 5th–6th eds. (Greek). *Translator or author:* Karl Friedrich Ameis; Carl Hentze. Leipzig, Germany.

1874–78— Odyssea edidit Guilielmus Dindorf; 4th ed. (Greek). Leipzig, Germany: B. G. Teubner.

1875— Homeri Odyssea; edidit Guilielmus Dindorf; 4th ed. (Greek). Leipzig, Germany: B. G. Teubner.

1875—[H]omerou Odysseia = The Odyssey of Homer; according to the text of Wolf; with notes for the use of schools and colleges by John J[ason] Owen (Greek). New York, N.Y.: David Appleton.

1875— Ilias (Greek). Oxford, England.

1875—[H]omerou Odysseia = Homers Odyssee; erklarende Schulausgabe von Heinrich Duntzer; 2nd ed. (Greek). Paderborn, Germany: Ferdinand Schoningh.

1875—[H]omerou Odysseia = L'Odyssee d'Homere; texte Grec revu et corrige d'apres les diorthoses Alexandrines, accompagne d'un commentaire critique et explicatif, precede d'une introduction et suivi de la Batrochomyomachie, des Hymnes Homeriques (Greek). Paris, France; London, England: L. Hachette.

1875— Ilias Homerii; edidit Guilielmus Dindorf; 4th ed. (Greek). Leipzig, Germany: B. G. Teubner.

1875— The First Six Books of Homer's Iliad; with English notes, critical and explanaory, a metrical index, and Homeric glossary (Greek). *Translator or author:* Charles Anthon. New York, N.Y.: Harper and Brothers.

1875— Das zehnte Lied vom Zorne des Achilleus, nach Karl Lachmann, aus [lambda], [xi], [omicron] der Homerische Ilias; herausgeben von Hans Karl Benicken; beigegeben sind Homerische Kleinigkeiten (German). *Translator or author:* Hans Carl Benicken. Gutersloh, Germany: C. Bertelmann.

1875— Homer's Iliad; translation of book I; also passages from Virgil (English). *Translator or author:* Matthew Piers Watt Boulton. London, England: Chapman and Hall.

1875— The Iliad of Homer; translated into English blank verse (English). *Translator or author:* William Cullen Bryant. Boston, Mass.: James R. Osgood; Fields.

1875— The Odyssey of Homer; translated into English blank verse (English). *Translator or author:* William Cullen Bryant. Boston, Mass.: James R. Osgood.

1875— The Iliad of Homer; literally translated, with explanatory notes (English). *Translator or author:* Theodore Alois Buckley. New York, N.Y.: Harper and Brothers.

1875— Homer's Iliad and Odyssey; edited with notes by Richard Herne Shepherd (English). *Translator or author:* George Chapman. London, England: Chatto and Windus.

1875— Homer's Odyssey (English). *Translator or author:* William Lucas Collins. Philadelphia, Pa.: J. B. Lippincott.

1875— L'Iliade; traduction de Mme. Dacier, suivie des petits poemes attribues a Homere; 9th ed. (French). *Translator or author:* Anne LeFevre Dacier. Paris, France: Garnier Freres.

1875— Homers Odyssee; ubersetzt und erklart (German). *Translator or author:* Wilhelm Jordan. Frankfurt am Main, Germany: Wilhelm Jordan.

1875— Odissea di Omero, Poema Epico. *Translator or author:* Ippolito Pindemonte.

1875— The Iliad of Homer [reprint of the 1715–20 edition] (English). *Translator or author:* Alexander Pope. New York, N.Y.

1875— Homers Werke (German). *Translator or author:* Johann Heinrich Voss. Stuttgart, Germany: J. G. Cotta Buchhandlung.

1875–81— The Odyssey; with English notes, critical and explanatory by T[homas] H[umphry] L[indsay] Leary; [according to the text of Baeumlein] (Greek). London, England: C. Lockwood.

1875–81—[H]omerou Odysseia; emmetros metaphrasis Iakovou Polyla (Greek, Modern). *Trans-*

lator or author: Iakovos Polylas. Athens, Greece: Ephemeridos ton Syzeteseon.

1875–82— Ilias; Pt. 1–4. pt 1–2, 2nd ed. (German). *Translator or author:* Karl Friedrich Ameis. Leipzig, Germany.

1875–87— [H]omerou Ilias; ekdotheisa (Greek, Modern). *Translator or author:* Georgiov Mistriotov. Athens, Greece: Sakellariou.

1876— L'Iliade; edition classique, precedee d'une notice litteraire par T. Bude. Paris, France: Jules Delalain et Fils.

1876— Homeri Ilias (Greek). Leipzig, Germany: Otto Holtze.

1876— Homeri Odyssea; edidit Guilielmus Dindorf; 4th ed. Leipzig, Germany: B. G. Teubner.

1876— Odyssey; edited by William Walter Merry; 4th ed. (Greek). Oxford, England.

1876— Iliade; precedee d'une etude sur Homere, et accompagnee de sommaires et de notes philologiques, litteraires et grammaticales en Francais par M. P. -A Brach (Greek). Paris, France: E. Belin.

1876— Iliad and Odyssey (English). *Translator or author:* M. Barnard.

1876— The Iliad of Homer; translated into English blank verse (English). *Translator or author:* William Cullen Bryant. Boston, Mass.: James R. Osgood.

1876— The Odyssey (English). *Translator or author:* Theodore Alois Buckley. New York, N.Y.

1876— The Iliad of Homer; literally translated, with explanatory notes (English). *Translator or author:* Theodore Alois Buckley. London, England: George Bell.

1876— The Iliad of Homer; literally translated, with explanatory notes (English). *Translator or author:* Theodore Alois Buckley. New York, N.Y.: Harper and Brothers.

1876— Iliad; homometrically translated (English). *Translator or author:* Charles Bagot Cayley. Longmans.

1876— The Iliad of Homer; rendered into English blank verse; 10th ed. (English). *Translator or author:* Edward George Geoffrey Smith Stanley, Earl of Derby. London, England: John Murray.

1876— Homers Frogschmausekrieg; Deutsch im Vermasse der Urschrift mit Vorwort (German). *Translator or author:* Max Oberbreyer. Leipzig, Germany: Philipp Reclam jun.

1876— The Iliad (Greek). *Translator or author:* Owen. New York, N.Y.

1876— Iliad, Book VI; edited with notes (Greek). *Translator or author:* J. Surtees Phillpotts. Rivingtons.

1876— Iliad and Odyssey; translated (English). *Translator or author:* Alexander Pope. George Routledge.

1876— The Odyssey of Homer; translated; to which are added the Battle of the Frogs and Mice by Parnell; and the Hymns by Chapman and others; with observations and brief notes, by J[ohn] S[elby] Watson; illustrated with the entire series of Flaxman's designs (English). *Translator or author:* Alexander Pope. London, England: George Bell.

1876— Homer's Odyssey; translated; with valuable notes and commentaries, and several papers not contained in any other edition; ed. By W. C. Armstrong (English). *Translator or author:* Alexander Pope. New York, N.Y.: World Publishing House.

1876— Homers Odyssee; ins Deutsche ubertragen (German). *Translator or author:* Heinrich Schwarzschild. Frankfurt am Main, Germany: Moritz Diesterweg.

1876— Homers Werke (Ilias und Odyssee); ubersetzt; mit 25 Radirungen nach Zeichnungen von Bonaventura Genelli (German). *Translator or author:* Johann Heinrich Voss. Stuttgart, Germany: J. G. Cotta Buchhandlung.

1876— Iliad, First Book; vocabulary [series: White's Grammar School Texts] (Greek). *Translator or author:* J. T. White. Longmans.

1876— Lesebuch aus Homer; eine Vorschule zur Geschichte und Mytthologie; 3rd ed. (German). *Translator or author:* Otto Willmann. Leipzig, Germany: G. Grabner.

1876–77— L'Iliade; traduction (French). *Translator or author:* Paul Jeremie Bitaube.

1876–79— Homers Iliade; erklart von J[ohann] U[lrich] Faesi; 6th ed. (Greek). Berlin, Germany: Weidmannsche Buchhandlung.

1876–80— Odyssee, I–IV (Greek). *Translator or author:* Karl Friedrich Ameis. Leipzig, Germany.

1877— Odyssey; 5th ed. (Greek). Oxford, England.

1877— Polemata kai ta tou Kyklou Leipsana = Carmina et Cycli Epici Reliquiae, Graece et Latine; cum indice nominum et rerum (Greek; Latin). Paris, France: Ambrosio Firmin Didot.

1877—[H]omerou Ilias = The Iliad of Homer, According to the Text of Wolf; with notes for the use of schools and colleges by John J[ason] Owen (Greek). New York, N.Y.: David Appleton.

1877—Homeri Odyssea; edidit Guilielmus Dindorf; 4th ed. (Greek). Leipzig, Germany: B. G. Teubner.

1877—Homeri Ilias; edidit Guilielmus Dindorf; 4th ed. Corrected (Greek). Leipzig, Germany: B. G. Teubner.

1877—Hymni Homerici Accedentibus Epigrammatis et Batrachomyomachia Homero vulgo attributis; ex recensione Augusti Baumeister (Greek). Leipzig, Germany: B. G. Teubner.

1877—The Iliad; with English notes, critical and explanatory, by T[homas] H[umphry] L[indsay] Leary (Greek). London, England: C. Lockwood.

1877—Die Alteste Odyssee in Ihrem Verhaltnisse zur Redaction des Onomakritus und der Odyssee-Ausgabe Zenodots (Greek). *Translator or author:* L. Adam.

1877—Ilias (Greek). *Translator or author:* Karl Friedrich Ameis; Carl Hentze. Leipzig, Germany.

1877—Odyssey [reprint of the 1869 edition] (English). *Translator or author:* Lovelace Bigge-Wither.

1877—The First Six Books of Homer's Iliad; 8th ed (Greek). *Translator or author:* Boise. Chicago, Il.

1877—The Iliad of Homer; translated into English blank verse (English). *Translator or author:* William Cullen Bryant. Boston, Mass.: James R. Osgood.

1877—The Odyssey of Homer, with the Hymns, Epigrams, and Battle of the Frogs and Mice; literally translated, with explanatory notes (English). *Translator or author:* Theodore Alois Buckley. New York, N.Y.: Harper.

1877—Odisea; version Espanola con sumarios y notasa esplicativas (Spanish). *Translator or author:* Ricardo Canales. Barcelona, Spain: Jane Hermanos.

1877—The Iliad of Homer; homometrically translated (English). *Translator or author:* Charles Bagot Cayley. London, England: Longmans.

1877—Iliad; first three books, with notes etc. *Translator or author:* B. Davies. London, England: W. Tegg.

1877—The Similes of Homer's Iliad; translated with an introduction and notes (Greek, English).

Translator or author: William Charles Green. London, England.

1877—L'Odyssee; traduction nouvelle; 2nd ed. (French). *Translator or author:* Leconte de Lisle. Paris, France: Alphonse Lemerre.

1877—The Iliad of Homer, Book I; translated into English hexameters, verse for verse (English). *Translator or author:* James A. Martling. St. Louis, Mo.: R. P. Shelley Company.

1877—Odyssee; 3rd ed. (German). *Translator or author:* Friedrich Preller. Leipzig, Germany.

1877—Iliad, Books I and II. *Translator or author:* Arthur Sidgwick. Rivingtons.

1877—The Odyssey of Homer; translated into English verse in the Spenserian stanza; 3rd ed. (English). *Translator or author:* Philip Stanhope Worsley. London, England: William Blackwood and Sons.

1877—The Odyssey; translated into Spenserian stanza [3rd ed; reprint of the 1861–62 edition] (English). *Translator or author:* Philip Stanhope Worsley. Edinburgh, Scotland.

1877–79—Carmina ad Optimorum Librorum Fidem Expressa (Greek). Leipzig, Germany.

1877–79—Homeri Ilias; cum potiore lections varietate, edidit Augustus Nauck. Berlin, Germany: Weidmannsche Buchhandlung.

1877–83—Homers Ilias; fur den Schulgebrauch erklart von J[acob] La Roche (Greek). Leipzig, Germany: B. G. Teubner.

1877–88—Ilias (Greek). *Translator or author:* Karl Friedrich Ameis; Carl Hentze. Leipzig, Germany.

1878—Ilias; edidit Guilielmus Dindorf; 4th ed. Leipzig, Germany: B. G. Teubner.

1878—Homer, Iliad, Book I; with an essay on Homeric grammar and notes by D[avid] B[inning] Monro. Oxford, England: Clarendon Press.

1878—The First Six Books of Homer's Iliad; with explanatory notes and references to the grammars of Goodwin and Hadley by James Robinson Boise (Greek). Chicago, Il.: S. C. Griggs.

1878—Homers Odysse; erklart von J[ohann] U[lrich] Faesi. Berlin, Germany: Weidmannsche Buchhandlung.

1878—The First Six Books of Homer's Iliad; with English notes, critical and explanatory, a metrical index, and Homeric glossary (Greek). *Translator or author:* Charles Anthon. New York, N.Y.: Harper and Brothers.

1878— The Odyssey (English). *Translator or author:* Barnard. London, England.

1878— Ilias (Greek). *Translator or author:* Immanuel Bekker. Oxford, England.

1878— The Odyssey of Homer, with the Hymns, Epigrams and Battle of the Frogs and Mice; literally translated, with explanatory notes (English). *Translator or author:* Theodore Alois Buckley. New York, N.Y.: Harper and Brothers.

1878— The Odyssey of Homer, with the Hymns, Epigrams, and Battle of the Frogs and Mice; literally translated (English). *Translator or author:* Theodore Alois Buckley. London, England: George Bell.

1878— Stories from Homer; with twenty-four illustrations from Flaxman's designs (English). *Translator or author:* Alfred John Church. New York, N.Y.: David Appleton.

1878— Homers Ilias im Versmass der Urschrift; ubersetzt (German). *Translator or author:* F. W. Ehrenthal. Leipzig, Germany: Bibliographisches Institut.

1878— Homer. *Translator or author:* W. E. Gladstone. New York, N.Y.

1878— Homer. *Translator or author:* W. E. Gladstone. London, England.

1878— La Iliada; traducida del Griego al Castellano (Spanish). *Translator or author:* D. Jose Gomez Hermosilla. Paris, France: Garnier Freres.

1878— Odyssey; with notes. *Translator or author:* T. H. L. Leary. C. Lockwood.

1878— Iliad, Book I; with grammar and notes (Greek). *Translator or author:* David Binning Monro. Macmillan.

1878— Odyssee et Poesies Homeriques; traduites en Francais; 4th ed. (French). *Translator or author:* Dugas Montbel. Paris, France: Ambrosio Firmin Didot.

1878— Homeri Quae Nunc Exstant. *Translator or author:* F. A. Paley. London, England.

1878— Odissea Omero; tradotta; ed illustrate dai primari artisti (Italian). *Translator or author:* Ippolito Pindemonte. Milan, Italy: Tipografia Editrice Lombarda.

1878— Odyssee; ubersetzung; mit 6 original-Compositionen von Friedrich Preller; in Holzschnitt ausgefuhrt von K. Oertel (German). *Translator or author:* Johann Heinrich Voss. Leipzig, Germany: A. Durr.

1878— Homers Werke (German). *Translator or author:* Johann Heinrich Voss. Stuttgart, Germany.

1878— Homers Iliade; oversat; 4th ed. (Danish). *Translator or author:* Christian Frederik Emil Wilster. Copenhagen, Denmark: C. A. Reitzel.

1878–80— Iliad, Books I–IV; V–VIII; IX–XII; XIII–XX. *Translator or author:* Kelly. London, England: James Cornish.

1878–95— Odyssey; with introduction, notes, etc. by W[illiam] W[alter] Merry (Greek). Oxford, England: Clarendon Press.

1879—[H]omerou Ilias; The Iliad of Homer, according to the text of Wolf; with notes for the use of schools and colleges by John J[ason] Owen (Greek). New York, N.Y.: American Book Company.

1879— Odyssea; 4th ed (Greek). Leipzig, Germany.

1879— Die Homerische Odyssee; 2nd ed.; von A. Kirchhoff (Greek). Berlin, Germany: Wilhelm Hertz.

1879— The First Six Books of Homer's Iliad (Greek). *Translator or author:* Boise. Chicago, Il.

1879— The Iliad of Homer; translated into English blank verse (English). *Translator or author:* William Cullen Bryant. Boston, Mass.: Houghton, Osgood.

1879— The Iliad of Homer; literally translated, with explanatory notes (English). *Translator or author:* Theodore Alois Buckley. New York, N.Y.: Harper and Brothers.

1879— The Iliad of Homer; literally translated, with explanatory notes (English). *Translator or author:* Theodore Alois Buckley. London, England: George Bell and Sons.

1879— The Odyssey of Homer; done into English prose; with an introduction by Andrew Lang (English). *Translator or author:* Samuel Henry Butcher; Andrew Lang. New York, N.Y.: Macmillan.

1879— Iliad, Deeds and Death of Patroclos: Book XVI. *Translator or author:* H. Dunbar. Marshall Simpkin.

1879— Ilias; 6th ed. (Greek). *Translator or author:* Franke Faesi. Berlin, Germany.

1879— Studj Sulle Opere Latine del Boccaccio con Paticolare Riguardo alla Storia della Erudizione nel Medio evo e alle Letterature Straniere; aggiuntavi la bibliografia delle edizioni (Latin). *Translator or author:* Attilio Hortis. Treste [location?]: J. Dase.

1879— Iliad, Book XXII; with introductory notes etc. *Translator or author:* P. Sandford. Marshall Simpkin.

1879— The Iliad of Homer, Books I–III. *Translator or author:* Arthur Sidgwick; Robert P. Keep. Boston, Mass.: J. Allyn.

1879— Homers Ilias; ubersetzt (German). *Translator or author:* Ferdinand Leopold Stolberg. Leipzig, Germany: A. Durr.

1879— Homers Ilias (German). *Translator or author:* Johann Heinrich Voss. Berlin, Germany: G. Hempel.

1879— Homers Odyssee (German). *Translator or author:* Johann Heinrich Voss. Berlin, Germany: F. Dummler.

1879— The First Book of Homer's Iliad (Greek). *Translator or author:* White. London, England.

1879–80— Homers Odyssee; fur den Schulgebrauch erklart von Karl Friedrich Ameis; besorgt von C. Hentze (Greek). Leipzig, Germany: B. G. Teubner.

1879–80— Odyssey (English). *Translator or author:* Roscoe Mongan.

1879–80— Iliad. *Translator or author:* Roscoe Mongan. London, England: James Cornish.

1879–82— The Odyssey of Homer, Books I–XXIV; rendered into English verse (English). *Translator or author:* George Augustus Schomberg. London, England: John Murray.

1879–91— Homers Ilias; fur den Schulgebrauch erklart von J. La Roche; 3rd ed. (Greek). Leipzig, Germany: B. G. Teubner.

1880— The First Three Books of Homer's Iliad; according to the text of Dindorf, with notes critical and explanatory by Henry Clark Johnson. New York, N.Y.: David Appleton.

1880— The First Six Books of Homer's Iliad; with English notes, critical and explanatory, a metrical index, and Homeric glossary by Charles Anthon (Greek). New York, N.Y.: Harper and Brothers.

1880— Homeri Carmina ad Optimorum Librorum Fidem Expressa; curante Guilielmo Dindorfio; 4th ed. Leipzig, Germany: B. G. Teubner.

1880— Iliad, Book XXI; with introduction and notes, by Herbert Hailstone (Greek). Oxford, England: Clarendon Press.

1880— [H]omerou Odysseias; The Odyssey of Homer, According to the Text of Wolf; with notes; for the use of schools and colleges, by John J[ason] Owen (Greek). New York, N.Y.: David Appleton.

1880— The First Six Books of Homer's Iliad; with explanatory notes, and references to the grammar of Goodwin and Hadley by James Robinson Boise; 12th ed. (Greek). Chicago, Il.: S. C. Griggs.

1880— The Odyssey of Homer [reprint of the 1725–26 edition; series: Lovell's Library] (English). *Translator or author:* Alexander Pope, W. Broome, E. Fenton. New York, N.Y.

1880— The Iliad of Homer; literally translated, with explanatory notes (English). *Translator or author:* Theodore Alois Buckley. New York, N.Y.: Harper and Brothers.

1880— The Iliads of Homer, Prince of Poets; never before in any language truly translated; done according to the Greek (English). *Translator or author:* George Chapman. London, England: Marshall Simpkin.

1880— The Odyssey, or, The Adventures of Ulysses (English). *Translator or author:* Alfred John Church. Rochester, N.Y.: G. W. Fitch.

1880— The Iliad, or, The Siege of Troy (English). *Translator or author:* Alfred John Church. Rochester, N.Y.: G. W. Fitch.

1880— Homer, The Odyssey (English). *Translator or author:* William Lucas Collins. Philadelphia, Pa.: J. B. Lippincott.

1880— Homer, The Iliad. *Translator or author:* William Lucas Collins. Edinburgh, Scotland.

1880— The Iliad; rendered into English blank verse [reprint of the 1864 edition] (English). *Translator or author:* Edward George Geoffrey Smith Stanley, Earl of Derby. Philadelphia, Pa.

1880— The Odyssey (English). *Translator or author:* Charles Du Cane. Edinburgh, Scotland.

1880— Iliad, Book I; in graduate lessons, with notes. *Translator or author:* E. Fowle. Longmans.

1880— Iliad, Books XIII and XIV (English). *Translator or author:* Herbert Hailstone. Cambridge, England.

1880— Iliad, Book XXI; with introduction and notes. *Translator or author:* Herbert Hailstone. London, England; New York, N.Y.: Henry Frowde.

1880— Odissea di Omero; traduzione; 4th ed. (Italian). *Translator or author:* Paolo Maspero. Milan, Italy: R. Stab. Musicale Ricordi.

1880— The Phaeacian episode of the Odyssey (Greek). *Translator or author:* A. C. Merriam. New York, N.Y.

1880— Iliade; traduzione, con le osservazioni di Andrea Mustoxidi e le notizie della vita e dell'opera del traduttore; 4th ed. (Italian). *Translator or author:* Vincenzo Monti. Milan, Italy: Edoardo Sonzogno.

1880—Homeri Odysseae Epitome. *Translator or author:* Francueus Pauly.

1880—Iliade [d']Homere; publiee avec un argument analytique et des notes en Francais (Greek; French). *Translator or author:* A. Pierron. Paris, France: L. Hachette.

1880—The Iliad and Odyssey; with notes by W. C. Armstrong (English). *Translator or author:* Alexander Pope. Philadelphia, Pa.

1880—The Odyssey of Homer; translated (English). *Translator or author:* Alexander Pope. New York, N.Y.: American Book Exchange.

1880—Hector and Andromache from Pope's translation (English). *Translator or author:* Alexander Pope. Marshall Simpkin.

1880—The Iliad of Homer [reprint of the 1715–20 edition; series: Seaside Library] (English). *Translator or author:* Alexander Pope. New York, N.Y.

1880—Iliada Homer; przelozyl wierszem miarowym (Polish). *Translator or author:* Pawel Popiel. Krakow, Poland: Nakladem Tlomacza.

1880—The Story of Achilles from the Iliad (Greek). *Translator or author:* John Henry Pratt; Walter Leaf. London, England.

1880—Iliad, Book XXI. *Translator or author:* Arthur Sidgwick. Rivingtons.

1880—Iliad I (English). *Translator or author:* Stone. Cambridge, England.

1880—De Ilias van Homeros; vertaald (Dutch). *Translator or author:* Carel Vosmaer. Leiden (Leyden), Netherlands: A. W. Sijthoff.

1880—The Odyssey; translated by Avia (English). *Translator or author:* Arthur Sanders Way. London, England.

1880–10—Homers Odyssee; erklart von J[ohann] U[lrich] Faesi (Greek). Berlin, Germany: Weidmannsche Buchhandlung.

1880–18—Homers Iliade; erklart von J[ohann] U[lrich] Faesi. Berlin, Germany: Weidmannsche Buchhandlung.

1880–84—Homers Odyssee; fur den Schulgebrauch erklart von Dr. Karl Friedrich Ameis; besorgt von Dr. C. Hentze (Greek). Leipzig, Germany: B. G. Teubner.

1880s—The Iliad of Homer; with English notes by F[rederick] A[pthorp] Paley; 2nd ed. (Greek). London, England: George Bell Whittaker.

1880s—La Odisea Homero; traducida directamenta del Griego en verso Castellano (Spanish). *Translator or author:* Federico Baraibar y Zumarrage. Madrid, Spain: Libreria de Perlado.

1880s—The Iliad; 14th ed. (English). *Translator or author:* William Cullen Bryant. Boston, Mass.

1881—Iliad, Books XVI–XVIII; XIX–XXI; construed with text. London, England: James Cornish.

1881—The Phaeacian Episode of the Odyssey; as comprised in the sixth, seventh, eighth, eleventh, and thirteenth books; with introduction, notes and appendix by Augustus C[hapman] Merriam (Greek). New York, N.Y.: Harper and Brothers.

1881—Analekta fur Schule und Leben. Leipzig, Germany: T. Grieben.

1881—Flores Homerici, sive, Loci Memoriales ex Homeri Carminibus Selecti; cum brevi commentario et appendice edidit Dr. Lazarewicz (Greek). Leipzig, Germany: B. G. Teubner.

1881—[H]omerou Ilias = Homeri Ilias (Greek). Oxford, England: Jacob Parker and Friends.

1881—The Iliad of Homer, According to the Text of Wolf; with notes for the use of schools and colleges by John J. Owen [reprint of the Wolf's text printed in Leipzig in 1839] (Greek). New York, N.Y.: David Appleton.

1881—[H]omerou Poiemata kai ta tou Kyklou Leipsana = Homeri Carmina et Cycli Epici Reliquiae; Graece et Latine; cum indice nominum et rerum (Greek; Latin). Paris, France: Ambrosio Firmin Didot.

1881—The Odyssey of Homer (English). Boston, Mass.: Houghton Mifflin.

1881—Ilias; edidit Guilielmus Dindorf; 4th ed. (Greek). Leipzig, Germany: B. G. Teubner.

1881—Iliad; complete; Books I–VIII translated by Charles William Bateman; Books IX–XXIV translated by Roscoe Mongan (English). *Translator or author:* Charles William Bateman; Roscoe Mongan.

1881—The Iliad of Homer; translated into English blank verse (English). *Translator or author:* William Cullen Bryant. Boston, Mass.: Houghton Mifflin.

1881—The Odyssey of Homer; done into English prose; 3rd ed. (English). *Translator or author:* Samuel Henry Butcher; Andrew Lang. London, England: Macmillan.

1881—Opere [chpt. 6–16 is La Iliade de Omero].

Translator or author: Melchiorre Cesarotti. Pisa, Italy: Tipografia della Societa Lett.

1881—Stories from Homer; with twenty-four illustrations from Flaxman's designs (English). *Translator or author:* Alfred John Church. London, England: Seeley, Jackson, and Halliday.

1881—The Iliad of Homer; rendered into English blank verse; 11th ed. (English). *Translator or author:* Edward George Geoffrey Smith Stanley, Earl of Derby. London, England: John Murray.

1881—Homer. *Translator or author:* Karl Frey. Bern, Switzerland.

1881—The Iliad; a literal prose translation (English). *Translator or author:* Herbert Hailstone. Cambridge, England: Johnson.

1881—Homers Ilias; ubersetzt und erklart (German). *Translator or author:* Wilhelm Jordan. Frankfurt am Main, Germany; Leipzig, Germany: Wilhelm Jordan; F. Volckmar.

1881—Iliad; complete, literally translated (English). *Translator or author:* Kelly. London, England: James Cornish.

1881—Homer, Analekta fur Schule und Leben; hrsg (German). *Translator or author:* Carl Sylvio Kohler. Leipzig, Germany: T. Grieben.

1881—Iliad, Book I; with English notes (Greek). *Translator or author:* F. A. Paley. London, England: George Bell and Sons.

1881—The Odyssey of Homer; translated, with notes and introduction by the Rev. T[heodore] A[lois] Buckley and Flaxman's designs (English). *Translator or author:* Alexander Pope. New York, N.Y.: John W. Lovell.

1881—The Odyssey of Homer; translated, with notes and introduction by the Rev. Theodore Alois Buckley; and Flaxman's designs (English). *Translator or author:* Alexander Pope. Philadelphia, Pa.: J. B. Lippincott.

1881—The Odyssey of Homer; translated; to which are added the Battle of the Frogs and Mice, by Parnell and the Hymns by Chapman and others; with observations and brief notes by the Rev. J. S. Watson; Illus. with the entire series of Flaxman's designs (English). *Translator or author:* Alexander Pope. London, England: George Bell and Sons.

1881—Odyssee-Landschaften; in Holzschnitt ausgefuhrt von R. Brend'amour; mit einer Biographis des Kunstlers. *Translator or author:* Friedrich Preller. Leipzig, Germany: A. Durr.

1881—Iliad, Books I and II; 2nd edition. *Translator or author:* Arthur Sidgwick. Rivingtons.

1881—Homers Odyssee; abdruck der ersten Ausgabe vom Jahre 1781, mit einer Einleitung von Michael Bernays (German). *Translator or author:* Johann Heinrich Voss. Stuttgart, Germany: J. G. Cotta Buchhandlung.

1881—The Odyssey of Homer; done into English verse; 2nd ed. (English). *Translator or author:* Arthur Sanders Way. London, England: Kegan, Paul, Trench.

1881—Odyssey. *Translator or author:* Arthur Sanders Way. Low.

1881–86—The Iliad; with English notes, critical and explanatory, by T[homas] H[umphry] L[indsay] Leary (Greek). London, England: C. Lockwood.

1882—Odyssey; 2nd ed. (Greek). Oxford, England.

1882—Hymni Homerici Accedentibus Epigrammatis et Batrachomyomachia Homero; vulgo attributis ex recensione Augusti Baumeister (Greek). Leipzig, Germany: B. G. Teubner.

1882—The Iliad of Homer. Macmillan.

1882—Iliad, Book VI; with introduction and notes, by Herbert Hailstone (Greek). Oxford, England: Clarendon Press.

1882—Odyssey, Book IX; with introduction and notes for schools; by Malcolm Montgomrey (Greek). Dublin, Ireland: Browne and Nolan et al.

1882—Iliade, Texte Grec, d'Homere; publie avec une introduction, des arguments analytiques et des notes en Francais par A. Pierron (Greek). Paris, France: L. Hachette.

1882—The First Six books of Homer's Iliad; with explanatory notes, and references to the grammar of Goodwin and Hadley; by James Robinson Boise with notes revised and largely rewritten; 14th ed. Chicago, Il.: S. C. Griggs.

1882—The Odyssey of Homer, with the Hymns, Epigrams, and Battle of the Frogs and Mice; literally translated, with explanatory notes (English). *Translator or author:* Theodore Alois Buckley. New York, N.Y.: Harper and Brothers.

1882—The Odyssey of Homer; done into English prose; 3rd ed. (English). *Translator or author:* Samuel Henry Butcher; Andrew Lang. Boston, Mass.: D. Lothrop.

1882—The Odyssey; 3rd ed. (English). *Translator or author:* Samuel Henry Butcher; Andrew Lang. New York, N.Y.: Macmillan.

1882—Iliad; literal prose translated (English). *Translator or author:* Herbert Hailstone. London, England: James Cornish.

1882—Iliad, Book XVII; The Arms of Achilles. *Translator or author:* Sydney R. James. Macmillan.

1882—The Iliad of Homer; done into English prose (English). *Translator or author:* Andrew Lang; Walter Leaf; Ernest Myers. Boston, Mass.: D. Lothrop.

1882—Homere Iliade; traduction nouvelle; 3rd ed. (French). *Translator or author:* Leconte de Lisle. Paris, France: Alphonse Lemerre.

1882—Homerova Odysseja; preveo, uvod napisao I tumac dodao (Croatian). *Translator or author:* Tomislav Maretiac. Zagreb, Croatia: Matica Hrvatska.

1882—Odyssey, Book IX; with notes. *Translator or author:* Montgomery. Marshall Simpkin.

1882—The Odyssey (English). *Translator or author:* Alexander Pope. New York, N.Y.

1882—The Iliad of Homer; translated; with notes and introduction by the Rev. Theodore Alois Buckley and Flaxman's designs (English). *Translator or author:* Alexander Pope. New York, N.Y.: American News Company.

1882—Iliada; przel. Wierszem miarowym; 2nd ed. (Polish). *Translator or author:* Popiel Pawer. Krakow, Poland: W. Anczyca.

1882—The Story of Achilles from Homer's Iliad; edited with notes and introduction; 2nd ed. (English). *Translator or author:* John Henry Pratt; Walter Leaf. London, England: Macmillan.

1882—Odyssey in English verse, Books XIII–XXIV (English). *Translator or author:* George Augustus Schomberg. London, England: John Murray.

1882—The Iliad (Greek). *Translator or author:* Arthur Sidgwick; Robert P. Keep. Boston, Mass.

1882—Iliad (Greek). *Translator or author:* White. London, England.

1882–83—Homeri Carmina. Leipzig, Germany: B. G. Teubner.

1882–83—La Iliada; traducida del Griego al Castellano (Spanish). *Translator or author:* D. Jose Gomez Hermosilla. Madrid, Spain: L. Navarro.

1882–84—Homer, Odyssey, Books I–XII; with introduction, notes, etc. by W[illiam] W[alter] Merry (Greek). Oxford, England: Clarendon Press.

1882–87—Homers Ilias; fur den Schulgebrauch erkart von Karl Friedrich Ameis; besorgt von Dr. C. Hentze (Greek). Leipzig, Germany: B. G. Teubner.

1883—Iliad; 2nd ed (Greek). Oxford, England.

1883—The First Six Books of Homer's Iliad; with explanatory notes, and references to the grammar of Goodwin and Hadley by James Robinson Boise; 15th ed. (Greek). Chicago, Il.: S. C. Griggs.

1883—Homere, L'Odyssee; avec une etude sur Homere, par Eugene Hins. Mons [location?]: H. Manceaux.

1883—Homeri Ilias Lib. I; ex novissima recensione Frederici A. Paley. Cambridge, England; London, England: Bell Deighton; Whittaker; George Bell and Sons.

1883—Iliad, Book XXIV; with introduction, notes etc. Marshall Simpkin.

1883—The Tale of Troy; scenes and tableaux from the Iliad and Odyssey of Homer; represented at Cromwell House for the benefit of the Building Fund for the King's College Lecture to Ladies, May 29 & 30 and June 4, 1883 (English). London, England: Spottiswoode.

1883—The Odyssey of Homer (English). New York, N.Y.: John B. Alden.

1883—The First Six Books of Homer's Iliad; with English notes, critical and explanatory, a metrical index and Homeric glossary (Greek). New York, N.Y.: Harper and Brothers.

1883—The Iliad of Homer, Books I–VI; with an introduction and notes by Robert P[orter] Keep (Greek). Boston, Mass; Chicago, Il.: Allyn and Bacon.

1883—Iliad; literal translation, Books I–V (English). Marshall Simpkin.

1883—A Literal Translation of the Iliad of Homer, Books I–V (English). *Translator or author:* Allen Blyth; Thomas Allen. Oxford, England: A. Thomas Shrimpton.

1883—Odyssey, Book I. *Translator or author:* J. Bond; A. S. Walpole. Macmillan.

1883—The Arms of Achilles (English). *Translator or author:* William Henry Salter Brooks. Dublin, Ireland: et al. Ponsonby.

1883—Homer's Odyssey [reprint of the 1871 edition] (English). *Translator or author:* William Cullen Bryant. Boston, Mass.

1883—Homer's Iliad; translated into English blank verse [reprint of the 1870 edition] (English). *Trans-

lator or author: William Cullen Bryant. Boston, Mass.

1883— The Odyssey of Homer; done into English prose; 4th ed. (English). *Translator or author:* Samuel Henry Butcher; Andrew Lang. London, England; New York, N.Y.: Macmillan.

1883— Iliad [short passage from Book I representing an attempt at a literal translation] (English). *Translator or author:* H. Dunbar. Oxford, England.

1883— Die Homerische Odyssee (Greek). *Translator or author:* August Fick. Gottingen, Germany.

1883— Oeuvres Completes d'Homere; traduction nouvelle, avec une introduction et des notes; 14th ed. (French). *Translator or author:* Pierre Giguet. Paris, France: L. Hachette.

1883— Odyssey (Greek). *Translator or author:* Hamilton. London, England.

1883— Odyssey, Books XXI–XXIV: the triumph of Odysseus. *Translator or author:* S. Hamilton. Macmillan.

1883— The Siege of Troy and the Wanderings of Ulysses [former title: Homer's Stories Simply Told] (English). *Translator or author:* Charles Henry Hanson. London, England: Nelson and Sons.

1883— Iliad (English). *Translator or author:* Andrew Lang; Walter Leaf; Ernest Myers. New York, N.Y.

1883— The Iliad of Homer; done into English prose (English). *Translator or author:* Andrew Lang; Walter Leaf; Ernest Myers. London, England: Macmillan.

1883— Homerova Iliada; preveo I tumac dodao (Croatian). *Translator or author:* Tomislav Maretiac. Zagreb, Croatia: Matica Hrvatska.

1883— L'Istoire de la Destruction de Troye la Grant; translatee de Latin en Francoys mise par personnages et composee (French). *Translator or author:* Jacques Milet; Edmund Stengel. Marburg and Leipzig, Germany; Paris, France: N. G. Elwert; H. le Soudier.

1883— The Iliad and Odyssey; translated into English verse; with obversations and an essay on the life, writings, and learning of Homer, etc. (English). *Translator or author:* Alexander Pope. London, England.

1883— The Iliad of Homer; translated; with notes and introduction by the Rev. Theodore Alois Buckley and Flaxman's designs (English). *Translator or author:* Alexander Pope. Philadelphia, Pa.: J. B. Lippincott.

1883— The Iliad of Homer; translated; with notes and introduction by Theodore Alois Buckley and Flaxman's designs (English). *Translator or author:* Alexander Pope. New York, N.Y.: John B. Alden.

1883— Ilias; ubers.; mit Einleitung von Prof. Jak. Mahly (German). *Translator or author:* Johann Heinrich Voss. Stuttgart, Germany: W. Spemann.

1883–84— L'Iliade d'Homere; texte Grec, revu et corrige d'apres les documents authentiques de la recension d'Aristarque, accompagne d'un commentaire critique, precede d'une introduction et suivi des prolegomenes de Villoison, des prolegomenes; 2nd ed. (Greek). Paris, France: L. Hachette.

1883–84— [Oeuvres d'Homere] traduites (French). *Translator or author:* J. B. F. Froment. Paris, France: Plon.

1883–91— Homers Ilias; fur den Schulgebrauch erklart von J[acob] la Roche; 3rd ed. (Greek). Leipzig, Germany: B. G. Teubner.

1884— The First Six Books of Homer's Iliad; with explanatory notes, and references to the grammars of Goodwin and Hadley, by James Robinson Boise; 16th ed. Chicago, Il.: S. C. Griggs.

1884— Ilias; 5th ed (Greek). Leipzig, Germany.

1884— The Iliad of Homer, Books I–VI; with an introduction and notes by Robert P. Keep; 2nd ed. Boston, Mass.: J. Allyn.

1884— Homeri Odyssea; edidit Guilielmus Dindorf; 5th ed. (Greek). Leipzig, Germany: B. G. Teubner.

1884— The First Six Books of Homer's Iliad; with English notes, critical and explanatory, a metrical index and Homeric glossary by Charles Anton (Greek). New York, N.Y.: Harper and Brothers.

1884— Homeri Odysseae Epitome; in usum scholarum; edidit Franciscus Pauly; 4th ed. Prague, Czechoslavakia: F. F. Tempsky.

1884— Homer[s] Odyssey, Books I–XII; with introduction, notes, etc.; edited by William Walter Merry (Greek). Oxford, England: Clarendon Press.

1884— Odyssee, Chants I et II; accompagnee de notes critiques, grammaticales et litteraires, et precedee d'une notice sur Homere, par Elie Leroux (Greek). Paris, France: P. Dupont.

1884— The Iliad of Homer; with English notes by F. A. Paley; 2nd ed. (Greek). London, England: Whittaker; George Bell and Sons.

1884— Ilias v. 1, pt. 1–4 (German). *Translator or author:* Karl Friedrich Ameis. Leipzig, Germany.

1884—Iliad, book 1. *Translator or author:* J. Bond; A. S. Walpole. Macmillan.

1884—The Iliad of Homer; literally translated, with explanatory notes (English). *Translator or author:* Theodore Alois Buckley. London, England: George Bell and Sons.

1884—Iliad and Odyssey [reprint of the 1851 edition] (English). *Translator or author:* Theodore Alois Buckley. New York, N.Y.

1884—The Odyssey of Homer, with the Hymns, Epigrams, and Battle of the Frogs and Mice; literally translated, with explanatory notes (English). *Translator or author:* Theodore Alois Buckley. London, England: George Bell and Sons.

1884—Iliad; with an introduction by Henry Morley [reprint of the 1611 edition; series: Morley's Universal Library]. *Translator or author:* George Chapman. George Routledge.

1884—Iliadis Carmina (Greek). *Translator or author:* Christ. Leipzig, Germany.

1884—Iliada Gomera (Russian). *Translator or author:* Nikolaaei Ivanovich Gnedich. St. Petersburg, Russia: A. S. Suvorina.

1884—Iliad; with a verse translation; vol. 1, books I–XII. *Translator or author:* William Charles Green. Longmans.

1884—The Seige of Troy, and The Wanderings of Ulysses; with ninety-seven illustrations (English). *Translator or author:* Charles Henry Hanson. London, England; New York, N.Y.: Thomas Nelson.

1884—Homere, Iliade; traduction nouvelle (French). *Translator or author:* Leconte de Lisle. Paris, France: Alphonse Lemerre.

1884—Odyssey, Book IX; with a commentary. *Translator or author:* John E. B. Mayor. Macmillan.

1884—Homer's Odyssey, Books I–XII; text and English version in rhythmic prose [completed in the 1891 edition] (Greek; English). *Translator or author:* George Herbert Palmer. Boston, Mass.

1884—The Iliad of Homer [reprint of the 1715–20; series: Lovell's Library] (English). *Translator or author:* Alexander Pope. New York, N.Y.

1884—The Iliad of Homer; translated; with notes and introduction by Theodore Alois Buckley, and Flaxman's designs (English). *Translator or author:* Alexander Pope. Chicago, Il.: Clarke Belford.

1884—The Odyssey of Homer [from the 1725–26 and 1880 editions] (English). *Translator or author:* Alexander Pope; W. Broome; E. Fenton. New York, N.Y.

1884–87—Homers Odyssee; erklart von J[ohann] U[lrich] Faesi (Greek). Berlin, Germany: Weidmannsche Buchhandlung.

1884–88—Iliad, Books I–XII; with brief notes. *Translator or author:* David Binning Monro. Oxford Warch.

1884–90—Homers Odyssey; fur den Schulgebrauch; erklart von Karl Friedrich Ameis; besorgt von Dr. C. Hentze (Greek). Leipzig, Germany; Berlin, Germany: B. G. Teubner.

1884–97—Iliad; Books I–XXIV [by] Homer; with an introduction, a brief Homeric grammar, and notes by D. B. Munro [from the 4th and 5th editions] (Greek). Oxford, England: Clarendon Press.

1885—The Odyssey of Homer; according to the text of Wolf; with notes for the use of schools and colleges by John J. Owen (Greek). New York, N.Y.: David Appleton.

1885—Iliad, Book I; with an essay on Homeric grammar and notes by D[avid] B[inning] Monro; 3rd ed. (Greek). Oxford, England: Clarendon Press.

1885—Iliad, Books XXI–XXII; with notes and literal translation by a Graduate (Greek; English). Marshall Simpkin.

1885—The First Three Books of Homer's Iliad; with lexicon; with notes critical and explanatory and references to Hadley's Crosby's, and Goodwin's Greek grammars and to Goodwin's Greek Moods and Tenses by Henry Clark Johnson; 2nd ed (Greek). New York, N.Y.: American Book Company.

1885—The First Six Books of Homer's Iliad; with explanatory notes, and references to the grammars of Goodwin and Hadley by James Robinson Boise; 17th ed. (Greek). Chicago, Il.: S. C. Griggs.

1885—Homers Ilias; fur den Schulgebraugh; erklart von Karl Friedrich Ameis (Greek). Leipzig, Germany: B. G. Teubner.

1885—Odyssee, Chants XXII et XXIII; annotes par Ch. Cucuel (Greek). Paris, France: Garnier Freres.

1885—Homeri Iliados, Liber XVIII; edited for the use of schools by Sydney R. James, with notes and vocabulary (Greek). London, England: Macmillan.

1885—The Odyssey of Homer; done into English prose; 3rd ed. (English). *Translator or author:* Samuel Henry Butcher; Andrew Lang. London, England; New York, N.Y.: Macmillan.

1885— Homers Odysseuslied; in der Nibelungen-
strophe nachgedichtet (German). *Translator or
author:* Ernst Johann Jakob Engel. Leipzig, Germany: Breitkopf and Hartel.

1885— Homers Achilleis aus der Ilias der Homeri-
den; herametrisch Deutsch (German). *Translator
or author:* Otto Jager. Stuttgart, Germany: P. Neff.

1885— The Iliad; 3rd ed (Greek). *Translator or author:* Robert P. Keep. Boston, Mass.

1885— Iliade di Omero; traduxione con le osservazioni di Andrea Mustozidi e le notizie della vita
e delle opere del tradultore; 5th ed. (Italian).
Translator or author: Vincenzo Monti. Milan,
Italy: Edoardo Sonzogno.

1885— Iliad; 2nd edition, revised, vol. 2. *Translator or author:* F. A. Paley. George Bell Whittaker.

1885— Lou Premie Cant de L'Iliado; revira dou
Gre. *Translator or author:* L. Piat. Montpellier,
France.

1885— Homers Werke; ubersetzt; mit einer lit-
terarhistorischen Einleitung von Joseph Lautenbacher (German). *Translator or author:* Johann
Heinrich Voss. Stuttgart, Germany: J. G. Cotta
Buchhandlung.

1885— The Iliad of Homer; done into English
verse (English). *Translator or author:* Arthur
Sanders Way. London, England: Sampson, Low,
Marston, Searle & Rivington.

1885— Iliad, Books I–IV (English). *Translator or
author:* Henry Smith Wright. Cambridge, England.

1885— The Wanderings of Ulysses (a sequel to The
Trojan War); translated from the German (English). *Translator or author:* Frances Younghusband. London, England: Green Longmans.

1885— The Wanderings of Ulysses, by Professor
C. Witt; translated (English). *Translator or au-
thor:* Frances Younghusband. New York, N.Y.:
Harper and Brothers.

1885— Odisseia Gomera; perevod (Russian). *Translator or author:* Vasilii Andreevich Zhukovskii. St.
Petersburg, Russia: Izdanie Glazunova.

1885–10— Odyssee (Greek). Berlin, Germany.

1885–86— Odyssea Homeri (Greek). Leipzig,
Germany: Otto Holtze.

1885–86— Ilias (Greek). Leipzig, Germany.

1885–87— Iliad, Book XXI; 2nd edition; Book
XXII, new edition. *Translator or author:* Arthur
Sidgwick. Rivingtons.

1886— Homeri Ilias; edidit Guilielmus Dindorf;

5th ed. (Greek). Leipzig, Germany: B. G. Teubner.

1886— Die Homerischen Hymnen; hrsg. Und erlautert von Albert Gemoll. Leipzig, Germany: B.
G. Teubner.

1886— The Odyssey of Homer; according to the
text of Wolf; with notes for the use of schools and
colleges by John J[ason] Owen (Greek). New
York, N.Y.: David Appleton.

1886— The First Six Books of Homer's Iliad; with
explanatory notes, and references to the grammars of Goodwin and Hadley, by James Robinson
Boise; 18th ed. (Greek). Chicago, Il.: S. C. Griggs.

1886— The First Six Books of Homer's Iliad; with
English notes, critical and explanatory, a metrical
index, and Homeric glossary by Charles Anthon
(Greek). New York, N.Y.: Harper and Brothers.

1886— Homer Without a Lexicon, for Beginners:
Iliad, book VI, with notes (Greek). Rivingtons.

1886— Homere Chants I, II, III et IV de l'Odyssee.
Paris, France: L. Hachette.

1886— Homeri Hymni, Epigrammata, Batrachomyomachia; edidit Eugenius Abel (Greek).
Leipzig, Germany: G. Freytag.

1886— The Iliad of Homer, Books XVI–XXIV;
with explanatory notes for the use of students in
colleges by W[illiam] S[eymour] Tyler (Greek).
New York, N.Y.: Harper.

1886— Homeri Ilias. Leipzig, Germany: Otto
Holtze.

1886— Die Homerische Ilias; nach ihrer Entste-
hung betrachtet und in der ursprunglichen
Sprachform wiederhergestellt, von August Fick
(Greek). Gottingen, Germany: Vendenhoeck und
Ruprecht.

1886— Iliad, [of] Homer, Books I–XII; with an
introduction, a brief Homeric grammar, and
notes by D[avid] B[inning] Monro; 2nd ed.
(Greek). Oxford, England: Clarendon Press.

1886— Homeri Odyssea. Leipzig, Germany: Otto
Holtze.

1886— The First Three Books of Homer's Iliad;
with explanatory notes, and references to the
grammars of Goodwin and Hadley by James
Robinson Boise; with notes revised and largely
rewritten (Greek). Chicago, Il.: S. C. Griggs.

1886— Hymni, Epigrammata, Batrachomyomachia
(Greek). *Translator or author:* Abel. Leipzig, Germany.

1886— La Odisea; traducida directamenta del

Griego en verso Castellano (Castilian Spanish). *Translator or author:* Federico Baraibar y Zumarraga. Madrid, Spain: L. Navarro.

1886— The Iliad of Homer; literally translated, with explanatory notes (English). *Translator or author:* Theodore Alois Buckley. New York, N.Y.: Harper and Brothers.

1886— The Odyssey of Homer, Books I–XII; translated into English verse (English). *Translator or author:* Henry Howard Molyneux, Earl of Carnarvon. London, England; New York, N.Y.: Macmillan.

1886— Homer's Iliad; translated; with an introduction by Henry Morley; 2nd ed. (English). *Translator or author:* George Chapman. London, England: George Routledge.

1886— The Iliad of Homer; a translation (with Greek text) (Greek; English). *Translator or author:* John Graham Cordery. London, England: Kegan Paul; Trench.

1886— Odyssee; im Versmass der Urschrift ubersetzt (German?). *Translator or author:* F. W. Ehrenthal. Leipzig, Germany: Bibliographisches Institut.

1886— Die Homerische Ilias (Greek). *Translator or author:* August Fick. Gottingen, Germany.

1886— Die Homerische Hymnen (Greek). *Translator or author:* Gemoll. Leipzig, Germany.

1886— Odissea di Omero; traduzione; 5th ed. (Italian). *Translator or author:* Paolo Massero. Milan, Italy: U. Hoepli.

1886— Iliad, Book XVI; with an introduction, notes, and translation (English). *Translator or author:* Augustus Constable Maybury.

1886— Odyssey, Books I–VI; literally translated [reprinted from the edition of 1879–80] (English). *Translator or author:* Roscoe Mongan. London, England: James Cornish.

1886— L'Iliade di Omero; traduzione; con note di Ferruccio Martini (Italian). *Translator or author:* Vincenzo Monti. Ancona, Italy: A. G. Morelli.

1886— The Odyssey (Greek, English). *Translator or author:* George Herbert Palmer. Boston, Mass.

1886— Iliade [d']Homere; vingt-quatre grandes compositions par M. Henri Motte; traduction (French). *Translator or author:* Emile Pessonneaux. Paris, France: Maison Quantin.

1886— L'Odyssee d'Homere; traduction Francaise avec le texte Grec en regard et des notes (Greek; French). *Translator or author:* Jean Edouard Albert Sommer. Paris, France: L. Hachette.

1886— The Tale of Troy; done into English (English). *Translator or author:* Aubrey Stewart. London, England; New York, N.Y.: Macmillan.

1886— Iliad, Books XVI–XXIV; with notes. *Translator or author:* W. S. Tyler. New York, N.Y.

1886— Homers Odyssee (German). *Translator or author:* Johann Heinrich Voss. Halle an der Saale, Germany: O. Hendel.

1886–01— Homer's Odyssey; edited with English notes, appendices, etc. by W[illiam] Walter Merry and James Riddell; 2nd ed. (Greek). Oxford, England: Clarendon Press.

1886–05— Homers Ilias; fur den Schulgebrauch erklart von Karl Friedrich Ameis; besorgt von Prof. Dr. C. Hentze. Leipzig, Germany; Berlin, Germany: B. G. Teubner.

1886–19— Homers Iliade; erklart von J[ohann] U[lrich] Faesi (Greek). Berlin, Germany: Weidmannsche Buchhandlung.

1886–87— Homeri Iliadis Carmina; edidit Aloisius Rzach (Greek). Leipzig, Germany: G. Freytag.

1886–87— [H]omerou Ilias = Homeri Ilias; scholarum in usum edidit Paulus Cauer (Greek; Latin). Vienna, Austria; Prague, Chechoslavakia: F. F. Tempsky.

1886–87— Odyssea (Greek). *Translator or author:* Paul Cauer. Leipzig, Germany.

1886–88— The Iliad; edited with English notes and introduction by Walter Leaf (Greek). London, England: Macmillan.

1886–88— The Iliad of Homer; done into English verse (English). *Translator or author:* Arthur Sanders Way. London, England: Sampson Low, Marston, Searle & Rivington.

1886–90— [H]omerou Odysseia; fur den Schulgebrauch erklart von Ferdinand Weck (Greek). Gotha, Germany: F. A. Perthes.

1886–91— Homeri Odyssea; edidit Guilielmus Dindorf; 5th ed. (Greek). Leipzig, Germany: B. G. Teubner.

1886–91— Ilias fur den Schulgebrauch; erklart von J[acob] La Roche; 3rd ed. Leipzig, Germany: B. G. Teubner.

1886–96— Homers Ilias; fur den Schulgebrauch erklart von Karl Friedrich Ameis; 5th ed. Leipzig, Germany: B. G. Teubner.

1887— The Story of Achilles, from Homer's Iliad; edited with notes and introduction by John Henry Pratt and Walter leaf; 3rd ed. London, England; New York, N.Y.: Macmillan.

1887—The First Book of Homer's Iliad; with a vocabulary, some account of Greek prosody and an appendix by John T. White (Greek). London, England: Green Longman.

1887—The Odyssey; with English notes critical and explanatory, by T. H. L. Leary. London, England: Crosby Lockwood.

1887—The Odyssey of Homer, Book IX; with introduction, notes and appendices by G[erald] M[aclean] Edwards. Cambridge, England: Cambridge University Press.

1887—The Phaeacian Episode of the Odyssey; as comprised in the sixth, seventh, eighth, eleventh, and thirteenth books; with introduction, notes, and appendix, by Augustus C[hapman] Merriam (Greek). New York, N.Y.: Harper and Brothers.

1887—Odyssey, Book I; with notes & table of poems; edited by William Walter Merry (Greek). Oxford Warch.

1887—Homer, Odyssey, Books I–XII; with introduction, notes, etc. by W[illiam] W[alter] Merry (Greek). Oxford, England: Clarendon Press.

1887—Homeri Iliadis Carmina; cum apparatu critico; ediderunt J. van Leeuwen et M[aurits] B[enjamin] Mendes da Costa. Leiden (Leyden), Netherlands: A. W. Sijthoff.

1887—Homeri Iliadis Carmina; edidit Aloisius Rzach (Greek). Leipzig, Germany: G. Freytag.

1887—Odyssey (Greek). Oxford, England.

1887—The Iliad of Homer, Books I–VI; with an introduction and notes by Robert P[orter] Keep. Boston, Mass.: J. Allyn.

1887—The Iliad of Homer, According to the Text of Wolf; with notes for the use of schools and colleges by John J[ason] Owen (Greek). New York, N.Y.: David Appleton.

1887—La Batracomiomaquia [de] Homero; tracida directamente del Griego (Spanish). *Translator or author:* Genaro Alenda y Mira. Madrid, Spain: L. Navarro.

1887—The Iliad of Homer; literally translated, with explanatory notes (English). *Translator or author:* Theodore Alois Buckley. New York, N.Y.: Harper.

1887—The Odyssey of Homer; done into English prose [3rd ed.] (English). *Translator or author:* Samuel Henry Butcher; Andrew Lang. London, England: Macmillan.

1887—Iliad done into English prose (English). *Translator or author:* Samuel Butler. Macmillan.

1887—Odyssey, Books I–XII, English verse (English). *Translator or author:* Earl of Carnarvon. Macmillan.

1887—Batrachomyomachia, Hymns and Epigrams [edited by Richard Hooper]. *Translator or author:* George Chapman. London, England: Reeves and Turner.

1887—Homer's Iliad; translated; with twenty-four illustrations designed by Henri Motte, printed in heliogravure; with an introduction by Henry Morley; 3rd ed. (English). *Translator or author:* George Chapman. London, England; New York, N.Y.: George Routledge.

1887—The Iliads of Homer, Prince of Poets; with an introduction by Henry Morley [reprint of the 1611 edition] (English). *Translator or author:* George Chapman. New York, N.Y.

1887—The Iliad; rendered into English blank verse; to which are appended translations of poems ancient and modern; 12th ed. (English). *Translator or author:* Edward George Geoffrey Smith Stanley, Earl of Derby. London, England: John Murray.

1887—Ilyada; mutercimi (Turkish). *Translator or author:* Naim Frasari. Istanbul, Turkey: Karabet ve Kasbar Matbaasi.

1887—Canti e Versioni di Giacomo Leopardi; publicati con numerose varianti di su gli autografi recanatesi, da Camillo Antona-Traversi. *Translator or author:* Giacomo Leipardi. Citta di Castello, Italy: S. Lapi.

1887—The Odyssey of Homer; done into English verse [1st ed.] (English). *Translator or author:* William Morris. London, England: Reeves and Turner.

1887—The Odyssey of Homer; translated (English). *Translator or author:* Alexander Pope. New York, N.Y.: Worthington Co.

1887—Homer's Iliad: First Three Books; adapted to the Hamiltonian system; with analytical-interlineal translation and notes (Greek; English). *Translator or author:* John William Underwood. London, England: Hodgson.

1887—Homers Ilias (German). *Translator or author:* Johann Heinrich Voss. Halle an der Saale, Germany: O. Hendel.

1887—Odyssey (Greek). *Translator or author:* White. London, England.

1887–88—[H]omerou Odysseia = L'Odyssee d'Homere; texte Grec, revu et corr. d'apres les diorthose Alexandrines, accompagne d'un commentaire critique et explicatig; precede d'une introd. Et suivi de la Batrachomyomachie, des Hymnes Homeriques, etc., par [Pierre] (Greek). Paris, France: L. Hachette.

1887–88—[H]omerou Odysseia = Homeri Odyssea; scholarum in usum edidit Paulus Cauer (Greek). Leipzig, Germany: G. Feytag.

1887–88—Echoes of Hellas: The Tale of Troy & The story of Orestes from Homer & Aeschylus; with introductory essay & sonnets by Prof. George C. Warr, presented in 82 designs by Walter Crane (English). *Translator or author:* George C. Warr. London, England; New York, N.Y.: W. Ward.

1887–91—Homer's Iliad, Books I–VI; edited on the basis of the Ameis-Hentze edition by Thomas D[ay] Seymour. Boston, Mass.: Ginn.

1888—Homer, Iliad. Oxford, England: Clarendon Press.

1888—The First Six Books of Homer's Iliad; with English notes, critical and explanatory, a metrical index, and Homeric glossary by Charles Anthon. New York, N.Y.: Harper and Brothers.

1888—Homer, Odyssey, Books XIII–XXIV; with introduction, notes, etc. by W[illiam] W[alter] Merry; 3rd ed. (Greek). Oxford, England: Clarendon Press.

1888—Homeri Carmina et Cycli Epici Reliquae; Graece et Latine cum indice nominum et rerum (Greek; Latin). Paris, France: Ambrosio Firmin Didot.

1888—The Iliad of Homer; with an interlinear translation; for the use of schools and private learners on the Hamiltonian system, as improved by Thomas Clark [series: Hamilton, Leeke and Clark] (English). Philadelphia, Pa.: David McKay.

1888—Homer's Iliad; with the plays of Aeschylus and Sophocles; with introductions by Henry Morley. London, England: Routledge and Sons.

1888—Iliad, Books XIII–XXIV; with notes by D[avid] B[inning] Monro (Greek). Oxford, England: Clarendon Press.

1888—[H]omerou Ilias; with prefatory note and introduction by James M[orton] Paton (Greek). London, England; New York, N.Y.: White and Allen.

1888—Odyssey, Books I–XII, with introductory notes etc. by William Walter Merry (Greek). Oxford Warch.

1888—The Iliad of Homer; with an interlinear translation, for the use of schools and private learners on the Hamiltonian system as improved

by Thomas Clark (Greek; English). Philadelphia, Pa.: C. De Silver and Sons.

1888—[H]omerou Odysseia; with an introduction by James M[orton] Paton (Greek). London, England: Pickering and Chatto.

1888—The Iliad, Book I; a metrical translation (English). *Translator or author:* A. W. Bacheler. Gloucester, England.

1888—Hymni Homerici Accedentibus Epigrammatis et Batrachomyomachia Homero; vulgo Attributis; ex recensione Augusti Baumeister (Greek). *Translator or author:* Augustus Baumeister. Leipzig, Germany: B. G. Teubner.

1888—The Iliad of Homer; literally translated, with explanatory notes (English). *Translator or author:* Theodore Alois Buckley. New York, N.Y.: Harper.

1888—The Odyssey of Homer; done into English prose (English). *Translator or author:* Samuel Henry Butcher; Andrew Lang. New York, N.Y.: Macmillan.

1888—The Iliads of Homer, Prince of Poets; with a comment on some of his chief places; done according to the Greek; with an introduction and notes by Richard Hooper; 3rd ed. (English). *Translator or author:* George Chapman. London, England: J. R. Smith.

1888—Homer's Batrachomyomachia, Hymns and Epigrams, Hesiod's Works and Days, Musaeus' Hero and Leander, Juvenal's Fifth satire, translated, with introduction and notes, by the Rev. Richard Hooper; 2nd ed (English). *Translator or author:* George Chapman. London, England: J. R. Smith.

1888—Odyssey, Book IX with notes. *Translator or author:* G. M. Edwards. Camb. Warch.

1888—Homer's Iliad [reprint of the 1855–58 edition] (English). *Translator or author:* Hamilton and Clark. Philadelphia, Pa.

1888—The Iliad; 5th ed (Greek). *Translator or author:* Robert P. Keep. Boston, Mass.

1888—Adventures of Ulysses; with notes by Alfred Ainger (English). *Translator or author:* Charles Lamb. New York, N.Y.: International Pub. Co.

1888—Iliade d'Omero, Poema Epico; tradotta; 6th ed. (Italian). *Translator or author:* Vincenzo Monti. Torino (Turin), Italy: Tipografia e Libreria Salesiana.

1888—Odysseia (Greek). *Translator or author:* Paton. London, England.

1888—Iliad, Book XXII; with notes; 2nd edition. *Translator or author:* P. Sandford. Marshall Simpkin.

1888—Homers Ilias in verkurzter Form; bearb. von Dr. Edmund Weissenborn (German). *Translator or author:* Johann Heinrich Voss. Leipzig, Germany: B. G. Teubner.

1888-—Iliade; erklart von J[ohann] U[lrich] Faesi; 7th ed. Berlin, Germany: Weidmannsche Buchhandlung.

1888-00—The Iliad; edited, with apparatus criticus, prolegomena, notes, and appendices by Walter Leaf (Greek). London, England; New York, N.Y.: Macmillan.

1888-90—Homeri Ilias; edidit Guilielmus Dindorf; 5th ed. (Greek). Leipzig, Germany: B. G. Teubner.

1888-96—Homers Ilias; fur den Schulgebrauch erklart von Karl Friedrich Ameis; 5th ed. (Greek). Leipzig, Germany: B. G. Teubner.

1888-96—Ilias (Greek). *Translator or author:* Karl Friedrich Ameis; Carl Hentze. Leipzig, Germany.

1889—The First Six Books of Homer's Iliad; with explanatory notes, and references to the grammar of Goodwin and Hadley; by James Robinson Boise; 19th ed. (Greek). Chicago, Il.: S. C. Griggs.

1889—The Phaeacian Episode of the Odyssey as Comprised in the Sixth, Seventh, Eighth, Eleventh, and Thirteenth Books; with introduction, notes, and appendix by Augustus C. Merriam (Greek). New York, N.Y.: Harper and Brothers.

1889—The First Three Books of Homer's Iliad; with lexicon; with notes critical and explanatory and references to Hadley's, Crosby's, and Goodwin's Greek Grammars and to Goodwin's Greek moods and tenses together with an appendix containing an outline of the "Homeric Question" (Greek). New York, N.Y.: David Appleton.

1889—Odyssey, Book X [edited by Gerald Maclean Edwards; 1st ed.] (Greek). Cambridge, England: Cambridge University Press.

1889—Homeri Odysseae Epitome; in usum scholarum edidit Franciscus Pauly; 7th ed. Vienna, Austria: F. F. Tempsky.

1889—Homers Odyssee; fur den Schulgebrauch erklart von Dr. K. F. Ameis; besorgt von Dr. C. Hentze; 8th ed. (Greek). Leipzig, Germany: B. G. Teubner.

1889—The Iliad of Homer, Books I–III; with an introduction and notes by Robert P[orter]

Keep; 6th ed. (Greek). Boston, Mass.: Allyn and Bacon.

1889—Homer's Iliad, Books I–VI [series: Handy Literal Translation] (English). New York, N.Y.

1889—Odyssey, Books I–XII; with introduction, notes, etc. by W[illiam] W[alter] Merry (Greek). Oxford, England: Clarendon Press.

1889—Homer's Odyssey, Books I–IV; edited on the basis of the Ameis-Hentze edition, by B[ernadotte] Perrin (Greek). Boston, Mass.: Ginn.

1889—The First Six Books of Homer's Iliad; with introduction, commentary, and vocabulary, for the use of schools, by Thomas D[ay] Seymour (Greek). Boston, Mass.: Ginn.

1889—La Batracomiomaquia [de] Homero; traducida directamente del Griego (Spanish). *Translator or author:* Genaro Alenda y Mira. Madrid, Spain: Tip. De "El Ejercito Espanol".

1889—Homer's Iliad: a Burlesque Translation; revised and modified by George A. Smith (English). *Translator or author:* Thomas Seymour Bridges. Philadelphia, Pa.: Gebbie.

1889—Ulysses among the Phaeacians [reprint of the 1871 edition] (English). *Translator or author:* William Cullen Bryant. Boston, Mass.

1889—Ulysses Among the Phaeacians; from the translation of Homer's Odyssey (English). *Translator or author:* William Cullen Bryant. New York, N.Y.; Cambridge, Oh.: Houghton Mifflin ; Riverside Press.

1889—The First Six Books of Homer's Iliad; literally translated with explanatory notes (English). *Translator or author:* Theodore Alois Buckley. Reading, Pa.: Handy Book.

1889—The Iliad of Homer; literally translated, with explanatory notes (English). *Translator or author:* Theodore Alois Buckley. New York, N.Y.: American Book Company.

1889—La Iliada; traducida del Griego al Castellano (Castilian Spanish). *Translator or author:* Jose Gomez Hermosilla. Madrid, Spain: Libreria de la Viuda de Hernando y Ca.

1889—Homer's Iliad, Books I and VI; metrical translation; with notes (English). *Translator or author:* George Howland. New York, N.Y.: E. Maynard.

1889—Homer's Iliad; metrical translation (English). *Translator or author:* George Howland. Boston, Mass.

1889—Homers Odyssee; ubersetzt und erklart;

2nd ed. (German). *Translator or author:* Wilhelm Jordan. Leipzig, Germany; Frankfurt am Main, Germany: Wilhelm Jordan.

1889—The Iliad of Homer; done into English prose (English). *Translator or author:* Andrew Lang; Walter Leaf; Ernest Myers. London, England; New York, N.Y.: Macmillan.

1889—Homer, Vol. 1 [series: Bibliotheca Classica]. *Translator or author:* F. A. Paley. George Bell Whittaker.

1889—The Odyssey of Homer, Books I–XII; text and an English version in rhythmic prose (Greek; English). *Translator or author:* George Herbert Palmer. Boston, Mass.: Houghton Mifflin.

1889—Odyssey (Greek). *Translator or author:* H. Perrin. Boston, Mass.

1889—The Odyssey; translated; to which are added the Battle of the Frogs and Mice, by Parnell and the Hymns by Chapman and others; with observations and brief notes, by J. S. Watson; illustrated with the entire series of Flaxman's designs (English). *Translator or author:* Alexander Pope. London, England: George Bell.

1889—The Iliad of Homer; translated; with observations on Homer and his works, and brief notes, by the Rev. J. S. Watson; illustrated with the entire series of Flaxman's designs (English). *Translator or author:* Alexander Pope. London, England: George Bell and Sons.

1889—Iliad and Odyssey, translated, edited by Carey; new edition (English). *Translator or author:* Alexander Pope. George Routledge.

1889—Iliad done into English verse; vol. 2, books 13–24 (English). *Translator or author:* Arthur Sanders Way. Low.

1889—The Trojan War; by Professor C. Witt, translated from the German; with a preface by the Rev. W. Gunion Rutherford; 3rd ed. (English). *Translator or author:* Frances Younghusband. London, England; New York, N.Y.: Green Longmans.

1889–07—Homeri Carmina; recensuit et selecta lectionis varietate instruxit Arthurus Ludwich. Leipzig, Germany: B. G. Teubner.

1889–91—Homeri Odyssea; edidit Guilielmus Dindorf; 5th ed. (Greek). Leipzig, Germany: B. G. Teubner.

1889–92—Homeri Odyssea; edidit Guilielmus Dindorf; 4th ed. Leipzig, Germany: B. G. Teubner.

1889–92—Homerova Odysseia; heksametrom na movu ukrainsko-rus'ku perevirshuvav Petro Baida [Petro Nishchyns'kyi] (Ukrainian). *Translator or author:* Petro Nishchyns'kyi. L'viv (Lwow), Ukraine: Nakl. Red. "Pravdy".

1890—Iliad; 3rd ed (Greek). Oxford, England.

1890—The Iliad of Homer, Book XXII; with introduction, notes and appendices by G[erald] M[aclean] Edwards (Greek). Cambridge, England: Cambridge University Press.

1890—Homer's Odyssey, Book I; edited for the use of schools; by J. Bond and A. S. Walpole; with notes and vocabulary (Greek). London, England: Macmillan.

1890—Iliad; 5th ed (Greek). Leipzig, Germany.

1890—The First Six Books of Homer's Iliad; with English notes, critical and explanatory, a metrical index, and Homeric glossary, by Charles Anthon (Greek). New York, N.Y.: Harper.

1890—[H]omerou Odysseia = Homeri Odyssea; edidit Paulus Cauer (Greek). London, England: Cassell.

1890—Homeric Birthday book: Gems from Iliad and Odyssey of Homer (English). Marshall Simpkin.

1890—Homer's Iliad and Odyssey; designs by Flaxman. Frederick Warne.

1890—The Iliad of Homer, Books I–VI; with an introduction and notes by Robert P[orter] Keep. Boston, Mass.: Allyn and Bacon.

1890—Homeri Iliadis Carmina; edidit Aloisius Rzach (Greek). London, England: Cassell.

1890—Homer, Iliad, Books I–XII; with an introduction, a brief Homeric grammar, and notes, by D[avid] B[inning] Monro; 3rd ed. (Greek). Oxford, England: Clarendon Press.

1890—Hymnvs Homericvs in Mercvrvm; ab Arthvro Lvdwich editvs; adiectis animadversionibvs criticis in Phlegontis Oracvla Sibyllina. Konigsburg [location?]: Hartungiana.

1890—The Iliad of Homer; according to the text of Wolf; with notes for the use of schools and colleges by John J[ason] Owen (Greek). New York, N.Y.: David Appleton.

1890—The Iliad of Homer; with an interlinear translation, for the use of schools and private learners, on the Hamiltonian system as improved by Thomas Clark (Greek; English). Philadelphia, Pa.: David McKay.

1890—Homeri Odysseae Carmina; cum apparatu critico; ediderunt J. van Leeuwen et M. B. Mendes da Costa. Leiden (Leyden), Netherlands: A. W. Sijthoff.

1890—The Return of Ulysses: a Drama in Five Acts in a Mixed Manner (English). *Translator or author:* Robert Seymour Bridges. London, England: E. Bumpus.

1890—The Story of the Iliad; or, The Siege of Troy (English). *Translator or author:* Edward Brooks. Philadelphia, Pa.: Penn Publishing.

1890—The Iliad of Homer; literally translated, with explanatory notes (English). *Translator or author:* Theodore Alois Buckley. London, England: George Bell and Sons.

1890—The Odyssey of Homer; done into English prose (English). *Translator or author:* Samuel Henry Butcher; Andrew Lang. New York, N.Y.; London, England: Macmillan.

1890—Tales from the Odyssey for Boys and Girls (English). *Translator or author:* C.M.B. New York, N.Y.: Harper and Brothers.

1890—Homer's Iliad; translated, with an introduction by Henry Morley; 4th ed. (English). *Translator or author:* George Chapman. London, England: Rutledge.

1890—Stories from Homer; with twenty-four illustrations from Flaxman's designs (English). *Translator or author:* Alfred John Church. London, England: Seeley.

1890—The Iliad of Homer; a translation (English). *Translator or author:* John Graham Cordery. London, England: Kegan Paul.

1890—Homer's Odyssey, Book XXI; introduction, notes, appendices. *Translator or author:* G. M. Edwards. Cambridge University Press.

1890—Homers Odyssee; in freier Umdichtung fur das Deutsche Haus (German). *Translator or author:* Emil Engelmann. Stuttgart, Germany: P. Neff.

1890—Homer's Iliad, Books XXII [and] XXIV; literally translated, with notes. *Translator or author:* John Henry Freese. Marshall Simpkin.

1890—Iphigenia in Delphi: a Dramatic Poem; with Homer's "Shield of Achilles" and other translations from the Greek (English). *Translator or author:* Richard Garnett. London, England: T. Fisher Unwin.

1890—Homers Ilias; erster bis neunter Gesang (German). *Translator or author:* Herman Grimm. Berlin, Germany: Wilhelm Hertz.

1890—The Adventures of Ulysses; with an intro-

duction by Andrew Lang (English). *Translator or author:* Charles Lamb. New York, N.Y.: Edward Arnold.

1890—The Adventures of Ulysses; with a preface by Andrew Lang; illustrated with thirty-four designs by Frederick Preller (English). *Translator or author:* Charles Lamb. Philadelphia, Pa.: Gebbie.

1890—Iliade d'Omero, Poema Epico; tradotto; 7th ed. (Italian). *Translator or author:* Vincenzo Monti. Torino (Turin), Italy: Tipografia e Libreria Salesiana.

1890—Odyssee; texte Grec publie avec une introduction, des arguments analytiques et des notes en Francais (Greek). *Translator or author:* Pierre Alexis Pierron. Paris, France: L. Hachette.

1890—Homer's Iliad and Odyssey; edited by H. F. Cary (English). *Translator or author:* Alexander Pope. George Routledge.

1890—The Iliad of Homer; translated; with notes and introduction by Rev. Theodore Alois Buckley (English). *Translator or author:* Alexander Pope. New York, N.Y.: A. L. Burt.

1890—Homer's Odyssey; translated; with valuable notes and commentaries and several papers not contained in any other edition; edited by W. C. Armstrong (English). *Translator or author:* Alexander Pope. Philadelphia, Pa.: Keystone Pub. Co.

1890—Homer's Iliad (Books I, VI, XXII, XXIV) (English). *Translator or author:* Alexander Pope. New York, N.Y.; Cambridge, Oh.: American Book Company.

1890—The Iliad and Odyssey of Homer; translated; with valuable notes and commentaries, and several incidental literary papers, not contained in any other edition; edited by W. C. Armstrong (English). *Translator or author:* Alexander Pope. New York, N.Y.: Leavitt and Allen.

1890—Iliad [reprint of the 1885 edition] (English). *Translator or author:* Arthur Sanders Way.

1890—Homers Iliade; oversat; 5th ed. (Danish). *Translator or author:* Christian Frederik Emil Wilster. Copenhagen, Denmark: C. A. Reitzel.

1890—Homers Odyssee; 5. opl. (Danish). *Translator or author:* Christian Frederik Emil Wilster. Copenhagen, Denmark.

1890–07—Homeri Ilias; edidit Guilielmus Dindorf (Greek). Leipzig, Germany.

1890–91—[H]omerou Ilias = Homeri Ilias; scholarum in usum edidit Paulus Cauer (Greek). Vienna, Austria; Leipzig, Germany: F. F. Tempsky; G. Freytag.

1890–91— Homeri Odyssea; recensuit A[rthur] Ludwich. Leipzig, Germany: B. G. Teubner.

1890–93— Homeri Ilias, Homeri Odyssea; edidit Guilielmus Dindorf; 5th ed. (Greek). Leipzig, Germany: B. G. Teubner.

1890–93— Iliad, Books XIII–XXIV, [of] Homer; with notes by D[avid] B[inning] Monro; 2nd ed. (Greek). Oxford, England: Clarendon Press.

1890–93— Ilias; edidit Guilielmus Dindorf; 5th ed. (Greek). Leipzig, Germany: B. G. Teubner.

1890–95— Odyssee (Greek). *Translator or author:* Karl Friedrich Ameis; Carl Hentze. Leipzig, Germany.

1890–97— Iliad [of] Homer. Oxford, England: Clarendon Press.

1890s— Iliade; text Grec [de] Homere; publie avec und introduction, des arguments analytiques et des notes en Francais par [Pierre] A[lexis] Pierron (Greek). Paris, France: L. Hachette.

1890s— Homer's Iliad; translated; with valuable notes and commentaries and several papers not contained in any other edition, edited by W. C. Armstrong (English). Philadelphia, Pa.: Keystone Pub. Co.

1890s— Homers Ilias; ubersetzt und erklart; 3rd ed. (German). *Translator or author:* Wilhelm Jordan. Frankfurt am Main, Germany: Moritz Diesterweg.

1890s— The Iliad of Homer; translated; with notes and introduction by the Rev. Theodore Alois Buckley (English). *Translator or author:* Alexander Pope. New York, N.Y.: T. Y. Crowell.

1890s— Odyssey; translated (English). *Translator or author:* Alexander Pope. New York, N.Y.: John W. Lovell.

1890s— The Iliad of Homer (Books I, VI, XXII, XXIV); translated; edited by Warwick James Price (English). *Translator or author:* Alexander Pope. Boston, Mass.: Sibley and Drucker.

1890s— The Iliad of Homer; translated (English). *Translator or author:* Alexander Pope. New York, N.Y.: Hurst.

1890s— Odyssey of Homer; translated (English). *Translator or author:* Alexander Pope. New York, N.Y.: American News Company.

1890s— Homers Ilias; abdruck der ersten Ausgabe (German). *Translator or author:* Johann Heinrich Voss. Leipzig, Germany: Philipp Reclam.

1890s— Homers Werke in zwei Banden; ubersetzt; mit einer literarhistorischen Einleitung von Joseph Lautenbacher (German). *Translator or author:* Johann Heinrich Voss. Stuttgart, Germany: J. G. Cotta Buchhandlung.

1890s— Odisseia Gomera; v pervodeiie; s risunkami v teksteiie I 16 otdeiienymi kartinami F. Prellera; s predisloviem V. Zeiielinskago (Russian). *Translator or author:* Vasilii Andreevich Zhukovskii. St. Petersburg, Russia: A. F. Devriena.

1891— The Iliad of Homer, Book XXII; with introduction, notes, and appendices by G[erald] M[aclean] Edwards. Cambridge University Press.

1891— Odyssey, Books I–XXIV [of] Homer; with introduction, notes, and table of Homeric forms by W[illiam] W[alter] Merry (Greek). Oxford, England: Clarendon Press.

1891— Ilias; sun tois sholiois pseudepigrafois, Didumou (Greek). Oxford, England: Clarendon Press.

1891— The Iliad of Homer, Book XXIII; with introduction, notes, and appendices by G[erald] M[aclean] Edwards (Greek). Cambridge, England: Cambridge University Press.

1891— Homer's Odyssey, Books XI, XII, XIII, XIV; edited with introduction, notes, and appendix on the dialect by J[ohn] H[ampten] Haydon and F[rances] G[iffard] Plaistowe (Greek). London, England: W. B. Clive.

1891— The First Six Books of Homer's Iliad; with introduction, commentary, and vocabulary; for the use of schools; edited on the basis of the Ameis-Hentze edition, by Thomas D[ay] Seymour. Boston, Mass.: Ginn.

1891— Homer's Odyssey, Books IX–X; edited by John Hampden Haydon and Arthur Hadrian Allcroft. London, England: W. B. Clive.

1891— Homer's Odyssey, Book IV; edited by A. F. Burnett and John Thompson. London, England: W. B. Clive.

1891— Odyssee; 5th ed (Greek). Leipzig, Germany.

1891— The Story of Odyssey, or, The Adventure of Ulysses (English). *Translator or author:* Edward Brooks. Penn Publishing.

1891— The First Six Books of Homer's Iliad; literally translated with explanatory notes (English). *Translator or author:* Theodore Alois Buckley. New York, N.Y.: Arthur Hinds.

1891— The Odyssey of Homer, with the Hymns, Epigrams, and Battle of the Frogs and Mice; literally translated, with explanatory notes (English). *Translator or author:* Theodore Alois Buckley. London, England: George Bell and Sons.

1891— The Iliad of Homer; literally translated, with explanatory notes (English). *Translator or author:* Theodore Alois Buckley. New York, N.Y.: Harper.

1891— The Story of the Iliad; with an introduction and notes by Albert F[ranklin] Blaisdell; with illustrations after Flaxman (English). *Translator or author:* Alfred John Church. New York, N.Y.: Macmillan.

1891— A Daughter of the Gods; ballads from the first, second and third books of the Iliad; etchings by Tristram Ellis (English). *Translator or author:* Joseph Cross. London, England: Leadenhall Press.

1891— The Homeric Hymns; translated into English prose (English). *Translator or author:* John Edgar. Edinburgh, Scotland: Thin.

1891— Homers Odyssee; in freier Umdichtung fur das Deutsche Haus (German). *Translator or author:* Emil Engelmann. Stuttgart, Germany: P. Neff.

1891— Odyssey, Books IX–XIV. *Translator or author:* John Hamilton Haydon; Arthur Hadrian Scott.

1891— Homer's Odyssey, Book I, V, IX, X; metrical translation; with notes (English). *Translator or author:* George Howland. New York, N.Y.: E. Maynard.

1891— The Iliad of Homer; done into English prose (English). *Translator or author:* Andrew Lang; Walter Leaf; Ernest Myers. New York, N.Y.: Macmillan.

1891— Batrachomyomachia, or the Battle of the Frogs and the Mice (English). *Translator or author:* H. Morgan-Brown. North Finchley, [England?].

1891— Homer's Odyssey; translated into English rhythmic prose [completion of the 1884 edition] (English). *Translator or author:* George Herbert Palmer. Boston, Mass.: Houghton Mifflin.

1891— Homer's Odyssey; in English rhythmic prose (English). *Translator or author:* George Herbert Palmer. London, England.

1891— L'Odissea; tradotta; con pref. e commento di Vittorio Turri (Italian). *Translator or author:* Ippolito Pindemonte. Florence, Italy: G. C. Sansoni.

1891— Iliad and Odyssey of Homer; translated; edited by H[enry] F[rancis] Cary, with an intro-

duction by Sir John Lubbock (English). *Translator or author:* Alexander Pope. London, England: George Routledge.

1891— The Iliad of Homer; translated; with notes and introduction by the Rev. Theodore Alois Buckley, and Flaxman's designs (English). *Translator or author:* Alexander Pope. London, England: W. W. Gibbings.

1891— The Odyssey of Homer; translated; with notes by Theodore Alois Buckley and Flaxman's designs (English). *Translator or author:* Alexander Pope. London, England: W. W. Gibbings.

1891— Choix de Rhapsidies; illustrees d'apres l'art antique et l'archaeologie moderne et mises en vers (French). *Translator or author:* Charles Potvin. Brussels, Belgium.

1891— The Iliad of Homer; translated into English prose; edited with an introduction by Evelyn Abbott (English). *Translator or author:* John Purves. London, England: Percival.

1891— Die Homerische Odyssee; bei Scheidung des Inhalts derselben in zwei Hauptabteilungen und sechs Unterabteilungen aus dem Griechischen metrisch ins Deutsche ubertragen und mit erlauternden Bemerkungen versehen (German). *Translator or author:* Friedrich Soltau. Berlin, Germany: Norddeutscher Verlag.

1891— Qua in re Hymni Homerici Quinque Maiores Inter se Different Antiquitate vel Homeritate Investigavit J. R. S. Sterret (Greek). *Translator or author:* John Robert Sitlington Sterret. Boston, Mass.: Heath Ginn.

1891— Homers Odyssey; ubersetzt; fur Schule und Haus bearbeitet von Bernhard Kuttner; 2nd ed. (German). *Translator or author:* Johann Heinrich Voss. Frankfurt am Main, Germany: J. D. Sauerlander.

1891— Ilias, I–VIII; nach der auswahl von Kammer; ubersetzt in gereinten trochasichen tetrametern (German). *Translator or author:* Julius Zimmermann. Zeitz, Germany.

1891–96— Ilias; fur den Schulgebrauch erklart D. F. Ameis; besorgt, C. Hentze (Greek). Leipzig, Germany.

1892— The Phaeacian Episode of the Odyssey as Comprised in the Sixth, Seventh, Eighth, Eleventh, and Thirteenth Books; with introduction, notes, and appendix, by Augustus C[hapman] Merriam (Greek). New York, N.Y.: Harper.

1892— Homer's Iliad, Book III for Beginners; edited, with introduction and notes, by M. T.

Tatham (Greek). Oxford, England: Clarendon Press.

1892— The First Six Books of Homer's Iliad; with introduction, commentary, and vocabulary, for the use of schools, by Thomas D[ay] Seymour. Boston, Mass.: Ginn.

1892— The Odyssey of Homer; edited by Arthur Platt (Greek). Cambridge, England: Cambridge University Press.

1892— Homeri Odyssea; in usum scholarum edidit et commentario instruxit J. La Roche. Vienna, Austria: F. F. Tempsky.

1892— The First Three Books of Homer's Iliad; with introduction, commentary, and vocabulary for the use of schools by Thomas D[ay] Seymour (Greek). Boston, Mass.: Ginn.

1892— Homer for beginners— Iliad, book VIII, with notes (Greek). London, England; New York, N.Y.: Henry Frowde.

1892— The First Book of Homer's Iliad; with a vocabulary by John T[albot] White (Greek). London, England: Green Longmans.

1892— Homer's Odyssey, Books IX, X; edited, with introduction, notes, and appendix on the dialect, by J[ohn] H[amden] Haydon and A[rthur] H[adrian] Allcroft (Greek). London, England: W. B. Clive.

1892— The Iliad of Homer, Book VI; with introduction, notes and appendices by G[erald] M[aclean] Edwards; edited for the syndics of the University Press (Greek). Cambridge, England: Cambridge University Press.

1892— Homer's Odyssey, Books VI, VII; with notes; edited by William Walter Merry (Greek). London, England; New York, N.Y.: Henry Frowde.

1892— Odyssey; with introduction, notes, etc. by W[illiam] W[alter] Merry (Greek). Oxford, England: Clarendon Press.

1892— The Odyssey of Homer; literally translated with explanatory notes (English). *Translator or author:* Theodore Alois Buckley. New York, N.Y.: Arthus Hinds.

1892— The Odyssey of Homer; literally translated (English). *Translator or author:* Theodore Alois Buckley. New York, N.Y.: Harper.

1892— Homer's Iliad and Odyssey; edited, with notes, by Richard Herne Shepherd [reprint of the 1612 edition] (English). *Translator or author:* George Chapman. London, England: Chatto and Windus.

1892— Pictorial Atlas to Homer's Iliad and Odyssey; containing 225 illustrations from works of ancient art,... and an epitome of the contents of each book (English). *Translator or author:* Richard Engelmann; William Cliffe Foley Anderson. London, England; New York, N.Y.: Grevel; B. Westermann.

1892— Iliada Gomera; perevod; redizhirovannyaei S. I. Ronomarevym; 2nd ed. (Russian). *Translator or author:* Nikolaaei Ivanovich Gnedich. St. Petersburg, Russia: A. S. Suvorina.

1892— Homer's Iliad, Book VI [series: Tutorial]. *Translator or author:* B. J. Hayes. London, England: W. B. Clive.

1892— Homers Ilias; ubersetzt und erklart; 2nd ed. (German). *Translator or author:* Wilhelm Jordan. Frankfurt am Main, Germany: Wilhelm Jordan.

1892— The Adventures of Ulysses; edited, with notes, for schools (English). *Translator or author:* Charles Lamb. Boston, Mass.: Ginn.

1892— The Iliad of Homer; done into English prose (English). *Translator or author:* Andrew Lang; Walter Leaf; Ernest Myers. London, England; New York, N.Y.: Macmillan.

1892— Tales of Ancient Troy, and The Adventures of Ulysses; edited (English). *Translator or author:* Walter Montgomery. Boston, Mass.: Estes and Lauriat.

1892— L'Iliade; traduzione; ed. scolastica con note dichiarative di Gustavo Boralevi (Italian). *Translator or author:* Vincenzo Monti. Livorno, Italy: Raffaello Giusti.

1892— He Iliada, Mer. 1, 1–6; metaphrasmene (Greek, Modern). *Translator or author:* Alexander Anastasius Pallis. Athens, Greece: S. K. Vlastou.

1892— The Iliad of Homer; translated (English). *Translator or author:* Alexander Pope. Chicago, Il.: A. C. McClurg.

1892— Homers Odyssee (German). *Translator or author:* Johann Heinrich Voss. Leipzig, Germany: Philipp Reclam jun.

1893— The Iliad of Homer, Books XVI–XXIV; with explanatory notes for the use of students in college by W[illiam S[eymour] Tyler (Greek). New York, N.Y.: Harper.

1893— The First Six Books of Homer's Iliad; the original text reduced to the natural English order; with a literal interlinear translation (Greek; English). New York, N.Y.: Arthur Hinds.

1893— The Iliad of Homer, Books I–III; with an introduction and notes by Robert P[orter] Keep; 7th ed. (Greek). Boston, Mass.: Allyn and Bacon.

1893— Iliad; with notes by D[avid] B[inning] Monro; 3rd ed. (Greek). Oxford, England: Clarendon Press.

1893— The Iliad of Homer; literally translated, with explanatory notes (English). *Translator or author:* Theodore Alois Buckley. New York, N.Y.: Harper and Brothers.

1893— The Odysseys of Homer; done into English prose; 3rd ed. (English). *Translator or author:* Samuel Henry Butcher; Andrew Lang. New York, N.Y.: Macmillan.

1893— The Iliads of Homer, Prince of Poets; done into English (English). *Translator or author:* George Chapman. New York, N.Y.: G. P. Putnam.

1893— Homer's Odyssey, Books V–VIII (English). *Translator or author:* William Cudworth. Darlington, England.

1893— Oeuvres Completes [d'Homere]; trad. nouv. (French). *Translator or author:* Pierre Giguet. Paris, France: L. Hachette.

1893— Hymni Homerici (Greek). *Translator or author:* Goodwin. Oxford, England.

1893— The Iliad of Homer; done into English prose (English). *Translator or author:* Andrew Lang; Walter Leaf; Ernest Myers. London, England; New York, N.Y.: Macmillan.

1893— Homere, Odysee; traduction nouvelle; 5th ed. (French). *Translator or author:* Leconte de Lisle. Paris, France: Alphonse Lemerre.

1893— Homer's Odyssey translated into English rhythmic prose [reprint of the 1891 edition] (English). *Translator or author:* George Herbert Palmer. Boston, Mass.

1893— Odyssey, Book IX (Greek; English). *Translator or author:* Talbot Sydenham Peppin.

1893— The Iliad of Homer [reprint of the 1715–20 edition] (English). *Translator or author:* Alexander Pope. Chicago, Il.

1893— Iliad, Book XXII (Greek; English). *Translator or author:* Richard Williams Reynolds.

1893–94— Homeri Ilias; edidit Guilielmus Dindorf; 5th ed. (Greek). Leipzig, Germany: B. G. Teubner.

1893–95— Odyssee; 8–10 aufl (Greek). *Translator or author:* Karl Friedrich Ameis; Carl Hentze. Leipzig, Germany.

1893–97— Odyssea. Leipzig, Germany: B. G. Teubner.

1894— Hymni Homerici Accedentibus Epigrammatis et Batrachomyomachia Homero Vulgo Attributis; ex recensione Augusti Baumeister (Greek). Leipzig, Germany: B. G. Teubner.

1894— Homer's Iliad, Book IX, from "The Story of Achilles"; edited with notes by John Henry Platt and Walter Leaf. London, England: Macmillan.

1894— Homer's Odyssey, Books V–VIII; edited on the basis of the Ameis-Hentze edition, by B[ernadotte] Perrin (Greek). Boston, Mass; London, England: Ginn.

1894— Homeri Ilias; ed. Guilielmus Baumlein (Greek). Leipzig, Germany: Car. Tauchnitz.

1894— [H]omerou Ilias = Homers Ilias; Schulausgabe von Paul Cauer; 2nd ed. Prague, Czech.; Vienna, Austria; Leipzig, Germany: F. F. Tempsky; G. Freytag.

1894— Iliad; with an introduction, a brief Homeric grammar, and notes, by D[avid] B[inning] Monro; 4th ed (Greek). Oxford, England: Clarendon Press.

1894— The Iliad of Homer, Book XXIV; with introduction, notes and appendices by G[erald] M[aclean] Edwards (Greek). Cambridge, England: Cambridge University Press.

1894— The Iliad of Homer, Books I–VI; with an introduction and notes by Robert P[orter] Keep; 7th ed. Boston, Mass.: J. Allyn.

1894— Batrachomyomachie Homericae Archetyppon; ad fidem codicum antiquissimorum ab Arthuro Ludwich restitutum (Greek). Konigsburg [location?]: Hartungiana.

1894— The Iliad of Homer, Books XVI–XXIV; with explanatory notes for the use of students in college by W[illiam] S[eymour] Tyler. New York, N.Y.: Harper.

1894— The Iliad of Homer; edited by Arthur Platt. Cambridge, England: Cambridge University Press.

1894— Homer's Odyssey; edited by Arthur Platt. Cambridge University Press.

1894— Die Gedichte Homers (Greek). Leipzig, Germany: B. G. Teubner.

1894— The Phaeacian Episode of the Odyssey as Comprised in the Sixth, Seventh, Eighth, Elevnth, and Thirteenth Books; with introduction, notes, and appendix by Augustus C. Merriam (Greek). New York, N.Y.: Harper.

1894—Iliade; extraits, avec une introduction, un index et des notes (French). *Translator or author:* F. Allegre. Paris, France.

1894—The Battle of the Frogs and Mice; rendered into English; pictured by Francis C. Bedford (English). *Translator or author:* Jane Barlow. New York, N.Y.: Frederick A. Stokes.

1894—The Battle of the Frogs & Mice; rendered into English; pictured by Francis D. Bedford (English). *Translator or author:* Jane Barlow. London, England: Methuen.

1894—Ulisses und der Kyklop; edited by W. S. Lyon; elementary text with vocabulary (German???). *Translator or author:* Karl Friedrich Becker. New York, N.Y.: Merrill Maynard.

1894—The Iliad of Homer; literally translated, with explanatory notes (English). *Translator or author:* Theodore Alois Buckley. New York, N.Y.: Harper and Brothers.

1894—Sample Passages from a New Prose Translation of the Odyssey (English). *Translator or author:* Samuel Butler. Edinburgh, Scotland: T. and A. at Edinburgh University Press Constable.

1894—Homeri Odyssea; scholarum in usum von Paulus Cauer (Greek; German). *Translator or author:* Paul Cauer. Prague, Czech.; Vienna, Austria; Leipzig, Germany: F. F. Tempsky; Freytag, G.

1894—Die Odyssee; in Deutschen Stanzen; fur das Deutsche Volk bearbeitet (German). *Translator or author:* Theodor Dann. Stuttgart, Germany: Kohlhammer.

1894—The Iliad of Homer; rendered into English blank verse to which are appended translations of poems ancient and modern; 13th ed. (English). *Translator or author:* Edward George Geoffrey Smith Stanley, Earl of Derby. London, England: John Murray.

1894—Gereimte Ubersetzung des Neunten Gesanges der Odyssee (German). *Translator or author:* B. Fahland.

1894—Odysseae Liber Sextus; Latinis versibus expressit (Latin). *Translator or author:* Christain Alfred Fahlcrantz. Uppsala, Sweden.

1894—Iliad, Book XXII and XXIV [reprint of the 1890 edition] (English). *Translator or author:* John Henry Freese.

1894—Adventures of Ulysses; edited, with an introduction and notes, by John Cooke; 5th ed. (English). *Translator or author:* Charles Lamb. Dublin, Ireland: Browne and Nolan.

1894—Homer's Iliad, Book XXIV [series: Elementary Classics]. *Translator or author:* Walter Leaf; Matthew Albert Bayfield. Macmillan.

1894—Homer's Iliad; grammar, notes; 3rd edition (Greek). *Translator or author:* David Binning Monro. London, England; New York, N.Y.: Henry Frowde.

1894—The Odyssey of Homer; translated; 4th ed. (English). *Translator or author:* George Herbert Palmer. Boston, Mass.; New York, N.Y.; Cambridge, Mass.: Houghton Mifflin; Riverside Press.

1894—Odissea di Omero, Poema Epico; tradotta; ed annotato ad uso delle scuole da Giuseppe Puppo (Italian). *Translator or author:* Ippolito Pindemonte. Torino (Turin), Italy: Tipografia e Libreris Salesiana.

1894—Homer's Odyssey; translated; to which are added the Battle of the Frogs and Mice by Parnell and the Hymns by Chapman and others; with observations and brief notes by J. S. Watson; illustrated with the entire series of Flaxman's designs (English). *Translator or author:* Alexander Pope. London, England: George Bell and Sons.

1894—The Iliad and Odyssey; edited by T[heodore] A[lois] Buckley [series: Albion Poets] (English). *Translator or author:* Alexander Pope. New York, N.Y.

1894—The Iliad and the Odyssey of Homer; translated; with notes and introduction by the Rev. Theodore Alois Buckley; Flaxman's designs (English). *Translator or author:* Alexander Pope. London, England; New York, N.Y.: Frederick Warne.

1894—Pope's Iliad of Homer; translated; with introduction and notes by the H. L Earl (English). *Translator or author:* Alexander Pope.

1894—Homer's Nostos, or The Wanderings of Ulysses; selected from the Odyssey; edited by E. D. Stone (English). *Translator or author:* E. D. Stone. London, England: Methuen.

1894—Homer's Iliad, Book XXIV. *Translator or author:* Richard Moody Thomas. London, England: W. B. Clive.

1894—Homer's Iliad; done into English verse [reprint of the 1885–88 edition] (English). *Translator or author:* Arthur Sanders Way. Macmillan.

1894—Odisseia Gomera; perevod (Russian). *Translator or author:* Vasilii Andreevich Zhukovskii. St. Petersburg, Russia: Izdanie Glazunova.

1894–03—Homers Ilias; fur den Schulgebrauch erklart von Karl Friedrich Ameis; besorgt von Prof. Dr. C. Hentze; 6th ed. (Greek). Leipzig, Germany; Berlin, Germany: B. G. Teubner.

1894–19—Homers Odyssee; fur den Schulgebrauch erklart von Karl Friedrich Ameis; besorgt von C. Hentze (Greek). Leipzig, Germany: B. G. Teubner.

1894–95—Homers Odyssee; zum Schulgebrauch bearbeitet und erlautert von Dr. Ernst Naumann. Beilefeld, Germany: Velhagen und Klasing.

1894–96—Homeri Ilias; edidit Guilielmus Dindorf; 5th ed. (Greek). Leipzig, Germany: B. G. Teubner.

1894–96—Homers Ilias; fur den Schulgebrauch erklart von Karl Friedrich Ameis; 5th ed. Leipzig, Germany: B. G. Teubner.

1894–96—Homers Odyssee; 2nd ed. *Translator or author:* Paul Cauer. Vienna, Austria; Leipzig, Germany: F. F. Tempsky; G. Freytag.

1895—The Story of Achilles from Homer's Iliad; edited with notes and introduction by John Henry Pratt and Walter Leaf (Greek). London, England; New York, N.Y.: Macmillan.

1895—The Sixth Book of Homer's Odyssey; edited for the use of schools by Char[les] W[esley] Bain. Boston, Mass.: Ginn.

1895—Odyssee; texte Grec publie avec des arguments analytiques et des notes en Francais, par A. Pierron, Chant XI (Greek). Paris, France: L. Hachette.

1895—Odyssey [edited by William Walter Merry] (Greek). Oxford, England.

1895—The Iliad of Homer, Books I–VI; with an introduction and notes by Robert P[orter] Keep. Boston, Mass.: Allyn and Bacon.

1895—Homer's Odyssey, Books XIII–XVIII; with notes etc. [edited by William Walter Merry] (Greek). London, England; New York, N.Y.: Henry Frowde.

1895—Homers Odyssee; fur den Schulgebrach in verkurzter Form bearbeitet und herausgegeben von Joseph Bach (Greek). Munster, Germany: Aschendorffschen Verlagsbuchhandlung.

1895—Homer, Odyssey, Books I–XII; with introduction, notes, etc. by W[illiam] W[alter] Merry (Greek). Oxford, England: Clarendon Press.

1895—Homer's Iliad, Book 23; literally translated (English). Marshall Simpkin.

1895—Homers Odyssee; fur den Schulgebrauch erklart von Karl Friedrich Ameis; besorgt von C. Hentze (Greek). Leipzig, Germany: B. G. Teubner.

1895—La Nekyia Ossia il Libro XI dell'Odissea; considerato dal Lato linguistico e sinattico e confrontato col resto delle poesie di Omero (Greek; Italian). *Translator or author:* Nicolo Batistiac. Zara, Turkey: Pietro Jankovic.

1895—The Story of the Odyssey, or, The Adventures of Ulysses; for boys and girls; with seventeen illustrations from Flaxman's designs (English). *Translator or author:* Edward Brooks. Philadelphia, Pa.: Penn Publishing.

1895—The Odyssey of Homer, with the Hymns, Epigrams, and Battle of the Frogs and Mice; literally translated, with explanatory notes (English). *Translator or author:* Theodore Alois Buckley. New York, N.Y.: Harper and Brothers.

1895—The Iliad of Homer; literally translated, with explanatory notes (English). *Translator or author:* Theodore Alois Buckley. New York, N.Y.: Harper.

1895—The Odyssey of Homer; done into English prose; 3rd ed. (English). *Translator or author:* Samuel Henry Butcher; Andrew Lang. New York, N.Y.: Macmillan.

1895—Homer's Iliad; translated, with an introduction by Henry Morley; 5th ed. (English). *Translator or author:* George Chapman. London, England; New York, N.Y.: George Routledge.

1895—The Iliads of Homer, Prince of Poets [reprint of the 1611 edition; series: Ballads of the Nations] (English). *Translator or author:* George Chapman. New York, N.Y.

1895—The Stories of the Iliad and the Aeneid (English). *Translator or author:* Alfred John Church. London, England: Seeley.

1895—Iliad, Books I, VI, and IX (English). *Translator or author:* William Cudworth. Darlington, England.

1895—Homers Ilias; in Niederdeutscher poetischer Ubertragung (German, Low). *Translator or author:* August Duhr. Kiel, Germany; Leipzig, Germany: Lipsius und Tischer.

1895—[H]omerou Ilias; meta scholion kai hermeneias (Greek, Modern). *Translator or author:* A. X. Karapanagiotes. Athens, Greece: Typographeiou Paraskeua Leone.

1895—The Adventures of Ulysses; edited, with notes, for schools; with additional notes by Edward Manley (English). *Translator or author:* Charles Lamb. Boston, Mass.: Ginn.

1895—The Iliad of Homer; done into English prose (English). *Translator or author:* Andrew Lang; Walter Leaf; Ernest Myers. London, England; New York, N.Y.: Macmillan.

II. Printed Editions of the Homeric Texts, 1470 to 2000 C.E.

280

1895—Homer's Wine etc, poems (English). *Translator or author:* G. Laura. Ackroyd.

1895—Die Ursprungliche Gestalt von Ilias (Greek). *Translator or author:* Ludwig. Prague, Czechoslavakia.

1895—The Odyssey of Homer; the text, and an English version in rhythmic prose (Greek; English). *Translator or author:* George Herbert Palmer. Boston, Mass; New York, N.Y.: Houghton Mifflin.

1895—L'Iliade [d']Homerre; illustrations de G. Picard (French). *Translator or author:* J. -H Rosny. Paris, France: L. Borel.

1895—Homers Odyssee, Vossische Ubersetzung; mit 40 Original-Compositionen von Friedrich Preller; in Holzschnitt ausgefuhrt von R. Brend'Amour und K. Oertel; 4th ed. (German). *Translator or author:* Johann Heinrich Voss. Leipzig, Germany: Breitkopf and Hartel.

1895—The Odyssey of Homer; translated into English verse in the Spenserian stanza (English). *Translator or author:* Philip Stanhope Worsley. Edinburgh, Scotland: William Blackwood.

1895–01—Odyssey; with introduction, notes, etc. by W[illiam] W[alter] Merry (Greek). Oxford, England: Clarendon Press.

1895–01—Homers Odyssee; fur den Schulgebrauch erklart von Karl Friedrich Ameis (Greek). Leipzig, Germany: B. G. Teubner.

1895–96—Homeri Iliadis Carmina cum Apparatu Critico; edidit J. van Leeuwen J. F. et M. B. Mendes da Costa. Leiden (Leyden), Netherlands: A. W. Sijthoff.

1895–98—[H]omerou Ilias = The Iliad of Homer; edited with general and grammatical introductions, notes, and appendices, by Walter Leaf and M[atthew] A[lbert] Bayfield (Greek). London, England; New York, N.Y.: Macmillan; St. Martin's Press.

1896—Odyssey, Book X [edited by Gerald Maclean Edwards; 2nd ed.] (Greek). Cambridge, England: Cambridge University Press.

1896—The First Six Books of Homer's Iliad; with introduction, commentary, and vocabulary for the use of schools, by T[homas] D[ay] Seymour. Boston, Mass.: Ginn.

1896—The First Six Books of Homer's Iliad; the original text reduced to the natural English order, with a literal interlinear translation (Greek; English). New York, N.Y.: Noble & Eldredge Hinds.

1896—Die Homerische Batrachomyomachia des

Karers Pigres; nebst Scholien und Paraphrase; hrsg. und erlautert von Arthur Ludwich. Leipzig, Germany: B. G. Teubner.

1896—Odyssey, Book XXI; edited with introduction, notes and appendices by G[erald] M[aclean] Edwards (Greek). Cambridge, England: Cambridge University Press.

1896—The Iliad of Homer, Books I–VI; with an introduction and notes by Robert P. Keep (Greek). Boston, Mass.: Allyn and Bacon.

1896—The Iliad of Homer; literally translated, with explanatory notes (English). *Translator or author:* Theodore Alois Buckley. London, England: George Bell and Sons.

1896—First Thirteen Books of the Odyssey of Homer; literally translated with explanatory notes; with an introduction by Edward Brooks, Jr. (English). *Translator or author:* Theodore Alois Buckley. Philadelphia, Pa.: David McKay.

1896—First Nine Books of the Iliad of Homer; literally translated; with an introduction by Edward Brooks, Jr. (English). *Translator or author:* Theodore Alois Buckley. Philadelphia, Pa.: David McKay.

1896—The Iliad (English). *Translator or author:* Theodore Alois Buckley. New York, N.Y.

1896—Homere (French). *Translator or author:* Maurice Croiset. Paris, France.

1896—Homer's Iliad [reprint of the 1855–58 edition] (English). *Translator or author:* Hamilton and Clark. Philadelphia, Pa.

1896—Odyssee, Buch VI; Nachdichtung, und Festgedicht zur Bismarckfeier (German). *Translator or author:* Emil Irmscher. Dresden, Germany: Butzmann.

1896—Homers Odyssee, Buch VI; Nachtung von Emil Irmscher (German). *Translator or author:* Emil Irmscher. Leipzig, Germany: G. Fock.

1896—The Homeric Hymns; a new prose translation, and essays, literary and mythological (English). *Translator or author:* Andrew Lang. New York, N.Y.; London, England: Green Longman; G. Allen.

1896—Odysseus in Phaeacia [Odyssey VI] (English). *Translator or author:* John William Mackail. London, England: David Nutt.

1896—Homeri Opera et Reliquiae. *Translator or author:* David Binning Monro. London, England; New York, N.Y.: Henry Frowde.

1896—Iliade di Omero; traduzione; con le osservazioni di Andrea Mustoxidi e le notizie della bita e delle opera del tradultore (Italian). *Translator or author:* Vincenzo Monti. Milan, Italy: Edoardo Sonzogno.

1896— Iliade d'Omero, Poema Epica; tradotto; 12th ed. (Italian). *Translator or author:* Vincenzo Monti. Torino (Turin), Italy: Tipografia e Libreria Salesiana.

1896— Four Books of Pope's Iliad, I, VI, XXII, XXIV; with an introduction, the story of the Iliad, and notes (English). *Translator or author:* Alexander Pope. Boston, Mass.: Houghton Mifflin.

1896— The Iliad of Homer, Books I, VI, XXII, XXIV; translated; edited by Warwick James Price (English). *Translator or author:* Alexander Pope. Boston, Mass.: Leach, Shewell, & Sanborn.

1896— Pope's The Iliad of Homer, Books I, VI, XXII and XXIV; edited with notes and an introduction by William H. Maxwell [reprint from the 1715–20; series: Riverside Literature] (English). *Translator or author:* Alexander Pope. New York, N.Y.; London, England: Green Longmans.

1896— Homer's Iliad (Books I, VI, XXII, XXIV); translated [series: Eclectic English Classics] (English). *Translator or author:* Alexander Pope. New York, N.Y.: American Book Company.

1896— Homer's Iliad [Books I, VI, XXII, XXIV; edited by W. H. Maxwell and Percival Chubb; series: Longman's English Classics] (English). *Translator or author:* Alexander Pope. New York, N.Y.

1896— The Iliad of Homer; ed. by Warwick James Price [reprint of the 1715–20 edition; series: Student's Series of English Classics] (English). *Translator or author:* Alexander Pope. Boston, Mass.

1896— L'Inno Omerico a Demetra (Greek). *Translator or author:* Puntoni. Livorno, Italy.

1896— L'Odyssee d'Homere Melesigene; tr. vers pour vers (French). *Translator or author:* Ulysse Francois Ange de Sequier. Paris, France: Ambrosio Firmin Didot.

1896— In Lust un Leed: Plattdeutsche Gedichte nebst Nachdistungen zu Horaz und Scenen aus Homer. *Translator or author:* Felix Stillfried. Wismar, Germany: Hinstorff'sche Hofbuchhandlung Verlagsconto.

1896— Homers Ilias; ubersetzt; fur Schule und Haus bearbeitet von Bernhard Kuttner; mit einem erklarenden Anhang (German). *Translator or author:* Johann Heinrich Voss. Frankfurt am Main, Germany: J. D. Sauerlander.

1896— Homers Ilias; nach der Ubersetzung von

Joh[ann] Heinr]ich] Voss; fur den Schulgebrauch hrsg. Von Bruno Stehle (German). *Translator or author:* Johann Heinrich Voss. Leipzig, Germany: G. Freytag.

1896–05— L'Iliade; commentata da C. O. Zuretti (Greek). Torino (Turin), Italy: Loescher.

1896–99— Odyssey; with introduction, notes, etc. by W[illiam] W[alter] Merry (Greek). Oxford, England: Clarendon Press.

1897— Odyssey, Books XIII–XXIV; edited, introduction, notes. London, England; New York, N.Y.: Henry Frowde.

1897— Homers Odyssee; in Niederdeutscher poetischer Ubertragung; Proben aus den ersten Buchern [von] Dr. Duhr. (German, Low). Nordhausen, Germany: C. Kirchner.

1897— Homer's Odyssey, Books V–VIII; edited on the basis of the Ameis-Hentze edition by B. Perrin. Boston, Mass.: Ginn.

1897— Homeri Odysseae Carmina; cum apparatu critico; ediderunt J[an] van Leeuwen et M[aurits] B[enjamin] Mendes da Costa. Leiden (Leyden), Netherlands: A. W. Sijthoff.

1897— Iliad, Books XIII–XXIV [of] Homer; with note by D[avid] B[inning] Monro; 4th ed. (Greek). Oxford, England: Clarendon Press.

1897— The Odyssey of Homer, Book XIX. Cambridge, England: Cambridge University Press.

1897— Iliad of Homer, Books I–VI; with an introduction and notes by Robert P. Keep. Boston, Mass.: Allyn and Bacon.

1897— L'Odyssee [d']Homere; illustrations de A. Calbet (French). Paris, France: L. Borel.

1897— Odyssey, Book X; edited by G[erald] M[aclean] Edwards. Cambridge, England: Cambridge University Press.

1897— Hymni Homerici Accedentibus Epigrammatis et Batrachomyomachia Homero Vulgo Attributis; ex recensione Augusti Baumeister (Greek). Leipzig, Germany: B. G. Teubner.

1897— Homeric Birthday book: setting of gems from Iliad and Odyssey of Homer; selected by V. E. Gonsales (English). Frederick Warne.

1897— Homeri Odysseae Carmina cum Apparatu Critico; ediderunt J. Van Leeuwen J. F., et M. B. Mendes da Costa (Greek).

1897— Homer, Iliad. Oxford, England: Clarendon Press.

1897— Four Books of Homer's Odyssey; with introduction, commentary and vocabulary for the use of schools by Bernadotte Perrin and Thomas Day Seymour (Greek). Boston, Mass.: Ginn.

1897—Eight Books of Homer's Odyssey; with introduction, commentary, and vocabulary; for the use of schools, by Bernadotte Perrin and Thomas Day Seymour (Greek). Boston, Mass; London, England: Athenaeum Press; Ginn.

1897—The Iliad; translated into English verse; student's edition (English). *Translator or author:* William Cullen Bryant. London, England.

1897—Homer; translated into English verse (English). *Translator or author:* William Cullen Bryant. Boston, Mass.

1897—The Odysseys of Homer Translated According to the Greek; with introduction and notes by the Rev. Richard Hooper; 2nd ed. (English). *Translator or author:* George Chapman. London, England: Reeves and Turner.

1897—The Odysseys of Homer Translated According to the Greek; 2nd ed. (English). *Translator or author:* George Chapman. London, England: J. M. Dent.

1897—The Odysseys of Homer, Prince of Poets, Never Before in any Language Truly Translated Done According to the Greek; with an introduction and notes by Richard Hooper (English). *Translator or author:* George Chapman. London, England: W. W. Gibbings.

1897—The Iliads of Homer, Prince of Poets, Never Before in any Language truly Translated, Done According to the Greek; with an introduction and notes by Richard Hooper; 2nd ed. (English). *Translator or author:* George Chapman. London, England: W. W. Gibbings.

1897—The Story of Troy (English). *Translator or author:* Michael Clarke. Cincinnati, Oh.: American Book Company.

1897—The Story of Troy (English). *Translator or author:* Michael Clarke. New York, N.Y.: Franklin.

1897—Iliad [reprint of the 1869 edition] (English). *Translator or author:* William Lucas Collins.

1897—The Odyssey of Homer; translated (English). *Translator or author:* John Graham Cordery. London, England: Methuen.

1897—Homers Odyssee, Im Versmass der Urschrift; übersetzt (German). *Translator or author:* F. W. Ehrenthal. Leipzig, Germany: Bibliographisches Institut.

1897—Homers Ilias, im Versmass der Urschrift;

ubersetzt; 2nd ed. (German). *Translator or author:* F. W. Ehrenthal. Leipzig, Germany: Bibliographisches Institut.

1897—Odyssee, Buch XXII; Nachdichtung und "Die Lieblingsblumen Kaiser Wilhelms I", gedicht von Emil Irmscher (German). *Translator or author:* Emil Irmscher. Dresden, Germany: Gutzmann.

1897—Homers Odyssee, Buch XXII; Nachdichtung (German). *Translator or author:* Emil Irmscher. Leipzig, Germany: G. Fock.

1897—Helen of Troy, Her Life and Translation Done into Rhyme from the Greek Books (English). *Translator or author:* Andrew Lang. Portland, Me.: T. B. Mosher.

1897—The Iliad of Homer; done into English prose (English). *Translator or author:* Andrew Lang; Walter Leaf; Ernest Myers. London, England; New York, N.Y.: Macmillan.

1897—Odyssey, Anc. Clas. *Translator or author:* Walter Leaf. Collins.

1897—Iliad. *Translator or author:* W. Lucas. Collins.

1897—The Odyssey of Homer; done into English verse (English). *Translator or author:* William Morris. London, England; New York, N.Y.: Green Longmans.

1897—Pope's Homer, Books I, VI, XXII, and XXIV; edited with introduction and notes by Alexanders S[tevenson] Twombly (English). *Translator or author:* Alexander Pope. New York, N.Y.; Boston, Mass.: Silver Burdett.

1897—The Iliad and Odyssey; edited by H. F. Cary; introduction by Sir J. Lubbock [series: Best Books] (English). *Translator or author:* Alexander Pope. George Routledge.

1897—Iliadis Epitome Francisci Hocheggeri; 6th ed. *Translator or author:* Augustinus Scheindler. Vienna, Austria: Carolus Gerold.

1897—Die Odyssee; nachgebildet in achtzeiligen Strophen (German). *Translator or author:* Hermann von Schelling. Munich, Germany; Leipzig, Germany: R. Oldenbourg.

1897—Homers Odyssee; übersetzt; fur Schule und Haus bearb. Von Bernhard Kuttner; 3rd ed. (German). *Translator or author:* Johann Heinrich Voss. Frankfurt am Main, Germany: J. D. Sauerlander.

1897–00—Homeri Odyssea; edidit Guilielmus Dindorf; 5th ed. (Greek). Leipzig, Germany: B. G. Teubner.

1897–98— The Whole works of Homer [reprint of the 1612 edition; series: Temple Classics] (English). *Translator or author:* George Chapman. London, England; New York, N.Y.

1897–99— Iliad (Greek). Oxford, England.

1898— The First Book of Homer's Odyssey; with a vocabulary and some account of Greek prosody by John T. White (Greek). London, England; New York, N.Y.: Green Longmans.

1898— Homer's Odyssey, Books I–VIII; edited on the basis of the Ameis-Hentze edition, by B[ernadotte] Perrin. Boston, Mass.: Ginn.

1898— Homer's Iliad, Book I; edited for the use of schools, with notes and vocabulary by John Bond and A[rthur S[umner] Walpole (Greek). Toronto, Canada; New York, N.Y.: Clark Copp; Macmillan.

1898— Eight Books of Homer's Odyssey; with introduction, commentary, and vocabulary; for the use of schools, by Bernadotte Perrin and Thomas Day Seymour. Boston, Mass; London, England: Athenaeum Press; Ginn.

1898— The Odyssey (English). London, England.

1898— Homers Odyssee; erzahlt von Ferdinand Schmidt; illustriert nach W. von Kaulbach und Flaxman; 10th ed. (German). Leipzig, Germany: A. Oehmigke.

1898— The Story of the Odyssey, or The Adventures of Ulysses; for boys and girls (English). *Translator or author:* Edward Brooks. Philadelphia, Pa.: Penn Publishing.

1898— Odyssey; translated into English verse; student's edition (English). *Translator or author:* William Cullen Bryant. London, England.

1898— The Iliad of Homer; translated into English blank verse [reprint of the 1871 edition; series: Student's Edition] (English). *Translator or author:* William Cullen Bryant. Boston, Mass; New York, N.Y.: Houghton Mifflin.

1898— The Iliad of Homer; literally translated, with explanatory notes (English). *Translator or author:* Theodore Alois Buckley. New York, N.Y.: Harper and Brothers.

1898— Odysseus, the Hero of Ithaca; adapted from the third book of the primary schools of Athens, Greece (English). *Translator or author:* Mary Elizabeth Burt; Zenaeide Alexeievna Ragozin. New York, N.Y.: Charles Scribner Sons.

1898— The Odyssey of Homer; done into English prose (English). *Translator or author:* Samuel Henry Butcher; Andrew Lang. London, England: Macmillan.

1898— The Iliad of Homer; rendered into English prose for the use of those who cannot read the original (English). *Translator or author:* Samuel Butler. London, England; New York, N.Y.: Green Longmans.

1898— The Iliad of Homer; rendered into English for the use of those who cannot read the original (English). *Translator or author:* Samuel Butler. New York, N.Y.: E. P. Dutton.

1898— The Iliads; translated according to the Greek (English). *Translator or author:* George Chapman. London, England: J. M. Dent.

1898— The Iliads of Homer, Prince of Poets, Never Before in any Language Truly Translated; with a comment on some of his chief places done according to the Greek; with an introduction and notes by Richard Hooper; 3rd ed. (English). *Translator or author:* George Chapman. London, England: J. R. Smith.

1898— Odyssee in Niederdeutscher poetischer Ubertragung; proben aus den ersten Buchern zweiter teil (German, Low). *Translator or author:* August Duhr. Nordhausen, Germany.

1898— Centones, etc. *Translator or author:* Harris. J. Rendel.

1898— Iliad, Book XXIV; introduction, text, notes [series: University Tutorial] (Greek). *Translator or author:* John Hampden Haydon. London, England: W. B. Clive.

1898— The Adventures of Ulysses; with additional notes by Edward Manley (English). *Translator or author:* Charles Lamb. Boston, Mass.: Ginn.

1898— The Iliad of Homer; done into English prose (English). *Translator or author:* Andrew Lang; Walter Leaf; Ernest Myers. London, England; New York, N.Y.: Macmillan.

1898— The Iliad of Homer; edited with general and grammatical introductions, notes, and appendices [1st ed.]. *Translator or author:* Walter Leaf; Matthew Albert Bayfield. London, England; New York, N.Y.: Macmillan; St. Martin's Press.

1898— The Odyssey, Book VII; in English verse; 1st ed. (English). *Translator or author:* John William Mackail. London, England: Chiswick Press.

1898— The Odyssey of Homer; translated (English). *Translator or author:* George Herbert Palmer. Boston, Mass.: Houghton Mifflin.

1898— Homer's Odyssey, Book IX. *Translator or author:* Talbot Sydenham Peppin. Hoddes.

1898— The Iliad of Homer; translated; edited by

J[ohn] S[elby] Watson; and illustrated with the entire series of Flaxman's desings (English). *Translator or author:* Alexander Pope. London, England: George Bell.

1898—Pope's The Iliad of Homer, Book I, VI, XXII, XXIV; edited with notes and introduction by William H[enry] Maxwell and Percival Chubb (English). *Translator or author:* Alexander Pope. New York, N.Y.: Green Longmans.

1898—Pope's Translation of Homer's Iliad, Books I, VI, XXII, XXIV; edited with introduction and notes by William Tappan [series: Standard English Classics] (English). *Translator or author:* Alexander Pope. Boston, Mass; New York, N.Y.: Ginn; Merrill Maynard.

1898—Homer's Iliad; Pope's translation (laurel-crowned verse) (English). *Translator or author:* Alexander Pope. London, England.

1898—Homer's Iliad, Book XXII; with translation. *Translator or author:* Richard Williams Reynolds. Hoddes.

1898–02—L'Odyssee; traduction (French). *Translator or author:* Paul Jeremie Bitaube. Paris, France: Librarie de la Bibliotheque nationale.

1899—The Seventh Book of Homer's Odyssey; edited for the use of schools by Cha[rles] W[esley] Bain. Boston, Mass.: Ginn.

1899—Homeri Ilias; edidit Guilielmus Dindorf; correctior quam curavit C. Hentze 5th ed. Leipzig, Germany: B. G. Teubner.

1899—Odyssea; edidit Guilielmus Dindorf; 5th ed. (Greek). Leipzig, Germany: B. G. Teubner.

1899—Homers Iliade; erzahlt von Ferdinand Schmidt; illustriert von W. V. Kaulbach und Flaxman; 10th ed. (German). Leipzig, Germany: A. Oehmigke.

1899—The Twelfth Book of Homer's Odyssey; edited for the use of schools by Richard A[lexander von] Minckwitz. Boston, Mass.: Ginn.

1899—Homer, Odyssey, Books I–III, XIII–XXIV; with introduction, notes, etc. by W[illiam] W[alter] Merry. Oxford, England: Clarendon Press.

1899—Iliad, Books I–XII; with an introduction, a brief Homeric grammar, and notes, by D[avid] B[inning] Monro; 5th ed. (Greek). Oxford, England: Clarendon Press.

1899—The Odyssey of Homer [reprint of the 1871 edition; series: Riverside Literature] (English). *Translator or author:* William Cullen Bryant. New York, N.Y.

1899—Four Books of the Iliad: I, VI, XXII, XXIV; translated, with introduction and notes (English). *Translator or author:* William Cullen Bryant. Boston, Mass.: Houghton Mifflin.

1899—The Odyssey of Homer; translated into English blank verse (English). *Translator or author:* William Cullen Bryant. Boston, Mass; New York, N.Y.: Houghton Mifflin.

1899—Ulysses Among the Phaeacians; from the translation of Homer's Odyssey (English). *Translator or author:* William Cullen Bryant. Boston, Mass; New York, N.Y.: Houghton Mifflin.

1899—The Odyssey of Homer; translated into English blank verse (English). *Translator or author:* William Cullen Bryant. Boston, Mass.: Houghton Mifflin.

1899—The Odyssey; arranged from the translations of Bryant, Worsley, Cowper, Pope, and Chapman; with a prose narrative by A[lfred] J[ohn] Church; edited by Frederick B[righam] De Berard (English). *Translator or author:* William Cullen Bryant; Worsley et al. New York, N.Y.: I. H. Blanchard.

1899—Odysseus, the Hero of Ithaca; adapted from the third book of the primary schools of Athens, Greece (English). *Translator or author:* Mary Elizabeth Burt; Zenaeide Ragozin. New York, N.Y.: Charles Scribner Sons.

1899—The Iliad of Homer; arranged from the translations of Chapman, Pope, Derby, and Bryant, with a parallel prose narrative by Church; edited by Frederick B[righam] De Berard (English). *Translator or author:* George Chapman; Alexander Pope et al. New York, N.Y.: International Book.

1899—The Story of the Iliad; with illustrations after Flaxman (English). *Translator or author:* Alfred John Church. New York, N.Y.: Macmillan.

1899—Homer's Iliad, Books XIX–XXIV; edited on the basis of the Ameis-Hentze edition [series: College Series of Greek Authors]. *Translator or author:* Edward Bull Clapp. Boston, Mass.: Edward Ginn Arnold.

1899—Odysseia; changed into common parlance with pictures; 4th ed. (Greek, Modern). *Translator or author:* Anestis Constantinidos. Athens, Greece: Constantinidos.

1899—Odyssey, Book IX; edited, introduction, notes. *Translator or author:* A. Douglas-Thomson. Black.

1899—Oeuvres Completes d'Homere; traduction nouvelle avec une introduction et des Notes par

P. Giguet (French). *Translator or author:* Pierre Giguet. Paris, France: L. Hachette.

1899— The Homeric Hymns; a new prose translation, and essay, literay and mythological (English). *Translator or author:* Andrew Lang. New York, N.Y.; London, England: Green Longmans; G. Allen.

1899— Nausikaa; traduction; compositions decoratives par Gaston de Latenay (French). *Translator or author:* Leconte de Lisle. Paris, France: H. Piazza Edition d'Art.

1899— The Phaeacians of Homer; The Phaeacian episode of the Odyssey as comprised in the sixth, seventh, eighth, eleventh, and thieteenth books, with introduction, notes and appendix. *Translator or author:* A. C. Merriam. New York, N.Y.: Harper and Brothers.

1899— The Odyssey of Homer; translated (English). *Translator or author:* George Herbert Palmer. Boston, Mass; New York, N.Y.: Houghton Mifflin.

1899— The Iliad of Homer [Books I, VI, XXII, XXIV]; ed. by P. Storey [reprint of the 1715–20 edition; series: English Classics] (English). *Translator or author:* Alexander Pope. Boston, Mass.

1899— The Iliad of Homer, Books I, VI, XXII, XXIV; translated; edited for school use by W[ilfred] W[esley] Cressy and W [illiam] V[augh] Moody [reprint of the 1715–20 edition; series: Lake English Classics] (English). *Translator or author:* Alexander Pope. Chicago, Il.; New York, N.Y.: Foresman Scott.

1899— The Iliad of Homer; translated; with a critical introduction by W. C. Wilkinson (English). *Translator or author:* Alexander Pope. New York, N.Y.: David Appleton.

1899— Pope, The Iliad of Homer, Books, I, VI, XXII, and XXIV; edited with introduction and notes by Philip Gentner [series: Cambridge Literature] (English). *Translator or author:* Alexander Pope. Boston, Mass.: Benj. H. Sanborn.

1899— The Iliad of Homer [Books I, VI, XXII, XXIV]; ed. by A. H. Smyth [reprint of the 1715–20 edition; series: Pocket English Classics] (English). *Translator or author:* Alexander Pope. New York, N.Y.

1899— Pope's The Iliad of Homer, Books I, VI, XXII, and XXIV; edited with notes by Margaret A[bbott] Eaton (English). *Translator or author:* Alexander Pope. Boston; New York; Chicago; San Francisco: Educational Pub. Co.

1899— The Iliad of Homer; translated; with notes by the Rev. Theodore Alois Buckley and Flaxman's designs (English). *Translator or author:* Alexander Pope. London, England: C. Arthur Pearson.

1899— Pope, The Iliad of Homer, Books I, VI, XXII, XXIV; edited with notes and an introduction by Albert [Henry] Smyth (English). *Translator or author:* Alexander Pope. New York, N.Y.; London, England: Macmillan.

1899— Pope's Iliad of Homer, Books, I, VI, XXII, and XXIV; edited with an introduction and notes by Paul Shorey (English). *Translator or author:* Alexander Pope. Boston, Mass.: D. C. Heath.

1899— Pope's The Iliad of Homer, Books I, VI, XXII, and XXIV; edited, with notes and an introduction, by William H[enry] Maxwell and Percival Chubb (English). *Translator or author:* Alexander Pope. New York, N.Y.: Green Longmans.

1899— Homers Odyssee; mit einer Einleitung von Jakob Mahly (German). *Translator or author:* Johann Heinrich Voss. Berlin, Germany; Stuttgart, Germany: W. Spemann.

1899–00— Homeri Ilias; edidit Guilielmus Dindorf; correctior quam curavit C. Hentze; 5th ed. (Greek). Leipzig, Germany: B. G. Teubner.

1899–01— Odyssey; with introduction, notes, etx. By W[illiam] W[alter] Merry. Oxford, England: Clarendon Press.

1899–03— Homer, Iliad (Greek). Oxford, England: Clarendon Press.

1899–19— Homeri Odyssea; edidit Guilielmus Dindorf; 5th ed. (Greek). Leipzig, Germany: B. G. Teubner.

1900— Die Batrachomyomachie, Froschmausekampf; im Versmasse der Ursprache wiedergegeben und mit Bemerkungen versehen von R. Bertin. Langenberg: Rheinland.

1900— The First Three Books of Homer's Iliad; with introduction, commentary, and vocabulary for the use of schools by Thomas D[ay] Seymour (Greek). Boston, Mass.: Ginn.

1900— Odyssey, Book XI; edited with introduction, notes, and appendices by J. A. Nairn. London, England: Cambridge University Press.

1900— The Story of Achilles from Homer's Iliad; edited with notes and introduction by John Henry Pratt and Walter Leaf (Greek). London, England; New York, N.Y.: Macmillan.

1900— Ilias; 2nd ed. (German). *Translator or author:* Karl Friedrich Ameis. Leipzig, Germany.

1900—Homeric Similes from the Iliad (Greek, English). *Translator or author:* Edgar Barclay. London, England: George Bell and Sons.

1900—La Odisea, La Batracomiomaquia, Himnos, Epigramas Homero; version Castellana; 5th ed. (Spanish). *Translator or author:* Juan Bautista Bergua. Madrid, Spain: Ediciones Ibericas.

1900—The First Six Books of Homer's Iliad; literally translated with explanatory notes (English). *Translator or author:* Theodore Alois Buckley. New York, N.Y.: Arthur Hinds.

1900—Al-Iliyadhah Humirus; naqalatha ila al-Arabiyah (Arabic). *Translator or author:* Sulayman Khaototar Bustani. Beirut, Lebanon: Dar al-Maarifah.

1900—The Odyssey of Homer; done into English prose (English). *Translator or author:* Samuel Henry Butcher; Andrew Lang. London, England: Macmillan.

1900—Odyssey of Homer; done into English prose (English). *Translator or author:* Samuel Henry Butcher; Andrew Lang. New York, N.Y.: Modern Library.

1900—Odyssey of Homer; done into English prose; with a critical and biographical profile of Homer by Herbert J. Rose (English). *Translator or author:* Samuel Henry Butcher; Andrew Lang. New York, N.Y.: F. Watts.

1900—The Odyssey; rendered into English prose for the use of those who cannot read the original (English). *Translator or author:* Samuel Butler. London, England: A. C. Fifield.

1900—The Iliad; rendered into English prose for the use of those who cannot read the original (English). *Translator or author:* Samuel Butler. New York, N.Y.

1900—The Odyssey; rendered into English prose for the use of those who cannot read the original (English). *Translator or author:* Samuel Butler. New York, N.Y.: E. P. Dutton.

1900—The Odyssey; rendered into English prose for the use of those who cannot read the original (English). *Translator or author:* Samuel Butler. London, England; New York, N.Y.; Bombay; Cambridge: Green Longmans; Metcalfe.

1900—The Story of Eros and Psyche from Apuleius; the First Book of the Iliad of Homer; done into English (English). *Translator or author:* Edward Carpenter. London, England: Sonnenschein.

1900—The Iliad of Homer; retold; illustrated by John Flaxman (English). *Translator or author:* Alfred John Church. Biblo; Moser.

1900—The Story of Ulysses (English). *Translator or author:* Michael Clarke. New York, N.Y.: American Book Company.

1900—L'Odyssee; tr. (French). *Translator or author:* Anne LeFevre Dacier. Paris, France: Garner Freres.

1900—The Iliad of Homer; rendered into English blank verse; 5th ed. (English). *Translator or author:* Edward George Geoffrey Smith Stanley, Earl of Derby. New York, N.Y.: Porter and Coates.

1900—Gl'inni; dichiarati e tradotti (Italian). *Translator or author:* Egisto Gerunzi. Florence, Italy: L. Monnier.

1900—L'Iliade et l'Odyssee (French). *Translator or author:* Pierre Giguet. Paris, France.

1900—The Adventures of Ulysses; adapted from George Chapman's translation of the Odyssey; introduction by W. P. Trent (English). *Translator or author:* Charles Lamb. Boston, Mass.: D. C. Heath.

1900—The Homeric Hymns; an new prose translation; and essays, literary and mythological, with illustrations (English). *Translator or author:* Andrew Lang. New York, N.Y.: Green Longmans.

1900—The Iliad of Homer; done into English prose (English). *Translator or author:* Andrew Lang; Walter Leaf; Ernest Myers. London, England; New York, N.Y.: Macmillan.

1900—Iliad; edited with apparatus criticus; vol. 1: Books I–XII; 2nd ed. *Translator or author:* Walter Leaf. Macmillan.

1900—Homer's Iliad, Book One; from the original Greek in heroic hexameter; translated (English). *Translator or author:* Albert James Lonney. Bloomington, Ill.: Lloyd & Miller.

1900—The Adventures of Odysseus; retold in English; illustrated by Chas. Robinson (English). *Translator or author:* Francis Sydney Marvin; Robert John Grote Mayor; Florence Melian Stawell. London, England: J. M. Dent.

1900—Odyssey, Book XI; edited, introduction, notes, appendices [series: Pitt Press] (Greek). *Translator or author:* J. A. Nairn. C. J. Clay.

1900—The Odyssey of Homer; translated (English). *Translator or author:* George Herbert Palmer. Boston, Mass; New York, N.Y.: Houghton Mifflin.

1900—Iliad; Pope's translation; introductory

notes by H. L. Earl etc. [series: English Classics for Schools] (English). *Translator or author:* Alexander Pope. Rivington.

1900—The Iliad of Homer; with notes and introduction by Theodore Alois Buckley and Flaxman's designs (English). *Translator or author:* Alexander Pope. New York, N.Y.: Frederick Warne.

1900—Pope's Translation of Homer's Iliad, Books I,VI, XXII, XXIV; edited by William Cranston Lawton (English). *Translator or author:* Alexander Pope. New York, N.Y.: Globe School Book Co.

1900—The Iliad of Homer; translated; with notes and introduction by Theodore Alois Buckley (English). *Translator or author:* Alexander Pope. New York, N.Y.: Hurst.

1900—The Iliad of Homer; translated (English). *Translator or author:* Alexander Pope. Chicago, Il.: A. C. McClurg.

1900—Odysseus, Pope's translation (English). *Translator or author:* Alexander Pope. Martin.

1900—The Iliad of Homer (English). *Translator or author:* Alexander Pope. New York, N.Y.: David Appleton.

1900—The Iliad of Homer (Books I, VI, XXII, XXIV); edited with notes and an introduction by Albert H. Smyth (English). *Translator or author:* Alexander Pope. New York, N.Y.: Macmillan.

1900—Odysseae Epitome; 2nd ed. (Greek). *Translator or author:* Augustinus Scheindler. Vienna, Austria.

1900—Odyssey, Book VI. *Translator or author:* E. E. Sikes. Edinburgh, Scotland: William Blackwood.

1900—De Ilias; vertaald; 7th ed. (Dutch). *Translator or author:* Carel Vosmaer. Leiden (Leyden), Netherlands: A. W. Sijthoff.

1900—De Odussee; vertaald; 5th ed. (Dutch). *Translator or author:* Carel Vosmaer. Leiden (Leyden), Netherlands: A. W. Sijthoff.

1900—[H]omerou Odysseia = Homers Odyssee; Deutsch; bearbeitet von E. R. Weiss (Greek; German). *Translator or author:* Johann Heinrich Voss. Berlin, Germany: Der Tempel.

1900—Homers Werke; ubersetzt; Abdruck der eresten Ausgaben; mit Abbildung einer Homerbuste, Bildnis und Unterschrift von Joh[anne] H[einrich] Voss, sowie einer literar-historischen Einleitung von Gotthold Klee (German). *Translator or author:* Johann Heinrich Voss. Leipzig, Germany: Max Hesse.

1900—The Trojan War; translated from the German by Frances Younghusband; with the preface by W. Gunion Rutherford (English). *Translator or author:* C. Witt. London, England; New York, N.Y.: Green Longmans.

1900—Iliad, Books XXII–XXIV; translated with test papers [series: University Tutorial] (English). *Translator or author:* W. J. Woodhouse; R. M. Thomas. London, England: W. B. Clive.

1900?—The Odyssey of Homer. New York, N.Y.: Carlton House.

1900–02—The Iliad of Homer; edited with apparatus criticus, prolegomena, notes, and appendices by Walter Leaf; 2nd ed. (Greek). London, England; New York, N.Y.: Macmillan.

1900–02—[H]omerou Ilias; fur den Schulgebrauch erklart von Gottl. Stier; 2nd ed. (Greek). Gotha, Germany: F. A. Perthes.

1900–10—Odyssee; 3rd ed. (Greek). *Translator or author:* Karl Friedrich Ameis; Carl Hentze. Leipzig, Germany.

1900–19—Odyssea; edidit Guilielmus Dindorf; 5th ed. (Greek). Leipzig, Germany: B. G. Teubner.

1901 to 1950

1901—The First Six Books of Homer's Iliad; with introduction, commentary, and vocabulary for the use of the schools by Thomas D[ay] Seymour (Greek). Boston, Mass.: Ginn.

1901—Homeri Ilias; edidit Guilielmus Dindorf; correctior quam curavit C. Hentze; 5th ed. Leipzig, Germany: B. G. Teubner.

1901—Homer's Odyssey, Book I; edited for the use

of schools with introduction, notes and vocabulary by John Bond and A[rthur] S[umner] Walpole. London, England; New York, N.Y.: Macmillan.

1901—Homer's Odyssey, Books XIII–XXIV; edited with English notes and appendices by D[avid] B[inning] Monro (Greek). Oxford, England: Clarendon Press.

1901—Odyssey, Books XIII–XXIV; with introduction, notes, etc. by W[illiam] W[alter] Merry (Greek). Oxford, England: Clarendon Press.

1901—Opera et Reliquiae; recensuit D[avid] B[inning] Monro (Greek). Oxford, England: Clarendon Press.

1901—Hymni Homerici Accedentibus Epigrammatis et Batrachomyomachie Homero Vulgo Attributis; ex recensione Augusto Baumeister (Greek). Leipzig, Germany: B. G. Teubner.

1901—The First Three Books of Homer's Iliad; with introduction, commentary, and vocabulary, for the use of schools by Thomas D[ay] Seymour (Greek). Boston, Mass.: Ginn.

1901—Homers Odyssee; erklart von J[ohann] U[lrich] Faesi; 9th ed. (Greek). Berlin, Germany: Weidmannsche Buchhandlung.

1901—Odyssee; in verkurzter Ausgabe; fur den Schulgebrauch, von A[ugustin] Th[eodor] Christ; 3rd ed. Prague, Czechoslavakia: F. F. Tempsky.

1901—Iliad Alpha; done into English hexameters by Richard F. Biedermann [and other] members of class one of the graduating class of 1901 of the De Witt Clinton high school (English). *Translator or author:* Richard F. Biedermann. New York, N.Y.

1901—The Story of the Odyssey (English). *Translator or author:* Edward Brooks. Philadelphia, Pa.: Penn Publishing.

1901—The Iliads of Homer; translated according to the Greek; 2nd ed. (English). *Translator or author:* George Chapman. London, England: J. M. Dent.

1901—The Odysseys; 2nd ed. (English). *Translator or author:* George Chapman. London, England.

1901—[H]omerou Odysseia; metenechtheisa eis ten kathomilemenen mata semeioseon (Greek, Modern). *Translator or author:* Simon Chiotelles. Athens, Greece: Ekdotikos Oikos Georgiou D. Phexe.

1901—Gedichte (Greek). *Translator or author:* Henke. Leipzig, Germany.

1901—The Adventures of Ulysses; adapted from George Chapman's translation of the Odyssey; introduction by W. P. Trent; with fourteen illustrations after Flaxman by C. E. Atwood, and a map (English). *Translator or author:* Charles Lamb. Boston, Mass.: D. C. Heath.

1901—The Adventures of Ulysses; adapted from George Champman's translation of the Odyssey; edited by E. E. Speight, with an introduction by Sir George Birdwood; 2nd ed. (English). *Translator or author:* Charles Lamb. London, England: Horace Marshall.

1901—The Iliad of Homer; done into English prose [reprint of the 1883 edition] (English). *Translator or author:* Andrew Lang; Walter Leaf; Ernest Myers. London, England: Macmillan.

1901—Homer's Odyssey, Book I; edited with introduction and notes (Greek). *Translator or author:* Edgar Cardew Marchant. London, England: George Bell.

1901—Odyssey, Books XIII–XXIV. *Translator or author:* David Binning Monro. London, England; New York, N.Y.: Henry Frowde.

1901—The Odyssey of Homer; done into English verse (English). *Translator or author:* William Morris. London, England: Chiswick Press.

1901—The Odyssey of Homer; done into English Verse; first printed in 1887 and now reprinted at the Chiswick Press with Morris type designed for Kelmscott Press] (English). *Translator or author:* William Morris. London, England; New York, N.Y.: Green Longmans.

1901—The Odyssey of Homer; edited. *Translator or author:* E. C. Everard Owen. London, England: Blackie.

1901—The Iliad of Homer [Books 1, 6, 22, 24]; ed. by F. E. Shoup & I. Ball [reprinted from the 1715–20 edition] (English). *Translator or author:* Alexander Pope. Baltimore, Md.

1901—Pope's Translation of Homer's Iliad, Books I, VI, XXII, XXIV; edited with introduction and notes by William Tappan (English). *Translator or author:* Alexander Pope. Boston, Mass.: Athenaeum Press.

1901—The Iliad of Homer, Books I, VI, XXII, XXIV; edited with notes and introduction by Albert H. Smyth (English). *Translator or author:* Alexander Pope. New York, N.Y.: Macmillan.

1901—Pope's The Iliad of Homer, Books I, VI, XXII, and XXIV; edited with introduction and notes by Paul Shorey (English). *Translator or author:* Alexander Pope. Boston, Mass.: D. C. Heath.

1901—Pope's The Iliad of Homer, Books I, VI, XXII, and XXIV; edited with introduction and notes by Francis Elliott Shoup and Isaac Ball (English). *Translator or author:* Alexander Pope. Richmond, Va.: B. F. Johnson.

1901—Das Lied vom Zorn Achills; aus unserer Ilias hergestellt und in Deutsche Nibelungenzeilen ubertragen (German). *Translator or author:* Julius Schultz. Berlin, Germany: Wiegand & Grieben.

1901—Homer's Iliad, Books I–III; edited on the basis of the Ameis-Hentze edition (English). *Translator or author:* Thomas Day Seymour. Boston, Mass.: Ginn.

1901–19—Die Gedichte Homers; bearb. Von Oskar Henke. Leipzig, Germany: B. G. Teubner.

1902—The Iliad of Homer, Books IX and X; edited by J[ohn] C[uthbert] Lawson (Greek). Cambridge, England: Cambridge University Press.

1902—Homeri Odyssea; edidit Guilielmus Dindorf; edition quinta correctior quam curavit C. Hentze; 5th ed. Leipzig, Germany: B. G. Teubner.

1902—Odyssey, Books XIII–XXIV; with introduction, notes, and table of Homeric forms by W[illiam] W[alter] Merry (Greek). Oxford, England: Clarendon Press.

1902—Iliad; edited by D[avid] B[inning] Monro and T[homas] W[illiam] Allen; 3rd ed. (Greek). Oxford, England: Clarendon Press.

1902—Homers Odyssee; Schulausgabe von Paul Cauer; 3rd ed. (Greek). Leipzig, Germany: C. Freytag.

1902—[H]omerou Ilias = Homers Ilias; schulausgabe von Paul Cauer; 2nd ed. (Greek). Leipzig, Germany; Vienna, Austria: G. Freytag; F. Tempsky.

1902—The Story of the Iliad (English). *Translator or author:* Edward Brooks. Philadelphia, Pa.: Penn Publishing.

1902—The Odyssey of Homer, with the Hymns, Epigrams, and Battle of the Frogs and Mice; literally translated (English). *Translator or author:* Theodore Alois Buckley. London, England: George Bell.

1902—The Iliad; literally translated with explanatory notes (English). *Translator or author:* Theodore Alois Buckley. London, England: George Bell and Sons.

1902—La Batrachomyomachie ou le Combat des Rats et des Grenouilles; traduit d'Homere et illustre (French). *Translator or author:* Eugene Chalon. Paris, France: Alphonse Lemerre.

1902—The Whole Works of Homer, Prince of Poets, in his Iliads and Odysseys; translated according to the Greek (English). *Translator or author:* George Chapman. London, England: Chatto and Windus.

1902—The Story of the Iliad; with illustrations after Flaxman (English). *Translator or author:* Alfred John Church. London, England: Seeley.

1902—Das alte Lied vom Zorne Achills (Urmenis) aus der Ilias; ausgeschieden und metrisch ubersetzt (German). *Translator or author:* August Fick. Gottingen, Germany: Vanderhoeck and Ruprecht.

1902—The Adventures of Ulysses the Wanderer, an Old Story Retold; illustrated by W. G. Mein (English). *Translator or author:* Cyril Arthur Edward Ranger Gull. London, England: Greening.

1902—Homeros Iliasa; az eredeti versmertekben forditotta (Hungarian). *Translator or author:* Jozsef Kempf. Budapest, Hungary: Lampel.

1902—The Adventures of Ulysses; with illustrations by M. H. Squire & E. Mars (English). *Translator or author:* Charles Lamb. New York, N.Y.: Platt and Peck.

1902—Iliad; edited, with apparatus criticus, prolegomena notes, and appendices; vol. 2, Books XIII–XXIV; 2nd ed. (Greek). *Translator or author:* Walter Leaf. Macmillan.

1902—Odyssey, Book I. *Translator or author:* E. C. Everard Owen. London, England: Blackie.

1902—The Song of Demeter and her Daughter Persephone, an Homeric Hymn; translation (English). *Translator or author:* Walter Pater. Chicago, Il.: R. F. Seymour.

1902—The Boy's Iliad; with illustrations by Jacomb Hood [George Percy] (English). *Translator or author:* Walter Copland Perry. London, England; New York, N.Y.: Macmillan.

1902—Homer: Song of Demeter and her Daughter Persephone (English). *Translator or author:* Peter. Chicago, Il.

1902—The Iliad of Homer; translated (English). *Translator or author:* Alexander Pope. London, England; New York, N.Y.: Henry Frowde.

1902—The Iliad of Homer; translated; with notes and introduction by Theodore Alois Buckley (English). *Translator or author:* Alexander Pope. New York, N.Y.: A. L. Burt.

1902—The Iliad of Homer, Books I, VI, XXII, XXIV; translated; edited for school use by Wilfred Wesley Cressy and William Vaughn Moody (English). *Translator or author:* Alexander Pope. Chicago, Il.: Foresman Scott.

1902—Iliad [series: World Classics] (English). *Translator or author:* Alexander Pope. London, England: G. Richards.

1902—The Iliad and the Odyssey [series: Bohn's Classical Library] (English). *Translator or author:* Alexander Pope. London, England: George Bell.

II. Printed Editions of the Homeric Texts, 1470 to 2000 C.E.

290

1902–04— Homerova Ileieiiada; pereklav (Ukrainian). *Translator or author:* Petro Nishchynskyaei. Ulvovi [location?]: Knyharni Haukovoho t-va im. Shevchenka.

1902–07— Homeri Carmina; recensuit et selecta lectionis varietate instruxit Arthurus Ludwich (Greek). Leipzig, Germany: B. G. Teubner.

1902–12— Homeri Opera; recognoverunt brevique adnotatione critica instruxerunt David B[inning] Monro et Thomas W. Allen (Greek). Oxford, England: Clarendon Press.

1902–12— The Odyssey of Homer; Pope Translation (English). *Translator or author:* Alexander Pope. Chicago, Il.: Henneberry.

1903— The First Three Books of Homer's Iliad; with introduction, commentary, and vocabulary, for the use of schools, by Thomas D[ay] Seymour (Greek). Boston, Mass.: Ginn.

1903— Selections from Homer's Iliad; with an introduction, notes, a short Homeric grammar, and a vocabulary by Allen Rogers Benner (Greek). New York, N.Y.: David Appleton.

1903— Odyssee in Verkurzter Ausgabe; fur den schulgebrauch von A. Th[eodor] Christ; 4th ed. (Greek). Vienna, Austria: F. F. Tempsky.

1903— Iliad, Books XIII–XXIV; with notes by D[avid] B[inning] Monro; 4th ed. (Greek). Oxford, England: Clarendon Press.

1903— The First Six Books of Homer's Iliad; with introduction, commentary, and vocabulary for the use of schools, by Thomas D. Seymour (Greek). Boston, Mass.: Ginn.

1903— The Sixth Book of Homer's Odyssey (English). Boston, Mass.: Ginn.

1903— Iliada. Krakow, Poland.

1903— Nausicaa, Piece en un Acte, en Vers, Tiree de l'Odyssee. *Translator or author:* Maurice Bouchor. Paris, France: Armand Colin.

1903— The Story of Odysseus; selected from the prose translation of Samuel Henry Butcher and Andrew Lang; introduction by Nathan Haskell Dole (English). *Translator or author:* Samuel Henry Butcher; Andrew Lang. Boston, Mass.

1903— The Odyssey of Homer; done into English prose (English). *Translator or author:* Samuel Henry Butcher; Andrew Lang. London, England: Macmillan.

1903— Iliad and Odyssey; translated according to the Greek; edited, with notes, by Richard Herne Shepherd (English). *Translator or author:* George

Chapman. London, England: Chatto and Windus.

1903— Homer's Iliad; translated, with an introduction by Henry Morley (English). *Translator or author:* George Chapman. London, England: George Routledge and Sons.

1903— Stories from Homer; with twenty-four illustrations from Flaxman's designs (English). *Translator or author:* Alfred John Church. London, England: Seeley.

1903— Homer. *Translator or author:* E. Drerup. Munich, Germany.

1903— Achilles & Hector: Iliad Stories Retold for Boys and Girls (English). *Translator or author:* Agnes Spofford Cook Gale. Chicago, Il.; New York, N.Y.: McNally Rand.

1903— Homeric Stories for Young Readers (English). *Translator or author:* Frederic Aldin Hall. New York, N.Y.; Cambridge, Oh.: American Book Company.

1903— Homer's Battle of the Frogs and Mice; arranged for young people, illustrated by Frederick Ehrlich (English). *Translator or author:* Oscar Herrmann. New York, N.Y.: Everitt & Francis.

1903— The Iliad of Homer; done into English prose (English). *Translator or author:* Andrew Lang; Walter Leaf; Ernest Myers. London, England; New York, N.Y.: Macmillan.

1903— Iliad, Book XVIII; with vocabulary (Greek). *Translator or author:* Arthur Platt. London, England: Blackie.

1903— The Odyssey of Homer; translated [series: World Classics] (English). *Translator or author:* Alexander Pope. London, England: G. Richards.

1903— The Odyssey of Homer; translated (English). *Translator or author:* Alexander Pope. London, England; New York, N.Y.: Henry Frowde; Oxford University Press.

1903— The Iliad of Homer, Books I, VI, XXII, XXIV; edited with notes by Margaret A. Eaton (English). *Translator or author:* Alexander Pope. Boston, Mass.: Educational Pub. Co.

1903— Odysseja; przeklad (Polish). *Translator or author:* Lucjan Hipolit Siemienski. Warsaw, Poland: Naklad Gebethnera I Wolffa.

1903— [H]omerou Ilias; Lloimo, meni. Homera Iliada; pomor, gniew; [tekst Grecki opracowal Leon Sternbach; jako tekstu polskiego uzlo parafrazy poetyckiej Juliusza Slowackiego z r. 1846; tlumaczenie to, pierwszej ksiegi od wiersza 1–492, przytoczono z tomu I-go (Greek; Polish).

Translator or author: Juliusz Slowacki. Cracow, Poland.

1903— Homers Ilias (in verkurzter form); nach der Ubersetzung von Johann Heinrich Voss fur den Schulgebrauch bearbeitet von Dr. A. Primozic und K. A. Schmidt (German). *Translator or author:* Johann Heinrich Voss. Leipzig, Germany; Berlin, Germany: B. G. Teubner.

1903— Homers Odyssee in Auszuge; in der Ubersetzung von J. H. Voss (German). *Translator or author:* Johann Heinrich Voss. Bielefeld, Germany: Velhagen und Klasing.

1903— Iliad, Book I [series: Illustrated Classics]. *Translator or author:* L. D. Wainwright. London, England: George Bell.

1903–06— Iliad; with an introduction, a brief Homeric Grammar, and notes by D[avid] B[inning] Monro; 5th ed. (Greek). Oxford, England: Clarendon Press.

1903–10— The Odyssey; translated into English verse (English). *Translator or author:* John William Mackail. London, England; Edinburgh, Scotland: John Murray; Ballantyne, Hanson.

1904— Homeri Ilias; edidit Guilielmus Dindorf; 4th ed. (Greek). Leipzig, Germany: B. G. Teubner.

1904— The Homeric Hymns; edited, with preface, apparatus criticus, notes, and appendices by Thomas W. Allen and E. E. Sikes (Greek). London, England; New York, N.Y.: Macmillan.

1904— Die Gedichte Homers; bearbeitet von Professor Dr. Oskar Henke. Leipzig, Germany: B. G. Teubner.

1904— Odyssea; 5th ed. (Greek). Leipzig, Germany.

1904— The First Three Books of Homer's Iliad; with introduction, commentary, and vocabulary, for the use of schools by Thomas D[ay] Seymour (Greek). Boston, Mass.: Ginn; Athenaeum Press.

1904— Homeri Ilias (Latin). Oxford, England: J. Parker.

1904— Selections from Homer's Iliad; with an introduction, notes, a short Homeric grammar, and a vocabulary by Allen Rogers Benner (Greek). New York, N.Y.: Appleton-Century-Crofts.

1904— Odyssee. Paris, France: L. Hachette.

1904— The Homeric Hymns (Greek). *Translator or author:* Sikes Allen. London, England.

1904— Ilyadhat Humirus; muarrabah naozman wa-alayha sharon tarikhi adabi; bi-qalam Sulayman al-Bustani; L'Iliade d'Hommere traduite en vers Arabes par Sulaeman al-Bustany (Arabic). *Translator or author:* Sulayman Khaototar Bustani. Cairo, Egypt: Al-Hilal.

1904— The Story of Odysseus in the Land of the Phaeacians, Being the Sixth and a Part of the Seventh Book of the Odyssey; translated (English). *Translator or author:* Samuel Henry Butcher; Andrew Lang. Boston, Mass.: N. H. Dole.

1904— The Odysseys of Homer; together with the shorter poems; translated according to the Greek (English). *Translator or author:* George Chapman. London, England; New York, N.Y.: G. Newnes; C. Scribner.

1904— The Iliads of Homer; translated according to the Greek (English). *Translator or author:* George Chapman. London, England: Simpkin, Marshall, Hamilton, Kent.

1904— The Iliads of Homer, Prince of Poets, Never Before in any Language Truly Translated; done according to the Greek (English). *Translator or author:* George Chapman. London, England; New York, N.Y.: G. Newnes; C. Scribner's Sons.

1904— Achilles & Hector, Iliad Stories Retold for Boys and Girls (English). *Translator or author:* Agnes Spofford Cook Gale. Chicago, Il.; New York, N.Y.: McNally Rand.

1904— L'Iliade di Omero; traduzione; con note dichiarative di Gustavo Boralevi; 3rd ed. (Italian). *Translator or author:* Vincenzo Monti. Livorno, Italy: Raffaello Giusti.

1904— The Odyssey of Homer; done into English verse (English). *Translator or author:* William Morris. London, England: Longmans.

1904— Ilias; in der Sprache der zehnjahrigen erzahlt; mit 6 Vollbildern von C. Bertling. *Translator or author:* Helene Otto. Leipzig, Germany: R. G. T. Scheffer.

1904— Homer. *Translator or author:* Willy Pastor. Berlin, Germany.

1904— The Iliad of Homer; translated; edited by the Rev. J. S. Watson (English). *Translator or author:* Alexander Pope. London, England: George Bell.

1904— Peraihody Odysseovy; Z Odysseie pereloezil (Czech). *Translator or author:* Otmar Vaenorny. Prague, Czechoslavakia: J. Laichter.

1904— Homerus' Ilias; in proza vertaald en met korte ophelderingen voorzien (Dutch). *Translator or author:* W. G. Van Der Weerd. Amsterdam, Netherlands: S. L. Van Looy.

1904— The Odyssey of Homer in English Verse;

3rd ed. (English). *Translator or author:* Arthur Sanders Way. London, England; New York, N.Y.: Macmillan.

1904— The Odyssey; translated by Avia [reprint of the 1880 edition] (English). *Translator or author:* Arthur Sanders Way. New York, N.Y.

1904— Odysseja Homer; streasci (Polish). *Translator or author:* A. Wrzesiean. Warsaw, Poland: M. Arcta.

1904–06— The Complete Works of Percy Bysshe Shelley; edited by Nathan Haskell Dole (English). *Translator or author:* Percy Bysshe Shelley. London, England; Boston, Mass.: Virtue.

1904–11— Odyssee; fur den Schulgebrauch erklart von Karl Friedrich Ameis; besorgt von C. Hentze. Leipzig, Germany: B. G. Teubner.

1904–15— Homers Odyssee; im Versmass der Urschrift ubersetzt (German). *Translator or author:* F. W. Ehrenthal. Leipzig, Germany: Bibliographisches Institut.

1905— [H]omerou Odysseia = Homers Odyssee; Schulausgabe von Paul Cauer; 4th ed. (Greek). Leipzig, Germany; Vienna, Austria: G. Freytag; F. Tempsky.

1905— Homers Ilias; fur den Schulgebrauch in verkurzter form; bearb. und hrsg. Von Joseph Bach; 2nd ed. (Greek). Munster, Germany: Aschendorffschen Verlagsbuchhandlung.

1905— L'Odissea, Libro I; testo, costruzione, versione letterale e argomenti Omero; 3rd ed. (Greek). Rome, Italy: Sega Societa Editrice Dante Alighieri di Albrighi.

1905— The Sixth Book of the Iliad; edited with notes, introduction, and vocabulary by Walter Leaf and M[atthew] A[lbert] Bayfield (Greek). London, England; New York, N.Y.: Macmillan.

1905— Homer['s] Odyssey, Books VII–XII; with introduction, notes ... by W[illiam] W[alter] Merry (Greek). Oxford, England: Clarendon Press.

1905— Il Libro XVII dell'Odissea; con note Italiane del Pasquale Giardelli (Greek). Rome; Milan: Sega Societa Editrice Dante Alighieri di Albrighi.

1905— Ilias Latina; edited by W[illiam] H[enry] S[amuel] Jones (Latin). London, England: Blackie.

1905— The Twenty-Fourth Book of the Iliad; edited with notes, introduction and vocabulary by Walter Leaf and M[atthew] A[lbert] Bayfield (Greek). London, England; New York, N.Y.: Macmillan.

1905— The Odyssey of Homer; translated into blank verse; with Flaxman's illustrations (English). *Translator or author:* William Cullen Bryant. Boston, Mass; New York, N.Y.: Houghton Mifflin.

1905— The Iliad of Homer; translated into blank verse; with Flaxman's illustrations (English). *Translator or author:* William Cullen Bryant. Boston, Mass; New York, N.Y.: Mifflin Houghton.

1905— The Odyssey of Homer; done into English prose (English). *Translator or author:* Samuel Henry Butcher; Andrew Lang. New York, N.Y.: Macmillan.

1905— The Iliads of Homer, Prince of Poets [reprint of the 1611 edition] (English). *Translator or author:* George Chapman. New York, N.Y.

1905— The Odysseys of Homer; together with the shorter poems; translated according to ye Greeke [reprint of the 1615 edition] (English). *Translator or author:* George Chapman. London, England; New York, N.Y.: Simpkin, Marshall, Hamilton, Kent; Charles Scribner.

1905— The Story of the Iliad; with illustrations after Flaxman (English). *Translator or author:* Alfred John Church. London, England: Seeley.

1905— The Story of the Iliad; edited for school use (English). *Translator or author:* Alfred John Church. New York, N.Y.: Macmillan.

1905— Iliad, Book XXIV; literally translated with notes (English). *Translator or author:* E. S. Crooke. Marshall Simpkin.

1905— Homeros Odysseiaja; az eredeti versmertekben forditotta Kemenes Jozsef (Hungarian). *Translator or author:* Jozsef Kemenes. Budapest, Hungary: Lampel.

1905— Iliad [reprint of the 1883 edition; series: Pocket English and American Classics] (English). *Translator or author:* Andrew Lang; Walter Leaf; Ernest Myers. New York, N.Y.

1905— The Iliad of Homer; done into English prose (English). *Translator or author:* Andrew Lang; Walter Leaf; Ernest Myers. New York, N.Y.; London, England: Macmillan.

1905— Homer, in translation (English). *Translator or author:* Matthew. Edward Arnold.

1905— Homers Odyssee; Deutsch (German). *Translator or author:* Hans Georg Meyer. Berlin, Germany: J. Springer.

1905— Iliade di Omero; traduzione, con le osservazioni di Andrea Mustoxidi e le notizie della vita e dell'opere dal traduttore (Italian). *Translator or author:* Vincenzo Monti. Milan, Italy: Societa Editrice Sonzogno.

1905— The Iliad; translated (English). *Translator or author:* Alexander Pope. New York, N.Y.: Hurst.

1905— Pope, The Iliad of Homer, Books I, VI, XXII, XXIV; edited with notes and an introduction by Albert H. Smyth (English). *Translator or author:* Alexander Pope. New York, N.Y.: Macmillan.

1905— Die Odyssee; nachgebildet in achtzeiligen iambischen Strophen; 2nd ed. (German). *Translator or author:* Hermann von Schelling. Munich, Germany: R. Oldenbourg.

1905–13— Homers Ilias; fur den Schulgebrauch erklart von Carl Friedr[ich] Ameris und Carl Hentze (Greek). Leipzig, Germany: B. G. Teubner.

1905–13— The Iliad of Homer; translated into English prose (English). *Translator or author:* Edward Henry Blakeney. London, England: George Bell.

1906— Homeri Odyssea; edidit Guilielmus Dindorf; 4th ed. (Latin). Leipzig, Germany: B. G. Teubner.

1906— The Iliad, Book XXIII; edited with introduction, notes and appendices by G[erald] M[aclean] Edwards; 2nd ed. Cambridge, England: Cambridge University Press.

1906— Homer. J. W. Mackail.

1906— Iliad [of] Homer; with an introduction, a brief Homeric grammar, and notes by D[avid] B[inning] Monro. Oxford, England: Clarendon Press.

1906— Hymni Homerici Accedentibus Epigrammatis et Batrachomyomachia Homero Vulgo Attributis; ex recensione Augusti Baumeister (Greek). Leipzig, Germany: B. G. Teubner.

1906— Homer, Iliad, Books I–XII; with an introduction, a brief Homeric grammar, and notes by D[avid] B[inning] Monro; 5th ed. (Greek). Oxford, England: Clarendon Press.

1906— The Odyssey of Homer, with the Hymns, Epigrams, and Battle of the Frogs and Mice; literally translated (English). *Translator or author:* Theodore Alois Buckley. London, England: George Bell.

1906— The Odyssey of Homer; done into English prose (English). *Translator or author:* Samuel Henry Butcher; Andrew Lang. New York, N.Y.: Macmillan.

1906— The Odyssey of Homer [series: Pocket English and American Classics] (English). *Translator or author:* Samuel Henry Butcher; Andrew Lang. New York, N.Y.

1906— The Odysseys of Homer; translated according to the Greek (English). *Translator or author:* George Chapman. London, England: J. M. Dent.

1906— The Story of the Iliad; with illustrations after Flaxman (English). *Translator or author:* Alfred John Church. New York, N.Y.: Macmillan.

1906— The Odyssey for Boys and Girls; told from Homer (English). *Translator or author:* Alfred John Church. New York, N.Y.: Macmillan.

1906— Homer's Odyssey, Books IX, X. *Translator or author:* John Hampden Haydon; Arthur Hadrian Allcroft. London, England: W. B. Clive.

1906— The Odyssey of Homer; translated (English). *Translator or author:* Alexander Pope. London, England; New York, N.Y.: Henry Frowde; Oxford University Press.

1906— The Odyssey of Homer; translated; to which are added the Battle of the Frogs and Mice, by Parnell, and the Hymns, by Chapman and others; edited by the Rev. J[ohn] S[elby] Watson; illustrated with the entire series of Flaxman's designs (English). *Translator or author:* Alexander Pope. London, England: George Bell and Sons.

1906— The Iliad of Homer; translated; with notes and introduction by Theodore Alois Buckley (English). *Translator or author:* Alexander Pope. New York, N.Y.: A. L. Burt.

1906–07— The Iliad and Odyssey; ed. by A. J. Church (English). *Translator or author:* Alexander Pope.

1906–08— Homeri Carmina cum Prolegomenis et Annotatione Critica; tertium ediderunt J. Van Leeuwen, J. F. et M. B. Mendes da Costa (Greek). Leiden (Leyden), Netherlands: A. W. Sijthoff.

1906–24— Homers Ilias; fur den schulgebrauch erklart von Karl Friedrich Ameis; besorgt von Prof. Dr. C. Hentze; 6th ed. Leipzig, Germany: B. G. Teubner.

1907— Odyssey; with introduction, notes, etc. by W[illiam] W[alter] Merry (Greek). Oxford, England: Clarendon Press.

1907— [H]omerou Ilias = Homeri Ilias; schulausgabe von Paul Cauer; 2nd ed. (Greek). Leipzig, Germany: G. Freytag.

1907— Les Auteurs Grecs Expliques d'apres une Methode Nouvelle par Deux Traductions Francaises: Homere. Paris, France: L. Hachette.

1907— The Iliad, Book VI; edited with introduction, notes and appendices by G[erald] M[aclean] Edwards [reprint of the 1892 edition]. Cambridge, England: Cambridge University Press.

1907— Homer's Iliad, First Three Books and Selections; edited for the use of schools, by J[ohn] R[obert] Sitlington Sterrett. New York, N.Y.; Cambridge, Oh.: American Book Company.

1907— Ilias; 2nd ed. (German). *Translator or author:* Paul Cauer. Leipzig, Germany.

1907— The Iliad for Boys and Girls; told from Homer in simple language; with twelve illustrations in colour (English). *Translator or author:* Alfred John Church. New York, N.Y.: Macmillan.

1907— The Children's Odyssey; told from Homer in simple language (English). *Translator or author:* Alfred John Church. London, England: Seeley.

1907— Stories from Homer; with twenty-four illustrations from Flaxman's designs (English). *Translator or author:* Alfred John Church. London, England: Seeley.

1907— The Story of the Odyssey; with illustrations after Flaxman; 4th ed. (English). *Translator or author:* Alfred John Church. London, England: Seeley.

1907— The Iliad; rendered into English blank verse [reprint of the 1864 edition; series: New Universal Library] (English). *Translator or author:* Edward George Geoffrey Smith Stanley, Earl of Derby. New York, N.Y.; London, England: George Routledge.

1907— Das erste Buch der Ilias in Prosa ubersetzt; ein Versuch (German). *Translator or author:* Georg Finsler. Bern, Switzerland: Steampfli.

1907— L'Iliade et l'Odyssee [d']Homere; abregees et annotees par Alph. Feillet sur la traduction de P. Giguet; ouvrage illustre de 33 vignettes par Olivier (French). *Translator or author:* Pierre Giguet. Paris, France: L. Hachette.

1907— Stories from the Odyssey; told to the children; with pictures by W. Heath Robinson (English). *Translator or author:* Jeanie Lang. London, England; New York, N.Y.: T. C. and E. C. Jack; E. P. Dutton.

1907— Homers Ilias; Deutsch (German). *Translator or author:* Hans Georg Meyer. Berlin, Germany: Trowitzsch.

1907— Pope's Iliad of Homer; edited with an introduction by Professor A[lfred] J. Chruch; with 24 full-page illustrations by Wal Paget (English). *Translator or author:* Alexander Pope. New York, N.Y.: John Land.

1907— L'Oudissaeio d'Oumaero; revirado au Prouvenocau paer Charloun Riaeu, daou Paradou. *Translator or author:* Charles Rieu. Marsiho [location?]: P. Ruat.

1907— The Iliad of Homer; to which is added an appendix containing poems selected from twenty-six languages, all translated (English). *Translator or author:* Edgar Alfred Tibbetts. Boston, Mass.: R. G. Badger.

1907–08— Odyssea; cum prolegomenis et annotatione critica ediderunt J. Van Leeuwen J. F. et M. B. Mendes da Cosat; 3rd ed. (Greek). Leiden (Leyden), Netherlands: A. W. Sijthoff.

1907–08— Homeri Odyssea; edidit Guilielmus Dindorf; 5th ed. (Latin). Leipzig, Germany: B. G. Teubner.

1907–08— Homeri Ilias; edidit Guilielmus Dindorf; 5th ed. Leipzig, Germany: B. G. Teubner.

1907–10— Die Odyssee; neu ins Deutsche ubertragen [Cranach Presse] (German). *Translator or author:* Rudolf Alexander Schroder. Leipzig, Germany: Insel-Verlag.

1907–12— Homeri Opera; recognovervnt breviqve adnotatione critica instrvxervnt David B[inning] Monro et Thomas W[illiam] Allen. Oxford, England: Clarendon Press.

1908— The Iliad; edited by A. R. Benner. New York, N.Y.: David Appleton.

1908— Selections from Homer's Iliad; with an introduction, notes, a short Homeric grammar and a vocabulary by Allen Rogers (Greek). New York, N.Y.: David Appleton.

1908— L'Odyssee (French). Paris, France: E. Flammarion.

1908— L'Iliade (French). Paris, France: E. Flammarion.

1908— Homeri Odyssea; edidit Guilielmus Dindorf; 5th ed. Leipzig, Germany: B. G. Teubner.

1908— Der ursprungliche und echte Schluss der Odyssee Homers (Greek). *Translator or author:* Ludwig Adam. Wiesbaden, Germany: C. Ritter.

1908— The Iliad of Homer; literally translated, with explanatory notes (English). *Translator or author:* Theodore Alois Buckley. London, England: George Bell.

1908— The Children's Iliad; told from Homer in

simple language (English). *Translator or author:* Alfred John Church. London, England: Seeley.

1908—Odyssey, Books IX–X; literally translated from the Pitt Press, text by A. Jagger (English). *Translator or author:* A. Jagger. Cambridge, England: Marshall Simpkin.

1908—Homeros' Odyssee; fran Grekiskan (Swedish). *Translator or author:* Erland L. Lagerlof. Stockholm, Sweden: Ljus.

1908—The Odyssey of Homer; translated (English). *Translator or author:* George Herbert Palmer. Boston, Mass; New York, N.Y.: Houghton Mifflin.

1908—L'Odissea; tradotta, con prefazione e commento di V[ittorio] Turri; 2nd ed. (Italian). *Translator or author:* Ippolito Pindemonte. Florence, Italy: G. C. Sansoni.

1908—The Iliad of Homer; tr. by Alexander Pope, esq.; in two volumes, ornamented with wood cuts, originally designed and engraved by Dr. A. Anderson, of New York... (English). *Translator or author:* Alexander Pope. New York, N.Y.: J. Suymour.

1908—Homero, La Iliada; version directa y literal del Griego; ilustraciones de Flaxman y A[lfred] J[ohn] Church (Spanish). *Translator or author:* Luis Segala y Estalella. Barcelona, Spain: Montaner and Simon.

1908—Homerova Odysseia Homer; prelozil (Czech). *Translator or author:* Antonin Skoda. Prague, Czechoslavakia.

1908—Homers Ilias; in Deutscher Ubersetzung; hrsg. von Hans Feigl, vorwort von Willy Paster (German). *Translator or author:* Johann Heinrich Voss. Vienna, Austria: Carl Konegen; Ernst Stulpnagel.

1908–11—[H]omerou Ilias = The Iliad of Homer; edited with general and grammatical introductions, notes, and appendices, by Walter Leaf and M[atthew] A[lbert] Bayfield; 2nd ed. London, England: Macmillan.

1908–11—Homers Odyssee; fur den Schulgebrauch erklart von Karl Friedrich Ameis; besorgt von C. Hentze (Greek). Leipzig, Germany: B. G. Teubner.

1908–11—Odyssee (Greek). *Translator or author:* Karl Friedrich Ameis; Carl Hentze. Leipzig, Germany.

1909—[H]omerou Odysseia = Homeri Odyssea (Greek). Oxford, England: Oxford University Press.

1909—The Twenty-Second Book of the Iliad; with critical notes by Alex[ander] Pallis (Greek). London, England: David Nutt.

1909—Studies in Epics, with Questions and Aids; edited by Hubert M. Skinner. Minneapolis, Minn.: Cree.

1909—Odyssey. Oxford, England: Clarendon Press.

1909—Die Homerische Batrachomyomachia des Karers Pigres; hrsg. Von J. Greoschl (German). Friedid.

1909—Odysseus, the Hero of Ithaca; adapted from the third book of the primary schools of Athens, Greece (English). *Translator or author:* Mary Elizabeth Burt. New York, N.Y.: Charles Scribner.

1909—The Greek Classics, Epic Literature; Marion Mills Miller, editor (English). *Translator or author:* Samuel Henry Butcher; Andrew Lang. New York, N.Y.: Vincent Parke.

1909—The Odyssey; translated; with introduction, notes and illustrations [series: The Harvard Classics] (English). *Translator or author:* Samuel Henry Butcher; Andrew Lang. New York, N.Y.: P. F. Collier & Son.

1909—The Odyssey for Boys and Girls, Told from Homer; with twelve illustrations (English). *Translator or author:* Alfred John Church. New York, N.Y.: Macmillan.

1909—The Homeric Stories: Iliad and Odyssey; done into English prose (English). *Translator or author:* Andrew Lang; Walter Leaf; E. Myers; S. H. Butler. Chautauqua, N.Y.: Chautauqua Press.

1909—The Iliad of Homer; done into English prose; with an introduction by W. Lucas Collins (English). *Translator or author:* Andrew Lang; Walter Leaf; Ernest Myers. New York, N.Y.; London, England: Macmillan.

1909—The Odyssey; printed at the Oxford University Press with Greek types designed by Robert Proctor; the text is that of Dr. D. B. Monro issued by the Oxford Press in 1901 (Greek). *Translator or author:* David Binning Monro. Oxford, England: Oxford University Press.

1909—Homer's Odyssey; translated into English rhythmic prose [series: Riverside Literature and Abridged School] (English). *Translator or author:* George Herbert Palmer. Boston, Mass.: Houghton.

1909—The Iliad of Homer; translated; edited by J. S. Watson; and illustrated with the entire series of Flaxman's designs (English). *Translator or au-*

thor: Alexander Pope. London, England: George Bell.

1909— The Iliad of Homer; translated [series: People's Library] (English). *Translator or author:* Alexander Pope. London, England; New York, N.Y.: Cassell.

1909— Hector and Achilles, a Tale of Troy; rendered into English after the chronicle of Homer (English). *Translator or author:* Richard Sheepshanks. Edinburgh, Scotland: William Blackwood.

1909— Homers Odyssee; ubers.; hrsg. Von Paul Brandt (German). *Translator or author:* Johann Heinrich Voss. Leipzig, Germany; Vienna, Austria: Bibliographisches Institut.

1909–13— Iliad; literally translated in prose [reprint of the 1851 edition] (English). *Translator or author:* Theodore Alois Buckley.

1910— Hymni Homerici Accedentibus Epigrammatis et Batrachomyomachia Homero Vulgo Attributis; ex recensione Augusti Baumeister (Greek). Leipzig, Germany: B. G. Teubner.

1910— Selections from Homer's Iliad (Greek). *Translator or author:* Benner. New York, N.Y.

1910— The Story of the Iliad (English). *Translator or author:* Edward Brooks. Philadelphia, Pa.: Penn Publishing.

1910— The Odyssey of Homer; done into English prose (English). *Translator or author:* Samuel Henry Butcher; Andrew Lang. London, England; New York, N.Y.: Macmillan.

1910— The Odyssey of Homer; translated (English). *Translator or author:* William Cowper. London, England; New York, N.Y.: J. M. and Sons Dent; E. P. Dutton.

1910— The Iliad of Homer; translated into English hexameter verse; an abridgment which includes all the main story and the most celebrated passages (English). *Translator or author:* Prentiss Cummings. Boston, Mass.: Little Brown.

1910— The Iliad of Homer; translated; series: Everyman's Library (English). *Translator or author:* Edward George Geoffrey Smith Stanley, Earl of Derby. London, England; New York, N.Y.: J. M. Dent; E. P. Dutton.

1910— Ilias; das Lied vom Zorn des Achilleus; rekonstruiert und ubers. (German). *Translator or author:* Stephan Gruss. Strasbourg, France: Heitz.

1910— Stories from the Iliad; retold (English). *Translator or author:* Herbert Lord Havell. London, England: George G. Harrap.

1910— Lamb's Adventures of Ulysses (English). *Translator or author:* Charles Lamb. London, England; New York, N.Y.: Thomas Nelson and Sons.

1910— Stories from the Odyssey; told to the children; with pictures by W. Heath Robinson (English). *Translator or author:* Jeanie Lang. London, England; New York, N.Y.: T. C. & E. C. Jack; E. P. Dutton; T. Nelson and Sons.

1910— L'Iliade; tradotta; con commento do Vittoria Turri; 3rd ed. (Italian). *Translator or author:* Vincenzo Monti. Florence, Italy: G. C. Sansoni.

1910— Homero, La Odisea; version directa y literal del Griego; ilustraciones de Flaxman y de Wal Paget (Spanish). *Translator or author:* Luis Segala y Estalella. Barcelona, Spain: Montaner and Simon.

1910— Homers Ilias im Auszuge nach der Ubersetzung von J. H. Voss; bearbeitet von Granz Kern; mit sieben Abbildungen nach den Umrisszeichnungen von John Flaxmann [sic.] (German). *Translator or author:* Johann Heinrich Voss. Bielefeld, Germany: Velhagen und Klasing.

1910— The Iliad of Homer; done into English verse (English). *Translator or author:* Arthur Sanders Way. London, England: Macmillan.

1910— Bilder aus der Odyssee (freie ubertragungen) (German). *Translator or author:* G. Wille. Sangerhausen.

1910— Homeros Ilias; proze-bewerking (Dutch). *Translator or author:* Karel van de Woestijne. Amsterdam, Netherlands: Maatschappij voor Doede en Doedkoope Lectuur.

1910–11— Homeri Ilias; edidit Guilielmus Dindorf; 5th ed. (Greek). Leipzig, Germany: B. G. Teubner.

1910–13— Iliad; translated into English prose [reprint of the 1905–13 edition] (English). *Translator or author:* Edward Henry Blakeney. New York, N.Y.

1911— Homers Odyssee; zum schulgebrauch bearb. und erlautert con Dr. Ernst Maumann (Greek). Bielefeld, Germany; Leipzig, Germany: Velhagen und Klasing.

1911— Odyssee; texte Grec publie avec une introduction, des arguments analytiques et des notes en Francais par A. Pierron (Greek). Paris, France: L. Hachette.

1911— Selections from Homer; edited with introductory notes and vocabulary, by W. Rennie (Greek). London, England: Edward Arnold.

1911— Homeri Iliados Liber XVIII, The Arms of

Achilles; edited, for the use of schools with notes and vocabulary, by Sydney R. James; with illustrations (Greek). London, England: Macmillan.

1911—Odiseja; prosto po Homerju prestavil; 1st ed. (Slovenian). *Translator or author:* Blazij Bevk. V. Gorici [location?]: G. Juch.

1911—The Odyssey of Homer, Books VI–XIV, XVIII–XXIV; translation; edited with an introduction and notes by Edwin Fairley (English). *Translator or author:* Theodore Alois Buckley. New York, N.Y.: C. E. Merrill.

1911—Homer's Odyssey; a line-for-line translation in the metre of the original; with twenty-four illustrations by Patten Wilson (English). *Translator or author:* Henry Bernard Cotterill. London, England; Boston, Mass.: George G. Harrap; Dana Estes.

1911—Homere, L'Iliade, L'Odyssee; un volume orne de deux cartes et de plusieurs reproductions de Flaxman; 4th ed. (French). *Translator or author:* Auguste Henri Couat. Paris, France: H. and H. Oudin Lecaene.

1911—La Iliada Homero; version Castellana (Castilian Spanish). *Translator or author:* Juan B. Gergua. Madrid, Spain: Libreria Bergua.

1911—Homeri Iliakan Homer; bnagren targmanets (Armenian). *Translator or author:* Arsen Ghazaros Ghazikian. Venetik [location?]: Mkhitarean Tpagrutyun.

1911—Stories from the Odyssey; retold (English). *Translator or author:* Herbert Lord Havell. London, England: George G. Harrap.

1911—Homers Odyssee und Ilias im Auszuge; in neuer Ubersetzung (German). *Translator or author:* Oskar Hubatsch. Bielefeld, Germany; Leipzig, Germany: Velhagen und Klasing.

1911—Homeros Odyssee; Ubersetzung; herausgegeben und mit Anmerkungen versehen von Professor Dr. Ed[uard] Prigge (German). *Translator or author:* Wilhelm Jordan. Frankfurt am Main, Germany: Moritz Diesterweg.

1911—The Homeric Hymns; a new prose translation; and essays, literary and mythological (English). *Translator or author:* Andrew Lang. London, England: G. and Unwin Allen.

1911—The Iliad of Homer; done into English prose (English). *Translator or author:* Andrew Lang; Walter Leaf; Ernest Myers. London, England: Macmillan.

1911—The Iliad of Homer; translated into English blank verse (English). *Translator or author:* Arthur Gardner Lewis. New York, N.Y.: Baker and Taylor.

1911—The Odyssey of Homer; translated into English verse; edited, with introduction and notes by Edgar S. Shumway and Waldo Shumway (English). *Translator or author:* Alexander Pope. New York, N.Y.: Macmillan.

1911—The Iliad of Homer; translated; edited by Charles Elbert Rhodes with an introduction, notes, and a glossary (English). *Translator or author:* Alexander Pope. New York, N.Y.: Macmillan.

1911—The Odyssey of Homer; translated (English). *Translator or author:* Alexander Pope. London, England; New York, N.Y.: Henry Frowde.

1911—Schaidenreissers Odyssea, Augsburg, 1537; neudruck hrsg. von Friedrich Weidling (German). *Translator or author:* Simon Schaidenreisser. Leipzig, Germany: Kommission bei E. Avenarius.

1911—Homers Odyssee; neu ubertragen (German). *Translator or author:* Rudolf Alexander Schroder. Leipzig, Germany: Erschienen im Inselverlag.

1911—Homers Werke; ubersetzt; mit Einleitung, Anmerkungen, Namenregister und einer Darstellung der Homerischen Welt hrsg. Von Eduard Stemplinger (German). *Translator or author:* Johann Heinrich Voss. Berlin, Germany: Deutsches Verlagshaus Bong.

1911–12—The Iliad and Odyssey; edited by E. S. Shumway and Waldo Shumway [Odyssey] and C. Elbert Rhodes [Iliad] (English). *Translator or author:* Alexander Pope. New York, N.Y.

1911–12—Homerova Ilias; pereloezil (Czech). *Translator or author:* Antonin Skoda. Prague, Czechoslavakia: Ceska Akademie Caisaere Frantieska Josefa.

1911–13—[H]omerou Ilias; metaphrasis (Greek, Modern). *Translator or author:* Ioannes Spyridonos Zerbos. Athens, Greece: Ekdotikos Oikos Georgiou D. Phexe.

1911–15—Homeri Ilias; edidit Guilielmus Dindorf; 5th ed. (Greek). Leipzig, Germany: B. G. Teubner.

1911–19—Homeri Opera; recognovervnt breviqve adnotatione critica instrvxervnt David B. Monro et Thomas W. Allen (Greek). Oxford, England: Clarendon Press.

1912—Iliada Homer; utoazy A. Lange (Polish). Brody, Poland: Naktadem Kisnegarni F. Westa.

1912—Homeri Opera, Tom. V, Hymns, etc. [series: Oxford Classical Texts] (Greek). *Translator or author:* T. W. Allen. Oxford, England: Clarendon Press.

1912— Ulysses of Ithaca; translated from the German by George P[utnam] Upton (English). *Translator or author:* Karl Friedrich Becker. Chicago, Il.: A. C. McClurg.

1912— The Story of the Iliad (English). *Translator or author:* Edward Brooks. Penn Publishing.

1912— The Odyssey of Homer, with the Hymns, Epigrams, and Battle of the Frogs and Mice; literally translated, with explanatory notes (English). *Translator or author:* Theodore Alois Buckley. London, England: George Bell and Sons.

1912— The Odyssey of Homer; done into English prose (English). *Translator or author:* Samuel Henry Butcher; Andrew Lang. New York, N.Y.; London, England: Macmillan.

1912— The Whole Works of Homer [reprint of the 1612 edition; series: Caxton] (English). *Translator or author:* George Chapman. New York, N.Y.

1912— Odyssey; a line-for-line translation in the metre of the original; illus by Patten Wilson (English). *Translator or author:* Henry Bernard Cotterill. Boston, Mass.: George G. Harrap.

1912— The Iliad of Homer; translated into English hexameter verse: an abridgement which includes all the main story and the most celebrated passages (English). *Translator or author:* Prentiss Cummings. Boston, Mass.: Little Brown.

1912— The Iliad of Homer; translated; series: Everyman's Library (English). *Translator or author:* Edward George Geoffrey Smith Stanley, Earl of Derby. London, England; New York, N.Y.: J. M. Dent; E. P. Dutton.

1912— Homers Odysseifs-kvida; islenzkadi. *Translator or author:* Sveinbjorn Egilsson. Kaupmannahofn [location?]: S. L. Muller.

1912— Poemy Gomera v perevodakh Fneiiedicha I Zhukovskago; red. A. E. Gruzinskiaei; vstup. Ceteiiud Veiiach. Ivanova; slovar I 50 risunkov D. Flaksmana (Russian). *Translator or author:* Nikolaaei Ivanovich Gnedich. OKTO.

1912— Ilias; paraphrased in modern Greek; new ed. (Greek, Modern). *Translator or author:* A. Konstantinidos. Athens, Greece: I. Sideris.

1912— Lamb's Adventures of Ulysses (English). *Translator or author:* Charles Lamb. London, England: Thomas Nelson.

1912— The Iliad of Homer; done into English prose; abridged ed. (English). *Translator or author:* thor: Andrew Lang; Walter Leaf; Ernest Myers. New York, N.Y.; London, England: Macmillan.

1912— La Odisea; relatada a los nianos; con ilustraciones de W[illiam] Heath Robinson (Spanish). *Translator or author:* Jeanie Lang. Barcelona, Spain: R. de S. N. Araluce.

1912— The Iliad of Homer; translated into English blank verse (English). *Translator or author:* Arthur Gardner Lewis. New York, N.Y.

1912— The Odyssey (English). *Translator or author:* John William Mackail. London, England: John Murray.

1912— Iliade di Omero; tradotta; con riscontri su le varie stampe e con note per cura del Prof. Enrico Mestica (Italian). *Translator or author:* Vincenzo Monti. Florence, Italy: G. Barbera.

1912— The Odyssey of Homer; done into English verse (English). *Translator or author:* William Morris. New York, N.Y.: Green Longmans.

1912— The Odyssey of Homer (English). *Translator or author:* George Herbert Palmer. Boston, Mass; New York, N.Y.: Mifflin Houghton.

1912— [H]omerou Odysseia; metaphrasis (Greek, Modern). *Translator or author:* Iakovos Polylas. Athens, Greece: Ekdotikos Oikos Georgiou D. Phexe.

1912— Homer's Odyssey; translated, to which are added the Battle of the Frogs and Mice, by Parnell and The Hymns by Chapman and others, edited by J. S. Watson (English). *Translator or author:* Alexander Pope. London, England: George Bell.

1912— The Iliad (English). *Translator or author:* Alexander Pope. Macmillan.

1912— The Women of the Iliad; a metrical translation of the first book and of other passages in which women appear (English). *Translator or author:* Hugh Woodruff Taylor. New York, N.Y.

1912— Achilles; translated and abridged from the German of Carl Friedrich Becker (English). *Translator or author:* George Putnam Upton. Chicago, Il.: A. C. McClurg.

1912— Homers Ilias, ubersetzt; herausgegeben von Dr. Paul Brandt; dritsch Durchgesehene und erlauterte ausgabe (German). *Translator or author:* Johann Heinrich Voss. Leipzig, Germany: Bibliographisches Institut.

1912— Ilias; ubersetzt (German). *Translator or author:* Johann Heinrich Voss. Berlin, Germany: Spamersche Buchdruckerei.

1912–17— Homeri Carmina; cum prolegomenis,

notic criticis commentariis exegeticis, edidit J[an] Van Leeuwen. Leiden (Leyden), Netherlands: A. W. Sijthoff.

1912–20— Opera Homeri; recognoverunt brevique adnotatione critica instruxerunt David B[inning] Monro et Thomas W[illiam] Allen; 3rd ed. (Greek). Oxford, England: Clarendon Press.

1913— L'Odissea Libro XIV; con note Italiane del Prof. Giuseppe Bazzarin (Greek). Padova (Padua), Italy: Tipografia Edit. Del Seminario.

1913— The Iliad; translated into English prose; vol. II, Books XIII–XXIV [series: Bohn's Library] (English). London, England: George Bell.

1913— Himnos Homericos; vertidos directa y literalmente del Griego por vez primera a la prose Castellana (Castilian Spanish). *Translator or author:* Jose Banque y Faliu. Barcelona, Spain: De Serra Hnos. y Russel.

1913— Homers Odyssee; nach der Deutschen Ubersestzung des Johann Heinrich Voss neu bearbeitet; Volksausgabe mit 20 Textbildern von Alfred Renz (German). *Translator or author:* Jakob Bass. Stuttgart, Germany: Loewe.

1913— The Odyssey of Homer; translated (English). *Translator or author:* William Cowper. London, England; New York, N.Y.: J. M. and Sons Dent; E. P. Dutton.

1913— Ilias; ubersetzt (German). *Translator or author:* Thassilo Fritz Sheffer. Munich, Germany: G. Muller.

1913— Homers Odyssee [reprint of the 1781 edition] (German). *Translator or author:* Johann Heinrich Voss. Dusseldorf, Germany: E. Ohle.

1913— Homer (English). *Translator or author:* Arthur Sanders Way.

1913–24— Homerus Ilias; fur die Schulgebrauch erkart; 7th ed. *Translator or author:* Karl Friedrich Ameis; Carl Hentze. Leipzig, Germany; Berlin, Germany: B. G. Teubner.

1914— Ilias; cum annot. Heyn. Humphrey Milford.

1914— Die Gedichte Homers; bearbeitet von Oskar Hende; 5th ed. (Greek). Leipzig, Germany: B. G. Teubner.

1914— Il Libro VII dell'Odissea; con note Italiane del Prof. Luigi Cisorio; 2nd ed. (Greek). Milan, Italy; Rome, Italy: Sega Societe Editrice Dante Alighieri di Albrighi.

1914— L'Odissea Lib. XI; con note Italiane di Vincenzo Costanzi; 2nd ed. (Greek). Milan, Italy; Rome, Italy: Sega Societe Editrice Dante Alighieri di Albrighi.

1914— The Iliad of Homer, Book XXIV; edited by G[erald] M[aclean] Edwards [reprint of the 1894 edition]. Cambridge, England: Cambridge University Press.

1914— Homeri Iliadis Epitome Francisci Hocheggeri; in usum scholarum sextum edidit Augustinus Scheindler (Latin). Vienna, Austria: Carolus Gerold.

1914— Odyssea. Humphrey Milford.

1914— Odyssee, Gesange 1–6; fur den Schul- und privatge-brauch erklart von Richard Mollweide [no more were published]. St. Ludwig [location?]: Mollweide.

1914— The Odyssey of Homer, Book IX; edited by G[erald] M[aclean] Edwards. Cambridge, England: Cambridge University Press.

1914— The Iliad of Homer; rendered into English prose for the use of those who cannot read the original (English). *Translator or author:* Samuel Butler. London, England: A. C. Fifield.

1914— The Story of the Iliad; with illus. after Flaxman (English). *Translator or author:* Alfred John Church. New York, N.Y.: Macmillan.

1914— The Story of the Odyssey [of] Homer (English). *Translator or author:* Alfred John Church. New York, N.Y.: Macmillan.

1914— The Story of the Odyssey; with illustrations after Flaxman; 5th ed. (English). *Translator or author:* Alfred John Church. London, England: Service Seeley.

1914— L'Iliade [d']Homere; (textes choisis), avec des analyses et des notes (French). *Translator or author:* Maurice Croiset. Paris, France: Armand Colin.

1914— The Iliad of Homer; translated; series: Everyman's Library (English). *Translator or author:* Edward George Geoffrey Smith Stanley, Earl of Derby. London, England; New York, N.Y.: J. M. Dent; E. P. Dutton.

1914— Hesiod, the Homeric Hymns, and Homerica; with an English tranlsation (Greek; English). *Translator or author:* Hugh Gerard Evelyn-White. London, England; New York, N.Y.: William Heinemann; Macmillan.

1914— Iliad; done into English prose; Globe edition (English). *Translator or author:* Andrew Lang; Walter Leaf; Ernest Myers. London, England: Macmillan.

1914— Des Odysseus Erbe: Eine Tragodie in Drei

Aufzeugen (German). *Translator or author:* Georg Terramare. Berlin, Germany: E. Reiss.

1914—Odyssee; Deutsch; bearb. von E. R. Weiss (German). *Translator or author:* Johann Heinrich Voss. Leipzig, Germany: Tempel-Verlag.

1914–15—Ilias; edidit Guilielmus Dindorf, editio quinta correctier quam curavit C. Hentse; Editio Stereotypa. Leipzig, Germany: B. G. Teubner.

1914–27—Ilias. *Translator or author:* E. Bethe. Leipzig, Germany.

1915—Homer's Iliad, Book I; edited for the use of schools by John Bond and A[rthur] S[umner] Walpole; with notes and vocabulary; with illustrations (Greek). London, England; Glasgow, Scotland: Macmillan; University Press.

1915—Hymni Homerici Accedentibus Epigrammatis et Batrachomyomachia Homero Vulgo Attributis; ex recensione Augusti Baumeister; Editio Stereotypa (Greek). Leipzig, Germany: B. G. Teubner.

1915—Il Libro XIV dell'Odissea Omero; con note Italiane del Salvatore Rossi (Greek). Livorno, Italy: Raffaello Giusti.

1915—The Odyssey of Homer, Books VI and VII; with notes and vocabulary by G[erald] Maclean] Edwards [series: Cambridge Elementary Classics] (Greek). London, England; New York, N.Y.: Cambridge University Press.

1915—The Iliad of Homer; translated into English hexameter verse; an abridgment (English). *Translator or author:* Prentiss Cummings. Boston, Mass.: Little.

1915—aUrvals'mttir aur Odysseifskviu Haomers eptir'ay ingu Sveinbjarnar Egilssonar me nokkrum athugasemdum og skayringum [Odyssey, selections] (Icelandic). *Translator or author:* Sveinbjorn Egilsson. Reykjavik, Iceland: Sigfausar Eymundssonar.

1915—Homeric Hymns and Homerica; Hesiod [series: Loeb Classical Library] (Greek; English). *Translator or author:* Hugh Gerard Evelyn-White. New York, N.Y.: G. P. Putnam.

1915—Stories from the Odyssey, Retold (English). *Translator or author:* Herbert Lord Havell. London, England: George G. Harrap.

1915—The Homeric Hymns; a new prose translation, and essays, literary and mythological (English). *Translator or author:* Andrew Lang. New York, N.Y.; London, England: Green Longmans; George Allen & Unwin.

1915—The Iliad of Homer; done into English

prose; revised ed. [reprinted from the 1883 edition printed in London] (English). *Translator or author:* Andrew Lang; Walter Leaf; Ernest Myers. New York, N.Y.: Macmillan.

1915—Homerova Odiseja; preveo T. Maretiac; treace (matiacino drugo) izdanje (Serbo-Croatian). *Translator or author:* Tomislav Maretiac. Zagreb, Croatia: Matica Hrvatska.

1915—The Battle in the River Scamander and the Death of Hector; Books XXI and XXII of Pope's translation of the Iliad (English). *Translator or author:* Alexander Pope. Humphrey Milford.

1915—Homers Ilias im Auszuge nach der Ubersetzung von J[ohann] H[einrich] Voss; bearbeitet von Franz Kern (German). *Translator or author:* Johann Heinrich Voss. Bielefeld, Germany: Velhagen und Klasing.

1915–21—Homeri Ilias; edidit Guilielmus Dindorf; quam curavit C. Hentze; 5th ed., Stereotype Ed. (Greek). Leipzig, Germany: B. G. Teubner.

1916—Odyssee, mit einer ubersicht der handschriftlichen Lesarten und mit erklarenden Anmerkungen, heraugeben von N. Wecklein (Greek). Hamburg, Germany: C. C. Buchners.

1916—Odyssey, Books XIII–XXIV; with introduction, notes, etc. by W[illiam] W[alter] Merry (Greek). Oxford, England: Clarendon Press.

1916—Odysseun harharetket (Finnish). Porvoo, Finland: W. Soderstrom.

1916—Il Libro XX dell'Iliade, con note Italiane del prof. Luigi Cognasso (Greek). Livorno, Italy: Raffaello Giusti.

1916—Homeri Opera (Greek). *Translator or author:* Allen. Oxford, England.

1916—Iliad Ibant Obsevri; an Experiment in the Classical Hexameter (English). *Translator or author:* Robert Seymour Bridges. Oxford, England: Clarendon Press.

1916—The Iliad of Homer; translated into English blank verse; with illustrations by John Flaxman [reprint of the 1870 edition] (English). *Translator or author:* William Cullen Bryant. Boston, Mass.; Cambridge, Engand: Houghton Mifflin; Riverside Press.

1916—Odyssey (English). *Translator or author:* Samuel Henry Butcher; Andrew Lang. New York, N.Y.

1916—The Story of the Iliad; with illustrations after Flaxman (English). *Translator or author:* Alfred John Church. New York, N.Y.: Macmillan.

1916—The Iliad and the Odyssey [reprint of the

1791 edition] (English). *Translator or author:* William Cowper. J. M. Dent.

1916— Odyssey, Books IX–XIV [reprinted from the 1891 edition] (English). *Translator or author:* John Hampden Haydon; Arthur Hadrian Allcroft.

1916— The Iliad of Homer; done into English prose; abridged edition (English). *Translator or author:* Andrew Lang; Walter Leaf; Ernest Myers. New York, N.Y.; London, England: Macmillan.

1916— Homers Ilias; 2nd ed. (German). *Translator or author:* Hans Georg Meyer. Berlin, Germany: Trowitzsch and Son.

1916— The Toils and Travels of Odysseus (English). *Translator or author:* Cyril Arthington Pease. London, England: Wells, Gardner, Darton.

1916— L'Odissea; tradotta; con prefazzione e commento di Vittorio Turri; 6th ed con saggi delle versioni di G. Leopardi, P. Maspero, G. Mazzoni, G. Pascoli; con illustrazioni di monumenti antichi (Italian). *Translator or author:* Ippolito Pindemonte. Florence, Italy: G. C. Sansoni.

1916— Odysseen oversat af Christian Wilster; Ny udgave, gennemset og rettet af M. C. Gertz; 2nd ed. (Danish). *Translator or author:* Christian Frederik Emil Wilster. Copenhagen, Denmark: Gyldendalske.

1916–19— Homeri Opera; recognovit brevique adnotatione critica instruxerunt David B[inning] Monro ... et Thomas W[illiam] Allen; 3rd ed. (Greek). Oxford, England: Clarendon Press.

1917— Odyssea; cum notis criticis, commentariis exegeticis, indicibus ad ultrumque epos pertinentibus, edidit J[an] van Leeuwen (Latin). Leiden (Leyden), Netherlands: A. W. Sijthoff.

1917— The First Book of Homer's Iliad; with a vocabulary; some account of Greek prosody and an appendix by John T. White (Greek). New York, N.Y.: Green Longmans.

1917— The Iliad, Book XXII; edited with introduction, notes and appendices, by G[erald] M[aclean] Edwards (Greek). Cambridge, England: Cambridge University Press.

1917— Homer's Iliad [series: Student's Interlinear Translation] (English). New York, N.Y.

1917— Iliad, XXIV; ibant obscuri; exper. in classical hexameter. *Translator or author:* Robert Seymour Bridges.

1917— The Odyssey of Homer; done into English prose (English). *Translator or author:* Samuel Henry Butcher; Andrew Lang. New York, N.Y.; London, England: Macmillan.

1917— The Adventures of Ulysses; edited by Francis Kingsley Ball; illustrated Otho Cushing (English). *Translator or author:* Charles Lamb. Boston, Mass; New York, N.Y.: Ginn.

1917— The Iliad of Homer; done into English prose; abridged edition (English). *Translator or author:* Andrew Lang; Walter Leaf; Ernest Myers. New York, N.Y.: Macmillan.

1917— The Toils and Travels of Odysseus (English). *Translator or author:* Cyril Arthington Pease. London, England: Wells, Gardner, Darton.

1918— Homeri Odyssea; 5th ed. (Greek). Leipzig, Germany: B. G. Teubner.

1918— The Odyssey of Homer; done into English prose (English). *Translator or author:* Samuel Henry Butcher; Andrew Lang. London, England: Macmillan.

1918— The Odyssey of Homer; done into English prose (English). *Translator or author:* Samuel Henry Butcher; Andrew Lang. New York, N.Y.: Carlton House.

1918— The Children's Homer: the Adventures of Odysseus and the Tale of Troy; illustrated by Willy Pogany [1st ed.] (English). *Translator or author:* Padriac Colum; Willy Pogany. New York, N.Y.: Macmillan.

1918— Homers Ilias; met Anmerkingen von Ed. Prigge; als Anhang: Goethes Achilleis; 2nd ed. (German). *Translator or author:* Wilhelm Jordan. Frankfurt am Main, Germany: Moritz Diesterweg.

1918— Iliada; prevod. *Translator or author:* Georgi Popov. Sofija (Sofia), Bulgaria: S. D. Kazankalov.

1918— First book of the Iliad. *Translator or author:* W. H. A. Quilliam.

1918— Homers Odyssee; neu ubertragen (German). *Translator or author:* Rudolf Alexander Schroder. Leipzig, Germany: Insel-Verlag.

1918— Prigodi Odisseia; opovidanne dlia molodizhi. *Translator or author:* Mikhailo Sonevitskii. L'viv (Lwow), Ukraine.

1918— Odyssee Homer; ubersetzt (German). *Translator or author:* Thassilo Von Scheffer. Munich, Germany: G. Muller.

1918— Die Batrachomyomachia in England [includes early texts]. *Translator or author:* Friedrich Wild. Vienna, Austria: W. Braumuller.

1918–19— Ilias; quartum ediderunt J. van Leeuwen et M. B. Mendes da Costa. *Translator or author:* Jan van Leeuwen; Maurits Benjamin

Mendes da Costa. Leiden (Leyden), Netherlands: A. W. Sijthoff.

1919—Ilias; Schulausgabe von Paul Caucer; 3rd printing of 2nd ed. (Greek). Vienna, Austria; Leipzig, Germany: F. F. Tempsky; G. Freytag.

1919—Il Libro XIX dell'Odissea; con introduzione e note di Frederico Carlo Wick (Greek). Torino (Turin), Italy; Milan, Italy: G. B. Paravia.

1919—Homers Iliade; erklart von J[ohann] U[lrich] Faesi; besorgt von J. Sitzler; 7th ed. (Greek). Berlin, Germany: Weidmannsche Buchhandlung.

1919—Il Libro XVIII dell'Iliade; con note grammaticali lessicali ed esegetiche a cura de Antonio Lantrua (Greek). Torino (Turin), Italy: Libreria Editrice Internazionale.

1919—Iliade; tradotta e annotata (Italian). *Translator or author:* Nicola Festa. Milan, Italy: R. Sandron.

1919—Odyssevskvaedet Homer; paa norskt; 2nd ed. (Norwegian). *Translator or author:* Arne Garborg. Kristiania [Norway?]: Aschehoug.

1919—The Iliad of Homer; done into English prose; rev. ed. [reprint of the 1914 edition] (English). *Translator or author:* Andrew Lang; Walter Leaf; Ernest Myers. London, England: Macmillan.

1919—Ilias; suomentanut (Finnish). *Translator or author:* Otto Manninen. Porvoo, Finland: W. Soderstrom.

1919—Homeri Opera; recognovervnt breviqve adnotatione critica instrvxervnt; 3rd ed. (Greek). *Translator or author:* David Binning Monro; Thomas William Allen. Oxford, England: Clarendon Press.

1919—L'Iliade; tradotta, con commento di Vittorio Turri; con illustrazioni di Monumenti Antichi; 6th ed. (Italian). *Translator or author:* Vincenzo Monti. Florence, Italy: G. C. Sansoni.

1919—The Odyssey; with an English translation (Greek; English). *Translator or author:* Augustus Taber Murray. London, England: William Heinemann.

1919—The Odyssey; with an English translation [series: Loeb Classical Library] (Greek; Latin). *Translator or author:* Augustus Taber Murray. Cambridge, Mass.; New York, N.Y.: Harvard University Press; G.P. Putnam's Sons.

1919—The Iliad of Homer; translated [reprint of the 1902 edition] (English). *Translator or author:* Alexander Pope. London, England; New York,

N.Y.: Humphrey Milford; Oxford University Press.

1919—Idissea; tradducio (Catalan). *Translator or author:* Carles Riba. Mallorca, Spain: Editorial Catalana.

1919—Homero Iliada; version Castellana (Spanish). *Translator or author:* Manuel Vallve. Barcelona, Spain: Editorial Iberica.

1920—Homer's Odyssey; Book I, edited for the uses of schools with introduction, notes and vocabulary by John Bond and A[rthur] S[umner] Walpole (Greek). London, England: Macmillan.

1920—Odyssey, Book X; edited by G[erald] M[aclean] Edwards (Greek). Cambridge, England: Cambridge University Press.

1920—Il Libro VII dell'Iliade; con note Italiane del Prol Salvatore Rossi; 2nd ed. (Greek). Livorno, Italy: Raffaello Giusti.

1920—Iliad, Vol. I, Books I–XII; edited by D[avid] B[inning] Monro and T[homas] W[illiam] Allen; 3rd ed. (Greek). Oxford, England: Clarendon Press.

1920—Die Odyssee; bearbeitet von Prof. Dr. Oskar Henke; besorgt von Prof. Dr. George Siefert (Greek). Leipzig, Germany; Berlin, Germany: B. G. Teubner.

1920—The Odyssey of Homer; done into English prose; abridged ed. (English). *Translator or author:* Samuel Henry Butcher; Andrew Lang. New York, N.Y.: Macmillan.

1920—The Iliad and the Odyssey; a prose translation [reprint of the 1898 edition] (English). *Translator or author:* Samuel Butler. London, England: Jonathan Cape.

1920—Homers Ilias in verkurzter Ausgabe fur den Schulgebrauch; 4th ed. *Translator or author:* Augustin Theodore Christ. Vienna, Austria: F. F. Tempsky.

1920—The Iliad for Boys and Girls; told from Homer in simple language, with twelve illustrations in colour (English). *Translator or author:* Alfred John Church. New York, N.Y.: Macmillan.

1920—The Children's Homer: the Adventures of Odysseus and the Tale of Troy; illustrated by Willy Pogany [reprint of the 1918 edition] (English). *Translator or author:* Padraic Colum; Willy Pogany. London, England: George G. Harrap.

1920—The Odyssey of Homer; translated (English). *Translator or author:* William Cowper. London, England; New York, N.Y.: J. M. and Sons Dent; E. P. Dutton.

1920—Hesiod, the Homeric Hymns, and Homerica; with an English translation (Greek; English). *Translator or author:* Hugh Gerard Evelyn-White. London, England; New York, N.Y.: William Heinemann; G. P. Putnam.

1920—Homara Gatha (Indian). *Translator or author:* Giraja Kumara Ghoska. Prayaga, India: Sahitya Bhavana.

1920—Stories from the Iliad (English). *Translator or author:* Herbert Lord Havell.

1920—Homeros' Odyssee; fran Grekisan; 2nd ed. *Translator or author:* Erland L. Lagerlof. Lund, Sweden: C. W. K. Gleerup.

1920—Adventures of Odysseus; re-told from Homer in English prose (English). *Translator or author:* Francis Sydney Marvin. J. M. Dent.

1920—Homeri Opera; recognoverunt brevique adnotatione critica instruxerunt; 3rd ed. (Greek). *Translator or author:* David Binning Monro; Thomas William Allen. Oxford, England: Clarendon Press.

1920—L'Iliade, tradotta, con commento di Vittorio Turri; con illustrazioni di Monumenti Antichi; 6th ed. (Italian). *Translator or author:* Vincenzo Monti. Florence, Italy: G. C. Sansoni.

1920—The Odyssey of Homer; translated into English verse; edited, with introduction and notes by Edgar S[olomon] Shumway and Waldo Shumway (English). *Translator or author:* Alexander Pope. New York, N.Y.: Macmillan.

1920—Ilias Homer; ubersetzt; 2nd ed. (German). *Translator or author:* Thassilo Fritz H. von Scheffer. Berlin, Germany: Propylaen-Verlag.

1920—Odissea; traduzione e note (Italian). *Translator or author:* Marino de Szombathely. Bologna, France: L. Cappelli.

1920—Odyssee; Abdruck der 1. Ausg. (German). *Translator or author:* Johann Heinrich Voss. Leipzig, Germany: Philipp Reclam jun.

1920—Die Irrfahrten des Odysseus (German). *Translator or author:* Johann Heinrich Voss. Berlin, Germany: Heyder.

1920—Homers Ilias (German). *Translator or author:* Johann Heinrich Voss. Leipzig, Germany: Philipp Reclam jun.

1920—Homers Odyssee ubersetzt; mit 24 Originallithographien und Buchschmuck von Alois Kolb (German). *Translator or author:* Johann Heinrich Voss. Frankfurt am Main, Germany: Frankfurter Verlags.

1920–28—Odysee fur den Schulgebrauch, erklart von Karl Friedr[ich] Ameis und Carl Hentze (Greek). Berlin, Germany: B. G. Teubner.

1920s—Odisea; traduccion nueva del Griego por Leconte de Lisle; version Espanola de Nicasio Hernandez Luquero (Spanish). *Translator or author:* Nicasio Hernandez Luquero. Valencia [Spain?]: Prometeo.

1920s—L'Iliade [di] Omero; traduzione; precede uno studio di Ermanno Grimm (Italian). *Translator or author:* Vincenzo Monti. Milan, Italy: Istituto Editoriale Italiano.

1920s—Odyssee, auf Grund der Ubersetzungen von Johann Heinrich Voss; bearb. von E[mil] R[udof] Weiss (Greek; German). *Translator or author:* Johann Heinrich Voss. Berlin, Germany: Tempel-Verlag.

1920s—Homers Werke in zwei Banden; ubersetzt; sowie einer literarhistorischen Einleitung von Gotthold Klee (German). *Translator or author:* Johann Heinrich Voss. Leipzig, Germany: Hesse & Becker.

1921—L'Odyssee, Principaux Chants (I, II, V, VI, IX, XI, XXII, XXIII); avec une introduction et des notes par Maurice Croiset; 6th ed. (Greek). Paris, France: Armand Colin.

1921—Pages Choisies des Grandes Ecrivains: Homere; avec une introduction par Maurice Croiset. Paris, France: Armand Colin.

1921—Iliad, Book XXI; with introduction, notes and vocabulary by A[ubrey] C[harles] Price (Greek). Cambridge, England: Cambridge University Press.

1921—Homere Illustre: Iliade, Odyssee; poemes Homerique, avec index et remarques sur la grammaire, la versification et le style Homerique par Ch[arles] Georgin (Greek). Paris, France: A. Hatier.

1921—[H]omerou Epe: Ilias, Odysseia (Greek). Leipzig, Germany: Insel-Verlag.

1921—Homero, La Iliada. Universidad Nacional de Mexico.

1921—The Homeric Catalogue of Ships [Iliad, Book II]; edited with a commentary by Thomas W. Allen (Greek). Oxford, England: Clarendon Press.

1921—La Odisea (Spanish). Universidad Nacional de Mexico.

1921—The Odyssey, Books I–XII; literally translated with explanatory notes (English). *Translator or author:* Theodore Alois Buckley. Harrisburg, Pa.: Handy Book.

1921— The Odyssey of Homer; done into English prose (English). *Translator or author:* Samuel Henry Butcher; Andrew Lang. New York, N.Y.: Modern Library.

1921— The Odyssey of Homer; done in English prose (English). *Translator or author:* Samuel Henry Butcher; Andrew Lang. New York, N.Y.; London, England: Macmillan.

1921— The Odyssey; rendered into English prose for the use of those who cannot read the original; 2nd ed. (English). *Translator or author:* Samuel Butler. New York, N.Y.: E. P. Dutton.

1921— The Iliad of Homer; rendered into English prose for the use of those who cannot read the original (English). *Translator or author:* Samuel Butler. London, England: Jonathan Cape.

1921— The Odyssey; translated into English, in the original metre; with a preface by the Rev. A. A. Davis (English). *Translator or author:* Francis Caulfeild. London, England: George Bell.

1921— The Story of the Iliad; edited for school use (English). *Translator or author:* Alfred John Church. New York, N.Y.; London, England: Macmillan.

1921— The Iliad of Homer; translated; series: Everyman's Library (English). *Translator or author:* Edward George Geoffrey Smith Stanley, Earl of Derby. London, England; New York, N.Y.: J. M. Dent; E. P. Dutton.

1921— Stories from the Odyssey, Retold [series: Told Through the Ages] (English). *Translator or author:* Herbert Lord Havell. London, England: George G. Harrap.

1921— The Adventures of Ulysses; edited by Ernest A[rthur] Gardner (English). *Translator or author:* Charles Lamb. Cambridge, England: Cambridge University Press.

1921— The Iliad of Homer; done into English prose; revised ed. (English). *Translator or author:* Andrew Lang; Walter Leaf; Ernest Myers. London, England: Macmillan.

1921— Homerova Ilijada; preveo i protumaecio T. Maretiac. *Translator or author:* Tomislav Maretiac. Zagreb, Croatia: Matica Hrvatska.

1921— Homer forsog til en ny oversaettelse; Iliadens f'irste sang (Danish). *Translator or author:* Carl V. Ostergaard. Copenhagen, Denmark: A. Marcus.

1921— The Odyssey of Homer; revised ed. (English). *Translator or author:* George Herbert Palmer. Boston, Mass.: Houghton Mifflin.

1921— The Iliad of Homer, Books I, VI, XXII, XXIV; edited for school use by W[ilfred] W[esley] Cressy and W[illiam] V[aughn] Moody; revised ed. (English). *Translator or author:* Alexander Pope. Chicago, Il.: Foresman Scott.

1921— Iliad, Book XXI; with introduction, notes and vocabulary (Greek). *Translator or author:* Aubrey Charles Price. Cambridge University Press.

1921— Odisceja; vertce d-ras J. Ralys. *Translator or author:* J. Ralys. Kaunas, Lithuwania: eSvietimo Ministerijos Leidinys.

1921— Odysseia (Czech). *Translator or author:* Otmar Vaenorny; Ferdinand Stieblitz. Prague, Czechoslavakia: J. Laichter.

1921— [H]omeros; emmetre kai piste metaphrasis me scholia dai semeioseis (Greek, Modern?). *Translator or author:* Paulos Valdasseridis. Larnaca (Larnax), Cyprus: Skala.

1921–22— L'Iliade d'Omero; introduzione e note di Roberto d'Alfonso (Italian). *Translator or author:* Vincenzo Monti. Torino (Turin), Italy: Unione Tipografico-Editrice Torinese.

1921–23— L'Iliade; commentata da C. O. Zuretti (Greek). Torino (Turin), Italy: G. Chiantore.

1922— [H]omerou Odysseia = Homers Odyssee; schulausgabe von Paul Cauer; 5th ed. (Greek). Leipzig, Germany: G. Freytag.

1922— Ilias; Odyssea. New York, N.Y.: Knopf.

1922— Ilias; erzahlt von Ferdinand Schmidt; illustriert von M. von Kaulback und Flaxman; mit einem Vorwort von A. Huhnhauser; 13th ed. (German). Rostock, Germany: A. Oehmigke.

1922— The Odyssey of Homer; done into English prose (English). *Translator or author:* Samuel Henry Butcher; Andrew Lang. London, England: Macmillan.

1922— The Odyssey; rendered into English prose for the use of those who cannot read the original (English). *Translator or author:* Samuel Butler. New York, N.Y.: E. P. Dutton.

1922— The Odyssey; rendered into English prose for the use of those who cannot read the original; 2nd ed. (English). *Translator or author:* Samuel Butler. London, England: Jonathan Cape.

1922— Iliada; w przekiadzie; zrewidowai, wstnepem i komentarzem opatrzyi Tadeusz Sinko (Polish). *Translator or author:* Franciszek Ksawery Dmochowski. Krakow, Poland: Nakiadem Kradowskiej Spoiki Wydawniczej.

1922— The Wrath of Achilles; translated from the Iliad into quantitative hexameters (English). *Translator or author:* George Ernle. London, England: Humphrey Milford; Oxford University Press.

1922— Hesiod, the Homeric Hymns, and Homerica; with an English translation (Greek, English). *Translator or author:* Hugh Gerard Evelyn-White. London, England; New York, N.Y.: William Heinemann; G. P. Putnam's Sons.

1922— Homers Iliade; ubersetzung [von Holderlin] der ersten zwei Bucher, herausgeben von Ludwig von Pigenot (German). *Translator or author:* Friedrich Holderlin. Berlin, Germany: Propylaen-Verlag.

1922— Wawatjan Praboe Odysseus Karaganana Homerus; disoendakeun koe Kartadinata. *Translator or author:* Kartadinata. Weltevreden [location?]: Commissie voor de Volkslectuur.

1922— The Iliad of Homer; done into English prose; revised ed. (English). *Translator or author:* Andrew Lang; Walter Leaf; Ernest Myers. London, England: Macmillan.

1922— The Iliad of Homer; done into English prose; abridged ed. (English). *Translator or author:* Andrew Lang; Walter Leaf; Ernest Myers. New York, N.Y.; London, England: Macmillan.

1922— Thirty-two Passages from the Iliad, in English Rhymed Verse (English). *Translator or author:* C. D. Locock. London, England: G. and Unwin Allen.

1922— Odyssey; revised edition [series: Riverside Literature] (English). *Translator or author:* George Herbert Palmer. Constable.

1922— Ilias; auf Grund der Ubersetzungen von Johann Heinrich Voss verdeutscht von Hans Rupe (Greek, German). *Translator or author:* Hans Rupe. Berlin, Germany: Tempel-Verlag.

1922— Odyssee; 2nd ed. (German). *Translator or author:* Thassilo Fritz H. von Scheffer. Berlin, Germany: Propylaen-Verlag.

1922— Odysseja, przekiadzie wstnepem i objanieniami zaopatrzyi Tadeusz Sinko (Polish). *Translator or author:* Lucjan Hipolit Siemienski. Krakow, Poland: Nakiadem Krakowskiej Spoiki Wydawniczej.

1922— Homer's Iliad; 3rd ed. *Translator or author:* D. J. Snider. St. Louis, Mo.

1922— Homerowa Ilijada; Z originala a z jeho meeru zeserbesacii a wudai M. Ruban-Turjan. *Translator or author:* Matej Urban. W Budyesinje [Poland?]: Z naki.wudawarja.

1922— Homers Ilias; mit 24 Originallithographien und Buchschmuck von Alois Kolb (German). *Translator or author:* Johann Heinrich Voss. Frankfurt am Main, Germany: Frankfurter Verlags.

1923— Ein Kerngedicht der Ilias; aufgebaut auf den Zusammenhang der Ilias mit dem Prometheus Mythos (German). Freiburg, Switzerland: B. J. Bielefeld.

1923— Il Libro X dell'Odissea; con note Italiane del Prof. Salvatore Rossi; 2nd ed. (Greek). Livorno, Italy: Raffaello Giusti.

1923— The Iliad of Homer; edited with general and grammatical introductions, notes and appendices by Walter Leaf and M. A. Bayfield (Greek). London, England: Macmillan.

1923— Iliada lui Homer. Bucuresti (Bucharest), Romania: Casa Scoalelor.

1923— Ilias, Vierundzwanzigster Gesang; wie Hektor beweint und bestattet wurde (German). Stuttgart, Germany: Julius Hoffmann.

1923— Homer's Iliad, Books I–VI; literally translated with explanatory notes; with a brief introduction by James Kendrick (English). *Translator or author:* Theodore Alois Buckley. New York, N.Y.: Translation Publishing.

1923— The Odyssey of Homer; done into English prose; abridged ed. (English). *Translator or author:* Samuel Henry Butcher; Andrew Lang. New York, N.Y.; London, England: Macmillan.

1923— The Iliad of Homer; rendered into English prose for the use of those who cannot read the original (English). *Translator or author:* Samuel Butler. New York, N.Y.: E. P. Dutton.

1923— The Odyssey; translated into English, in the original metre; with a preface by A. A. David [series: Bohn's Popular Library] (English). *Translator or author:* Francis Caulfeild. London, England: George Bell.

1923— The Odyssey for Boys and Girls; told from Homer (English). *Translator or author:* Alfred John Church. New York, N.Y.: Macmillan.

1923— The Story of the Odyssey (English). *Translator or author:* Alfred John Church. New York, N.Y.: Macmillan.

1923— Ulysses' Tale of Wanderings; ballad version from Homer's Odyssey (English). *Translator or author:* Isaac Flagg. East Aurora, N.Y.: Roycrofters.

1923— Stories from the Odyssey; retold (English). *Translator or author:* Herbert Lord Havell. New York, N.Y.: T. Y. Crowell.

1923— La Iliada; traducida (Spanish). *Translator or author:* Jose Gomez Hermosilla. Madrid, Spain: Hernando.

1923— The Iliad of Homer; done into English prose; rev. ed. (English). *Translator or author:* Andrew Lang; Walter Leaf; Ernest Myers. London, England: Macmillan.

1923— Odyssee; traduit d'Homere (French). *Translator or author:* Leconte de Lisle. Paris, France: Alphonse Lemerre.

1923— Thirty-two Passages from the Odyssey; in English rhymed verse (English). *Translator or author:* C. D. Locock. London, England: G. and Unwin Allen.

1923— Un Paladin de la Iliade. *Translator or author:* Leopoldo Lugones. Buenos Aires, Argentina: Babel.

1923— Homers Odyssee; Deutsch; 4th ed. (German). *Translator or author:* Hans Georg Meyer. Berlin, Germany: J. Springer.

1923— Homers Odyssee; new ubertragen (German). *Translator or author:* Rudolf Alexander Schroder. Leipzig, Germany: Insel-Verlag.

1923— Ilias und Odyssee Homer[s]; Deutsch; mit Bildern von Bonaventura Genelli und einer Einleitung von Max von Boehn (German). *Translator or author:* Johann Heinrich Voss. Berlin, Germany: Askanischen Verlag.

1923— Ilias; ubersetzt; text der ersten Ausgabe; mit einem Nachwort von Curt Woyte; new ed. (German). *Translator or author:* Johann Heinrich Voss. Leipzig, Germany: Philipp Reclam jun.

1923–24— [H]omerou Poiesis. Florence, Italy: Leonem S. Olschki.

1923–24— [H]omerou Poiesis (Greek). Munich, Germany: Bremer Presse.

1923–28— Odyssey; with introduction, notes, etc. by W[illiam] W[alter] Merry (Greek). Oxford, England: Clarendon Press.

1924— The Iliad of Homer; edited with general and grammatical introductions, notes, and appendices by Walter Leaf and M[atthew] A[lbert] Bayfield (Greek). London, England: Macmillan.

1924— Il Libro XXII dell'Iliade; con note Italiane del Prof. Salvatore Rossi; 3rd ed. (Greek). Livorno, Italy: Raffaello Giusti.

1924— Homeri Ilias; edidit Guilielmus Dindorf; 5th ed. (Greek). Leipzig, Germany: B. G. Teubner.

1924— The Odyssey of Homer, Book XI; edited with introduction, notes, vocabulary, and appen-

dices by J[ohn] A[rbuthnot] Nairn (Greek). Cambridge, England: Cambridge University Press.

1924— Homeri Odyssea; edidit Guilielmus Dindorf; 5th ed. (Greek). Leipzig, Germany: B. G. Teubner.

1924— Homere, Poesie Homerique [Oeuvres; texte et traduction] (Greek; French). *Translator or author:* Victor Berard. Paris, France: Societe d'Edition "Les Belles Lettres".

1924— Altionische Gotterlieder unter dem Namen Homers; Deutsch von Rudolf Borchardt (German). *Translator or author:* Rudolf Borchardt. Munich, Germany: Bremer Presse.

1924— The Story of the Iliad (English). *Translator or author:* Edward Brooks. Philadelphia, Pa.: Penn Publishing.

1924— The Iliad of Homer; translated into English blank verse (English). *Translator or author:* William Cullen Bryant. Boston, Mass.: Houghton Mifflin.

1924— The Odyssey of Homer; done into English prose; with twenty plates in colour after the water-colour drawings by W. Russell Flint (English). *Translator or author:* Samuel Henry Butcher; Andrew Lang. London, England; Boston, Mass.: Medici Society.

1924— Omero, l'Iliade; con incisioni di A. de Carolis (Italian). *Translator or author:* A. de Carolis. Bologna, France: N. Zanichelli.

1924— The Whole Works of Homer ... in his Iliads, and Odysseys; translated according to the Greek (English). *Translator or author:* George Chapman. London, England: Chatto and Windus.

1924— Homer's Odyssey; a line-for-line translation in the metre of the original; with an introduction by Walter Leaf (English). *Translator or author:* Henry Bernard Cotterill. London, England: George G. Harrap.

1924— Homeri Odisakan; bnagren targmanets (Armenian). *Translator or author:* Arsen Gharzaros Ghazikian. Venetik-S Ghazar [location?]: Mkhitarean Tpagrutyun.

1924— Iliad un Odyssey; ausderwelte ilustrirte derzeilungen far kinder (Yiddish). *Translator or author:* Golda [or Gilda Patz] Katz. Berlin, Germany: Gescher.

1924— Iliade; tradotta (Italian). *Translator or author:* Vincenzo Monti. Florence, Italy: A. Salani.

1924— The Odyssey [of] Homer; with an English translation (Greek; English). *Translator or author:*

Augustus Taber Murray. London, England; New York, N.Y.: William Heinemann; G. P. Putnam's Sons.

1924— The Iliad; with an English translation (Greek; English). *Translator or author:* Augustus Taber Murray. London; New York, N.Y.; Cambridge, Mass.: William Heinemann; G. P. Putnam's Sons; Harvard U.

1924— Iliad, 22nd Book. *Translator or author:* Alexander Anastasius Pallis.

1924— Boy's Iliad and Odyssey (English). *Translator or author:* Walter Copland Perry.

1924— The Iliad of Homer translated; edited by Charles Elbert Rhodes; with an introduction, notes, and a glossary (English). *Translator or author:* Alexander Pope. New York, N.Y.: Macmillan.

1924— Odysseja; z Greckiego przei i przedm poprzedzii; Rzecz o Homerze napisai Ryszard Ganszyniec (Polish). *Translator or author:* Jozef Wittlin. L'viv (Lwow), Ukraine: H. Alterberg.

1925— Homer's Iliad, Book 1; edited for the use of schools with notes and vocabulary, by Rev. John Bond and A. S. Walpole (Greek). London, England: Macmillan.

1925— Homer, Odyssey, Books VII–XII; with introduction, notes, and table of Homeric forms by W[illiam] W[alter] Merry (Greek). Oxford, England: Clarendon Press.

1925— [H]omerou Poiemata; text aus der Uberlieferung hergestellt von August Scheindler (Greek). Vienna, Austria: Osterreichischer Bundesverlag.

1925— Il Libro I dell'Odissea; con note Italiane del Prof. Salvatore Rossi; 3rd ed. (Greek). Livorno, Italy: Raffaello Giusti.

1925— Ilias; edidt Guilielmus Dindorf; 5th ed. (Greek). Leipzig, Germany: B. G. Teubner.

1925— L'Odyssee; traduction nouvelle (Greek; French). *Translator or author:* Victor Berard. Paris, France: Societe d'Edition "Les Belles Lettres".

1925— The Odyssey of Homer; done into English prose (English). *Translator or author:* Samuel Henry Butcher; Andrew Lang. New York, N.Y.: Macmillan.

1925— The Odyssey; rendered into English prose (English). *Translator or author:* Samuel Butler. London, England; New York, N.Y.: Jonathan Cape; E. P. Dutton.

1925— The Iliad of Homer; rendered into English

prose (English). *Translator or author:* Samuel Butler. London, England; New York, N.Y.: Jonathan Cape; E. P. Dutton.

1925— The Odyssey of Homer; translated (English). *Translator or author:* William Cowper. London, England; New York, N.Y.: J. M. and Sons Dent; E. P. Dutton.

1925— Odyssee (German). *Translator or author:* Ruter Dorpfeld. Munich, Germany.

1925— Odissea; traduzione in versi esametri (Italian). *Translator or author:* Manlio Faggella. Bari, Italy: G. Laterza.

1925— Humir va iliyad, nigarish-i Mahmud-i Irfan (Iranian?). *Translator or author:* Mahmud Irfan. Tihran Tehran?: Kitabkhana-yi Sharq.

1925— The Iliad of Homer; done into English prose; rev. ed. (English). *Translator or author:* Andrew Lang; Walter Leaf; Ernest Myers. London, England: Macmillan.

1925— Iliade [d']Homere; traduction nouvelle (French). *Translator or author:* Leconte de Lisle. Paris, France: Alphonse Lemerre.

1925— The Odyssey of Homer; translated (English). *Translator or author:* William Sinclair Marris. London, England; New York, N.Y.: Oxford University Press.

1925— The Iliad; with an English translation (Greek; English). *Translator or author:* Augustus Taber Murray. London; New York, N.Y.; Cambridge, Mass.: William Heinemann; G.P. Putnam's Sons.

1925— Pope, The Iliad of Homer, Books XXII–XXIV; edited by F. H. Colson (English). *Translator or author:* Alexander Pope. Cambridge, England: Cambridge University Press.

1925— The Odyssey of Homer; translated (English). *Translator or author:* Alexander Pope. London, England; New York, N.Y.: Humphrey Milford; Oxford University Press.

1925— Homers Odyssee; die wiederherstellung der ursprunglichen epos von der heimkehr des Odysseus nach dem tageplan, mit beigaben uber Homerische geographie und kulture, von Wilhelm Dorpfeld. *Translator or author:* Heinrich Ruter. Munich, Germany: Buchenau and Reichert.

1925— Ilias in Auswahl Homer; ubersetzt und ausgewahlt (German). *Translator or author:* Thassilo Fritz H. von Scheffer. Munich, Germany: R. Oldenbourg.

1925— Odyssee in Auswahl Homer; ubersetzt und

ausgewahlt (German). *Translator or author:* Thassilo Fritz H. von Scheffer. Berlin, Germany: Propylaen-Verlag.

1925—Il Paziente Odisseo; con ... illustrazioni ricavate da vasi antichi e da monumenti (Italian). *Translator or author:* Gherardo Ugolini. Brescia, Italy: La Scuola.

1926—L'Odissea; con incisioni di A. de Carolis (Italian). Bologna, France: N. Zanichelli.

1926—The Odyssey of Homer; done into English prose; abridged ed. (English). *Translator or author:* Samuel Henry Butcher; Andrew Lang. London, England; New York, N.Y.: Macmillan.

1926—L'Epica di Omero e di Virgilio, Canti Scelti dell'Iliade, dell'Odissea e dell'Eneide; in traduzione classiche e moderne; Caro, Monti, Pindemonte, Leopardi, Bignone; con introd. e commento di Ettor Bignone; in conformita dei vigenti programmi per le scuole (Italian). *Translator or author:* Caro, Monti, Pindemonte. Florence, Italy: G. C. Sansoni.

1926—The Odyssey for Boys and Girls, Told from Homer (English). *Translator or author:* Alfred John Church. New York, N.Y.: Macmillan.

1926—Hesiod, the Homeric Hymns and Homerica; with an English Translation (Greek; English). *Translator or author:* Hugh Gerard Evelyn-White. London, England; New York, N.Y.: William Heinemann; G. P. Putnam.

1926—Achilles & Hector, Iliad Stories Retold for Boys and Girls (English). *Translator or author:* Agnes Spofford Cook Gale. Chicago, Il.; London, England: McNally Rand.

1926—Stories from the Iliad, Retold (English). *Translator or author:* Herbert Lord Havell. London, England: George G. Harrap.

1926—The Adventures of Ulysses; with illustrations by Doris Pailthorpe & T. H. Robinson (English). *Translator or author:* Charles Lamb. New York, N.Y.: Frederick A. Stokes.

1926—Musa Epica, Episodii Scelti de l'Iliade e da l'Odissea; commentati per le scuole medie (Italian). *Translator or author:* Vincenzo Monti. Palermo, Sicily, Italy: A. Trimarchi.

1926—La Iliada, o, El Sitio de Troya; relatada a los nianos (Spanish). *Translator or author:* Maria Luz Morales. Barcelona, Spain: R. de S. N. Araluce.

1926—The Toils and Travels of Odysseus; translated; edited by Stella Stewart Center (English). *Translator or author:* Cyril Arthington Pease. Boston, Mass.: Allyn and Bacon.

1926—Achille e Patroclo, dall'Iliade de Omero (Italian). *Translator or author:* Gherardo Ugolini. Brescia, Italy: La Scuola.

1926—Homerova Ilias; perel [z ereectiny, uvodem, poznamkami a slovnieckem opateril] (Czech). *Translator or author:* Otmar Vaenorny; Ferdinand Stieblitz. Prague, Czechoslavakia: J. Laichter.

1926—Homers Odyssee. *Translator or author:* Johann Heinrich Voss. Munich, Germany: Bremer Presse.

1926–32—Homeri Opera; recognoverunt brevique adnotatione critica instruxerunt David B[inning] Monro et Thomas W[illiam] Allen (Greek). Oxford, England: Clarendon Press.

1927—Odissea Libro Ventiduesimo; introduzione e commento di Flaminio Nencini (Greek). Milan, Italy: Carlo Signorelli.

1927—Homer, Dichtung und Sage, Bd. 3: Die Sage vom troischen Kriege (German). Leipzig, Germany: B. G. Teubner.

1927—Odyssea Homeri; edidit Guilielmus Dindorf; 5th ed. (Greek). Leipzig, Germany: B. G. Teubner.

1927—Homeri Ilias, Pars I, Iliadis I–XII; edidit Guilielmus Dindorf; 5th ed. (Greek). Leipzig, Germany: B. G. Teubner.

1927—Homere; 2nd ed. (French). *Translator or author:* Maurice Bouchor. Paris, France: Delagrave.

1927—The Odyssey of Homer; done into English prose (English). *Translator or author:* Samuel Henry Butcher; Andrew Lang. London, England: Macmillan.

1927—The Story of the Odyssey; edited for school use (English). *Translator or author:* Alfred John Church. New York, N.Y.: Macmillan.

1927—The Story of Achilles and the Story of Aeneas; from the Elson readers, book six; arranged for sight-saving class use by Robert B. Irwin (English). *Translator or author:* Alfred John Church. Upper Montclair, N.J.: Clear Type Publishing Committee.

1927—Hymns to Aphrodite (English). *Translator or author:* John Edgar. San Francisco, Ca.: Grabhorn Press.

1927—A Bujdoso Kiraly; Muhlbeck Karoly rajzaival. *Translator or author:* Mozes Gaal. Budapest, Hungary: Singer es Wolfner Kiadada.

1927—The Odyssey of Homer; translated into English prose (English). *Translator or author:* Robert Henry Hiller. Philadelphia, Pa.; Chicago, Il.: John C. Winston.

1927— The Iliad of Homer; done into English prose; rev. ed. (English). *Translator or author:* Andrew Lang; Walter Leaf; Ernest Myers. London, England; New York, N.Y.: Macmillan.

1927— Playbook of Troy; illustrations by Esther Peck (English). *Translator or author:* Susan Meriwether. New York, N.Y.: Harper and Brothers.

1927— L'Iliade d'Omero; introduzione e note di Roberto d'Alfonso (Italian). *Translator or author:* Vincenzo Monti. Torino (Turin), Italy: Unione Tipografico-Editrice Torinese.

1927— The Odyssey [of] Homer; with an English translation (Greek; English). *Translator or author:* Augustus Taber Murray. London, England; New York, N.Y.: William Heinemann; G. P. Putnam.

1927— The Odyssey of Homer; with notes by the Rev. Theodore Alois Buckley, and Flaxman's designs [series: Chandos Classics] (English). *Translator or author:* Alexander Pope. London, England; New York, N.Y.: Frederick Warne.

1927— The Iliad of Homer (English). *Translator or author:* Alexander Pope. London, England: Oxford University Press.

1927— The Iliad; with notes by Rev. T. A. Buckley and Flaxman's designs [series: Chandos Classics] (English). *Translator or author:* Alexander Pope. Frederick Warne.

1927— De Homeriska Hymnerna; of versatta fran Grekiskan (Swedish). *Translator or author:* Rudolf Roding. Goteborg, Sweden: Elanders Boktryckeri Aktiebolag.

1927— Odyssee, Drei Gesange (German). *Translator or author:* Albrecht Schaeffer. Leipzig, Germany: P. List.

1927— Die Odyssee Homers; Deutsch erneuert (German). *Translator or author:* Albrecht Schaeffer. Berlin, Germany: Deutsche Buch-Gemeinschaft.

1927— Die Odyssee Homers; Deutsch erneuert (German). *Translator or author:* Albrecht Schaeffer. Berlin, Germany; Grunewald, Germany: Horen-Verlag.

1927— Die Homerischen Gotterhymnen; verdeutscht (German). *Translator or author:* Thassilo Fritz H. von Scheffer. Jena, Germany: Diederichs.

1927— Obras Completas de Homero; version directa y literal del Griego (Spanish). *Translator or author:* Luis Segala y Estalella. Barcelona, Spain: Montaner and Simon.

1927— Iliyad: Iliade; en eski yunan osairi; in epopesi (Turkish). *Translator or author:* Omer Seyfeddin. Istanbul, Turkey: Devlet Matbaas.

1927— Achilleus, das Homerische Ur-Epos; wiederhergestellt und verdeutscht (German). *Translator or author:* Emil Wendling. Karlsruhe, Germany: Boltze.

1928— Iliad; with an introduction, a brief Homeric grammar, and notes by D[avid] B[inning] Monro (Greek). Oxford, England: Clarendon Press.

1928— Odissea Libro Ventesimo; introduzione e commento di Francesco Guglielmo (Greek). Milan, Italy: Carlo Signorelli.

1928— Homers Odyssee; fur den Schulgebrauch; erklart von Karl Friedr[ich] Ameis und Carl Hentze [und Paul Cauer] (Greek). Leipzig, Germany; Berlin, Germany: B. G. Teubner.

1928— Homere Iliade; texte Grec publie avec une introduction, des arguments analytiques, des notes explicatives et des illustrations documentaires par Victor Magnien (Greek). Paris, France: L. Hachette.

1928— Odyssey [of] Homer; with introduction, notes, etc. by W[illiam] W[alter] Merry (Greek). Oxford, England: Clarendon Press.

1928— The Shorter Iliad (Books I–XII); selected and arranged by H[enry] H[arrison] Hardy (Greek). London, England: George Bell and Sons.

1928— Odissea Libro Diciannovesimo; introduzione e commento di Silvio Colangelo (Greek). Milan, Italy: Carlo Signorelli.

1928— Odissea Libro None; introduzione e commento di Angelo Maggi (Greek). Milan, Italy: Carlo Signorelli.

1928— Four Books of the Iliad, I, VI, XXII, XXIV; translated; new ed. (English). *Translator or author:* William Cullen Bryant. Boston, Mass.: Houghton Mifflin.

1928— The Odyssey of Homer; translated (English). *Translator or author:* William Cowper. New York, N.Y.: E. P. Dutton.

1928— The Iliad of Homer; translated; series: Everyman's Library (English). *Translator or author:* Edward George Geoffrey Smith Stanley, Earl of Derby. London, England; New York, N.Y.: J. M. Dent; E. P. Dutton.

1928— [H]omerou Ilias; 8th ed. (Greek, Modern). *Translator or author:* Demetrios N. Goudes. Athens, Greece: P. D. Kyriakou.

1928— The Iliad of Homer; the first twelve staves; translated into English (English). *Translator or author:* Maurice Hewlett. London, England: Cresset Press.

1928—The Iliad of Homer; done into English prose; abridged ed. (English). *Translator or author:* Andrew Lang; Walter Leaf; Ernest Myers. New York, N.Y.; London, England: Macmillan.

1928—Iliad Homer; cyfieithiadau; gyda chwanegiadau, rhagair, a nodiadau gan T. Gwynn Jones (Welsh). *Translator or author:* R. Morris Lewis. Wrexham (Wrecsam), England: Hughes.

1928—Opere Drammatiche e Poesie Varie; a cura di Antonio Avena (Italian). *Translator or author:* Scipione Maffei. Bari, Italy: G. and Sons Laterza.

1928—Odyssea de Homero; em verso Portuguez (Portuguese). *Translator or author:* Manuel Odorico Mendes. Rio de Janeiro, Brazil: Freitas:Depositorios Livraria Leite Ribeir Bastos.

1928—The Odyssey of Homer; with an English translation (Greek; English). *Translator or author:* Augustus Taber Murray. London, England; New York, N.Y.: William Heinemann; G. P. Putnam.

1928—L'Odissea di Omero; introduzione e note di Giulio Teichenbach; con due tavole (Italian). *Translator or author:* Ippolito Pindemonte. Torino (Turin), Italy: Unione Tipografico-Editrice Torinese.

1929—[H]omerou Batrachomyomachia = Homeri Batrachomyomachia (Greek). Haarlem, Netherlands: Halcyon Press.

1929—Il Libro IX dell'Odissea; con note Italiane del Prof. Salvatore Rossi; 4th ed. (Greek). Livorno, Italy: Raffaello Giusti.

1929—Iliad [series: Cardinal]. Macmillan.

1929—The First Six Books of Homer's Iliad; with introduction, commentary, and vocabulary for the use of schools by Thomas D. Seymour; revised ed. (Greek). Boston, Mass.: Ginn.

1929—The Odyssey of Homer; translated into English verse (English). *Translator or author:* Herbert Bates. New York, N.Y.: McGraw-Hill.

1929—The Odyssey of Homer; translated into English verse (English). *Translator or author:* Herbert Bates. New York, N.Y.; London, England: Harper and Brothers.

1929—The Odyssey of Homer; done into English prose (English). *Translator or author:* Samuel Henry Butcher; Andrew Lang. New York, N.Y.: Modern Library.

1929—The Odyssey of Homer; done into English prose (English). *Translator or author:* Samuel Henry Butcher; Andrew Lang. London, England: Macmillan.

1929—Ao-te-sai [The Odyssey] (Chinese). *Translator or author:* Tung-hua Fu.

1929—The Iliad; done into English prose; revised ed. (English). *Translator or author:* Andrew Lang; Walter Leaf; Ernest Myers. London, England: Macmillan.

1929—The Iliad of Homer; done into English prose (English). *Translator or author:* Andrew Lang; Walter Leaf; Ernest Myers. New York, N.Y.: Modern Library.

1929—Homer's Hymns to Aphrodite; translated (English). *Translator or author:* Jack Lindsay. London, England: Fanfrolico Press.

1929—Iliade [da] Omero; tradotte; annotata per il popolo e per le scuole; a cura di Ettore Fabietti; new ed. (Italian). *Translator or author:* Vincenzo Monti. Milan, Italy: A. Barion.

1929—The Odyssey of Homer; translated; with illustrations by N. C. Wyeth (English). *Translator or author:* George Herbert Palmer. Boston, Mass: Houghton Mifflin.

1929—The Odyssey of Homer; translated; with illustrations by N. C. Wyeth (English). *Translator or author:* George Herbert Palmer. Cambridge, Mass.: Riverside Press.

1929—Iliad Homeri; die Bucher von dem Khrig so zwischen den Grichen und Troianern vor der Stat Troja beschehen; Homeri des viertreflichen weitberumbten Poeten und Geschichtschreibers in Griechischer Sprach von im gar woll und Herrlich beschriben und durch mich (German). *Translator or author:* Johann Baptista Rexius. Berlin, Germany: Walter De Gruyter.

1929—Homers Ilias; Versuch einer Wiederherstellung des urgedichtes vom Zorn des Achilleus in Deutscher Prosa (German). *Translator or author:* Heinrich Ruter. Munich, Germany; Grafelfing, Germany: R. Uhde.

1929—Die Ilias; Deutsch (German). *Translator or author:* Albrecht Schaeffer. Berlin, Germany: L. Schneider.

1929—Six Hymns of Homer; the English translation facing the original Greek; [edited by Paul can de Woestijne] (Greek; English). *Translator or author:* Percy Bysshe Shelley. Maastricht, Netherlands: Halcyon Press.

1929–30—The Iliad; with an English translation (Greek; English). *Translator or author:* Augustus Taber Murray. London, England; New York, N.Y.: William Heinemann; G. P. Putnam.

1929–31—Die Ilias; bearbeitet von Prof. Dr. Oskar

Henke ... besorgt von Prof. Dr. George Siefert (Greek). Leipzig, Germany; Berlin, Germany: B. G. Teubner.

1930—Homere, Iliade; text Grec publie avec une introduction, des arguments analytiques, des notes explicatives et des illustrations documentaires par Victor Magnien (Greek). Paris, France: L. Hachette.

1930—L'Odyssee [d']Homere, Principaux Chants (I, II, V, VI, IX, XI, XXII, XXIII); avec une introduction et des notes par Maurice Croiset. Paris, France: Armand Colin.

1930—The Odyssey of Homer, Book IX; edited by G[erald] M[aclean] Edwards (Greek). Cambridge, England: Cambridge University Press.

1930—Selections from Homer's Iliad; with an introduction, notes, a short Homeric grammar, and a vocabulary by Allen Rogers Benner (Greek). New York, N.Y.: Appleton-Century.

1930—The Sigma Rhapsody of the Iliad; annotated by Alexander Pallis (Greek). London, England; New York, N.Y.: Humphrey Milford; Oxford University Press.

1930—Ilias; septimum ediderunt J. van Leeuwen et M[aurits] B[enjamin] Mendes da Costa; 7th ed. Leiden (Leyden), Netherlands: A. W. Sijthoff.

1930—The Iliad, Book XXII; edited with introduction, notes, appendices and vocabulary by G[erald] M]aclean] Edwards [reprint of 1890 edition] (Greek). Cambridge, England: Cambridge University Press.

1930—Odyssey, Book IX; edited by G[erald] M[aclean] Edwards; re-issue with vocabulary [series: Pitt Press] (Greek). Cambridge University Press.

1930—Il Primo Libro dell'Iliade; commentato da marcello Torta (Greek). Naples, Italy: Societa Anonima Editrice Francesco Perrella.

1930—Homer Ilias; fur den Schulgebrauch erklart von Karl Friedrich Ameis; Gesange XXII–XXIV; bearbeitet von C. Hentze; 6th ed. (Greek). Leipzig, Germany: B. G. Teubner.

1930—Homer's Iliad; twelve books literally translated, with explanatory notes (English). *Translator or author:* Theodore Alois Buckley. New York, N.Y.: Excelsior.

1930—The Odyssey of Homer; done into English prose; abridged and edited by Wallace B. Moffett; illustrated by Norman Roberts (English). *Translator or author:* Samuel Henry Butcher; Andrew lang. New York, N.Y.: Macmillan.

1930—The Odyssey, rendered into English prose; illustrated by W. Russell Flint (English). *Translator or author:* Samuel Henry Butcher; Andrew Lang. London, England; Boston, Mass.: Medici Society.

1930—The Odyssey of Homer; rendered into English prose; illustrated after drawings by W. Russell Flint (English). *Translator or author:* Samuel Henry Butcher; Andrew Lang. Boston, Mass; London, England: Cushman & Flint Hale; Medici Society.

1930—The Iliad of Homer; rendered into English prose for the use of those who cannot read the original (English). *Translator or author:* Samuel Butler. London, England; Toronto, Canada: Jonathan Cape.

1930—The Whole Works of Homer, Prince of Poetts, in his Iliads, and Odysses; translated according to the Greeke (English). *Translator or author:* George Chapman. Oxford, England: Shakespeare Head Press.

1930—The Iliad for Boys and Girls; told from Homer in simple language; new ed. (English). *Translator or author:* Alfred John Church. New York, N.Y.: Macmillan.

1930—The Story of the Iliad; edited for school use (English). *Translator or author:* Alfred John Church. New York, N.Y.; London, England: Macmillan.

1930—L'Odyssee [d']Homere (French). *Translator or author:* Anne LeFevre Dacier. Paris, France: Ambroise Vollard.

1930—The Iliad, Book XXII; edited with introduction, notes, etc. *Translator or author:* G[erald] M[aclean] Edwards. Cambridge University Press.

1930—The Iliad, Homer; with introduction by Louise Pound; translation (English). *Translator or author:* Andrew Lang; Walter Leaf; Ernest Myers. New York, N.Y.: Macmillan.

1930—The Iliad of Homer; done into English prose; abridged and edited by Wallace B., Moffett; illustrated by W[allace] B. Berger; revised ed. (English). *Translator or author:* Andrew Lang; Walter Leaf; Ernest Myers. New York, N.Y.; London, England: Macmillan.

1930—The Iliad; done into English prose (English). *Translator or author:* Andrew Lang; Walter Leaf; Ernest Myers. New York, N.Y.: Modern Library.

1930—Hymns to Aphrodite (English). *Translator or author:* Jack Lindsay. London, England: Fanfrolico Press.

1930—Iliade; traduction Francaise (French). *Translator or author:* Victor Magnien. Paris, France: Payot.

1930— Odusseias de Homeros; el la antikva Greka lingvo tradukis (Esperanto). *Translator or author:* W. J. A. Manders. Zutphen, Netherlands: W. J. Thieme.

1930— The Story of the Iliad; retold (English). *Translator or author:* Francis Sydney Marvin; R.J.G. Mayor; F.M. Stawell. New York, N.Y.; London, England; Toronto, Canada: E. P. Dutton; J. M. Dent & Sons.

1930— The Odyssey; with an English translation (Greek; English). *Translator or author:* Augustus Taber Murray. London, England; New York, N.Y.: William Heinemann; G. P. Putnam.

1930— L'Iliade d'Homere; etude et analyse (French). *Translator or author:* Aime Puech. Paris, France: Mellottee.

1930— L'Odissea: Il Ritorno di Ulisse; commentata da Angelo Taccone (Greek). *Translator or author:* Marino de Szombathely. Torino (Turin), Italy: Societa Editrice Internazionale.

1930— Sefer Ilias, Homerus; oheleok rishon, Shirim 1–12; metugarmim mi-Yeovanit al-yede (Hebrew). *Translator or author:* Saul Tchernichowsky. Vilnius (Vilna), Lithuania: Hotsaat Shotibel.

1930— Ilyas, Shirim 1–12; meturgamim mi-Yeovanit al yede Shaul o Tsherniohovsoki (Hebrew). *Translator or author:* Saul Tchernichowsky. Berlin, Germany: A. Y. Shotibel.

1930— Homers Odyssey = [H]omerou Odysseia; auf Grund der Ubersetzungen von Johann Heinrich Voss; bearbeitet von E. R. Weiss (Greek; German). *Translator or author:* Johann Heinrich Voss. Leipzig, Germany: Tempel-Verlag.

1930— Homers Ilias im Auszuge; bearb. von Franz Kern (German). *Translator or author:* Johann Heinrich Voss. Bielefeld, Germany; Leipzig, Germany: Velhagen und Klasing.

1930— Ho-ma (Chinese). *Translator or author:* Hsi-ho Wang.

1930–31— Ilias; fur den Schulgebrauch in verkurzter Form bearbeitet und herausgegen von Joseph Bach; 5th ed. (Greek). Munster, Germany: Aschendorffschen Verlagsbuchhandlung.

1930–31— Homeri Odyssea; edidit Guilielmus Dindorf; 5th ed. (Greek). Leipzig, Germany: B. G. Teubner.

1930–33— L'Odyssee [d']Homere; traduction; il-lustrations et decors de Francois-Louis Schmied (French). *Translator or author:* Victor Berard. Paris, France: La Compagnie des Bibliophiles de l'Automobile-Club.

1930–35— The Whole Works of Homer [based on the 1616 edition] (English). *Translator or author:* George Chapman. Oxford, England: Shakespeare Head Press.

1931— The Odyssey of Homer, Books VI and VII; with notes and vocabulary by G[erald] M[aclean] Edwards (Greek). Cambridge, England: Cambridge University Press.

1931— Selections from Homer's Iliad; with an introduction, notes, a short Homeric grammar, and a vocabulary by Allen Rogers Benner (Greek). New York, N.Y.: Irvington Publishers.

1931— La Odisea, Homero (Spanish). Mexico (City), Mexico: Universidad Nacional de Mexico.

1931— Der Homerische Hermeshymnus; erlautert und untersucht von L. Radermacher. Vienna, Austria: Holder-Pichler-Tempsky.

1931— Selections from Homer's Iliad; with an introduction, notes, a short Homeric grammar, and a vocabulary by Allen Rogers Benner (Greek). New York, N.Y.: Appleton-Century-Crofts.

1931— Homeri Ilias; edidit Thomas W[illiam] Allen (Greek). Oxford, England: Clarendon Press.

1931— L'Iliade (French). Paris, France: E. Flammarion.

1931— Odyssee; fur den Schulgebrauch in verkurzter Form, beareitet und herausgeben von Dr. Joseph Bach; besorgt von Dr. Herm. Widmann (Greek). Munster, Germany: Aschendorffschen Verlagsbuchhandlung.

1931— Homeri Ilias. *Translator or author:* T. W. Allen. Oxford University Press.

1931— The Whole Works of Homer; translated according to the Greeke (English). *Translator or author:* George Chapman. Blackman.

1931— The Story of the Iliad; edited for school use (English). *Translator or author:* Alfred John Church. New York, N.Y.; London, England: Macmillan.

1931— Sotto le Mura de Troia (Italian). *Translator or author:* Alba Cinzia. Torino (Turin), Italy: Societa Editrice Internazionale.

1931— The Odyssey of Homer; translated (English). *Translator or author:* William Cowper. London, England; New York, N.Y.: J. M. and Sons Dent; E. P. Dutton.

1931—The Iliad of Homer; translated; series: Everyman's Library (English). *Translator or author:* Edward George Geoffrey Smith Stanley, Earl of Derby. London, England; New York, N.Y.: J. M. Dent; E. P. Dutton.

1931—Sonette nach der Odyssee (German). *Translator or author:* Michael Foerster. Lausanne, Switzerland: E. Frankfurter.

1931—[H]omerou Ilias = The Iliad of Homer; edited with general and grammatical introduction, notes, and appendices, by Walter Leaf and M[atthew] A[lbert] Bayfield; 2nd ed. (Greek; English). *Translator or author:* Walter Leaf; Matthew Albert Bayfield. London, England: Macmillan.

1931—L'Iliade Omero; nella traduzione; introduzione, commento e appendice a cura di Giuseppe Raniolo (Italian). *Translator or author:* Vincenzo Monti. Milan, Italy: Arnoldo Mondadori.

1931—The Rhapsody of the Dead; annotated by Alexander Pallis. *Translator or author:* Alexander Anastasius Pallis. Oxford University Press.

1931—L'Odissea; nella traduzione; introduzione, commento e appendice a cura di Biuseppe Raniolo (Italian). *Translator or author:* Ippolito Pindemonte. Milan, Italy: Arnoldo Mondadori.

1931—Iliad; with Pope's translation (English). *Translator or author:* Alexander Pope. London, England: Nonesuch Press.

1931—Odyssey; limited edition (English). *Translator or author:* Alexander Pope. London, England: Nonesuch Press.

1931—The Odyssey of Homer [series: Limited Editions Club] (English). *Translator or author:* Alexander Pope. J. Enschede.

1931—The Iliad of Homer; translated; with the introduction by Mr. Pope (English). *Translator or author:* Alexander Pope. Haarlem, Netherlands: Limited Editions Club.

1931—The Odyssey; translated; with an introduction by Carl Van Dorn (English). *Translator or author:* Alexander Pope. Haarlem, Netherlands: Limited Editions Club.

1931—The Odyssey of Homer; translated (English). *Translator or author:* Alexander Pope. London, England: Oxford University Press.

1931—Homera Odysseja; z Greckiego Przelozyl i przedmwa pooprzedzil; rzecz o Homerze napisal Ryszard Ganszyniec; 2nd ed. (Polish). *Translator or author:* Jozef Wittlin. Warsaw, Poland: J. Mortkowicz.

1931—Der Froschmausekrieg; Deutsch; mit Zeichnungen von Gerolf Steiner (German). *Translator or author:* Werner Wolf. Buhl-Baden, Germany: Konkordia.

1932—Iliad; texte Grec, publie avec une introduction, des arguments analytiques, des notes explicatives, et des illustrations documentaires, par Victor Magnien (Greek). Paris, France: L. Hachette.

1932—Odyssey, Books I–XII; with introduction, notes, etc. by W[illiam] W[alter] Merry (Greek). Oxford, England: Clarendon Press.

1932—Les XXIV Chants de l'Odyssee (French). *Translator or author:* Victor Berard. Paris, France: Armand Colin.

1932—The Odyssey of Homer; done into English prose (English). *Translator or author:* Samuel Henry Butcher; Andrew Lang. London, England: Macmillan.

1932—The Iliad for Boys and Girls, told from Homer in simple language (English). *Translator or author:* Alfred John Church. New York, N.Y.: Macmillan.

1932—L'Iliade; traduction nouvelle avec une introduction et des notes (French). *Translator or author:* Eugene Lasserre. Paris, France: Garnier Freres.

1932—The Odyssey of Homer; limited edition (English). *Translator or author:* Thomas Edward Lawrence. London, England: Emery Walker; Wilfred Merton; Bruce Rogers.

1932—The Odyssey of Homer; newly translated into English by T. E. Shaw (English). *Translator or author:* Thomas Edward Lawrence. New York, N.Y.: Editions for the Armed Services.

1932—The Odyssey of Homer; newly translated from the Greek into English prose by T. E. Shaw (Lawrence of Arabia); with an introduction (English). *Translator or author:* Thomas Edward Lawrence. New York, N.Y.: Oxford University Press.

1932—The Bride of Achilles, a Garland of Lines from Homer (English). *Translator or author:* Henry Bertram Lister. Boston, Mass.: Christopher Publishing House.

1932—The Odyssey; translated in verse (English). *Translator or author:* John William Mackail. Oxford, England: Clarendon Press.

1932—Slownik Grecko-Polski; do wyboru z piesni Homera Opracowal Artur Rapaport, z 36 rycinami [Homeric Hymns] (Polish). *Translator or author:* Artur Rapaport. L'viv (Lwow), Ukraine: Ksiaznica Atlas.

1932— The Adventures of Ulysses (English). *Translator or author:* William Henry Denham Rouse. London, England: Macmillan.

1933— Iliad and Odyssey; re-issued [series: Dent's Double Volumes] (English). London, England: J. M. Dent.

1933— L'Odyssee, Poesie Homerique; texte etabli et traduit par Victor Berard; 2nd ed. (Greek; French). *Translator or author:* Victor Berard. Paris, France: Societe d'Edition "Les Belles Lettres".

1933— La Iliada; 2nd ed. (Spanish). *Translator or author:* Juan Bautista Bergua. Madrid, Spain: Liberaia Bergua.

1933— The Odyssey; done into English prose; abridged and edited by W. B. Moffett; illustrated by Norman Roberts (English). *Translator or author:* Samuel Henry Butcher; Andrew Lang. New York, N.Y.: Macmillan.

1933— The Iliad and Odyssey of Homer; introductions by F[lorence] Melian Stawell; series: Dent's Double Volumes (English). *Translator or author:* Derby Edward, Earl of Derby; William Cowper. London, England: J. M. Dent.

1933— The Tenth Book of Homer's Odyssey; translated into Esperanto hexameters (Esperanto). *Translator or author:* Giles Dixey. London, England: British Experanto Association.

1933— Stories from the Iliad; retold by H. L. Havell (English). *Translator or author:* Herbert Lord Havell. London, England: George G. Harrap.

1933— The Iliad of Homer; done into English prose; abridged and edited by William B. Moffett, illustrated by W. M. Berger (English). *Translator or author:* Andrew Lang; Walter Leaf; Ernest Myers. New York, N.Y.: Macmillan.

1933— Translation from Homer's Iliad, Book 24, Lines 478–676 [in Delta Kappa Epsilon Quarterly, vol. 52, no. 2, May] (English). *Translator or author:* Edgar Lee Master. New York, N.Y.: Council of Delta Kappa Epsilon.

1933— The Iliad of Homer; rendered into English hexameters (English). *Translator or author:* Alexander Falconer Murison. London, England; New York, N.Y.: Green Longmans.

1933–34— Odyssea; nonum ediderunt J. van Leeuwen (Greek). Leiden (Leyden), Netherlands: A. W. Sijthoff.

1934— Hector's Ransoming: a translation of Iliad

XXIV, with a note on the metre (English). *Translator or author:* Samuel Ogden Andrew. Oxford, England: Shakespeare Head Press.

1934— The Odyssey by Homer; done into English prose; with introduction by John A. Scott (English). *Translator or author:* Samuel Henry Butcher; Andrew Lang. New York, N.Y.: Macmillan.

1934— The Odyssey of Homer; together with the shorter poems, translated according to the Greek (English). *Translator or author:* George Chapman. London, England: Simpkin, Marshall, Hamilton, Kent.

1934— The Odyssey for Boys and Girls; told from Homer (English). *Translator or author:* Alfred John Church. New York, N.Y.: Macmillan.

1934— Ao-te-sai [The Odyssey] (Chinese). *Translator or author:* Tung-hua Fu. Shang-hai, China: Shang wu yin shu kuan.

1934— Antologia Omerica: Iliade; scelta, commento e indici analitici (Italian). *Translator or author:* Antonio Giusti. Milan, Italy: Carlo Signorelli.

1934— The Odyssey of Homer; newly translated into English prose (English). *Translator or author:* Thomas Edward Lawrence. New York, N.Y.: Oxford University Press.

1934— Bellezze dell'Iliade dell'Odissea e dell' 'Eneide; con l'epilogo dei tre poemi; a cura adi Enrico Mestica; nuovmente annotate e commentate in conformita dei programmi governativi (Italian). *Translator or author:* Nissim Rossi Lea, and Aldo Bruscaglioni. Florence, Italy: G. Barbera.

1934— The Iliad of Homer (English). *Translator or author:* William Sinclair Marris. London, England; New York, N.Y.: Oxford University Press.

1934— L'Iliade; annotata e commentata in conformita dei programmi governativi dalla Prof. Lea Nissim Rossi (Italian). *Translator or author:* Vincenzo Monti. Florence, Italy: G. Barbera.

1934— Odissea nella traduzione di Ippolito Pindemonte; con note e analisi critiche di M. Valgimigli; new tiratura (Italian). *Translator or author:* Ippolito Pindemonte. Florence, Italy: Felice Le Monnier.

1934— The Iliad of Homer (English). *Translator or author:* Alexander Pope. London, England; New York, N.Y.: Oxford University Press.

1934— La Guerre de Troie; 4 planches hors texte en couleurs et 50 compositions en noir par Henri de Nolhac (French). *Translator or author:* Ch. Gailly de Taurines. Paris, France: Larousse.

1934— Odissea; versione poetica (Italian). *Translator or author:* Guido Vitali. Messina, Sicily, Italy: G. Principato.

1934— The Homeric Hymns, with Hero and Leander; in English verse (English). *Translator or author:* Arthur Sanders Way. London, England: Macmillan.

1934–35— Ilias; octavum ediderunt J[an] van Leeuwen ... et M[aurits] B[enjamin] Mendes da Costa.... Leiden (Leyden), Netherlands: A. W. Sijthoff.

1934–39— The Iliad with an English translation [series: Loeb Classical Library] (Greek, English). *Translator or author:* Augustus Taber Murray. London, England; Cambridge, Mass.: Harvard University Press; William Heinemann.

1935— Ilias; edidit Guilielmus Dindorf; editio quinta correctrior quam curavit C. Henze; stereotype ed. (Greek). Leipzig, Germany: B. G. Teubner.

1935— The Iliad of Homer; from the text of Wolf, with English notes; edited by C. C. Felton; stereotype ed. (English). Boston, Mass.: Gray Hilliard.

1935— Homer's Odyssey, Book XIII–XXIV; edited with English notes and appendices by W[illiam] W[alter] Merry (Greek). Oxford, England: Clarendon Press.

1935— Ilias; erste rhapsodie (German). *Translator or author:* Gottfried August Burger. Leipzig, Germany.

1935— The Odyssey by Homer; with introduction by John A. Scott (English). *Translator or author:* Samuel Henry Butcher; Andrew Lang. New York, N.Y.: Macmillan.

1935— The Iliad and the Odyssey of Homer; retold; illustrated by John Flaxman (English). *Translator or author:* Alfred John Church. New York, N.Y.: Macmillan.

1935— The Odyssey of Homer (English). *Translator or author:* William Cowper. London, England; New York, N.Y.: J. M. Dent; E. P. Dutton.

1935— The Iliad of Homer; translated; series: Everyman's Library (English). *Translator or author:* Edward George Geoffrey Smith Stanley, Earl of Derby. London, England; New York, N.Y.: J. M. Dent; E. P. Dutton.

1935— L'Odyssee; traduction nouvelle avec introduction, notes et index (French). *Translator or author:* Mederic, Dufour, Jeanne Raison. Paris, France: Garnier Freres.

1935— Iliada, Gomer; perevod N. I. Gnedicha; redaketisieilai i kommentarii I. M. Troetiskogo pri uchastii I. I. Tolstogo (Russian). *Translator or author:* Nikolaaei Ivanovich Gnedich. Moscow, Russia: Academia.

1935— The Complete Works of Homer; the Iliad and the Odyssey; the Iliad done into English prose by Andrew Lang, Walter Leaf, Ernest Myers; the Odyssey done into English prose by S. H. Butcher and Andrew Lang (English). *Translator or author:* Andrew Lang; Walter Leaf; E. Myers; S. H. Butler. New York, N.Y.: Random House.

1935— The Complete Works of Homer; the Iliad and the Odyssey; the Iliad done into English prose by Andrew Lang, Walter Leaf, Ernest Myers; the Odyssey done into English prose by S. H. Butcher and Andrew Lang (English). *Translator or author:* Andrew Lang; Walter Leaf; E. Myers; S. H. Butler. New York, N.Y.: Modern Library.

1935— The Iliad of Homer; done into English prose; revised ed. (English). *Translator or author:* Andrew Lang; Walter Leaf; Ernest Myers. London, England: Macmillan.

1935— The Odyssey (English). *Translator or author:* Thomas Edward Lawrence. New York, N.Y.

1935— The Odyssey of Homer; translated by T. E. Shaw (English). *Translator or author:* Thomas Edward Lawrence. London, England: Oxford University Press.

1935— Iliada, Gomer; perevod N. M. Minskogo; redaketisieila i vstuputel#naeila stat#eila P. F. Preobrazhenskogo (Russian). *Translator or author:* Nikolaaei Maksimovich; Fedorovich, Petr. Moscow, Russia: Gos. Izd-vo Khudozh Lit-ry.

1935— Iliad. *Translator or author:* William Sinclair Marris. Oxford University Press.

1935— L'Iliade di Omero nella traduzione di Vincenzio Monti; passi scelti, annotati e collegati col racconto del poema da Francesco Luigi Mannucci (Italian). *Translator or author:* Vincenzo Monti. Torino (Turin), Italy: S. Lattes.

1935— Der Wahre, Grosse und Unvergangliche Homer; Deutsch (mit aufschliessenden Erlauterungen) (German). *Translator or author:* Dietrich Mulder. Leipzig, Germany: O. R. Reisland.

1935— I Iliada; metaphrazmeni (Greek, Modern (Pontic dialect)). *Translator or author:* Aleks. Pali. Rostov-na-Donu, Russia: Ekdotiko Komynistis.

1935— Odyssee, Funfter Gesang (German). *Translator or author:* Johann Heinrich Voss. Leipzig, Germany.

1935— Travellers' Tales, from the Odyssey and

Baron Munchausen (English). *Translator or author:* Michael West. London, England: Greens Longmans.

1935—Odisseia; perevod; stat ia, redaktsiia i kommentarii I. M. Trotskogo, pri uchastii l.l. Tolstogo; graveiiury P. A. Shillingovskogo [series: Antichnaia Literatura] (Russian). *Translator or author:* Vasilii Andreevich Zhukovskii. Moscow, Russia: Academia.

1935–38—Iliad (Greek). Oxford, England: Clarendon Press.

1936—The Homeric Hymns; edited T[homas] W[illiam] Allen … W[illiam] R[eginald] Halliday … and E[dward] E[rnest] Sikes (Greek). Oxford, England: Clarendon Press.

1936—The Odyssey of Homer; rendered into English prose…; illustrated after drawings by Sir W[illiam] Russell Flint; popular ed. (English). *Translator or author:* Samuel Henry Butcher, Andrew Lang. London, England: Medici Society.

1936—The Odyssey of Homer; rendered into English (English). *Translator or author:* Samuel Butler. Washington, D.C.: National Homer Library Foundation.

1936—The Iliad of Homer; rendered into English prose for the use of those who cannot read the original (English). *Translator or author:* Samuel Butler. London, England: Jonathan Cape.

1936—The Odyssey for Boys and Girls, Told from Homer (English). *Translator or author:* Alfred John Church. New York, N.Y.: Macmillan.

1936—Hesiod, the Homeric Hymns, and Homerica, with an English translation; new and revised ed. [series: Loeb Classical Library] (Greek, English). *Translator or author:* Hugh Gerard Evelyn-White. London, England; New York, N.Y.: William Heinemann; Macmillan.

1936—Hesiod, the Homeric Hymns, and Homerica; new and revised ed. (Greek; English). *Translator or author:* Hugh Gerard Evelyn-White. Harvard University Press.

1936—Odissea (Italian). *Translator or author:* Hilda Montesi Festa. Florence, Italy: Vallecchi.

1936—Homera Iliada; no grieku valodas tulkojis A. Giezens (Latvian). *Translator or author:* Augusts Giezens. Riga, Latvia: Izglitibas Ministrijas Izdevums.

1936—Homers Odyssee in Auszuge; in neuer Ub. hrsg. (German). *Translator or author:* Oskar Hubatsch. Leipzig, Germany: Velhagen und Klasing.

1936—Hymnes; texte etabli et traduit par Jean Humbert … (Greek, French). *Translator or author:* Jean Humbert. Paris, France: Societe d'Edition "Les Belles Lettres".

1936—The Iliad and the Odyssey; extracts from the translations by Lang, Leaf and Myers and Butcher and Lang; edited by H. M. King and H. Spooner (English). *Translator or author:* Andrew Lang; Walter Leaf; Ernest Myers; Butcher. Macmillan.

1936—Iliade-Omero; episodi e canti peincipali; traduzione; commentati e collegati ad uso delle scuole medie inferiori da M[anara] Valgimigli; new ed. (Italian). *Translator or author:* Vincenzo Monti. Florence, Italy: Felice Le Monnier.

1936—L'Iliade di Omeronei Passi Migliori Della; traduzione; [a cura di] A[rturo] Avelardi [e] L[uigi] Papandrea (Italian). *Translator or author:* Vincenzo Monti. Florence, Italy: Nemi.

1936—Armi Ed Eroi Nell'Epopea Classica; episode dell'Iliade; traduzione, col riassunto delle parti omnesse e con note di Lea Nissim Rossi (Italian). *Translator or author:* Vincenzo Monti. Florence, Italy: G. Barbera.

1936—"La Odisea": tradedia muy tragica en tres actos y en verso (es un decir) adaptada de la conocida (por algunos) epopeya del mismo nombre que hace algun tiempo escribio Homero para poder presumir de hombre celebre (el autor no aspira a tanto) original del r (Spanish). *Translator or author:* Juan B. de Oyarzabal. Havana, Cuba: Fernandez Cia Seoane.

1936—[H]e Iliada; metaphrasmene (Greek, Modern). *Translator or author:* Alexander Anastasius Pallis. Athens, Greece: I. D. Kollaros.

1936—Armi Ed Eroi Nell'Epopea Classica; episodi dell'Odissea nell traduzione di Ippolito Pindemonte, col riassunto delle parti Omesse e con note di Lea Nissim Rossi (Italian). *Translator or author:* Ippolito Pindemonte. Florence, Italy: G. Berbera.

1936—L'Odissea; tradotta … con introd. e note in conformita dei programmi governativi, a cura di Lea Nissim Rossi (Italian). *Translator or author:* Ippolito Pindemonte. Florence, Italy: G. Barbera.

1936—The Odyssey of Homer; translated … with notes and introduction by Theodore A[lois] Buckley (English). *Translator or author:* Alexander Pope. Chicago, Il.: Clarke Belford.

1936—La Vie d'Achille Illustree par les Vases Grecs; recits tires de l'Iliade d'Homere et des poemes cycliques, traduits librement (French). *Translator or author:* Anne Rivier. Payot et al. Lausanne etc.

1936— L'Odissea; traduzione … con note di Giovanni Lattanzi; new ed. (Italian). *Translator or author:* Ettore Romagnoli. Bologna, France: N. Zanichelli.

1937— The Sixth Book of the Iliad; edited with notes, introduction, and vocabulary by Walter Leaf and M. A. Bayfield (Greek). London, England: Macmillan.

1937— Carmina et Cycli Epici Reliquae, Graece et Latine; cum indice nominum et rerum (Greek; Latin). Paris, France: Ambrosio Firmin Didot.

1937— Homeri Ilias, Odyssea; ediderunt [J. C.] Bruyn [und] [Cornelius S.] Spoelder (Greek). Haarlem, Netherlands: H. D. Tjeenk & Zoon Willink.

1937— Homer. *Translator or author:* W. Aly. Frankfurt am Main, Germany.

1937— Homeros' Odyssee; in Nederlandsche hexameters overgebracht (Dutch). *Translator or author:* P. C. Boutens. Haarlem, Netherlands: F. Bohn.

1937— Tantalus (Greek, English). *Translator or author:* William Broome. Cambridge, England.

1937— Ilias; Odyssea. *Translator or author:* Bruyn Spoelder. Oxford University Press.

1937— The Odyssey of Homer; translated from the Greek (English). *Translator or author:* Samuel Henry Butcher; Andrew Lang. New York, N.Y.: President Publishing.

1937— The Odyssey of Homer; with introduction and notes (English). *Translator or author:* Samuel Henry Butcher; Andrew Lang. New York, N.Y.: P. F. Collier & Son.

1937— The Odyssey by Homer; with introduction by John A[dams] Scott (English). *Translator or author:* Samuel Henry Butcher; John Adams Scott. New York, N.Y.: Macmillan.

1937— [H]omerou Ilias = Homers Ilias; Schulausgabe; 8th ed. (Greek; German). *Translator or author:* Paul Cauer. Leipzig, Germany: G. Freytag.

1937— Les Hymnes Homeriques; nouvellement traduites du Grec avec une preface et des notes (French). *Translator or author:* Louis Dimier. Paris, France: Garnier Freres.

1937— Homers Odyssee und Ilias im Auszuge; in neuer Ubersetzung (German). *Translator or author:* Oskar Hubatsch. Bielefeld, Germany; Leipzig, Germany: Velhagen und Klasing.

1937— Obras de Homero; traducidas en versos Castellanos (Castilian Spanish). *Translator or author:* Leopoldo Lopez Alvarez. Pasto, Spain: El Centenario.

1937— Ewen Maclachlan's Gaelic Verse; comprising a translation of Homer's Iliad, books I–VIII, and original compositions, edited by John Macdonald (Gaelic). *Translator or author:* Ewen Maclachlan. Inverness, Scotland: R. and Sons Carruthers.

1937— Iliade; texte etabli et traduit par Paul Mason, avec la collaborations de P. Chantraine, P. Collart et R. Langumier (French). *Translator or author:* Paul Mazon. Paris, France: Societe d'Edition "Les Belles Lettres".

1937— Iliade, Omero; nella traduzione Italiana di Vincenzo Monti, con note e commento di Manfredo Vanni e Angelo Ottolini (Italian). *Translator or author:* Vincenzo Monti. Milan, Italy: Carlo Signorelli.

1937— Odiseye, Homer; fun Grikhish, M. L. Petshenik; mit an araynfir fun Shelomoh Shaynberg (Yiddish). *Translator or author:* M. L. Petshenik; Shelomoh Shaynberg. Varshe [location?]: Yidishe Universal Bibliotek.

1937— Odissea; tr., a cura di Onorato Castellino e Vincenzo Peloso; 2nd ed. (Italian). *Translator or author:* Ippolito Pindemonte. Torino (Turin), Italy: Societa Editrice internazionale.

1937— The Story of Odysseus; a new translation; with decorations by Lynd Ward (English). *Translator or author:* William Henry Denham Rouse. New York, N.Y.: Modern Age Books.

1937— The Story of Achilles (English). *Translator or author:* William Henry Denham Rouse. London, England.

1937— The Story of Odysseus; a translation of Homer's "Odyssey" into plain English (English). *Translator or author:* William Henry Denham Rouse. London, England; New York, N.Y.: Thomas Nelson and Sons.

1937— The Odyssey: the Story of Odysseus, Homer (English). *Translator or author:* William Henry Denham Rouse. New York, N.Y.: Penguin Books.

1937— The Story of Odysseus; a new translation (English). *Translator or author:* William Henry Denham Rouse. New York, N.Y.: Mentor Books.

1937— The Odyssey: the Story of Odysseus (English). *Translator or author:* William Henry Denham Rouse. New York, N.Y.: New American Library.

1937— Die Odyssee Homers; Deutsch erneuert

(German). *Translator or author:* Albrecht Schaeffer. Leipzig, Germany: P. List.

1937— The Original Iliad; translated into English prose (English). *Translator or author:* Robinson Smith. Nice, France.

1937— Z Homerovy Odysseie (Czech). *Translator or author:* Vladimir Sramek; Jaroslav Benda; Antonin Strnadel. V. Praze [location?]: Klub zameestnanceu Leecebneho.

1937— The Odyssey of Homer; edited with general and grammatical introduction, commentary, and indexes (English). *Translator or author:* William Bedell Stanford. London, England: Macmillan.

1938— Odissea, Libro V; con introduzione e commento di Gino Massoni (Greek). Florence, Italy: Vallecchi.

1938— Odyssea Homeri; edidit Guilielmus Dindorf; 5th ed. corr. quam curavit C. Hentze (Greek). Leipzig, Germany: B. G. Teubner.

1938— The Wrath of Achilles; translated from Iliad I, XI, XVI–XXIV, with a note on the metre; preface by Sir Arthur Quiller-Couch (English). *Translator or author:* Samuel Odgen Andrew. London, England: J. M. and Sons Dent.

1938— The Odyssey of Homer (English). *Translator or author:* Samuel Henry Butcher; Andrew Lang. New York, N.Y.: P. F. Collier.

1938— The Odyssey of Homer; done into English prose (English). *Translator or author:* Samuel Henry Butcher; Andrew Lang. New York, N.Y.: Macmillan.

1938— The Odyssey of Homer; translated into English prose (English). *Translator or author:* Robert Henry Hiller. Book League of America.

1938— Homere Iliade; traduction nouvelle (French). *Translator or author:* Leconte de Lisle. Paris, France: Alphonse Lemerre.

1938— Himnos; traducidas directamenta del Griego en versos Castellanos (Spanish). *Translator or author:* Leopoldo Lopez Alvarez. Pasto, Spain: Tipografia Athene.

1938— Nausikaa, a Love Story; the sixth book of the Odyssey, done into English hexameters; 2nd ed. (English). *Translator or author:* Annette Meakin. Oxford, England: Shakespeare Head Press.

1938— Iliade; traduzione (Italian). *Translator or author:* Vincenzo Monti. Florence, Italy: A. Salani.

1938— L'Iliade; tradotta; con commento di Vit-

torio Turri; con 56 illustrazioni; 6th ed. (Italian). *Translator or author:* Vincenzo Monti. Florence, Italy: G. C. Sansoni.

1938— L'Odissea; con commento di Vittorio Turri; con 92 illustrazioni; 7th ed. (Italian). *Translator or author:* Ippolito Pindemonte. Florence, Italy: G. C. Sansoni.

1938— The Odyssey; translated (English). *Translator or author:* Alexander Pope. London, England: Oxford University Press.

1938— The Story of Achilles; a translation of Homer's "Iliad" (English). *Translator or author:* William Henry Denham Rouse. London, England; Toronto, Canada; New York, N.Y.: Thomas Nelson and Sons.

1938— The Story of Odysseus; a translation of Homer's "Odyssey" into plain English; illustrated by Norman Hall; 2nd ed. (English). *Translator or author:* William Henry Denham Rouse. London, England; New York, N.Y.: Thomas Nelson.

1938— The Iliad; the story of Achilles (English). *Translator or author:* William Henry Denham Rouse. New York, N.Y.; Toronto, Canada; London, London: New American Library; New English Library.

1938— Ilias; verdeutscht; neu gestaltete Ausgabe (German). *Translator or author:* Thassilo Fritz H. von Scheffer. Bremen, Germany: C. Schunemann.

1938— Odysse; verdeutscht; neu gestaltete Ausg. (German). *Translator or author:* Thassilo Fritz H. von Scheffer. Leipzig, Germany: Fieterich.

1938— La Odisea Homero (Spanish). *Translator or author:* Luis Segala y Estalella. Buenos Aires, Argentina: Losada.

1938— Himnon el Demeter mi-Yevanit (Hebrew). *Translator or author:* Shelomoh Shpan. Tel Aviv, Israel: Gazit.

1938— The Original Iliad; text and translation (Greek; English). *Translator or author:* Robinson Smith. London, England: Grafton.

1938–39— Homeri Opera; recognovervnt breviqve adnotatione critica instrvxervnt David B[inning] Monro ... et Thomas W[illiam] Allen; ed. altera (Greek). Oxford, England: Clarendon Press.

1938–39— Odisseia; traducao do Grego; prefacio e notas dos E. Dias Palmeira e M. Alves Correia (Portuguese). *Translator or author:* E. Dias Palmeira. Lisbon, Portugal: Sa da Costa.

1938–42— The Odyssey; with an English translation (Greek; English). *Translator or author:* Augustus Taber Murray. London, England; Cambridge, Mass.: Harvard University Press; William Heinemann.

1939— L'Odyssee, Poesie Homerique; texte etabli et traduit par Victor Berard; 3rd ed. (Greek; French). *Translator or author:* Victor Berard. Paris, France: Societe d'Edition "Les Belles Lettres".

1939— The Iliad for Boys and Girls; told from Homer in Simple Language (English). *Translator or author:* Alfred John Church. New York, N.Y.: Macmillan.

1939— De Dolinge van Ulysse; Homerus' Odysseia I–XVIII in Nederlandse; verzorgd door Th[eodoor] Weevers (Dutch). *Translator or author:* Dirk Volkertszoon Coornhert. Amsterdam, Netherlands: Elsevier.

1939— The Iliad of Homer, Book XI; edited (Greek; English). *Translator or author:* E[dward] S[eymour] Forster. London, England: Methuen.

1939— Ao-te-sai Ho-ma chu [The Odyssey] (Chinese). *Translator or author:* Tung-hua Fu. Ch'angsha, China: Shang wu yin shu kuan.

1939— L'Odyssee d'Homere, Aventures d'Ulysse (French). *Translator or author:* Robert Klaerr. Paris, France: L. Hachette.

1939— Odysseia A–D [H]omerou; archeion keimenon, emmetros metaphrasis Zesimou Sidere; prolegomena eis to [H]omerikon zetema Gianne Kordatou (Greek, Modern). *Translator or author:* Gianes Konstantinou Kordatos. Athens, Greece: Ioannou & P. Zacharopoulos.

1939— The Odyssey of Homer; newly translated into English prose (English). *Translator or author:* Thomas Edward Lawrence. New York, N.Y.: Oxford University Press.

1939— La Odisea; traducidas directamente del Griego en versos Castellanos (Greek; Spanish). *Translator or author:* Leopoldo Lopez Alvarez. Pasto, Narino, Colombia: Tipografia Athene.

1939— L'Odissea di Omero; nei passi migliipri della traduzione di Ippolito Pindemonte, collegati con las narrazione di tutto il poema [a cura di] Luigi Papandrea (Italian). *Translator or author:* Ippolito Pindemonte. Florence, Italy: Nemi.

1939— The Poetical Works of Alexander Pope, Esq.; to which is prefixed the life of the author, by Dr. Johnson; new ed. (English). *Translator or author:* Alexander Pope. Philadelphia, Pa.: Crissy and Markley.

1939— Iliada, Odisea; seleccion prologos y notas

de Roberto F. Giusti; 3rd ed. *Translator or author:* Luis Segala y Estalella. Buenos Aires, Argentina: A. y cia Estrada.

1939— Homers Ilias; Deutsch, mit Holzschnitten von Ludwig von Hofmann und einer Einleitung "Homer in der Kunst" von Max von Boehn und Wolfgang Bruhn (German). *Translator or author:* Johann Heinrich Voss. Berlin, Germany: Askanischen Verlag.

1939— Homers Ilias in Auszuge (German). *Translator or author:* Johann Heinrich Voss. Bielefeld, Germany; Leipzig, Germany: Velhagen und Klasing.

1940— Homers Odyssee; fur den Schulgebrauch erklart bon Karl Friedr[ich] Ameis und Carl Hentze (Greek). Leipzig, Germany: B. G. Teubner.

1940— Homers Ilias; fur den Schulgebrauch erklart von Karl Friedrich Ameis; Gesang IV–VI; bearb. von C. Hentze; 9th ed. (Greek). Leipzig, Germany: B. G. Teubner.

1940— Auswahl aus Homers Odyssee; herausgeben von Eduard Bornemann (Greek). Frankfurt am Main, Germany: Moritz Diesterweg.

1940— The Iliad for Boys and Girls; told from Homer in simple language (English). *Translator or author:* Alfred John Church. New York, N.Y.: Macmillan.

1940— The Iliad of Homer, Book XI; edited (Greek; English). *Translator or author:* E[dward] S[eymour] Forster. London, England: Methuen.

1940— Iliada, Odisea Homero; seleccion, prologo y notas de Roberto F. Giusti; 4th ed. *Translator or author:* Roberto Fernando Giusti. Buenos Aires, Argentina: A. y Cia Estrada.

1940— The Odyssey of Homer; newly translated into English prose by T. E. Shaw (English). *Translator or author:* Thomas Edward Lawrence. New York, N.Y.: Editions for the Armed Forces.

1940— The Odyssey of Homer; translated from the Greek by T. E. Shaw (English). *Translator or author:* Thomas Edward Lawrence. New York, N.Y.: Oxford University Press.

1940— La Odisea Homero; version compendiada (Spanish). *Translator or author:* Lauro Palma. Buenos Aires, Argentina: Editorial Atlantida.

1940— L'Odissea; con introd. e note a cura di Carmone di Pierro (Italian). *Translator or author:* Ippolito Pindemonte. Florence, Italy: G. Barbera.

1940— [H]omerou Ilias kai Odysseia; eisagoge eis to [H]omerikon epos [h]ypo Vilamovits; metaphrasis kai semeiosis Nik[os] I. Sephaki kai alloi (Greek; Modern Greek). *Translator or author:* Nikos I. Sephakis. Athens, Greece: Epistemonike Hetaireia ton Hellenikon Grammaton Papyros.

1940— Odysseia [Z reckeho originalu pro dnesniho cloveka pretlumocil Vladimir Sramek; preklad prohledl a doslov napsal Ferdinand Stieblitz]. *Translator or author:* Vladimir Sramek. Prague, Czechoslavakia: Evropsky Literarni Klub.

1940— Homers Odyssee; nach der ersten Ausgabe von Joh[ann] Heinrich Voss; mit achtzehn illustrationen nach Zeichnungen von Bonaventura Genelli und ornamentalem von J. V. Cissarz (German). *Translator or author:* Johann Heinrich Voss. Stuttgart, Germany: J. G. Cotta Buchhandlung.

1940–41— Odyssee ... Homere; trad. Francaise (French). *Translator or author:* Ch. and H. Berthaut Georgin. Paris, France: A. Hatier.

1941— Odyssey; with introduction, notes, etc. by W[illiam] W[alter] Merry (Greek). Oxford, England: Clarendon Press.

1941— The Odyssey of Homer, Books VI and VII; with notes and vocabulary by G[erald] M[aclean] Edwards (Greek). Cambridge, England: Cambridge University Press.

1941— L'Iliade, Homere (French). Paris, France: E. Flammarion.

1941— Vorrimi I Hektorit; libri XXIV I Iliades; perkethyeshgyp (Albanian). *Translator or author:* Frano Alkaj. Shkoder: A. Gjergy Fishta.

1941— Hymes; texts etabli et traduit par Jean Humbert (Greek; French). *Translator or author:* Jean Humbert. Paris, France: Societe d'Edition "Les Belles Lettres".

1941— The Iliad by Homer; with introduction by Louise Pound; translation (English). *Translator or author:* Andrew Lang; Walter Leaf; Ernest Myers. New York, N.Y.: Macmillan.

1941— The Odyssey; translated from the Greek (English). *Translator or author:* Thomas Edward Lawrence. Oxford University Press.

1941— Oddyseifur; aefintyralegar frasagnir ur Oddyseifskviou Homers; endursagoar vio haefi barna og unlinga af Henrik Pontoppidan; Steinbor Guomundsson islenzkaoi (Icelandic). *Translator or author:* Henrik Pontoppidan; Steinbor Guomundsson. Reykjavik, Iceland: Vikingsutgafan.

1941— The Story of Odysseus, Shortened from Homer's Odyssey; translated into plain English (English). *Translator or author:* William Henry

Denham Rouse. London, England: Thomas Nelson.

1941— Der Frosch-Mause-Krieg (Batrachomyomachia); verdeutscht (German). *Translator or author:* Thassilo Fritz H. von Scheffer. Munich, Germany: Ernst Heimeran.

1941— Homerus, Odiseyah; meturgemah mi-Yevonit le-Ivrit al yede Sha'ul Tshernihovski (Hebrew). *Translator or author:* Saul Tchernichowsky. Jerusalem, Israel: he-Hevrah le-hotsa'at sefarim al yad ha-Universita.

1941— Odiseyah; meturgemah mi-Yevanit le-ivrit al yede Sha'ul Tshernihovski (Hebrew). *Translator or author:* Saul Tchernichowsky. Tel Aviv, Israel: Be-siyu'a keren Yitshak Leyb ve-Rahel.

1941–42— Odusseia: Odise, Homeros; ceviren Ahmet Cevat Emre (Turkish). *Translator or author:* Ahmeet Cevar Emre. Ankara, Turkey: Recep Ulusoglu Basimevi.

1942— Iliade, Libro I; con introduzione e commento di Angelo Taccone; 2nd ed. Torino (Turin), Italy: Editrice Libraria Italiana.

1942— The Odyssey, Homer; including also passages from Homer's Iliad; also Norse legends and American Indian legends (English). Syracuse, N.Y.: L. W. Singer.

1942— Odissea, Libro V; introduzione e commento di Aniello Notaro (Greek). Torino (Turin), Italy: Editrice Libraria Italiana.

1942— Odissea, Libro IX; con introduzione e note di Goffredo M. Lattanzi; 2nd ed. (Greek). Torino (Turin), Italy: Editrice Libraria Italiana.

1942— The Iliad of Homer; translated; edited by Louise Ropes Loomis (English). *Translator or author:* Samuel Butler; Louise Ropes Loomis. Princeton, N.J.: D. Van Nostrand.

1942— The Iliad of Homer; translated; edited by Louise R[opes] Loomis (English). *Translator or author:* Samuel Butler; Louise Ropes Loomis. New York, N.Y.: Classics Club by W. J. Black.

1942— The Iliad of Homer; translated; edited by Louise Ropes Loomis (English). *Translator or author:* Samuel Butler; Louise Ropes Loomis. Toronto, Canada; New York, N.Y.: D. Van Nostrand.

1942— The Odyssey for Boys and Girls; told from Homer (English). *Translator or author:* Alfred John Church. New York, N.Y.: Macmillan.

1942— Achilleeis, Homers Ur-Ilias; ubersetzt in sieben Gesangen (German). *Translator or author:* Bernd Isemann. Strasbourg, France: Hunenburg.

1942—Iliaden och Odysseen; utdrag ur Erland Lagerleofs eoverseattning; utgivna jeamte inledning och feorklaringar av Einar Pontan (Swedish). *Translator or author:* Erland L. Lagerlof; Einar Pontan. Lund, Sweden: C. W. K. Gleerup.

1942—Iliade, Homere; traduction nouvelle (French). *Translator or author:* Leconte de Lisle. Paris, France: Alphonse Lemerre.

1942—The Iliad; with an English translation (Greek; English). *Translator or author:* Augustus Taber Murray. London, England; Cambridge, Mass.: Harvard University Press; William Heinemann.

1942—The Odyssey of Homer; in the English verse translation; illustrated with the classical designs of John Flaxman (English). *Translator or author:* Alexander Pope. New York, N.Y.: Heritage Press.

1942—L'Odyssee, Homere; texte Francais etabli par Emile Ripert d'apres la traduction de Madame Dacier; avec une preface de Emile Ripert (French). *Translator or author:* Emile Ripert. Paris, France: Bibliotheque de l'Etoile.

1942—The Story of Achilles, Shortened from Homer's Iliad; translated into plain English (English). *Translator or author:* William Henry Denham Rouse. London, England; Edinburgh, Scotland: Thomas Nelson and Sons.

1942—Himnon el Hermes; mi-Yeovanit (Hebrew). *Translator or author:* Shelomoh Shpan. Tel Aviv, Israel: Hotsarat Gazit.

1942—Odiseah; tirgem mi-yeovanit Sha'ul Tsherniohovsoki okitsur ove-he arot me-et Yehoshu'a Guotman (Hebrew). *Translator or author:* Saul Tchernichowsky. Tel Aviv, Israel: Hotsa'at Shooken.

1942—Homerova Ilias; pereloezil (Czech). *Translator or author:* Otmar Vaenorny; Ferdinand Stieblitz. Prague, Czechoslavakia: J. Laichter.

1942–45—The Odyssey; with an English translation (Greek; English). *Translator or author:* Augustus Taber Murray. London, England; Cambridge, Mass.: Harvard University Press; William Heinemann.

1943—The Iliads of Homer, Prince of Poets; translated; introduction and notes by W. Cooke Taylor (English). *Translator or author:* George Chapman. London, England: Charles Knight.

1943—Hesiod, the Homeric Hymns, and Homerica; with an English translation; new ed. (Greek; English). *Translator or author:* Hugh Gerard Evelyn-White. Cambridge, Mass.; London, England: Harvard University Press; William Heinemann.

1943—Homere, Odyssee; traduction nouvelle (French). *Translator or author:* Leconte de Lisle. Paris, France: Alphonse Lemerre.

1943—The Iliad of Homer; in the English verse translation; illustrated with the classical designs of John Flaxman (English). *Translator or author:* Alexander Pope. New York, N.Y.: Heritage Press.

1943—The Iliad of Homer; translated (English). *Translator or author:* Alexander Pope. New York, N.Y.: Oxford University Press.

1943—L'Iliade; con incisioni di A. de Carolis (Italian). *Translator or author:* Ettore Romagnoli. Bologna, France: N. Zanichelli.

1943—Homere, l'Iliade (French). *Translator or author:* Gabriel de Roton. Bordeaux, France.

1943—Ilias; Deutsch (German). *Translator or author:* Rudolf Alexander Schroder. Berlin, Germany: Suhrkamp.

1943—Iliada, Odisea, Himnos (Spanish). *Translator or author:* Luis Segala y Estalella. Barcelona, Spain: Raiz y Rama.

1943—De Odusseia; bewerkt naar de vertaling van C. Vosmaer. *Translator or author:* Carel Vosmaer. Brugge-Brussel, Belgium: De Kinkhoren.

1943–46—Homers Werke; ubersetz; herausgeben von Peter Von der Muhll (German). *Translator or author:* Johann Heinrich Voss. Basel, Switzerland: Birkhauser.

1944—Odyssee; traduction; photographies de Fred. Boissonnas; 2nd ed. (French). *Translator or author:* Victor Berard. Paris, France: Armand Colin.

1944—L'Iliade di Omero; tradotta (Italian). *Translator or author:* Jolanda de Blasi. Florence, Italy: G. C. Sansoni.

1944—The Iliad of Homer; translated into English blank verse; abridged edition, edited by Sarah E[mma] Simons (English). *Translator or author:* William Cullen Bryant. Boston, Mass.; Cambridge, Mass.: Houghton Mifflin; Riverside Press.

1944—The Odyssey of Homer; done into English prose; abridged and edited by Wallace B. Moffett; illustrated by Norman Roberts (English). *Translator or author:* Samuel Henry Butcher; Andrew Lang. New York, N.Y.: Macmillan.

1944—The Odyssey of Homer; translated (English). *Translator or author:* Samuel Butler. Toronto, Canada; New York, N.Y.: D. Van Nostrand.

1944— The Odyssey of Homer; translated; edited by Louise Ropes Loomis (English). *Translator or author:* Samuel Butler; Louise Ropes Loomis. New York, N.Y.: Classics Club.

1944— The Story of the Iliad (English). *Translator or author:* Alfred John Church. New York, N.Y.: Macmillan.

1944— The Iliad of Homer; translated; series: Everyman's Library (English). *Translator or author:* Edward George Geoffrey Smith Stanley, Earl of Derby. London, England; New York, N.Y.: J. M. Dent; E. P. Dutton.

1944— The Odyssey of Homer; newly translated into English prose by T. E. Shaw (English). *Translator or author:* Thomas Edward Lawrence. New York, N.Y.: Oxford University Press.

1944— L'Iliade d'Omero; introduzione e note di Roberto d'Alfonso (Italian). *Translator or author:* Vincenzo Monti. Torino (Turin), Italy: Unione Tipografico-Editrice Torinese.

1944— Ilias, Zangen I, VI, XXII; in het nederlandsch vertaald door R. de Pauw ... en bewerkt door A. Clerckx. *Translator or author:* R. de Pauw. Antwerp, Belgium: Standaard-Boekhandel.

1944— L'Odissea d'Omero (Italian). *Translator or author:* Ippolito Pindemonte. Torino (Turin), Italy: Arnoldo Mondadori.

1944— L'Odissea d'Omero; a cura di Giulio Reichenbach (Italian). *Translator or author:* Ippolito Pindemonte. Torino (Turin), Italy: Utet.

1944— La Odisea, Homero; traduccion; prologo y ed. cuidada por Pedro Henriquez (Spanish). *Translator or author:* Luis Segala y Estalella. Buenos Aires, Argentina: Losada.

1944— Homere. *Translator or author:* Albert Severyna. Brussels, Belgium.

1944— The Iliad of Homer; a line for line translation in dactylic hexameters; illustrated with the classical designs of John Flaxman; 1st ed. (English). *Translator or author:* William Benjamin Smith; Walter Miller. New York, N.Y.: Macmillan.

1944— De Ilias; bewerkt naar de vertaling van C. Vosmaer. *Translator or author:* Carel Vosmaer. Brugge-Brussel, Belgium: De Kinkhoren.

1945— Homer, Iliad, Books I–XII; with an introduction, a brief Homeric grammar, and notes, by D. B. Monro; 5th ed. (Greek). Oxford, England: Clarendon Press.

1945— La Morte di Ettore, Iliade, Libro XXII; introduzione e commento di Gregorio Munno. Citta di Castello, Italy: Macri.

1945— Les Amusements Naturels, l'Iliade, les Eumenides, le Mystere d'Adam et Cent Cinquante Poems Nouveaux (French). *Translator or author:* Pierre Albert-Birot. Paris, France: Denoel.

1945— Homere, l'Iliade (French). *Translator or author:* Y. Bequignon. Paris, France.

1945— The Odyssey of Homer; done into English prose (English). *Translator or author:* Samuel Henry Butcher; Andrew Lang. London, England: Macmillan.

1945— The Odyssey for Boys and Girls; told from Homer (English). *Translator or author:* Alfred John Church. New York, N.Y.: Macmillan.

1945— Homer's Iliad; long selections, with a brief introduction [by] Helen Pope (English). *Translator or author:* Edward George Geoffrey Smith Stanley; Earl of Derby. Girard, Ks.: Haldeman-Julius Publications.

1945— The Iliad of Homer; done into English prose; abridged and edited by Wallace B. Moffett; illustrated by W. M. Berger (English). *Translator or author:* Andrew Lang; Walter Leaf; Ernest Myers. New York, N.Y.: Macmillan.

1945— The Odyssey, Homer; translated (English). *Translator or author:* Emile Victor Rieu. London, England: Penguin Books.

1945— Inni, Batracomiomachia, Epigrammi, Margite; con incisioni di A. de Carolis (Italian). *Translator or author:* Ettore Romagnoli. Bologna, France: N. Zanichelli.

1945— The Iliad of Homer; a line for line translation in dactylic hexameters; illustrated with the classical designs of John Flaxman (English). *Translator or author:* William Benjamin Smith; Walter Miller. New York, N.Y.: Macmillan.

1945— Homers Ilias; ubersetzt (German). *Translator or author:* Johann Heinrich Voss. Basel, Switzerland: Birkhauser.

1945— Homers Odyssee; ubersetzt (German). *Translator or author:* Johann Heinrich Voss. Basel, Switzerland: Birkhauser.

1946— Homeri Odyssea; recognovit P[eter] von der Meuhll. Basel, Switzerland: Helbing & Lichtenhahn.

1946— Odissea, Libro XIII; con introduzione e commento do Domenico Martella (Greek). Torino (Turin), Italy: S. Lattes.

1946— Batrachomyomachia; heroico Latino carmine (Latin). *Translator or author:* D. Barresi. Rhegii in Bruttiis [location?]: J La Roccae.

1946— L'Odyssee, Poesie Homerique; texte etabli et traduit; 4th ed. (Greek; French). *Translator or author:* Victor Berard. Paris, France: Societe d'Edition "Les Belles Lettres".

1946— The Odyssey by Homer; with an introduction by John A. Scott; 3rd ed. (English). *Translator or author:* Samuel Henry Butcher; John Adams Scott. New York, N.Y.: Macmillan.

1946— The Children's Homer: the Adventures of Odysseus and the Tale of Troy; illustrated by Willy Pogany [reprint of the 1918 edition] (English). *Translator or author:* Padraic Colum; Willy Pogany. New York, N.Y.: Macmillan.

1946— Hymne a Demeter [d']Homere; traduit selon le rythme; burins originaux de Roger Vieillard (Greek; French). *Translator or author:* P. L. Couchoud. Paris, France: Nouvelle Edition.

1946— Odysseia [H]omerou (Greek, Modern). *Translator or author:* Argyres Ephtaliotes. Athens, Greece: Vivliopoleio tes "Hestias".

1946— Homeros' Iliad; frean Grekiskan (Swedish). *Translator or author:* Erland L. Lagerlof. Lund, Sweden: C. W. K. Gleerup.

1946— L'Iliade; traduction nouvelle avec une introduction et des notes (French). *Translator or author:* Eugene Lasserre. Paris, France: Garnier Freres.

1946— The Odyssey of Homer; newly translated into English prose by T. E. Shaw (English). *Translator or author:* Thomas Edward Lawrence. New York, N.Y.: Oxford University Press.

1946— The Iliad; with an English translation (Greek; English). *Translator or author:* Augustus Taber Murray. Cambridge, Mass.; London, England: Harvard University Press; William Heinemann.

1946— The Odyssey; with an English translation (Greek; English). *Translator or author:* Augustus Taber Murray. Cambridge, Mass.; London, England: Harvard University Press; William Heinemann.

1946— The Odyssey [of] Homer; translated (English). *Translator or author:* Emile Victor Rieu. Harmondsworth, England: Penguin Books.

1946— The Story of Achilles, Shortened from Homer's Iliad; translated into plain English (English). *Translator or author:* William Henry Denham Rouse. London, England; Edinburgh, Scotland: Nelson.

1946— La Odisea Homero; version directa y literal del Griego; ilustraciones de Cenni (Spanish).

Translator or author: Luis Segala y Estalella. Buenos Aires, Argentina: Jose Ballesta.

1946— Obras Completas; version directa y literal del Griego; ed. ilus ... con 72 grandes composiciones de John Flaxman (Spanish). *Translator or author:* Luis Segala y Estalella. Buenos Aires, Argentina: Gil.

1946— Ha-Himnonot ha-Homeriyim (Hebrew). *Translator or author:* Shelomoh Shpan. Jerusalem, Israel: Ha-oHevrah le-hotsaat sefarim al-yad ha-universiot.

1946—[Homers] Werke; ubers; [heraugeben von Peter von der Muhll] (German). *Translator or author:* Johann Heinrich Voss. Basel, Switzerland: Birkhauser.

1947— Auswahl aus Homers Odyssee; von Dr. Eduard Bornemann; new ed. (Greek). Frankfurt am Main, Germany: Hirschgraben-Verlag.

1947— Homero; nueva version directa. Barcelona, Spain: Ed. Labor.

1947— Poemetos e Fragmentos; traducao do Grego; introducao e notas (Portuguese). *Translator or author:* Pe. M. Alves Correia. Lisbon, Portugal: Livraria Sa da Costa.

1947— Odysee Homero; 3rd ed. (Spanish???). *Translator or author:* Victor Berard. Paris, France: Armand Colin.

1947— The Children's Homer: the Adventures of Odysseus and the Tale of Troy; illustrated by Willy Pogany [reprint of the 1918 edition] (English). *Translator or author:* Padraic Colum; Willy Pogany. New York, N.Y.: Macmillan.

1947— Odysseia Homeros; forditotta (Hungarian). *Translator or author:* Gabor Devecseri. Budapest, Hungary: Singer es Wolfner Kiadada.

1947— Iliada; w przekladzie (Polish). *Translator or author:* Franciszek Ksawery Dmochowski. Krakow, Poland: Zaklad Narodowego Imienia Ossolinskich.

1947— L'Odyssee; traduction nouvelle, avec introduction, notes et index (French). *Translator or author:* Mederic Dufour; Jeanne Raison. Paris, France: Garnier Freres.

1947— Hesiod, the Homeric Hymns, and Homerica; new and revised ed. (Greek; English). *Translator or author:* Hugh Gerard Evelyn-White. Cambridge, Mass.: Harvard University Press.

1947— Ao-te-sai Homer Chu [The Odyssey] (Chinese). *Translator or author:* Tung-hua Fu. Shang-hai, China: Shang wu yin shu kuan.

1947—Homer's Odyssey; a new translation for children; with drawings by Ann Buckmaster (English). *Translator or author:* George P. Kerr. London, England: P. Lunn.

1947—The Iliad by Homer; with introduction by Louise Pound; translation (English). *Translator or author:* Andrew Lang; Walter Leaf; Ernest Myers. New York, N.Y.: Macmillan.

1947—The Iliad; with an English translation (Greek; English). *Translator or author:* Augustus Taber Murray. Cambridge, Mass.; London, England: Harvard University Press; William Heinemann.

1947—Odissea; riassunti. *Translator or author:* Angelo Nucciotti. Bologna, France: L. Cappelli.

1947—Ilias [von] Homer; verdeutscht (German). *Translator or author:* Thassilo Fritz H. von Scheffer. Wiesbaden, Germany: Dieterich'sche Verlagbuchhandlung.

1947–48—The Odyssey of Homer; edited, with general and grammatical introduction, commentary, and indexes, by W[illiam] B[edell] Stanford (Greek). London, England: Macmillan.

1947–49—Iliade [d'] Homere; texte etabli et traduit par Paul Mazon (Greek; French). *Translator or author:* Paul Mazon. Paris, France: Societe d'Edition "Les Belles Lettres".

1948—Iliade, Libro XXIV (Il Riscatto di Ettore); introduzione e commento di Umberto Boella. Torino (Turin), Italy: G. B. Paravia.

1948—Iliade, Libro XXIV; a cura di Folco Martinazzoli. Rome, Italy: Casa Editrice Gismondi.

1948—Homer's Odyssey; translated (English). *Translator or author:* Samuel Ogden Andrew. London, England: J. M. Dent.

1948—Auswahl aus Homers Ilias; neue Ausgabe. *Translator or author:* Eduard Bornemann. Frankfurt am Main, Germany: Hirschgraben-Verlag.

1948—The Iliad of Homer and the Odyssey; rendered into English prose (English). *Translator or author:* Samuel Butler. Chicago, Il.: Encyclopedia Britannica.

1948—The Odyssey of Homer; adapted; illustrated by Thomas Fraumeni (English). *Translator or author:* Henry Irving Christ. New York, N.Y.: Globe Book Co.

1948—The Odyssey for Boys and Girls, Told from Homer (English). *Translator or author:* Alfred John Church. New York, N.Y.: Macmillan.

1948—The Iliad of Homer; translated; series: Everyman's Library (English). *Translator or author:* Edward George Geoffrey Smith Stanley, Earl of Derby. London, England; New York, N.Y.: J. M. Dent; E. P. Dutton.

1948—Homeros' Odysse; frn Grekiskan; 3rd ed. (Swedish). *Translator or author:* Erland L. Lagerlof. Lund, Sweden: C. W. K. Gleerup.

1948—The Odyssey [of] Homer; translated in selection; illustrations engraved on copper by John Buckland-Wright (English). *Translator or author:* Frank Laurence Lucas. London, England: Folio Society.

1948—Aphrodite, the Homeric Hymn to Aphrodite and the Pervigilium Veneris; translated into English (Greek; English). *Translator or author:* Frank Laurence Lucas. Cambridge, England: Cambridge University Press.

1948—The Homeric Hymn to Aphrodite; a new translation; with 10 engravings by Mark Severin (English). *Translator or author:* Frank Laurence Lucas. London, England: Golden Cockerel Press.

1948—L'Odissea; novament traslladada en versos Catalans; ornada amb gravats sobre fusta de E. C. Ricart (Catalan). *Translator or author:* Carles Riba. Barcelona, Spain.

1948—The Odyssey; translated (English). *Translator or author:* Emile Victor Rieu. Harmondsworth, England: Penguin Books.

1948—The Story of Odysseus; a translation of Homer's "Odyssey" into plain English; 2nd ed. (English). *Translator or author:* William Henry Denham Rouse. London, England; New York, N.Y.: R. Nelson.

1948—Die Homerischen Gotterhymnen (German). *Translator or author:* Thassilo Fritz H. von Scheffer. Leipzig, Germany.

1948—Homers Odyssee; Deutsch (German). *Translator or author:* Rudolf Alexander Schroder. Berlin, Germany: S. Fischer.

1948—Odyseja; w prekladzie; wstepem i objasnieniami zaopatrzyl Tadeusz Sinko; 4th ed. (Polish). *Translator or author:* Lucjan Hipolit Siemienski. Warsaw, Poland: Wydawn.

1948—Odyssee; ubersetzt; mit eimen Nachwort von Karl Reinhardt (German). *Translator or author:* Johann Heinrich Voss. Leipzig, Germany: Insel-Verlag.

1948–49—Kviour Homers; bjuggu til prentunar (Icelandic). *Translator or author:* Sveinbjorn Egilsson; Kristinn Armansson; Jon Gisl. Reykjavik, Iceland: Bokautgafa Menningarsjos.

1949—La Yliada en Romance; segun la impresion de Arnao Guillen de Brocar (Valladolid, 1519); ed., prologo y glosario por Martin de Riquer (Latin; Spanish). Barcelona, Spain.

1949—Odyssey; with introduction, notes, etc. by W[illiam] W[alter[Merry (Greek). Oxford, England: Clarendon Press.

1949—Odysseus und Nausikaa; ein Idyll aus Homers Odyssee nach der Deutschen Ubertragung von Johann Heinrich Voss mit Originalzeichnungen von Karl List (German). Lahr, Germany: Internationalen Bibliothek.

1949—Homer. *Translator or author:* Ernst Bickel. Bonn, Germany.

1949—The Odyssey; rendered into English prose; illustrated after drawings by Sir W. Russell Flint (English). *Translator or author:* Samuel Henry Butcher; Andrew Lang. Medici Society.

1949—The Odyssey of Homer; done into English prose (English). *Translator or author:* Samuel Henry Butcher; Andrew Lang. London, England: Macmillan.

1949—The Iliad for Boys and Girls; Told from Homer in Simple Language (English). *Translator or author:* Alfred John Church. New York, N.Y.: Macmillan.

1949—De Dolinge van Ulysse; Homerus' Odysseia I–XVIII in Nederlandse verzen (Dutch). *Translator or author:* Dirk Volkertszoon Coornhert. Amsterdam, Netherlands: Elsevier.

1949—The Coming of Ulysses; A Play in Four Acts (English). *Translator or author:* Philip Dorf. New York, N.Y.: Oxford Book Co.

1949—Hymns to Aphrodite; translated (English). *Translator or author:* John Edgar. New York, N.Y.: Valenti Angelo.

1949—Ilias en Odyssee; een keuze van fragmenten, metrisch vertaald en van verbindenden tekst voorien (Dutch). *Translator or author:* Wolter Everard Kuiper. Haarlem, Netherlands: N.V. Drukkerij De Spaarnestad.

1949—Iliaden och Odysseen; utdrag ur Erland Lagerlofs oversattning, utgivna jamte inledning och forklaringar av Einar Pontan. *Translator or author:* Erland L. Lagerlof. Lund, Sweden: C. W. K. Gleerup.

1949—The Iliad of Homer; done into English prose (English). *Translator or author:* Andrew Lang; Walter Leaf; Ernest Myers. London, England: Macmillan.

1949—The Odyssey; translated (English). *Trans-lator or author:* George Herbert Palmer. Boston, Mass.: Houghton Mifflin.

1949—The Odyssey of Homer; translated (English). *Translator or author:* Alexander Pope. London, England: Oxford University Press.

1949—The Iliad of Homer; translated (English). *Translator or author:* Alexander Pope. London, England; New York, N.Y.: Oxford University Press.

1949—Iliada; prevede. *Translator or author:* Asen Raztsvetnikov. Sofija (Sofia), Bulgaria: Narodna Prosveta.

1949—The Odyssey; the Story of Ulysses [by] Homer; translated (English). *Translator or author:* William Henry Denham Rouse. New York, N.Y.: New American Library.

1949—Iliada Gomer; perevod (Russian). *Translator or author:* Vikentii Vikentevich Veresaeva. Moscow, Russia: Gos. izd-vo Khuodozh Lit-ry.

1950—Ilias, Odyssee; J. C. Bruijn [et] C. Spoelder [ed.]; 4th ed. Haarlem, Netherlands: H. D. Tjeenk Willink.

1950—Ilias Atheniensium; the Athenian Iliad of the Sixth Century B.C.; edited by George Melville Bolling (Greek). Lancaster, Pa.: American Philological Association.

1950—The Iliad of Homer, Books I–VI; rev. ed. Boston, Mass.: J. Allyn.

1950—Homeri Opera; recognovit brevique adnotatione critica instrvxit Thomas W. Allen; 2nd ed. [from the 1917 edition] (Greek). Oxford, England: Clarendon Press.

1950—Homer's Iliad, Book 1; vocabulary; edited for the use of schools by John Bond and A.S. Walpole (Greek).

1950—Iliadis; recognovit adnotationeqve instruxit Harushige Kozu. Tokyo, Japan: Iwanami Shoten.

1950—The Iliad by Homer; illustrated by Alex A. Blum [comic book] (English). New York, N.Y.: Gilberton.

1950—Iliyadah ove-Odiseyah me ubadim al yede Yan oVerner oVesoton; ivrit (Hebrew). *Translator or author:* Anda Amir-Pinkerfeld. Tel Aviv, Israel: Amos.

1950—The Odyssey [of] Homer (English). *Translator or author:* Samuel Henry Butcher; Andrew Lang. Chicago, Il.: Great Books Foundation.

1950—The Odyssey of Homer (English). *Translator or author:* Samuel Henry Butcher; Andrew Lang. New York, N.Y.: Carlton House.

1950— The Odyssey; translated (English). *Translator or author:* Samuel Henry Butcher; Andrew Lang. New York, N.Y.: Modern Library.

1950— The Iliad; translated; with illustrations by Steele Savage (English). *Translator or author:* Alston Hurd Chase; William Graves Perry, Jr. Boston, Mass.: Little Brown.

1950— The Iliad; translated from Homer; with illustrations by Steele Savage (English). *Translator or author:* Alston Hurd Chase; William Graves Perry, Jr. New York, N.Y.: Grosset and Dunlap.

1950— Iliada; w przek.; zrewidowai, wstiepem i komentarzem oipatrzyi Tadeusz Sinko; 7th ed. (Polish). *Translator or author:* Franciszek Ksawery Dmochowski. Warsaw, Poland: Wydawnictwo.

1950— Hesiod, the Homeric Hymns, and Homerica; with an English translation (Greek; English). *Translator or author:* Hugh Gerard Evelyn-White. London, England; Cambridge, Mass.: Harvard University Press; William Heinemann.

1950— La Iliada Homero; traduccion directa del Griego; 3rd ed. (Greek; Spanish). *Translator or author:* Hermosilla D. Jose Gomez. Buenos Aires, Argentina: Editorial Sopena Argentina.

1950— The Iliad of Homer; done into English prose (English). *Translator or author:* Andrew Lang; Walter Leaf; Ernest Myers. New York, N.Y.: Carlton House.

1950— The Iliad; translated (English). *Translator or author:* Andrew Lang; Walter Leaf; Ernest Myers. New York, N.Y.: Random House.

1950— The Iliad of Homer; done into English prose; abridged and edited by Wallace B. Moffett; illustrated by W. M. Berger (English). *Translator or author:* Andrew Lang; Walter Leaf; Ernest Myers. New York, N.Y.; London, England: Macmillan.

1950— The Complete Works of Homer; translated (English). *Translator or author:* Andrew Lang; Walter Leaf; Ernest Myers; Butcher. New York, N.Y.: Modern Library.

1950— The Iliad; translated; illustratrations engraved on copper by John Buckland-Wright (English). *Translator or author:* Frank Laurence Lucas. London, England: Folio Society.

1950— Odiseja; preveo i protumaecio; 4th ed. (Croatian). *Translator or author:* Tomislav Maretiac. Zagreb, Croatia: Matica Hrvatska.

1950— [H]e Iliada; metephrasmene (Greek, Modern). *Translator or author:* Alexander Anastasius Pallis. Athens, Greece: I. D. Kollaros.

1950— Iliad; archaion keimenon metaphrasis-semeioseis (Greek; Modern Greek). *Translator or author:* Io Protopappas. Athens, Greece: Papyros.

1950— The Wrath of Achilles; the Iliad of Homer; shortened and in a new translation; 1st ed. (English). *Translator or author:* Ivor Armstrong Richards. New York, N.Y.: W. W. Norton.

1950— The Iliad [of] Homer; translated (English). *Translator or author:* Emile Victor Rieu. Harmondsworth, England: Penguin Books.

1950— The Iliad [of] Homerus; translated (English). *Translator or author:* Emile Victor Rieu. Baltimore, Md.: Penguin Books.

1950— Homere (French). *Translator or author:* F. Robert. Paris, France.

1950— The Odyssey; the Story of Odysseus; translated (English). *Translator or author:* William Henry Denham Rouse. New York, N.Y.: New American Library; Mentor Books.

1950— The Iliad; the Story of Achilles; translated (English). *Translator or author:* William Henry Denham Rouse. New York, N.Y.: New American Library.

1950— Homers Odyssee; Deutsch (German). *Translator or author:* Rudolf Alexander Schroder. Berlin, Germany: S. Fischer.

1950— Odisea Homero; version directa y literal del Griego; nota preliminar de F. S. R.; 2nd ed. (Spanish). *Translator or author:* Luis Segala y Estalella. Madrid, Spain: Aguilar.

1950— Odysseus the Wanderer (English). *Translator or author:* Aubrey de Selincourt. London, England: George Bell and Sons.

1950— Iliada; prevedel (Slovenian). *Translator or author:* Anton Sovrae. Ljubljana, Slovenia: Drezavna Zaloezba Slovenije.

1950— Ilias Homerus; metrische vertaling; 3rd ed. (Dutch). *Translator or author:* Aegidius W. Timmerman. Amsterdam, Netherlands: H. J. Paris.

1950— Odyssee, Homerus; metrische vertaling; 2nd ed. (Dutch). *Translator or author:* Aegidius W. Timmerman. Amsterdam, Netherlands: H. J. Paris.

1951 to 2000

1951— The Odyssey by Homer [comic book format]; Classics Illustrated No. 81 (English). New York, N.Y.: Gilberton.

1951— Odyssevs' Rejser og Eventyr; saaledes som jeg har fortalt dem for mine Birn; med illustrationer af Niels Skovgaard; 4th ed. Copenhagen, Denmark: Gldendalske Boghandel.

1951— La Iliada de Homero, Sequn adaptacion de Jose Montero Alonso; con ilustraciones de Zarageueta (Spanish). *Translator or author:* Jose Montero Alonso. Madrid, Spain: Boris Bureba Ediciones.

1951— The Iliad of Homer; retold (English). *Translator or author:* Alfred John Church. New York, N.Y.: Macmillan.

1951— The Odyssey of Homer; retold (English). *Translator or author:* Alfred John Church. New York, N.Y.: Macmillan.

1951— Hymnes (Greek, French). *Translator or author:* Jean Humbert. Paris, France.

1951— The Iliad; translated with an introduction (English). *Translator or author:* Richmond Alexander Lattimore. Chicago, Il.: University of Chicago Press.

1951— The Iliad; translated (English). *Translator or author:* Richmond Alexander Lattimore. London, England: Routledge and Kegan Paul.

1951— The Iliad of Homer; translated (English). *Translator or author:* Richmond Alexander Lattimore. Garden City, N.Y.: International Collector's Library.

1951— Iliade; traduit d'Homere (French). *Translator or author:* Leconte de Lisle. Paris, France: Alphonse Lemerre.

1951— Odyssee; traduit d'Homere (French). *Translator or author:* Leconte de Lisle. Paris, France: Alphonse Lemerre.

1951— La Iliada; segun la traduccion de Leconte de Lisle (Spanish). *Translator or author:* Leconte de Lisle. Buenos Aires, Argentina: Ed. Tor.

1951— I Poemi Omerici (Italian). *Translator or author:* Giuseppe Pavano. Palermo, Sicily, Italy: G. Priulla.

1951— Traduzioni dall'Odissea; 1st ed. (Italian). *Translator or author:* Salvatore Quasimodo. Verona, Italy; Milan, Italy: Arnoldo Mondadori.

1951— La Iliada de Homero, Primera Parte, Aquiles Agraviado; traslado; 1st ed. (Spanish). *Translator or author:* Alfonso Reyes. Mexico (City), Mexico; Buenos Aires: Fondo de Cultura Economica.

1951— The Wrath of Achilles; the Iliad of Homer shortened and in a new translation (English). *Translator or author:* Ivor Armstrong Richards. London, England: Routledge and Kegan Paul.

1951— Homere (French). *Translator or author:* Gabriel de Roton. Bordeaux, France.

1951— La Iliada Homero (Spanish). *Translator or author:* Luis Santullano. Mexico (City), Mexico: Cia. General de Ediciones.

1951— La Odisea Homero (Spanish). *Translator or author:* Luis Santullano. Mexico (City), Mexico: Cia. General de Ediciones.

1951— Odisea Homero; version directa y literal del Griego (Spanish). *Translator or author:* Luis Segala y Estalella. Madrid, Spain: Espasa-Calpe.

1951— La Iliada Homero; 3rd ed. (Spanish). *Translator or author:* Luis Segala y Estalella. Buenos Aires, Argentina: Editorial Losada.

1951— Odiseai; prevedel (Slovenian). *Translator or author:* Anton Sovrae. Ljubljana, Slovenia: Drezavna Zaloezba Slovenije.

1951— Omero, Iliade; versione poetica (Italian). *Translator or author:* Guido Vitali. Torino (Turin), Italy: G. B. Paravia.

1951— Ilias, Homeros; ubersetzt (German). *Translator or author:* Johann Heinrich Voss. Stuttgart, Germany: Philipp Reclam jun.

1951— Homerische Hymnen; herausgeben (Greek; German). *Translator or author:* Anton Weiher. Munich, Germany: Ernst Heimeran.

1951— Iliade, Chant 1er [et VIe]; notes, commentaire et traduction (French). *Translator or author:* Albert Willem. Brussels, Belgium: Editions "Labor".

1952— The Iliad of Homer; with an interlinear translation, for the use of schools and private learners of the Hamiltonian system as improved by Thomas Clark (Greek; English). New York, N.Y.: David McKay.

1952— The Iliad of Homer; edited with general and grammatical introductions, notes, and appendices by Walter Leaf ... and M. A. Bayfield (Greek). London, England: Macmillan.

1952—The Odyssey of Homer, Book IX; edited by G[erald] M[aclean] Edwards (Greek). Cambridge, England: Cambridge University Press.

1952—[H]omerou Odysseia (Greek). Munich, Germany: Keosel.

1952—Odyssee, Chants I, V–VII, IX–XII, XIV, XXI–XXIII; presentes par Jean Berard, Henri Goube, et Rene Langumier (Greek). Paris, France: L. Hachette.

1952—L'Odyssee (French). *Translator or author:* Victor Berard. Paris, France: Creuzevault.

1952—The Iliad and the Odyssey; rendered into English prose (English). *Translator or author:* Samuel Butler. Chicago, Il.: Encyclopedia Britannica.

1952—Priece o Ahilu, Odiseju i Eneji. *Translator or author:* Milene ESafarik. Belgrade (Beograd), Yugoslavia: Znanje.

1952—Navigations d'Ulysse; Fragments de l'Odyssee (French). *Translator or author:* Henri Gaberel. Lausanne, Switzerland: Rencontre.

1952—The Trojan War; adapted [from Homer]; illustrated by Douglas Brown (English). *Translator or author:* William Kottmeyer. St. Louis, Mo.: Webster Division McGraw-Hill.

1952—The Iliad and the Odyssey; extracts from the translations by Lang, Leaf and Myers & Butcher and Lang (English). *Translator or author:* Andrew Lang; Walter Leaf; Ernest Myers; Butcher. London, England: Macmillan; Walter Leaf; Ernest Myers; Butcher.

1952—L'Iliade [d']Homere; traduction nouvelle avec une introduction et des notes (French). *Translator or author:* Eugene Lasserre. Paris, France: Garnier Freres.

1952—The Iliad (English). *Translator or author:* Richmond Alexander Lattimore. Chicago, Il.

1952—Poesia d'Omero (Iliade — Odissea); scelta, commento e analisi critiche per la scuola media inferiore (Italian). *Translator or author:* Mansueto Lombardi-Lotti; A. Paladini. Treviso, Italy: Canova.

1952—Iliade [da] Omero; tradotta (Italian). *Translator or author:* Vincenzo Monti. Milan, Italy: Rizzoli.

1952—The Odyssey of Homer; retold; illustrated by Joan Kiddell-Monroe (English). *Translator or author:* Barbara Leonie Picard. New York, N.Y.: J. Z. Walck.

1952—The Return of King Odysseus, Based on the Odyssey of Homer; illustrated by Joan Kiddell-Monroe (English). *Translator or author:* Barbara Leonie Picard. London, England: Oxford University Press.

1952—The Wrath of Achilles; the Iliad of Homer; shortened and in a new translation (English). *Translator or author:* Ivor Armstrong Richards. Tokyo, Japan: Kenkyusha.

1952—Homer. *Translator or author:* M. Riemschneider. Leipzig, Germany.

1952—The Odyssey; translated (English). *Translator or author:* Emile Victor Rieu. London, England: Methuen.

1952—The Odyssey [of] Homer; translated (English). *Translator or author:* Emile Victor Rieu. Harmondsworth, England; New York, N.Y.: Penguin Books.

1952—Homer's Iliad; translated (English). *Translator or author:* William Henry Denham Rouse. London, England; New York, N.Y.: Thomas Nelson.

1952—Homer's Odyssey; translated (English). *Translator or author:* William Henry Denham Rouse. New York, N.Y.; London, England: Thomas Nelson.

1952—Guir og menn; urval ur kvium Homers; sveinbjeorn Egilsson yddi; Jon Gislason sa um utgafuna (Icelandic). *Translator or author:* Egilsson Sveinbjeorn; Jan Gislason. Reykjavik, Iceland: Bokautgafa Menningarsjos.

1952—Iliadah ve Odisiyah; shirim nivharim im mavo kolel, biurim ve-he arot meturgamim mi-yiovanit, al-yide; 2nd ed. (Hebrew). *Translator or author:* Saul Tchernichowsky. Tel Aviv, Israel: Devir.

1952—Prikleiiuchenieiia Odisseeiia; prozaich-eskiaei pereskaz [Konsultant akademik I. I. Tolstoaei; Risunki V. Vlasova] (Russian). *Translator or author:* Elena Aleksandrovna Tudorovskaeiia. Leningrad, Russia: Gos. Izd-vo Khudozh Lit-ry.

1952—Die Ilias; uit die oorspronklike Grieks vertaal (Afrikaans). *Translator or author:* J. P. J. Van Rensburg. Stellenbosch, South Africa: Pro Ecclesia-Drukkery.

1952—Homers Odysee, der Zehnte Gesang; mit zwolf Holzstichen von Karl Reossing (German). *Translator or author:* Johann Heinrich Voss. Frankfurt am Main, Germany: Verlag der Goldene Brunnen.

1953—Iliad, Books I–XII; with an introduction, a brief Homeric grammar, and notes, by D[avid]

B[inning] Monro; 5th ed. (Greek). Oxford, England: Clarendon Press.

1953— Istories apo ton [H]omero; [edited by Maria Kolyda] (Greek, Modern). Athens, Greece.

1953— Odyssee in Auswahl; herausgeben von Julius Tambornino; 2nd ed. (Greek). Paderborn, Germany: Ferdinand Schoningh.

1953— Homer's Odyssey; translated; with an introduction by John Warrington (English). *Translator or author:* Samuel Ogden Andrew. London, England; New York, N.Y.: J. M. Dent; E. P. Dutton.

1953— Odisseu; illustracions de J. M. Gimenez Botey. *Translator or author:* Agusti Bartra. Mexico (City), Mexico: Edicions Catalanes.

1953— L'Odyssee; Poesie Homerique; texte etabli et traduit par Victor Berard; 5th ed. (Greek; French). *Translator or author:* Victor Berard. Paris, France: Societe d'Edition "Les Belles Lettres".

1953— Iliada, Homero; traslacion en verso; 1st ed. (Spanish). *Translator or author:* Fernando Gutierrez. Barcelona, Spain: Jose Janes.

1953— Iliade, Libro XXIV; 2nd ed. (Italian). *Translator or author:* Folco Martinazzoli. Rome, Italy: Gismondi.

1953— Iliade [di] Omero; commento di Eugenio Treves; 5th ed. (Italian). *Translator or author:* Vincenzo Monti. Florence, Italy: Nuova Italia Editrice.

1953— The Odyssey; with an English translation (Greek; English). *Translator or author:* Augustus Taber Murray. Cambridge, Mass.: Harvard University Press.

1953— Odyseja, Homer; przekiad; 1st ed. (Polish). *Translator or author:* Jan Parandowski. Warsaw, Poland: Czytelnik.

1953— L'Odissea, Homer; novament traslladada en versos Catalans (Catalan). *Translator or author:* Carles Riba. Barcelona, Spain: Editorial Alpha.

1953— The Iliad; translated (English). *Translator or author:* Emile Victor Rieu. Harmondsworth, England: Penguin Books.

1953— The Odyssey; translated (English). *Translator or author:* Emile Victor Rieu. London, England; Baltimore, Md.: Penguin Books.

1953— The Iliad; translated (English). *Translator or author:* Emile Victor Rieu. London, England: Methuen.

1953— The Odyssey; the Story of Odysseus; translated (English). *Translator or author:* William Henry Denham Rouse. New York, N.Y.: New American Library.

1953— Iliada, Homero; version directa y literal del Griego; nota preliminar de F. S. R.; 3rd ed. (Spanish). *Translator or author:* Luis Segala y Estalella. Madrid, Spain: Aguilar.

1953— Pocemy; illeiiustraetisii I. Arkhipova (Russian). *Translator or author:* A. A. Takho-Godi. Moscow, Russia: Gos. Izd-vo Khudozh Lit-ry.

1953— Odisseeiia, Homer; perevod V. Veresaeva; [redaktsiia I. I. Tolstogo] (Russian). *Translator or author:* I. I. Tolstogo. Moscow, Russia: Gosudarstvennoe izd-vo Khudozhestvennoaei lit-ry.

1953— Iliade di Omero; versione poetica; ed. integrale (Italian). *Translator or author:* Guido Vitali. Milan, Italy: Arnoldo Mondadori.

1953— Werke; ubersetzt; herausgeben von Peter von der Muhll (German). *Translator or author:* Johann Heinrich Voss. Basel, Switzerland: Birkhauser.

1953–55— The Works of William Cowper; comprising his poems, correspondence, and translations with a life of the author by the editor, Robert Southey (English). *Translator or author:* William Cowper. London, England: Henry G. Bohn.

1954— The Odyssey of Homer, Books VI and VII; with notes and vocabulary by G[erald] Maclean] Edwards, M. A. (Greek). Cambridge, England: Cambridge University Press.

1954— Ilias in Auswahl; bearb. von Kock, Bernhard (Greek). Paderborn, Germany: Ferdinand Schoningh.

1954— Ilias; [edited by Hans Farber] (Greek). Munich, Germany: Kosel.

1954— Iliade, Chants V et VI; publie par Victor Martin (Greek). Geneva, Switzerland: Bodmer.

1954— Di Adisi Homara; anubada (Bengali). *Translator or author:* Kshitindranarayan Bhattacarya. Kalakata, Bengal: Abhyudaya Prakasamandira.

1954— The Odyssey [braille edition] (English). *Translator or author:* Samuel Henry Butcher; Andrew Lang. Louisville, Ky.: American Printing House for the Blind.

1954— The Odyssey of Homer; done into English prose; abridged and edited by Wallace B. Moffett; illustrated by Norman Roberts (English). *Translator or author:* Samuel Henry Butcher; Andrew Lang. New York, N.Y.: Macmillan.

1954—L'Odyssee Homere; traduction nouvelle, avec introduction, notes et index (French). *Translator or author:* Mederic Dufour; Jeanne Raison. Paris, France: Garnier Freres.

1954—Hesiod, the Homeric Hymns, and Homerica; with an English translation (Greek; English). *Translator or author:* Hugh Gerard Evelyn-White. London, England: William Heinemann.

1954—[H]omerou Ilias; archaion keimenon eisagoge metaphrasis scholia (Greek; Modern Greek). *Translator or author:* Olgas Komnenos-Kakrides. Athens, Greece: Ioannos N. Zacharopoulos.

1954—L'Odyssee d'Ulysse; racontee par Jacques Le Marchand; illus. par Andre Francois (French). *Translator or author:* Jacques Le Marchand. Paris, France: G. Le Prat.

1954—The Iliad; with an English translation (Greek; English). *Translator or author:* Augustus Taber Murray. Cambridge, Mass.: Harvard University Press.

1954—The Iliad; the Story of Achilles; translated (English). *Translator or author:* William Henry Denham Rouse. New York, N.Y.: New American Library.

1954—La Iliada; version directa y literal del Griego (Spanish). *Translator or author:* Luis Segala y Estalella. Madrid, Spain: Espasa-Calpe.

1954—La Iliada; version directa y literal del Griego; 13th ed. (Spanish). *Translator or author:* Luis Segala y Estalella. Mexico (City), Mexico: Espasa-Calpe Mexicana.

1954—Ili'adah, Odiseyah; tirgem mi-Yevonit, Sha'ul Tshernihovski (Hebrew). *Translator or author:* Saul Tchernichowsky. Jerusalem, Israel: Shoken.

1954—The Story of the Odyssey, Simply Told (English). *Translator or author:* Herman Davis Turner. New York, N.Y.: Vantage Press.

1955—[H]omerou Ilias; eklogai Nikephorou kai Kallirroes Eleopoulou; 5th ed. (Greek). Athens, Greece: Organismos Ekdoseos Scholikon Vivlion.

1955—Iliados; recognoverunt brevique adnotatione critica instruxerunt David B[inning] Monro et Thomas W[illiam] Allen; 3rd ed. (Greek). Oxford, England: Clarendon Press.

1955—Odysseen; oversat af Otto Gelsted; illustreret af Axel Salto. Copenhagen, Denmark: Thaning and Appel.

1955—Ilias, Odyssee; [uitg. door] J. C. Bruijn [en] C. Spoelder; 5th ed. (Greek). Haarlem, Netherlands: H. D. Tjeenk & Zoon Willink.

1955—La Iliada o el Sirio de Troya a los Ninos por Maria Luz Morales; con ilus. de Jose Segrelles; 8th ed. Barcelona, Spain: Editorial Araluce.

1955—Die Schonsten Stellen aus der Ilias Homer; ausgewahlt und bearb. von Alfre Heubeck (Greek). Hamberg, Germany: C. C. Buchners.

1955—Iliad; translated; with an introduction by John Warrington; preface by M. J. Oakley (English). *Translator or author:* Samuel Ogden Andrew; Michael Oakley. London, England; New York, N.Y.: J. M. and Sons Dent; E. P. Dutton.

1955—Iliade [et] Odyssee; Iliade introd. et notes de Robert Flaceliere; Odyssee introd. et notes de Jean Berard; index par Rene Langumier (French). *Translator or author:* Victor Berard. Paris, France: Gallimard.

1955—Trojanska Kriget (Swedish). *Translator or author:* Fridtjuv Berg. Stockholm, Sweden: Svensk Leararetidnings.

1955—The Odyssey [from the 1888 edition] (English). *Translator or author:* Samuel Henry Butcher; Andrew Lang. Chicago, Il.: Great Books Foundation.

1955—The Iliad and the Odyssey; rendered into English prose (English). *Translator or author:* Samuel Butler. Chicago, Il.: Encyclopedia Britannica.

1955—[H]omerou Iliada (Greek, Modern). *Translator or author:* Nikos Kazantzakis; Kakridis, Johannes Th. Athens, Greece.

1955—L'Iliade; traduction nouvelle avec une introduction et des notes par Eugene Lasserre (French). *Translator or author:* Eugene Lasserre. Paris, France: Garnier Freres.

1955—The Odyssey; translated from the Greek by T. E. Shaw (Lawrence of Arabia) with an introduction by Maurice Bowra (English). *Translator or author:* Thomas Edward Lawrence. London, England: Oxford University Press.

1955—Iliada Homer; ain romainoste de G. Murnu; studiu introductiv ose comentarii de D. M. Pippidi (Romanian). *Translator or author:* G. Murnu; D. M. Pippidi. Bucuresti (Bucharest), Romania: Ed. de stat Pentru Literaturaea ost artaea.

1955—The Wrath of Achilles; the Iliad of Homer, shortened and in a new translation (English). *Translator or author:* Ivor Armstrong Richards. New York, N.Y.: W. W. Norton.

1955—The Odyssey [series: Penguin Classics] (English). *Translator or author:* Emile Victor Rieu. Harmondsworth, England: Penguin Books.

1955— Bilder zur Odyssee (German). *Translator or author:* Karl Rossing. Frankfurt am Main, Germany: Bauersche Giesserei Boldene Brunnen.

1955— La Iliada; 2nd ed. (Spanish). *Translator or author:* Luis Santullano. Mexico (City), Mexico: Compania General de Ediciones.

1955— Obras Completas de Homer; version directa y literal del Griego por Luis Segala Estalella (Spanish). *Translator or author:* Luis Segala y Estalella. Barcelona, Spain: Montaner and Simon.

1955— Odyssee; Griechisch und Deutsch; mit erlauterndem Anhang und Namenverzeichnis (Greek; German). *Translator or author:* Anton Weiher. Munich, Germany: Ernst Heimeran.

1955— Homeros Odysseus Irrfarder; [Aterberattad av Beppe Wolgers efter Alfred J. Church]; illustrerad av John Flaxman (Danish). *Translator or author:* Beppe Wolgers. Stockholm, Sweden: Natur och Kultur.

1955–56— The Iliad of Homer; edited with general and grammatical introductions, notes and appendices (English). *Translator or author:* Walter Leaf; Matthew Albert Bayfield. London, England; New York, N.Y.: Macmillan; St. Martin's Press.

1955–57— Iliade; texte etabli et traduit par Paul Mazon avec la collaboration de Pierre Chantraine, Paul Collart, et Rene Languimer (Greek; French). *Translator or author:* Paul Mazon. Paris, France: Societe d'Edition "Les Belles Lettres".

1955–59— Opera; recognoverunt brevique adnotatione critica instruxerunt David B. Monro et Thomas W. Allen (Greek). Oxford, England: Clarendon Press.

1955–59— L'Odyssee, "Poesie Homerique"; texte etabli et traduit par Victor Berard (Greek; French). *Translator or author:* Victor Berard. Paris, France: Societe d'Edition "Les Belles Lettres".

1956— La Odisea; [traduccion respetuosamenta abreviada, prologo e indice de nombres por Luis Santullano]; 2nd. ed. (Spanish). Mexico (City), Mexico: Compania General de Ediciones.

1956— Iliade, Libro XXII; introduzione e commento di Angelo Maggi; 2nd ed. (Greek). Torino (Turin), Italy: S. Lattes.

1956— Ilias und Odysse; Nacherzahlt von Walter Jens; Bilder von Alice und Martin Provensen; 2nd ed. Ravensburg, German: O. Maier.

1956— Iliade, Libro XII Omera; a cura di Raffaele Argenio (Greek). Rome, Italy: Sega Societa Editrice Dante Alighieri di Albrighi.

1956— Iliade, Libro VII Omera; a cura di Andrea di Benedetto (Greek). Rome, Italy: Sega Societa Editrice Dante Alighieri di Albrighi.

1956— Homeri Odyssea; recognovit P[eter] von der Meuhll (Greek). Basel, Switzerland: Helbing & Lichtenhahn.

1956— The Odyssey of Homer; done into English prose (English). *Translator or author:* Samuel Henry Butcher; Andrew Lang. London, England; New York, N.Y.: Macmillan; St. Martin's Press.

1956— The Odyssey of Homer; translated; with introduction and notes (English). *Translator or author:* Samuel Henry Butcher; Andrew Lang. New York, N.Y.: P. F. Collier.

1956— Chapman's Homer: The Iliad, the Odyssey, and the Lesser Homerica; edited, with introductions, textual notes, commentaries, and glossaries, by Allardyce Nicoll (English). *Translator or author:* George Chapman. New York, N.Y.: Pantheon Books.

1956— Chapman's Homer: The Iliad, the Odyssey, and the Lesser Homerica; edited, with introductions, textual notes, commentaries, and glossaries, by Allardyce Nicoll (English). *Translator or author:* George Chapman. Princeton, N.J.: Princeton University Press.

1956— The Odyssey of Homer; retold; illustrated by John Flaxman [from the 1908 edition titled The Odyssey for Boys and Girls] (English). *Translator or author:* Alfred John Church. New York, N.Y.: Macmillan.

1956— The Children's Homer: the Adventures of Odysseus and the Tale of Troy; illustrated by Willy Pogany [reprint of the 1918 edition] (English). *Translator or author:* Padraic Colum; Willy Pogany. New York, N.Y.: Macmillan.

1956— Ilias und Odysse; Nacherzahlt von Walter Jens; Bilder von Alice und Martin Provensen (German). *Translator or author:* Walter Jens. Ravensburg, Germany: O. Maier.

1956— The Iliad, by Homer; with an introduction by Louise Pound (English). *Translator or author:* Andrew Lang; Walter Leaf; Ernest Myers. New York, N.Y.: Macmillan; Ernest Myers.

1956— The Odyssey of Homer; translated into English prose by T. E. Shaw (English). *Translator or author:* Thomas Edward Lawrence. New York, N.Y.: Oxford University Press.

1956— A Iliada; prefacio do Silveira Bueno. *Translator or author:* Manuel Odorico Mendes. Sao Paulo, Brazil: Atena Editora.

1956— L'Iliade; traduction nouvelle rev. et corrigee (French). *Translator or author:* Mario Meunier. Paris, France: A. Michel.

1956— The Iliad for Children; told and illustrated (English). *Translator or author:* Ernest Moss. Sussex,England: Ditchling Press.

1956— Odyseja Homer; przekiad; 2nd ed. (Polish). *Translator or author:* Jan Parandowski. Warsaw, Poland: Czytelnik.

1956— Wybor z Odysei Homera; tekst Grecki z przekiadem polskim Jana Parandowskiego; wstoepem i objasnieniami opatrzyli Wiadysiaw Madyda i Jan Safarewicz; 1st ed. (Greek; Polish). *Translator or author:* Jan Parandowski. Warsaw, Poland: Panstwowe Wydawn.

1956— Homer's Odyssey; translated and with an introduction by Thomas Yoseloff (English). *Translator or author:* Alexander Pope. New York, N.Y.: Fine Editions Press.

1956— The Odyssey; translated (English). *Translator or author:* Emile Victor Rieu. Baltimore, Md.: Penguin Books.

1956— The Iliad, the Story of Achilles; translated (English). *Translator or author:* William Henry Denham Rouse. New York, N.Y.: New American Library.

1956— The Odyssey, the Story of Ulysses; translated (English). *Translator or author:* William Henry Denham Rouse. New York, N.Y.: New American Library.

1956— The Iliad; translated from the Greek; 2nd ed. [series: Mentor Books] (English). *Translator or author:* William Henry Denham Rouse. F. Muller.

1956— The Odyssey; translated from the Greek [series: Mentor Books] (English). *Translator or author:* William Henry Denham Rouse. F. Muller.

1956— Odysseus and Calypso; introduction by Edith Hamilton; line drawings by Richard Hall (English). *Translator or author:* Herbert Frans Schaumann. Orange, N.J.: Omnibus Studio Enterprises.

1956— Odyssee (Greek, German). *Translator or author:* Weiss Schwartz. Berlin, Germany.

1956— La Iliada Homero; traduccion; introduccion e aindices de Guillermo Thiele (Spanish). *Translator or author:* Luis Segala y Estalella. San Juan, Puerto Rico; Madrid, Spain: Ediciones de la Universidad de Puerto Rico.

1956— Odysseus the Wanderer; illustrated by Norman Meredith (English). *Translator or author:*

Aubrey de Selincourt. New York, N.Y.: Criterion Books.

1956— Shirm Homeriyim, Himnonot, Epigramot, Milohemet Ha-tsefarde im ovehaakhbarim tirgem mi-Yeovait, Shelomoh Shpan (Hebrew). *Translator or author:* Shelomoh Shpan. Jerusalem, Israel: Mosad Byaliok.

1956— [H]omerou Odysseia; archaion keimenon, emmetros metraphrasis; eisagoge Gianne Kordatou (Greek; Modern Greek). *Translator or author:* Zesimos Sideres. Athens, Greece: Ioannos N. Zacharopoulos.

1956— Prikleiiuchenieiia Odisseeiia; prozaicheskiaei (Russian). *Translator or author:* Elena Aleksandrovna Tudorovskaeiia. Leningrad, Russia: Gos. Izd-vo Khudozh Lit-ry.

1956— Odysseia Homer; pereloezili; ilustroval Karel Vodak (Czech). *Translator or author:* Otmar Vaenorny; Ferdinand Stieblitz. Prague, Czechoslavakia: Statni Nakladatelstvi Krasne Literatury.

1956— Ilias (Greek; German). *Translator or author:* Johann Heinrich Voss. Berlin, Germany: Tempel-Verlag.

1956— Odyssee (Greek; German). *Translator or author:* Johann Heinrich Voss. Berlin, Germany: Tempel-Verlag.

1956— Odyssee [translated from the Greek; series: Goldmanns Gelbe Taschenbucher] (German). *Translator or author:* Johann Heinrich Voss. Barmerlea.

1956— L'Iliade et l'Odyssee; le recit de la guerre de Troie et des fabuleuses aventures d'Ulysse; adapte d'Homere; illustrations de A. et M. Provensen (French). *Translator or author:* Jane Werner Watson. Paris, France: Editions Graphiques Internationales.

1956— The Iliad and the Odyssey: the Heroic Story of the Trojan War [and] the Fabulous Adventures of Odysseus; adapted from the Greek classics of Homer; pictures by Alice and Martin Provensen (English). *Translator or author:* Jane Werner Watson. New York, N.Y.: Golden Press.

1957— Opera; recognoverunt brevique adnotatione critica instruxerunt David B. Monro et Thomas W. Allen; 3rd ed. Oxford, England: Clarendon Press.

1957— The Odyssey of Homer; translated into English verse (English). *Translator or author:* Herbert Bates. New York, N.Y.: McGraw-Hill.

1957— Odyssee [de] Homere; version Francaise; lithographies originales de Hans Erni (French).

Translator or author: Victor Berard. Lausanne, Switzerland: Andre Gonin.

1957— Chapman's Homer: The Iliad, the Odyssey, and the Lesser Homerica; edited, with introductions, textual notes, commentaries, and glossaries, by Allardyce Nicoll (English). *Translator or author:* George Chapman. London, England: Routledge and Kegan Paul.

1957— The Odyssey of Homer; retold; illustrated by John Flaxman (English). *Translator or author:* Alfred John Church. New York, N.Y.: Macmillan.

1957— The Iliad of Homer; retold; illustrated by John Flaxman (English). *Translator or author:* Alfred John Church. New York, N.Y.: Macmillan.

1957— Iliasz; forditotta. *Translator or author:* Gabor Devecseri. Budapest, Hungary: Europa Konyvkiado.

1957— L'Odyssee; traduction nouvelle avec introduction, notes, et index par Medric Dufour et Jeanne Raison (French). *Translator or author:* Mederic Dufour; Jeanne Raison. Paris, France: Garnier Freres.

1957— Odysseia; ceviren; yakup Kadri Karaosmanoglu ve A. C. Emre nin birer onsozu ile. *Translator or author:* Ahmet Cevat Emre. Istanbul, Turkey: Varlik Yayinevi.

1957— Iliada: Ilias Destani; ceviren. *Translator or author:* Ahmet Cevat Emre. Istanbul, Turkey: Varlik Yayinevi.

1957— Odysszeia Homerosz (Hungarian). *Translator or author:* Devecseri Gabor. Europa Konyvkiado.

1957— Odisakan Homeros; hunaren bnagrits t'argmanets Simon Grk'asharyan; khmbagrut'yamb Suren Vahunu (East Armenian, Modern). *Translator or author:* Simon Grk'asharian; Suren Vahuni. Yerevan (Erevan), Armenia: Haypethrat.

1957— Odysseia; 2nd ed. [a sequel to Homer] (Greek, Modern). *Translator or author:* Nikos Kazantzakis. Athens, Greece.

1957— The Iliad; translated with an introduction (English). *Translator or author:* Richmond Alexander Lattimore. Chicago, Il.: University of Chicago Press.

1957— Odisseai; trad; prefacio de Karl Otfried Muller. *Translator or author:* Manuel Odorico Mendes. Salvador, Brazil: Bahia Livraria Progresso Editora.

1957— The Iliad; with an English translation (English). *Translator or author:* Augustus Taber Murray. Cambridge, Mass.; London, England: Harvard University Press; William Heinemann.

1957— The Odyssey of Homer; a Twi translation of Book VIII line 461 to the end of Book XII (Twi). *Translator or author:* L. H. Ofosu-Appiah. Accra, Ghana; London, England: Scottish Mission Book Depot; Longmans, Green.

1957— The Return of Odysseus, for Baritone, Narrator, Chorus, and Orchestra (English). *Translator or author:* Burrill Phillips. Urbana, Il.: University of Illinois.

1957— The Odyssey; translated (English). *Translator or author:* Emile Victor Rieu. Baltimore, Md.: Penguin Books.

1957— The Iliad; translated (English). *Translator or author:* Emile Victor Rieu. Harmondsworth, England: Penguin Books.

1957— Obras Completas Homero; prologo de Arturo Marasso; traduccion; 2nd ed. *Translator or author:* Luis Segala y Estalella. Buenos Aires, Argentina: El Ateneo.

1957— Ilias; Odyssee Homer; in der Ubertragung von Johann Heinrich Voss (German). *Translator or author:* Johann Heinrich Voss. Stuttgart, Germany: Deutscher Bucherbund.

1957— Odyssee Homer[s]; ubersetzt; text der ersten Ausgabe; mit einem nachwort von Hans Kleinstuck (German). *Translator or author:* Johann Heinrich Voss. Wiesbaden, Germany: Vollmer Verlag.

1957— Iliad [series: Goldmanns Gelbe Taschenbucher] (German). *Translator or author:* Johann Heinrich Voss. Barmerlea.

1957— Ilias Homer[s]; ubersetzt; text der ersten Ausgabe; met einem Nachwort von Hans Kleinstuck (Greek; German). *Translator or author:* Johann Heinrich Voss. Wiesbaden, Germany: Vollmer Verlag.

1957— Ilias, Odyssee; in der Ubertragung von Johann Heinrich Voss (German). *Translator or author:* Johann Heinrich Voss. Munich, Germany: Winkler.

1957— Odyseja; przeklad z Greckiego; 3rd ed. (Polish). *Translator or author:* Jozef Wittlin. W Londynie [Poland?]: Veritas.

1957— Odyssea, Liber Primus; a Guilelmo Zappacosta translatus atque editus (Latin). *Translator or author:* Guilelmo Zappacosta. Terni, Italy: Thyrus.

1958— Ilias. Bremen, Germany: C. Scheunemann.

1958—Iliade, Libro X Omero; a cura di Bruno Zucchelli (Greek). Milan, Italy: Sega Societa Editrice Dante Alighieri di Albrighi.

1958—The Odyssey; edited by R. D. Wormald; illustrated by J. C. Knight [series: Heritage of Literature]. Longmans; Green.

1958—Iliade, Libro IX Omero; a cura di Umberto Scatena (Greek). Milan, Italy: Sega Societa Editrice Dante Alighieri di Albrighi.

1958—The Sixth Book of the Iliad; edited with notes, introduction and vocabulary by Walter Leaf and M. A. Bayfield (Greek). London, England: Macmillan.

1958—Odyssey, Book X [by] Homer; edited by G[eorge] M[aclean] Edwards (Greek). Cambridge, England: Cambridge University Press.

1958—The Odyssey; edited with general and grammatical introduction, commentary, and indexes by W. B. Stanford; 2nd ed. (Greek). London, England; New York, N.Y.: Macmillan; St. Martin's Press.

1958—Odissea, Libro XI; col commento di Mario Untersteiner. Florence, Italy: G. C. Sansoni.

1958—Odyssee. Bremen, Germany: C. Scheunemann.

1958—Iliada kai Odyssea; eklekta mere gia paidia; ikloge (Greek, Modern). *Translator or author:* D. V. Akrita. Athens, Greece: Astis.

1958—Epica Antica; antologia Omerico-Virgiliana (Italian). *Translator or author:* Walter Binni; Lanfranco Caretti. Florence, Italy: La Nuova Italia.

1958—The Iliad of Homer; literally translated (English). *Translator or author:* Theodore Alois Buckley. New York, N.Y.: Harper.

1958—The Odyssey of Homer; retold; illustrated by John Flaxman (English). *Translator or author:* Alfred John Church. New York, N.Y.: Macmillan.

1958—Odysseen; oversatt av P. Østbye; 3rd ed. (Norwegian). *Translator or author:* Peter Nilsen Østbye. Oslo, Norway: Gyldendal Norsk Forlag.

1958—Ilyada; Teurkoceye oceviren (Turkish). *Translator or author:* Arn Engin. Istanbul, Turkey.

1958—Ilyada, Beoleum I–VI; Teurkocesi (Turkish). *Translator or author:* Azra Erhat; A. Kadir. Istanbul, Turkey: oCituri Biraderler bas mevi.

1958—Homere (French). *Translator or author:* G. Germain. Paris, France.

1958—Odisakan; hin honaren bnagrits t argmanets

(Armenian). *Translator or author:* Mamazasp Asaturi Hambardzumian. Yerevan (Erevan), Armenia: Haykakan SSoR GA.

1958—The Odyssey; a Modern Sequel; translation into English verse, introduction, synopsis, and notes by Kimon Friar; illustrated by Ghika (English). *Translator or author:* Nikos Kazantzakis. New York, N.Y.: Simon and Schuster.

1958—The Odyssey; a Modern Sequel; translation into English verse, introduction, synopsis, and notes by Kimon Friar; illustrations by Ghika (English). *Translator or author:* Nikos Kazantzakis. London, England: Secker and Warburg.

1958—The Odyssey; an abridged translation; with illustrations by John Verney; rev. ed. (English). *Translator or author:* George P. Kerr. London, England; New York, N.Y.: Frederick Warne.

1958—The Iliad; done into English prose; rev. ed. (English). *Translator or author:* Andrew Lang; Walter Leaf; Ernest Myers. London, England; New York, N.Y.: Macmillan; St. Martin's Press; Ernest Myers.

1958—The Iliad (English). *Translator or author:* Frank Laurence Lucas. London, England.

1958—Iliade; tradotta (Italian). *Translator or author:* Vincenzo Monti. Florence, Italy: A. Salani.

1958—Odissea; nella traduzione, con note e analisi critiche di Manara Valgimigli; new ed. (Italian). *Translator or author:* Ippolito Pindemonte. Florence, Italy: Felice Le Monnier.

1958—Odyssee Homero (German). *Translator or author:* Wolfgang Schadewaldt. Hamburg, Germany: Rowohlt.

1958—Die Odyssee [translated from the Greek; series: Rowohlts Klassiker] (German). *Translator or author:* Wolfgang Schadewaldt. Barmerlea.

1958—Odisseia Gomer; perevod; 5th ed. (Russian). *Translator or author:* Vasilii Andreevich Zhukovskii. Moscow, Russia: Gos. Izd-vo Khudozh Lit-ry.

1958–62—Homeri Opera; recognoverunt brevique adnotatione critica instruxerunt David B. Monro et Thomas W. Allen; Iliad with an introduction, a brief Homeric grammar and notes by Monro; Odyssey with introduction, notes, etc. by W[illiam] W[alter] Merry. Oxford, England: Clarendon Press.

1959—Ilias, Odyssee; [Uitg. Door] J. C. Bruijn [en] C. Spoelder; 6th ed. (Greek). Haarlem, Netherlands: H. D. Tjeenk Willink.

1959—Il Libro VI dell'Iliade; a cura di Giuseppe

Bonaccorsi, e con una introd. sul dialetto Omerico di Giovanni Decia; 3rd ed. (Greek). Florence, Italy: Felice Le Monnier.

1959— Ulisszes, azaz Homeros Odisszeaja magyarul. Budapest, Hungary: Kiadja a Terra.

1959— Odissea, Libro I; test, introduzione e note a cura di M. Nicosia Margani; 2nd ed. Torino (Turin), Italy: S. Lattes.

1959— The Odyssey of Homer, Books VI and VII; with notes and vocabulary by G[erald] M[aclean] Edwards. Cambridge, England: Cambridge University Press.

1959— Thetis and Achilles: Homer, Iliad, XVIII, 1–147; translated (in Texas Quarterly) (English). *Translator or author:* William Arrowsmith.

1959— Odyssee; traduction et introduction de Victor Berard; postface de Alphonse Dain (French). *Translator or author:* Victor Berard. Paris, France: Club du Meilleur Livre.

1959— Homera Odyssea; przekladal z Greckiego. *Translator or author:* Antoni Bronilowski.

1959— The Odyssey; translated; with a portrait of a bust of Homer and reproductions of early drawings of the narrative together with an introduction by James I. Armstrong (English). *Translator or author:* Samuel Henry Butcher; Andrew Lang. New York, N.Y.: Mead Dodd.

1959— The Odyssey of Homer; translated; with introduction and notes; registered ed. (English). *Translator or author:* Samuel Henry Butcher; Andrew Lang. New York, N.Y.: P. F. Collier.

1959— La Iliada Homero; traduccion revisada y cotejada con las mas modernas ediciones Europeas, prologo y notas por Montserrat Casamada; new ed. (Spanish). *Translator or author:* Montserrat Casamada. Barcelona, Spain: Editorial Iberia.

1959— Hesiod, the Homeric Hymns, and Homerica; with an English translation (Greek; English). *Translator or author:* Hugh Gerard Evelyn-White. London, England; Cambridge, Mass.: Harvard University Press; William Heinemann.

1959— Odysseen; illustreret af Axel Salto (Danish). *Translator or author:* Otto Gelsted. Copenhagen, Denmark: Thaning and Appel.

1959— La Iliada, Poema Epico Homero; traduccion nueva del Griego por Leconte de Lisle; version Espanola de German Gomez de la Mata (Spanish). *Translator or author:* German Gomez de la Mata. Mexico (City), Mexico: Editora Latino Americana.

1959— The Anger of Achilles; Homer's Iliad,

translated; illustrated by Ronald Searle; 1st ed. (English). *Translator or author:* Robert Graves. Garden City, N.Y.: Doubleday.

1959— Hymnes [d']Homere; texte etablie et traduit par Jean Humbert (Greek; French). *Translator or author:* Jean Humbert. Paris, France: Societe d'Edition "Les Belles Lettres".

1959— Ilias und Odyssee; Nacherzahlt von Walter Jens; Bilder von Alice und Martin Provensen (German). *Translator or author:* Walter Jens. Ravensburg, Germany: O. Maier.

1959— Homeros' Iliad; frean Grekiskan av Erland Lagerleof; I bearbetning ock med inledning av Gerhard Bendz (Swedish). *Translator or author:* Erland L. Lagerlof. Malmo, Sweden: C. W. K. Gleerup.

1959— Iliade; texte etabli et traduit par Paul Mazon, avec la collaboration de Pierre Chantraine, Paul Collart, et Rene Langumier (Greek; French). *Translator or author:* Paul Mazon. Paris, France: Societe d'Edition "Les Belles Lettres".

1959— Homer. *Translator or author:* Gerhard Nebel. Stuttgart, Germany.

1959— Odyseja Homer; przeioczyi I wstnepem poprzedzi Jan Parandowski (Polish). *Translator or author:* Jan Parandowski. Warsaw, Poland: Paanstwowy Instytut Wydawn.

1959— The Iliad of Homer; translated (English). *Translator or author:* Alexander Pope. London, England: Oxford University Press.

1959— Homer and the Aether (English). *Translator or author:* John Cowper Powys. New York, N.Y.: Colgate University Press.

1959— Homer and the Aether (English). *Translator or author:* John Cowper Powys. London, England: Macdonald.

1959— The Iliad [of] Homer; translated (English). *Translator or author:* Emile Victor Rieu. Harmondsworth, England: Penguin Books.

1959— La Iliada Homero; version directa y literal del Griego por Luis Segala y Estalella; prologo de Alfonso Reyes (Spanish). *Translator or author:* Luis Segala y Estalella. Mexico (City), Mexico: Editorial Porrua.

1959— Odisseia; perevod (Russian). *Translator or author:* Vasilii Andreevich Zhukovskii. Moscow, Russia: Gos. Izd-vo Khudozhestvennoaei lit-ry.

1959–60— The Iliad of Homer; edited with general and grammatical introductions, notes, and appendices by Walter Leaf and M[atthew]

A[lbert] Bayfield. London, England; New York, N.Y.: Macmillan; St. Martin's Press.

1959–74—[H]omerou Odysseia, The Odyssey of Homer; edited with general and grammatical introduction, commentary and indexes by W. B. Stanford; 2nd ed. London, England; New York, N.Y.: Macmillan; St. Martin's Press.

1960—La Odisea Homer. Bilbao, Spain: Ediciones Moreton.

1960—[H]omerou Iliada; apodose P. Tsimikale; eikonographese, A. Korogiannake (Modern Greek). Athens, Greece: M. Pechlivanides.

1960—The Iliad; edited, with apparatus criticus, prolegommena, notes, and appendices by Walter Leaf; 2nd ed. [from the 1900–02 edition] (Greek). Amsterdam, Netherlands: Adolf M. Hakkert.

1960—Iliade, Libro I; a cura di Guglielmo Quaglia (Greek). Milan, Italy: Sega Societa Editrice Dante Alighieri di Albrighi.

1960—The Odyssey; selected readings (English). New York, N.Y.: Jesuit Educational Association.

1960—La Iliada Homer; prologo y preparacioin de la obra por Enrique Rull. Bilbao, Spain: Ediciones Moreton.

1960—Homer's Iliad, Book I; edited for the use of schools by John Bond and A[rthur] S[umner] Walpole; with notes and vocabulary (Greek).

1960—Iliad. Oxford, England: Clarendon Press.

1960—Iliade, Libro XXIII Omero; a cura di Mari Mocci (Greek). Rome, Italy: Sega Societa Editrice Dante Alighieri di Albrighi.

1960—Iliada Homero; traduocao do Grego; prefacio e notas de M. Alves Correia; 3rd ed. (Portuguese). Translator or author: Manuel Alves Correia. Lisbon, Portugal: Livraria Sa da Costa.

1960—Ilias. Translator or author: August Annist. Tallinn, Estonia: Eesti Riiklik Kirjastus.

1960—Odyssee; traduction; introduction et notes de Jean Berard (French). Translator or author: Victor Berard. Paris, France: Armand Colin.

1960—The Odyssey of Homer; done into English prose (English). Translator or author: Samuel Henry Butcher; Andrew Lang. New York, N.Y.: F. Watts.

1960—The Iliad; translated; with a selection, "Troy: the Bible of Greece" by Herbert J. Muller (English). Translator or author: Alston Hurd Chase; William Graves Perry, Jr. New York, N.Y.: Bantam Books.

1960—The Odyssey of Homer; adapted; illustrated by Thomas Fraumeni; revised ed. (English). Translator or author: Henry Irving Christ. New York, N.Y.: Globe Book Co.

1960—The Odyssey of Homer; retold; illustrated by John Flaxman (English). Translator or author: Alfred John Church. New York, N.Y.: Macmillan.

1960—Iliada, w przekiadzie zrewidowai, wstnepem I komentarzem opatrzyi Tadeusz Sinko; 9th ed. (Polish). Translator or author: Franciszek Ksawery Dmochowski. Breslau (Wroclaw), Poland: Zaksad Narodowy.

1960—Odysseia; emmetre metaphrase Argyre Ephtaliote (Greek, Modern). Translator or author: Argyres Ephtaliotes. Athens, Greece: Vivliopoleio tes "Hestias".

1960—Gomer Iliada; perevod N. M. Gnedicha; predislovie I. Shtali (Russian). Translator or author: Nikolaaei Ivanovich Gnedich. Moscow, Russia: Gos. Izd-vo Khudozh Lit-ry.

1960—The Anger of Achilles; Homer's Iliad; translated (English). Translator or author: Robert Graves. London, England: Cassell.

1960—Achilles Vrede, Homeros Iliad; I tolkning (Swedish?). Translator or author: Robert Graves; Nils Holmberg. Stockholm, Sweden: Tidens.

1960—L'Iliade; [traduction nouvelle avec une introduction et des notes] (French). Translator or author: Eugene Lasserre. Paris, France: Garnier Freres.

1960—The Odyssey of Homer; translated into English prose by T. E. Shaw (English). Translator or author: Thomas Edward Lawrence. London, England; New York, N.Y.: Oxford University Press.

1960—La Guerra dei Re e degli Eroi; tradizioni elleniche; illus. De Piero Bernardini (Italian). Translator or author: Giannino Marescalchi. Florence, Italy: Felice Le Monnier.

1960—Homer Bearndeutsch: Odyssee, Gesange I–XXIV (Bernese German). Translator or author: Albert Meyer. Bern, Switzerland: Francke.

1960—The Iliad; with an English translation (Greek?; English). Translator or author: Augustus Taber Murray. London, England; New York, N.Y.: William Heinemann; G. P. Putnam.

1960—[H]omerou Iliada kai Odysseia; te metaphrase kai syndese ton keimenon ekame [h]o logotechnes Giannes Oikonomides (Greek, Modern). Translator or author: Giannes Th. Oikonomides. Athens, Greece: Edkoseis Chresima Vivlia.

1960— The Iliad of Homer; retold; illustrated by Joan Kiddell-Monroe (English). *Translator or author:* Barbara Leonie Picard. Oxford, England: Oxford University Press.

1960— Odissea; nella versione; passi scelti e commentati da Eugenio Treves; 9th ed. (Italian). *Translator or author:* Ippolito Pindemonte. Florence, Italy: La Nuova Italia.

1960— Traduzioni dall'Odissea; 2nd ed. (Italian). *Translator or author:* Salvatore Quasimodo. Milan, Italy: Arnoldo Mondadori.

1960— The Odyssey; translated (English). *Translator or author:* Ennis Rees. New York, N.Y.: Random House.

1960— The Odyssey; translated (English). *Translator or author:* Ennis Rees. New York, N.Y.: Modern Library.

1960— I Poemi di Omero (Italian). *Translator or author:* Ettore Romagnoli. Bologna, France: N. Zanichelli.

1960— The Iliad, the Story of Achilles; translated (English). *Translator or author:* William Henry Denham Rouse. New York, N.Y.: New American Library.

1960— The Odyssey, the Story of Ulysses [by] Homer; translated (English). *Translator or author:* William Henry Denham Rouse. New York, N.Y.: New American Library.

1960— Irrhahrt und Heimkehr: Homers Odyssee nach dem Text des Lager 437 von Heinz Schwitzke; Zeichnungen von Richard Seewald (German). *Translator or author:* Heinz Schwitzke. Olten, Switzerland: Walter.

1960— Odisea Homero; version directa y literal del Griego; illustraciones de Jaime Azpelicueta (Spanish). *Translator or author:* Luis Segala y Estalella. Barcelona, Spain: Juventud.

1960— La Odisea [de] Homero; version directa y literal del Griego; prologo de Manuel Alcala; 1st ed. (Spanish). *Translator or author:* Luis Segala y Estalella. Mexico (City), Mexico: Editorial Porrua.

1960— Ilias; Deutsch; Vorwort von Eckart Peterich (German). *Translator or author:* Friedrich Leopold Stolberg. Munich, Germany: Droemersche Verlagsanstalt Th. Knaur Nachf.

1960— Ilias und Odyssee Homer[s]; in der Ubersetzung von Johann Heinrich Voss; mit einem Geleitwort von Max Rychner (German). *Translator or author:* Johann Heinrich Voss. Gutersloh, Germany: Bertelsmann.

1960— Ilias Homer[s]; nach der Ubertragung von Johann Heinrich Voss (German). *Translator or author:* Johann Heinrich Voss. Munich, Germany: Goldmann.

1960— Odyssee (Greek; German). *Translator or author:* Johann Heinrich Voss. Berlin, Germany: Tempel-Verlag.

1960–62— [H]omerou Ilias; The Iliad; edited with general and grammatical introductions, notes, and appendices by Walter Leaf and M[atthew] A[lbert[Bayfield. London, England; New York, N.Y.: Macmillan; St. Martin's Press.

1960–63— The Iliad; with an English translation (English). *Translator or author:* Augustus Taber Murray. London, England; Cambridge, England: Harvard University Press; William Heinemann.

1960–66— The Odyssey; with an English translation (Greek; English). *Translator or author:* Augustus Taber Murray. Cambridge, Mass.; London, England: Harvard University Press; William Heinemann.

1961— La Odisea; adaptacion del texto original por A. J. M.; ilus. De J. A. Sanchez-Prieto (Spanish). Madrid, Spain: Aguilar.

1961— The Odyssey of Homer, Books VI and VII; with notes and vocabulary by G[erald] M[aclean] Edwards (Greek). Cambridge, England: Cambridge University Press.

1961— Iliada, Homer; no Grieku valodas tulkojis A. Giezens; A. Feldhuna ievads; A. Giezena un A. Feldhuna komentari. Riga, Latvia: Latvijas Valsts isdevnieciba.

1961— The Iliad (English). Grosset & Dunlap.

1961— Odyssey; translated; with an introduction by John Warrington (English). *Translator or author:* Samuel Ogden Andrew. London, England: J. M. Dent.

1961— The Odyssey by Homer; with introduction by John A. Scott (English). *Translator or author:* Samuel Henry Butcher; Andrew Lang. New York, N.Y.: Macmillan.

1961— The Odyssey of Homer; translated; with introduction and notes (English). *Translator or author:* Samuel Henry Butcher; Andrew Lang. New York, N.Y.: P. F. Collier.

1961— The Odyssey of Homer; retold; illustrated by John Flaxman (English). *Translator or author:* Alfred John Church. New York, N.Y.: Macmillan.

1961— L'Odyssee; traduction, introduction, notes et index par Mederic Dufour et Jeanne Raison

(French). *Translator or author:* Mederic Dufour; Jeanne Raison. Paris, France: Garnier Freres.

1961 — Odiseja, Homer; ilustrovao Boris Anastasijevic (Serbo-Croatian). *Translator or author:* Uros Dzonic. Belgrade (Beograd), Yugoslavia: Mlado Pokolenje.

1961 — The Odyssey, Homer; translated (English). *Translator or author:* Robert Fitzgerald. Garden City, N.Y.: Anchor Press; Doubleday.

1961 — The Odyssey, Homer; translated; 1st ed. (English). *Translator or author:* Robert Fitzgerald. Atlanta, Georgia: Communication and Studies.

1961 — The Odyssey; in contemporary verse; with drawings by W. T. Mars (English). *Translator or author:* Robert Fitzgerald. Franklin Center, Pa.: Franklin Library.

1961 — The Odyssey; translated (English). *Translator or author:* Robert Fitzgerald. Garden City, N.Y.: International Collectors Library.

1961 — The Odyssey, Homer; translated (English). *Translator or author:* Robert Fitzgerald. New York, N.Y.: Vintage Books.

1961 — Iliade [et] Odyssee; Iliade traduction, intr. et notes par Robert Flaceliere; Odyssee traduction par Victor Berard; intr. par Jean Berard; index par Rene Langumier (French). *Translator or author:* Robert Flaceliere; Victor Berard. Paris, France: Gallimard.

1961 — Esperimenti di Traduzione dell'Iliade; ed. Critica (Italian). *Translator or author:* Ugo Foscolo. Florence, Italy: Felice Le Monnier.

1961 — Iliaden; oversat; illustreret af Axel Salto; 3rd ed. (Danish). *Translator or author:* Otto Gelsted. Copenhagen, Denmark: Thaning and Appel.

1961 — The Anger of Achilles (English). *Translator or author:* Robert Graves. London, England: New English Library.

1961 — The Anger of Achilles; Homer's Iliad; translated (English). *Translator or author:* Robert Graves. London, England: Cassell.

1961 — The Luck of Troy (English). *Translator or author:* Roger Lancelyn Green. London, England: Bodley Head.

1961 — Ilias; herausgeben (German). *Translator or author:* Walther Killy. Frankfurt am Main, Germany: Fischer Bucherei.

1961 — The Iliad of Homer; translated with an introduction (English). *Translator or author:* Richmond Alexander Lattimore. Garden City, N.Y.: International Collector's Library.

1961 — The Iliad of Homer; translated with an introduction (English). *Translator or author:* Richmond Alexander Lattimore. Chicago, Il.: University of Chicago Press.

1961 — L'Odyssey; traduction nouvelle rev. et corr. (French). *Translator or author:* Mario Meunier. Paris, France: A. Michel.

1961 — L'Iliade; tradotta; a cura di Vittorio Turri; nuova presentazione di Iginio de Luca (Italian). *Translator or author:* Vincenzo Monti. Florence, Italy: G. C. Sansoni.

1961 — Homar Iliyatham; edited by M. Periyaswami and P. Tirukutasundarum (Tamil). *Translator or author:* M. P. Periaswamythooran; P. Tirukutasundaram. Chennai (Madras), India: Government Oriental Manuscripts Library.

1961 — The Poems of Alexander Pope (English). *Translator or author:* Alexander Pope. London, England; New Haven, Conn.: Methuen; Yale University Press.

1961 — The Iliad, Homer; translated (English). *Translator or author:* Emile Victor Rieu. Baltimore, Md.: Penguin Books.

1961 — The Odyssey; translated (English). *Translator or author:* Emile Victor Rieu. Baltimore, Md.: Penguin Books.

1961 — Ilias; ubertragen; mit Urtext, Anhang und Registern; 2nd ed. (Greek; German). *Translator or author:* Hans Rupe. Munich, Germany: Ernst Heimeran.

1961 — Homerisches Gelachter; eine Auswahl antiker Epik (German). *Translator or author:* Rudolf Alexander Schroder. Zurich, Switzerland: Origo.

1961 — La Iliada, Homero; version directa y literal del Griego; ilustraciones de Jaime Azpelicueta (Spanish). *Translator or author:* Luis Segala y Estalella. Barcelona, Spain: Juventud.

1961 — Odysseus the Wanderer; illustrated by Norman Meredith (English). *Translator or author:* Aubrey de Selincourt. Eau Claire, Wis.: Hale.

1961 — Odyssee, Homer; Deutsch; Vorwort von Eckart Peterich (German). *Translator or author:* Johann Heinrich Voss. Munich, Germany; Zurich, Switzerland: Droernersche Verlagsanstalt Th. Knaur Nachf.

1961 — Homerische Hymnen; Griechisch und Deutsch; herausgeben von Anton Weiher (Greek; German). *Translator or author:* Anton Weiher. Munich, Germany: Ernst Heimeran.

1961 — Odyssee; Griechisch und Deutsch; ubertragung; mit erlauterndem Anhang und Namenverzeichnis; 2nd (Greek; German). *Translator or author:* Anton Weiher. Munich, Germany: Ernst Heimeran.

1961— Iliada, Homer; prseloyl oraz opatrzyl wstepem i slowniczkiem imion wlasnych Ignacy Wieniewski; rysunki Tadeusza Terleckiego. *Translator or author:* Ignacy Wieniewski. London, England: B. Swiderski.

1961–63— Iliade; texte etabli et traduit par Paul Mazon avec la collaboration de Pierre Chantraine, Paul Collart et Rene Langumier; 5th ed. (Greek; French). *Translator or author:* Paul Mazon. Paris, France: Societe d'Edition "Les Belles Lettres".

1961–64— The Odyssey; with introduction, notes, etc. by W[illiam] W[alter] Merry (Greek). Oxford, England: Clarendon Press.

1961–65— The Odyssey of Homer; edited, with general and grammatical introductions, commentary, and indexes by W[illiam] B[edell] Stanford; 2nd ed. (Greek). London, England; New York, N.Y.: Macmillan; St. Martin's Press.

1961–66— Homeri Opera; recognovervnt breviqve adnotatione critica instrvxervnt D[avid] B[inning] Monroe et T. W. Allen (Greek). Oxford, England: Clarendon Press.

1962— Iliada y Odisea [por] Homero (Spanish). Barcelona, Spain: Editorial Juventud.

1962— Odyssea; recognovit P[eter] vonj der Muhil (Greek). Basel, Switzerland: Helbing & Lichtenhahn.

1962— The Iliad [of] Homer (English). Chicago, Il.: Great Books Foundation.

1962— La Iliada Homero. Caracas, Venezuela: Edime.

1962— A Bedside Odyssey. Paris, France: Olympai Press.

1962— Iliade, Chants VII–XXIV; texte presente et annote par Fernand Houbrexhe. Paris, France: H. Dessain.

1962— La Odisea Homero; [Joaquin Aguirre Bellver; illustraciones, Balbuena, Fortun, Masberger] (Spanish). *Translator or author:* Joaquin Aguirre Bellver. Madrid, Spain: Graficas Expres.

1962— La Odisea Homero; traduccion directa del Griego; sequida de La Batracomiomaquia, traduccion; 3rd ed. (Spanish). *Translator or author:* Federico Baraibar y Zumarraga. Buenos Aires, Argentina: Sopena Argentina.

1962— Odyssee; traduction; introduction et notes de Jean Berard (French). *Translator or author:* Victor Berard. Paris, France: Le Livre de Poche.

1962— L'Odyssee, Poesie Homerique; texte etabli et traduit par Victor Berard; 6th ed. (Greek; French). *Translator or author:* Victor Berard. Paris, France: Societe d'Edition "Les Belles Lettres".

1962— Auswahl aus Homers Ilias (Greek; German). *Translator or author:* Eduard Bornemann. Frankfurt am Main, Germany: Moritz Diesterweg.

1962— Ilias; Odyssee; 7th ed. (Dutch). *Translator or author:* J. C. Bruijn; Cornelis Spoelder. Haarlem, Netherlands.

1962— The Odyssey; translated (English). *Translator or author:* Robert Fitzgerald. London, England: William Heinemann.

1962— The Anger of Achilles; translated from the Greek (English). *Translator or author:* Robert Graves. London, England: New English Library.

1962— The Siege and Fall of Troy (English). *Translator or author:* Robert Graves. Garden City, N.Y.: Doubleday.

1962— Iliada, [tou] [H]omerou; metaphrase (Greek, Modern Greek). *Translator or author:* Nikos Kazantzakis; Ioannes Theophanous Kakrides. Athens, Greece.

1962— The Songs of Homer (English). *Translator or author:* G. S. Kirk. Cambridge, England: Cambridge University Press.

1962— Iliaden; Odysseen; erland Lagerlofs oversattning; I urval och bearbetning med inledning och forklaringar av Einar Pontan och Gerhard Bendz. *Translator or author:* Erland L. Lagerlof. Lund, Sweden: C. W. K. Gleerup.

1962— The Iliad of Homer; translated with an introduction (English). *Translator or author:* Richmond Alexander Lattimore. Atlanta, Georgia: Communication and Studies.

1962— The Iliad; translated with an introduction (English). *Translator or author:* Richmond Alexander Lattimore. Garden City, N.Y.: International Collectors Library.

1962— The Iliad; translated with an introduction; drawings by Leonard Baskin (English). *Translator or author:* Richmond Alexander Lattimore. Chicago, Il.: University of Chicago Press.

1962— Patrocleia, Book XVI of Homer's "Iliad"; freely adapted into English; designed by Germano Facetti; photograph by Mirella Ricciardi (English). *Translator or author:* Christopher Logue. London, England: Scorpion Press.

1962—La Odisea; adaptacion del texto original (Spanish). *Translator or author:* A. J. M. Madrid, Spain: Aguilar.

1962—Homer Barndeutsch Odyssee, Gesange V–XIII (German). *Translator or author:* Albert Meyer. Bern, Switzerland: Stampfli.

1962—Odisseia; traducao; 4th ed. (Portuguese). *Translator or author:* Carlos Alberto Nunes. Sao Paulo, Brazil: Edicoes Melhoramentos.

1962—Iliada; traducao; 4th ed. (Portuguese). *Translator or author:* Carlos Alberto Nunes. Sao Paulo, Brazil: Edicoes Melhoramentos.

1962—Homeros Ilias; prelozil Miloslav Okal; [Valal Slovensky spisovatel; zodpovedny redaktor Milan Kraus]. *Translator or author:* Miloslav Okal. Bratislava, Slovakia: Svaz slovenskyych spisovatelovv.

1962—The Odyssey; translated; edited by Howard Porter (English). *Translator or author:* George Herbert Palmer. New York, N.Y.: Bantam Books.

1962—Odyssey of Homer; retold (English). *Translator or author:* Barbara Leonie Picard. New York, N.Y.: J. Z. Walck.

1962—The Odyssey, the Story of Odysseus; translated (English). *Translator or author:* William Henry Denham Rouse. New York, N.Y.: New American Library.

1962—La Iliada Homero; traduccion; edicion e indices de Guillermo Thiele; 2nd ed. (Spanish). *Translator or author:* Luis Segala y Estalella. San Juan, Puerto Rico: Ediciones de la Universidad de Puerto Rico.

1962—Homer. *Translator or author:* George M. Steiner. Englewood, Canada.

1962—Homeri Idyssea Liber Sextus; translatus (Latin). *Translator or author:* Guilelmo Zappacosta. Terni, Italy: Edizioni Thyrus.

1963—The Odyssey: Selection: [of] Homer, Rhetoric: Selections: [of] Aristotle, How Many "Causes"; The Sole Good [of] Seneca, Lives: Marcus Cato: Plutarch (English). Chicago, Il.: Great Books Foundation.

1963—The Sixth Book of the Iliad; edited with notes, introduction and vocabulary by Walter Leaf and M. A. Bayfield. London, England; New York, N.Y.: St. Martin's Press.

1963—Iliaden; i urval av Carl Theander (Greek). Lund, Sweden: C. W. K. Gleerup.

1963—Homers Ilias in Auswahl; herausgegeben von Bernhard Kock (Greek). Paderborn, Germany: Ferdinand Schoningh.

1963—The Homeric Hymns; edited by T[homas] W[illiam] Allen, W[illiam] R[eginald] Halliday, and E[dward] E[rnest] Sikes; 2nd ed. Amsterdam, Netherlands; New York, N.Y.: Adolf M. Hakkert; Oxford University Press.

1963—Iliad; translated; with an introduction by John Warrington; preface by M. J. Oakley (English). *Translator or author:* Samuel Ogden Andrew; Michael Oakley. London, England; New York, N.Y.: J. M. Dent and Sons; E. P. Dutton.

1963—Odeusseia (Estonian). *Translator or author:* August Annist. Tallinn, Estonia: Eesti Riiklik Kirjastus.

1963—Odyssee; traduit et presente (French). *Translator or author:* Victor Berard. Paris, France: Armand Colin.

1963—The Compact Homer; The Iliad and the Odyssey; illustrated with reproductions of Greek vase paintings; abridged, with summaries of the omitted books, notes and an introduction by Mildred E. Marcett (English). *Translator or author:* Samuel Butcher et al. Great Neck, N.Y.: Barron's Educational Series.

1963—Odissea; prefacione di Fausto Codino (Italian). *Translator or author:* Rosa Calzecchi Onesti. Torino (Turin), Italy: Giulio Einaudi.

1963—Iliade; prefazione di Fausto Codino (Italian). *Translator or author:* Rosa Calzecchi Onesti. Torino (Turin), Italy: Giulio Einaudi.

1963—Odisseia Homero; traduocao do Grego, prefacio e notas; 3rd ed. (Portuguese). *Translator or author:* E. Dias Palmeira; Manuel Alves Correia. Lisbon, Portugal: Livraria Sa da Costa.

1963—The Odyssey; translated (English). *Translator or author:* Robert Fitzgerald. New York, N.Y.: Anchor Books; Doubleday.

1963—The Iliad, Homer; translated (English). *Translator or author:* Robert Fitzgerald. Garden City, N.Y.: Anchor Books.

1963—La Iliada; Poema Epico; traduccion nueva del Griego por Leconte de Lisle; version Espanola de German Gomez de la Mata; 3rd ed. (Spanish). *Translator or author:* German Gomez de la Mata. Latino Americana.

1963—Las Aventuras de Ulises; traduccion; ilustraciones, Mario Logli y Gabriele Santini (Spanish). *Translator or author:* Pilar Grimaldo Tormos. Barcelona, Spain: Editorial Teide.

1963—La Odisea, Poema Epico Homero; traduccion nueva del Griego por Leconte de Lisle; version Espanola; 3rd ed. (Spanish). *Translator or author:* Nicasio Hernandez Luquero. Mexico (City), Mexico: Latino Americana.

1963—Iliaden, Odysseen; oversattning i urval och bearbetning med inledning och forklaringar; 3rd ed. (Swedish). *Translator or author:* Erland L. Lagerlof; Gerhard Bendz. Lund, Sweden: C. W. K. Gleerup.

1963—Iliada, Homero; traduccion nueva del Griego; version Espanola de German Gomez de la Mata (Spanish). *Translator or author:* Leconte de Lisle. Mexico (City), Mexico: Libro Epanol.

1963—Patrocleia; a new version; foreword and postscript by D. S. Carne-Ross (English). *Translator or author:* Christopher Logue. Ann Arbor, Mi.: University of Michigan Press.

1963—Pax: Episodes from the Iliad, book XIX; translated (English). *Translator or author:* Christopher Logue. Austin, Texas: University of Texas.

1963—Iliade, Homere; traduction et presentation de Paul Mazon; notes et index de Rene Langumier; preface de Jean Giono (French). *Translator or author:* Paul Mazon. Paris, France: Livre de Poche.

1963—Iliade; traduction et presentation de Paul Mazon; notes et index de Rene Langumier; preface de Jean Giono (French). *Translator or author:* Paul Mazon. Paris, France: Brodard et Taupin.

1963—Versione dell'Iliade di Vincenzo Monti; con introduction e commento di Gian Franco Chiodaroli; nuova ed. (Italian). *Translator or author:* Vincenzo Monti. Torino (Turin), Italy: Unione Tipografico-Editrice Torinese.

1963—Odissea (Italian). *Translator or author:* Ippolito Pindemonte. Florence, Italy: A. Salani.

1963—The Iliad; translated (English). *Translator or author:* Ennis Rees. New York, N.Y.: Random House.

1963—The Iliad of Homer; translated (English). *Translator or author:* Ennis Rees. New York, N.Y.: Modern Library.

1963—The Iliad; translated (English). *Translator or author:* Emile Victor Rieu. Baltimore, Md.: Penguin Books.

1963—The Iliad, the Story of Achilles; translated (English). *Translator or author:* William Henry Denham Rouse. New York, N.Y.: New American Library.

1963—Tales From the Odyssey; adapted; illustrations by Severino Baraldi (English). *Translator or author:* Walter Shad. Oldbourne [England?].

1963—Odisseia Homer; pereklav iz starohretskoi I Sklav prymitky; peredmova Oleksandra Deicha (Ukrainian). *Translator or author:* Borys Ten. Kiev (Kyyir), Ukraine: Derzhavne vyd-vo khudozhnoi literatury.

1963—Die Odusseia; uit die oorsprinklike Grieks vertaal deur J. P. J. van Rensburg (Afrikaans). *Translator or author:* J. P. J. Van Rensburg. Capetown (Kaapstad), South Africa: Human and Rousseau.

1963—Irrfahrten und Heimkehr des Odysseus; nach der Erzahlung von Thassilo von Scheffer neubearbeitet von Eugen Wolf; mit zahlreichen Farbbildern von J. A. Sanchez-Prieto (German). *Translator or author:* Thassilo Von Scheffer; Eugen Wolf. Stuttgart, Germany: Union Verlag.

1963—Odyssee [von] Homer; Deutsch; [mit einem Nachwort von Uvo Holscher] (German). *Translator or author:* Johann Heinrich Voss. Frankfurt am Main, Germany: Fischer Bucherei.

1963—Funf Gesange der Odyssee, Homer; holzschnitte von Gerhard Marcks (German). *Translator or author:* Johann Heinrich Voss. Hamburg, Germany: Galerie Rudolf Hoffmann.

1964—La Odisea; adaptacion del texto original por A. J. M.; illustraciones de J A. Sanchez-Prieto; 2nd ed. (Spanish). Madrid, Spain: Aguilar.

1964—Antologia de la "Iliada"; 3rd ed. Madrid, Spain: Sociedad Espanola de Estudios Classicos.

1964—Iliade, Chant XXIII; ed., introd. et commentaire de Pierre Chantraine et Henri Goube; 1st ed. Paris, France: Presses Universitaires de France.

1964—Odyssey, Book X [of] Homer; edited by G[erald] M[aclean] Edwards (Greek). Cambridge, England: Cambridge University Press.

1964—Homers Odyssee; fur den Schulgebrauch; erklart von Dr. Karl Friedrich Ameis; besorgt von Dr. Carl Hentze (Greek). Amsterdam, Netherlands: Adolf M. Hakkert.

1964—La Iliada (Spanish). Mexico (City), Mexico: Editorial Porrua.

1964—Sipure ha-Odiseah; mesuparim li-yeladim al yede Zani Lang (Hebrew). *Translator or author:* Asher Barash. Tel Aviv, Israel: Yosef Sreberok.

1964—Terre des Dieux; citations de l'Odyssee d'Homere traduites par Felix Germain; commentaires des illustrations de John Lindsay Opie; traduction Francaise de Felix Germain (French).

Translator or author: Roloff Beny. Paris, France: Arthaud.

1964— The Iliad; translated; revised and with an introduction by Malcolm M. Willcock (English). *Translator or author:* Samuel Butler; Malcolm M. Willcock. New York, N.Y.: Washington Square Press.

1964— Stories from the Iliad and Odyssey; edited and translated from the French by Barbara Whelpton (English). *Translator or author:* G. Chandon. World Publishing Co.

1964— The Iliad and the Odyssey of Homer; re-told; illustrated by Eugene Karlin; afterword by Clifton Fadiman (English). *Translator or author:* Alfred John Church. New York, N.Y.: Macmillan.

1964— La Iliada [por] Homero; introduccion, se-leccion, version y notes, Jose Alsina Clota & Victor Bort Casanovas (Spanish). *Translator or author:* Jose Alsina Clota; Victor Bort Casanovas. Barcelona, Spain: Edotorial Vincens-Vives.

1964— The Children's Homer: the Adventures of Odysseus and the Tale of Troy; illustrated by Willy Pogany [reprint of the 1918 edition] (English). *Translator or author:* Padraic Colum; Willy Pogany. New York, N.Y.: Macmillan.

1964— Hesiod, the Homeric Hymns, and Home-rica; with English translation (Greek; English). *Translator or author:* Hugh Gerard Evelyn-White. London, England; Cambridge, Mass.: William Heinemann; Harvard University Press.

1964— The Iliad of Homer, Book XI; edited (Greek; English). *Translator or author:* E[dward] S[eymour] Forster. London, England: Methuen.

1964— Ilias und Odyssee; Nacherzahlt von Walter Jens; Bilder von Alice und Martin Provensen (German). *Translator or author:* Walter Jens. Ravensburg, German: O. Maier.

1964— Streandernas Svall; en roman om det near-varande (Swedish). *Translator or author:* Eyvind Johnson. Stockholm, Sweden: Bonnier.

1964— Homere, Iliad; texte preface etabli et traduit par Paul Mazon ... avec la collaboration de Pierre Chantraine ... Paul Collart ... et Rene Langumier (French). *Translator or author:* Paul Mazon. Paris, France: Club Francaise du Livre.

1964— Odissea; nella versions di Ippolito Pinde-monte; comento di Eugenio Treves (Italian). *Translator or author:* Ippolito Pindemonte. Florence, Italy: La Nuova Italia.

1964— Odissea tradotta; a cura di Vittorio Turri; nuova presentazione di Emilio Faccioli (Italian).

Translator or author: Vittorio Pindemonte. Florence, Italy: G. C. Sansoni.

1964— The Odyssey; translated (English). *Translator or author:* Emile Victor Rieu. Baltimore, Md.: Penguin Books.

1964— The Odyssey, the Story of Odysseus; translated (English). *Translator or author:* William Henry Denham Rouse. New York, N.Y.: New American Library.

1964— Die Odyssee, Homer; ubersetzt in Deutsche Prosa (German). *Translator or author:* Wolfgang Schadewaldt. Schleswig, Germany: Rowohlt.

1964— Homers Ilias und Odyssee; 3rd ed. (German). *Translator or author:* Johann Heinrich Voss. Basel, Switzerland: Birkhauser.

1964— The Iliad and the Odyssey, the Heroic Story of the Trojan War [and] the Fabulous Adventures of Odysseus; adapted from the Greek classics of Homer; pictures by Alice and Martin Provensen (English). *Translator or author:* Jane Werner Watson. New York, N.Y.: Golden Press.

1964–66— Odyssey, Books I–XXIV; with introduction, notes, etc., by W[illiam] W[alter] Merry (Greek). Oxford, England: Clarendon Press.

1964–67— [H]omerou Odysseia; The Odyssey of Homer; edited, with general and grammatical introductions, commentary, and indexes by W[illiam] B[edell] Stanford; 2nd ed. (Greek). London, England; New York, N.Y.: Macmillan; St. Martin's.

1965— La Odisea (Spanish). Mexico (City), Mexico: Editorial Porrua.

1965— La Iliada. Caracas, Venezuela: Edime.

1965— Homers Ilias; fur den Schulgebrauch erklart von Carl Friedrich Ameis und Carl Hentze [reprint of the Teubner text] (Greek). Amsterdam, Netherlands: Adolf M. Hakkert.

1965— Nueva Antologia de la "Iliada" y la "Odisea" Homero (Spanish). Madrid, Spain: Sociedad Espanola de Estudios Clasicos.

1965— Iliada; seleccion; estudio literario, notas y vacabulario [por] Fiorentino Castanos Garay [y] Santiago Segura Mungia. Salamanca, Spain: Anaya.

1965— The Iliad of Homer; edited with general and grammatical introductions, notes, and appendices by Walter Leaf and M[atthew] A[rnold] Bayfield (Greek). London, England: Macmillan.

1965— Iliade, Libro VI, Omero; a cura di Franco

Robecchi (Greek). Milan, Italy: Sega Societa Editrice Dante Alighieri di Albrighi.

1965— Odyssee [door] Homeros; vertaald. *Translator or author:* Bertus Aafjes. Amsterdam, Netherlands: Meulenhoff.

1965— La Iliade Homero; adaptacion del texto original; ilustraciones de Sanchez Prieto (Spanish). *Translator or author:* Martin Alonso Pedraz. Madrid, Spain: Aguilar.

1965— The Odyssey of Homer; translated into English prose (English). *Translator or author:* Samuel Henry Butcher; Andrew Lang. New York, N.Y.: Airmont Publishing.

1965— The Odyssey; translated (English). *Translator or author:* Samuel Butler; Malcolm M. Willcock. New York, N.Y.: Washington Square Press.

1965— L'Odyssee; traduction, introduction, notes et index (French). *Translator or author:* Mederic Dufour; Jeanne Raison. Paris, France: Garnier Freres.

1965— [H]omerou Odysseia; emmetre metaphrase (Greek, Modern). *Translator or author:* Argyres Ephtaliotes; Nikolaos Poriotes. Athens, Greece: Organismos Ekdoseos Didaktikon Biblion.

1965— The Odyssey; translated from the Greek; study materials prepared by James J. Garvey (English). *Translator or author:* Preston Herschel Epps. New York, N.Y.: Macmillan.

1965— The Odyssey; translated (English). *Translator or author:* Robert Fitzgerald. London, England: Panther Books.

1965— The Odyssey [of] Homer; translated; with an introduction by Dudley Fitts; suggestions for reading and discussion by Frederick A. Peterson (English). *Translator or author:* Robert Fitzgerald. New York, N.Y.: Houghton Mifflin.

1965— [H]omerou Odysseia; metaphrase (Greek, Modern). *Translator or author:* Nikos Kazantzakis; Johannes Th. Kakridis. Athens, Greece.

1965— Homeros' Odysse; fran Grekiskan; med foretal av Harry Martinson (Swedish). *Translator or author:* Erland L. Lagerlof. Lund, Sweden: C. W. K. Gleerup.

1965— The Iliad of Homer; done into English prose (English). *Translator or author:* Andrew Lang; Walter Leaf; Ernest Myers. London, England; New York, N.Y.: St. Martin's Press; Ernest Myers.

1965— L'Iliade; traduction nouvelle avec une introduction et des notes (French). *Translator or author:* Eugene Lasserre. Paris, France: Garnier Freres.

1965— The Iliad of Homer; translated with an introduction (English). *Translator or author:* Richmond Alexander Lattimore. Chicago, Il.: University of Chicago Press.

1965— Die Odyssee; Homers Epos in Bildern erzahlt. *Translator or author:* Erich Lessing. Freiburg, Switzerland: Herder.

1965— El Libro de Odiseo. *Translator or author:* Jorge Guillermo Llosa. Santiago, Chile: Zig-Zag.

1965— Odseja; przekad (Polish). *Translator or author:* Jan Parandowski. Warsaw, Poland: Cztelnik.

1965— [H]omerou Ilias; metaphrasis (Greek, Modern). *Translator or author:* Iakovos Polylas. Athens, Greece: Organismos Edkoseos Didaktikon Vivlion.

1965— The Iliad of Homer; translated; edited, with an introduction and textual notes by Reuben A. Brower and W. H. Bond [series: Classics of Greece and Rome] (English). *Translator or author:* Alexander Pope. New York, N.Y.: Collier-Macmillan.

1965— Les Voyages d'Ulysse; resume de l'Odyssee par Louis Duplessis; illustrations de Mario Logli et G. Santini (French). *Translator or author:* Louis Francois Armand du Plessis Richelieu. Paris, France: F. Nathan.

1965— Iliada; version directa y literal del Griego; nota preliminar de F. S. R.; 10th ed. (Spanish). *Translator or author:* Luis Segala y Estalella. Madrid, Spain: Aguilar.

1965— La Iliada Homero; version directa y literal del Griego; prologo de Alfonso Reyes; 5th ed. (Spanish). *Translator or author:* Luis Segala y Estalella. Mexico (City), Mexico: Editorial Porrua.

1965— Odissea, Brani Scelti; versione poetica. *Translator or author:* Vera Settembri. Bologna, France: Calderini.

1965— [H]omerou Odysseia; archaion keimenon, emmetros metraphrasis (Greek; Modern Greek). *Translator or author:* Zesimos Sideres. Athens, Greece: Organismos Ekdoseos Didaktikon.

1965— Obras Completas; prologo por Arturo Marasso; traduccion directa del Griego por Luis Segala y Estalella; 3rd ed. (Spanish). *Translator or author:* Manuel B. Trias. Buenos Aires, Argentina: El Ateneo.

1965— Ilias, Odyssee; in der Ubertragung von Johann Heinrich Voss (German). *Translator or author:* Johann Heinrich Voss. Munich, Germany;

Darmstadt, Germany: Winkler; Wissenschaftliche Buchgesellschaft.

1965— The Iliad and the Odyssey, the Heroic Story of the Trojan War [and] the Fabulous Adventures of Odysseus; adapted from the Greek classics of Homer; pictures by Alice and Martin Provensen (English). *Translator or author:* Jane Werner Watson. Hamlyn [location?].

1965–67— Iliade [d']Homere; texte etabli et traduit par Paul Mazon, avec la collaboration de Pierre Chantraine, Paul Collart et Rene Langumier (Greek; French). *Translator or author:* Paul Mazon. Paris, France: Societe d'Edition "Les Belles Lettres".

1965–67— The Iliad; with an English translation (Greek; English). *Translator or author:* Augustus Taber Murray. Cambridge, Mass.: Harvard University Press.

1965–68— The Iliad of Homer; edited, with general and grammatical introductions, and appendices by Walter Leaf and M[atthew] A[lbert] Bayfield (Greek). London, England: Macmillan.

1965–74— [H]omerou Odysseia; The Odyssey of Homer; edited, with general and grammatical introductions, commentary, and indexes by W[illiam] B[edell] Stanford; 2nd ed. (Greek). New York, N.Y.: St. Martin's Press.

1966— Iliade, Libro XXIV; a cura di Folco Martinazzoli; 3rd ed. (Greek). Rome, Italy: V. Bonacci.

1966— Ilias (Greek; German). Berlin, Germany; Darmstadt, Germany: Tempel-Verlag.

1966— The Iliad by Homer; illustrated by Alex A. Blum (comic book) (English). New York, N.Y.: Gilberton.

1966— Ilias; verzorgd door J[ohan] W[ilhelmus] Fuchs (Greek). The Hague, Netherlands: G. B. Van Goor Zonen.

1966— The Odyssey (English). Chicago, Il.: Great Books Foundation.

1966— Odyssee (Greek; German). Berlin, Germany; Darmstadt, Germany: Tempel-Verlag.

1966— Homeri Opera; recognovervnt breviqve adnotatione critica instrvxervnt David B. Monro et Thomas W. Allen (Greek). Oxford, England: Clarendon Press.

1966— A Bedside Odyssey (English). New English Library.

1966— L'Odyssee; l'epopee d'Homere racontee en images. Paris, France: A. Hatier.

1966— La Odisea (Spanish). Mexico (City), Mexico: Compania General de Ediciones.

1966— Ilyadhat Humirus [mu arrabah naozman bi-qalam] Sulayman al-Bustani; dars wa-muntakhabat bi-qalam Fu ad Afram al-Bustani; tab ah 2 munaqqaohah wamazid alayha (Lebanese?). *Translator or author:* Sulayman Khaototar Bustani. Beirut, Lebanon: Al-Maotba ah al-Kathuli-kiyah.

1966— The Odyssey by Homer; with an introduction by John A. Scott; translation; 3rd ed. (English). *Translator or author:* Samuel Henry Butcher; John Adams Scott. New York, N.Y.: Macmillan.

1966— La Odisea Homero; seleccion on y adaptacion (Spanish). *Translator or author:* Ramon Conde Obregon. Barcelona, Spain: I.D.A.G.

1966— Odiseea; traducere; editie ingrijitea de I. Sfeteasi Cazimir; prefatea de St. Cazimir (Polish). *Translator or author:* George Cosbuc. Bucuresti (Bucharest), Romania: Editura Pentru Literaturea.

1966— La Iliada y la Odisea; adaptacion de Julia Daroqui; Illustraciones de Santos Martinez Koch (Spanish). *Translator or author:* Julia Daroqui. Buenos Aires, Argentina: Editorial Sigmar.

1966— Iliada; w przekadzie; zrewidowai, wstepem i komentarzem opatrzyi Tadeusz Sinko; 10th ed. (Polish). *Translator or author:* Franciszek Ksawery Dmochowski. Warsaw, Poland: Zakiad Narodowy Im. Ossolianskich.

1966— Ao-te-sai [The Odyssey] (Chinese). *Translator or author:* Tung-hua Fu. Taipei, Taiwan: Taiwan shang wu yin shu kuan.

1966— Iliada, [H]omerou; eikonographese P. Rotsou; diaskeue T. Kavvadia; metaphrastes (Greek, Modern). *Translator or author:* N. Giannopoulos. Athens, Greece: Ekdoseis Leon.

1966— The Anger of Achilles: Homer's Iliad; translated (English). *Translator or author:* Robert Graves. New York, N.Y.: Pyramid Books.

1966— The English Works of Thomas Hobbes of Malmesbury; Now First Collected and Edited by Sir William Molesworth [reprint of the 1839 edition] (English). *Translator or author:* Thomas Hobbes. Darmstadt, Germany: Scientia Verlag Aalen.

1966— The Odyssey; 2nd ed. *Translator or author:* Nikos Kazantzakis. Simon and Schuster.

1966— [H]omerou Iliada; metaphrase (Greek, Modern). *Translator or author:* Nikos Kazantzakis; Johannes Th. Kakridis. Athens, Greece.

1966— Ilyadhat Humirus; naqalataha ila al-Arabiyah Anbarah Salam al-Khalidi (Arabic). *Trans-*

lator or author: Anbarah Salam Khalidi. Al-Quds [Lebanon?]: Al-Maotbah al-Aosriyah.

1966— The Iliad of Homer; translated into English prose (English). *Translator or author:* Andrew Lang; Walter Leaf; Ernest Myers. New York, N.Y.: Airmont Publishing; Ernest Myers.

1966— The Iliad and the Odyssey; extracts from the translations by Lang, Leaf and Myers and Butcher and Lang; selected and edited by H. M. King and H. Spooner (English). *Translator or author:* Andrew Lang; Walter Leaf; Ernest Myers; Butcher. New York, N.Y.: St. Martin's Press; Walter Leaf; Ernest Myers; Butcher.

1966— The Odyssey of Homer; translated into English prose by T. E. Shaw (English). *Translator or author:* Thomas Edward Lawrence. New York, N.Y.: Oxford University Press.

1966— Homer. *Translator or author:* Andre Michalopoulos. New York, N.Y.

1966— The Odyssey (Greek, English). *Translator or author:* Augustus Taber Murray. London, England.

1966— Homeros Odysseia; preloezil (Slovak). *Translator or author:* Miloslav Okal. Bratislava, Slovakia: Slovensky Spisovateil.

1966— The Iliad; translated (English). *Translator or author:* Emile Victor Rieu. Harmondsworth, England: Penguin Books.

1966— The Iliad, Homer; translated (English). *Translator or author:* Emile Victor Rieu. London, England: Folio Society.

1966— The Iliad, Homer; translated (English). *Translator or author:* Emile Victor Rieu. Baltimore, Md.: Penguin Books.

1966— The Odyssey; translated (English). *Translator or author:* Emile Victor Rieu. Baltimore, Md.: Penguin Books.

1966— Die Odyssee, Homer; Deutsch (German). *Translator or author:* Wolfgang Schadewaldt. Zurich, Switzerland; Stuttgart, Germany: Artemis Verlag.

1966— La Iliada Homero; estudio preliminar por David Garcia Bacca; traduccion; 2nd ed. (Spanish). *Translator or author:* Luis Segala y Estalella. Mexico (City), Mexico: W. M. Jackson.

1966— La Odisea Homero; version directa y literal del Griego; prologo de manuel Alcala; 5th ed. (Spanish). *Translator or author:* Luis Segala y Estalella. Mexico (City), Mexico: Editorial Porrua.

1966— The Golden Sandals; a Play for Young People Adapted from Homer's Odyssey (English). *Translator or author:* Ellen Stuart. New York, N.Y.: New Play for Children.

1966— Ilias [und] Odyssee, Griechisch und Deutsch (Greek; German). *Translator or author:* Johann Heinrich Voss. Berlin, Germany: Tempel-Verlag.

1966— Der Ilias; gedichtet von Homer aber aus der unverstandlichen Sprache der alten Griechen in die schone Sprache der Schwaben ubertragen und mit gangigen Evergreens garniert von Alfred Weitnauer; Bildberichterstatter, F. J. Tripp (Schwabian=German?). *Translator or author:* Alfred Weitnauer. Kempte (Allgau), Germany: Heimatpflege.

1966–74— The Odyssey; with an English translation [reprint of the 1919 edition] (Greek; English). *Translator or author:* Augustus Taber Murray. Cambridge, Mass.; London, England: Harvard University Press; William Heinemann.

1967— Iliada, Odisseeiia Gomer; perevod s grevnegrecheskogo (Russian). Moscow, Russia: Khudozhestvennaiia literatura.

1967— Odissea, libro XD; col. commento di Mario Untersteiner. Florence, Italy: G. C. Sansoni.

1967— Odissea Libro I; a cura di Anthos Ardizzoni (Greek). Rome, Italy: V. Bonacci.

1967— Odysseia [door] Homeros; verzorgd door J. W. Fuchs (Greek). The Hague, Netherlands: G. B. Van Goor Zonen.

1967— Odiseja (Latvian). Riga, Latvia: Izdevnieciba "Liesma".

1967— Homer's Odyssey; translated; with an introduction by John Warrington [reprint of the 1953 edition] (English). *Translator or author:* Samuel Ogden Andrew. New York, N.Y.: E. P. Dutton.

1967— The Odyssey of Homer; translated; introduction by Gilbert Highet (English). *Translator or author:* Samuel Henry Butcher; Andrew Lang. New York, N.Y.: Modern Library.

1967— La Iliada Homero; traduccion revisada y cotejada con las mas modernas ediciones Europeas, prologo y notas (Spanish). *Translator or author:* Montserrat Casamada. Barcelona, Spain: Obras Maestras.

1967— Chapman's Homer: The Iliad, the Odyssey, and the Lesser Homerica; edited, with introductions, textual notes, commentaries, and glossaries; edited by Allardyce Nicoll; 2nd ed. (English).

Translator or author: George Chapman. Princeton, N.J.: Princeton University Press.

1967—Chapman's Homer: The Iliad, the Odyssey, and the Lesser Homerica; edited, with introductions, textual notes, commentaries, and glossaries; edited by Allardyce Nicoll; 2nd ed. (English). *Translator or author:* George Chapman. London, England: Routledge and Kegan Paul.

1967—The Iliad; translated; with a selection , "Troy: the Bible of Greece" by Herbert J. Muller (English). *Translator or author:* Alston Hurd Chase; William Graves Perry, Jr. New York, N.Y.: Bantam Books.

1967—The Iliad and the Odyssey of Homer, retold; illustrated by Eugene Karlin; afterword by Clifton Fadiman (English). *Translator or author:* Alfred John Church. New York, N.Y.: Macmillan.

1967—The Odyssey; a new verse translation; 1st ed. (English). *Translator or author:* Albert Spaulding Cook. New York, N.Y.: W. W. Norton.

1967—Iliaden; overs. Fra Graesk til Norsk af P. Cstbye, fordanskning ved Mogens Boisen; 2nd ed. (Danish). *Translator or author:* Peter Nilsen Cstbye; Mogens Boisen. Copenhagen, Denmark: S. Vendelkaers.

1967—Ilyada, Teurkocesi (Turkish). *Translator or author:* Azra Erhat; A. Kadir. Istanbul, Turkey: Sander Kitabevi.

1967—Hesiod, the Homeric Hymns, and Homerica, with an English translation; new and revised ed. (Greek; English). *Translator or author:* Hugh Gerard Evelyn-White. Cambridge, England; London, England: Harvard University Press; William Heinemann.

1967—The Luck of Troy (English). *Translator or author:* Roger Lancelyn Green. London, England: Puffin Books.

1967—Hymnes; texte etabli et traduit; 5th ed. (Greek, French). *Translator or author:* Jean Humbert. Paris, France: Societe d'Edition "Les Belles Lettres".

1967—The Iliad, with introduction by Louis Poind; translation (English). *Translator or author:* Andrew Lang; Walter Leaf; Ernest Myers. New York, N.Y.: Macmillan; Ernest Myers.

1967—The Iliad of Homer; translated with an introduction (English). *Translator or author:* Richmond Alexander Lattimore. Chicago, Il.: Phoenix Books.

1967—The Odyssey of Homer; translated with an introduction (English). *Translator or author:* Richmond Alexander Lattimore. New York, N.Y.: Harper and Row.

1967—Pax; from Book XIX of the Iliad; translated; 1st limited ed. (English). *Translator or author:* Christopher Logue. London, England: Turret Books.

1967—Pax; Book XIX of the Iliad; translated (English). *Translator or author:* Christopher Logue. London, England: Rapp & Carroll.

1967—L'Odyssee [par] Homere; traduction nouvelle revue et corrigee (French). *Translator or author:* Mario Meunier. Levallois-Perret, France: Cercle du Bibliophile.

1967—Diary of a Warrior King; adventures from the Odyssey; consultant: M. A. Jagendorg [and] Carolyn W. Field; illustrated by Bill Shields (English). *Translator or author:* Frederick James Moffitt. Morristown, N.J.: Silver Burdett.

1967—Iliad; with an introduction, a brief Homeric grammar, and notes (Greek). *Translator or author:* David Binning Monro. Oxford, England: Clarendon Press.

1967—Versione dell'"Iliade" di Vincenzo Monti; con introd e commento di Gian Franco Chiodaroli; new ed. (Italian). *Translator or author:* Vincenzo Monti. Torino (Turin), Italy: Unione Tipografico-Editrice Torinese.

1967—Odissea: Canto Primo Omero; a cura di Franco Mosino; 1st ed. (Greek). *Translator or author:* Franco Mosino. Torino (Turin), Italy: G. B. Paravia.

1967—The Odyssey of Homer; edited by Maynard Mack (English). *Translator or author:* Alexander Pope. London, England; New Haven, Conn.: Methuen; Yale University Press.

1967—The Iliad of Homer; translated; edited by Maynard Mack (English). *Translator or author:* Alexander Pope. London, England; New Haven, Conn.: Methuen; Yale University Press.

1967—Dall'Odissea; traduzione (Greek; Italian). *Translator or author:* Salvatore Quasimodo. Milan, Italy: Arnoldo Mondadori.

1967—Dall'Odissea; traduzione; 1st ed. (Greek; Italian). *Translator or author:* Salvatore Quasimodo. Verona, Italy: Arnoldo Mondadori.

1967—The Odyssey; translated (English). *Translator or author:* Emile Victor Rieu. Harmondsworth, England: Penguin Books.

1967—Iliad; translated (English). *Translator or author:* Emile Victor Rieu. Baltimore, Md.: Penguin Books.

1967—La Iliada; con unestudio preliminar y bibliografia seleccionada por D. Julio Palli Bonet, catedratico; verion Castellana (Castilian Spanish). *Translator or author:* Luis Segala y Estalella. Barcelona, Spain: Editorial Bruguera.

1967—La Iliada; version directa y literal del Griego; illustraciones de Flaxman y A. J. Church (Spanish). *Translator or author:* Luis Segala y Estalella. Mexico (City), Mexico: Editora Nacional.

1967—La Iliada Homero; traduccion; edicion e indices de Guillermo Thiele; 4th ed. (Spanish). *Translator or author:* Luis Segala y Estalella. San Juan, Puerto Rico: Editorial de la Universidad de Puerto Rico.

1967—Odysseia; pereloezil Otmar Vaneornay; illust. Arnoest Paderlaik. *Translator or author:* Otmar Vaenorny; Ferdinand Stieblitz. Prague, Czechoslavakia: Odeon.

1967—A Bedside Odyssey, Homer & Associates; translated (English). *Translator or author:* Gerald Williams. New York, N.Y.: Traveller's Companion in assoc. with Olympia Press.

1967–68—L'Odyssee; "Poesie Homerique"; texte etabli et traduit (Greek; French). *Translator or author:* Victor Berard. Paris, France: Societe d'Edition "Les Belles Lettres".

1967–70—Iliade; texte etabli et traduit par Paul Mazon avec la collaboration de Pierre Chantraine, Paul Collart, et Rene Langumier; 6th ed. (Greek; French). *Translator or author:* Paul Mazon. Paris, France: Societe d'Edition "Les Belles Lettres".

1967–71—The Iliad, with an English translation (Greek; English). *Translator or author:* Augustus Taber Murray. London, England: William Heinemann.

1967–71—The Iliad [of] Homer; with an English translation (Greek; English). *Translator or author:* Augustus Taber Murray. Cambridge, Mass.: Harvard University Press.

1967–71—The Odyssey of Homer; edited, with general and grammatical introduction, commentary, and indexes, by W[illiam] B[edell] Stanford; 2nd ed. (English). *Translator or author:* William Bedell Stanford. London, England; New York, N.Y.: Macmillan; St. Martin's.

1968—Ilias (Eklogai) (Greek). Athens, Greece: Organisme d'Editions Scolaires.

1968—Iliad, Book XXI; with introduction notes and vocabulary by A[ubrey] C[harles] Price. Cambridge, England: Cambridge University Press.

1968—Odissea, Libro XXIV [di] Omero; col commento di Mario Untersteiner (Greek). Florence, Italy: G. C. Sansoni.

1968—Odissea Libro IX; commento di Franco Serpa. Rocca San Casciano [location?]: Cappelli.

1968—Pseudo-Homer: Der Froschmausekrieg; Theodoros Prodromos: Der Katzenmausekrieg; Griechisch und Deutsch von Helmut Ahlborn (Greek; German). *Translator or author:* Helmut Ahlborn. Berlin, Germany: Akademie-Verlag.

1968—Odissea [di] Omero; versione di Giovanna Bemporad; prefazione di Giovanni Battista Pighi; sceneggiatura e dialoghi di Giampiero Bona, Vittorio Bonicelli, Fabio Carpi, Luciano Codignola, Mario Prosperi, Renzo Rosso per lan coproduzione televisiva Rai, Ort (Italian). *Translator or author:* Giovanna Bemporad. Torino (Turin), Italy: ERI.

1968—Iliade, Canto XXIV; 1st ed. (Greek). *Translator or author:* Umberto Boella. Torino (Turin), Italy: G. B. Paravia.

1968—Ilias; Odyssee. *Translator or author:* J. C. Bruijn; Cornelis Spoelder. Haarlem, Netherlands: H. D. Tjeenk & Zoon Willink.

1968—The Odyssey [of] Homer; done into English prose by S. H. Butcher and Andrew Lang; with a critical and biographical profile of the author by Herbert J. Rose (English). *Translator or author:* Samuel Henry Butcher; Andrew Lang. Danbury, Conn.: Grolier Enterprises.

1968—The Iliad of Homer; rendered into English prose (English). *Translator or author:* Samuel Butler. New York, N.Y.: AMS Press.

1968—The Odyssey, rendered into English prose; 1st ed. (English). *Translator or author:* Samuel Butler. New York, N.Y.: AMS Press.

1968—Odissea [di] Omero; versione di Rosa Calzecchi Onesti; con la cronologia dell'epoca dei fatti dell'Odissea, la cronologia dei tempi Omerici e un'introduzione all'opera; in appendice indice dei nomi (Italian). *Translator or author:* Rosa Calzecchi Onest. Milan, Italy: Arnoldo Mondadori.

1968—The Odyssey of Homer; adapted; illustrated by Thomas Fraumeni (English). *Translator or author:* Henry Irving Christ. New York, N.Y.: Globe Book Co.

1968—La Odisea Homero; adaptacion; cubierta e ilustraciones interiores, Vincente Segrelles; 7th ed. (Spanish). *Translator or author:* Ramon Conde Obregon. Barcelona, Spain: AFHA Internacional.

1968—La Iliada Homero, adaptacion; cubierta e

ilustraciones interiores Vicente Segrelles; 3rd ed. (Spanish). *Translator or author:* Ramon Conde Obregon. Madrid, Spain: AFHA Internacional.

1968— La Odisea Homero; adaptacion (Spanish). *Translator or author:* Ramon Conde Obregon. Barcelona, Spain: Veron.

1968— [H]omerou Odysseia (diaskeue); eikonographese (Greek, Modern). *Translator or author:* Phok. Demetriade. Athens, Greece: Ph. Demetriades.

1968— [H]omerou Ilias (Eklogai) (Greek, Modern). *Translator or author:* Nikephoros and Kallirroe Eleopoulos. Athens, Greece: Organismos Ekdoseos Didaktikin Vivlion.

1968— The Milesian Intrusion: a Restoration Comedy Version of Iliad XIV (English). *Translator or author:* Ian Fletcher. Nottingham, Eng.: Byron P.

1968— Obras: Iliada, Odisea; introduccion y notas de Jose Alsina; traslacion en verso (Spanish). *Translator or author:* Fernando Gutierrez. Barcelona, Spain: Editorial Planeta.

1968— Ilias und Odyssee; Nacherzahlt von Walter Jens; Bilder von Alice und Martin Provensen (German). *Translator or author:* Walter Jens. Ravensburg, German: O. Maier.

1968— The Iliad and Odyssey: extracts from the translations by Lang, Leaf and Myers and Butcher and Lang; selected and edited; 1st American ed. (English). *Translator or author:* H. M. King; H. Spooner. New York, N.Y.: St. Martins Press.

1968— The Iliad; translated; introduction by Gilbert Highet (English). *Translator or author:* Andrew Lang; Walter Leaf; Ernest Myers. New York, N.Y.: Modern Library; Ernest Myers.

1968— The Odyssey of Homer; translated with an introduction (English). *Translator or author:* Richmond Alexander Lattimore. New York, N.Y.: Harper and Row.

1968— L'Odyssee [par] Homere; traduction nouvelle revue et corrigee (French). *Translator or author:* Mario Meunier. Paris, France: Club des Classiques.

1968— L'Iliade; 2nd ed revised (Italian). *Translator or author:* Ugo Enrico Paoli. Torino (Turin), Italy: E.R.I.

1968— Odissea [di] Omero; introduzione e note di Carlo Del Grande; traduzione (Italian). *Translator or author:* Ippolito Pindemonte. Milan, Italy: Bietti.

1968— Inni Omerici; tradotti; don un saggio di

Giorgio Seferis & dieci illustrazioni originali di Corrado Cagli (Italian). *Translator or author:* Filippo Mjaria Pontani. Rome, Italy: Edizioni dell'Elefante.

1968— Iliade; Episodi scelti e tradotti; con 26 tavole di Giorgio De Chirico (Italian). *Translator or author:* Salvatore Quasimodo. Milan, Italy: Arnoldo Mondadori.

1968— The Iliad [of] Homer; translated (English). *Translator or author:* Emile Victor Rieu. Baltimore, Md.: Penguin Books.

1968— Odissea Omero; traduzione (Italian). *Translator or author:* Carlo Saggio. Milan, Italy: R. Ricciardi.

1968— La Iliada Homero; traduccion; prologo y edicion cuidada por Pedro Henriquez Ureana (Spanish). *Translator or author:* Luis Segala y Estalella. Buenos Aires, Argentina: Editorial Losada.

1968— La Iliada Homero; version directa y literal del Griego; 8th ed. (Spanish). *Translator or author:* Luis Segala y Estalella. Madrid, Spain: Espasa-Calpe.

1968— La Odisea Homero; traduccion; prologo y edicion cuidada por Pedro Henriquez Urena (Spanish). *Translator or author:* Luis Segala y Estalella. Buenos Aires, Argentina: Editorial Losada.

1968— Odisseeiia; pereklav iz starohreetiskoei I sklav prymitky ta slovnyk Boris Ten (Ukrainian). *Translator or author:* Borys Ten. Kiev (Kyyir), Ukraine: Dnipro.

1968— Odissea [di] Omero; versione di Giuseppe Tonna; 1st ed. (Italian). *Translator or author:* Giuseppe Tonna. Milan, Italy: Garzanti.

1968— Odysseus Comes Home from the Sea; told by Anne Terry While; illustrated by Arthur Shilstone (English). *Translator or author:* Anne Terry White. New York, N.Y.: T. Y. Crowell.

1968— Pseudo-Homera Boj Zabiomysi [Batrochomyomachia] (Polish). *Translator or author:* Ignacy Wieniewski. Nakladem [Poland?]]: Polskiej Fundacji.

1968–69— Odysse Homer; 80 Tafeln nach Monotypien von Professor Walter Ritter; text nach Thassilo von Scheffer (German). Bad Goisern, Germany: Neugebauer Press.

1968–71— [H]omerou Ilias; the Iliad of homer; edited with general and grammatical introductions, notes and appendices; 1st ed. (English). *Translator or author:* Walter Leaf; Matthew Albert Bayfield. London, England: Macmillan.

1968–75— The Iliad [of] Homer; done into English prose; with a critical and biographical profile of the author by Herbert J. Rose (English). *Translator or author:* Andrew Lang; Walter Leaf; Ernest Myers. Danbury, Conn.: Grolier Enterprises; Ernest Myers.

1969— Odyssee, Chants I, V–VII, IX–XII, XIV, XXI–XXIII, Homere; present. par Jean Berard, Henri Boube, et Rene Langumier; 4th ed. Paris, France: L. Hachette.

1969— The Odyssey by Homer [comic book format] (English). New York, N.Y.: Gilberton.

1969— Poetica e Poesia; antologia a cura di Marcello Gigante e Fabio Bonino; 2nd ed. (Greek). Naples; Florence: Il Tripode.

1969— Odissea: Canto Primo [di] Omero; a cura di Franco Mosino; 2nd ed. (Greek). Torino (Turin), Italy: G. B. Paravia.

1969— La Iliada; Compania General de Ediciones (Spanish). Mexico (City), Mexico: Sayrols.

1969— Di Adisi Homara; anubada (Bengali). *Translator or author:* Kshitindranarayan Bhattacarya. Kalakata, Bengal: Abhyudaya Prakasamandira.

1969— The Odyssey; done into English prose; with a critical and biographical profile of Homer by Herbert J. Rose (English). *Translator or author:* Samuel Henry Butcher; Andrew Lang. New York, N.Y.: F. Watts.

1969— The Odyssey of Homer; done into English prose (English). *Translator or author:* Samuel Henry Butcher; Andrew Lang. Danbury, Conn.: Grolier Enterprises.

1969— The Iliad; translated; and with an introduction by Malcolm M. Willcock (English). *Translator or author:* Samuel Butler; Malcolm M. Willcock. New York, N.Y.: Washington Square Press.

1969— The Odyssey [of] Homer; translated by Samuel Butler, revised by Malcolm M. Willcock; supplementary materials prepared by Walter James Miller (English). *Translator or author:* Samuel Butler; Malcolm M. Willcock. New York, N.Y.: Washington Square Press.

1969— The Odyssey [of] Homer; supplementary materials prepared by Walter James Miller (English). *Translator or author:* Samuel Butler; Malcolm M. Willcock. New York, N.Y.: Pocket Books.

1969— The Iliad; translated; revised by Malcolm M. Willcock; supplementary materials prepared by Walter James Miller; rev. ed. (English). *Translator or author:* Samuel Butler; Malcolm M. Willcock. New York, N.Y.: Pocket Books.

1969— The 'Iliad' and 'Odyssey' of Homer: radio plays; illustrated by Swiethlan Kraczyna, Charles Keeping (English). *Translator or author:* Kenneth Cavander. London, England: British Broadcasting Corporation.

1969— The Iliads of Homer, Prince of Poets; neuer before in any language truly translated; with a coment uppon some of his chiefe places; donne according to the Greek [reprint of the 1611 edition] (English). *Translator or author:* George Chapman. Amsterdam, Netherlands; New York, N.Y.: Theatrum Orbis Terrarum.

1969— The Odyssey; translated; with drawings by Hans Erni (English). *Translator or author:* Robert Fitzgerald. Garden City, N.Y.: Anchor Books.

1969— Las Aventuras de Ulises; traduccion; ilustraciones, Mario Logli y Gabriele Santini; 3rd ed. (Spanish). *Translator or author:* Pilar Grimaldo Tormos. Barcelona, Spain: Editorial Teide.

1969— Homerova "Odisseeiia" dleiia diteaei perekazala Kateryna Hlovaetiska (Russian). *Translator or author:* Kateryna Hlovaetiska. Kiev (Kyyir), Ukraine: Veselka.

1969— The Iliad; done into English prose; with a critical and biographical profile of the author by Herbert J. Rose (English). *Translator or author:* Andrew Lang; Walter Leaf; Ernest Myers. Danbury, Conn.: Grolier Enterprises; Ernest Myers.

1969— The Iliad of Homer; translated with an introduction; drawings by Leonard Baskin (English). *Translator or author:* Richmond Alexander Lattimore. Chicago, Il.: University of Chicago Press.

1969— The Odyssey of Homer; translated into English prose by T. E. Shaw (English). *Translator or author:* Thomas Edward Lawrence. London, England: Oxford University Press.

1969— Homeri Opera; recognovervnt breviqve adnotatione critica instrvxervnt; 3rd ed. (Greek). *Translator or author:* David Binning Monro; Thomas William Allen. Oxford, England: Clarendon Press.

1969— Iliade, Canto VI (Italian). *Translator or author:* Giuseppe Norcio. Torino (Turin), Italy: G. B. Paravia.

1969— Stories from the Odyssey; retold; illustrated by Ann Riley (English). *Translator or author:* Jocelyn Phillips. London, England: Tyndall Mitchell.

1969— Homer's Iliad; translated; with an introduction and appreciation by Andrew Sinclair; original illustrations by Janos Kass (English).

Translator or author: William Henry Denham Rouse. London, England: Heron.

1969—La Odisea [de] Homero; traduccion respetuosamente abreviada, prologo e indice de nombres; 8th ed. (Spanish). *Translator or author:* Luis Santullano. Mexico (City), Mexico: Compania General de Ediciones.

1969—Odyssee; Deutsch (German). *Translator or author:* Wolfgang Schadewaldt. Reinbeck bei Hamberg, Germany: Rowohlt.

1969—La Iliada; version directa y literal del Griego; prologo de Alfonso Reyes; 10th ed. (Spanish). *Translator or author:* Luis Segala y Estalella. Mexico (City), Mexico: Editorial Porrua.

1969—Odisea Homero; 7th ed. (Spanish). *Translator or author:* Luis Segala y Estalella. Buenos Aires, Argentina: Espasa-Calpe.

1969—La Odisea por Homero; version directa y literal del Griego; prologo de Manuel Alcala (Spanish). *Translator or author:* Luis Segala y Estalella. Mexico (City), Mexico: Editorial Porrua.

1969—Iliada, Odisea Homero; traduccion; edicion y prologo de Jose Alsina Clota (Spanish). *Translator or author:* Luis Segala y Estalella. Barcelona, Spain: Editorial Vergara.

1969—Homer's Iliad and Vergil's Aeneid [abridged]; edited, in new translations and with introductions (English). *Translator or author:* David Silhanek. New York, N.Y.: Dell Publishing.

1969—La Iliada Homero; traduccion (Spanish). *Translator or author:* Vincente Lopez Soto. Barcelona, Spain: Editorial Ramon Sopena.

1969—Odyssee [von] Homer; Urfassung der Odyssee-Ubersetzung von Johann Heinrich Voss; mit den Lithographien von Oskar Kokoschka (German). *Translator or author:* Johann Heinrich Voss. Lucerne (Luzern), Switzerland; Frankfurt, Germany: C. J. Bucher.

1969—Leibeshubungen bei Homer; Quellen zur Geschichte der Leibeshubungen in der Antike; Zusammengestellt und eingeleitet [contains The Iliad, Book XXIII and The Odyssey, Book VIII] (German). *Translator or author:* Klaus Willimczik. Schorndorf bei Stuttgart, Germany: K. Hogmann.

1969–72—Homers Odyssee; fur den Schulgebrauch erklart von Dr. Karl Friedrich Ameis (Greek). Leipzig, Germany: B. G. Teubner.

1970—La Iliada; La Odisea; La Batracomiomaquia; Himnos, Homer (Spanish). Madrid, Spain: EDAF.

1970—Selections from Homer's Iliad; with an introduction, notes, a short Homeric grammar, and a vocabulary by Allen Rogers Benner (Greek). New York, N.Y.: David Appleton.

1970—Iliada Homero (Spanish). Miami, Fl.: Ediciones Universal.

1970—Ilias; Odyssee; [herzien door] J. C. Bruijn [en] C. Spoelder; 3rd ed. (Greek). Haarlem, Netherlands: H. D. Tjeenk Willink.

1970—La Odisea [por] Homero (Spanish). Mexico (City), Mexico: Compania General de Ediciones.

1970—Odysseia Homerou; eikonographese P. Rotsou; diaskeue T. Kavvadia; metaphrases N. Giannopoulos (Modern Greek). Athens, Greece: Ekdoseis Leon.

1970—La Guerra de Troya: adaptacion de "La Iliada" de Homero; traduccion; ilustraciones, Gabriele Santini (Spanish). *Translator or author:* Rodolfo Arevalo. Barcelona, Spain: Teide.

1970—Odissea; versione di Giovanna Bemporad; prefazione di Umberto Albini; 2nd ed. (Italian). *Translator or author:* Giovanna Bemporad. Torino (Turin), Italy: ERI.

1970—The Homeric Hymns (English). *Translator or author:* Charles Boer. Chicago, Il.

1970—The Homeric Hymns; translated; 2nd ed., rev. (English). *Translator or author:* Charles Boer. Dallas, Tx.: Spring Publications.

1970—The Iliad of Homer; translated; edited by Louise R. Loomis (English). *Translator or author:* Samuel Butler. New York, N.Y.: W. J. Black.

1970—The Iliad; translated from Homer; with illustrations by Steele Savage (English). *Translator or author:* Alston Hurd Chase; William Graves Perry, Jr. New York, N.Y.: Grosset and Dunlap.

1970—Hesiod, the Homeric Hymns, and Homerica, with an English translation (Greek; English). *Translator or author:* Hugh Gerard Evelyn-White. London, England; Cambridge, Mass.: Harvard University Press; William Heinemann.

1970—The Iliad, Book Eight, Lines 553–565; translated (English). *Translator or author:* Robert Fitzgerald. Iowa City, Io.: Windhover Press.

1970—Me Tous Eroes tou Homerou: Iliada-Odysseia keimeno S. Marantou; eikonographese Zanet kai Annas Gkracham Tzonston (Greek, Modern). *Translator or author:* S. Marantos. Athens, Greece: I. Sideris.

1970—[H]e Iliada; metaphrasmene (Greek, Modern). *Translator or author:* Alexander Anastasius Pallis. Athens, Greece: Estias.

1970— Deux Amis d'Homere au XVII Siecle; textes inedits de Paul Pellisson et de Claude Fleuty (French). *Translator or author:* Paul Pellisson. Paris, France: Klincksieck.

1970— The Odyssey of Homer in the English Verse Translation by Alexander Pope; illus. with the classical designs of John Flaxman (English). *Translator or author:* Alexander Pope. Avon, Ct.: Heritage Press.

1970— The Odyssey; translated (English). *Translator or author:* Emile Victor Rieu. Baltimore, Md.: Penguin Books.

1970— Ilias; Ubertragen; mit Urtext, Anhang und Registern; 2nd ed. (German). *Translator or author:* Hans Rupe. Munich, Germany: Ernst Heimeran.

1970— Die Odyssee Homer; Deutsch (German). *Translator or author:* Wolfgang Schadewaldt. Lausanne, Switzerland; Cologne, Germany: Editions Rencontre.

1970— Odisea [de] Homero; traduccion; introduccion de Angel Luis Fernandez y Ana Victoria Fon (Spanish). *Translator or author:* Luis Segala y Estalella. Havana, Cuba: Instituto del Libro.

1970— La Iliada; version directa y literal del Griego; prologo de Alfonsa Reyes (Spanish). *Translator or author:* Luis Segala y Estalella. Mexico (City), Mexico: Editorial Porrua.

1970— Iliada, Odisea Homero; version directa y literal del Griego; con 73 ilustraciones de John Flaxman (Spanish). *Translator or author:* Luis Segala y Estalella. Madrid, Spain: Aguilar.

1970— La Odisea [de] Homero; traduccion; prologo y edicion cuidada por Pedro Henriquez Ureana; 2nd ed. (Spanish). *Translator or author:* Luis Segala y Estalella. Buenos Aires, Argentina: Editorial Losada.

1970— Odisea; version directa y literal del Griego; 8th ed. (Spanish). *Translator or author:* Luis Segala y Estalella. Madrid, Spain: Espasa-Calpe.

1970— La Odisea [de] Homero; version directa y literal del Griego; prologo de Manuel Alcala; 10th ed. (Spanish). *Translator or author:* Luis Segala y Estalella. Mexico (City), Mexico: Editorial Porrua.

1970— Homerische Hymnen, Griechisch und Deutsch; 3rd ed. (Greek; German). *Translator or author:* Anton Weiher. Munich, Germany: Ernst Heimeran.

1970s— The Odyssey of Homer; 3rd ed. (English). New York, N.Y.; Paris, France: L. Amiel.

1970s— Odysseia Homeros; prolegomena sto Homeriko zetema, Giannes Kordatos; eisagoge, metaphrase, scholia, Zesimos Sideres; ipimeleia ekdoseos, Giannes Kordatos (Greek). Athens, Greece: Ioannos N. Zacharopoulos.

1970s— The Odyssey of Homer; done into English prose (English). *Translator or author:* Samuel Henry Butcher; Andrew Lang. New York, N.Y.: F. Watts.

1970s— The Odyssey: the Story of Odysseus [by] Homer; translated (English). *Translator or author:* William Henry Denham Rouse. New York, N.Y.: New American Library.

1971— I-li-ya-te hsuan I [The Iliad] (Chinese). Taipei, Taiwan: Cheng wen shu chu.

1971— La Iliada [de] Homero (Spanish). Bilbao, Spain: Editorial Vasco Americana.

1971— Iliada kai Odysseia: eklektta mere gia paidia Omerou; ekdoge, D. B. Akrita (Greek, Modern). Athens, Greece: Papademetriou.

1971— The Iliad; edited, with apparatus criticus, prolegomena notes, and appendices by Walter Leaf; 2nd ed. (Greek). Amsterdam, Netherlands: Adolf M. Hakkert.

1971— La Odisea [de] Homero (Spanish). Bilbao, Spain: Editorial Vasco Americana.

1971— Homeri Odyssea, recognovit P[eter] von der Muhll (Greek). Basel, Switzerland: Helbing & Lichtenhahn.

1971— La Iliada; traduccio integra, directe del Grec en hexametres Catalans; 1st ed. (Catalan). *Translator or author:* Manuel Balasch. Barcelona, Spain: Editorial Selecta.

1971— Le Voyage d'Ulysse; s'apres l'oeuvre d'Homere (French). *Translator or author:* Georges Chappon. Paris, France: L. Hachette.

1971— La Iliada [de] Homero; adaptacion; 3rd ed. (Spanish). *Translator or author:* Ramon Conde Obregon. Barcelona, Spain: Veron.

1971— Werke (German). *Translator or author:* Dietrich Ebener. Berlin, Germany.

1971— Homers Ilias. *Translator or author:* Friedrich Eichhorn. Horn [location?].

1971— The Adventures of Ulysses: the Odyssey of Homer; retold (English). *Translator or author:* Bernard Evslin. New York, N.Y.: Bantam Books.

1971— Odissea: 24 Acqueforti Originali di David Wurtzel (English; Italian). *Translator or author:* Robert Fitzgerald; R. C. Onesti. Florence, Italy: Centro Grafico Santa Reparata.

1971—Die Irrfahrten des Odysseus: die Sage vom Untergang Trojans und von der Heimkehr des Odysseus nach Homer und anderen Quellen neu erzahlt; mehrfarbige Linoschnitte von Eberhard und Elfriede Binder (German). *Translator or author:* Franz Fuhmann. Recklinghausen, Germany: G. Bitter.

1971—La Odisea (Spanish). *Translator or author:* Juan Godo. Barcelona, Spain: Ediciones Zeus.

1971—La Iliada Homero; traduccion; Carlos Ayala notas prologales; 2nd ed. (Spanish). *Translator or author:* Juan Godo. Barcelona, Spain: Ediciones Zeus.

1971—Il Mondo di Omero: antologia dall'Iliade e dall'Odissea a cura di Pietro Janni (Italian). *Translator or author:* Pietro Janni. Bari, Italy: Editori Laterza.

1971—Ilias und Odyssee; Nacherzahlt von Walter Jens; Bilder von Alice und Martin Provensen (German). *Translator or author:* Walter Jens. Ravensburg, German: O. Maier.

1971—The Compact Homer; in the translations of Andrew Lang, Walter Leaf and Ernest Myers [from the 1963 edition] (English). *Translator or author:* Andrew Lang; Walter Leaf; Ernest Myers. Woodbury, N.Y.: Barron's Educational Series; Ernest Myers.

1971—The Iliad of Homer; done into English prose; abridged ed. (English). *Translator or author:* Andrew Lang; Walter Leaf; Ernest Myers. New York, N.Y.; London, England: Macmillan; Ernest Myers.

1971—The Iliad; translated with an introduction (English). *Translator or author:* Richmond Alexander Lattimore. Chicago, Il.: University of Chicago Press.

1971—The Iliad; an abridgement consisting of selections from the complete translation, connected by prose narrative to present a reasonably comprehensive story of the great epic (English). *Translator or author:* Charles E. MacBean. Seattle, Wa.: Mayfair Press.

1971—Homerikoi Hymnoi: Vatrachomyomachia, eisagoge emmetre metaphrase (Greek, Modern). *Translator or author:* Paikos Nikolaides. Athens, Greece.

1971—The Odyssey [of] Homer; translated; edited by Howard Porter (English). *Translator or author:* George Herbert Palmer. New York, N.Y.: Bantam Books.

1971—The Iliad of Homer in the English Verse translation by Alexander Pope; illustrated with the classical designs of John Flaxman (English). *Translator or author:* Alexander Pope. Norwalk, Conn.: Heritage Press.

1971—Hermes, Lord of Robbers; Homeric Hymn Number Four; translated and adapted; illustrated by Barbara Cooney; 1st ed. (English). *Translator or author:* Penelope Proddow. Garden City, N.Y.: Doubleday.

1971—La Iliada Homero; version directa y literal del Griego; prologo de Alfonso Reyes (Spanish). *Translator or author:* Luis Segala y Estalella. Mexico (City), Mexico: Editorial Porrua.

1971—La Odisea [de] Homero; version directa y literal del Griego; prologo de Manuel Alsala; 12th ed. (Spanish). *Translator or author:* Luis Segala y Estalella. Mexico (City), Mexico: Editorial Porrua.

1971—Obras Completas; version del Griego (Spanish). *Translator or author:* Luis Segala y Estalella. Barcelona, Spain: Juventud.

1971—Iliada, Odisea Homero; traduccion; con ilustraciones de Vicente B. Ballestar (Spanish). *Translator or author:* Luis Segala y Estalella. Barcelona, Spain: Circulo de Lectores.

1971—La Iliada Homero; traduccion; prologo y edicion cuidada por Pedro Henriquez Ureana; 2nd ed. (Spanish). *Translator or author:* Luis Segala y Estalella. Buenos Aires, Argentina: Editorial Losada.

1971—Iliada Homeri; e perktheu Gjon Shllaku (Albanian). *Translator or author:* Gjon Shllaku. Prishtinee [location?]: Rilindja.

1971—Hymnos eis ten Demetran = Hymne an Demeter; ubersezt und erlautert (Greek; German). *Translator or author:* Johann Heinrich Voss. Heidelberg, Germany: C. F. Winter.

1971—Sing Me, Goddess; being the first recitation of Homer's Iliad translated (English). *Translator or author:* Martin Litchfield West. London, England: Duckworth.

1971–72—Odusseia Homerosu (Japanese). *Translator or author:* Shigeichi Kure. Tokyo, Japan: Iwanami Shoten.

1971–85—La Iliada Homero; revision del texto Griego y traduccion, con introduccion, bibliografia, notas, critica textual, glosario e indice (Spanish). *Translator or author:* Francisco Sanz Franco. Barcelona, Spain: Ediciones Avesta.

1972—Iliasz Homerosz. Budapest, Hungary: Magyar Helikon.

1972—Odisea [de] Homero (Spanish). Miami, Fl.: Ediciones Universal.

1972—Iliade: Chant XXIII [d']Homere; edition, introduction et commentaire de Pierre Chantraine et Henri Goube; 2nd ed (Greek). Paris, France: Presses Universitaires de France.

1972—La Iliada; la Odisea [de] Homero (Spanish). Barcelona, Spain: CREDSA.

1972—Odeusszeia Homerosz. Budapest, Hungary: Szepirodalmi Keonyvkiado.

1972—Odyssee [d']Homere; preface de Paul Claudel; traduction; introduction et notes de Jean Berard (French). *Translator or author:* Victor Berard. Paris, France: Gallimard.

1972—Odyssee [d']Homere; traduit et presente par Victor Berard; preface de Fernand Robert; index et notes de Luc Durst (French). *Translator or author:* Victor Berard. Paris, France: Livre de Poche.

1972—Homer. *Translator or author:* C. M. Bowra. London, England.

1972—The Odyssey of Homer; done into English prose (English). *Translator or author:* Samuel Henry Butcher; Andrew Lang. Danbury, Conn.: Grolier Enterprises.

1972—The Iliad, translated; with a selection "Troy: the Bible of Greece" by Herbert J. Muller (English). *Translator or author:* Alston Hurd Chase; William Graves Perry, Jr. New York, N.Y.: Bantam Books.

1972—La Iliada [de] Homer; traduccion y adaptacion; illustraciones de J. A. Sanchez Prieto; 2nd ed. (Spanish). *Translator or author:* Ramon Conde Obregon. Barcelona, Spain: Veron.

1972—La Odisea [de] Homero; traduccion y adaptacion; ilustraciones de J. A. Sanchez Prieto; 1st ed. (Spanish). *Translator or author:* Ramon Conde Obregon. Barcelona, Spain: Veron.

1972—La Iliada [de] Homero; adaptacion; cubiertas e illustraciones interiores, Vicente Segrelles (Spanish). *Translator or author:* Ramon Conde Obregon. Barcelona, Spain: AFHA Internacional.

1972—The Works of Mr. John Dryden [reprint of the 1700 edition] (English). *Translator or author:* John Dryden. London, England: Jacob Tonson.

1972—The Homeric Hymns; and, The Battle of the Frogs and the Mice; translated from the Greek (English). *Translator or author:* Daryl Hine. New York, N.Y.: Atheneum.

1972—The Trojan War; adapted; illustrated by Douglas Brown (English). *Translator or author:* William Kottmeyer. St. Louis, Mo.: McGraw-Hill Webster Division.

1972—The Odyssey of Homer Translated into English Prose by T. E. Shaw (English). *Translator or author:* Thomas Edward Lawrence. London, England; New York, N.Y.: Oxford University Press.

1972—Ao-te-sai [The Odyssey] (Chinese). *Translator or author:* Lieh-wen Li. Taipei, Taiwan: Cheng wen shu cheu.

1972—Odyssea; proen Vasilea tes Ithakes, a pomnjemoneumate (Greek, Modern). *Translator or author:* Angelos Dem Phouriotes. Athens, Greece: Dodone.

1972—Odissea Omero; traduzione; nota e commento a cura di Giavardi Luigi [from the 1712 edition] (Italian). *Translator or author:* Ippolito Pindemonte. Milan, Italy: Editrice Lucchi.

1972—Odysseia; suomentanut Pentti Saarikoski. *Translator or author:* Pentti Saarikoski. Helsinki, Finland.

1972—Ilias [ins Prosa ubertragen; ill. Werner Klemke]; 1st ed. (German). *Translator or author:* Gerhard Scheibner. Berlin, Germany; Weimar, Germany: Aufbau-Verlag.

1972—La Iliada [de] Homero; traduccion (Catalan). *Translator or author:* Luis Segala y Estalella. Lima, Peru: Editorial Universo.

1972—Iliada Homero; traduccion; introduccion de Enrique Sainz (Spanish). *Translator or author:* Luis Segala y Estalella. Havana, Cuba: Instituto Cubano del Libro.

1972—La Odisea [de] Homero; version directa y literal del Griego; prologo de Manuel Alcala; 13th ed. (Spanish). *Translator or author:* Luis Segala y Estalella. Mexico (City), Mexico: Editorial Porrua.

1972—La Iliada [de] Homero; con un estudio preliminar y bibliografia seleccionada por Julio Palli Bonet; version Castellana (Spanish). *Translator or author:* Luis Segala y Estalella. Barcelona, Spain: Editorial Bruguera.

1972—La Odisea [de] Homero; traduccion (Spanish). *Translator or author:* Luis Segala y Estalella. Lima, Peru: Editorial Universo.

1972—Homers Frosch- und Mauskrieg; Deutsch (German). *Translator or author:* Christian Stolberg. Munich, Germany: William Heinemann.

1972—Ilias und Odyssee Homer; in der Ubertragung von Johann Heinrich Voss; herausgeben von Peter Von der Muhll (German). *Translator or au-*

thor: Johann Heinrich Voss. Wiesbaden, Germany: R. Leowit.

1972–87 — Iliade [d']Homere; texte etabli et traduit par Paul Mazon; avec la collaboration de Pierre Chantraine, Paul Collart et Rene Langumier (Greek; French). *Translator or author:* Paul Mazon. Paris, France: Societe d'Edition "Les Belles Lettres".

1973 — The Cave of the Cyclops; adapted from the story by Homer; illustrations by Ron Sandford (English). Harmondsworth, England: Penguin Education.

1973 — Epica Spontanea ed Epica Riflessa: Omero, Virgilio; a cura di Nuncia Pizzuto (Greek). Messina, Sicily, Italy; Florence, Italy: G. D'Anna.

1973 — La Iliada; 6th ed. (Spanish). Madrid, Spain: Editorial Mediterraneo.

1973 — Iliada [de] Homero. Rio Piedras, Puerto Rico: Edil.

1973 — The Wooden Horse of Troy; adapted and retold; illustrated by Denis Manton; based on the epic poems 'The Iliad' by Homer and 'The Aeneid' by Virgil (English). *Translator or author:* Alan Blackwood. London, England; North Cheam [England?]: Nelson; Young World Productions.

1973 — Illiaseu, Odisseia Homereoseu; Cheong Pyeong-jo, Kim Pyong-ik yeok (Korean). *Translator or author:* Pyeong-jo Cheong; Kim, Pyeong-ik. Seoul, South Korea: Tonghwa Chulpan Kongsa Teukpyeolsi.

1973 — L'Odyssee [d']Homere; traduction, introduction, notes et index (French). *Translator or author:* Mederic Dufour; Jeanne Raison. Paris, France: Garnier Freres.

1973 — The Death of Hector; a version after Iliad XXII; with drawings by Peter Campbell (English). *Translator or author:* Rene Hague. Wellingborough, Eng.: Christopher Skelton.

1973 — The Odyssey; an abridgement, consisting of selections from the complete translation; with an introduction by Lyle E. Daniel (English). *Translator or author:* Charles E. MacBean. Vashon, Wash.: Charles E. MacBean.

1973 — The Iliad [of] Homer; an abridgement, consisting of selections from the complete translation, connected by prose narrative to present a reasonably comprehensive story of the great epic (English). *Translator or author:* Charles E. MacBean. Seattle, Wa.: Iliad Abridgement Committee.

1973 — Homeros, Ilias (English, German, Hungarian). *Translator or author:* Jenio Medveczky.

Budapest, Hungary: Kepziomiuveszeti Alap Kiadovallalata.

1973 — L'Odyssee, Homer; traduction (French). *Translator or author:* Mario Meunier. Paris, France: Les Chef-d'Oeuvres des Lettres.

1973 — La Iliada; relatos ilustrados; adaptacion Jose Maria Osorio; dibujante; Teo (Spanish). *Translator or author:* Jose Maria Osorio. Leon: Editorial Everest.

1973 — Stories from Homer; adapted and translated (English). *Translator or author:* David Raven. London, England: Oxford University Press.

1973 — The Iliad; translated (English). *Translator or author:* Emile Victor Rieu. Baltimore, Md.: Penguin Books.

1973 — The Odyssey [by] Homer; translated (English). *Translator or author:* Emile Victor Rieu. London, England: Allen Lane.

1973 — The Iliad; translated (English). *Translator or author:* Emile Victor Rieu. London, England: Allen Lane.

1973 — La Odisea, Homero; trad. Respetuosamente abreviada; prologo e indice de nombres; 12 ed. (Spanish). *Translator or author:* Luis Santullano. Mexico (City), Mexico: Cia. General de Ediciones.

1973 — The Homeric Hymns; 1st ed (English). *Translator or author:* Sargent. New York, N.Y.

1973 — La Odisea, Homero; version directa y literal del Griego; prologo de Manuel Alcala; 15th ed. (Spanish). *Translator or author:* Luis Segala y Estalella. Mexico (City), Mexico: Editorial Porrua.

1973 — La Iliada, Homero; version directa y literal del Griego; 2nd ed. (Spanish). *Translator or author:* Luis Segala y Estalella. Barcelona, Spain: Veron.

1973 — La Odisea, Homero; version directa y literal del Griego; 10th ed. (Spanish). *Translator or author:* Luis Segala y Estalella. Madrid, Spain: Espasa-Calpe.

1973 — La Odisea, Homero; version directa y literal del Griego (Spanish). *Translator or author:* Luis Segala y Estalella. Barcelona, Spain: Veron.

1973 — La Odisea, Homero; traduccion; 4th ed. (Spanish). *Translator or author:* Luis Segala y Estalella. Lima, Peru: Editorial Universo.

1973 — La Iliada Homero; version directa y literal del Griego (Spanish). *Translator or author:*

Luis Segala y Estalella. Madrid, Spain: Espasa-Calpe.

1973— Iliada Homero; version directa y literal del Griego; prologo de Alfonso Reyes (Spanish). *Translator or author:* Luis Segala y Estalella. Mexico (City), Mexico: Editorial Porrua.

1973— Odisea Homero; version directa y literal del Griego; illustraciones de Jaime Azpelicueta; 5th ed. (Spanish). *Translator or author:* Luis Segala y Estalella. Barcelona, Spain: Editorial Juventud.

1973— Iliada Homero; version Castellana (Spanish). *Translator or author:* Manuel Vallve. Mexico (City), Mexico: D. F. Editora Nacional.

1973— Odisea Homeri, Keengeet I–XII; e peerktheu nga origjinali Spiro Comora. *Translator or author:* Andrea Varfi. Tiranee [location?]: Naim Frasheeri.

1974— Iliados Rapsoidiai kappa delta = La Guerre de Troie, Poeme du XIVe Siecle en Vers Octosyllabes; publie d'apres les manuscrits de Leyde et de Paris, par Emile Legrand (Greek). Athens, Greece: B. N. Gregoriades.

1974—[H]omerou Odysseia; emmetre metaphrase Angelikes Panophoropoulou-Sigala (Modern Greek). Athens, Greece: Ekdoseis Mnemosyne.

1974— La Odisea; 7th ed. (Spanish). Madrid, Spain: Editorial Mediterraneo.

1974— Iliasz, Odeusszeia; Homeroszi keoltmenyek Homerosz (Hungarian). Budapest, Hungary: Magyar Helikon.

1974—[H]omerou Ilias (Rapsodiai I, II, III, IV, VI); Odysseia (Rapsodiai I, V, Vi); eisagoge, keimenon, scholia, glossika, pragmatika, aisthetika Demetriou N. Goude (Greek). Athens, Greece: Dem. N. Papademas.

1974—[H]omerou Odysseia = The Odyssey of Homer; edited with general and grammatical introduction, commentary, and indexes by W[illiam] B[edell] Stanford; 2nd ed. (Greek). London, England: Macmillan.

1974—[H]omerou Odysseia; The Odyssey of Homer; edited, with general and grammatical introductions, commentary, and indexes by W[illiam] B[edell] Stanford (Greek). New York, N.Y.: St. Martins Press.

1974— The Odyssey of Homer; with an introduction by John A. Scott; translation (English). *Translator or author:* Samuel Henry Butcher; Andrew Lang. New York, N.Y.: Macmillan.

1974— Akroama: Euripedes-Homer, Two Greek

Poets (English). *Translator or author:* Howard Callas. Austin, Texas: University Stores.

1974— The Odyssey; a new verse translation, backgrounds, the Odyssey in antiquity, criticism; translated and edited; 1st ed. (English). *Translator or author:* Albert Spaulding Cook. New York, N.Y.: W. W. Norton.

1974— The Iliad [of] Homer; translated (English). *Translator or author:* Robert Fitzgerald. Garden City, N.Y.: International Collectors Library.

1974— The Iliad; translated; with drawings by Hans Erni (English). *Translator or author:* Robert Fitzgerald. Garden City, N.Y.: Anchor Press; Doubleday.

1974— Homer, Wyd (Polish). *Translator or author:* Kazimierz T. Kumaniecki. Warsaw, Poland.

1974— Iliade, Tome III, Chants XIII–XVII [d']Homere; texte etabli et traduit par Paul Mazon; avec la collaboration de Pierre Chantraine, Paul Collart et Rene Langumier (Greek; French). *Translator or author:* Paul Mazon. Paris, France: Societe d'Edition "Les Belles Lettres".

1974— Odusseus; wokyeree ase fi hela kasa mu (Twi). *Translator or author:* L. H. Ofosu-Appiah. Accra, Ghana: Bureau of Ghana Languages.

1974— L'Uomo nel Mondo Omerico (Italian). *Translator or author:* Rosa Calzecchi Onesti. Torino (Turin), Italy: Marietti.

1974— Ilias [H]omerou; metaphrasis (Greek, Modern). *Translator or author:* Iakovos Polylas. Athens, Greece: Organismos Ekdoseos Didaktikon Vivlion.

1974— The Odyssey; translated; lithographs by Elisabeth Frink (English). *Translator or author:* Emile Victor Rieu. London, England: Folio Society.

1974— La Iliada Homero; version directa al Castellano; 1st ed. (Spanish). *Translator or author:* Luis Segala y Estalella. Mexico (City), Mexico: Editora Latino Americana.

1974— La Iliada, Homero; traduccion; edicion e indices de Guillermo Thiele; 5th ed. (Spanish). *Translator or author:* Luis Segala y Estalella. San Juan, Puerto Rico: Ediciones de la Universidad de Puerto Rico.

1974— La Odisea, Homero; version directa al Castellano; 1st ed. (Spanish). *Translator or author:* Luis Segala y Estalella. Mexico (City), Mexico: Editora Latino Americana.

1974— La Iliada Homero; estudio preliminar por

David Garcia Bacca; traduccion; 7th ed. (Spanish). *Translator or author:* Luis Segala y Estalella. Mexico (City), Mexico: W. M. Jackson.

1974— La Iliada, Homero; Julio Palli Bonet, estudio preliminar; traduccion (Spanish). *Translator or author:* Luis Segala y Estalella. Barcelona, Spain: Editorial Bruguera.

1974— La Iliada Homero; version directa y literal del Griego; prologo de Alfonso Reyes; 16th ed. (Spanish). *Translator or author:* Luis Segala y Estalella. Mexico (City), Mexico: Editorial Porrua.

1974— Die Heimkehr des Odysseus; eine altgriechische Heldensaga Homer; Deutsch mit erlauterungen; und mit 175 handzeichnungen von Jacques Pecnard (German). *Translator or author:* Otto Zeller. Osnabruck, Germany: Biblio Verlag.

1974–89— L'Odyssee, Poesie Homerique, Homere; texte etabli et traduit par Victor Berard (Greek; French). *Translator or author:* Victor Berard. Paris, France: Societe d'Edition "Les Belles Lettres".

1975— La Odisea, Homero; 6th ed. (Spanish). Barcelona, Spain: AFHA International.

1975— The Homeric Hymn to Demeter (Greek). Oxford, England: Clarendon Press.

1975— Odisea Homero (Spanish). Barcelona, Spain: Editorial Vosgos.

1975— Iliada [H]omeros; eisagoge, metaphrase, scholia O. Komnenou-Kakride (Greek). Athens, Greece: Ioannos N. Zacharopoulos.

1975— Sangen om Odysseus; Odysseen av Homeros; oversattning fran Grekiska samt inledning och kommentar (Swedish). *Translator or author:* Tord Baeckstrom. Stockholm, Sweden: Forum.

1975— Inni Omerici; a cura di Filippo Cassola; 1st ed. (Greek; Italian). *Translator or author:* Filippo Cassola. Milan, Italy: Arnoldo Mondadori; Fondazione Lorenzo Valla.

1975— L'Odyssee, Homere; lithographies originales de Marc Chagall (French). *Translator or author:* Anne LeFevre Dacier. Fernand Mourlot.

1975— The Odyssey, Homer; translated; with drawings by Hans Erni (English). *Translator or author:* Robert Fitzgerald. Garden City, N.Y.: Anchor Books.

1975— The Iliad [of] Homer; translated (English). *Translator or author:* Robert Fitzgerald. Garden City, N.Y.: Anchor Books.

1975— Teoria Nova da Antiguidade, Sampaio Bruno (Portuguese). *Translator or author:* Antonio Barahona da Fonseca. Lisbon, Portugal: Minerva.

1975— L'Iliade [d']Homere; traduction nouvelle avec une introduction et des notes (French). *Translator or author:* Eugene Lasserre. Paris, France: Garnier Freres.

1975— The Odyssey of Homer; translated with an introduction (English). *Translator or author:* Richmond Alexander Lattimore. New York, N.Y.: Harper and Row.

1975— The Odyssey of Homer; a modern translation (English). *Translator or author:* Richmond Alexander Lattimore. New York, N.Y.: Harper Torchbooks.

1975— The Odyssey of Homer; translated with an introduction (English). *Translator or author:* Richmond Alexander Lattimore. New York, N.Y.: Perennial Library.

1975— Versions de l'Obra Completa d'Horaci; I de quinze rapsodies de la Iliade d'Homer; traduccio directa en eis metres original (Catalan). *Translator or author:* Josep Maria Lovera. Sabadell, Spain: Academia Catolica.

1975— Iliade [d']Homere; preface de Pierre Vidal-Naquet; traduction (French). *Translator or author:* Paul Mazon. Paris, France: Gallimard.

1975— The Iliad [of] Homer; translated (English). *Translator or author:* Emile Victor Rieu. London, England: Folio Society.

1975— Ilias [von] Homer; neue Ubertragen; mit zwolf antiken Vasenbildern (German). *Translator or author:* Wolfgang Schadewaldt. Frankfurt am Main, Germany: Insel-Verlag.

1975— La Iliada Homero; version directa literal del Griego; prologo de Alfonso Reyes; 17th ed. (Spanish). *Translator or author:* Luis Segala y Estalella. Mexico (City), Mexico: Editorial Porrua.

1975— La Odisea, Homero; version directa y literal del Griego; prologo de Manuel Alcala; 16th ed. (Spanish). *Translator or author:* Luis Segala y Estalella. Mexico (City), Mexico: Editorial Porrua.

1975— Odyseja, (wybor) Homer; przeioczyi; wstnepem poprzedziia Zofia Abramowiczowna; wybor opracowai I objasnieniami opatrzyi Jerzy janowski; 8th ed. (Polish). *Translator or author:* Lucjan Hipolit Siemienski. Warsaw, Poland: Zakiad Narodowy im. Ossolinskich.

1975–76— The Odyssey, Homer; with an English translation (Greek; English). *Translator or author:* Augustus Taber Murray. Cambridge, Mass.; London, England: Harvard University Press; William Heinemann.

1975–79—Homeri Opera; recognoverunt brevique adnotatione critica instruxerunt David B[inning] Monro et Thomas W[illiam] Allen (Greek). Oxford, England: Clarendon Press.

1975–80—[H]omerou Odysseia; meta scholion [h]ypo K[arl] F[riedrich] Ameis kai [h]ermeneias [h]ypo A. X. Karapanagiotou (Greek; Modern Greek). *Translator or author:* A. X. Karapanagiotes; Giannakopoulos, P. E. Athens, Greece: Dem. N. Papademas.

1976—La Iliada (Spanish). Barcelona, Spain: Ramon Sopena.

1976—Odisea Homero; asesor, Arturo Del Hoyo; 1st ed. (Spanish). Mexico (City), Mexico: Aguilar.

1976—Odisea Homero; version Castellana, prologo y notas de Raul Biengio Brito (Spanish). *Translator or author:* Raul Blengio Brito. Montevideo, Uruguay: Ediciones del Partenon.

1976—L'Odyssee [d']Homere; extraits; traduction, adaption et presentation (French). *Translator or author:* Michelle Brier. Paris, France: Bordas.

1976—La Odisea; seleccion y adaptacion; cubierta e ilustraciones: Vicente Segrelles; 7th ed. (Spanish). *Translator or author:* Ramon Conde Obregon. Barcelona, Spain: Ediciones AFHA Internacional.

1976—La Iliada Homero; adaptacion; cubierta e ilustraciones interiores, Vicente Segrelles; 6th ed. (Spanish). *Translator or author:* Ramon Conde Obregon. Barcelona, Spain: AFHA Internacional.

1976—L'Odyssee [d']Homere; trad., introd., notes et index (French). *Translator or author:* Mederic Dufour; Jeanne Raison. Paris, France: Garnier Freres.

1976—Greek Bearing Gifts, the Epics of Achilles and Ulysses; illustrated by Lucy Martin Bitzer (English). *Translator or author:* Bernard Evslin. New York, N.Y.: Four Winds Press.

1976—The Iliad [of] Homer; in contemporary verse [illustrated by Quentin Fiore] (English). *Translator or author:* Robert Fitzgerald. Franklin Center, Pa.: Franklin Library.

1976—The Odyssey [of] Homer; in contemporary verse (English). *Translator or author:* Robert Fitzgerald. Franklin Center, Pa.: Franklin Library.

1976—Pages from the Iliad; Robert Fitzgerald, translator; K. K. Merker, printer prefacer (English). *Translator or author:* Robert Fitzgerald. Iowa City, Io.: Windhover Press.

1976—Odiseja Homeri; e peerktheu Pashko Gjeci (Albanian). *Translator or author:* Pashko Gjeci. Tiranee [location?]: Shteepia Botuese "Naim Frasheeri".

1976—Hymnes [d']Homere; texte etabli et traduit; 6th ed. (Greek; French). *Translator or author:* Jean Humbert. Paris, France: Societe d'Edition "Les Belles Lettres".

1976—[H]omerou Iliada; metaphrase (Greek, Modern). *Translator or author:* Nikos Kazantzakis; Ioannes Theophanous Kakrides. Athens, Greece.

1976—The Iliad of Homer; translated with an introduction (English). *Translator or author:* Richmond Alexander Lattimore. Chicago, Il.: University of Chicago Press.

1976—Obras Selectas de homero: La Odisea (Spanish). *Translator or author:* Leconte de Lisle; Louis Palemeque. Mexico (City), Mexico: Editorial del Valle de Mexico.

1976—Odusseia Homair; eadar-theangaichte (Gaelic). *Translator or author:* Iain Mac Gilleathain. Glasgow, Scotland: Gairm.

1976—Odisea Homero; traduccion, introduction y notas (Spanish). *Translator or author:* Jose Luis Calvo Martinez. Madrid, Spain: Editora Nacional.

1976—Iliade[d']Homere; traduit et presente par Mario Meunter; preface de Fernand Robert; index et notes de Luc Duret (French). *Translator or author:* Mario Meunier. Paris, France: Livre de Poche.

1976—Iliada Omir; preveli ot starograeuetiski Aleksandaeur Milev I Blaga Dimitrova; 3rd ed. (Bulgarian). *Translator or author:* Aleksandaeur Milev; Blaga Dimitrova. Sofija (Sofia), Bulgaria: Narodna Kultura.

1976—Homeri Opera; recognoverunt brevique adnotatione critica instruxerunt; 3rd ed. (Greek; English). *Translator or author:* David Binning Monro; Thomas William Allen. Oxford: Clarendon Press.

1976—Iliad Homer: cyfaddasiad radio ynghyd ag ysgrif ar "Apel Homer" (Welsh). *Translator or author:* Derec Llwyd Morgan. Llandysul, Wales: Gwasg Gomer.

1976—[H]omerou Odysseia; eleuthere apodose tou archaiou keimenou se pezo logo (Greek, Modern). *Translator or author:* Georgios D. Papaioannos. Athens, Greece: Ekdoseis Dorikos.

1976—Iliade Omero; episodi scelti; illustrati con 26 tavole da Giorgia De Chirico (Greek; Italian).

Translator or author: Salvatore Quasimodo. Rome, Italy: Delfino.

1976— The Odyssey [of] Homer; translated (English). *Translator or author:* Emile Victor Rieu. Harmondsworth, England; Baltimore, Md.: Penguin Books.

1976— La Odisea Homero; version directa y literal del Griego; prologo de Manuel Alsala; 17th ed. (Spanish). *Translator or author:* Luis Segala y Estalella. Mexico (City), Mexico: Editorial Porrua.

1976— La Iliada Homero; estudio preliminar: Julio Palli Bonet; traduccion Castellana; 9th ed. (Castilian Spanish). *Translator or author:* Luis Segala y Estalella. Barcelona, Spain: Editorial Bruguera.

1976— La Odisea Homero; estudio preliminar de Angeles Cardona de Gibert; traduccion; 9th ed. (Spanish). *Translator or author:* Luis Segala y Estalella. Barcelona, Spain: Editorial Bruguera.

1976–78— The Iliad [of] Homer, with an English translation (Greek; English). *Translator or author:* Augustus Taber Murray. Cambridge, Mass.: Harvard University Press.

1976–80— The Odyssey [of] Homer; with an English translation (Greek; English). *Translator or author:* Augustus Taber Murray. Cambridge, Mass.: Harvard University Press.

1977— La Iliada (English). Barcelona, Spain: AFHA Internacional.

1977— Iliade Omero; prefazione di Fausto Codino; versione di Rosa Calzecchi Onesti (Italian). *Translator or author:* Rosa Calzecchi Onesti. Torino (Turin), Italy: Giulio Einaudi.

1977— Lettura di Omero: il canto quinto dell' "Odissea"; introduzione, testo critico, traduzione, commento, appendice su testo e linguaggio, indici Gennaro D'Ippolito (Greek; Italian). *Translator or author:* Gennaro D'Ippolito. Palermo, Sicily, Italy: Manfredi.

1977— Hesiod, the Homeric Hymns, and Homerica; with an English translation (Greek; English). *Translator or author:* Hugh Gerard Evelyn-White. Cambridge, Mass.; London, England: Harvard University Press; William Heinemann.

1977— Homers Ilias; new gefasst; mit 13 Holzschnitten von Hella Ackermann (German). *Translator or author:* Hermann Hoepke. Baden-Baden, Cologne, Germany; New York, N.Y.: Witzstrock.

1977— Iliada Homero; asesor: Arturo Del Hoyo;

1st ed. (Spanish). *Translator or author:* Arturo del Hoyo. Mexico (City), Mexico: Aguilar.

1977— Homer's Iliad; translated (English). *Translator or author:* J. P. Kirton. Lowestoft, England: J. P. Kirton.

1977— The Odyssey of Homer; translated with an introduction (English). *Translator or author:* Richmond Alexander Lattimore. New York, N.Y.: Harper and Row.

1977— I-li-ya-te; Lo Tu-hsiu, An Chia-fang I [The Iliad] (Chinese). *Translator or author:* Tu-hsiu Lo. Tao-yeuan, China: Min kuo Lo Tu-hsiu.

1977— The Iliad by Homer; Elliot Maggin, script; Yong Montano, artist [comic book format] (English). *Translator or author:* Elliot Maggin. New York, N.Y.: Marvel Comics Group.

1977— The Odyssey by Homer; Bill Mantlo, writer; Jess Jodloman, artist [comic book] (English). *Translator or author:* Bill Mantlo. New York, N.Y.: Marvel Comics Group.

1977— The Adventures of Ulysses; retold; from Homer's Odyssey; illustrations by Tom Barling (English). *Translator or author:* John Marsden. London, England: Pan Books.

1977— Odysseus Returns: Homer's Odyssey Retold (English). *Translator or author:* Kenneth McLeish. London, England: Longman.

1977— Odisea Homero; con ilustraciones de Roberto Paez; 2nd ed. (Spanish). *Translator or author:* Lauro Palma. Buenos Aires, Argentina: Atlantida.

1977— Odissea Omero; episodi scelti; illustrati con 20 tavole da Giacomo Manzu (Greek; Italian). *Translator or author:* Salvatore Quasimodo. Rome, Italy: Delfino.

1977— The Iliad of Homer; translated; 1st ed. (English). *Translator or author:* Ennis Rees. Indianapolis, In.: Bobbs-Merrill Educational Pub.

1977— The Odyssey of Homer; translated; 1st ed. (English). *Translator or author:* Ennis Rees. Indianapolis, In.: Bobbs-Merrill Educational Pub.

1977— La Odisea; version directa y literal del Griego; prologo de Manuel Alcala (Spanish). *Translator or author:* Luis Segala y Estalella. Mexico (City), Mexico: Editorial Porrua.

1977— La Iliada Homero; version directa y literal del Griego; prologo de Alfonso Reyes; 18th ed. (Spanish). *Translator or author:* Luis Segala y Estalella. Mexico (City), Mexico: Editorial Porrua.

1978— Ao-te-sai, Ho-ma chu [The Odyssey]

(Chinese). Taipei, Taiwan: Yeuan Ching chu pan shih yeh kung ssu.

1978— Odisea Homero; 4th ed. (Spanish). Barcelona, Spain: Vosgos.

1978— Iliada: prvi, esesti, deveti, enajsti, esest-najsti, osemnahsti, dvaindvajseti, in estiriindva-jseti spev Homer; prevedel Anton Sovrae; uredil Kajetan Gantar. Ljubljana, Slovenia: Mladinska Knjiga.

1978— The Iliad of Homer, Books I–XII; edited with introduction and commentary by M[alcolm] M. Willcock (Greek). Basingstoke, England: Macmillan Education.

1978— La Odisea Homero (Spanish). Mexico (City), Mexico: Editora Nacional.

1978— La Odisea Homero; 9th ed. (Spanish). Barcelona, Spain: AFHA International.

1978— Homere l'Iliade; extraits, traduction, adaptation et presentation (French). *Translator or author:* Michelle Brier. Paris, France: Bordas.

1978— The Odyssey [of] Homer; done into English prose; with a critical and biographical profile of the author by Herbert J. Rose (English). *Translator or author:* Samuel Henry Butcher; Andrew Lang. Danbury, Conn.: Grolier Enterprises.

1978— The Odyssey of Homer [adapted] (English). *Translator or author:* Kenneth Cavander. London, England: Macmillan Education.

1978— The Iliad of Homer [adapted] (English). *Translator or author:* Kenneth Cavander. London, England: Macmillan Education.

1978— The Odyssey of Homer; [adapted from the 1969 edition] (English). *Translator or author:* Kenneth Cavander. Basingstoke, England: Macmillan.

1978— The Odyssey of Homer; adapted; illustrated by Thomas Fraumeni; 2nd ed. (English). *Translator or author:* Henry Irving Christ. New York, N.Y.: Globe Book Co.

1978— The Odyssey: a dramatization (English). *Translator or author:* Gregory A. Falls; Kurt Beattie. Seattle, Wa.: Contemporary Theatre.

1978— The Odyssey [of] Homer; in contemporary verse; illustrated by Walter Brooks (English). *Translator or author:* Robert Fitzgerald. Franklin Center, Pa.: Franklin Library.

1978— Iliada Gomer; perevod s drevnegrech-eskogo; vstup. Stateiia V. eliArkho; primech. S. Osherova (Russian). *Translator or author:* Nikolaaei Ivanovich Gnedich. Moscow, Russia: Khudozh Lit-ra.

1978— Odysseus, the Complete Adventures (English). *Translator or author:* D. J. Hartzell. Wellesley Hills, Mass.: Independent School Press.

1978— Odysseus: the Complete Adventures (English). *Translator or author:* D. J. Hartzell. New York, N.Y.: Longman.

1978— Homer's Odyssey; a translation with an introduction (English). *Translator or author:* Denison Bingham Hull. Greenwich, Conn.: D. B. Hull.

1978— Homer's Odyssey; a translation with an introduction (English). *Translator or author:* Denison Bingham Hull. Athens, Ohio: Ohio University Press.

1978— Ulysses [of] Homer, Lob, Pichard; translated [from French; comic book format] (English). *Translator or author:* Sean Kelly; Valerie Marchant. New York, N.Y.: Heavy Metal.

1978— The Iliad [of] Homer; done into English prose; with a critical and biographical profile of the author by Herbert J. Rose (English). *Translator or author:* Andrew Lang; Walter Leaf; Ernest Myers. Danbury, Conn.: Grolier Enterprises; Ernest Myers.

1978— The Odyssey of Homer; translated into English by T. E. Shaw (English). *Translator or author:* Thomas Edward Lawrence. New York, N.Y.: Oxford University Press.

1978— Homer Barndutsch Odyssee, Gesange I–XXIV; ubersetzt; 3rd ed (Bernese German). *Translator or author:* Albert Meyer. Bern, Switzerland: Brancke.

1978— The Odyssey of Homer; in the English translation by Alexander Pope; illustrated with the classical designs of John Flaxman (English). *Translator or author:* John Pope. Norwalk, Conn.: Easton Press.

1978— La Odisea Homero; version directa y literal del Griego; prologo de Manuel Alsala; 19th ed. (Spanish). *Translator or author:* Luis Segala y Estalella. Mexico (City), Mexico: Editorial Porrua.

1978— Trojan Mahayuddha; lekhakaru (Kannada). *Translator or author:* K. M. Sitaramayya. Bengaluru: Bengaluru Visvavidyalaya.

1978— Iliada Homer; pereklav iz starohreetis'koei; vstup. Statteiia I prymitky Andrieiia Bileetis'koho (Ukranian). *Translator or author:* Borys Ten. Kiev (Kyyir), Ukraine: Dnipro.

1978— Travellers' Tales from the Odyssey and Baron Munchausen; simplified; revised by D. K

Swan; illustrated by David Perry; 3rd ed. (English). *Translator or author:* Michael West. London, England: Longman.

1978–84— The Iliad of Homer, Books I–XII; edited with introduction and commentary by M[alcolm] M. Willcock (Greek). Houndsmills, England: St. Martin's Press.

1978–85— The Iliad [of] Homer; with an English translation (Greek; English). *Translator or author:* Augustus Taber Murray. Cambridge, Mass.; London, England: Harvard University Press; William Heinemann.

1979— A World of Heroes: selection from Homer, Herodotus, and Sophocles; text and running vocabulary (Greek). Cambridge, England; New York, N.Y.: Cambridge University Press.

1979— Dios Odysseus, Szenen aus der Odyssee; fur den Unterricht bearbeitet von Karl Heinz Eller; ilustrationen von Siegfried Bauer (Greek; German). Frankfurt am Main, Germany: Moritz Diesterweg.

1979— De Stora Eaventyren Odysseen, av Homeros Odysseen [translated from the 1977 Marvel Comics edition; comic book format] (Swedish). Sundbyberg, Sweden: Semic Press.

1979— L'Odyssée: une Oeuvre [d']Homere; les aventures sur mer: un theme [de] Hugo, Bombard, Monfreid; presentation de Martine Gaillot et de Raoul Mas (French). Paris, France: A. Hatier.

1979— The Iliad [of] Homer (English). West Haven, Conn.: Pendulum Press.

1979— A World of Heroes; selections from Homer, Herodotus and Sophocles; text and running vocabulary (Greek). Cambridge, England: Cambridge University Press.

1979— La Odisea Homero (Spanish). Mexico (City), Mexico: Concepto.

1979— Homeri Carmina ad Optimorum Librorum Fidem Expressa Curante Guilielmo Dindorfio (Greek). Leipzig, Germany: B. G. Teubner.

1979— La Odisea Homero (Spanish). Mexico (City), Mexico: Salvat Mexicana de Ediciones.

1979— Iliad III [of] Homer; with introduction, notes & vocabulary by J. T. Hooker (Greek). Bristol, England: Bristol Classical Press.

1979— Homeri Ilias; edidit Thomas W[illiam] Allen (Greek). New York, N.Y.: Arno Press.

1979— The Iliad of Homer; translated into English blank verse (English). *Translator or author:* William Cullen Bryant. Boston, Mass.: Houghton, Osgood.

1979— [H]e Odysseia tou [H]omerou; mythos dai morphe, paramythiko [h]ypostroma, mythos, ploke meron, historiles epidraseis, politismika stoicheia, aisthetikes kai ethikes axies, kritike (Greek, Modern). *Translator or author:* Triantaphyllos I. Deles. Athens, Greece: Gutenberg.

1979— L'Odyssee [d']Homere; trad., introd., notes et index (French). *Translator or author:* Mederic Dufour; Jeanne Raison. Paris, France: Garnier Freres.

1979— The Odyssey [of] Homer; [adapted by John Norwood Fago, illustrated by Nestor Redondo] (English). *Translator or author:* John Norwood Fago. West Haven, Conn.: Pendulum Press.

1979— The Odyssey [of] Homer; in contemporary verse; illustrated by W[itold] T. Mars (English). *Translator or author:* Robert Fitzgerald. Franklin Center, Pa.: Franklin Library.

1979— The Iliad [of] Homer, in contemporary verse; illustrated by Walter Brooks (English). *Translator or author:* Robert Fitzgerald. Franklin Center, Pa.: Franklin Library.

1979— The Dolphin's Path, a Bookman's Sequel to the Odyssey of Homer; assisted by P. R. Goodfellow and Kasiphones (English). *Translator or author:* Harry Gold. Chapel Hill, N.C.: Harry (Aberdeen Book Co.) Gold.

1979— Odyssee Homer; neue Ubersetzung, Nachwort und Register von Roland Hampe (German). *Translator or author:* Roland Hampe. Stuttgart, Germany: Philipp Reclam jun.

1979— The Iliads and Odysses of Homer; translated out of Greek into English, with a large preface concerning the vertues of an heroick poem, written by the translator [reprint of the 1677 edition printed in London] (English). *Translator or author:* Thomas Hobbes. New York, N.Y.: AMS Press.

1979— Homer Odyssee; ubersetzt; mit den Holzstichen von Karl Rossing (German). *Translator or author:* Friedrich Georg Junger. Stuttgart, Germany: J. G. Cotta Buchhandlung.

1979— Al-lliyadhah, Humirus; naqalaha ila al-Arabiyah (Arabic). *Translator or author:* Anbarah Salam Khalidi. Beirut (Beyreut, Bayrut), Lebanon: Dar al-Ilm lil-Malayin.

1979— al-Udhisah; haqalatha ila al- Arabiyah (Arabic). *Translator or author:* Anbarah Salam Khalidi. Beirut (Beyreut, Bayrut), Lebanon: Dar al-Ilm lil-Malayin.

1979— L'Iliade [d']Homere; traduction (French). *Translator or author:* P. Lagrandville. Paris, France: Gallimard.

1979—[H]omerou Ilias; Nikolaou Loukane; eisa-goge, Francis R. Walton; metaphrase eisagoges Sophe Papageorgiou (Greek, Modern). *Translator or author:* Nikolaos Loukanes. Athens, Greece: Gennadeios Vivliotheke Amerikanike Schole Klassiko.

1979— Les Plus Belles Legendes de l'Odyssee; Ill. De Jean Retailleau (French). *Translator or author:* Andre Massepain. Paris, France: L. Hachette.

1979— Odysseus Returns: Homer's Odyssey retold (English). *Translator or author:* Kenneth McLeish. London, England: Longman.

1979— The Iliad of Homer; in the English verse translation by Alexander Pope; illustrated with the classical designs of John Flaxman (English). *Translator or author:* Alexander Pope. Norwalk, Conn.: Easton Press.

1979—[H]omerou Odysseia; metaphrase (Greek, Modern). *Translator or author:* Georgio Psychountakes. Athens, Greece: G. Psychountakes.

1979— Lirici Greci dall'Odissea, dall'Iliade; traduzione; introduzione di Gilberto Finzi; 1st ed. (Greek; Italian). *Translator or author:* Salvatore Quasimodo. Milan, Italy: Arnoldo Mondadori.

1979— La Iliada Homero; version directa y literal del Griego; prologo de Alfonso Reyes; 19th ed. (Spanish). *Translator or author:* Luis Segala y Estalella. Mexico (City), Mexico: Editorial Porrua.

1979— La Odisea por Homero [illustrated with comic strips by Manuel] (Spanish). *Translator or author:* Eugenio Sotillos. Barcelona, Spain: Toray.

1979— Ilias, Odyssee Homer; in der Ubertragung von Johann Heinrich Voss (German). *Translator or author:* Johann Heinrich Voss. Munich, Germany: Deutscher Taschenbuch Verlag.

1979— Homerische Hymnen; Griechisch und Deutsch; herausgegeben; 4th ed. (Greek; German). *Translator or author:* Anton Weiher. Munich, Germany: Ernst Heimeran.

1979— Ao-te-hsiu chi, Ho-ma shih shih [Odyssey]; Yang Hsien-I I; Wai kuo wen hseueh ming chu tsung shu pien chi wei yeuan hui pien (Chinese). *Translator or author:* Hsien-I Yang. Shang-hai, China: Shang-hai I wen chu pan she.

1979— Illieodeu, Oditsei Houmeo chak; Yu Yeong yeok (Korean). *Translator or author:* Yeong Yu. Seoul, South Korea: Cheongeumsa.

1980— La Odisea Homero [cartoon format] (French). West Haven, Conn.: Pendulum Press.

1980— La Iliada; 18th ed. Mexico (City), Mexico: Cia . General de Ediciones.

1980— Iliad III [of] Homer; with introduction, notes and vocabulary by J. T. Hooker (Greek). Bristol, England: Bristol Classical Press.

1980— Odyssey IX [of] Homer; with introduction and running vocabulary by J[ohn] V[ictor] Muir (Greek). Bristol, England: Bristol Classical Press.

1980— La Iliada y Otros Textos Homero (Spanish). Mexico (City), Mexico: Fernandez.

1980— La Iliada Homero (Spanish). Mexico (City), Mexico: Editorial Concepto.

1980— The Homeric Hymns; edited [reprint of the 1936 edition printed at Oxford] (Greek). *Translator or author:* T. E. Allen; W. R. Halliday; E. E. Sikes. Amsterdam, Netherlands: Adolf M. Hakkert; E. E. Sikes.

1980— Ilyadhat Humirus Muarrabah naozman wa-alayha sharoh tarikhi adabi; bi-qalam Sulayman al-Bustani [facsimile of the 1904 edition] (Arabic). *Translator or author:* Sulayman Khaototar Bustani. Beirut, Lebanon: Dar Iohya al-Turath al-Arabai.

1980— The Odyssey [of] Homer; translated (English). *Translator or author:* Samuel Henry Butcher; Andrew Lang. Danbury, Conn.: Grolier Enterprises.

1980— La Iliada Homero; [adaptacion]; 10th ed. (Spanish). *Translator or author:* Ramon Conde Obregon. Barcelona, Spain: AFHA Internacional.

1980— Homer's The Odyssey: a Dramatization (English). *Translator or author:* Gregory Falls; Kurt Beattie. New Orleans, La.: Anchorage Press.

1980— Odisea Homero; introduccion y notas de Jose Alsina; traslacion en verso (Spanish). *Translator or author:* Fernando Gutierrez. Barcelona, Spain: Planeta.

1980— Homerova "Odisseeiia" (Ukranian). *Translator or author:* Kateryna Hlovaetiska. Kiev (Kyyir), Ukraine: Veselka.

1980— Udhisah Humirus; naqalatha ila al-Arabiyah Anbarah Salam al-Khalidi (Arabic). *Translator or author:* Anbarah Salam Khalidi. Beirut, Lebanon: Dar al-Ilm lil-Malayin.

1980— Allian Homer; Z erec. Orig. perel. Rudolf Mertlik; Doslov Homer a jeho allias a pozn. Naps, a jmennay rejsterik sest. Ladislav Vidman (Czech). *Translator or author:* Rudolf Mertlik. Prague, Czechoslavakia: Odeon.

1980— La Iliada; adaptacion; dibujante Teo; 2nd ed. (Spanish). *Translator or author:* Jose Maria Osorio. Leon [location?]: Editorial Everest.

1980—The Illustrated Odyssey; translated from Homer; introduction by Jacquetta Hawkes; original photographs by Tim Mercer (English). *Translator or author:* Emile Victor Rieu. London, England: Sidgwick and Jackson.

1980—Iliad Homer; ubertragen; mit Urtext, Anhang und Registern; 7th ed. (German). *Translator or author:* Hans Rupe. Munich, Germany: Ernst Heimeran.

1980—Die Odyssee in Scherenschnitten; [begleitender Text, Framente aus Homer's "Odyssee" in der Ubersetzung von Johann Heinrich Voss] (German). *Translator or author:* Jurgen Schwendy. Munich, Germany: Langen-Muller.

1980—La Odisea Homero; version directa y literal del Griego; prologo de Manuel Alcala; 20th ed. (Spanish). *Translator or author:* Luis Segala y Estalella. Mexico (City), Mexico: Editorial Porrua.

1980—La Iliada Homero; [version directa y literal del Griego]; 4th ed. (Spanish). *Translator or author:* Luis Segala y Estalella. Mexico (City), Mexico: Editores Mexicanos Unidos.

1980—Odisea y Otros Textos; seleccion de textos y adaptacion: Francisco Serrano; revision de textos: Rosanela Alvarez; ilustraciones: Elena Climent (Spanish). *Translator or author:* Francisco Serrano. Mexico (City), Mexico: Fernandez.

1980—The Odyssey of Homer; translated, with an epiloque on translation; introduction by G. S. Kirk (English). *Translator or author:* Walter Shewring. Oxford, England; New York, N.Y.: Oxford University Press.

1980—The Odyssey: Selected Adventures; by Homer; adapted; illustrated by Konrad Hack (English). *Translator or author:* Diana Stewart. Milwaukee, Wis.: Raintree Publishers.

1980—Odyssee aus dem Griechischen; herausgegeben von Peter von der Muhll; mit einem Nachwort von Egon Friedell (German). *Translator or author:* Johann Heinrich Voss. Zurich, Switzerland: Diogenes.

1980—Ilias Homer (German). *Translator or author:* Johann Heinrich Voss. Munich, Germany: Goldmann.

1980—Ur-Odyssee [von] Homer; nach der Ubersetzung von Johann Heinrich Voss; mit Bildern von Friedrich Preller; herausgegeben von Ulrich Creamer (German). *Translator or author:* Johann Heinrich Voss. Tubingen, Germany: Grabert-Verlag.

1980—Odyssee: Griechisch und Deutsch [von] Homer; Ubertragung; Einfuhrung von A. Heubeck; mit Urtext, Anhang und Registern; 6th ed. (Greek; German). *Translator or author:* Anton Weiher. Munich, Germany: Ernst Heimeran.

1980–84—The Odyssey [of] Homer; with an English translation (Greek; English). *Translator or author:* Augustus Taber Murray. Cambridge, Mass.; London, England: Harvard University Press; William Heinemann.

1980–97—Odysseia Metaphrase; [prologiko semeioma, Giorgos maurogiannes] (Greek, Modern). *Translator or author:* Stauros Kampourides. Athens, Greece: Ekdoseis Pella.

1980s—Odisseia Homero. Mem Martins [location?]: Publiccoes Europa-America.

1980s—Mu ma t'u ch'eng chi; [yeuan tso che Homa; pien che Shih cheueh ts'ung shu pien chi pu] (Chinese). *Translator or author:* Chih cheueh t'u ch'eng chi yeuan I. Hong Kong (Hsiang Kang), China: Ming hsin ch'u pan she.

1980s—[H]omerou Odysseia (Greek, Modern). *Translator or author:* Antonella Damianou. Athens, Greece: Ekdoseis N. Damianou.

1980s—[H]omerou Iliada (Greek, Modern). *Translator or author:* Antonella Damianou. Athens, Greece: Ekdoseis N. Damianou.

1980s—The Odyssey: the Story of Odysseus [by] Homer; translated (English). *Translator or author:* William Henry Denham Rouse. New York, N.Y.: New American Library.

1980s—La Iliada y Otros Textos; seleccion de textos y adaptacion: Francisco Serrano; revision de textos: Rosanela Alvarez; ilustraciones: Elena Climent. *Translator or author:* Francisco Serrano. South Pasadena, Ca.: Bilingual Educational Services.

1981—Odyssee Homer. Ottobrunn bei Munchen, Germany: Franklin Bibliothek.

1981—Odissea Omero; prefazione di Fausto Codino; versione di Rosa Calzecchi (Italian). *Translator or author:* Rosa Calzecchi Onesti. Torino (Turin), Italy: Giulio Einaudi.

1981—The Iliad of Homer, Book XI; edited (Greek; English). *Translator or author:* E[dward] S[eymour] Forster. Letchworth, England: Bradda.

1981—Odisea; edicion escolar, texto integro; traduccion directa del Griego por Mario Frias Infante, estudios por Carlos Coello Vila (Spanish). *Translator or author:* Mario Frias Infante. La Paz, Bolivia: Editorial Don Bosco.

1981—La Odisea: Aventuras Seleccionadas

Homero; adaptado por Diana Stewart; illustrado por Konrad Hack; tracuido al Castellano por Ella C. de Gedovius (Castilian Spanish). *Translator or author:* Ella C. de Gedovius. Mexico (City), Mexico: Raintree de Mexico Editores.

1981— Homer Bearndeutsch Ilias (Bernese German). *Translator or author:* Walter Gfeller. Bern, Switzerland: Francke.

1981— Iliada Gomer; perevod s drevnegrecheskogo; [khudozhnik R. Danetisig; posleslovie V. eliArkho; primechaniia S. Osherova (Russian). *Translator or author:* Nikolaaei Ivanovich Gnedich. Moscow, Russia: Moskovskii Rabochii.

1981— Ta Taxidia tou Odyssea; stichoi Renas Karthaiou; eikonographese, Tasou Kouphou (Anaskos); 2nd ed. (Greek, Modern). *Translator or author:* Alke Goulime. Athens, Greece: G. K. Eleutheroudakes.

1981— Homerova "Iliada"; dleiia seredn'oho shkil'noho viku (Ukranian). *Translator or author:* Kateryna Hlovaetiska. Kiev (Kyyir), Ukraine: Veselka.

1981— Iliada Homer; przeoczya Kaximiera Jeczewska; wstnepem I przpisami opatrz Jerzy janowski; 13th ed. (Polish). *Translator or author:* Kazimiez Jexzewski; Jerzy Janowski. Warsaw, Poland: Zakad Narodowy im. Ossolinskich.

1981— Homers Odyssee; ubersetzt (German). *Translator or author:* Friedrich Georg Junger. Stuttgart, Germany: Klett-Cotta.

1981— lriasu Homerosu [cho]; Kure Shigeichi yaku (Japanese). *Translator or author:* Shigeichi Kure. Tokyo, Japan: Iwanami Shoten.

1981— The Odyssey of Homer; translated by T. E. Shaw, Lawrence of Arabia; wood engravings by Berry Moser; preface by Jeremy M. Wilson (English). *Translator or author:* Thomas Edward Lawrence. New York, N.Y.: Limited Editions Club.

1981— Ulysse; [texte de] Homere [et] Lob; [dessins de] Pichard [comic book] (French). *Translator or author:* Jacques Lob. Grenoble, France: Editions Glenat.

1981— War Music; An Account of Books 16 to 19 of Homer's Iliad (English). *Translator or author:* Christopher Logue. London, England: Jonathan Cape.

1981— Alliad Hoimear, Leabhair I–VIII; reamhaiste le Breandan O Doibhlin (Irish). *Translator or author:* Sean Mac Heil. Galway [Gaillimh], Ireland: Officina Typographica.

1981— Nuova Traduzione Metrica di Iliade, XIV; da una miscellanea umanistica di Agnolo Manetti [a cura di] Renata Fabbri; con la tavola del Codice magliab. XXV, 626 (Latin). *Translator or author:* Agnolo Manetti. Rome, Italy: Edizioni di Storia e Letteratura.

1981— La Iliada y la Odisea; ilustraciones de Laszlo Gal. *Translator or author:* Carlo Montella. Madrid, Spain: Ediciones Montena.

1981— Dastani Raspotin berhemi zamey nuseri ferensa Sarl Biti; Homer le 'erebiyewe kirduye be Kurdi; Raspotin kesiseki dawenpis u falbaz [Kurdish translation from Arabic from French] (Kurdish). *Translator or author:* Charles Petit. Baghdad (Bexdad), Iraq: Capxaney al-Hawadith.

1981— The Odyssey of Homer, a Dramatization for Radio in Eight One-Hour Episodes (English). *Translator or author:* Yuri Rasovsky. Chicago, Il.: National Radio Theatre.

1981— The Illustrated Odyssey; translated from Homer; introduction by Jacquette Hawkes; original photographs by Tim Mercer (English). *Translator or author:* Emile Victor Rieu. New York, N.Y.: A and W Publishers.

1981— The Illustrated Odyssey; translated from Homer; introduction by Jacquetta Hawkes; original photographs by Tim Mercer (English). *Translator or author:* Emile Victor Rieu. London, England: Book Club Associates.

1981— La Odisea Homero; traduccion, respetuosamente abreviada, prologo e indice de nombres de Luis Santullano; 16th ed. (Spanish). *Translator or author:* Luis Santullano. Mexico (City), Mexico: Compania General de Ediciones.

1981— La Iliada Homero; version directa y literal del Griego; prologo de Alfonso Reyes (Spanish). *Translator or author:* Luis Segala y Estalella. Mexico (City), Mexico: Editorial Porrua.

1981— La Iliada Homero; [version directa y literal del Griego]; 5th ed. (Spanish). *Translator or author:* Luis Segala y Estalella. Mexico (City), Mexico: Mexicanos Unidos.

1981— La Iliada Homero; estudio preliminar por David Garcia Bacca; traduccion (Spanish). *Translator or author:* Luis Segala y Estalella. Mexico (City), Mexico: Editorial Cumbre.

1981— The Iliad by Homer; adapted; illustrated by Charles Shaw (English). *Translator or author:* Diana Stewart. Milwaukee, Wis.: Raintree Publishers.

1981— La Odisea Homero; [prologo de Manuel Vivero]; 5th ed. (Spanish). *Translator or author:* Manuel Vivero. Mexico (City), Mexico: Editores Mexicanos Unidos.

1981—The Amazing Adventures of Ulysses [by] Homer; retold; illustrated by Stephen Cartwright (English). *Translator or author:* Vivian Webb; Heather Amery. London, England; Tulsa, Ok: Hayes.

1981—The Amazing Adventures of Ulysses; retold; illustrated by Stephen Cartwright (English). *Translator or author:* Vivian Webb; Heather Amery. Adelaide, Australia: Rigby.

1981—La Odisea Homero; introduccion de Alberto Bernabe; [traduccion] (Spanish). *Translator or author:* Felipe Ximenez de Sandoval. Madrid, Spain: EDAF.

1981—Odisseia Gomer; rerevod s drevnegrecheskogo (Russian). *Translator or author:* Vasilii Andreevich Zhukovskii. Moscow, Russia: Izd-vo "Khudozhestvennaeiia literatura".

1981–86—Odissea Omero; introduzione generale di Alfred Heubeck e Stephanie West, testo e commento a cura di Stephanie West, traduzione di G. Aurelio Privitera; 1st ed. (Greek; Italian). *Translator or author:* G. Aurelio Privitera. Rome; Milan: Fondazione Lorenzo Valla; Arnoldo Mondadori.

1982—La Odisea (Spanish). Madrid, Spain: Europa-Ediexport.

1982—Odyssey VI & VII [of] Homer; with notes and vocabulary by G[erald] M[aclean] Edwards [reprint of the 1915 edition printed at Cambridge] (Greek). Bristol, England: Bristol Classical Press.

1982—La Odisea Homero; [prologo de Manuel Vivero]; 6th ed. (Spanish). Mexico (City), Mexico: Editores Mexicanos Unidos.

1982—Iliad Latina; introduzione, edizione critica, traduzione Italiana e commento a cura Marco Scaffai (Latin; Italian). *Translator or author:* Baebius Italicus; Marco Scaffai. Bologna, Italy: Patron.

1982—Iliade; prefazione di Fausto Codino (Italian). *Translator or author:* Rosa Calzecchi Onesti. Torino (Turin), Italy: Giulio Einaudi.

1982—The Children's Homer: the Adventures of Odysseus and the Tale of Troy; illustrated by Willy Pogany [reprint of the 1918 edition] (English). *Translator or author:* Padraic Colum. New York, N.Y.: Collier Books.

1982—The Children's Homer: the Adventures of Odysseus and the Tale of Troy; illustrated by Willy Pogany [reprint of the 1918 edition] (English). *Translator or author:* Padraic Colum. New York, N.Y.: Aladdin Paperbacks.

1982—Hesiod, the Homeric Hymns, and Homerica; with an English translation (Greek; English). *Translator or author:* Hugh Gerard Evelyn-White. Cambridge, Mass.; London, England: Harvard University Press; William Heinemann.

1982—Ao-te-sai Homer chu [The Odyssey] (Chinese). *Translator or author:* Tung-hua Fu. Taiwan (Tai-nan): Li ta chu pan she.

1982—Homara Racanasamagra; amubada (Bengali). *Translator or author:* Sudhamsuranhan Ghosh. Kalakata, Bengal: Tuli-kalama.

1982—Iliada Homero; introduccion y notas de Jose Alsina; tr. en verso; 2nd ed. (Spanish). *Translator or author:* Fernando Gutierrez. Barcelona, Spain: Planeta.

1982—Homer's Iliad; a translation, with an introduction (English). *Translator or author:* Denison Bingham Hull. Scottsdale, Ar.: D. B. Hull.

1982—Homer's Iliad; a translation with an introduction (English). *Translator or author:* Denison Bingham Hull. Athens, Ohio: Ohio University Press.

1982—Homer: die Odyssee; Zeichnungen nach antiken Motiven von Brinna Otto (German). *Translator or author:* Eva Jantzen. Mainz, Germany: P. Von Zabern.

1982—[H]omerou Iliada; hermeneutike ekdose me vase te metaphrase Kazantzake-Kakride (Greek, Modern). *Translator or author:* Kostas Kalokairinos. Athens, Greece: Ekdoseis Gregore.

1982—Ilyadhad Humirus; naqalatha ila al-Arabiyah Anbarah Salam al-Khalidi (Arabic). *Translator or author:* Anbarah Salam Khalidi. Beirut, Lebanon: Dar al-Ilm lil-Malayin.

1982—The Meeting of Achilleus and Priam from The Iliad: Book Twenty-Four; in the translation by Richmond Lattimore (English). *Translator or author:* Richmond Alexander Lattimore. New York, N.Y.: Kelly/Winterton Press.

1982—Iliad, Book XXIV; edited (Greek). *Translator or author:* Colin Macleod. Cambridge, England; New York, N.Y.: Cambridge University Press.

1982—Odisea Homero; introduccion de Manuel Fernandez-Galiano; traduccion (Spanish). *Translator or author:* Jose Manuel Pabon. Madrid, Spain: Editorial Gredos.

1982—Odisea Homero; introduccion de Manuel Fernandez-Galiano; traduccion (Spanish). *Translator or author:* Jose Manuel Pabon. Madrid, Spain: Editorial Gredos.

1982—Przygody Odyseusza; Opowiadanie dla mlodziezy wedlug "Odysei" (Polish). *Translator or author:* Jan Parandowski. Warsaw, Poland: Krajowa Agencja Wydawnicza.

1982—The Odyssey [of] Homer; translated (English). *Translator or author:* Emile Victor Rieu. New York, N.Y.: Greenwich House.

1982—Baebii Italici Ilias Latina; introduzione, edizione critica, traduzione Italiana e commento a cura di Marco Scaffai; 1st ed. (Latin; Italian). *Translator or author:* Marco Scaffai. Bologna, France: Patron.

1982—Ilias & Odyssee Homerus; vertaald (Dutch). *Translator or author:* M. A. Schwartz. Amsterdam, Netherlands: Polak & Van Gennep Athenaeum.

1982—Iliada Homero; edicion, introduccion y notas de Javier Lopez Facal; 1st ed. (Spanish). *Translator or author:* Luis Segala y Estalella. Madrid, Spain: Sociedad General Espanola de Libreria.

1982—La Odisea Homero; version directa y literal del Griego (Spanish). *Translator or author:* Luis Segala y Estalella. Mexico (City), Mexico: Editorial Epoca.

1982—Odisea Homero; edicion, introduccion y notas de Luis Alberto de Cuenca (Spanish). *Translator or author:* Luis Segala y Estalella. Madrid, Spain: Sociedad General Espana de Libreria.

1982—La Iliada Homero; estudio preliminar por David Garcia Bacca; tr. (Spanish). *Translator or author:* Luis Segala y Estalella. Barcelona, Spain: Oceano.

1982—La Iliada Homero; version directa y literal del Griego; illustraciones de Flaxman y A. J. Church [reprint of the 1908 edition printed at Barcelona] (Spanish). *Translator or author:* Luis Segala y Estalella. Mexico (City), Mexico: Editorial Epoca Ediciones Selectas.

1982—Iliade Omero; [versione di Giuseppe Tonna; introduzione di Fauto Codino]; 5th ed. (Italian). *Translator or author:* Giuseppe Tonna. Milan, Italy: Garzanti.

1982—Las Asombrosas Aventuras de Ulises [de] Homero; version de Vivian Webb y Heather Amery; ilustraciones de Stephen Cartwright; [translation by Jose Ferrer Aleu of The Amazing Adventures of Ulysses]. *Translator or author:* Vivian Webb; Heather Amery. Esplugues de Llobregat [location?]: Plaza and Janes.

1982—Odyssee; Griechisch und Deutsch; Ubertragen; mit Urtext, Anhang und Registern; Ein-fuhrung von A. Heubeck (Greek; German). *Translator or author:* Anton Weiher. Munich, Germany: Artemis Verlag.

1982—Odisseia Gomer; perevod s drevnegrecheskog; predislovie A. A. Sodomory, khudozhnik V. M. Dozorets (Russian). *Translator or author:* Vasilii Andreevich Zhukovskii. Kiev (Kyyir), Ukraine: Izd-vo TSK LKSMU "molod".

1982—Odisseia Gomer; perevod s drevnegrecheskogo; [posleslovie A. Takho-Godi; primechanieiia S. Osherova] (Russian). *Translator or author:* Vasilii Andreevich Zhukovskii. Moscow, Russia: Moskovshii Rabochii.

1982–92—Iliade Homere; texte etabli et traduit par Paul Mazon avec la collaboration de Pierre Chantraine, Paul Collart, et Rene Langumier; 8th ed. (Greek; French). *Translator or author:* Paul Mazon. Paris, France: Societe d'Edition "Les Belles Lettres".

1983—Homerowej Iliady pomor-gniew (reprint of the 1903 edition) (Greek; Polish). Warsaw, Poland: WAIF.

1983—Iliad I [by] Homer; with introduction, notes and vocabulary by J. A. Harrison and R. H. Jordan (Greek). Bristol, England: Bristol Classical Press.

1983—Yullisiijeu: Odissei Homeo Chieum; Song Myeong-ho olmgim (Korean). Seoul, South Korea: Kyerim Ch'ulp'ansa.

1983—T'euroi eui Mokma: Illiadeu (Korean). Seoul, South Korea: Kyerim Ch'ulp'ansa.

1983—Ho-ma shih shih ti ku shih: I-li-ya-t'e, Ao-te-sai ti kushih; Ho-ma yuan chu (Chinese). Taipei, Taiwan: Chih wen ch'u pan she.

1983—Homerou Iliada (Greek, Modern). Athens, Greece: Ekdoseis Ladia.

1983—The Odyssey of Homer; done into English prose (English). *Translator or author:* Samuel Henry Butcher; Andrew Lang. New York, N.Y.: Modern Library.

1983—Stories from the Iliad and Odyssey; edited and translated from the French by Barbara Whelpton; illustrated by Rene Peron (English). *Translator or author:* George Chapman. London, England; New York, N.Y.: Burke.

1983—Werke in zwei Banden [von] Homer; [aus dem Griechischen ubersetzt]; 3rd ed. (German). *Translator or author:* Dietrich Ebener. Berlin, Germany: Aufbau-Verlag.

1983—The Iliad [of] Homer; in contemporary verse (English). *Translator or author:* Robert

Fitzgerald. New York, N.Y.; Franklin Center, Pa.: Oxford University Press; The Franklin Library.

1983—Homeric Hymn to Hermes [includes the Oxford Classical Text] (Greek). *Translator or author:* Julia Haig Gaisser. Bryn Mawr, Pa.: Bryn Mawr College.

1983—[H]omerou Iliada, metaphrase; [epimeleia Adamantios St. Anestides, A E. Vantares, I. N. Basles (Greek, Modern). *Translator or author:* Nikos Kazantzakis. Athens, Greece: Scholike Vivliotheke Killegiou Athenon.

1983—Homer's Odyssey; as translated (English). *Translator or author:* Memas Kolaitis. Santa Barbara, Ca.: M. Kolaitis.

1983—The Odyssey of Homer; done into English verse (English). *Translator or author:* William Morris. London, England: Reeves and Turner.

1983—La Iliada Homero; traduccion, respetuosamente abreviada prologo a indice de nombres; 21st ed. (Spanish). *Translator or author:* Luis Santullano. Mexico (City), Mexico: Compania General de Ediciones.

1983—Homerische Hymnen, Griechisch-Deutsch; ubertragung; Nachbemerkung von Georg Schoeck; mit einer Radierung von Helmut Ackermann (Greek; German). *Translator or author:* Konrad Schwenck. Zurich, Switzerland; Verona, Italy: Manesse Verlag; Stamperia Valdonega.

1983—La Odisea Homero; traduccion; prologo y edicion cuidada por Pedro Heniquez Ureana; 6th ed. (Spanish). *Translator or author:* Luis Segala y Estalella. Buenos Aires, Argentina: Editorial Losada.

1983—La Iliada Homero; edicion de Julio Palli; traduccion (Spanish). *Translator or author:* Luis Segala y Estalella. Barcelona, Spain: Bruguera.

1983—Ashobiyyah; razmiyyah Homer's Iliad manzum tarjamah (Urdu). *Translator or author:* Shaukat Vasiti. Pishavar, Pakistan: Idarah-yi 'Ilm o Fann-I Pakistan.

1983—Iliada Homerou; metaphrasis (Greek, Modern). *Translator or author:* Ioannou Zervou. Athens, Greece: Ekdoseis Ladia.

1984—The Odyssey [of] Homer [comic strip] (English). West Haven, Conn.: Academic Industries.

1984—Homeo Iyagi Homeo Chieum; Chang Mun-pyeong omgim] (Korean). Seoul, South Korea: Keumseong Chulpansa.

1984—[H]omerou Iliada; metaphrase se aigaiopelagitiko demotiko tragoudi Alexes I. Poulianos

(Greek, Modern). Athens, Greece: G. Maurogeorges; K. Pournatzes.

1984—Homarana Iliyad; Grikara sahasa kathegalu; prathama bhaga; Bi. Gopalarav (Kannada). Maisura: Sailasri Sahitya Prakasana.

1984—The Iliad of Homer; edited with introduction and commentary by M[alcolm] M. Willcock (Greek). New York, N.Y.: St. Martin's Press.

1984—La Iliada Homero (Spanish). San Sabastian, Spain: Txertoa.

1984—The Iliad [of] Homer [comic strip] (English). West Haven, Conn.: Academic Industries.

1984—La Odisea Homero (Spanish). Mexico (City), Mexico: Editores Mexicanos Unidos.

1984—La Odisea Homero; [introduccion por Juan Manuel Rodriguez] (Spanish). Madrid, Spain: Alba.

1984—Homeri Odyssea; recognovit P[eter] von der Muhll; 3rd stereotype ed. (Greek). Stuttgart, Germany: B. G. Teubner.

1984—Odisea Homero (Spanish). Managua, Nicaragua: Editorial Nueva Nicaragua.

1984—Iliada Homero (Spanish). Santiago, Chile: Editorial Ercilla.

1984—The Iliad of Homer, Books XIII–XXIV; edited with an introduction and commentary by M[alcolm] M. Willcock (Greek). Basingstoke, England: Macmillan Education.

1984—The Odyssey of Homer; adapted; [illustrated by Thomas Fraumeni]; 3rd ed. (English). *Translator or author:* Henry Irving Christ. New York, N.Y.: Globe Book Co.

1984—Ho-ma Shih shih Ti Ku Shih: I-li-ya-te, Ao-to-sai Ti Ku Shih; Alfred J Church, Charles Lamb chu; Chi Hsia-fei I; He-ma shi shi de gu shi I-li-ya te, Ao-te-sai ti ku shih (Chinese). *Translator or author:* Alfred John Church. Taipei, Taiwan: Chih Wen Shu Pan She.

1984—The Odyssey; in contemporary verse; illustrated by W. T. Mars (English). *Translator or author:* Robert Fitzgerald. New York, N.Y.: Oxford University Press.

1984—The Iliad [of] Homer; translated (English). *Translator or author:* Robert Fitzgerald. Oxford, England; New York, N.Y.: Oxford University Press.

1984—Iliade, Odyssee [d']Homere; "Iliade" traduction, introduction et notes par Robert Flaceliere; "Odyssee" traduction par Victor Berard, introduction et notes par Jean Berard, index par

Tene Langumier (French). *Translator or author:* Robert Flaceliere; Victor Berard. Paris, France: Gallimard.

1984— Mu Ma Tu Cheng Chi; [yeuan tso che Homa]; pien chu Hua Yung (Chinese). *Translator or author:* Yung Hua. Taiwan (Tai-nan): Ta Chien Chu Pan Shih Yeh Kung Ssu.

1984— Ao te sai mi hang chi; Hua Yung pien chi (Chinese). *Translator or author:* Yung Hua. Taiwan (Tai-nan): Ta Chien Chu Pan Shih Yeh Kung Ssu.

1984— The Nostos of Odysseus: the Warrior's Return (Phaecian episode from the Odyssey); translated (English). *Translator or author:* J. P. Kirton. J. P. Kirton.

1984—[H]e Aspida tou Achillea: [H]omerou Iliada, Rapsodia 18, Stichoi 468–608 = Le Bouclier d'Achille: Homere, L'Iliade, Rhapsodie XVIII, Vers 468–608 = the Shield of Achilles: Homer, The Iliad, Book XVIII, Verses 468–608; 2nd ed. (Greek). *Translator or author:* Lalaounis. Athens, Greece.

1984— War Music: an Account of Books XVI to XIX of Homer's Iliad (English). *Translator or author:* Christopher Logue. Harmondsworth, England: Penguin Books.

1984— Odisea, Aventuras de Ulises; adaptacion; ilustraciones de Libico Maraja; traduccion de Ma. Luz Gonzalez (Spanish). *Translator or author:* Stelio Martelli. Madrid, Spain: EDAF.

1984— Iliada, la Guerra de Troya/Odisea, Aventuras de Ulises; adaptacion; ilustraciones de Libico Maraja; traduccion de Ma. Luz Gonzalez (Spanish). *Translator or author:* Stelio Martelli. Madrid, Spain: EDAF.

1984— Odisi; Homara likhita 'Odisi' ce bhashantara (Marathi). *Translator or author:* S. N. Oak. Mumbai: Maharashtra Rajya Sahitya Sanskrti Mandala.

1984— Iliade Omero; prefazione di Fausto Codino; testo originale a fronte; 9th ed. (Greek; Italian). *Translator or author:* Rosa Calzecchi Onesti. Torino (Turin), Italy: Giulio Einaudi.

1984— Odissea Omero; traduzione; 1st ed. (Greek; Italian). *Translator or author:* G. Aurelio Privitera. Milan, Italy: Fondazione Lorenzo Valla; Arnoldo Mondadori.

1984— The Voyage of Odysseus; illustrated by Hal Frenck [v. 2 of series: Tales from the Odyssey] (English). *Translator or author:* I. M. Richardson. Mahwah, N.J.: Troll Associates.

1984— The Return of Odysseus; illustrated by Hal Frenck [v. 7 of series: Tales from the Odyssey] (English). *Translator or author:* I. M. Richardson. Mahwah, N.J.: Troll Associates.

1984— The Wooden Horse; illustrated by Hal Frenck [v. 1 of series: Tales from the Odyssey] (English). *Translator or author:* I. M. Richardson. Mahwah, N.J.: Troll Associates.

1984— Odysseus and the Magic of Circe; illustrated by Hal Frenck [v. 5 of series: Tales from the Odyssey] (English). *Translator or author:* I. M. Richardson. Mahwah, N.J.: Troll Associates.

1984— Odysseus and the Cyclops; illustrated by Hal Frenck [v. 3 of series: Tales from the Odyssey] (English). *Translator or author:* I. M. Richardson. Mahwah, N.J.: Troll Associates.

1984— Odysseus and the Giants; illustrated by Hal Frenck [v. 4 of series: Tales from the Odyssey] (English). *Translator or author:* I. M. Richardson. Mahwah, N.J.: Troll Associates.

1984— Odysseus and the Great Challenge; illustrated by Hal Frenck [v. 6 of series: Tales from the Odyssey] (English). *Translator or author:* I. M. Richardson. Mahwah, N.J.: Troll Associates.

1984— La Iliada Homero; version directa y literal del Griego; illus. de Jaime Azpelicueta; 6th ed. (Spanish). *Translator or author:* Luis Segala y Estalella. Barcelona, Spain: Editorial Juventud.

1984— Odisea Homero; traduccion (Spanish). *Translator or author:* Luis Segala y Estalella. Mexico (City), Mexico: OMGSA Origen.

1984— Iliada Homero (Spanish). *Translator or author:* Luis Segala y Estalella. Mexico (City), Mexico: OMGSA Origen.

1984— L'Odyssee; desnario, Seron et Homere [comic book] (French). *Translator or author:* Seron. Marcinelle-Charleroi [France?]: Dupuis.

1984— Iliados, Libri I, II; Latine versi; primum edidit Renata Fabbri (Latin). *Translator or author:* Raffaele Maffei Volaterrano. Padova (Padua), Italy: Antenore.

1985— La Iliada Homero; [traduccion en prosa del Griego] (Spanish). Barcelona, Spain: S. A. Editors.

1985— La Iliada Homero; [introduccion, Juan Manuel Rodriguez]; 2nd ed. (Spanish). Madrid, Spain: Ediciones y Distribuciones Alba.

1985— Iliad VI [of] Homer; with introduction, notes & vocabulary by R. H. Jordan and J[ames] A[lexander] Harrison (Greek). Bristol, England: Bristol Classical Press.

1985— Ilijada Homer; preveo Milos N. Duric; 4th ed. Novi Sad, Yugoslavia: Matica Srpska.

1985— La Odisea Homero; 9th ed. (Spanish). Mexico (City), Mexico: Editores Mexicanos Unidos.

1985— Chun tien tsui chu ti wei hsiao Ho-ma chu; Chien Chun-chi (Chinese). *Translator or author:* Chun-chi Chien. Shang-hai, China: Changhar I wen chu pan she.

1985— Odisuja Homer; preveo; 4th ed. *Translator or author:* Milos N. Duriac. Novi Sad, Yugoslavia: Matica Srpska.

1985— The Iliad [of] Homer; translated (English). *Translator or author:* Robert Fitzgerald. London, England: Collins Harvill.

1985— The Odyssey [of] Homer; translated (English). *Translator or author:* Robert Fitzgerald. London, England: Collins Harvill.

1985— To Menyma tou [H]omerou (Greek, Modern). *Translator or author:* Johannes Th. Kakridis. Athens, Greece: Vivliopoleio tes "Hestias".

1985— La Odisea Homero; traduccion (Spanish). *Translator or author:* Vicente Lopez Soto. Barcelona, Spain: Editorial Ramon Sopena.

1985— Carmina Homeri; recensuit et selecta lectionis varietate instruxit Arthurus Lubwich [reprint of the 1978 edition printed in Athens] (Greek). *Translator or author:* Arthur Ludwich. Chicago, Il.: Ares Publishers.

1985— Odisseila Gomer; prevod s drevnegrecheskogo V. Khukovskogo; [predislovie A. Neeikhardt; Illeilustraetisii I oformlenie D. Bisti] (Russian). *Translator or author:* Aleksandra Aleksandrovna Neaikhardt. Moscow, Russia: Pravda.

1985— Odisea Homero; itzultzaille (Basque). *Translator or author:* Santiago de Onaindia. Bilbo: Euskerazaintza'ren Argitalpena.

1985— La Iliada; [adaptacion; dibujante Teo]; 2nd ed. (Spanish). *Translator or author:* Jose Maria Osorio. Madrid, Spain: Editorial Everest.

1985— La Iliada; [adaptacion; dibujante Teo]; 3rd ed. (Spanish). *Translator or author:* Jose Maria Osorio. Madrid, Spain: Editorial Everest.

1985— Odissea Omero; libero adattamento di Gianni Padoan; illustrazione Cesare Colombo; 1st ed. (Italian). *Translator or author:* Gianni Padoan. Milan, Italy: Arnoldo Mondadori.

1985— Pope's Iliad: a Selection with Commentary; edited by Felicity Rosslyn (English). *Translator or author:* Alexander Pope. Bristol, England: Bristol Classical Press.

1985— Odisea Homero; [traduccion] (Spanish). *Translator or author:* Luis Segala y Estalella. Havana, Cuba: Editorial Arte y Literatura.

1985— La Odisea Homero; [traduccion] (Spanish). *Translator or author:* Luis Segala y Estalella. Santiago, Chile: Editorial Ercilla.

1985— La Iliada Homero; nota preliminar de Fernando Diez de Urdanivia; [version directa y literal del Griego por Luis Sagala y Estalella]; 8th ed. (Spanish). *Translator or author:* Luis Segala y Estalella. Mexico (City), Mexico: Editores Mexicanos Unidos.

1985— The Iliad: Stories of the Trojan Wars; [English translation; illustrated by Libico Maraja] (English). *Translator or author:* Karin Sisti. Twickenham, England: Hamlyn.

1985— The Odyssey: the Adventures of Odysseus; illustrated by Libico Maraja; translated from the Italian (English). *Translator or author:* Karin Sisti. Twickenham, England: Hamlyn.

1985— Odysseus and the Enchanters; retold; illustrated by Mike Codd (English). *Translator or author:* Catherine Storr. Milwaukee, Wis.: Raintree Childrens Books.

1985— I-li-ya Wei Cheng Chi Homer Yeuan Chu; E. V. Riew Ying I; Tsao Hung-chao I (Chinese). *Translator or author:* Hung-chao Tsao. Taipei, Taiwan: Lien Ching Chu Pan Shih Yeh Kung Ssu.

1985–88— The Iliad [of] Homer; with an English translation [reprint of the 1924–25 edition] (Greek; English). *Translator or author:* Augustus Taber Murray. Cambridge, Mass.; London, England: Harvard University Press; William Heinemann.

1986— La Iliada Homero (Spanish). Bogota, Columbia: Editorial Bedout.

1986— [H]omerou Iliada, Rapsodia O; scholia kai hermeneia A. X. Karapanagiote; metaglottise scholion, metaphrase, Alex. Ath. Baltas (Greek; Modern Greek). Athens, Greece: Dem. N. Papademas.

1986— Iliada e Odisseia Homero; narrativas escolhidas e condensadas por G. Chandon; versao Portuguese; ilustracoes de J. Kuhn-Regnier; com uma breve enciclopedia (Portuguese). *Translator or author:* Roberto Alberty. Lisbon, Portugal: Verbo.

1986— Homer's Hymns to Ceres (English). *Translator or author:* Robert Anderson.

1986— The Odyssey; a children's play based upon Homer's Odyssey; book and lyrics by Maurice

Breslow; music by Norm Nurmi; 1st ed. (English). *Translator or author:* Maurice Breslow. Ontario, Canada: Playwrights Union of Canada.

1986— The Odyssey of Homer; done into English prose (English). *Translator or author:* Samuel Henry Butcher; Andrew Lang. New York, N.Y.: Modern Library.

1986— The Odyssey of Homer; done into English prose (English). *Translator or author:* Samuel Henry Butcher; Andrew Lang. New York, N.Y.: F. Watts.

1986— The Odyssey of Homer; adapted; [illustrated by Thomas Fraumeni]; 4th ed. (English). *Translator or author:* Henry Irving Christ. New York, N.Y.: Globe Book Co.

1986— La Leyenda de Ulises; traducido por Juan Manuel Ibeas (Spanish). *Translator or author:* Peter Connolly. Madrid, Spain: Ediciones General Anaya.

1986— The Legend of Odysseus (English). *Translator or author:* Peter Connolly. Oxford, England; New York, N.Y.: Oxford University Press.

1986— Odusszeia Homerosz; forditotta (Hungarian). *Translator or author:* Gabor Devecseri. Budapest, Hungary: Europa Konyvkiado.

1986— Stories from Homer (English). *Translator or author:* E. F. Dodd. London, England: Macmillan.

1986— The Iliad [of] Homer; translated; with drawings by Hans Erni (English). *Translator or author:* Robert Fitzgerald. London, England: Collins.

1986— Iliada Gomer; perevod s drevnegrecheskogo (Russian). *Translator or author:* Nikolaaei Ivanovich Gnedich. Moscow, Russia: Khudozh Lit-ra.

1986— Iliada Homero; introduccion y notas de Jose Alsina; traslacion en verso; 3rd ed. (Spanish). *Translator or author:* Fernando Gutierrez. Barcelona, Spain: Planeta.

1986— The Iliads and Odysses of Homer (English). *Translator or author:* Thomas Hobbes.

1986— [H]omerou Iliada; metaphrase (Greek, Modern). *Translator or author:* Nikos Kazantzake; Johannes Th. Kadrides. Athens, Greece: Vivliopoleio tes "Hestias".

1986— al-Awthisih la-sha air al-kalud Humirus; [tarjumah] Darini Khashbah (Arabic). *Translator or author:* Darini Khasbah. Beirut, Lebanon: Dar al-Awdah.

1986— Epos e Civilta del Mondo Antico (Italian).

Translator or author: Antonio La Penna. Torino (Turin), Italy: Loescher.

1986— The Odyssey of Homer; translated by T. E. Shaw (English). *Translator or author:* Thomas Edward Lawrence. Gloucester, England: Sutton.

1986— L'Iliade d'Homere; traduction en vers (French). *Translator or author:* Frederic Mugler. Carpentras, France: Odice-rencontres.

1986— Odysseia Homeros; epos XXIV spevov, preloezil; ilustroval Gabriel Strba; typografia Lubomir Kratky; 2nd ed. (Slovak). *Translator or author:* Miloslav Okal. Bratislava, Slovakia: Slovensky Spisovateil.

1986— Ilias Homeros; epos XXIV spevov, preloezil; ilustroval Gabriel Strba; typografia Lubomir Kratky; 2nd ed. (Slovak). *Translator or author:* Miloslav Okal. Bratislava, Slovakia: Slovensky Spisovateil.

1986— The Iliad and Odyssey of Homer; retold for children, illustrated by Joan Kiddell-Monroe (English). *Translator or author:* Barbara Leonie Picard. London, England: Chancellor Press.

1986— The Works of Homer; translated into English verse (English). *Translator or author:* Alexander Pope.

1986— [H]omerou Odysseia; metaphrase se aigaiopelagitiko demotiko tragoudi (Greek, Modern). *Translator or author:* Alexes I. Poulianos. Athens, Greece: Graphikes Technes Nikotyp.

1986— Odissea Omero; traduzione; 2nd ed. (Greek; Italian). *Translator or author:* G. Aurelio Privitera. Rome; Milan: Fondazione Lorenzo Valla; Arnoldo Mondadori.

1986— La Iliada Homero; traduccion, introduccion y notas (Spanish). *Translator or author:* Alberto Pulido Silva. Mexico (City), Mexico: SEP/Cultura.

1986— The Voyage of Odysseus: Homer's Odyssey Retold; [illustrated by Eric Fraser]; 1st Am. ed. (English). *Translator or author:* James Reeves. New York, N.Y.: Bedrick/Blackie.

1986— Iliada, Odisseia Homer; [tearjcumea Mikaiyl Rzaguluzadea; Aleakbear Ziatai] (Azerbaijani). *Translator or author:* Mikaiyl Rzaguluzadea; Alakbar Ziiatai. Baky: Lazychy.

1986— Die Odyssee [von] Homer; Deutsch (German). *Translator or author:* Wolfgang Schadewaldt. Hamburg, Germany: Rowohlt.

1986— Odyssea; das seind die allerzierlichsten und lustigsten vier und zwaintzig Bucher des eltisten kunstreichesten Vatters aller Poeten

Hoeri; zu Teutsch transsferiert, mit argumentun und kurtzen Scholijs erklaret durch Simon Schaidenreisser [facsimile of e (German). *Translator or author:* Simon Schaidenreisser. Munster, Germany: Grimmelshausen-Gesellschaft.

1986— Odyssee Homer; [in prosa ubertragen]; 1st ed. (German). *Translator or author:* Gerhard Scheibner. Berlin, Germany: Aufbau-Verlag.

1986— La Odisea Homero; version directa y literal del Griego; prologo de Manuel Alcala (Spanish). *Translator or author:* Luis Segala y Estalella. Mexico (City), Mexico: Editorial Porrua.

1986— Hymns to the Gods, Ascribed to Homer (English). *Translator or author:* Percy Bysshe Shelley.

1986— Homerische Hymnen; Griechisch und Deutsch hrsg. von Anton Weiher; 5th ed. (Greek; German). *Translator or author:* Anton Weiher. Munich, Germany: Artemis Verlag.

1986— Odisseila Gomer; perevod s drevnegrecheskogo (Russian). *Translator or author:* Vasilii Andreevich Zhukovskii. Moscow, Russia: Izd-vo "Khudozhestvennaeiia Literaturea".

1987— Homer's Odyssey; W[illiam] Walter Merry, David Binning Monro and James Riddell, editors (Greek). New York; London: Garland.

1987— Homer's Odyssey [edited by William Walter Merry; reprint of the 1886 edition] (English). New York, N.Y.: Garland.

1987—[H]omerou Odysseia; The Odyssey of Homer; edited, with general and grammatical introductions, commentary, and indexes by W[illiam] B[edell] Stanford; 2nd ed. (Greek). New York, N.Y.: St. Martin's Press.

1987— La Iliada Homero (Spanish). Santiago, Chile: Sociedad Comercial y Editorial Santiago Limitada.

1987—[H]omerou Iliada, Rapsodia Ch; scholia A. X. Karapanagiote; eisagoge, apodose scholion ste demotike, metaphrase keimenou (Greek; Modern Greek). *Translator or author:* Alex. Ath. Baltas. Athens, Greece: Dem. N. Papademas.

1987—[H]omerou Iliada, Rapsodia A; scholia, hereneia A. X. karapanagiote; eisagoge, apodose scholion ste demotike, metaphrase keimenou (Greek; Modern Greek). *Translator or author:* Alex. Ath. Baltas. Athens, Greece: Dem. N. Papademas.

1987— La Morte di Ettore: Iliade XXII Omero; a cura di Maria Grazia Ciani; commento di Elisa Avezau; 1st ed. (Greek; Italian). *Translator or author:* Maria Grazia Ciani. Venice, Italy: Marsilio.

1987— La Odisea Homero; [traduccion y adaptacion; ilustraciones de J. A. Sanchez Prieto]; 1st ed. (Spanish). *Translator or author:* Ramon Conde Obregon. Mexico (City), Mexico: Noriega Editores.

1987— La Odisea Homero; seleccion y adaptacion; cubierta ilustraciones interiores, Vicente Segrelles; 15th ed. (Spanish). *Translator or author:* Ramon Conde Obregon. Madrid, Spain: Ediciones Auriga.

1987— La Iliada Homero; [traduccion y adaptacion; ilustraciones de J. A. Sanchez Prieto]; 1st ed. (Spanish). *Translator or author:* Ramon Conde Obregon. Mexico (City), Mexico: Noriega Editores; Ediciones Ciencia y Tecnica.

1987— La Iliada Homero; seleccion y adaptacion, Ramon Conde Obregon; cubierta ilustraciones interiores, Vicente Segrelles (Spanish). *Translator or author:* Ramon Conde Obregon. Madrid, Spain: Ediciones Auriga.

1987— Odysseus; tekst og billeder af Ritva Nybacka; pea dansk ved Jakob Gormsen (Danish). *Translator or author:* Jakob Gormsen. Ridekro, Denmark: ARNIS.

1987— The Iliad [of] Homer; translated with an introduction (English). *Translator or author:* Martin Hammond. London, England; New York, N.Y.: Penguin Books.

1987—[H]omerou Iliada; metaphrase N. Kazantzake, I. Th. Kakride; eisagoge, hermeneutikes semioseis Helenes Kakride; 7th ed. (Greek, Modern). *Translator or author:* Nikos Kazantzakis; Johannes Th. Kakrides. Athens, Greece: Organismos Ekdoseos Didaktikon Vivlion.

1987— Iliakan Homeros; grabarits targmanets Mkrtich Kheranyan (Armenian). *Translator or author:* Mkrtich Kheranyan. Yerevan (Erevan), Armenia: Erevani Hamalsarani hratarakch ut yun.

1987— The Odyssey; retold; illustrated by Alan Baker (English). *Translator or author:* Robin Lister. London, England: Kingfisher.

1987— War Music: An Account of Books 16 to 19 of Homer's Iliad (English). *Translator or author:* Christopher Logue. New York, N.Y.: Farrar, Straus Giroux.

1987— Iliade, Tome I, Chants I–VI [d']Homere; texte etabli et traduit par Paul Mazon; avec la collaboration de Pierre Chantraine, Paul Collart et Rene Langumier (Greek; French). *Translator or author:* Paul Mazon; Pierre Chantraine, Paul Collart, Rene. Paris, France: Societe d'Edition "Les Belles Lettres".

1987—Odysseus Polutropos: Intertextual Readings in the Odyssey and the Iliad (English). *Translator or author:* Pietro Pucci. Ithaca, N.Y.: Cornell University Press.

1987—The Odyssey: the Story of Odysseus [by] Homer; translated (English). *Translator or author:* William Henry Denham Rouse. New York, N.Y.: New American Library.

1987—Odisea Homero; version directa y literal del Griego; ilustraciones de Jaime Azpelicueta (Spanish). *Translator or author:* Luis Segala y Estalella. Barcelona, Spain: Juventud.

1987—Homerove Odiseja; J. Bass; preveo s njemaeckogo Baldo Soljan; [ilustrirao Alfred Renz] (Serbo-Croatian). *Translator or author:* Baldo Soljan. Zagreb, Croatia: SNL.

1987—Odiseyah Homerus; tirgem mi-Yevanit, Sha'ul Tshernihovski; kitsur ve-he'arot me-et Yehoshua' Gutman (Hebrew). *Translator or author:* Saul Tchernichowsky. Tel Aviv, Israel: Hotsa'at 'Am 'oved.

1987—Iliadah Homerus; tirgem mi-Yeovanit, Shaul o Tsherniohovsoki (Hebrew). *Translator or author:* Saul Tchernichowsky. Tel Aviv, Israel: Hotsaat Am oved.

1987—Iliada; Odisseia Gomer (Russion). *Translator or author:* Vikentii Vikentevich Veresaeva. Moscow, Russia: Prosveschenie.

1987—Odisseia: cepicheskaeila pocema Gomer; perevod s drevnegrecheskogo; [vstupitelnaeila stateila I kommentarii I. Nakhova] (Russian). *Translator or author:* Vasilii Andreevich Zhukovskii. Moscow, Russia: Detskaeila lit-ra.

1987–92—L'Odyssee: Poesie Homerique [d'] Homere; texte etablie et traduit par Victor Berard (Greek; French). *Translator or author:* Victor Berard. Paris, France: Societe d'Edition "Les Belles Lettres".

1988—Shih chieh Wen Hseueh Min Chu; I [Chi ssu shih chieh min chu pien chi tsu]; chi jie wen xue min zhu; 1st ed. (Chinese). Taipei, Taiwan: Chi Ssu Wen Hua Shih Yeh Yu Hsien Kung Ssu.

1988—La Iliada Homero; texto adaptado, illustraciones de Andres Jullian; 4th ed. (Spanish). Santiago, Chile: A. Bello.

1988—Odisakan Homeros; hin hunarenits targmanets Hamazasp Hambardzumyanee (Armenian). Yerevan (Erevan), Armenia: Erevani Hamalsarani Hratrakchutyun.

1988—La Iliada Homero; prologo de Alberto Bernabe (Spanish). *Translator or author:* Emiliano Aguado. Madrid, Spain: EDAF.

1988—Der Froschmausekrieg [von] Pseudo-Homer; Der Katzenmausekrieg [von] Theodoros Prodromos; Griechisch und Deutsch; 4th ed. (Greek; German). *Translator or author:* Helmut Ahlborn. Berlin, Germany: Akademie-Verlag.

1988—The Odyssey [of] Homer; with reader's guide [by] Abrahmam Ponemon (English). *Translator or author:* Samuel Butler; Abraham Ponemon. New York, N.Y.: Amsco School Publications.

1988—L'Ira di Achille (Iliade I) Omero; commento di Elisa Avezzau; 1st ed. (Greek; Italian). *Translator or author:* Maria Grazia Ciani. Venice, Italy: Marsilio.

1988—La Odisea Homero; [traduccion y adaptacion]; 1st ed. (Spanish). *Translator or author:* Ramon Conde Obregon. Mexico (City), Mexico: Editorial Limusa.

1988—The Legend of Odysseus (English). *Translator or author:* Peter Connolly. Oxford, England; New York, N.Y.: Oxford University Press.

1988—L'Odyssee [d]Homere; traduction, introduction, notes et index (French). *Translator or author:* Mederic Dufour; Jeanne Raison. Paris, France: Garnier Freres.

1988—A Iliada Homero; traducao de versao Francesca e nota introdutoria de Cascais Franco (Portuguese). *Translator or author:* Cascais Franco. Portugal: Publiocoes Europa-America.

1988—Odysseia: ett modernt epos; prologen och forsta sangen; [av Nikos Kazantzakis]; oversattning, Gottfried Grunewald; under medverkan av Stig Rudberg och Christos Tsiparis (Swedish). *Translator or author:* Nikos Kazantzakis. Partille, Sweden: P. Astrom.

1988—L'Iliade [d']Homere; traduction nouvelle avec une introduction et des notes (French). *Translator or author:* Eugene Lasserre. Paris, France: Garnier Freres.

1988—L'Odyssee [d']Homere; traduction du Grec; illustree de dessins de Notor a partir de ceramiques Grecques (French). *Translator or author:* Leconte de Lisle; Bruno Remy. Paris, France: L'Ecole des Loisirs.

1988—The Odyssey; retold; illustrated by Alan Baker; 1st U.S. ed. (English). *Translator or author:* Robin Lister. New York, N.Y.: Doubleday.

1988—War Music: An Account of Books 16 to 19 of Homer's Iliad (English). *Translator or author:* Christopher Logue. London, England: Faber.

II. Printed Editions of the Homeric Texts, 1470 to 2000 C.E.

372

1988—Odysseos Schedia: [h]e pempte rapsodia tes Odysseias; metaphrase, scholia (Greek; Modern Greek). *Translator or author:* D. N. Maronites. Athens, Greece: Stigme.

1988—Iliade Omero; tradotta; a cura di Vittorio Turri; nrova presentazione di Ignio De Luca (Italian). *Translator or author:* Vincenzo Monti. Florence, Italy: G. C. Sansoni.

1988—The Battle of the Frogs and Mice; illustrated by Fiona MacVicar; translated (Greek; English). *Translator or author:* Thomas Parnell. Marlborough, Eng.: Libanus Press.

1988—The Odyssey; translated [reprint of the 1946 edition] (English). *Translator or author:* Emile Victor Rieu. London, England; New York, N.Y.: Penguin Books.

1988—Iliada Homero; trad.; edicion e indices de Guillermo Thiele; 4th ed. (Spanish). *Translator or author:* Luis Segala y Estalella. Rio Piedras, Puerto Rico: Editorial Universidad.

1988—Iliade Omero; introduzione di Fausto Codino; versione di Giuseppe Tonna; 10th ed. (Italian). *Translator or author:* Giuseppe Tonna. Milan, Italy: Garzanti.

1988—Illiaseu, Odiseia Homeroseu (Korean). *Translator or author:* Cheong-hyeok Yun. Seoul, South Korea: Teukpyeolsi: Samseongdang.

1989—A World of Heroes; selections from Homer, Herodotus, and Sophocles; text and running vocabulary (Greek). Cambridge, England; New York, N.Y.: Cambridge University Press.

1989—A Odisseia de Homero; adaptaocao em prosa; illustraocaoes de Martins Barata; 14th ed. (Portuguese). *Translator or author:* Joao de Barros. Lisbon, Portugal: Libraria Sa da Costa Editora.

1989—L'Odyssee [d']Homere (French). *Translator or author:* Victor Berard. Paris, France: Gallimard.

1989—Andromache's Hector and Helenus: a Trojan War Novel; based on Homer's Iliad (English). *Translator or author:* Richard McCulloch Byers. Baltimore, Md.: Fairfield House.

1989—Odissea Omero (Greek; Italian). *Translator or author:* Rosa Calzecchi Onesti. Torino, Italy: Einaudi.

1989—Il Canto do Patroclo (Iliade XVI) Omero; a cura di Maria Grazia Ciani; commento do Elisa Avezzau; 1st ed. (Greek; Italian). *Translator or author:* Maria Grazia Ciani. Venice, Italy: Marsilio.

1989—L'Iliade; texte bilingue presente par Claude

Michel Cluny (Greek; French). *Translator or author:* Claude Michel Cluny. Paris, France: Editions de la Difference.

1989—Iliada Homer; przeo (Polish). *Translator or author:* Franciszek Ksawery Dmochowski. Warsaw, Poland: Zaksad Narodowy im. Ossolianskich.

1989—The Iliad [of] Homer; translated (English). *Translator or author:* Robert Fitzgerald. New York, N.Y.: Doubleday Anchor Books.

1989—Esperimento di Traduzione della Iliade di Omero; a cura di Arnaldo Bruni (Italian). *Translator or author:* Ugo Foscolo. Parma, Italy: Edizioni Zara.

1989—Homer's Odyssey (Czech). *Translator or author:* Jaroslav Hulak. Hamlyn [location?].

1989—Perilous Voyage: an Adaptation of Homer's Odyssey (English). *Translator or author:* Oliver Hunkin. Marshall Pickering.

1989—Odyssee Homere; traduction; preface et commentaires de Paul Wathelet (French). *Translator or author:* Leconte de Lisle. Paris, France: Presses Pocket.

1989—Odisea Homero; 17th ed. (Spanish). *Translator or author:* Antonio Lopez Eire. Madrid, Spain: Espasa-Calpe.

1989—Iliada Homero; edicion y traduccion de Antonio Lopez Eire (Spanish). *Translator or author:* Antonio Lopez Eire. Madrid, Spain: Catedra.

1989—Oeuvres d'Homere; texte bilingue; traduits du Grec (Greek; French). *Translator or author:* Frederic Mugler. Paris, France: Editions de la Difference.

1989—Omero Napoletano; a cura di Enrico Malato e Emanuele A. Giordano (Italian (Neopolitan dialect)). *Translator or author:* Nunziante Pagano; Nicolo Capasso. Rome, Italy: Benincasa.

1989—Ilias [von] Homer; ubertragen; mit Urtext, Anhang und Registern; 9th ed. (Greek; German). *Translator or author:* Hans Rupe. Munich, Germany: Artemis Verlag.

1989—Den Berumte Odysseus; illustreret af Andy Li Jurgensen; 2nd ed. *Translator or author:* Villy Sorensen. Copenhagen, Denmark: Gyldendal.

1989—Ilyada Homeros; Turkocesi, Celaal Uster; resimier, Alice ve Martin Provensen; uyarlayan, Jane Werner Watson (Turkish). *Translator or author:* Celal Uster. Istanbul, Turkey: Can Yay.

1989—Odisseya Homeros; Turkocesi, Celal Uster; resimler, Alice ve Martin Provensen; uyarlayan,

Jane Werner Watson (Turkish). *Translator or author:* Celel Uster. Istanbul, Turkey: Can Yay.

1989— Homerische Hymnen; Griechisch und Deutsch; herausgegeben von Anton Weiher; 6th ed. (Greek; German). *Translator or author:* Anton Weiher. Munich, Germany: Artemis Verlag.

1990— La Odisea; texto adaptado Homero (Spanish). Santiago, Chile: Editorial Andres Bello.

1990— La Iliada Homero; produccion editorial y adaptacion Martin Concha (Spanish). Chile: E.T.E.

1990—[H]omerou Iliada, Rapsodia Z; eisagoge, metaphrase; hermeneutika scholia keimenou, A. X. Karapanagiote (Greek, Modern Greek). *Translator or author:* Alex. Ath. Baltas. Athens, Greece: Dem. N. Papademas.

1990— Odissea Omero; nella versione poetica di Giovanna Bemporad; tutti I canti, per intero o a frammenti; introduzione di Maurizio Perugi (Italian). *Translator or author:* Giovanna Bemporad. Florence, Italy: Lettere.

1990— Odisea Homero; edicion de Jose Luis Calvo; traduccion; 3rd ed. (Spanish). *Translator or author:* Jose-Luis Calvo Carilla. Madrid, Spain: Catedra.

1990— Inni Omerici e Batracomiomachia; a cura di Enzio Cetrangolo; con un'introduzione di Franco Montanari (Italian). *Translator or author:* Enzio Cetrangolo. Florence, Italy: G. C. Sansoni.

1990— Ettore a Andromaca (Iliade VI) Omero; a cura di maria Grazia Ciani; commento do Eliza Avezzau; 1st ed. (Greek; Italian). *Translator or author:* Maria Grazia Ciani. Venice, Italy: Marsilio.

1990— Il Riscatto do Ettore (Iliade XXIV) Omero; a cura di Maria Grazia Ciani; commento di Elisa Avezzau; 1st ed. (Greek; Italian). *Translator or author:* Maria Grazia Ciani. Venice, Italy: Marsilio.

1990— Iliade Omero; a cura di Maria Grazia Ciani; commento di Elisa Avezzau; 1st ed. (Greek; Italian). *Translator or author:* Maria Grazia Ciani. Venice, Italy: Marsilio.

1990— Iliade Omero; prefazione di Fausto Codino; versione di Rosa Calzecchi Onesti; testo originale a fronte; 12th ed. (Greek; Italian). *Translator or author:* Fausto Codini. Torino (Turin), Italy: Giulio Einaudi.

1990— An Odaisae an Paadraig de Braun, a d'aistrigh; Ciaraan O Coigligh, a chuir in eagar; Maire Mhac an Saoi, a scraiobh an Brollach (Irish). *Translator or author:* Paadraig De Braun. Dublin (Baile Atha Cliath), Ireland: Coiscaeim.

1990— Iliada Homer; prezecoczyc; z orygyinacem skloacjonowac opracowac, komentarzem opatrzyc I aneks zestawic Zygmunt Kubiak; 1st ed. (Polish). *Translator or author:* Franciszek Ksawery Dmochowski. Warsaw, Poland: Panstwowy Instytut Wydawniczy.

1990— The Iliad [of] Homer; translated; introduction and notes by Bernard Knox (English). *Translator or author:* Robert Fagles. New York, N.Y.: Viking.

1990— The Odyssey [of] Homer; translated; illustrated by Jackie Schuman (English). *Translator or author:* Robert Fitzgerald. New York, N.Y.: Vintage Books.

1990— Iliada Gomer; perevod; izdanie podgotovil A. I Zaeietisev; [otvetstvennyei redaktor eli A. M. Borovskiei] (Russian). *Translator or author:* Nikolaaei Ivanovich Gnedich. Leningrad, Russia: Nauka.

1990— Homero Odysea; introduccion y notas de Jose Alsina; traslacion eb verso (Greek?). *Translator or author:* Fernando Gutierrez. Barcelona, Spain: Planeta.

1990— Epos e Civilta del Mondo Antico; con saggi di traduzioni famose e dizionarietto mitologico (Italian). *Translator or author:* Antonio La Penna. Torino (Turin), Italy: Loescher.

1990— The Iliad; and, The Odyssey of Homer; translated; 2nd ed. (English). *Translator or author:* Richmond Alexander Lattimore. Chicago, Il.; London, England: Encyclopaedia Britannica.

1990— Homeroon Odysseian Kuudes Runoilemo Homer; suomentanut ja esipuheen kirjoittanut Elias Leonnrot (Finnish). *Translator or author:* Elias Leonnrot. Helsinki, Finland: Suomalaisen Kirjallisuuden Seuera.

1990— Ilionu: Chand Pora Homer; Taronacho Blitis (Tajik). *Translator or author:* Pierre Loueys. Dushanbe, Tajikistan: Adib.

1990— The Odyssey of Homer; a new verse translation; with twelve engravings by Marialuisa de Romans (English). *Translator or author:* Allen Mandelbaum. Berkeley, Ca.: University of California Press.

1990— Epsilon = Simple E: Fragments from the Fifth Book of Homer's Odyssey. *Translator or author:* Thomas Meyer. Edinburgh, Scotland: Morning Star Publications.

1990— L'Odyssee: Epopee Homerique; traduction intetrale; illustree par Francoise Soulier (French). *Translator or author:* Louise Mistral. Nice, France: Z Editions.

1990— Iliade di Omero; introduzione e commento di Michele Mari; 1st ed. (Italian). *Translator or author:* Vincenzo Monti. Milan, Italy: Rizzoli.

1990— Odyssey by Homer; translated into Persian by Saaid Nafidi (Persian). *Translator or author:* Saaid Nafisi. Scientic and Cultural Publications.

1990— Iliad by Homer; translated into Persian (Persian). *Translator or author:* Saaid Nafisi. Scientific and Cultural Publications.

1990— Odyseja Homer; przekl (Polish). *Translator or author:* Jan Parandowski. Warsaw, Poland: Czytelnik.

1990— The Iliad for Speaking (English). *Translator or author:* Michael Reck. Breitbrunn am Ammersee, Germany: Porpentine Press.

1990— The Iliad: the Story of Achilles [by] Homer; translated (English). *Translator or author:* William Henry Denham Rouse. New York, N.Y.: Penguin Books.

1990— La Iliada Homero; version directa y literal del Griego; prologo de Alfonso Reyes; 23rd ed. (Spanish). *Translator or author:* Luis Segala y Estalella. Mexico (City), Mexico: Editorial Porrua.

1990— Odisea Homero; introduccion, Carles Miralles; traduccion; 1st ed. (Spanish). *Translator or author:* Luis Segala y Estelella. Barcelona, Spain: Ediciones B.

1990— A Iliada Homero; version Galega (Galician-Portuguese). *Translator or author:* Evaristo de Sela. Galicia, Spain: Consello da Cultura Galega.

1990— O Proiskhozhdenii Bogov; [sostavlenie I vstupitelnaeils statiils] I. V. Shtal (Russian). *Translator or author:* Irina Vladimirovna Shtal. Moscow, Russia: Sov. Rossieiia.

1990— Odyseja Homer; przeoczy Lucjan Siemieanski; z orginaem skolacjonowa, opracowa, komentarzem opatrzy I aneks zestaw Zygmunt Kubiak (Polish). *Translator or author:* Lucjan Hipolit Siemienski. Warsaw, Poland: Panstwowy Instytut Wydawniczy.

1990— Ilias, Odyssee [von] Homer; in der Ubertragung von Johann Heinrich Voss; 1st ed. (German). *Translator or author:* Johann Heinrich Voss. Frankfurt am Main, Germany: Insel-Verlag.

1990— Odyssee, Griechisch und Deutsch [von] Homer; Ubertragung; mit Urtext, Anhang und Registern; Einfuhrung von A. Heibeck; 9th ed. (Greek; German). *Translator or author:* Anton Weiher. Munich, Germany: Artemis Verlag.

1990s— The Iliad: the Story of Achilles; translated (English). *Translator or author:* William Henry Denham Rouse. New York, N.Y.: Mentor Books.

1991— The Iliad and the Odyssey (English). New York, N.Y.: Dorset Press.

1991— The Iliad and the Odyssey. Montreal, Canada: Tormont Publications.

1991— The Iliad and the Odyssey (English). New York, N.Y.: Barnes and Noble.

1991— Ho-ma Shih Shih Ti Ku Shih Ho-ma Yeuan Chu; Chi Hsia-fei I (Chinese). Taipei, Taiwan: Chih Wen Chu Pan She.

1991— Homeri Odyssea; recognovit Helmut van Thiel (Greek). Hildesheim, Germany; New York, N.Y.: George Olms.

1991— Ilias: Text [von] Homer; eingeleitet, ausgewahlt und kommentiert von Manfred Kretschmer (Greek). Munich, Germany: Aschendorffschen Verlagsbuchhandlung.

1991— The Odyssey [of] Homer; original lithographs by Marc Chagall (English). Buffalo Grove, Il.: Merrill Chase Galleries.

1991— [H]omerou Odysseia, Rapsodia S; archaio keimeno, eisagoge, metaphrase, scholia, Alex. Ath. Baltas (Greek; Modern Greek). *Translator or author:* Alex. Ath. Baltas, Athens, Greece: Dem. N. Papademas.

1991— Odyssee Homer; mit einem Nachwort, einer Zeittafel zur mukenischen Zeit und zur Geschichte de Odussee-Testes bis zum Hellenismus, Anmerkungen und bibliographischen Hinweisen von Marian Giebel; 5th ed. (German). *Translator or author:* Johann Heinrich Voss. Munich, Germany: Goldmann.

1991— D Jeronimo Osorio: Tradutor da Iliada; 1st ed. (Portuguese). *Translator or author:* Joaquim Mendes de Castro. Lisbon, Portugal: Instituto Nacional de Investigaocao Cientaifica.

1991— The Legend of Odysseus (English). *Translator or author:* Peter Connolly. Oxford, England; New York, N.Y.: Oxford University Press.

1991— Iliada Homero; traduccion; prologo y notas (Spanish). *Translator or author:* Emilio Crespo. Madrid, Spain: Editoral Gredos.

1991— The Iliad [of] Homer; translated (English). *Translator or author:* Robert Fagles. Harmondsworth, England: Penguin Books.

1991— Iliada Homero; texto, introduccion, traccion y notas por Jose Garcia Blanco y Luis M. Macia Aparicio (Greek; Spanish). *Translator or* *author:* Jose Garcia Blanco; Luis M. Macia Aparicio. Madrid, Spain: Consejo Superior de Investigaciones Cientaificas.

1991— The Story of Yuriwaka: a Japanese Odyssey; translated and retold; illustrated by Birgitta Saflund (English). *Translator or author:* Erik and Masako Haugaard. Nowot, Colo.: Roberts Rinehart Publishers.

1991— The Odyssey I and II [of] Homer; with an introduction, translation and commentary (English). *Translator or author:* Peter V. Jones. Warminster, England: Aris and Phillips.

1991— Ulysses, v. 1, Pichard, Homer, Lob; [lettered by Monish Sheth] (English). *Translator or author:* Michael Kock. New York, N.Y.: Eurotica.

1991— Yu-li-his-ssu Li Hsien Chi = The Adventures of Ulyssee (Chinese; English). *Translator or author:* Charles Lamb. Taiwan (Tai-nan): Ta Hsia Chu Pan She.

1991— The Odyssey of Homer; translated with an introduction (English). *Translator or author:* Richmond Alexander Lattimore. New York, N.Y.: Harper Perennial.

1991— The Odyssey of Homer Newly Translated into English Prose by T. E. Lawrence; with an introduction by Bernard Knox (English). *Translator or author:* Thomas Edward Lawrence. New York, N.Y.: Oxford University Press.

1991— L'Odyssee [d']Homere; d'apres la traduction de Leconte de Lisle; images de Florence Koenig (French). *Translator or author:* Leconte de Lisle. Paris, France: L. Hachette.

1991— Kings: an Account of Books 1 and 2 of Homer's Iliad (English). *Translator or author:* Christopher Logue. New York, N.Y.: Farrar, Straus Giroux.

1991— The Odyssey of Homer; a new verse translation (English). *Translator or author:* Allen Mandelbaum. New York, N.Y.: Bantam Books.

1991— Odysseia, Rapsodia VII [i.e. VI], Odysseos kai Nausikas [H]omilia [H]omerou; metaphrase-epilegomena (Greek; Modern Greek). *Translator or author:* D. N. Maronites. Athens, Greece: Stigme.

1991— Oeuvres d'Homere, 2: L'Odyssee; traduites; texte bilingue presente par Michel Butor (Greek; French). *Translator or author:* Frederic Nugler. Paris, France: Editions de la Difference.

1991— The Odyssey of Homer; retold; illustrated by Joan Kiddell-Monroe (English). *Translator or author:* Barbara Leonie Picard. New York, N.Y.: Oxford University Press.

1991— The Iliad of Homer; translated (English). *Translator or author:* Ennis Rees. New York, N.Y.; Oxford, England: Oxford University Press.

1991— The Odyssey of Homer; translated (English). *Translator or author:* Ennis Rees. New York, N.Y.; Toronto, Canada: Macmillan; Collier Macmillan Canada.

1991— The Odyssey [of] Homer; translated by E. V. Rieu; revised by his son D. C. H. Rieu in consultation with Peter V. Jones (English). *Translator or author:* Emile Victor Rieu; D. C. H. Rieu. Harmondsworth, England: Penguin Books.

1991— The Odyssey [of] Homer; translated by E. V. Rieu; revised [translation] by D. C. H. Rieu, in consultation with Peter V. Jones (English). *Translator or author:* Emile Victor Rieu; D. C. H. Rieu. London, England; New York, N.Y.: Penguin Books.

1991— Odyssea; illustrated by Barbara M. Wolff (English). *Translator or author:* Stella Sands. Fort Lee, N.J.: W. W. Publishers.

1991— La Odisea Homero; version directa y literal del Griego; 24th ed. (Spanish). *Translator or author:* Luis Segala y Estalella. Mexico (City), Mexico: Editorial Porrua.

1991— La Iliada Homero; traduccion; edicion e indices de Guillermo Thiele (Spanish). *Translator or author:* Luis Segala y Estalella. Rio Piedras, Puerto Rico: Editorial de la Universidad de Puerto Rico.

1991—[H]omerou "Iliada"; poietike piste metaphrase, eisagoge, stererotypo, scholia (Greek; Modern Greek). *Translator or author:* Demetres Ioannou Siatopoulos. Athens, Greece: Edkoseis Chrysaphe Paneze.

1991— The Odyssey: Selected Adventures; by Homer; adapted; illustrated (English). *Translator or author:* Diana Stewart. Austin, Texas: Steck-Vaughn.

1991— The Iliad by Homer; adapted (English). *Translator or author:* Diana Stewart. Austin, Texas: Steck-Vaughn.

1991— Ao-ti-sai; liu lang hai shang ti ying hsiung; Kai-se-lin Shih-to kai hsieh; [hui hua che Mike Codd] (Chinese). *Translator or author:* Catherine Storr. Taipei, Taiwan: Lu Chiao Wen Hua Shih Yeh Yu Hsien Kung Ssu.

1991— Otwitseia Homeroseu Chieum (Korean). *Translator or author:* Yu Yeong. Seoul, South Korea: Peomusa.

1991–93— Odissea Omero; introduzione generale

di Alfred Heubeck e Stephanie West; traduzione; 5th ed. (Greek; Italian). *Translator or author:* G. Aurelio Privitera. Milan, Italy: Fondazione Lorenzo Valla; Arnoldo Mondadori.

1992—La Odisea Homero; relatada a los Niannos por Maria Luz Morales; con ilustraciones de Jose Segrelless; 1st ed. (Spanish). Mexico (City), Mexico: Editorial Porrua.

1992—Iliad [of] Homer (English). Everyman's Library.

1992—The Iliad and the Odyssey (English). Award Publications.

1992—La Iliada, o, El Sitio de Troya; relatada a los nianos por Maria Luz Morales; con ilustraciones de Jose Segrelles; 1st ed. (Spanish). Mexico (City), Mexico: Editorial Porrua.

1992—La Odisea Homero; 9th ed., 5th printing (Spanish). Mexico (City), Mexico: Editores Mexicanos Unidos.

1992—Homer, Odyssey. Award Publications.

1992—Odyssey, Books XIX and XX; edited by R. B. Rutherford (Greek). Cambridge, England: Cambridge University Press.

1992—Odyssey, Books XIX and XX [by] Homer; edited by R. B. Rutherford (Greek). Cambridge, England; New York, N.Y.: Cambridge University Press.

1992—L'Odyssee: Poesie Homerique, Tome II, Chants VIII–XV; texte etabli et traduit par Victor Berard (Greek; French). *Translator or author:* Victor Berard. Paris, France: Societe d'Edition "Les Belles Lettres".

1992—Odissea, Libro XXIII Omero (Greek; Italian). *Translator or author:* Giuseppe Brizi. Milan, Italy: Mursia.

1992—Prolegomeni all'Omero Latino. *Translator or author:* Giuseppe Broccia. Macerata, Italy: Universita degli stude di macerata.

1992—Iliade di Omero; tradotta in Ottava rima; a cura di Paolo De Angelis (Italian). *Translator or author:* Giacomo Casanova. Palermo, Sicily, Italy: Novecento.

1992—The Odyssey of Homer; adapted; [illustrated by Thomas Fraumeni] (English). *Translator or author:* Henry Irving Christ. Englewood Cliffs, N.J.: Globe Book Co.

1992—The Odyssey [of] Homer; translated; introduced by Peter Levi; consultant for this volume Richard Stoneman (English). *Translator or author:* William Cowper. London, England; Rutland, Vt.: Tuttle.

1992—Iliad [of] Homer; translated from the Greek (English). *Translator or author:* Robert Fagles. Penguin Books.

1992—The Odyssey [of] Homer; translated; illustrated by Barnaby Fitzgerald (English). *Translator or author:* Robert Fitzgerald. London, England: Everyman's Library.

1992—The Odyssey [of] Homer; translated; with an introduction by Seamus Heaney (English). *Translator or author:* Robert Fitzgerald. New York, N.Y.: Knopf.

1992—The Iliad [of] Homer; translated; with an introduction by Gregory Nagy (English). *Translator or author:* Robert Fitzgerald. New York, N.Y.: Knopf.

1992—Ilias [H]omeros; eisagoge, metaphrase, scholia (Greek; Modern Greek). *Translator or author:* Panagiotes E. Giannakopoulos. Athens, Greece: Kaktos.

1992—The Trojan Horse; retold and illustrated; 1st ed. (English). *Translator or author:* Warwick Hitton. New York, N.Y.: Margaret K. McElderry Books.

1992—The Collected Works of Thomas Hobbes; collected and edited by Sir William Molesworth; with new introduction by G. A. J. Rogers (English). *Translator or author:* Thomas Hobbes. London, England: Routledge Thoemmes Press.

1992—L'Odyssee [d']Homere; traduction, notes et postface; suivi de: Des Lieux et des Hommes, par Francois hartog (French). *Translator or author:* Philippe Jaccottet. Paris, France: Editions La Decouverte.

1992—Ilias und Odyssee; Nacherzahlt von Walter Jens; Bilder von Alice und Martin Provensen; 15th ed. (German). *Translator or author:* Walter Jens. Ravensburg, Germany: O. Maier.

1992—Odwitseia Homeroseu Chieum (Korean). *Translator or author:* Yeong-gil Kang. Seoul, South Korea: Hongsin Munhwasa.

1992—Ulysses, v. 2, Pichard, Homer. Lob; [lettered by Rachael Rodrigo] (English). *Translator or author:* Michael Kock. New York, N.Y.: Eurotica.

1992—The Odyssey [of] Homer; translated by T. E. Shaw (English). *Translator or author:* Thomas Edward Lawrence. Ware, England: Wordsworth Classics.

1992—L'Iliade [d']Homere; d'apres la traduction de Leconte de Lisle; images de Daniel Henon (French). *Translator or author:* Leconte de Lisle. Paris, France: L. Hachette.

1992— Kings: an Account of Books One and Two of Homer's Iliad; revised edition (English). *Translator or author:* Christopher Logue. London, England: Turret Books.

1992— Kings: an Account of Books One and Two of Homer's Iliad; rev. ed. (English). *Translator or author:* Christopher Logue. London, England: Faber and Faber.

1992— Odysseia, Rapsodia A, Athena pros Telemachon, [H]omerou; metaphrase-epilegomena (Greek; Modern Greek). *Translator or author:* D. N. Maronites. Athens, Greece: Stigme.

1992— Odysseia, Rapsodia Th, Odysseoa Systasis, [H]omerou; metaphrase-epilegomena (Greek; Modern Greek). *Translator or author:* D. N. Maronites. Athens, Greece: Stigme.

1992— Odysseia, Rapsodia [H]e, Odysseoa eisodos, [H]omerou; metaphrase-epilegomena (Greek; Modern Greek). *Translator or author:* D. N. Maronites. Athens, Greece: Stigme.

1992— Iriasu Homerosu; Matsudaira Chiaki yaku (Japanese). *Translator or author:* Chiaki Matsudaira. Tokyo, Japan: Iwanami Shoten.

1992— Odisseia Homero; traduocaao; ediocaao de Antonio Medina Rodriques (Portuguese). *Translator or author:* Manuel Odorico Mendes. Sao Paulo, Brazil: EDUSP: Ars Poetica.

1992— The Collected Works of William Morris; with introductions by his daughter, May Morris [facsimile of the 1912 edition printed by Longmans, Green] (English). *Translator or author:* William Morris. London, England: Routledge Thoemmes Press.

1992— Tales Frae the Odyssey o Homer; owreset intil Scots; prints by Barbara Robertson (Scottish). *Translator or author:* William Neill. Edinburgh, Scotland: Saltire Society.

1992— The Odyssey; adapted; illustrated by Roger Payne (English). *Translator or author:* Peter Oliver. Newmarket [England?]: Brimax.

1992— La Iliada Homero; traduccion (Spanish). *Translator or author:* Luis Segala y Estalella. Barcelona, Spain: Edicomunicacion.

1992— The Odyssey of Homer; edited with general and grammatical introduction, commentary, and indexes; 2nd ed. (English). *Translator or author:* William Bedell Stanford. Victoria, Australia; Ontario, Canada: Nelson.

1992— Odysseus and the Enchanters; retold; illustrated by Mike Codd (English). *Translator or author:* Catherine Storr. Milwaukee, Wis.: Raintree Steck-Vaughn.

1992— [H]omerou Ilias; me emmetre apodose ste nea Hellenike (Greek; Modern Greek). *Translator or author:* Theodoro Tsochale. Athens, Greece: Lithographeio tes Hetairias M. A. Moatsos.

1993— La Odisea Homero; texto adaptado (Spanish). Santiago, Chile: A. Bello.

1993— Homeri Odyssea; recognovit P. von der Huehll (Greek). Stuttgart, Germany: B. G. Teubner.

1993— Odwitseia Homeroseu Chieum; Yu Yeong omgim (Korean). Seoul, South Korea: Peomusa.

1993— The Iliad of Homer; translated into English blank verse; edited by Sarah E. Simons [facsimile of the 1916 edition printed by Houghton Mifflin] (English). *Translator or author:* William Cullen Bryant. Irvine, Ca.: Reprint Services.

1993— The Iliad and the Odyssey [of] Homer; translated (English). *Translator or author:* Samuel Henry Butcher; Andrew Lang. Stamford, Ct.: Longmeadow Press.

1993— The Odyssey [of] Homer; trans. (English). *Translator or author:* Samuel Butler. New York, N.Y.: Barnes and Noble.

1993— The Children's Homer: the Adventures of Odysseus and the Tale of Troy; illustrated by Willy Pogany [reprint of the 1918 edition] (English). *Translator or author:* Padraic Colum. New York, N.Y.: Macmillan/McGraw Hill School Pub.

1993— The Legend of Odysseus (English). *Translator or author:* Peter Connolly. Oxford, England; New York, N.Y.: Oxford University Press.

1993— The Odyssey [of] Homer; a verse translation, backgrounds, criticism; translated and edited; 2nd ed. (English). *Translator or author:* Albert Spaulding Cook. New York, N.Y.: W. W. Norton.

1993— The Bending of the Bow: a Version of the Closing Books of Homer's Odyssey; with images by Jim Dine (English). *Translator or author:* Neil Curry. London, England; Chester Springs, Pa.: Enitharmon Press; Dufour Editions.

1993— The Odyssey; translation and analysis (English). *Translator or author:* Roger David Dawe. Lewes, England: Book Guild.

1993— Prikleiiuchenieiia Odisseeiia; po motivam mifov drevneei Greetisi pereskaz Leonida eli-Akhnina; khudozhnig Aleksandr Dobrietisyn (Russian). *Translator or author:* Aleksandr Dobrietisyn. Moscow, Russia: Kristina I. Olga.

1993— Irrfahrt und Heimkehr des Odysseus; Prometheus; Der Geliebte der Morgenrote und andere Erzahlungen; Redaktion, Ingrid Prignitz (German). *Translator or author:* Franz Fuhmann. Rostock, Germany: Hinstorff.

1993— Odysseen Homer; oversat (Swedish). *Translator or author:* Otto Gelsted. Copenhagen, Sweden: Taning & Appel.

1993— Iliada Gomer; perevod s drevnegrech-eskogo; [illeiiustraetisil D. Bisti] (Russian). *Translator or author:* Nikolaaei Ivanovich Gnedich. Moscow, Russia: TOO "Deiiuna".

1993— Mu Ma Tu Cheng Shi (Chinese). *Translator or author:* Yung Hua. Taiwan (Tai-nan): Ta Chien Chu Pan Shih Yeh Kung Ssu.

1993— Ao-te-sai Mi Hang Chi [The Odyssey] (Chinese). *Translator or author:* Yung Hua. Taiwan (Tai-nan): Ta Chien Chu Pan Shih Yeh Kung Ssu.

1993— The Odyssey [of] Homer; translated from the classical Greek into English hexameter verse (English). *Translator or author:* Brian Kemball-Cook. Hitchin, England: Calliope Press.

1993— These Two Came into the Presence of Zeus (English). *Translator or author:* Richmond Alexander Lattimore. Berkeley, Ca.: Mayacamas Press.

1993— Odysseia, Rapsodia I, Kikones, Lotophagoi, Kyklopes [H]omerou; metaphrase-epilegomena (Greek; Modern Greek). *Translator or author:* D. N. Maronites. Athens, Greece: Stigme.

1993— The Odyssey; illustrated by Victor G. Ambrus (English). *Translator or author:* Geraldine McCaughrean. New York, N.Y.: Checkerboard Press.

1993— Homara krta Iliyada; anuvadaka (Gujarati). *Translator or author:* Jayant Pandya. Gandhinagara: Gujarata Sahitya Akadami.

1993— The Iliad of Homer; edited by Maynard Mack (reprint of the 1967, Methuen edition) (English). *Translator or author:* Alexander Pope. London, England: Routledge.

1993— L'Odissea Homer; 1st ed. (Catalan). *Translator or author:* Carles Riba. Barcelona, Spain: Edicions de la Magrana.

1993— Las Aventuras de Ulises Homero; adaptacion; ilustraciones de Fina Rifaa; 1st ed. (Spanish). *Translator or author:* Carles Riba. Barcelona, Spain: La Galera.

1993— The Long Way Home: an Adaptaion of Homer's Odyssey (English). *Translator or author:* Carl Schwaber. Croitwich [England?]: Hanbury Plays.

1993— Odisea Homero; [traduccion] (Spanish). *Translator or author:* Luis Segala y Estalella. Havana, Cuba: Editorial Arte y Literatura.

1993— La Iliada Homero; version directa y literal del Griego; ilustraciones de Jaime Azpelicueta; 7th ed. (Spanish). *Translator or author:* Luis Segala y Estalella. Barcelona, Spain: Editorial Juventud.

1993— Black Ships Before Troy: the Story of the Iliad; illustrated by Alan Lee (English). *Translator or author:* Rosemary Sutcliff. Pymble, New South Wales: Angus and Robertson.

1993— Die Orationes Homeri des Leonardo Bruni Aretino; kritische Edition der Lateinischen und Kastilianischen Ubersetzung mit Prolegomena und Kommentar (Latin; Castilan). *Translator or author:* Peter Thiermann. Leiden (Leyden), Netherlands; New York, N.Y.: E. J. Brill.

1993— Illiaseu Homeroseu Chieum (Korean). *Translator or author:* Yeong Yu. Seoul, South Korea: Peomusa.

1993–98— The Iliad [of] Homer; with an English translation (Greek; English). *Translator or author:* Augustus Taber Murray. Cambridge, Mass.: Harvard University Press.

1994— Ao-te-sai Ho-ma Chu [The Odyssey] (Chinese). Taipei, China: Shu Hua Chu Pan Shih Yeh Yu Hsien Kung Ssu.

1994— Odyssey, Books VI–VIII [of] Homer; edited by A. F. Garvie (Greek). Cambridge, England; New York, N.Y.: Cambridge University Press.

1994— The Odyssey, Book One (English). Hereford, England: Thormynd Press.

1994— The Odyssey (English). Hereford, England: Thormynd.

1994— Odyssey, Books VI–VIII; edited by A. F. Garvie (Greek). Cambridge, England: Cambridge University Press.

1994— Menis: A Ira de Aquiles; canto I da Iliada de Homero; [traducaao]; transcricaao visual de Jose Roberto Aquilar (Greek; Portuguese). *Translator or author:* Haroldo de Campos; Trajano Vieira. Sao Paulo, Brazil: Nova Alexandria.

1994— I-li-ya-te Ho-ma Chu [The Iliad] (Chinese). *Translator or author:* Chen Chung-mei. Kuang-chou [China?]: Hua Cheng Chu Pan She.

1994— Odissea Omero; introduzione e traduzione di Maria Grazia Ciani; commento do Elisa Avezzau; 1st ed (Greek; Italian). *Translator or author:* Maria Grazia Ciani. Venice, Italy: Marsilio.

1994—Iliade Omero; a cura di Maria Grazia Ciani. *Translator or author:* Maria Grazia Ciani. Venice, Italy: Marsilio.

1994—The Children's Homer: the Adventures of Odysseus and the Tale of Troy; illustrated by Willy Pogany [reprint of the 1918 edition] (English). *Translator or author:* Padraic Colum. Edinburgh, Scotland: Floris.

1994—La Iliada Homero; traduccion y adaptacion; illustracion de Washington Rodriquez; 8th ed. (Spanish). *Translator or author:* Ramon Conde Obregon. Mexico (City), Mexico: Editorial Limusa.

1994—La Iliada y La Odisea Homero; [adaptacion de Julia Daroqui; ilustraciones de Santos Martinez Koch; (Spanish). *Translator or author:* Julia Daroqui. Buenos Aires, Argentina: Editorial Sigmar.

1994—The Odyssey; adapted; illustrated by Nestor Redondo; a Vincent Fago Production (English). *Translator or author:* John Norwood Fago. Belmont, Ca.: Lake Education.

1994—The Iliad; adapted; illustrated by E. R. Cruz; a Vincent Fago production (English). *Translator or author:* John Norwood Fago. Belmont, Ca.: Lake Education.

1994—Ha-Odiseah me-et Homeros; targum le-ivrit mi-Germanit (al-pi Yohan Hainrikh Fos) ove-hosif mavo, he arot u-musafim Yosef Ha uben (Nevo) (Hebrew). *Translator or author:* Joseph Hauben. Tel Aviv, Israel: Yaron Golan.

1994—Homer's Iliad; retold; translated by Vladimir Varecha from the Czech; illustrations by Jiri Behounek (English). *Translator or author:* Vitezslav Kocourek. London, England: Sunburst.

1994—The Odyssey; retold; illustrated by Alan Baker (English). *Translator or author:* Robin Lister. New York, N.Y.: Kingfisher.

1994—Ho-ma Shih Shih Yen Chiu; shih hum kuan ku chin (Chinese). *Translator or author:* Ching Lo. Taipei, Taiwan: Tai-wan Hseueh Sheng Shu Cheu.

1994—Odysseia, Rapsodia M, Seirenes, Planktes, Skylla, Charyvde, Thrinakia [H]omerou; metaphrase-epilegomena (Greek; Modern Greek). *Translator or author:* D. N. Maronites. Athens, Greece: Stigme.

1994—Odysseia, Rapsodia K, Aiolos, Laistrygones, Kirke [H]omerou; metaphrase-epilegomena (Greek; Modern Greek). *Translator or author:* D. N. Maronites. Athens, Greece: Stigme.

1994—Odysseia, RapsodiaI, Nekyia Homerou; metaphrase-epilegomena (Greek; Modern Greek). *Translator or author:* D. N. Maronites. Athens, Greece: Stigme.

1994—[H]omerou Odysseia; apologoi; seirenes planktes-skylla-charyvde, thrinakia; rapsodia m metaphrade-epilegomena; (Greek; Modern Greek). *Translator or author:* D. N. Maronites. Athens, Greece: Stigme.

1994—[H]ektoros kai Andromaches [H]omilia: [H]omeros, Sappho, Sophocles; metaphrase-epimetro (Greek; Modern Greek). *Translator or author:* D. N. Maronites. Athens, Greece: Diatton.

1994—Iliada, Wojna Trojaanska; [adaptacja tekstu; ilustracje Libico Maraja; trumaczenie Ewa Patczyanska] (Polish). *Translator or author:* Stelio Martelli. Bielsko-Biata, Poland: Debit.

1994—Odusseia Homerosu (Japanese). *Translator or author:* Chiaki Matsudaira. Tokyo, Japan: Iwanami Shoten.

1994—La Iliada, o, El Sitio de Troya; relatada a los nianos; con ilustraciones de Jose Segrelles (Spanish). *Translator or author:* Maria Luz Morales. Mexico (City), Mexico: Editorial Porrua.

1994—The Odyssey, Book Two (English). *Translator or author:* D. W. Myatt. Hereford, England: Thormynd Press.

1994—The Iliad [of] Homer; translated, and with an introduction; 1st ed. (English). *Translator or author:* Michael Reck. New York, N.Y.: IconEditions.

1994—La Odisea Homero; adaptacion (Spanish). *Translator or author:* Manuel Rojas. Santiago, Chile: Zig-Zag.

1994—La Odisea Homero; traduccion (Spanish). *Translator or author:* Luis Segala y Estalella. Barcelona, Spain: Edicomunicacion.

1994—Den Berumte Odysseus; illustreret af Andy Li Jurgensen. *Translator or author:* Villy Sorenson. Copenhagen, Denmark: Gyldendals Bogklubber.

1995—Homeri Ilias; recensvit Arthurus Ludwich (Greek). Stuttgart, Germany; Leipzig, Germany: B. G. Teubner.

1995—Odyseja; adapatacja Peter Oliver; ilustracje Roger Payne; prektad z angielskiego Krzysztof Zarzecki; 2nd ed. (Polish). Warsaw, Poland: Grafag.

1995—The Iliad [of] Homer (English). Ware, England: Wordsworth Classics.

II. Printed Editions of the Homeric Texts, 1470 to 2000 C.E.

380

1995—Iliad, Book Nine [of] Homer; edited by Jasper Griffin (Greek). New York, N.Y.: Oxford University Press.

1995—Iliad, Book Nine; edited by Jasper Griffin (Greek). Oxford, England: Clarendon Press.

1995—La Odisea Homero; prologo y notas, Juan Alcarcon Benito (Spanish). Madrid, Spain: M. E. Editores.

1995—La Iliada Homero; prologo y notas (Spanish). *Translator or author:* Juan Alarcon Benito. Madrid, Spain: M. E. Editores.

1995—L'Iliade; L'Odyssee [d']Homere; edition etablie et traduite (French). *Translator or author:* Louis Bardollet. Paris, France: Laffont.

1995—The Iliad [of] Homer; translated (English). *Translator or author:* Samuel Butler. New York, N.Y.: Barnes and Noble.

1995—The Odyssey (English). *Translator or author:* John Escott. Newmarket [England?]: Brimax.

1995—The Rage of Achilles from the Iliad [of] Homer; translated; introduction by Bernard Knox (English). *Translator or author:* Robert Fagles. New York, N.Y.: Penguin Books.

1995—Ha-Iliadah Me-et Homeros; targum le-Ivrit mi-Vermanit (al-pi Yohan Hainikh Fos) ove-hosif mavo, he arot u-musafim Yosef Ha uben (Nevo) (Hebrew). *Translator or author:* Joseph Hauben. Tel Aviv, Israel: Yaron Golan.

1995—Odyseja Homer; z ilustracjami Stanistawa Hiszpanskiego; w przedtadzie Lucjana Siemiean-skiego; 9th ed. (Polish). *Translator or author:* Stanistzwa Hiszpanskiego. Warsaw, Poland: Wydawnictwo Alfa.

1995—L'Iliade [d']Homere; traduction, introduction et notes (French). *Translator or author:* Eugene Lasserre. Paris, France: Garnier-Flammarion.

1995—The Husbands: an Account of Books III and IV of Homer's Iliad; 1st ed. (English). *Translator or author:* Christopher Logue. London, England; Boston, Mass.: Faber and Faber.

1995—The Husbands: an Account of Books III and IV of Homer's Iliad; 1st Amer. Ed. (English). *Translator or author:* Christopher Logue. New York, N.Y.: Farrar, Straus, Giroux.

1995—Iliada: Troeilanskaeiia Voeina; [adap-taetisieia Stelio Marteli, Ill. Libiko mareiia; perevod s Italeiianskogo] (Russian). *Translator or author:* Stelio Martelli. Minsk, Belarus: Belfaks.

1995—Iliade, Tome III, Chants XIII–XVIII [d']Homere; texte etabli et traduit par Paul Mazon; avec la collaboration de Pierre Chantraine, Paul Collart et Rene Langumier (Greek; French). *Translator or author:* Paul Mazon. Paris, France: Societe d'Edition "Les Belles Lettres".

1995—Odyssee, Gesank I–III; op leetzebuergesch dem Homer seng; iwersat aus dem al-griichescheen (Luxembourgish?). *Translator or author:* Henri Muller. Luxembourg: Imprimerie Centrale.

1995—The Odyssey [of] Homer; with an English translation; revised by George E. Dimock; 2nd ed. (Greek; English). *Translator or author:* Augustus Taber Murray. Cambridge, Mass.: Harvard University Press.

1995—Przygody Odyseusza; Wojna Trojanska Jan Parandowski [ilustrache na motywach z waz greckich, Zbigniew Parandowski] (Polish). *Translator or author:* Jan Parandowski. Warsaw, Poland: Nasza Ksinegarnia.

1995—[H]omerou Iliada; metaphrase; prologos Stylianos Alexiou; philologike epimeleia Tasoula Markomichelake-Mintza (Greek, Modern). *Translator or author:* Giorgos Psychountakes. Herakleio [Greece?]: Panepistemiakes Edkoseis Kretes.

1995—The Iliad [of] Homer; translated, and with an introduction (English). *Translator or author:* Michael Reck. New York, N.Y.: IconEditions.

1995—Priamos im Zelt des Achilleus; ein Ausschnitt aus dem 24. Gesang von Homers Ilias; ausgewahlt und ausgelegt von Hans-Friedrich Bartig (German). *Translator or author:* Wolfgang Schadewaldt. Mainz, Germany: Dieterich'sche Verlagsbuchhandlung.

1995—La Iliada Homero; version directa y literal del Griego; 3rd ed. (Spanish). *Translator or author:* Luis Segala y Estalella. Barcelona, Spain: Veron.

1995—The Wanderings of Odysseus: the Story of the Odyssey; illustrated by Alan Lee (English). *Translator or author:* Rosemary Sutcliff. Pymble, New South Wales: Harper Collins.

1995—Ilias; Odyssee; in der Ubertragung von Johann Heinrich Voss; [Vollstandige Ausg., mit einem Nachwort von Wolf Hartmut Friefrich]; 19th ed. (German). *Translator or author:* Johann Heinrich Voss. Munich, Germany: Artemis and Winkler.

1996—Odwiseia Homeroseu Chieum; Cheon Pyeong Heui omgim (Korean). Seoul, South Korea: Tanguk Taehakkyo Chulpanbu.

1996— La Iliada Homero. Madrid, Spain: Alba.

1996— Odisea Homero. Madrid, Spain: Alba.

1996— The Triumph of Odysseus, Homer's Odyssey Books 21 and 22 with introduction, text and running vocabulary; The Joint Association of Classical Teachers' Greek Course (Greek). Cambridge, England: Cambridge University Press.

1996— Odyssey Humir; tarjumih-I Saaid Nafisi (Persian). Tehran, Iran: Intisharat-I Ilmi va Farhangi.

1996— The Triumph of Odysseus: Homer's Odyssey, Books XXI–XXII; introduction, text, and running vocabulary (Greek). Cambridge, England; New York, N.Y.: Cambridge University Press.

1996— Iliad, Books I–XII; edited with introduction and commentary by M[alcolm] M. Willcock (Greek). London, England: Bristol Classical Press.

1996— Homeri Ilias; recognovit Helmut van Thiel (Greek). Hildesheim, Germany; New York, N.Y.: George Olms.

1996— Odyssey; edited with introduction and commentary by W[illiam] B[edell] Stanford (Greek). London, England: Bristol Classical Press.

1996— Beginning Greek with Homer: an Elementary Course Based on Odyssey V (Greek). *Translator or author:* Frank Beetham. London, England: Bristol Classical Press.

1996— Odyssee [d']Homere; trad.; introduction de Paul Demont, notices, index et notes de Marie-Pierre Noel (French). *Translator or author:* Victor Berard. Paris, France: Librairie Generale Francaise.

1996— Iliade Omero; introduzione e traduzione; commento di Antonietta Gostoli; con un saggio di Wolfgang Schadewaldt (Greek; Italian). *Translator or author:* Giovanni Cerri. Milan, Italy: Rizzoli.

1996— L'Odyssee: La Vengeance d'Ulysse, Chants XIII a XXIV [d']Homere; traduction revue et adaptee; edition dy Francoise Colmez (French). *Translator or author:* Mederic Dufour. Paris, France: E. Flammarion.

1996— The Iliad [of] Homer; translated; introduction and notes by Bernard Knox; illustrated by Grahame Baker (English). *Translator or author:* Robert Fagles. London, England: Folio Society.

1996— The Odyssey [of] Homer; translated; introduction and notes by Bernard Knox (English). *Translator or author:* Robert Fagles. New York, N.Y.: Viking.

1996— The Odyssey: a dramatization; revisions by Kurt Beattie (English). *Translator or author:* Gregory A. Falls; Kurt Beattie. Seattle, Wa.: Rain City Projects.

1996— Dateline: Troy (English). *Translator or author:* Paul Fleischman. Cambridge, Mass.: Candlewick Press.

1996— Odiseah Homeros; targum, Ahuvyah Kahana; arikhah madait, Uoohanan Glioker (Hebrew). *Translator or author:* John Glucker. Jerusalem, Israel: Keter.

1996— Canti e Aedi Nei Poemi Omerici; edizione e commento. *Translator or author:* Simonetta Grandolini. Pisa, Italy: Istuti Editoriali e Poligrafici Internazionali.

1996— The Luck of Troy (English). *Translator or author:* Roger Lancelyn Green. London, England: Puffin Books.

1996— Odisea Homero; introduccion y notas de Jose Alsina; traslacion en verso; 8th ed. (Spanish). *Translator or author:* Fernando Gutierrez. Barcelona, Spain: Planeta.

1996— [H]omerou Odysseia; metaphrase (Greek, Modern). *Translator or author:* Nikos Kazantzake; Johannes Th. Kakridis. Athens, Greece: Vivliopoleio tes "Hestias".

1996— [H]omerou Odysseia: ta en Lakedaimoni, Rapsodia d; metaphrase-epilegomena (Greek; Modern Greek). *Translator or author:* D. N. Maronites. Athens, Greece: Edkoseis Kastaniote.

1996— [H]omerou Odysseia, Rapsodies a–m; metaphrase (Greek; Modern Greek). *Translator or author:* D. N. Maronites. Athens, Greece: Ekdoseis Kantaniote.

1996— [H]omerou Odysseia: Telemachos Pros Eumaion Aphixis, Rapsodia O; metaphrase-e;ilegomena (Greek; Modern Greek). *Translator or author:* D. N. Maronites. Athens, Greece: Ekdoseis Kastaniote.

1996— [H]omerou Odysseia, Odysseos Apoplous, Aphixis eis Ithaken, Rapsodia N; metaphrase-epilegomena (Greek; Modern Greek). *Translator or author:* D. N. Maronites. Athens, Greece: Edkoseis Kastaniote.

1996— The Odyssey by Homer; retold; interior illustrations by Hokanson/Cichetti; Wishbone illustrations by Kathryn Yingling (English). *Translator or author:* Joanne Mattern. New York, N.Y.: Harper Paperbacks.

1996— The Iliad of Homer; edited by Steven Shankman (English). *Translator or author:* Alexander Pope. London, England; New York, N.Y.: Penguin Books.

1996— Homer in English; edited with an introduction and notes; with the assistance of Aminadav Dykam (English). *Translator or author:* George M. Steiner. London, England; New York, N.Y.: Penguin Books.

1996— The Wanderings of Odysseus: the Story of the Odyssey; illustrated by Alan Lee (English). *Translator or author:* Rosemary Sutcliff. New York, N.Y.: Delacorte Press.

1996— Ilias; Odyssee [von] Homer; in der Ubertragung von Johann Heinrich Voss (German). *Translator or author:* Johann Heinrich Voss. Dusseldorf, Germany; Zurich, Switzerland: Artemis and Winkler.

1996— The Iliad and the Odyssey; retold and illustrated [comic strip]; 1st U.S. ed. (English). *Translator or author:* Marcia Williams. Cambridge, Mass.: Candlewick Press.

1996— The Iliad and the Odyssey; retold and illustrated [comic strip] (English). *Translator or author:* Marcia Williams. London, England: Walker.

1996— Iliad, Books VIII and IX [of] Homer; edited with an introduction, translation and commentary; advisory editor, M. M. Wilcock (Greek; English). *Translator or author:* Christopher H. Wilson. Warminster, England: Aris and Phillips.

1996–97— Iliada Homero; introduccion, version Raitmica y notas de Ruben Bonifaz Nuano; 1st ed. (Greek; Spanish). *Translator or author:* Ruben Bonifaz Nuano. Mexico (City), Mexico: Universidad Nacional Autonoma de Mexico.

1997— The Odyssey [of] Homer (English). New York, N.Y.: Pocket Books.

1997— Cearti Celebre; repovestite pe scurt pentru copiisi tineret; [repovestite di Mos Ene (Mihail Drumes); ilustratii, Gabriela Savin]. Lasi [location?]: Casa Editorialea Regina.

1997— The Odyssey [of] Homer (English). Los Angeles, Ca.: Cyber Classics.

1997— The Odyssey [of] Homer; [art by Harley Griffiths]; essay by Maurice A. Randall [comic strip style] (English). New York, N.Y.: Acclaim Books.

1997— Homeo Iyagi Illiadeu, Homeo Chieum; Sin Cheong-gi omgim; 1st ed. (Korean). Seoul, South Korea: Taeil Chulpansa.

1997—[H]omerou Iliada, Rapsodia I; scholia kai hermeneia, A. X. Karapanagiote; metaglosttise

scholion, metaphrase; 2nd ed. (Greek; Modern Greek). *Translator or author:* Alex. Ath. Baltas. Athens, Greece: Dem. N. Papademas.

1997— The Iliad [of] Homer; essay by Maurice A. Randall; art by Alex Blum [comic strip] (English). *Translator or author:* Alex Blum. New York, N.Y.: Acclaim Books.

1997— The Iliad by Homer; translated (English). *Translator or author:* Samuel Butler. Los Angeles, Ca.: Cyber Classics.

1997— Iliade di Omero in Veneziano; tradotta in Ottava rima (Italian (Venetian dialect)). *Translator or author:* Giacomo Casanova. Venice, Italy: Editoria Universitaria.

1997— Inni Omerici; a cura di Filippo Cassola; 6th ed. (Greek; Italian). *Translator or author:* Filippo Cassola. Milan, Italy: Arnoldo. Mondadori; Foundazione Lorenzo Valle.

1997— The Trojan War and the Adventures of Odysseus; illustrated by Barry Moser; afterword by Peter Glassman (English). *Translator or author:* Padraic Colum. New York, N.Y.: Morrow.

1997— Nessuno: l'Odissea Raccontata ai Lettori d'Oggi; 1st ed. *Translator or author:* Luciano de Crescenzo. Milan, Italy: Arnoldo Mondadori.

1997— The Odyssey [of] Homer; translated; introduction and notes by Bernard Knox (English). *Translator or author:* Robert Fagles. New York, N.Y.: Penguin Books.

1997— The Odyssey [of] Homer; translated; introduction and notes by Bernard Knox (English). *Translator or author:* Robert Fagles. London, England: Penguin Books.

1997— The Collected English Works of Thomas Hobbes; collected and edited by Sir William Molesworth; with new introduction by G. A. J. Robers (English). *Translator or author:* Thomas Hobbes. London, England: Routledge/Thoemmes Press.

1997— Hymnes [d']Homere; texte etabli et traduit (French). *Translator or author:* Jean Humbert. Paris, France: Societe d'Edition "Les Belles Lettres".

1997— Odiseia Homeroseu (Korean). *Translator or author:* Yeong-gil Kang. Seoul, South Korea: Hongsin Munhwasa.

1997— Iliadeu Homeroseu (Korean). *Translator or author:* Yeong-gil Kang. Seoul, South Korea: Hongsin Munhwasa.

1997—[H]omerou Iliada; metaphrase (Greek, Modern). *Translator or author:* Nikos Kazantzakis; Johannes Th. Kakridis. Athens, Greece: Vivliopoleio tes "Hestias".

1997— The Iliad of Homer; translated with an introduction (English). *Translator or author:* Richmond Alexander Lattimore. Chicago, Il.: University of Chicago Press.

1997— I-li-ya-te Ho-Ma Chu [The Iliad] (Chinese). *Translator or author:* Nien-sheng Lo; Huansheng Wang. Beijing, China: Jen Min Wen Hseueh chu Pan She.

1997— Iliad [of] Homer; translated (English). *Translator or author:* Stanley Lombardo. Indianapolis, In.: Hackett Pub.

1997— Odysseia, Rapsodia X, Odysseoa Pros Eumain [H]omilia [H]omerou; metaphrase-epilegomena (Greek; Modern Greek). *Translator or author:* D. N. Maronites. Athens, Greece: Kastaniote.

1997— The Odyssey [of] Homer; retold; illustrated by Victor G. Ambrus (English). *Translator or author:* Geraldine McCaughrean. London, England; New York, N.Y.: Puffin Books; Oxford University Press.

1997— La Iliada, o, El Sitio de Troya; relatada a los nianos; con ilustraciones de Jose Segrelles; 4th ed. (Spanish). *Translator or author:* Maria Luz Morales. Mexico (City), Mexico: Editorial Porrua.

1997— Iliade [di] Omero; traduzione e saggio introduttivo di Guido Paduano; commento di Maria Serena Mirto (Greek; Italian). *Translator or author:* Guido Paduano. Torino (Turin), Italy: Einaudi-Gallimard.

1997— The Adventures of Odysseus; retold; illustrated by Peter Malone; 1st Amer. Ed. (English). *Translator or author:* Neil Philip. New York, N.Y.: Orchard Books.

1997— Baebii Italici Ilias Latina; introduzione, edizione critica, traduzione Italiana e commento; 2nd ed. (Latin; Italian). *Translator or author:* Marco Scaffai. Bologna, France: Patron.

1997— Odisea [di] Homero; traduccion; edicion, Antonio Lopez Eire; 24th ed. (Spanish). *Translator or author:* Luis Segala y Estalella. Madrid, Spain: Espasa-Calpe.

1997— Odyseja: Wybor dia Szkot Homer; 1st ed. (Polish). *Translator or author:* Lucjan Hipolit Siemienski. Warsaw, Poland: Wydawnictwo Kama.

1997— The Iliad; retold; illustrated by Victor Ambrus; 1st ed. (English). *Translator or author:* Ian Strachan. New York, N.Y.; London, England: Kingfisher.

1997— Naves Negras Ante Troya; la historia de la Iliada de Homero (Spanish). *Translator or author:* Rosemary Sutcliff. Barcelona, Spain: Vicens Vives.

1997— Pocemy Gomer (Russian). *Translator or author:* Vikentii Vikentevich Veresaeva. Rostovna-Donu, Russia: Feniks.

1998— Homeri Odyssea; recensvit Arthurus Ludwich (Greek). Stuttgart, Germany; Leipzig, Germany: B. G. Teubner.

1998— Homeri Ilias; recensuit, testimonis congessit Martin L. West (Greek). Stuttgart, Germany: B. G. Teubner.

1998— La Odisea [di] Homero; texto adaptado; 11th ed. (Spanish). Barcelona, Spain: Editorial Andres Bello.

1998— La Iliada; text adapto Homero; ilistraciones de andres Julian; 8th ed. (Spanish). Barcelona, Spain: Editorial Andres Bello.

1998— Beginning Greek with Homer: an Elementary Course Based on Odyssey V (Greek). *Translator or author:* Frank Beetham. London, England: Bristol Classical Press.

1998— Iliade, In Lingua Veneta e in Ottava Rima (Padova 1784 e Venezia 1788) (Italian (Venetian dialect)). *Translator or author:* Francesco Boaretti. Venice, Italy: Editoria Universitaria.

1998— The Iliad of Homer; translated into English blank verse [facsimile of the 1916 edition printed by Houghton Mifflin] (English). *Translator or author:* William Cullen Bryant. Temecula, Ca.: Reprint Services Corp.

1998— The Iliad; edited, with introduction and glossary; edited by Allardyce Nicoll; with a new preface by Gary Wills [series: Bollingen Series] (English). *Translator or author:* George Chapman. Princeton, N.J.: Princeton University Press.

1998— Chapman's Homer: The Iliad; edited, with introduction and glossary by Allsrdyce Nicoll; with a new preface by Garry Wills (English). *Translator or author:* John Chapman. Princeton, N.J.: Princeton University Press.

1998— Iliade di Omero; a cura di Maria Grazia Ciani e Elisa Avezzau (Greek; Italian). *Translator or author:* Maria Grazia Ciani; Elisa Avezzau. Torino (Turin), Italy: Unione Tipografico-Editrice Torinese.

1998— Lettura di Omero, Canto X dell'Iliade (Greek; Italian). *Translator or author:* Amalia Margherita Cirio. Palermo, Sicily, Italy: L'Epos.

1998— The Iliad [of] Homer; translated; introduction and notes by Bernard Knox (English).

Translator or author: Robert Fagles. New York, N.Y.: Penguin Books.

1998— The Iliad [of] Homer; translated; with an introduction by G. S. Kirk (English). *Translator or author:* Robert Fitzgerald. Oxford, England: Oxford University Press.

1998— Recits Inedits sur la Guerre de Troie (Latin; French). *Translator or author:* Gerard Fry; Dictys Cretensis. Paris, France: Societe d'Edition "Les Belles Lettres".

1998— Iliada, Odisseiia Gomer. *Translator or author:* Nikolaaei Ivanovich Gnedich. St. Petersburg, Russia: Kristall Respeks.

1998— L'Extraordinaire Voyage d'Ulysse, d'Apres l'Odyssee d'Homere; un recit d'Helene Kerillis; illustre par Erwan Fages (French). *Translator or author:* Helene Kerillis. Paris, France: A. Hatier.

1998— Prikleiiuchenieiia Odisseeiia; v pereskaze dleiia deteaei (Russian). *Translator or author:* Andreai Fedorovich Konev. Minsk, Belarus: Literatura.

1998— L'Iliade: Dal Nostro Inviato al Fronte Troiano (Italian). *Translator or author:* Piero Magi. Florence, Italy: Bonechi.

1998— [H]omerou Odysseia: Anagorismos Odysseos hypo Telemachou, Rapsodia P; metaphrase-epilegomena (Greek; Modern Greek). *Translator or author:* D. N. Maronites. Athens, Greece: Edkoseis Kastaniote.

1998— Iliade [d']Homere; preface de Pierre Vidal-Naquet (French). *Translator or author:* Paul Mazon. Paris, France: Gallimard.

1998— Iliade, Chants IX a XVI [d']Homere; texte etablie et traduit par Paul Mazon; notes par Helene Monsacre (French). *Translator or author:* Paul Mazon. Paris, France: Societe d'Edition "Les Belles Lettres".

1998— Versione dell'Iliade di Vincenzo Monti; a cura di Gennaro Barbarisi; con introduzione e commento di Gian Franco Chiodaroli (Italian). *Translator or author:* Vincenzo Monti. Torino (Turin), Italy: Unione Tipografico-Editrice Torinese.

1998— The Odyssey [of] Homer; with an English translation; revised by George E. Dimock; 2nd ed. (Greek; English). *Translator or author:* Augustus Taber Murray. Cambridge, Mass.: Harvard University Press.

1998— Ao-ti-sai Ho-ma; [rewritten; cartoon format] (Chinese). *Translator or author:* David Oliphant. Taipei, Taiwan: Lu Chiao Wen Hus Shih Yeh Yu Hsien Kung Ssu.

1998— Odyseja Homer; przetoczy I opracowat; 1st ed. (Polish). *Translator or author:* Jan Parandowski. Warsaw, Poland: Proszyanski I s-ka.

1998— L'Odissea di Omero; [traduzione; a cura di Valerio Marucci] (Italian). *Translator or author:* Ippolito Pindemonte. Rome, Italy: Salerno.

1998— The Odyssey [of] Homer; translated, with an epilogue on translation; introduced by G. S. Kirk (English). *Translator or author:* Walter Shewring. Oxford, England; New York, N.Y.: Oxford University Press.

1998— La Aventuras de Ulises: La Historia de la Odisea de Homero; ilustrado por Alan Lee; introduccion, Carlos Garcia Gual; notas, glosarios y actividades, Manuel Otero; traduccion, Jose Luis Lopez Munoz; 1st ed. (Spanish). *Translator or author:* Rosemary Sutcliff. Barcelona, Spain: Vicens Vives.

1998— Odisseia, Batrakhomiomakhiia, Gomerovskie Gimny; perevod s drevnegrecheskogo [series: Pamiatniki Antichnoi Literatury] (Russian). *Translator or author:* Vasilii Andreevich Zhukovskii. Moscow, Russia: Terra-Knizhniyi Klub.

1999— Sui Sentieri Pescosi: I Viaggi per Mare nell'Odissea; traduzione e saggi (Greek; Italian). Rome, Italy: Logart Press.

1999— Opera Homeri; recognovit brevique adnotatione critica instruxit David B. Munro et Thomas W. Allen; 4th ed. (Greek). Oxford, England: Clarendon Press.

1999— The Odyssey (English). New York, N.Y.; London, England: Dover; Constable.

1999— The Iliad [of] Homer; translated (English). *Translator or author:* Samuel Butler. Mineola, N.Y.: Dover Publications.

1999— The Iliad and the Odyssey [of] Homer; translated (English). *Translator or author:* Samuel Butler; Andrew Lang. New York, N.Y.: Barnes and Noble.

1999— Ulysses and the Trojan War; retold; illustrated by Jeff Anderson; designed by Kathy Ward and Zoe Wray; edited by Anna Claybourne (English). *Translator or author:* Anna Claybourne; Kamini Khanduri. Tulsa, Ok.: EDC Publ.

1999— The Odyssey [of] Homer; abridged and adapted; illustrated by Karen Locisano (English). *Translator or author:* Mark Falstein. Upper Saddle River, N.J.: Globe Fearon Education Publisher.

1999— The Odyssey [of] Homer; translated; introduction by D. S. Carne-Ross (English). *Trans-*

lator or author: Robert Fitzgerald. New York, N.Y.: Farrar, Straus, Giroux.

1999—Iliada, Odisea Homero; edicion de Carlos Garcia Gual; traducciones; apendice de Oscar Martinez (Greek; Spanish). *Translator or author:* Emilio Crespo Geuemes; Jose Manuel Pabon. Madrid, Spain: Espasa-Calpe.

1999—Iliada Homer; prezetoczyta Kazimiera Jeczewska; wstnepem I przpisami opatrzy Jerzy janowski; 3rd ed. (Polish). *Translator or author:* Jeczewska Kazimiera. Warsaw, Poland: Proszyanski I S-ka.

1999—The Odyssey of Homer; translated with an introduction (English). *Translator or author:* Richmond Alexander Lattimore. New York, N.Y.: HarperPerennial.

1999—War Music: an Account of Books 16–19 of Homer's Iliad (English). *Translator or author:* Christopher Logue. Nevada City, Cal.: Harold Berliner.

1999—Iliad [of] Homer; with an English translation; 2nd ed., revised by William F. Wyatt (Greek; English). *Translator or author:* Augustus Taber Murray. Cambridge, Mass.: Harvard University Press.

1999—The Odyssey [of] Homer; translated (English). *Translator or author:* George Herbert Palmer. Mineola, N.Y.: Dover Publications.

1999—Homer: Selected Verse from the Iliad and the Odyssey; translated; edited by David Hopkins (English). *Translator or author:* Alexander Pope. London, England: Everyman.

1999—The Odyssey: the Story of Odysseus [of] Homer; translated (English). *Translator or author:* William Henry Denham Rouse. New York, N.Y.: Signet Classic.

1999—The Iliad: the Story of Achilles [of] Homer; translated (English). *Translator or author:* William Henry Denham Rouse. New York, N.Y.: Signet Classic.

1999—Odisea Homero; version directa y literal del Griego; ilustraciones de Jaime Azpelicueta; 8th ed. (Spanish). *Translator or author:* Luis Segala y Estalella. Barcelona, Spain: Juventud.

1999—Iliada Homero; traduccion; introduccion y edition de Pedro Enriquez Ureana; 1st ed. (Spanish). *Translator or author:* Luis Segala y Estalella. Buenos Aires, Argentina; Mexico (City), Mexico: Losada; Editorial Oceano de Mexico.

1999—Odisea [di] Homero; traduccion; introduccion y edicion de Pedro Enriquez Ureana; 1st ed. (Spanish). *Translator or author:* Luis Segala y Estalella. Buenos Aires, Argentina; Mexico (City), Mexico: Losada; Editorial Oceano de Mexico.

1999—Oditsei Homer (Korean). *Translator or author:* Chi-hye So. Seoul, South Korea: No wa Na Midio.

2000—Homeri Ilias; recensuit, testimonia congessit Martin L[itchfield] West (series: Bibliotheca Scriptorum Graecorum et Romanorum Teubneriana). Munich, Germany: Saur.

2000—The Odyssey by Homer (English). Evanston, Ill.: Nextext.

2000—The Odyssey (English). *Translator or author:* Samuel Butler. Nashville, Tn.: Sun Hill Rose.

2000—The Odyssey; translated; with an introduction by Jasper Griffin (English). *Translator or author:* Martin Hammond. London, England: Duckworth.

2000—War Music: an Account of Books 16 to 19 of Homer's Iliad (English). *Translator or author:* Christopher Logue. London, England: Faber and Faber.

2000—The Essential Homer: Selections from the Iliad and Odyssey; translated and edited; introduction by Sheila Murnaghan (English). *Translator or author:* Stanley Lombardo. Indianapolis, In.: Hackett Pub.

2000—The Odyssey [of] Homer; translated; introduction by Sheila Murnaghan (English). *Translator or author:* Stanley Lombardo. Indianapolis, In.: Hackett Pub.

2000—The Iliad; retold; 1st ed. (English). *Translator or author:* Nick McCarty. New York, N.Y.: Kingfisher.

2000—Waiting for Odysseus: a Novel (English). *Translator or author:* Clemence McLaren. New York, N.Y.: Atheneum Books for Young Readers.

2000—The Odyssey; [adapted]; illustrated by Stuart Robertson; 1st U.S. ed. (English). *Translator or author:* Adrian Mitchell. London, England; New York, N.Y.: Dorling Kindersley.

2000—The Odyssey; retold; illustrated by Stuart Robertson (English). *Translator or author:* Adrian Mitchell. London, England: Dorling Kindersley.

2000—Iliad I [of] Homer; commentary (English). *Translator or author:* Samuel Pulleyn. Oxford, England: Oxford University Press.

Part III

Appendices

APPENDIX A:
COMMENTS ON THE
PRINTINGS LISTS OF PART II

The lists of Homeric printings provided in Part II, while not perfect (see discussion below), do provide remarkable statistical data about the printing history of the Homeric text during the era of printing. As seen in Chapter 6, the figures present graphically the numbers of printings in several ways: by year, by decade, and by century. Although there were variations from era to era, the graphs clearly show a rather steady number of printings from the sixteenth through eighteenth centuries, and then the explosion of printings during the nineteenth century coinciding with the new discovery of Homeric oral poetry. The other most significant revelation of the graphical data is the dramatic drop in numbers of Homeric printings during the first half of the twentieth century, almost certainly a reflection of the general turmoil in Europe and America as a result of two world wars which caused a startling adjustment of public and scholarly attention. The final figures shown on the graphs are the drop-off in numbers in the last decades of the twentieth century, a warning that the fears of Hanson and Heath, as well as myself, that "Homer" (both the Homeric text and classical studies), is being "killed" are warranted, as the world turns away from the successes of Western civilization. How sad it is that Homer may be lost when, as we have seen, "he" has just been found by classical scholarship and by the creation of computer databases which only recently have made possible the compilation of printings lists.

Readers will want to know how the Homeric printings lists were compiled. It is fair to say that compiling a complete list of printings of the Homeric text is impossible; however, the lists provided in chapter 6 of this book are the most complete and up-to-date that have been attempted. The reasons why a completely inclusive list is impossible are many, including the following:

- there is no universal bibliography of books held in all libraries (the best, by far, is the OCLC database "Worldcat" which is a common cataloging utility widely used by libraries of all types and locations)

- some early editions could have vanished with no copy surviving
- early editions could be held in private hands and not be included in any public bibliography
- it would be humanly impossible to visit every library holding copies of Homeric texts; thus, the compiler must rely on the bibliographies and lists created by others, and they include errors, assumptions and other problems, including short or cryptic descriptions that make it hard to spot duplicates or outright mistakes
- printers often changed texts slightly from printing to printing, so that one copy varies slightly from another but is, essentially, the same thing
- published bibliographies and lists are biased in favor of American and European scholarship and library holdings which means that the compiler is blind to possible non–Western editions unavailable to mainstream lists
- sometimes ambitious publishers advertise books in advance that, in fact, never get published (so-called phantom editions)
- a personal judgement must be made by the compiler as to what is a Homeric text — at what point on the continuum from actual words of the *Iliad* and *Odyssey* to parodies, imitations, selections, etc., does the listing stop?

To illustrate the complexity of compiling listings of Homer printings from existing bibliographies, one example, the popular translations of the *Iliad* by Lord Derby, will suffice. The first step is to compile a list of all known printings the particulars of which, after removing obvious duplicates, are shown in the following chart:

Year	London Printer	Edition Statement	U.S. Printings	Edition Statement
1860			NY: Scribner	3rd
1864	Murray; Routledge			
1865	Murray	5th revised	NY: Scribner	2nd
			Phila: Porter	5th
1866			NY: ?	3rd
1867	Murray	6th	NY: Scribner	3rd fr. Eng 5th
			Phila: Coates	5th fr. Eng 9th
1868	Murray	7th		
1869			Phila: Winston	5th fr. Eng 9th
			NY: Scribner	3rd
1870	Murray	10th	Phila: Porter/Coates	5th fr. Eng 9th
1871	Murray	8th	NY: Scribner	4th
1872–76			Phila: Coates	5th fr. Eng 9th
1873		Phila: Porter/Coates	5th	
1874	Murray		9th	

Year	London Printer	Edition Statement	U.S. Printings	Edition Statement
1876	Murray		10th	
1880		Phila: ?		
1881	Murray		11th	
1887	Murray		12th	
1894	Murray		13th	
1900		Phila: Coates	5th	
1907		NY: Routledge		
1910	Dent	NY: Dutton		
1912	Dent	NY: Dutton		
1914	Dent	NY: Dutton		
1921	Dent	NY: Dutton		
1928	Dent	NY: Dutton		
1931	Dent	NY: Dutton		
1933	Dent	NY: Dutton		
1935	Dent	NY: Dutton		
1944	Dent	NY: Dutton		
1945		Girard, Ks: Haldeman-Julius		
1948	Dent	NY: Dutton		

Several problems are immediately evident, and there also is a conflict with biographical sources about Lord Derby which state that the first edition was published in 1864. So, the purported 1860 printing is likely to be a mistake, perhaps resulting from a typographical error for 1866 which would square with the edition statement. With this change, we correctly have 1864 as the first edition, but the sources list two separate publishers, Murray and Routledge. Looking at the subsequent publishing record makes the Routledge listing look very suspicious because all other London printings until 1910 were by Murray, but this is not good enough evidence to throw it out. Now, another puzzle appears— if 1864 was the first edition, why do we have Murray claiming a "5th edition, revised" the very next year? Looking at the U.S. column leads one to suspect that the Scribner publication in 1865 marked "2nd edition" led the English publisher to jump his numbering ahead, thus omitting editions two through four. His note that his 1865 edition is "revised" and not just reprinted is a clear indication of his intent to set this new edition apart. Murray, then, follows with a 6th edition in 1867, 7th in 1868, 8th in 1871, 9th in 1874, 10th in 1876, 11th in 1881, 12th in 1887 and 13th in 1894. In New York Scribner begins with the 2nd edition in 1865, 3rd in 1866 and 1869, and 4th in 1871; it would seem that Murray agreed to let Scribner use the edition numbers 2 through 4! But what about the Murray edition of 1870 said to be "10th" when that edition is also claimed for 1887, which is a better fit with the sequence? This is almost certainly another outright mistake in the sources— surely, both references are to an 1876 10th edition.

The Philadelphia printings of Porter/Coates and Winston are peculiar in that they all claim to be 5th editions, which would work if they derive from the Murray second effort of 1865 which we have seen was labeled "5th edition, revised." However, the 1867,

1869, 1870, and 1873 printings claim to derive from the English 9th edition, which we have established was not printed until 1874! Could Murray have supplied the Philadelphia printers with an advance copy of their 9th edition before they themselves got to it? This would seem rather unlikely, leading one to suspect that the Philadelphia assertions are nothing more than advertising rhetoric to make their works appear more up-to-date than those of their New York competitor Scribner. Two other interesting items emerge from the latter part of the chart. From 1910 to 1948 there was a partnership between the London printer Dent and the New York printer Dutton to produce simultaneous editions—in fact, these were works in the popular series called "Everyman's Library." The 1933 Dent printing lacks the Dutton partnership because it was an independent effort in the series "Dent's Double Volumes" where Lord Derby's *Iliad* was paired with William Cooper's *Odyssey*. The other curious item in the chart is the 1945 single printing of the Earl of Derby's translation in Girard, Kansas, apparently just a one-time effort. Thus, our analysis results in a corrected version of the printing history for this translation which can be summarized as follows:

Year	*Murray Ed.*	*Scribner Ed.*	*Porter/Coates Ed.*	*Other Printers*
1864	[1st]			Routledge
1865	5th revised	2nd	5th	
1866	3rd			
1867	6th	3rd fr. Eng 5th	5th fr. Eng 9th	
1868	7th			
1869	3rd			Winston 5th fr. Eng 9th
1870			5th fr. Eng 9th	
1871	8th	4th		
1873			5th	
1874	9th			
1876	10th			
1880			?	
1881	11th			
1887	12th			
1894	13th			
1900		5th		
1907				Routledge
1910				Dent/Dutton
1912				Dent/Dutton
1914				Dent/Dutton
1921				Dent/Dutton
1928				Dent/Dutton
1931				Dent/Dutton
1933				Dent
1935				Dent/Dutton
1944				Dent/Dutton
1945				Haldeman-Julius
1948				Dent/Dutton

The term "printing" has been used to indicate the uncertainty of how various Homeric printed books relate to one another. Librarians and bibliographers have specific definitions for the term "edition" which indicates a complete resetting of type or other significant change from the previous printing (a new printing with no or only minor changes being termed a "reprint"). However, one cannot assume such accuracy when using a wide varieties of checklists and bibliographies and, thus, the term "printing" seemed preferable to avoid unwarranted bibliographical implications. It should be noted that in the listings themselves the abbreviation "ed." has been used for brevity but has only the validity of "printing" as defined here.

Along with the qualitative decision required for inclusion or exclusion from the lists for each book discovered is the decision of how to count the printings by year. The counts and graphs which show the fluctuations of Homeric printings are made possible by these data but consistency and reasonableness are required to inform them with value. It would be possible to count the Homeric printings in a variety of ways; my count is based on the following rules:

- each single Homeric title entry (e.g. *Iliad*) in each single year gets one count
- braille printings have not been included in the lists or counted
- when two printers seem to have printed the same book, it is counted twice
- a multi-volume set whose sections were printed over a range of years gets only one count in the first year of the series
- one count is given to each entry with the realization that a printed section, e.g. a translation of one book of the *Iliad*, would receive the same count as a listing of a set of Homer's works which in reality might have consisted of many volumes printed over many years

In the lists the actual wording of each book's title is given as closely as possible. Thus, in early printings the old spellings and grammar may show up, although sometimes the sources used have already modernized them in which case this list can only follow. The language of the printings is given wherever known or implied from the available bibliographic data. It should be noted that this is the language of the text itself, not of notes, introductions or commentary. Unlike for titles, names of printers and cities of publication have been modernized and Anglicized wherever possible (see Appendix C for Latin cities).

APPENDIX B:
SOURCES USED
FOR PART II

Adams, H(erbert) M(ayow). *Catalogue of Books Printed on the Continent of Europe, 1501–1600 in Cambridge Libraries*. Cambridge: University Press, 1967.

The British Library catalog (Internet)

Brunet, Jacques-Charles. *Manuel du Libraire et de l'Amateur de Livres*. Paris: Firmin Didot Freres, Fils, etc., 1862 (5 vols. 1860–64).

Catalog of Books in the American Philosophical Society Library, Philadelphia, Pennsylvania. Westport, Conn.: Greenwood Publishing Corporation, n.d.

Catalogue de la Bibliothèque de l'École Biblique et Archéologique Française, Jerusalem, Israel. Boston: G.K. Hall & Co., 1975.

Catalogue of Manuscripts in the Houghton Library, Harvard University. Alexandria: Chadwyck-Healey, Inc., 1986.

Dictionary Catalog of the Research Libraries of the New York Public Library 1911–1971. New York: The New York Public Library, 1979.

Dictionary Catalogue of the Library of the Pontifical Institute of Medieval Studies, Toronto, Canada. Boston: G.K. Hall & Co., 1972.

Goff, Frederick Richmond, and Margaret Bingham Stillwell. *Incunabula in American Libraries: A Third Census of Fifteenth-Century Books Recorded in North American Collections*. New York: Bibliographical Society of America, 1964.

Goldsmith, V(alentine) F(ernande). *A Short Title Catalogue of French Books 1601–1700 in the Library of the British Museum*. Folkstone and London: Dawsons of Pall Mall, 1973.

Graesse, Jean George Théodore (alt.: Johann Georg Theodor) Graesse (alt.: Grässe). *Trésor de Libres Rares et Précieux ou Nouveau Dictionnaire Bibliographique*. Milano: Görlich, 1950.

Harvard University Library, Widener Library Shelflist, 58. *Ancient Greek Literature*. Cambridge, Mass.: Harvard University Library, 1979.

Hoffman, Samuel Friedrich Wilhelm *Bibliographisches Lexicon der Gesammten Literatur der Griechen*. Leipzig: A. F. Bohme, 1845.

_____. *Lexicon Bibliographicum sive Index Editionum et Interpretationum Scriptorum Graecorum tum Sacrorum tum Profanorum*. Leipzig: I. A. G. Weigel, 1833.

Incunabula Graeca. Rome: Aedibus Athenaei, 1961–.

Index Aureliensis: Catalogus Librarum Sedecimo Saeculo Impressorum. Aurelias Aquensis: Koerner, 1962–.

John Crerar Library Author-Title Catalog. Boston: G.K. Hall & Co., 1967.

New York Public Library, Astor, Lenox & Tilden Foundations, the Research Libraries, *Dictionary Catalog of The Rare Book Division.* Boston: G.K. Hall & Co., 1971.

New York Public Library, the Research Libraries, *Dictionary Catalog of the Slavonic Collection*, 2nd edition, revised and enlarged. Boston: G.K. Hall & Co., 1974.

OCLC, "WorldCat" database (Internet).

Peddie, Robert Alexander. *The English Cataloque of Books … Issued in the United Kingdom of Great Britain and Ireland 1801–1836* (continued up to 1965). London: The Publishers Circular, 1914 (reprinted by Kraus reprint Company, 1963).

Pollard, Alfred William, and G.R. Redgrave, *A Short-Title Catalogue of Books Printed in England, Scotland and Ireland and of English Books Printed Abroad, 1475–1640.* London: Bibliographical Society, 1926.

Rath, Erich von, and Ernst Crous. *Gesamtkatalog der Wiegendrucke.* New York: F. W. Hiersemann; H. P. Kraus, 1925–.

Stillwell, Margaret Bingham, *Incunabula and Americana 1450–1800: A Key to Bibliographical Study.* New York: Columbia University Press, 1931.

Swarthmore College Peace Collection. *Catalog of the Peace Collection.* Boston: G.K. Hall & Co., 1982.

Union Theological Seminary Library, New York City, Alphabetical Arrangement of Main Entries from the Shelf List. Boston: G.K. Hall & Co., 1960.

Wing, Donald. *Short-Title Catalogue of Books Printed in England, Scotland, Ireland, Wales, and British America, and of English Books Printed in Other Countries 1641–1700.* New York: Modern Language Association of America, 1982–1998.

APPENDIX C:
LATIN CITY NAMES AND
THEIR MODERN EQUIVALENTS

Aberdoniis	Aberdeen, Scotland
Albiorium	Wittenburg, Germany
Anvers	Antwerp, Belgium
Argentina	Strasbourg, France
Argentoratum	Strasbourg, France
Avenione	Avignon, France
Basilaea	Basel, Switzerland
Berolinum	Berlin, Germany
Bononia	Bologna, Italy
Bonna	Bonn, Germany
Brixia	Brescia, Italy
Cantabrìgìa	Cambridge, England
Chemnicium	Chemnitz, Germany
Colonia Agrippina	Cologne, Germany
Colonia Allobrogum	Geneva, Switzerland
Erfordiae	Erfurt, Germany
Flexia	La Fleche, France
Glasgua	Glasgow, Scotland
Halae Saxonum	Halle an der Salle, Germany
Helmaestadium	Helmstedt, Germany
Helsingoforsa	Helsinki, Finland
Lincopia	Schweden, Germany
Lipsiae	Leipzig, Germany
Louanium	Leuven, Belgium
Lugduni Batavorum	Leiden, Netherlands
Lutetia Parisiorum	Paris, France

Moguntia	Mainz, Germany
Mediolarium	Milan, Germany
Misenae	Meissen, Germany
Monachium	Munich, Germany
Mutina	Modena, Italy
Norimbergae	Nuremberg, Germany
Novi Eboraci	New York, N.Y.
Padavium	Padua, Italy
Parrhisiis	Paris, France
Patavii	Padova, Italy
Petropolis	St. Petersburg, Russia
Regimonti	Konigsberg, Germany
Traiectum ad Rhenum	Utrecht, Netherlands
Traiectum Batavorum	Batenburg, Netherlands
Vindobona	Vienna, Austria
Vinegia	Venice, Italy

APPENDIX D:
PRINTINGS LISTED BY TRANSLATOR OR AUTHOR

Aafjes, Bertus 1965
Abel 1886
Adam, Ludwig 1877
Adam, Ludwig 1908
Adams, W. Marsham 1873
Aedicollius, Servatius 1511?
Aedicollius, Servatius 1516
Aesop 1584
Aesop 1593
Aguado, Emiliano 1988
Aguirre Bellver, Joaquin 1962
Ahlborn, Helmut 1968
Ahlborn, Helmut 1988
Aignan, E. 1809
Aignan, E. 1812
Akrita, D. V. 1958
Alarcon Benito, Juan 1995
Albert-Birot, Pierre 1945
Alberty, Roberto 1986
Aldus Manutius 1530
Alegrius, Xav. 1760
Alegrius, Xav. 1776
Alegrius, Xav. 1788
Alenda y Mira, Genaro 1887
Alenda y Mira, Genaro 1889
Alkaj, Frano 1941
Allegre, F. 1894
Allen 1916
Allen, Sikes 1904
Allen, T. E.; W. R. Halliday; E. E.
  Sikes 1980
Allen, T. W. 1912
Allen, T. W. 1931
Almack 1874
Alonso Pedraz, Martin 1965
Alonso, Jose Montero 1951
Alter, Car. 1789–94
Alves Correia, Manuel 1960

Alves Correia, Pe. M. 1947
Aly, W. 1937
Ameis, Karl Friedrich 1861–65
Ameis, Karl Friedrich 1868–71
Ameis, Karl Friedrich 1868–86
Ameis, Karl Friedrich 1870–84
Ameis, Karl Friedrich 1875–82
Ameis, Karl Friedrich 1876–80
Ameis, Karl Friedrich 1884
Ameis, Karl Friedrich 1900
Ameis, Karl Friedrich; Carl Hentze
  1869–72
Ameis, Karl Friedrich; Carl Hentze
  1872–76
Ameis, Karl Friedrich; Carl Hentze
  1874–77
Ameis, Karl Friedrich; Carl Hentze
  1877
Ameis, Karl Friedrich; Carl Hentze
  1877–88
Ameis, Karl Friedrich; Carl Hentze
  1888–96
Ameis, Karl Friedrich; Carl Hentze
  1890–95
Ameis, Karl Friedrich; Carl Hentze
  1893–95
Ameis, Karl Friedrich; Carl Hentze
  1900–10
Ameis, Karl Friedrich; Carl Hentze
  1908–11
Ameis, Karl Friedrich; Carl Hentze
  1913–24
Ameis, L. Fr. 1856
Amir-Pinkerfeld, Anda 1950
Anderson, Robert 1986
Andrea Divo; Conrad Heresbach
  1534
Andrew, Samuel Odgen 1938

Andrew, Samuel Ogden 1934
Andrew, Samuel Ogden 1948
Andrew, Samuel Ogden 1953
Andrew, Samuel Ogden 1961
Andrew, Samuel Ogden 1967
Andrew, Samuel Ogden; Michael
  Oakley 1955
Andrew, Samuel Ogden; Michael
  Oakley 1963
Annist, August 1960
Annist, August 1963
Anthon, Charles 1844
Anthon, Charles 1845
Anthon, Charles 1854
Anthon, Charles 1868
Anthon, Charles 1870
Anthon, Charles 1872
Anthon, Charles 1874
Anthon, Charles 1875
Anthon, Charles 1878
Anthon, Charles; B. Davies 1846
Anthon, Charles; B. Davies
  1858–59
Anthon, Charles; B. Davies 1860
Anthon, Charles; Major 1857
Anton, K. G. 1772
aPasse, Crespin de 1613
Aretino, Bali Gregorio Redi 1751
Aretinus, Karolus 1492
Aretinus, Karolus 1498
Aretinus, Karolus 1508
Aretinus, Karolus 1512
Arevalo, Rodolfo 1970
Argyriades, N. 1867
Arnold 1850
Arnold 1852
Arnold 1856
Arnold 1857

Bornemann, Eduard 1962
Bothe, Fridericus Henricus
  1832–35
Bouchor, Maurice 1903
Bouchor, Maurice 1927
Boulton, Matthew Piers Watt 1875
Boutens, P. C. 1937
Boutmy, E. 1829
Boutmy, E. 1829–30
Bowra, C. M. 1972
Bozoli, Guiseppe 1769–70
Bozoli, Guiseppe 1772
Bozoli, Guiseppe 1778
Brandreth, T. S. 1846
Brandreth, T. S. 1849
Brassicano, D. Jo. Alex. 1523
Breslow, Maurice 1986
Bridges, Robert Seymour 1762–64
Bridges, Robert Seymour 1890
Bridges, Robert Seymour 1916
Bridges, Robert Seymour 1917
Bridges, Thomas Seymour 1889
Brier, Michelle 1976
Brier, Michelle 1978
Brizi, Giuseppe 1992
Broccia, Giuseppe 1992
Bronilowski, Antoni 1959
Brooks, Edward 1890
Brooks, Edward 1891
Brooks, Edward 1895
Brooks, Edward 1898
Brooks, Edward 1901
Brooks, Edward 1902
Brooks, Edward 1910
Brooks, Edward 1912
Brooks, Edward 1924
Brooks, William Henry Salter
  1883
Broome, William 1722
Broome, William 1750
Broome, William 1937
Bruijn, J. C.; Cornelis Spoelder
  1962
Bruijn, J. C.; Cornelis Spoelder
  1968
Bruyn Spoelder 1937
Bryant, William Cullen 1870
Bryant, William Cullen 1871
Bryant, William Cullen 1871–72
Bryant, William Cullen 1872
Bryant, William Cullen 1873
Bryant, William Cullen 1875
Bryant, William Cullen 1876
Bryant, William Cullen 1877
Bryant, William Cullen 1879
Bryant, William Cullen 1881
Bryant, William Cullen 1883
Bryant, William Cullen 1889
Bryant, William Cullen 1897
Bryant, William Cullen 1898
Bryant, William Cullen 1899
Bryant, William Cullen 1905
Bryant, William Cullen 1916
Bryant, William Cullen 1924
Bryant, William Cullen 1928

Bryant, William Cullen 1944
Bryant, William Cullen 1979
Bryant, William Cullen 1993
Bryant, William Cullen 1998
Bryant, William Cullen; Worsley
  et al. 1899
Bryce 1847
Brydges, Thomas; Francis Grose
  1772
Brydges, Thomas 1762–64
Brydges, Thomas 1764
Brydges, Thomas 1767
Brydges, Thomas 1770
Brydges, Thomas 1797
Bucheler 1869
Buckingham, D. D.; et al. 1800
Buckley, Theodore Alois 1851
Buckley, Theodore Alois 1853
Buckley, Theodore Alois 1854
Buckley, Theodore Alois 1855
Buckley, Theodore Alois 1856
Buckley, Theodore Alois 1857
Buckley, Theodore Alois 1858
Buckley, Theodore Alois 1859
Buckley, Theodore Alois 1860
Buckley, Theodore Alois 1861
Buckley, Theodore Alois 1863
Buckley, Theodore Alois 1867
Buckley, Theodore Alois 1870
Buckley, Theodore Alois 1871
Buckley, Theodore Alois 1872
Buckley, Theodore Alois 1872–76
Buckley, Theodore Alois 1873
Buckley, Theodore Alois 1874
Buckley, Theodore Alois 1875
Buckley, Theodore Alois 1876
Buckley, Theodore Alois 1877
Buckley, Theodore Alois 1878
Buckley, Theodore Alois 1879
Buckley, Theodore Alois 1880
Buckley, Theodore Alois 1882
Buckley, Theodore Alois 1884
Buckley, Theodore Alois 1886
Buckley, Theodore Alois 1887
Buckley, Theodore Alois 1888
Buckley, Theodore Alois 1889
Buckley, Theodore Alois 1890
Buckley, Theodore Alois 1891
Buckley, Theodore Alois 1892
Buckley, Theodore Alois 1893
Buckley, Theodore Alois 1894
Buckley, Theodore Alois 1895
Buckley, Theodore Alois 1896
Buckley, Theodore Alois 1898
Buckley, Theodore Alois 1900
Buckley, Theodore Alois 1902
Buckley, Theodore Alois 1902
Buckley, Theodore Alois 1906
Buckley, Theodore Alois 1908
Buckley, Theodore Alois 1909–13
Buckley, Theodore Alois 1911
Buckley, Theodore Alois 1912
Buckley, Theodore Alois 1921
Buckley, Theodore Alois 1923
Buckley, Theodore Alois 1930
Buckley, Theodore Alois 1958

Bugge, M. 1852
Bugliazzini, Bernardino 1703
Burger, Gottfried August 1767
Burger, Gottfried August 1776
Burger, Gottfried August 1783
Burger, Gottfried August 1835
Burger, Gottfried August 1844
Burger, Gottfried August 1935
Burt, Mary Elizabeth 1909
Burt, Mary Elizabeth; Zenaeide
  Alexeievna Ragozin 1898
Burt, Mary Elizabeth; Zenaeide
  Ragozin 1899
Bustani, Sulayman Khaototar
  1900
Bustani, Sulayman Khaototar
  1904
Bustani, Sulayman Khaototar
  1966
Bustani, Sulayman Khaototar
  1980
Butcher, Samuel et al. 1963
Butcher, Samuel Henry, Andrew
  Lang 1936
Butcher, Samuel Henry; Andrew
  Lang 1879
Butcher, Samuel Henry; Andrew
  Lang 1881
Butcher, Samuel Henry; Andrew
  Lang 1882
Butcher, Samuel Henry; Andrew
  Lang 1883
Butcher, Samuel Henry; Andrew
  Lang 1885
Butcher, Samuel Henry; Andrew
  Lang 1887
Butcher, Samuel Henry; Andrew
  Lang 1888
Butcher, Samuel Henry; Andrew
  Lang 1890
Butcher, Samuel Henry; Andrew
  Lang 1893
Butcher, Samuel Henry; Andrew
  Lang 1895
Butcher, Samuel Henry; Andrew
  Lang 1898
Butcher, Samuel Henry; Andrew
  Lang 1900
Butcher, Samuel Henry; Andrew
  Lang 1903
Butcher, Samuel Henry; Andrew
  Lang 1904
Butcher, Samuel Henry; Andrew
  Lang 1905
Butcher, Samuel Henry; Andrew
  Lang 1906
Butcher, Samuel Henry; Andrew
  Lang 1909
Butcher, Samuel Henry; Andrew
  Lang 1910
Butcher, Samuel Henry; Andrew
  Lang 1912
Butcher, Samuel Henry; Andrew
  Lang 1916
Butcher, Samuel Henry; Andrew
  Lang 1917

Butcher, Samuel Henry; Andrew Lang 1918

Butcher, Samuel Henry; Andrew Lang 1920

Butcher, Samuel Henry; Andrew Lang 1921

Butcher, Samuel Henry; Andrew Lang 1922

Butcher, Samuel Henry; Andrew Lang 1923

Butcher, Samuel Henry; Andrew Lang 1924

Butcher, Samuel Henry; Andrew Lang 1925

Butcher, Samuel Henry; Andrew Lang 1926

Butcher, Samuel Henry; Andrew Lang 1927

Butcher, Samuel Henry; Andrew Lang 1929

Butcher, Samuel Henry; Andrew Lang 1930

Butcher, Samuel Henry; Andrew Lang 1932

Butcher, Samuel Henry; Andrew Lang 1933

Butcher, Samuel Henry; Andrew Lang 1934

Butcher, Samuel Henry; Andrew Lang 1935

Butcher, Samuel Henry; Andrew Lang 1937

Butcher, Samuel Henry; Andrew Lang 1938

Butcher, Samuel Henry; Andrew Lang 1944

Butcher, Samuel Henry; Andrew Lang 1945

Butcher, Samuel Henry; Andrew Lang 1949

Butcher, Samuel Henry; Andrew Lang 1950

Butcher, Samuel Henry; Andrew Lang 1954

Butcher, Samuel Henry; Andrew Lang 1955

Butcher, Samuel Henry; Andrew Lang 1956

Butcher, Samuel Henry; Andrew Lang 1959

Butcher, Samuel Henry; Andrew Lang 1960

Butcher, Samuel Henry; Andrew Lang 1961

Butcher, Samuel Henry; Andrew Lang 1965

Butcher, Samuel Henry; Andrew Lang 1967

Butcher, Samuel Henry; Andrew Lang 1968

Butcher, Samuel Henry; Andrew Lang 1969

Butcher, Samuel Henry; Andrew Lang 1972

Butcher, Samuel Henry; Andrew Lang 1974

Butcher, Samuel Henry; Andrew Lang 1978

Butcher, Samuel Henry; Andrew Lang 1980

Butcher, Samuel Henry; Andrew Lang 1983

Butcher, Samuel Henry; Andrew Lang 1986

Butcher, Samuel Henry; Andrew Lang 1993

Butcher, Samuel Henry; John Adams Scott 1937

Butcher, Samuel Henry; John Adams Scott 1946

Butcher, Samuel Henry; John Adams Scott 1966

Butler, Samuel 1887

Butler, Samuel 1894

Butler, Samuel 1898

Butler, Samuel 1900

Butler, Samuel 1914

Butler, Samuel 1920

Butler, Samuel 1921

Butler, Samuel 1922

Butler, Samuel 1923

Butler, Samuel 1925

Butler, Samuel 1930

Butler, Samuel 1936

Butler, Samuel 1948

Butler, Samuel 1952

Butler, Samuel 1955

Butler, Samuel 1968

Butler, Samuel 1970

Butler, Samuel 1993

Butler, Samuel 1995

Butler, Samuel 1997

Butler, Samuel 2000

Butler, Samuel; Abraham Ponemon 1988

Butler, Samuel; Andrew Lang 1999

Butler, Samuel; Louise Ropes Loomis 1942

Butler, Samuel; Louise Ropes Loomis 1944

Butler, Samuel; Malcolm M. Willcock 1964

Butler, Samuel; Malcolm M. Willcock 1965

Butler, Samuel; Malcolm M. Willcock 1969

Butsch, Johan Albert; Johannes Lundblad; et al. 1821

Byers, Richard McCulloch 1989

C.M.B. 1890

Caccavello, Giovanni Paolo 1618

Caldcleugh, W. G. 1870

Calentius, Elisius 1521

Calentius, Elisius 1534

Calentius, Elisius 1546

Calenzio, Elisius 1535

Callas, Howard 1974

Calvo Carilla, Jose-Luis 1990

Calzecchi Onest, Rosa 1968

Calzecchi Onesti, Rosa 1963

Calzecchi Onesti, Rosa 1977

Calzecchi Onesti, Rosa 1981

Calzecchi Onesti, Rosa 1982

Calzecchi Onesti, Rosa 1989

Camerarius, Joachim 1538

Camerarius, Joachim 1540

Camerarius, Joachim 1584

Campos, Haroldo de; Trajano Vieira 1994

Canales, Ricardo 1877

Capasso, Nicc. 1761

Capnione, Johanne 1510

Carlet de Marivaux 1716

Carlowitz, Alb. De 1844

Carnarvon, Earl of 1887

Carnarvon, Henry Howard Molyneux, Earl of 1886

Caro, Monti, Pindemonte 1926

Carolis, A. de 1924

Carpenter, Edward 1900

Carrafa, Ferrante 1578

Cary, Henry Francis 1797

Cary, Henry Francis 1821

Cary, Henry Francis 1823

Cary, Henry Francis 1828

Cary, Henry Francis 1833

Casamada, Montserrat 1959

Casamada, Montserrat 1967

Casanova, Giacomo 1778

Casanova, Giacomo 1992

Casanova, Giacomo 1997

Cassola, Filippo 1975

Cassola, Filippo 1997

Castelion, Sebastien 1561

Castelion, Sebastien 1567

Castelion, Sebastien 1582

Castro, Joaquim Mendes de 1991

Cauer, Paul 1886–87

Cauer, Paul 1894

Cauer, Paul 1894–96

Cauer, Paul 1907

Cauer, Paul 1937

Caulfeild, Francis 1921

Caulfeild, Francis 1923

Cavander, Kenneth 1969

Cavander, Kenneth 1978

Cayley, Charles Bagot 1876

Cayley, Charles Bagot 1877

Cerri, Giovanni 1996

Certon, Salomon 1604

Certon, Salomon 1615

Certon, Salomon 1616

Certon, Salomon 1756

Ceruti 1776

Ceruti 1787

Ceruti 1805

Ceruti 1820

Ceruti 1825

Ceruti, Giacinto; Gius. Bossoli 1793

Ceruti, Giacinto; Gius. Bossoli 1805

Ceruti, Hyac. 1775–87

Cesarotti, Melchiorre 1786–94

Cesarotti, Melchiorre 1798–02

Cesarotti, Melchiorre 1800–13

Conde Obregon, Ramon 1966
Conde Obregon, Ramon 1968
Conde Obregon, Ramon 1971
Conde Obregon, Ramon 1972
Conde Obregon, Ramon 1976
Conde Obregon, Ramon 1980
Conde Obregon, Ramon 1987
Conde Obregon, Ramon 1988
Conde Obregon, Ramon 1994
Confiniacum, Franc. Villerium 1573
Confiniacus, Franciscus Villerius 1543
Congreve, William 1753
Congreve, William 1779–81
Connolly, Peter 1986
Connolly, Peter 1988
Connolly, Peter 1991
Connolly, Peter 1993
Constantinidos, Anestis 1899
Cook, Albert Spaulding 1967
Cook, Albert Spaulding 1974
Cook, Albert Spaulding 1993
Coornhert, Dirk Volkertszoon 1598
Coornhert, Dirk Volkertszoon 1605
Coornhert, Dirk Volkertszoon 1606
Coornhert, Dirk Volkertszoon 1609
Coornhert, Dirk Volkertszoon 1939
Coornhert, Dirk Volkertszoon 1949
Cordery, John Graham 1870
Cordery, John Graham 1871
Cordery, John Graham 1886
Cordery, John Graham 1890
Cordery, John Graham 1897
Cordier de Launay-Valeris, L. G. R. 1782–85
Cosbuc, George 1966
Cotterill, Henry Bernard 1911
Cotterill, Henry Bernard 1912
Cotterill, Henry Bernard 1924
Couat, Auguste Henri 1911
Couchoud, P. L. 1946
Cowper, William 1791
Cowper, William 1792
Cowper, William 1802
Cowper, William 1810
Cowper, William 1814
Cowper, William 1816–17
Cowper, William 1817
Cowper, William 1820
Cowper, William 1836
Cowper, William 1837
Cowper, William 1838
Cowper, William 1843
Cowper, William 1847
Cowper, William 1849
Cowper, William 1850
Cowper, William 1853
Cowper, William 1855

Cowper, William 1855–58
Cowper, William 1858
Cowper, William 1862
Cowper, William 1872–76
Cowper, William 1910
Cowper, William 1913
Cowper, William 1916
Cowper, William 1920
Cowper, William 1925
Cowper, William 1928
Cowper, William 1931
Cowper, William 1935
Cowper, William 1953–55
Cowper, William 1992
Crescenzo, Luciano de 1997
Crespo, Emilio 1991
Creuzer, C. F. 1848
Croiset, Maurice 1896
Croiset, Maurice 1914
Crooke, E. S. 1873
Crooke, E. S. 1905
Cross, Joseph 1891
Crusius, Gottlieb Christian 1840–42
Crusius, Gottlieb Christian 1842
Crusius, Gottlieb Christian 1844–53
Crusius, Gottlieb Christian 1852–64
Crusius, Gottlieb Christian 1852–72
Crusius, Gottlieb Christian 1856
Cstbye, Peter Nilsen 1958
Cstbye, Peter Nilsen; Mogens Boisen 1967
Cudworth, William 1893
Cudworth, William 1895
Cummings, Prentiss 1910
Cummings, Prentiss 1912
Cummings, Prentiss 1915
Cunichio, Raym. 1784
Cunichio, Raymundo 1776
Curry, Neil 1993
Dacier, Anne LeFevre 1709
Dacier, Anne LeFevre 1711–20
Dacier, Anne LeFevre 1712–17
Dacier, Anne LeFevre 1716–20
Dacier, Anne LeFevre 1717
Dacier, Anne LeFevre 1719
Dacier, Anne LeFevre 1731
Dacier, Anne LeFevre 1741–56
Dacier, Anne LeFevre 1756
Dacier, Anne LeFevre 1766
Dacier, Anne LeFevre 1779
Dacier, Anne LeFevre 1805
Dacier, Anne LeFevre 1811
Dacier, Anne LeFevre 1815
Dacier, Anne LeFevre 1816
Dacier, Anne LeFevre 1817
Dacier, Anne LeFevre 1818
Dacier, Anne LeFevre 1819
Dacier, Anne LeFevre 1825
Dacier, Anne LeFevre 1826
Dacier, Anne LeFevre 1841
Dacier, Anne LeFevre 1845

Dacier, Anne LeFevre 1850
Dacier, Anne LeFevre 1872
Dacier, Anne LeFevre 1875
Dacier, Anne LeFevre 1900
Dacier, Anne LeFevre 1930
Dacier, Anne LeFevre 1975
Dacier, Anne LeFevre; Mm. Trianon; E. Falconnet 1846
Dacier, Anne LeFevre; Mm. Trianon; E. Falconnet 1855
Damianou, Antonella 1980s
Damianou, Antonella 1980s
Damm, Christian Tobias 1769–71
Dankowszky, Gregor 1829–31
Dann, Theodor 1894
Daroqui, Julia 1966
Daroqui, Julia 1994
Dart, J. H. 1862
Dart, J. H. 1865
Davies, B. 1877
Davies, J. 1846
Dawe, Roger David 1993
De Braun, Paadraig 1990
Deles, Triantaphyllos I. 1979
Demetriade, Phok. 1968
Denham, John 1709
Denman, G. 1873
Derby, Edward George Geoffrey Smith Stanley, Earl of of 1862
Derby, Edward George Geoffrey Smith Stanley, Earl of 1864
Derby, Edward George Geoffrey Smith Stanley, Earl of 1865
Derby, Edward George Geoffrey Smith Stanley, Earl of 1866
Derby, Edward George Geoffrey Smith Stanley, Earl of 1867
Derby, Edward George Geoffrey Smith Stanley, Earl of 1868
Derby, Edward George Geoffrey Smith Stanley, Earl of 1869
Derby, Edward George Geoffrey Smith Stanley, Earl of 1870
Derby, Edward George Geoffrey Smith Stanley, Earl of 1871
Derby, Edward George Geoffrey Smith Stanley, Earl of 1873
Derby, Edward George Geoffrey Smith Stanley, Earl of 1874
Derby, Edward George Geoffrey Smith Stanley, Earl of 1876
Derby, Edward George Geoffrey Smith Stanley, Earl of 1880
Derby, Edward George Geoffrey Smith Stanley, Earl of 1881
Derby, Edward George Geoffrey Smith Stanley, Earl of 1887
Derby, Edward George Geoffrey Smith Stanley, Earl of 1894
Derby, Edward George Geoffrey Smith Stanley, Earl of 1900
Derby, Edward George Geoffrey Smith Stanley, Earl of 1907
Derby, Edward George Geoffrey Smith Stanley, Earl of 1910

Derby, Edward George Geoffrey
Smith Stanley, Earl of 1912
Derby, Edward George Geoffrey
Smith Stanley, Earl of 1914
Derby, Edward George Geoffrey
Smith Stanley, Earl of 1921
Derby, Edward George Geoffrey
Smith Stanley, Earl of 1928
Derby, Edward George Geoffrey
Smith Stanley, Earl of 1931
Derby, Edward George Geoffrey
Smith Stanley, Earl of 1935
Derby, Edward George Geoffrey
Smith Stanley, Earl of 1944
Derby, Edward George Geoffrey
Smith Stanley; Earl of 1945
Derby, Edward George Geoffrey
Smith Stanley, Earl of 1948
Derby, Edward, Earl of; William
Cowper 1933
Dethou, A. 1865
Devecseri, Gabor 1947
Devecseri, Gabor 1957
Devecseri, Gabor 1986
Dias Palmeira, E. 1938–39
Dias Palmeira, E.; Manuel Alves
Correia 1963
Didot 1845
Dimier, Louis 1937
D'Ippolito, Gennaro 1977
Divus, Andreas 1537
Divus, Andreas 1538
Divus, Andreas 1540
Divus, Andreas 1638
Divus, Andreas; Aldus Manutius,
Georgius Dartona 1537
Divus, Andreas; Aldus Manutius,
Georgius Dartona 1538
Divus, Andreas; Conrad Heres-
bach 1538
Dixey, Giles 1933
Dmochowski, Franciszek Ksawery
1800
Dmochowski, Franciszek Ksawery
1804–05
Dmochowski, Franciszek Ksawery
1922
Dmochowski, Franciszek Ksawery
1947
Dmochowski, Franciszek Ksawery
1950
Dmochowski, Franciszek Ksawery
1960
Dmochowski, Franciszek Ksawery
1966
Dmochowski, Franciszek Ksawery
1989
Dmochowski, Franciszek Ksawery
1990
Dmochowskiego, Francziskiego
Xaweriusa 1791
Dobremes, M. 1784
Dobrietisyn, Aleksandr 1993
Dodd, E. F. 1986
Doederlein 1863–64

Doehler, E. 1864
Dolce, Lucovico 1571
Dolce, Lucovico 1572
Dolce, Lucovico 1573
Donner, Johann Jakob Christian
1864–74
Donner, Johann Jakob Christian
1874
Donner, Johann Jokob Christian
1858
Dorf, Philip 1949
Dorpfeld, Ruter 1925
Douglas-Thomson, A. 1899
Drerup, E. 1903
Dryden, John 1700
Dryden, John 1713
Dryden, John 1721
Dryden, John 1734
Dryden, John 1743
Dryden, John 1745
Dryden, John 1752
Dryden, John 1754
Dryden, John 1755
Dryden, John 1764
Dryden, John 1771
Dryden, John 1772
Dryden, John 1773
Dryden, John 1774
Dryden, John 1776
Dryden, John 1810
Dryden, John 1972
Du Cane, Charles 1880
Duckett, George 1716
Dudner, Friedrich 1865
Dufour, Mederic 1996
Dufour, Mederic, Jeanne Raison
1935
Dufour, Mederic; Jeanne Raison
1947
Dufour, Mederic; Jeanne Raison
1954
Dufour, Mederic; Jeanne Raison
1957
Dufour, Mederic; Jeanne Raison
1961
Dufour, Mederic; Jeanne Raison
1965
Dufour, Mederic; Jeanne Raison
1973
Dufour, Mederic; Jeanne Raison
1976
Dufour, Mederic; Jeanne Raison
1979
Dufour, Mederic; Jeanne Raison
1988
Dugas-Montbel, M. Jean-Baptiste
1815–18
Dugas-Montbel, M. Jean-Baptiste
1818
Dugas-Montbel, M. Jean-Baptiste
1825
Dugas-Montbel, M. Jean-Baptiste
1828–34
Dugas-Montbel, M. Jean-Baptiste
1853

Duhr, August 1895
Duhr, August 1898
Dumoulin, L.; A. Goujon, Ch.-
Martin Rousselet 1852
Dumoulin, L.; A. Goujon, Ch-
Martin Rousselet 1832
Dunbar, H. 1879
Dunbar, H. 1883
Duntzer 1863–64
Duport, Jac. 1660
Duriac, Milos N. 1985
Dzonic, Uros 1961
Ebener, Dietrich 1971
Ebener, Dietrich 1983
Edgar, John 1891
Edgar, John 1927
Edgar, John 1949
Edgington, G. W. 1869
Edwards, Gerald Maclean 1888
Edwards, Gerald Maclean 1890
Edwards, Gerald Maclean 1930
Egilsson, Sveinbjorn 1829–40
Egilsson, Sveinbjorn 1835–40
Egilsson, Sveinbjorn 1855
Egilsson, Sveinbjorn 1856
Egilsson, Sveinbjorn 1912
Egilsson, Sveinbjorn 1915
Egilsson, Sveinbjorn; Kristinn
Armansson; Jon Gisl 1948–49
Ehrenthal, F. W. 1878
Ehrenthal, F. W. 1886
Ehrenthal, F. W. 1897
Ehrenthal, F. W. 1904–15
Eichhorn, Friedrich 1971
Eleopoulos, Nikephoros and
Kallirroe 1968
Emre, Ahmeet Cevar 1941–42
Emre, Ahmet Cevat 1957
Engel, Ernst Johann Jakob 1885
Engelmann, Emil 1890
Engelmann, Emil 1891
Engelmann, Richard; William
Cliffe Foley Anderson 1892
Engin, Arn 1958
Ephtaliotes, Argyres 1946
Ephtaliotes, Argyres 1960
Ephtaliotes, Argyres; Nikolaos
Poriotes 1965
Epps, Preston Herschel 1965
Erhat, Azra; A. Kadir 1958
Erhat, Azra; A. Kadir 1967
Ernle, George 1922
ESafarik, Milene 1952
Eschen, F. A. 1797
Eschen, F. A. 1798
Eschen, F. A. 1799
Escott, John 1995
Eton 1860
Eust. Fiocci 1812
Eust. Fiocci 1823
Eustathius 1542–50
Eustathius 1558
Eustathius 1559–60
Evelyn-White, Hugh Gerard 1914
Evelyn-White, Hugh Gerard 1915

Evelyn-White, Hugh Gerard 1920
Evelyn-White, Hugh Gerard 1922
Evelyn-White, Hugh Gerard 1926
Evelyn-White, Hugh Gerard 1936
Evelyn-White, Hugh Gerard 1943
Evelyn-White, Hugh Gerard 1947
Evelyn-White, Hugh Gerard 1950
Evelyn-White, Hugh Gerard 1954
Evelyn-White, Hugh Gerard 1959
Evelyn-White, Hugh Gerard 1964
Evelyn-White, Hugh Gerard 1967
Evelyn-White, Hugh Gerard 1970
Evelyn-White, Hugh Gerard 1977
Evelyn-White, Hugh Gerard 1982
Evslin, Bernard 1971
Evslin, Bernard 1976
Eyth, Ed. 1834–35
Eyth, Ed. 1851
Faesi, Franke 1879
Faesi, Johann Ulrich 1853
Faesi, Johann Ulrich 1855–56
Faggella, Manlio 1925
Fagles, Robert 1990
Fagles, Robert 1991
Fagles, Robert 1992
Fagles, Robert 1995
Fagles, Robert 1996
Fagles, Robert 1997
Fagles, Robert 1998
Fago, John Norwood 1979
Fago, John Norwood 1994
Fahland, B. 1894
Fahlcrantz, Christain Alfred 1894
Falbe, G. S. 1840
Falls, Gregory A.; Kurt Beattie 1978
Falls, Gregory A.; Kurt Beattie 1996
Falls, Gregory; Kurt Beattie 1980
Falstein, Mark 1999
Fausset, Andrew Robert 1864
Fausset, Andrew Robert 1869
Felton, Cornelius Conway 1833
Felton, Cornelius Conway 1835
Felton, Cornelius Conway 1844
Felton, Cornelius Conway 1847
Felton, Cornelius Conway 1848
Felton, Cornelius Conway 1852
Felton, Cornelius Conway 1854
Felton, Cornelius Conway 1857
Fenton, Elijah 1717
Fenton, Elijah 1779
Ferentz, Nagy 1810
Ferian, St. Ange 1776
Festa, Hilda Montesi 1936
Festa, Nicola 1919
Fibiger, P. G. 1825
Fibiger, P. G. 1827
Fick, August 1883
Fick, August 1886
Fick, August 1902
Finsler, Georg 1907
Fiocchi, Eustathius 1816
Fitz-Cotton, H. 1749
Fitzgerald, Robert 1961

Fitzgerald, Robert 1962
Fitzgerald, Robert 1963
Fitzgerald, Robert 1963
Fitzgerald, Robert 1965
Fitzgerald, Robert 1969
Fitzgerald, Robert 1970
Fitzgerald, Robert 1974
Fitzgerald, Robert 1975
Fitzgerald, Robert 1976
Fitzgerald, Robert 1978
Fitzgerald, Robert 1979
Fitzgerald, Robert 1983
Fitzgerald, Robert 1984
Fitzgerald, Robert 1985
Fitzgerald, Robert 1986
Fitzgerald, Robert 1989
Fitzgerald, Robert 1990
Fitzgerald, Robert 1992
Fitzgerald, Robert 1998
Fitzgerald, Robert 1999
Fitzgerald, Robert; R. C. Onesti 1971
Flaceliere, Robert; Victor Berard 1961
Flaceliere, Robert; Victor Berard 1984
Flagg, Isaac 1923
Flaxman, John 1805
Fleischman, Paul 1996
Fletcher, Ian 1968
Floridus, Franciscus Sabinus 1545
Foerster, Michael 1931
Follenius, A.; Conr. Schwenck 1814
Fonseca, Antonio Barahona da 1975
Fontana, Fel. 1784
Forster, E[dward] S[eymour] 1939
Forster, E[dward] S[eymour] 1940
Forster, E[dward] S[eymour] 1964
Forster, E[dward] S[eymour] 1981
Foscolo, Ugo 1807
Foscolo, Ugo 1871
Foscolo, Ugo 1961
Foscolo, Ugo 1989
Foscolo, Ugo; Melchiorre Cesarotti; Vincenzo Monti 1807
Fouldes, William 1603
Fouldes, William 1613
Fouldes, William 1634
Fowle, E. 1880
Francini, Antonio 1537
Francino, Antonio 1519
Franco, Cascais 1988
Franke, F. 1828
Frasari, Naim 1887
Freese, John Henry 1890
Freese, John Henry 1894
Frenzel, K. 1852
Frey, Karl 1881
Freytagius, Theod. Frideric. 1837
Frias Infante, Mario 1981
Froment, J. B. F. 1883–84
Fromm 1750
Fry, Gerard; Dictys Cretensis 1998

Fu, Tung-hua 1929
Fu, Tung-hua 1934
Fu, Tung-hua 1939
Fu, Tung-hua 1947
Fu, Tung-hua 1966
Fu, Tung-hua 1982
Fuhmann, Franz 1971
Fuhmann, Franz 1993
G. V. S. 1651
G. V. S. 1720
Gaal, Mozes 1927
Gaberel, Henri 1952
Gabor, Devecseri 1957
Gail, Jean-Baptiste 1801
Gail, Jean-Baptiste 1803
Gaisser, Julia Haig 1983
Gale, Agnes Spofford Cook 1903
Gale, Agnes Spofford Cook 1904
Gale, Agnes Spofford Cook 1926
Garborg, Arne 1919
Garcia Blanco, Jose; Luis M. Macia Aparicio 1991
Garioni, P. 1793
Garnett, Richard 1890
Gaze, Theodorus 1810–12
Gebhardt, H. 1862
Geddes, Alexander 1792
Gedovius, Ella C. de 1981
Gelsted, Otto 1959
Gelsted, Otto 1961
Gelsted, Otto 1993
Gemoll 1886
Georgin, Ch. and H. Berthaut 1940–41
Georgius Maxillus, alias Ubelin 1510
Gergua, Juan B. 1911
Germain, G. 1958
Gerunzi, Egisto 1900
Gesner, Konrad 1542
Gesner, Konrad 1586
Geuemes, Emilio Crespo; Jose Manuel Pabon 1999
Gfeller, Walter 1981
Ghazikian, Arsen Gharzaros 1924
Ghazikian, Arsen Ghazaros 1911
Ghosh, Sudhamsuranhan 1982
Ghoska, Giraja Kumara 1920
Giannakopoulos, Panagiotes E. 1992
Giannopoulos, N. 1966
Giezens, Augusts 1936
Giguet, Pierre 1854
Giguet, Pierre 1857
Giguet, Pierre 1860
Giguet, Pierre 1861
Giguet, Pierre 1863
Giguet, Pierre 1866
Giguet, Pierre 1869
Giguet, Pierre 1870
Giguet, Pierre 1873
Giguet, Pierre 1883
Giguet, Pierre 1893
Giguet, Pierre 1899
Giguet, Pierre 1900

Hobbes, Thomas 1845
Hobbes, Thomas 1966
Hobbes, Thomas 1979
Hobbes, Thomas 1986
Hobbes, Thomas 1992
Hobbes, Thomas 1997
Hoepke, Hermann 1977
Hoffmann 1864
Hofmann, J. Jak. 1799
Holderlin, Friedrich 1922
Hole, Richard 1781
Holl, P. J. 1858
Hoogstraten, David van 1739
Hoogstraten, David van 1740
Hortis, Attilio 1879
Howland, George 1889
Howland, George 1889
Howland, George 1891
Howse, Francis 1810
Hoyo, Arturo del 1977
Hua, Yung 1984
Hua, Yung 1993
Hubatsch, Oskar 1911
Hubatsch, Oskar 1936
Hubatsch, Oskar 1937
Hugues Salel 1545
Hugues Salel 1555
Hulak, Jaroslav 1989
Hull, Denison Bingham 1978
Hull, Denison Bingham 1982
Hulle, Hedwig Hoffmeier 1826
Humbert, Jean 1936
Humbert, Jean 1941
Humbert, Jean 1951
Humbert, Jean 1959
Humbert, Jean 1967
Humbert, Jean 1976
Humbert, Jean 1997
Hunkin, Oliver 1989
Hygyes, M; Lamin, Amadis 1577
Irfan, Mahmud 1925
Irmscher, Emil 1896
Irmscher, Emil 1897
Isemann, Bernd 1942
Jaccottet, Philippe 1992
Jacobi, A. W. L. 1844
Jacobi, A. W. L. 1846
Jacobus Micyllus, Joachim Camerarius 1541
Jager, Otto 1885
Jagger, A. 1908
James, Lord Scudamore 1665
James, Sydney R. 1882
Jamyn, Amadis 1574
Jamyna, Amadis; Hugues Salel 1580
Janni, Pietro 1971
Jantzen, Eva 1982
Jay, Matthew 1652
Jens, Walter 1956
Jens, Walter 1959
Jens, Walter 1964
Jens, Walter 1968
Jens, Walter 1971
Jens, Walter 1992

Jexzewski, Kazimiez; Jerzy Janowski 1981
Jlgen., C. D. 1796
Johannson, J. Fr. 1846
Johansson, J. Fr. 1844–45
Johnson, Christopher 1580
Johnson, Eyvind 1964
Johnson, P. Roosevelt 1872–76
Jones, Peter V. 1991
Jordan, Wilhelm 1875
Jordan, Wilhelm 1881
Jordan, Wilhelm 1889
Jordan, Wilhelm 1890s
Jordan, Wilhelm 1892
Jordan, Wilhelm 1911
Jordan, Wilhelm 1918
Juan de Mena, Juan 1519
Junger, Friedrich Georg 1979
Junger, Friedrich Georg 1981
Kakridis, Johannes Th. 1985
Kalokairinos, Kostas 1982
Kammerer, F. 1815
Kampourides, Stauros 1980–97
Kang, Yeong-gil 1992
Kang, Yeong-gil 1997
Kannegiesser, K. L. 1822
Karapanagiotes, A. X. 1895
Karapanagiotes, A. X.; Giannakopoulos, P. E. 1975–80
Kartadinata 1922
Katz, Golda [or Gilda Patz] 1924
Kazantzake, Nikos; Johannes Th. Kadrides 1986
Kazantzake, Nikos; Johannes Th. Kakridis 1996
Kazantzakis, Nikos 1957
Kazantzakis, Nikos 1958
Kazantzakis, Nikos 1983
Kazantzakis, Nikos 1988
Kazantzakis, Nikos; Ioannes Theophanous Kakrides 1962
Kazantzakis, Nikos; Ioannes Theophanous Kakrides 1976
Kazantzakis, Nikos; Johannes Th. Kakrides 1987
Kazantzakis, Nikos; Johannes Th. Kakrides 1965
Kazantzakis, Nikos; Johannes Th. Kakrides 1966
Kazantzakis, Nikos; Johannes Th. Kakrides 1997
Kazantzakis, Nikos; Kakridis, Johannes Th. 1955
Kazimiera, Jeczewska 1999
Keckman, Karl Niklas 1832
Keep, Robert P. 1885
Keep, Robert P. 1888
Kelle, K. G. 1826
Kelly 1872–80
Kelly 1878–80
Kelly 1881
Kelly, Sean; Valerie Marchant 1978
Kemball-Cook, Brian 1993
Kemenes, Jozsef 1905
Kempf, Jozsef 1902

Kenealy, Edward Vaughan 1864
Kennedy, James 1834
Kennedy, James 1839
Kerillis, Helene 1998
Kern, Joh. 1848
Kerr, George P. 1947
Kerr, George P. 1958
Khalidi, Anbarah Salam 1966
Khalidi, Anbarah Salam 1979
Khalidi, Anbarah Salam 1980
Khalidi, Anbarah Salam 1982
Khasbah, Darini 1986
Kheranyan, Mkrtich 1987
Kicinshki, Bruno Comes 1820
Kickvorschen 1636
Killy, Walther 1961
King, H. M.;H. Spooner 1968
Kirk, G. S. 1962
Kirton, J. P. 1977
Kirton, J. P. 1984
Klaerr, Robert 1939
Klopstock 1781
Knight, Richard Payne 1820
Koch 1868–70
Kock, Michael 1991
Kock, Michael 1992
Kocourek, Vitezslav 1994
Koechly 1861
Kohler, Carl Sylvio 1881
Kohler, K. Ldw. 1768
Kolaitis, Memas 1983
Komnenos-Kakrides, Olgas 1954
Konev, Andreai Fedorovich 1998
Konstantinidos, A. 1912
Kooten, Theodorus van 1806
Kooten, Theodorus van 1809
Kopievich, Il'ya Fedorovich 1700
Koraes, Adamantios 1811–20
Kordatos, Gianes Konstantinou 1939
Korodi, L. 1863
Kosegarten, L. T. 1780
Kottmeyer, William 1952
Kottmeyer, William 1972
Kremerom, I. A. 1871–74
Kuiper, Wolter Everard 1949
Kumaniecki, Kazimierz T. 1974
Kure, Shigeichi 1971–72
Kure, Shigeichi 1981
Kuttner, C. A. 1771–73
Kuttner, C. A. 1781
La Badessa, Paolo 1564
La Penna, Antonio 1986
La Penna, Antonio 1990
La Roche 1867–68
La Roche 1870–71
Lagerlof, Erland L. 1908
Lagerlof, Erland L. 1920
Lagerlof, Erland L. 1946
Lagerlof, Erland L. 1948
Lagerlof, Erland L. 1949
Lagerlof, Erland L. 1959
Lagerlof, Erland L. 1962
Lagerlof, Erland L. 1965
Lagerlof, Erland L.; Einar Pontan 1942

Lagerlof, Erland L.; Gerhard Bendz 1963
Lagrandville, P. 1871
Lagrandville, P. 1979
Lalaounis 1984
Lamb, Charles 1808
Lamb, Charles 1819
Lamb, Charles 1839
Lamb, Charles 1841–44
Lamb, Charles 1867
Lamb, Charles 1888
Lamb, Charles 1890
Lamb, Charles 1892
Lamb, Charles 1894
Lamb, Charles 1895
Lamb, Charles 1898
Lamb, Charles 1900
Lamb, Charles 1901
Lamb, Charles 1902
Lamb, Charles 1910
Lamb, Charles 1912
Lamb, Charles 1917
Lamb, Charles 1921
Lamb, Charles 1926
Lamb, Charles 1991
Lamberti, Luigi 1805
Landon, James T. B. 1863
Lang, Andrew 1896
Lang, Andrew 1897
Lang, Andrew 1899
Lang, Andrew 1900
Lang, Andrew 1911
Lang, Andrew 1915
Lang, Andrew; Walter Leaf; E. Myers; S. H. Butler 1909
Lang, Andrew; Walter Leaf; E. Myers; S. H. Butler 1935
Lang, Andrew; Walter Leaf; Ernest Myers 1882
Lang, Andrew; Walter Leaf; Ernest Myers 1883
Lang, Andrew; Walter Leaf; Ernest Myers 1889
Lang, Andrew; Walter Leaf; Ernest Myers 1891
Lang, Andrew; Walter Leaf; Ernest Myers 1892
Lang, Andrew; Walter Leaf; Ernest Myers 1893
Lang, Andrew; Walter Leaf; Ernest Myers 1895
Lang, Andrew; Walter Leaf; Ernest Myers 1897
Lang, Andrew; Walter Leaf; Ernest Myers 1898
Lang, Andrew; Walter Leaf; Ernest Myers 1900
Lang, Andrew; Walter Leaf; Ernest Myers 1901
Lang, Andrew; Walter Leaf; Ernest Myers 1903
Lang, Andrew; Walter Leaf; Ernest Myers 1905
Lang, Andrew; Walter Leaf; Ernest Myers 1911

Lang, Andrew; Walter Leaf; Ernest Myers 1912
Lang, Andrew; Walter Leaf; Ernest Myers 1914
Lang, Andrew; Walter Leaf; Ernest Myers 1915
Lang, Andrew; Walter Leaf; Ernest Myers 1916
Lang, Andrew; Walter Leaf; Ernest Myers 1917
Lang, Andrew; Walter Leaf; Ernest Myers 1919
Lang, Andrew; Walter Leaf; Ernest Myers 1921
Lang, Andrew; Walter Leaf; Ernest Myers 1922
Lang, Andrew; Walter Leaf; Ernest Myers 1923
Lang, Andrew; Walter Leaf; Ernest Myers 1925
Lang, Andrew; Walter Leaf; Ernest Myers 1927
Lang, Andrew; Walter Leaf; Ernest Myers 1928
Lang, Andrew; Walter Leaf; Ernest Myers 1929
Lang, Andrew; Walter Leaf; Ernest Myers 1930
Lang, Andrew; Walter Leaf; Ernest Myers 1933
Lang, Andrew; Walter Leaf; Ernest Myers 1941
Lang, Andrew; Walter Leaf; Ernest Myers 1945
Lang, Andrew; Walter Leaf; Ernest Myers 1947
Lang, Andrew; Walter Leaf; Ernest Myers 1949
Lang, Andrew; Walter Leaf; Ernest Myers 1956
Lang, Andrew; Walter Leaf; Ernest Myers 1958
Lang, Andrew; Walter Leaf; Ernest Myers 1965
Lang, Andrew; Walter Leaf; Ernest Myers 1967
Lang, Andrew; Walter Leaf; Ernest Myers 1968
Lang, Andrew; Walter Leaf; Ernest Myers 1968–75
Lang, Andrew; Walter Leaf; Ernest Myers 1969
Lang, Andrew; Walter Leaf; Ernest Myers 1971
Lang, Andrew; Walter Leaf; Ernest Myers 1978
Lang, Andrew; Walter Leaf; Ernest Myers; Butcher 1936
Lang, Andrew; Walter Leaf; Ernest Myers; Butcher 1950
Lang, Andrew; Walter Leaf; Ernest Myers; Butcher 1952
Lang, Andrew; Walter Leaf; Ernest Myers; Butcher 1966
Lang, Jeanie 1907

Lang, Jeanie 1910
Lang, Jeanie 1912
Langley, Samuel 1767
Lasserre, Eugene 1932
Lasserre, Eugene 1946
Lasserre, Eugene 1952
Lasserre, Eugene 1955
Lasserre, Eugene 1960
Lasserre, Eugene 1965
Lasserre, Eugene 1975
Lasserre, Eugene 1988
Lasserre, Eugene 1995
Lattimore, Richmond Alexander 1951
Lattimore, Richmond Alexander 1952
Lattimore, Richmond Alexander 1957
Lattimore, Richmond Alexander 1961
Lattimore, Richmond Alexander 1962
Lattimore, Richmond Alexander 1965
Lattimore, Richmond Alexander 1967
Lattimore, Richmond Alexander 1968
Lattimore, Richmond Alexander 1969
Lattimore, Richmond Alexander 1971
Lattimore, Richmond Alexander 1975
Lattimore, Richmond Alexander 1976
Lattimore, Richmond Alexander 1977
Lattimore, Richmond Alexander 1982
Lattimore, Richmond Alexander 1990
Lattimore, Richmond Alexander 1991
Lattimore, Richmond Alexander 1993
Lattimore, Richmond Alexander 1997
Lattimore, Richmond Alexander 1999
Launay-Valery, L. G. R. Cordier de 1784–85
Launay-Valery, L. G. R. Cordier de 1785
Launay-Valery, L. G. R. Cordier de 1795
Launay-Valery, L. G. R. Cordier de 1800
Laura, G. 1895
Lavagnoli, Ant. 1744
Lavagnoli, Ant. 1788
Lawrence, Thomas Edward 1932
Lawrence, Thomas Edward 1934
Lawrence, Thomas Edward 1935
Lawrence, Thomas Edward 1939

Lawrence, Thomas Edward 1940
Lawrence, Thomas Edward 1941
Lawrence, Thomas Edward 1944
Lawrence, Thomas Edward 1946
Lawrence, Thomas Edward 1955
Lawrence, Thomas Edward 1956
Lawrence, Thomas Edward 1960
Lawrence, Thomas Edward 1966
Lawrence, Thomas Edward 1969
Lawrence, Thomas Edward 1972
Lawrence, Thomas Edward 1978
Lawrence, Thomas Edward 1981
Lawrence, Thomas Edward 1986
Lawrence, Thomas Edward 1991
Lawrence, Thomas Edward 1992
Le Marchand, Jacques 1954
Lea, Nissim Rossi, and Aldo
  Bruscaglioni 1934
Leaf, Walter 1897
Leaf, Walter 1900
Leaf, Walter 1902
Leaf, Walter; Matthew Albert
  Bayfield 1894
Leaf, Walter; Matthew Albert
  Bayfield 1898
Leaf, Walter; Matthew Albert
  Bayfield 1931
Leaf, Walter; Matthew Albert
  Bayfield 1955–56
Leaf, Walter; Matthew Albert
  Bayfield 1968–71
Leary, T. H. L. 1857–59
Leary, T. H. L. 1864
Leary, T. H. L. 1870
Leary, T. H. L. 1878
Lebrun 1822
Lebrun 1825
Lebrun, Charles-Francois 1776
Lebrun, Charles-Francois 1809
Lebrun, Charles-Francois 1812
Lebrun, Charles-Francois 1819
Lebrun, Charles-Francois 1826
Lebrun, Charles-Francois 1836
Leconte de Lisle 1867
Leconte de Lisle 1868
Leconte de Lisle 1877
Leconte de Lisle 1882
Leconte de Lisle 1884
Leconte de Lisle 1893
Leconte de Lisle 1899
Leconte de Lisle 1923
Leconte de Lisle 1925
Leconte de Lisle 1938
Leconte de Lisle 1942
Leconte de Lisle 1943
Leconte de Lisle 1951
Leconte de Lisle 1963
Leconte de Lisle 1989
Leconte de Lisle 1991
Leconte de Lisle 1992
Leconte de Lisle; Bruno Remy 1988
Leconte de Lisle; Louis Palemeque
  1976
Leeuwen, Jan van; Maurits Ben-
  jamin Mendes da Costa 1918–19

Lefevre, Raoul 1475
Lefevre, Raoul 1676
Lefevre, Raoul 1684
Lefevre, Raoul 1708
Lefevre, Raoul; William Caxton
  1596
Lefevre, Raoul; William Caxton
  1663
Lefevre, Raoul; William Caxton
  1670
Lefevre, Raoul; William Caxton
  1680
Lefevre, Raoul; William Caxton;
  William Phiston 1636
Lehmann, H. 1869
Leipardi, Giacomo 1887
Lemnius, Simon 1549
Lemnius, Simon 1581
Leoni, Mich. 1823-25
Leoni, Mich. 1833
Leonnrot, Elias 1990
Leopardi, C. 1816
Leprevost, C. 1843–79
Leprevost, M. C. 1848
Lessing, Erich 1965
Lewis, Arthur Gardner 1911
Lewis, Arthur Gardner 1912
Lewis, R. Morris 1928
Li, Lieh-wen 1972
Lindsay, Jack 1929
Lindsay, Jack 1930
Link, Gli. Ch. O. 1781
Liska, Ant. 1844
Lister, Henry Bertram 1932
Lister, Robin 1987
Lister, Robin 1988
Lister, Robin 1994
Llosa, Jorge Guillermo 1965
Lloyd, C. 1807
Lo, Ching 1994
Lo, Nien-sheng; Huan-sheng
  Wang 1997
Lo, Tu-hsiu 1977
Lob, Jacques 1981
Locock, C. D. 1922
Locock, C. D. 1923
Loewe 1828
Logue, Christopher 1962
Logue, Christopher 1963
Logue, Christopher 1967
Logue, Christopher 1981
Logue, Christopher 1984
Logue, Christopher 1987
Logue, Christopher 1991
Logue, Christopher 1992
Logue, Christopher 1995
Logue, Christopher 1999
Logue, Christopher 2000
Lombardi-Lotti, Mansueto; A. Pal-
  adini 1952
Lombardo, Stanley 1997
Lombardo, Stanley 2000
Longhi, Francesco Maria 1838
Lonitzer, Johann 1525
Lonitzer, Johann 1534

Lonney, Albert James 1900
Lopez Alvarez, Leopoldo 1937
Lopez Alvarez, Leopoldo 1938
Lopez Alvarez, Leopoldo 1939
Lopez Eire, Antonio 1989
Lopez Soto, Vicente 1985
Loque, Christopher 1988
Loredano, S. Gio. Franc. 1653
Loredano, S. Gio. Franc. 1654
Loredano, S. Gio. Franc. 1662
Loredano, S. Gio. Franc. 1668
Loueys, Pierre 1990
Loukanes, Nikolaos 1526
Loukanes, Nikolaos 1979
Loukanos 1870
Lovera, Josep Maria 1975
Lowe, G. Ed.; F. A. Ad. Heinichen
  1822–28
Lucano, Nic. 1640
Lucanus, Nicolaus 1556
Lucas, Frank Laurence 1948
Lucas, Frank Laurence 1950
Lucas, Frank Laurence 1958
Lucas, Robert 1781
Lucas, W. 1897
Luce de Lancival, J.-Ch.-J. 1818
Ludwich, Arthur 1985
Ludwig 1895
Lugones, Leopoldo 1923
Lunicer, Philipp 1534
Luquero, Nicasio Hernandez
  1920s
Lycio, Leonhart 1550
Lycio, Leonhart.; S. Lemnius
  1570?
M., A. J. 1962
Mac Gilleathain, Iain 1976
Mac Heil, Sean 1981
Macault, Ant. 1540
MacBean, Charles E. 1971
MacBean, Charles E. 1973
MacHale, John 1844–69
Mackail, John William 1896
Mackail, John William 1898
Mackail, John William 1903–10
Mackail, John William 1912
Mackail, John William 1932
Maclachlan, Ewen 1937
Macleod, Colin 1982
Macpherson, James 1773
Macpherson, James 1808
Macpherson, James 1818–19
Maffei, Marchese Scipione 1752
Maffei, Scipione 1736
Maffei, Scipione 1928
Maggin, Elliot 1977
Magi, Piero 1998
Maginn, W. 1849
Maginn, W. 1850
Maginn, W. 1856
Magnien, Victor 1930
Maittaire, Mich. 1722
Maittaire, Mich. 1726
Maittaire, Mich. 1747
Maittaire, Mich. 1781

Monti, Vincenzo 1888
Monti, Vincenzo 1890
Monti, Vincenzo 1892
Monti, Vincenzo 1896
Monti, Vincenzo 1904
Monti, Vincenzo 1905
Monti, Vincenzo 1910
Monti, Vincenzo 1912
Monti, Vincenzo 1919
Monti, Vincenzo 1920
Monti, Vincenzo 1921–22
Monti, Vincenzo 1924
Monti, Vincenzo 1926
Monti, Vincenzo 1927
Monti, Vincenzo 1929
Monti, Vincenzo 1931
Monti, Vincenzo 1934
Monti, Vincenzo 1935
Monti, Vincenzo 1936
Monti, Vincenzo 1937
Monti, Vincenzo 1938
Monti, Vincenzo 1944
Monti, Vincenzo 1952
Monti, Vincenzo 1953
Monti, Vincenzo 1958
Monti, Vincenzo 1961
Monti, Vincenzo 1963
Monti, Vincenzo 1967
Monti, Vincenzo 1988
Monti, Vincenzo 1990
Monti, Vincenzo 1998
Moor, James; George Muirhead
    1756–58
Moor, James; George Muirhead
    1758
Morales, Maria Luz 1926
Morales, Maria Luz 1994
Morales, Maria Luz 1997
Morgan, Derec Llwyd 1976
Morgan-Brown, H. 1891
Morrice, James 1809
Morris, William 1887
Morris, William 1897
Morris, William 1901
Morris, William 1904
Morris, William 1912
Morris, William 1983
Morris, William 1992
Mosino, Franco 1967
Moss, Ernest 1956
Motte, M. de la 1701
Motte, M. de la 1714
Motte, M. de la 1720
Mugler, Frederic 1986
Mugler, Frederic 1989
Mulder, Dietrich 1935
Muller, Gf. Ephr. 1745
Muller, Henri 1995
Muller, Johann August 1788–93
Munford, William 1846
Munford, William 1852–55
Murison, Alexander Falconer 1933
Murnu, G.; D. M. Pippidi 1955
Murray, Augustus Taber 1919
Murray, Augustus Taber 1924

Murray, Augustus Taber 1925
Murray, Augustus Taber 1927
Murray, Augustus Taber 1928
Murray, Augustus Taber 1929–30
Murray, Augustus Taber 1930
Murray, Augustus Taber 1934–39
Murray, Augustus Taber 1938–42
Murray, Augustus Taber 1942
Murray, Augustus Taber 1942–45
Murray, Augustus Taber 1946
Murray, Augustus Taber 1947
Murray, Augustus Taber 1953
Murray, Augustus Taber 1954
Murray, Augustus Taber 1957
Murray, Augustus Taber 1960
Murray, Augustus Taber 1960–63
Murray, Augustus Taber 1960–66
Murray, Augustus Taber 1965–67
Murray, Augustus Taber 1966
Murray, Augustus Taber 1966–74
Murray, Augustus Taber 1967–71
Murray, Augustus Taber 1975–76
Murray, Augustus Taber 1976–78
Murray, Augustus Taber 1976–80
Murray, Augustus Taber 1978–85
Murray, Augustus Taber 1980–84
Murray, Augustus Taber 1985–88
Murray, Augustus Taber 1993–98
Murray, Augustus Taber 1995
Murray, Augustus Taber 1998
Murray, Augustus Taber 1999
Murray, John 1862
Murville 1776
Musaeus; Marcus Musurus 1519
Musgrave, George 1865
Musgrave, George 1869
Myatt, D. W. 1994
Nadermann, H. L. 1818
Nafisi, Saaid 1990
Nairn, J. A. 1900
Nauverk, L. 1840
Neaikhardt, Aleksandra Aleksan-
    drovna 1985
Neandrum, Mich. 1570
Nebel, Gerhard 1959
Neill, William 1992
Nejedleho, J. 1801
Neumann, C. G. 1826
Nevizano, Francesco 1572
Newman, F. W. 1856
Newman, F. W. 1871
Nikolaides, Demetros; Gregoras,
    Chr. 1863
Nikolaides, Paikos 1971
Nishchynskyaei, Petro 1902–04
Nishchyns'kyi, Petro 1889–92
Norcio, Giuseppe 1969
Norgate, Thomas Starling 1862
Norgate, Thomas Starling 1863
Norgate, Thomas Starling 1864
Norgate, Thomas Starling 1865
Novara, L. B. 1827
Nucciotti, Angelo 1947
Nugler, Frederic 1991
Nunes, Carlos Alberto 1962

Oak, S. N. 1984
Oberbreyer, Max 1876
Obsopoeum, Vinc. 1527
Oertel, E. F. Ch. 1822–23
Oesterheld 1865
Ofosu-Appiah, L. H. 1957
Ofosu-Appiah, L. H. 1974
Ogilby, John 1656
Ogilby, John 1660
Ogilby, John 1665
Ogilby, John 1669
Oikonomides, Giannes Th. 1960
Okal, Miloslav 1962
Okal, Miloslav 1966
Okal, Miloslav 1986
Oliphant, David 1998
Oliver, Peter 1992
Onaindia, Santiago de 1985
Onesti, Rosa Calzecchi 1974
Onesti, Rosa Calzecchi 1984
Osorio, Jose Maria 1973
Osorio, Jose Maria 1980
Osorio, Jose Maria 1985
Ostergaard, Carl V. 1921
Ostobek 1869
Otto, Helene 1904
Owen 1845
Owen 1851
Owen 1852
Owen 1855
Owen 1856
Owen 1857
Owen 1862
Owen 1867
Owen 1868
Owen 1876
Owen, E. C. Everard 1901
Owen, E. C. Everard 1902
Owen, J. J. 1847
Oyarzabal, Juan B. de 1936
Pabon, Jose Manuel 1982
Paci, Gianfr. 1747
Padoan, Gianni 1985
Paduano, Guido 1997
Pagano, Nunziante; Nicolo
    Capasso 1989
Pagnini, Gius. 1791
Paley, F. A. 1878
Paley, F. A. 1881
Paley, F. A. 1885
Paley, F. A. 1889
Palgrave, Frank 1797
Pali, Aleks. 1935
Pallis, Alexander Anastasius 1892
Pallis, Alexander Anastasius 1924
Pallis, Alexander Anastasius 1931
Pallis, Alexander Anastasius 1936
Pallis, Alexander Anastasius 1950
Pallis, Alexander Anastasius 1970
Palma, Lauro 1940
Palma, Lauro 1977
Palmer, George Herbert 1884
Palmer, George Herbert 1886
Palmer, George Herbert 1889
Palmer, George Herbert 1891

Palmer, George Herbert 1893
Palmer, George Herbert 1894
Palmer, George Herbert 1895
Palmer, George Herbert 1898
Palmer, George Herbert 1899
Palmer, George Herbert 1900
Palmer, George Herbert 1908
Palmer, George Herbert 1909
Palmer, George Herbert 1912
Palmer, George Herbert 1921
Palmer, George Herbert 1922
Palmer, George Herbert 1929
Palmer, George Herbert 1949
Palmer, George Herbert 1962
Palmer, George Herbert 1971
Palmer, George Herbert 1999
Pandya, Jayant 1993
Pannonium, Io. 1522
Pantaleon, Heinricus 1551
Paoli, Ugo Enrico 1968
Papaioannos, Georgios D. 1976
Parandowski, Jan 1953
Parandowski, Jan 1956
Parandowski, Jan 1959
Parandowski, Jan 1965
Parandowski, Jan 1982
Parandowski, Jan 1990
Parandowski, Jan 1995
Parandowski, Jan 1998
Parker, Samuel 1700
Parnell, Chapman, Shelley, Con-
    greve, Hole 1872
Parnell, Thomas 1717
Parnell, Thomas 1727
Parnell, Thomas 1760
Parnell, Thomas 1772
Parnell, Thomas 1806
Parnell, Thomas 1810
Parnell, Thomas 1988
Pastor, Willy 1904
Pater, Walter 1902
Paton 1888
Patricius (Bishop) 1515
Pauly, Francueus 1880
Pauw, R. de 1944
Pavano, Giuseppe 1951
Paynell, Thomas; Mathurin Heret;
    Dares 1553
Pazzi, Ant. 1820
Pease, Cyril Arthington 1916
Pease, Cyril Arthington 1917
Pease, Cyril Arthington 1926
Peletier, Jacques 1574
Pellisson, Paul 1970
Peppin, Talbot Sydenham 1893
Peppin, Talbot Sydenham 1898
Perez, Gonzalo 1550
Perez, Gonzalo 1553
Perez, Gonzalo 1556
Perez, Gonzalo 1562
Perez, Gonzalo 1767
Perez, Gonzalo 1785
Periaswamythooran, M. P.; P.
    Tirukutasundaram 1961
Perrin, H. 1889

Perrodil, Victor de 1835
Perry, Walter Copland 1902
Perry, Walter Copland 1924
Pessonneaux, Emile 1861
Pessonneaux, Emile 1865
Pessonneaux, Emile 1866
Pessonneaux, Emile 1869
Pessonneaux, Emile 1886
Peter 1902
Petit, Charles 1981
Petro to Pinello, Ioannes 1640
Petshenik, M. L.; Shelomoh
    Shaynberg 1937
Philip, Neil 1997
Phillips, Burrill 1957
Phillips, Jocelyn 1969
Phillpotts, J. Surtees 1876
Philymno 1513
Phorcensi, Johanne Capnione 1510
Phorcensi, Johanne Capnione 1516
Phouriotes, Angelos Dem 1972
Piat, L. 1885
Picard, Barbara Leonie 1952
Picard, Barbara Leonie 1960
Picard, Barbara Leonie 1962
Picard, Barbara Leonie 1986
Picard, Barbara Leonie 1991
Picou, Henri de 1650
Picou, Henri de 1653
Pierron 1869
Pierron, A. 1880
Pierron, Pierre Alexis 1890
Pindemonte, Ippolito 1785
Pindemonte, Ippolito 1809
Pindemonte, Ippolito 1817
Pindemonte, Ippolito 1822
Pindemonte, Ippolito 1823
Pindemonte, Ippolito 1827
Pindemonte, Ippolito 1829
Pindemonte, Ippolito 1830
Pindemonte, Ippolito 1831
Pindemonte, Ippolito 1837
Pindemonte, Ippolito 1845
Pindemonte, Ippolito 1853
Pindemonte, Ippolito 1868
Pindemonte, Ippolito 1873
Pindemonte, Ippolito 1875
Pindemonte, Ippolito 1878
Pindemonte, Ippolito 1891
Pindemonte, Ippolito 1894
Pindemonte, Ippolito 1908
Pindemonte, Ippolito 1916
Pindemonte, Ippolito 1928
Pindemonte, Ippolito 1931
Pindemonte, Ippolito 1934
Pindemonte, Ippolito 1936
Pindemonte, Ippolito 1937
Pindemonte, Ippolito 1938
Pindemonte, Ippolito 1939
Pindemonte, Ippolito 1940
Pindemonte, Ippolito 1944
Pindemonte, Ippolito 1958
Pindemonte, Ippolito 1960
Pindemonte, Ippolito 1963
Pindemonte, Ippolito 1964

Pindemonte, Ippolito 1968
Pindemonte, Ippolito 1972
Pindemonte, Ippolito 1998
Piper, Theophilus Calestinus 1775
Planche 1850
Planudes, Maximus 1657
Platt, Arthur 1903
Politius, Alex. 1730–35
Polylas, Iakovos 1875–81
Polylas, Iakovos 1912
Polylas, Iakovos 1965
Polylas, Iakovos 1974
Ponceau, Doigne de 1776
Pontani, Filippo Maria 1968
Pontoppidan, Henrik; Steinbor
    Guomundsson 1941
Pope, Alexander 1715–20
Pope, Alexander 1718
Pope, Alexander 1720
Pope, Alexander 1720–26
Pope, Alexander 1725–26
Pope, Alexander 1728
Pope, Alexander 1729
Pope, Alexander 1732
Pope, Alexander 1733
Pope, Alexander 1736
Pope, Alexander 1738
Pope, Alexander 1743
Pope, Alexander 1751
Pope, Alexander 1752
Pope, Alexander 1753
Pope, Alexander 1754
Pope, Alexander 1756
Pope, Alexander 1758
Pope, Alexander 1759
Pope, Alexander 1760
Pope, Alexander 1761
Pope, Alexander 1763
Pope, Alexander 1766
Pope, Alexander 1767
Pope, Alexander 1768
Pope, Alexander 1769
Pope, Alexander 1770
Pope, Alexander 1771
Pope, Alexander 1771–72
Pope, Alexander 1773
Pope, Alexander 1774
Pope, Alexander 1775–76
Pope, Alexander 1776
Pope, Alexander 1777
Pope, Alexander 1778
Pope, Alexander 1779–81
Pope, Alexander 1783
Pope, Alexander 1784
Pope, Alexander 1790
Pope, Alexander 1792
Pope, Alexander 1795
Pope, Alexander 1796
Pope, Alexander 1797
Pope, Alexander 1800
Pope, Alexander 1801
Pope, Alexander 1802
Pope, Alexander 1805
Pope, Alexander 1805–06
Pope, Alexander 1806

Pope, Alexander 1807
Pope, Alexander 1808
Pope, Alexander 1809
Pope, Alexander 1810
Pope, Alexander 1811
Pope, Alexander 1812
Pope, Alexander 1813
Pope, Alexander 1816
Pope, Alexander 1817
Pope, Alexander 1818
Pope, Alexander 1819
Pope, Alexander 1820
Pope, Alexander 1821–22
Pope, Alexander 1822
Pope, Alexander 1824
Pope, Alexander 1825
Pope, Alexander 1826
Pope, Alexander 1827
Pope, Alexander 1828
Pope, Alexander 1830
Pope, Alexander 1832–33
Pope, Alexander 1833
Pope, Alexander 1834
Pope, Alexander 1835
Pope, Alexander 1836
Pope, Alexander 1837
Pope, Alexander 1839
Pope, Alexander 1840
Pope, Alexander 1842
Pope, Alexander 1842
Pope, Alexander 1844
Pope, Alexander 1845
Pope, Alexander 1846
Pope, Alexander 1847
Pope, Alexander 1848
Pope, Alexander 1849
Pope, Alexander 1849
Pope, Alexander 1850
Pope, Alexander 1851
Pope, Alexander 1853
Pope, Alexander 1854
Pope, Alexander 1855
Pope, Alexander 1857
Pope, Alexander 1858
Pope, Alexander 1859
Pope, Alexander 1860
Pope, Alexander 1862
Pope, Alexander 1863
Pope, Alexander 1864
Pope, Alexander 1865
Pope, Alexander 1866
Pope, Alexander 1867
Pope, Alexander 1868
Pope, Alexander 1870
Pope, Alexander 1871
Pope, Alexander 1872
Pope, Alexander 1872–73
Pope, Alexander 1873
Pope, Alexander 1874–75
Pope, Alexander 1875
Pope, Alexander 1876
Pope, Alexander 1880
Pope, Alexander 1881
Pope, Alexander 1882
Pope, Alexander 1883

Pope, Alexander 1884
Pope, Alexander 1887
Pope, Alexander 1889
Pope, Alexander 1890
Pope, Alexander 1891
Pope, Alexander 1892
Pope, Alexander 1893
Pope, Alexander 1894
Pope, Alexander 1896
Pope, Alexander 1897
Pope, Alexander 1898
Pope, Alexander 1899
Pope, Alexander 1900
Pope, Alexander 1901
Pope, Alexander 1902
Pope, Alexander 1902–12
Pope, Alexander 1903
Pope, Alexander 1904
Pope, Alexander 1905
Pope, Alexander 1906
Pope, Alexander 1906–07
Pope, Alexander 1907
Pope, Alexander 1908
Pope, Alexander 1909
Pope, Alexander 1911
Pope, Alexander 1911–12
Pope, Alexander 1912
Pope, Alexander 1915
Pope, Alexander 1919
Pope, Alexander 1920
Pope, Alexander 1921
Pope, Alexander 1924
Pope, Alexander 1925
Pope, Alexander 1927
Pope, Alexander 1931
Pope, Alexander 1934
Pope, Alexander 1936
Pope, Alexander 1938
Pope, Alexander 1939
Pope, Alexander 1942
Pope, Alexander 1943
Pope, Alexander 1949
Pope, Alexander 1956
Pope, Alexander 1959
Pope, Alexander 1961
Pope, Alexander 1965
Pope, Alexander 1967
Pope, Alexander 1970
Pope, Alexander 1971
Pope, Alexander 1979
Pope, Alexander 1985
Pope, Alexander 1986
Pope, Alexander 1993
Pope, Alexander 1996
Pope, Alexander 1999
Pope, Alexander; Richard Hole;
  Henry J. Pye 1820
Pope, Alexander; W. Broome, E.
  Fenton 1745
Pope, Alexander; W. Broome, E.
  Fenton 1758
Pope, Alexander; W. Broome, E.
  Fenton 1768
Pope, Alexander; W. Broome, E.
  Fenton 1771

Pope, Alexander; W. Broome, E.
  Fenton 1778
Pope, Alexander; W. Broome, E.
  Fenton 1811
Pope, Alexander; W. Broome, E.
  Fenton 1861
Pope, Alexander; W. Broome, E.
  Fenton 1880
Pope, Alexander; W. Broome; E.
  Fenton 1852–55
Pope, Alexander; W. Broome; E.
  Fenton 1884
Pope, Alexander; W. Broome; E.
  Fenton; J.S.Watson 1872–76
Pope, Alexander; W. Broome;
  E.Fenton 1873
Pope, John 1978
Pope; Buckley 1874
Popiel Pawer 1882
Popiel, Pawel 1880
Popov, Georgi 1918
Porson, Richard 1801
Portus, Aemilius 1574–80
Portus, Aemilius 1629
Portus, Aemilius 1639
Portus, Franciscus 1570
Portus, Franciscus 1589
Portus, Inumeris 1580
Postel, Christ. Henr. 1700
Potvin, Charles 1891
Poulianos, Alexes I. 1986
Powys, John Cowper 1959
Powys, John Cowper 1959
Prassinus, Joh. 1539
Pratt, John Henry; Walter Leaf
  1880
Pratt, John Henry; Walter Leaf
  1882
Preller, Friedrich 1877
Preller, Friedrich 1881
Price, Aubrey Charles 1921
Price, H. 1736
Privitera, G. Aurelio 1981–86
Privitera, G. Aurelio 1984
Privitera, G. Aurelio 1986
Privitera, G. Aurelio 1991–93
Proddow, Penelope 1971
Protopappas, Io 1950
Przybylskiego, Hiacynth. 1789
Przybylskiego, Hiacynth. 1814–16
Przybylskiego, Hiacynth. 1815
Psychountakes, Georgio 1979
Psychountakes, Giorgos 1995
Pucci, Pietro 1987
Puech, Aime 1930
Pulido Silva, Alberto 1986
Pulleyn, Samuel 2000
Puntoni 1896
Purton, William 1862
Purves, John 1891
Pye, H. J. 1810
Quasimodo, Salvatore 1951
Quasimodo, Salvatore 1960
Quasimodo, Salvatore 1967
Quasimodo, Salvatore 1968

Schaeffer, Albrecht 1810
Schaeffer, Albrecht 1927
Schaeffer, Albrecht 1929
Schaeffer, Albrecht 1937
Schaidenraisser, Simon 1537
Schaidenraisser, Simon 1570
Schaidenreisser, Simon 1911
Schaidenreisser, Simon 1986
Schaumann, E. 1828–36
Schaumann, E. 1830
Schaumann, Herbert Frans 1956
Scheffer, Thassilo Fritz H. von 1920
Scheffer, Thassilo Fritz H. von 1922
Scheffer, Thassilo Fritz H. von 1925
Scheffer, Thassilo Fritz H. von 1927
Scheffer, Thassilo Fritz H. von 1938
Scheffer, Thassilo Fritz H. von 1941
Scheffer, Thassilo Fritz H. von 1947
Scheffer, Thassilo Fritz H. von 1948
Scheibner, G. T. 1834
Scheibner, Gerhard 1972
Scheibner, Gerhard 1986
Scheindler, Augustinus 1897
Scheindler, Augustinus 1900
Schelling, Hermann von 1897
Schelling, Hermann von 1905
Schermer, L. 1709
Schmidt, Ferdinand 1870
Schomberg, George Augustus 1879–82
Schomberg, George Augustus 1882
Schroder, Rudolf Alexander 1907–10
Schroder, Rudolf Alexander 1911
Schroder, Rudolf Alexander 1918
Schroder, Rudolf Alexander 1923
Schroder, Rudolf Alexander 1943
Schroder, Rudolf Alexander 1948
Schroder, Rudolf Alexander 1950
Schroder, Rudolf Alexander 1961
Schultz, Julius 1901
Schulze 1829
Schunck, E. 1861
Schwaber, Carl 1993
Schwartz, M. A. 1982
Schwartz, Weiss 1956
Schwarzschild, Heinrich 1876
Schwenck, Konrad 1822
Schwenck, Konrad 1825
Schwenck, Konrad 1826
Schwenck, Konrad 1829
Schwenck, Konrad 1834
Schwenck, Konrad 1835
Schwenck, Konrad 1841
Schwenck, Konrad 1983
Schwendy, Jurgen 1980

Schwenk, Conrad 1830
Schwitzke, Heinz 1960
Scott, Joseph Nicol 1755
Scudamore, James 1664
Sebaldi detto l'Elicona, Gio. Batt. 1620
Seckendorf, F. K. L. Frnhn. Von 1800
Segala y Estalella, Luis 1908
Segala y Estalella, Luis 1910
Segala y Estalella, Luis 1927
Segala y Estalella, Luis 1938
Segala y Estalella, Luis 1939
Segala y Estalella, Luis 1943
Segala y Estalella, Luis 1944
Segala y Estalella, Luis 1946
Segala y Estalella, Luis 1950
Segala y Estalella, Luis 1951
Segala y Estalella, Luis 1953
Segala y Estalella, Luis 1954
Segala y Estalella, Luis 1955
Segala y Estalella, Luis 1956
Segala y Estalella, Luis 1957
Segala y Estalella, Luis 1959
Segala y Estalella, Luis 1960
Segala y Estalella, Luis 1961
Segala y Estalella, Luis 1962
Segala y Estalella, Luis 1965
Segala y Estalella, Luis 1966
Segala y Estalella, Luis 1967
Segala y Estalella, Luis 1968
Segala y Estalella, Luis 1969
Segala y Estalella, Luis 1970
Segala y Estalella, Luis 1971
Segala y Estalella, Luis 1972
Segala y Estalella, Luis 1973
Segala y Estalella, Luis 1974
Segala y Estalella, Luis 1975
Segala y Estalella, Luis 1976
Segala y Estalella, Luis 1977
Segala y Estalella, Luis 1978
Segala y Estalella, Luis 1979
Segala y Estalella, Luis 1980
Segala y Estalella, Luis 1981
Segala y Estalella, Luis 1982
Segala y Estalella, Luis 1983
Segala y Estalella, Luis 1984
Segala y Estalella, Luis 1985
Segala y Estalella, Luis 1986
Segala y Estalella, Luis 1987
Segala y Estalella, Luis 1988
Segala y Estalella, Luis 1990
Segala y Estalella, Luis 1991
Segala y Estalella, Luis 1992
Segala y Estalella, Luis 1993
Segala y Estalella, Luis 1994
Segala y Estalella, Luis 1995
Segala y Estalella, Luis 1997
Segala y Estalella, Luis 1999
Seguier, F. 1813
Sela, Evaristo de 1990
Selincourt, Aubrey de 1950
Selincourt, Aubrey de 1956
Selincourt, Aubrey de 1961
Selwyn 1865

Semusovio, Joanne Stariconio 1568
Sephakis, Nikos I. 1940
Sequier, Ulysse Francois Ange de 1896
Seron 1984
Serrano, Francisco 1980
Serrano, Francisco 1980s
Settembri, Vera 1965
Settle, Elkanah 1700
Settle, Elkanah 1791
Settle, Elkanah 1794
Severyna, Albert 1944
Seyfeddin, Omer 1927
Seymour, Thomas Day 1901
Shad, Walter 1963
Shadwell, Lancelot 1844
Shaw, Brandreth; Thomas Shaw 1841
Sheepshanks, Richard 1909
Shelley, Percy Bysshe 1821
Shelley, Percy Bysshe 1904–06
Shelley, Percy Bysshe 1929
Shelley, Percy Bysshe 1986
Shewring, Walter 1980
Shewring, Walter 1998
Shllaku, Gjon 1971
Shpan, Shelomoh 1938
Shpan, Shelomoh 1942
Shpan, Shelomoh 1946
Shpan, Shelomoh 1956
Shtal, Irina Vladimirovna 1990
Siatopoulos, Demetres Ioannou 1991
Sickler, F. K. 1820
Sideres, Zesimos 1956
Sideres, Zesimos 1965
Sidgwick, Arthur 1877
Sidgwick, Arthur 1880
Sidgwick, Arthur 1881
Sidgwick, Arthur 1885–87
Sidgwick, Arthur; Robert P. Keep 1879
Sidgwick, Arthur; Robert P. Keep 1882
Siegenbeek 1808
Siemienski, Lucjan Hipolit 1903
Siemienski, Lucjan Hipolit 1922
Siemienski, Lucjan Hipolit 1948
Siemienski, Lucjan Hipolit 1975
Siemienski, Lucjan Hipolit 1990
Siemienski, Lucjan Hipolit 1997
Sikes, E. E. 1900
Silhanek, David 1969
Silius Italicus; Tiberius Catius 1496?
Simcox, Edwin W. 1865
Simms, C. S. 1866
Simms, C. S. 1873
Sisti, Karin 1985
Sitaramayya, K. M. 1978
Sjostrom, Axelius Gabr. 1842
Skalides, A. 1871
Skoda, Antonin 1908
Skoda, Antonin 1911–12

APPENDIX E:
PRINTINGS LISTED BY PRINTER OR PUBLISHER

A and W Publishers 1981
A. G. and J. P. 1679
A. Gjergy Fishta 1941
Abbaziana 1763
Abhyudaya Prakasa-mandira 1954
Abhyudaya Prakasa-mandira 1969
Academia 1935
Academia Catolica 1975
Academic Industries 1984
Acclaim Books 1997
Ackroyd 1895
Adib 1990
AFHA Internacional 1968
AFHA Internacional 1972
AFHA Internacional 1975
AFHA Internacional 1976
AFHA Internacional 1977
AFHA Internacional 1978
AFHA Internacional 1980
Aguilar 1950
Aguilar 1953
Aguilar 1961
Aguilar 1962
Aguilar 1964
Aguilar 1965
Aguilar 1970
Aguilar 1976
Aguilar 1977
Airmont Publishing 1965
Airmont Publishing 1966
Akademie-Verlag 1968
Akademie-Verlag 1988
Aladdin Paperbacks 1982
Alba 1984
Alba 1996
Alberghetti 1863–66
Albinus, Ioannes 1600

Albrizzi q. Girolamo, Gio. Battista 1744
Albrizzini, Gaetano 1741
Alden, John B. 1883
Alessandro, Marino d' 1578
Al-Hilal 1904
Allan, W. 1862
Allen, G. and Unwin 1911
Allen, G. and Unwin 1922
Allen, G. and Unwin 1923
Allman, T. 1834
Allman, T. 1837
Allman, T. 1842
Allman, T. 1858
Allyn and Bacon 1883
Allyn and Bacon 1889
Allyn and Bacon 1890
Allyn and Bacon 1893
Allyn and Bacon 1895
Allyn and Bacon 1896
Allyn and Bacon 1897
Allyn and Bacon 1926
Allyn, J. 1879
Allyn, J. 1884
Allyn, J. 1887
Allyn, J. 1894
Allyn, J. 1950
Al-Maotba ah al-Kathuli-kiyah 1966
Al-Maotbah al-Aosriyah 1966
Alopecium, Heronem 1522
Alopecium, Heronem 1524
Alsop, B. and T. Fawcet 1636
Alterberg, H. 1924
American Book Company 1846
American Book Company 1879
American Book Company 1885
American Book Company 1889

American Book Company 1890
American Book Company 1896
American Book Company 1897
American Book Company 1900
American Book Company 1903
American Book Company 1907
American Book Exchange 1880
American News Company 1882
American News Company 1890s
American Philological Association 1950
American Printing House for the Blind 1954
Amiel, L. 1970s
Amos 1950
Amrosio, Firmin Didot 1861
AMS Press 1968
AMS Press 1979
Amsco School Publications 1988
Anaya 1965
Anchor Books 1963
Anchor Books 1969
Anchor Books 1975
Anchor Books; Doubleday 1963
Anchor Books; Doubleday 1989
Anchor Press; Doubleday 1961
Anchor Press; Doubleday 1974
Anchorage Press 1980
Anczyca, W. 1882
Andreoni, Antonio 1752
Andrus, S. 1848
Andrus, S. 1851
Andrus, S. 1853
Andrus, S. 1854
Andrus, S. and Son 1849
Angelo, Valenti 1949
Angus and Robertson 1993
Anisson, Jean 1700

Benard, Simon 1674
Benedictis, Hieronymus de 1522
Bengaluru Visvavidyalaya 1978
Benincasa 1989
Bensley 1802
Bensley, T. 1810
Berbera, G. 1936
Berjon, Math. 1621
Berjon, Math. 1622
Berliner, Harold 1999
Bernardinum Benetum de Vital-
   ibus 1516
Bernat Bosc 1664
Bertelmann, C. 1875
Bertelsmann 1960
Bertramus, Antonius 1601
Bertrand, Arth. 1823
Bertrand, Arth. 1837
Be-siyu'a keren Yitshak Leyb ve-
   Rahel 1941
Bettenham, J. 1721
Bettoni, Nicolo 1807
Bettoni, Nicolo 1810
Bettoni, Nicolo 1825
Biblio Verlag 1974
Bibliographisches Institut 1878
Bibliographisches Institut 1886
Bibliographisches Institut 1897
Bibliographisches Institut 1904–15
Bibliographisches Institut 1909
Bibliographisches Institut 1912
Bibliotheque de l'Etoile 1942
Biblo; Moser 1900
Bielefeld, B. J. 1923
Bietti 1968
Bilingual Educational Services
   1980s
Biorckegranianis 1776
Birckmannica, sumptibus Arnoldi
   Mylij 1588
Birkhauser 1781
Birkhauser 1943–46
Birkhauser 1945
Birkhauser 1946
Birkhauser 1953
Birkhauser 1964
Bisagni 1661
Bishop, George 1591
Bitter, G. 1971
Black 1899
Black, W. J. 1970
Blackie 1901
Blackie 1902
Blackie 1903
Blackie 1905
Blackman 1931
Blackwood, William 1861–62
Blackwood, William 1895
Blackwood, William 1900
Blackwood, William 1909
Blackwood, William, and Sons
   1861–62
Blackwood, William, and Sons
   1877
Blackwoods 1868

Blackwoods 1869
Blackwoods 1870
Bladus, Antonius Asulanus; Giun-
   tam 1542–50
Blaise, T. 1615
Blanchard, I. H. 1899
Bliss 1810
Bliss, N. 1811
Bobbs-Merrill Educational Pub.
   1977
Bodley Head 1961
Bodmer 1954
Bodoni 1805
Bodoni 1808
Boehme, A. F. 1806
Bogard, Iac. 1543
Bohn 1854
Bohn 1855
Bohn, F. 1937
Bohn, Henry G. 1846
Bohn, Henry G. 1851
Bohn, Henry G. 1853
Bohn, Henry G. 1857
Bohn, Henry G. 1858
Bohn, Henry G. 1859
Bohn, Henry G. 1860
Bohn, Henry G. 1862
Bohn, Henry G. 1863
Bohn, Henry G. 1865
Bohn, Henry G. 1953–55
Bohn, John 1839
Bohn, John 1843
Bohn, John 1845
Bokautgafa Menningarsjos
   1948–49
Bokautgafa Menningarsjos 1952
Boldene Brunnen, Bauersche
   Giesserei 1955
Boltze 1927
Bonacci, V. 1966
Bonacci, V. 1967
Bonechi 1998
Bonk, P.; J. W. de Groot 1745
Bonnier 1964
Bonsal and Niles 1804
Book Club Associates 1981
Book Guild 1993
Book League of America 1938
Bordas 1976
Bordas 1978
Borel, L. 1895
Borel, L. 1897
Boris Bureba Ediciones 1951
Bossange 1809
Bossange 1825
Bossange 1826
Bossange and Masson 1812
Bossange and Masson 1819
Bouret, A. 1874
Boutier, Anth. 1603
Bowyer, G. 1726
Bowyer, J, and H. Clements 1714
Bowyer, William 1714
Bowyer, William 1715–20
Bowyer, William 1720

Bowyer, William 1721
Boyle, John 1774
Boyle, John 1778
Brach, P. A. 1872
Bradda 1981
Brancke 1978
Brandolese 1798–02
Brandolese 1810
Braumuller, W. 1918
Brayer, Lucas 1577
Breitkopf 1774
Breitkopf and Hartel 1885
Breitkopf and Hartel 1895
Bremer Presse 1923–24
Bremer Presse 1924
Bremer Presse 1926
Breyer, Lucas 1574
Breyer, Lucas 1580
Brill, E. J. 1851
Brill, E. J. 1993
Brill, John 1624
Brimax 1992
Brimax 1995
Brindley, Giovanni 1736
Brindley, J. 1750
Brislo 1775–87
Bristol Classical Press 1979
Bristol Classical Press 1980
Bristol Classical Press 1982
Bristol Classical Press 1983
Bristol Classical Press 1985
Bristol Classical Press 1996
Bristol Classical Press 1998
British Broadcasting Corporation
   1969
British Experanto Association
   1933
Brocas, Jean-Baptiste 1640?
Brocas, Jean-Baptiste 1744
Brocas, Jean-Baptiste 1747–48
Brockhaus 1822
Brodard et Taupin 1963
Bronner 1825
Bronner 1826
Brown, A.; Longman, Hurst et al.
   1813
Browne and Nolan 1894
Browne and Nolan et al. 1882
Brubacchius, Petrus 1534
Brubacchius, Petrus 1541
Bruguera 1983
Brunet 1708–09
Brunet 1777
Brunet, Michel 1709
Bruzelius, E. 1818
Bryling, Nicolaus 1561
Bryling, Nicolaus 1567
Bryling, Nicolaus 1582
Bryling, Nicolaus 1584
Bryling, Nicolaus and Barthol.
   Calybaeus 1553
Bryling, Nicolaus; Bartholomaeus
   Calybaeus 1551
Brylinger 1582
Bryn Mawr College 1983

Buchenau and Reichert 1925
Bucher, C. J. 1969
Buchners, C. C. 1916
Buchners, C. C. 1955
Buckland, J; T. Longman 1777
Buckley, T. A. 1797
Bulmer 1808
Bumpus, E. 1890
Bunney and Gold 1802
Burchoorn, Js. 1636
Bureau of Ghana Languages 1974
Burgofrancho, D. Iacob a 1534
Burgofrancho, D. Iacob a 1537
Burke 1983
Burleigh, R. 1716
Burt, A. L. 1890
Burt, A. L. 1902
Burt, A. L. 1906
Buschel 1768
Butter, Nathaniell 1603–14
Butter, Nathaniell 1613
Butter, Nathaniell 1640
Butzmann 1896
Bye and Law 1802
Bye and Law 1806
Byron P. 1968
Cabinet du Roi 1784
Calderini 1965
Caldoriana Societas 1610
Calliope Press 1993
Calve 1826–27
Calve, J. C. (F. Tempsky) 1859
Camb. Warch. 1888
Cambridge University Press 1887
Cambridge University Press 1889
Cambridge University Press 1890
Cambridge University Press 1891
Cambridge University Press 1892
Cambridge University Press 1894
Cambridge University Press 1896
Cambridge University Press 1897
Cambridge University Press 1900
Cambridge University Press 1902
Cambridge University Press 1906
Cambridge University Press 1907
Cambridge University Press 1914
Cambridge University Press 1915
Cambridge University Press 1917
Cambridge University Press 1920
Cambridge University Press 1921
Cambridge University Press 1924
Cambridge University Press 1925
Cambridge University Press 1930
Cambridge University Press 1931
Cambridge University Press 1941
Cambridge University Press 1948
Cambridge University Press 1952
Cambridge University Press 1954
Cambridge University Press 1958
Cambridge University Press 1959
Cambridge University Press 1961
Cambridge University Press 1962
Cambridge University Press 1964
Cambridge University Press 1968
Cambridge University Press 1979

Cambridge University Press 1979
Cambridge University Press 1982
Cambridge University Press 1989
Cambridge University Press 1992
Cambridge University Press 1994
Cambridge University Press 1996
Can Yay 1989
Candlewick Press 1996
Canova 1952
Cape, Jonathan 1920
Cape, Jonathan 1921
Cape, Jonathan 1922
Cape, Jonathan 1930
Cape, Jonathan 1936
Cape, Jonathan 1981
Cape, Jonathan; E. P. Dutton 1925
Capito, Wolfgang [Vuolffgangus
    Cephalaeus] 1525
Capito, Wolfgang [Vuolffgangus
    Cephalaeus] 1534
Capito, Wolfgang [Vuolffgangus
    Cephalaeus] 1542
Capito, Wolfgang [Vuolffgangus
    Cephalaeus] 1550
Capito, Wolfgang [Vuolffgangus
    Cephalaeus] 1563
Cappelli 1968
Cappelli, L. 1920
Cappelli, L. 1947
Capxaney al-Hawadith 1981
Carey, M. 1794
Carli, Fr. 1784
Carli, Nic. 1810–12
Carlton House 1900?
Carlton House 1918
Carlton House 1950
Caroli, Pazzini, Fratres 1777
Carruthers, R. and Sons 1937
Casa Editorialea Regina 1997
Casa Editrice Gismondi 1948
Casa Scoalelor 1923
Caselli, P. 1823
Cassell 1890
Cassell 1909
Cassell 1960
Cassell 1961
Castel de Courval 1825
Castel-Courval 1826
Castilla 1788
Catedra 1989
Catedra 1990
Cavalier, Henrico Giblet 1653
Cawood, John 1553
Centro Grafico Santa Reparata 1971
Cercle du Bibliophile 1967
Cervicornus, Euchahrius 1523
Cervicornus, Euchahrius 1527
Cervicornus, Euchahrius 1534
Ceska Akademie Caisaere
    Frantieska Josefa 1911–12
Chalmers 1806
Chambeau 1820
Chancellor Press 1986
Chang-har I wen chu pan she 1985
Chapman and Hall 1875

Chappelet, Sebastian 1619
Chappelet, Sebastian 1626
Chappelet, Sebastian 1639
Charpentier 1845
Charpentier 1846
Charpentier 1855
Charpentier 1861
Charpentier 1865
Charpentier 1866
Charpentier 1869
Chatto and Windus 1875
Chatto and Windus 1892
Chatto and Windus 1902
Chatto and Windus 1903
Chatto and Windus 1924
Chautauqua Press 1909
Checkerboard Press 1993
Cheng wen shu cheu 1972
Cheng wen shu chu 1971
Cheongeumsa 1979
Chez tous les libraries 1865
Chi Ssu Wen Hua Shih Yeh Yu
    Hsien Kung Ssu 1988
Chiantore, G. 1921–23
Chierici 1838
Chih Wen Chu Pan She 1991
Chih wen ch'u pan she 1983
Chih Wen Shu Pan She 1984
Chiswick Press 1898
Chiswick Press 1901
Christopher Publishing House 1932
Ch'ulp'ansa, Kyerim 1983
Cia .General de Ediciones 1980
Cia. General de Ediciones 1951
Cia. General de Ediciones 1973
Ciardetti, L. 1821
Ciardetti, L. 1823
Ciardetti, L. 1825
Ciardetti, L. 1826
Circulo de Lectores 1971
Ciuffetti, D. 1703
Clarendon Press 1583
Clarendon Press 1780
Clarendon Press 1800
Clarendon Press 1808
Clarendon Press 1811
Clarendon Press 1817
Clarendon Press 1821
Clarendon Press 1827
Clarendon Press 1834
Clarendon Press 1870–78
Clarendon Press 1873
Clarendon Press 1878
Clarendon Press 1878–95
Clarendon Press 1880
Clarendon Press 1882
Clarendon Press 1882–84
Clarendon Press 1884
Clarendon Press 1884–97
Clarendon Press 1885
Clarendon Press 1886
Clarendon Press 1886–01
Clarendon Press 1887
Clarendon Press 1888
Clarendon Press 1889

Crampton, P. 1737
Crapelet 1822
Cratonis Mylii 1540
Cravotto, Martin 1572
CREDSA 1972
Cree 1909
Creech, William et al. 1809
Creede, Thomas 1596
Cresset Press 1928
Creutziger, Johann 1567
Creuzevault 1952
Crispinus, Ioannis 1559
Crispinus, Ioannis 1567
Crispinus, Ioannis 1570
Crissy and Markley 1850
Crissy and Markley 1853
Crissy and Markley 1939
Crissy, J. 1845
Criterion Books 1956
Crook, William 1673
Crook, William 1675
Crook, William 1677
Crook, William 1684
Crook, William 1686
Crosby Lockwood 1887
Crowell, T. Y. 1853
Crowell, T. Y. 1890s
Crowell, T. Y. 1923
Crowell, T. Y. 1968
Crownfield, Corn. 1711
Crukshank, J. 1795
Crusius 1790
Cuelens, G. 1829
Cumming and Ferguson 1846
Cumming, J. (at University Press) 1833
Cumming, J. at the Hibernia Press 1819
Cuthell, J. 1815
Cuthell, J. 1825
Cuthell, J., etc. 1821
Cuthell, J.; J. Nunn, Lackington et al. 1815
Cyber Classics 1997
Czytelnik 1953
Czytelnik 1956
Czytelnik 1965
Czytelnik 1990
D. F. Editora Nacional 1973
Daniel, Roger 1657
D'Anna, G. 1973
Dar al-Awdah 1986
Dar al-Ilm lil-Malayin 1979
Dar al-Ilm lil-Malayin 1980
Dar al-Ilm lil-Malayin 1982
Dar al-Maarifah 1900
Dar Iohya al-Turath al-Arabai 1980
Dase, J. 1879
Davies, T. et al. 1773
Davies, T. et al. 1774
Davison, T. 1808
de Gourmont, Gilles 1507
de Gourmont, Gilles 1521
de Gourmont, Gilles 1523

De Gruyter, Walter 1929
De Kinkhoren 1943
De Kinkhoren 1944
De La Compagnie 1712–17
De La Compagnie 1717
De Serra Hnos. y Russel 1913
De Silver, C. 1860
De Silver, C. 1863
De Silver, C., and Sons 1888
de Tournes, Ioan. 1629
de Tournes, Ioan. 1639
Debit 1994
Debrett 1792
Deel I. 1810
Deighton, Bell; Whittaker; George Bell and Sons 1883
Deis 1828
Delacorte Press 1996
Delagrave 1927
Delalain, Aug. 1815
Delalain, Aug. 1816
Delalain, Aug. 1816–18
Delalain, Aug. 1818
Delalain, Aug. 1826–28
Delalain, Aug. 1827
Delalain, Aug. 1828
Delalain, Aug. 1829
Delalain, Aug. 1832
Delalain, Jules, et Fils 1876
Delf 1852
Delfino 1976
Delfino 1977
Dell Publishing 1969
Demetriades, Ph. 1968
Demonville 1776
Denham, A. 1872
Denoel 1945
Dent, J. M. 1897
Dent, J. M. 1898
Dent, J. M. 1900
Dent, J. M. 1901
Dent, J. M. 1906
Dent, J. M. 1916
Dent, J. M. 1920
Dent, J. M. 1933
Dent, J. M. 1948
Dent, J. M. 1961
Dent, J. M. and Sons 1938
Dent, J. M. and Sons; E. P. Dutton 1910
Dent, J. M. and Sons; E. P. Dutton 1913
Dent, J. M. and Sons; E. P. Dutton 1920
Dent, J. M. and Sons; E. P. Dutton 1925
Dent, J. M. and Sons; E. P. Dutton 1931
Dent, J. M. and Sons; E. P. Dutton 1955
Dent, J. M. and Sons; E. P. Dutton 1963
Dent, J. M.; E. P. Dutton 1910
Dent, J. M.; E. P. Dutton 1912
Dent, J. M.; E. P. Dutton 1914

Dent, J. M.; E. P. Dutton 1921
Dent, J. M.; E. P. Dutton 1928
Dent, J. M.; E. P. Dutton 1931
Dent, J. M.; E. P. Dutton 1935
Dent, J. M.; E. P. Dutton 1944
Dent, J. M.; E. P. Dutton 1948
Dent, J. M.; E. P. Dutton 1953
Dentu, J. G. 1804
Dentu, J. G. 1810
Der Tempel 1900
Derzhavne vyd-vo khudozhnoi literatury 1963
Desbordes, R. J. 1755
Desilver, C. 1872
Dessain, H. 1962
Detskaeila lit-ra 1987
Deutsche Buch-Gemeinschaft 1927
Deutscher Bucherbund 1957
Deutscher Taschenbuch Verlag 1979
Deutsches Verlagshaus Bong 1911
Devir 1952
Devriena, A. F. 1890s
Diatton 1994
Didot 1789
Didot l'aine 1787–88
Didot, Ambrosio Firmin 1786
Didot, Ambrosio Firmin 1828–34
Didot, Ambrosio Firmin 1837–38
Didot, Ambrosio Firmin 1843
Didot, Ambrosio Firmin 1856
Didot, Ambrosio Firmin 1860
Didot, Ambrosio Firmin 1862
Didot, Ambrosio Firmin 1864
Didot, Ambrosio Firmin 1866
Didot, Ambrosio Firmin 1871
Didot, Ambrosio Firmin 1877
Didot, Ambrosio Firmin 1878
Didot, Ambrosio Firmin 1881
Didot, Ambrosio Firmin 1888
Didot, Ambrosio Firmin 1896
Didot, Ambrosio Firmin 1937
Didot, Ambrosio Firmin, Freres 1833
Didot, Ambrosio Firmin, Freres 1837
Didot, Ambrosio Firmin, Freres 1853
Diederichs 1927
Diesterweg, Moritz 1876
Diesterweg, Moritz 1890s
Diesterweg, Moritz 1911
Diesterweg, Moritz 1918
Diesterweg, Moritz 1940
Diesterweg, Moritz 1962
Diesterweg, Moritz 1979
Dieterich'sche Verlagbuchhandlung 1947
Dieterich'sche Verlagsbuchhandlung 1835
Dieterich'sche Verlagsbuchhandlung 1844
Dieterich'sche Verlagsbuchhandlung 1995

Dilly 1781
Diogenes 1980
Ditchling Press 1956
Dnipro 1968
Dnipro 1978
Dodd, Mead 1959
Dodone 1972
Dodsley 1767
Dole, N. H. 1904
Domin. Rocociolum 1498
Donaldson, Alexander 1767
Donaldson, Alexander 1778
Donaldson, Alexander; J. Reid 1763
Dorffling & Francke; Williams & Norgate 1865
Dorling Kindersley 2000
Dorset Press 1991
Doubleday 1959
Doubleday 1962
Doubleday 1971
Doubleday 1988
Dove, J. F. 1720
Dove, J. F. 1824
Dover Publications 1999
Dover; Constable 1999
Drezavna Zaloezba Slovenije 1950
Drezavna Zaloezba Slovenije 1951
Droemersche Verlagsanstalt Th. Knaur Nachf. 1960
Droernersche Verlagsanstalt Th. Knaur Nachf 1961
Du Roveray, F. J. 1805–06
Du Villard Fils and Nouffer 1779
Duckworth 1971
Duckworth 2000
Dummler, F. 1879
Duncan 1819
Duncan, Andr. 1814
Duncan, J. [etc.] 1838
Dupont, P. 1884
Dupuis 1984
Dupuis, Greg. 1714
Durell, William; C. S. Van Winkle 1812
Durell, William; D. and G. Bruce 1812
Durell, William; Elliot's Press 1808
Durell, William; J. Seymour 1808
Durr, A. 1872
Durr, A. 1878
Durr, A. 1879
Durr, A. 1881
Dutton, E. P. 1898
Dutton, E. P. 1900
Dutton, E. P. 1921
Dutton, E. P. 1922
Dutton, E. P. 1923
Dutton, E. P. 1928
Dutton, E. P. 1967
Dutton, E. P.; J. M. Dent & Sons 1930
Duvv, Alphonse 1873
Duyckinck 1814

Dyk 1771–73
Dyk 1781
E.R.I. 1968
E.T.E. 1990
Easton Press 1978
Easton Press 1979
Ebeling, H, & C. Plahn 1870
Ed. de stat Pentru Literaturaea ost artaea 1955
Ed. Tor 1951
EDAF 1970
EDAF 1981
EDAF 1984
EDAF 1988
EDC Publ. 1999
Ediciones AFHA Internacional 1976
Ediciones Auriga 1987
Ediciones Avesta 1971–85
Ediciones B 1990
Ediciones de la Universidad de Puerto Rico 1956
Ediciones de la Universidad de Puerto Rico 1962
Ediciones de la Universidad de Puerto Rico 1974
Ediciones del Partenon 1976
Ediciones General Anaya 1986
Ediciones Ibericas 1900
Ediciones Montena 1981
Ediciones Moreton 1960
Ediciones Selectas, Editorial Epoca 1982
Ediciones Universal 1970
Ediciones Universal 1972
Ediciones y Distribuciones Alba 1985
Ediciones Zeus 1971
Edicins Catalanes 1953
Edicins de la Magrana 1993
Edicoes Melhoramentos 1962
Edicomunicacion 1992
Edicomunicacion 1994
Edil 1973
Edime 1962
Edime 1965
Edition d'Art, H. Piazza 1899
Editions "Labor" 1951
Editions de la Difference 1989
Editions de la Difference 1991
Editions for the Armed Forces 1940
Editions for the Armed Services 1932
Editions Glenat 1981
Editions Graphiques Internationales 1956
Editions La Decouverte 1992
Editions Rencontre 1970
Editora Latino Americana 1959
Editora Latino Americana 1974
Editora Nacional 1967
Editora Nacional 1976
Editora Nacional 1978
Editoral Gredos 1991

Editores Mexicanos Unidos 1980
Editores Mexicanos Unidos 1981
Editores Mexicanos Unidos 1982
Editores Mexicanos Unidos 1984
Editores Mexicanos Unidos 1985
Editores Mexicanos Unidos 1992
Editori Laterza 1971
Editoria Universitaria 1997
Editoria Universitaria 1998
Editorial Alpha 1953
Editorial Andres Bello 1990
Editorial Andres Bello 1998
Editorial Araluce 1955
Editorial Arte y Literatura 1985
Editorial Arte y Literatura 1993
Editorial Atlantida 1940
Editorial Bedout 1986
Editorial Bruguera 1967
Editorial Bruguera 1972
Editorial Bruguera 1974
Editorial Bruguera 1976
Editorial Catalana 1919
Editorial Concepto 1980
Editorial Cumbre 1981
Editorial de la Universidad de Puerto Rico 1967
Editorial de la Universidad de Puerto Rico 1991
Editorial del Valle de Mexico 1976
Editorial Don Bosco 1981
Editorial Epoca 1982
Editorial Ercilla 1984
Editorial Ercilla 1985
Editorial Everest 1973
Editorial Everest 1980
Editorial Everest 1985
Editorial Gredos 1982
Editorial Iberia 1959
Editorial Iberica 1919
Editorial Juventud 1962
Editorial Juventud 1973
Editorial Juventud 1984
Editorial Juventud 1993
Editorial Limusa 1988
Editorial Limusa 1994
Editorial Losada 1951
Editorial Losada 1968
Editorial Losada 1970
Editorial Losada 1971
Editorial Losada 1983
Editorial Mediterraneo 1973
Editorial Mediterraneo 1974
Editorial Nueva Nicaragua 1984
Editorial Planeta 1968
Editorial Porrua 1959
Editorial Porrua 1960
Editorial Porrua 1964
Editorial Porrua 1965
Editorial Porrua 1966
Editorial Porrua 1969
Editorial Porrua 1970
Editorial Porrua 1971
Editorial Porrua 1972
Editorial Porrua 1973
Editorial Porrua 1974

Gleerup, C. W. K. 1949
Gleerup, C. W. K. 1959
Gleerup, C. W. K. 1962
Gleerup, C. W. K. 1963
Gleerup, C. W. K. 1965
Globe Book Co. 1948
Globe Book Co. 1960
Globe Book Co. 1968
Globe Book Co. 1978
Globe Book Co. 1984
Globe Book Co. 1986
Globe Book Co. 1992
Globe Fearon Education Publisher 1999
Globe School Book Co. 1900
Gluck, Johannes; Bartholomaei Voigt 1622
Glykus, Nikolaos 1803
Glykus, Nikolaos 1805
Glykus, Nikolaos 1821
Godfridum Back 1495
Godsche 1809–14
Godsche 1820
Godwin, J. J., and Co. 1819
Goedsche, F. W. 1788–93
Goedsche, F. W. 1818–19
Golan, Yaron 1994
Golan, Yaron 1995
Gold, Harry (Aberdeen Book Co.) 1979
Golden Cockerel Press 1948
Golden Press 1956
Golden Press 1964
Goldmann 1960
Goldmann 1980
Goldmann 1991
Gomer, Gwasg 1976
Gonin, Andre 1957
Gorchs, T. 1851
Gos. Izd-vo Khudozh Lit-ry 1935
Gos. Izd-vo Khudozh Lit-ry 1952
Gos. Izd-vo Khudozh Lit-ry 1953
Gos. Izd-vo Khudozh Lit-ry 1956
Gos. Izd-vo Khudozh Lit-ry 1958
Gos. Izd-vo Khudozh Lit-ry 1960
Gos. Izd-vo Khudozhestvennoaei lit-ry 1959
Gos. izd-vo Khuodozh Lit-ry 1949
Goschen, G. I. 1804–07
Goschen, G. I. 1806
Goschen, G. I. 1807
Goschen, G. I. 1817
Gosudarstvennoe izd-vo Khu-dozhestvennoaei lit-ry 1953
Goujon, A. 1832
Goujon, A. 1852
Government Oriental Manuscripts Library 1961
Grabert-Verlag 1980
Grabhorn Press 1927
Grabner, G. 1876
Grafag 1995
Graficas Expres 1962
Grafton 1938
Graham & Son 1818–19

Grahn 1814–15
Graisberry, R. 1834
Grant 1843
Grapheum, Io. 1528
Graphikes Technes Nikotyp 1986
Grasse, Nic. 1634
Great Books Foundation 1950
Great Books Foundation 1955
Great Books Foundation 1962
Great Books Foundation 1963
Great Books Foundation 1966
Greening 1902
Greenwich House 1982
Gregoriades, B. N. 1974
Grevel; B. Westermann 1892
Grieben, T. 1881
Griffin 1853
Griggs, S. C. 1872
Griggs, S. C. 1878
Griggs, S. C. 1880
Griggs, S. C. 1882
Griggs, S. C. 1883
Griggs, S. C. 1884
Griggs, S. C. 1885
Griggs, S. C. 1886
Griggs, S. C. 1889
Grignani, Lodovico; Lorenzo Lupis 1620
Grimmelshausen-Gesellschaft 1986
Griveav, Georgius 1619
Grolier Enterprises 1968
Grolier Enterprises 1968–75
Grolier Enterprises 1969
Grolier Enterprises 1972
Grolier Enterprises 1978
Grolier Enterprises 1980
Gronenberg, Joannem 1511
Groombridge and Sons 1867
Grosset & Dunlap 1961
Grosset and Dunlap 1950
Grosset and Dunlap 1970
Grouleau, Estienne 1555
Gryphius, Sebastian 1541
Gudmhain 1844–69
Guigoni, M. 1873
Guillard, Carolas 1545
Guillemot, Math. 1619
Guillemot, Math. 1639
Guillemot, Math. 1681
Gujarata Sahitya Akadami 1993
Gutenberg 1979
Gutzmann 1897
Gyldendal 1830
Gyldendal 1989
Gyldendal Norsk Forlag 1958
Gyldendals Bogklubber 1994
Gyldendalske 1916
Gyorb 1788
Gyorgy, Kilian 1857
Haas, F. 1800
Haasische Buchhandlung 1814
Haasische Buchhandlung 1816
Hachette 1829
Hachette, L. 1843–79

Hachette, L. 1848
Hachette, L. 1849
Hachette, L. 1850
Hachette, L. 1854–59
Hachette, L. 1856
Hachette, L. 1857
Hachette, L. 1860
Hachette, L. 1861
Hachette, L. 1863
Hachette, L. 1866
Hachette, L. 1869
Hachette, L. 1869–75
Hachette, L. 1870
Hachette, L. 1873
Hachette, L. 1875
Hachette, L. 1880
Hachette, L. 1882
Hachette, L. 1883
Hachette, L. 1883–84
Hachette, L. 1886
Hachette, L. 1887–88
Hachette, L. 1890
Hachette, L. 1890s
Hachette, L. 1893
Hachette, L. 1895
Hachette, L. 1899
Hachette, L. 1904
Hachette, L. 1907
Hachette, L. 1911
Hachette, L. 1928
Hachette, L. 1930
Hachette, L. 1932
Hachette, L. 1939
Hachette, L. 1952
Hachette, L. 1969
Hachette, L. 1971
Hachette, L. 1979
Hachette, L. 1991
Hachette, L. 1992
Hackett Pub. 1997
Hackett Pub. 2000
Hackius, Fr. 1656
Haenlinius, Gregorius 1637
Hahn 1832–35
Hahn 1837–39
Hahn 1842
Hahn 1843–49
Hahn 1844–53
Hahn 1845–49
Hahn 1848–57
Hahn 1849–57
Hahn 1863
Hahn 1872–75
Hahn 1872–93
Hakkert, Adolf M. 1960
Hakkert, Adolf M. 1964
Hakkert, Adolf M. 1965
Hakkert, Adolf M. 1971
Hakkert, Adolf M. 1980
Hakkert, Adolf M.; Oxford University Press 1963
Halcyon Press 1929
Haldeman-Julius Publications 1945
Hale 1961

International Collectors Library
1974
International Collector's Library
1951
International Pub. Co. 1888
Internationalen Bibliothek 1949
Intisharat-I Ilmi va Farhangi 1996
Irvington Publishers 1931
Istituto Editoriale Italiano 1920s
Istuti Editoriali e Poligrafici Inter-
nazionali 1996
Izdevnieciba "Liesma" 1967
Izd-vo "Khudozhestvennaeiia lit-
eratura" 1981
Izd-vo "Khudozhestvennaeiia Lit-
eraturea" 1986
Izd-vo TSK LKSMU "molod"
1982
Izglitibas Ministrijas Izdevums
1936
J., T. 1718
J., T. 1728
Jack, T. C. and E. C.; E. P. Dutton
1907
Jack, T. C. and E. C.; E. P. Dutton;
T. Nelson and S 1910
Jackson, W. M. 1966
Jackson, W. M. 1974
Jackson, Walford and Hodder
1865
Janes, Jose 1953
Jankovic, Pietro 1895
Jean de (Wittemberg)Wiridimon-
tanus or Frunenberger 1513
Jen Min Wen Hseueh chu Pan She
1997
Jesuit Educational Association
1960
Johnsen, Th; E. Poroarson; E. Jon-
sson; J. Arnason 1855
Johnson 1788
Johnson 1881
Johnson, B. F. 1901
Johnson, J. 1791
Johnson, J. 1801
Johnson, J. 1802
Johnson, J. 1806
Johnson, J. 1810
Jones and Company 1824
Jones and Company 1826
Jordan, Wilhelm 1875
Jordan, Wilhelm 1889
Jordan, Wilhelm 1892
Jordan, Wilhelm; F. Volckmar
1881
Juch, G. 1911
Junge 1799
Junta, Luca Antonius 1537
Juste, Francois 1534
Juventud 1960
Juventud 1961
Juventud 1971
Juventud 1987
Juventud 1999
Juvenum, Martin 1581

Kaktos 1992
Karabet ve Kasbar Matbaasi 1887
Kastaniote 1997
Kayser 1826–28
Kazankalov, S. D. 1918
Kegan, Paul, Trench 1881
Kelly 1867
Kelly/Winterton Press 1982
Kenkyusha 1952
Keosel 1952
Kepziomiuveszeti Alap Kiadoval-
lalata 1973
Kesselring 1820
Keter 1996
Keumseong Chulpansa 1984
Keystone Pub. Co. 1890
Keystone Pub. Co. 1890s
Khudozh Lit-ra 1978
Khudozh Lit-ra 1986
Khudozhestvennaiia literatura
1967
Kiadja a Terra 1959
Kincaid, A. and W. Creech and J.
Balfour 1733
Kindersley, Dorling 2000
Kingfisher 1987
Kingfisher 1994
Kingfisher 1997
Kingfisher 2000
Kirchner, C. 1897
Kirton, J. P. 1977
Kirton, J. P. 1984
Kitabevi, Sander 1967
Kitabkhana-yi Sharq 1925
Klett-Cotta 1981
Klincksieck 1970
Klub zameestnanceu Leecebneho
1937
Knapton, Jac. And Joa. 1729–40
Knapton, John and Paul 1740
Knapton, John and Paul 1754
Knapton, John and Paul 1802
Knight, C. 1843
Knight, Charles 1943
Knoblouch, Joh. 1523
Knopf 1922
Knopf 1992
Knott and Lloyd 1805
Knott and Lloyd 1807
Knott and Lloyd 1810
Knyharni Haukovoho t-va im.
Shevchenka 1902–04
Kohles, J. G. 1707
Kohlhammer 1894
Kolaitis, M. 1983
Kollaros, I. D. 1936
Kollaros, I. D. 1950
Kommission bei E. Avenarius 1911
Konegen, Carl; Ernst Stulpnagel
1908
Konkordia 1931
Koromela, Andreas 1872
Korte 1778
Korte 1787
Korte 1793

Kosel 1954
Kostnao Bessastaoa Skola 1829–40
Krais and Hoffmann 1864–74
Krajowa Agencja Wydawnicza
1982
Krieger 1815
Krieger 1822
Krieger 1826
Kristall Respeks 1998
Ksiaznica Atlas 1932
Kummer 1781–87
Kyriakou, P. D. 1928
La Compagnie des Bibliophiles de
l'Automobile-Club 1930–33
La Galera 1993
La Nuova Italia 1958
La Nuova Italia 1960
La Nuova Italia 1964
La Roccae, J 1946
La Scuola 1925
La Scuola 1926
Labor, Ed. 1947
Lackington, Allen 1806
Laffont 1995
Laichter, J. 1904
Laichter, J. 1921
Laichter, J. 1926
Laichter, J. 1942
Lake Education 1994
Lampel 1902
Lampel 1905
Land, John 1907
Landes 1829–31
Landsberg, Martin 1496?
Lane, Allen 1973
L'Angelier, Abel 1584
L'Angelier, Abel 1597
L'Angelier, Abel 1604
Langen-Muller 1980
Langenscheidt, G. 1866–98
Langenscheidt, G. 1874
Lanneau 1825
Lapi, S. 1887
Larousse 1934
Lasneau 1825
Laterza, G. 1925
Laterza, G. and Sons 1928
Latino Americana 1963
Lattes, S. 1935
Lattes, S. 1946
Lattes, S. 1956
Lattes, S. 1959
Latvijas Valsts isdevnieciba 1961
Laurentius, Henricus 1648
Lausanne etc, Payot et al. 1936
Lavigne 1842–43
L'Avocat 1823
Law, Charles H. 1854
Lazychy 1986
Le Livre de Poche 1962
Le Monnier, Felice 1861
Le Monnier, Felice 1934
Le Monnier, Felice 1936
Le Monnier, Felice 1958
Le Monnier, Felice 1959

Lovell, John W. 1890s
Low 1870
Low 1881
Low 1889
Lownes, H. 1609?
Loys, Jehan 1545
Lu Chiao Wen Hua Shih Yeh Yu
  Hsien Kung Ssu 1991
Lu Chiao Wen Hus Shih Yeh Yu
  Hsien Kung Ssu 1998
Lucas, R.; N. G. Maxwell 1819
Luchtmanniensis and Holtropianis
  1809
Luchtmans 1808
Luchtmans, Samuel and Joann.
  1780
Luchtmans, Samuel and Joann.
  1782
Luchtmans, Samuel and Joann.
  1802
Luchtmans, Samuel and Joann.
  1823
Lucius, Jacob 1598–01
Lunn, P. 1947
M. E. Editores 1995
Maatschappij voor Doede en
  Doedkoope Lectuur 1910
MacBean, Charles E. 1973
Macdonald 1959
Macham, S. 1610
Mackail, J. W. 1906
Macmillan 1844
Macmillan 1858
Macmillan 1864
Macmillan 1866
Macmillan 1871
Macmillan 1878
Macmillan 1879
Macmillan 1881
Macmillan 1882
Macmillan 1883
Macmillan 1884
Macmillan 1885
Macmillan 1886
Macmillan 1886–88
Macmillan 1887
Macmillan 1888
Macmillan 1888–00
Macmillan 1889
Macmillan 1890
Macmillan 1891
Macmillan 1892
Macmillan 1893
Macmillan 1894
Macmillan 1895
Macmillan 1897
Macmillan 1898
Macmillan 1898
Macmillan 1899
Macmillan 1900
Macmillan 1900–02
Macmillan 1901
Macmillan 1902
Macmillan 1903
Macmillan 1904

Macmillan 1905
Macmillan 1906
Macmillan 1907
Macmillan 1908–11
Macmillan 1909
Macmillan 1910
Macmillan 1911
Macmillan 1911
Macmillan 1912
Macmillan 1914
Macmillan 1915
Macmillan 1916
Macmillan 1917
Macmillan 1918
Macmillan 1919
Macmillan 1920
Macmillan 1921
Macmillan 1922
Macmillan 1923
Macmillan 1924
Macmillan 1925
Macmillan 1926
Macmillan 1927
Macmillan 1928
Macmillan 1929
Macmillan 1930
Macmillan 1931
Macmillan 1932
Macmillan 1933
Macmillan 1934
Macmillan 1935
Macmillan 1936
Macmillan 1937
Macmillan 1938
Macmillan 1939
Macmillan 1940
Macmillan 1941
Macmillan 1942
Macmillan 1944
Macmillan 1945
Macmillan 1946
Macmillan 1947
Macmillan 1947–48
Macmillan 1948
Macmillan 1949
Macmillan 1950
Macmillan 1951
Macmillan 1952
Macmillan 1954
Macmillan 1956
Macmillan 1957
Macmillan 1958
Macmillan 1960
Macmillan 1961
Macmillan 1964
Macmillan 1965
Macmillan 1965–68
Macmillan 1966
Macmillan 1967
Macmillan 1968–71
Macmillan 1971
Macmillan 1974
Macmillan 1978
Macmillan 1986
Macmillan Education 1978

Macmillan Education 1984
Macmillan/McGraw Hill School
  Pub. 1993
Macmillan; Collier Macmillan
  Canada 1991
Macmillan; St. Martin's Press
  1895–98
Macmillan; St. Martin's Press 1898
Macmillan; St. Martin's Press
  1955–56
Macmillan; St. Martin's Press 1956
Macmillan; St. Martin's Press 1958
Macmillan; St. Martin's Press
  1959–60
Macmillan; St. Martin's Press
  1959–74
Macmillan; St. Martin's Press
  1960–62
Macmillan; St. Martin's Press
  1961–65
Macmillan; St. Martin's Press
  1964–67
Macmillan; St. Martin's Press
  1967–71
Macmillan; University Press 1915
Macri 1945
Madden, J. 1868
Magyar Helikon 1972
Magyar Helikon 1974
Maharashtra Rajya Sahitya San-
  skrti Mandala 1984
Maier, O. 1956
Maier, O. 1959
Maier, O. 1964
Maier, O. 1968
Maier, O. 1971
Maier, O. 1992
Maire, Ioannis 1632
Maison Quantin 1800
Maison Quantin 1886
Malatesta, Francesco 1753
Manceaux, H. 1883
Mandar; Devaux 1827
Manesse Verlag; Stamperia Val-
  donega 1983
Manfre, Giovanni 1742
Manfre, Joannes 1740
Manfre, Joannes 1760
Manfre, Joannes 1769
Manfre, Joannes; Typis Seminarii
  1777
Manfredi 1977
Mangen, Christoff; Elias Willers
  1617
Mangen, Christoph 1610
Mansut 1829
Manutius, Aldus Pius 1504
Manutius, Aldus Pius 1537
Manutius, Aldus Pius; Andreae
  Asvlani soceri 1517
Manutius, Aldus Pius; Andreae
  Asvlani soceri 1524
Marcus, A. 1921
Marcus, Adolph 1863–72
Margaret K. McElderry Books 1992

Oxford Warch. 1884–88
Oxford Warch. 1887
Oxford Warch. 1888
Paanstwowy Instytut Wydawn 1959
Paefraed, Albertus 1516
Pan Books 1977
Panepistemiakes Edkoseis Kretes 1995
Panstwowe Wydawn 1956
Panstwowy Instytut Wydawniczy 1990
Pantheon Books 1956
Panther Books 1965
Papademas, Dem. N. 1974
Papademas, Dem. N. 1975–80
Papademas, Dem. N. 1986
Papademas, Dem. N. 1987
Papademas, Dem. N. 1990
Papademas, Dem. N. 1991
Papademas, Dem. N. 1997
Papademetriou 1971
Paperinium, Bern. 1730–35
Papyros 1950
Paravia, G. B. 1919
Paravia, G. B. 1948
Paravia, G. B. 1951
Paravia, G. B. 1967
Paravia, G. B. 1968
Paravia, G. B. 1969
Paris, H. J. 1950
Parke, John W. 1846
Parke, Vincent 1909
Parker and Son 1849
Parker and Son 1857
Parker, H. 1855–56
Parker, J. 1868
Parker, J. 1869
Parker, J. 1904
Parker, Jacob, and Friends 1881
Parker, John Henry and Jacob 1849
Parker, John Henry and Jacob 1851
Parker, John Henry and Jacob 1860
Parker, John Henry and Jacob 1861
Parker, John Henry and Jacob 1864
Pasquali q. Mario 1803–4
Passaei, Cr. 1613
Passare, N. G. 1871
Passenger, T. 1670
Passenger, T. 1676
Passenger, T. 1680
Passenger, T. 1684
Passigli, Borghi 1831–32
Patrick 1811
Patron 1982
Patron 1997
Paul, Kegan 1890
Paul, Kegan; Trench 1886
Pauli Gulpen 1511?
Pavoni, Taddeo 1642

Payne 1804
Payot 1930
Pearson, C. Arthur 1899
Pechlivanides, M. 1960
Pelt 1798
Penada 1786–94
Pendulum Press 1979
Pendulum Press 1980
Penguin Books 1937
Penguin Books 1945
Penguin Books 1946
Penguin Books 1948
Penguin Books 1950
Penguin Books 1952
Penguin Books 1953
Penguin Books 1955
Penguin Books 1956
Penguin Books 1957
Penguin Books 1959
Penguin Books 1961
Penguin Books 1963
Penguin Books 1964
Penguin Books 1966
Penguin Books 1967
Penguin Books 1968
Penguin Books 1970
Penguin Books 1973
Penguin Books 1976
Penguin Books 1984
Penguin Books 1987
Penguin Books 1988
Penguin Books 1990
Penguin Books 1991
Penguin Books 1992
Penguin Books 1995
Penguin Books 1996
Penguin Books 1997
Penguin Books 1998
Penguin Education 1973
Penn Publishing 1890
Penn Publishing 1891
Penn Publishing 1895
Penn Publishing 1898
Penn Publishing 1901
Penn Publishing 1902
Penn Publishing 1910
Penn Publishing 1912
Penn Publishing 1924
Peomusa 1991
Peomusa 1993
Perault 1764
Perchacino, Gratioso 1564
Percival 1891
Perennial Library 1975
Pernas, Petrus 1573
Perthes 1823
Perthes, F. A. 1886–90
Perthes, F. A. 1900–02
Petit, Jehan 1530
Petrus de Nicolinis de Sabio, sumptu Melchioris Se 1547
Petrus de Nicolinis de Sabio, sumptu Melchioris Se 1551
Peypus, Frid. 1527
Pharson, W. 1791

Philippe 1829
Philippe 1830
Philippe le Noir 1526
Philippi, Johannis, de Lignamie 1474
Phoenix Books 1967
Pickering 1831
Pickering 1849
Pickering and Chatto 1888
Pickering, Marshall 1989
Pickering, William 1830
Pickering, William 1850
Pinelli, P. 1640
Pirotta 1847
Pitra, Samuel 1762
Pitteri, F. 1739
Plancher 1815
Planeta 1980
Planeta 1982
Planeta 1986
Planeta 1990
Planeta 1996
Plantin, Christopher 1568
Plantin, Christopher 1581–89
Plantin, Christopher 1585
Plantin, Christopher 1588
Plantin, Christopher 1589
Platt and Peck 1902
Playwrights Union of Canada 1986
Plaza and Janes 1982
Plon 1883–84
Pocket Books 1969
Pocket Books 1997
Poilleux 1830
Pokolenje, Mlado 1961
Polskiej Fundacji 1968
Pomba, G. 1829
Pomba, Vedova, e Figli 1816
Pomeroy, R. W. 1839
Ponsonby, et al. 1883
Poolsum, Georgius a 1685
Poolsum, Georgius a 1699
Pope, M. 1797
Porpentine Press 1990
Porter and Coates 1865
Porter and Coates 1870
Porter and Coates 1873
Porter and Coates 1900
Portonariis, Andrea de 1550
Portonariis, Vinc. de. 1538
Poussielgue, Ch. 1866
Powell, S. 1716
Prato 1790
Prault, Pierre 1716
Pravda 1985
President Publishing 1937
Presses Pocket 1989
Presses Universitaires de France 1964
Presses Universitaires de France 1972
Presso Turchi, Veroli e comp. 1825
Prevosteau, Steph. 1582
Priestley 1819

Priestley 1820
Priestley 1822
Priestley 1834
Priestly 1823
Prince; Elmsley 1788
Princeton University Press 1956
Princeton University Press 1967
Princeton University Press 1998
Principato, G. 1934
Priulla, G. 1951
Pro Ecclesia-Drukkery 1952
Prometeo 1920s
Propylaen-Verlag 1920
Propylaen-Verlag 1922
Propylaen-Verlag 1925
Prost, C; J. Bapt De Venet 1645
Prostant, J. R. 1722
Prosveschenie 1987
Proszyanski I s-ka 1998
Proszyanski I S-ka 1999
Psychountakes, G. 1979
Publiccoes Europa-America 1980s
Publiocoes Europa-America 1988
Puffin Books 1967
Puffin Books 1996
Puffin Books; Oxford University
  Press 1997
Purfoote, Thomas 1580
Pustet 1823
Putnam, G. P. 1850
Putnam, G. P. 1893
Putnam, G. P. 1915
Pyramid Books 1966
R. Stab. Musicale Ricordi 1880
Ragoczy 1830
Rain City Projects 1996
Raintree Childrens Books 1985
Raintree de Mexico Editores 1981
Raintree Publishers 1980
Raintree Publishers 1981
Raintree Steck-Vaughn 1992
Raiz y Rama 1943
Ralph Nevvbarie 1581
Ramanzini, Dionigi 1749
Rampazato, Francesco 1562
Rand, McNally 1903
Rand, McNally 1904
Rand, McNally 1926
Random House 1935
Random House 1950
Random House 1960
Random House 1963
Rapheleng, Fr. 1588
Rapp & Carroll 1967
Ravenstein, Joannes 1650
Ravesteyniuni, Joannes 1672
Recep Ulusoglu Basimevi 1941–42
Reclam, Philipp, jun. 1848
Reclam, Philipp, jun. 1872
Reclam, Philipp, jun. 1876
Reclam, Philipp, jun. 1890s
Reclam, Philipp, jun. 1892
Reclam, Philipp, jun. 1920
Reclam, Philipp, jun. 1923
Reclam, Philipp, jun. 1951

Reclam, Philipp, jun. 1979
Recurti, Battista 1751
Redmayne, John 1671
Redmayne, John 1679
Redmayne, John 1713
Redmayne, William 1706
Reeves and Turner 1864
Reeves and Turner 1887
Reeves and Turner 1897
Reeves and Turner 1983
Reeves and Turner; OR Smith
  1874
Regiae Acad. Typographi 1821
Reisland, O. R. 1935
Reiss, E. 1914
Reitzel, C. A. 1865
Reitzel, C. A. 1878
Reitzel, C. A. 1890
Rencontre 1952
Rendel, J. 1898
Renouard, A. A. 1815–18
Renouard, A. A. 1818
Reprint Services 1993
Reprint Services Corp. 1998
Rescius, Rutg. 1535
Rheinland 1900
Ricciardi, R. 1968
Richard 1560
Richards and Mallory, etc. 1816
Richards and Mallory; P. H. Nick-
  lin 1813
Richards, G. 1902
Richards, G. 1903
Richardson, G. Innys and J. et al.
  1755
Richardson, H. 1807
Richardus, Thd. 1562
Rigaud 1709
Rigaud 1711–20
Rigby 1981
Rihelius, Theodosius 1567
Rihelius, Theodosius 1572
Rihelius, Theodosius 1579?
Rilindja 1971
Ris, T. 1871
Ris, T. 1871–74
Ritter, C. 1908
Riverside Press 1929
Rivington 1819
Rivington 1827
Rivington 1836
Rivington 1850
Rivington 1851
Rivington 1859
Rivington 1860
Rivington 1861
Rivington 1862
Rivington 1871
Rivington 1900
Rivington, Charles 1774
Rivington, Charles; T. Osborne
  1760
Rivington, etc. 1861
Rivington, F. & J. 1853
Rivington, F. & J. [etc.] 1847

Rivington, F. C. and J. 1821–22
Rivington, F. C. and J., etc. 1818
Rivington, F. C. and J.; J. Walker
  1811
Rivington, J. & F. H. 1866
Rivingtons 1857
Rivingtons 1864
Rivingtons 1870
Rivingtons 1873
Rivingtons 1876
Rivingtons 1877
Rivingtons 1880
Rivingtons 1881
Rivingtons 1885–87
Rivingtons 1886
Rizzoli 1952
Rizzoli 1990
Rizzoli 1996
Robbins 1817
Roberts Rinehart Publishers 1991
Roberts, J. 1717
Robertson 1824
Robertson 1825
Robertson, J. 1773
Robertsons, E. and J. 1761
Robson, J. 1781
Rocca, Simon 1570
Roger Daniel 1648
Romangini 1788
Rooman, A. 1611
Rossieiia, Sov. 1990
Rossium, Jo. 1568
Roussin, Jacques 1602
Routledge 1993
Routledge and Kegan Paul 1951
Routledge and Kegan Paul 1957
Routledge and Kegan Paul 1967
Routledge and Sons 1888
Routledge Thoemmes Press 1992
Routledge, George 1720
Routledge, George 1858
Routledge, George 1860
Routledge, George 1864
Routledge, George 1876
Routledge, George 1884
Routledge, George 1886
Routledge, George 1887
Routledge, George 1889
Routledge, George 1890
Routledge, George 1891
Routledge, George 1895
Routledge, George 1897
Routledge, George 1907
Routledge, George, and Sons 1872
Routledge, George, and Sons 1903
Routledge, Warne, and Routledge
  1864
Routledge/Thoemmes Press 1997
Routledge; Warne and Routledge
  1864
Roveray, F. J. 1813
Rowohlt 1958
Rowohlt 1964
Rowohlt 1969
Rowohlt 1986

Simpkin, Marshall 1860
Simpkin, Marshall 1862
Simpkin, Marshall 1866
Simpkin, Marshall 1872–73
Simpkin, Marshall 1873
Simpkin, Marshall 1879
Simpkin, Marshall 1880
Simpkin, Marshall 1882
Simpkin, Marshall 1883
Simpkin, Marshall 1885
Simpkin, Marshall 1888
Simpkin, Marshall 1890
Simpkin, Marshall 1895
Simpkin, Marshall 1905
Simpkin, Marshall 1908
Simpkin, Marshall, Hamilton, Kent 1904
Simpkin, Marshall, Hamilton, Kent 1934
Simpkin, Marshall, Hamilton, Kent; Charles Scribne 1905
Sincino, Hieronymo 1515
Singer es Wolfner Kiadada 1927
Singer es Wolfner Kiadada 1947
Singer, L. W. 1942
Skala 1921
Skelton, Christopher 1973
Smesmannus, Abraham 1591
Smith, J. R. 1857
Smith, J. R. 1865
Smith, J. R. 1888
Smith, J. R. 1898
Smith, Samuel 1685
Smith, Samuel 1686
Smith, Samuel 1726
Smith, Samuel 1733
Smith, W. and W. et al. 1770
Smith, William 1839
SNL 1987
Soc. tipogr. 1822
Sociedad Comercial y Editorial Santiago Limitada; 1987
Sociedad Espanola de Estudios Classicos 1964
Sociedad Espanola de Estudios Classicos 1965
Sociedad General Espanola de Libreria 1982
Societa Anonima Editrice Francesco Perrella 1930
Societa Editrice Dante Alighieri di Albrighi, Sega 1905
Societa Editrice Dante Alighieri di Albrighi, Sega 1914
Societa Editrice Dante Alighieri di Albrighi, Sega 1956
Societa Editrice Dante Alighieri di Albrighi, Sega 1958
Societa Editrice Dante Alighieri di Albrighi, Sega 1960
Societa Editrice Dante Alighieri di Albrighi, Sega 1965
Societa Editrice Internazionale 1930
Societa Editrice Internazionale 1931

Societa Editrice internazionale 1937
Societa Editrice Sonzogno 1905
Societa Tipografica dei Classici Italiani 1820
Societe d'Edition "Les Belles Lettres" 1924
Societe d'Edition "Les Belles Lettres" 1925
Societe d'Edition "Les Belles Lettres" 1933
Societe d'Edition "Les Belles Lettres" 1936
Societe d'Edition "Les Belles Lettres" 1937
Societe d'Edition "Les Belles Lettres" 1939
Societe d'Edition "Les Belles Lettres" 1941
Societe d'Edition "Les Belles Lettres" 1946
Societe d'Edition "Les Belles Lettres" 1947–49
Societe d'Edition "Les Belles Lettres" 1953
Societe d'Edition "Les Belles Lettres" 1955–57
Societe d'Edition "Les Belles Lettres" 1955–59
Societe d'Edition "Les Belles Lettres" 1959
Societe d'Edition "Les Belles Lettres" 1961–63
Societe d'Edition "Les Belles Lettres" 1962
Societe d'Edition "Les Belles Lettres" 1965–67
Societe d'Edition "Les Belles Lettres" 1967
Societe d'Edition "Les Belles Lettres" 1967–68
Societe d'Edition "Les Belles Lettres" 1967–70
Societe d'Edition "Les Belles Lettres" 1972–87
Societe d'Edition "Les Belles Lettres" 1974
Societe d'Edition "Les Belles Lettres" 1974–89
Societe d'Edition "Les Belles Lettres" 1976
Societe d'Edition "Les Belles Lettres" 1982–92
Societe d'Edition "Les Belles Lettres" 1987
Societe d'Edition "Les Belles Lettres" 1987–92
Societe d'Edition "Les Belles Lettres" 1992
Societe d'Edition "Les Belles Lettres" 1995
Societe d'Edition "Les Belles Lettres" 1997
Societe d'Edition "Les Belles Lettres" 1998

Soderstrom, W. 1916
Soderstrom, W. 1919
Soncinam, Hieronymus 1508
Soncinam, Hieronymus 1509
Sonnenschein 1900
Sonzogno, Edoardo 1880
Sonzogno, Edoardo 1885
Sonzogno, Edoardo 1896
Sopena Argentina 1962
Sopena, Ramon 1976
Soter, Ioannes 1540
Spamersche Buchdruckerei 1912
Speed, Samuel 1663
Spemann, W. 1883
Spemann, W. 1899
Spisovateil, Slovensky 1966
Spisovateil, Slovensky 1986
Spottiswoode 1883
Spring Publications 1970
Springer, J. 1905
Springer, J. 1923
Sreberok, Yosef 1964
Srpska, Matica 1985
St. Martin's Press 1963
St. Martin's Press 1965
St. Martin's Press 1965–74
St. Martin's Press 1966
St. Martin's Press 1968
St. Martin's Press 1974
St. Martin's Press 1978–84
St. Martin's Press 1984
St. Martin's Press 1987
Stafford, S. 1613
Stamperia del Seminario 1746
Stamperia delle Muse 1821–28
Stamperia Francese 1825
Stampfli 1962
Standaard-Boekhandel 1944
Stanford 1873
Starke 1819
Starkium, William 1813
Starkium, William 1815
Starkium, William 1821–22
Statni Nakladatelstvi Krasne Literatury 1956
Steampfli 1907
Steck-Vaughn 1991
Steelsio, Juan 1550
Steelsio, Juan 1553
Steelsio, Juan 1556
Stella 1825
Stephanus, Henricus 1566
Stephanus, Henricus 1573
Stephanus, Henricus 1578
Stephanus, Henricus 1588
Stephanus, Paul 1604
Stigme 1988
Stigme 1991
Stigme 1992
Stigme 1993
Stigme 1994
Stoer, Iac. 1617
Stoesselios 1767
Stoesselios, Fratres 1745–53
Stokes, Frederick A. 1894

Stokes, Frederick A. 1926
Strahan 1867
Strahan 1869
Straub, L. 1667
Stricker, Nicolai 1874
Suhrkamp 1943
Sumptibus Librariae Scholarum
  Regiae 1839
Sun Hill Rose 2000
Sunburst 1994
Suomalaisen Kirjallisuuden Seuera
  1990
Suttaby, Evance 1805
Suttaby, Evance 1818
Suttaby, Evance; Crosby 1811
Suttaby, W. et al. 1809
Suttaby, W.; C. Corral 1805
Suttaby, W.; Crosby et al. 1808
Sutton 1986
Suvorina, A. S. 1884
Suvorina, A. S. 1892
Suymour, J. 1908
Svaz slovenskyych spisovatelovv
  1962
Svensk Leararetidnings 1955
Swiderski, B. 1961
Sylvanus, George 1685
Szepirodalmi Keonyvkiado 1972
Ta Chien Chu Pan Shih Yeh Kung
  Ssu 1984
Ta Chien Chu Pan Shih Yeh Kung
  Ssu 1993
Ta Hsia Chu Pan She 1991
Tacuini, Ioannis, de Tridino 1502
Taeil Chulpansa 1997
Tai-wan Hseueh Sheng Shu Cheu
  1994
Taiwan shang wu yin shu kuan
  1966
Talboys; Pickering 1831
Tanguk Taehakkyo Chulpanbu
  1996
Taning & Appel 1993
Tauchnitz 1826
Tauchnitz, Bernhardi 1854
Tauchnitz, Car. 1810
Tauchnitz, Car. 1818
Tauchnitz, Car. 1819
Tauchnitz, Car. 1825
Tauchnitz, Car. 1826-27
Tauchnitz, Car. 1828-29
Tauchnitz, Car. 1894
Taylor, J. 1827-28
Tegg, W. 1846
Tegg, W. 1854
Tegg, W. 1858-59
Tegg, W. 1860
Tegg, W. 1877
Teide 1970
Tempel-Verlag 1914
Tempel-Verlag 1920s
Tempel-Verlag 1922
Tempel-Verlag 1930
Tempel-Verlag 1956
Tempel-Verlag 1960

Tempel-Verlag 1966
Tempsky, F. F. 1856-58
Tempsky, F. F. 1884
Tempsky, F. F. 1886-87
Tempsky, F. F. 1889
Tempsky, F. F. 1892
Tempsky, F. F. 1901
Tempsky, F. F. 1903
Tempsky, F. F. 1920
Tempsky, F. F.; G. Freytag 1890-91
Tempsky, F. F.; G. Freytag 1894
Tempsky, F. F.; G. Freytag
  1894-96
Tempsky, F. F.; G. Freytag 1919
Terra-Knizhniyi Klub 1998
Teubner 1828
Teubner 1871
Teubner, B. G. 1824-61
Teubner, B. G. 1826-69
Teubner, B. G. 1850-55
Teubner, B. G. 1851
Teubner, B. G. 1851-53
Teubner, B. G. 1853-56
Teubner, B. G. 1855-57
Teubner, B. G. 1855-58
Teubner, B. G. 1858
Teubner, B. G. 1858-60
Teubner, B. G. 1861-65
Teubner, B. G. 1865-71
Teubner, B. G. 1867-69
Teubner, B. G. 1869
Teubner, B. G. 1870
Teubner, B. G. 1870-72
Teubner, B. G. 1870-74
Teubner, B. G. 1871-73
Teubner, B. G. 1872-74
Teubner, B. G. 1873
Teubner, B. G. 1873-74
Teubner, B. G. 1873-76
Teubner, B. G. 1874
Teubner, B. G. 1874-78
Teubner, B. G. 1875
Teubner, B. G. 1876
Teubner, B. G. 1877
Teubner, B. G. 1877-83
Teubner, B. G. 1879-80
Teubner, B. G. 1879-91
Teubner, B. G. 1880
Teubner, B. G. 1880-84
Teubner, B. G. 1881
Teubner, B. G. 1882
Teubner, B. G. 1882-83
Teubner, B. G. 1882-87
Teubner, B. G. 1883-91
Teubner, B. G. 1884
Teubner, B. G. 1884-90
Teubner, B. G. 1885
Teubner, B. G. 1886
Teubner, B. G. 1886-05
Teubner, B. G. 1886-91
Teubner, B. G. 1886-96
Teubner, B. G. 1888
Teubner, B. G. 1888-90
Teubner, B. G. 1888-96
Teubner, B. G. 1889

Teubner, B. G. 1889-07
Teubner, B. G. 1889-91
Teubner, B. G. 1889-92
Teubner, B. G. 1890-91
Teubner, B. G. 1890-93
Teubner, B. G. 1893-94
Teubner, B. G. 1893-97
Teubner, B. G. 1894
Teubner, B. G. 1894-03
Teubner, B. G. 1894-19
Teubner, B. G. 1894-96
Teubner, B. G. 1895
Teubner, B. G. 1895-01
Teubner, B. G. 1896
Teubner, B. G. 1897
Teubner, B. G. 1897-00
Teubner, B. G. 1899
Teubner, B. G. 1899-00
Teubner, B. G. 1899-19
Teubner, B. G. 1900-19
Teubner, B. G. 1901
Teubner, B. G. 1901-19
Teubner, B. G. 1902
Teubner, B. G. 1902-07
Teubner, B. G. 1903
Teubner, B. G. 1904
Teubner, B. G. 1904-11
Teubner, B. G. 1905-13
Teubner, B. G. 1906
Teubner, B. G. 1906-24
Teubner, B. G. 1907-08
Teubner, B. G. 1908
Teubner, B. G. 1908-11
Teubner, B. G. 1910
Teubner, B. G. 1910-11
Teubner, B. G. 1911-15
Teubner, B. G. 1913-24
Teubner, B. G. 1914
Teubner, B. G. 1914-15
Teubner, B. G. 1915
Teubner, B. G. 1915-21
Teubner, B. G. 1918
Teubner, B. G. 1920
Teubner, B. G. 1920-28
Teubner, B. G. 1924
Teubner, B. G. 1925
Teubner, B. G. 1927
Teubner, B. G. 1928
Teubner, B. G. 1929-31
Teubner, B. G. 1930
Teubner, B. G. 1930-31
Teubner, B. G. 1935
Teubner, B. G. 1938
Teubner, B. G. 1940
Teubner, B. G. 1969-72
Teubner, B. G. 1979
Teubner, B. G. 1984
Teubner, B. G. 1993
Teubner, B. G. 1995
Teubner, B. G. 1998
Teubner, B., G. 1878
Teubner, G. B. 1873
Teukpyeolsi, Tonghwa Chulpan
  Kongsa 1973
Teukpyeolsi: Samseongdang 1988

Thaning and Appel 1955
Thaning and Appel 1959
Thaning and Appel 1961
Thanner, Jacobus 1504
Theatrum Orbis Terrarum 1969
Theissing 1818
Thiboust, Viduam Claudii;
  Petrum Esclassan 1697
Thieme, W. J. 1930
Thierry le Chasseur 1658
Thin 1891
Thompson, George 1847
Thordason, E. 1856
Thormynd 1994
Thormynd Press 1994
Thorn, B., and Son 1781
Thurneisen, Eman. 1779
Thyrus 1957
Tidens 1960
Tip. De "El Ejercito Espanol" 1889
Tipografia Athene 1938
Tipografia Athene 1939
Tipografia della Sibilla 1833
Tipografia della Societa Lett.
  1800–13
Tipografia della Societa Lett. 1881
Tipografia e Libreria Salesiana
  1888
Tipografia e Libreria Salesiana
  1890
Tipografia e Libreria Salesiana
  1896
Tipografia e Libreris Salesiana
  1894
Tipografia Edit. Del Seminario
  1913
Tipografia Editrice Lombarda
  1878
Tipografia Fraticelli 1844
Tjeenk Willink, H. D. 1950
Tlomacza, Nakladem 1880
Tonson, Jacob 1700
Tonson, Jacob 1713
Tonson, Jacob 1721
Tonson, Jacob 1734
Tonson, Jacob 1972
Tonson, Jacob and R. 1760
Tonson, Jacob and R.; S. Draper
  1755
Tonson, Jacob and R; S. Draper
  1745
Tonson, Jacob.; J. Watts 1747
Tonson, Jacob; J. Watts 1721
Tonson, Jacob; J. Watts 1722
TOO "Deiiuna" 1993
Toray 1979
Tormont Publications 1991
Tornaesivs, Joannus 1619
Toussaint Quinet 1650
Tracey, E. 1708
Translation Publishing 1923
Trattner 1789–94
Traveller's Companion in assoc.
  with Olympia Press 1967
Treuttel and Wurtz 1812

Treuttel and Wurz 1820
Trimarchi, A. 1926
Troll Associates 1984
Trow and Company 1851
Trowitzsch 1907
Trowitzsch and Son 1916
Tuli-kalama 1982
Turnbull, Thomas 1806
Turnebus, Adrian 1554
Turret Books 1967
Turret Books 1992
Tuttle 1992
Txertoa 1984
Typis Academicis 1821–22
Typis Regiae Academiae 1780
Typographeiou Paraskeua Leone
  1895
Typographeo Academico 1855
Typographeo Academico 1856
Typographia Guttemberg 1874
Typographia Seminarii 1819–20
Typographia Seminarii 1820
U Izdatelia Knigoprodavtsa
  Lisenkova 1839
Ugoletus, Angelus 1492
Uhde, R. 1929
Union Verlag 1963
Unione Tipografico-Editrice Tori-
  nese 1921–22
Unione Tipografico-Editrice Tori-
  nese 1927
Unione Tipografico-Editrice Tori-
  nese 1928
Unione Tipografico-Editrice Tori-
  nese 1944
Unione Tipografico-Editrice Tori-
  nese 1963
Unione Tipografico-Editrice Tori-
  nese 1967
Unione Tipografico-Editrice Tori-
  nese 1998
Universidad Nacional Autonoma
  de Mexico 1996–97
Universidad Nacional de Mexico
  1921
Universidad Nacional de Mexico
  1931
Universita degli stude di macerata
  1992
University of California Press
  1990
University of Chicago Press 1951
University of Chicago Press 1957
University of Chicago Press 1961
University of Chicago Press 1965
University of Chicago Press 1969
University of Chicago Press 1971
University of Chicago Press 1976
University of Chicago Press 1997
University of Illinois 1957
University of Michigan Press 1963
University of Texas 1963
University Stores 1974
Unwin, T. Fisher 1890
Urie, R. 1754

Utet 1944
Valade, chez Laurent 1784–85
Vallarsi, Jacopo 1737
Vallecchi 1936
Vallecchi 1938
Valpianis 1817
Valpianis; Longman, Whittaker,
  Simpkin etc. 1832
Valpy 1826
Valpy 1832–33
Van Goor Zonen, G. B. 1966
Van Goor Zonen, G. B. 1967
Van Looy, S. L. 1904
Van Nostrand, D. 1942
Van Nostrand, D. 1944
Vanderhoeck and Ruprecht 1902
Vantage Press 1954
Varisci, J. 1593
Varlik Yayinevi 1957
Varlik Yayinevi 1957
Vascosanus, Michael 1545
Velhagen und Klasing 1894–95
Velhagen und Klasing 1903
Velhagen und Klasing 1910
Velhagen und Klasing 1911
Velhagen und Klasing 1915
Velhagen und Klasing 1930
Velhagen und Klasing 1936
Velhagen und Klasing 1937
Velhagen und Klasing 1939
Vendelkaers, S. 1967
Vendenhoeck und Ruprecht 1886
Venturini 1703
Verbo 1986
Verdiere 1816
Verheyden, Jac. 1720
Veritas 1957
Verlag der Goldene Brunnen
  1952
Veron 1968
Veron 1971
Veron 1972
Veron 1973
Veron 1995
Veselka 1969
Veselka 1980
Veselka 1981
Vicens Vives 1997
Vicens Vives 1998
Vietorus, Hieronymus 1510
Vietorus, Hieronymus 1513
Vietorus, Hieronymus 1516
Vieusseux 1828
Vignon, Eustathius 1574
Vignon, Eustathius 1580
Vignon, Eustathius 1586
Vignon, Eustathius 1590
Vignon, Eustathius 1609
Vigo, Francesco 1871
Viking 1990
Viking 1996
Vikingsutgafan 1941
Vincent, J. 1863
Vintage Books 1961
Vintage Books 1990

APPENDIX F:
PRINTINGS LISTED BY
PLACE PRINTED

Aberdeen, Scotland 1774
Aberdeen, Scotland 1778
Aberdeen, Scotland 1806
Aberdeen, Scotland; London,
    England 1813
Accra, Ghana 1974
Accra, Ghana; London, England
    1957
Adelaide, Australia 1981
Al-Quds [Lebanon?] 1966
Altdorf, Germany 1707
Altdorf, Germany 1781
Altona, Germany 1751
Altona, Germany 1752
Altona, Germany 1754
Altona, Germany 1756
Altona, Germany 1793
Amsterdam, Netherlands 1605
Amsterdam, Netherlands 1609
Amsterdam, Netherlands 1648
Amsterdam, Netherlands 1650
Amsterdam, Netherlands 1651
Amsterdam, Netherlands 1656
Amsterdam, Netherlands 1672
Amsterdam, Netherlands 1707
Amsterdam, Netherlands 1712–17
Amsterdam, Netherlands 1714
Amsterdam, Netherlands 1717
Amsterdam, Netherlands 1720
Amsterdam, Netherlands 1731
Amsterdam, Netherlands 1734
Amsterdam, Netherlands 1743
Amsterdam, Netherlands 1806
Amsterdam, Netherlands 1808
Amsterdam, Netherlands 1809
Amsterdam, Netherlands 1818–19
Amsterdam, Netherlands 1904
Amsterdam, Netherlands 1910

Amsterdam, Netherlands 1939
Amsterdam, Netherlands 1949
Amsterdam, Netherlands 1950
Amsterdam, Netherlands 1960
Amsterdam, Netherlands 1964
Amsterdam, Netherlands 1965
Amsterdam, Netherlands 1971
Amsterdam, Netherlands 1980
Amsterdam, Netherlands 1982
Amsterdam, Netherlands; New
    York, N.Y. 1963
Amsterdam, Netherlands; New
    York, N.Y. 1969
Ancona, Italy 1886
Andover, Mass. 1822
Andover, Mass. 1856
Ankara, Turkey 1941–42
Ann Arbor, Mi. 1963
Antwerp, Belgium 1495
Antwerp, Belgium 1528
Antwerp, Belgium 1550
Antwerp, Belgium 1553
Antwerp, Belgium 1556
Antwerp, Belgium 1568
Antwerp, Belgium 1581–89
Antwerp, Belgium 1585
Antwerp, Belgium 1588
Antwerp, Belgium 1944
Athens, Greece 1869
Athens, Greece 1870
Athens, Greece 1871
Athens, Greece 1872
Athens, Greece 1875–81
Athens, Greece 1875–87
Athens, Greece 1892
Athens, Greece 1895
Athens, Greece 1899
Athens, Greece 1901

Athens, Greece 1911–13
Athens, Greece 1912
Athens, Greece 1928
Athens, Greece 1936
Athens, Greece 1939
Athens, Greece 1940
Athens, Greece 1946
Athens, Greece 1950
Athens, Greece 1953
Athens, Greece 1954
Athens, Greece 1955
Athens, Greece 1956
Athens, Greece 1957
Athens, Greece 1958
Athens, Greece 1960
Athens, Greece 1962
Athens, Greece 1965
Athens, Greece 1968
Athens, Greece 1970
Athens, Greece 1970s
Athens, Greece 1971
Athens, Greece 1972
Athens, Greece 1974
Athens, Greece 1975
Athens, Greece 1975–80
Athens, Greece 1976
Athens, Greece 1979
Athens, Greece 1980–97
Athens, Greece 1980s
Athens, Greece 1981
Athens, Greece 1982
Athens, Greece 1983
Athens, Greece 1984
Athens, Greece 1985
Athens, Greece 1986
Athens, Greece 1987
Athens, Greece 1988
Athens, Greece 1990

Athens, Greece 1991
Athens, Greece 1992
Athens, Greece 1993
Athens, Greece 1994
Athens, Greece 1996
Athens, Greece 1997
Athens, Greece 1998
Athens, Ohio 1978
Athens, Ohio 1982
Atlanta, Georgia 1961
Atlanta, Georgia 1962
Augsburg, Germany 1537
Augsburg, Germany 1610
Augsburg, Germany 1617
Austin, Texas 1963
Austin, Texas 1974
Austin, Texas 1991
Austin, Texas 1991
Avignon, France 1741
Avignon, France 1805
Avignon, France 1811
Avignon, France 1819
Avignon, France 1820
Avignon, France 1826
Avon, Ct. 1970
Bad Goisern, Germany 1968–69
Baden-Baden, Cologne, Germany;
  New York, N.Y. 1977
Baghdad (Bexdad), Iraq 1981
Baky 1986
Baltimore, Md. 1819
Baltimore, Md. 1901
Baltimore, Md. 1950
Baltimore, Md. 1956
Baltimore, Md. 1957
Baltimore, Md. 1961
Baltimore, Md. 1963
Baltimore, Md. 1964
Baltimore, Md. 1966
Baltimore, Md. 1967
Baltimore, Md. 1968
Baltimore, Md. 1970
Baltimore, Md. 1973
Baltimore, Md. 1989
Baltimore, Md.; New York, N.Y.
  1812
Bamberg, Germany 1818
Barcelona, Spain 1851
Barcelona, Spain 1877
Barcelona, Spain 1908
Barcelona, Spain 1910
Barcelona, Spain 1912
Barcelona, Spain 1913
Barcelona, Spain 1919
Barcelona, Spain 1926
Barcelona, Spain 1927
Barcelona, Spain 1943
Barcelona, Spain 1947
Barcelona, Spain 1948
Barcelona, Spain 1949
Barcelona, Spain 1953
Barcelona, Spain 1955
Barcelona, Spain 1955
Barcelona, Spain 1959
Barcelona, Spain 1960

Barcelona, Spain 1961
Barcelona, Spain 1962
Barcelona, Spain 1963
Barcelona, Spain 1964
Barcelona, Spain 1966
Barcelona, Spain 1967
Barcelona, Spain 1968
Barcelona, Spain 1969
Barcelona, Spain 1970
Barcelona, Spain 1971
Barcelona, Spain 1971–85
Barcelona, Spain 1972
Barcelona, Spain 1973
Barcelona, Spain 1974
Barcelona, Spain 1975
Barcelona, Spain 1976
Barcelona, Spain 1977
Barcelona, Spain 1978
Barcelona, Spain 1979
Barcelona, Spain 1980
Barcelona, Spain 1982
Barcelona, Spain 1983
Barcelona, Spain 1984
Barcelona, Spain 1985
Barcelona, Spain 1986
Barcelona, Spain 1987
Barcelona, Spain 1990
Barcelona, Spain 1992
Barcelona, Spain 1993
Barcelona, Spain 1994
Barcelona, Spain 1995
Barcelona, Spain 1996
Barcelona, Spain 1997
Barcelona, Spain 1998
Barcelona, Spain 1999
Bari, Italy 1925
Bari, Italy 1928
Bari, Italy 1971
Barmen, Germany 1872
Basel, Switzerland 1518
Basel, Switzerland 1530
Basel, Switzerland 1535
Basel, Switzerland 1540
Basel, Switzerland 1541
Basel, Switzerland 1542
Basel, Switzerland 1544
Basel, Switzerland 1549
Basel, Switzerland 1551
Basel, Switzerland 1553
Basel, Switzerland 1557
Basel, Switzerland 1558
Basel, Switzerland 1559–60
Basel, Switzerland 1561
Basel, Switzerland 1567
Basel, Switzerland 1573
Basel, Switzerland 1582
Basel, Switzerland 1583
Basel, Switzerland 1584
Basel, Switzerland 1603
Basel, Switzerland 1606
Basel, Switzerland 1651
Basel, Switzerland 1686
Basel, Switzerland 1779
Basel, Switzerland 1781
Basel, Switzerland 1943–46

Basel, Switzerland 1945
Basel, Switzerland 1946
Basel, Switzerland 1953
Basel, Switzerland 1956
Basel, Switzerland 1962
Basel, Switzerland 1964
Basel, Switzerland 1971
Basingstoke, England 1978
Basingstoke, England 1984
Bassano, Italy 1785
Beijing, China 1997
Beilefeld, Germany 1894–95
Beirut, Lebanon 1900
Beirut, Lebanon 1966
Beirut, Lebanon 1979
Beirut, Lebanon 1980
Beirut, Lebanon 1982
Beirut, Lebanon 1986
Belgrade (Beograd), Yugoslavia
  1952
Belgrade (Beograd), Yugoslavia
  1961
Belmont, Ca. 1994
Bengaluru 1978
Benzlau, Germany 1828–36
Bergen, Norway 1852
Berkeley, Ca. 1990
Berkeley, Ca. 1993
Berlin, Germany 1735
Berlin, Germany 1736
Berlin, Germany 1762
Berlin, Germany 1797
Berlin, Germany 1798
Berlin, Germany 1819
Berlin, Germany 1837
Berlin, Germany 1840
Berlin, Germany 1843
Berlin, Germany 1844
Berlin, Germany 1846
Berlin, Germany 1854–55
Berlin, Germany 1855–56
Berlin, Germany 1858
Berlin, Germany 1859
Berlin, Germany 1860–62
Berlin, Germany 1861
Berlin, Germany 1862–67
Berlin, Germany 1864–65
Berlin, Germany 1865
Berlin, Germany 1866–98
Berlin, Germany 1867–73
Berlin, Germany 1869–73
Berlin, Germany 1870
Berlin, Germany 1870–71
Berlin, Germany 1871–74
Berlin, Germany 1871–77
Berlin, Germany 1873
Berlin, Germany 1874
Berlin, Germany 1874–77
Berlin, Germany 1876–79
Berlin, Germany 1877–79
Berlin, Germany 1878
Berlin, Germany 1879
Berlin, Germany 1880–10
Berlin, Germany 1880–18
Berlin, Germany 1884–87

Berlin, Germany 1885–10
Berlin, Germany 1886–19
Berlin, Germany 1888–
Berlin, Germany 1890
Berlin, Germany 1891
Berlin, Germany 1900
Berlin, Germany 1901
Berlin, Germany 1904
Berlin, Germany 1905
Berlin, Germany 1907
Berlin, Germany 1911
Berlin, Germany 1912
Berlin, Germany 1914
Berlin, Germany 1916
Berlin, Germany 1919
Berlin, Germany 1920
Berlin, Germany 1920–28
Berlin, Germany 1920s
Berlin, Germany 1922
Berlin, Germany 1923
Berlin, Germany 1924
Berlin, Germany 1925
Berlin, Germany 1927
Berlin, Germany 1929
Berlin, Germany 1930
Berlin, Germany 1939
Berlin, Germany 1943
Berlin, Germany 1948
Berlin, Germany 1950
Berlin, Germany 1956
Berlin, Germany 1960
Berlin, Germany 1966
Berlin, Germany 1968
Berlin, Germany 1971
Berlin, Germany 1983
Berlin, Germany 1986
Berlin, Germany 1988
Berlin, Germany; Darmstadt, Germany 1966
Berlin, Germany; Grunewald, Germany 1927
Berlin, Germany; Schoneberg, Germany 1874
Berlin, Germany; Stuttgart, Germany 1899
Berlin, Germany; Weimar, Germany 1972
Bern, Switzerland 1881
Bern, Switzerland 1907
Bern, Switzerland 1960
Bern, Switzerland 1962
Bern, Switzerland 1978
Bern, Switzerland 1981
Berwick, England 1791
Berwick, England 1807
Besancon, France 1828
Bielefeld, Germany 1903
Bielefeld, Germany 1910
Bielefeld, Germany 1915
Bielefeld, Germany; Leipzig, Germany 1911
Bielefeld, Germany; Leipzig, Germany 1930
Bielefeld, Germany; Leipzig, Germany 1937

Bielefeld, Germany; Leipzig, Germany 1939
Bielsko-Biata, Poland 1994
Bilbao, Spain 1960
Bilbao, Spain 1971
Bilbo 1985
Birmingham, England 1805
Birmingham, England 1807
Birmingham, England 1810
Bloomington, Ill. 1900
Bogota, Columbia 1986
Bologna, France 1522
Bologna, France 1568
Bologna, France 1821–28
Bologna, France 1825
Bologna, France 1828
Bologna, France 1838
Bologna, France 1839
Bologna, France 1920
Bologna, France 1924
Bologna, France 1926
Bologna, France 1936
Bologna, France 1943
Bologna, France 1945
Bologna, France 1947
Bologna, France 1960
Bologna, France 1965
Bologna, France 1982
Bologna, France 1997
Bologna, Italy 1982
Bonn, Germany 1776
Bonn, Germany 1822
Bonn, Germany 1858
Bonn, Germany 1863–72
Bonn, Germany 1949
Bordeaux, France 1943
Bordeaux, France 1951
Boston, Mass 1929
Boston, Mass. 1806
Boston, Mass. 1808
Boston, Mass. 1814
Boston, Mass. 1834
Boston, Mass. 1835
Boston, Mass. 1837
Boston, Mass. 1838
Boston, Mass. 1839
Boston, Mass. 1841
Boston, Mass. 1844
Boston, Mass. 1846
Boston, Mass. 1847
Boston, Mass. 1848
Boston, Mass. 1852
Boston, Mass. 1854
Boston, Mass. 1857
Boston, Mass. 1860
Boston, Mass. 1870
Boston, Mass. 1871
Boston, Mass. 1871–72
Boston, Mass. 1872
Boston, Mass. 1872–76
Boston, Mass. 1873
Boston, Mass. 1875
Boston, Mass. 1876
Boston, Mass. 1877
Boston, Mass. 1879

Boston, Mass. 1880s
Boston, Mass. 1881
Boston, Mass. 1882
Boston, Mass. 1883
Boston, Mass. 1884
Boston, Mass. 1885
Boston, Mass. 1886
Boston, Mass. 1887
Boston, Mass. 1887–91
Boston, Mass. 1888
Boston, Mass. 1889
Boston, Mass. 1890
Boston, Mass. 1890s
Boston, Mass. 1891
Boston, Mass. 1892
Boston, Mass. 1893
Boston, Mass. 1894
Boston, Mass. 1895
Boston, Mass. 1896
Boston, Mass. 1897
Boston, Mass. 1898
Boston, Mass. 1899
Boston, Mass. 1900
Boston, Mass. 1901
Boston, Mass. 1903
Boston, Mass. 1904
Boston, Mass. 1907
Boston, Mass. 1909
Boston, Mass. 1910
Boston, Mass. 1912
Boston, Mass. 1915
Boston, Mass. 1921
Boston, Mass. 1924
Boston, Mass. 1926
Boston, Mass. 1928
Boston, Mass. 1929
Boston, Mass. 1932
Boston, Mass. 1935
Boston, Mass. 1949
Boston, Mass. 1950
Boston, Mass. 1979
Boston, Mass.; Cambridge, Engand 1833
Boston, Mass.; Cambridge, Engand 1916
Boston, Mass.; Cambridge, Mass. 1944
Boston, Mass.; New York, N.Y.; Cambridge, Mass. 1894
Boston, Mass; Chicago, Il. 1883
Boston, Mass; London, England 1894
Boston, Mass; London, England 1897
Boston, Mass; London, England 1898
Boston, Mass; London, England 1930
Boston, Mass; New York, N.Y. 1871
Boston, Mass; New York, N.Y. 1895
Boston, Mass; New York, N.Y. 1898

Boston, Mass; New York, N.Y. 1899
Boston, Mass; New York, N.Y. 1900
Boston, Mass; New York, N.Y. 1905
Boston, Mass; New York, N.Y. 1908
Boston, Mass; New York, N.Y. 1912
Boston, Mass; New York, N.Y. 1917
Boston, Mass; Philadelphia, Pa. 1872–76
Boston; New York; Chicago; San Francisco 1899
Bratislava, Slovakia 1962
Bratislava, Slovakia 1966
Bratislava, Slovakia 1986
Breitbrunn am Ammersee, Germany 1990
Bremen, Germany 1796
Bremen, Germany 1826
Bremen, Germany 1938
Bremen, Germany 1958
Brescia, Italy 1474
Brescia, Italy 1497
Brescia, Italy 1807
Brescia, Italy 1810
Brescia, Italy 1925
Brescia, Italy 1926
Breslau (Wroclaw), Poland 1848
Breslau (Wroclaw), Poland 1960
Bristol, England 1979
Bristol, England 1980
Bristol, England 1982
Bristol, England 1983
Bristol, England 1985
Brody, Poland 1912
Brugge-Brussel, Belgium 1943
Brugge-Brussel, Belgium 1944
Brussels, Belgium 1780
Brussels, Belgium 1891
Brussels, Belgium 1944
Brussels, Belgium 1951
Bryn Mawr, Pa. 1983
Bucuresti (Bucharest), Romania 1923
Bucuresti (Bucharest), Romania 1955
Bucuresti (Bucharest), Romania 1966
Budapest, Hungary 1902
Budapest, Hungary 1905
Budapest, Hungary 1927
Budapest, Hungary 1947
Budapest, Hungary 1957
Budapest, Hungary 1959
Budapest, Hungary 1972
Budapest, Hungary 1973
Budapest, Hungary 1974
Budapest, Hungary 1986
Buenos Aires, Argentina 1923
Buenos Aires, Argentina 1938
Buenos Aires, Argentina 1939
Buenos Aires, Argentina 1940

Buenos Aires, Argentina 1944
Buenos Aires, Argentina 1946
Buenos Aires, Argentina 1950
Buenos Aires, Argentina 1951
Buenos Aires, Argentina 1957
Buenos Aires, Argentina 1962
Buenos Aires, Argentina 1965
Buenos Aires, Argentina 1966
Buenos Aires, Argentina 1968
Buenos Aires, Argentina 1969
Buenos Aires, Argentina 1970
Buenos Aires, Argentina 1971
Buenos Aires, Argentina 1977
Buenos Aires, Argentina 1983
Buenos Aires, Argentina 1994
Buenos Aires, Argentina; Mexico (City), Mexico 1999
Buffalo Grove, Il. 1991
Buhl-Baden, Germany 1931
Cairo, Egypt 1904
Cambridge, England 1648
Cambridge, England 1655
Cambridge, England 1660
Cambridge, England 1664–65
Cambridge, England 1672
Cambridge, England 1679
Cambridge, England 1686
Cambridge, England 1689
Cambridge, England 1711
Cambridge, England 1810
Cambridge, England 1828
Cambridge, England 1833
Cambridge, England 1834
Cambridge, England 1843
Cambridge, England 1859
Cambridge, England 1861–65
Cambridge, England 1866
Cambridge, England 1880
Cambridge, England 1881
Cambridge, England 1885
Cambridge, England 1887
Cambridge, England 1889
Cambridge, England 1890
Cambridge, England 1891
Cambridge, England 1892
Cambridge, England 1894
Cambridge, England 1896
Cambridge, England 1897
Cambridge, England 1902
Cambridge, England 1906
Cambridge, England 1907
Cambridge, England 1908
Cambridge, England 1914
Cambridge, England 1917
Cambridge, England 1920
Cambridge, England 1921
Cambridge, England 1924
Cambridge, England 1925
Cambridge, England 1930
Cambridge, England 1931
Cambridge, England 1937
Cambridge, England 1941
Cambridge, England 1948
Cambridge, England 1952
Cambridge, England 1954

Cambridge, England 1958
Cambridge, England 1959
Cambridge, England 1961
Cambridge, England 1962
Cambridge, England 1964
Cambridge, England 1968
Cambridge, England 1979
Cambridge, England 1992
Cambridge, England 1994
Cambridge, England 1996
Cambridge, England; London, England 1883
Cambridge, England; London, England 1967
Cambridge, England; New York, N.Y. 1979
Cambridge, England; New York, N.Y. 1982
Cambridge, England; New York, N.Y. 1989
Cambridge, England; New York, N.Y. 1992
Cambridge, England; New York, N.Y. 1994
Cambridge, England; New York, N.Y. 1996
Cambridge, Mass. 1929
Cambridge, Mass. 1947
Cambridge, Mass. 1953
Cambridge, Mass. 1954
Cambridge, Mass. 1965–67
Cambridge, Mass. 1967–71
Cambridge, Mass. 1976–78
Cambridge, Mass. 1976–80
Cambridge, Mass. 1993–98
Cambridge, Mass. 1995
Cambridge, Mass. 1996
Cambridge, Mass. 1998
Cambridge, Mass. 1999
Cambridge, Mass.; London, England 1943
Cambridge, Mass.; London, England 1946
Cambridge, Mass.; London, England 1947
Cambridge, Mass.; London, England 1957
Cambridge, Mass.; London, England 1960–66
Cambridge, Mass.; London, England 1966–74
Cambridge, Mass.; London, England 1975–76
Cambridge, Mass.; London, England 1977
Cambridge, Mass.; London, England 1978–85
Cambridge, Mass.; London, England 1980–84
Cambridge, Mass.; London, England 1982
Cambridge, Mass.; London, England 1985–88
Cambridge, Mass.; New York, N.Y. 1919

Capetown (Kaapstad), South
Africa 1963
Caracas, Venezuela 1962
Caracas, Venezuela 1965
Carlsruhe, Germany 1821
Carpentras, France 1986
Catskill [location?] 1822
Ch'angsha, China 1939
Chapel Hill, N.C. 1979
Chautauqua, N.Y. 1909
Chemnitz, Germany 1745–53
Chemnitz, Germany 1767
Chemnitz, Germany 1776–77
Chemnitz, Germany 1785
Chemnitz, Germany 1809
Chemnitz, Germany 1813
Chemnitz, Germany 1815
Chemnitz, Germany 1819
Chemnitz, Germany 1821–22
Chennai (Madras), India 1961
Chester, England 1834
Chicago, Il. 1850s
Chicago, Il. 1869
Chicago, Il. 1872
Chicago, Il. 1874
Chicago, Il. 1877
Chicago, Il. 1878
Chicago, Il. 1879
Chicago, Il. 1880
Chicago, Il. 1882
Chicago, Il. 1883
Chicago, Il. 1884
Chicago, Il. 1885
Chicago, Il. 1886
Chicago, Il. 1889
Chicago, Il. 1892
Chicago, Il. 1893
Chicago, Il. 1900
Chicago, Il. 1902
Chicago, Il. 1902–12
Chicago, Il. 1912
Chicago, Il. 1921
Chicago, Il. 1936
Chicago, Il. 1948
Chicago, Il. 1950
Chicago, Il. 1951
Chicago, Il. 1952
Chicago, Il. 1955
Chicago, Il. 1957
Chicago, Il. 1961
Chicago, Il. 1962
Chicago, Il. 1963
Chicago, Il. 1965
Chicago, Il. 1966
Chicago, Il. 1967
Chicago, Il. 1969
Chicago, Il. 1970
Chicago, Il. 1971
Chicago, Il. 1976
Chicago, Il. 1981
Chicago, Il. 1985
Chicago, Il. 1997
Chicago, Il.; London, England
1926
Chicago, Il.; London, England 1990

Chicago, Il.; New York, N.Y. 1899
Chicago, Il.; New York, N.Y. 1903
Chicago, Il.; New York, N.Y. 1904
Chile 1990
Chiswick, England 1818
Chiswick, England 1819
Chiswick, England 1820
Chiswick, England 1825
Christ. [Norway?] 1835
Cincinnati, Oh. 1897
Citta di Castello, Italy 1887
Citta di Castello, Italy 1945
Clausthal, Germany 1864
Cologne, Germany 1522
Cologne, Germany 1523
Cologne, Germany 1524
Cologne, Germany 1527
Cologne, Germany 1534
Cologne, Germany 1588
Cologne, Germany 1742
Cologne, Germany 1808
Copenhagen, Denmark 1825
Copenhagen, Denmark 1827
Copenhagen, Denmark 1836
Copenhagen, Denmark 1837
Copenhagen, Denmark 1857
Copenhagen, Denmark 1865
Copenhagen, Denmark 1878
Copenhagen, Denmark 1890
Copenhagen, Denmark 1890
Copenhagen, Denmark 1916
Copenhagen, Denmark 1921
Copenhagen, Denmark 1951
Copenhagen, Denmark 1955
Copenhagen, Denmark 1959
Copenhagen, Denmark 1961
Copenhagen, Denmark 1967
Copenhagen, Denmark 1989
Copenhagen, Denmark 1994
Copenhagen, Sweden 1993
Cracow, Poland 1903
Croitwich [England?] 1993
Curia, Germany 1786
Dallas, Tx. 1970
Danbury, Conn. 1968
Danbury, Conn. 1968–75
Danbury, Conn. 1969
Danbury, Conn. 1972
Danbury, Conn. 1978
Danbury, Conn. 1980
Darlington, England 1893
Darlington, England 1895
Darmstadt, Germany 1770–71
Darmstadt, Germany 1966
Daventrie [location?] 1516
Delft, Netherlands 1598
Delft, Netherlands 1606
Dresden, Germany 1745
Dresden, Germany 1826
Dresden, Germany 1896
Dresden, Germany 1897
Dublin (Baile Atha Cliath), Ireland
1844–69
Dublin (Baile Atha Cliath), Ireland
1990

Dublin, Ireland 1716
Dublin, Ireland 1717
Dublin, Ireland 1737
Dublin, Ireland 1770
Dublin, Ireland 1773
Dublin, Ireland 1787
Dublin, Ireland 1792
Dublin, Ireland 1799
Dublin, Ireland 1808
Dublin, Ireland 1815
Dublin, Ireland 1818–19
Dublin, Ireland 1819
Dublin, Ireland 1821–22
Dublin, Ireland 1833
Dublin, Ireland 1834
Dublin, Ireland 1839
Dublin, Ireland 1846
Dublin, Ireland 1847
Dublin, Ireland 1856
Dublin, Ireland 1856
Dublin, Ireland 1867
Dublin, Ireland 1869
Dublin, Ireland 1882
Dublin, Ireland 1883
Dublin, Ireland 1894
Dushanbe, Tajikistan 1990
Dusseldorf, Germany 1913
Dusseldorf, Germany; Zurich,
Switzerland 1996
East Aurora, N.Y. 1923
Eau Claire, Wis. 1961
Edinburgh, Scotland 1733
Edinburgh, Scotland 1758
Edinburgh, Scotland 1761
Edinburgh, Scotland 1763
Edinburgh, Scotland 1767
Edinburgh, Scotland 1769
Edinburgh, Scotland 1773
Edinburgh, Scotland 1777
Edinburgh, Scotland 1778
Edinburgh, Scotland 1779
Edinburgh, Scotland 1790
Edinburgh, Scotland 1792
Edinburgh, Scotland 1806
Edinburgh, Scotland 1808
Edinburgh, Scotland 1809
Edinburgh, Scotland 1810
Edinburgh, Scotland 1845
Edinburgh, Scotland 1846
Edinburgh, Scotland 1861–62
Edinburgh, Scotland 1865–68
Edinburgh, Scotland 1867
Edinburgh, Scotland 1868
Edinburgh, Scotland 1870
Edinburgh, Scotland 1871
Edinburgh, Scotland 1877
Edinburgh, Scotland 1880
Edinburgh, Scotland 1891
Edinburgh, Scotland 1894
Edinburgh, Scotland 1895
Edinburgh, Scotland 1900
Edinburgh, Scotland 1909
Edinburgh, Scotland 1990
Edinburgh, Scotland 1992
Edinburgh, Scotland 1994

Istanbul, Turkey 1989
Ithaca, N.Y. 1987
Jena, Germany 1812
Jena, Germany 1865
Jena, Germany 1927
Jerusalem, Israel 1941
Jerusalem, Israel 1946
Jerusalem, Israel 1954
Jerusalem, Israel 1956
Jerusalem, Israel 1996
Kalakata, Bengal 1954
Kalakata, Bengal 1969
Kalakata, Bengal 1982
Karlsruhe, Germany 1834–35
Karlsruhe, Germany 1927
Kaunas, Lithuwania 1921
Kaupmannahofn [location?] 1854
Kaupmannahofn [location?] 1912
Kempte (Allgau), Germany 1966
Kiel, Germany; Leipzig, Germany
 1895
Kiev (Kyyir), Ukraine 1963
Kiev (Kyyir), Ukraine 1968
Kiev (Kyyir), Ukraine 1969
Kiev (Kyyir), Ukraine 1978
Kiev (Kyyir), Ukraine 1980
Kiev (Kyyir), Ukraine 1981
Kiev (Kyyir), Ukraine 1982
Konigsburg [location?] 1802
Konigsburg [location?] 1890
Konigsburg [location?] 1894
Kotet. [Hungary?] 1788
Krakow, Poland 1789
Krakow, Poland 1814-16
Krakow, Poland 1815
Krakow, Poland 1880
Krakow, Poland 1882
Krakow, Poland 1903
Krakow, Poland 1922
Krakow, Poland 1947
Kristiania [Norway?] 1919
Kuang-chou [China?] 1994
La Fleche, France 1619
La Paz, Bolivia 1981
La Rochelle, France 1755
Lahr, Germany 1949
Lancaster, Pa. 1950
Langenberg 1900
Larnaca (Larnax), Cyprus 1921
Lasi [location?] 1997
Lausanne, Switzerland 1931
Lausanne, Switzerland 1952
Lausanne, Switzerland 1957
Lausanne, Switzerland; Cologne,
 Germany 1970
Leiden (Leyden), Netherlands
 1538
Leiden (Leyden), Netherlands
 1541
Leiden (Leyden), Netherlands
 1588
Leiden (Leyden), Netherlands
 1589
Leiden (Leyden), Netherlands
 1632

Leiden (Leyden), Netherlands
 1636
Leiden (Leyden), Netherlands
 1645
Leiden (Leyden), Netherlands
 1653
Leiden (Leyden), Netherlands
 1766
Leiden (Leyden), Netherlands
 1771
Leiden (Leyden), Netherlands
 1780
Leiden (Leyden), Netherlands
 1782
Leiden (Leyden), Netherlands
 1802
Leiden (Leyden), Netherlands
 1808
Leiden (Leyden), Netherlands
 1821
Leiden (Leyden), Netherlands
 1851
Leiden (Leyden), Netherlands
 1880
Leiden (Leyden), Netherlands
 1887
Leiden (Leyden), Netherlands
 1890
Leiden (Leyden), Netherlands
 1895-96
Leiden (Leyden), Netherlands
 1897
Leiden (Leyden), Netherlands
 1900
Leiden (Leyden), Netherlands
 1906-08
Leiden (Leyden), Netherlands
 1907-08
Leiden (Leyden), Netherlands
 1912-17
Leiden (Leyden), Netherlands
 1917
Leiden (Leyden), Netherlands
 1918-19
Leiden (Leyden), Netherlands
 1930
Leiden (Leyden), Netherlands
 1933-34
Leiden (Leyden), Netherlands
 1934-35
Leiden (Leyden), Netherlands;
 Amsterdam, Netherlan 1809
Leiden (Leyden), Netherlands;
 New York, N.Y. 1993
Leipzig, Germany 1496?
Leipzig, Germany 1504
Leipzig, Germany 1507
Leipzig, Germany 1509
Leipzig, Germany 1512
Leipzig, Germany 1515
Leipzig, Germany 1518
Leipzig, Germany 1537
Leipzig, Germany 1549
Leipzig, Germany 1550
Leipzig, Germany 1566

Leipzig, Germany 1570?
Leipzig, Germany 1607-22
Leipzig, Germany 1622
Leipzig, Germany 1750
Leipzig, Germany 1759-64
Leipzig, Germany 1765
Leipzig, Germany 1768
Leipzig, Germany 1771
Leipzig, Germany 1771-73
Leipzig, Germany 1772
Leipzig, Germany 1773
Leipzig, Germany 1775
Leipzig, Germany 1781
Leipzig, Germany 1781-87
Leipzig, Germany 1787
Leipzig, Germany 1790
Leipzig, Germany 1793
Leipzig, Germany 1804
Leipzig, Germany 1805
Leipzig, Germany 1806
Leipzig, Germany 1807
Leipzig, Germany 1810
Leipzig, Germany 1814
Leipzig, Germany 1816
Leipzig, Germany 1817
Leipzig, Germany 1818
Leipzig, Germany 1819
Leipzig, Germany 1822
Leipzig, Germany 1822-24
Leipzig, Germany 1822-28
Leipzig, Germany 1824
Leipzig, Germany 1824-61
Leipzig, Germany 1825
Leipzig, Germany 1826
Leipzig, Germany 1826-27
Leipzig, Germany 1826-28
Leipzig, Germany 1826-69
Leipzig, Germany 1827
Leipzig, Germany 1828
Leipzig, Germany 1828-29
Leipzig, Germany 1830
Leipzig, Germany 1832-35
Leipzig, Germany 1837
Leipzig, Germany 1839
Leipzig, Germany 1843
Leipzig, Germany 1844
Leipzig, Germany 1848
Leipzig, Germany 1849-50
Leipzig, Germany 1850-55
Leipzig, Germany 1851
Leipzig, Germany 1851-53
Leipzig, Germany 1852
Leipzig, Germany 1853
Leipzig, Germany 1853-56
Leipzig, Germany 1854
Leipzig, Germany 1854-56
Leipzig, Germany 1855-57
Leipzig, Germany 1855-58
Leipzig, Germany 1856
Leipzig, Germany 1858
Leipzig, Germany 1858-60
Leipzig, Germany 1860
Leipzig, Germany 1861
Leipzig, Germany 1861-63
Leipzig, Germany 1861-65

Leipzig, Germany 1863-64
Leipzig, Germany 1864
Leipzig, Germany 1865
Leipzig, Germany 1865-71
Leipzig, Germany 1865-77
Leipzig, Germany 1867-68
Leipzig, Germany 1867-69
Leipzig, Germany 1868-71
Leipzig, Germany 1868-86
Leipzig, Germany 1869
Leipzig, Germany 1869-72
Leipzig, Germany 1870
Leipzig, Germany 1870-72
Leipzig, Germany 1870-74
Leipzig, Germany 1870-84
Leipzig, Germany 1871
Leipzig, Germany 1871-73
Leipzig, Germany 1872
Leipzig, Germany 1872-74
Leipzig, Germany 1872-76
Leipzig, Germany 1873
Leipzig, Germany 1873-74
Leipzig, Germany 1873-76
Leipzig, Germany 1874
Leipzig, Germany 1874-18
Leipzig, Germany 1874-77
Leipzig, Germany 1874-78
Leipzig, Germany 1875
Leipzig, Germany 1875-82
Leipzig, Germany 1876
Leipzig, Germany 1876-80
Leipzig, Germany 1877
Leipzig, Germany 1877-79
Leipzig, Germany 1877-83
Leipzig, Germany 1877-88
Leipzig, Germany 1878
Leipzig, Germany 1879
Leipzig, Germany 1879-80
Leipzig, Germany 1879-91
Leipzig, Germany 1880
Leipzig, Germany 1880-84
Leipzig, Germany 1881
Leipzig, Germany 1882
Leipzig, Germany 1882-83
Leipzig, Germany 1882-87
Leipzig, Germany 1883-91
Leipzig, Germany 1884
Leipzig, Germany 1885
Leipzig, Germany 1885-86
Leipzig, Germany 1886
Leipzig, Germany 1886-87
Leipzig, Germany 1886-91
Leipzig, Germany 1886-96
Leipzig, Germany 1887
Leipzig, Germany 1887-88
Leipzig, Germany 1888
Leipzig, Germany 1888-90
Leipzig, Germany 1888-96
Leipzig, Germany 1889
Leipzig, Germany 1889-07
Leipzig, Germany 1889-91
Leipzig, Germany 1889-92
Leipzig, Germany 1890
Leipzig, Germany 1890-07
Leipzig, Germany 1890-91

Leipzig, Germany 1890-93
Leipzig, Germany 1890-95
Leipzig, Germany 1890s
Leipzig, Germany 1891
Leipzig, Germany 1891-96
Leipzig, Germany 1892
Leipzig, Germany 1893-94
Leipzig, Germany 1893-95
Leipzig, Germany 1893-97
Leipzig, Germany 1894
Leipzig, Germany 1894-19
Leipzig, Germany 1894-96
Leipzig, Germany 1894-96
Leipzig, Germany 1895
Leipzig, Germany 1895-01
Leipzig, Germany 1896
Leipzig, Germany 1897
Leipzig, Germany 1897-00
Leipzig, Germany 1898
Leipzig, Germany 1899
Leipzig, Germany 1899-00
Leipzig, Germany 1899-19
Leipzig, Germany 1900
Leipzig, Germany 1900-10
Leipzig, Germany 1900-19
Leipzig, Germany 1901
Leipzig, Germany 1901-19
Leipzig, Germany 1902
Leipzig, Germany 1902-07
Leipzig, Germany 1904
Leipzig, Germany 1904-11
Leipzig, Germany 1904-15
Leipzig, Germany 1905-13
Leipzig, Germany 1906
Leipzig, Germany 1906-24
Leipzig, Germany 1907
Leipzig, Germany 1907-08
Leipzig, Germany 1907-10
Leipzig, Germany 1908
Leipzig, Germany 1908-11
Leipzig, Germany 1910
Leipzig, Germany 1910-11
Leipzig, Germany 1911
Leipzig, Germany 1911-15
Leipzig, Germany 1912
Leipzig, Germany 1914
Leipzig, Germany 1914-15
Leipzig, Germany 1914-27
Leipzig, Germany 1915
Leipzig, Germany 1915-21
Leipzig, Germany 1918
Leipzig, Germany 1920
Leipzig, Germany 1920s
Leipzig, Germany 1921
Leipzig, Germany 1922
Leipzig, Germany 1923
Leipzig, Germany 1924
Leipzig, Germany 1925
Leipzig, Germany 1927
Leipzig, Germany 1927
Leipzig, Germany 1930
Leipzig, Germany 1930-31
Leipzig, Germany 1935
Leipzig, Germany 1936
Leipzig, Germany 1937

Leipzig, Germany 1938
Leipzig, Germany 1940
Leipzig, Germany 1948
Leipzig, Germany 1952
Leipzig, Germany 1969-72
Leipzig, Germany 1979
Leipzig, Germany; Berlin, Germany 1884-90
Leipzig, Germany; Berlin, Germany 1886-05
Leipzig, Germany; Berlin, Germany 1894-03
Leipzig, Germany; Berlin, Germany 1903
Leipzig, Germany; Berlin, Germany 1913-24
Leipzig, Germany; Berlin, Germany 1920
Leipzig, Germany; Berlin, Germany 1928
Leipzig, Germany; Berlin, Germany 1929-31
Leipzig, Germany; Frankfurt am Main, Germany 1889
Leipzig, Germany; Goshen [Germany?] 1804-07
Leipzig, Germany; Goshen [Germany?] 1806
Leipzig, Germany; Leiden (Leyden), Germany 1820
Leipzig, Germany; Leiden (Leyden), Germany 1823
Leipzig, Germany; London, England 1802-22
Leipzig, Germany; London, England 1865
Leipzig, Germany; Paris, France 1868
Leipzig, Germany; Vienna, Austria 1902
Leipzig, Germany; Vienna, Austria 1905
Leipzig, Germany; Vienna, Austria 1909
Lemgo, Germany 1769-71
Lemgo, Germany 1789
Lemgo, Germany 1798
Lemovicis 1644
Lenae [location?] 1860
Leningrad, Russia 1952
Leningrad, Russia 1956
Leningrad, Russia 1990
Leon [location?] 1973
Leon [location?] 1980
Leonica (Liegnitz), Poland 1839
Leovardiae [location?] 1747
Letchworth, England 1981
Leuven (Louvain), Belgium 1523
Leuven (Louvain), Belgium 1535
Leuven (Louvain), Belgium 1555
Leuven (Louvain), Belgium 1829
Levallois-Perret, France 1967
Lewes, England 1993
Lexington 1834
Liiae [location?] 1857-59

Liiae [location?] 1860
Lima, Peru 1972
Lima, Peru 1972
Lima, Peru 1973
Lisbon, Portugal 1835
Lisbon, Portugal 1938-39
Lisbon, Portugal 1947
Lisbon, Portugal 1960
Lisbon, Portugal 1963
Lisbon, Portugal 1975
Lisbon, Portugal 1986
Lisbon, Portugal 1989
Lisbon, Portugal 1991
Livorno, Italy 1805
Livorno, Italy 1822
Livorno, Italy 1823
Livorno, Italy 1853
Livorno, Italy 1871
Livorno, Italy 1892
Livorno, Italy 1896
Livorno, Italy 1904
Livorno, Italy 1915
Livorno, Italy 1916
Livorno, Italy 1920
Livorno, Italy 1923
Livorno, Italy 1924
Livorno, Italy 1925
Livorno, Italy 1929
Ljubljana, Slovenia 1950
Ljubljana, Slovenia 1951
Ljubljana, Slovenia 1978
Llandysul, Wales 1976
London, England 1486
London, England 1553
London, England 1580
London, England 1581
London, England 1591
London, England 1596
London, England 1598
London, England 1600
London, England 1603-14
London, England 1609?
London, England 1613
London, England 1616
London, England 1624
London, England 1629
London, England 1631
London, England 1633
London, England 1634
London, England 1636
London, England 1640
London, England 1652
London, England 1657
London, England 1660
London, England 1663
London, England 1665
London, England 1669
London, England 1670
London, England 1671
London, England 1673
London, England 1675
London, England 1676
London, England 1677
London, England 1679
London, England 1680

London, England 1681
London, England 1684
London, England 1685
London, England 1686
London, England 1689
London, England 1694
London, England 1700
London, England 1702
London, England 1706
London, England 1708
London, England 1709
London, England 1712
London, England 1713
London, England 1714
London, England 1715
London, England 1715-20
London, England 1716
London, England 1717
London, England 1718
London, England 1720
London, England 1720-26
London, England 1721
London, England 1722
London, England 1725-26
London, England 1726
London, England 1727
London, England 1728
London, England 1729-40
London, England 1733
London, England 1734
London, England 1736
London, England 1736-43
London, England 1738
London, England 1740
London, England 1741
London, England 1743
London, England 1745
London, England 1747
London, England 1749
London, England 1750
London, England 1751
London, England 1752
London, England 1753
London, England 1754
London, England 1755
London, England 1756
London, England 1758
London, England 1760
London, England 1760-68
London, England 1762-64
London, England 1763
London, England 1764
London, England 1766
London, England 1767
London, England 1768
London, England 1769
London, England 1770
London, England 1771
London, England 1772
London, England 1773
London, England 1774
London, England 1775-76
London, England 1777
London, England 1779
London, England 1781

London, England 1782
London, England 1783
London, England 1784
London, England 1785
London, England 1788
London, England 1789
London, England 1790
London, England 1791
London, England 1792
London, England 1794
London, England 1796
London, England 1797
London, England 1801
London, England 1802
London, England 1805
London, England 1805-06
London, England 1806
London, England 1807
London, England 1808
London, England 1809
London, England 1810
London, England 1811
London, England 1813
London, England 1815
London, England 1816
London, England 1816-17
London, England 1817
London, England 1818
London, England 1819
London, England 1820
London, England 1821
London, England 1821-22
London, England 1822
London, England 1823
London, England 1824
London, England 1825
London, England 1826
London, England 1827
London, England 1828
London, England 1830
London, England 1831
London, England 1832
London, England 1833
London, England 1834
London, England 1836
London, England 1837
London, England 1838
London, England 1839
London, England 1840
London, England 1841
London, England 1841-44
London, England 1842
London, England 1843
London, England 1844
London, England 1845
London, England 1846
London, England 1847
London, England 1850
London, England 1851
London, England 1852
London, England 1853
London, England 1854
London, England 1855
London, England 1856
London, England 1857

London, England 1857-58
London, England 1857-59
London, England 1858
London, England 1858-59
London, England 1858-60
London, England 1859
London, England 1860
London, England 1861
London, England 1861-62
London, England 1862
London, England 1863
London, England 1864
London, England 1865
London, England 1866
London, England 1866-71
London, England 1866-82
London, England 1867
London, England 1868
London, England 1869
London, England 1870
London, England 1871
London, England 1872
London, England 1872-80
London, England 1873
London, England 1874
London, England 1875
London, England 1875-81
London, England 1876
London, England 1877
London, England 1878
London, England 1878-80
London, England 1879
London, England 1879-80
London, England 1879-82
London, England 1880
London, England 1880s
London, England 1881
London, England 1881-86
London, England 1882
London, England 1883
London, England 1884
London, England 1885
London, England 1886
London, England 1886-88
London, England 1887
London, England 1888
London, England 1889
London, England 1890
London, England 1891
London, England 1892
London, England 1894
London, England 1895
London, England 1896
London, England 1897
London, England 1898
London, England 1899
London, England 1900
London, England 1901
London, England 1902
London, England 1903
London, England 1904
London, England 1905
London, England 1905-13
London, England 1906
London, England 1907

London, England 1908
London, England 1908-11
London, England 1909
London, England 1910
London, England 1911
London, England 1912
London, England 1913
London, England 1914
London, England 1915
London, England 1916
London, England 1917
London, England 1918
London, England 1919
London, England 1920
London, England 1921
London, England 1922
London, England 1923
London, England 1924
London, England 1925
London, England 1926
London, England 1927
London, England 1928
London, England 1929
London, England 1929
London, England 1930
London, England 1931
London, England 1932
London, England 1933
London, England 1934
London, England 1935
London, England 1936
London, England 1937
London, England 1938
London, England 1939
London, England 1940
London, England 1941
London, England 1943
London, England 1945
London, England 1947
London, England 1947-48
London, England 1948
London, England 1949
London, England 1950
London, England 1951
London, England 1952
London, England 1953
London, England 1953-55
London, England 1954
London, England 1955
London, England 1957
London, England 1958
London, England 1959
London, England 1960
London, England 1961
London, England 1962
London, England 1964
London, England 1965
London, England 1965-68
London, England 1966
London, England 1967
London, England 1967-71
London, England 1968-71
London, England 1969
London, England 1971
London, England 1972

London, England 1973
London, England 1974
London, England 1975
London, England 1977
London, England 1978
London, England 1979
London, England 1980
London, England 1981
London, England 1983
London, England 1985
London, England 1986
London, England 1987
London, England 1988
London, England 1992
London, England 1993
London, England 1994
London, England 1996
London, England 1997
London, England 1998
London, England 1999
London, England 2000
London, England; Baltimore, Md.
   1953
London, England; Boston, Mass.
   1904-06
London, England; Boston, Mass.
   1911
London, England; Boston, Mass.
   1924
London, England; Boston, Mass.
   1930
London, England; Boston, Mass.
   1995
London, England; Cambridge,
   England 1844
London, England; Cambridge,
   England 1960-63
London, England; Cambridge,
   Mass. 1934-39
London, England; Cambridge,
   Mass. 1938-42
London, England; Cambridge,
   Mass. 1942
London, England; Cambridge,
   Mass. 1942-45
London, England; Cambridge,
   Mass. 1950
London, England; Cambridge,
   Mass. 1959
London, England; Cambridge,
   Mass. 1964
London, England; Cambridge,
   Mass. 1970
London, England; Chester Springs,
   Pa. 1993
London, England; Edinburgh,
   Scotland 1903-10
London, England; Edinburgh,
   Scotland 1942
London, England; Edinburgh,
   Scotland 1946
London, England; Edinburgh,
   Scotland; York, Englan 1815
London, England; Glasgow, Scot-
   land 1915

London, England; New Haven, Conn. 1961

London, England; New Haven, Conn. 1967

London, England; New York, N.Y. 1864

London, England; New York, N.Y. 1880

London, England; New York, N.Y. 1883

London, England; New York, N.Y. 1884

London, England; New York, N.Y. 1885

London, England; New York, N.Y. 1886

London, England; New York, N.Y. 1887

London, England; New York, N.Y. 1887-88

London, England; New York, N.Y. 1888

London, England; New York, N.Y. 1888-00

London, England; New York, N.Y. 1889

London, England; New York, N.Y. 1892

London, England; New York, N.Y. 1893

London, England; New York, N.Y. 1894

London, England; New York, N.Y. 1894

London, England; New York, N.Y. 1895

London, England; New York, N.Y. 1895-98

London, England; New York, N.Y. 1896

London, England; New York, N.Y. 1897

London, England; New York, N.Y. 1897-98

London, England; New York, N.Y. 1898

London, England; New York, N.Y. 1898

London, England; New York, N.Y. 1900

London, England; New York, N.Y. 1900-02

London, England; New York, N.Y. 1901

London, England; New York, N.Y. 1902

London, England; New York, N.Y. 1903

London, England; New York, N.Y. 1904

London, England; New York, N.Y. 1905

London, England; New York, N.Y. 1906

London, England; New York, N.Y. 1907

London, England; New York, N.Y. 1909

London, England; New York, N.Y. 1910

London, England; New York, N.Y. 1911

London, England; New York, N.Y. 1912

London, England; New York, N.Y. 1913

London, England; New York, N.Y. 1914

London, England; New York, N.Y. 1915

London, England; New York, N.Y. 1919

London, England; New York, N.Y. 1920

London, England; New York, N.Y. 1921

London, England; New York, N.Y. 1922

London, England; New York, N.Y. 1924

London, England; New York, N.Y. 1926

London, England; New York, N.Y. 1927

London, England; New York, N.Y. 1928

London, England; New York, N.Y. 1929-30

London, England; New York, N.Y. 1930

London, England; New York, N.Y. 1931

London, England; New York, N.Y. 1933

London, England; New York, N.Y. 1934

London, England; New York, N.Y. 1935

London, England; New York, N.Y. 1936

London, England; New York, N.Y. 1937

London, England; New York, N.Y. 1938

London, England; New York, N.Y. 1944

London, England; New York, N.Y. 1948

London, England; New York, N.Y. 1949

London, England; New York, N.Y. 1952

London, England; New York, N.Y. 1953

London, England; New York, N.Y. 1955

London, England; New York, N.Y. 1955-56

London, England; New York, N.Y. 1956

London, England; New York, N.Y. 1958

London, England; New York, N.Y. 1959-60

London, England; New York, N.Y. 1959-74

London, England; New York, N.Y. 1960

London, England; New York, N.Y. 1960-62

London, England; New York, N.Y. 1961-65

London, England; New York, N.Y. 1963

London, England; New York, N.Y. 1964-67

London, England; New York, N.Y. 1965

London, England; New York, N.Y. 1967-71

London, England; New York, N.Y. 1972

London, England; New York, N.Y. 1983

London, England; New York, N.Y. 1987

London, England; New York, N.Y. 1988

London, England; New York, N.Y. 1991

London, England; New York, N.Y. 1996

London, England; New York, N.Y. 1997

London, England; New York, N.Y. 2000

London, England; New York, N.Y.; Bombay; Cambridge 1900

London, England; North Cheam [England?] 1973

London, England; Paris, France; Strasbourg, France 1820

London, England; Rutland, Vt. 1992

London, England; Toronto, Canada 1930

London, England; Toronto, Canada; New York, N.Y. 1938

London, England; Tulsa, Ok 1981

London, England; Winton [England?] 1817

London; New York, N.Y.; Cambridge, Mass. 1924

London; New York, N.Y.; Cambridge, Mass. 1925

Londra [Italy?] 1736

Los Angeles, Ca. 1997

Los Angeles, Ca. 1997

Louisville, Ky. 1954

Lovanij 1521

Lowestoft, England 1977

Lucca, Italy 1703

Lucca, Italy 1745

Lucerne (Luzern), Switzerland; Frankfurt, Germany 1969

Lund, Sweden 1920

Lund, Sweden 1942

Lund, Sweden 1946
Lund, Sweden 1948
Lund, Sweden 1949
Lund, Sweden 1962
Lund, Sweden 1963
Lund, Sweden 1965
Luxembourg 1995
L'viv (Lwow), Ukraine 1889-92
L'viv (Lwow), Ukraine 1918
L'viv (Lwow), Ukraine 1924
L'viv (Lwow), Ukraine 1932
Lyons, France 1486
Lyons, France 1534
Lyons, France 1559
Lyons, France 1602
Lyons, France 1607
Lyons, France 1656
Lyons, France 1745
Lyons, France 1796
Lyons, France 1810
Lyons, France 1819
Lyons, France 1820
Lyons, France 1822
Lyons, France 1827-28
Maastricht, Netherlands 1929
Macerata, Italy 1825
Macerata, Italy 1992
Madrid, Spain 1767
Madrid, Spain 1785
Madrid, Spain 1787
Madrid, Spain 1788
Madrid, Spain 1827
Madrid, Spain 1831
Madrid, Spain 1880s
Madrid, Spain 1882-83
Madrid, Spain 1886
Madrid, Spain 1887
Madrid, Spain 1889
Madrid, Spain 1900
Madrid, Spain 1911
Madrid, Spain 1923
Madrid, Spain 1933
Madrid, Spain 1950
Madrid, Spain 1951
Madrid, Spain 1953
Madrid, Spain 1954
Madrid, Spain 1961
Madrid, Spain 1962
Madrid, Spain 1964
Madrid, Spain 1965
Madrid, Spain 1968
Madrid, Spain 1970
Madrid, Spain 1973
Madrid, Spain 1974
Madrid, Spain 1976
Madrid, Spain 1981
Madrid, Spain 1982
Madrid, Spain 1984
Madrid, Spain 1985
Madrid, Spain 1986
Madrid, Spain 1987
Madrid, Spain 1988
Madrid, Spain 1989
Madrid, Spain 1990
Madrid, Spain 1991

Madrid, Spain 1995
Madrid, Spain 1996
Madrid, Spain 1997
Madrid, Spain 1999
Magdeburg, Germany 1661
Mahwah, N.J. 1984
Mainz, Germany 1600
Mainz, Germany 1982
Mainz, Germany 1995
Maisura 1984
Mallorca, Spain 1919
Malmo, Sweden 1959
Managua, Nicaragua 1984
Mannheim, Germany 1826
Mantova (Mantua), Italy 1778
Marburg and Leipzig, Germany;
    Paris, France 1883
Marburg, Germany 1815
Marburg, Germany 1822
Marburg, Germany 1826
Marcinelle-Charleroi [France?]
    1984
Marlborough, Eng. 1988
Marseilles, France 1865
Marsiho [location?] 1907
Meissen, Germany 1788-93
Meissen, Germany 1809-14
Meissen, Germany 1818-19
Meissen, Germany 1820
Mem Martins [location?] 1980s
Messina, Sicily, Italy 1934
Messina, Sicily, Italy; Florence,
    Italy 1973
Mexico (City), Mexico 1931
Mexico (City), Mexico 1951
Mexico (City), Mexico 1953
Mexico (City), Mexico 1954
Mexico (City), Mexico 1955
Mexico (City), Mexico 1956
Mexico (City), Mexico 1959
Mexico (City), Mexico 1960
Mexico (City), Mexico 1963
Mexico (City), Mexico 1964
Mexico (City), Mexico 1965
Mexico (City), Mexico 1966
Mexico (City), Mexico 1967
Mexico (City), Mexico 1969
Mexico (City), Mexico 1970
Mexico (City), Mexico 1971
Mexico (City), Mexico 1972
Mexico (City), Mexico 1973
Mexico (City), Mexico 1974
Mexico (City), Mexico 1975
Mexico (City), Mexico 1976
Mexico (City), Mexico 1977
Mexico (City), Mexico 1978
Mexico (City), Mexico 1979
Mexico (City), Mexico 1980
Mexico (City), Mexico 1981
Mexico (City), Mexico 1982
Mexico (City), Mexico 1983
Mexico (City), Mexico 1984
Mexico (City), Mexico 1985
Mexico (City), Mexico 1986
Mexico (City), Mexico 1987

Mexico (City), Mexico 1988
Mexico (City), Mexico 1990
Mexico (City), Mexico 1991
Mexico (City), Mexico 1992
Mexico (City), Mexico 1994
Mexico (City), Mexico 1996-97
Mexico (City), Mexico 1997
Mexico (City), Mexico; Buenos
    Aires 1951
Miami, Fl. 1970
Miami, Fl. 1972
Milan, Italy 1753
Milan, Italy 1784
Milan, Italy 1793
Milan, Italy 1812
Milan, Italy 1815
Milan, Italy 1816
Milan, Italy 1817
Milan, Italy 1820
Milan, Italy 1821
Milan, Italy 1825
Milan, Italy 1827
Milan, Italy 1829
Milan, Italy 1830
Milan, Italy 1831
Milan, Italy 1833
Milan, Italy 1839
Milan, Italy 1840
Milan, Italy 1841
Milan, Italy 1842
Milan, Italy 1845
Milan, Italy 1847
Milan, Italy 1873
Milan, Italy 1878
Milan, Italy 1880
Milan, Italy 1885
Milan, Italy 1886
Milan, Italy 1896
Milan, Italy 1905
Milan, Italy 1919
Milan, Italy 1920s
Milan, Italy 1927
Milan, Italy 1928
Milan, Italy 1929
Milan, Italy 1931
Milan, Italy 1934
Milan, Italy 1937
Milan, Italy 1952
Milan, Italy 1953
Milan, Italy 1958
Milan, Italy 1960
Milan, Italy 1965
Milan, Italy 1967
Milan, Italy 1968
Milan, Italy 1972
Milan, Italy 1975
Milan, Italy 1979
Milan, Italy 1982
Milan, Italy 1984
Milan, Italy 1985
Milan, Italy 1988
Milan, Italy 1990
Milan, Italy 1991-93
Milan, Italy 1992
Milan, Italy 1996

Milan, Italy 1997
Milan, Italy; Rome, Italy 1914
Milwaukee, Wis. 1980
Milwaukee, Wis. 1981
Milwaukee, Wis. 1985
Milwaukee, Wis. 1992
Mineola, N.Y. 1999
Minneapolis, Minn. 1909
Minsk, Belarus 1995
Minsk, Belarus 1998
Modena, Italy 1498
Mons [location?] 1883
Montevideo, Uruguay 1976
Montpellier, France 1885
Montreal, Canada 1991
Morristown, N.J. 1967
Moscow, Russia 1871
Moscow, Russia 1871-74
Moscow, Russia 1935
Moscow, Russia 1949
Moscow, Russia 1953
Moscow, Russia 1958
Moscow, Russia 1959
Moscow, Russia 1960
Moscow, Russia 1967
Moscow, Russia 1978
Moscow, Russia 1981
Moscow, Russia 1982
Moscow, Russia 1985
Moscow, Russia 1986
Moscow, Russia 1987
Moscow, Russia 1990
Moscow, Russia 1993
Moscow, Russia 1998
Mumbai 1984
Munich, Germany 1537
Munich, Germany 1647
Munich, Germany 1667
Munich, Germany 1782
Munich, Germany 1805
Munich, Germany 1818
Munich, Germany 1822-23
Munich, Germany 1839
Munich, Germany 1903
Munich, Germany 1905
Munich, Germany 1913
Munich, Germany 1918
Munich, Germany 1923-24
Munich, Germany 1924
Munich, Germany 1925
Munich, Germany 1926
Munich, Germany 1941
Munich, Germany 1951
Munich, Germany 1952
Munich, Germany 1954
Munich, Germany 1955
Munich, Germany 1957
Munich, Germany 1960
Munich, Germany 1961
Munich, Germany 1970
Munich, Germany 1972
Munich, Germany 1979
Munich, Germany 1980
Munich, Germany 1982
Munich, Germany 1986

Munich, Germany 1989
Munich, Germany 1990
Munich, Germany 1991
Munich, Germany 1995
Munich, Germany 2000
Munich, Germany; Darmstadt, Germany 1965
Munich, Germany; Grafelfing, Germany 1929
Munich, Germany; Leipzig, Germany 1897
Munich, Germany; Zurich, Switzerland 1961
Munster, Germany 1895
Munster, Germany 1905
Munster, Germany 1930-31
Munster, Germany 1931
Munster, Germany 1986
Nakladem [Poland?]] 1968
Nantes, France 1817
Nantes, France 1857
Naples, Italy 1556
Naples, Italy 1578
Naples, Italy 1618
Naples, Italy 1747
Naples, Italy 1761
Naples, Italy 1763
Naples, Italy 1776
Naples, Italy 1815
Naples, Italy 1815
Naples, Italy 1825
Naples, Italy 1828
Naples, Italy 1833
Naples, Italy 1860
Naples, Italy 1930
Naples; Florence, Italy 1969
Nashville, Tn. 2000
Neustettin [Germany?] 1869
Nevada City, Cal. 1999
New Orleans, La. 1980
New York, N.Y. 1808
New York, N.Y. 1812
New York, N.Y. 1814
New York, N.Y. 1822
New York, N.Y. 1825
New York, N.Y. 1826
New York, N.Y. 1832
New York, N.Y. 1834
New York, N.Y. 1836
New York, N.Y. 1837
New York, N.Y. 1840
New York, N.Y. 1842
New York, N.Y. 1844
New York, N.Y. 1845
New York, N.Y. 1846
New York, N.Y. 1847
New York, N.Y. 1848
New York, N.Y. 1849
New York, N.Y. 1850
New York, N.Y. 1851
New York, N.Y. 1853
New York, N.Y. 1854
New York, N.Y. 1855
New York, N.Y. 1855-58
New York, N.Y. 1856

New York, N.Y. 1857
New York, N.Y. 1858
New York, N.Y. 1859
New York, N.Y. 1859-60
New York, N.Y. 1860
New York, N.Y. 1860s
New York, N.Y. 1861
New York, N.Y. 1862
New York, N.Y. 1863
New York, N.Y. 1864
New York, N.Y. 1865
New York, N.Y. 1866
New York, N.Y. 1867
New York, N.Y. 1868
New York, N.Y. 1869
New York, N.Y. 1870
New York, N.Y. 1870s
New York, N.Y. 1870s
New York, N.Y. 1870s
New York, N.Y. 1871
New York, N.Y. 1872
New York, N.Y. 1872-76
New York, N.Y. 1873
New York, N.Y. 1874
New York, N.Y. 1875
New York, N.Y. 1876
New York, N.Y. 1877
New York, N.Y. 1878
New York, N.Y. 1879
New York, N.Y. 1880
New York, N.Y. 1881
New York, N.Y. 1882
New York, N.Y. 1883
New York, N.Y. 1884
New York, N.Y. 1885
New York, N.Y. 1886
New York, N.Y. 1887
New York, N.Y. 1888
New York, N.Y. 1889
New York, N.Y. 1890
New York, N.Y. 1890s
New York, N.Y. 1891
New York, N.Y. 1892
New York, N.Y. 1893
New York, N.Y. 1894
New York, N.Y. 1895
New York, N.Y. 1896
New York, N.Y. 1897
New York, N.Y. 1898
New York, N.Y. 1899
New York, N.Y. 1900
New York, N.Y. 1901
New York, N.Y. 1902
New York, N.Y. 1903
New York, N.Y. 1904
New York, N.Y. 1905
New York, N.Y. 1906
New York, N.Y. 1907
New York, N.Y. 1908
New York, N.Y. 1909
New York, N.Y. 1910
New York, N.Y. 1910-13
New York, N.Y. 1911
New York, N.Y. 1911-12
New York, N.Y. 1912

New York, N.Y. 1914
New York, N.Y. 1915
New York, N.Y. 1916
New York, N.Y. 1917
New York, N.Y. 1918
New York, N.Y. 1920
New York, N.Y. 1921
New York, N.Y. 1922
New York, N.Y. 1923
New York, N.Y. 1924
New York, N.Y. 1925
New York, N.Y. 1926
New York, N.Y. 1927
New York, N.Y. 1928
New York, N.Y. 1929
New York, N.Y. 1930
New York, N.Y. 1931
New York, N.Y. 1932
New York, N.Y. 1933
New York, N.Y. 1934
New York, N.Y. 1935
New York, N.Y. 1936
New York, N.Y. 1937
New York, N.Y. 1938
New York, N.Y. 1939
New York, N.Y. 1940
New York, N.Y. 1941
New York, N.Y. 1942
New York, N.Y. 1943
New York, N.Y. 1944
New York, N.Y. 1945
New York, N.Y. 1946
New York, N.Y. 1947
New York, N.Y. 1948
New York, N.Y. 1949
New York, N.Y. 1950
New York, N.Y. 1951
New York, N.Y. 1952
New York, N.Y. 1953
New York, N.Y. 1954
New York, N.Y. 1955
New York, N.Y. 1956
New York, N.Y. 1957
New York, N.Y. 1958
New York, N.Y. 1959
New York, N.Y. 1960
New York, N.Y. 1961
New York, N.Y. 1962
New York, N.Y. 1963
New York, N.Y. 1964
New York, N.Y. 1965
New York, N.Y. 1965-74
New York, N.Y. 1966
New York, N.Y. 1967
New York, N.Y. 1968
New York, N.Y. 1969
New York, N.Y. 1970
New York, N.Y. 1970s
New York, N.Y. 1970s
New York, N.Y. 1971
New York, N.Y. 1972
New York, N.Y. 1973
New York, N.Y. 1974
New York, N.Y. 1975
New York, N.Y. 1976

New York, N.Y. 1977
New York, N.Y. 1978
New York, N.Y. 1979
New York, N.Y. 1980s
New York, N.Y. 1981
New York, N.Y. 1982
New York, N.Y. 1983
New York, N.Y. 1984
New York, N.Y. 1986
New York, N.Y. 1987
New York, N.Y. 1988
New York, N.Y. 1989
New York, N.Y. 1990
New York, N.Y. 1991
New York, N.Y. 1992
New York, N.Y. 1993
New York, N.Y. 1994
New York, N.Y. 1995
New York, N.Y. 1996
New York, N.Y. 1997
New York, N.Y. 1998
New York, N.Y. 1999
New York, N.Y. 2000
New York, N.Y.; Boston, Mass.
1897
New York, N.Y.; Cambridge, Oh.
1889
New York, N.Y.; Cambridge, Oh.
1890
New York, N.Y.; Cambridge, Oh.
1903
New York, N.Y.; Cambridge, Oh.
1907
New York, N.Y.; Franklin Center,
Pa. 1983
New York, N.Y.; London, England
1869
New York, N.Y.; London, England
1890
New York, N.Y.; London, England
1896
New York, N.Y.; London, England
1899
New York, N.Y.; London, England
1905
New York, N.Y.; London, England
1907
New York, N.Y.; London, England
1909
New York, N.Y.; London, England
1912
New York, N.Y.; London, England
1915
New York, N.Y.; London, England
1916
New York, N.Y.; London, England
1917
New York, N.Y.; London, England
1921
New York, N.Y.; London, England
1922
New York, N.Y.; London, England
1923
New York, N.Y.; London, England
1928

New York, N.Y.; London, England
1929
New York, N.Y.; London, England
1930
New York, N.Y.; London, England
1931
New York, N.Y.; London, England
1950
New York, N.Y.; London, England
1952
New York, N.Y.; London, England
1971
New York, N.Y.; London, England
1997
New York, N.Y.; London, England
1999
New York, N.Y.; London, England;
Toronto, Canada 1930
New York, N.Y.; Oxford, England
1991
New York, N.Y.; Paris, France
1970s
New York, N.Y.; Philadelphia, Pa.
1872-76
New York, N.Y.; Toronto, Canada
1991
New York, N.Y.; Toronto, Canada;
London, London 1938
New York; London 1987
Newmarket [England?] 1992
Newmarket [England?] 1995
Neyss [location?] 1567
Nice, France 1937
Nice, France 1990
Nordhausen, Germany 1897
Nordhausen, Germany 1898
North Finchley, [England?] 1891
Norwalk, Conn. 1971
Norwalk, Conn. 1978
Norwalk, Conn. 1979
Nottingham, Eng. 1968
Novi Sad, Yugoslavia 1985
Nowot, Colo. 1991
Nuremberg, Germany 1527
Oerebro, Sweden 1842
Oerebro, Sweden 1844-45
Oerebro, Sweden 1846
Oldbourne [England?] 1963
Olten, Switzerland 1960
Ontario, Canada 1986
Orange, N.J. 1956
Oslo, Norway 1958
Osnabruck, Germany 1974
Ottobrunn bei Munchen, Ger-
many 1981
Oxford, England 1583
Oxford, England 1664
Oxford, England 1665
Oxford, England 1670
Oxford, England 1674
Oxford, England 1676
Oxford, England 1695
Oxford, England 1696-98
Oxford, England 1698
Oxford, England 1702

Oxford, England 1705
Oxford, England 1706
Oxford, England 1708
Oxford, England 1714
Oxford, England 1739
Oxford, England 1743
Oxford, England 1750-58
Oxford, England 1758
Oxford, England 1765
Oxford, England 1767
Oxford, England 1772
Oxford, England 1774
Oxford, England 1775
Oxford, England 1780
Oxford, England 1782
Oxford, England 1792-97
Oxford, England 1797
Oxford, England 1800
Oxford, England 1801
Oxford, England 1802
Oxford, England 1808
Oxford, England 1810
Oxford, England 1811
Oxford, England 1814
Oxford, England 1815
Oxford, England 1817
Oxford, England 1821
Oxford, England 1821-25
Oxford, England 1821-34
Oxford, England 1823
Oxford, England 1825
Oxford, England 1827
Oxford, England 1831
Oxford, England 1833
Oxford, England 1834
Oxford, England 1855
Oxford, England 1855-56
Oxford, England 1856
Oxford, England 1861
Oxford, England 1863
Oxford, England 1864
Oxford, England 1868
Oxford, England 1870-78
Oxford, England 1871
Oxford, England 1873
Oxford, England 1874
Oxford, England 1875
Oxford, England 1876
Oxford, England 1877
Oxford, England 1878
Oxford, England 1878-95
Oxford, England 1880
Oxford, England 1881
Oxford, England 1882
Oxford, England 1882-84
Oxford, England 1883
Oxford, England 1884
Oxford, England 1884-97
Oxford, England 1885
Oxford, England 1886
Oxford, England 1886-01
Oxford, England 1887
Oxford, England 1888
Oxford, England 1889
Oxford, England 1890

Oxford, England 1890-93
Oxford, England 1890-97
Oxford, England 1891
Oxford, England 1892
Oxford, England 1893
Oxford, England 1894
Oxford, England 1895
Oxford, England 1895-01
Oxford, England 1896-99
Oxford, England 1897
Oxford, England 1897-99
Oxford, England 1899
Oxford, England 1899-01
Oxford, England 1899-03
Oxford, England 1901
Oxford, England 1902
Oxford, England 1902-12
Oxford, England 1903
Oxford, England 1903-06
Oxford, England 1904
Oxford, England 1905
Oxford, England 1906
Oxford, England 1906
Oxford, England 1907
Oxford, England 1907-12
Oxford, England 1909
Oxford, England 1911-19
Oxford, England 1912
Oxford, England 1912-20
Oxford, England 1916
Oxford, England 1916-19
Oxford, England 1919
Oxford, England 1920
Oxford, England 1921
Oxford, England 1923-28
Oxford, England 1925
Oxford, England 1926-32
Oxford, England 1928
Oxford, England 1930
Oxford, England 1930-35
Oxford, England 1931
Oxford, England 1932
Oxford, England 1934
Oxford, England 1935
Oxford, England 1935-38
Oxford, England 1936
Oxford, England 1938
Oxford, England 1938-39
Oxford, England 1941
Oxford, England 1945
Oxford, England 1949
Oxford, England 1950
Oxford, England 1953
Oxford, England 1955
Oxford, England 1955-59
Oxford, England 1957
Oxford, England 1958-62
Oxford, England 1960
Oxford, England 1961-64
Oxford, England 1961-66
Oxford, England 1964-66
Oxford, England 1966
Oxford, England 1967
Oxford, England 1969
Oxford, England 1975

Oxford, England 1975-79
Oxford, England 1976
Oxford, England 1995
Oxford, England 1998
Oxford, England 1999
Oxford, England 2000
Oxford, England; London, England 1776
Oxford, England; London, England 1788
Oxford, England; London, England 1862
Oxford, England; London, England 1869
Oxford, England; New York, N.Y. 1980
Oxford, England; New York, N.Y. 1984
Oxford, England; New York, N.Y. 1986
Oxford, England; New York, N.Y. 1988
Oxford, England; New York, N.Y. 1991
Oxford, England; New York, N.Y. 1993
Oxford, England; New York, N.Y. 1995
Oxford, England; New York, N.Y. 1998
Paderborn, Germany 1863-64
Paderborn, Germany 1866
Paderborn, Germany 1873-78
Paderborn, Germany 1875
Paderborn, Germany 1953
Paderborn, Germany 1954
Paderborn, Germany 1963
Padova (Padua), Italy 1564
Padova (Padua), Italy 1740
Padova (Padua), Italy 1740
Padova (Padua), Italy 1742
Padova (Padua), Italy 1744
Padova (Padua), Italy 1760
Padova (Padua), Italy 1769
Padova (Padua), Italy 1777
Padova (Padua), Italy 1786-94
Padova (Padua), Italy 1798-02
Padova (Padua), Italy 1802
Padova (Padua), Italy 1810
Padova (Padua), Italy 1819-20
Padova (Padua), Italy 1820
Padova (Padua), Italy 1832
Padova (Padua), Italy 1913
Padova (Padua), Italy 1984
Palermo, Sicily, Italy 1661
Palermo, Sicily, Italy 1926
Palermo, Sicily, Italy 1951
Palermo, Sicily, Italy 1977
Palermo, Sicily, Italy 1992
Palermo, Sicily, Italy 1998
Paris, France 1507
Paris, France 1510
Paris, France 1516
Paris, France 1521
Paris, France 1523

Paris, France 1526	Paris, France 1708	Paris, France 1835
Paris, France 1530	Paris, France 1708-09	Paris, France 1836
Paris, France 1535	Paris, France 1709	Paris, France 1837
Paris, France 1538	Paris, France 1711-20	Paris, France 1837-38
Paris, France 1538	Paris, France 1714	Paris, France 1841
Paris, France 1540	Paris, France 1716	Paris, France 1842-43
Paris, France 1541	Paris, France 1716-20	Paris, France 1843
Paris, France 1542	Paris, France 1717	Paris, France 1843-79
Paris, France 1543	Paris, France 1719	Paris, France 1845
Paris, France 1545	Paris, France 1720	Paris, France 1846
Paris, France 1546	Paris, France 1741-56	Paris, France 1848
Paris, France 1547	Paris, France 1744	Paris, France 1849
Paris, France 1550	Paris, France 1747-48	Paris, France 1850
Paris, France 1554	Paris, France 1756	Paris, France 1852
Paris, France 1555	Paris, France 1764	Paris, France 1853
Paris, France 1558	Paris, France 1766-70	Paris, France 1854
Paris, France 1560	Paris, France 1772-77	Paris, France 1854-59
Paris, France 1562	Paris, France 1776	Paris, France 1855
Paris, France 1566	Paris, France 1777	Paris, France 1856
Paris, France 1570	Paris, France 1780-85	Paris, France 1857
Paris, France 1573	Paris, France 1781	Paris, France 1860
Paris, France 1574	Paris, France 1781-82	Paris, France 1861
Paris, France 1577	Paris, France 1782-85	Paris, France 1862
Paris, France 1578	Paris, France 1783	Paris, France 1863
Paris, France 1580	Paris, France 1784	Paris, France 1864
Paris, France 1581	Paris, France 1784-85	Paris, France 1865
Paris, France 1582	Paris, France 1785	Paris, France 1866
Paris, France 1584	Paris, France 1786	Paris, France 1867
Paris, France 1588	Paris, France 1786-88	Paris, France 1868
Paris, France 1597	Paris, France 1787-88	Paris, France 1869
Paris, France 1599	Paris, France 1789	Paris, France 1869-75
Paris, France 1604	Paris, France 1795	Paris, France 1870
Paris, France 1610-27	Paris, France 1796	Paris, France 1871
Paris, France 1614	Paris, France 1800	Paris, France 1872
Paris, France 1615	Paris, France 1801	Paris, France 1873
Paris, France 1616	Paris, France 1803	Paris, France 1874
Paris, France 1617	Paris, France 1804	Paris, France 1875
Paris, France 1619	Paris, France 1804-05	Paris, France 1876
Paris, France 1620	Paris, France 1809	Paris, France 1877
Paris, France 1620-28	Paris, France 1810	Paris, France 1878
Paris, France 1622	Paris, France 1811	Paris, France 1880
Paris, France 1622-24	Paris, France 1811-20	Paris, France 1881
Paris, France 1624	Paris, France 1812	Paris, France 1882
Paris, France 1625	Paris, France 1815	Paris, France 1883
Paris, France 1626	Paris, France 1815-18	Paris, France 1883-84
Paris, France 1627	Paris, France 1816	Paris, France 1884
Paris, France 1628	Paris, France 1816-18	Paris, France 1885
Paris, France 1631	Paris, France 1817	Paris, France 1886
Paris, France 1634	Paris, France 1818	Paris, France 1887-88
Paris, France 1636	Paris, France 1819	Paris, France 1888
Paris, France 1637	Paris, France 1822	Paris, France 1890
Paris, France 1638	Paris, France 1823	Paris, France 1893
Paris, France 1639	Paris, France 1823-24	Paris, France 1894
Paris, France 1640?	Paris, France 1825	Paris, France 1895
Paris, France 1642	Paris, France 1826	Paris, France 1896
Paris, France 1650	Paris, France 1826-28	Paris, France 1897
Paris, France 1657	Paris, France 1827	Paris, France 1898-02
Paris, France 1658	Paris, France 1828	Paris, France 1899
Paris, France 1665	Paris, France 1828-34	Paris, France 1900
Paris, France 1674	Paris, France 1829	Paris, France 1902
Paris, France 1681	Paris, France 1829-30	Paris, France 1903
Paris, France 1697	Paris, France 1830	Paris, France 1904
Paris, France 1699	Paris, France 1831	Paris, France 1907
Paris, France 1700	Paris, France 1832	Paris, France 1908
Paris, France 1701	Paris, France 1833	Paris, France 1911

Paris, France 1914
Paris, France 1921
Paris, France 1923
Paris, France 1924
Paris, France 1925
Paris, France 1927
Paris, France 1928
Paris, France 1930
Paris, France 1930-33
Paris, France 1931
Paris, France 1932
Paris, France 1933
Paris, France 1934
Paris, France 1935
Paris, France 1936
Paris, France 1937
Paris, France 1938
Paris, France 1939
Paris, France 1940-41
Paris, France 1941
Paris, France 1942
Paris, France 1943
Paris, France 1944
Paris, France 1945
Paris, France 1946
Paris, France 1947
Paris, France 1947-49
Paris, France 1950
Paris, France 1951
Paris, France 1952
Paris, France 1953
Paris, France 1954
Paris, France 1955
Paris, France 1955-57
Paris, France 1955-59
Paris, France 1956
Paris, France 1957
Paris, France 1958
Paris, France 1959
Paris, France 1960
Paris, France 1961
Paris, France 1961-63
Paris, France 1962
Paris, France 1963
Paris, France 1964
Paris, France 1965
Paris, France 1965-67
Paris, France 1966
Paris, France 1967
Paris, France 1967-68
Paris, France 1967-70
Paris, France 1968
Paris, France 1969
Paris, France 1970
Paris, France 1971
Paris, France 1972
Paris, France 1972-87
Paris, France 1973
Paris, France 1973
Paris, France 1974
Paris, France 1974-89
Paris, France 1975
Paris, France 1976
Paris, France 1978
Paris, France 1979

Paris, France 1982-92
Paris, France 1984
Paris, France 1987
Paris, France 1987-92
Paris, France 1988
Paris, France 1989
Paris, France 1991
Paris, France 1992
Paris, France 1995
Paris, France 1996
Paris, France 1997
Paris, France 1998
Paris, France (?) 1650?
Paris, France; Amsterdam, 1624-50
Paris, France; Barbin, Holland 1682
Paris, France; Berlin, Germany 1827
Paris, France; London, England 1875
Parma, Italy 1492
Parma, Italy 1805
Parma, Italy 1807
Parma, Italy 1808
Parma, Italy 1872
Parma, Italy 1989
Partille, Sweden 1988
Passau [location?] 1823
Pasto, Narino, Colombia 1939
Pasto, Spain 1937
Pasto, Spain 1938
Pavia, Italy 1805
Pavia, Italy 1812
Pavia, Italy 1823
Pesaro, Italy 1508
Pesaro, Italy 1509
Pesaro, Italy 1760
Pest, Hungary 1846
Pest, Hungary 1857
Petersburg and Leipzig, Germany 1774
Philadelphia, PA 1794
Philadelphia, Pa. 1795
Philadelphia, Pa. 1800-75
Philadelphia, Pa. 1812
Philadelphia, Pa. 1822
Philadelphia, Pa. 1828
Philadelphia, Pa. 1830
Philadelphia, Pa. 1835
Philadelphia, Pa. 1836
Philadelphia, Pa. 1838
Philadelphia, Pa. 1839
Philadelphia, Pa. 1845
Philadelphia, Pa. 1847
Philadelphia, Pa. 1850
Philadelphia, Pa. 1853
Philadelphia, Pa. 1855-58
Philadelphia, Pa. 1860
Philadelphia, Pa. 1863
Philadelphia, Pa. 1865
Philadelphia, Pa. 1865
Philadelphia, Pa. 1867
Philadelphia, Pa. 1870
Philadelphia, Pa. 1872
Philadelphia, Pa. 1872-76

Philadelphia, Pa. 1875
Philadelphia, Pa. 1880
Philadelphia, Pa. 1881
Philadelphia, Pa. 1883
Philadelphia, Pa. 1888
Philadelphia, Pa. 1889
Philadelphia, Pa. 1890
Philadelphia, Pa. 1895
Philadelphia, Pa. 1896
Philadelphia, Pa. 1898
Philadelphia, Pa. 1901
Philadelphia, Pa. 1902
Philadelphia, Pa. 1910
Philadelphia, Pa. 1924
Philadelphia, Pa. 1939
Philadelphia, Pa.; Chicago, Il. 1927
Piiarow, Poland 1804-05
Pisa, Italy 1800-13
Pisa, Italy 1802
Pisa, Italy 1881
Pisa, Italy 1996
Pishavar, Pakistan 1983
Pistoia, Italy 1791
Poitiers, France; Lyon, France 1535
Portland, Me. 1897
Portugal 1988
Porvoo, Finland 1916
Porvoo, Finland 1919
Prague, Czech.; Vienna, Austria; Leipzig, Germany 1894
Prague, Czechoslavakia 1826-27
Prague, Czechoslavakia 1856-58
Prague, Czechoslavakia 1859
Prague, Czechoslavakia 1884
Prague, Czechoslavakia 1895
Prague, Czechoslavakia 1901
Prague, Czechoslavakia 1904
Prague, Czechoslavakia 1908
Prague, Czechoslavakia 1911-12
Prague, Czechoslavakia 1921
Prague, Czechoslavakia 1926
Prague, Czechoslavakia 1940
Prague, Czechoslavakia 1942
Prague, Czechoslavakia 1956
Prague, Czechoslavakia 1967
Prague, Czechoslavakia 1980
Prato, Italy 1863-66
Prayaga, India 1920
Praze [location?] 1801
Praze [location?] 1842
Praze [location?] 1844
Prenzlau 1830
Presburg [?] 1829-31
Princeton, N.J. 1847
Princeton, N.J. 1942
Princeton, N.J. 1956
Princeton, N.J. 1967
Princeton, N.J. 1998
Prishtinee [location?] 1971
Pymble, New South Wales 1993
Pymble, New South Wales 1995
Ravensburg, Germany 1956
Ravensburg, Germany 1964

Ravensburg, Germany 1968
Ravensburg, Germany 1971
Ravensburg, Germany 1992
Ravensburg, Germany 1959
Reading, Pa. 1889
Recklinghausen, Germany 1971
Reinbeck bei Hamberg, Germany
   1969
Reutlingen, Germany 1819
Reykjavik, Iceland 1855
Reykjavik, Iceland 1856
Reykjavik, Iceland 1915
Reykjavik, Iceland 1941
Reykjavik, Iceland 1948-49
Reykjavik, Iceland 1952
Rhegii in Bruttiis [location?] 1946
Rheims, France 1776
Richmond, Va. 1852-55
Richmond, Va. 1901
Ridekro, Denmark 1987
Riga, Latvia 1936
Riga, Latvia 1961
Riga, Latvia 1967
Rio de Janeiro, Brazil 1874
Rio de Janeiro, Brazil 1928
Rio Piedras, Puerto Rico 1973
Rio Piedras, Puerto Rico 1988
Rio Piedras, Puerto Rico 1991
Rocca San Casciano [location?]
   1968
Rochester, N.Y. 1880
Rome, Italy 1474
Rome, Italy 1510
Rome, Italy 1512
Rome, Italy 1517
Rome, Italy 1542-50
Rome, Italy 1573
Rome, Italy 1739
Rome, Italy 1769-70
Rome, Italy 1772
Rome, Italy 1776
Rome, Italy 1783
Rome, Italy 1788
Rome, Italy 1789
Rome, Italy 1790
Rome, Italy 1830
Rome, Italy 1905
Rome, Italy 1948
Rome, Italy 1953
Rome, Italy 1956
Rome, Italy 1960
Rome, Italy 1966
Rome, Italy 1967
Rome, Italy 1968
Rome, Italy 1976
Rome, Italy 1977
Rome, Italy 1981
Rome, Italy 1989
Rome, Italy 1998
Rome, Italy 1999
Rome; Milan, Italy 1905
Rome; Milan, Italy 1981-86
Rome; Milan, Italy 1986
Ronciglione, Italy 1620
Rostock, Germany 1922

Rostock, Germany 1993
Rostov-na-Donu, Russia 1935
Rostov-na-Donu, Russia 1997
Rouen, France 1595
Rouen, France 1603
Rouen, France 1605
Sabadell, Spain 1975
Salamanca, Spain 1550
Salamanca, Spain 1965
Salingiaci [location?] 1540
Salvador, Brazil 1957
Salzwedel, Germany 1815
San Francisco, Ca. 1927
San Juan, Puerto Rico 1962
San Juan, Puerto Rico 1967
San Juan, Puerto Rico 1974
San Juan, Puerto Rico; Madrid,
   Spain 1956
San Sabastian, Spain 1984
Santa Barbara, Ca. 1983
Santiago, Chile 1965
Santiago, Chile 1984
Santiago, Chile 1985
Santiago, Chile 1987
Santiago, Chile 1988
Santiago, Chile 1990
Santiago, Chile 1993
Santiago, Chile 1994
Sao Paulo, Brazil 1956
Sao Paulo, Brazil 1962
Sao Paulo, Brazil 1992
Sao Paulo, Brazil 1994
Schleswig, Germany 1964
Schorndorf bei Stuttgart, Germany
   1969
Schweden [location?] 1776
Scottsdale, Ar. 1982
Seattle, Wa. 1971
Seattle, Wa. 1973
Seattle, Wa. 1978
Seattle, Wa. 1996
Senis [location?] 1777
Senis [location?] 1784
Seoul, South Korea 1973
Seoul, South Korea 1979
Seoul, South Korea 1983
Seoul, South Korea 1984
Seoul, South Korea 1988
Seoul, South Korea 1991
Seoul, South Korea 1992
Seoul, South Korea 1993
Seoul, South Korea 1996
Seoul, South Korea 1997
Seoul, South Korea 1999
Shang-hai, China 1934
Shang-hai, China 1947
Shang-hai, China 1979
Shang-hai, China 1985
Shkoder [location?] 1941
Sofija (Sofia), Bulgaria 1918
Sofija (Sofia), Bulgaria 1949
Sofija (Sofia), Bulgaria 1976
Soroe, Denmark 1830
South Pasadena, Ca. 1980s
St. Louis, Mo. 1877

St. Louis, Mo. 1922
St. Louis, Mo. 1952
St. Louis, Mo. 1972
St. Ludwig [location?] 1914
St. Petersburg, Russia 1771
St. Petersburg, Russia 1829
St. Petersburg, Russia 1837
St. Petersburg, Russia 1839
St. Petersburg, Russia 1884
St. Petersburg, Russia 1885
St. Petersburg, Russia 1890s
St. Petersburg, Russia 1892
St. Petersburg, Russia 1894
St. Petersburg, Russia 1998
Stamford, Ct. 1993
Stellenbosch, South Africa 1952
Stendal, Germany 1786
Stockholm, Sweden 1814-15
Stockholm, Sweden 1818
Stockholm, Sweden 1864
Stockholm, Sweden 1865
Stockholm, Sweden 1908
Stockholm, Sweden 1955
Stockholm, Sweden 1960
Stockholm, Sweden 1964
Stockholm, Sweden 1975
Stolberg, Germany 1776
Strasbourg, France 1489
Strasbourg, France 1510
Strasbourg, France 1512
Strasbourg, France 1516
Strasbourg, France 1517
Strasbourg, France 1523
Strasbourg, France 1525
Strasbourg, France 1530
Strasbourg, France 1534
Strasbourg, France 1538
Strasbourg, France 1540
Strasbourg, France 1542
Strasbourg, France 1550
Strasbourg, France 1567
Strasbourg, France 1572
Strasbourg, France 1579?
Strasbourg, France 1601
Strasbourg, France 1910
Strasbourg, France 1942
Stuttgart, Germany 1781-93
Stuttgart, Germany 1793
Stuttgart, Germany 1801
Stuttgart, Germany 1814
Stuttgart, Germany 1821
Stuttgart, Germany 1830-43
Stuttgart, Germany 1833
Stuttgart, Germany 1839
Stuttgart, Germany 1840
Stuttgart, Germany 1842
Stuttgart, Germany 1851
Stuttgart, Germany 1852
Stuttgart, Germany 1853
Stuttgart, Germany 1854
Stuttgart, Germany 1856
Stuttgart, Germany 1858
Stuttgart, Germany 1869
Stuttgart, Germany 1870
Stuttgart, Germany 1872

Stuttgart, Germany 1875
Stuttgart, Germany 1876
Stuttgart, Germany 1878
Stuttgart, Germany 1881
Stuttgart, Germany 1883
Stuttgart, Germany 1885
Stuttgart, Germany 1890
Stuttgart, Germany 1891
Stuttgart, Germany 1894
Stuttgart, Germany 1913
Stuttgart, Germany 1923
Stuttgart, Germany 1940
Stuttgart, Germany 1951
Stuttgart, Germany 1957
Stuttgart, Germany 1959
Stuttgart, Germany 1963
Stuttgart, Germany 1979
Stuttgart, Germany 1981
Stuttgart, Germany 1984
Stuttgart, Germany 1993
Stuttgart, Germany 1998
Stuttgart, Germany; Leipzig, Germany 1995
Stuttgart, Germany; Leipzig, Germany 1998
Stuttgart, Germany; Nubling [Germany?] 1864-74
Stuttgart, Germany; Tubingen, Germany 1822
Stuttgart, Germany; Tubingen, Germany 1844
Stuttgart, Germany; Tubingen, Germany 1847
Stuttgart, Germany; Tubingen, Germany 1853
Sundbyberg, Sweden 1979
Sussex,England 1956
Syracuse, N.Y. 1942
Taipei, Taiwan 1994
Taipei, Taiwan 1966
Taipei, Taiwan 1971
Taipei, Taiwan 1972
Taipei, Taiwan 1978
Taipei, Taiwan 1983
Taipei, Taiwan 1984
Taipei, Taiwan 1985
Taipei, Taiwan 1988
Taipei, Taiwan 1991
Taipei, Taiwan 1991
Taipei, Taiwan 1998
Taiwan (Tai-nan) 1982
Taiwan (Tai-nan) 1984
Taiwan (Tai-nan) 1984
Taiwan (Tai-nan) 1991
Taiwan (Tai-nan) 1993
Tallinn, Estonia 1960
Tallinn, Estonia 1963
Tao-yeuan, China 1977
Tehran, Iran 1996
Tel Aviv, Israel 1938
Tel Aviv, Israel 1941
Tel Aviv, Israel 1942
Tel Aviv, Israel 1950
Tel Aviv, Israel 1952
Tel Aviv, Israel 1964

Tel Aviv, Israel 1987
Tel Aviv, Israel 1994
Tel Aviv, Israel 1995
Temecula, Ca. 1998
Terni, Italy 1957
Terni, Italy 1962
The Hague, Netherlands 1966
The Hague, Netherlands 1967
Tihran Tehran? 1925
Tiranee [location?] 1973
Tiranee [location?] 1976
Tokyo, Japan 1950
Tokyo, Japan 1952
Tokyo, Japan 1971-72
Tokyo, Japan 1981
Tokyo, Japan 1992
Tokyo, Japan 1994
Torino (Turin), Italy 1572
Torino (Turin), Italy 1775-87
Torino (Turin), Italy 1787
Torino (Turin), Italy 1816
Torino (Turin), Italy 1823-25
Torino (Turin), Italy 1829
Torino (Turin), Italy 1833
Torino (Turin), Italy 1841
Torino (Turin), Italy 1848
Torino (Turin), Italy 1852
Torino (Turin), Italy 1888
Torino (Turin), Italy 1890
Torino (Turin), Italy 1894
Torino (Turin), Italy 1896
Torino (Turin), Italy 1896-05
Torino (Turin), Italy 1919
Torino (Turin), Italy 1921-22
Torino (Turin), Italy 1921-23
Torino (Turin), Italy 1927
Torino (Turin), Italy 1928
Torino (Turin), Italy 1930
Torino (Turin), Italy 1931
Torino (Turin), Italy 1935
Torino (Turin), Italy 1937
Torino (Turin), Italy 1942
Torino (Turin), Italy 1942
Torino (Turin), Italy 1944
Torino (Turin), Italy 1946
Torino (Turin), Italy 1948
Torino (Turin), Italy 1951
Torino (Turin), Italy 1956
Torino (Turin), Italy 1959
Torino (Turin), Italy 1963
Torino (Turin), Italy 1967
Torino (Turin), Italy 1968
Torino (Turin), Italy 1969
Torino (Turin), Italy 1970
Torino (Turin), Italy 1974
Torino (Turin), Italy 1977
Torino (Turin), Italy 1981
Torino (Turin), Italy 1982
Torino (Turin), Italy 1984
Torino (Turin), Italy 1986
Torino (Turin), Italy 1990
Torino (Turin), Italy 1997
Torino (Turin), Italy 1998
Torino (Turin), Italy; Milan, Italy 1919

Torino (Turin), Italy 1989
Toronto, Canada; New York, N.Y. 1898
Toronto, Canada; New York, N.Y. 1942
Toronto, Canada; New York, N.Y. 1944
Toulouse (Toloso), France 1664
Toulouse (Toloso), France 1830
Toulouse, France 1828
Treste [location?] 1879
Treviso, Italy 1841
Treviso, Italy 1952
Tubingen, Germany 1799
Tubingen, Germany 1806
Tubingen, Germany 1980
Tulsa, Ok. 1999
Twickenham, England 1985
Ulvovi [location?] 1902-04
Upper Montclair, N.J. 1927
Upper Saddle River, N.J. 1999
Uppsala, Sweden 1821
Uppsala, Sweden 1894
Uppsala, Sweden 1800
Urbana, Il. 1957
Utrecht, Netherlands 1613
Utrecht, Netherlands 1685
Utrecht, Netherlands 1699
V. Gorici [location?] 1911
V. Praze [location?] 1937
Valencia [Spain?] 1920s
Valladolid, Spain 1519
Varshe [location?] 1937
Vashon, Wash. 1973
Venetik [location?] 1847
Venetik [location?] 1864
Venetik [location?] 1911
Venetik-S Ghazar [location?] 1924
Venice (?) 1540
Venice, Italy 1486
Venice, Italy 1490?
Venice, Italy 1502
Venice, Italy 1504
Venice, Italy 1516
Venice, Italy 1517
Venice, Italy 1524
Venice, Italy 1526
Venice, Italy 1534
Venice, Italy 1537
Venice, Italy 1542
Venice, Italy 1543
Venice, Italy 1547
Venice, Italy 1551
Venice, Italy 1553
Venice, Italy 1556
Venice, Italy 1562
Venice, Italy 1570
Venice, Italy 1571
Venice, Italy 1572
Venice, Italy 1573
Venice, Italy 1593
Venice, Italy 1640
Venice, Italy 1642
Venice, Italy 1643
Venice, Italy 1653

Venice, Italy 1739
Venice, Italy 1741
Venice, Italy 1744
Venice, Italy 1751
Venice, Italy 1765
Venice, Italy 1776
Venice, Italy 1778
Venice, Italy 1788
Venice, Italy 1793
Venice, Italy 1794
Venice, Italy 1803
Venice, Italy 1803-4
Venice, Italy 1805
Venice, Italy 1818
Venice, Italy 1821
Venice, Italy 1825
Venice, Italy 1830
Venice, Italy 1837
Venice, Italy 1843-47
Venice, Italy 1987
Venice, Italy 1988
Venice, Italy 1989
Venice, Italy 1990
Venice, Italy 1994
Venice, Italy 1997
Venice, Italy 1998
Verona, Italy 1470
Verona, Italy 1737
Verona, Italy 1746
Verona, Italy 1749
Verona, Italy 1752
Verona, Italy 1788
Verona, Italy 1809
Verona, Italy 1822
Verona, Italy 1967
Verona, Italy; Milan, Italy 1951
Victoria, Australia; Ontario, Canada 1992
Videyar Klaustri, Iceland 1829-40
Videyar Klaustri, Iceland 1838-40
Vienna, Austria 1510
Vienna, Austria 1513
Vienna, Austria 1516
Vienna, Austria 1783
Vienna, Austria 1784
Vienna, Austria 1789
Vienna, Austria 1789-94
Vienna, Austria 1814
Vienna, Austria 1816
Vienna, Austria 1817
Vienna, Austria 1827-28
Vienna, Austria 1828
Vienna, Austria 1838

Vienna, Austria 1844
Vienna, Austria 1870-76
Vienna, Austria 1889
Vienna, Austria 1892
Vienna, Austria 1897
Vienna, Austria 1900
Vienna, Austria 1903
Vienna, Austria 1908
Vienna, Austria 1914
Vienna, Austria 1918
Vienna, Austria 1920
Vienna, Austria 1925
Vienna, Austria 1931
Vienna, Austria; Leipzig, Germany 1890-91
Vienna, Austria; Leipzig, Germany 1894-96
Vienna, Austria; Leipzig, Germany 1919
Vienna, Austria; Prague, Chechoslavakia 1800
Vienna, Austria; Prague, Chechoslavakia 1886-87
Vilnius (Vilna), Lithuania 1930
Vioey, Iceland 1835-40
W Budyesinje [Poland?] 1922
W Londynie [Poland?] 1957
Ware, England 1992
Ware, England 1995
Warminster, England 1991
Warminster, England 1996
Warsaw, Poland 1780
Warsaw, Poland 1791
Warsaw, Poland 1800
Warsaw, Poland 1819
Warsaw, Poland 1903
Warsaw, Poland 1904
Warsaw, Poland 1931
Warsaw, Poland 1948
Warsaw, Poland 1950
Warsaw, Poland 1953
Warsaw, Poland 1956
Warsaw, Poland 1959
Warsaw, Poland 1965
Warsaw, Poland 1966
Warsaw, Poland 1974
Warsaw, Poland 1975
Warsaw, Poland 1981
Warsaw, Poland 1982
Warsaw, Poland 1983
Warsaw, Poland 1989
Warsaw, Poland 1990
Warsaw, Poland 1995

Warsaw, Poland 1995
Warsaw, Poland 1995
Warsaw, Poland 1997
Warsaw, Poland 1998
Warsaw, Poland 1999
Washington, D.C. 1936
Weimar, Germany 1800
Wellesley Hills, Mass. 1978
Wellingborough, Eng. 1973
Weltevreden [location?] 1922
West Haven, Conn. 1979
West Haven, Conn. 1980
West Haven, Conn. 1984
Wiesbaden, Germany 1908
Wiesbaden, Germany 1947
Wiesbaden, Germany 1957
Wiesbaden, Germany 1972
Wilmington, DE 1804
Wismar, Germany 1896
Wittenburg, Germany 1511
Wittenburg, Germany 1513
Wittenburg, Germany 1539
Wittenburg, Germany 1545
Wittenburg, Germany 1566
Woodbury, N.Y. 1971
Worms, Germany 1563
Wrexham (Wrecsam), England 1928
Yerevan (Erevan), Armenia 1957
Yerevan (Erevan), Armenia 1958
Yerevan (Erevan), Armenia 1987
Yerevan (Erevan), Armenia 1988
Zabomyszwoyna, Poland 1588
Zagreb, Croatia 1882
Zagreb, Croatia 1883
Zagreb, Croatia 1915
Zagreb, Croatia 1921
Zagreb, Croatia 1950
Zagreb, Croatia 1987
Zara, Turkey 1895
Zeitz, Germany 1891
Zurich, Switzerland 1755
Zurich, Switzerland 1760
Zurich, Switzerland 1763
Zurich, Switzerland 1778
Zurich, Switzerland 1961
Zurich, Switzerland 1980
Zurich, Switzerland; Stuttgart, Germany 1966
Zurich, Switzerland; Verona, Italy 1983
Zurich, Switzerland 1767
Zutphen, Netherlands 1930

APPENDIX G:
FIRST PRINTINGS IN
VERNACULAR LANGUAGES

Afrikaans 1952
Albanian 1941
Arabic 1900
Armenian 1843
Azerbaijani 1986
Basque 1985
Bengali 1954
Bernese German
   1978
Bohemian 1801
Bulgarian 1976
Castilian Spanish
   1886
Catalan 1919
Chinese 1929
Croatian 1950
Czech 1904
Danish 1825
Dutch 1880
East Armenian 1957

English 1553
Esperanto 1930
Estonian 1963
Finnish 1832
Flemish 1561
French 1475
Gaelic 1937
Galician-Portuguese
   1990
German 1537
German, Low 1895
Greek 1488
Greek, Modern
   1526
Gujarati 1993
Hebrew 1930
Hungarian 1788
Icelandic 1829
Indian 1920
Iranian 1925

Irish 1990
Italian 1470
Italian (Bolognese
   Dialect) 1838
Italian (Neopolitan
   Dialect) 1700s
Italian (Venetian
   Dialect) 1872
Japanese 1971
Kannada 1978
Korean 1973
Kurdish 1981
Languedoc 1664
Latin 1474
Latvian 1936
Lebanese 1966
Luxembourgish 1995
Marathi 1984
Norwegian 1835
Persian 1990

Platt-Deutsch 1869
Polish 1588
Portuguese 1835
Romanian 1955
Russian 1805
Schwabian 1966
Scottish 1992
Serbo-Croatian 1915
Slovak 1966
Slovenian 1911
Spanish 1519
Swedish 1814
Tajik 1990
Tamil 1961
Turkish 1887
Twi 1957
Ukrainian 1889
Urdu 1983
Welsh 1928
Yiddish 1924

NOTES

Chapter 1

1. There has been much scholarly discussion about the distinction between the Greek words "rhapsode" and "aoidos," meaning literally "singer." I will follow the opinion of Gregory Nagy, *Pindar's Homer: The Lyric Possession of an Epic Past* (Baltimore: The Johns Hopkins University Press, 1990), p. 54: "Whereas the oral poet [aoidos] recomposes as he performs, the rhapsode simply performs [poems composed by aoidoi]." For a different interpretation see Martin L. West, *Studies in the Text and Transmission of the Iliad* (Munich, Leipzig: K. G. Saur, 2001), p.5, n.5.

2. M. L. West, "The Invention of Homer," *Classical Quarterly* (vol. 49, no. 2: 1999), p. 364.

3. *Ibid.*, pp.374–376.

4. *Ibid.*, p. 369–372.

5. Translation by Apostolos N. Athanassakis (London: The Johns Hopkins University Press, 1976).

6. Denton J. Snider, *Homer in Chios* (St. Louis: Sigma Publishing, 1891).

7. *Ibid.*, p. 16.

8. Thomas W. Allen, *Homer: the Origins and the Transmission* (Oxford: The Clarendon Press, 1924), p. 12.

9. Diodorus Siculus 1.96. Mary Lefkowitz, *Not Out of Africa: How Afrocentrism Became an Excuse to Teach Myth as History* (New York: BasicBooks, 1996), pp. 82, 85.

10. It is likely that the extent of literacy in antiquity has been overrated: William V. Harris, *Ancient Literacy* (Cambridge, Mass.: Harvard University Press, 1989).

11. M. L. West, "Invention," p. 367.

12. Nagy, *Homeric Questions* (Austin: University of Texas Press, 1996), pp. 89–90.

13. Allen, p. 13.

14. *Ibid.*, p. 14.

15. Minna Skafte Jensen, *The Homeric Question and the Oral-Formulaic Theory* (Copenhagen: Museum Tusculanum Press, 1980), p. 125.

16. Joachim Latacz, *Homer: His Art and World* (Ann Arbor: The University of Michigan Press, 1996), pp. 28–29.

17. Jan Paul Crielaard, "A 'Dutch' Discoverer of Homer's Tomb" in Crielaard *Homeric Questions: Essays in Philology, Ancient History and Archaeology* (Amsterdam: J. C. Gieben, 1995), pp. 313–315.

18. K. Rhomaios, "The Pseudo-Herodotean Life of Homer and Chios," in John Boardman and C. E. Vaphopoulou-Richardson, *Chios: A Conference at the Homereion in Chios 1984* (Oxford: Clarendon Press, 1986), pp. 21–26.

19. G. S. Kirk, *Homer and the Oral Tradition* (New York: Cambridge University Press, 1976), pp.202–203.

20. John A. Scott, *Homer and His Influence* (New York: Longmans, Green, 1931), p. 25.

21. J. A. Davison, "The Transmission of the Text," chapter 6 of Alan J. B. Wace and Frank H. Stubbings, *A Companion to Homer* (New York: St. Martin's Press, 1962), p. 235.

22. Peter Green, "War and Peace: Reading, Translating, and Speaking Homer," *The New Republic* (vol. 216, no. 8: 1997), p. 2.

Chapter 2

1. Bernard Knox, *Backing Into the Future: The Classical Tradition and Its Renewal* (New York: W. W. Norton, 1994), pp. 43–44.

2. David Denby, *Great Books: My Adventures with Homer, Rousseau, Woolf, and Other Indestructible Writers of the Western World* (New York: Simon & Schuster, 1996), p. 51.

3. Nagy, *The Best of the Achaeans: Concepts of the Hero in Archaic Greek Poetry* (Baltimore: Johns Hopkins University Press, 1979), p. x.

4. Denby, *Great Books*, pp. 80–81.

5. Green, pp. 5–6.

6. Iman Wilkens, *Where Troy Once Stood* (New York: St. Martin's Press, 1990).

7. Elizabeth Riorden, "Visions of Troy," *Archaeology* (vol. 53, no. 1: January/February, 2000), pp. 52–59.

8. Jane B. Carter and Sarah P. Morris, eds. *The Ages of Homer: A Tribute to Emily Townsend Vermeule* (Austin: University of Texas Press, 1995), p. 4.

9. J. V. Luce, *Celebrating Homer's Landscapes: Troy and Ithaca Revisited* (New Haven: Yale University Press, 1998), p. 1. See also: Carl W. Blegen, *Troy and the Trojans* (New York: Barnes & Noble Books, 1995 [originally published 1963]; and Luce, *Homer and the Heroic Age* (New York: Harper & Row, 1975).

10. Kurt A. Raaflaub, "Homer, the Trojan War, and History," *The Classical World* (vol. 91, no. 5: 1998), p. 399.

11. George Steiner, "Homer and the Scholars" in Steiner and Robert Fagles, eds. *Homer: A Collection of Critical Essays* (Englewood Clifts, N.J.: Prentice-Hall, 1962), p. 9.

12. Samuel Butler, *The Authoress of the* Odyssey*: Where and When She Wrote, Who She Was, the Use She Made of the* Iliad*, and How the Poem Grew Under Her Hands* (London: A. C. Fifield, 1897), p. 9.

13. M. L. West, *Studies*, p. 11.

14. Kirk, *The Songs of Homer* (Cambridge: The University Press, 1962), p. 223.

15. Horace, *De Arte Poetica*.

16. Maurice Bowra in Wace and Stubbings, p. 26.

17. Kirk, *The Songs of Homer*, p. 67.

18. M. I. Finley, *The World of Odysseus* (New York: The Viking Press, 1965, revised edition), p. 21.

19. *Prolegomena ad Homerum sive de Operum Homericorum Prisca et Genuina Forma Variisque Mutationibus et Probabili Ratione Emendandi* (Halle, 1795).

20. Davison, p. 246.

21. *Ibid.*, p. 247.

22. De Jong, "Homer as Literature: Some Current Areas of Research" in Crielaard, *Homeric Questions*, pp. 127–128.

23. Johann Wolfgang Goethe quoted in Ernst Vogt, "Homer — ein grosser Schatten? Die Forschungen zur Person Homers" in Latacz, *Zweihundert Jahre Homer-Forschung: Ruckblick und Ausblick* (Stuttgart and Leipzig: B. G. Teubner, 1991), p. 365.

24. *Ibid.*, pp. 128–129.

25. Albin Lesky, *A History of Greek Literature*; translated by James Willis and Cornelius de Heer (Indianapolis: Hackett, 1996, c1963), pp. 36–36.

26. *Ibid.*, p. 39.

27. Milman Parry, "Studies in the Epic Technique of Oral Verse-Making I: Homer and the Homeric Style," *Harvard Studies in Classical Philology* (41: 1930).

28. Steiner, "Homer and the Scholars," p. 5.

29. Bowra, p. 46.

30. Albert B. Lord, *The Singer of Tales* (Cambridge, Mass.: Harvard University Press, 1960), p. 28.

31. Lord, "Homer" in Steiner and Fagles, p. 68.

32. Jensen, p. 60.

33. Bowra, p. 25.

34. Nagy, *Homeric Questions*, p. 40.

35. *Ibid.*, p. 53.

36. *Ibid.*, p. 55.

37. *Ibid.*, p. 79.

38. Nagy, *Homeric Questions*, pp. 77–80.

39. Jensen, p. 9.

40. Latacz, *Homer*, p. 21.

41. Steiner, "Homer and the Scholars," p. 6.

42. Nagy, *Homeric Questions*, p. 30.

43. Jensen, p. 37.

44. Bernard C. Fenik, ed. *Homer: Tradition and Invention* (Leiden: E. J. Brill, 1978), pp. vii–viii.

45. James M. Redfield, *Nature and Culture in the Iliad: The Tragedy of Hector* (Chicago: The University of Chicago Press, 1975), pp. 222–223.

46. W. H. D. Rouse, "Introduction" to Matthew Arnold, *On Translating Homer* (London: John Murray, 1905, new edition), p. 4.

47. Nagy, *Best of the Achaeans*, p. 41.

48. Alfred Heubeck, "Homeric Studies Today; Results and Prospects" in Fenik, p. 16.

49. Latacz, *Homer*, p. 11.

50. James P. Holoka, "Homer, Oral Poetry Theory, and Comparative Literature" in Latacz, *Zweihundert*, p. 481.

51. Richard Janko, "The *Iliad* and Its Editors: Dictation and Redaction," *Classical Antiquity*, vol. 9, no. 2 (October, 1990), pp. 326–334.

52. Kirk, *The Songs of Homer*, p. 159.

53. Jensen, p. 10.

54. Davison, p. 257.

55. Nils Berg and Dag Haug, "Innovation vs. Tradition in Homer — an Overlooked Piece of Evidence," *Symbolae Osloenses* (vol. 75, no. 1: 9-1-2000), p. 6.

56. A. Lord, "Homer," p. 69.

57. Davison, p. 257.

58. Jensen, p. 87.

59. *Ibid.*

60. Oliver Taplin, "The Division of the *Iliad* into Twenty-Four Books," Appendix to his *Homeric Soundings The Shaping of the* Iliad (Oxford: The Clarendon Press, 1992), pp. 285–293.

61. De Jong, "Homer as Literature," p. 132.

62. Steiner, "Homer and the Scholars," pp. 6–7.

63. Kirk, *The Songs of Homer*, pp. 145–156.

64. Crielaard, "Homer, History and Archaeology Some Remarks on the Date of the Homeric World" in Crielaard, *Homeric Questions*.

65. Nagy, *Best of the Achaeans*, p. 3.

66. C. J. Ruijgh, "D'Homère aux Origines Proto-Mycèniennes de la Tradition Épique" in Crielaard, *Homeric Questions*, pp. 91–92. See also: Denys Page, *History and the Homeric Iliad* (Berkeley: University of California Press, 1972).

67. J. Griffin, "Heroic and Unheroic Ideas in Homer" in Boardman and Vaphopoulou-Richardson, pp. 3–13.

68. Crielaard, "Homer, History," p. 230.

69. *Ibid.*, p. 245.

70. *Ibid.*, pp. 208–209.

71. Ian Morris, "The Use and Abuse of Homer,"

Classical Antiquity, vol. 5, no. 1 (April, 1986), pp. 81–138.

72. Barry B. Powell, *Homer and the Origin of the Greek Alphabet* (Cambridge: University Press, 1991).

73. Jensen, p. 10.

74. Powell, p. 9.

75. P. Kyle McCarter, Jr., *The Antiquity of the Greek Alphabet and the Early Phoenician Scripts* (Missoula: Harvard, 1975), pp. 123–124.

76. Nagy, *Homeric Questions*, p. 65.

77. Berg and Haug.

78. The following discussion is based on: Anthony Snodgrass, *Homer and the Artists Text and Picture in Early Greek Art* (Cambridge: Cambridge University Press, 1998).

79. See Susan Woodford, *The Trojan War in Ancient Art* (Ithaca, N.Y.: Cornell University Press, 1993).

80. Snodgrass, p. ix.

81. *Ibid.*, p. 76.

82. George Melville Bolling, ed., *Ilias Atheniensium: The Athenian Iliad of the Sixth Century B.C.* (n.pl.: American Philological Association, 1950).

83. H. A. Shapiro "Hipparchos and the Rhapsodes" in Carol Dougherty and Leslie Kurke, *Cultural Poetics in Archaic Greece: Cult, Performance, Politics* (New York: Oxford University Press, 1998), p. 104.

84. Jensen, p. 149.

85. *Ibid.*, p. 10.

86. *Ibid.*, p. 142.

87. *Ibid.*, pp. 153–154.

88. Erwin F. Cook, *The* Odyssey *in Athens: Myths of Cultural Origins* (Ithaca: Cornell University Press, 1995).

89. Nagy in "Foreword" to Cook, p. x.

90. *Ibid.*

91. Cook, p.4.

92. *Ibid.*, p. 8.

93. Based especially on the work of Nagy.

94. See note 3.

95. Jensen.

96. Ken Dowden, "Homer's Sense of Text," *Journal of Hellenic Studies* (vol. 116: 1996).

97. Nagy, *Homeric* Questions, p. 21.

98. Luigi Enrico Rossi, "Dividing Homer: When and How Were the *Iliad* and the *Odyssey* Divided into Songs?" *Symbolae Osloenses* (vol. 76: 2001).

Chapter 3

1. Finley, p. 3.

2. Davison, p. 235.

3. *Nemean* 7, 20f.

4. Nagy, *Pindar's Homer*, p. 202.

5. Rupert Mann, "Pindar's Homer and Pindar's Myths," *Greek, Roman and Byzantine Studies* (vol. 35, issue 4: Winter, 1994), pp. 313–337.

6. *The Persian Wars* 2.112–117; *The Peloponnesian War* 2.41.4.

7. H. J. Richardson, "Aristotle's Reading of Homer and Its Background" in Robert Lamberton and John J. Keaney, eds., *Homer's Ancient Readers: The Hermeneutics of Greek Epic's Earliest Exegetes* (Princeton, N.J.: Princeton University Press, 1992), p. 32.

8. Nagy, *Pindar's Homer*, p. 228.

9. Scott, p. 98.

10. Richardson, p. 33; A. A. Long, "Stoic Readings of Homer," in Lamberton and Keaney, p. 44.

11. *Protagoras* 316d.

12. Richardson, p. 33.

13. R. Chandran Madhu, "Plato's Homer," *Ancient Philosophy* 19 (1999), p. 94.

14. "Introduction" to Lamberton and Keaney, p. xi.

15. Richardson, p. 37.

16. *Ibid.*, p. 38.

17. Davison, p. 221.

18. Jensen, pp. 107–108.

19. Quoted in Scott, p. 105.

20. Scott, pp. 97–98.

21. Long, pp. 41–42.

22. *Ibid.*, pp. 44–50.

23. *Ibid.*, p. 61.

24. "Introduction" to Lamberton and Keaney, p. xix.

25. Davison, p. 224; see also the Internet Web site "Homer and the Papyri" at The University of California, Irvine — http://eee.uci.edu/%7epapyri/.

26. Commentaries, paraphrases, summaries, vocabularies, lexica, glossaries, *scholia*, catechims, epitomes, dialogs, explanations of Homeric words, allegorical interpretations, discussions on topics, and Homeric Hymns.

27. Roger A. Pack, *The Greek and Latin Literary Texts from Greco-Roman Egypt* (Ann Arbor: The University of Michigan Press, 1965, second edition).

28. Finley, p. 11.

29. M. L. West, *Studies*, p. 86.

30. Stephanie West, *The Ptolemaic Papyri of Homer*, Vol. III of *Papyrologica Coloniensa* (Koln: Westdeutscher Verlag, 1967), p. 5.

31. *Ibid*, p. 14.

32. Robert Browning "The Byzantines and Homer" in Lamberton and Keaney, p. 134.

33. Davison, pp. 222–223.

34. Davison, p. 223. However, it should be noted that M. L. West argues that textual criticism by comparing multiple manuscripts cannot be projected back as far as Zenodotus and Aristarchos (*Studies*, pp. 36ff).

35. *Ibid.*

36. Jensen (p. 109) follows this theory but says it is that of B. A. van Groningen.

37. Jensen, p. 109.

38. S. West, p. 16.

39. Davison, p. 225.

40. S. West, p. 17.

41. Nagy, *Homeric Questions*, p. 98.

42. S. West, p. 18.

43. Virginia Knight, *The Renewal of Epic:*

Responses to Homer in the Argonautica of Apollonius (New York: E. J. Brill, 1995), p. 4.

44. *Ibid.*, p. 5.

45. *Ibid.*, pp. 5–8.

46. Dennis Ronald MacDonald, *The Homeric Epics and the Gospel of Mark* (New Haven and London: Yale University Press, 2000).

47. Scott, pp. 102–107.

48. Duncan F. Kennedy, "Virgilian Epic" in Charles Martindale, ed. *The Cambridge Companion to Virgil* (Cambridge: Cambridge University Press, 1997), p. 151.

49. *Ibid.*, p. 151.

50. *Ibid.*, p. 146.

51. Peter Levi, *Virgil: His Life and Times* (London: Duckworth, 1998), p. 206.

52. Michael C. J. Putnam, *Virgil's Aeneid: Interpretation and Influence* (Chapel Hill: University of North Carolina Press, 1995), p. 4.

53. Levi, p. 223.

54. R. J. Tarrant, "Aspects of Virgil's Reception in Antiquity" in Martindale, p. 58.

55. Scott, p. 121.

56. Long, p. 45.

57. Felix Buffiere, tr. *Heraclite: Allegories d'Homere* (Paris: Société d'Édition "Les Belles Lettres" 1962), p. xix.

58. Lamberton, "The Neoplatonists and the Spiritualization of Homer" in Lamberton and Keaney, p. 115.

59. I follow Lamberton, pp. 126–127.

60. Lamberton, p. 132.

61. "Introduction," Lamberton and Keaney, p. xx.

62. Davision, p. 226.

63. MacDonald, *Christianizing Homer: The Odyssey, Plato, and the Acts of Andrew* (New York: Oxford University Press, 1994), p. 5.

64. *Ibid.*, p. 5.

65. *Ibid.*, p. 314.

66. *Ibid.*, p. 8.

67. *Ibid.*, p. 316.

68. G. H. R. Horsley, *Homer in Pisidia: Degrees of Literateness in a Backwards Province of the Roman Empire* (Australia: University of New England, 1999).

69. McDonald, *The Homeric Epics and the Gospel of Mark*, p. 4.

Chapter 4

1. M. L. West, *Studies*, p. 139.

2. Scott, pp. 122–123.

3. J. A. K. Thomson, "Homer and His Influence" in Wace and Stubbings, p. 5.

4. *Ibid.*, pp. 5–6.

5. Mark David Usher, *Texts and Their Transformations: Continuity and Change in the Classical Tradition* (Chicago: The University of Chicago Library, 1994), p. 7.

6. Walter Berschin, *Greek Letters and the Latin Middle Ages: From Jerome to Nicholas of Cusa* (Washington, D.C.: The Catholic University of America Press, 1988, revised and expanded edition), pp. 1–35.

7. *Ibid.*, p. 45.

8. *Ibid.*, p. 205.

9. *Cliges* 28–33, quoted in Berschin, p. 207.

10. Browning, "Homer in Byzantium," *Viator: Medieval and Renaissance Studies* vol. 6 (1975), p. 16.

11. Browning, "The Byzantines and Homer," p. 134.

12. *Ibid.*, p. 135.

13. MacDonald, *Christianizing Homer*, pp. 20–25.

14. Usher, *Homeric Stitchings: The Homeric Centos of the Empress Eudocia* (Lanhan, Md: Rowman & Littlefield, 1998), p. 2.

15. Nagy, "Foreword" to Usher, *Homeric Stitchings*, p. x.

16. Usher, *Homeric Stitchings*, pp. 93–139.

17. *Ibid.*, p. 2.

18. *Ibid.*, p. 12.

19. Browning, "The Byzantines and Homer," pp. 146–147.

20. Browning, "Homer in Byzantium," p. 19; the quote is from Michael Psellus, *Chronographia* 6.61.

21. Browning, "The Byzantines and Homer," p. 137.

22. Browning, "Homer in Byzantium," p. 25.

23. Ranuccio Bianchi Bandinelli, *Hellenistic-Byzantine Miniatures of the Iliad (Ilias Ambrosiana)* (Olten, Switzerland: Urs Graf-Verlag, 1955).

24. Davison, p. 227.

25. Gareth Morgan, "Homer in Byzantium: John Tzetzes," in Carl A. Rubino and Cynthia W. Shelmerdine, editors, *Approaches to Homer* (Austin: University of Texas Press, 1983), p. 165.

26. Browning, "The Byzantines and Homer," pp. 148–151.

27. Quoted in Morgan, p. 169.

28. Quoted *Ibid.*, p. 170.

29. Browning, "Homer in Byzantium," p. 26.

30. *Ibid.*

31. Browning, "The Byzantines and Homer," p. 142.

32. MacDonald, *Christianizing Homer*, p. 19.

33. cod. Ven. Marc. 421 quoted and translated by Browning, "The Byzantines and Homer," p. 136.

Chapter 5

1. Deno John Geanakoplos, *Byzantium and the Renaissance: Studies in the Dissemination of Greek Learning from Byzantium to Western Europe* (Hamden, Conn.: Archon Books, 1973), p. 1.

2. Scott, pp. 4–5.

3. Geanakoplos, p. 39.

4. *Ibid.*, pp. 1–38.

5. Berschin, p. 270.

6. Aldo S. Bernardo and Saul Levin, eds. *The Classics in the Middle Ages* (Binghamton, N.Y.: Center for Medieval and Early Renaissance Studies, 1990), p. 5.

7. Quoted in Scott, pp. 123–124.

8. Berschin, p. 269.

9. *Ibid.*, p. 273.

10. *Ibid.*, p. 279.

11. *Ibid.*, pp. 270–280.

12. Anthony Grafton, "Renaissance Readers of Homer's Ancient Readers" in Lamberton and Keaney, p. 150.

13. *Ibid.*, p. 153.

14. *Ibid.*, pp. 156–157.

15. *Ibid.*, p. 158.

16. *Ibid.*, p. 164.

17. "Introduction," Lamberton and Keaney, p. xxii.

18. Grafton, p. 166.

19. *Ibid.*, p. 171.

20. John Ozell quoted in Usher, *Texts*, p. 7.

21. Thomson, p. 10.

22. Elizabeth Asmis in the "Foreword" to Usher, *Texts*, p. xi.

23. Daniel J. Webster, "Insomnia and Homer: A Comparative Study of Translations into English of an Early Poem by Osip Mandelstam," *Translation Review* (volume 60: 2000), p. 20.

24. George deF. Lord, *Homeric Renaissance: The* Odyssey *of George Chapman* (Hamden, Conn.: Archon Books, 1972, c1956), p. 30.

25. Scott, p. 32; John Cooper Powys, "Preface" to *Homer and the Aether* (1959); reprinted in Steiner and Fagles, p. 145.

26. Rouse, pp. 21–22.

27. Steven Shankman, *Pope's* Iliad*: Homer in the Age of Passion* (Princeton, NJ: Princeton University Press, 1983), p.xiv.

28. Douglas Knight, *Pope and the Heroic Tradition: A Critical Study of His* Iliad (New Haven: Yale University Press, 1951), pp. 5–6.

29. Simeon Underwood, *English Translations of Homer from George Chapman to Christopher Logue* (Plymouth, U. K.: Northcote House, 1998), p. 6.

30. Redfield, p. xi.

31. Andre Michalopoulos, *Homer* (New York: Twayne Publishers, 1966), p. 5.

32. Fern Farnham, *Madame Dacier: Scholar and Humanist* (Monterey, Cal.: Angel Press, 1976), p. 147.

33. Martin L. West, *Sing Me, Goddess: Being the First Recitation of Homer's Iliad* (London: Duckworth, 1971), p. v.

34. Thomson, p. 14.

35. Arnold, p. 10.

36. Michalopoulos, p. 6.

37. Arnold, p. 4.

38. Brean S. Hammond, *Pope* (Atlantic Highlands, N.J.: Humanities Press International, 1986), pp. 119–120.

39. Rouse, p. 9.

40. Scott, p. 38.

41. H. A. Mason, *To Homer Through Pope: An Introduction to Homer's* Iliad *and Pope's Translation* (London: Chatto and Windus), p. 181.

42. William Cowper quoted *ibid.*, pp. 185–6.

43. Knox, pp. 298–299.

44. F. Melian Stawell, "Introduction" to *The Iliad of Homer Translated by Edward Earl of Derby* (London: J. M. Dent, 1917).

45. S. H. Steinberg, *Five Hundred Years of Printing* (New York: Penguin Books, 1974, third edition), p. 119.

46. Sesto Prete, *The Humanists and the Discovery of Printing* (Krefeld: Scherpe Verlag, 1982), pp. 1–22.

47. Kirsti Simonsuuri, *Homer's Original Genius: Eighteenth-Century Notions of the Early Greek Epic (1688–1798)* (Cambridge: Cambridge University Press, 1979), p. 10.

48. *Ibid.*, p. 11.

49. Davison, p. 228.

50. Flodr.

Chapter 6

1. Elizabeth Asmis in the "Foreward" to Usher, *Texts*, p. xi.

2. Daniel J. Webster, "Insomnia and Homer: A Comparative Study of Translations into English of an Early Poem by Osip Mandelstam," *Translation Review* (volume 60: 2000), p. 20.

3. George deF. Lord, *Homeric Renaissance: The* Odyssey *of George Chapman* (Hamden, Conn.: Archon Books, 1972, c1956), p. 30.

4. Scott, p. 32; John Cooper Powys, "Preface" to *Homer and the Aether* (1959); reprinted in Steiner and Fagles, p. 145.

5. Rouse, pp. 21–22.

6. Steven Shankman, *Pope's* Iliad*: Homer in the Age of Passion* (Princeton, NJ: Princeton University Press, 1983), p.xiv.

7. Douglas Knight, *Pope and the Heroic Tradition: A Critical Study of His* Iliad (New Haven: Yale University Press, 1951), pp. 5–6.

8. Simeon Underwood, *English Translations of Homer from George Chapman to Christopher Logue* (Plymouth, U. K.: Northcote House, 1998), p. 6.

9. Redfield, p. xi.

10. Andre Michalopoulos, *Homer* (New York: Twayne Publishers, 1966), p. 5.

11. Fern Farnham, *Madame Dacier: Scholar and Humanist* (Monterey, Cal.: Angel Press, 1976), p. 147.

12. Martin L. West, *Sing Me, Goddess: Being the First Recitation of Homer's Iliad* (London: Duckworth, 1971), p. v.

13. Thomson, p. 14.

14. Arnold, p. 10.

15. Michalopoulos, p. 6.

16. Arnold, p. 4.

17. Brean S. Hammond, *Pope* (Atlantic Highlands, N.J.: Humanities Press International, 1986), pp. 119–120.

18. Rouse, p. 9.

19. Scott, p. 38.

20. H. A. Mason, *To Homer Through Pope: An Introduction to Homer's* Iliad *and Pope's Translation* (London: Chatto and Windus), p. 181.

21. William Cowper quoted *ibid.*, pp. 185–6.

22. Knox, pp. 298–299.

23. F. Melian Stawell, "Introduction" to *The Iliad of Homer Translated by Edward Earl of Derby* (London: J. M. Dent, 1917).

24. S. H. Steinberg, *Five Hundred Years of Printing* (New York: Penguin Books, 1974, third edition), p. 119.

25. Sesto Prete, *The Humanists and the Discovery of Printing* (Krefeld: Scherpe Verlag, 1982), pp. 1–22.

26. Kirsti Simonsuuri, *Homer's Original Genius: Eighteenth-Century Notions of the Early Greek Epic (1688–1798)* (Cambridge: Cambridge University Press, 1979), p. 10.

27. *Ibid.*, p. 11.

28. Davison, p. 228.

29. Flodr.

30. Scott, p. 126.

31. Davison, p. 242.

32. Steiner, *Homer in English* (London; Penguin Books, 1996), p. xv.

33. Underwood, pp. 18–19.

34. Herbert Gladstone Wright, *The Life and Works of Arthur Hall of Grantham, Member of Parliament, Courtier and First Translator of Homer into English* (Manchester: University of Manchester Press, 1919), p. 160; quoted in Underwood, p. 19.

35. Underwood, p. 20.

36. *Ibid.*

37. G. Lord, p. 128.

38. *Ibid.*, p. 127.

39. Steinberg, p. 244.

40. Quoted in Scott, p. 35.

41. Usher, *Texts*, p. 4.

42. Scott, p. 35.

43. G. Lord, p. 41.

44. *Ibid.*, 129.

45. G. Lord, p. 16.

46. Sinonsuuri, p. 59.

47. G. Lord, p. 56.

48. Scott, p. 32.

49. Samuel Sheppard, quoted in Underwood, p. 26.

50. Underwood, pp. 27–28.

51. Scott. p. 33.

52. G. Lord, p. 9.

53. Simonsuuri, p. 12.

54. Paul Davis, "Thomas Hobbes's Translations of Homer: Epic and Anticlericalism in Late Seventeenth-Century England," *The Seventeenth Century* (12: 1997), pp. 231–255; refuted by A. P. Martinich, "Hobbes's Translations of Homer and Anticlericalism," *The Seventeenth Century* (16: 2001), pp. 147–157.

55. Usher, *Texts*, p. 8.

56. Steiner, *Homer in English*, p. 65.

57. Simonsuuri, p. 4.

58. Davison, p. 242.

59. Simonsuuri, p. 19.

60. Thomson, p. 10.

61. Farnham, p. 10.

62. *Ibid.*, p. 47.

63. *Ibid.*, p. 48.

64. My translation from French quote *ibid.*, p. 143.

65. Fabienne Moore, "Homer Revisited: Anne Le Fevre Dacier's Preface to her Prose Translations of the Iliad in Early Eighteennth-Century France," *Studies in the Literary Imagination* (vol. 33, no. 2: Fall, 2000), p. 89.

66. Farnham, p. 94.

67. *Ibid.*, p. 171.

68. *Ibid.*, p. 158.

69. Usher, *Texts*, p. 5.

70. Simonsuuri, pp. 51–52.

71. Quoted in Usher, *Texts*, p.5.

72. Farnham, p. 145.

73. *Ibid.*, p. 16.

74. Hammond, p. 9.

75. Felicity Rosslyn, *Alexander Pope: A Literary Life* (London: Macmillan, 1990), p. 8.

76. From a letter quoted in Carolyn D. Williams, *Pope, Homer, and Manliness: Some Aspects of Eighteenth-Century Classical Learning* (New York: Routledge, 1993), p. 59.

77. *Ibid.*, p. 57.

78. *Ibid.*, pp. 66–67.

79. *Ibid.*, p. 69.

80. Rosslyn, pp. 62–63.

81. Simonsuuri, p. 58.

82. Rosslyn, p. 77.

83. Hammond, p. 120.

84. David Foxon, *Pope and the Early Eighteenth-Century Book Trade* (Oxford: Clarendon Press, 1991), p. 51.

85. Underwood, p. 41.

86. Hammond, p. 101.

87. *Ibid.*, p. 117.

88. Quoted in Usher, *Texts*, p.5.

89. Simonsuuri, p. 63.

90. *Letters of Sir Thomas Fitzosborne* (=Melmoth), 4th edition (London, 1754), p. 82; quoted in Lewis William Bruggemann, *A View of the English Translations and Illustrations of the Ancient Greek and Latin Authors* (New York: Burt Franklin, 1797), pp. 25–26.

91. *Biographia Literaria* vol. II, p. 2; quoted in Scott, p. 38

92. Quoted in Farnham, p. 147.

93. Quoted in Scott, p. 38.

94. Usher, *Texts*, p. 5.

95. Williams, p. 5.

96. Shankman, p. 131.

97. In the *Critical Review* for June 1797, pp. 200–204; quoted in Bruggemann, vol. 2, p. 8.

98. Stawell, p. viii.

99. From *The Flying Post* for April 13, 1728; quoted in J. V. Guerinot *Pamphlet Attacks on Alexander Pope 1711–1744: A Descriptive Bibliography* (New York: New York University Press, 1969), p. 120.

100. From the *Monthly Chronicle* for June 26, 1728; quoted in Guerinot, p. 127.

101. In *The Gentleman's Magazine* (London, 1785, p. 610); quoted by Shankman, p. 131.

102. Scott, p. 35.

103. *Ibid.*, pp. 36–37.

104. Thomas Bentley, *A Letter to Mr. Pope, Occasioned by Sober Advice from Horace* (1735); quoted in Williams, p. 77.

105. Quoted in Arnold, p. 5.

106. Mason, pp. 192–195.

107. D. Knight, p. 34.

108. Thomson, p. 11.

109. Shankman, p. 162; 164.

110. Colley Cibber, *Lives of the Poets of Great Britain and Ireland* (London, 1753), vol. 5, p. 22; quoted in Bruggemann, p. 25.

111. Rudolf Pfeiffer, *History of Classical Scholarship from 1300 to 1850* (Oxford: The Clarendon Press, 1976), p. 157.

112. Davison, p. 244.

113. In the *Monthly Review* for June, 1762, pp. 454–458; quoted in Bruggemann, p. 27.

114. Thomas Burnet and George Duckett, *Homerides* (1716); quoted in Williams, p. 129.

115. Jack Broughton was in 1765 a noted prize-fighter in England.

116. In the *Monthly Review* for March, 1759, p. 233; quoted in Bruggemann, p. 20.

117. David Bindman, ed., *John Flaxman* (London: Thames and Hudson, 1979).

118. Stawell, p. viii.

119. In the appendix to the *Critical Review*, New arrangement, vol. 4, p. 569; quoted in Bruggemann, p. 28.

120. In the *Monthly Review* enlarged for August 1792, pp. 431–443; quoted in Bruggemann, p. 28.

121. Arnold, pp. 7–8.

122. Sir John F. Herschel in the "Preface" to his *Iliad* (London: Macmillan, 1866), pp. xi–xii.

123. Rouse, p. 1.

124. Steiner, *Homer in English*, p.197.

125. Rouse, p. 18.

126. Michalopoulos, p. 6.

127. Rouse, p. 20.

128. Knox, pp. 294–295.

129. Usher, *Texts*, p. 8.

130. Stawell, p. ix.

131. Steiner, *Homer in English*, p. 195.

132. Knox, p. 295.

133. Stawell, p. ix.

134. Steiner, *Homer in English*, p. 181.

135. Rouse, p. 17.

136. From Hewlett's draft of a Preface, quoted by M. L. West, *Sing Me, Goddess*, pp. vii–viii.

137. Jeremy Wilson, *Lawrence of Arabia: The Authorized Biography of T. E. Lawrence* (New York: Atheneum, 1990), p. 3.

138. Knox, p. 283.

139. The page numbers for each quote in the text refer to the Wilson biography.

140. Knox, p. 296.

141. *Ibid.*, p. 299.

142. Underwood, p. 49.

143. *Ibid.*, p. 296.

144. Quoted in Underwood, p. 55.

145. D. Carne-Ross, R. Rutherford, M. S. Silk, and H. A. Mason quoted in Underwood, p. 55.

146. Steiner, *Homer in English*, p. 250.

147. Mason, p. 179.

148. Andrew Szegedy-Maszak, "Why Do We Still Read Homer?" *American Scholar* (vol. 71, issue 1: Winter, 2002), p. 100.

149. Underwood, pp. 61 and 64.

150. *Ibid.*, p. 58.

151. Mason, p. 189.

152. Underwood, p. 58.

153. Steiner, *Homer in English*, p. 266.

154. Kostas Myrsiades, *Approaches to Teaching Homer's* Iliad *and* Odyssey (New York: The Modern Language Association of America, 1987), p. 17.

155. Steiner, *Homer in English*, p. 324.

156. *Ibid.*, p. xxv.

157. *Ibid.*, p. xx.

158. Shankman, p. xiv.

159. M. L. West, *Sing Me, Goddess*, p. 10.

160. Myrsiades, p. 3.

161. M. L. West, *Sing Me, Goddess*, pp. v–vi.

Chapter 7

1. Lesky, p. 39.

2. Denby, Does Homer Have Legs?" (*The New Yorker*, September 6, 1993), pp. 56, 69.

3. Jonathan Shay, *Achilles in Vietnam: Combat Trauma and the Undoing of Character* (New York: Atheneum, 1994).

4. Steiner, "Homer and Scholars," p. 3.

5. *Ibid.*, p. 9.

6. Michalopoulos, p. 139.

7. I. A. Richards in his "Introduction" to his *Iliad*, p. 5.

8. Latacz, *Homer*, p. 2.

9. J. A. Symonds, *Studies of the Greek Lyric Poets* I, 123; noted in Scott, p. 51, n. 15.

10. Thomson, p. 12.

11. London: John Murray, 1999.

12. G. Lord, p. 13.

13. Steven S. Tigner, "Homer, Teacher of Teachers" (*Journal of Education*, vol. 175, issue 3, 1993), pp. 42–65.

14. Thomson, p. 1.

15. Frank Budgen, "James Joyce: An Encounter with Homer" in *James Joyce and the Making of Ulysses* (1960); reprinted in Steiner and Fagles.

16. Carol Dougherty, "Homer After *Omeros*: Reading a H/Omeric Text," *South Atlantic Quarterly* (vol. 96, no. 2: Spring, 1997), pp. 355–356.

17. Horsley, p. 3.

18. Latacz, *Homer*, p. xi.

19. Leo Tolstoy, "Homer and Shakepeare" in *Recollections and Essays* (Oxford University Press, 1937); reprinted in Steiner and Fagles.

20. Powys in Steiner and Fagles, p. 140.

21. Arnold, p. 1.

22. Knox, pp. 12–13.

23. How many people today would understand?

24. Knox, p. 14.

25. *Ibid.*, pp. 304–305.

26. Denby, *Great Books, p.* 12.

27. *Ibid.*, p. 85.

28. Mary Whitlock Blundell and Kirk Ormand, "Western Values, or the People's Homer: *Unforgiven* as a Reading of the *Iliad*," *Poetics Today* (volume 18, number 4: winter, 1997), p. 535.

29. *Ibid.*, p. 536.

30. Knox, p. 306.

31. *Ibid.*, p. 310.

32. Szedgedy-Maszak, p. 105.

33. George P. Landow, *Hypertext: The Covergence of Contemporary Critical Theory and Technology* (Baltimore: Johns Hopkins University Press, 1992), p. 2.

34. Crossman in Charles Martell, "The Disembodied Librarian in the Digital Age, Part II," *College & Research Libraries* (vol. 61, num. 2: March, 2000).

35. Heim, p. 30; Turkle, p. 52; Gaggi, p. 13 — all in Martell.

BIBLIOGRAPHY OF
SOURCES CITED

Allen, Thomas W. *Homer: The Origins and the Transmission*. Oxford: Clarendon Press, 1924.

Arnold, Matthew. *On Translating Homer*. New edition with introduction and notes by W. H. D. Rouse: London: John Murray, 1905.

Berg, Nils, and Dag Haug. "Innovation vs. Tradition in Homer — an Overlooked Piece of Evidence." *Symbolae Osloenses* 75, no. 1 (9-1-2000): 5–23.

Bernardo, Aldo S., and Saul Levin, eds. *The Classics in the Middle Ages*. Binghamton, N.Y.: Center for Medieval and Early Renaissance Studies, 1990.

Berschin, Walter. *Greek Letters and the Latin Middle Ages: From Jerome to Nicholas of Cusa*. Revised and expanded edition. Washington, D.C.: Catholic University of America Press, 1988.

Bianche Bandinelli, Ranuccio. *Hellenistic-Byzantine Miniatures of the Iliad (Ilias Ambrosiana)*. Olten, Switzerland: Urs Graf-Verlag, 1955.

Bindman, David, ed. *John Flaxman*. London: Thames and Hudson, 1979.

Blegen, Carl W. *Troy and the Trojans*. New York: Barnes & Noble Books, 1995 (originally published 1963).

Blundell, Mary Whitlock and Kirk Ormand. "Western Values, or the People's Homer: *Unforgiven* as a Reading of the *Iliad*." *Poetics Today* 18, no. 4 (winter, 1997): 533–568.

Boardman, John, and C. E. Vaphopoulou-Richardson eds. *Chios: A Conference at the Homereion in Chios 1984*. Oxford: Clarendon Press, 1986.

Bolling, George Melville. *Ilias Atheniensium: The Athenian Iliad of the Sixth Century B.C.* American Philological Association, 1950.

Bowra, Maurice, chapters 1 to 3 in Wace and Stubbings.

Browning, Robert. "The Byzantines and Homer," in Lamberton and Keaney.

_____. "Homer in Byzantium," *Viator: Medieval and Renaissance Studies*, vol. 6, pp. 15–33. Berkeley: University of California Press, 1975.

Bruggemann, Lewis William. *A View of the English Editions, Translations and Illustrations of the Ancient Greek and Latin Authors*. New York: Burt Franklin, 1797.

Budgen, Frank. "James Joyce: An Encounter with Homer," in *James Joyce and the Making of Ulysses* (1960), reprinted in Steiner and Fagles.

Buffiere, Felix, trans. *Heraclite, Allegories d'Homère*. Paris: Société d'Édition "Les Belles Lettres," 1962.

Butler, Samuel. *The Authoress of the* Odyssey: *Where and When She Wrote, Who She Was, the Use She Made of the* Iliad, *and How the Poem Grew Under Her Hands*. London: A. C. Fifield, 1897.

Carter, Jane B., and Sarah P. Morris. *The Ages of Homer: A Tribute to Emily Townsend Vermeule*. Austin: University of Texas Press, 1995.

Cook, Erwin F. *The* Odyssey *in Athens: Myths of Cultural Origins*. Ithaca, N.Y.: Cornell University Press, 1995.

Crielaard, Jan Paul. "A 'Dutch' Discoverer of Homer's Tomb," in Crielaard, *Homeric Questions*.

_____. "Homer, History and Archaeology: Some Remarks on the Date of the Homeric World," in Crielaard, *Homeric Questions*.

_____. *Homeric Questions: Essays in Philology, Ancient History and Archaeology*. Amsterdam: J. C. Gieben, 1995.

Davis, Paul. "Thomas Hobbes's Translations of Homer: Epic and Anticlericalism in Late Seventeenth-Century English." *The Seventeenth Century*, vol. 12 (1997): 231–235.

Davison, J. A. "The Transmission of the Text," in Wace and Stubbings.

De Jong, Irene J. F. "Homer as Literature: Some Current Areas of Research," in Crielaard, *Homeric Questions*.

_____, ed. *Homer: Critical Assessments*. New York: Routledge, 1999.

Denby, David. "Does Homer Have Legs." *The New Yorker*, September 6, 1993, pp. 52–69.

_____. *Great Books: My Adventures with Homer, Rousseau, Woolf, and Other Indestructible Writers of the Western World*. New York: Simon & Schuster, 1996.

Dougherty, Carol. "Homer After *Omeros*: Reading a H/Omeric Text." *South Atlantic Quarterly* 96, no. 2 (spring, 1997): 335–357.

_____, and Leslie Kurke. *Cultural Poetics in Archaic Greece: Cult,Performance, Politics*. New York: Oxford University Press, 1998.

Dowden, Ken. "Homer's Sense of Text." *Journal of Hellenic Studies*, vol. 116 (1996): 47–61.

Farnham, Fern. *Madame Dacier: Scholar and Humanist*. Monterey, Calif.: Angel Press, 1976.

Fenik, Bernard C., ed. *Homer: Tradition and Invention*. Leiden: E. J. Brill, 1978 .

Finley, M. I. *The World of Odysseus*, revised edition New York: Viking Press, 1965.

Foxon, David. *Pope and the Early Eighteenth-Century Book Trade*. Oxford: Clarendon Press, 1991.

Geanakoplos, Deno John. *Byzantium and the Renaissance: Studies in the Dissemination of Greek Learning from Byzantium to Western Europe*. Hamden, Conn.: Archon Books, 1973.

Grafton, Anthony. "Renaissance Readers of Homer's Ancient Readers," in Lamberton and Keaney.

Green, Peter. "War and Peace: Reading, Translating, and Speaking Homer." *The New Republic* 216, no. 8 (1997).

Griffin, J. "Heroic and Unheroic Ideas in Homer," in Boardman and Vaphopoulou-Richardson, pp. 3–13.

Guerinot, J. V. *Pamphlet Attacks on Alexander Pope 1711–1744: A Descriptive Bibliography*. New York: New York University Press, 1969.

Hammond, Brean S. *Pope*. Atlantic Highlands, N.J.: Humanities Press International, 1986.

Hanson, Victor Davis, and John Heath. *Who Killed Homer? The Demise of Classical Education and the Recovery of Greek Wisdom*. New York: Free Press, 1998.

Harris, William V. *Ancient Literacy*. Cambridge, Mass.: Harvard University Press, 1989.

Heubeck, Alfred. "Homeric Studies Today: Results and Prospects," in Fenik.

Holoka, James P. "Homer, Oral Poetry Theory, and Comparative Literature," in Latacz, *Zweihundert*.

Horsley, G. H. R. *Homer in Pisidia: Degrees of Literateness in a Backwoods Province of the Roman Empire*. Australia: University of New England, 1999.

Janko, Richard. "The *Iliad* and Its Editors: Dictation and Redaction." *Classical Antiquity* 9, no. 2 (October, 1990): 326–334.

Jensen, Minna Skafte. *The Homeric Question and the Oral-Formulaic Theory*. Copenhagen: Museum Tusculanum Press, 1980.

Kennedy, Duncan F. "Virgilian Epic," in Martindale, pp. 145–154.

Kirk, G. S. *Homer and the Oral Tradition*. New York: Cambridge University Press, 1976.

_____. *The Songs of Homer*. Cambridge, England: Cambridge University Press, 1962.

Knight, Douglas. *Pope and the Heroic Tradition: A Critical Study of his* Iliad. New Haven: Yale University Press, 1951.

Knight, Virginia. *The Renewal of Epic: Responses to Homer in the Argonautica of Apollonius*. New York: E. J. Brill, 1995.

Knox, Bernard. *Backing into the Future: The Classical Tradition and Its Renewal*. New York: W. W. Norton, 1994.

Lamberton, Robert. "The Neoplatonists and the Spiritualization of Homer," in Lamberton and Keaney.

_____, and John J. Keaney, eds. *Homer's Ancient Readers: The Hermeneutics of Greek Epic's Earliest Exegetes*. Princeton, N.J.: Princeton University Press, 1992.

Landow, George P. *Hypertext: The Convergence of Contemporary Critical Theory and Technology*. Baltimore: Johns Hopkins University Press, 1992.

Latacz, Joachim. *Homer: His Art and His World*. Ann Arbor: University of Michigan Press, 1996.

_____. *Zweihundert Jahre Homer-Forschung: Ruckblick und Ausblick*. Stuttgart: B. G. Teubner, 1991.

Lefkowitz, Mary. *Not Out of Africa: How Afrocentrism Became an Excuse to Teach Myth as History*. New York: Basic Books, 1996.

Lesky, Albin. *A History of Greek Literature*. Translated by James Willis and Cornelius de Heer. Indianapolis: Hackett, 1996, c1963.

Levi, Peter. *Virgil: His Life and Times*. London: Duckworth, 1998.

Long, A. A. "Stoic Readings of Homer," in Lamberton and Keaney.

Lord, Albert B. "Homer," in Steiner and Fagles.

_____. *The Singer of Tales*. Cambridge, Mass.: Harvard University Press, 1960.

Lord, George deF. *Homeric Renaissance: The* Odyssey *of George Chapman*. Hamden, Conn.: Archon Books, 1972, c1956.

Luce, J. V. *Celebrating Homer's Landscapes: Troy and Ithaca Revisited*. New Haven: Yale University Press, 1998.

_____. *Homer and the Heroic Age*. New York: Harper & Row, 1975.

MacDonald, Dennis Ronald. *Christianizing Homer: The Odyssey, Plato, and the Acts of Andrew*. New York: Oxford University Press, 1994.

_____. *The Homeric Epics and the Gospel of Mark*. New Haven: Yale University Press, 2000.

Madhu, R. Chandran. "Plato's Homer." *Ancient Philosophy* 19 (1999): 87–95.

Mann, Rupert. "Pindar's Homer and Pindar's Myths." *Greek, Roman and Byzantine Studies* 35, no. 4 (winter, 1994): 313–337.

Martell, Charles. "The Disembodied Librarian in the Digital Age, Part II." *College & Research Libraries* 61, no. 2 (March, 2000): pp. 99–113.

Martindale, Charles, ed. *The Cambridge Companion to Virgil*. Cambridge, England: Cambridge University Press, 1997.

Martinich, A. P. "Hobbes's Translations of Homer and Anticlericalism." *The Seventeenth Century*, 16 (2001): 147–157.

Mason, H. A. *To Homer Through Pope: An Introduction to Homer's* Iliad *and Pope's Translation*. London: Chatto and Windus, 1972.

McCarter, P. Kyle, Jr. *The Antiquity of the Greek Alphabet and the Early Phoenician Scripts*. Harvard, Mass.: Scholars Press for Semitic Museum, 1975.

Michalopoulos, Andre. *Homer*. New York: Twayne Publishers, 1966.

Moore, Fabienne. "Homer Revisited: Anne Le Favre Dacier's Preface to Her Prose Translation of the Iliad in Early Eighteenth-Century France." *Studies in the Literary Imagination* 33, no. 2 (fall, 2000): 87f.

Morgan, Gareth. "Homer in Byzantium: John Tzetzes," in Rubino and Shelmerdine.

Morris, Ian. "The Use and Abuse of Homer." *Classical Antiquity* 5, no. 1 (April, 1986): 81–138.

Myrsiades, Kostas, ed. *Approaches to Teaching Homer's* Iliad *and* Odyssey. New York: Modern Language Association of America, 1987.

Nagy, Gregory. *The Best of the Achaeans: Concepts of the Hero in Archaic Greek Poetry*. Baltimore: Johns Hopkins University Press, 1979.

_____. "Foreword" to Cook.

_____. "Foreword" to Usher, *Homeric Stitchings*.

_____. *Homeric Questions*. Austin: University of Texas Press, 1996.

_____. *Pindar's Homer: The Lyric Possession of an Epic Past*. Baltimore: Johns Hopkins University Press, 1990.

Pack, Roger A. *The Greek and Latin Literary Texts from Greco-Roman Egypt*, second edition. Ann Arbor: University of Michigan Press, 1965.

Page, Denys L. *History and the Homeric Iliad*. Berkeley: University of California Press, 1972.

Parry, Milman. "Studies in the Epic Technique of Oral Verse-Making I: Homer and the Homeric Style." *Harvard Studies in Classical Philology* 41 (1930).

Pfeiffer, Rudolf. *History of Classical Scholarship from 1300 to 1850*. Oxford: Clarendon Press, 1976.

Powell, Barry B. *Homer and the Origin of the Greek Alphabet*. Cambridge, England: Cambridge University Press, 1991.

Powys, John Cowper. "Preface" to *Homer and the Aether* (1959), reprinted in Steiner and Fagles.

Prete, Sesto. *The Humanists and the Discovery of Printing*. Krefeld: Scherpe Verlag,1982.

Putnam, Michael C. J. *Virgil's Aeneid: Interpretation and Influence*. Chapel Hill: University of North Carolina Press, 1995.

Raaflaub, Kurt A. "Homer, the Trojan War, and History." *The Classical World* 91, no. 5 (1998): 386–403.

Redfield, James M. *Nature and Culture in the Iliad: The Tragedy of Hector*. Chicago: University of Chicago Press, 1975.

Rhomaios, K. "The Pseudo-Herodotean Life of Homer and Chios," in Boardman and Vaphopoulou-Richardson, pp. 21–26.

Richardson, H. J. "Aristotle's Reading of Homer and Its Background," in Lamberton and Keaney.

Riorden, Elizabeth. "Visions of Troy." *Archaeology* 53, no. 1 (January/February, 2000): 52–59.

Rossi, Luigi Enrico. "Dividing Homer: When and How Were the *Iliad* and the *Odyssey* Divided into Songs?" *Symbolae Osloenses* 76, no. 1 (9-1-2001): 103–112.

Rosslyn, Felicity. *Alexander Pope: A Literary Life*. London: Macmillan, 1990.

Rouse, W. H. D. "Introduction" to Arnold.

Rubino, Carl A., and Cynthia W. Shelmerdine, eds. *Approaches to Homer*. Austin: University of Texas Press, 1983, pp. 165–188.

Ruijgh, C. J. "D'Homère aux Origines Proto-Mycèniennes de la Tradition Épique," in Crielaard, *Homeric Questions*.

Scott, John A. *Homer and His Influence*. New York: Longmans, Green, 1931.

Shankman, Steven. *Pope's* Iliad: *Homer in the Age of Passion*. Princeton, N.J.: Princeton University Press, 1983.

Shapiro, H. A. "Hipparchos and the Rhapsodes," in Dougherty and Kurke.

Shay, Jonathan. *Achilles in Vietnam: Combat Trauma and the Undoing of Character*. New York: Atheneum, 1994.

Shaw, T. E. "Translator's Note" in *The Odyssey of Homer*. Oxford: Oxford University Press, 1932, in Steiner and Fagles.

Simonsuuri, Kirsti. *Homer's Original Genius: Eighteenth-Century Notions of the Early Greek Epic (1688–1798)*. Cambridge, England: Cambridge University Press, 1979.

Snider, Denton J. *Homer in Chios*. St. Louis: Sigma Publishing, 1891.

Snodgrass, Anthony. *Homer and the Artists: Text and Picture in Early Greek Art*. Cambridge: Cambridge University Press, 1998.

Stawell, F. Melian. "Introduction" to *The Iliad of Homer Translated by Edward Earl of Derby*. London: J. M. Dent, 1917.

Steinberg, S. H. *Five Hundred Years of Printing*, third edition. New York: Penguin Books, 1974.

Steiner, George. "Homer and the Scholars," in Steiner and Fagles.

_____. *Homer in English*. London: Penguin Books, 1996.

_____, and Robert Fagles, eds. *Homer: A Collection of Critical Essays*. Englewood Clifts, N.J.: Prentice-Hall, 1962.

Szegedy-Maszak: Andrew. "Why Do We Still Read Homer?" *American Scholar* 71, no. 1 (winter, 2002): 95–105.

Taplin, Oliver. "The Division of the *Iliad* into Twenty-Four Books"; Appendix to his *Homeric Soundings: The Shaping of the* Iliad. Oxford: Clarendon Press, 1992.

Tarrant, R. J. "Aspects of Virgil's Reception in Antiquity," in Martindale, pp. 56–72.

Thomson, J. A. K. "Homer and his Influence," in Wace and Stubbings, pp. 1–15.

Tigner, Steven S. "Homer, Teacher of Teachers." *Journal of Education* 175, no. 3 (1993).

Tolstoy, Leo. "Homer and Shakespeare" in *Recollections and Essays*. Oxford University Press, 1937, in Steiner and Fagles.

Tuchman, Barbara W. *The March of Folly: From Troy to Vietnam*. New York: Knopf, 1984.

Underwood, Simeon. *English Translators of Homer from George Chapman to Christopher Logue*. Plymouth, England: Northcote House Publishers, 1998.

Usher, Mark David. *Homeric Stitchings: The Homeric Centos of the Empress Eudocia*. Lanham, Md.: Rowman and Littlefield, 1998.

_____. *Texts and Their Transformations: Continuity and Change in the Classical Tradition*. Chicago: University of Chicago Library, 1994.

Vogt, Ernst. "Homer — ein grosser Schatten? Die Forschungen zur Person Homers," in Latacz, *Zweihundert*.

Wace, Alan J. B., and Frank H. Stubbings. *A Companion to Homer*. New York: St. Martin's Press, 1962.

Webster, Daniel J. "Insomnia and Homer: A Comparative Study of Translations into English of an Early Poem by Osip Mandelstam." *Translation Review* 60 (2000): 20–30.

West, Martin L. "The Invention of Homer." *Classical Quarterly* 49, no. 2 (1999): 364–382.

_____. *Sing Me, Goddess: Being the First Recitation of Homer's Iliad*. London: Duckworth, 1971.

_____. *Studies in the Text and Transmission of the Iliad*. Munich: K. G. Saur, 2001.

West, Stephanie. *The Ptolemaic Papyri of Homer*. Volume III of *Papyrologica Coloniensa*. Köln: Westdeutcher Verlag, 1967.

Wilkens, Iman. *Where Troy Once Stood*. New York: St. Martin's Press, 1990.

Williams, Carolyn D. *Pope, Homer, and Manliness: Some Aspects of Eighteenth-Century Classical Learning*. New York: Routledge, 1993.

Wilson, Jeremy. *Lawrence of Arabia: The Authorized Biography of T. E. Lawrence*. New York: Atheneum, 1990.

Wolf, F. A. *Prolegomena ad Homerum sive de Operum Homericorum Prisca et Genuina Forma Variisque Mutationibus et Probabili Ratione Emendandi*. Halle, 1795.

Wood, Michael. *In Search of the Trojan War*. New York: Facts on File, 1985

Woodford, Susan. *The Trojan War in Ancient Art*. Ithaca, N.Y.: Cornell University Press, 1993.

Wright, Herbert Gladstone. *The Life and Works of Arthur Hall of Grantham, Member of Parliament, Courtier and First Translator of Homer into English*. Manchester: University of Manchester Press, 1919.

INDEX